Experiencing:

A Humanistic Theory
of Psychology and Psychiatry

Experiencing:

A Humanistic Theory of Psychology and Psychiatry

by

Alvin R. Mahrer, Ph.D.

Professor of Psychology
School of Psychology
University of Ottawa, Canada

BRUNNER/MAZEL, Publishers • New York

Wingate College Library

Library of Congress Cataloging in Publication Data

Mahrer, Alvin R
  Experiencing: a humanistic theory of psychology and psychiatry

  Includes bibliographical references and index.
  1. Humanistic psychology. 2. Developmental psychology. I. Title.
BF204.M34   150′.19′2   77-27269
ISBN 0-87630-160-X

Published by
BRUNNER/MAZEL, INC.
19 Union Square West, New York, N.Y. 10003

Distributed in Canada by BOOK CENTER
1140 Beaulac St., Montreal, Quebec H4R-1R8

MANUFACTURED IN THE UNITED STATES OF AMERICA

Contents

I

Humanistic Theory

1

The Context and the Scope

I have puzzled about the answers to many simple questions about human beings, questions which have been around for centuries. These questions are central to so-called helping professions such as psychoanalysis, clinical psychology, psychiatry, and social work. They are also central to fields such as psychology, philosophy, education, sociology, biology. Some of the questions are:

1. There are times when I have bad feelings. These are referred to by words such as scared and tense, lonely and depressed, anguished and distressed, bewildered and confused. How may I describe and understand these bad feelings? What accounts for these bad feelings?

2. There are times when I have the most delightful feelings—when I feel happy and alive and giddy and buoyant, when I feel whole and all together and peaceful and harmonious. How may I describe and understand these good feelings?

3. There are many phenomena happening in and to my body. I become fatter or I become thinner. I have aches in my head or in my stomach. Strange growths appear in my insides. How may I describe and understand the phenomena happening in and to my body?

4. I live in worlds of people and things and relationships. I exist in and am part of complexes of group relationships and social phenomena. How may I describe and understand myself and the personal-social worlds in which I exist?

5. I am continuously behaving. Sometimes I behave in ways which make me feel anguished and torn apart. At other times I behave in ways which make me feel wonderfully enriched and delightfully alive. How may I describe and understand the ways in which human beings behave, sometimes for better and sometimes for worse?

6. Occasionally I meet special persons who raise in me the hope that human beings can reach greater heights than we have ordinarily

achieved. I think of the possibilities for optimal human beings. How may I describe and understand what human beings can become and can achieve?

7. I am fascinated and curious about infants, the ways in which infants behave, the wondrous ways in which infants change into children and adults. How may I describe and understand these infant phenomena?

RELATIONS AMONG THEORY, RESEARCH AND PRACTICE

These are the kinds of simple questions this book addresses. Here is yet another attempt to describe and understand persons, their behavior and their feelings, their social relationships, their development from infancy, their problems and their possibilities. It is relatively easy to tell another theoretical story. What is difficult is to propose a theoretical description which goes beyond prolix verbiage and which is interrelated with research and practice. In this sense, good theory advances good research and good practice and, in turn, is itself moved ahead by advances in our knowledge (research) and in what we can do (practice). My aim is to articulate a theory about certain human phenomena, a theory which has an alive, systematic relationship with what we already know and can do about these phenomena, and which has heuristic value in promoting advances in what we can know and can do about these phenomena. Good theory promotes research and practice; it does not quarrel with other theories (Zilboorg, 1941, 1956).

The degree of relationship to research and practice is a harsh criterion for a theoretical proposal. How would we assess Freud's theory of dreams under this criterion? What did Freudian dream theory enable us to do that is new? What knowledge did it enable us to gain that we did not know before? Did Freud's theory enable us to make sense of dreams by means of free association? There is some evidence that we already had that knowledge and a refined method of free association nearly two thousand years ago. In 140 A.D. Artemidorus of Daldi put forth a comprehensive theory of dreams, including a thorough review of past dream literature (Wolff, 1952). What is more important, he provided rules for interpreting dreams, including a method of interpreting dreams on the basis of free associations. I am not denigrating Freud's contribution. I am suggesting that any theory be evaluated on the basis of its interrelationships with research and practice. What does the theory enable us to do now that we could not do before? What does the theory enable us to discover that we had not already discovered?

Quite often, theory contributes little or nothing to advances in practice. Kalinowsky and Hoch (1961), for example, assert that psychiatric therapies *first* arose through empirical clinical work, and *then* were coupled haphazardly to theoretical rationales. These authors are especially assertive in regard to the field of chemotherapy wherein theory is held as playing practically no role in the development and use of drugs in psychiatric treatment.

By itself, I believe, no one area—theory, research, or practice—can make substantially significant forward strides. It has, for example, taken a thousand years to bring meditation exercises to their present state. Although these exercises are embedded in a belief structure (Ornstein, 1971), they are essentially unrelated to theory and research. As practice alone, these meditation exercises may muddle forward through the next thousand years, still unrefined, still entwined in a religio-cultural belief system which keeps them stuck at their present level. Progress in these exercises will occur when the person who practices the exercise starts to theorize, to wonder and speculate, and also starts to study them, to engage in research about meditation. If not, if practitioners do their exercises without dipping into theory and research, we will have poor practice, poor theory, and poor research. Each of the three can muddle forward, but the real forward strides will flow out of the contributions of each to the others.

In other words, progress in practice requires scientific coupling with theory and research. Implicit theories are dangerous, for they make us carry out this practice or that practice without our ever really knowing why we are doing what we are doing. Because the guiding theory is implicit, we are prevented from envisioning other kinds of practices. As a result, we spend centuries carrying out practices on criminals and offenders without really knowing what we are doing or why we are doing them or what else we might be doing (cf. Hawkinshire, 1963). To the extent that much of our theory of the human body is implicit, we are terribly limited in what we seek to accomplish—without ever knowing that we are limited, and without knowing other possible horizons of what might be accomplished. The same is true of theories of psychotherapy and of the so-called "mental health" field. The theories which dictate practice are predominantly implicit and move us toward goals of which we are unaware, while closing off other goals we are in no position to consider. Regardless of the area, genuine advances in practice call for linkages to both theory and research. Similarly, theory and research can be understood as contributing to each other's mutual development. Of all the ways in which the two can be related to one another, I am of the opinion that the most robust relationship is one in which advances in one contribute directly to advances in the other. For example, I hope that the theory proposed in this book will illuminate new phenomena which then can be investigated. We may have studied infants in the past, but this theory may suggest that researchers look over here or study that aspect of infants or describe this new bit of infant behavior. A new theory will tell researchers where to look, and good researchers can help us see more than we saw before. Humanistic theory, like other theories, will pass in and out of favor. It is my hope that while it is around, it points toward a number of phenomena and invites researchers to take a closer look over here and over there. This is one relationship between advances in theory and research. But there are more.

Advances in humanistic theory can lead also to advances in humanistic research tools and methodologies. Certainly the history of research in the social sciences illuminates the need for more effective research tools and methodologies. In my own field of psychotherapy, Kiesler (1966) concludes that the predominant theories have failed to produce an adequate paradigm for research. This is a serious indictment. Yet, if humanistic theories are to offer significant contributions, they *must* deliver research paradigms, methodologies, and tools—not only in the field of psychotherapy, but also in each field which humanistic theories seek to describe and understand. Although humanistic research approaches are beginning (e.g. Child, 1973; Giorgi, 1970), they have hardly reached their infancy. One reason, I suspect, that humanistic theories have failed to produce research is that their contours do not fit into the grooves of the natural sciences' meaning of research. Before humanistic theories can generate research, they must develop their own systematic framework for scientific research. When that task is more or less accomplished, I suspect the whole fabric of research paradigms will bear very little resemblance to our present research paradigms. It is my hope that this book inches us in that direction.

However, no such research paradigms will be developed until the various pockets of humanistic and existential thought coalesce into a comprehensive theory of personality. Most of our contemporary big schools grew up in the early 1900's, and they did not include any of the humanistic-existential variety. In the 1950's, there occurred a kind of acknowledged moratorium on the further growth and development of big schools of psychology and psychiatry. The need was to make sense of smaller bodies of empirical data, and thus to generate low order mini-theories, reassuringly linked rather closely to known data (cf. Koch, 1951; MacKinnon, 1953). For better or for worse, I see that trend as winding into ever tighter spirals of empirical data—mini-theory—empirical data—mini-theory. Furthermore, I believe the moratorium and the consequent trend toward mini-theories are independent of the particular train of historical forces spawning humanistic-existential theories as an emerging big school. It is time for humanistic-existential theories to develop and to make large-scale sense of the research data we now have available to us. The purpose of this book is to propose a comprehensive humanistic theory and to relate that theory to much of the research knowledge generated by other theories.

Within the sciences which seek to understand human beings, much of what we consider progress consists in self-reassurance of the reasonableness of the regnant theoretical approaches. Scientists are exceedingly human, and, as a collective, work hard at justifying the current popular theories (cf. Maslow, 1970b). The popular research flows from the popular theories and panders to them in unctuous confirmation. Instead of a mutual admiration between popular theory and research, marching along in lock-step, I believe it is time to open up our research data to other, less popular theories. My aim is to invite humanistic theory, one of these less popular theories, to take a look at our research data. I am curious to see what emerges when humanistic theory is allowed to reformulate itself in relationship to some of what we believe we know about human beings.

Theorogenic questions. Just as our research data belong to the public domain and not to some theory of personality, the seven questions at the beginning of this chapter were phrased so as to be free of the jargon or technical vocabulary of any particular theory of personality. I see these as questions puzzling people, not just personality theoreticians. These are questions of concern to human beings who have no knowledge of the technical vocabulary of learning theory or phenomenology or psychoanalysis. I wish to respect simple questions such as these. They were there before our theories, and they will still be there after our present theories pass into history.

Many questions are *not* fundamental. Too many questions have meaning only within some given theoretical approach. When I read, I try to articulate the questions to which that piece of work is addressed. I try to phrase the question in words free of the technical meaning of a given theoretical system. At times this is easy to do. Sometimes, however, the question can be phrased only in the language system of a given approach. For example, a piece of work might seek to address itself to the following question: What are the distinguishing characteristics of paranoid schizophrenics? That is a most meaningful question to persons who accept the concept of schizophrenia. I do not. Therefore, it is not a jargon-free, simple question belonging to the public domain. When the concept of schizophrenia passes away, so will nearly all the work addressed to that question. Today we seldom pay much attention to works addressed to questions meaningful only within a theoretical system which is no longer espoused. For example, we seldom pay heed to pieces of work addressed to questions such as: How many basic body humours are there? Is a witch susceptible to common illnesses? These are what I term *theorogenic* questions, i.e. questions made meaningful by a specific theory, and having meaningfulness only within that theory. In the same way, we frequently ask theorogenic questions today: What are the stages of development of the *ego*? How prevalent is *mental illness*? What is the reliability of the *neuroticism* scale? What are the determinants of *drive reduction*? Can parents serve as *secondary reinforcers*? What are the sources of *psychic energy*? What is the relationship between *internal control* and the *Manifest Hostility Scale*? In contrast, the focus of this book includes a series of questions which concerned us long before our contemporary theories developed, and which will be there long after our contemporary theories have ended their careers.

A theory of the interior. The rationale of common sense assumes that there is some sort of inner world. Call it subjective, call it private experience—I assume its existence. Indeed, in contrast to the tradition of Watsonian behaviorism, and following in the tradition of theorists such as George Herbert Mead (1934) and others, the subjectively private is held to be of central importance in the understanding of human beings. Practitioners know that there is this inner world, but know very little about that world; research has been pleased to leave this world largely untouched. Some say that the explanation lies in the difficulty of getting a research foothold, complete with research equipment, measures, and procedures (e.g. von Eckartsberg, 1971). Perhaps an even more telling consideration is that we have no theory of this region, no conceptual map of the territory. Many of our theories of human beings either ignore or minimize the role of this territory. One of the intents of this book is to provide such a theory of the inner world, a way of conceptualizing what goes on within the person. I hope this theoretical map opens the way to better maps, and that research can then flow out of our having adequate conceptual maps of this inner region.

An emphasis on theory, not research or practice. When psychoanalysis was in its heyday, it enjoyed a multiplicity of distinctiveness. Psychoanalysis referred to (a) a method of psychological investigation; (b) a body of empirical observations in such areas as dreams, the "psychopathology of everyday life," and child development; (c) a set of techniques for therapeutic personality and behavior change; and (d) a theory of human personality and behavior (Hartmann, 1959; Hendrick, 1939). The purpose of this book is less ambitious, for the aim is to describe a theory of human personality and behavior, and *not* any distinctive method of investigation, body of empirical observations, or set of therapeutic techniques.

Yet research and practice are always over my shoulder. In the attempt to set forth a theory, we will back into some very heavy concerns—such as issues of determinism and free will, mind-body issues, and questions out of the heart of the philosophy of science. Our major purpose is to propose a theory of human personality and behavior; it is not to discuss these other issues and questions. When we back into these issues and questions in the course of our major work, we will discuss them. But our discussion will be incomplete—partly because I am far from knowledgeable in many of these topics, and partly because they are secondary to our major purpose.

HUMANISTIC THOUGHT AND A HUMANISTIC THEORY

I am seeking to articulate a theory of personality from a pool of humanistic thought. The pool of humanistic thinking does not spring from a single resource, like Sigmund Freud for psychoanalysis or Carl Rogers for client-centered therapy. It is much more a part of the public domain. From this general pool of humanistic thought, I am seeking to articulate one humanistic theory of personality. My conviction is that what we know as humanistic thought is not yet a formal theory of personality. Without going into either a formal critique or a panegyric on humanistic thought as a theory of personality, it seems to me that humanism is far from achieving the stature of a comprehensive theory of personality. My aim is to take the basic conceptions of humanistic thinking and to stretch them into a full-fledged personality theory.

I believe that a few key principles underlie the various approaches and movements which fall under the humanistic umbrella. My early attraction to psychoanalysis was in part due to its elegance in making sense out of apparently unrelated sets of phenomena by articulating a few key principles (cf. Loevinger, 1966). It is my conviction that a small set of *humanistic* principles also can make heuristically good sense of the phenomena of interest to students of human behavior, personality, human interaction, development and change.

Humanistic theory is, then, an attempt to formalize one comprehensive theory of human personality upon the foundations of humanistic thought. I believe it is the very comprehensiveness of applied professionalism which currently is pulling for comprehensive theories. A few generations ago, it seemed that applied social work, psychology, and psychiatry found the extant big theories generally inadequate. Koch (1951) pronounced those years as the crisis in theoretical psychology and prescribed *mini-theories* on mini-problems. In the last few generations the continued growth of applied work has pressed increasingly for *comprehensive theories* to provide answers for myriads of practical, applied questions. How can the patients in one institution be mutually helpful toward the patients at another institution? Why do so many therapists seek to *reduce* anxiety when other therapists aim at *opening up* the patient's anxiety? Why do large scale mental health centers seem to fail? How does chemotherapy work? What can be accomplished with "mental retardates"? What kinds of training programs will be most effective for volunteers? How should "mental health teams" best be organized? What can we do to assist parents in infant care? What is the most effective next step in mental health legislation? What new paradigms are needed for applied research? These and hundreds of questions made meaningful by the growth of applied professional work constitute challenges to the theories we have available. Little wonder that theories either fall under the strain or new ones are invited to help the professional live effectively in the world of applied work.

It is my impression, one which has been expressed by other writers (e.g. Farber, 1964), that humanistic thought has yet to provide a systematic basis for a rigorous framework of human behavior and a rigorous framework for applied practice (Vespe, 1969). Indeed, the term "humanistic" has come to include only minute traces of intellectual *thought* so that the phrase "humanistic theory" is almost a contradiction in terms. What Kinget (1975) terms the "scholarly wing of humanistic psychology" has, nevertheless, struggled to develop a scientific theory of human beings based upon humanistic thought. In order to develop such a rigorously comprehensive humanistic theory, a number of steps must be taken. One step consists of trying to apply humanistic thought to many of the questions to which other theories are addressed, for example, the seven questions presented in the opening of this chapter. A second step is to define clear position statements on some of the more basic issues that comprise much of the philosophy of science (e.g., as discussed in Chapter 4). A set of position statements on these issues is required of a pool of humanistic ideas which seeks to become a serious humanistic theory. By following at least these two steps, we will be working toward a comprehensive humanistic theory even if we take a little humanistic thinking from here and a little from there in a kind of loosely woven humanistic eclecticism (cf. McGeoch, 1933).

Working toward a systematic humanistic theory means applying rigor wisely. At the present time I see humanistic thought as growing, but growing in a loose and lumpy way. I do not believe it is strong enough to withstand high doses of rigor. There must be, at this point in the career of humanistic theorizing, a reasoned balance between rigor and growth. The implication here is that rigor is a tool, and scientists can use that tool however they are inclined. I eschew the use of rigor as a means of attacking other theories and defending one's own. In the long run, the only one to benefit from such practices is the wielder of the weapon; neither one's own theory nor the theories of others benefit from such defensive-aggressive use of rigor, regardless of excuses given in the name of science. I prefer rigor wielded by friends—by those whose aim is to help humanistic thought to produce a good humanistic theory.

Too often the demand for rigor is a mere weapon against the concepts of others. When Eysenck (1952, 1954, 1955b) tweaked psychotherapists with his wry summary of findings on the inefficacy of psychotherapy, the concept of spontaneous remission was pushed into the embarrassed faces of psychotherapists. Almost immediately, that concept was attacked as failing to meet the demands of rigor (e.g. Cartwright, 1955; de Charms, Levy, & Wertheimer, 1954; Luborsky, 1954; Strupp, 1963). Suddenly that concept was put through rigorous scientific hazing. It is all too human to attack enemy concepts with whatever standards we hope they will fail to meet, and to withdraw our own concepts from such attack.

For example, humanistic thought has practically nothing to say about infancy and the processes of personality development. Humanistic thought has led to no substantive research in these areas. In order to frame out a humanistic theory of infancy and personality development, the criterion of rigor needs to be gentled a bit. Our humanistic theory seeks to cover two prongs of the study of personality as laid down by Watson (1919), namely, personality as structure and personality as processes of developmental change. As implied in the seven questions set forth in the beginning of this chapter, I am interested in describing human beings in the cross-section of the immediate here and now (i.e. structure), and in the scope of the developmental processes which precede and follow this moment. Yet, as Schachtel (1959) has pointed out so lucidly, humanistic thought is simply too frail to generate tough notions of the structure and process of personality development. Accordingly, with too few exceptions (e.g. Buhler & Massarik, 1968) humanistic thought has not even ventured any serious attempts to offer a theory of personality development. My aim is to propose a humanistic theory of infancy and child development. At this point, I believe the need is more for carefully reasonable approximation than pinpoint rigor.

Even at this point in the development of a humanistic theory of the origin, behavior, and development of infants, our point of departure differs from that of most approaches. Our theory provides us with a formulation in which human beings (generally parenting human beings) "originate" infants; *human beings* elicit infant behavior, and human beings are the active developmental agents of infants. Infants do

not originate; they *are originated* by human beings. Infants do not behave; behavior is moulded by human beings. Infants do not develop
or grow or mature; human beings develop, grow, and mature *infants*.
In our formulation, we can describe and understand infants only after
we have a framework for describing and understanding human beings
in general. It is quite in order, then, that the final chapters of this
book turn to infants, although it may strike the reader as odd, especially since most theories of human behavior and development *open*
with chapters on infancy. Our departures from contemporary theories
may be necessary to the development of humanistic-existential
thought, whether or not these departures are taken as evidence of
rigorous science-building or loose thinking.

There is, I believe, quite a distinction between *espousing* scientific
rigor and *being* scientifically rigorous. Before my graduate school
years, I was attracted by the careful thinking of psychoanalytic writers;
then I was fortunate to become part of a graduate school energized by
the scientific spirit of a burgeoning social learning approach to human
personality and behavior. Although the various learning theories and
their filial behavior modification therapies apotheosize rigorous scientific methodology, I found an enormous hiatus between *proclaiming*
the value of a rigorous scientific approach and *providing* one. To reduce the chasm between my scientific party chant and the effective
understanding of myself and my professional work, I turned increasingly to the teachings of the humanists. I am now of the opinion that
humanistic thought contains the wherewithall for a rigorous theory of
personality and behavior. Furthermore, I am convinced that no single
approach or school is the chosen repository of scientific principles of
human personality and behavior. My suspicion is that learning
theorists and behavior modificationists characteristically identify *their*
scientific principles as *the* scientific principles—a position which the
history of science finds inhospitable to the progress of science and
more suitable to regnant political and religious dogma than to the
progressive development of scientific knowledge. On this score,
Farber is representative of those who see the development of humanistic theories as inimical to the attempt to discover behavioral predictability through the laws of learning theories. From that perspective, humanism ". . . emerges as a flat denial . . . that behavior is predictable . . . At the other extreme it consists of the condemnation and
proscription of attempts to discover the laws of behavior" (Farber,
1964, p. 12). If this *is* a parameter of humanistic thought, I am hardly
excited by that sort of humanism. On the other hand, my excitement
is in helping to articulate a humanistic theory which contributes to
knowledge about human personality and behavior, even if this process

adds little or nothing to the learning theories' own brand of behavioral laws.

Toward Definitions of a Humanistic Theory

This is a *humanistic* theory in that it rests on what may be identified as humanistic conceptions of human beings. It does not rest on what may be roughly identified as psychoanalytic conceptions of human beings, nor does it rest on behavioristic conceptions of human beings. The humanistic family includes such members as Gestalt, phenomenology, Daseinsanalysis, existentialism, and experientialism. One way of defining humanistic theory, then, is that it is a theory derived from the body of humanistic thought. Another is that it is a theory expressing much of the substantial commonality across such humanistic conceptions as Gestalt, phenomenology, Daseinsanalysis, existentialism, and experientialism.

Humanistic theory seeks to provide answers to many questions about human beings, just as the psychoanalytic theories, the behavioral theories, and other theories of human beings do. The seven questions cited at the beginning of this chapter are central to nearly all theories of human personality and behavior. They are among the questions to which humanistic theory, behavior theory, psychoanalytic theory, and other theories give characteristically different answers. I define *humanistic* theory as a cohesive body of concepts relating to human beings, their personality and their behavior. This meaning of humanistic theory rests upon writings of persons such as Kierkegaard, Husserl, Allport, Laing, Murray, Bakan, Buhler, Maslow, Binswanger, Bugental, Merleau-Ponty, Hampden-Turner, Jourard, Angel, Buytendijk, Frankl, Boss, Heideggar, Gendlin, Giorgi, May, Polanyi, Mahrer, Rogers, Straus, von Kaam, Jaspers, Framo, Kantor, Watts, Shostrom, Sartre, Perls, Fagan, Ellenberger, Mullen, Combs and others.

Humanistic theory is also defined in terms of a body of practice which is called humanistic—whether in psychotherapy, organizational development, social change, small groups, education, or any other area of practice. Humanistic practices will change. They will grow, expand, replace one another, find new areas of application. I do not weld humanistic theory to its current practices because these will change and still be humanistic in that they relate logically to humanistic theory.

Too often a theory is *constrained* to the definition of one particular expression of its practices. For example, psychoanalysis has been constrained to narrowly specific modes of practice: individual psychoanalysis with adults, methods of free association and interpretation of transference, and so on. I believe this is regrettable because I would prefer to allow psychoanalysis (or any other theory) to generate successive waves of practice, and to develop varying practices for various contexts—e.g. for infants, groups, adolescents, institutional change, and so on, all conceptually related to psychoanalysis. Humanistic theories have generated particular kinds of psychotherapies for some persons under some circumstances. But quite different modes of practice can be generated for use with infants, and for groups, and for institutional change, and for lots of other things. I do not constrain the meaning of humanistic to its present body of practices, whatever they are.

Humanistic theory also refers to a way of knowing, a body of methods of inquiring, a system of research. There is a methodology in its initial stages of development. Because this meaning derives from a developing theory, and because humanistic ways of knowing will evolve and change, this is certainly not the most stalwart definition of humanistic theory.

One can view the comings and goings of theories from the perspective of a historian who stands in any of the fields of applied work. One of these fields is psychotherapy. Standing in the field of psychotherapy, it seems that one of the major generators of new theories is the dialectic movement away from Freudian psychoanalysis. "Lately, psychotherapy seems to be moving with great speed in two directions away from Freudianism. The one direction is an attempt to find a more 'rigorous' natural-scientific basis for curing patients. Chemotherapy and what has been called 'behavior therapy' are clear examples of this tendency. In the other direction we find many schools of thought going under the name of 'existentialist,' 'phenomenological,' 'humanistic,' etc . . . " (Needleman, 1967a, p. viii). I hope that the predominant impetus toward humanistic theory is more than that of merely moving away from Freudianism. Yet I appreciate the history of our theories enough to see the humanistic school of thought as living out a defined career with a beginning and an end. It is my hope that humanistic theory plays a substantial role in generating the better theories of the future.

PSYCHOTHERAPY AND HUMANISTIC THEORY

I am a psychotherapist. Out of my bewilderments and puzzlings with what occurs in psychotherapy comes my preoccupation with the seven questions defined above. Psychotherapy is both the wellspring for my concerns with a humanistic theory, and the area of research and practice to which I hope to apply what humanistic theory illuminates about human beings.

Some theories of human beings, especially those of a biological heritage, come out of general psychology and speak mainly to students of general psychology. On this score, the present venture will be different. Our illustrative material and implications will be linked far more to the field of psychotherapy. I cannot help stating this with some satisfaction, for the genesis of humanistic theory is through the field of psychotherapy, and owes its heritage to psychotherapy. It is through this field that glimpses into the nature of human beings are found—at least for me. The bias of humanistic theory, its distortions and skewed perceptions of human beings, come out of its genesis from my experiences in psychotherapy.

I have been in the practice of psychotherapy for over 25 years. In addition to my therapeutic work in clinics, hospitals and universities, I have engaged in private practice continuously during all of this time. In a way, psychotherapy has served as a kind of laboratory, with the processes of psychotherapy as sets of research instruments. "Here is a method of research that offers singular opportunities for gaining incomparable insight into the dynamics of emotional and mental life . . . It reaches the remotest recesses and makes transparent what stirs and moves in the hiding places of the netherworld. No other psychological method shows us how thousands of emotional verities follow the same laws, laws as valid as those of physics and chemistry. To find the laws that govern the unconscious processes, to discover what is concealed behind the psychical facade—these are the satisfactions a psychoanalyst may experience" (Reik, 1948, p. viii). I am a psychotherapist during the therapy hours. Afterwards, by myself in my office, I think about the person, about myself, and about us human beings. These hours constitute much of the wellsprings of humanistic theory, and are its virtue as well as its limitation.

Our data base is more from the field of psychotherapy than from experiments on animals. Questions pertaining to the comparative study of human beings and animals are also beyond the scope of this book. Indeed, human beings are taken as we are, and not as a product of Darwinian evolutionary continuity or as a discontinuous evolutionary threshold (Teilhard de Chardin, 1965). I am not concerned with the issue of whether the distinctiveness of human beings, as compared with animals, lies in our capacity for self-reflective thinking or the use of symbols in human communication (e.g. Bertalanffy, 1965). Yet the pursuit of ways in which we are different from animals is fed by a deeper quest for understanding ourselves, for knowing what human beings are like, and *that is* a central concern of this book.

A large chunk of the evidential base for humanistic theory derives from my own work in psychotherapy, and from that sector of the lit-

erature which studies human beings through intensive psychotherapy.
Psychoanalysis rested upon the same kind of evidential foundation
(Farrell, 1955), and the risk is the same, viz. that a depth understanding of persons in psychotherapy illuminates a distorted picture
of human beings in general. I think that is a well-taken consideration.
Yet it is nevertheless accurate that psychotherapeutic writings and experience constitute a large part of the evidential base of humanistic
theory.

This is not a book on *how to do* psychotherapy or counselling. There
is no discussion of methods of personality change. We will talk about
bad feelings and good feelings, but not the methods of moving from
the former to the latter. We will discuss human behavior which is
filled with pain, and what human behavior can be like under optimal
personality states, but we will not investigate *how* to bring about these
changes. Although this book is filled with hintings and implications of
the processes of change, there is no attempt to frame out a systematic
theory of change.

Chapter 2 sets forth the general contours of humanistic theory, and
introduces the basic building blocks: potentials and the relationships
among potentials. Chapter 3 further describes personality structure,
and focuses on an explanation of bad feelings in the course of outlining the topography of personality structure. Having sketched out a
humanistic theory of personality, the position of that theory is compared and contrasted with the positions of other theories of personality on some of the issues of a philosophy of science (Chapter 4). Many
of these issues involve the place of the body, the role of bodily events,
and the nature of bodily phenomena. These are discussed in Chapter
5. Turning from the person to the encompassing world in which the
person exists, Chapter 6 describes the ways in which the person constructs his external world and the functions served by the constructed
external world. The thesis of Chapter 7 is that social phenomena are
generated by collective persons engaged in constructing their own
external worlds to serve their own functions. With some understanding of individual personality structures (Chapters 2-5) and the constructed external worlds in which they exist (Chapters 6-7), the next
focus is on the description of human behavior. Chapters 8 and 9 describe the basic principles of human behavior (Chapter 8) and the
ways in which these principles are orchestrated (Chapter 9). One class
of human behavior includes behavior which is painful or which may
be considered as problem behavior or "psychopathology." This class of
behavior is described in Chapter 10. Turning from painful or problem behavior to optimal ways of being, Chapters 11 and 12 describe
the optimal states of integration (Chapter 11) and actualization
(Chapter 12). Given a general theoretical framework for understand-

ing human beings, we are now ready to describe how human beings construct infants. This is why a discussion of infants and children occurs at the end of the book rather than at the beginning. Chapter 13 focuses upon a humanistic theory of infancy. The factors which account for infant behavior are discussed in Chapter 14, and further development of the child is described in Chapter 15. Movement throughout the course of life occurs as transitions from one plateau to another. The five plateaus of human development are described in the final chapter.

2

Some Basic Concepts of Humanistic Theory

The purpose of this chapter is to introduce some of the basic concepts of humanistic theory. Other basic concepts will be introduced in subsequent chapters, and each of the concepts introduced here will be discussed more fully in subsequent chapters.

POTENTIALS FOR EXPERIENCING

I have experiencings which I describe as love, curiosity, aggression, passivity. For me, each of these is a different experience. Each constitutes a potential within me, a potential for experiencing love or curiosity or aggression or passivity or whatever else can be described with the right words. In Figure 2.1 each *potential for experiencing* is indicated as a circle. Circle 1 might indicate my potential for experiencing what can be described as creative expression, and circle 3 my potential for experiencing love and affection. I will refer to these circles as *potentials*, on the understanding that each *is a different potential for experiencing*.

If we could speak with these potentials, we would be impressed that they only know experiencing—raw simple experiencing or "function pleasure," as Karl Buhler (Buhler & Massarik, 1968) described what potentials do. Each potential for experiencing, in one sense, ". . . knows no other aim than the fulfillment of wishes and . . . has at its command no other force than wishful impulses" (Freud 1953d). There is a commonality between wish fulfillment and function pleasure which is included in our meaning of potential for experiencing. Yet experiencing simply is. It is a process of itself; it does not accomplish something further or lead to some end such as gratifying something or filling some deficiency or quieting some tension or whatever. Experiencing is the fulfilling; it is not something whose aim is to fulfill another something.

18

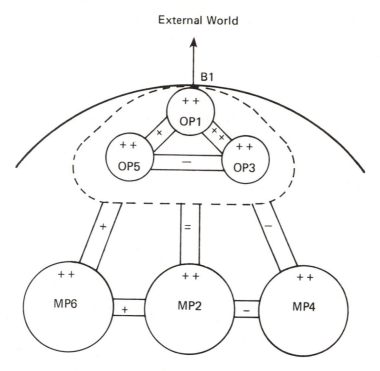

Figure 2.1 Operating and Mediating Potentials for Experiencing

Potentials for experiencing do not *push* the person into experiencing. They merely stand ready (potential) to experience love or curiosity or whatever. In contrast with concepts such as libido, drive, motivation, energy, need, actualization, growth force, arousal, activation or press, our potentials do not possess any character of shoving, pushing, pulling or driving (cf. Appleton, 1910; Freeman, 1948; Freud, 1959; Hull, 1943; Lewin, 1935; Maslow, 1970; Rogers, 1959). They are only potentials, nothing more. We can speak of a potential for experiencing sex or a potential for experiencing aggression, but these are quite different from psychoanalytic *drives* for sex or aggression. Unlike psychoanalytic drives, potentials for experiencing are not presumed to have a characteristic of being displaced or transformed into various human activities; they do not shove a person along the pathway from birth to maturity; they do not push or pull behavior, and they do not require consummation in human object relationships (cf. Hartmann, 1959).

Within the psychoanalytic family, one group has more or less abandoned the concept of drive as based ultimately on a system of energetics. Instead of energized drives, this group turned toward more social determinants of human behavior. Prominent in this group are Adler, Fromm, and Sullivan. A second group is represented by Holt and George Klein. According to these theorists, the concept of drives is more profitably entertained by divorcing it from the whole system of energetics. Drives are not replaced by social forces, but the meaning of drive has no connection to energy. Our concept is similar to such a concept of drive, i.e., merely a potential for experiencing, devoid of any intrinsic energy component, and not operating on the basis of homeostasis or reduction of energy. Unlike a physiological need, unlike Maslow's conception of some needs, potentials have no characteristic of a deficiency which can be filled or satisfied or gratified.

When a person experiences love or leadership or passivity or any other kind of experiencing, we can speak of a bodily locus of the experience. It can occur in the head or in the stomach or all over the body or just generally "inside." The *potential* for experiencing is an idea, a concept, but *experiencing* itself is felt in the body. Yet, unlike the concept of physiological needs, experiencing is not tied to a particular body part, such as sexual needs referring to the genitals or hunger referring to the stomach (Maslow, 1970b). Nevertheless, experiencing always includes a "feelinged" bodily component. If I refer to a potential for experiencing love, the referent includes some bodily process. When we describe a specific experiencing, the words imply some kind of behavior and some sort of situational context. But the nub of experiencing is the experiencing in itself, and not the behavior or the situational context. For example, the experiencing of loving is that which occurs when I am with my wife, and we are saying special words while holding and touching one another. But no matter how much I describe the behaviors and the situational context, something is left out. That something is the feelinged bodily component which stands as the experience of loving. Without this, the behaviors occurring in the appropriate situational context lack the core of experiencing. A potential for experiencing, then, when its structure is studied, must include a feelinged bodily component.

The basic unit in our conception of personality is the potential for experiencing. In large measure, description and understanding consist of grasping the nature of the particular potential. By accepting experiencing as the formal basis of personality description, humanistic theory leaves behind wishes, drives, needs, goals, impulses, and other constructs which draw attention away from the specific nature of sheer human experiencing.

If the potential for experiencing is the basic unit, it becomes quite difficult to identify a paradigm for human motivation. When we think of a potential for experiencing, a mere potential devoid of the characteristic of drive or force, we cannot turn to familiar disciplines for our paradigm. Typically we have more or less accepted physiological needs as our paradigm. Hunger has served as a paradigm of human motivation. Although we have taken little steps away from biology and physiology, we still retain the idea that human beings are driven or pushed by something. The something may be real or unreal, internal or external, an explanatory or descriptive concept. Yet the central core of push or drive is there, exactly as it is in the paradigm of hunger. However, there is no easy or ready paradigm for a potential for experiencing. What are available as possible paradigms consist of one's own actual experiencings, such as intimacy or rejection or being comforted. In place of a paradigm, we have descriptions, usually phenomenological descriptions, of concrete human experiencing. Our paradigm, then, will be found in the neighborhood of naive, simple, phenomenological description of common human experiencing. The paradigm is the experiencing of what specific human beings have available as experiencing: being the special one, being intimate, being entered into, being left out, being alone, being independent. When we understand human experiencing, our paradigm shall come from human experiencing, and we will be ready to go beyond physiological hunger or thirst as workable paradigms.

In accepting such potentials as the unit for human personality description, humanistic theory rejects such other basic units as "the psychiatric category." According to the psychiatric approach, the person is an anxiety reaction, hebephrenic, delinquent, homosexual, manic-depressive, and so on. Where psychiatric conceptions would describe the person as delinquent, our perspective would seek to describe the nature of the person's potentials for experiencing. Instead of saying that she is a lesbian or a delinquent or a paranoid, we would be seeking to describe the nature of her experiencing. Instead of the question being, "What psychiatric category do you fall under?," the question is, "What are you experiencing?"

When the field moved from psychiatric intrapsychic illness to the cleaner air of sheer behavior description, the endeavor promised us the gift of scientific simplicity. Humanistic theory cannot offer such a promise. Indeed, we do not know how to describe our experiencing adequately; our present repertoire of descriptions is embarrassingly primitive. It is easier to accept sheer behavior as the unit of description. It is even easier to be satisfied with psychiatric labels as units of description. Nevertheless, in our perspective, the nature of the potentials is proposed as the basic unit for describing human beings.

Potentials vary in the degree to which they are being experienced at this moment. A given potential may be experienced to a heightened degree, or to a minimal extent, or not at all. Thus I may have a *potential* for experiencing love, yet it is quite another matter to consider the actual degree to which I am experiencing love at this very moment. Potentials for experiencing vary in their degree of actual, here-and-now experiencing.

When we find good ways to describe potentials—their nature and their depths of experiencing—we will be focusing upon the experiencing itself and not on sheer behavior. I agree with those theorists who say that nothing of serious scientific merit is added to our understanding of behavior by postulating something inside (like "potential") which is held as nothing more than that behavior (Farber, 1964; Skinner, 1953, 1967; Watts, 1961). We really know very little more about eating behavior or sexual behavior by postulating motivations (or needs or drives) for eating and for sex. Postulating some inner motivation for protecting one's survival hardly helps us understand behaving in a way which seems to protect our survival. The description of a potential is a description of the precise nature of the experience, and *not* a naming of behaviors. A potential for experiencing love is more than a behavior of being caressed by a caring person. It is more than all the *behaviors* which qualify as loving behaviors. Although behaviors will be described (Chapter 8) as the *means* whereby potentials are experienced, there is a vast difference between looking deeply into another's eyes as a *behavior*, and the *experiencing* which is occurring. Thus, humanistic theory accepts arguments against the definition of personality constructs as sheer behavior. "There is no use saying that a person runs away because he is afraid, if the fear is inferred wholly from his running away . . . If (intervening variables) do no more than account for the particular behavior from which they are adduced, they are fatuitous" (Farber, 1964, pp. 28-29).

In an important sense, the behaviorists' argument against the usefulness of personality constructs is an extension of arguments against radical operationalism. The argument is that the meaning of a scientific construct cannot be identified with its confirming evidence (Feigl, 1953). The meaning of a construct or scientific statement, according to this argument, cannot be coterminal with the state of affairs which is to serve as evidence of the construct or scientific statement. From this line of reasoning, it is a relatively short step to the behavioristic position that a personality construct (e.g. motivation) cannot be coterminal with sheer behavior. Thus, asserts the behaviorist, hunger is not eating behavior, a drive for sex is not the same as sex behavior, and so on. The position of humanistic theory is in accord with the behavioristic argument and with the arguments against radical operationalism. We arrive at the same conclusion, viz. a potential for experiencing is not sheer behavior.

Farber, Skinner, and Watts conclude that since most inner concepts (like drive or need) are restatements of behavior, we can easily do without any postulated inner concepts. The conclusion I would draw is that potentials are beyond sheer behavior and are not to be defined in behavioral terms. When I behave in a way which is called sexual, the aim is to describe the *nature* of the experience and not to explain the behavior. Our focus is on the description of that sexual experience rather than the explanation of my sexual behavior. On this score, humanistic theory must reject the behaviorist's identification of *behavior* with *personality* (cf. Farber, 1964). Within a behavioristic framework it is consistent to reject personality constructs which are restatements of behavior, and to conclude that behavior is, then, personality. In our approach, there is room for *both* behavior and personality constructs; personality is far more than sheer behavior.

When a person behaves, that behavior has a presence, an immediate presence. As scientists, we are comfortable with this quality of behavior because we can do systematic things with such "present" behavior. We can observe it and we can record it. What existential, phenomenological, and humanistic theoreticians contend is that behavior is not the *whole* of what is there. Something else is also present, something which we as scientists do not yet know how to handle in systematic fashion. It is a presence of a *person*. It is an *experiencing* person which organizes the behavior and is there with it. If we exclude everything which is not present—all the vacuous personality constructs which are not right there at all—then behavior alone does not fill the whole present stage. That something more is referred to as the potential for experiencing (Boss, 1963).

Operating and Mediating Potentials

Some potentials are coupled directly to behavior. If I have a potential for creating, building, and expressing, that potential may link directly with my painting a picture or designing a home. That potential is experienced more or less directly. I refer to these as *operating potentials*. They are indicated as OP in Figure 2.1. Thus, operating potential 1 may refer to the potential for experiencing creative expression, operating potential 3 may refer to my potential for experiencing love and affection, and operating potential 5 may refer to my potential for experiencing domination and control.

Other potentials for experiencing are deeper in my personality. They are not directly connected with behavior and are not the potentials on which I operate. For example, I may be described as having a deeper potential for experiencing manliness and virility, independence, and hostility and aggression. Yet these three potentials do not link directly to ways of behaving. They are not the potentials on which I operate. Compared with operating potentials, I less frequently am them; I less frequently experience them "from within." In effect, these are *deeper* potentials. I refer to these as *mediating potentials*, and they are indicated in Figure 2.1 as MP2, MP4, and MP6.

If a potential for independence were at the operating level, it would be experienced to a greater degree than if the potential for independence were at a deeper or mediating level. In general, the "higher" the potential in Figure 2.1, the more it is experienced; the "lower" the potential, the less it is experienced—directly, "from within," and in direct linkage to behavior.

In Figure 2.1, the operating potential may be a potential for experiencing creative expression (OP1), and the deeper potential may be a potential for experiencing manliness and virility (MP2). If Figure 2.1 were used to schematicize another person, the two might well be reversed, and the *operating* potential might be manliness and virility, while the *deeper* potential is a potential for creative expression. Any potential for experiencing can be at the operating level or at a deeper level. When I come to know the person's operating potential, I still cannot be at all certain what deeper potential lies beneath it. I might make some decent guesses, but I have found essentially the same potential on the operating surface for some persons, and far down into the deeper levels for others.

Some approaches posit a more or less fixed hierarchy of personality parts (needs, drives, motivations) so that "deeper" parts are of certain kinds and more functional parts are of other kinds. This is not the position of humanistic theory. In our framework, for example, it is perfectly conceivable that aggression (MP6, Figure 2.1) might occur at any level. This conception is in accord with that of Anna Freud (1936) for whom aggression, as one example, can occur at any level within a psychoanalytic schema of personality, from an instinctual status to serving as part of the functioning ego.

Like the relationship between the psychoanalytic ego and unconscious instinctual processes, the operating potential is closer to the realities of the external world, and the deeper potential is "deeper" within the personality structure. But unlike the psychoanalytic conception, operating and deeper potentials are composed of the same stuff. There are no qualitative differences between the operating and the deeper potentials, nor do they function according to qualitatively different principles. For example, in psychoanalytic theory, the ego functions on a secondary process form of energy distribution, while the unconscious functions on a qualitatively different form of energy distribution, i.e., primary process, with its tendency toward immediate discharge. Related to these two forms of psychoanalytic energy distribution are qualitatively different functions, so that such functions as perception, memory, thinking, and so on are located within the ego rather than within the unconscious. Furthermore, the ego functions on the basis of a reality principle, while the unconscious functions on the basis of the pleasure principle. While these sets of differences are organized with one another—pleasure principle, primary process of energy distribution, and immediate discharge all go with one another—the psychoanalytic picture has ego and unconscious as qualitatively different kinds of entities, functioning on the basis of different principles. In humanistic theory these differences do not exist. As will be discussed shortly, the operating and deeper potentials differ primarily in the roles they play at a particular moment. What is operating now can be deeper shortly, and the deeper potential can become the operating potential. In humanistic theory, the stuff of which operating and deeper potentials are made is one and the same; only their immediate functional roles differ.

Variability of operating potentials. At the present moment I may be behaving on the basis of operating potential 1, the potential for experiencing creative expression (Figure 2.1). An hour from now, I may be experiencing operating potential 3, love and affection. Operating potential 3 has exchanged places with operating potential 1, and it is now operating potential 3 which is linked directly to behavior. Each of the three operating potentials in Figure 2.1 can vary position so as to click into the place occupied in Figure 2.1 by operating potential 1.

It is even possible for a *deeper* potential to step into the role of the operating potential. Although my daily waking behavior may be determined by my potential for creative expression (OP1, Figure 2.1), in my dream life I may operate on the basis of my potential for experiencing manliness and virility (MP2, Figure 2.1). Yet that potential may never be operating in my daily waking life, and I may seldom if ever experience manliness and virility in my daily waking life. Recent research on the study of rapid eye movement and the "D-state" of sleep (Jones, 1970) seems to suggest that the "person" (I would refer to this as the person-who-is-the-operating-potential-of-the-moment) disengages from the waking "self," and slowly moves by stages into being the dreaming person. Here is a dramatic instance of shifting from one being into another. Just as in sleep we move into and out of our various "selves" or "potentials," in waking state we likewise can and do move into and out of several (operating) potentials. Any potential conceivably can fulfill the role of an operating potential. In other words, the operating potential has variability.

If we slow down the process of varying operating potentials, it is as if the person is one potential now, moves out of being that one, and finally becomes another one. Until this process is completed, there is an intervening stage when no potential is "engaged" as the operating site. It is a stage of transition. This transition is shown in the movement from wakefulness to dreaming. When I am awake I may be my operating potential for creative expression. When I dream, I have shifted into being my deeper potential for manliness and virility. In between there would be a transition. I have left being creative expression; I am not yet manliness and virility. During this transition, there would not be any dream or dream-related body movements (cf. Dement & Kleitman, 1957a, 1957b) since no potential is yet engaged.

RELATIONSHIPS AMONG POTENTIALS

Humanistic theory is a language system, and as such it rests on the implicit assumptions ingrained in our Indo-European languages. One of these implicit assumptions is that the world is divided into two classes —it is not *nature* which is divided into these two classes; it is our *language system* which bifurcates nature. As described by Whorf (1956), our language divides the world into subject and predicate, objects and their attributes, quantities and operations, actors and actions, things and relations between things. I have described personality in terms of potentials; these are the parts or the things of which personality is constructed. Now I would like to turn to the idea that there are *relations* between these things or parts. It is within the implicit assumptive base of our own language that this division exists: things (potentials) and the relationships among things.

It is a very ancient idea that the state of the human being depends on the way its "parts" relate to one another. For example, Hippocrates conceived of these parts as blood, black bile, yellow bile, and phlegm. The way these parts *related* to one another was an important determinant of the state of the person. This same basic idea is present in some of the thinking of modern personality theorists who likewise hold that our state depends a great deal upon the way our parts relate to one another (Kierkegaard, 1944; Maslow, 1963, 1970b; Rogers, 1961). Within the language system of psychoanalysis, the relationship between the ego and instinctual excitations is crucial to the state of psychopathology. If the relationship is a poor one of mistrust and protest, the ego must ward off the instinctual excitations and the way is set for the development of neurosis (Fenichel, 1954c, p. 44). Psychoanalysis accepts the importance of the relationship among personality processes.

Approaches which speak of self-awareness and self-concept assume a personality structure composed of parts in relationship to one another. The person is one part, the self is another, and the awareness or nature of one's concept of the self is an expression of the relationship among these parts. It makes no difference of what the person is aware. Regardless whether the person is aware of the potentialities of his existence, unconscious impulses, the opportunity for choice, or the voice of the superego, there is a person and a self. The concept of personality parts in relationship has a long and distinguished history in the understanding of human beings.

Although acknowledgment can be made of the importance of the relationships among personality parts, what is needed seems to be an explicit articulation of the principles whereby these relationships exert their effects upon human behavior. "We are faced then with the necessity for studying the relationships of all the motivations to each other and we are concomitantly faced with the necessity of giving up the motivational units in isolation if we are to achieve the broad understanding that we seek for" (Maslow, 1970b, p. 24).

Shostrom (1967, p. 54) describes the nature of these relationships as varying along a dimension of goodness of fit, from opposed to complementary. Borrowing this dimension, we can consider two potentials as relating together in a way which is complementary, harmonious, unified, organized, peaceful, loving, accepting. I term this kind of relationship *integrated*. For example, my potential for creative expression (OP1, Figure 2.1) may relate to my potential for dominance and control (OP3, Figure 2.1) in an integrated fashion. This integrated relationship is indicated by the two positive signs in the channel between these two potentials (Figure 2.1). In the same way, there may be *integrated relationships* between my potential for dominance and control (OP5, Figure 2.1) and my deeper potential for hostility and aggression (MP6, Figure 2.1), and also between my potential for hostility and aggression (MP6, Figure 2.1) and my potential for manliness and virility (MP2, Figure 2.1). This means that these pairs of potentials get along well, they relate together harmoniously and peacefully. It means that when I am being dominant and controlling (OP5, Figure 2.1), my deeper potential for hostility and aggression relates to that way of being in an integrated fashion.

When potentials are *disintegrated*, their relationships are fractionated, abrasive, disjunctive, opposed, disorganized. Instead of accepting and loving one another, they fear and hate each other. For example, the relationship between my potential for creative expression (OP1, Figure 2.1) and my potential for manliness and virility (MP2, Figure 2.1) is a disintegrative one. This is indicated by the two negative signs in the channel of the relationships between these two potentials. It means that whenever I begin to experience creative expression, the relationship with the potential for manliness and virility is disjunctive, opposed, disorganized, and even fearful and hateful. Whenever I begin to experience manliness and virility, my potential for creative expression is likewise torn apart, disjunctive, disorganized.

When potentials are disintegratively related, they regard each other as enemies. Under these circumstances, the deeper potential seeks to overcome and destroy the person (operating potential), and the person seeks to fend off and destroy the deeper potential. The person regards the deeper potential as bad; it must be cauterized or kept in place or at least guarded against.

Humanistic theory holds that the nature of the relationships among potentials is the major determinant of problems. A disintegrative relationship among potentials is probably the major factor in the occurrence of bad feelings (Chapter 3), in the occurrence of bodily pain and suffering (Chapter 5), in the construction of a person's unhappy world (Chapter 6) and in the social construction of social problems (Chapter 7). In the description of human behavior (Chapters 8 and 9), human problem behavior (Chapter 10), and infancy and child development (Chapters 13, 14, 15), disintegrative relationships among potentials are held as the key determinant of human problems and pain. Where Freudian psychoanalysis submits that repression of infantile fears and experiences is the ultimate wellspring of neurosis (Wolberg, 1954), our theory turns to the disintegrative relationship among potentials, not merely for "neurosis," but for the whole spectrum of human suffering.

If two potentials are related integratively, they get along with one another. If two potentials are related disintegratively, they have poor relationships with one another. The *nature* of the two potentials makes no difference at all. In Figure 2.1, the potential for love and affection (OP3) and the potential for independence (MP4) are related disintegratively. When I experience love and affection, the potential for independence is aggravated, disjunctive, disorganized. Yet there is nothing about the *nature* of these two potentials which necessitates that state of affairs. It is quite possible that relationships among these two potentials could be integrative. If they were, then my experiencing love and affection (OP3) would be regarded tranquilly by the potential for independence (MP4). Whether or not potentials get along well depends entirely on the nature of their relationships, and *not at all on the nature* of the potentials. Potentials for experiencing whose natures *seem* opposed or logically disjunctive may relate together integratively *or* disintegratively. Thus dominance and submission do not necessarily conflict with one another. Neither do being active and being passive, being outgoing and being pulled in, being sexually attracted to one's own sex and to the "opposite" sex, or any other pair of apparently conflicting potentials. Contemporary theories of conflict tend to assume that such potentials conflict with one another because of their nature. On the assumption that the nature of the potentials (or motivations or drives or behavioral tendencies) causes conflict, Brown (1942, 1948) and Miller (1944) devised a schema of approach-approach, approach-avoidance, and avoidance-avoidance conflicts. But this schema rests on the firm notion that the *nature* of the two potentials causes the nature of the relationships, whereas, in humanistic theory, not only is this proposition rejected, but it is held that the nature of the potentials themselves is *not* a factor in determining the nature of the relationships. If relationships are disintegrative, then potentials for dominance and submission—or any other pair—will be poor and marked with fractionated relationships. If the relationships are integrative, then dominance and submission—or any other pair—will get along smoothly.

The nature of the relationships is a two-way street. Each potential has a feelinged relationship toward its neighbor, one which is either integrative or disintegrative. If you will permit this anthropomorphizing of potentials and their relationships, we may imagine the attitude of the deeper potential for manliness and virility (MP2, Figure 2.1) toward the picture painted by the operating potential for creative expression (OP1, Figure 2.1): "Painting a picture! My God! What kind of a sissy act is that? I'd like to kick it in!" At the same time, the operating motivation for creative expression tends to recoil disintegratively from its deeper potential for manliness and virility: "There. That shows I'm not gross and brusque. Such a sensitive piece of work could never come from someone who is rough and awkward."

Each Potential as its Own Zone of Experiencing

The experiencing of creative expression occurs at operating potential 1 (Figure 2.1), and the experiencing of manliness and virility occurs at mediating potential 2 (Figure 2.1). Each potential constitutes its own zone of experiencing, more or less distinct and independent of the other potentials. It is as if each potential is its own mini-world of experiencing. In this sense, we are indeed multiple selves, multiple consciousnesses, even multiple personalities. Each potential is its own center, its own self system, its own personality. "They are quite independent. Each center has its memory, its own imagination and its own will" (Ouspensky, 1957, p. 8). One may be characterized by a zealous enthusiasm while another is deceptively mendacious. One may be intellectually dull while another is cerebrally sparkling (Mahrer, 1957, 1958; Mahrer & Bernstein, 1959; Mahrer & Thorp, 1959).

The way a person predominantly is may come from one or two operating potentials. She complains about her husband. How he mistreats her, and makes her feel miserable; She is devoted, depressed, nervous at times, wanting to love him. Nearly all of her whole way of being flows out of one or two operating potentials. There is no "solution" to her "problem." The operating potential is the problem. It is a being unhappy with him. Nothing can be done "for" that person even though she asks for help, writhes in anguish, talks about love and having a good family, wants to solve "the problem," cries about it, is thankfully pleased during the brief periods when they get along. Yet, deeper within the larger structure is another person, with quite different experiencing. That person thinks this way: "How bored I am with her. How utterly tiresome she is, on and on for years in that unhappy wailing. She is a most unhappy person. Frankly, I have little sympathy for her and her problems. I have other things I'd like to do." These two personalities are quite different and quite separate. The woman who is the operating potential never knows that deeper self, she never is the deeper self. The two personalities live as if in separate worlds, each in its own zone of experiencing.

Operating potential 1 may therefore be engaged in creative expression. Yet, within its neighbor, operating potential 3, the experiencing of love and affection is going on. We might observe the person in the behavioral process of creative expression—e.g. playing a clarinet, painting a picture, writing a poem. We may not be able to observe potential 3, the potential for love and affection. Yet within potential 3 there is occurring, perhaps right now, the experiencing of love and affection.

My deeper potential for hostility and aggression might well be sensitive to your sarcastic slights to me, while the operating potentials are pristinely unaware. When I shut the door on you, my deeper potential for independence might snicker and "know" what is happening, while my operating potential for love and affection might not even comprehend what is occurring. Two matronly women may be walking home from the grocery store. One glances up at a sunshine-drenched billboard and sees an image of a young girl, nude, legs spread, left hand covering the vaginal area. The older woman's *deeper* potential may be "aware" of that sexual image, while her operating potentials might not be aware at all.

Humanistic theory pictures human beings as composed of multiple selves (potentials), each living in its own world of experiencing. Our picture is quite in accord with Darwin's and McDougall's antirationalism, Bergson's elan, and Freud's unconscious determinism. That is, the wellsprings of experiencing (and consciousness) are typically hidden from other zones of experiencing. Each potential is itself; it knows pitifully little about other potentials; it has its own zone of consciousness and awareness. Each zone is more or less limited to the perimeter of the potential, and extends outward only along its channels of relationships to neighboring potentials. "We may then assert that sound motivational theory cannot possibly afford to neglect the unconscious life" (Maslow, 1970b, p. 22). Regardless of which potential we select, it is described as unconscious of other potentials.

In the psychoanalytic model, the ego and the unconscious ordinarily are unaware of the existence of the other. Translated into our model, a given personality structure may include several "ego potentials" and several "unconscious potentials" as separate systems within the larger universe of the overall personality structure. In no way do relationships radiate from one potential throughout the whole person. Our theory flatly disagrees with the notion that the occurrence of a given motivational state "... has repercussions throughout the whole organism both in its somatic and psychic aspects" (Maslow, 1970, p. 23). The experiencing of creative expression or independence or love has repercussions only within its own perimeter and along its relationships with immediate neighbors.

The psychoanalytic theory of repression is often criticized as requiring some little person within us who is conscious and aware while we ourselves are unconscious. If your sexual overtures toward me are threatening and I am unaware of them, does that not mean that something within me is aware while "I" am unaware? How can a person be both aware and unaware at the same time? Does that not imply some sort of perpetually vigilant homunculus? Humanistic theory is quite vulnerable to these criticisms because it assumes *multiple* homunculi. While one potential is experiencing, another may be also experiencing—but experiencing something quite different.

Psychotherapists know that patients are frequently aware of what they are unaware. That is, when the person in psychotherapy remembers the lost memory or discovers a childhood event or recollects a lost feeling about something, many times the patient will report that somehow, strangely, he knew it all the time (May, 1967, p. 97). It is frequently reported as if the memory or the knowledge were always there, half-sensed. Is this because you knew it earlier and then "repressed" it? Our suggestion is that there is more than one you, or that each potential is a separate you, or that you can be within the domain of each of the potentials which comprise the structure of your personality.

Each potential is the center of its own nearly complete world. When I am any potential, everything swings about me. That is how the sun moves about the earth, it is how the child is truly the center of the world, and it is how we persist in believing that we determine and control our behavior. I agree with White's (1947) citation of this overweening narcissism as a major obstacle to our understanding of behavior.

Conscious self. Yet in all of this, where am "I"? I must be more than a loose collection of potentials bearing relationships to one another. There is a sense of "I am," a sense of self or identity. At any moment, "I" exist within the circumference of the operating potentials. The possible outer limits of my I-ness are indicated by the dotted elipse (Figure 2.1), and this sense of "I" lies somewhere within that elipse.

This model of human beings limits consciousness to my own immediate sense of self. Suppose that you notice my hand tighten and loosen, clench and unclench. That is behavior coming from me, but it is behavior of which I am not conscious or aware. According to our conceptualization, one potential may be in dialogue with you, experiencing some threat as we discuss your negative reaction to the idea I had proposed. That is the operating potential in the region of my consciousness and awareness. Yet it may very well be another (deeper) potential which is clenching and unclenching. That potential is here, immediate, and doing something, though its experience is quite different from mine, for it is experiencing a sense of fight, attack, strength, choke, toughness, hit. While my region of I-ness may include one or two operating potentials, the hand clenching and unclenching may come out of a third potential, perhaps from outside my region of I-ness, beyond the zone of my conscious self.

It is important to distinguish this from the psychoanalytic concept of unconscious determinism. The clenching behavior is an expression of another me, another potential which is right here on the behavioral surface, doing things. To state that this is unconscious means that it is not an expression of the conscious self where I am at the moment. That "unconscious" potential has its own center of consciousness; its existence and its behavior are only unconscious relative to the region of conscious self where "I" am in this immediate moment.

Typically the sense of I-ness is centered in a region which includes the operating potentials. What is outside this region is beyond the consciousness of the sense of "I." From the vantage of this "I," the sense of what may be termed intentionality is beyond consciousness. Holt describes this as follows: ". . . although consciousness is intentional, people are far from being always conscious of these intentions. They do not know why they react as they normally do; they do not know the purposes served by the structures of their consciousness . . ." (1968, p. 244).

That region of conscious self can shift in at least two directions. First it can shift its center from one potential system to another. Thus, when in my dream world, who I am may be potential 6 (Figure 2.1), a being hostile and aggressive. In that world "I" may be a person whose self-consciousness is that of a hostile and aggressive individual. Who and what I am, my self-identity, can thereby take some radical leaps from one potential system to another, jumping out of the skin of one region and into that of another. Consider the transition from being a given person as you *enter* the sleep state and becoming another person *in* the dream state. Your center of I-ness has shifted from one center to a second center. In the waking state the potential for experiencing hostility and aggression (MP6, Figure 2.1) is outside the region of I-ness. In the dream state, however, that potential may be the center of your immediate sense of self. Thus, the person who you are, your consciousness, can shift from one experiential potential to another. Moving in and out of the dream state is merely one example of shifting the center of your being. We have that possibility in our waking state too. Always, every moment, the person who you are *can* move out of one potential for experiencing and into another.

Ordinarily, the center of my I-ness resides within the domain of the operating potentials. This sense of I is relatively stable even though the immediate operating potential may rotate from operating potential 1 to operating potentials 3 and 5. Here is a self with enduringness across three operating potentials which serve as the referent for I. Yet, there are times, although fleeting perhaps, when the sense of I-ness shifts dramatically into one or another of the *deeper* potentials. It is the same *sense* of I-ness, and therein lies the illusion of a single and permanent self. For, even though the *sense* of I-ness remains stable, the nature and site of the I who is speaking are qualitatively new and different. From such a perspective of multiple I's, ". . . the principal mistake we make about ourselves is that we consider ourselves one; we always speak about ourselves as 'I' and we suppose that we refer to the same thing all the time . . . At one moment when I say 'I,' one part of me is speaking, and at another moment when I say 'I,' it is quite another 'I' speaking. We do not know that we have not one 'I,' but many different 'I's, connected with our feelings and desires, and have no controlling 'I.' These 'I's' change all the time; one suppresses another, one replaces another, and all this struggle makes up our inner life" (Ouspensky, 1957, p. 3).

Second, the region of I-ness can dilate or constrict. As indicated in Figure 2.1, the region of I-ness includes operating potentials 1, 3, and 5. Those three operating potentials are included in defining me, in being my identity, my conscious self. When my conscious self goes ever so slightly beyond these operating potentials, it can include some of the disintegrative and integrative feelings which are the relationships between operating and mediating potentials. Thus, the region of I-ness can include some disquieting disintegrative feelings which mark relationships between operating potential 1 and mediating potential 3. On the other hand, the region of I-ness can constrict to include only operating potentials 1 and 3—or nothing at all. There is also the possibility that "I" can expand into being every bit of me, all the potentials which are present within me. That is a possibility of becoming.

Jung likewise sees the conscious self as having the characteristic of expanding and contracting, and also of moving its center. The center can move into what Jung considers a more optimal point between the operating and deeper potentials: ". . . if the unconscious can be recognized as a co-determining quality along with the conscious, and if we can live in such a way that conscious and unconscious, or instinctive demands, are given recognition as far as possible, the center of gravity of the total personality shifts its position. It ceases to be in the ego, which is merely the center of consciousness, and instead is located in a hypothetical point between the conscious and the unconscious, which might be called the self" (Jung, 1962, p. 124).

When Jung speaks of the "center of gravity" of the person being located in a hypothetical point between the ego and the unconscious, I interpret Jung's statements as assuming, at a necessary minimum, at least two separate potentials which occupy the region in which the center exists. In other words, one of the necessary conditions for the sense of self is two separated potentials. Sense of conscious self is essentially a being within a region created by a minimum of two potentials.

When I am nothing more than a constricted region of I-ness, I exist with blinders, living in a myopic, shrunken world. I am aware and conscious of little. You might subtly ridicule me, and I will not be able to grasp that. I might sense a dim glow of what you are doing, perhaps sense that what is happening is alien or outside, but I will not know, and will be confined to shadowy sensings. However, if my conscious self is *dilated*, then I am more fully with you. I am most aware of how you are being. I can grasp what you are. No longer a scrunched-up self, I am now a dilated person whose outer perimeter of what *I* am is enlarged to include more of my potentials.

The outer periphery of what I sense myself to be is indicated by the dotted line (Figure 2.1). When I am being the potential for creative expression (operating potential 1), "I" am located within this dotted zone and sense the love and affection (operating potential 3) and dominance and control (operating potential 5) which are there. The sense of "I"—the center of my self, the center of my consciousness—is within the dotted line, and never fully in the ongoing, functioning operating potential which is behaving and being right now. This I-ness ordinarily shifts from place to place, but always within the dotted line. As far as "I" know, and genuinely believe, there is no more to me than the collection of operating potentials. When I am being creatively expressive (operating potential 1), and I am confronted with love and affection or dominance and control, I can sense those as being parts of me. What I cannot sense, what is genuinely alien, are the deeper potentials beyond the dotted line, beyond the outer periphery of the collection of operating potentials. These I do not know. These are too far beyond me.

It is inconceivable to this "I" that there are deeper potentials for experiencing. Indeed, the ordinary conception of change is limited to the compass of the operating potentials. From the perspective of "I," being fully me, changing, growing, becoming, means no more than being the other operating potentials within me. That is the ultimate. I know no more. I sense nothing further. Beyond is nothing but sheer emptiness and dark nothingness. When I strain to know all that I am and all that I can be, the ordinary outer limit is the periphery of the dotted line (Figure 2.1).

There are, then, at least two meanings of "person." One refers to my conscious self. That is the region of my I-ness, and that might be very small or very large. It is what I sense is me, right now. It is who and what I am. It is the self of which I am conscious, and no more. That center of my consciousness is, as Jung asserts, far from being the center of my whole personality (Jung, 1962; Wheelwright, 1956). Another meaning of me, of who and what I am, includes *all* of my potentials: ". . . the patient's being includes, apart from overtly admitted and accepted modes of behavior, a great many other modes of being, some of which the patient is trying hard not to become aware of, and many of which contrast with the overtly expressed modes" (Boss, 1963, p. 235). The definition of I, me, self, person—this refers both to what is included within the narrower region of I-ness (the dotted lines, Figure 2.1) and also the broader contents of the entire personality structure.

What a strange picture of what we are like! Here are multiple selves living in multiple worlds (Ellenberger, 1958, p. 121). And yet there is a *sense* of I-ness which continues along, perhaps even as "I" move from being one self to another. As Ellenberger says, mainstream theories, especially those of general psychology, argue for a continuing sameness in who I am. Yet, from our perspective, the self can shift from one potential to another, can "be" quite different and even contrasting selves, can live in quite different and even contradictory worlds, and still there is the illusion of continuity. I still am myself through all this. It is one of the grand illusions under which human beings live.

More than an illusion, a bizarre characteristic of human beings is that whatever insignificant portion of the whole personality is the region of I-ness is assumed to be the whole personality. "I" is assumed to be *permanent*, to be *all of me*, and to be something *precious*—to be maintained and defended at all costs. These assumptions are little more than fictitious illusions (Maupin, 1965) which must exist as rock bottom unquestioned truths as long as the sense of I-ness is limited to such an insignificant portion of the larger universe which is my personality.

In describing the plight of modern human beings, May (1958b) speaks of what he terms "compartmentalization." Human beings are segmented, fractionated, compartmentalized in many aspects: into compartments of static mechanisms; into compartments of reason, will, and emotions; into compartments separated from other human beings and the group and the nation state. I picture the personality structure of nearly all persons in terms of these compartments. Each potential constitutes its own compartment, its own mini-world, living out its own existence. Not only is each potential a compartment in this sense, but it is also a compartment in the sense of being predominantly cut off from other compartments so that there are vast moats between compartments, without any compartment knowing about the existence of moats. The region of I-ness is our sense of only one of these compartments, and it is kept separate by our unquestioned acceptance of this compartment as our permanent self, as all of me, and as terribly precious.

Most human beings can be described in terms of conscious self, a sense of I-ness. My impression is that most animals are not aptly described in the same way. To the extent that most animals and most human beings do indeed differ in this way, I am strongly inclined to turn away from either engaging in animal research or paying much attention to the results of animal research. To the extent that human beings can be described profitably in terms of I-ness and conscious self, and animals cannot, animals and human beings differ in significant ways. As will be discussed in subsequent chapters, the sense of I-ness is coupled with the occurrence of bad feelings, many phenomena of the body, many ways in which the human being will construct an external world, much of the explanation of human behavior, the kinds of persons we human beings can become, and the ways in which we develop infants. Thus the difference in I-ness or sense of self is coupled with a larger package of differences.

THE FUNCTIONS OF OPERATING POTENTIALS

Enhancing the Experiencing of Deeper Potentials

One major function of operating potentials is to enhance the experiencing of deeper potentials. In this function, the operating potential serves as the instrumental means whereby the deeper potentials gain experiencing. The operating potential is the avenue of expression for its deeper underlying potential. Suppose that mediating potential 6 (Figure 2.1) is a potential for experiencing hostility and aggression. How can this be experienced? Operating potential 5 (Figure 2.1) might consist of the experiencing of dominance and control, and this may serve as a means of experiencing the deeper potential for hostility and aggression. Thus the experiencing of dominance and control (OP5, Figure 2.1) may serve to enhance the experiencing of the deeper potential for hostility and aggression.

In effect, the operating potential serves as the gateway through which the deeper potential gets out into the world of experience. The operating potential gives the deeper its "here-ness." In this sense, the deeper potential is like the psychoanalytic unconscious; ". . . the unconscious in the strict psychoanalytic sense . . . may point to a being but by no means to an existence. For the latter means a being which is Here and has its Here . . ." (Binswanger, 1958a, p. 326). The operating potential provides that sense of Here for the deeper potential.

Whereas the operating potential gives the deeper potential its "hereness" and serves as its gateway into experiencing, the latter rounds out the meaning of the former. Being creatively expressive (OP1, Figure 2.1) has one meaning if the deeper potential relates to manliness and virility; it acquires a different meaning if its deeper potential relates to being fertile and frugivorous. In effect the deeper potential sets the larger contours for the operating potential. The style of creative expression differs under these two different deeper potentials. Thus the nature of what is deeper rounds out the meaning, gives depth and purposive distinction to the operating potential.

In some ways, the relationship between operating and deeper potentials has been described by the relationship between ego and unconscious. As articulated by psychoanalytic theory, the deeper potential spawned the operating potential, and the latter has the function of serving the former. The operating region of my conscious self is the servant of deeper potentials about which I am not conscious—precisely as in the psychoanalytic paradigm. I am conscious of being and behaving this way or that way. But the conscious "I" which is here and doing all this is a mere servant of an unknown master—the deeper potential of humanistic theory, and the unconscious of psychoanalytic theory.

Feelings of experiencing. When a potential is opened up to experiencing, there are special feelings which occur, bodily sensations (Gendlin, 1962, 1964). The kinds of feelings are given in such words as pleasure, aliveness, excitement, vitality, energy, buoyancy, joy, ecstasy, thrill, exhilaration, giddiness, merriment, happiness, and satisfaction. All it takes is sheer raw experiencing and I have these kinds of feelings. I have the same kinds of feelings whether I experience creative expression, dominance and control, love and affection, hostility and aggression, manliness and virility, independence, or any other potential.

Such good feelings are the feelings of "function-pleasure," as Karl Buhler referred to them—the sheer pleasure of activity-experiencing (Buhler & Massarik, 1968; Murray & Kluckhohn, 1956), and the activity of engagement in and with the world (Schachtel, 1959). Ego psychology also recognizes these pleasurable feelings as epiphenomenal accompaniments to sheer functioning. As articulated by writers such as Kris, Lowenstein, and Hartmann, pleasure occurs in the sheer functioning of the ego, in its doing, in its exploring, moving, remembering, thinking and perceiving. Pleasure resides in the sheer doing itself, rather than in some secondary or derived process such as the gratifying of supposedly deeper libidinous impulses.

Such feelings are epiphenomena which accompany the increased experiencing of any potential, regardless of the content of the potential. Such feelings are devoid of any property of goal direction or intention or purpose (Buytendijk, 1950). Feelings which accompany experiencing are characterized by a non-directiveness, an absence of goal-direction, a lack of intention or aim; they are also characterized by a kind of heightened energy level, an aliveness, vitality, excitement. It is noteworthy that old accounts of the play of children cite these as the two defining characteristics of such play (Schiller, 1873; Spencer, 1873). That is, these writers saw the play of children as the goalless outpouring of a surplus of energy. Although these theories of children's play are no longer fashionable, I suggest that these writers were describing a very special aspect of behavior, viz. the nature of feelings of sheer experiencing. The raw feelings of experiencing which take place when the child is zooming down a slide or throwing a snowball or kicking a can in play can be seen as reflective of excitement, vitality, aliveness, high energy.

It will be noted that these are good feelings, not bad ones. In Figure 2.1 the feelings of experiencing are indicated by the two positive signs within the circle of each potential. Thus the positive or negative signs in the channels between potentials signify the integrative (positive) or disintegrative (negative) nature of the *relationship*, whereas the two positive signs within each potential signify the good feelings of experiencing.

Good feelings of experiencing are the same whether the potential which is being experienced is a pretty one or an ugly one, a socially heralded one or a socially disapproved one. If I am fully experiencing a potential by stalking the streets at night for a solitary elderly person to strangle, or setting the match to the gasoline in the basement of the old tenement, I am filled with the same good feelings of aliveness and excitement as when I fully experience nicer potentials by rescuing a child from drowning, helping a neighbor paint a house, or scoring the winning goal in the key hockey game.

In the same way, these good feelings occur whether relationships with the experienced potential are integrative or disintegrative. If I am being dominant and controlling, there will be good feelings of experiencing (pleasure, aliveness, excitement) whether the neighboring potentials bear an accepting integrative relationship or an avoidant disintegrative relationship. In a very strong sense, these good feelings simply cling to the experiencing of any potential regardless of its nature, regardless of where it sits in the personality, and regardless of how it is regarded by the other potentials.

If deeper potentials have these good feelings of experiencing, and if each potential is its own zone of experiencing, then picture what it would be like if we could listen directly to an experiencing deeper potential. Suppose that the operating potential perceived the deeper one as ugly, slothful obesity, as something to be feared, hated, avoided. What feelings would occur if the deeper potential could experience directly, without gaining its experiencing through the operating potential? I suggest that it would come forth in a way which would be filled with the good feelings of experiencing. "Oh it feels so good to run my hands over this belly and these hips. I'm built big, and my hips are wide—and solid. (Smiles) I'm a lot of woman!" Now that the deeper potential is experiencing, it feels good. It enjoys itself.

The sheer degree of these good feelings is a function of the extent of experiencing. At any one moment, then, the degree of experiencing the good feelings depends upon the degree to which that particular potential is experienced. If sheer experiencing is curtailed, then the person will seldom if ever experience a high degree of these good feelings.

The capacity to surrender. The function of the operating potential is to serve the deeper potential by providing for its experiencing. Yet at any moment, the operating potential can provide for *complete* experiencing by *fully surrendering* to the deeper potential. No longer would the operating potential stand between the deeper potential and the external world. It would be swallowed up by the deeper potential. Instead of dominance and control (OP5, Figure 2.1) serving as a means of enhancing the experiencing of the potential for hostility and aggression (MP6, Figure 2.1), the operating potential would dissolve into the deeper one.

The capacity for choosing to surrender or not to surrender is a characteristic of operating potentials. Each moment that the operating potential acts, it has chosen not to surrender. Indeed, the operating potential might devote an entire lifetime to serving the deeper potential and *never* surrender. But the choice is there from moment to moment. The operating potential cannot escape its freedom to surrender to its "ground," as Binswanger calls it (1958b, p. 225); "Although its history is determined by the themes it has been assigned and on which it works and even though its history consists in having and working out those themes, still its historicity rests upon its attitude toward its 'ground.' Although existence does not lay its own ground itself but takes it over as its being and heritage, it still is left with freedom in relation to the ground."

It is important to define the limits of that to which the person can surrender. Those limits are very narrow: All the person has to surrender to is the deeper potential. Binswanger and Kierkegaard express the same notion, viz. all that one has available to surrender to is that authentic mode of existence, the ground, one's own deeper potential; nothing more is available. Nor is there any force which predetermines whether or not the operating potential will surrender (Binswanger, 1958a; Bugental, 1965, 1968). For better or for worse, the person always owns this capacity.

Reducing the Experiencing of Deeper Potentials.

The second function of the operating potential is to *reduce* the sheer degree of experiencing of the deeper potential. Thus the operating potential acts to dampen, mollify, narrow and avoid what the deeper potential can experience. The sheer presence of the operating potential acts to dilute and reduce this degree of experiencing, so that, in Figure 2.1, operating potentials 1, 3 and 5 act to cut off the potential for experiencing independence (MP4), manliness and virility (MP2), and hostility and aggression (MP6). Thus the operating potential carries out two functions which seem paradoxical—to both enhance and reduce the experieicing of deeper potentials, to provide for their experiencing, but in a diluted manner.

One of the problems in this arrangement is that the sheer presence of the operating potential closes down the likelihood of experiencing the deeper potentials. Homosexuality is a problem when it is the working way of being which, by its very presence, restricts the experiencing of such deeper potentialities as heterosexuality (Ellis, 1959a). By the same logic, heterosexuality as an operating potential is a problem when its presence restricts the experiencing of deeper potentialities such as homosexuality.

Because the operating potential curtails direct expression of the deeper potential, this function can easily culminate in an operating potential which bears a curious polar relationship toward the deeper potential. A deeper potential for experiencing exhibitionism then leads to a polar operating potential for experiencing timidity and inhibition; a deeper potential for uncooperativeness can lead to the development of an operating potential for sweetness and unassertiveness (cf. Levitsky & Perls, 1970). These polarities are designed to dilute the experiencing of the deeper potential.

On the other hand, if the operating potential throws itself too energetically into enhancing the experiencing of the deeper potential, the operating potential could endanger its very existence. It might become swallowed up by the deeper potential. Therefore, in acting to reduce the degree of experiencing of the deeper potential, it is acting to preserve itself. We could even say that the operating potential is protecting its self esteem (McCall, 1968). Thus the two functions of the operating potential could be described as (a) providing for the heightened experiencing of the deeper potential (and endangering its own existence), and (b) truncating the degree of experiencing of the deeper potential (thereby preserving its own existence).

Typically, the operating potential combines its two functions. It provides for the experiencing of the deeper potential, but in a diluted way. By means of dominance and control (OP 5, Figure 2.1), there is some experiencing of the deeper potential for hostility and aggression (MP 6), more than if no avenue into experiencing were present, but less than a direct expression of hostility and aggression. Within a psychoanalytic vocabulary, I am describing the partial expression of unconscious impulses (akin to the function of *enhancing* the experiencing of deeper potentials) which are, at the same time, defended against (akin to the function of *reducing* the experiencing of deeper potentials) (Munroe, 1955, pp. 175-176; Wolberg, 1967, p. 212).

CHANGING THE NATURE OF DEEPER POTENTIALS

The Nature and Structure of Deeper Potentials

Each deeper potential is a potential for experiencing. It is exceedingly difficult to describe the precise nature of that experiencing. The words we use almost always have a valence. They are nice acceptable words or bad nasty words. How may I describe a deeper potential in a way which tells about the nature of that experiencing without falling into some value laden words? I would have to use neutral words, yet I find it very difficult to locate precise descriptive words free of any implied goodness or badness. The basic nature of deeper potentials is neutral, value-free experiencing, almost always described in a good or bad way, as wonderful or hideous, preferred or detested—as if the deeper potential were perceived through a channel which is integrative or disintegrative.

Relationships among potentials: The determinant of invested nature. Relationships among potentials can be integrative or disintegrative. If the relationships are integrative, the operating potential will see the deeper potential as good, acceptable. On the other hand, if relationships are disintegrative, the operating potential will see the deeper potential as bad, something to be feared and hated, dangerous, menacing. Within a psychoanalytic vocabulary, the ego is already predisposed to regard instincts as dangerous under the predisposition that ". . . instinctual excitation is dangerous" (Fenichel, 1954b, p. 19) so that there is a preestablished ". . . fear by the ego of the quantity of its instincts in general, a primary hostility to instinct on the part of the ego" (Fenichel, 1954d, p. 61). Once the relationship is sufficiently disintegrative, the operating potential may draw back from the deeper potential as crazy or "psychotic." It must defend lest the awful "primary process" material erupt. Yet the nature of the deeper potential is *made* awful, crazy, "psychotic" because of the disintegrative relationship which was present.

What is within is *not* bad. Rather, we are afraid and hateful toward our insides, and thereby *make* them bad. Psychoanalysis assumes that what is within ("the unconscious") *is* bad; that is built into the theory. Many approaches call what is within "drives," and invest them with bad characteristics—being implacable and insatiable, stubbornly demanding, wildly raging to get out of control. According to such approaches, the human being ". . . is at bottom a driven or drive-dominated creature, his nature is driven instinctively . . . we deal here with a one-sided distortion of the human image in the form of a scientific theory of man" (Binswanger, 1958c, pp. 315, 328). Such a drive-dominated caricature of human beings derives out of an assumption that our insides are bad—an assumption rejected by humanistic theory.

Once we consider our insides through a relationship which is disintegrative, we can perceive these inner contents as a base pit of culturally opposed wishes, terrible impulses, and awful thoughts (May, 1967, p. 248), as blind cravings which inevitably must be opposed by massive social forces (Asch, 1952). Through the disintegrative relationship we know our insides as monstrous, evil, twisted, demonic, grotesque. Early Egyptians, Hebrews, Chinese and Greeks shared a conception of basically evil forces owning our insides. They must be flogged, exorcized, trephined, to be gotten rid of.

Today we still treat what is within as bad—dangerous, evil, crazy. Therefore, we must defend against what is within, perhaps by imposing controls upon the awful insides. We might even arrange for guarded expression in ways which prevent our insides from their natural bent, for open expression would be interfering and dangerous to one's fellows (Fromm-Reichmann, 1958).

As long as the relationships are disintegrative, what is within *will* be regarded as dangerous and bad. The very goal of defending against what is within *preserves* our insides as dangerous and evil. In this picture, viewed from a psychoanalytic perspective, the ego is ". . . at the mercy of the relentless automaticity of the unconscious pattern . . ." (Saul, 1958, p. 6). The goal is to free the ego from these tyrannical deeper forces. Winning the battle is supposed to defeat the bad inner processes, but the battle itself *preserves* them in their (assumed) awful evilness.

Humanistic theory takes a different stance toward the nature of our deeper personality processes. We describe them as neutral potentials for experiencing. It is the disintegrative or integrative relationship which invests them with their supposed badness or goodness. Human "nature" is conceptualized as neither good nor bad (Asch, 1952; Binswanger, 1958c; May, 1967) in a wholesale rejection of both the doctrine of essential human goodness or essential evilness. The goodness or evilness of human beingness derives out of the integrative or disintegrative relationships among potentials. The fearing and hating of what is within *invest* it with its badness. This is a reversal of the attitude that we fear and hate what is within *because* of its badness.

To go even further, the disintegrative relationship *causes* the deeper potential to take a form which is monstrous and bad. The way (form) in which our insides appear to us is caused by our attitude of fearing and hating them. The attitudinal relationship comes first, and invests the insides with a form which appears to us as grotesque, evil, monstrous, demonic, crazy, twisted. As a consequence, we know our particular deeper potentials as grasping ambition, power strivings, perverse sex, sadism, rage, violence, brutality. The names we have invented for what is within betray our fearful and hateful attitudes toward them.

The form of a deeper potential. Each deeper potential is attributed a *pictorialized behavioral image* which is in accord with the nature of the relationship. Our relationship to what is within causes it to assume some form (Gendlin, 1966, p. 242). What I recoil from is not the intrinsic nature of what is within, but rather the form which is evoked by my own relationship with it (Jung, 1933, p. 17), a pictorialized behavioral image of it. If my relationship to the deeper potential for hostility and aggression is disintegrative, I will picture it as certain *behaviors*—such as murdering, slashing, killing, choking—within defined *situations*—such as murdering my child with a hammer, slashing the throat of an enemy, unbridled killing of innocent people with a machine gun, choking a puppy to death. The *form* of the deeper potential also includes specific thoughts, ideas, or cognitions. If the relationship with the deeper potential for hostility and aggression is disintegrative, its form may include ideas that pushing others around is bad, or the world will stomp all over the nice guy, or if I get too angry I will go beserk. These cognitive ideas are merely a part of the behavioral form taken by the deeper potential under a disintegrative relationship. Yet such cognitive ideas bear the stamp of transcendent truths only insofar as they are made to occur by the disintegrative relationship.

One way of describing the form of a deeper potential is to identify the precise words which express the cognitive idea. A good clinician or a sensitive listener might "hear" a deeper potential "saying": "I must be loved in order to be worth anything at all." All inner cognitions (and thoughts and ideas) are part of the pictorialized behavioral image or form of the deeper potential, and, as such, are distinguishable from the core potential for experiencing.

If I fear and hate my deeper potential for sexuality, I conceive of it in a bad form which is composed of fearful and hateful pictorialized behavioral images. That bad form is *made* awful by the disintegrative relationship. Thus the bad pictorialized behavioral image may be a scene of sexually ravaging a young girl in a dark alley; it may be an idea that there is sexual perversity in me which could erupt into my attacking my older sister; it may include monstrous images of exhibiting my penis to the sexy secretary at work. It is my disintegrative relationship with the deeper potential which causes the fearful and hateful pictorialized behavioral images.

The magnificent difference is between a deeper potential's *potential for experiencing* and the *form* in which you see it. Even in the sheer naming of it, you must distinguish a *description* of the form in which it might appear from the *nature* of the potential for experiencing. Imagine the experience of being light and airy, ephemeral, and without substance. If these words referred to a deeper potential, consider the form in which it can be perceived by an operating potential. If the relationship is integrative, the good form might include ballet dancing, slender and feminine, to a lovely lilting classical strain. If the relationship is disintegrative, then it may be seen in its bad form, e.g., being overlooked by others, being pushed aside as if I were not even there. The form of the deeper potential is quite distinct from the central nature of its experiencing.

The *form* in which a deeper potential is seen is changeable, while the core potential for experiencing remains the same. Whatever pictorialized behavioral image is maintained by the operating potential, it is merely one among many, and is not to be confused with the deeper experiencing itself. Yet most persons see only the form and confidently treat the deeper potential as existing more or less permanently in that form.

I submit that nearly all attempts at describing what exists within ourselves are predominantly descriptions of their bad forms, the pictorialized behavioral images which stand between us and their experiential cores. Almost everyone who has disintegrative misgivings about what he houses within himself sees only the bad form in which it is feared. The very words we use tell us about these awful possibilities and not about the nature of the experiencing itself. Thus we speak of sadism, dependency, homosexuality, homicidal impulses, suicidal tendencies, hostility. We only see bad forms—and bad forms are neither the deeper potential itself nor the good form in which it can occur.

Yet, aside from its immediate specific form, our picture of deeper potentials is one in which the form can stretch all the way from many disintegrated bad forms to many integrated good forms. The breadth is enormous. A potential for experiencing light airiness and unsubstantiality can vary all the way from various bad forms (e.g. being overlooked by others) to various good forms (e.g. a floating ballet step). Because of the breadth of possible forms, our deeper potentials are neither static contents nor fixed entities.

From Bad Form to Good Form

If the deeper potentials are potentials for experiencings—neither intrinsically good nor intrinsically bad—and if they assume their *form* (pictorialized behavioral images) because of the nature of our relationships with them, then *we can change the very form of our deeper potentials*! If a disintegrative relationship calls forth the bad form, the change to an integrative relationship can call forth the good form of that same deeper potential. This can be a profound change in the contents of our personalities. We are able to change the very way in which our deeper potentials exist, their pictorialized behavioral images, the warp and woof of the way they occur in actual, daily life experience. Here is the distinct possibility for a genuine change in the very nature of what we are. One's personality can be altered profoundly, and the key is the qualitative change in the nature of the relationships.

What a power this is! If I choose, I *can* alter my insides! I have the power to change the form from bad to good. The key is the change from a disintegrative fearing and hating to an integrative loving unity with it. Then so much of what can be opens up, like the releasing of effulgent power. That same power to make my insides twisted and crazy by fearing and hating what was within can transform what is within, can change it from bad form to good form.

The change is not in the core nature of the experiencing. That remains unaltered. Instead, the change is in the way it appears to me, in its expressible form, its material flesh and blood. When I fear and hate my insides, I fear and hate their *form*—the awful possibilities within me, the behaviors which lie within me, the terrible thoughts and ideas which are there. All of this is altered when I integrate with them. The miraculous transformation is that of dissolving the evilness with which we drench our insides (Jung, 1933, p. 17), and bringing forth its new and wonderful good form. That good form includes a whole new set of thoughts and ideas and cognitions. There are new inner convictions and beliefs—all comprising the good form of the altered deeper potential.

Suppose that the bad form of a particular deeper potential includes a cognitive notion that I must be the leader in order to be of worth, otherwise I am a worthless nothing. That is my basic premise or life style. It may be one I hate. It may be surrounded with all sorts of bad feelings. That cognitive notion (or basic premise or life style) is only one form—the bad form—of the deeper potential. If it is to exist in its good form, the wellsprings of that good form reside within the person's own deeper potential. Thus humanistic theory objects to disengaging the *person's* cognitive notions (or basic premises or life styles) and replacing them with *your* cognitive notions. We do not aim at "correcting" a person's basic life style by giving him a "better" one (cf. Dreikurs, 1956). Instead, we seek the replacement in the good form of the person's own *integrated* deeper potential—the very same one, incidentally, which gave rise to the bad form.

What is changed is the person's relationship with the deeper potential—and not the cognitive idea which is its bad form. Thus the focus is not on attacking, desensitizing, and replacing an idea that I must be loved in order to be of worth (cf. Ellis, 1959b). That idea, which plagues me from within, is only the bad form of what is deeper. When the process of integration occurs, the bad form slides out of existence, and with it the cognitive notion that I must be loved to be of worth.

Integration does not mean accepting or living with the bad form of the deeper potential. If that appears as a violent temper, the integrative transformation goes beyond accepting it, for the violent temper is only the bad form. If you sense that your deeper potential includes a suicidal tendency, the change does not mean coming to live with that looming possibility. The suicidal tendency is not the way your insides are; it is only their form, their pictorialized behavioral image. So many persons' visions of what they can become are limited to existing with what they now see as the way they "really" are. What pitifully truncated visions! All they know of their insides is the bad form which appears through disintegrative relationships. They have not the slightest hint of what form those same insides can take when they undergo a major shift toward integration. I have seen so many persons whose faint hope from psychotherapy is to learn to live with what they see as a frightening "homosexuality." They enter a whole new world when they become truly integrated with the deeper potential which appeared to them as some sort of vile "homosexuality." Integration is not at all a matter of coming to accept or tolerate one's fear-laden, hate-laden conception of what one's insides are.

Nor is it a matter, as Maslow (1963) says, of moving into a loving acceptance of the humanness of what is inside and, perhaps, seeing one's insides as a beautiful glory. From our perspective, the change is much more audacious. The deeper potentials undergo a radical transformation in their expressible nature, their form.

Before this relationship changes, the person may know "it" as a monstrous homosexuality. He may have vivid pictures of what his inner homosexuality is like, and no hint of what he would be like were that homosexuality converted to a good form. Nor is it possible to stand aside and think about what he would be like if he no longer had to struggle with this terrible homosexuality which has him in its grip. The person cannot get outside himself to see what he would be like if the bad form were changed to the good form. What can the person do who is plagued with an awful inner pool of loneliness? That person can try to consider what he would be like if that loneliness were converted to its good form, but he will fail. He is still an alone person trying to consider a possibility of being something different. Whatever you *think* you will be like is almost undoubtedly an error. In other words, what that deeper potential becomes after integration forever is hidden from our view.

The good form of the deeper potential is *your* good form. When you alter the relationship to one of integration, what emerges as the good form is one which is peaceful and tranquil *to you*, which is at one with you, and which feels right and unified in you. This by no means is a promise that others will like the emerged good form. Your spouse, children, family, friends, neighborhood and society might love the good form. Or they might well recoil from it. It may or may not take the form of rose gardens, filial piety, patriotism, sweetness, affection, understanding—or any other way of being which others (even you, now) might regard as desirable. The good form of your deeper potential might be prized or loathed by society, but it will be that form about which you feel loving and welcoming, and with which you are integrated.

Since all you know of your own deeper potentials is what you see through your own relationships with them, it is difficult to describe changes from bad form to good form. Perhaps it would help if I describe real instances of persons seeking psychotherapy, and the change in form of *their* particular deeper potentials.

One person struggled for years to defend against a deeper potential

which he feared as an all-encompassing irresponsibility and abandonment of commitments. He was driven to behave responsibly, to be
hard working, trustworthy, stable and consistent. Yet he feared
something within, something which he viewed as moving him inexorably toward a slothfulness, a withdrawing of concerns, an inner restless dissatisfaction about which he was becoming most anxious. Following integration, that same deeper potential took on a good form,
with pictorialized behavioral images of owning his own business, having confidence in his own ideas, not engaging in automatic social
dialogue, paying off the long-term financial debt he owed his father.
These were altogether new pictorialized behavioral images which had
never emerged before he became integrated with the deeper potentials. In a strange way he had only dimly sensed the deeper independence, the experiencing of being on his own—even in its form of the
previous irresponsibility, abandoning of commitments, withdrawing of
concerns. Yet the potential is unchanged; only the form changed from
a bad, disintegrative one to a good, integrative one.

Kevin was a young married fellow who was terrified of "impulses"
(by using that word he meant that he had not done "it," but had to
struggle hard against doing "it") to drive to a high density part of the
city and to expose his penis while sitting in the car. Such thoughts had
been there for years and now he was frightened because they were
becoming increasingly compelling. When Kevin finally achieved a relationship of genuine integration with that same deeper potential, he
not only was free of the bad form, but he enjoyed carrying out the
good form in actual behavior: "I used to be so scared. Remember?
Those awful fears of exhibiting myself? Remember? . . . Well I just
never even think like that anymore. But you know what? I love
parading around and so does Ellen. I lie there with a stiff erection,
and she salutes it! (laughs) Yeah! Can you imagine! She salutes it!
What a difference. What a huge huge difference! I love sex! Everything's so different!"

For an older nurse, the bad form of her deeper potential appeared
as monstrous scenes of being sexually mauled, ravaged, raped. She
had struggled since adolescence against these frightening possibilities.
Yet these were only the bad form of the deeper potential, which, following integration, could emerge as welcomed pictorial behavioral images of giving herself fully to the peaks of pleasure, a whole new
spectrum of experiencings which had been tucked away behind the
frightening bad form.

The middle-aged man confessed to terrible worries about being
homosexual. He envisaged awful scenes of being called a queer by acquaintances, being recognized and made sexual overtures to by gay
men, and possibilities of having anal intercourse with overt homosex-

uals. All of these were products of his disintegrative relationships with a deeper potential whose core experiencing involved intimacy and oneness. When he achieved integration with that deeper potential it was as if he had lifted a veil between himself and other men, a veil he had never known was there. For the first time in his life he saw its good form—images of man-to-man closeness and brotherliness, of deep oneness with men, of comradeship and loyalty among men. At its core, the potential for experiencing intimacy and oneness remained; its form was drastically altered.

Boss (1963, pp. 186-208) describes the treatment of a young man struggling against deeper compelling tendencies whose bad form occurred as stalking the streets at night in search of an older woman to strangle. If this was the bad form, what would be the core nature of the deeper potential? Homicidal sadism? Latent homosexuality? Oedipal conflicts? It is easy to jump too quickly from the bad form to some hypothesis about its deeper nature. That is, knowing only how a deeper part looms in a bad and fearsome way, we often make errors in inferring what the deeper part could be like in its good form. In this instance, what emerged as the good form was the fire of strong attachment to a nurturant, motherly woman. This came forth as the good face of the deeper potential—the good face which could show only after the relationship changed to one of integration.

The woman feared and hated what seemed to her to constitute her "maleness." In therapy she cried in agonizing frustration over what she labeled her "penis envy." All through her psychiatric residency training she had believed that she had come to understand and accept that maleness. Yet recently she had nearly given in to brutal impulses toward her baby son, and this opened up a flood of recent memories which now seemed to push in on her as evidence of a looming unresolved "maleness." Under a deepening integrative relationship, that deeper potential revealed itself as the wonderful earthiness of the baby; the having of unfettered temper tantrums, the ease and naturalness of urination and defecation, the openness of grabbing what she wanted. All occurred as the good form of that which she had feared and hated within her as maleness.

A deeper potential can take the bad form of pushiness, controlling, dominance, an uncaring using of others. I draw back from such tendencies within myself, and try hard not to be that way. Yet I sense that is what is within, and I recoil from my propensity for egregious over-assertiveness. What can come forth when my relationship becomes one of integration? Under such a changed relationship the good form contains a forthrightness, a sense of leadership, a dedication to firm action.

When the older man feared and hated what he sensed within, it appeared as monstrous propensities for hostility. The bad form included scenes of carrying out physical violence, heinous acts of cruelty. When he achieved a new state of integration with the deeper potential, he was filled with a whole new passionate energy toward effecting social change. As a judge, he was in a position to champion radical changes in the way young offenders were treated. It was as if the hostility within became transformed into an energetic cracking of barriers. The "breaking through" was only the good (integrative) form of the deeper potential which had presented itself as the feared hostility.

John was a 34-year-old barber struggling against what seemed to be lifelong inner tendencies toward being tossed about by external forces beyond his control, a helpless pawn of the whims of others, a victim of inner passivity and impotence. That was the ineluctable destiny. Yet that was only the bad face of the deeper potential. When he achieved integration, the good face offered itself as a wholly new propensity for being reached, being understandingly empathic, being able to entrust himself dependently onto others, a newfound gentleness. The profound change was in the nature of the form taken by the deeper potential.

The attorney was torn apart by thoughts of becoming lazy, without ambition, being an old man, penniless, a bum. He became increasingly worried by such thoughts. Under an integrated relationship, the deeper potential acquired a wholly new form: being casual and easy going, rising above petty jealousies and ambitions, not falling into fruitless competitions and graspings. What he had feared now sprang forth in its integrative form and took its place as a wholly new way of being.

When the married woman began psychotherapy, she described a life of barricading herself against the threat of loss of security. She dated her troubles from the wrenching divorce of her parents when she was 11 years old. From then on, her life was a constant series of recoilings against the terrible possibility of being abandoned and lost. Each separation was a crisis. To be bereft of love was her personal hell. As the process of therapy continued, the deeper potential now came forth in its good form. This included welcomed and positive pictorialized behavioral images of being intact, self-sufficient, independent, an "emergence from embeddedness" (Schachtel, 1959). This was the good form of that which she had feared and hated for most of her life, and against which she had recoiled in utter catastrophic anxiety. Its form had changed significantly, the form in which it moved toward expression, the form to which she reacted, the form in which she could know it.

Sandra worried about giving in to the inner edge of rigidity. Both her physical body and her daily life were plagued with a tight band of paralysis. It was getting so that she was terrified that soon she would spend her whole life in her bed, rigid and unmoving. Under her lifelong disintegrative relationship, that was the bad form of a deeper potential which became transformed when the relationship was changed to one of integration. What had occurred as the threat of paralytic rigidity became the welcomed inner potential for a stout in-tactness, a being her own person, a willingness to take a given stand, a firm position. At the inner core of the experiencing, nothing was al-tered. But the form taken by the deeper potential underwent a radical transformation.

The family physician, in his early fifties, found himself increasingly in periods of aloneness. The accompanying feelings were gradually worsening until he found himself deeper and deeper in a bottomless pit of racking aloneness. A process of integration finally transformed this bad form of the potential. Under the integrated good form, he now could *be* alone in a wholly new mode. As he described it, a screen seemed to have lifted between himself and the world. He had never even suspected the screen had been there. His new aloneness gave him the gift of seeing what was around him. He saw colors for almost the first time. He listened to music which had become vivid to him. His aloneness was now a fertile oasis where before it had been a cof-fin. As described by Moustakas (1961), the new aloneness came forth as a way of being which offers its own new experiencings.

The young man confessed to a sense of anxiety whenever he caught himself sucking his thumb. Beginning one evening at dinner when he licked gravy off his thumb, that silly act occurred repeatedly in secret, surrounded by embarrassment and rising anxiety. By now he was ex-tremely upset about that behavior, not so much as an act in itself, but somehow what it meant to him. Early in his psychotherapy he found increasing inner tendencies of a persistent babyness. Basically, he sob-bed, he was just a very little boy who might be "found out." In the course of psychotherapy, this disintegrative bad form of the potential converted into a naive curiosity, a capacity for being surprised, an eager freshness for living, a delight in the simple—and a rediscovery of the world of innocent sexuality: touchings, suckings, smellings, see-ings, caressings. When he feared and hated that deeper potential, it was thereby called forth in a bad form; its way of being was trans-formed by his coming into an integrative relationship with it.

When the husband brought his wife to psychotherapy, she was a drawn woman, frail and emaciated. As she revealed the inner life, a picture emerged of a battle against a terrifying possibility of bloated obesity. This loomed as the devilish essence of ugliness, the enemy against which she was continuously struggling. When the fearing and hating of the deeper potential were converted to an integrative loving and assimilative fusion, the pictorialized behavioral images took the radical new form of ripeness, fertility, motherliness. The old bad form was gone, and with it the driven struggles against falling into being that bad form.

3

Bad Feelings

The purpose of this chapter is to answer the first of the seven questions set forth in the first chapter: How may I describe and understand bad feelings? How may I describe and understand such bad feelings as being scared or terribly gloomy or mixed up or anxious? Two major categories of bad feelings are presented. The first is labeled "disintegrative feelings," and the second has the inelegant title of "unfeeling."

DISINTEGRATIVE FEELINGS

Some bad feelings share the following characteristics: (a) They include a sense of being in pieces, fractionated, incomplete, disjointed. This feeling state is the opposite of being an organized whole, of being unified, of oneness and being internally together. (b) They include a sense of one's parts being at war, in turmoil, fighting, torn apart. This is the opposite of a feeling of internal peace, tranquility, harmony, positive self-regard, self-acceptance. Not only is the person broken into parts, but these parts are set against one another. (c) Bad feelings come in such kinds as anxiety, threat, tension, dread, fear; helplessness, smallness, pawnness; shame, guilt, self-punishment; separation, alienation, aloneness; meaninglessness, hollowness; depression, gloom; bodily pains and distresses; and hostility and anger. These feelings are termed *disintegrative feelings*, and are indicated by the negative signs in the channel of the relationships between potentials (Figures 2.1, 3.1).

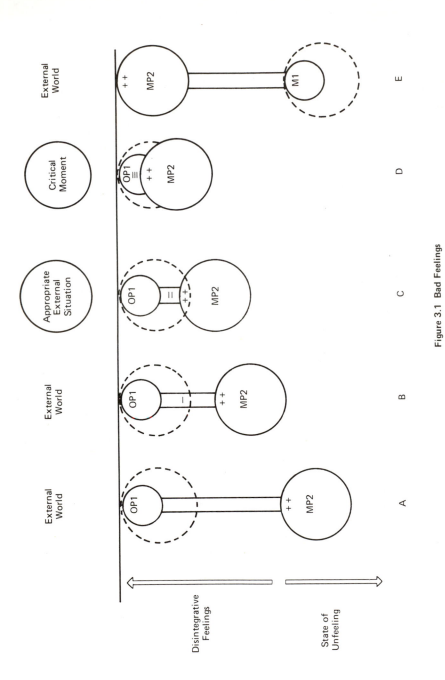

Figure 3.1 Bad Feelings

Disintegrative Feelings vs. Behaviors vs. Potentials for Experiencing

Humanistic theory distinguishes between a feeling, a behavior, and a potential. It is unfortunate that we so often use the same word to mean all three. In our system, they mean quite different things. Feelings include certain kinds of felt bodily sensations (Gendlin, 1962). For example, we can speak about a *feeling* of anxiety which refers to certain kinds of felt bodily sensations—perhaps a hot hollowness in the stomach, a tense sensation of the musculature, a bodily felt apprehension, clutching up, tension. On the other hand, we can speak of anxious *behaviors* such as shaking, breathing hard, perspiring, running this way and that, fidgety and restless movements, a quivering voice, and perhaps even saying that one is anxious. The bodily felt *feeling* of anxiety is to be differentiated sharply from anxious *behaviors*.

We draw a distinction between depressed *behaviors* (e.g. sitting and walking dejectedly, a gloomy facial expression, sitting lifelessly with a vacant stare on one's face, saying how very depressed one is, a heavy monotonous voice quality) and a *feeling* of depression (e.g., that felt bodily sensation of being pulled in and down, saturnine gloom, an awful bodily felt heaviness). In the same way that a feeling is to be differentiated from a behavior, a feeling must also be differentiated from a potential. For example, a *feeling* of anger can refer to defineable felt bodily sensations; angry *behaviors* can refer to having a ferocious visage, screaming profanities in a fury, pushing another individual in wrath, attacking another individual while in a rage. We can also describe anger as a *potential* for experiencing. Thus, a person may be described as having a potential for experiencing anger, and this potential may be linked to various kinds of behaviors and accompanied with various kinds of feelings.

Potentials are continuously at work carrying out functions. But feelings are different. They accompany what the rest of the personality does, while having little or no responsibilities themselves. Unlike potentials or behaviors, feelings cannot be described as having any properties like intentionality, purpose, drive or wish (Buytendijk, 1950). A feeling is not a potential is not a behavior. The non-intentionality of feelings applies to any kind of feeling: to disintegrative feelings, to integrative feelings, to feelings attendant to sheer experiencing. Bodily felt feelings are not goal-directed; they are not toward something or some state; there is no purpose or aim to their occurrence.

Feelings refer only to the immediately ongoing bodily sensations. These are to be distinguished from *words about* feelings. For example, the person may be saying, "I feel angry," and those words may or may not be accompanied with feelings of anger. The verbal content of the words is not the same as the bodily felt feelings. The person who says that he feels angry may be actually experiencing quite different bodily sensations—trembling anxiety, dead depression, or perhaps even fear. Fenichel (1953a) describes a woman who expresses a pervasive sense of doubt. Yet the bad feeling is not one of doubt. Although she speaks *about* doubt, Fenichel identifies the key feelings as those of helplessness, depression, and fear. These are the bodily felt feelings which occur as she talks about that doubt which will plague her the rest of her life, and from which she can never escape. The sensitive clinician or research investigator must draw a careful distinction between the actual, ongoing, bodily felt feelings and the content of the verbal behavior. I refer to the failure to make the proper distinction as the *content error*, i.e. confusing the manifest content, the words themselves, with the actual ongoing bodily felt feelings.

A certain amount of conceptual confusion is cleared away by describing feelings in terms of bodily felt feelings and physical sensations. Our definition of feelings, for example, would not allow for a search for the differences between specific anxiety and generalized or pervasive anxiety. The words "specific" and "generalized or pervasive" refer to the *external situation* and not to the nature of the bodily felt event. Thus we are talking about the *situation* in which the *feeling* of anxiety occurs, one being a specific one (e.g. on top of a tall building) and the other a general one. Or, the distinction between specific and generalized anxiety could refer to behaviors and not to feelings. Once you extend the feeling of anxiety to include the nature of the situation (specific or generalized), or once you equate the feeling of anxiety with specific or generalized behaviors, you can begin looking for all sorts of factors which account for the difference between "specific" and "generalized" or "pervasive" anxiety (cf. Wolpe, 1958). In humanistic theory, the feeling is the feeling, a bodily felt event, and not to be confused with behavior or various situational contexts in which the feeling occurs.

There can be various couplings between, for example, angry feelings, angry behavior, and anger as a potential. I can *feel* angry while experiencing a potential other than anger—e.g., competition or sexuality. I can *feel* angry while carrying out a behavior which is not angry behavior—such as riding my bicycle or reading a book. I can also feel angry while I am carrying out angry behavior under a potential for experiencing anger. Cattell and Scheier (Cattell, 1963; Cattell & Scheier, 1958, 1961), on the other hand, conclude from their research that anxiety is more or less a single package, with anxious behavior as its outside face and anxious feelings as its inside face. But from the perspective of humanistic theory there is no *necessary* relationship between what we term anxiety as a feeling and as a behavior. I can distinguish anxious feelings as occurring *without* the presence of anxious behavior (such as body trembling or fidgety movements). I can distinguish anxious behavior occurring *without* an accompanying feeling of anxiety (such as a sense of inner apprehension or that hot hollow feeling in the region of the stomach). Thus I find it most helpful to distinguish between the feeling, the behavior, and the potential—even though our common vocabulary often uses the same word for all three.

Older theories of emotions postulated a necessary linkage between the emotion and its instinct. Thus James, McDougall, Shand, and Driver all adhered to a position that, for example, the emotion of anger corresponded to the instinct of pugnacity (Burt, 1955). Such a position is not at all that of humanistic theory, in which a clear distinction is drawn between feelings, behaviors, and potentials—with no necessary correspondences among them. Indeed, the failure to draw clear distinctions among feelings, behavior, and potentials partly explains why it is that we have so many different "theories" of anxiety (Fischer, 1970; Levitt, 1967), anger (Buss, 1961), and depression (Beck, 1967). I am strongly inclined to hypothesize that much of the differences reflect a failure to distinguish feelings, behaviors, and potentials so that some theories of anxiety (or depression or anger) focus on anxiety as a feeling, others on anxiety as a potential, and others on anxiety as a class of behaviors.

It seems that there is a gloomy scientific future for a word which refers to a behavior, a feeling, and a potential. Such a word is on its way into the scientific trash bin. A word such as "depression," for example, comes at the scientific theoretician and researcher from so many places, with such evanescent diversity and bewildering overlap, that it is exceedingly difficult to keep the sorting process organized (cf. Wittenborn, 1965). Humanistic theory seeks to dismiss such words and to adopt a vocabulary which cleanly differentiates between feeling, behavior and potential.

NECESSARY AND SUFFICIENT CONDITIONS FOR DISINTEGRATIVE FEELINGS

What are the necessary and sufficient conditions under which there will occur bad feelings which (a) include that sense of being disorganized and in pieces, (b) include that sense of one's parts being set against one another, and (c) are referred to by words such as anxiety, threat, tension, dread, fear; helplessness, smallness, pawnness; shame, guilt, self-punishment; separation, alienation, aloneness; meaninglessness, hollowness; depression, gloom; bodily pains and distresses; and hostility and anger? There are three conditions which we hold as necessary and sufficient. That is, when these three conditions are present, disintegrative feelings will occur.

1. Disintegrative Relationships Between Potentials

In order for bad feelings to occur, the relationship between potentials must *already* be disintegrative, with elements of fearfulness, hatred and distrust. It is disjunctive and fractionated, disorganized and menacing. This disintegrative relationship is indicated by the negative signs in the channel of the relationship between operating potential 1 and mediating potential 2 (Figure 3.1).

Ann was a 27-year-old teacher. Her operating potential (OP1, Figure 3.1) consisted of shy sweetness. As this operating potential, Ann was already apprehensive (that is, bore a disintegrative relationship) toward a deeper potential for experiencing vibrant sexuality. Under this disintegrative relationship, the bad form of this deeper potential loomed as scenes of vile lewdness, sexual dirtiness, and cheap lust. She feared and hated what seemed to her to be a hidden possibility of ugly carnality (MP2, Figure 3.1). Here is the disintegrative relationship necessary for Ann to have painfully bad feelings.

When the nature of the relationships is mildly disintegrative, the operating potential does not *feel* that disintegrative relationship. This state is indicated in stage B (Figure 3.1), in which the nature of the relationship is mildly disintegrative (indicated by the single negative sign in the channel of the relationships), but the deeper potential is so far down that the person barely senses any bad disintegrative feeling. The shy sweet Ann (OP1, Figure 3.1) is hardly aware of any bad feelings in relation to the deeper potential for ugly carnality (MP2). Yet one of the conditions is fulfilled, viz. the existence of disintegrative relations.

Some existential theorists assert that human beings carry about an irreducible, residual pocket of bad feelings, generally those of anxiety and guilt. These feelings are simply there, and it is difficult to explain their basis. Perhaps we know that we have deeper, unrealized potentialities, and the fact of not fulfilling these potentialities accounts for a sense of guilt (May, 1967, p. 107). I suspect that the *sheer presence* of a disintegrative relationship accounts for what existential writers describe as these irreducible residual pockets of bad feelings. The sheer disintegrative relationship means that the operating potential is engaged in fighting what is deeper, blockading it, resisting its expression. What existentialists describe as residual bad feelings is understood from our perspective as the ever present disintegrative relationship between potentials.

2. Appropriate External Situation

In order to have bad feelings, the person *must be in an external situation which can provide for the experiencing of the deeper potential.* How did such an appropriate external situation occur with regard to Ann's deeper potential for ugly carnality? In order for her bad feelings to occur, she must be in some situation which offers a reasonably good opportunity for the experiencing of that toward which she bears a disintegrative relationship. It happened at a party attended by five or six young married couples and a few single women. Ann found herself talking with two husbands, and sensed a mutual attractiveness. From the general external world in which Ann lived (stage B, Figure 3.1), that kind of interaction with those particular men in the context of the party evolved into an appropriate external situation (stage C, Figure 3.1). The second of the necessary and sufficient conditions was now in motion. She was now in a situation which was devilishly appropriate for her to experience what lies within. I cannot agree with Goldstein's (1939) description of the right situation as one which is *inadequate* for the "organism's pursuit of self-actualization." According to Goldstein, bad feelings such as anxiety require a situation which does *not* allow the organism to unfold its deeper possibilities. In contrast, humanistic theory holds that the right situation is one which *provides* for the experiencing of what is deeper in the personality—as long as what is deeper is characterized by disintegrative relationships.

In Chapter 6 we will discuss how the person can be an *active participant* in the *construction* of such appropriate external situations. At this point, we must be content with describing the appropriate external situation as merely a necessary condition for the occurrence of bad feelings. Sometimes the person actively constructs these appropriate situations, and sometimes the appropriate external situation more or less presents itself to the person. For example, the college student with disintegrative relations toward a deeper homosexuality is presented with an appropriate external situation when he is sitting on the toilet and the man in the adjoining stall slides him a note inviting him to a "party" that evening. On the other hand, there are times when it is clear that the person has worked hard to construct the appropriate external situation. The devout husband with disintegrative relationships toward a deeper potential for adultery can actively construct an appropriate external situation by making sexual overtures to the attractive girl in the office and secretly arranging a weekend trip together. Nevertheless, even when the appropriate external situation presents itself to the person, its occurrence is the product of organized, directed work. The person is continually at work, fashioning such appropriate situations. Even though the person will feel frustrated or torn apart or terribly depressed in a given situation, the situation has itself been more or less constructed by the person.

Such appropriate external situations are *necessary* but not *sufficient* for the occurrence of bad feelings (Boss, 1963, p. 20). Without an appropriate external situation the bad feeling cannot occur. But by itself, the appropriate external situation cannot bring about the bad feeling (Goldstein, 1951). Yet, as one of the conditions, the bad feeling will not occur unless the person is engaged in the appropriate situational context (Goldstein, 1963). Research and clinical anecdotes seem to imply that the right external situation *is* sufficient to bring about bad feelings. Bad feelings of inner disturbance and restlessness are described as occurring in mental hospital patients when there is a change in ward personnel (Caudill, Redlich, Gilmore & Brody, 1952); a bad feeling of depression occurs when the situation forces the person to know that infantile paradise can never be recaptured (Arieti, 1962); a bad feeling of bodily pain may occur when the external situation makes the person fatigued and emotionally stressed (Alexander, 1950). Hundreds of investigations are taken as confirming evidence of direct causal linkages between the external situation and the occurrence of bad feelings. But such research does not explain how the situation is linked with bad feelings in some persons and not in others, nor does such research uncover the mechanisms whereby the situation is linked systematically with the occurrence of the bad feelings.

When we identify that a woman is anxious when she is alone in a closed elevator, we are defining only one condition—the nature of the appropriate situation. We have not yet specified the other conditions which must occur for the anxiety to take place. Our approach is in contrast to one in which the anxiety is held as bonded to the situation alone (rather than merely occurring in the situation as one of the necessary and sufficient conditions). Wolpe (1958), for example, conceptualizes the anxiety as conditioned to external stimulus configurations so that the paramount actors in the drama include only the anxiety response and the external anxiety cues to which the anxiety responses are conditioned. From our perspective, the external cues (the situational context) are merely one necessary but highly insufficient condition for the occurrence of anxiety.

The past: neither necessary nor sufficient. In order for a bad feeling to occur, the person (a) must bear a disintegrative relationship with a deeper potential and (b) must be in an appropriate external situation which allows for the experiencing of that potential. For these two conditions, the past occurrence of that appropriate external situation is neither necessary nor sufficient.

There are advantages to be gained from an uncovering of past situations in which the bad feeling occurred. One advantage is to identify dramatic earlier appropriate external situations in which the bad feeling was more intense and in which the deeper potential came much closer to open experiencing. It would be helpful, for example, to know that the most intense bad feeling with regard to Ann's deeper potential for ugly carnality occurred when she was 14 years old and she was taking a nap with her stepfather who proceeded to stimulate her and pressured her to masturbate him. During that situation, her deeper potential was even more intensely experienced than during the party situation. We can search the past for external situations which were *more* appropriate, but the history of past situations is neither instrumental to the present disintegrative relations nor to the presence of the immediate appropriate external situation.

When I go with the person into the details of a present appropriate external situation, we are nearly always led to an earlier situation. It is as if the present appropriate situation were a package containing earlier appropriate situations. Entering with Ann into the details of the present party situation opened the door to the situation which had occurred when she was 14. I prize those earlier situations as therapeutically invaluable when they exceed the present one in appropriateness—that is, when the intensity of feeling was even stronger, and when the earlier situation was even more cordial for the experiencing of the deeper potential. Even in the initial occurrence of the bad feelings in an earlier situation, the relationship among potentials was *already* disintegrative, and that initial situation must have contained the appropriate constituents. Thus the initial situations can be exceedingly valuable for therapeutic purposes, but they are not *required* for the occurrence of the present bad feeling.

Even in the initial early occurrence of the bad feeling, the situation must have been appropriate for the experiencing of the disintegrative deeper potential. To identify a bad feeling as occurring in some earlier situation is to beg the question: What were the conditions which accounted for its occurrence even in the first situation? We may trace the initial occurrence of Ann's anxiety back to that situation when she was 14 years old, or find an earlier one when she was 10, 6 or 4 years old. Yet, whenever the bad feeling first occurred, the situational context must have been appropriate to the experiencing of her deeper potential.

3. Rise of Deeper Potential

The third condition is the rising of the deeper potential. It comes closer to the person, closer to the possibility of experiencing. When operating and mediating potentials are related disintegratively, and when the person is in an external situation appropriate for the experiencing of the deeper potential, the *problem* resides within, not out in the external situation. Indeed, the problem is that the deeper potential is beginning to rise toward heightened experiencing. In stage C (Figure 3.1), mediating potential 2 is now high enough that the person can just begin to experience it. If the person is ordinarily a jokester with his girl friend, and, in this particular situation, is unable to be funny, does the problem reside out there in the nature of the external situation? No, the locus of the "problem" is a rising deeper potential which is saying, "I've had enough of being the jokester! Now I am ready to talk to her straight, to meet directly with her, person to person!" Nor is the problem the bad *feeling* itself. If a young woman is finding herself tense and much less attentive to her mother's slightest overtures, is the tense feeling or the diminishing attentiveness the problem? No, the problem lies in the rising deeper potential which is voicing the following: "It's time that we both had lives of our own. You are *some* daughter! You have made your mother into an invalid with your suffocating over-attentiveness. You must free her and yourself too!" In the appropriate external situation, the disintegratively fended off deeper potential has begun to rise (stage C, Figure 3.1), and *this* constitutes the problem—rather than the bad *feeling* itself or the external *situation*.

When Ann was at the party talking with the attentive husbands, the situation was appropriate for an increase in the experiencing of her deeper sexual potential. This deeper potential was not brought into *intense* experiencing. She was not *flooded* with sexual experiencing. But there was some measure of an experiential opening up of this deeper potential. In Figure 3.1, this change is indicated by the reduced distance between the deeper potential (MP2) and the external world (stage C).

The middle aged, Spanish-American father is waiting on the street for the bus to take him home. Work is over and he is tired and looking forward to wine and evening talk with his wife who is waiting for him to come home. When the bosomy prostitute approaches, she whispers the ancient invitation and runs her fingers lightly over his cheek. With this act, in this appropriate external situation, there is a rise of his deeper potential for sexual experiencing and transgression. Such an upward movement (from stage B to stage C, Figure 3.1) is just what the deeper potential wants. Existential writers describe this as "... some possibility opening up, some potentiality crying to be 'born' ..." (May, 1958b, p. 52). As far as the deeper potential is concerned, this change is a desirable one. But when we shift to the perspective of the person (the operating potential), what is starting to occur is very ominous indeed. Within a psychoanalytic vocabulary, the dangerous instinctual force is verging toward the ego (Freud, 1936, p. 18).

As long as the relationship is disintegrative, the deeper potential can be of any nature. It is not the rising up of any particular inner tendencies which account for our bad feelings. As long as I bear a disintegrative relationship with it, and as long as I begin to experience it, I will have bad feelings. It is an error to elevate to a universal characteristic of human beings some special kind of human quality about which many of us can feel awful. For example, at one time or another many of us might have bad feelings as we come to experience the possibility of our inevitable death. By the same token, we might feel terrible about experiencing failure, impotence, physical ailment, old age, or loneliness. It is, I believe, an error to describe all human beings as vulnerable to all of that as a kind of unhappy fateful "humanness." I do not consider, for example, loneliness as some inevitable, inescapable condition of human life (cf. Moustakas, 1961). It is neither necessary nor universal. I see loneliness as a particular potentiality for experiencing, found in some persons and not necessarily in all persons, and, like any other potential, capable of being accompanied with bad feelings under the right conditions.

The person is now confronted with some ominous possibilities:

Radical intrusion of the deeper potential. In Figure 2.1, the domain of the operating potentials is signified by a dotted elipse. Within this domain lies the sense of I-ness. What is outside this domain (e.g. the mediating potentials) is not a part of my self or my personhood. What lies within this domain is my I-ness, my self, my personhood. Although the center of this I-ness may move about, it stays within the perimeter of this domain. In Figure 3.1, this domain is signified by the dotted circle encompassing the operating potential. The dotted circle signifies the perimeter of my I-ness, my sense of self, my personhood.

If the upward movement of the deeper potential continues, it will enter into the domain of the operating potential. As far as the person is concerned, that upward movement signals the end of his existence. His very self will undergo a wrenching change. It will be eclipsed and radically altered. I am faced with the utterly real imminence of nothingness and nonbeing (Goldstein, 1939). Jungian analytical psychology, existentialism, and Daseinsanalysis are especially eloquent in describing the monstrous terror of the imminent dissolving away of what I am (Boss, 1963; May, 1958a; Wheelwright, 1956).

A part of this awfulness is that my basic convictions about the world, life, and myself are murdered. They are simply overpowered and no longer mean anything at all. Every last shred of the way I made sense of the world is torn away. My "world design" is virtually cracked (Binswanger, 1958a, p. 204). My mother will be there to love me—that conviction is wrenched to pieces. I am basically a decent person—but now that image is shattered. One must be fair; research is necessary to science; some persons are evil. My whole way of making sense of the world passes away as the operating potential is radically intruded into by the rising deeper potential.

The possibility of such a radical intrusion is a crucial component of the existential emphasis upon one's confrontation with death, for the continued rise of the deeper potential can mean the very death of the person's heart. It surely will collapse. The intrusion of the deeper potential at worst will kill the person himself, and at the least will mean his radical transformation as the deeper potential overwhelms him. This state is indicated in stage D (Figure 3.1), in which the operating potential is already invaded and its existence is in the process of being eclipsed. When Ann is invaded by the rising mediating potential for sexuality, the beginning of the end is near for Ann as sweetness and shyness. The shy, sweet operating person will be wrenchingly transformed or dissolved out of existence. Its very life will come to a close.

It is difficult to comprehend that the operating potential is correct in its worst fears. The intrusion of the deeper potential *does* mean its end. What I am will die and never be any more. The world design will crack asunder. The shell which is me will be broken into pieces, and all the king's horses and all the king's men will not be able to put me together again. Worse than being broken, worse than being a fractured person, I simply will be gone. Never more will I be. So the person's absolute fears are grounded in hard reality.

Now we can describe more of what the disintegrative feeling is. We undergo disintegrative feelings when the deeper potential is moving into us and ending our very existence. The bad feeling is the wail we emit at that point when we sense the closing off of our existence. In Figure 3.1, the operating potential is safe from the deeper potential in stage B. However, in stage C, the deeper potential is coming closer, and *that* signals the beginning of the closing off of existence; the two negative signs in stage C indicate the increase in bad feelings. The increase to three negative signs in stage D means that the operating potential is now having intense bad feelings as its domain is invaded, its nature is being dissolved away, and its existence coming to a certain end.

Behavioral expression of the bad form. Ann's shy sweet self had more or less successfully avoided the feared and hated deeper potential. She may have dimly sensed what it was like, but she never really saw it up close. Now the bad form of that ugly carnality is right against her, is shoving at her in a way which can hardly be avoided. Here is that against which the person has been struggling. She does not want to know the deeper part. She certainly does not want to see it. Yet here it is, up so very close. As indicated in stage D (Figure 3.1), the deeper potential is shoving itself right up against the bowels of the person, who is confronted with every ugly detail of that which she struggled to avoid and fend off!

There are enormous differences between the nature of the deeper potential from the perspective of the person and from the perspective of a concerned observer such as a parent or psychotherapist. From the perspective of an outside observer, the deeper part is frequently described as a repressed impulse, some rising inner tendency. The person is observed as coping with "sexual impulses," "hostility," "sibling rivalry," "latent homosexual impulses," "aggression." Such descriptions ordinarily carry the subtle flavor of animal-ness, of arcane wickedness and excitement. The person is coping with impulses which would be sheer delight in a world of utter freedom and abandonment. The external observer can appreciate this parameter of the rising deeper potential far more than the poor wretch who is undergoing the experiencing. Furthermore, the observer ordinarily describes these wicked impulses in terms that fall far short of the specificity and concreteness which they hold for the person. To the person, sexual impulses take the form of exquisite detail. One may be unaffected by "sexual or aggressive impulses," but go right to pieces when confronted with the deeper potential in its concretely specific behavioral form.

In concrete specificity, the terrible behaviors which constitute the bad form of the deeper potential are now close enough actually to come forth! The very imminent possibility is that behavioral expressions of Ann's cheap and vile lewdness, sexual dirtiness, and monstrous lust will now burst forth. That pictorialized behavioral image might include slow tantalizing pelvic movements, a look of sexual abandon, and inviting whisperings to the husbands. Bad feelings occur when the deeper potential rises to that point where it is on the verge of behavioral happening. That is the point when what we have avoided within ourselves is now pressing into experiencing (Fenichel, 1954d; Gendlin, 1964, p. 16) as specific behaviors. A moment ago the Spanish-American father was standing at the intersection waiting for a bus. Now the deeper potential for sexual experiencing and transgression is on the verge of behavioral expression: returning the lascivious glance of the prostitute, asking her where to go and how much she charges for various services, walking away with her, going to her bed. In this moment, the bad form of the deeper potential is going to happen. The person *is* going to do it! Disintegrative feelings are the expression of the shy, sweet Ann (OP1, Figure 3.1) as it knows she is about to behave in a sexual way by moving her pelvis slowly and tantalizingly, exuding a look of sexual abandonment, and letting the husbands know how much she craves them sexually.

Pleasurable experiencing of the deeper potential. As described in Chapter 2, the sheer experiencing of a potential is accompanied with feelings of pleasure, aliveness, excitement, vitality, buoyancy, joy, ecstasy, thrill, exhilaration, happiness and satisfaction. These good feelings are indicated by the two positive signs within the circle of the deeper potential (MP2, Figure 3.1). As the deeper potential rises closer, the person is presented with the looming possibility of experiencing these good feelings. Indeed, a point is reached (stage D, Figure 3.1), in which the person *is* feeling the pleasure attached to the experiencing of the deeper potential.

When Ann is chatting with the husbands at the party, the shy, sweet Ann (OP1, stage D, Figure 3.1) is presented from below with feelings of pleasure as the deeper potential for sexuality crowds into her. There is the good feeling of aliveness, excitement, vitality, buoyancy, joy, a thrilling exhilarating happiness and satisfaction of raw sexual experiencing. All of these good feelings are actually starting to fill shy, sweet Ann.

At least as far back as the fifteenth century, a distinction was drawn between being seized willingly or unwillingly by the devil. Under this sagacious distinction, the person is acknowledged as having some degree of choice. Either the person resists the devil or willingly submits. In either condition the devil possesses the person. Borrowing this medieval notion, the person who bears a disintegrative relationship with the deeper potential is always the unwilling victim. While the person does experience the devilish pleasure, she always resists submitting willingly to its enjoyment. Thus the shy, sweet Ann recoils disintegratively from the intruding deeper sexuality and its accompanying inner, devilish, pleasurable feelings.

The net effect is that the person struggles against the good feelings of pleasure, joy, aliveness, exictement. As Fenichel describes this in a patient, ". . . the anxiety was experienced not as a fear of punishment, but as a fear of excitement, as an incapacity to allow the excitation to proceed further" (1954d, p. 58). Stated more carefully, the person will avoid the feelings of pleasure accompanying the experiencing of the deeper potential when (a) there are disintegrative relationships between the person and the deeper potential, and (b) the deeper potential has risen sufficiently high in an appropriate external situation. Stated more bluntly, persons tend to *avoid* pleasure! Quite the reverse of the pleasure-*seeking* which is axiomatic in most of our theories of personality!

When these good feelings are experienced under such conditions, we can speak of surreptitious inner pleasure, covert excitement, wicked thrills, evil joy, arcane exhilaration, devilish happiness, and demonic hidden satisfaction. This is the desire to become that which we dread (Kierkegaard, 1944). We are undergoing the good feelings of experiencing, but we dare not let them happen fully. The deeper potential is filled with these good feelings, but the person does not join in. As a result, the feelings are hidden and covert, even from oneself, and they are then wicked and arcane, not welcomed or fully experienced. The person is being invaded by a new I, a new person who is the rising deeper potential. To surrender to this invading person is to experience the deeper potential and its attendant good feelings of joy, pleasure, and the like. It is this state which Kierkegaard describes as the desire for what is dreaded, as a kind of fascination with what is looming up from within, an inability to tear one's self away from that which lays hold, a fearing of what is desired (1944). As long as the two personhoods are separate, the I who I am right now does not know what it is like to be the other deeper I. But when the deeper potential is right here, that other I is claiming hold of me, and that other I loves and enjoys itself, exhilarates and revels in being what it is. This is the state in which I and the invading I exist.

During those special moments when I have a rising up of bad feelings, during those instances when I am filled with tension or despair or fright or agony, there are lambent tongues of these good feelings of experiencing. Look for them. Search around and underneath the bad feeling; you will always discover a hidden delight, a joy, an arcane feeling of utter aliveness and excitement. All of this is available to the person who minutely examines the moments when bad feelings occur.

Mother is in the kitchen when she hears her baby cry. The deeper potential wishes to avoid the baby. Don't hasten to him. Let him cry. Ignore that demanding thing. For just a moment that deeper potential begins to have its way, and there is a sense of giddy excitement. To neutralize such good feelings and prevent their occurrence, the mother *feels bad instead*. She suddenly feels tense and frustrated. She feels bad in place of feeling pleasure!

The young woman liked him, even considered living with him. They were alone in her small apartment when something strange came over him. He wrestled her to the floor and seemed to turn into a sexual animal. Good feelings started to present themselves to her, marvelous new feelings of delirious thrill, as he manhandled her and set himself upon her. The moment these good feelings of raw inner experiencing started to press toward her, she was filled with a disintegrative mixture of loathing and terror. Such disintegrative feelings constituted a defensive mask on the verging good feelings, and occurred *instead of* the rising good feelings of thrilling excitement.

In all of this, the person ("I") is nestled within the domain of the self. Indeed, the occurrence of the bad feelings requires that the person remain within the perimeter of the circle encompassing the operating potential (Figure 3.1). Once the person moves from the domain of the operating potential and enters into the deeper part, disintegrative feelings cannot occur. Instead, the person will undergo the good feelings of sheer experiencing. Paradoxical as it sounds, the occurrence of these bad feelings requires that the person must cling to being who he is, within the domain of his present self.

The Critical Moment

There is always a final moment in which the person must carry out one of two options. Either the person succumbs to or resists the rising deeper potential. If he resists, then the radical intrusion of the deeper potential will mean that the person's existence will be ended. If he surrenders, it means the actual behavioral expression of the bad form of the deeper potential, the behaviors feared and hated by the person. If he surrenders, he will be filled with the good feelings of experiencing—the pleasure, joy, ecstasy, and excitement. I term this the *critical moment* (stage D, Figure 3.1).

Critical moments are brief, usually very brief. They last perhaps as long as a second. In that brief critical moment, the deeper potential is right on the very brink of bursting into experience. The slightest movement toward surrender, and it will eclipse the operating potential, the feared and hated behavior will happen, and the good feelings of experiencing will explode into the person.

During this critical moment, I know that my very life is in real danger of ending, that I must fight to the death against letting the awful behavior happen, and must somehow insure that the good feelings of experiencing do not mushroom. On the other hand, the other, deeper "I" is coming alive, smells the possibility of actual experiencing, is rushing headlong into being. The net result is that "I" am on both sides of this struggle (May, 1967, p. 276). I am torn apart, at war with myself. In this critical moment the decision is made as to whom "I" shall be.

For Ann, a critical moment occurred when she and the husbands were conversing. There was a moment when she was acutely aware of their sexual sensing of her body. They were not talking in that moment, yet all were caught in the sexual envelopment. Ann was looking rather frankly into the eyes of one of the men, yet sensing the heavy gaze of the other. In this moment of shared sexual silence, Ann's body swayed almost imperceptibly toward the men. The look on her face was almost not her look, but rather the expression of the sexual satisfaction in the silent acknowledgement of their attraction for one another. Yet nothing was said. Inside, Ann's body was filled to the brim with two sets of feelings: the wonderful feelings of experiencing—the pleasure and aliveness of experiencing the deeper sexuality; and the disintegrative feelings of risen anxiety. This was a critical moment for Ann.

While the young woman was having tea with her newfound female acquaintance, her invalid mother was sitting upstairs in the bedroom. The daughter was chatting with her friend when mother pounded twice with the cane. At the sound of the pounding, the daughter put down the tea pot and excused herself, arising to inquire what her mother wanted. The event was mild and over in an instant. But it was a critical moment. What had attracted the acquaintance to the daughter was the air of quiet inward resignation. They met at the bookstore where the daughter worked part-time. For just a (critical) moment, that quiet resignation was shattered by the rising of a deeper potential for freedom and independence, shattered by the sound of mother's pounding cane. In that instant a jaw muscle tightened almost imperceptibly; her heart pounded in resonant response to the pounding of the cane; her eyes hardened for a flicker. That was all that showed. Yet within, and over in a critical moment, the daughter was suddenly invaded by a feeling of excitement, her usual quiet resignation was almost exploded away, and an oath nearly escaped ("Damn you. Leave me alone!"). All of this occurs in critical moments which come and pass within an instant.

Identifying these critical moments requires carefully detailed investigation. That evening the daughter complained of strong feelings of depression filled with a kind of restless aggressiveness. She knew it began in the afternoon, perhaps while she was having tea with her friend. Only through incisive probing into the precise moment was she able to locate that instant when the critical moment took place. Whether the critical moment is a fleeting upsurge of mild bad feeling or the peak of catastrophic crisis, the identification is an act of deftly systematic precision.

Determinants of bad feelings are internal, not external. Now that we have isolated the critical moment, we can look for the locus of the threat. That is, when I have a bad feeling, is the threat internal or external? Is it the external situation which houses the threat? If I feel anxious or fearful or alienated or depressed or angry, is it not about something in the external situation? According to humanistic theory, there are three ways of describing the threat. First, the person is having a bad feeling about the radical intrusion of the deeper potential; the very existence of the operating person is coming to a close. This is internal, not external. Second, the person is terribly concerned that the feared and hated bad form of the deeper part is going to happen;

very specific behaviors will erupt out of the person. This, too, is an internal state of affairs. Third, the bad feelings occur in place of the looming good feelings of experiencing; in effect, the bad feelings occur instead of the good feelings. This, too, is internal, not external.

In our theory, the direct and immediate causes of bad feelings are always internal. These internal variables can construct something in the *external* situation, and our bad feelings *require* that in order to occur, but the causes lie within. In contrast, for example, learning theories understand the person as a reactor to what is external, with bad feelings as responses to external stimuli (e.g., Shoben, 1949).

Suppose that an external examiner or experimenter tells you words and asks you to associate to them, or uses a tachistoscope to flash words or objects or scenes, and asks you to identify what has been flashed. It seems likely that you might take longer (or distort to a greater extent) those external presentations which are threatening to you. How may this be understood? From our perspective, it is the deeper part which recognizes the threatening word (or object or scene). The rising up of the deeper potential (toward seeing it or saying it) leads to the above three threats. To avoid these threats the person does *not* see the scene or object clearly, does *not* think of the nasty association. In general, these steps would likely require more time than responding to external presentations which are not threatening to you. In each case, the locus of the threat is internal, not external, within the person, not in the external situation.

This is our way for accounting for what has been described as perceptual defense, repression, security operations, and other terms indicating that the person somehow is aware and is not aware of the threat which seems to exist out there. Some theorists have argued against the notion of a person both perceiving and not perceiving, as if the person contained some inner homunculus which sees what is out there, while the person himself is largely unaware (Gendlin, 1964). Our theory is precisely that. Under these conditions, the deeper homunculus *does* see accurately, while the person does not. Recall a recent critical moment in which you experienced the rising up of bad feelings. In that moment, you wanted to pull back from the threat, to not see it clearly, to make it vague and cloudy. In precisely the same way, you will freeze the external critical situation, be unable to see in lapidary detail what is happening out there. You will be unable to take in all that is there in its detailed entirety. You will see through a kind of haze, a cloudy pulling away. But the deeper homunculus will see in concrete pinpoint detail what you do not and cannot.

When a person has a bad feeling, the locus of the bad state of affairs is *internal*. The appropriate *external* situation only offers the proper conditions for the rising up of the deeper potential. This point seems innocent enough until we come to implications which can be perplexing. I would like to give two examples of the implications which follow from this point.

Since the threat is internal, the external situation can no longer be treated as if *it* housed the threat. *I* house the threat. All the external situation can do is offer the appropriate conditions for the internal play to begin. You cannot cause me to have bad feelings; only the particular state of my insides can cause me to have bad feelings. Miller and Dollard (1941) classify some *situations* as dangerous; but from our perspective, the danger lies *within*. All the situation can provide are the conditions appropriate for the occurrence of the internal danger. It is the internal state which is anxious, fearful, oppressive, stressing, depressing. In no way is the external situation to be labelled as anxious, fearful, oppressive, stressing, depressing; it only provides the proper conditions for the rising deeper potential, and *that internal state of affairs* causes the bad feelings. The determinants of my bad feelings are internal, not within the external situation.

Social roles do not and cannot cause internal conflict. Due to sociocultural evolution, it is said, the roles of wife and mother are becoming increasingly conflict-laden, especially since the wife is also supposed to be educated, intelligent, informed, and vocationally capable (e.g. Leighton & Hughes, 1961). Conflict is held as residing in the *social roles*. I reject such an approach and propose, instead, that the bad feelings of conflict reside *in the person*, not in the roles. These specific social roles, together with the "conflict" between them, constitute no more than portions of an appropriate situational context, and are not at all included in the internal state of affairs which causes the bad feeling (e.g. conflict).

There is a second implication which flies in the face of the way we usually think, and, unfortunately, the way we usually behave. Disintegrative feelings are brought about because of the changes occurring within the person with the bad feelings—and not some other person who is part of the external situation. The person with the bad feelings is the one housing the immediate causes of that bad feeling. When the little boy in the back row is fidgeting and the teacher experiences the bad feeling of frustrated anger, the little boy is part of the appropriate external situation, while the immediate causes of the teacher's bad feeling lie stoutly within her. Where is the problem? Within the little boy or within the teacher? From our perspective, the immediately determining factors lie within the person with the bad feelings, and *not* in the external situation. What this means is that the *problem* (that is, the cause of the bad feelings in the teacher) is *not* the little boy and his fidgeting. If the teacher is free of the little boy's fidgeting, the situation is no longer appropriate and the bad feelings would be alleviated. Stated somewhat more bluntly, this means that the person with the bad feelings is the one who houses the problem. Changing the external situation relieves the bad feelings but leaves unchanged the direct immediate causes of the bad feelings, for these reside within the person with the bad feelings.

From this vantage point, what a colossal error it is to seek changes in some other person when *I* have bad feelings! When the teacher tells the school psychologist about the little boy's "problem," it is the *teacher* who houses the problem, not the little boy. When you and I get ourselves into an argument, and I am distressingly annoyed, I am the one to change, not you. When the mother is disturbed by her child's aggressiveness, it is the mother who houses the problem. When my wife's failure to understand me makes me unhappy, changes ought to occur in me. When the nurse is angered by the patient's demandingness, it is the nurse who has the internal problem. When father is upset by his adolescent son's language, it is the father who is ready for change. In each instance, if the other person is made to change, I will not have bad feelings because the appropriate external situation has been disrupted. But the immediate causes of my disintegrative feelings still lie within me, not within you.

Dollard and Miller (1950) tell us about parental reaction to the child's masturbating. The anxiety, they say, resides in the parent, not in the child. Where is the sexual conflict? According to Dollard and Miller the sexual conflict resides in the parents, and not in the child. While the child is busily masturbating, it is the parents' own sexual conflict which accounts for the anxiety—in the parent, not in the behaving child. Since the determinants of bad feelings are internal (that is, lie within the parents) and not external (how frequently the child is identified as the "problem"!), the road to change lies in the *parent*, not in the child.

Critical moment: a unit of study has personality change. I look upon critical moments as wonderful possibilities. Some deeper potential is coming alive. It means that you can bring into experiencing some new potential within you. And it means that you have the chance to come to know and understand something new within you. During these critical moments your deeper potentials are moving close enough for you to view what potentialities lie within you (Mahrer, 1971a). You can almost touch your own inner potentialities (cf. Figure 3.1, stage D). You are close enough to smell it, touch it, feel it, and even experience a bit of what it is like. For purposes of knowing what we are like, the critical moment is invaluable because the deeper potentials are close to the surface, and most available for grasping.

Because the person and deeper potentials are in such close proximity during the critical moment, it is as if the person is charged up, is

in a state of tension, is exceedingly open and vigilant to the encroaching potential. Maslow describes this as a strange kind of unity
(1970), a state in which one knows what one is. You are a person with
a deeper craziness. It is there, and you will or will not be that craziness, but now you know it is there. "Every kind of emotional moment,
emotional shock, makes you realize 'I am.' You realize it without any
theory behind it: if you find yourself in a very unexpected place, you
have a feeling of 'I' and 'here'; when you are in unusual circumstances
it always reminds you of your existence" (Ouspensky, 1957, p. 114).
During these critical moments you have the opportunity to experience
the more or less specific contours of your very personhood in a very
strange kind of unity with the immediate parts of your self. What is
included within the dotted elipse (Figure 2.1) comes into explicit illumination during these critical moments.

On the other hand, the glorification of critical moments flies in the
face of the person who is in the throes of it all. When I am in the
midst of being utterly depressed or scared or torn apart, that is precisely what is going on. I am all depression or fright or being torn
apart. It is from the vantage point of some *other* person that these
moments are regarded as wonderful possibilities. That other person
might be a far off part of my own personality or it might be someone
else, such as my friend or therapist or lover. Yet such moments are at
one and the same time, from different vantage points, moments of
awful feelings and moments of wonderful possibility.

One kind of awful feeling is that of utter boredom where everything turns stale and pale and meaningless. To the person, the critical
moment is saturated with awfulness, yet such moments hold the precious possibility of significant personality change. These are the moments ". . . when goals and projects turn stale; when money can no
longer buy anything that the person wants; when the fame that was
once the person's glory has turned to ashes; and when the love of that
woman, long pursued, is now experienced as cloying, suffocating pos-
sessiveness. The lack of fulfillment when long enjoyed goals are
achieved signifies, however indirectly, that *our personal being* has
changed, unnoticed by us . . . The boredom signifies the imminence of
growth. The time is ripe for the experience of new goals, and new
unfoldings of our being . . . We may undergo this new experience (if
we let it happen) in delight, or in the terrifying realization that we are
going out of our minds . . . When we meet impasses and failure in the
pursuit of our projects, then our habits, concepts . . . and expectations
are challenged, or upended. Failure of our projects gives us a whiff of
the stink of chaos, and this can be terrifying . . . I am also ready to
grow when I experience boredom, despair, depression, and anxiety"
(Jourard, 1968, pp. 155, 165, 166). Here are critical moments, pos-

sibilities of change, when the bad feelings betray the utter imminence of the exploding deeper potentials.

Existentialists tell us that the way out of one's problems lies buried in the very heart of the difficulties themselves. "Neurosis is an adjustment activity which has within it the creative potential of the individual that must in one way or another be shifted to the constructive goals in his process of overcoming his problems . . . the neurosis has within it the potentialities which we hope will be called forth . . ." (May, 1967, p. 95). How do we illuminate these deeper emerging potentialities? Under what conditions can we best see the contours of these deeper possibilities? I suggest that during these critical moments the deeper possibilities are straining closest to expression, and the doorway to the "neurosis" is the critical moment. This is the moment in which we are divided, and sense this division into various parts, or selves, or "I's": ". . . when we begin to divide ourselves and know that at every moment it is only one 'I' or one group of 'I's' speaking, then we are nearly to self-consciousness, nearer to objective facts" (Ouspensky, 1957, p. 106), nearer to the way out of the problems.

Consider what it would be like if the critical moment could be frozen. If this moment were held, the person could disengage from being the operating potential and could step inside the rising deeper part. Ann, the shy sweet self, would be able to step inside the deeper potential for sexuality, and be filled with the experiencing of sexuality. In the actual critical moment, she was on the very edge of being sexual, but did not take that next plunging step. Now, in the safety of the frozen critical moment, she has the opportunity to go forth with the sexual experiencing—and thereby to know intimately that which she has avoided with fear and hatred. In that moment Ann has the opportunity to let the throbbing in her breasts happen, to engage the eyes of the men and let her sexual longing pour forth. She can reach forward and run her fingers down the chests of the men, exuding her sexual wantonness. No longer drawing back from a shadowy cloud of sexuality, she becomes engulfed in the exact behaviors which constitute the bad form of that deeper potential. Only then can Ann see the deeper potential right here, up close—and relate to the specific reality of what that sexuality is. Now she can see the sexuality for what it is—very specific ways of behaving in that critical moment, and the wonderful pleasurable feelings attached to it. Here it is up close and exact, and she can relate to what it really is in that critical moment.

How often do you have such critical moments? For many persons little critical moments occur five or ten times a day. Unfortunately, there are many persons for whom critical moments are rare. Perhaps once every day or so their deeper potentials rise up enough for them to have even a mild thrust of feeling. In order to use critical moments, we must develop systematic ways of identifying them the instant they occur. I foresee the development of hardware attached to our bodies, sensitive to the heightened physical experiencings which occur as we enter into critical moments. We must find ways of recording these moments so that later they can be utilized for effective personality change. It is important to devise ways in which we will be able systematically to identify critical moments as they occur. These critical moments are entry points into personality change.

Psychoanalysis counts upon a fully blown "transference neurosis" to reveal the deeper personality processes of the person (Bergman, 1949). In the peak of a transference neurosis, the analysand is filled with the burgeoning inner personality processes. I consider critical moments as the larger category which includes not only the peak moments of a transference neurosis, but all those moments when the deeper processes are filling the person to the brim. Some of these critical moments occur in the therapeutic relationship; others happen when the person crosses the street or merely talks with a friend.

I suspect that one avenue toward progress in psychotherapy is the systematic analysis of the critical moments when something therapeutically special occurs. Here are the instants, the important five to ten seconds, when feelings are high and personality-behavior change seems to be most within reach. Progress in psychotherapy will occur by going deeper and deeper into the parameters of these turning points. Practically no use has been made of this method. A notable exception is that of Rogers (1970, p. 128), who listened diligently to therapy tapes in an effort to probe into these "moments of movement," as he refers to them. I strongly urge psychotherapy investigators to utilize these moments of movement as data, to subject these moments to intensive and systematic analysis. Something is occurring in these moments. We have a need to know what is happening.

For purposes of personality change, the key is this precious instant. All of the possibilities last but a moment. Ouspensky (1957) describes both this momentary nature and a special kind of critical moment as necessary for personal change: " . . . when we begin to awake we realize the state in which we are in now. It is necessary to find moments of self-remembering and then, at these moments, you will see the difference" (p. 106). Ouspensky has a special meaning to moments of self-remembering, but shares our precious valuing of the momentary nature of events which open the door to one's process of change.

In the investigation of psychotherapy, one of the desiderata is a reasonable, definable unit of study. "Meaningful units require a proper definition of a critical event, and ways of determining the beginning and ending of such an event" (Leary & Gill, 1959, p. 76). I propose that the critical event is our critical moment, and that the definition of the critical moment serves as the definition of the meaningful unit of study in investigations of psychotherapy. When we are able to offer rigorous definitions of those moments when feelings are high, we shall have provided one unit of study for the systematic investigation of psychotherapy.

Beyond the field of psychotherapy, critical moments can serve as the unit for a systematic study of personality and personality change. The identification, analysis, and investigation of critical moments can provide the unit of investigation in such areas as family systems, small group processes, peer relations, creative thinking, problem solving, organizational development, and others. Indeed, the study of critical moments is proposed as one component of the phenomenological method of investigation (Buytendijk, 1950). Consider a young man who is bothered by his tendency to dress secretly in female garments. With our unit of study as the critical moment, we are interested in the description of the precise moment when the feeling is high. We expect that a study of his critical moments will open up what is important for our description and understanding. Suppose we may find that the feeling rises high when, having secretly dressed himself in female garments, he reaches orgiastic heights through masturbating while in a favorite fantasy of being seduced by his father. That person is enormously different from the fellow who reaches the height of feeling when he is on the verge of successfully stealing an item of women's clothing from a store. The salient differences lie in the nature of the emerging deeper potential. In the first instance, it may consist of incestuous seduction, while in the second it may consist of aggressively taking that which has been denied him. In any sense, this approach to the unit of study (i.e. the critical moment) is quite different from one in which the very general, vague class of behaviors (transvestism) is predefined as a syndrome having some sort of symbolic meaning or meanings. Thus, for example, Fenichel (1954a) organizes an entity called "transvestism," and identifies its core as the twofold meaning: being seen and admired for one's penis, and being seen and admired as a beautiful girl. To adopt the critical moment as a unit of investigation is to open the way for new conceptualizations of behavior.

Crisis. Each critical moment is a mini-crisis. In its own quiet way, every upsurge of disintegrative feeling carries with it all the characteristics of an actual miniature crisis. When a wife goes to pieces as she watches the plane explode with her husband and three children inside, when the adolescent girl sees her father pounding her mother into insensibility, the same three conditions are necessary and sufficient: (a) There must be disintegrative relations between the operating and deeper potentials. (b) The person must be in an appropriate external situation. (c) The deeper potential must rise up toward actual occurrence, bringing with it the imminence of radical transformation or death of the person, the imminent actual behavioral expression of the rising deeper potential, and the "having" of the good feelings of experiencing attendant to the deeper potential. All of this occurs in each critical moment, and also in every crisis situation.

What, then, are the differences? A crisis is a critical moment in which the disintegrative relations between the operating and deeper potentials are of major proportions. In Figure 3.1, the disintegrative relationships are such that in the critical moment (stage D), they reach a moderate height, indicated by the three negative signs. If the disintegrative relations were such that the critical moment included six negative signs, the person would be in a crisis. The number of negative signs is not so very important; what *is* important is that a moderately disintegrative relationship will not evolve into a crisis situation, whereas a highly disintegrative relationship can lead to a crisis. From this consideration, we can begin predicting what sorts of crises are available for you and for me. Neither Harry nor Brian had ever been in an out-and-out physical fight with another adult. Both were in their twenties. Both bore disintegrative relations toward deeper potentials for experiencing physical aggression. But for Harry the disintegrative relation was enormous, while for Brian the relationship was only moderately disintegrative. When the three necessary and sufficient conditions occurred for both men, Harry was plunged into the throes of the greatest crisis in his life, and Brian was involved in a moderately strong critical moment. Harry collapsed in a quivering mass and plunged deeply into a profound depressed withdrawal; Brian avoided the fight by talking his way out, and was thoroughly disgusted with himself.

Except for the difference in sheer degree of disintegrative relationships, the crisis is merely a kind of critical moment. From this perspective, crises are golden possibilities for significant personality change (Forer, 1963). In the heavy preponderance of crises, these opportunities are bypassed in the effort to reduce the massive distress of the disintegrative relationships. Yet the possibilities are there in every instance of crisis.

THE CONTENT OF DISINTEGRATIVE FEELINGS

So far we have been discussing disintegrative feelings in general. Now we turn to specific disintegrative feelings. Sometimes I feel anxiety, and not anger or depression. At other times I feel guilt, and not anxiety or anger or depression. How may we describe the occurrence of a disintegrative feeling of one content rather than another? We

turn now to some common disintegrative feelings, and to some of the
features which distinguish each. The purpose is to illustrate how some
specific disintegrative feelings can be described and distinguished in
terms of the three conditions proposed above. The purpose is not an
exhaustive analysis of every kind of disintegrative feeling.

Anxiety

As one disintegrative feeling, anxiety occurs when the three necessary and sufficient conditions are present. But certain features of
these three conditions lead to anxiety rather than to any of the other
kinds of disintegrative feelings.

Radical intrusion of the deeper potential. Anxiety is the common feeling
which occurs when the deeper potential intrudes into the domain of
the operating potential to such a point that the person is in imminent
danger of being radically transformed or eclipsed. "Anxiety occurs at
the point where some emerging potentiality or possibility faces the individual, some possibility of fulfilling his existence; but this very possibility involves the destroying of present security, which thereupon
gives rise to the tendency to deny the new potentiality" (May, 1958b,
p. 52). One's whole world view is threatened with collapse. "Heideg-
ger's answer is that Dasein is anxious in the face of the collapse of its
world, the gradual dissolution into insignificance of the totality of its
involvements. Dasein is anxious in the face of the meaninglessness of
its activities and understandings . . . Those ways in which Dasein had
previously grasped itself, even taken itself for granted, no longer
make sense" (Fischer, 1970, p. 95). The very foundation of the way I
make sense of my world is on the verge of shattering; my "world-de-
sign" is being basically disrupted (Binswanger, 1958a, p. 204).

There is a point where the deeper potential has risen so far that it
is offering the person the most serious proposition to carry out the
action, be it, experience it. This is the point at which I know, with a
newfound certainty, that I *can* do it, I can carry it out, I can surrender into experiencing it, I have that choice and that freedom to be it
(Kierkegaard, 1944). And with that ominous realization comes the certainty that to be the deeper potential means no longer being what I
am. The ultimatum is either to face destruction of the foundation of
my personhood or to surrender into the being of the intruding
deeper potential. In either instance, not only I am seized by the alien
deeper potential, but it is about to dissolve away my very existence,
and I feel dread and catastrophic anxiety about that. "For dread is the
inevitable result only when the existence has 'at bottom' become prey
to or been seized by that of which it is afraid" (Binswanger, 1958c, p.
287). When that happens I know that my existence *is* ended, I will

never return, never again return, never wake up. This is the meaning of a radically intrusive deeper potential, and the anxiety to which it leads.

Appropriate external situation. One of the three necessary and sufficient conditions for the occurrence of any disintegrative feeling is an appropriate external situation. Anxiety is the concrete disintegrative feeling when the external situation is of two kinds. First, the external situation leads to anxiety to the extent that what is occurring externally reflects point by point what is occurring internally. The deeper potential is pressing in, overpowering me. In the same way, the external situation is appropriate for anxiety when it too is pressing in and overpowering me. The deeper potential is going to harm me, and I try to pull back away from it; in the same way, the kind of external situation which links up with anxiety contains imminent harm, and the person tends to move back and away from the impending situation (Miller & Dollard, 1941). The external situation is appropriate for anxiety when it is isomorphic with the internal situation.

It is common for anxiety to occur in an external situation in which the person is being overpowered, inundated, overwhelmed. Indeed, for many psychoanalytic writers, the paradigm of anxiety includes the newborn infant confronted with an environment supercharged with an overabundance of stimuli, far too much for the undeveloped newborn's nervous system to handle (Greenacre, 1952). The neonate simply cannot cope with the inundation of excitations (Fenichel, 1954d; Freud, 1936). A situation is appropriate for anxiety when it does to the person what the deeper potential does to the person, viz. when both the external and the internal are radically intruding, forcing a collapse, on the verge of overwhelming, too much to handle. In other words, the appropriate external situation is one which is an isomorphic externalization of what is happening internally.

Greenacre, Fenichel, and Freud identify birth as the ultimate origin of anxiety. From our perspective, birth is not the origin of anxiety at all, but the way birth is *described* by psychoanalysts *is* important, for it identifies salient characteristics of anxiety. I do not regard the basic cause of anxiety as the undeveloped neonate suddenly bombarded with an overabundance of inundating external stimuli, far in excess of the capacity of its nervous system. On the other hand, I do regard one condition for anxiety to be an appropriate external situation described along the same lines as psychoanalysts describe the external world faced by the neonate.

This same characteristic of an external situation, appropriate for the occurrence of anxiety, is described yet another way in many approaches. Anxiety occurs when there is excessive external *stress and pressure* on the person. This is merely another set of words to describe what the rising deeper potential is doing to the person. The radical intrusion into the heart of the operating potential, and its imminent breakdown and dissolution constitute stress and pressure. In a mirror image of this *internal* state of affairs, the appropriate *external* situation likewise is characterized by excessive stress and pressure. Thus anxiety is regularly observed as an accompaniment of an external situation which is stressing and pressuring, and the result is stuttering (Freud, 1953b), headache (Friedman et al., 1954), or any of a myriad of expressions of heightened inner anxiety. Under all these circumstances, that external stress and pressure are a mirror image of the internal stress and pressure exerted by the rising deeper potential.

One kind of appropriate external situation does to the person what the deeper potential is doing to the person, i.e., exerting stress and pressure, being overpowering, inundating. A second kind of appropriate external situation compellingly invites experiencing of the deeper potential. If the deeper potential relates to the experiencing of physical violence, the situation is appropriate to the extent to which it pulls for that particular kind of experiencing. If the situation is ripe for actions of physical violence, then the external situation *is* an appropriate one.

Nature of deeper potentials. The disintegrative feeling will tend to be that of anxiety when the rising deeper potential involves (a) a concerted muscular bodily act, (b) helpless dependency, or (c) independence (Mahrer, 1972b). Although these are by no means the only deeper potentials whose intrusions lead to anxiety, they are proposed as rather common ones, accounting for the preponderance of anxiety, and reasonably supported by research and clinical analysis.

In his clinical study of the roots of anxiety, Freud (1936) typically found a charged up physical body, with increased muscular tension, bunched up and on the verge of a concerted physical act. "We cannot long escape noting a relationship which inhibition bears to anxiety. Many inhibitions are obvious renunciations of function, because the exercise of the function would give rise to the anxiety" (p. 12). Concerted muscular bodily acts include screamings, bodily wrenchings, physical attacks, violent encounters, acts of physical defiance, muscular explosions. When the person feels anxious, one likelihood is that the rising deeper potential involves some concerted muscular bodily act. There is some research support here. Thus such cardiovascular changes as elevated blood pressure and heart palpitations are understood as components of the rising deeper potential *about which* the person is anxious, and not as a component of the anxious feeling itself (cf. Gunn, 1962).

A second deeper potential, often underlying the feeling of anxiety, is that of experiencing helpless dependency. It is as if the person senses being on the verge of sheer helplessness, powerlessness, limpness, fecklessness, dependence, weakness. Freud (1936, pp. 76-77) also uncovered this helpless dependency at the foundation of cases of anxiety so frequently that it can be named as a second common deeper potential whose upward rise leads to anxiety.

A third deeper potential is what Fenichel (1954d), Freud (1936), and Schachtel (1959) describe as the sense of being abandoned, lost, separated, bereft of love and basic security. From the perspective of humanistic theory, these psychoanalytic writers are describing the bad form of a deeper potential for intactness, self-sufficiency, independence, or "emergence from embeddedness" (Schachtel, 1959). When such a deeper potential intrudes, the person experiences anxiety. Clearly, there are other deeper potentials whose heightening leads to anxiety, but these three seem to be especially common.

Fear

Fear and anxiety are brought about by the same three necessary and sufficient conditions. What, then, can we understand as the differences between conditions leading to anxiety and those leading to fear?

Appropriate external situation. The disintegrative feeling of fear requires that (a) the external situation include a concrete manifestation of the bad form of the deeper potential, and (b) the externalized bad form be directed toward attacking the person. To meet the first condition, the person's deeper potential for aggressive sexuality would have to be in the bad form of, for example, a poisonous snake. To meet the second condition, that snake would have to be attacking the person.

Perhaps the most traditional way of discriminating fear and anxiety is on the basis of the concrete specificity of the external threat. In fear, it is traditionally held, the external threat is concrete and specific, whereas in anxiety the threat is vague and nonspecific. However, from the perspective of humanistic theory, in *anxiety* the external situation must either be doing what the deeper potential is doing (viz. radically intruding into the operating potential), or the external situation must be compellingly pulling for the experiencing of certain defined deeper potentials. In anxiety, the degree of explicitness of the external situation can vary all the way from concretely specific to vaguely nonspecific. With regard to *fear*, however, the very specific bad form of the deeper potential must be present in the external situation. The conclusion, from our perspective, is that fear would always be accompanied by anxiety, but that anxiety can occur without fear.

Nature of the deeper potential. I have not found (in my own work or in the literature) any particular kinds of deeper potentials especially associated with the feeling of fear. What I *have* found is that the key to the *nature* of the deeper potential always lies in the nature of the feared external object and the action it carries out. When the young girl is filled with fear at the vision of her deceased grandmother, as a hooded evilness intent on attacking her, the nature of the deeper potential may be either (a) the experiencing of physical attacking or (b) the experiencing of being physically attacked. The man was enormously fearful of grasshoppers. More specifically, he was fearful of a grasshopper grabbing hold of his skin and sticking to him no matter how frantically he tried to brush it off. That grasshopper was the manifest bad form of his own deeper potential to be grabbed at and unshakably clung to. Dollard and Miller (1950) describe the fear of one's vital parts being damaged. For example, how may we understand the fear that many persons have at the prospects of receiving electric shock therapy, or the fear of damage to some vital part such as the heart, brain, spinal cord, or genitals? Our guideline tells us that the nature of the deeper potential is given in the nature of the feared external object and the action it carries out. According to this guideline, the nature of the deeper potential is either (a) to inflict damage to some vital part, or (b) to experience one's own vital parts as damaged—the heart attacked, brain smashed, spinal cord cracked, genitals cut.

Anger

Appropriate external situation. Anger is conventionally understood as occurring in a situational context characterized by frustration. According to Dollard and his colleagues (1939) and Miller and Dollard (1941), aggression is understood as the consequence of the blocking or frustration of a goal-response in a behavioral sequence. Probably a major difference between their formulation and ours is the question of the origin of the frustrating situation. According to humanistic theory, the *person* is the major architect of the frustrating situation, whereas in the frustration-aggression hypothesis, the person plays little or no role in the construction of the frustrating situation. Aside from this difference, the commonality lies in the presence of a frustrating element in the appropriate external situation.

Disintegrative clash between potentials. In the upward movement of the deeper potential, there is a point *after* the deeper potential becomes threateningly imminent (stage C, Figure 3.1) and *before* the operating potential has had its existence substantially cut off (stage D). This is the point of aggressive encounter. From the perspective of the operating potential, this is the point beyond which the deeper potential's continued rise means the almost certain end of one's very existence, the radical insult into one's very being. Anger is the expression of the actual grappling encounter of these disintegrative potentials.

Helplessness

Other words and phrases to describe the disintegrative feeling of helplessness include feeling weakness, impotence, or feeling controlled and driven. This feeling occurs at that point when the operating potential knows that it has lost the struggle against the rising deeper potential. Although the existence of the person is not yet completely closed off, it is now rendered ineffective. It has been seized and overpowered by the deeper part. Mandate and control are now in the hands of the deeper potential. That is the point of feeling helpless. It occurs well into stage D (Figure 3.1).

When the person locates the threat as *internal*, the helpless feeling is that awful *internal* forces have me in their coercive control (Whitehorn, 1959). Saul (1958) describes this feeling as one in which overwhelmingly powerful internal forces exert an automatic, relentless tyranny over me. Inner forces control me, are ominous and menacing, and I am no longer capable of resistance. I am in the grip of controlling inner forces—raging impulses, neuroses, psychoses, perverse tendencies, primary process material, crazy thoughts, insanity, drugs, liquor, genetic endowment, neurophysiological forces. All of these are various internal costumes worn by a deeper potential which can render the person helpless.

On the other hand, the seized operating potential may localize the awful controlling force as *external*. On the external stage, the controlling deeper potential takes the form of social forces which leave the person helpless under the controlling influence of the group, mores, external pressures, social pulls and pushes, immutable social laws. I am helpless, floating in a sea of controlling external influences. Whether the deeper potential is identified as internal or external, the helpless feeling occurs at that point when the person *is* helpless in the control of the deeper potential.

Shame

As with every disintegrative feeling, shame requires the same three necessary and sufficient conditions. If we ask what is specific about these conditions which lead to shame rather than some other disintegrative feeling, the following considerations seem to be paramount.

Disengagement of the operating potential. In order for the person to have a feeling of shame, the rising deeper potential must go beyond the point where it has intruded into the operating potential (stage D, Figure 3.1). In order for shame to occur, the deeper potential must proceed to the point where it has *disengaged* the operating potential and actually taken its place. That is, the deeper potential must pour forth in actual behavior. Some existential theorists hold that the feeling of shame will occur when the person *fails* to fulfill potentialities (May, 1958b, p. 52). In contrast, humanistic theory holds that shame requires that the person *be taken over* by the potentialities so that they *are* expressed in real behavior!

I was sitting in the passenger's seat in the front of the small car. My friend was driving, and his wife was sitting in the rear seat, holding their baby on her lap. I was very fond of the baby, and my left arm was draped over the back of my seat, my hand lightly patting and fondling the baby. When I turned slightly to my left, I saw that my hand was not patting and fondling the baby at all. I was patting and fondling the wife's knee! In order for a feeling of shame to occur, the deeper potential must disengage the operating potential and burst forth in a real behavioral actuality. The staid married businessman must actually put on the female undergarments in secrecy. The graduate student must actually give in to a secret wild homosexual spree. The wealthy physician must actually become the night burglar. The person must actually experience what it is like to let the deeper potential take over and commit the "slip of the tongue," or fondle the wife's knee.

The good feelings of experiencing. In stages B and C (Figure 3.1), the person does not have the good feelings of experiencing, indicated as the two positive signs within the deeper potential. But when the deeper part actually comes forth and does the act, the person has a full measure of the good feelings of pleasure and excitement, the thrill, the satisfaction, the joy, the ecstasy, the good feelings of actual experiencing. I feel that which I struggle against, but secretly enjoy, because "... shame shows to the other precisely what it wants to hide from him ... whether I blush because I myself have touched the inner border of sin, or because another has touched it, I always show him by blushing something which at bottom I do not wish to show at all, namely the 'point' where the inner border of sin 'in me' is touched" (Binswanger, 1958c, p. 337).

What I have betrayed is my complicity with the deeper part against which I have struggled. Always we return to the two functions of the operating potential: to truncate the experiencing of the deeper potential, and to provide for its experiencing. In the case of the feeling of shame, we witness the "surreptitious alliance" (Fingarette, 1962) between me and that against which I have struggled: my providing for its experiencing while, at the same time, seeking to truncate its experiencing. There is no gainsaying the pleasure upon fondling the wife's knee, verbalizing the "slipped out" word, doing all those deliciously wicked things of which the awful deeper potential is capable.

Reengagement of the operating potential. The feeling of shame does not occur while the deeper potential is behaving and the good feelings of experiencing are happening. The feeling of shame can occur only when the person takes over mandate once again. This is indicated in stage C (Figure 3.1) where the person has returned to more or less normal, and the deeper part has resumed its ordinary position once again. All of these changes may occur within an instant. For example, an instant after the deeper potential fondled the wife's knee and enjoyed it, *I* took over once again (stage C, Figure 3.1), and only then did "I" have the feeling of shame. Or it may require several moments, even five or ten minutes or more. For example, while the wealthy physician was being the burglar, there was no shame. The feeling of shame could only occur later when his typical self again was reengaged. Only then did he have the bad feeling of agonizing shame. Shame occurs in the intervals between thrilling transgressions, and not in the midst of the thrilling transgression when the deeper part is regnant.

Depression

The good feeling of experiencing. Disintegrative feelings occur in place of a full measure of the good feelings of experiencing. When the person begins to feel the inner pleasure and excitement, disintegrative feelings occur in their place, and ward off or neutralize the inner arcane pleasurable feelings. Feelings of depression are effective instruments for neutralizing inner feelings of joy and excited aliveness. It is as if depression is the other side of these good feelings which accompany the experiencing of the deeper potential.

Nature of deeper potentials. There are two kinds of deeper potentials especially linked to depressed feelings. One, as was found in anxiety, involves a concerted muscular bodily act (Cameron, 1947). To go a bit further, the concerted muscular bodily act characteristically relates to sexual immorality or explosive aggression (Mahrer & Bornstein, 1969; Maslow & Mittelmann, 1941) directed either toward oneself or toward others (Beck, 1967). The second deeper potential relates to withdrawal, pulling within oneself, getting away, not being involved (Mahrer & Bornstein, 1969). It is as if the deeper potential is saying, "This life is all wrong. I am going in the wrong direction. Get me out of here!" It is a deeper experiencing of leaving the whole scene, closing down, getting away from all of the gluey mess.

Depression can occur *when* a person is caught in a dilemma, in problems and choices with no way out. But the depression is not *because* of being caught. Here is the person who is stuck between awful heterosexuality and awful homosexuality (Serban, 1968) or between being straight, cerebral, ever watchful and, on the other hand, being wild and impulsive and crazy. This kind of depression comes from the stirrings of something deeper, something which is on neither side of the dilemma, something which is held down by being stuck. The person who is suffering from being stuck is clinging to being the person who *is* stuck, and is thereby averting any possible knowing of what the deeper alternative is.

Meaninglessness

Existential writers have probed especially deeply into the feeling of meaninglessness—the bodily sense of emptiness, hollowness, boredom and monotony, the feeling of being a void, the sense of not being oneself, inauthenticity. It is the feeling of slowing down, lacking alive experience, being clogged with the unexpressed (Enright, 1970). It is a sinking into the death of unexperiencing.

According to existential theorists, this is an exceedingly common bad feeling. Indeed, Ellenberger (1958) considers this feeling of meaninglessness as an essential determinant of nearly all bad feelings, psychological pain and general distress. Within humanistic theory, meaninglessness is not held as such an essential determinant. Although common, it is described as merely another kind of bad feeling, subject to the same three conditions which are necessary and sufficient for any bad feeling.

However, in contrast to the bad feelings we have so far discussed, the sense of meaninglessness is felt as much by the *deeper* potential as the operating potential. This is an important distinction, for, with regard to the other bad feelings, it was the person-as-operating-potential whose perspective was uppermost and who experienced the bad feeling. But with regard to meaninglessness, the feeling starts from down below, and from there expands outward to fill the person.

This bad feeling occurs when the person and the deeper potential sense that the inner potential will not be realized. It is as if the deeper potential now says: "I have been blocked off too successfully. I know I shall never be experienced. I have tried to rise time after time. The way is too difficult. My avenue is so congealed that I now know that I shall never penetrate out into real experiencing. I have been hurled back so often and so forcefully that I am content simply to languish here, far from experiencing. I am unable to come forth." Where other disintegrative feelings occur as the process moves from stage B to C to D (Figure 3.1), meaninglessness occurs as the process moves from stage B toward stage A. In this movement, there are two things the operating potential can do to bring about the bad feeling of meaninglessness:

1. *The external pursuit of internal integration.* Given a state of internal disintegration, the person-as-operating potential can set out on a long and fruitless *external* quest for internal integration. Instead of pursuing integration by turning inward, the fatal error is to turn one's face to the outside world in a fruitless effort after oneness, loving acceptance, fusion, unity, belongingness, harmony, peacefulness, tranquility. Integration can only be achieved by turning inward to one's own deeper potentials. If one turns outward, the deeper potential and the person sooner or later arrive at the certainty that the quest is hopeless. With that comes the feeling of meaninglessness.

If I fear and hate what is within, I can dedicate years to my attempt to get *you* to love me, to be warm and close to me. But in the end, I fail, and I am filled with the sense of meaninglessness. I may search for others who will surround me with perfect acceptance and welcoming positive regard. I may find intermittent oases in my personal relations, in a marriage, a friendship, a relation with a clergyman or psychotherapist. But in the end the internal disintegration endures, and the deeper potential undergoes the utter meaninglessness of it all. The person can never erase *internal* disintegration by *external* acceptance from one's group, family, organization, party, circle of friends. When the group acceptance plays out its career, the ineluctable end is the swelling up of the ever-present *inner* disintegration, and the ensuing feelings of meaninglessness and hollowness.

One searches in vain for *external* pools of oneness and unity. There is no recapturing of what Fromm (1947) describes as the yearning for mystical reunion and oceanic loving acceptance of infancy. It is a lost state, forever beyond recapturing. No right person is available. Mother and father are gone or unaccountably different. The old days have dissolved away and will never be found in pathetic wanderings throughout the external world. Endless recountings of the past are bedeviling thin promises for an unattainable reunion. In the end, one is always overtaken with the feeling of meaninglessness from external pursuits for what is missing internally.

Even when the person manages to capture a brief moment of unifying fusion, the feeling of meaninglessness rushes in to fill the void. Some persons wring from sexual intercourse that yearned sense of integrative assimilation. For a climactic instant, the bodies blend into one; boundaries melt in the flash of fusion. Yet that instant is over, and the person is once again filled with meaninglessness because the pursuit after internal integration has been carried into the external world.

To the extent that the person surges after integration by rushing out into the *external* world, the inevitable result, sooner or later, is the feeling of meaninglessness and hollowness. It is as if the deeper potential, feared and hated by the person, sees the person going further and further into the external world, while inside the deeper potential is increasingly confronted with the truth that no real integration will ever happen. The result is meaninglessness, hollowness, an empty void.

2. *Successful barricading of the deeper potential.* That feeling of meaninglessness also occurs when the person is agonizingly *successful* in erecting an effective barricade against the deeper potential. Sensing that the deeper potential consists of loathsome insignificance and inadequacy, the person sets out to prove that he is *not* insignificant and *not* inadequate—and thereby builds a barricade against the deeper potential. If the person is smashingly successful then the deeper potential is shoved further and further down, with diminishing chances of ever being experienced. If the person is sufficiently successful in proving what he is not, if the deeper potential is pushed down far enough, a point will be reached when it will be locked within its cell, unable to come forth, never to reach the level of experiencing. When that happens, the deeper potential will exude huge waves of meaninglessness and hollowness and nothingness.

All the disintegrative feelings described heretofore increase with the rise of the deeper potential from stage B to stage C to stage D (Figure 3.1). The feeling of meaninglessness occurs at stage B, *after* the deeper potential has failed repeatedly to reach stage D, or even C, and, instead, found the channel increasingly congealed and impenetrable. In effect, the deeper potential is forced further and further down, more and more unable to rise upwards. The person has managed to prove to himself that he is not insignificant and inadequate. In accomplishing this successfully, the potential for experiencing insignificance and inadequacy has been almost completely worn out and shut down. From *its* perspective, the life he has managed to carve out for himself *is* hollow! Nothing in his present life provides for the experiencing of the deeper insignificance and inadequacy. Furthermore, what he has managed to achieve means that the potential for insignificance and inadequacy will probably never be experienced. Hence the feeling of meaninglessness.

Many psychotherapists, catching a glimpse of grotesque and threatening deeper potentials, explicitly set out to reinforce the barricade by building up opposing operating potentials. Fromm-Reichmann, for example, builds up defenses against some inner impulses by directing the mentally ill person into a productive life of creativity (Bullard, 1959). The person with misogynistic deeper tendencies can be directed through psychoanalytic methods into a life of creative poetic expression of glorified femininity. The success of such attempts only serves to seal off the deeper potential. The result is a pervasive sense of meaninglessness.

What adds to the tragedy is that the life which is pursued is frequently one of very high personal and social value. In fending off the deeper potential, the person usually seeks precisely what so many consider highly prized—becoming healthy and vigorous, hardworking, attractive, dedicated, honest, loving, good-humored, understanding, capable, ambitious, patriotic, heroic, successful, influential, intelligent, faithful, pious, humble. When achievement of these ways of being serves to suffocate the deeper potential, the result is a greater likelihood of eventual meaninglessness.

In this process of pushing down the deeper potential, sheer time is a most powerful ally. So many women and men fight hard against deeper sexual potentials from their adolescent years until they are well into their forties, fifties, and sixties. At that time, advancing age joins with them against the deeper sexual potentials, and the Pyrrhic victory is achieved. The result is a feeling of utter meaninglessness and hollowness. The army sergeant had managed to hide his sexual fetishes for the past 30 years. No one knew of his secret practices. Then, in his late fifties, there was a diminishing craving for these sexual practices. At last the inner tendencies receded. Age and the operating potential had defeated the deeper potential. But the final scene in this drama is inevitably the rising sense of meaninglessness.

She was the youngest sister, and only with her did father step out of the role of martinet. While her deeper potential yearned to be father's loved one, the appealing and attractive one, the operating potential mounted a lifelong campaign against being this way. Throughout adolescence and adulthood she successfully avoided being the appealing and attractive special darling to father by becoming a self-sufficient free agent. Marriage was essentially asexual. Never was she anyone's special darling. Finally, in her late fifties, her father died, and aging reality presented her with testimony that she was old, no longer attractive, unsexual, never to be anyone's sexual darling. That deeper potential, continuously barricaded, finally gave up, and the consequence was a pervading sense of meaninglessness and hollowness—the hallmark of her final years.

What has been described as menopause and involutional melancholia are not consequences of sexual juices running dry. Biology did not do it; the operating potential had an assist from sheer aging in its successful struggle to barricade the deeper potential. The feeling of meaninglessness, frequently associated with menopause and involutional melancholia, is a function of the successful effort of the operating potential to close down the deeper potential.

Unfeeling

So far, we have discussed disintegrative feelings, the necessary and sufficient conditions for their occurrence, and the content of several disintegrative feelings. In the beginning of this chapter I said that humanistic theory recognizes *two* major kinds of bad feelings. The first is disintegrative feeling. Now we turn to the second.

The Nature of the State of Unfeeling

One reason why it is difficult to describe this state is that so many of us live in it so much of the time. I consider unfeeling as the characteristic state of human beings. Furthermore, since we unknowingly achieve and exist in this state, we are skilled at insuring that nothing shall disturb what we have managed to achieve. It is difficult to describe because existing in it forecloses the possibility of acknowledging it.

The state of unfeeling can be described in a number of ways: (a) It is a state of sheer deadness, a living in numbness, an absence of any bodily felt sensations, a state of nothingness. (b) Sheer experiencing is closed off, sealed, narrowed nothingness. (c) The lack of feelings applies even to those of disintegration. In this state the person does not feel anxiety, tension, anger, depression, or other disintegrative feelings. (d) It is like being asleep, behaving automatically without knowing what you are doing, moving about in a hypnotic-like state, not fully present, spending one's life in a fog, not experiencing that one is not experiencing. Persons know the state of unfeeling only *after* they have emerged *out of* that state. Once having emerged, the person grasps the change as a kind of awakening, a coming out of a sleep that he had been in throughout his life, without knowing that he had been sleeping. Unfeeling is a state in which the person has no feeling, and has no feeling about having no feeling. This is the insidious characteristic of the state, viz. that while the person is in it, there can be no awareness of being in it. If the person were aware of being in the sleep of unfeeling, the person would not be asleep! Instead, the person would be feeling depression or boredom or meaninglessness or even some disintegrative feeling. This is why it is so difficult to describe the sleep of unfeeling to persons who are themselves in that state. To them, they *seem* awake, there is no sense at all of being an automaton. There is no awareness of having no awareness. The only way persons in such a state can know they are in such a state is by being in some other state.

When I am in this state, I talk to my friends, I have disagreements with my children, I eat meals, I make love, I write letters, I tell jokes.

But I do not know that I am in a state of unfeeling. Worse, I act as if I *am* in a feelinged state. Once I sink into the state of unfeeling, I am unable to know that I am in the state of unfeeling; indeed, I am convinced that I am fully feeling.

There are two avenues by which the person can enter the state of unfeeling:

1. *Closing Down the Deeper Potential*

In describing disintegrative feelings, I spoke of the way in which the disintegrative feeling ordinarily increases as the deeper potential rises closer and closer to the operating potential. In stage B (Figure 3.1), the deeper potential has risen close enough to help bring about a mild degree of disintegrative feeling. This mild degree is indicated by the single negative sign in the channel of the relationships between the two potentials. We can identify a threshold *above* which disintegrative feelings occur. *Below* that threshold is the domain of unfeeling. When the deeper potential falls (or is pushed) below that threshold, the state of unfeeling is entered. This point is indicated at the left in Figure 3.1. Deeper potential 2 enters the state of *unfeeling* when it falls below that point (stage A), and it leads to mild feelings of *disintegration* when it rises above that point into stage B. In other words, the more successful is the person in sealing off (curtailing, shoving down) the deeper potential, the more likely it is that the person will enter the state of unfeeling.

Above that threshold, in stages B-D, the person will *feel something*, even though the feelings are disintegrative. The feeling of meaninglessness is still a feeling. Being depressed or angry or frustrated or anxious is a bad feeling, but it is a feeling. Once the deeper potential falls below that threshold, such feelings are gone, and the person is a mechanical automaton, behaving while in a state of sleep, not having bad feelings. For example, if the deeper potential relates to rage, and if a headache is the manifestation of a disintegrative relationship, pushing down the rage sufficiently will result in the dissolving away of the headache (Lustman, 1951). Closing the deeper potential down into the state of unfeeling extinguishes evidence of disintegrative relationships, and the bad feeling (e.g. the headache) goes away.

Critical moments commonly consist of tiny bursts of (disintegrative) feelings as the person moves from the dead sleep state (stage A) into mild disintegrative feelings (stage B). This is the person who starts to come alive with a feeling of depression or meaninglessness or perhaps even a prick of anxiety. At least they are having *some* (bad) feeling! When this is happening, the deeper potential is still alive and struggling to avoid falling into the quicksand of an unfeelinged state. Sullivan (1953) has described persons who struggle to construct anxiety-arousing experiences to escape from such an unfeelinged state. It is the deeper potential which is struggling for its very existence by constructing such experiences, for the next step is a kind of death, an utter burial in which there is no chance for the deeper potential to come to life. The next step is the sleep of death. Slapping oneself or being slapped may shock the person, but it also might waken him out of the state of sleep. Falling into a lake or hitting oneself with a hammer on the thigh or screaming just as loud as one can might serve to pull the person out of the unfeelinged deadness.

In fending off the deeper potential for insignificance and inadequacy, the operating potential may push the deeper potential down to stage B by acquiring wealth, social prestige, influence, power. When that deeper potential has been fully sealed off (stage A), almost without knowing what has happened, the person will become an automaton, moving about in the state of sleep, not having real feelings, existing in a numbed life, never fully there—and without any awareness of having become enveloped in this state. Another person may so struggle against his deeper potential for experiencing affectionate warmth, that he becomes a stoically cool individual. When that deeper affectionate warmth has been pushed below the threshold, the person has died, and lives his life in a state of death sleep. There are no real feelings, and the person lives within an illusory world of being fully feelinged!

When this state is reached, there is truly a hiatus between the person and the deeper potentials. Behind this gap, the operating potentials exist inauthentically, mere half-persons out of touch with their deeper insides. They are puppets who have no inkling of their puppethood, persons who do not even know of their lack of personhood.

2. *Disengagement of the Operating Potential*

The state of unfeeling can be entered when a strong operating potential wages a successful war against the deeper potential. This is given in stage A (Figure 3.1). The second avenue into the state of unfeeling is indicated in stage E in Figure 3.1. Suppose, for example, that the mediating potential involved a sadistic hostility toward women. In stage D, that mediating potential is crowding so close that the person is all but enveloped. He is in his room, struggling *not* to put on his leather jacket and his soft leather boots and to set out into the night in search of an older woman to strangle. The deeper potential is right on the verge of taking him over. The second avenue into the state of unfeeling occurs at this point. It is entered when the person *disengages* in the state of unfeeling, and permits the deeper potential to take over the determination of behavior. In effect, the person goes to sleep while the deeper potential takes his place. As indicated in stage E (Figure 3.1), the person now enters into the state of unfeeling. When that happens, the deeper potential (not the person) takes over behavior, puts on the appropriate clothes, and leaves the room in search of a solitary older woman suitable for strangling. The person feels nothing, exists in a state of dead numbness, does not have any bad feelings of disintegration. The struggle against the deeper potential (stages B-D) is over, and the person is fully asleep, disengaged from his ordinary position and existing in the state of unfeeling (stage E).

Most persons, however, do not spend their lives coping in this way with a dramatic potential to strangle others. But in less dramatic ways, this is how we are most of the time. Every day we come near critical moments from which we preserve ourselves by quickly falling asleep while our deeper potentials momentarily take over. Then, moments later, we wake up again in charge of behavior (stages D, C, B). In undramatic ways, across days stretching into years, our conscious selves automatically disengage, leaving the deeper potentials in charge for a moment. In its dramatic form we speak of multiple personalities, or being in a fugue state, or being amnesic. But there is no label for the thousands of times we momentarily disengage ourselves and let the deeper potential behave for us, while we fall into the momentary state of sleeping unfeeling. During that moment (stage E), the person is in a state of limbo—intact, preserved, not really alive, but not dead. Existence is held in limbo for a while, without knowing.

Reduction of Bad Feelings: A Self-Defeating Course of Life.

If a person is having bad feelings (as indicated in stages C and D in Figure 3.1), the most common course is either toward stage E (in which the person disengages and the deeper potential takes over), or toward stages B and A (in which the deeper potential is pushed downward). Either course enjoys some undeniable advantages: (a) There is a reduction in bad feelings. No longer does the person feel so fractionated and torn apart. There is an unquestionable reduction in anxiety, alienation, hostility or meaninglessness. (b) No longer does the rising deeper potential threaten to eclipse the person and bring his very existence to a close. (c) No longer is the person in danger of the feelings accompanying the experiencing of the deeper potential —feelings of pleasure and joy, excitement and aliveness.

These are powerful advantages. Small wonder that either course is nearly universal in the helping professions. This is the course promised by our pharmaceutical cornucopia. It is the course upheld as a professional value by nearly every helping profession in the field of human relations—from psychology to psychiatry to religion. How eager are one's acquaintances, family, community and society to serve as powerful allies in the diminishing of these bad feelings! The common effort is *against* the upward rise of the deeper potential and its consequent disintegrative feelings. Under the guise of helping, the disintegrative feelings are to be reduced, and the person welcomes any and all allies in the struggle.

Suppose that the mother is terribly upset by persistent thoughts which come to her, nasty thoughts of getting rid of her baby. Wolpe (1958) is representative of approaches which seek to reduce the bad upset feelings, and succeed in doing so at the expense of the deeper potential. For Wolpe, the central target is the mother's uncomfortable feeling about her persistent thoughts. "The feature of any example of obsessional behavior is not its inevitability but its *intrusiveness*. Its elicitation or the impulse toward it is an encumbrance and an embarrassment to the patient" (1958, p. 89). The paramount therapeutic focus is the woman's disintegrative feelings in relationship to this thought, feelings which are intrusive, embarrassing, and tension-producing. Wolpe's aim is to reduce these bad feelings, and to do so by joining with the woman (OP1, stage C or D, Figure 3.1) in getting rid of the bad feelings. In other words, the direction is back to stage A in which the deeper potential is overwhelmed and buried. If a person is anxious. one behavioristic approach aims at reducing the anxiety by helping the person to experience that feeling in the absence of the actual, real "phobic" object (Hogan & Kirchner, 1967). The result is the successful extinguishing of the anxiety. But in addition, from our perspective, that way also succeeds in burying the rising deeper potential so that it no longer is capable of generating the anxiety. It is a way of reducing the anxiety, but the price paid is rather stiff: viz. the suffocation of the deeper potential.

Behavioral approaches have dedicated themselves to winning the fight against the rising deeper potential. Each new technique has been in the service of pushing it down. In outlining the broad scope of a learning approach to psychotherapy, Shoben (1949) cited the goal as the neutralizing of anxiety-invoking stimuli. The patient is to be helped to react in a non-anxious way to cues previously associated with anxiety. In the encounter or struggle between the person and that about which the person is anxious, the therapist regularly sides with the person and wages war against the source of anxiety. Never is the choice of sides questioned. Never is there any choice of sides.

Behavioral learning theories employ any methods which directly reduce the anxiety and whatever the person is anxious about. In this battle against the anxiety and that about which the person is anxious, ". . . we may use rational-emotive therapy, role playing, systematic desensitization, shaping, modeling or the like. We will aim in this instance to reduce interfering responses or responses to stimuli that are irrelevent or not even present in the situation, that is, if you wish, behavior whose stimuli are the individual's own anxiety responses" (Ullmann, 1972, p. 200). War is waged against the rising deeper potential. The goal is to bury it, seal it off, push it down. From the perspective of humanistic theory, such a course is always self-defeating; its implicit or explicit goal is to bury, if not downright murder, one's self. Whether the course is toward stage E or back toward stage A (Figure 3.1), the person is driven toward a state of unfeeling, a living death, a limbo of sleep. One becomes a part-person, frozen into a state of numbness, sleeping while not even knowing that one is asleep. When the course is constantly back toward stage A, the disintegrative feelings *are* reduced, the threat *is* over, the good feelings of experiencing *are* shut off, but at what a price! If the operating potential does not maneuver the deeper one *all the way* to stage E or stage A, then the possibility of a career of ebb and flow is always present. One has reduced the bad feeling, but nothing has been done to the conditions which will again and again produce the bad feeling. Indeed, one has prevented the person from engaging the genuine causes of the bad feeling (Solomon & Wynne, 1954), with the result that the conditions are thereby preserved. Never does the person *meet* the deeper potential. From our perspective, either of these courses is downright sinful and self-defeating.

I am often impressed by the particular part of the personality which drags the person into therapy. Shah (1969) describes the case of a woman who alternated between violent aggressive outbursts and struggles to acquire control over the outbursts. The two parts of the woman were at war with one another. When the former was uppermost, that person felt good. But when the latter was uppermost, that person felt terrible guilt over what had been done. When the woman sought therapy, the presenting part was that which wished to gain control over the part which engaged in the periodic aggressive outbursts. The therapist worked within a behavior modification framework and took the role of the ally of the part which sought control over the part which engaged in the periodic outbursts. Accordingly, the therapist became the external agent of control: ". . . specific instructions were given to Mrs. Smith that physical punishment was no longer to be used . . . In step-by-step fashion a detailed program was outlined . . . for regulating the mother's own behavior . . . the mother was urged to get to bed earlier, to use progressive relaxation to stop and to alleviate tension at other times, and to wake up with the children in the mornings . . ." (1969, pp. 404, 405). Such an approach effectively joins with one operating potential in shoving the deeper potential down below the threshold of unfeeling. It preserves and enhances the person to a point where the deeper potential is buried. This regime successfully reduces the bad feelings of guilt. At the same time, it ends the possibilities of the deeper potential. And, in this enterprise, the therapist is an effective accomplice in the final sealing off of the deeper potentials.

Those who aim at reducing bad feelings by suppressing the rising deeper potential espouse a theoretical conception which is quite compatible with their practice. Their conception of what causes the bad feelings and what is going on as they feed the pills, or support the ego, or defend against the awful inner instincts, or control the behavior, is quite consistent with their practices. Yet the net result is, nevertheless, murder of the deeper potential. It would require a wholesale change in conceptualization to illuminate the murder occurring on the stage of the helping professions. Perhaps this is too much to ask. Perhaps it is better not to invite such committed practitioners to put on another theoretical conceptualization which would disclose what they have been doing as murder.

The pity is that the occurrence of bad feelings can mean that the person is *alive* (not in a deadened state of unfeeling), and that the deeper potential is *starting* to come forth. Indeed, the presence of bad feelings can mean that the person *is undergoing* genuine personality change, including a direct meeting of the inner process in the course of transformation (Goldstein, 1939). The presence of bad feelings can mean the person is now ready for the next step. It is an opportunity which can be capitalized upon.

Humanistic theory invites a radical posture toward one's own bad feelings. These bad feelings occur within a personality structure which welcomes their occurrence as a talisman of *constructive* personality change. The bad feeling hurts, but the context accepts the pain as part of the process of forward movement. This is the difference between what existentialists refer to as neurotic bad feelings and normal bad feelings. "The goal of therapy is not the absence of anxiety, but rather the changing of neurotic anxiety into normal anxiety, and the development of the capacity to live with and to use normal anxiety. The patient after therapy may well bear more anxiety than he had before, but it will be conscious anxiety and he will be able to use it constructively. Nor is the goal the absence of guilt feeling, but rather the transformation of neurotic guilt into normal guilt, together with the development of the capacity to use this normal guilt creatively (May, 1967, p. 109). Our aim is to facilitate the process which brings with it an epiphenomenological bad feeling, and not to defend against bad feelings in the course of a descent into a state of unfeeling.

4

The Position of Humanistic Theory on Some Issues of the Philosophy of Science

Chapters 2 and 3 introduced some of the concepts and principles of humanistic theory, and these permitted us to describe bad feelings. In order to present further concepts and principles, we must turn to the philosophy of science. It is necessary to set humanistic theory within its proper place on some of the issues in the philosophy of science in order to proceed to a description of the human body, the person and the external world, and subsequent human phenomena.

Theories of human behavior and personality rest on a foundation of basic assumptions about science. Sometimes these basic assumptions are explicit; usually they are implicit. Our various theories grow out of such diverse beds of assumptions that there often is no common communication base. Or worse, apparent discourse on questions of mutual scientific interest has only the illusionary air of communication when in actuality the participants live in different worlds which slide past one another without touching. The purpose of this chapter is to discuss the position of humanistic theory on some of the issues of the philosophy of science on which theories of human behavior and personality depart from one another. More particularly, the purpose is to define the position of humanistic theory on the premise that its basic scientific foundation offers a uniquely worthwhile departure for the description and understanding of human phenomena.

Among these issues in the philosophy of science, one cluster is referred to as mind-body issues. It has been generally accepted that a comprehensive theory is obligated to take some position on these mind-body issues, even if this consists of a rationale for avoiding the issues themselves (e.g. McGeoch, 1933).

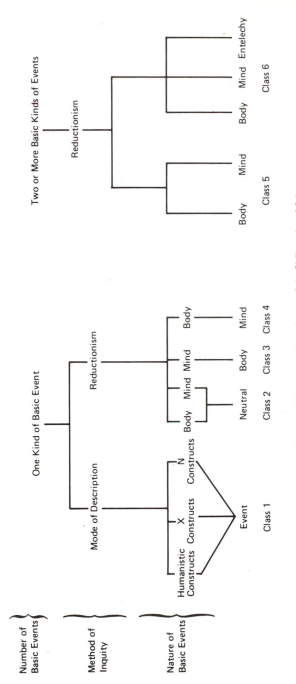

Figure 4.1 Classes of Theories on Some Issues of the Philosophy of Science

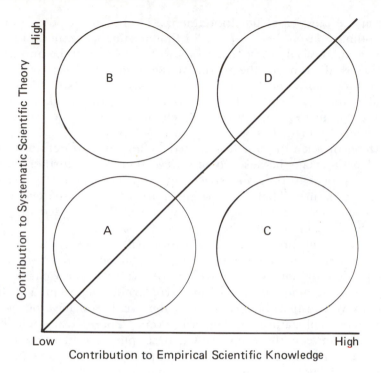

Figure 4.2 Two Dimensions for Evaluating the Scientific Worth of Research

THE FUNDAMENTAL NATURE OF BASIC EVENTS

Let us consider some everyday, common events: a person riding a bicycle, a person grinning and feeling happy, a person sitting in a chair and remembering his father throwing him up in the air and catching him. Suppose we are dedicated to rigorously systematic description and understanding of these events. How do we go about describing and understanding the events which are basic to riding a bicycle, grinning and feeling happy, or remembering an incident from one's childhood?

Events and Descriptive Constructions of Events

When I try to get at the most basic nature of those events, all I can state is that they are occurrences, localizable in time and space (Kantor, 1942; Stevens, 1935). That may sound very disappointing—to get right down to the basic foundation of what is going on, and to say for certain nothing more than that. It might leave the inquirer first a bit puzzled, and then prone to ask, "But what is *really* going on there, down at the most basic and fundamental level of description and understanding?" From the viewpoint of humanistic theory, nothing more can be said. Basically these are *events* with a locus in time and space, and that is all. Indeed, the secret of the strength of this position *is* that nothing more *can* be said. To try to say more about the fundamental nature of basic events is, from the approach taken here, a mistake. No matter what an approach offers to the description of basic events, an error has been committed—I believe.

Nothing of scientific worth is added by attempts to define the nature of basic events because, in our view, there *is* no further nature. Beyond its locus in time and space, an event is treated as possessing no further nature. There is nothing more to what basic events are like—at least from our perspective. Whatever else is added (in other approaches) is not an intrinsic property of basic events. It is a surplus. It is an attributed property. It is a *construction* of basic events, a mode of description about the event. Change the mode of description and the supposed fundamental nature of the event will also change. All you have is one mode of describing or construing the event. You have a descriptive construction *of* and *about* the event; you have not seized the fundamental nature of the basic event! There is a tremendous distinction between the event and a descriptive construction of the event. When I try to grasp the fundamental nature of the event, I can say practically nothing (except that it has locus in time and space). When I indulge in a descriptive construction of the event, *then* I can be utterly free to select *any* mode of description.

The enterprise of finding descriptions of events is a means of studying or knowing them. Descriptive constructs are ways of trying to make sense of them by conceptualizing about them. "Events may be simply described as anything that happens which may or may not become known or studied" (Kantor, 1957, p. 56). To add anything else is engaging in further knowing or studying of them, but it is not a grasping of them. I can describe a person riding a bicycle from the viewpoint of humanistic theory. I can adopt any mode of descriptive construction I wish. I can describe that event sociologically, artistically, physiologically, psychoanalytically, endocrinologically, spiritualistically, neurologically, economically, politically, kinesiologically, legally—just to name a few of the available modes of description. The error, or so it seems from our viewpoint, is to confuse the mode of description with the essential nature of that event. The person riding the bicycle is *not basically or fundamentally* a sociological event—although it can be described sociologically. Neither is it an artistic or a physiological event—though it certainly can be described artistically or physiologically. Only one approach accepts the distinction between events and descriptive constructions about events. This approach is indicated as class 1 in Figure 4.1. All other approaches infuse (and confuse) events with descriptive constructs about events, so that the basic event is assumed to have a basic nature such as a mental or physical basic nature. "Of course no scientist would admit that he confuses events with his own creations, his own constructs . . . But we insist that much bad thinking in science is traceable to just this admixture of events and constructs" (Kantor, 1957, p. 56). What makes matters perhaps even worse, those scientists who confuse events with their own constructions about the events live in worlds in which it is not possible to grasp what it is like to differentiate events from descriptive constructs about events. It is the old story of now knowing and not knowing about not knowing.

Scientists who hold to the class 1 position live in worlds in which they are the constructors of theories. Theories are sets of descriptive constructs about events. On the other hand, scientists who hold to the positions of classes 2-6 live in worlds of real, actual events. Scientists who live in class 1 worlds adopt or modify their theories because of personal considerations. The theory fits in with their beliefs about the nature of things, or the theory provides personal satisfaction, or the theory is held on grounds of sheer personal faith. This acceptance of the final and ultimate role of the *person* in constructing (adopting, modifying) theories is exemplified by Boulding, Teilhard de Chardin, and Polanyi. It is exemplified in Einstein's adoption of a theory of relativity because, succinctly, he liked it better than a theory of quantum physics. This is not to deny all other considerations for preferring one theory over another. But scientists who fall in the class 1 position acknowledge that they are the constructors of their theories; they are the ones who invent the constructs, and the final ultimate selection is a matter of faith, an accepted set of assumptions about the world, and simple personal preference. In contrast, the worlds in which scientists of classes 2-6 live dictate that a different package of considerations accounts for one's preference for a given theory, viz. because it is more correct, because that is the way events really are. These are two essentially different sets of final ultimate reasons for accepting, adopting, or modifying theories.

Scientists are not the only ones who confuse events with their own concepts, their own creations. Most human beings live their lives one giant step removed from raw events. They can stretch only to the furthest reaches of their concepts, and they mistakenly interact with those furthest conceptualizations of the event as if they were in actual contact with the event itself. Our own position on this issue is already articulated in Zen Buddhism, wherein concepts are easily recognized as the creation of human beings, and the sharpest possible differentiation is drawn between descriptive constructs *about* events and actual engagement *with* the events themselves (e.g. Suzuki, 1949). Here, in the writings of Zen Buddhism, lies our own position on the distinction between events and descriptive constructs about events.

We *can* say that basic events have a locus in time and space. But because we are talking from the perspective of one particular mode of description, we cannot say that basic events are *fundamentally* neurological or electronic or chemical or mental or physical or musical or nuclear. These are not the essential intrinsic natures of basic events; they are modes of construction attributed to basic events. At its essential core, that event which I refer to with words like "a person riding a bicycle" is no more than a raw event in time and space. That is all. It is no more a chemical event than it is a social event, no more a mental event than it is a physical event.

Human beings are basically and fundamentally events. We are not *fundamentally* anything—not mental nor anatomical, not nuclear nor physiological. These are arbitrary categories from various modes of description of human beings. Our philosophical position ". . . categorically refrains . . . from imposing some arbitrary idea of being and reality—however customary or 'self-evident'—on the 'particular being' we call 'man.' We must be able to abstain from forcing man into any preconceived or prejudicial categories beforehand, such as 'soul,' 'person,' or 'consciousness' " (Boss, 1963, pp. 31-32). This is one implication of our starting point, viz. the distinction between events and our descriptive constructs about events. We may quietly assert that ". . . constructs in any form or style are not to be confounded with the events . . ." (Kantor, 1957, p. 56), but there are sets of profound implications from holding to this position, or embracing some other position. It has enormously far-reaching implications when we live in a world in which the categories, concepts, descriptions, and constructs are taken as the events themselves.

The word "psychotherapy" is a very high level, sophisticated construct. From our theoretical stance, there is a profound distinction between the construct "psychotherapy" and the events to which that word refers. For purposes of research, the events to which psychoanalytic psychotherapy refers must be cleanly differentiated from the events to which *behavior modification* psychotherapy, *experiential* psychotherapy, *Adlerian* psychotherapy, *reality* therapy, or *implosive* psychotherapy refer. Each of these referred-to domains of events can differ significantly from one another. To throw all of these events into a hodgepodge melange under the label "psychotherapy" is to commit a gross error, one which sharply curtails what psychotherapy research can hope to accomplish (Kiesler, 1966). There is no single organized body of events called psychotherapy, and the longer we refuse to acknowledge this the more muddled will research on psychotherapy become. When we finally give up the confusion of "psychotherapy" with the events to which that word refers, we will no longer pursue research based on the assumption that all psychotherapies refer to some single organized body of events. One consequence will be a redirection of a considerable proportion of our psychotherapy research energy!

It is my intent to outline a language of humanistic theory which escapes the trap of an implicit mind-body duality, i.e. which does not include a hidden assumption of basic events divided into mental and physical. "It is common enough to find others deploring the body-mind dualism and yet at the same time continuing to use a language which inevitably commits them to it. If we wish to avoid this result we must devise or find a language which carries with it no such commitments; that is to say, we must find a *pre-dualistic language*" (Woodger, 1952, pp. 256-257). Our language system seeks to avoid such traps by embracing assumptions which clearly distinguish between events and constructions of those events.

I have expressed a point of view which rests upon three assumptions: (a) With regard to the *number* of basic events, our assumption is that "The human being is assumed to be a single, unitary thing, with only a single kind of event, stuff, or substance at its base" (Mahrer, 1962a, p. 54). How many basic events are there? One, just one. (b) With regard to the *nature* of basic events, all we can say is that events have a locus in time and space (Feigl, 1955; Rotter, 1954). "Beyond its status as an event, the human being has no intrinsic nature, such as a mental or bodily nature" (Mahrer, 1962a, p. 55). (c) With regard to the *method of describing* basic events, our assumption is that all further properties of basic events are attributed by means of a set of constructs which comprise a mode of description. These descriptive constructs are *about* the event; they are not the event itself.

Here is an event which we *describe* as a person riding a bicycle, a person grinning and feeling happy, a person sitting in a chair and remembering his father throwing him up in the air and catching him. Here is an event which we *describe* as a nerve; it is not basically or fundamentally a nerve. Here is an event which we describe as a schizophrenic individual; it is not basically or fundamentally a schizophrenic individual. Riding a bicycle is merely an event. It is not basically a physical event; "physical" is a construct within some particular (although very common) mode of description. Remembering one's father is merely an event. It is not basically a "mental" event; "mental" is itself a construct within some particular mode of description.

Humanistic theory may be interested in events which we describe as riding bicycles. It is quite interested in events described as remembering earlier incidents; it is not concerned with "mental" events as such, but rather with the events which other modes of description *label* as "mental" events. Humanistic theory is likewise interested in events which other modes of description label as "physical"—nerves, miscarriages, cancer, ulcers, bronchitis. It is not interested in "physical" events; the label "physical" belongs to other modes of description, not to ours. Humanistic theory is also interested in persons who seem unreachable, who act in bewildering ways, who talk in ways which seem scrambled and incomprehensible. Other approaches term such persons "schizophrenic." We are interested in those events, but not in "schizophrenia," a construct belonging to a mode of description which is not that of humanistic theory.

How do we try to identify and describe the raw events of interest to us? We do this by seeking to stick as closely as possible to the raw neutral event. We talk about our events as immediate, observable, behavioral. Our descriptions are carefully restricted to what is immediate, observable, and behavioral. In describing behavioral events, our ". . . statements never want to be anything more than 'mere,' of extremely strict, careful, and subtle descriptions and expositions of the essential aspects and features" (Boss, 1963, p. 29). We eschew labels such as schizophrenia, but fix our attention on strict, careful, subtle description of the immediate, observable behavioral events tucked under the label "schizophrenia."

When we seek to describe a phenomenon, whether for clinical work or for research, our aim is to nudge up against the raw events, to get as close as possible to the events. The event may be described as verbalizing that one is depressed, or looking gloomy and depressed, or sitting alone and dejected. Once the events are grouped into some abstract class, you have lost proximity with the events themselves, and all you have left is your category. Thus we describe the phenomenon with mere simple descriptions; we do not use a big, lumpy construct like "depression." It would be an even further loss of contact with the events to employ a *scale* for "depression." And it would compound the infraction even further to select items for the scale from psychiatrists' notions of what "depression" is like (cf. Wechsler & Busfield, 1963). Because we respect a major distinction between the event and our descriptive constructions of that event, we try to stick as closely as possible to the event itself, even when we use mere descriptions.

Depression is a construct. It refers to events. Because we must be quite alert to distinguish as sharply as possible between depression and the events to which it refers, we can acknowledge that depression is merely a ". . . term . . . variously applied to designate: a particular type of feeling or symptom; a symptom complex (or syndrome); and a well-defined disease entity" (Beck, 1967, p. 6). Like humours of the body, schizophrenia, and witches, depression may well pass out of scientific respect when we no longer have need for such a construct, and all we will lose will be the construct. As with "witches," we will still have the events to which the construct "depression" refers.

A similar gap is present between the event and the theoretical constructs we employ *in guiding us toward describing that event.* Already we have used theoretical constructs such as potential, relationships among potentials, and so on. A deeper potential is not an event. It is a high level construct used to help us negotiate closer descriptions of the event. I would never expect to touch a deeper potential, nor would I see one or consider it real in the sense that an event is real. Even psychoanalysis (which has been grossly misinterpreted on this point) acknowledges the difference between events and theoretical constructs: ". . . the fact remains that the unconscious still remains a *working hypothesis*; our only reason for believing in an unconscious is that by assuming it *phenomena* become explicable" (Fenichel, 1953c, p. 16).

In seeking to move our description into intimate contact with the events themselves, we must admit that our descriptive constructs will nevertheless be saturated by the theoretical perspective which does the describing. Try as I may, I will describe events with my own constructs from my own perspective. Consider, as an example, an attempt to describe the basic events called psychotherapy. One may attempt to be "factual," to be free of the bias of any particular approach to psychotherapy and, instead, to describe the basic commonalities across all approaches—mere factual descriptions of the set of simple observations which comprise what psychotherapy is. The attempt is made by a learning theorist whose effort is saturated with the learning perspective. Neutral, factual, "mere" observation is drenched by the perspective of learning theory: "In summary, then, one might say that clinical cases share in common (a) anxiety touched off by (b) unverbalized, unsuccessfully repressed impulses to act in ways that have met with punishment, and (c) persistent nonintegrative behavior of many kinds, which reduces the anxiety but does nothing about eliminating its objective causes" (Shoben, 1949, p. 372). Far from being simple, perspective-free, common observations, this description of the simple, common "facts" of psychotherapy is testimony to the seductive fusion of events with descriptive perspectives. We seek to differentiate our descriptions from the events themselves, and to get as close as we can to the events. But no matter how close we believe we are to the events themselves, we are trapped by our own perspective. It is infuriatingly difficult to get close to the basic events; our theoretical perspectives keep us too far away.

The difficulty is magnified even further when a high level construct is taken as if it were the event itself, or even as if it were some simple, theory-free, empirical, close-to-the-event-itself, raw description. In to-day's research market, with its interdisciplinary flair, we often launch research programs as if we were studying raw events, when in actu-ality we are studying sophisticated constructs which are lodged within some single approach. For example, a considerable body of research-ers has been drawn to answering the question of what factors account for the relatively greater prevalence of psychiatric disorder among the lower class. We may answer this question by studying interdisciplinary psychological factors, genetic factors, social factors, economic factors, cultural factors, political factors, and more. We can study a melange of factors from various approaches. For example, we can investigate the interrelationships between sociocultural factors and genetic factors in producing a higher incidence of "psychiatric disorder" among the "lower classes" (Leighton & Hughes, 1961). But "psychiatric disorder" is very far from an event, and is, moreover, an extremely sophisti-cated construct like schizophrenia, witch, God, or humours of the body. I suggest that psychiatric disorder is a high level construct from one theoretical perspective—mistakenly given the status of a real event. When we progress beyond that theoretical approach, the career of that construct will be ended, and, together with its demise, we will witness the demise of all research investigating its supposed preva-lence in the lower class. The careful distinction between an event and constructions of that event requires precautions against such errors.

The Number of Basic Events

Humanistic theory adopts the position that there is only one kind of basic event. As indicated in Figure 4.1, some other approaches also as-sume that there is one fundamental kind of basic event. Whereas basic events are assumed, in our theory, to have no special fundamental nature (beyond a locus in time and space), other approaches (classes 2, 3, and 4, Figure 4.1) *do* endow basic events with a single, fundamental intrinsic nature. They assume, for example, that basic events are physical as opposed to mental. Included here are approaches (class 3, Figure 4.1) which assume that basic events are neurophysiological, or biochemical, or composed basically of electrons, or the single basic stuff may consist of ceaseless movement, back and forth, to and fro. This is referred to as phyit-pyet in Vipassana meditation (Byles, 1962). According to Klein (Jones, 1970), Freud's theory rested squarely on an assumption of a single kind of basic event whose na-ture is physiological. The assumption is ". . . that ultimately, the regu-larities described with purposive concepts will be *explainable* through the use of purely physiological models which disclose the causes of which the purposive principle is simply a descriptive expression"

(Jones, 1970, p. 112). Other approaches also assume a fundamental nature to basic events, but their basic events are nonphysical, mental, psychic (class 4, Figure 4.1). Still other approaches assume a third kind of fundamental nature to basic events. For them, basic events consist of a force, entelechy, Kapp's "diathetes," or elan vital (class 2, Figure 4.1). This third kind of basic event is a descendent of some of the primitive roots of animism. Like these other approaches, humanistic theory assumes one kind of basic event. Unlike these, however, our assumption is that the one kind of basic event merely has locus in time and space, and is not physical, mental, or composed of some vital force.

Still other approaches hold to an assumption that there are two or three different basic kinds of events (classes 5 and 6, Figure 4.1). In these approaches, basic events can be divided into two equally fundamental kinds, one being physical and the other mental. Class 5 approaches assume that human beings are composed of these two irreducible basic events. In Plato's formulation, for example, one of these two basic events includes matter or things. The other basic event is mind, composed of ideas and faculties such as courage and reason. A few approaches (class 6) even hold to a division into three basic kinds of events: physical, mental, and a vital third force—all equally basic and fundamental.

Theorogenic problems. When an approach assumes a fundamental division into two or more kinds of basic events, it has thereby created a set of problems which it must solve. The problems are created by the content of the theory, i.e., they are "theorogenic." Having divided events into those which are basically *matter* (physical, bodily) and those which were basically *soul* (psychic, mental), Descartes handed centuries of thinkers such corollary questions as which of these two kinds of fundamental events is more basic, and what is the process by which they interact with one another; if events are basically either physical or mental, then the problem is how to define a physical event as differentiated from a mental event. Huxley (Burt, 1955), reasoning from such an assumption, divided human states into those which were basically physical-neurological ("neuroses") and those which were basically psychic-conscious ("psychoses"). The generated problem is how to differentiate physical-neurological states from psychic-conscious states. Once a basic division is made between the physical (neurological) and the mental (psychic, conscious), we are confronted with differentiating much more than neuroses and psychoses. What are the differences between the physical and the mental? Mental states were supposed to be purposeful and intentional, whereas physical states lacked those qualities; but that distinction didn't work. What is physical is public, and mental events were private; but that way of distinguishing the two has not paid off. Mental states are characterized by free choice and reason, whereas physical states are characterized by causal chains and determinism. The search for the differences between the mental and the physical has a long history and a long (though fruitless) future. Once an approach accepts the assumption of a distinction between mental and physical basic events (and classes 2-6 accept such an assumption), the endless search has begun for the "real" differences between the two. None has proved satisfactory. None will.

One way of solving this problem is to hold that body events are those which follow bodily principles, and mental events are those which follow mental principles. Let us select an example and see how this differentiation works. Suppose that we are interested in separating psychological and neurophysiological events in the area of sensory quality. How do we distinguish between nerve impulses and psychological events, on the assumption that some events are basically either one or the other? One way is to accept that the event is a nerve impulse if it follows certain *neurophysiological* principles (Osgood, 1953): (a) If the event conforms to the all-or-none principle, it is a nerve impulse, viz. ". . . if a stimulus is sufficient to excite nervous tissue, the response of this tissue is an all-or-none affair" (Osgood, 1953, p. 33). (b) The event is a nerve impulse if it conforms to the essential identity principle whereby the nature of all nervous impulses is identical. Thus nerve impulses traveling in optic or cutaneous fibers do not differ in quality from each other. (c) The event is a nerve impulse if it conforms to the refractory principle whereby nervous tissue is limited in the rate at which it can react, recover, and react once again. An event, on the other hand, is a psychological one if it conforms to *psychological* principles. With regard to sensory experience, psychological events vary in quality (e.g. distinguishing pressure at the fingertips or distinguishing the fragrance of geraniums) and in sensory intensity (e.g., with quality held constant, pressure may be 'heavy' or 'light'; pinkness of a flower may vary in brightness) (Osgood, 1953). Once you assume that basic events are either psychological or nervous, principles must be created whereby each is distinguished from the other. Hence the problem is "theorogenic," i.e. created by the assumptions accepted by the theory itself, and restricted to theories accepting those assumptions.

Another "theorogenic" problem has to do with the number of basic kinds of any entity—such as the number of basic kinds of headaches, stutterings, heart problems, blindnesses or depressions. If your theory accepts the assumption that there are basically *two* kinds of events, psychic events and organic events, then you will be compelled to assume that there are two basic kinds of depression—"psychic" depression and "organic" depression. If you hold to the assumption that there is only one kind of basic event, and that is psychic in nature, then you are inclined to assume that basically there is only one kind of depression, and it is psychogenic. By the very same token, if you hold that your single kind of basic event is of an organic nature, then you will lean hard toward an assumption of one kind of depression, an organically based one. This is the precise state of affairs found by Beck (1967) in his excellent review of theories and research in the area of depression. "Some authorities contend that depression is primarily a psychogenic disorder; others maintain just as firmly that it is caused by organic factors. A third group supports the concept of two different types of depression: a psychogenic type and an organic type" (p. 4). Identifying the number of basic kinds of depression is a question of squaring the assumption on which your theory rests (i.e. number of basic events and their nature) with the data. The number of basic kinds of depression is a theorogenic problem, caused by the particular theory which you hold.

If your theory assumes that basic events are either mental or physical, then another problem is created: Is a particular phenomenon caused by mental factors or by physical factors? During the late 1800's, such a raging controversy occurred over the basic explanation of such phenomena as "hysterical" paralysis of an arm, "hysterical" blindness, and "hysterical" experiencing, or absence of experiencing, of pain. Was "hysteria" a mental phenomenon or a physical phenomenon? Bernheim and Liebeault argued that the basic causes were mental; Charcot insisted that the basic causes were physical. Bernheim and Liebeault tried to find the mental basic causes in the bedrock of suggestion and self-hypnosis; Charcot countered by seeking basic causes in organic deterioration. The same argument is alive today. Instead of arguing about hysteria, we have progressed to hundreds of phenomena: from headaches to schizophrenia, mental deficiency to moods, ulcers to mental deficiency, stomach pains to educability. Are the basic causes mental or physical? We are still enmeshed in this theorogenic problem, one which ineluctibly arises from an assumption that there are two kinds of basic events, one mental and one physical. On this assumption, all the opponents agree, otherwise there could be no basis for fighting. Humanistic theory does not accept the invitation to fight, because it does not accept the assumption of two or more basic kinds of events. Our theory does not bifurcate basic events into mental and physical. Therefore, our theory does not argue that such phenomena are either mental or physical.

Hospitals are filled with staff who hold that events are composed of mental (functional) components and physical (organic) components. Without really thinking about these issues, such personnel operate on the formula that an event (e.g. a headache or a stomach pain) is composed of so many parts physical plus so many parts mental. With regard to a headache, the formula runs as follows:

$$\text{Headache} = x \text{ parts organic} + y \text{ parts functional}$$

If a "physical" examination uncovers reasons to believe that there are organic factors of sufficient magnitude, then the headache is considered "organic," and the residual "functional" factors are considered minimal. Under these conditions, there is little basis for a "functional" examination, and organic treatment is carried out. The implicit formula has been filled in:

$$\text{Headache} = 95\% \text{ organic} + 5\% \text{ functional}$$

If a "physical" examination reveals *some* organic factors, but not sufficient to account for the headache, then the formula leads to the conclusion that a substantial amount of the causal factors must, therefore, be functional in nature. That is, if organic factors total approximately 40%, then 60% of the causal factors are likely of a functional nature. Under these circumstances, the patient with the headache would likely be referred for a "functional" examination. This line of implicit reasoning is quite common, and follows from a conception of two kinds of basic events, one being mental (functional) and the other physical (organic). How much of a given event is physical and how much (usually by exclusion) is mental is a problem created by and appropriate only to a particular set of assumptions. It is another example of a theorogenic problem, one which occupies considerable time, creates jobs, requires diagnostic conferences, and generally maintains psychologists, psychiatrists, psychoanalysts, physicians, psychometrists, and about a dozen subspecialists unwittingly perpetuating a rather simplistic and primitive level of conceptual thinking—aside from the potentially deleterious effects on untold thousands of "patients."

Another "theorogenic" problem is to identify the *real* level of explanation. Is this real or is that real? Is a synapse more real than an intention? Which is more real: a chemical bond or a reinforcement? The answers vary with the position taken on the three assumptions (cf. Figure 4.1). From our position (class 1, Figure 4.1), all we can say about the realness of an event is that it is an event, with no further qualities, parameters, essences, or essential characteristics. To go beyond this and to describe an event as an intention or a synapse is to invoke descriptive constructs. Thus the construct "intention" is no more and no less *real* than the construct "synapse."

But another, equally viable position is class 3 (Figure 4.1). According to this position, what is "real" is bodily. Let us say, as an example, that what is real is neurophysiological. From that assumptive system, an intention is not real. A synapse is more real than an intention. Another approach (class 5) assumes that the basic ("real") level of events is composed of body stuff *and* mind stuff. These are of equal stature. Therefore, according to this position, intentions, synapses, chemical bonds and reinforcements *can be* equally real.

The following statement, from Klein, is in accord with our position on this problem: "An intention and a function are as directly observable, no less specifiable, than a neurological discharge and, in that sense, just as 'real' " (in Jones, 1970, p. 115). Yet we can make such an assertion because, from our assumptions, constructs such as intention and neurological discharge are equally unreal in the sense that they are both constructs, and, as constructs, different from a basic level of events to which those constructs refer.

These are some of the problems created by an assumption that there are *two or more* basic kinds of events. It must be clear that these problems exist only for approaches which accept such an assumption. Let us turn now to some of the problems which exist for approaches which hold to a different assumption, viz. there is only *one* kind of basic event, and its nature is fundamentally physical or biological (class 3 approaches).

Once basic events are assumed to be physical or biological, then a field such as psychology becomes essentially a biological domain of study, and the particular nature of the mind-body problem is more or less set (Money, 1956): body is basic, mind derives from body. Accordingly, the range of possible solutions to the version of mind-body problems relevant to this third class of approaches is fairly well defined. In other words, the nature of the approach defines its own mind-body problem and the range of possible solutions.

Our position is that there is no "basic nature" of human beings. We can elect to describe human beings psychologically or biologically, yet the description is not of some assumed *basic* nature. In contrast, the mainstream of contemporary theorizing assumes that there *is* a basic nature to human beings, and that basic nature is biological. That is why contemporary theories of psychology are convinced of the existence of basic biological "needs" of the human "organism." "They are inherent in the structure of the living organism" (Maher, 1966, p. 60). Once it is assumed that basic events are, for example, of a biological nature, then it follows that the human organism has basic biological drives which operate on biological principles. "We cannot, of course, deny that basic drives seem to seek 'reduction of tension.' Oxygen need, hunger, thirst, elimination, are examples . . ." (Allport, 1965, p. 46). Our position is that the human being is not basically biological (or anything else), and that basic biological needs are not at all inherent in the structure of the living organism (Asch, 1952). We are free to take up that mode of *description*—or any other mode of description—but to search for basic biological needs inherent in the living organism is to set out to solve a problem which exists only for approaches which accept that particular assumption. In other words, it is a theorogenic problem.

If human beings are basically biological in their fundamental nature, then it is an easy step to the problem of identifying the basic biological needs or drives. We can, for example, identify basic biological needs for food, water, oxygen, rest, excretion, and sex (e.g. Vinacke, 1948). A next step is to presume that human beings share the same basic biological needs with all biological organisms, especially those of vertebrates and mammals (Asch, 1952). Yet we are solving a problem which was created by accepting the assumption that there is one basic event whose nature is biological. This problem is "theorogenic," created solely by the theory's own assumption. It is neither a problem in general, nor is it a problem for all or even most theories—just for those which embrace that particular assumption. Humanistic theory accepts none of these particular assumptions, and therefore does not find such problems meaningful or relevant. In effect, these problems were solved by bypassing the assumptions from which they arise.

Many psychologists and psychiatrists have come to a working compromise between the model of human beings suited to their basic theoretical assumptions, and the model of human beings suited to their professional work and even to their research. For example, when engaged in theoretical analyses of human beings, many psychologists and psychiatrists adopt a class 3 approach (Figure 4.1) in which the "primary motives" of human beings are of a biophysiological nature. Yet, in understanding the everyday interaction and interpersonal relationships of human beings, such biophysiological primary motives are disregarded. "In middle-class Western society much, if not most, behavior seems to be motivated by states which are not primary. Many men work for money, prestige, a sense of social worth, a feeling of personal accomplishment, etc . . . we may say that much behavior seems to occur without any correlated change in bodily state which we may identify as a motive" (Maher, 1966, p. 61). Primary biophysiological motives often are disregarded in actual clinical and research work with human beings. It is as if the theoretician believes that the human being is basically and fundamentally of a biophysiological nature, while the researcher and clinician often operate on other assumptions.

In the same vein, some approaches to psychotherapy claim to be "deep" and "intensive"; they claim to get at the *basic roots* of personality. It is difficult for me to picture the psychotherapist, having penetrated to the rock bottom of the patient's personality, exclaiming: "I see it all. Now I understand what you are like at the very core—hungry! thirsty! sleepy!" In our approach there is no theoretical necessity whatsoever to assume that human beings are basically *biophysiological*. One gets stuck into that position by having accepted specific assumptions about human beings.

If these assumptions are those of class 3 (Figure 4.1), then not only are personality foundations biological in nature, but the general contours of personality change are already predetermined. If it is assumed that personality consists of a biological foundation, the directions of optimal development and change must be in accord with such a biological nature for the basic stuff of personality (Mahrer, 1967b). Accordingly, personality development or change faces particular questions such as: (a) How may we remove, reduce, or eliminate blocks or interferences to biologically given capacities and potentialities for normal, healthy growth? (b) How may we assist biologically given capacities for maturity, health, and normality? These are *theorogenic* questions, applicable *only* to theories within the class 3 approach. In no way are these questions necessarily pertinent to theories falling in other classes.

Positions on the question of the nature of basic events lead easily to positions on the degree to which we can truly understand the particular person by seeking general laws about human beings. To what degree is it fruitful to search for general statements about human beings if our aim is to gain a full understanding of a particular person? Our position is that it is illusory to search for general "laws" of the *contents* of everybody's personality. We can, according to our approach, never get anywhere by trying to frame general laws about supposedly universal human needs or drives or motivations. To study the personality contents of the average person or to search for the contents of group norms brings us no closer to understanding the specific person or the parameters of the specific group. "If I want to understand an individual human being, I must lay aside all scientific knowledge of the average man and discard all theories in order to adopt a completely new and unprejudiced attitude. I can only approach the task of *understanding* with a free and open mind, whereas *knowledge* of man presupposes all sorts of knowledge about mankind in general" (Jung, 1957, p. 10).

On this question of a nomothetic or idiosyncratic approach to understanding the particular person or group of persons, one's stand has more or less already been determined by the position on the fundamental nature of basic events. Our position allows us to use increasingly systematic and precise descriptions of the contents—the fundamental nature—of the *individual* human being. But other approaches assume that there does exist an identifiable fundamental and basic nature of human beings *in general*. Therefore, other positions legitimate the search for what human beings are like in general, and act as if by identifying the basic nature of human beings we can then know the basic nature of every individual person. A stand on these assumptions, then, will automatically incline the theorist toward a given position on the question of nomothetic versus idiographic understanding of the particular person.

OPEN DESCRIPTION

When I seek to describe you, my descriptive statements are not a grasping of what you *are*. They are merely descriptive constructions *of* you. Since I elect to adopt a particular system of constructs in describing you, that system of constructs is far from absolute impartiality; it constrains me to that particular mode of description and to the assumptions of that system (Whorf, 1956). Therefore I can describe you, but that description *is not you*; I describe you by using a mode of description with its own built in set of constraints.

The Openness of Events to Any Mode of Description

From the position adopted by humanistic theory, any event is simply open to any mode of description. If we focus on those events we refer to as stuttering, then stuttering events are quite cordial to description from a physiological point of view, a linguistic point of view, and from such other viewpoints as cultural anthropology, psychoanalysis, semantics, anatomy, learning theory, chemistry, and so on. Indeed, stuttering is a good example of an event with a wide spectrum of workable modes of description. The same holds for events such as brushing one's teeth, sawing a piece of lumber, making love, or having a backache, viz. any event is simply open to any mode of description.

In the scientific pursuit of knowledge about the phenomena we study, it is desperately important to maintain this openness to various descriptive perspectives. Whether we are trying to understand the way infants knock a glass off a table, family interaction, a group of persons setting out to hate another group, or a person becoming obese, these phenomena beautifully lend themselves to description and understanding from many perspectives. It may be that our particular phenomena are special in some way that makes them especially open to various modes of description. It may be that good scientific methods of description and understanding are coming to be applied to our phenomena. It may be that the modes of description used by psychology, social work, and psychiatry are so primitive that just about any new mode of description is practically as good as the traditional ones. Whatever the explanation, our data seem marvelously open to various modes of description. According to Fiske (1971), we are in a different state than other sciences with regard to our data. "In most other sciences, the problem of multiple perspectives does not exist. The scientists in each of these disciplines have arrived at an unspoken consensus that their data shall consist of observations made by publically stated operations that are, both in principle and in practice, replicable by any qualified worker in the field" (p. 63). Not so in the field of human behavior. Each approach can claim a long and distinguished history. For example, there is a venerable history to the description of human behavior from the perspective of biochemistry. We can go back at least to Hippocrates' theory of humoural temperaments in which sanguine, choleric, melancholic, and phlegmatic temperaments are understood as corresponding to the relative predominance of the four different body biochemistries. Every mode of description of human personality and behavior has an ancient heritage of respectability. Each mode of grasping our data—be it medical, social, psychoanalytic, biophysiological, psychological or whatever—can dress itself in a respectable scientific heritage.

There are so many interlocking modes of description that it is difficult to organize them into categories. For example, is psychoanalytic description to be classified as a physiological mode? Many theoreticians consider psychoanalysis as resting squarely upon a physiological base of assumptions. A good case can be made that both the early and later versions of psychoanalysis rest upon a base of physiological assumptions common in the 19th century. In his early theorizing, Freud was candid about his reliance upon a physiological model to account for the phenomena he was encountering in his clinical practice. Even later, after supposedly abandoning the physiological model, his theory remained rooted in basic physiological assumptions. For example, the concept of regression to earlier stages of development grew straight out of the assumptive base of 19th century physiology (Hartmann, 1959). I consider psychoanalytic theory as resting squarely on physiological assumptions about human beings and their functioning, but others may find reasons for distinguishing between psychoanalytic and physiological modes of description. We have many modes of description to sort out. Indeed, there are so many respectable modes of description that careers are spent in the sheer cataloguing of the various modes. For example, one way of contributing to the field of psychotherapy is to know the compass of the respectable descriptive approaches. At present it is fair to say that there are from 10 to 20 respectable modes of description in this field. The same is characteristic of other bodies of data. In their study of separate and intact modes of description of the treatment of hospitalized patients, Strauss and his colleagues (1964) identified three large groupings:

sociotherapeutic approaches, somatotherapeutic approaches, and psychotherapeutic approaches—each with its own body of theory, research, and practice. The same story of multiple modes of description is true for nearly every defined area of study in the behavioral and social sciences, from stuttering to ulcers, from riots to educational change.

All of the various ways of describing our events are, from the perspective of class 1 approaches, nothing more than that—various sets of descriptive accounts. In Figure 4.1 they are indicated as X and N constructs under class 1 approaches. Any event is open to description from these several modes. It is as if several persons are using several different language systems to describe the same event. It is the *systems of language* (modes of description) which vary, even though the *designata* of the languages are identical. Feigl refers to this as the double-language solution of the mind-body problem (1955, pp. 319-321). Suppose that we limit these descriptive languages to two: a behavioristic descriptive language and a neurophysiological descriptive language. "Relative to the 'molar' (or macro-) account given by behavioristic psychology, the neurophysiological account is a micro-description of the very same events and processes . . . We contend that the designata of the mentalistic language are identical with . . . the designata of the neurophysiological language . . ." (Feigl, 1953, pp. 623-624). Events are open and cordial to multiple modes of description. This is the position adopted by humanistic theory as one of the class 1 approaches (Figure 4.1).

The event itself does not belong in any particular mode of description, for each mode invests the event with a different intrinsic nature. Class 1 approaches do not sort events into different basic kinds. Because it is the *modes of description* which vary, and not the *events*, class 1 approaches hold that their particular events are also open to description from the perspective of other language systems such as sociology, physics, or music. "If we confine attention strictly to behavior, described exclusively in physiological language, then the study of behavior whether animal or human remains within the boundaries of biology" (Woodger, 1956, p. 117). If we confine attention strictly to behavior, described exclusively in sociological, musical, or chemical languages, then the study of behavior exists within the boundaries of sociology, music, or chemistry. "Each has its characteristic vocabulary. Whether a statement belongs to a given science depends therefore on whether it can be expressed in the existing vocabulary of that science (p. 118). Given these various language systems (or modes of description or theories), any event is wholly open to any relevent mode of description—according to the class 1 approaches.

When the event we seek to describe is assumed (i.e., in class 1) to possess no intrinsic nature, only that of being a mere event, then there can be no "right" mode of description. The focus shifts from the event to the descriptive constructs themselves. Differences in ways of accounting for events can then reflect sober differences in theoretical constructs, and not errors in measurement. If you describe an event called stuttering from a physiological mode, and I describe that event from a psychological mode, what can we conclude about our differences? Are you right and I wrong? Do our differences mean that you have grasped stuttering more veridically than I have? "Some people say that the difference among observations by several people are simply due to the presence of errors of measurement, and that within such observations there is a core of consensus; there is a common variance that can be utilized for scientific work. An alternative view is that these differences among observations are fundamental. They are systematic rather than random. Hence observations from different points of view should be treated as different data, not as approximations of identical data" (Fiske, 1971, p. 61). I am arguing in favor of openness of scientific modes of description. My mode of description can differ from yours without one of ours being necessarily in error. The worthwhileness of our respective modes of description can be judged on grounds other than deciding which is in error with respect to the criteria of the other.

When the scientific viability of multiple modes of description gets out of hand, we can easily have several modes melting into one another. Unless each mode is kept intact, we will have a disorganized swirl of theoretical viewpoints in which everything is related to everything. What is the relationship between a person's "problems" and the "society in which he lives"? We must be careful, for there are many attractive theories to deal with these events. If they are not allowed to be respected as separate theories, separate modes of description, then all we can assert is that everything is loosely related to everything else: "The illnesses are a result or an expression of disharmonies within a person and between him and his society . . . Moreover, the cause-effect sequence runs both ways. A person's internal harmony or conflict affects his relationships with others, and his interpersonal experiences influence his internal state" (Frank, 1961, p. 216). All of these statements seem reasonable. When we allow each mode of description to melt into every other mode, the transcendent statements which emerge all seem quite reasonable. Yet on closer inspection, such statements leave one handcuffed. Such statements almost defy anyone to do anything. Where do you start? What do you do? According to these statements, you can start anywhere and go in any direction. You can start with the person's "problems" and you can also start with the "society in which he lives." It does not matter, because everything is related loosely and generally to everything else. Under conditions whereby each descriptive mode is blended into every other descriptive mode, nothing moves ahead—not theory, not research, and not practice. When we consider an event or set of events, the class 1 position leaves plenty of room for various modes of description, but each is respected as having its own independent integrity.

Accessibility to description is not ownership. Humanistic theory *owns* no events. It is free to describe whatever it wishes, but it has no territorial mandate over any set of events, no exclusive rights of ownership. Indeed, *no* theoretical mode of description owns any set of events. What occurs in groups is not the exclusive property of sociology or social psychology, or chemistry or physics. Human behavior is neither the exclusive property of psychology, political science, law, psychiatry, or history. Bodily events are not the property of anatomy, biology, neurology, physiology, or heredity to any greater extent than they are open to description from the perspectives of psychology, physics, religion, mathematics, or economics. No mode of theoretical description owns the *body*. No mode of theoretical description has any greater claim to bodily territoriality than other modes of description.

Until relatively recently, the body was owned by theology, and intrusion by any other discipline met with massive resistance from the church. Then medicine challenged theology's ownership rights and waged a bitter war for control. Medicine won the war. From then on, medicine declared itself king of the body. Medicine lusted for exclusive ownership, and stands guard against any intrusion. Today medicine remains firmly in power, and wages war on many fronts—legally, administratively, professionally, educationally, economically, and even scientifically and academically. Medicine guards the body as vigilantly as theology once did, but its weapons are far more effective. In flat opposition, our position is that *no* scientific mode of description can own the body, just as no scientific mode of description can own *any* set of events. The body stands open to description from any relevant set of theoretical constructs. Our position likewise wages war, but not to acquire ownership of the body, or any event. Instead, we wage war against any single, exclusive mode of description. Our position challenges any *exclusive* rights to description and calls for a thorough-going *openness* to description. I object to a position that because an event is *accessible* to description from some viewpoint, it should *only* be described from that viewpoint. Because the body is accessible to neurophysiological description, some writers (e.g. Vinacke, 1948) argue that the body *should only* be described in neurophysiological terms. "Every manifestation of behavior in an organism . . . occurs in association with some physiological change . . . the organism functions in terms of its structure and the properties of its organized tissues. Even a thought, however original or untraceable in origin it may seem, nevertheless depends upon some activity of the nervous tissues. Even an emotional response is somehow a chemicophysico response" (p. 112). In flat contrast, our position is that any event, behavior, thought, or emotion, is open to description from any relevant perspective; description shall never be restricted to the constructs of any single viewpoint! Because bodily events *can* be described physiologically does not mean that a physiological mode of description is either exclusive or predominant. I can describe every bodily manifestation poetically, but I would not conclude that a poetic language of the body is either exclusive or predominant.

The success of a given mode of description does not justify exclusive ownership of the events. A neurophysiological mode of describing human behavior is uppermost today, and therefore, neurophysiologically based research dominates today's scene. "Normal inductive extrapolation from the successes of psychophysiology to date makes it plausible that an adequate theory of animal and human behavior can be provided on a neurophysiological basis" (Feigl, 1958, p. 382). But the current vogue of any mode of description is hardly evidence of its ultimate scientific utility or worth. Accessibility to neurophysiological description is no surprise to our position. Nor is current popularity evidence that human behavior is solely or best described from that vantage point.

From a class 4 position (Figure 4.1), Alexander argues in the very same way for a *psychological* description of the body. "The fact that the mind rules the body is . . . the most fundamental fact which we know about the process of life . . . The body . . . carries out the most complex and refined motor activities under the influence of such psychological phenomena as ideas and wishes" (Alexander, 1950, p. 37). Because the body *can* be described psychologically (or neurophysiologically), we cannot agree that it should only or exclusively be described in those terms. No mode of description owns the events it describes. An event (e.g., the body) is merely open to various modes of description.

Binswanger (1958b, p. 234) describes a woman's act of inserting her arm into a burning stove. That act is described first using the perspective of existentialism, then from a psychiatric perspective in which the act is a symptom of a mental disease, and from still a third perspective of ethical morality. He might have added other perspectives, of course. The point is that existentialism does not own that act. Nor is that act exclusively psychiatric. Nor does ethical morality own such an act. No mode of description can, according to our position, claim ownership over the events it finds convenient to describe.

Nearly every mode of description can identify events where it works better and events where it has little or nothing to say. To use Kelly's apt phrase, each theory carves out its own "area of convenience" (1955, p. 22). Family interrelationships may be more effectively described from the viewpoint of psychology than from the viewpoints of mathematics or chemistry. But the current relative effectiveness of various modes of description is one issue quite distinct from that of sheer openness to description. I can describe the setting of a broken bone from the viewpoints of law, psychology, and medicine, but I would prefer the bone to be set by an experienced physician, rather than an attorney or a psychologist. With regard to sheer accessibility to scientific description, no mode of description owns family relationships, broken bones or any other events.

A theoretical system ordinarily will define the content area or field to which it applies. Thus, sociology is understood as the study of one set of events, and physics is understood as the study of another set of events. Nevertheless, several theoretical systems may pertain to the same or similar fields of events, and, conversely, the same field of events can be legitimately open to several theoretical systems. Theoretical systems differ primarily in the nature of their conceptual components rather than in the nature of the fields they study. This is the position of class 1 (Figure 4.1) approaches on the question of the definition of fields of study. But this is not the position of approaches falling under classes 2-6. According to those classes, the nature of the basic events *is* identifiable, and therefore fields of study *can* be differentiated one from the other. Indeed, for theorists operating within classes 2-6, a theoretical system *must* define its own set of events, its own distinctive field of investigation; it must have its own independent set of problems *and* individual field of study (McGeoch, 1933). Clearly, the position on this issue varies with the class in which the theoretical system falls.

When we adopt our perspective and consider a steak, a potato, and a salad, these events can be described from various viewpoints. For example, it is possible to describe them artistically—in terms of color, form and organization on a plate, placement and beauty and symmetry. It is possible to describe them economically—how much each item cost. It is possible to describe food from many viewpoints, and each may be a legitimate and reasonable mode of description. Food is not owned by physiology any more than it is owned by agriculture or artistry or business or history or cultural anthropology or psychology or physics. When a person is seeking food, the food may therefore be described as an event within many modes of description. *What* a person is seeking is no evidence at all that one mode is prepotent over others. That a person seeks food is not evidence that he is operating artistically, psychologically, or physiologically. Yet other approaches do indeed classify food as a *physiological* event, and the seeking of food is taken as evidence of the presence of a physiological "need." Such reasoning proceeds as follows: "Undoubtedly these physiological needs are the most prepotent of all needs. What this means specifically is that in a human being who is missing everything in life in an extreme fashion, it is most likely that the major motivation would be the physiological needs rather than any others. A person who is lacking food, safety, love, and esteem would most probably hunger for food more strongly than for anything else" (Maslow, 1970, p. 36). Is food a physiological thing? From our perspective, food is not owned exclusively by physiology, and the seeking of food is no evidence at all of either the existence or the prepotence of physiological needs. We are left only with the bare observation that persons who miss everything in life in an extreme fashion tend to seek food, and *that* empirical observation is itself open to understanding from all relevant descriptive modes. In the same way, water and rest are not exclusively physiological any more than seeking money is exclusively economic or seeking a breast is exclusively psychological.

Freedom of scientific movement. When an event is held to be open to multiple modes of description, the event also becomes open to multiple modes of scientific inquiry and research. Under such a regime, the pursuit of knowledge about family interrelationships (or bicycle riding or stomach pains) leaves investigators free to use the scientific methods of sociology, systems analysis, semantics and linguistics, psychology, or any other relevent science. In the study of any set of events, methods of rigorous research inquiry are not to be restricted to those of any single science. In studying the events in our field, we eschew restriction of research methods to those of the so-called "natural sciences." Much of psychology has adopted a biological mode of description, and equates rigorous research methods with those which psychology understands as those of the natural sciences. The problem arises when psychologists committed to the natural sciences approach strive to *restrict* scientific methods to those which are congruent with *their* particular mode of description. I object to constraining scientific methods to those of the natural sciences, and adopt a position which welcomes rigorous methods of inquiry congruent with the whole spectrum of relevent modes of description. "If 'scientific' is used in this unprejudiced manner, the claim that the methods of natural science alone can yield precise information becomes unwarranted" (Boss, 1963, p. 29).

Our criteria for a good method of research inquiry include its fruitfulness, its ability to offer a significant yield. The history of the natural sciences shows the magnificent fruitfulness of one particular approach to research, viz. the quantitative, experimental method. But science is not necessarily coterminal with the fruitful methods of the natural sciences (Giorgi, 1966). If we adopt a position outside that of the natural sciences—and humanistic theory *is* outside of the natural sciences—then *our* scientific approach is by no means constrained to the quantitative, experimental method of the natural sciences. We seek scientific methods which *are* fruitful, rather than defining science in terms of the methods which the *natural sciences* accept as *their* fruitful methods. Our definition of scientific methods *includes* the quantitative, experimental method, but is not restricted to it. As long as other methods are fruitful, they may be non-quantitative and non-experimental yet qualify as rigorously scientific methodology.

Each mode of description has its own set of constructs. Psychoanalysis employs its own constructs, as do humanistic theory, Gestalt psychology, social learning theory, and every other mode of description. It is quite legitimate to pursue research inquiry which is tied to the particular constructs of a specific mode of description. However, to the degree that a line of research has meaning primarily within a given theoretical system, I term it *house research*. Thus it is quite legitimate to utilize systematic methods of inquiry to gain knowledge about constructs of meaning within a particular theoretical house. If a theory employs the construct "superego," it can use rigorous methods of research to study the degree to which superego is related to suicide, or to find how early in child development superego functions appear. But it is quite another matter to equate house research with public scientific knowledge. The results of such research inquiry are of far more value to the parent theory than they are to a cumulative body of scientific knowledge. It is, I believe, an error to parade such research findings as factual empirical knowledge. It is an error of even greater proportions to *restrict* scientific inquiry to the constructs of any particular theoretical mode of description.

Research which employs a construct of *schizophrenia* is therefore of legitimate meaningfulness to theoretical modes of description employing the concept of schizophrenia. It is more house research than a contribution to scientific factual knowledge. The life span of the research findings is tied to the life span of the parent theory; when the theory is replaced by the succeeding wave of regnant theories, the research findings on schizophrenia will atrophy. In no way can research on the *events* to which the construct *schizophrenia* refers be restricted to theories employing the word schizophrenia. These are the conclusions from a position (class 1, Figure 4.1) which calls for freedom of scientific movement.

A theory must hold dear the concept of schizophrenia before it sets out to search for the etiological roots of schizophrenia. The critical point comes when lines of research, generated by investigators employing the concept of schizophrenia, come up with virtually nothing.

What do we do when we study "schizophrenogenic mothers," and reviews of research point toward a conclusion that we are not only unable to define a schizophrenogenic mother, but the concept itself seems to be heuristically sterile (Frank, 1965)? If the research is carried out by persons wedded to the concept of schizophrenia, they typically follow every option except that of scrapping the concept. I see such investigators as stuck, forced into a myopic research avenue generated primarily by the theoretical position of their own particular house. Freedom of scientific movement means that other theories also have the scientific invitation to make sense of the empirical data *without* utilizing the concept of schizophrenia. Humanistic theory, for example, has no place for "schizophrenia" nor for "schizophrenogenic" mothers. Our position arrogates the right to pursue research without using such concepts from other theoretical houses. Progress in the pursuit of knowledge invites theories to be free of the conceptual handicaps of constructs which ought perhaps best be scrapped, or at least recognized as belonging to particular theoretical viewpoints. Schizophrenia is only one, but it is a prominent one.

The concept of schizophrenia also includes events to which that concept refers. These events are public events which are open to various modes of description. But the *concept* of schizophrenia is another matter. In one form or another, the concept of schizophrenia has been held for centuries. Its remarkable endurance has been due, in part, to the larger theory which invests it with life-protecting meaning. Schizophrenia is woven into a larger theoretical tapestry, and will endure as long as the theory is intact, with or without research confirmation. Even with inadequate and equivocal research support, schizophrenia will persist as long as we continue to use the theoretical framework of which schizophrenia is a part. After a half century of inquiry, the research support for schizophrenia is embarrassingly meager. "No generally agreed upon clinical criteria for the diagnosis of 'schizophrenia' have been discovered. No consistency for prepsychotic personality, course, duration, outcome, has been discovered. Every conceivable view is held by authoritative people as to whether 'schizophrenia' is a disease or a group of diseases; whether an identifiable organic pathology has been, or can be expected to be found. There are no pathological anatomical findings post mortem. There are no organic structural changes noted in the course of the 'illness.' There are no physiological-pathological changes that can be correlated with this illness" (Laing & Esterson, 1970, p. 17). The history of science suggests that the concept of schizophrenia will be laid aside only when we accept a theoretical framework which has no place for such a concept. The freedom of scientific movement allows for such changes to occur.

Similar conclusions hold for research tied to any construct whose meaning lies within regnant theoretical modes of description. That includes constructs such as learning, motivation, mental disorder, catatonia, reinforcement, operant conditioning, actualization, maturity, maladjustment, and the like.

I respect the construct "psychotic." It is a word which means something when I talk with my friends and colleagues. It is in the dictionaries. I also respect "psychotic" as a relatively systematic construct within a moderately defined body of psychiatric thought. I can use the word when I am with professional persons who talk about cases and research in psychopathology. But the word has systematic meaning only within particular theoretical approaches. It has no such place within humanistic theory, and, therefore, it will not be used in any systematic fashion in this book. In a similar way, I dismiss as irrelevant *to humanistic theory* all the attempts by theoreticians and researchers to discover the factorial dimensions of psychosis, to devise various diagnostic types of psychosis, to study ways of treating "psychotics," to discover behavioral and demographic characteristics of "psychotics," to find the historical and physio-chemical causes of psychosis, and to examine the ways in which various kinds of "psychotics" score on various psychological tests and measures (Mahrer, 1970d). The whole literature is about as relevant to humanistic theory as the pursuit of answers to the same questions with regard to witches, elves, goblins, or incubi. That literature is *house research* whose predominant worth is restricted to the old psychiatric house.

House research is legitimate—as long as it is considered no more than what it is, mere house research. It cannot pretend that it is the essence of scientific inquiry. In addition to this meaning of research, there are at least two other legitimate meanings. A second applies to inquiry coming out of a *different* house but directed toward studying the *events* to which a construct, e.g., schizophrenia, refers—utilizing scientific methods whose rigor equals or exceeds those employed by houses using the construct of schizophrenia. A third legitimate line of research utilizes methods of inquiry which place a premium on the pursuit of *simple empirical relationships*. Freedom of scientific movement is a legitimization of multiple avenues of research inquiry, within any house of theoretical constructs, and also at the level of simple empirical relationships.

It must be understood, however, that much of our research, far more than we may believe, is house research whose career of usefulness is tied to the career of its theoretical house. So much of our research relies on *personality dimensions* relevant only to a particular theoretical framework. Research endeavors utilizing scales, tests, and assessment measures risk short careers when such personality dimensions as the following are used: social quotient, reactive versus process schizophrenia, internal versus external control, psychasthenia, paranoia, verbal intelligence, authoritarianism, distress/relief quotient, manifest anxiety, ego strength, maturity, empathic ability, drive level, stereotypy, hysteria, intropunitiveness, latent anxiety, acquiescence, social desirability, test anxiety, impulse control, and literally hundreds upon hundreds of others. Once a shift in meaning occurs in the definition of any of these personality dimensions, once the house theory shifts just a bit or is replaced by another, the research utilizing these measures tends to fade into meaninglessness. Such is the scientific fate of mere house research. In contrast, freedom of scientific movement allows both for research flowing out of many houses and for empirical research whose career outlasts that of a given theoretical house from which a personality dimension emerges.

The personality constructs and dimensions underlying the standard psychiatric nomenclature are meaningful only within the framework of traditional psychiatry. Research utilizing the standard psychiatric nomenclature is predominantly meaningful *only* within this framework. In contrast, description and understanding of human beings from a humanistic perspective—even when this is akin to personality classification—involve a whole different set of personality constructs and dimensions (Mahrer, 1970d). Within humanistic theory, there is no place for any of the constructs or dimensions which comprise the standard psychiatric nomenclature. Our system has no place for, and flatly rejects, the standard psychiatric nomenclature. That category system, and the assumptive base upon which it rests, belongs to an approach which is substantially different from ours. Freedom of scientific movement allows for varying sets of constructs and dimensions about (the personality classification of) human beings.

Of all the possible ways of evaluating the worth of research, I have been discussing only two. One refers to the degree to which the research contributes to the open, public market place. This can be described as empirical research. It adds to a cumulative body of simple observations and its locus is down close to the events themselves (Figure 4.2). The second dimension refers to the degree to which the research contributes to the further systematization of the parent theory. Research is high on this dimension to the degree that it "tests" the theory, makes a difference to that theory, is logically linked to the theory, leads to some change in the theory. On the basis of these two intersecting dimensions we can evaluate the scientific worth of most research:

In quadrant A (Figure 4.2) falls research which is low in both dimensions. Such research offers very little to empirical scientific knowledge, tells us practically nothing about human beings and what we are like. It also bears very little linkage to any particular theory. It is neither systematically derived from theory, nor do its results have much impact on the structure of the theory itself.

Research in quadrant B is linked to a given theory and is highly meaningful to the further systematic development of the theory. Whereas its worth is high on that dimension, it offers very little to the pool of empirical knowledge. Such research typically investigates the relationships among variables whose meanings are restricted to the parent theory. Although its results make a difference within and to the theory itself, the results tell us precious little of interest to those outside the theory, and have little to offer once the theory completes its career and passes away.

Research in quadrant C provides us with knowledge which belongs in the public scientific marketplace. We now know something of an empirical nature that we did not know before. For example, we may now know that 18 percent of the students in the faculty of arts at a given university tend to prefer writing with their left hand. But these results may have very little systematic linkage to any particular theory, are not derived from any theory, and make little or no difference to any theory.

Research is high on both dimensions if it falls in quadrant D. Here is the research which bears systematic linkages to theories. It is derived and generated from theories, and it makes a difference to the content and structure of the theories. At the same time, this research offers a contribution to public scientific knowledge. It is part of the body of cumulative scientific knowledge even after the demise of the parent theory itself. Although freedom of scientific movement opens the way of multiple modes of description, understanding, and explanation, the various modes are not necessarily of interchangeable scientific worth. Dimensions such as these two properly are invoked to assess the scientific worth of the various modes of description.

Our position does not prejudge the potential scientific heuristic worth of any mode of description. By maintaining a stance of open description, the way is clear for the future growth of any mode of description. The fact that several modes of description are quite good for describing an event is no basis for denying the potential scientific merit of any *other* mode. Dreams had been described theologically until we found dreams to be quite cordial to a psychoanalytic mode of description. Who knows what other mode will carry a full load of future scientific heuristic value? Let us leave the way open for each succeeding wave of modes, for future ones will very likely contribute significantly to the scientific understanding of dream phenomena.

In effect, we do not close the doors to any approach. If we are concerned with the resolution of a particular social problem, would we close the door on an approach which is not directly relevant to that specific social problem? Our position would encourage and promote such an approach. I honor the theoretical right of a research program which is pointed toward the resolution of social problems through the investigation of animal social behavior (cf. Spence, 1956). This kind of attitude toward the freedom of scientific approaches follows from the openness of events to any mode of description.

Can we gain substantive knowledge about complex human behavior by studying simple biological organisms? Our answer to this question depends upon the nature of the variables comprising the specific theory. My strong impression is that the variables which comprise humanistic theory are not relevant to simple biological organisms (cf. Koch, 1956). It is my conviction that the constructs, variables, and principles of humanistic theory relate far more to complex human behavior than to simple biological organisms. Therefore, I doubt very much that humanistic theory can be furthered by research on simple biological organisms.

If the investigator follows an approach in which human behavior is a function of neurophysiological variables, the investigator will be inclined toward contributing to and utilizing research on animal neurophysiology. But humanistic theory does not rest upon such a neurophysiological base, and therefore our research will not be inclined toward work with animals. Theorists who hold to the importance of neurophysiology will tend to include animal research, while other theorists, including humanists, will be inclined away from animal research.

Such considerations lead me away from the research study of simple biological organisms as an avenue toward the understanding of complex human behavior. I am not impressed by the argument that we can approach complex human behavior by studying first the simple behavior of organisms (Havemann, 1957, Skinner, 1953). I am not impressed by the argument about the relative ease of investigating biological organisms as compared with complex human interaction. If a theory of human beings includes constructs and variables which are salient to simple biological organisms, then it seems most appropriate to pursue research on either organisms, humans, or both. It is the salience of the constructs and variables which holds the heaviest load for me—and this consideration leads me toward research on human beings, and away from research on biological organisms, as an avenue toward the understanding of human behavior.

While our approach accepts a sharp fundamental difference between human beings described from the viewpoint of humanistic theory and human beings described from the viewpoint of the natural sciences, many scientists are busy arguing that our understanding of human beings *can best* be furthered by studying "nature." Can we understand a human being best by studying the way a computer works? Or by studying pigeons and rats and earthworms? Or by studying flowers and trees? Or by studying wind currents and oceans? These are serious questions on whose answers depend the careers of scientists, the rise and fall of disciplines, jobs, university departments, government agencies, and research support. From our perspective, the answer lies in the nature of the *theory*, its *construct system*, the language of science adopted by the scientist. If the theoretical construct system lends itself fittingly to both human beings and rats, then the answer is yes. If the theoretical construct system lends itself fully to human beings and not at all to computers or earthworms or fish or pebbles or wind currents, then the answer is no. The error which so many perpetuate is to assume that the answer lies in a debate over the *intrinsic nature* of human beings, earthworms, trees, and computers. In this debate the humanists assert we are unique (e.g. Maslow, 1970), and the natural scientists find an essential commonality. As I see it, debating the essential, *intrinsic nature* of events is absolutely fruitless, for that consists in debating assumptions on which we erect theoretical systems. My position on these issues turns away from debating basic assumptions, and grants full access, full scientific entrance, to any event. By switching theoretical systems, we can switch completely from a yes answer to a no answer—and the basic nature of the events is left completely alone, because there isn't any! From the position of our class 1 approach (Figure 4.1), we can *not* further the understanding of human beings by studying rats and flowers. In every approach falling in classes 2-6, the answer to this question is gained by examining, not the *constructs* of the theory, but the *assumed intrinsic basic nature* of human beings. If human beings and rats and flowers share a common intrinsic basic nature, then by all means inquire into human beings through their rat-ness and flower-ness. You are living in the class 2-6 world and have no other choice.

Our position on all these issues is only one of at least six (Figure 4.1). Can we test our position against others by means of research? Can hard research confirm that one position on these issues is forever superior to another? I doubt it. Any position ". . . is not an issue that can be decided on evidence—one can only assert the reasonableness and fruitfulness of a point of view . . . it is a faith, a belief, a credo, and as such it is incapable of either proof or disproof by the methods of science. . . ." (Osgood, 1953, pp. 33, 40).

Fullness of Theoretical Description

Suppose that we are considering whether a particular description of one person's stuttering and a second person's headache is a *full* description. What do we mean by a full description?

The fullness of each mode of description. From the perspective of class 1 approaches, the stuttering and the headache are neutral events open to multiple modes of description such as those of psychology and neurophysiology and others. It is possible (class 1, Figure 4.1) to mount a fully neurophysiological description of stuttering and of a headache complete with nothing but neurophysiological constructs. In precisely the same way, the stuttering and the headache can be described using psychological constructs. Just as a *fully neurophysiological* description will use only neurophysiological constructs, a fully *psychological* description can be provided using only psychological constructs. The meaning of a full description is relative to the given mode of description. Thus stuttering and headaches can be *fully* described using neurophysiological constructs, and *fully* described using psychological constructs. For each mode of description, the aim is its own development toward fullness using its own constructs. Understand, however, that these assertions about full description are generated out of class 1 approaches only.

Within these class 1 approaches, various modes of description *can* each yield a complete, full description of an event. A headache can be *fully* described from a psychological mode of description. The fullness of a psychological mode of description has nothing to do with the possible fullness of a neurological (or anatomical or physiological) mode of description. Earlier we discussed the implicit formula used by many of the professional staff of hospitals, a formula in which an event is held as composed of a basic mental component and a basic physical component (e.g. class 5, Figure 4.1), with the whole event being the summation of the two. According to our position, the event is neither basically mental, basically physical, nor basically a summation or combination of the two. According to the traditional formula, if the headache lends itself cordially to an "organic" description, it *is* predominantly organic and only minimally "functional." In contrast, our position holds that any event, such as a headache, may be open simultaneously to any degree of fullness of description from any viewpoint. If the headache is fully described organically, it *may* be only partly described functionally, or it *might* be *fully* described functionally. According to our position, the headache can vary from 0-100% "organic" and, independently, from 0-100% "functional." Each mode of description does its own fitting to the headache or any other event, and we can accept descriptions of headache which are 100% functional *and* 100% organic *and* 100% social or historical or linguistic or whatever mode of description is adopted.

Each mode of description, then, grows and develops within its own frame of reference. I do not work within a neurophysiological mode of description. Yet my hope is that such a mode of description develops to its fullest scientific potential. Let each way of describing stuttering, headaches, and every other event develop as fully as possible within its own frame of reference. When this state is approximated, we shall have a full description and explanation of stuttering and headaches using a neurophysiological mode of description, a full description and explanation using a psychological mode of description, and a full description and explanation from any other relevant mode of description. We are nowhere near this state, in part because of the reluctance of approaches to grant this meaning of full description.

What does our position do to the war between the "mental" description and explanation of "hysterical" phenomena (led by Bernheim and Liebeault), and the "physical" description and explanation championed by Charcot? It means that the war would be ended by withdrawing the assumptions on which the controversy rests. Just as the phenomena were assumed to be *either* mental or physical (as in classes 2-6, Figure 4.1), description and explanation were held as *either* mental or physical. From our position (class 1), that assumption is dropped. Instead, the assumption is that so-called "hysterical" phenomena were merely events, neither basically mental nor physical. A full explanation can be framed within a mental mode of description, and an equally full explanation can be framed within a physical mode of description—as well as other descriptive modes!

Our meaning of a full description rejects the notion that there exists *the* accurate or correct description of any event. Because a headache is merely an event, it is open to multiple sets of equally correct and accurate modes of description. There is a very accurate and correct neurological mode of describing a headache, and there is an accurate and correct Gestalt mode of describing a headache, and there is an accurate and correct physiological description of a headache. If, on the other hand, one has adopted an approach (classes 2-6) in which the event headache does possess some basic nature, one which is, for example, neurophysiological, then there would exist only one truly correct and accurate mode of description, and that would be a neurophysiological one. Any other mode of description might be decent, even respectable, but it would always fall short of being *the* accurate and correct (neurophysiological) one.

Many researchers operate within a class 3 approach in which the basic level of explanation is of a neurophysiological nature. Yet these researchers have conducted much of their work at a level which does not dip down into the most basic neurophysiological variables, even though they have uncovered consistent and discriminating variables. This has left these researchers with a defensive sense of incompleteness because they could not point confidently to the substantiating organic basis, the real stuff underlying the behavior which they studied (Littman & Rosen, 1950). Once the researcher adopts a class 3 approach, a full description of a phenomenon *requires* inclusion of organic, neurophysiological variables.

Fullness as the total package of modes of description. The second meaning of a full description begins with some event (like stuttering or headache), and defines fullness in terms of the totality of what each mode of description offers. From this meaning, a full description is one which includes all relevant modes of description. If we sought a full description of stuttering or headaches, we would not be satisfied with only a psychoanalytic mode of description. Nor would we be satisfied with a biochemical mode of description, or only an anatomical or semantic or philosophical or physiological mode of description. Our aim would be to gain a full description and explanation by assembling every point of view which seemed to offer a significant contribution to the description and explanation of stuttering and headaches. This is the second meaning of a full description, a meaning with which humanistic theory also concurs.

Fullness as the coupling of description to practice and research. A third meaning of fullness refers to the degree to which description is coupled with a prescription of what to do, i.e., practice, application, therapy, intervention, change. A mode of describing stuttering or headache is full to the extent that it prescribes what to do about the stuttering or the headache. It is especially *not* full if it provides a description, but, in order to do anything about the stuttering or the headache, one must switch over to some other mode of description. Psychoanalytic consultants to mental hospitals spin fascinating *psychoanalytic* descriptions of patients' problems, yet, once the consultant leaves, "treatment" typically occurs within a *pharmacologic* frame of reference. A detailed *physiological* description of the stomach wall is not full when what is done for the patient's ulcer can only be described in a simplistic *social work* frame of reference. A *cognitive* mode of describing a young man's thinking processes is not full when treatment is determined by *neurosurgical* considerations of what is to be done to his brain.

A full description of the events referred to as "mental deficiency" provides both a way of understanding mental deficiency and a way to do something about it. "There is no denying that, in order to treat the 'mental defective' medically, the condition must be defined and conceptualized from a somatic, physiological point of view" (Cantor & Cromwell, 1957, p. 465). A full sociological mode of description of "mental deficiency" would tell us what to do about it sociologically. A full humanistic description of mental deficiency would offer humanistic constructs of what to do about it. If any mode of description is full, in this third sense, it is coupled with a description of what to do about the events it describes.

This meaning of fullness also considers the coupling of a mode of description to the domain of research. For example, full description refers to the extent to which a particular theoretical perspective grasps research knowledge about some phenomenon. Here is an arena on which various theoretical modes can be compared and contrasted with one another. To what extent can particular theories of personality make sense of the research on eye color? It seems that *genetic* theory would be in a decent position to make some sense of the research on eye color. But *personality* theories and eye color? I doubt whether psychoanalytic theory or social learning theory or the theories of Sullivan, Jung, or Adler can make much more than a joke of the research on eye color. On the other hand, proponents of genetic theory make claims about other phenomena, claims which are open to serious question. Do we wish to rely upon genetic theory to understand and predict human beings' temperamental characteristics, intelligence, variations in affective feeling, tolerance of psychological stress? Some proponents of genetic theory suggest we turn to genetic theory for the grasping of research in these areas (e.g. Kallman, 1956). I suggest, rather, that no clear superiority exists wherein genetic theory makes better sense of the research on these phenomena than other theories of personality. Theories can be compared and contrasted with one another on their relative abilities to grasp research knowledge on specific phenomena. A full mode of description makes sense of the good research on the events it seeks to describe. On this score, the family of humanistic theories (e.g. Gestalt, phenomenology, existentialism and the cadre of writers in the humanistic tradition) has a miserable showing. Except possibly for a bit of the research on client-centered therapy and sensitivity groups, the humanistic family has managed successfully to detach itself from thousands of good research investigations on hundreds of topics about which the humanistic family at least purports to have a generally avuncular interest. With regard to this meaning, the humanistic family not only fails to provide a *full* mode of description, its obliviousness to research indicates a mode of description which is painfully depleted.

RELATIONSHIPS AMONG MODES OF DESCRIPTION

There are many modes of description in our field of human phenomena: neurophysiological and psychological, genetic and sociological, Freudian and neo-analytic, mental and physical, and on and on. How do these theories, and the concepts and principles which comprise these theories, relate to each other? In answering this question, I will highlight the perspective of humanistic theory as one of the class 1 approaches.

Integrity versus Reductionism

Our class 1 perspective holds that the constructs of humanistic theory bear systematic logical relationships to other constructs within the theory. Psychological constructs have systematic meaning in relation to other psychological constructs. Sociological constructs have systematic meaning in relation to other sociological constructs. Within its own mode of description, each construct enjoys meaning, systematic definition, and logical relationships with other constructs. I refer to this as *integrity*. For example, in humanistic theory, we have a construct of "operating potential." That construct has integrity to the extent that it has meaning within humanistic theory, has a systematic definition, and is logically related to the network of other constructs within humanistic theory.

If the construct "operating potential" had a way of viewing constructs of other theories, it would see them as simply parts of other modes of description. For example, if "operating potential" were to look across at a chemical mode of description, and focus specifically on the construct "ion bond," it would consider that "ion bond" gains its integrity—its meaning and significance—within a chemical theory. Both are parts of different modes of description.

Furthermore, the construct "operating potential" gains its meaning and significance from more *basic* constructs within its parent theory. "Potential for experiencing" is one construct basic to "operating potential." Even more fundamental to the construct "operating potential" are assumptions such as: "The human being is assumed to be a single, unitary thing, with only a single kind of event, stuff, or substance at its base," and "Events have a locus in time and space; beyond its status as an event, the human being has no intrinsic nature, such as a mental or bodily nature." These are constructs and assumptions basic to "operating potential." The constructs of our theory are systematically related to and derived out of more basic constructs and assumptions within humanistic theory.

According to the position of class 1 theories, the constructs of our theory are neither reducible to, explained by, or derived out of the constructs of any *other* theory. Indeed, the general position is that the constructs of *any* theory (in the class 1 category) are neither reducible to, explained by, or derived out of the constructs of *any other* theory. In accord with Pratt, McDougall, Driesch, Ducasse and others, biological concepts and laws do not bear reduction to the concepts and laws of physics, nor can psychological constructs be reduced to the constructs of chemistry, physics, sociology or physiology. Behavior which is conceptualized psychologically ". . . can never be reduced to physiological processes and explained as a result of the integration of reflexes" (Buytendijk, 1950, p. 127). Behavior which is understood and described psychologically is not to be causally reduced to *neurophysiological* workings of the brain (cf. Eysenck & Rachman, 1965). In class 1 approaches, the constructs of any theory have integrity, and cannot be reduced (as in classes 2-6) to the constructs of any other theory.

Most theories act as if they are able to translate the constructs of other theories into their own vocabulary. Theoreticians who adhere strongly to psychoanalysis often act as if whatever seems robust must be translatable into psychoanalysis. If I cite theoretical propositions from Hull's learning theory, or technical research findings within the framework of learning theory, or some behavior modification procedures logically derived from specific propositions within learning theory, my psychoanalytic friends find it almost necessary to translate all of this into psychoanalytic theory. Today, it is even more common for learning theorists to share in the same hunger for translatability. My learning theory friends ask me to explain how experiential methods work and how I conceive of personality change. Then their task is to translate what I say into the vocabulary of their learning theory. As Jessor outlines the general propositions of a reductionistic approach, just this sort of translation occurs: ". . . the terms or concepts and the relations or laws of one discipline may fully and without loss of meaning be translated into or deduced from those of another discipline" (1958, p. 171). We are talking now of the theory—the constructs, terms, principles—and not of a particular event. Whereas, from *our* perspective, an event is open to *multiple* modes of description, theories are not necessarily open to inter-translatability from one to the other. Under a reductionistic approach, inter-translatability is a necessity; under the approach to which humanistic theory belongs, there is no necessary inter-translatability.

Integrity among constructs means that a psychological construct is not defined in terms of neurophysiological constructs, nor are neurophysiological constructs defined in terms of psychological constructs. This is the position held by class 1 approaches. Other positions (e.g. class 3, Figure 4.1), however, explicitly proclaim that psychological constructs must have neurophysiological reference, neurophysiological locus, and be defined in the terms of a neurophysiological language system (Krech, 1950). Psychological constructs such as needs, drives, cognitive structures, expectancies, reinforcements —and all other psychological constructs—are to be defined in neurophysiological terms. Here then are two approaches which differ sharply and fundamentally from one another.

Klein is keenly aware of these considerations in setting forth a psychoanalytic psychology whose constructs may bear *relationships* to the constructs of neurophysiology, but cannot be reduced to or derived from neurophysiological constructs. He uses the word "translation" in its meaning of "having relationships to" but *not* in the reductionistic sense of "being fully and without loss of meaning substituted for." Given this caution about translatability, Klein is voicing our own position in the following statements about a non-reductionistic psychoanalytic psychology: "Meaning, purpose, intentionality—unconscious and conscious—define principles of regularity that are translatable to, but not reducible to, physiological and neurophysiological specifications . . . (The constructs of a psychoanalytic psychology) cannot be known from or deduced from principles of physics and chemistry, or of mechanical, attentional or physiological models, and therefore, it is of secondary, not primary importance for psychoanalysts to concern themselves with translations to physiological models of explanation" (in Jones, 1970, p. 115). In contrast, attempts to translate *fully* from a psychological theory to a neurophysiological theory can be successful only when theories are arranged such that one is more basic, and the constructs of one are therefore reducible to and derivable from the constructs of the more basic theory (e.g. in class 2-6).

Because the constructs of one mode of description cannot be reduced to the constructs of any other mode of description (in class 1 approaches), the several modes of description are not arranged in any hierarchy. Human beings ". . . can be observed and conceptualized in legitimately different ways by behaviorists, phenomenologists, psychodynamicists, and biochemists . . . Processes may be described in terms of conditional habits, reaction formations, cognitive expectancies or neurochemical dysfunctions. These levels of conceptualization cannot be arranged in a hierarchy, with one level viewed as reducible to another" (Millon, 1967, pp. 6-7). In class 1 approaches, there is no basis for arranging scientific modes of description in any hierarchy. Psychology, from this view, cannot be considered a branch of the science of the mental life of living organisms, rooted in the "fundamental laws" of biology (cf. Burt, 1955). We flatly reject any conception of psychological processes as essentially biological or physiological in nature (cf. Maslow & Mittelmann, 1941; Maslow & Murphy, 1954). In accord with Allport (1937), psychological motivations have their roots in basic psychological motivations, and cannot be conceptualized as existing in any hierarchy with "primary" physiological drives at the foundation.

The sciences are organized into a hierarchy *only within reductionistic approaches*. As indicated in Figure 4.1, there are several classes which incorporate reductionism. In class 3, for example, it is assumed that there is only one basic kind of event, that basic event is bodily in nature, and the method of inquiry is through reducing higher units to their component lower units. Accordingly, once one accepts these assumptions, it follows that sciences *are* organized into a hierarchy. There are various hierarchies which fit the reductionistic framework, depending upon which class organizes theories into the hierarchy. Often the "hard" sciences (e.g. physics and chemistry) are at the bottom and the "soft" sciences (e.g. sociology, psychology) are at the top in the general reductionistic models (Jessor, 1958). Once one abandons the reductionistic model, however, as in class 1 approaches, the hierarchy of sciences washes completely away. Nevertheless, most sciences, even so-called "soft" sciences, accept a reductionistic approach in which sciences are arranged in a hierarchy. "Certainly anatomy is basic to physiology and biochemistry, and it may be logically presumed that it is also basic to psychology (Williams, 1967, p. 22-23). Such a position is held once one has accepted such assumptions as an intrinsic nature to basic events, and the nonmental, physical nature of these basic events.

Many theoreticians assume that there is a hierarchy of "needs," with physiological needs prepotent over psychological needs. "Undoubtedly these physiological needs are the most prepotent of all needs. What this means specifically is that in the human being who is missing everything in life in an extreme fashion, it is most likely that the major motivation would be the physiological needs rather than any others. A person who is lacking food, safety, love and esteem would most probably hunger for food more strongly than anything else" (Maslow, 1970b, p. 36). Within our own approach, such a hierarchy of sciences does not occur, and there is no assumption of a hierarchy of psychological and physiological needs.

Maslow's system is rooted within a class 3 biological framework, complete with an explicitly stated hierarchy of needs, resting squarely on physiological needs which are basic and whose gratification must come first (1968, 1970b). All of this is missing from our humanistic theory which is not rooted in biology, and has no assumption of any sort of hierarchy of needs (or drives or motivations). Here is a fundamental difference between our humanistic theory and that of Maslow.

Once we adhere to a class 1 approach and reject reductionism and hierarchies of the sciences, our search for causal variables takes us deeper within our own mode of description, and not into the variables of other modes of description. How do we understand that some children are very outgoing and others tend to pull back and withdraw? If we hold to the class 1 position of humanistic theory, a psychological perspective would seek basic causes in psychological variables, a chemical perspective in chemical variables, a sociological perspective in basic sociological variables, and so on. There would be no predefined hierarchy of the various perspectives. We must, then, reject such statements as the following: The fundamental variables underlying human behavior and individual differences consist of neurological-physiological-anatomical matrices of inherited structures (cf. Eysenck, 1970). That statement is meaningful only within class 3 approaches and the reductionistic assumptions which they alone accept.

Integrity versus Reductive Causality

According to the position accepted by humanistic theory, since the constructs of one mode of description are not reducible to the constructs of another mode of description, there is no causal relationship between the two modes. Each set of constructs enjoys integrity in bearing causal relationships only to other constructs within its own mode. An operating potential may be causally related to behavior and to its deeper potential. It is not causally related to constructs of synapse, ion bond, brain potential, or myelin sheath; an operating potential neither causes a brain potential nor is it caused by a brain potential. "Everything is an arbitrary construction imposed upon reality. Therefore, it would be meaningless to suggest that one construction causes another or is more real than another. This would be true, for example, whether one proposed that behavioral events constructed *psychologically* were caused by events constructed *physiologically*, or vice versa" (Cantor & Cromwell, 1957, p. 463). The causes of psychological constructs lie in other psychological constructs; the causes of biological constructs lie within other biological constructs. Thus ". . . psychological facts cannot be explained entirely in terms of physically defined stimuli or physically defined patterns of responses, but must be understood in terms of causation at the level of psychological facts" (Bucklew, 1960, p. 14).

From this vantage point, constructs within a single overall framework bear systematic causal relationships only with one another. It is not possible to establish systematic causal relationships between constructs from different modes of description. As an example, we may adopt various modes of describing events referred to by such words as human growth and maturation. If we adopt a sociological mode of description, we can study systematic causal relationships among sociological constructs. If we adopt a psychological or a cultural anthropological mode of description, we can study systematic causal relationships among psychological constructs or among the constructs of cultural anthropology. But it is not possible to study systematic causal relationships between constructs from a psychological mode, a sociological mode, and a cultural anthropological mode. To the extent that "gene" is a physiological construct, it is therefore possible to study relationships between genetic factors and other functions described physiologically. When human growth and maturation are seen from a physiological perspective, we can investigate systematic causal relationships between genetic constructs and human growth and maturation. Thus, all within a *physiological* framework, the following can be stated: ". . . only within the limits set by the genetic constitution of the organism can external factors have an effect on the dynamics of physiologic functions and interactions . . . Such basic phenomena as growth and maturation, homeostasis and maturation . . . remain chameleonlike allegories without the solid foundations of genetic principles" (Kallman, 1956, p. 496). This can be done when human growth and maturation are viewed from a physiological perspective. But from a *humanistic* perspective, no such relationships are to be presumed. From a humanistic perspective, human growth and maturation (i.e. the events to which these terms refer) bear no systematic relationship with the construct "gene," and no systematic relationship with "genetic principles."

If an event is described using a "mental" set of constructs, and also using a "physical" set of constructs, our position is that the mental constructs do not cause the physical constructs, and the physical constructs do not cause the mental constructs. We may observe *relationships* between mental and physical constructs, but the relationships are not considered *causal* relationships. Indeed, there may be relationships between the constructs of any modes of description, but, as is axiomatic in statistics, the correlational relationships are not to be treated as causal relationships. Changes in *disintegrative relationships among potentials* (a construct within a humanistic mode of description) may bear some relation to changes in *synaptic discharge* (a construct within a neurological mode of description). But psychological constructs do not cause neurophysiological constructs. If family discord, emotional shock, and neurotic home environment are constructs within a psychological mode of description, and if hypothalamus is a physiological construct, then it cannot be said that the former constructs cause changes in the latter construct. Accordingly, if a set of events tends to cluster together, those which are described neurologically are not held as causing those which are described humanistically. While constructs from several modes of description can be said to occur with some regularity, physical constructs are not held as causing mental constructs, nor are mental constructs held as causing physical constructs.

In contrast, many writers quietly assume that if constructs from several modes of description cluster or relate together, causality resides in the constructs from the mode of description which is more "basic" in the "hierarchy of the sciences." That is, in reductionistic approaches, it is likely that constructs in the higher are caused by, derived out of, and can be reduced back to, the more basic constructs of the more fundamental science. "Such deduction or derivability proceeds only in one direction, from lower to higher levels in the hierarchical ordering" (Jessor, 1958, p. 171). Thus, in reductionistic approaches, "anger" can be reduced down to, and derived out of more basic neurophysiological variables, but the neurophysiological variables cannot be reduced to the constructs of a psychological system. This one-way reducibility occurs in classes 2, 3, and 4 (Figure 4.1), in which the assumption is that one science is fundamental to another. If changes in blood chemistry (within a chemical mode of description) cluster regularly with changes in level of cognitive thought (within a psychological mode of description), then this line of reasoning holds that blood chemical changes bear a causal relationship with changes in level of cognitive thinking. Correlation *is* (held as) causality when the more basic construct system is related to the less basic construct system.

When we abandon a position in which one kind of construct causes another kind of construct, we abandon all forms of that causal relationship. There is, then, no basis for identifying psychological constructs as the outcome of neurophysiological causal "predispositions." For example, stuttering described psychologically can no longer be considered as the outcome of such neurophysiological "predispositions" as inherited blood chemical states, metabolic conditions, inherited neurological weaknesses, hypothalamic dysfunctioning or other causal predispositions described within the construct systems of neurophysiology, genetics, or chemistry. Our approach provides no theoretical basis for entertaining such causal predispositions across construct systems.

According to our position, "psychic" constructs and "physiological" constructs each possess their own integrity. One is not causally related to the other because of some assumed reductive relationship. By the same token, one cannot be a reflection or epiphenomenon or subjective reaction to the other. Thus we reject any positions which ". . . understand psychic phenomena as the subjective aspect of certain physiological (brain) processes . . ." (Alexander, 1950, p. 49).

Alexander's theory is given in Figure 4.1 as a class 3 theory. According to the assumptions of this class, there is only one basic kind of event, that basic event is physiological, and psychological events are derived out of the more basic physiological events. The relationships between psychological and physiological constructs are such that all psychological constructs are derived out of the more fundamental and basic physiological constructs. Psychological constructs have no integrity of their own, for they all are representations of the more basic physiological ones. Indeed, psychological phenomena arise out of very particular physiological processes, viz. brain processes, central excitations in the nervous system. Ultimately, all psychological constructs can be reduced to those relating to central nervous excitations.

In class 3 (Figure 4.1), mental phenomena are assumed to derive from basic bodily processes. Within this particular class of assumptions, the proper study of the roots of mental phenomena lies in rock bottom neurological processes. Those who fall within this class can then ". . . limit oneself to the question as to which parts of the brain are indispensable for those neural processes that are a prerequisite for the appearance of mental phenomena . . ." (Spiegel, 1957, p. 614). From within this approach, everything mental (e.g. consciousness and awareness) can be fully reduced to and understood in terms of neurophysiological processes. According to such a position of materialistic monism, ". . . there is only one 'stuff' and that is material. Mental events, in the final analysis, are compounded of the same materials-in-movement as physical events and are subject to the same laws, the laws of natural science. With regard to the nature of awareness, the materialistic monist says that any momentary state of consciousness 'is,' 'equals,' 'is identical with' the momentary pattern of activity existing in the sensory cortex" (Osgood, 1963, p. 34). Such an endeavor is both proper for *and limited to* class 3 approaches. Our approach is not theirs, and therefore we neither assume that neural processes are basic nor that we shall find the roots of "mental phenomena" in a study of the neurological aspects of the brain. From our perspective, theirs is only one of many approaches—and in no necessary way the most fruitful for science to follow.

Ultimately, what is the best domain for describing and understanding the phenomena in which we are interested? Our approach holds that this question cannot be answered by a study of the various theories. Biology might be best, or chemistry or any other kind of theory. We cannot say. But from a class 3 approach, the answer is already given. Ultimately, the most robust variables are those of neurophysiology. So-called psychological variables may be expedient right now. Thus, for example, in a psychoanalytic theory, we may speak of ego and libidinal energy and preconscious, but all of these psychological constructs will ultimately be reduced to neurophysiological constructs. Until then, it is merely expedient to use psychological constructs.

From the perspective of class 3 approaches, the human being is perceived as forever divided into mind and body, with the body as basic and the mind as derived out of and reducible back to the body. This is the approach of Watsonian behaviorism which assailed the mind-body problem by means of physical, mechanistic principles. Watson followed in the tradition of Wundt and Titchener, vigorously understanding mental phenomena in terms of basic neurophysiological mechanisms.

Methods of Inquiry

Because we assume that basic events possess no essential nature other than a locus in time and space, the process of inquiry—whether through research investigation or clinical understanding—consists of effective employment of constructs. Inquiry and understanding of an event are pursued by describing it better and better. In order to inquire further into headaches, I employ increasingly effective and systematic constructs. In contrast, the method of inquiry used in classes 2-6 involves a process of reduction further and further into presumably basic components. If psychological levels of analysis are assumed to rest upon more basic neurophysiological levels, then the proper method of inquiry into headaches will follow a process of reduction into its basic neurophysiological components.

The reductive approach assumes that everything can be analyzed down to an irreducible minimum, and the process of inquiry is the pursuit of the nature and workings of this assumed irreducible minimum. Arguments are thereby generated over what is to be the best working irreducible minimum for a particular field of study. For example, this line of reductionistic thinking will propose such irreducible working units as traditional sociology's "family," the "dyadic group" of recent sociology, the "cell" of 19th century general physiology, and the "stimulus-response reflex" of some learning theory psychologies (Schwab, 1960). Controversies are legitimated by an assumption that research inquiry ought to search out the best irreducible basic minimum in a given field of study, and ought to be guided by that basic working unit. In contrast, humanistic theory searches for no such irreducible basic unit because our assumptions understand only an event with no intrinsic given basic nature; everything is added by means of constructs. Therefore, we do not search for some irreducible basic unit, because, from our perspective, it is not there.

Our position views research as that which contributes to knowledge, and *that* can include contributing to our means of describing the phenomena in which we are interested. Because we do not construe events as reducible to basic causal relationships of more fundamental events, the purposes of our research go beyond that of seeking to discover the basic nature of events. We see no discoverable *basic* nature.

Our research seeks to contribute to knowledge, but through avenues other than the pursuit of some assumed fundamentally irreducible basic nature.

We can add at least two avenues of research inquiry to experimental procedures which seek to uncover the fundamental nature of irreducible basic events. One involves the construction of a method, a procedure, a means of telling us more about an event or describing that event more effectively. For example, a new statistic can be a research contribution to knowledge, for it serves as an instrumental means of more effectively describing our phenomena. A new piece of hardware qualifies as a research contribution to knowledge, for it too provides us with a means of describing our phenomenon. My favorite example here is some piece of hardware which would enable dreams to be recorded visually. A new method of therapy or behavior change also qualifies here as a research contribution to knowledge. All of these are instrumental means of describing, understanding, *doing* things with our phenomena. Admittedly they do not bring us closer to the "true" nature of our phenomena, but that is all right, because our position assumes no discoverable basic nature.

The second additional avenue of research inquiry is a theoretical analysis which constitutes a contribution to knowledge. For example, this can consist of a systematic analysis of the logical conclusions to what we already know. If the new conclusions more systematically fit our present knowledge, the method of theoretical analysis can qualify as a contribution to knowledge. In discussing this kind of research investigation, Giorgi (1966) cites Straus' work on memory traces, in which the conclusions drawn from prior investigations are to be replaced with new conclusions. The employment of theoretical analysis in this way constitutes a method of research inquiry, and contributes to our knowledge in the form of unfolded conclusions to be drawn from experimental work.

CLASSES OF THEORIES ON SOME ISSUES OF THE PHILOSOPHY OF SCIENCE

We can now identify the position of humanistic theory on some of these issues of the philosophy of science, and compare our position with those of other theories. The reference for the following statements is Figure 4.1.

Class 1. The human being is assumed to be a single, unitary thing, with only a single kind of event, stuff, or substance at its base. There is, then, only a single kind of basic event. Beyond their locus in time and space, basic events have no further intrinsic nature. Constructs are employed to abstract further descriptions of events. The systematic utilization of rigorous constructs constitutes the method of inquiry. Sets of constructs are organized into various modes of description. Humanistic theory is merely one mode of description. Other modes of description (e.g. psychoanalytic, social learning, neurological, sociological, and so on) are indicated in Figure 4.1 as "X constructs" and "N constructs." It is this class into which our theory falls.

Class 2. The human being is assumed to be a single, unitary thing, with only a single kind of event, stuff, or substance at its base. There is, then, only a single kind of basic event. Unlike class 1 theories, however, this basic event is expressly neutral in nature. Out of this neutral base is derived body and mind. Thus the fundamental factors are bodily and mental, but these derive from an even more basic neutral underlay. In contrast to class 1 theories, the method of inquiry is by means of reductionism in which a process of analysis seeks to uncover increasingly basic bodily and mental components.

Class 3. Like classes 1 and 2, the human being is assumed to be a single, unitary thing, with only a single kind of event, stuff, or substance at its base. Unlike class 1 and class 2 theories, however, this basic event is bodily (physical) in its essential nature. Out of this bodily base is derived mental events. The method of inquiry is by means of reductionism in which a process of analysis seeks to uncover increasingly basic components, the most basic level of which is bodily in nature. This is the most popular class of theories in the fields of human personality and the behavioral sciences.

Class 4. Like classes 1, 2, and 3, the human being is assumed to be a single, unitary thing, with only a single kind of event, stuff, or substance at its base. It is distinctive in its assumption that the basic event is mental in nature. Out of this mental base is derived bodily events. The method of inquiry is by means of reductionism in which a process of analysis seeks to uncover increasingly basic components, the most basic level of which is mental in nature.

Class 5. Unlike the first four classes of theories, the human being is assumed to be fundamentally composed of two irreducible basic components. One of these is essentially bodily and the other is essentially mental in nature. These are the two kinds of basic events. Although they interact with one another, neither is basic to the other. The method of inquiry is by means of reductionism in which a process of analysis seeks to uncover increasingly basic components, the most basic level of which is composed of two kinds of events, one bodily and the other mental.

Class 6. The human being is assumed to be fundamentally composed of three irreducible basic components. One is essentially bodily, one essentially mental, and the third is described as an entelechy, vital force or elan vital. Although these three kinds of basic events interact with one another, none is basic to the others. The method of inquiry is by means of reductionism in which a process of analysis seeks to uncover increasingly basic components, the most basic level of which is composed of these three irreducible kinds of basic events.

5

The Human Body

Having identified humanistic theory's position on some of the basic issues in the philosophy of science, we are able to take a closer look at the human body. Our position on the issues described in Chapter 4 opens the way to a distinctive way of grasping bodily phenomena. The purpose of this chapter is to answer the following question from the perspective of humanistic theory: How may I describe the various kinds of changes which occur in the human body? These changes include all manner of aches and pains, growth and development, changes in the structure of parts of the body, the entire realm of so-called illness and bodily pathology, individual differences in body structure and function, surface bodily changes and deep internal bodily changes. By describing these events from the perspective of humanistic theory, I am suggesting a radical reformulation of bodily phenomena. The intent, then, is to look at the human body from our perspective, and neither to *review* the various ways of describing the human body, nor to *compare* ours with other theories of the human body.

THE PLACE OF THE BODY IN HUMANISTIC THEORY

Against the backdrop of the previous chapter, we can make some sense of the place of the human body in humanistic theory. Chapter 4 gave us some general principles to call upon and apply specifically to the human body. These principles allow us to set the stage for answering the target question to which this chapter is addressed, viz. how may I describe the various kinds of changes which occur in the human body?

The Fundamental Nature of the Human Body

With regard to its basic nature, the human body is assumed to be merely an event. That is, it has a locus in time and space—but nothing more. We can say nothing further about its fundamental nature. Beyond this assumption, we seek only to employ good *constructs* to describe the body. We may employ constructs from various modes of description, modes such as those of biology, of chemistry, of neurology, of physiology, of anatomy, and so on. As modes of description, they respect the body as merely an event whose basic nature is not that of a biological thing, a physiological thing, a chemical thing, a psychological thing, or a neurological thing. It is fundamentally neither a "physical" nor a "mental" thing. These are each modes of description *about* the human body, scientific language systems used to help us describe the human body intelligently.

Our way of making sense of the human body rests on three assumptions (Mahrer, 1962a): (a) The human body is assumed to be a single, unitary thing, with only a single kind of event, stuff, or substance at its base. (b) The fundamental nature of basic bodily events is merely that of having a locus in time and space. Beyond that, the body has no further intrinsic nature, such as a biological, physiological, or neurochemical basic nature. (c) With regard to the method of describing basic bodily events, our assumption is that all further properties are attributed by means of sets of constructs comprising various modes of description. These modes of description (e.g. a physiological mode of description, a biological mode of description, or a humanistic mode of description) are *about* the human body; they are not grasping the "basic" human body itself.

The body can be carved up in many conceptual ways. Each way of carving up the body depends upon the constructs of its parent mode of description. Thus that thing over there is not an olfactory bulb; *olfactory bulb* is a construct used to describe those particular things. That is not a basilar membrane; *basilar membrane* is a construct employed to refer to particular events. That is not a myoneural junction; *myoneural junction* is a construct used to refer to certain bodily events. In the same way we employ descriptive constructs such as brain, nerve, stomach, cornea, hypothalamus, optic lobe, reticular activating system, nasal cavity, medulla and muscle. None of these are body events. They are all *constructs* from modes of description, such as a physiological or a neurological or an anatomic or chemical mode of description.

Humanistic theory is interested in the bodily *events* to which all of these constructs refer. We seek to get at the events beneath the constructs of other theories of the body. We are interested in the bodily events to which the construct *cancer* refers; but we are not interested in the construct *cancer*. That construct belongs to a medical mode of describing the body, not to our mode of description. In other words, humanistic theory seeks to make sense of the human body from its own perspective, using its own constructs and not those from other modes of description. We try to discard the constructs of other modes of description, and to get as close as possible to the raw bodily events. Thus we are drawn toward understanding this bodily phenomenon and that one and that other one—rather than carving up the body along contours set by constructs such as miscarriages, paralysis, and asthma.

Because our class 1 approach assumes that basic bodily events have no intrinsic nature beyond their status as an event, and because it welcomes various modes of description of which humanistic theory is only one, there is no fundamental division into two or more basic kinds of bodily events. Accordingly, bodily states are not assumed to be divided into those which are basically physical-neurological and those which are basically psychic-conscious. There is no fundamental division into physical (or organic or neurophysiological) and psychic (or functional or psychological) fatigue, agitation, ulcer, labor pains, backache, speech dysfunction, tumor, breathing problem, muscle spasm, or any other kind of body events. Instead of a division into so many organic parts and so many functional parts, humanistic theory holds that all body events are open to multiple modes of description. Thus the "cramping" of a "calf muscle" may be described from the viewpoints of humanistic theory, psychoanalytic theory, behavior modification, physiology, neurology, and any other mode of description.

Because our theory assumes no basically biological (or spiritual or psychological) nature of the body, it does not search for the basic biological needs which run the body, it does not search for universal bodily "needs," it does not engage in comparative analyses of human bodily "needs" and animal bodily "needs."

Openness of the Body to Description from the Humanistic Perspective

Any body event is open to description from the perspective of any system of constructs. Thus, *any body event* is open to description from our humanistic perspective. This applies to the events referred to by such words as cutting one's wrists, respiration, digestion, dying, headaches, thinking, hearing, heart problems, concussions, fatigue, skin eruptions, obesity, dysmenorrhea, urinary tract disorders, bone fractures, toxicities, comas, seizures, gastrointestinal disorders, vascular changes, intracranial infections, menstrual changes, endocrine disturbances, and *any other kind* of body event. Here is the exciting possible horizon: to approach the raw events of the human body from the thorough-going perspective of a psychological system of constructs (Strauss, 1966), unfettered with the language and conceptual baggage of neurophysiology.

From our perspective, the events referred to by a construct such as "enzyme" are open to description employing humanistic constructs. If we identify events which are referred to by the term "enzyme," these events can be described using our constructs, and are also open to description in terms of constructs of other perspectives, such as "genetic constitution," but openness to description from a genetic-physiochemical perspective *stands independent* of description of "enzyme" events from a humanistic perspective.

The events referred to by any neurophysiological words are cordial to description from *any* relevant mode of description. Fatigue, for example, is a bodily event and, as any bodily event, can be described physiologically, chemically, neurologically, *and* from the perspective of humanistic theory. Because no mode of description is held as superordinate, and because every mode of description has equal accessibility to the body, no mode of description *owns* the body. No theoretical system has squatter's rights over *any* part of the body. Dollard and Miller (1950), for example, applied a purely stimulus-response psychology to the description of what we refer to as urination and defecation. They spoke of the strong drive stimulus of a swelling bowel or bladder. When that drive stimulus reaches a certain strength, the response consists of the release of the urethral sphincter or an evulsion response of the anus. The human body is exceedingly open to description from any perspective, even stimulus-response, or humanistic theory.

If we approach the human body as open to any mode of description, we can consider the way in which humanistic theory construes what other theories refer to as basic bodily events. We have assumed that our descriptions are constructs *about* the basic bodily event, and in no way are to be taken as some "true" intrinsic nature of the supposed basic bodily event. Accordingly, humanistic theory naively ventures hither and yon throughout the body, even venturing to make sense of what other theories regard as basic and fundamental molecular bodily events which are referred to by such terms as "living cells," or "basic neurological cells" (cf. White, 1959).

Our insistence on a wholesale openness nevertheless acknowledges that some body events are much more *usefully* described from one point of view than from another. Yet it is one thing to assert that some body events are best described physiologically, and quite a different thing to *restrict* description to that of an exclusively physiological mode of description. I doubt that the scientific understanding of the body has arrived at that point where further development in modes of description can be barred. That is hardly congruent with scientific progress, although it is uncomfortably apt as a comment on current "scientific" ways of understanding the body.

By the same token, I doubt that scientific investigation of the human body has progressed to that point where the *methods of inquiry* can be restricted to those of the currently dominant natural sciences. Our position insists that scientific methods of investigating the human body must be open to those employed by any given mode of description—including those of psychology, and specifically those of humanistic theory. As Alexander states (1950, p. 50), any body event is to be fully open to any relevant method of investigation. Body events referred to as changes in gastric secretion can be investigated by the methods of physiology, chemistry, anatomy, systems theory, psychology, or any other appropriate research procedure (Alexander & French, 1946, p. viii).

Not only is any body event *open* to any mode of description, it is open to a *full description* from each relevant theoretical perspective. From cutting one's wrists to changes in gastric secretion, from headaches to endocrine dysfunctions—all are open to *full* description from a humanistic perspective, and from a physiological perspective, and from any other relevant perspective. Some time ago, thinkers sought to provide a full description of the human body from a perspective employing religious concepts such as "devils" and "possession." Later, a full description was attempted using a language system incorporating notions of various humours of the body. Yet, at any point in time, each relevant mode of description is endowed with the right to offer as full a description as possible. Klein puts this position into the following words: "A statement of function or intention is as adequate a basis for explanation as a neurophysiological one" (in Jones, 1970, p. 115). Our position is in agreement.

This principle allows us to account for actual bodily changes using the concepts of humanistic theory. All observable changes in the actual structure and function of every part of the human body are open to a full description from our viewpoint. Worded otherwise, humanistic principles of the human body can *fully* account for *actual* changes in bodily structure and function. Some of these changes are everyday processes labeled digestion, excretion, breathing, and the like; others are less common, like conceiving a baby, having skin eruptions, growing a tumor, or internal bleeding. Yet all these changes lend themselves to a full and complete description from our perspective (and also from any other relevant perspective). On this score, we are in accord with the thinking of Alexander (1950) and Laing and Esterson (1970).

If we describe from our perspective, we can remain wholly *within* that perspective, and follow a chain of events within the workings of the body. If we stay within our perspective, we can describe the person who goes to the medicine cabinet and ingests a number of phenothiazines. We can also remain within our construct system and describe what goes on within those bodily regions known as the thalamus, hypothalamus, reticular formation, and the balance of the extra-pyramidal system—all within the framework of humanistic theory—after ingestion of the phenothiazines. Obviously such events can also be described from a chemical perspective, and a neurophysiological one, and others.

This principle is a rather robust one, for it also enables us to provide a whole new map of the structure and function of parts of the body. The medical sciences have developed *one* way of dividing up the body, and describing these various parts with various functions. The medical sciences have given us one, but *only* one among potentially many ways of organizing the body and its component parts. The mode of organizing the body into parts, and the naming of the structure and functions of these parts, can be reconceptualized through humanistic theory. From our perspective, for example, each body part can be described as representing a potential for experiencing. If a dominant potential involves striking out aggressively, then some body region will be organized around that mode of experiencing. It may be in the head, knee, back or front. But that experiencing will define body parts, their structures and functions. It is as if the map of the body is defined in terms of experiential functions rather than biological functions (e.g. Grover, Mahrer & Bornstein, 1970).

It is the nature of the potential, then, which determines where the bodily changes will occur (cf. Alexander & French, 1948; Grinker & Robbins, 1954; Mahrer, 1970b). If the potential involves striking out aggressively, it will involve certain body parts rather than others. That is, it will involve whatever body parts are organized around the function of striking out aggressively. A potential for holding in can more appropriately occur at certain body sites organized around that experiential function. Thus, a potential for holding in might involve what other theories term the urethra, sweat glands, the anal orifice, and similar body parts organized around the function of holding in. A full description of the body from a humanistic perspective would enable us to map out parts of the body and the locus of bodily changes on the basis of principles derived from this theory.

If we focus on any bodily phenomenon, our perspective grants us the right to describe that phenomenon fully using the principles of humanistic theory. For example, on the basis of only the principles to be proposed in the balance of this chapter, I would expect vast dif-

ferences among the parts of the phenomenon termed "normal" human bodies. Research has already confirmed the presence of such vast
differences. Stomachs can vary as much as sixfold in size; anywhere
from two to six branch arteries arise from the aortic arch; thyroid
glands vary sixfold in weight; each person's endocrine system is u-
nique; the number of islets of Langerhans varies tenfold; the thickness
of the adrenal cortex varies tenfold, and on and on (cf. Williams,
1967). Here is an intriguing statement about the common everyday
human body. Each perspective can, under our approach, provide its
own full description of this intriguing phenomenon.

To assert the openness of the body to humanistic study goes beyond
mere *redescription* of the body from a humanistic perspective. Our
hunch is that we will discover more about the body by opening the
body to humanistic study. When we opened the body to the perspectives of the medical sciences, we learned a great deal beyond what we
had known to that point. Each new perspective may, and my faith is
that many will, tell us more about the body. When we force non-
medical perspectives to meet the body *only through* the medical
perspectives, we close off too much of what we might otherwise learn.
For example, in studying bodily differences between persons in a so-
called hypnotic state and in a so-called waking state, the only indices
which had been used were physiological indices. Dalal and Barber
(1970) summarized research which concluded that these two states are
not necessarily different. However, such a conclusion is restricted to
physiological indices. We do not know the differences or similarities
between these two states were we to devise indices from perspectives
other than those of the medical sciences. If we were to devise indices
from a psychological perspective of the human body, it may be found
that vast differences (or even greater similarities) may emerge between
a hypnotic and waking state. Thus an opening of the body to other
than the perspectives of the current medical sciences contains the
good possibility of revealing much more knowledge about the body.

Relationships Among Modes of Describing the Body

What kinds of theoretical relationships hold between a humanistic
mode of describing the human body and other modes of description?

A humanistic description of any bodily event has its own independent integrity. It is neither reducible to, basic to, explained by, nor
derived out of the constructs of any other mode of description. Thus
our description of a bodily event is not reduced to nor derived out of
the constructs of neurology, physiology, nor any other mode. No particular mode of describing the body is more fundamental than
another; the various modes of describing the body are not arranged

in any sort of hierarchy. Accordingly, neurophysiological body processes are not held as fundamental to humanistic processes. Nor is there
any presumed hierarchy of human "needs," with biological or
physiological needs as prepotent over and basic to psychological
needs. From our viewpoint, the biological construct "needs," and the
humanistic construct "potentials for experiencing" have independent
integrity with regard to one another. From a biological perspective,
physiological needs are basic in understanding the body; from a totally
different perspective of humanistic theory, *potentials for experiencing* are
basic in understanding the human body. Physiological and humanistic
constructs bear no hierarchical relationship toward one another; each
set enjoys independent integrity.

As a further extension of our position, constructs from one mode of
describing the body bear no necessary causal relationships to constructs from any other mode of description. Humanistic constructs
about the body do not cause, and are not caused by, constructs from
neurology, physiology, biochemistry, or any other mode of describing
the human body. For example, other approaches hold that im-
munological cellular processes defend the body against disease (a
string of *biological* constructs); when these biological defenses fail,
there are *psychological* consequences described in terms of psychological constructs: lowered intellectual functioning, depression or anxiety,
cognitive inefficiency, and so on. In short, biological constructs *cause*
psychological constructs. Under our position, no such causal relationships can occur across modes of description.

It is quite likely that constructs from different modes of description
might have common resemblances, but in no way are these common
resemblances to be considered as causal relationships. For example,
operating potentials were described as carrying out two functions, one
of experience-enhancement (or excitation) and one of experience-
reduction (or inhibition). In describing the *events* referred to by the
phrase "neural processes" the humanistic perspective holds that the
major parameters would be those congruent with experience-
enhancement and experience-reduction. Investigators who hold to a
neurological mode of describing the neural processes have similarly
found two major parameters, which they term excitation and inhibition. Although I expect such phenotypic resemblances in constructs
used to describe a body event, there is no implied causal relationship.
That is, humanistic excitation and inhibition do not cause neurological
excitation and inhibition, nor do neurological excitation and inhibition
cause humanistic excitation and inhibition.

Since constructs from different modes of describing the human
body bear no causal relationships to one another, they cannot be considered as reflections or epiphenomena of one another. Thus, our

perspective cannot agree with a psychosomatic position such as the following: "Whereas physiology approaches the functions of the central nervous system in terms of space and time, psychology approaches them in terms of various subjective phenomena which are *the subjective reflections of physiological processes*" (Alexander, 1950, p. 36). In the same way, our approach rejects the common conceptualization of psychological phenomena as the personality *responses* to organic changes in the body. This is a common view of the body as housing only neurophysiological processes which somehow attract the attention of a psyche so that there ensues a psychological response to the ongoing neurophysiological processes. As an example, organic agents (such as syphilis) do their organic work upon the organic body, and this is said to produce some organic damage to which the person responds psychologically (cf. Wallerstein, 1951). In contrast, our formulation is expressed by Goldstein (1939): Personality processes enter in fully right from the very beginning, so that the initial bodily *reception* to intrusive external agents is itself open completely to psychological description. Under our formulation, everything is fully open to humanistic description, including the amount, location, and kind of bodily damage. Once again, organic constructs do not cause humanistic constructs; instead, the whole chain of events is fully open to a complete description from the viewpoint of humanistic theory (or any other!).

Physiological description of the body is an established domain, complete with a long and distinguished history. The posture I take in framing principles of the human body is simply to set aside the traditional principles of physiology. For example, there are many proponents of a physiological principle of homeostasis whereby the body is understood as maintaining itself in a more or less normal state. Likewise, there are many proponents of a physiological principle that when the body lacks a given chemical, an appetite develops for that lacking element. I elect to set these well established physiological principles aside in articulating a humanistic set of principles. In this effort, I am not concerned whether our principles are consonant with or in opposition to the traditional principles of physiology.

HUMANISTIC PRINCIPLES OF THE HUMAN BODY

We can now turn to the target question of this chapter: How may I describe the various changes which occur in the human body? To do this, I would like to propose a number of principles which account for bodily phenomena from our perspective.

I submit that these principles are in accord with a growing recognition of a kind of unity of so-called "mental" phenomena and so-called "bodily" phenomena. It is our way of accounting for the totality of what occurs at and within the human body, as an acknowledgment that "... an analysis of the mind-body problem is to be sought which does justice to the arguments for the sort of mind-body unity which impresses itself increasingly upon the majority of psychologists, psychophysiologists, and psychiatrists of our time" (Feigl, 1958, p. 388). Furthermore, I submit that these principles, derived from our approach to some key issues of the philosophy of science, meet another requirement of an adequate solution to the mind-body problem, viz. to relate psychological variables to bodily events, states, and processes (Feigl, 1958, p. 389). In short, the following principles are submitted as our way of resolving the mind-body problem with regard to bodily events, states, and processes.

Bodily Events and Behaviors are Isomorphic Expressions of Operating Potentials

An operating potential can express itself both in the form of behavior and in the form of bodily events. Thus a behavior and a bodily event can share the same form (that is, can be isomorphic), and the form is given by the nature of the potential. This means that whenever the operating potential is expressed in some kind of behavior, there is typically an accompanying bodily event sharing the same form as the behavior. If the behavior does something, the body does that same something, and the nature of both somethings is given by the nature of the operating potential. Whenever any behavior is occurring, an isomorphic bodily event is typically occurring somewhere in the body. When the potential involves receiving lovingly, the person may be accepting the caresses of another or smiling in affectionate understanding, but somewhere in the body there also is a "receiving lovingly." Although the body process may be more commonly referred to in physiological or neurological terms, what is happening right there in the body (from a humanistic perspective) is a "receiving lovingly." The bodily event may be occurring in the outer skin or deep in the body. It may be a gross bodily event or a fine one. It may be a known bodily event or one about which we have no current knowledge. But the bodily event regularly co-participates with behavior in the expression of every operating potential.

The clearest examples are those in which an identifiable operating potential is expressed in two sets of events, one a behavioral event and the other a bodily event. An operating potential for experiencing bunching up, tightening up, can be expressed in behaviors such as crouching and in bodily events such as a cramped muscle. An operating potential for sexual aggression can be expressed behaviorally in the form of caustic sexual sarcasm and acid innuendoes, and can be expressed bodily in the form of chronic vaginal infections. The bodily and the behavioral are common conjoint avenues of expression of the same operating potential. Thus a potential for containment may be expressed in behavioral reluctance to spend money and in bodily anal constriction. Both behaviorally and bodily, one may express the operating potential for being unreachable: "I will never *really* be affected from the outside world. Nothing will get to my insides. There will be a separation between me and the outside world." Behaviorally a person may accomplish this by living a lonely life, by abrasively fending others off, and by keeping on the go to avoid intimate involvements. The body can manifest the same potential by swelling up with a protective moat of fat.

Let us suppose that the person is characterized by an operating potential to withdraw from an intolerable situation, and, further, that this potential is expressed through excessive sleeping behavior. Our principle suggests that isomorphic bodily events would also be present, and that these events—described from a humanistic perspective—would lend themselves to a description as following the same *form* as the sleeping behavior. That is, the body events would express withdrawal from an intolerable situation. Research has suggested that persons with a high proclivity for sleep also tend to be characterized by distinctive EEG patterns (Imlab, 1961), neurological changes (Yoss & Daly, 1960), and inflammatory lesions in the hypothalamus (Von Economo, 1930). If these bodily events were freed of their *neurophysiological* description, our principle suggests that a *humanistic* description of these selfsame bodily events would likewise reflect a withdrawal from an intolerable situation. Behavioral and bodily events would be isomorphic in expressing a common experiencing. In other words, the same experiential process would be occurring behaviorally and bodily.

Arieti (1961) reviews research by Denny-Brown indicating neurological changes in motor integration of persons who are labeled "catatonic." Arieti's interpretation rejects both the thesis that the behavioral changes cause the changes in motor apparatus, and the thesis that changes in motor apparatus cause the behavioral changes. Instead, Arieti proposes that underlying psychological principles account both for the behavioral *and* the bodily changes. Our position is precisely the same. Bodily events and behavioral events are isomorphic expressions of the same experiencing process.

If the operating potential consists of showing to others how tense and upset you are, then that potential would be expressed both behaviorally and bodily. The same potential is expressed *behaviorally* (.e.g. low hand-steadiness, inability to look a person in the eye, high irritability, decreased power of concentration, high emotionality in word choice, lack of readiness to try new tasks, tendency to jump at noises, tendency to report threatening objects in blots or unstructured drawings) *and in bodily changes* (e.g. a sinking feeling in the stomach, dryness of mouth, heightened muscle tension, heightened galvanic skin response). Cattell (1963) reports just such high positive intercorrelations and interprets the findings as pointing toward a single pervasive underlying factor. To us, this single factor is the operating potential expressed both behaviorally and in bodily changes.

As the underlying factor, the potential causes both the behavioral changes and the bodily events. The behavioral headache and the bodily constriction in blood vessels may go together, but both are expressions of a singly operating potential. It is not the headache which causes the vessel constriction, nor the vessel constriction which causes the headache. Bodily events are not causes (Kantor, 1953); they and behaviors are both modes of expression of potentials. When behavioral and bodily events occur together, the bodily do not cause the behavioral, nor do the behavioral cause the bodily; all are expressions of the underlying operating potential. Many researchers report linkages among clusters of behavioral and bodily events. It is erroneous (from a humanistic perspective) to interpret these findings as evidence of bodily events which are causally related to the behavioral events. Both sets of events can be interpreted as isomorphic expressions of underlying potentials.

Eysenck (1960) has investigated linkages between autonomic reactivity (a bodily event), and such behaviors as socialization, impulsive behavior, presence or absence of inner controls, and other behaviors. His theory places causal influence upon the excess or deficit of autonomic reactivity. In contrast, our principle holds that a given operating potential would be expressed both in the *bodily event*, described by the words "excess or deficit of autonomic reactivity," and also in the kinds of *behavioral events* Eysenck has studied. From our viewpoint, a potential for impulsiveness could well be expressed both in impulsive behavior and also in an "impulsive" autonomic reactivity. The bodily excess reactivity is merely another mode of expression of the potential.

Thus our principle would hypothesize linkages between, for example, bodily physique and personality-behavior. A given operating potential might well express itself in bodily obesity and in behavioral events. But whereas Sheldon (1954), for example, interprets these linkages as evidence of the causal influence of the *bodily* events, our principle sees both the bodily and the behavioral events as isomorphic expressions of a single potential. From our viewpoint, attributing causality to the bodily events is an error.

Theorists such as Laing and Esterson (1970) and Alexander (1950) commit the same kind of error—at least as I see it. Instead of attributing causality as proceeding from bodily events to behavioral events, they attribute causality as proceeding from psychological behavioral events to bodily events: "Clinicians began to suspect that functional disorders of long duration may gradually lead to serious organic disorders associated with morphological changes . . . One had to reckon, therefore with the possibility that a functional disturbance of long duration in any organ may lead finally to definite anatomical changes and to the clinical picture of severe organic illness. . . . Formerly every disturbed function was explained as the *result* of disturbed structure. Now another causal sequence has been established: disturbed function as the *cause* of altered structure" (Alexander, 1950, pp. 43, 44, 45). In the same vein, Laing and Esterson deem it ". . . highly likely that relatively enduring biochemical changes may be the consequence of relatively enduring interpersonal situations of particular kinds" (1970, p. 18). According to humanistic theory, causality flows neither from bodily to behavioral, nor from behavioral to bodily; causality resides in operating potentials which are expressed in *both* the behavioral and the bodily.

The problem becomes especially sticky when the actual behavior is so subtle and so pervasive that it is virtually not seen clearly. Nearly every person behaves in ways which are evasive, defensive, avoidant. Practically no one can stare at a fixed object to such an extent that the person "loses himself" in that object. We are always relating with what is external only up to a point; beyond that point we stop, lest we become assimilated into it or begin to lose our sense of self (see Chapter 9). Given that such ways of behaving are subtle and very common, it is understandable that the same phenomenon would occur in the body. That is, bodily processes would occur expressive of pulling away, jumping back, not staying still, evading—and these would occur in greater magnitude under conditions when the person is in danger of being assimilated or swallowed up into the external object. In the region of the eye, these small muscular movements are called "optical nystagmus," and they keep the eye in virtually constant motion. So many of us are in constant motion, evading, not getting too involved, not losing one's self in the external person or object, restlessly moving to it and away from it. When the body manifests the same characteristics, it is yet another example of operating potentials being expressed both in the realm of actual behavior and bodily processes.

Thus far we have been looking at behavioral and bodily events which occur in clusters. Our principle also helps us to understand bodily and behavioral events which are strung together in series or chains. Under these conditions, an operating potential is expressed in the bodily event and (generally later in the chain of events) also in the behavioral event. The child whose operating potential relates to impotence may express this in a *chain of bodily and behavioral events*. Not only is the physical body painfully thin and weak, but the child later draws back from athletic activities and engages in behaviors reflecting impotence and weakness, from a listless handshake to being unable to hammer a nail, from tiring quickly to seeking out physically strong friends. According to our principle, the potential can be responsible for both the (earlier) bodily weakness and the (later) behavioral weakness.

Other approaches interpret the earlier bodily events as causally related to the later behavioral events. For example, Williams (1967) places causality in earlier bodily events which effect later personality behavioral events: "Individual infants are endowed with far-reaching anatomical distinctiveness; each has a distinctive endocrine system, a highly distinctive nervous system, a highly distinctive brain. The same distinctiveness carries over into the sensory and biochemical realms, and into their individual psychologies. It is not surprising therefore that each individual upon reaching adulthood exhibits a distinctive pattern of likes and dislikes not only with respect to trivialities but also with respect to what may be regarded the most important things in life" (p. 26). Humanistic theory understands these bodily-behavioral linkages as reflections of a third factor, the potentials which are expressed in as seemingly disparate bodily and behavioral events as infant endocrine and nervous systems, and adult likes and dislikes. The robustness of such a principle is expressed in Buhler's ". . . assumption that the individual's course of life has a definite basic structure and that this structure is evident in his biological life cycle as well as in his psychophysical development . . ." (1968a, p. 12).

Our principle of isomorphism must clearly be differentiated from psychophysical parallelism, the Gestalt isomorphism of Wertheimer, Koffka, and Kohler, and the cybernetic isomorphism of Wiener. Naming these three bodies of thought may only confuse the issues, and since the issues outweigh the importance of the labels, I will discuss these issues without reference to the labels. According to humanistic theory, the nature of the potential can be expressed both in the way the person behaves and in the happenings within the body. Other philosophical positions also hold to the idea of isomorphism. These say that there is a one-to-one correspondence between the "mental" and the "physical." Further, they say that the phenomenal fields of persons are isomorphic with the configuration of the neurophysiological fields, especially as found in cerebral and cortical processes. Our principle is different from these philosophical positions in the following ways:

1. According to our principle, isomorphism is only *one* way of describing how the body works. There are other principles. In contrast, these philosophical positions hold that isomorphism is *the* way of describing bodily processes.

2. Our principle refers to *behavior* and bodily events. In contrast, these other philosophical positions are concerned with *mental* events and bodily events. Our principle of isomorphism is not a way of resolving the mind-body problem; these other philosophical approaches are ways of resolving the mind-body problem.

3. Our principle is a statement about behavior and about bodily events. It is not a statement about the nature of basic events. In contrast, these philosophical positions are describing the nature of basic events and the ways in which these two kinds of basic events (mind and body) relate to one another.

As long as there is a human being involved, it is legitimate to open description to humanistic theory. Not only does this apply to clusters or chains of associated behavioral and bodily events, but also to clusters and chains of sheer bodily events. For example, studies indicate that there are regular and consistent relationships between oral contraceptive pills and such so-called physiological "side" effects as breast tenderness, nausea, heightened fluid retention, weight change, menstrual irregularity, cramps, spotting, and hemorrhaging (Klein & Levitt, 1967; Westoff & Ryder, 1968; Ziegler, Rogers, Kriegsman, & Marton, 1968). It is easy to frame all of this in a physiological or chemical language system and to make sense of the interrelationships within those systems. But, in addition, we can submit these events to description from our perspective. What operating potential is related to such a cluster or chain of bodily events and makes conceptual sense of the whole array of events? I would suggest, for example, that one possible operating potential would relate directly to the experiencing of pregnancy, and that the above bodily events are direct expressions of the operating potential for pregnancy. Rather than physiological and chemical effects of the pill, all the events, including taking the pill, are related to an underlying experiential factor.

It is the potential for experiencing which makes sense of the whole scene—taking the drug (injection, chemical, alcohol, narcotic), bodily changes, and ways of behaving. It is the potential which makes all of these events understandable, and which makes it unnecessary to consider any subset as causally related to the others (Mahrer, Young, & Katz, 1960). When the potential is to collapse, it is the experiencing of collapse that accounts for the selection of the drug, the using of the drug, the physical changes in the body, the way the person behaves— everything is an expression of the collapse. The potential for collapsing is there right from the beginning, so that the very seeking of the drug is carried out in a way which expresses the theme of collapsing. In the same way, the nature of the physical changes in the body manifest the theme of collapsing, for the changes will be those of a collapse. In all of the changes which occur, the potential is the organizing resource. Lines of causality run to each change from the potential, and *not* from one change (e.g. the dose of the drug) to another (e.g. vascular decrease).

Bodily Events Are External Behavioral Expressions of Operating Potentials

Our first principle described bodily events as evidencing the same form as behavioral events. When behaviors express a given potential, that same form is occurring somewhere in the body. Now we turn to a second principle for describing bodily events: Bodily events are external behavioral expressions of operating potentials. Under this second principle, bodily events *are* behaviors. They do precisely what behaviors do. Indeed, these bodily events are legitimate behaviors in their own right.

Although we shall discuss behavior itself in a later chapter, it is perhaps sufficient to state that behavior can serve as a means of experiencing a potential. On this score, the body is a potent means of experiencing many kinds of potentials. If the potential is that of avoiding a threatening sex role, the body can (behaviorally) accomplish this by means of physical exhaustion, low back pains, muscular cramps, a blockading envelope of ugly fat, generalized body weakness, paralyses, diarrhea, or stomachaches (Mahrer, 1970c). If the potential is one of avoiding or reducing the threat of punishment, the body behaviors can include fugue states, painful physical illnesses, responsibility-avoidant neurological dysfunctions such as epileptoid fits and seizures. If the potential is one of appealing to others for generalized structure and control, effective bodily behaviors include those which signify loss of body integrity, e.g., loss of feeling, loss of power in hands and legs, chills and shaking, pounding sensations in the head. If the potential consists of dependency, some effective bodily behaviors include incontinence, ulcers, generalized bodily weakness. If the potential involves control over one's family, effective bodily behavior can utilize an appropriate illness or condition which requires bedridden invalidism from which the person wields authoritative control. What Freud (1959) has described as the "paranosic gain" of bodily illnesses is testimony to the effectiveness of bodily behavior.

Viewed in this way, the body is a magnificent warehouse of effective behaviors. How marvelously deft the body is at, for example, utilizing what we ordinarily label as stress! In the hands of the right potential, the body can utilize stress to become too sick to run the race or engage in the fight or help the family move the household or go to the airport to meet the visiting inlaws. Such an interpretation of how the body works is in contrast to a formulation of the body as possessing a limited amount of defense against stress, so that too much further stress will deplete the ability of the body to defend itself (Selye, 1956).

A variation on this theme is when the body serves as an instrumental member of the behavioral team. In this role, the body assists in the delivery of behavior. For example, if the potential involves the punishment of one's parents, one usually effective behavioral means is for the child to stutter. One way of stuttering requires that the body assist through chest laryngeal mechanisms which interfere with the production of breath (Kenyon, 1941). This bodily behavior assists in the delivery of stuttering. In this way, the body is not the whole behavior; the bodily behavior is a member of the cooperating behavioral team, all serving to provide for the experiencing of the operating potential.

If the body is conceptualized as a means of experiencing potentials, then what kind of body can provide for the experiencing of being just like father, or being "penis-like" (small, powerful, potent), or being bigger than one's parents? One way of being like father is being like him in bodily form and shape. One way of being penis-like is for one's body to be small, powerful, potent. Fenichel (1954a) describes the clown's body as just such a means of experiencing being exhibited, laughed at, omnipotent. One way of experiencing being bigger than one's parents is to be taller than father and mother. Bluntly stated, the overall form and shape of the body can be a function of the person's operating potentials. Operating potentials may be expressed through bodily characteristics, and therefore will cause the person to be tall or short, fat or skinny.

Bodily Events Are Feelings

Feelings are not mysterious happenings in "the mind." That feeling of joy or deep melancholy is not some "psychic" occurrence located in some unidentifiable crevice in an abstract world. A feeling is a construct. Its referent is a bodily event. Thus, when you come right down to what a feeling *is*, a feeling is a bodily event (Binswanger, 1958c, p. 282; Gendlin, 1962, 1964, 1966, 1968, 1969). Feelings do not cause bodily events, they do not reduce to bodily events, they are not accompanied with bodily events, and they are not reflected in bodily events; they *are* bodily events. All feelings occur as bodily happenings, processes, changes, phenomena, sensations.

Feelings of agonizing restlessness, for example, are bodily in nature. In his description of the case of Ellen West, Binswanger spells out the coterminality of such feelings and bodily events: ". . . Ellen herself now emphasizes the intimate connection, indeed oneness, of herself with her body . . . since she has no inner calm, it becomes torture for her to sit still (for sitting still would be imprisonment, the tomb, death); every nerve in her trembles, her body takes part in all the stirrings in her soul. The experience of this inner unity, this oneness of self and body, must constantly be kept in view" (Binswanger, 1958c, p. 282).

The coterminality of feelings as bodily events applies to all kinds of feelings. Good feelings of experiencing include joy, aliveness, excitement. These occur in the form of bodily events; they *are* bodily events. Good feelings of internal integration include the sense of oneness, inner peace, unity. These also occur as bodily events. So too with bad feelings of disintegration. There are bodily events which constitute each of the disintegrative feelings described in Chapter 3: anxiety, fear, anger, helplessness, shame, depression, and meaninglessness. Now we are ready to describe another disintegrative feeling: bodily pain.

Bodily pain as disintegrative feeling. Bodily pains include the whole range of physically felt aches and hurts—sharp, throbbing, cutting, and dull; feelings of terrible pressure and jagged tearing; localized and generalized bodily pains; superficial and deep pains; pains in the head, teeth, chest, legs, neck, ribs, anus, ear, nose, back, anywhere in the body. All bodily pains, from our perspective, are understood as merely another class of disintegrative feelings. To describe the occurrence of bodily pain, then, is to name the three necessary and sufficient conditions for the occurrence of any disintegrative feeling. Accordingly, bodily pain occurs when these three conditions are fulfilled:

1. First, any disintegrative feeling, including that of bodily pain, requires that the internal state be one of disintegration. The participating potentials must bear disintegrative relationships, a stance of menacing distrust toward one another (Figure 3.1). If, for example, the deeper potential (MP2, Figure 3.1) is a potential for experiencing rage, the operating potential must bear a disintegrative relationship toward that potential. From the viewpoint of the operating potential, rage is terrible, intolerable.

The distinction is between the bodily pain as expressive of the disintegrative *relationship*, rather than the pain as expressive of the deeper potential. When, for example, a person has a headache, the ache is in part a function of the *feelinged relationship* between the operating potential and the nature of the deeper potential—perhaps the rage (cf. Lustman, 1951). Thus the bodily pain is my relationship to whatever is percolating within me; the bodily pain is not to be construed as an expression of the inner potentiality itself. This condition calls for a disintegrative struggle generally occurring at the site of the bodily pain. Enright describes this as ". . . the general process of negating, holding back, or balancing the impulse tension by additional, opposing sensori-motor tension . . . since there is increased activity at the points of muscular opposition, awareness may develop there as pain or discomfort . . ." (1970, p. 112). Disintegrative relations between potentials constitute one condition for bodily pain.

2. The second condition is the presence of an appropriate external situation. The appropriateness of the external situation lies in its ability to provide the right context for the experiencing of the deeper potential. Whenever pain is to occur, the appropriate external situation is a *necessary* but not a *sufficient* condition. This is an important point because some pains are commonly considered as *unrelated* to an appropriate external situation, whereas other pains are often considered to be *wholly a function of* an appropriate external situation. With regard to the first kind, a dull ache in the back of the head always requires some sort of appropriate external situation for its occurrence. Such a condition is necessary. Yet many approaches to bodily pains ignore the situational context as if it were irrelevant. Not so within humanistic theory. It is necessary that the disintegrative feeling of bodily pain occur within a defined situational context—even dull headaches which seem to be just there, or whose waxings and wanings apparently dance to some internal tune. On the other hand, many approaches presume that some understanding of the external situation is *wholly* sufficient to describe the occurrence of some pains. The hammer hit my finger; nothing more is needed to account for the pain. I fell and twisted my leg; that accounts for my pain. See the pin stuck into my skin; that is sufficient to account for the pain! Not so within our theory. The occurrence of such situations are *more or less* appropriate for different persons. For some persons, such situations may perhaps *not* qualify as appropriate for the occurrence of pain. Also, it may not be the hammer, twisting fall, or pin which is the essential component of the appropriate external situation. The essential components of a situation appropriate for the occurrence of pain may not be so easily discerned. In every kind of bodily pain, the external situation must be appropriate (i.e. must provide for the experiencing of the deeper potential), and the presence of that appropriate external situation is necessary but not sufficient to account for the bodily pain.

Our theory holds that the way in which the appropriate external situation contributes to the bodily pain is by providing the conditions for the heightened experiencing of the deeper potential. This applies to every kind of bodily pain, from headaches to sharp pains in the stomach. It applies to every kind of appropriate external situation, from a punch in the stomach to a screaming spouse, from a hammer hitting one's finger to the movements of the fetus during labor.

3. The third condition is the rising up of the deeper potential. Bodily pain requires that the person gain some measure of experiencing the deeper potential. The deeper potential of the woman in labor may consist of the potential for experiencing a rending apart, a tearing, splitting, upthrusting movement. But the operating potential recoils against such a possibility. In order for bodily pain to occur, the person must at least begin to experience some measure of the rising deeper potential. She must *begin* to experience the rending apart, tearing, splitting, upthrusting movement. As this deeper potential rises, the operating potential is presented with three disruptive changes. Given the rising up of a disintegrative potential in an appropriate external situation, these three changes serve as the immediate working causes of bodily pain:

(a) The rising up of the deeper potential means the cracking apart of the person. If the deeper rage continues, it will dissolve away the person I am and bring about a wrenching end to my own existence. The deeper potential is my mortal enemy. Its rise into the very guts of me means the radical transformation or death of me. Bodily pain is the reactive expression of the operating potential as the rising deeper potential begins to eclipse its very existence. As the person I am begins to dissolve away under the intrusion of the rising deeper potential for rage, I have the disintegrative feeling of pain. As the rising potential for upthrusting, rending apart sears its way into what I am and begins to dissolve me away, I have the disintegrative feeling of bodily pain. Such an hypothesis would suggest that the process of damage to the operating potential would be manifested in demonstrable *localized* damage (dissolving away, radical transformation, breakdown) concurrent with pain. It is interesting, in this connection, that neurological research on pain *has* suggested the presence of tissue damage at the site of the nerve terminals during pain (Wolff & Wolf, 1958).

(b) As the deeper potential rises ever closer, the person is forced to be confronted by its bad form. That bad form can no longer be avoided or vaguely grasped, for here it is, in all its detailed relief. Furthermore, that bad form is on the verge of bursting forth in behavioral actuality. Now the person is confronted by the pictorialized behavioral image of the deeper rage—exploding physical violence, pent-up fury, smashings, and ugly brutalities in specific behavioral detail. The woman in labor is now confronted with the pictorialized behavioral image of actual tearings, rippings, rendings apart. There it is in bold relief, right on the verge of happening at the very threshold of actual behavioral occurrence. Bodily pain is the disintegrative feeling of the operating potential when the bad form of the deeper rising potential is immediately present.

(c) The sheer experiencing of the rising deeper potential carries with it feelings of pleasure, joy, aliveness, excitement, exhilaration and ecstasy. These feelings of raw experiencing are inevitable accompaniments which begin to fill the person. Now that the deeper potential has risen into the territory of the operating potential, the person *is* having these particular feelings. As paradoxical as it seems, the bodily pain is experienced *in place of* these pleasurable feelings. Bodily pain is experienced to ward off and to prevent the experiencing of pleasure! Underneath bodily pain is the rudimentary experiencing of the pleasure attached to the occurrence of the deeper potential. As the person is taken over by the rising deeper rage, that raw experiencing is accompanied with feelings of pleasure which are masked by the bodily pain of the headache. Underneath the bodily pain of the woman in labor is the feeling of hidden pleasure accompanying the experiencing of the deeper potential for tearing and rending apart. In the region of the anus is located a bodily pain which is felt in place of the pleasure accompanying the rising deeper potential for holding in, clenching up, not releasing. Underneath the irritated soreness in her throat is the thrilling delight of the act of fellatio, with the magical swallowing of the ejaculatory juice of her forbidden lover (cf. Freud, 1959). It is not the bodily pain which feels good; it is the experiencing of the rising deeper potential which brings with it feelings of pleasure and excitement. Thus the felt bodily pain occurs instead of the good feelings accompanying the experiencing of the rising deeper potential.

Are there any *characteristic* deeper potentials associated with bodily pain? Or, worded differently, are there certain kinds of deeper potentials for which the likely disintegrative feeling is one of bodily pain rather than melancholic gloom, a sense of meaninglessness, or a feeling of anxiety? I am not aware of research which could shed light on the nature of these particular potentials. In my own psychotherapeutic work I have found that *peripheral* pain is associated with a spectrum of deeper potentials too broad to fall into characteristic kinds. This impression is supported by some research. For example, hospitalized psychiatric patients with headaches do not seem to be characterized by any unique symptoms or syndromes (Mahrer, Mason & Rosenshine, 1966) indicative of the presence of any particular potentials, not even the widely accepted syndrome of repressed hostility (Alexander & French, 1948; Brenner, Friedman & Carter, 1949; Friedman, Von Storch & Houston, 1954; Grinker & Gottschalk, 1949; Lustman, 1951). Peripheral bodily pains tell us little about underlying potentials. But with regard to *deeper* bodily pains, I have been impressed with the predominance of a deeper potential which says: "Be concerned with *me.* Take care of me, minister to me. Attend to me, comfort me," and a second deeper potential which says: "I must pull back from what is happening out there. I must get away from the ominous situation. I must seek sanctuary." So common is this second kind of deeper potential (Mahrer, Mason, Kahn & Projansky, 1966; Rickels, Downing & Downing, 1966) that I have referred to this as "the retreat into the body" (Mahrer, 1970b).

These, then, are the necessary and sufficient conditions for the occurrence of pain. Except for some speculations about deeper potentials frequently associated with pain, I have not explained why it is that the outcome would be the experience of *pain* rather than some other disintegrative feeling. I cannot say why the person would experience pain, but I am disinclined to accept the explanation of pain-specific raw nerve terminals scattered throughout the body (Tower, 1943; Weddell, 1941).

Bodily pain lends itself to description as merely another instance of a disintegrative feeling. Bodily pain follows from the same three conditions necessary and sufficient for disintegrative feelings in general. Just as disintegrative feelings are bodily, all feelings are bodily. It is fair, then, to understand the body as the physical expression of feelings. That is, all feelings are bodily felt events. Understood in this way, it is my conviction that feelings can take their place among dependable scientific data.

Bodily Events Are Expressions of Deeper Potentials

I have proposed three principles to describe bodily events. First, whenever the person is behaving in any way, some bodily events express the same potentials as the behavior is expressing. If the behavior is a way of experiencing being firm, there is some (isomorphic) bodily event which likewise is described as a "being firm." Second, some bodily events take their place as sheer behaviors. That is, some bodily events *are* behaviors. In order to gain dependent care from another person, one behavior can be *verbally* asking the person to hold you in a cuddling way. Another behavior can be *bodily* being sick, weak, tired, and thereby inviting dependent care. Third, some bodily events constitute feelings, for, according to our theory, all feelings are bodily events. We now turn to the fourth principle for describing bodily events.

The body is the domain in which *deeper* potentials are experienced. Where operating potentials may be experienced *externally*, in the external world, deeper potentials are experienced *internally*, in the bodily world. In Figure 2.1, operating potential 1 lies at the juncture between the person and the external world. Its domain of experiencing opens up to include the actual external world. If the potential for experiencing hostility is an operating potential, hostility will take place at that juncture, in the *external* world of experience. On the other hand, if the potential for experiencing hostility is a *deeper* potential, it will be experienced in the *internal bodily* domain.

Experiencing occurs as bodily events to the degree that (a) the potential is a *deeper* one, (b) the relationship between the operating and deeper potential is disintegrative, and not integrative, and (c) experiencing of the deeper potential is not occurring at the operating level. Thus the body is an alien domain where I experience what I do not like, and what I dare not show in open actual behavior. Under these circumstances, our principle tells us that such deeper potentials will likely take some bodily form; that is, the deeper potential will occur somewhere in the body. What I hate and fear in my self will then take some bodily form. These are old ideas. For example, in 1936 McFarland and Huddelson described personality processes which, if absent from the expressed outer periphery of actual behavior, will occur in the form of deep bodily events—for example, in circulatory or gastrointestinal changes.

On the surface, the person is about to say something to the group. Whereas the *person* intends to speak, the deeper potential wishes to draw back into silence. That deeper potential is expressed in the bodily form of a closed throat. To gain its way, the person must drink some water, cough, clear the throat somehow, for the experiencing of the deeper potential has taken the form of the closed throat.

He works in the sales and promotion department, and is aggressively successful. In no way does his actual external behavior express anything relating to nurturance and physical comfort, the deeper potential. As a result, the deeper potential takes a bodily form, perhaps as an ulcer. In this form it says: "Now you must feed me the right foods. Baby me. Give me baby foods. Do not neglect feeding me or I will hurt." That part of the body is the manifest deeper potential, expressing itself in bodily changes. The person cannot and does not say what the deeper potential is saying.

On the behavioral surface, the person does the housework. Complaining is mild, and even though she is not wholly enthusiastic about the housework, she gets it done. The deeper potential, however, speaks with a different mind. It loathes housework and would do anything to prevent it. This deeper potential takes the form known as the inflammation of the bursa. In this bodily form it loudly proclaims its disgust, and it acts to prevent her from being able to carry out the housework.

She could never "own" the deeper tendency toward a full scale, uncontrolled release. That is simply not the way she is. Yet that was precisely the nature of the deeper potential. How could the *body* express such an experience without *her* being responsible? Simple. The body expresses all this in the form of "epileptic fits" and "seizures." She bears sufficient disintegrative relationship toward this deeper potential to let the body (and not her) carry this experiencing forth, while she accepts the role of the minimally responsible accomplice. Thus she "... often asked to have insulin shock, so that she could have a medically induced seizure—an explosion, but pharmacologically determined—where she could release herself in wild, passionate abandonment, provided it were kept non-personal and she herself were exempted from any responsibility in the matter" (Boss, 1963, p. 18). Here is the experience of what has been termed an "epileptic seizure," complete with wild and uncontrolled physical release, a kind of explosion of bodily abandonment. This occurs in the person who is behaviorally removed, not fully present, holding in, watchful—and never succumbing to the deeper potential for full physical explosive release.

Although he would recoil at any such intimation, his deeper potential involved the experiencing of being powerful, a big force to be reckoned with. Yet he ordinarily would try not to appear that way, and much of his behavior was a sheer denial of being this way. Under these conditions, the deeper potential assumed a very fitting bodily form: he became massive with fat. It was almost as if the deeper potential were saying: "I *am* big and powerful, something massive which must be reckoned with." In addition, obesity can be the bodily expression of other deeper potentials. For some persons, being truly fat is an expression of a deeper potential for being unmovable and absolutely resistant. Obesity is a way of not being easily moved about, not airily swept thither and yon with the slightest shift in opinion. It takes real force to alter that person's position. For still others, being fat is an expression of the deeper potential not to be too easily invaded, to be distant from others, to be intact and separated. In each case, the obese body expresses the deeper potential which is refused expression by the operating potential.

The cousins are now in their sixties. They had been in business for nearly 35 years, partners who never expressed their deeper hatred toward one another. Sam's deeper potential has nursed hundreds of grudges and slights, and capitalized on every sort of proper excuse for fanning the inner hatred. Yet none of this was shown at the operating surface—except for a constant trembling of his right hand. It was always there, the slightest and most muted bodily expression of the deeper potential which says: "I want to beat him, smash him, obliterate him!" The continuous quivering of the right hand is the visible peak of the inner iceberg. Another way in which the deeper potential expressed itself in bodily form was in the perpetual battle state indicated by his heightened blood pressure as an expression of the inner rage (cf. Alexander, 1950, p. 12). Sam's blood pounded, as if his blood were already in the battle.

The other cousin, Reuben, was characterized by a deeper potential for short bursts of fierceness, meanness. Yet he never fully was that way in actual behavior. That deeper potential had, early in the business partnership, taken the bodily form of an ulcer which jabbed *him* in short, tough hurts. It poked and cut him in a mean and fierce way, with ugly nasty bursts of aggressive thrusts. Yet, on the surface, Reuben was the soft, gentle one, always with a little smile on his face. Only inside, in the form of the ulcer, did the deeper potential come forth in bodily experiencing.

Alexander and French describe a woman with highly contained deeper tendencies toward violent rage (1946, pp. 268-277). Nowhere in her actual external life was she characterized by any show of this hidden violent rage. Yet she died of cancer. Why cancer? The bodily events which were referred to as cancer can be described in experiential terms as the bodily expression of destroying, killing, tearing apart. It was as if the deeper potential for violent rage, not showing itself on the surface, took the form of an inner bodily process, expressing violent rage in its own way. For such a person, what is termed "cancer" is the bodily expression of deeper, destructive, violent rage. The carcinoma is the bodily form of the malignancy which is the deeper potential.

During his adult years, he lived in a world in which there existed outside forces which must be watched, and guarded against, contained lest they ramify like a deadly fungus whose continued growth would surely threaten his very life. He lived in such a way that these forces were always kept at bay. Conniving competitors would surely suffocate the life of his small laundry and dry cleaning establishment. Evil sexual and aggressive forces would threaten the health and virtue of his children. He had to deal with the criminal element in his city, paying them off regularly for their protection. On and on he existed in a world of continual adjustment against such dangerous external forces. In his early sixties he ended that way of being and retired to his small apartment, living with his wife and two old cats. The deeper potentials which had been externalized upon the outer world now took bodily form. They were threatening to kill him, suffocate him, take away his life. They were vital and always growing, eating him away. They were dangerous, voracious, malignant. He died of "cancer" within five years.

Deeper potentials for experiencing sexuality can assume a variety of bodily forms. If the person is ashamed of the deeper sexuality, it may occur as embarrassingly unpredictable penile erections. For others, the hidden deeper sexual experiencing may take the bodily form of hard fecal impactions pressuring against the anal orifice. Throbbing aches in the whole head region can be another bodily form of deeper sexual potentials. For the middle-aged wife, desperately fighting against the deeper fertility, the inner bodily expression took the form of a growing, developing, fertile tumor; the tumor was the disintegrative bodily form of the baby which she would never experience in external actuality.

Although Brenda appeared invitingly seductive, she was a virgin, and her deeper potential clung to a non-adult immaturity. Inside, she was a little girl, abundantly non-sexual. What bodily form did this deeper potential take? What bodily locus expressed the potential for being a non-sexual little girl? This occurred in the form of a thick and prominent hymen which, in its own way, served as the expression of this deeper experiencing.

It is quite common for the person to maintain inner resentments and violent rages which take the bodily form of headaches. Experienced clinicians have described the immediate circumstances under which that ache ebbs and flows (e.g. Grinker & Gottschalk, 1949). Typically these circumstances consist of situational invitations fully entitling the person to experience resentments against someone, but the person struggles diligently to avoid expression of these resentments. Thus, Grinker and Gottschalk describe immediate interchanges in which the headache ebbs and flows, with the delicately changing degree of expressiveness of the resentment. Yet somewhere in the general region of the head is the locus of a potential which experiences the awful rage and intense resentment.

The headache may also express other potentials. For example, some persons house deeper potentials which, in their disintegrative form, occur as a state of being raw, exposed, laid open. This is an awful state, one which often is defended against in the way the person organizes his life. Yet this potential for experience can occur in a bodily form. Boss (1963, pp. 15-16) describes just such an individual in which the deeper potential occurred as terrible headaches, accompanied with that same awful sense of being laid open, and the vulnerable, raw, exposed brain fraught with the terrible pain of the headache.

All of these bodily phenomena are manifest expressions of a part of the person which is deeper, separate, alien. It lives its own existence. My voice can be expressing what I can not and do not experience, for I am the operating potential, whereas my voice betrays the deeper potential. The same can be true of my trembling hand, my florid face, my facial tic, my low back pain, the hole in my stomach. Inside and outside, my body expresses what I dare not.

There is a range of bodily experiences which seem strange and bizarre, especially to the person undergoing them. It is as if the body is being a dramatic expression of the deeper potential, and the person is struggling, either in the course of the bodily experiencing or afterward, to disengage from that potential. The experiencing of pulling back, distancing, disengaging, separating from something out there can take the unusual bodily form of a visual phenomenon in which things appear smaller and far away, as if you are looking through the large end of a telescope (tunnel vision). In the same way, strange and unusual bodily experiences, often associated with drugs, occur as bodily hypnagogic phenomena—one's body shrinking, disassembling, enlarging, becoming quite heavy or very light, parts of the body swelling or becoming numb and unreal (McKellar, 1963). In these ways the body manifests the deeper potential which the person denies.

Notice that there is a genuine, two-way interactive relationship between the person-as-operating-potential and the body-as-deeper-potential. Regardless whether the relationship is integrative or disintegrative, the operating potential and the deeper (bodily-situated) potential are active participants in their relationships. Conceivably, the person-as-operating-potential can express his thoughts and feelings *about* the deeper potential. Also, conceivably, the bodily-situated deeper potential can give voice to its *own* thoughts and feelings regarding the operating potential. The person can tell us about his stomach, and the stomach can tell us about the person. This is the perspective of humanistic theory. In contrast, a common way of understanding the person's relationship to these internal bodily events is not such a genuine interaction, but rather one in which internal events are merely another set of the total world of cues to which the person responds (Feigl, 1958). Within that approach, there are external and internal stimuli, external and internal cues; the person responds to stomach rumblings on the basis of the same principles whereby the person responds to a dog growling.

If the person undergoes full integration with the deeper potential, the bodily expression of the disintegrative deeper potential will evaporate. To the extent that the bodily event is the manifestation of the feared and hated deeper part, integration will culminate in the dissolution of the cancer, the tumor, the infection, the ulcer, the irritated throat—every bodily phenomenon of this nature. I believe that when we can view bodily phenomena through such a theoretical perspective, we will be in a position to develop rigorous methods of bringing about bodily changes to an extent we can not conceive today.

Assessing the experiential nature of the bodily event. I foresee the time when we will have rigorous ways of assessing the experiential nature of bodily events. There will be sets of hardware designed to listen to parts of the body speaking in an experiential language. At present, we have instruments which assess what we term an "ulcer" from *neurophysiological* points of view. Some day we will have an instrument which will listen to the *experiencing* which is expressed in the form of an ulcer. We will be able to discern that the ulcer is being fiercely competitive, or is calling for comfort, or whatever potential for experiencing it represents. In the same way, we will have instruments which will detect whatever kind of experiencing is happening in the lower back, the constricted throat, the tumor in the breast, the womb, the chest cavity. So far we have failed to recognize that the body can have its own experiential language system and that, if we learn how to listen and to communicate with parts of the body, we can know the nature of the deeper potentials.

Some day we will hear the voice of each "cell," speaking to us of the nature of its experiencing. Some day we will be able to detect experiencings going on throughout the body. We shall discern the bodily forms of deeper potentials in their pullings away from, in their enterings in to, in their experiencing of attack, affection, growth, anger, joinings in, forward movement—all the experiencings of which we human beings are capable. Someone will find a way for the dream to express itself in much more systematic form. We will see it in hard detail on a screen as it is actually occurring. As yet we have not permitted ourselves to conceptualize the human body in ways which will call for ingenious new methods of listening to what the body has to say—physiologically, neurologically, motivationally. We need research, and hardware, to assess psychological constructs about the body. These constructs will lead to research, and hardware, which stay with the psychological constructs rather than converting them to neurophysiological constructs which then are assessed by means of other hardware. Psychological practitioners have known about a state that one enters in a certain kind of thinking—in meditation, in contemplation, and when a person achieves a focused centering of attention. In order to study the further bodily nature of that state, researchers have switched over to a neurophysiological system in assessing tiny electrical potentials in the brain, potentials that are gauged by an electroencephalogram. Using such neurophysiological hardware, persons in the meditative-centered attention state have been found to have a characteristic alpha rhythm (Ornstein, 1971). I envision a time when psychological researchers will go to the body with hardware designed to assess *psychological* constructs descriptive of this state, and not neurophysiological constructs. These researchers will be investigating much more than tiny electrical potentials in the brain. In the future we will have our own ways of knowing what the body is like psychologically, and of measuring psychological constructs referring to the body.

Because the operating potential is frequently in dangerously close contact with the bodily form of the deeper potential, the person senses a great deal about the nature of the bodily event. In effect, the person can tell us about the deeper potential by locking in on its bodily form. The young mother complained about a headache which seemed to start in the eighth month of pregnancy, and was still with her when the baby was 12 weeks old. The more she entered into a description of the headache, the closer she came to a description of its personality, and that revealed its experiential nature. She spoke about the headache as "... always there, never really goes away ... Sometimes I think I will always have it, it will *never* go away ... Maybe it shifts about from here over to here, and sometimes it seems to get ... bigger. But I can't really get rid of it ... I don't want it anymore! Oh, I want to get rid of it. Why can't you get rid of it for me? It won't *ever* leave me, will it?" It is as if the deeper potential, in the form of the bodily headache, plagued her by its sheer presence, would never go away, will always be there to make her uncomfortable. Here is a framing in of the major contours of the deeper potential. But it is possible to go further in specifying the potential by identifying the situational context in which it is occurring. In one situational context, the young mother might be experiencing that deeper potential in relation to her baby. But that is only one situational context in which the potential starts to come forth. When she describes the headache, it is as if we are now in another situational context, one in which the young mother is experiencing that potential in regard to her *own* mother! It is as if the young mother as a little child were saying to *her* mother: "I am here now. I am born. You never wanted me, and now you hate me for being here. I never go away, and you wish that I would. You will always have me, but you never wanted me, and you don't want me now. You want to get rid of me. I'll always plague you with my presence! Always!" The "personality" of the headache is the voice of the deeper potential which has been inside her for 24 years or so. The headache is the bodily form of the deeper potential—when we posture ourselves to let it express itself and to present its experiential nature.

Indeed, some day we shall have a refined conceptual system which will enable us to convert the whole realm of bodily insides to public knowledge—our inner feelings, thoughts, sensations, and experiencings. This conceptual system will lead to hardware derived from a conceptual system distinct from physiology, neurology, anatomy, and the like. At the present time, such inner events are considered outside of our ways of research inquiry (Koestenbaum, 1966), outside of public verifiability and replicability.

Isomorphism of bodily event and external world event. Very frequently, what occurs in the body also occurs in the person's external world. In other words, when *body* events express a deeper potential, events in the *external* world frequently express that same potential. In still other words, what we (as operating potentials) push away from ourselves often appears somewhere in the *external* world and also somewhere in the *internal* bodily world. Since we are not used to such lines of external-internal isomorphism, some illustrations might be clarifying.

Being maternal was not her characteristic way of functioning. Indeed, it seemed that the middle-aged lady was anything but maternal, anything but caring, nurturant, providing. She was 34 years old, had never been pregnant, had never felt what it was like to be maternal to a baby. Yet maternalism occurred in its bad form in both her external world and within her body, for being maternal was a deeper potential against which she had been struggling for years. Although *she* had no direct contact with babies, she was regularly upset by women who seemed to her to fawn over their pregnancy and motherhood. Maternalness seemed ever-present in her world, and always seemed to serve as a focus of jabbing annoyance to her. She was as irritated by "mothers" now at 34 as she was at 16. Her external world was always filled with irritating motherhood and babyhood. Just seeing a woman bloated up in pregnancy was enough to release an automatic loathing. At the same time, the deeper maternalness expressed itself within her body in the form of naggingly persistent chronic breast and womb ailments. They had been her physical problems since her adolescence. She considered these body difficulties as her plague. Both the external world and her internal bodily world expressed the deeper potential for maternalness; both worlds served as the domains for expression of the deeper potential.

Jeffrey was a barber. His deeper potential for sheer hate occurred both in his external world and within his bodily world. Yet he himself never fully expressed the length and breadth of the pure hate within him. He filled his external world with hate-mongering groups. They filled his line of chatter at the shop, in his attentive preoccupation as he read the daily paper, and in his whole world in general. Yet he always remained on the outer periphery of expression, for hate was a deeper potential, one which he seldom allowed direct expression. In the internal bodily realm, Jeffrey's deeper potential was expressed in the form of traveling pockets of abscessed infections. For several years they were confined to his teeth. Then the abscesses appeared in other zones of his body. Because the hate was a *deeper* potential, it tended to occur both in the interior body and in the exterior world of his environment—but not at all in his direct behavior.

When we focus attention on the *operating* potential, we find an isomorphism between body processes and the person's own behavior; when we shift our focus to the *deeper* potential, we find isomorphism between body processes and the nature of the external environment in which the person lives.

Deeper potential as the determinant of how the body receives external intrusions. The nature of the deeper potential determines how the body will receive intrusions from the external world. It is the deeper potential which structures the body in its posture toward such external intrusions. What happens, for example, when the person receives a blow on the head from a falling pot or a hurled rock or a piece of metal? If the predominant deeper potential relates to the importance of distance from the external world, high "person-world barriers," and the maintenance of a moat of separation, that person might well pass out in connection with the blow. If another person, in relation to the *same* blow, is characterized by a deeper potential for rage, that person may not pass out, but instead be mobilized into a wild spree of aggressiveness. A third person whose deeper potential related to fragile vulnerability to the external world, may suffer serious fractures and internal bleeding, perhaps even death—all in relation to the ostensibly same kind of blow to the head.

It is the nature of the deeper potential which determines whether or not the body will posture itself so as to accept or reject what has been inserted into it from the intruding external world. The person with strong deeper potentials toward rejection, pulling within, regarding the external world as strange and alien, will tend toward rejecting the alien kidney or heart from a donor. Even if this means the person's death, that is the way the person will posture with regard to the alien organ. The body sets itself in accordance with the nature of the deeper potential.

The deeper potentials are the prepotent determinants of how any sort of external intrusion will be received. Included here are not only external objects such as pots, rocks, hammers, and fists, but the whole realm of viruses, bacteria, chemicals and injections, infections and illnesses. Some deeper potentials will posture the body so as to fall victim to these agents; others will determine that the body will respond constructively or be largely unaffected.

The refinement of somatotherapies has led to some puzzling findings in the treatment of general paresis. There seems to be a significant lack of relationship between observed serological and neurological improvement under somatotherapy, and changes in the patient's behavior, thinking, and general mental functioning (Wallerstein,

1951). Furthermore, this lack of relationship carries over to the absense of a linkage between clinical behavior and degree of bodily degeneration as revealed in post mortem examinations. When the person should improve, he often does not; when he ought to be functioning in a deteriorative fashion, he often does not. These findings are not puzzling if we accept the determining effects of the deeper potentials. According to our proposition, the manner and extent of bodily damage (or lack of it) from such external intrusions as "syphilis" or somatotherapies in general are functions of the nature of the deeper potentials. Under some deeper potentials, the person will deteriorate or be relatively unchanged in the face of the external intrusion. It is not the spirochete or the chemical which determines what will happen; it is the nature of the deeper potentials. What you inject into the body from the external world will have this effect or that effect depending upon the nature of the deeper potentials. You can force-feed the person, but what happens within the body depends upon the nature of the deeper potentials.

From this perspective, differences in deeper potentials will be associated with *differences* in precisely what occurs within the body when the person receives electric shock therapy, insulin therapy, drug therapy, psychosurgical therapy. There will be differences in the precise ongoing bodily processes and also in the precise bodily sites which participate. On the other hand, *similarities* in body changes reflect similarities in deeper potentials. I expect that a deeper potential for aggression will make for general similarities in how these therapies are received in the body. That is, ten patients, all of whom share similar deeper potentials for aggression, will manifest greater bodily similarity than ten patients representing a variety of deeper potentials. Little wonder that we have no systematic theories of the bodily mode of action or the bodily changes generally associated with electric shock therapy, insulin therapy, drug therapies, and psychosurgery (Kalinowsky & Hoch, 1961). There is practically no agreement on even the body sites involved in any of these therapies. Attempts at specifying the body sites which are involved consist of gross statements of major body zones, such as autonomic nervous system changes associated with electric shock. But the general conclusion of Kalinowsky and Hoch, in their review of the action of these somatic therapies, is that the mode of action remains obscure at best. I would invite research which brings the patient's deeper potentials into the causal arena. As long as research on the mode of action of these somatic therapies confines itself to neurological, chemical, and physiological variables, the field is destined to be comprised more of artful rules of thumb than scientific regularity.

6

The Person and the External World

You and I live in worlds. We sometimes refer to these worlds as the environment, or as society, or as interpersonal relationships, or as the aggregate of external influences. For me, all of these meanings are folded into the term "external world." The purpose of this chapter is to answer the following question: How may we understand the external world and our interrelationships? That is, how may I describe the environment in which we exist, the society with which we relate, and the complex of interpersonal relationships?

Chapters 2-5 have been concerned largely with what is going on within the person, including the internal structure of personality and the physical body. The guiding thesis has been that a single network of constructs can make sense of both the internal personality structure and the phenomena of the body. We now turn to the person and the external world. In expanding the focus of our discussion, we are loyal to the same thesis, viz. that a single network of constructs—humanistic theory—can be used to make sense of the "outside" phenomena of the person and the external world. Haley (1963, pp. 151-152) has stated that a shift from the internal to the external frames of reference requires a major change in thinking. I do not believe this is necessarily so. I believe that a single set of theoretical constructs *can* encompass both territories. I believe that a single set of constructs can describe internal personality structure, physical bodily events *and* the person and the external world.

MODES OF CONSTRUCTING AN EXTERNAL WORLD

The need for a humanistic theory of an external world. Humanistic theory takes one giant step away from the natural sciences' assumption of a given, separated reality out there. Such an assumption rules out the

177

MODE OF CONSTRUCTION	FUNCTION				
	Context for Experiencing	EXTENDED PERSONALITY			
		Operating Potential		Deeper Potential	
Receiving an Intrusive External World	Experiencing Potential	Experiencing Potential	Experiencing Relationship	Experiencing Potential	Experiencing Relationship
Utilizing a Readymade External World	Experiencing Potential	Experiencing Potential	Experiencing Relationship	Experiencing Potential	Experiencing Relationship
Conjoint Construction of External World	Experiencing Potential	Experiencing Potential	Experiencing Relationship	Experiencing Potential	Experiencing Relationship
Fabrication of an External World	Experiencing Potential	Experiencing Potential	Experiencing Relationship	Experiencing Potential	Experiencing Relationship

Figure 6.1 Modes and Functions of Constructing an External World

possibility of the reality of the very phenomena we seek to explain (Needleman, 1967a, p. viii). In turning away from such a natural science assumption, we require an alternate assumptive base for understanding the external world.

It is at this point that humanistic theory turns to existential phenomenology. Humanistic thinking has reacted vigorously against the natural sciences' way of understanding the relationship between the person and the external world. In this vigorous opposition, hu-

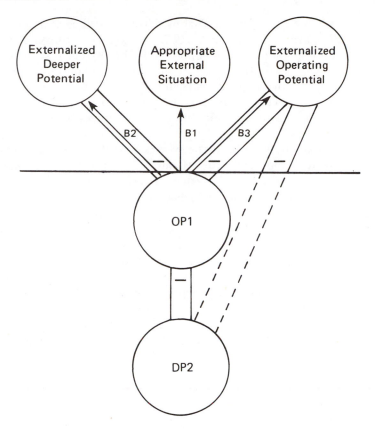

Figure 6.2 Functions of the External World

manistic theorists called the natural sciences approach mechanistic, un-humanistic, reductionistic, dualistic. In its attempt to provide a better conception of the person-world relationship, humanism focused too much of its concern on the person. In a curious twist which put humanistic thinking right back where it started, the external world was *preserved* as the mechanistic, un-humanistic, reductionistic, dualistic world against which humanism so strongly objected. It is as if humanism changed the whole conception of the *person*—but left the person in the same old world. "The irony of this position is that it occurs within a general trend of thought which violently disputes the Cartesian dualism of mind and matter and what is called the subject-object split. In fact, however, Humanism remains in essence Cartesian because fundamentally it never questions the Cartesian concept of nature, however much it criticizes the Cartesian concept of the self. Thus contemporary natural science still remains credited with the only reliable knowledge of nature, and thus nature is still seen as non-vital and non-purposive" (Needleman, 1967a, p. xii). In adopting an existential phenomenological conception of the external world, humanistic theory seeks to articulate an alternate conception of the ways in which external worlds are constructed. We turn to an understanding of external worlds different in kind from the mechanistic, stimulus-response, un-humanistic, mind-body approach of the natural sciences.

Our theory encompasses both the person and the world in the same terms. This is the same thesis underlying Chapter 5, where a single set of principles described both the person and the body. The person does not live in an alien body which conforms to a distinctive set of principles. Nor, I submit, does the person necessarily live in an alien world which follows still another distinctive set of principles. Both cosmos and person can be usefully described within a single theoretical perspective (Wilhelm, 1962). To take the traditional view, i.e., that human beings are to be described with one set of principles and the external reality with another set of principles, is to plunge into an inescapable and unresolvable morass of problems from which the science of human beings can hardly emerge.

Phenomenological construction of external worlds. The words used in the heading of this section tell the story: Each person *constructs* an external world. You and I are continuously at work constructing our own external worlds (Binswanger, 1958a; Holt, 1968; Maslow, 1970b; May, 1958a). Stated more ponderously, each person's potentials and their relationships are continuously engaged in *constructing* (creating, fashioning, causing, carving up, architecting, establishing, building, designing, moulding, bringing about, organizing) and *processing* (utilizing, perceiving, selecting out, giving meaning to, relating to, capitalizing upon) an external world. The person is building worlds through behaviors which may be active or passive. Even acts of willing or intending are world-building. That is why existentialists can describe consciousness as intentional (Holt, 1968). In every way, everything the person does is toward building a particular kind of world.

Human beings live in worlds of their own construction, endowing these worlds with specific functions, and constructing their worlds to serve those functions. Just as the individual person determines the nature of his effective environment, so collective persons determine the nature of their collective social environment (Mead, 1934). It is on this point that humanistic theory aligns with existentialism and parts company from the natural sciences, including contemporary psychology and psychiatry which accept the assumption of human beings and external worlds being separate and interacting.

Yet it must be noted that our position is no more than an assumption. Kant and Heideggar made the person into the constructor of his world by arbitrary fiat, by adopting a particular assumption. Our discussions of the modes by which persons construct their worlds are exfoliations of this fundamental fiat—and not statements of fact about the way things really are.

In our assumptive base, human beings are continuously at work fashioning and moulding the encompassing horizon—the world in which we live. What makes this enterprise complicated is that you and I can use different modes of constructing the worlds in which we live, and, furthermore, you and I may use modes which differ from those we used yesterday. How difficult it is to see that we are all building our worlds when one person is being bitten by a mosquito, or tossed about by the waves, or painting a picture, or building a house, or seeing a vision of God. Are these persons all constructing their worlds? Our answer is yes; although they are using quite different ways, each is busy constructing the world in which he is living. To be impressed with the *differences* in modes of constructing worlds only turns us away from the commonality in the world-building processes.

It is important to note that there are different modes of constructing external worlds. In this chapter we will discuss four modes. Many of the objections to Kantian phenomenology are essentially objections to a *particular* mode of constructing an external world. To object to a *particular* mode as incomplete and demonstrably non-universal does not argue against other modes of world-construction; objections to a particular mode need not imply the untenability of the whole position. In holding to a position of the person as constructor of his external world, it must be recognized that humanistic theory defines four distinct modes by which persons construct their external worlds.

Because there are at least four distinct modes by which we construct external worlds, and because most of us employ more than one mode, it is easy to slip from mode to mode without ever knowing that the common factor is our continuous construction of our own worlds. Yet there are special and rare moments when some rare persons achieve fusion with their own constructed external worlds, and in that state person and external world are indistinguishable. When this occurs, the typical ways of carving up the external world dissolve away, and are revealed as mere convenient units of perception (Watts, 1960). In that state there is no separate external world carved into bits, and we stand as the central creators of the worlds in which we exist.

The stuff of which the external world is created. We must distinguish quite carefully between the role of the person as constructor of his world, and the degree to which the mode of construction uses "real stuff." This chapter presents four *modes* by which persons construct their external worlds. Quite aside from the person as the world constructor is the degree of "reality" of the tools he uses. I can construct a world composed of things which meet all sorts of criteria of reality. I can construct a business which you can see, others can see, we all can touch it, assess its worth, compare it to other businesses, and so on. I can also construct a world of voices, whispering only to me. You cannot hear the voices at all. The degree to which my constructed world is real or unreal is independent of my being the constructor of that world. I constructed both the business and the voices, although the two differ on many of the criteria of what is real. You may build a cabin and demonstrate to me how *real* your cabin is, yet *you* have constructed the cabin.

A person may construct a business, voices whispering to him, a vision of God, a beautiful landscape, or a friend in need. In each of these, the paramount consideration is the nature of the potentials and relationships which engage in the construction of that particular external world. My aim is to grasp the nature of the person as constructor. This aim replaces a concern with the reality or unreality of the blocks with which the external world is constructed. Compared to a grasping of the nature of the person who constructs that world, it is of much lesser significance whether the business is really the way the person describes it, whether those are "paranoid" visions of God, whether the landscape is really there, or whether the friend is real or invented.

A group of persons may utilize different modes of constructing external worlds, yet collectively these persons can fashion a single, entire external world which is real! By perceiving or defining the world in any way (e.g. we live in a world which is changing at a dizzy pace—or, our present world is dominated by the products of technology—or, we live in a world of depleted natural resources) a group of persons can collectively construct a world which "really" is just that way. Nevertheless, all the evidence of the reality of the constructed world cannot dismiss our role as the architects. The world *is* changing at a rapid pace, yet that rapidly changing world is a product of the construction of collective persons, a sophisticated product of our collective personalities working together to define that particular kind of *real* world in which we live.

Whether individually or collectively, human beings can construct an external world by using elements which are quite real. For example, human beings can construct quite real *situations*. In a review of the role of the situation in determining behavior, Rotter (1955) concluded that nearly every theory of personality considers the situation as a significant determinant of the direction of human behavior. Yet, as Rotter indicates, the situation is always a given. That is, nearly every theory of personality starts with the person already in a defined situation, and proceeds from there to consider how the situation influences the direction of behavior. From our perspective, that situation is not a given, not simply there. It is constructed by the behaving person. Where do these situations come from? Although the human sciences have tried to answer this question, what is typically omitted is the role of the human being as the constructor of the situation. In our approach, human behavior is *always* at work doing something to redefine, reconstruct, rearchitect the situation.

To describe the situation as a determinant of human behavior is to come to the performance at the final act. The situation *does* determine human behavior. But let us not avoid the behaving person as a determinant of the situation. "I know of no way of defining or describing a field universally in such a way that this description can be independent of the particular organism functioning within it. Another way of saying this is, if we accept Koffka's distinction between the geographical and psychological environment, that the only satisfactory way of understanding how a geographical environment becomes a psychological environment is to understand that the principle of organization of the psychological environment as the current goal of the organism in that particular environment" (Maslow, 1970, p. 29). In a cautious statement, Maslow has shifted the causal center of gravity from the situational environment to the person. More bluntly, human beings construct situations which, in turn, serve to affect behavior.

If the external world, including the situation, is *constructed*, then the meaning of behavior must be enormously expanded to encompass an entire realm of behaviors engaged in *building external worlds*. Behavior is no longer confined to merely a way of behaving in some situation, or in relation to some external stimuli, or with regard to some configuration of cues in the external world. Behavior now includes that entire realm of behavior by which we *construct* all of those situations, build those external stimuli, fashion all the aspects of the external world in which we live and with which we relate. We may refer to this unacknowledged realm of behaviors as world-construction, for they are understood as building the external worlds in which we are. Once we open up the meaning of behavior to include the realm of world-construction, all kinds of behaviors leap forth. In this chapter I shall propose four classes of behavior which construct the external world, build it in a particular way, maintain or perpetuate a particular kind of external world. For example, the behavior of patients prior to admission to a mental hospital and following admission may be qualitatively different in their fundamental purposes and aims. As a generalization, the former behaviors may have a heavy component of world-building (i.e. constructing situations around hospital admission), while behaviors of the same patients *following* admission lack this component (Mahrer & Mason, 1965). In the same way, entire classes of behaviors are illuminated as dedicated to nothing more than constructing external worlds—using building materials which may be very real.

A humanistic science of person-world. The person's potentials and their relationships construct the encompassing external world and determine its functions. In humanistic theory, a sharp distinction is drawn between "I" (the center of my consciousness and awareness) and the potentials and their relationships which construct my world and assign its functions. Although existentialists assign such responsibility to one's own self (Frankl, 1959, 1969), in humanistic theory the behavior which constructs the external world can come from *any* system of "I." Our model of personality includes multiple "I's" which may or may not include my conscious "I" of the moment.

Is the scientific understanding of behavior increased or decreased by conceptualizing human beings as the architects in the design and construction of external worlds? Arguing from a behavioristic perspective, Farber (1964) asserts that the scientific understanding of behavior is *decreased* when such a concept is added to a model of human behavior. I must agree with Farber were I to approach the understanding of human beings from a *behavioristic* perspective. Yet, from a humanistic perspective, I submit that the scientific understanding of human behavior is *increased* through the inclusion of a concept of the person as the active agent in the designing and constructing of the external world.

Many theoreticians have sought to grasp the distinctiveness of a *psychological* conception of human behavior as residing somewhere in the nature of the human being's involvement with the external world. Human beings are held as distinctive in their relationship to the social context in which they exist, and therein, it is believed, lies the justification for a separate science of the psychology of human beings. There is, for example, a stream of theoreticians who see the distinctiveness of a science of psychology in just this interactional nature of the organism-environment relationship. I include in this stream theoreticians such as Adler, Sullivan, Kantor, Brunswick, Tolman, Rotter, and Haley. Precisely what is it about the interactional nature of human beings which makes for a distinct human science? I doubt very much if it is merely the relationship with the environment or psychosocial context—although many theoreticians stop at this. Jessor (1958), for example, assigns the distinctiveness of psychology to this interactional relationship with the environmental context, and argues that other scientific language systems—physiology, as one representative—have no terms which specify the nature of the relationship between the human organism and the external field. I do not consider the significance of the psychosocial context as a justification for a psychosocial science. Nor do I consider the human being's interactional relationship with this psychosocial context as distinctive. But I *do* consider as distinctive to a humanistic theory of human beings the assumption that human beings exist in worlds *of their own construction*.

Once the external world is grasped as a product of the person's own construction, the assumptions behind current approaches to research in the human sciences fall into question. No longer can it be assumed that person and external world are two separate fundamental elements (for a discussion of these assumptions and the several positions on these assumptions see Chapter 4). It does not matter how complicated are the interactions between person and world, the assumption behind most current research is that they are separate and equally fundamental elements—precisely the same way mind and body, although interacting, are assumed to be separate and equally fundamental elements. Given this assumption, research is confined to a pursuit of knowledge through theoretical analysis, laboratory analogues, controlled experimentation, systematic deduction from the principles and constructs of a given theory in the light of the results of careful research inquiry. Humanistic theory discards such assumptions, and with the discarding of those assumptions goes the necessity of pursuing research knowledge through such avenues alone. We can look for a humanistic science of person-world which uses other avenues for the pursuit of knowledge.

Receiving an Intrusive External World

In this mode, I construct the external world by the manner in which I receive it. I play no determining role in creating the components of the external world which intrude themselves upon me. I neither create these components of the external world, nor do I select which components of the external world act upon me, nor do I determine that they will act upon *me* rather than some other object. I have no role in the initial construction of any of these components of the situation. This is the mode adopted wholesale by classical learning theories such as that of Guthrie (1935), Skinner (1938), and Hull (1943, 1952) in the sense that (a) the external world is simply there, rather than being created by the person, (b) which aspect of the external world impinges on the person is a function of the external world rather than the person, and (c) impingement upon a particular person is a function of the external world rather than the person.

Scientific utility of this mode: useful but not universal. In this mode, and *only* in this mode, the external world houses that which gets the external world activated, e.g. that which turns a "stimulus" on. In this mode, it is a property of the external world to turn itself on, to get itself started. Why are you competitive? In this first mode the answer can be the same as that given by the learning theories: "... the stimuli necessary to initiate this behavior are to be found in the environment ... competitive behavior seems to be stimulated by the presence of someone to compete with ..." (Maher, 1966, p. 61). You receive that particular impression of the person you just met (he is competitive, he is a martinet, he is intellectually sparkling) because of the parameters of the cues presented *to you* by that individual. I find this first mode identical to that adopted by the learning model in several respects. First, the activation of the external world (stimulus) is up to the external world, and not up to the person. Second, the external world (stimulus) intrudes itself upon the person; *it* puts the stimulus *to* the person.

Most natural science psychologies adopt a theoretical framework in which the source of activation of external forces lies within the external forces themselves. Skinner, for example, explicitly adopts a natural sciences framework in which human behavior is turned on by external forces and events which house their own source of activation (1938, 1953). External cues may interfere with the more or less natural automatic functioning of the person, or they may constitute compelling discrepancies (e.g. Kanfer, 1970; Thoresen & Mahoney, 1974). In whatever way, stimuli-cues get the activation started in and of themselves. Our model differs in two respects. First, this mode is only *one* of at least four modes of constructing an external world. In Skinner's system, for example, this is *the* mode. Second, even within this mode, our system acknowledges the person's *active* role in using this particular mode. That is, the person plays a most active role in assuming that particular stance to the external world and therefore in receiving the intrusive external world with a given meaning. On both counts, therefore, our system rejects the model of external stimuli as the transcendent model of *all* human behavior. From the perspective of humanistic theory, some persons (but not all persons) do adopt a mode of constructing the world in which they are responders to activating stimuli. On the other hand, Williams (1967) is representative of many theorists who hold that human behavior in general is in the nature of responses *made to occur* by external stimuli.

Without notable exception, learning theories have wedded themselves to this single mode of person-world relationship, and its single mode of constructing an external world. Does systematic rigor lie only within this mode of person-world relationship? I cannot agree with Farber's (1964) arbitrary coupling of scientific rigor with an exclusive adherence to this single mode of person-world relationship. Furthermore, it is my conviction that any science which restricts itself to one mode of person-world relationship (whether that espoused by phenomenology, psychoanalysis, learning theories, or whatever) is condemning itself to a narrow and short-lived scientific career; any science which tries to call *its* single mode of person-world relationship *the* scientific one is operating more on the urge for guardianship than a dedication toward scientific progress. Humanistic theory includes that mode of person-world relationship adopted by the learning theories. But, in sharp contrast to the learning theories, humanistic theory accepts at least three other modes of person-world relationships, and submits that greater scientific precision lies in such a multiple approach than in clinging to any single exclusive mode of person-world relationship.

How does one do research based upon an exclusive single paradigm of human behavior? Farber provides the way: "... if one wants to know whether a given kind of behavior is some function of one, or, at most, a restricted set of these variables, one must either construct or find situations such that the effects of the one variable or the particular set of variables may be isolated. This can be done by eliminating the other relevant variables, holding them constant, or in some way measuring their effects" (1964, p. 19). Such a methodology is sound for a learning theory in which behavior is exclusively a function of determining variables which reside in the external world. For "stimulus-response persons," whether subjects or experimenters, this methodology is most appropriate. Yet such an approach to research will yield little of value to theories which are not confined to that model of human behavior. The fruits of decades of such a research methodology are of little value to humanistic theory, for example. From my perspective, such research sheds more and more light on less and less of human behavior—mainly because *our* determining variables are not restricted to the kinds of determining variables underlying such a research methodology.

The active selection of a passive mode of receiving an intrusive external world. Where our first mode *departs* from the classical learning paradigm is that once the external world ("stimulus") intrudes itself onto the person, everything which happens from there on is determined by the person. The external world is transformed by the person once it "meets" the person. When stimulus-response psychology grudgingly acknowledged the role of the person in receiving and making meaning of the intrusive stimulus, the S-R model was altered into the Woodworthian S-O-R model. In our paradigm, what is distinctive about this O (organism, person) lies in the active role of the person at the point where the stimulus intrudes. At that point, receiving the intrusive external world is a highly active enterprise. That is where my potentials and their relationships determine how I receive that intrusive external world. In order for me to behave in, for example, a competitive manner, I must receive those stimuli by an active process of acquiescence. There is a right and proper way of receiving a stimulus which invites me to be competitive.

One way of receiving the intrusive external world or stimulus is to shut off my own self and to respond automatically. In an important sense, I have made the choice to shut myself off, and the fact that I behave in the same automatic way over time means that the choice was made to go on automatic pilot. Yet the choice is always there, potentially to be called upon. I am the one who chose to receive the intrusive world in this way, and, by the same token, I can utilize that same capacity for choosing not to. I give meaning to the events which happen to me, whether I make full use or slight use of that capacity, or even elect to shut it off. This holds whether the intrusive external world is wrenchingly dramatic, such as an incurable disease or the certainty of death (Frankl, 1959), or subtly mundane, such as the knee reflex, a set of random digits (Mahrer, 1952), or rain falling upon my face. I choose my own particular way of meaningfully receiving that which occurs onto me. This is an active choice, even if I choose to shut myself off and to respond automatically.

For learning theorists to grant the person some choice in processing the intrusive external world is a nearly impossible request. About the closest many learning theorists have come is to acknowledge that there are meanings *attributed* to stimuli. Yet a closer inspection of the meaning of stimuli nearly always reveals that the *person* is still left out. In no way can the learning theorist tolerate in his system a conception of a person who plays any active role in giving meaning to the intrusive external world. In the following quotation, first the person is inserted as an active player, and then quickly withdrawn:

"From a behavioral standpoint, meanings are certainly important, and conceptualized as mediating processes, play a prominent role in current theoretical formulations. Thus, it is useful, in a variety of situations, to suppose that external events elicit some sort of implicit response whose stimulus components in one way or another modify the overt response to the external event" (Farber, 1964, p. 26). Meanings have been preserved as automatic, and the external world continues to elicit behavior quite independent of the person. In contrast, our position is that once the intrusive external world (i.e. the stimulus) enters into the person, it is the activating experiential properties of the person which are the predominant determiners of how it will be received.

Receiving the intrusive stimulus is a passive state. It is an active achievement to place oneself in this passive state. It requires that the person actively let the intrusive external world reach him. If we can slow down the impinging external world, we can see the person's ef-

forts of fitting himself in very precise ways to receive what the external world has sent. In other words, the proper passive posture is itself
an active achievement. Stimuli too are sophisticated achievements. The
person who lives in a world of external stimuli has already achieved a
great deal. No one lives in that kind of world sheerly by virtue of
simply being human. It requires patience, training, skill, and persistence to construct a world by receiving stimuli which intrude upon the
person from outside. In our system, the *person* defines and gives
meaning to external stimuli. Stimuli or cues are given their properties
by the persons who construct them. No stimulus or cue *has* a particular meaning or significance; it is invested with meaning or significance
by the persons who actively structure these intrusive components of
the external world (Mahrer, Thorp, & Sternlicht, 1960). The person
elects to live in a world of external stimuli created, constructed, given
meaning by the person. In contrast, most psychologists agree that the
formula goes the other way. That is, the *stimuli* cause the *person*. According to Kimble (1953), the predominance of scientific psychologists
fall into one of two variations of a model wherein stimuli effect the
person, rather than the reverse. Physiologically-minded psychologists
accept a paradigm in which stimuli produce some intervening
physiologic or organic change which in turn is responsible for behavior. This is the Woodworthian S-O-R paradigm introduced earlier.
The other large group of psychologists holds that antecedent stimulus
conditions define some sort of hypothetical intervening state (characterized by, for example, habit, symbolic processes, drives) which in
turn predicate behavior. This is the S-H-R paradigm. Our paradigm
differs from both, and holds that the *person* defines the stimulus,
rather than the stimulus defining the person either physiologically or
in terms of hypothetical constructs.

All those dots and tiny splotches on the sheet mean very little unless
some *person* is there to organize them into a portrait of a woman. All
of those people at the meeting mean very little unless the person is
there to organize it all into being an exciting prospect or a restless
situation or some other meaning. Whether we assert that the Gestalt is
more than its separate parts, whether we are impressed with the ways
in which stimuli or cues change meaning in varying contextual configurations, there is always the *person* who organizes it all together. In
a Gestalt approach, it is the *person* who adds that little bit more than
the sum of the parts. In the study of stimuli or cues in contextual
patterns or combinations, it is the *person* who organizes the separate
cues into patterns and combinations, or who provides the data
whereby cues can be combined so as to heighten predictability
(Mahrer & Young, 1961). Without persons, stimuli are nothing at all.
This is true in the whole career of a stimulus, from point of origin to

its change in meaning with use, from its solo performance to its role in combinations and patterns.

When the person is genuinely the naive receiver of the intrusive external impact, it is nevertheless the *person* who determines *how* that intrusion shall be received. We have sharply distinguished between the intrusive external world and the way it is received. In other words, there is a distinction between the stimulus *on its way* to the person and the meaning of the stimulus *to* the person. This distinction is in contrast to "... the crude and simple-minded identification of the stimulus-aspects with the mental qualities. Obviously we cannot say that a color sensation is identical with the radiation (of a certain intensity and frequency pattern) which, under certain conditions merely elicits that sensation" (Feigl, 1953, p. 620). There is a sharp and meaningful distinction between the way in which I receive (process, sense, or experience), and the stimulus aspect of the external world which intrudes itself into me.

In this mode of constructing a world, I add meaning to stimuli (cues) which intrude upon me from the *external* world and also to stimuli or cues arising *in my body*. "By internal cues I mean that the individual is responding to stimuli conditions, arising in the body, with learned associative meanings, such as to a parched throat, or a pain in the region of the stomach. By external cues I refer to any aspect of an individual's environment, outside of the body, to which he is responding at any given time, and which for him has acquired meanings as a result of previous experience" (Rotter, 1955, p. 251).

Whether the stimuli arise from outside or inside the body, the person who receives intrusive stimuli in this passive way is "in contact" with a real external world. In this mode, the person constructs a world which has all the characteristics of the "reality" of natural science and stimulus-response psychologies. The person does not live in a world constructed out of willy-nilly phenomenology. In this first mode, the person-world models of the natural sciences and of Taoism are friends: there is a real hard external reality which is known by receiving its intrusions. Yet the way in which the person receives the very real intrusions from the real world depends upon the *person*, and not on the strength of the stimulus. Some persons may receive an intrusive external world in a severe way, others may receive it mildly, and others may treat the intruding external world as a mere pecadillo and deprive it of its raw stimulus status. Where humanistic theory grants the *person* all this mandate, other approaches put the mandate in the hands of the external stimulus. For example, in other approaches there is a determining external stress and a behavioral response; if the stress is mild, the behavior is only neurotic, whereas if the stress exceeds a threshold, the behavioral response is psychotic

(Marmor & Pumpian-Mindlin, 1950). Our approach places the *person* squarely in the role of the one actively responsible for selecting this mode of constructing the world—of becoming "neurotic" or "psychotic."

Sitting with all the others in the warm crowded room above the grocery store, listening to the poetry, she had nothing to do with the bat coming into the open window and swooping down near her. But it was wholly her experiential system which determined whether she mobilized into sheer hilarity, rushed in panic out of the room, or burrowed into the protective comfort of the person to her left. In actuality, she screamed a mixture of fright and excitement, ran into the bathroom, grabbed a large beach towel, and flapped it at the bat until it was driven helter-skelter about the room and finally out the open window. She sank into the sofa, filled with gales of laughter, bewildered and pleased with her behavior and the fun of it all. Did she create "it"? We must be careful in identifying "it." No, she did not create the bat flying in the open window. However, once the bat intruded itself into her world, the meaning of the bat was encompassed within her own experiential significance. For her, this consisted of activation, doing something about it. She wrapped the bat in a context of meaning and acted in accordance with that immediate world which she constructed.

As described in the previous chapter, I may have nothing to do with the flower pot leaving the upstairs window and intruding itself onto my head. But my experiential system is active in processing all that into my fracturing, internally bleeding, dying, passing out, being forever fearful of such happenings, merely being bruised, or whatever.

The rapist, waiting excitedly for the right woman walking alone in the dark park, will be received one way by the woman whose potentials include heightened sexual sadism, and quite another way by a woman with dominant potentials for delicate fragility. Each will process the attack in her own distinctive way. At a large formal gathering, the back leg of the slender chair may give way, dumping the lady unceremoniously on the floor amidst the rapt attention of the other seated guests. Depending upon her experiential system, she may burst into tears, laughter, or the unmitigated horrors of traumatic embarrassment. As indicated in Figure 6.1, receiving an intrusive external world is one mode of constructing the external world. It is a common mode, but only one mode.

In this first mode of constructing an external world, it is the *person* who is the organizing center of it all. Psychologists, notably those who follow the various learning theories, have sought to make sense of human behavior by understanding the ways in which stimuli and cues organize or combine together. In general, learning theorists and researchers place their money on a study of the *cues* themselves. I submit that the most profitable scientific approach to understanding cue complexes and organizations is through the organizing *person* rather than through the pursuit of laws and principles of cues and cue organization and combination. To try to make sense of human behavior by seeking to discover laws and principles of cues and cue combinations is to enter a chaotic world of never-ending lawful possibilities which will fail to provide a way of understanding human behavior (Mahrer & Young, 1961) largely because these laws and principles omit the *person* as the organizing center of it all. In the pursuit of scientific understanding of human behavior, one approach looks to the stimuli, and tries to frame laws by which they combine together to construct the *person*. In contrast, humanistic theory follows an approach which looks to persons and seeks to frame principles by which *persons construct* external cues and cue complexes.

Utilizing a Ready-Made External World

In the first mode of constructing the external world, the person is active in *receiving* that which initiated in the external world. In the second mode, the person constructs the external world by a process of utilization (selection, capitalization) of what is ready-made. Although the person does not create anything new, the person constructs an external world by utilizing what is already lying about.

By using this mode, the person can construct his world through the ways in which he simply perceives what is there. Perception is a means of selecting out on the basis of one's own potentials and their relationships, and thereby building one's own world from what is already there (Enright, 1970). Dirt is there in the room. I utilize what is already there by means of my perceiving it. I have managed to construct a world of filth by means of sheer perceiving. I have utilized what is already there in the world, ready-made. Yet, as a science, we have yet to appreciate the extent to which simple perception is itself a means of world-construction. Not only is there a process of selecting something out, but much of what is selected is itself constructed. It is as if what is utilized is a little nub, and a whole process of construction builds upon that nub so that what is perceived has also been constructed. "The experience of the eclipse of the sun is not an absolute event that anyone, at any time in history, would experience in a similar way. An ancient Egyptian would not see a *sun* being covered by a shadow; he might see a threatening gesture of a god. And today, when we see an eclipse of the sun we cannot separate it from a world outlook that places the sun in the center of the solar system and the man as a satellite of the earth, a world outlook that isolates the sun and man as objects in themselves" (Needleman, 1967, p. 30). To perceive is to engage in a complicated process of construction by utilizing what is ready-made. Yet perceiving is only one of many ways of building worlds by utilizing what is ready-made.

Here is the person who builds worlds by *selectively engaging* with what is ready-made. In addition to perceiving it, you can place yourself in its path. An individual is scared and drawing back; if you choose, you can be the one of whom he is scared, and from whom he draws back. Here is someone exuding competitiveness; you can, if you wish, engage in competition with that person. Here is a flower issuing a fragrance; you can take in that fragrance if you wish. All of this is ready-made in your world. You can select from what is there; place yourself in its path. You can go forth and meet it. You can engage with whatever is there, presenting itself to you ready-made.

Anne constructed her external world by finding just the right men to mistreat and abuse her. She did not turn her men into being that way. They were there to be utilized by her, and she repeatedly constructed her world to include such a man. Donald was a high school senior who selected as a friend another boy marvelously equipped with characteristics of intense loyalty; Donald constructed his world by appropriate utilization of what was decently available. The family sought an external world which would prove downright inhospitable and antagonistic. Out of what was ready-made, they accurately selected a neighborhood of well-manicured lawns and carefully landscaped homes. a neighborhood ready-made to be antagonistic toward their exceedingly cavalier way of caring for their home. How could the eldest son utilize a ready-made part of the external world to provide him with a sense of being second rate, an outsider, looked down upon as not good enough? He met her at the tennis club, married her after a pregnant six months, and lived in the external world of her family—wealthy and erudite attorneys who enjoyed chamber music, philosophy and cultured ways. The eldest son had succeeded in utilizing the proper external world ready-made for making him feel second rate, an outsider, looked down upon as simply not good enough.

The young man was a graduate student in sociology, a complaining fellow who required external authorities about whom he could rail and complain. He found several such persons, professors who nicely served as the building blocks for constructing his particular kind of external world. Once having utilized these authoritarian professors in his world-schema, he asserted that the professors *really were* that way—and of course he was correct. In this mode of constructing the world, the building blocks are ready-made, and utterly real.

Where can you find a person who holds himself out as being concerned with you, who will put on all the accounterments of a most concerned person, but who will never really be *fully* concerned with you? For some persons, the answer consists of psychotherapists, ready-made building blocks for constructing that particular kind of external world. But, as Bergin (1963) points out, the person might also locate a clergyman, friend, teacher, physician, or anyone else who is ready-made to fit that specific requirement.

Both the authoritarian-seeking student and the authoritarian-being professor may use ready-made *roles* in constructing their worlds. It is easy for me to select a ready-made role to live in, and thereby to construct my world. Because I am the head of the family, they will come visit me at holidays. I am the sweet and understanding sister to so many people, and my sweetness and understandingness flow out of that role. I am the goat in the family, the one who gets blamed and ridiculed. Yet, in all this, I am the one who selects one or another role, and who deftly moves from one to the other. I am the one who decides whether or not to retain a ready-made role or to trade it for another. To understand my behavior as flowing from a given *role* is to fail to see *me* as the one who utilizes that ready-made role. There is a person here, a person who selects that particular role from which the behavior flows. Nor does conflict or stress come from any combination of roles which, in and of themselves, inherently conflict with one another. The conflict resides in the *person* who uses conflicting roles to create the conflict, rather than in the conflicting roles of loyal daughter and also angry left-wing protestor, or the altruistic leader who must be ruthless in the pursuit of humanitarian goals (cf. Leighton & Hughes, 1961). Roles can be described as cultural or social offerings, ready-made and available. Use of these roles is a means of constructing the external world by utilizing ready-made elements of the external world.

When you are ready to live in a world which has expectations of you, wishes to train you, or has plans for you, you will find such a world quite available. Many people will have expectancies about how you are to be. Many people will be ever so ready to have all sorts of plans for you. All you have to do is to utilize those parts of the external world which are ready-made with expectancies and anticipations for you. If you are a woman, you can find others who are ready-made to expect you to be a wife and a mother in ways which promise conflict in your trying to fulfill both roles. They will expect you to be polished and earthy, educated and unthinking, maternal and sexy, organized and silly, dedicated to both a home and a career, loyal and doggedly individualistic. You can select a ready-made world in such a way that the world will tear you to pieces—and then you can complain that the world really did all that to you.

Conjoint Construction of an External World

I can create an external world by the way in which I receive what impinges upon me, but the limits to the kind of world I can construct are quite narrow. It does not give me much room to paint an external world with dashingly broad strokes. The same is true for the second mode. How broadly I can construct an external world is limited by what the ready-made components can offer. Each component has a label indicating what it offers (such as belongingness, love, social action, an argument, sex, rebellion against authority, revolution, food and drink, and so on). I am sorely limited by the components which are available. But the third mode provides me with far greater creative possibilities. When you and I work together and pool our resources, we can construct all sorts of external worlds. Thus, as we move from the first to the second to the third mode, we are opening up greater and greater possibilities for the kinds of external worlds which can be constructed. In this sense, interpersonal and group relationships hold vast power to construct external worlds.

In the same fashion, my degree of *activity* as a world-constructor has also increased. I played an active role in receiving the intrusive external world, and an even more active role in constructing an external world by utilizing ready-made components. In this third mode, I play a still more active role. As we move down the four modes of constructing an external world (Figure 6.1), active involvement increases.

The conjoint construction of external worlds requires that two or more persons bring out what is potential in one another. You must seek something within me, and I must do the same with you. It is not right there, "hanging out" for direct use as in the second mode. We must find it inside each other and evoke it. I fashion you into being some way, and you do the same to me. We probe one another, searching our possibilities in each other. We slowly turn each other to see if there is a match between what I seek from you and what you seek from me. You and I go through a ritual dance together, carefully rotating one another to see if my dips and rises fit with your contours.

Existential phenomenology asserts that person and world (whether that world refers to another person or object) are to be described as forever working upon one another. Rather than being acted upon, a person is right there, building the world which is in turn building the person. "Man and universe are universally interdependent and co-defining" (Fischer, 1970, p. 84). This is the general proposition of this third mode, a statement of each person's role in constructing the world in which he lives. To describe a person as conjointly constructing a world with another person is to specify one particular mode by which "man and universe are universally interdependent and co-defining." It refers to one very particular mode in which the reality which emerges requires the conjoint efforts of the two parties. Without conjoint work, the reality does not exist; the reality only lurks there as a potential, until the two persons find the right alignment which brings it forth. In this process, the other object need not be another person. The other object can be a natural thing: a bird, a pen, a mountain, a stream, a sidewalk, a bicycle, a tree. Interaction with the physical object may be such that the physical object is altered by virtue of our interactive respondings to it (Mead, 1934), and thereby a new external world is created. Thus, in this mode of creating and constructing an external world, the person can interact with the objects of nature.

There are several areas of research which confirm the importance of this conjoint mutuality. One is the study of marriages which fit well or poorly, which last or break up. A second is the line of research examining variables which determine whether a mental patient will remain in a community or will return quickly back to the hospital. In both areas of investigation, the reasoning is similar: If the parties fit together well, the union persists; if there is a poor fit, there are problems; it is the goodness of fit or conjoint mutuality which plays the major determining role. For example, in their series of studies on the variables determining whether discharged male patients remain in their families or are returned to the hospital, Freeman and Simmons (1958b) find that ". . . the female relatives of low level mental patients tend to be frustrated, withdrawn, authoritarian, rigid, and anomic" (p. 157). Yet this reciprocity is an active one, not a mechanical fitting together. The returned male mental patients are actively at work inviting their wives and mothers to be a certain way, and the wives and mothers are equally hard at work building the returned mental patients into fulfilling particular roles. Each member is actively inducing the other to be very particular ways.

In the first mode, you are being dominant, and I construct my external world by the way in which I receive your dominance which intrudes itself upon me. In the second mode, you are still being dominant, and I construct my external world by selecting you out and utilizing your presented dominance. In the third mode, however, you are not *being* dominant. I must work upon you to bring forth your dominance, and that means you and I must work conjointly, for the bringing forth of your dominance requires our cooperation.

There are at least four modes by which we all construct our worlds. In mode one (Figure 6.1), we are more or less responders to external stimuli, receiving what comes to us from the external world. This is a most legitimate way, adopted by many persons much of the time. The third mode of working conjointly with another person in co-participating co-definition of the world is just another mode. In a review of Kierkegaard's thinking, Fischer (1970, p. 89) sets forth a description of human beings which closes off the former way of being and elevates the latter as the regnant principle for all human beings: "Man is not understood as an empiricistically conceived passive recipient of stimuli. Nor is he merely a respondent to his environment. Man and world are co-defining, and through an individual's choices, he makes both himself and his world." Humanistic theory rejects *any one* mode as the universal mode by which all human beings always build worlds and construct reality and meaning.

In this third mode, it is as if I have a number of possible roles which I can invite you to fulfill, and then I go about inducing you to fulfill one of them. Before we even come together, I am prepared to ask you to fulfill the role of my playmate, partner, tormentor, critic, or friend. When we are together, I "play" with you to see if you are inclined to fulfill one of these roles, and I try to induce such a role from you, if it is possible. Spiegel calls this process "role induction" (1957); it is an apt phrase, I believe. When a person enters a mental hospital and later behaves in ways that are considered as "regressed," I suggest that both patient and staff may have worked quite diligently to induce very particular roles from one another. When we attend to the patient, he had to work hard at inducing the staff to be in very special ways which welcome regressed behavior. When we look at the staff, they too had to work upon the patient in very special ways which would bring forth regressed behavior. Research has suggested that the hospital staff might well work upon the patient to become a "passive recipient" to their offerings: Such role induction appears likely to elicit regressed behavior from the patient (Polonsky, White, & Miller, 1957). Both parties, patient and staff, work upon each other to construct conjointly an external world of regression.

Mental hospitals are a wellspring of examples of two sets of persons rotating one another to produce a conjoint new external world in which they both live—for better or for worse. Here is a patient for whom it is important to be withdrawn in a situation in which others are non-giving, non-providing, non-satisfying. Here are staff personnel with the capacity to be separated, removed, distant from those who are not coming forth, not presenting themselves, withdrawn. How do these two sets of persons conjointly evoke behaviors from the other so as to construct a very explicit world for themselves? According to Schwartz, Schwartz and Staunton (1951), the former person (i.e. the patient in the mental hospital) must put forth a relatively small number of requests. Of these requests, a large proportion must be for simple material objects and services. Many of the requests must be for objects and services which are ungrantable. In such ways, the patients are inviting the hospital staff to behave in a way which provides for the patient's withdrawal. At the same time, the hospital staff, according to the findings of this study, must be individuals with a capacity for refusing, ignoring, and simply not hearing requests from such persons. When these two sets of persons work effectively with one another, they co-participate in conjointly constructing a world of a very specific kind—a world in which one person is withdrawn and the other is inviting such withdrawal.

Father and adolescent son are right now passing by each other. The son is looking for some matches and the father is going into the kitchen where his wife is doing the dishes. There is no defiance, no rebellion here. Now, less than five minutes later, the son is standing facing father, glaring at him, screaming that he will not do what father asks. Both are on edge, angry. Father looks menacing, contained, angry. These two persons worked conjointly together to create that happening. Father asked where the son was going. The son was going "out." Now the father steps toward the son and inquires sarcastically when he "intends" to be home, thereby communicating that the son seldom comes home when he says he does. The son pauses and looks cooly at the father. Pause. Father announces that the son will be home by ten. Son snorts with anger. He will not be home by ten! Back and forth and back and forth, until they have constructed the defiance and the rebelliousness. It was not there until they conjointly constructed it.

If we are observant, we can sense when we are being drawn into playing certain roles. The drawing power comes from the other person who is moving us about, trying us on for size, slowly rotating us. We must cooperate for this conjoint construction of an external world to be successful. Notice that point where you begin drawing me out, or where I begin to incline you in a particular direction. In my preliminary dance ritual, I move about the architect, looking for his appropriateness to fit a role of close working partner in a personally creative enterprise—the designing of a home. That is the role I want to induce him to play. My whole way of being with him is an asking of whether he is prepared to fulfill this role, whether it is within him and can be induced. In my being with the older woman, I can feel myself being induced to fulfill a role which she defines and seeks to draw from me. It is as if she is saying: "Although I may seem to be very 'real' and 'open,' all of this is strained and artificial. Please be annoyed at me for being transparent. I am asking you whether you have it in you to see me that way and treat me that way." I *do* have such a possibility within me, and I can sense my swaying into fulfilling that role.

Consider that when you and I first met 20 minutes or so ago, I was not withholding, withdrawn, removed, and you were not being hurt, disappointed, and sad. But now this is the way we are both being. We have succeeded in doing this to one another. Approximately 18 minutes ago you and I had worked upon each other so that you were trying hard to induce me to play a very definite role. You were handing me the role of being not fully with you, not disclosing to you, not sympatico. I acceded to that role which you induced me to play. But the key is that you and I both worked together to place us in this new situation in which you offer and I accept that particular role.

Now let us turn this process around. Instead of that moment when the other person is laying a role upon *me*, let us consider that other moment when *I* lay a role upon the other person. Suppose we analyze that moment when I finally stand up to my father and firmly tell him that mother is dying of cancer, she needs him now, and he must not follow his usual way of storming off on a vacation during every family crisis. Let us freeze that instant when I have said this to him. Here is a fraction of a second when I look at him. My father has always been seen by me as angry, blustery, defensive, fierce. Now, in this instant, I regard his face. How do I see him? I see him as angry, fierce, defensive. That is the role I place onto him. Is it even possible for me to "see" him as being some other way? Can I visualize him as being anything else? If the answer is no, then it is perhaps clear that my only way of seeing him is my effort at placing him in that single role, and if he indeed does respond to me by fighting back angrily, then he and I have succeeded in conjointly constructing this emergent external world *together*.

But suppose that I open up new possibilities for him. Suppose that I can "see" his face as registering something different. I look hard at his face, and, in this frozen instant, I am able to "see" him listening to me, receiving what I have to say, taking it in without anger or defensiveness. If I can see this, then I have opened up a new possibility, one which can offer him a new role. Now it becomes rather clear. If I really have at least two ways in which I can see him, then whichever I actually carry out is inviting him to be just that. I am constructing how he is to be, and doing this with him, conjointly.

In every instance of conjoint construction, the building blocks for the constructed external world can only be manufactured by the persons working together. The external world is not right there; it is a potential to be brought forth by our conjoint efforts. What I require for my external world lies right there in you, and what you require for your external world lies right here within me. Construction of our external worlds is a matter of conjoint bringing forth of what lies potentially within the other person. We both have potentials for delightful senses of humor. By conjointly constructing one another we are now successful in creating an external world of uproarious, knee-slapping good humor. I have the potential for being your good father, and you possess the possibilities for being my beholden little girl. If we are effective in working together we can fashion conjointly the right external worlds for one another.

The conjoint construction of a group. You and I can create a *group* with ourselves as members. What I need does not reside in *you*, and what you need does not reside in *me*; what *we* need can only be constructed by our being a group. If you and I both search for a sense of family, the family resides neither in me nor in you. But our being together can construct conjointly the group which offers us both the sense of family. If five or 20 or 300 of us have potentials for loyal allegiance, we can form the proper group and all maintain allegiance to it, and that to which we maintain loyal allegiance can only be constructed through our conjoint efforts.

You and I can construct an ingroup which bears a special relationship toward an outgroup—which you and I also construct. In all of this construction, we accomplish the work all by ourselves. We can create our own ingroup and outgroup from our own resources. We begin talking together and conjointly define an external situational context as one in which some of our teachers are crafty and mean to us. Soon you and I have drawn closer together against those awful teachers. As we experience more, as we construct the outgroup and our ingroup, we function as artists who have succeeded in painting our own picture of the external world. We have created crafty and mean teachers out there in the world. In our conjointly constructed situation of that bad outgroup, you and I have joined together as annoyed plotters against the teachers, as the angry students used by the teacher, or as comrades in frustrated helplessness. Before we talked with one another, that particular external world did not exist. Now that we have worked together, we have evoked something in one another which resulted in a defined external situation in which we exist together.

Responsibility for constructing external worlds lies with persons who participate conjointly. It requires conjoint effort for us to construct such dyads as majority-minority, student-teacher, dominant-submissive, black-white, we-they, male-female, haves and have-nots, parent-child, helper-helpee, strong-weak, employer-employee, management-labor, and so on. We ourselves are responsible for constructing the dyadic poles, the antimonies between them, and the impossibility of getting out of them.

Experimenters and subjects as conjoint constructers of an external world. I wish to construct a world in which I see things very clearly and accurately, with valid perceptions; I am superhuman in being beyond the laws and principles which govern the way you behave; I am part of the world of natural forces, owner of the power and the wisdom. You, on the other hand, must be the plaything of nature, a pawn of natural forces which dictate how you behave; you must be exceedingly human, complete with all the human frailties; your perceptions are invalid, what you see and do must be fraught with error. You need someone to be superhuman, beyond human frailty, Godlike, wise, the owner of natural forces, the repository of wisdom. When these persons come together and work upon each other conjointly, they may construct what we know as the experimenter-subject relationship. In this enterprise, the experimenter elevates himself to the role of scientist, a level above the subject, qualitatively different from the subject whom he studies (cf. Bergmann & Spence, 1944; Stevens, 1939). Here is another external world created by persons playing one role and inviting others to play the conjoint role.

When experimenters and subjects work together conjointly, the constructed world is a function of both groups. Accordingly, the results of the research must take into account the input of *both* groups. To interpret the results as a function of the subjects alone, or as reflecting only the world of the subjects, is to commit a serious methodological error. Yet traditional experimental methodologies and statistical procedures typically omit the conjoint efforts of experimenter and subject working together. Such methodologies rest on the presumption that the results are predominantly, if not exclusively, a function of subject variables. In contrast, our position is that the results are a *conjoint function* of subject *and* experimenter working conjointly together. What is needed is a package of experimental methodologies and statistical procedures to encompass *both* the subject variables *and* the experimenter variables! My best guess is that we can profitably study the movements of colliding pool balls without assuming that pool balls actively construct external worlds. However, we must understand *human beings* as constructing their own external worlds. This is a robust assumption with regard to humans as subjects—we are just beginning to learn this lesson—and also with regard to humans as experimenters. The latter lesson we have not yet begun to learn. Instead of designing methodologies which omit the impact of experimenters, new methodologies must be designed to acknowledge and assess the conjoint input of both experimenters and subjects.

Counselling and psychotherapy as the conjoint construction of external worlds. The field of counselling and psychotherapy is describable as therapists and patients conjointly constructing external worlds. In dyadic therapy and in groups (e.g. group therapy, family counselling, sensitivity groups) two or more persons come together and work hard at conjointly constructing external worlds. When counselor and client work together, they can create quite special kinds of external worlds valued quite highly by both participants. This is a delicate process requiring conjoint cooperation, for what they seek cannot be accomplished by counselor or client alone. Most of what goes on in therapy is a rather subtle process in which therapist and patient conjointly work together to construct very special kinds of external worlds. Each participant *needs* the other to construct something which is not present in either one, but can be constructed out of what may be potential in one another, providing they work together in effective conjoint fashion.

Virtually the entire psychotherapeutic literature is testimony to what patients seek from psychotherapy. They are easily understood as approaching the psychotherapeutic situation already programmed to turn psychotherapy into this or that kind of situation. Recently we are becoming aware of what the *therapist* also brings to that situation (e.g. Bugental, 1964; Frank, 1961; Lawton, 1958; Schofield, 1964). The next step is to recognize psychotherapy as merely another instance of *two persons* approaching one another with mutual readinesses conjointly to construct an external world for one another.

The therapist's contribution to the nature of the mutually constructed external world was first mentioned in the literature on countertransference. From then on, it was increasingly recognized that the therapist is an active co-participant with the patient in the construction of the psychotherapeutic mini-world. Unconsciously and consciously, the therapist works toward building a particular kind of relationship with the patient. Reviewing studies of the outcome of psychotherapy, Strupp suggests that ". . . the therapist's attitude toward the patient, as conveyed by his communications, may bring about a realization of the therapist's conscious as well as unconscious expectations concerning the course and outcome of therapy. For psychotherapy the crux of the matter is not the perceptions and clinical evaluations or even the therapist's conscious attitude toward the patient; rather it is the manner in which these variables influence and structure the therapeutic relationship" (1963, p. 7). Frequently these variables are very subtle. For example, the therapist is building a particular kind of relationship merely by having adopted a given theoretical approach. Suppose that the therapist's theory includes the idea that patients can have weak egos, that too much stress or pressure can result in the outbreak of primitive and psychotic material, that we must be careful not to present "too much for the patient to handle." These theoretical building blocks are just right for constructing very particular kinds of relationships. Without even thinking, just by having such a theory, the therapist is working very hard to construct a relationship in which he is strong, patient is weak; therapist can be cruel, patient is vulnerable; therapist has power, patient is fragile in the capable arms of the therapist. Without saying a word, merely by holding to such a theory, the therapist is contributing to such kinds of relationships. Yet neither therapist nor patient are fully aware of just what kinds of relationships they are (unconsciously) co-constructing.

The initial interviews between potential patients and potential therapists are saturated with these attitudes—metamessages exchanged behind ostensible communications with each other. A part of these metamessages often has to do with the question of whether the two parties will see each other again. Sometimes they decide that they will, and sometimes one or the other or both decide that this is the end. Often "... the therapist's attitude toward the patient may reinforce corresponding attitudes in the patient, leading to premature termination of therapy" (Strupp, 1963, p. 7). Yet the two parties nearly always discuss this question in some way and arrive at a conjoint conclusion. Here is an example of metamessages behind the actual words, metamessages whereby patient and therapist decide to construct a different external world for themselves. In their first hour together, neither therapist nor patient said these words, yet these constitute the metamessages whereby the two construct a special relationship:

Therapist: I am a professional therapist and a woman. A doctor. My office is in this clinic which is rather sterile, but I am warm and understanding, and I can do adequate therapy. I am a happily married woman, but my sex life isn't all that great.

Patient: I am scared because I am about to succeed. Soon I will expect myself to be a man. I want to snuggle up to a mother and sink down into that great oceanic feeling of not thinking—but not too much because I do want to finish law school.

Therapist: You don't terrify me, and that's a good start. Can we keep it safe and professional? Then I'll be warm and understanding, and, hopefully, that will make you feel good enough to give me a sense of being adequate as a therapist. Who knows, maybe that will even satisfy you.

Patient: Yes, oh yes. I do believe we will work out together.

Therapist: Me too. Oh good, you need me in just the way I want to be needed. . . . Next week at this time?

Patient: Yes, yes. I found you . . .

There are several common external worlds conjointly constructed by therapist and patient. Let us reformulate psychotherapy in this way, and describe a few typical conjointly created external worlds. In the first, the therapist seeks to be a very special person, saintly, the exemplar of virtue and maturity. This person is wise and paternal, omniscient and all-caring, giving and helping, understanding and empathic, strong. He requires a very special kind of partner—one who is a supplicant, craves help, places value on being enveloped in a relationship of caring, accepting, loving, strength-providing, sheltering, positive regarding, prizing, empathizing, wisdom-receiving. By the same token, the *patient* must seek someone who can really understand, can know him completely, can prize him as a person, attend lovingly to his inner feelings and sensings, be fully with him, give him a full measure of concern. Furthermore, he seeks this from a person who is all-wise, paternal, saintly, omniscient, virtuous, good, strong.

Studies of the effective ingredients of psychotherapy provide descriptions of this thematic relationship. Thus Rogers (1970, p. 130) concludes that in effective psychotherapeutic moments the client feels that he is being fully *received*, and the therapist senses that he is being fully receiving. Here is another manifestation of the conjoint construction of a very special and highly valued external world in which client and therapist conjointly construct a very special external world.

So subtle are these mutual influences that the therapist can construct a particular relationship only by working closely with a patient who is similarly inclined; the patient can construct a particular relationship only through equally careful conjoint working relationships with a therapist who is similarly inclined. So common are the inclinations to work conjointly in constructing these interlocking external worlds that the parameters of these relationships have become apotheosized as the essence of "the helping relationship" (Bordin, 1959; Goldstein, Heller & Sechrest, 1966; Kovaks, 1965; Mahrer, 1970a; May, 1958b; Mullan & Sangiuliano, 1964; Rogers, 1957; Schofield, 1964; Shoben, 1949; Truax, 1963).

In spelling out the "necessary and sufficient conditions for therapeutic personality change," Rogers (1957) has identified this same set of mutual seekings. That is, the conditions for personality change in Rogerian psychotherapy can be taken as a description of what the patient seeks for himself and for the therapist, and what the therapist seeks for himself and for the client. In Rogers' paraphrased words, the *therapist* seeks a role in which he is a congruent, integrated person, has unconditional positive regard for the client, has an empathic understanding of the client's frame of reference, and is successful in communicating the unconditional positive regard and empathic understanding to the client. The therapist seeks a client who is in a state of incongruence or anxiety, who seeks a relationship with someone who offers unconditioned positive regard and empathic understanding, and who seeks such a relationship with a person (therapist) who is congruent and integrated. The *client* seeks a role in which he is in a state of incongruence or anxiety, needs a therapist who is congruent and integrated, needs unconditioned positive regard and empathic understanding from the therapist. When the right kind of client meets the right kind of therapist, they can conjointly construct a highly valued external world together. Their mutual seekings and wantings constitute what Rogers describes as the necessary and sufficient conditions for therapeutic personality change, and which I would describe as the necessary and sufficient conditions whereby two kinds of persons work together to construct a relational world which is of importance and value to one another.

So much of what has been put forth as effective ingredients in psychotherapy can be understood, from this perspective, as ingredients in constructing this particular kind of very important external world. For example, Schofield (1964) cites two factors as key ingredients in the effectiveness of psychotherapy. One is ventilation, catharsis, sheer expression in which "... the patient, under the accepting, encouraging, and supportive friendship of the therapist, was enabled to give expression to his conflicts, his anxiety, his guilts, his resentments, to relieve his previously bottled up feelings ..." (p. 144). The second factor is acceptance and the lack of punishment. "In the prolonged relationships of intensive psychotherapy, it must be recognized that the patient has opportunity for repeated expressions of 'punishable' ideas and feelings which do not lead in therapy to punishment or rejection" (p. 145). I do not see these as leading to effective personality change in any direct fashion. Instead, I see these as components used by therapist and patient to conjointly construct a specific kind of external world. The patient and psychotherapist are working diligently at creating a world in which one person is supplicant, asking for help, pouring out his soul, pleading for loving acceptance—and the other person is highly valued, receiving what is deepermost in the other, kindly and accepting. It is the conjoint construction of this relational world which is crucial, and not the direct achievement of therapeutic effectiveness.

We have been describing the first common kind of external world conjointly constructed by the participants in psychotherapy. A second common external world is one consisting of a person seeking to have his behavior controlled (modified, adjusted, changed) and another person (therapist) seeking to control. To generalize this dyad a bit, the patient must be able to be in the role of sufferer, the one who has problems, the one who is displeased with the way he behaves. He must seek and find someone to control his behavior, change something about him, be the change-inducer. By the same token, the therapist must be willing to be the change-inducer, must want to change something about the other, must wish to change the other's behavior; this therapist requires a playmate who suffers, who has problems, who is displeased with the way he behaves. These two kinds of persons have sought and found one another throughout history (Frank, 1961, p. 215), and are continuously on the lookout for the appropriate partner. If we generalize these two roles even further, the person-as-patient seeks to establish a particular relationship with others, with the group, with the whole external world, with natural and supernatural forces; he requires someone who is, or who can stand as, all of that: Do something to me, try to do something to me, oppose me, accept me, be won over by me, show me your power. By the same token, the person-as-therapist must find it important to be in the role of the spokesman and representative of the group, the community, the society, natural forces, supernatural forces, mysterious forces of psychic healing. This person requires a companion who will see the person-as-therapist in this role, and who will seek to relate to him in some appropriate way: Change me, do to me, influence me. One is the individual and the other is the embodiment of influencing social forces.

Although many therapeutic approaches admirably outfit the therapist for the role of controller, the behavior therapies have especially suitable rationales and well-honed techniques to equip the therapist for this role. In discussing Wolpe's behavioral therapy methods, for example, Haley (1963) describes that therapeutic role as one of outright control of the patient's behavior. "Although the method as presented by Wolpe is a procedure focused upon the internal processes of the patient, a fuller description would indicate that the patient's behavior is 'taken over' by the therapist in the process of treatment" (p. 62). For many patients and therapists, such a role is precisely what is needed. At one extreme, the therapist may try to control the patient's personal behavior—such as being late for appointments or eating the piece of pie. At another extreme, the therapist may attempt to control the patient's active social participation; ". . . it is suggested that psychotherapists direct part of their efforts toward increasing the social contributiveness of patients in two ways: (a) by helping them develop broader social feelings, and (b) by encouraging active participation in the process of constructively changing their social environments" (Jessor, 1956, p. 226). In one form or another, many therapists and patients come to therapy programmed to construct this kind of external world.

Haley (1959) humorously describes the many ways that the stereotyped psychoanalyst and analysand construct this kind of conjoint relationship in which one is the controller, behavior changer, top-dog, superior one, and the other is the inferior, under-dog, mixed up, controlled one. The psychoanalyst has his own feet on the ground, while the patient's role is to lie on the couch with his feet in the air. The patient can never gain the superior position because the psychoanalyst refuses to compete or often even to respond. The psychoanalyst places the patient in an inferior position by proclaiming that the patient's behavior is determined by unconscious processes beyond the patient's awareness, but understood by the psychoanalyst. A part of the patient's role is to free associate, a maneuver which effectively insures that the patient can never successfully compete with the psychoanalyst for the superior position of controller. By means of such rules as these, the participants construct a very special relationship by conjointly working together.

On the basis of this second pair of relationships, therapists define characteristics of the "good" patient. In essence, these consist of qualities of a person who seeks and needs a therapist to provide control, to change him, to be a spokesman-representative of the powerful external world, who is the influencer. For this dyad, the qualities ". . . that make persons good candidates for psychotherapy are similar to those related to general accessibility to influence—a high degree of distress, anxiety, self-dissatisfaction, and feelings of social and personal insecurity" (Frank, 1961, p. 224). In groups where the "helper" (the leader, organizer, director) seeks to construct a controller-controllee relationship, good group members are those who are open to group influence and control. Thus the organizers of group treatment programs for adolescent offenders specifically exclude youths who are solitary "lone wolves," those who are uninspired by the potential controlling influences of the group (Pilnick, Elias, & Clapp, 1966). In order to construct a group which involves controlling and being controlled, taking over and being taken over, helpers are on the prowl for helpees (patients, group members, students, inmates) who are open to and seeking control by the right others.

The conjoint creation of controller-controllee is represented in its purest form in behavior modification approaches. But, as behavior modificationists are deft in pointing out, the control factor can be easily found in nearly all approaches to psychotherapy (Bandura, 1961). With some apology to the behavior modificationists, I cannot agree that the control parameter is a *necessary* ingredient of counselling or psychotherapy, though it appears necessary to a behavior modification approach. Yet I must agree with behavior modificationists in the sheer abundance of the controller-controllee relationship across most approaches. My explanation is that many persons seek an external world which controls them, and many other persons seek an external world willing to be controlled. When these two sets of persons conjointly work together, they successfully construct the sought after external worlds.

When one person seeks to be controlled, and another is most eager to control, the stage is set for methods based upon stimulus and response, and reward and punishment. When the patient is so postured to have an external world which controls, the patient has endowed the external world with a significant increment of reward-power and punishment-power (inelegant terms for such phrases as reinforcement value or contingency reinforcement). Bandura observed (1961) that rewards and punishments gain added value by virtue of the patient's seeking the interest and approval of the therapist. I would add that rewards and punishments are endowed with added value when the patient seeks to construct an external world which promises to control him—and this is a most common sort of person (client).

In addition to these two kinds of conjointly constructed external worlds, other writers have cited numerous additional worlds built by patients and therapeutic personnel. Caudill (1958) has described the hospital psychologist and psychiatrist who seek to construct special mini-worlds by working effectively and conjointly with hospitalized patients. For example, Caudill describes the doctor-patient context as a halcyon refuge in which the doctor can escape from the tension of the larger hospital network. In an insightful analysis of the kinds of gratifications offered to the psychotherapist by the therapeutic process, Bugental (1964) has described nine distinctive kinds of external worlds which psychotherapists set out to construct. Earlier, Lawton (1958) outlined 15 kinds of external worlds which the therapist often tries to construct in league with the right kind of patient. For example, the therapist may be programmed to resent the patient's excessive demands, and the patient is subtly moulded into making just such excessive demands. Or, the therapist may work conjointly with the patient to appease the patient's anger with mellifluous friendliness. Or the therapist may be geared toward outwitting the patient in a situation of competition, provided that the patient is the right sort of game player in the competitive sparring. Successful construction requires the conjoint cooperation of the right kind of client. In a way, I am denigrating what passes for much of counselling and psychotherapy as merely another example of persons conjointly constructing external worlds.

In this connection, both Bugental (1964) and Wheelis (1958) see the therapist and the patient as working diligently to establish a situation (called psychotherapy) in which the participants approximate a degree of safe experiencing of intimacy. The degree of success must be limited, however, else both therapist and patient become frightened by the implications of too serious an experiencing of intimacy. Little wonder that the participants create structures to insure safe limits, such as a 50-minute hour, physical contact taboos, payment of fees, living separate lives, and so on. Sensitivity and encounter groups are notorious contexts wherein trainers and group members alike establish sets of safeguards for experiencing the right degree of intimacy.

Much of what the therapist seeks to construct is usually embedded in and disguised as the goals of psychotherapy. For example, Felix (1961, p. 10) backs into a description of what psychotherapists seek by listing such goals as *reorganizing* the patient's personality, *removing* the patient's symptoms, *providing* needed counsel and support, *moving* the patient toward adjusting to society, *giving* the patient social protection. To be in this very special role requires that the psychotherapist work with a person whose seekings dovetail with those of the psychotherapist. The patient-to-be must seek personality reorganization, must have symptoms which ask to be removed, must be bent toward seeking social protection. Then the patient and the psychotherapist must work together conjointly in order to construct the right external worlds for one another.

A careful analysis of the goals common to many psychotherapies can be interpreted as a list of the common external worlds conjointly constructed by therapists and patients (Mahrer, 1970a). What have been articulated as the goals of psychotherapy are, in this sense, the experiences commonly constructed by therapists and patients working together. These common goals have been described by Knight (1941, 1952) with regard to the psychoanalytic psychotherapies, and by Mahrer (1967b) for psychotherapies in general. Following the schema proposed by Mahrer, it may be hypothesized that psychotherapy is a conjointly constructed situation whereby psychotherapists and patients may experience (a) the reduction of "psychopathology" such as symptoms and defenses; (b) the reduction of pain and suffering, primarily that of anxiety, hostility and a sense of meaninglessness; (c) increased pleasure; (d) increased experiencing; and (e) an enhanced self-relationship. The achievement of these goals requires both psychotherapist and patient in an effective, conjoint, working relationship.

Once the patient locates the therapist and lives in the channel of the relationship, the therapist and the relationship are going to be absolutely pivotal in the patient's constructed world. There is no way of avoiding this. But the patient is by no means working alone. The therapist is there, too, busy as can be, working hand in glove with the patient to construct that relationship. To describe this process as the patient's transference onto the therapist is to miss the conjoint participation of both partners. The phenomena referred to as transference (and countertransference) are conjointly produced by therapist and patient working together, and tell us about that particular dyad, not merely about the patient. It does not matter whether one or both participants are aware of what they are constructing together; my point is that both participants wittingly or unwittingly work together in constructing what is described as a transference and countertransference relationship. In the same way, therapist and patient conjointly construct many other relationships, from helper-helpee to romantic lovers, from father-child to complainer and wailing wall.

This relationship is so characteristic of psychotherapy that it has been accepted as its defining quality. "It is clear then that the vast majority of theoretical approaches to psychotherapeutic treatment, despite their marked diversity on other grounds, come together in the extent of their common emphasis on interpersonal constructs mediating between patient and therapist" (Goldstein, Heller, & Sechrest, 1966, p. 74). And in the same vein: "The key to the influence of psychotherapy on the patient is in his relationship with the therapist. Wherever psychotherapy is accepted as a significant enterprise, this statement is so widely subscribed to as to become trite" (Bordin, 1959, p. 235). To acknowledge the central importance of the interactional relationship is to grant that psychotherapy is yet another example of two persons conjointly constructing an external world.

Is there a way toward some alternative for the psychotherapist? Can a therapist function without co-participating in a conjointly constructed external world? Our solution is for the therapist to step out of the role of the conjoint co-participant. The patient can be freed to build a world which is not so centrally linked to the therapist and the therapeutic relationship. How may this be accomplished? Instead of being a conjoint partner, the therapist becomes a part of the *patient* as the patient actively works upon more meaningful aspects of his external world. The therapist can be more than someone who works together with him in constructing a mutually shared external world. He can be with that person without being a central part of his external world, and without placing him as a central part of his external world. He can be with that person without being a part of the external context in which the patient experiences what it is important for him to experience—and without making him into being a part of the therapist's external context in which he experiences what it is important for him to experience.

Once the therapist is freed to *not* be in the patient-therapist relationship, that relationship can be seen as very constricting. It is growth-hindering. Furthermore, it is illusory to consider this relationship as growth-enhancing. The only change which takes place is the construction of a new external world, a new relationship. Each partner approaches the relationship quite prepared to work with the partner in building this relationship together. Change is predefined by the nature of the two partners. Indeed, the only direction in which change *can* proceed is toward building the kind of world the partners are equipped to build. If the therapist and patient are drawn toward conjointly constructing a world of friend-friend (or parent-child or controller-controllee, or complainer-wailing wall, or saint-supplicant, or whatever), that is the only direction in which change can proceed. All other directions are blocked. Such a predefined direction of change is hardly growth-producing, is hardly "therapeutic," is hardly a way of opening up the person. It is delimiting, binding, truncating. Moreover, such a relationship can be painful. If I seek to be loved, and want the therapist to be my provider of love, but you are seeking to be a detached controller and want me to be in the role of one-down controllee, then trouble is brewing. At best, we can deflect off one another. But generally you will bend me out of my shape, punish me, and make me feel bad for being the way I am and for trying to have you fill a role you do not want to play. The typical therapeutic relationship is also growth-hindering in another way. If I am supplicant and you are saint, you and I mutually feed on only those parts of one another. All other potentials within me are cast aside. I become more and more the supplicant that you and I both want me to become. And nothing more. We have conjointly constructed a reality together, one which grows like a fungus to kill anything else I can be. That is hardly growth-*engendering*. It is time to progress beyond therapy as the (unwitting) construction of an external world by persons working conjointly together.

Fabrication of an External World

In the three modes of constructing an external world, the person has moved from minimal to mild to moderate degrees of active responsibility. Thus the person plays a more active role in conjointly constructing an external world than in utilizing a ready-made world, and construction by receiving an intrusive external world requires even less of an active role. We now turn to the most active role the person can play in constructing an external world, i.e., fabricating an external world out of whole cloth. In this mode, the person is the *complete* architect, designer, and builder. The fabrication of an external world is an act of personal artistry, calling upon true creative resources. It is the mode of creative inventiveness. When one fabricates an external world, the possibilities of what can be created exceed those of the first three modes. You can construct any kind of external world—from a new city to a new piece of art, from a political ideology to a God, from a vision of Christ to an image of your ancestor, from a voice calling to you out of the crowd to snakes surrounding your bed. All you require is your own personal resources. If you wish to construct a stand of trees where there was none, that can be fabricated out of your own personal resources. If you wish to construct an image of the devil where there was none, that too can be fabricated out of your own personal resources. Information theorists hold that human beings are limited to the information which is fed into them. In this fourth mode especially, human beings are held as *creating new information*, as inventing new horizons of information, as able to ask new questions. In this enterprise, the building blocks can be either internal or external.

From building blocks of internal reality. We can construct an external world with building blocks which are internal. Out of these internal building blocks we fabricate an external world which Freud called a "psychic reality," for ". . . psychic reality is a special form of existence which must not be confounded with factual reality" (Freud, 1938, p. 548). In one sense, an external world fabricated from internal building blocks is not real. When *I* see leering faces on the wall, you may not see them at all. No one else may discern those leering faces. They are my reality, mine alone. They are fabricated out of my internal reality, and the external world I construct may bear only slight relationships to your external reality.

When I am my sweet sexuality, touching and being touched by the lovely, gentle princess, I can fabricate this reality by means of fantasy. Then, in that external world, I do indeed gain a decent measure of sweet sexual experiencing. In my *non*-fantasy world there is no gentle princess. "The missing object which is wanted nevertheless is compensated for in the same way in which man can compensate for unsatisfying reality in general: by fantasy" (Fenichel, 1954e, p. 84). By drinking deeply of fantasy, I construct an external world from my own internal building blocks.

When I build an external world out of internal building blocks, it can be exceedingly fanciful and looked upon as quite strange. It differs quite a bit from *your* world. I fabricate an entire external world when I dream. That fabricated external world is strange and fanciful, and bears no relationship to your external world, even though you might be in the same bed with me. Furthermore, my dream-fabricated external world will be populated with foolish and bizarre stuff. There are other ways of fabricating strangely fanciful external worlds out of internal building blocks. If I place myself under conditions of heightened sensory or sleep deprivation, then I can fabricate a most unusual external world of squirrels which you cannot see (Bexton et al., 1954), or people hanging, or other strange and bizarre fillings-in (Edwards, 1941; Kleitman, 1939). Under these conditions I may fabricate an external world of "paranoid" delusions and ideation (Altman et al., 1960; Katz & Landis, 1935) or simple jets of water (Bliss, Clark & West, 1959). Persons labeled "psychotic" were found to evidence a return of old "symptoms" under such conditions of deprivation (Koranyi & Lehman, 1960) wherein the persons fully fabricated their own external worlds. Fabricating an external world predominantly from one's own internal resources can lead to worlds which are creative, fanciful, and sometimes strange and delightfully bizarre.

Yet worlds of deprivation, delusions and dreams are real. The fabricated world is a real world. Once we categorize the thing, event, or process, it has been granted the status of reality; what may or may not be "real" are the referents (or designata) of or about them (Feigl, 1953). In this sense, delusions, dreams, and the entire realm of fabricated worlds are real.

When I fabricate an external reality using only a mild measure of personal creativity, you may label that act a misperception or a parataxic distortion (Sullivan, 1953). To create a *rejecting* external world, I may only have to twist (or misperceive or distort) slightly the way you are to me. That is an easy fabrication, requiring only a slight degree of personal creativity. But when I construct what are termed delusions or hallucinations, these are audaciously resourceful and inventive acts of creative fabrication (Boss, 1963)! Fleischl (1958) describes how some persons (they are labeled "paranoid") fabricate an external world constructed to focus attention onto themselves. In their worlds the community may plot against them or plan to torture them or watch their every move—but the persons nevertheless have managed to be at the focal center of the concerns of others. Some may label these as delusional or hallucinatory mechanisms, pathological systems of defense against waves of inner anxiety (e.g. Boverman, 1953). Yet these persons are merely using another mode of doing what you and I are always doing, viz. constructing an external world—only they use building blocks of internal reality in fabricating their worlds.

Such construction requires skills, training, and effort. For example, it requires all of these qualities to construct a world *without meaning*. Yet I can construct such a world if I have the skills and if I work hard enough. If successful, I can then live in a world without real meaning. I will not see any meaning in my life; yet that itself is the mark of an achievement. Ellenberger (1958, p. 119) accounts for problems and difficulties as resulting from the person's *inability* to see meaning in his life. To have a life without meaning is not evidence of a *lack* of ability; it is the capstone of an *active enterprise*. It is a fabricated world, constructed by the architect. It is a positive achievement.

We all fabricate worlds out of internal building blocks when an inner insistence forces us to see-describe-prove that the world really is some particular way. I must describe the world as being a certain way, and will work hard at insisting that the world really is like that. I can work very diligently at describing you as untrustworthy or capable or patronizing or power-hungry. My description of you comes from an inner insistence on your being the way I describe you as being. I will argue that you really are that way. I will cite proof that you really are this way. It is terribly important that my world contain you as untrustworthy or capable or patronizing or power-hungry. It makes no difference whether you really are that way at all. All of the systematic methods of assessing whether you really are that way or not are irrelevant in this having-to-describe you as being like this or that.

Fabricated worlds are real worlds. Constructing the external world by fabrication, using internal building blocks, is the purest mode of personal reality-building. In this mode the person truly is building his own reality. Humanistic theory aligns with both existential phenomenology and some Eastern philosophies in the doctrine that we construct our own personal reality-worlds. Living in one's own constructed external reality is what we all do. This particular mode of constructing external reality is by no means restricted to crazy people. "This doctrine, as far as I can judge, was not meant to apply only to those we call psychotics or neurotics, but includes—indeed stresses— the illusory nature of the world and life of so-called 'normal' men" (Needleman, 1967, p. xv).

From building blocks of external reality. As a mode of constructing the external world, fabrication is more than making up a world out of one's fantasies and illusions. It is meant to include all the ways in which we actively manufacture worlds, build something where there was nothing. In doing this, we can use building blocks of *external* reality. I can build a shelter by putting rocks upon one another. In so doing I have fabricated an external world born out of the personal resources of what is within me. I am the complete architect. I created that world using the building blocks—pieces of reality—selected by me out of the external world. That was an act of my will. I fabricated that shelter. Yet, unlike an idea of reference or delusion or hallucination, that shelter *is* there. It is real. Anyone can see it, touch it, consensually validate its existence. It is testimony to my ability to fabricate an external world out of real external building blocks.

In the same way, if I am successful, I can make you into my servant. You obey me, and carry out nothing but my wishes. I can become your activator and the determiner of what you do and how you are to do it. I can deprive you of having any mandate over what you do (some refer to this as dehumanizing you) so that you are as subject to my will as those rocks. I have done this to you. I have made you into a real building block in the fabrication of my external world. The form and shape of that external world were fully a function of me. I did not *receive* a servant. I did not *utilize* servants who were already there in the external world. I did not work *conjointly* to create a servant. I personally created that servant all by myself. You were raw material which I shaped and moulded, designed and built to be what I wanted—a servant.

I can act upon the external world in ways which sculpt it into being a particular way. When I am done, I have created something by my very own efforts, something which was not there before. If I punish that dog in just the right ways, I can manufacture that animal into a nasty, cruel, angry dog. Although research has suggested the ineffectiveness of punishment as a means of *eliminating* socially disapproved behavior (Bandura, 1961), I see punishment as an effective means of *fabricating* socially disapproved behavior. By being punitive, I can hammer the punished behavior into its very existence. If we punish just right, we can fabricate a real piece of the external world.

Yet the restless urge to fabricate extends well beyond the personal and mundane. Most of traditional research is merely evidence of a person (the research scientist) fabricating an external world from building blocks of external reality. This person, in using our contemporary research methods, is as far away as possible from a naive receiver of the intrusive external world (the first mode of constructing an external world). The researcher is an *active fabricator* of the external world. Indeed, humanistic theory suggests that most of our contemporary research is sheer testimony to the effectiveness of the researcher's ability to fabricate the kind of external world he sets out to construct. Suppose that ten researchers set out to demonstrate that insight *is* a significant ingredient of psychotherapy, and ten other researchers set out to show that insight is *not* a significant ingredient of psychotherapy. Each of the two groups will select a methodology which enables them to accomplish what they intend to accomplish. Indeed, both groups will be rigorous and systematic in diligently fabricating their external worlds. Each researcher will perhaps fabricate an "experimental" group and a "control" group. The design and the procedure are usually not simply there; they must be created. When these two groups of researchers have completed their work, they will have fabricated a particular kind of external world to suit their purposes. That is, the first group of ten researchers will tend to fabricate external worlds which indicate that insight *is* a significant ingredient of psychotherapy, and the second group of ten researchers will tend to fabricate external worlds indicating that insight *is* *not* a significant factor in psychotherapy.

If we knew beforehand what sort of world the researcher was setting out to fabricate, we could predict decently well the outcome of the research. For example, if we studied the introductions to ten rigorous studies on the role of insight in psychotherapy (or any other issue), and could discern that these ten studies were done by researchers dedicated toward demonstrating that insight *is* a significant factor, and studied the introductions to ten other studies which revealed a commitment to showing that insight was *not* a significant factor, we should be able to predict the general run of the results of the studies.

We would predict that the researcher would select just that methodology which would provide the sought after results. For each set of researchers, the methodology and design could be equally tight. But the results would be predictable because each set of researchers fabricated their worlds. They used contemporary methodology (an external building block) to fabricate their external worlds.

What can be concluded from such results? Most research sets out to draw conclusions about the phenomenon studied. Humanistic theory flatly disagrees that such research tells us *anything* about those phenomena. I would see such research as being rather simplistic testimony to the ability of knowledgeable, clever persons (research investigators) to fabricate the kinds of external worlds they set out to fabricate. The conclusions I would draw would pertain to the *experimenters*, and not at all to the external phenomena (e.g., insight) they study! I would conclude that the results indicate that if you are inclined to show that insight is or is not a significant factor in psychotherapy, you can fabricate a world to confirm precisely that. In general, I would state that research done to prove or to disprove, to show this or that, to confirm or deny a held position (and that is the bulk of our research), tells us minimally about the investigated phenomenon, and tells us maximally about the researcher and his ability to fabricate an external world using building blocks of external reality.

When the researcher acts *upon* the external world, he is usually fabricating a particular kind of external world out of his own potentials. What he does to the external world tells us about *him*, and not about an objective, transcendent external reality. We know more of the kind of world *he* fabricates, and very little about the *phenomenon* about which he is talking. What do we know when a physician in a state mental hospital half a century ago proclaims that a mental patient is improved, or not improved, or is much improved? We know about the kind of world that physician is busy fabricating. We do *not* know about the phenomenon of improvement in that human being who was in the state mental hospital. When Eysenck (1952) accepts such results as indicating something about the phenomenon of improvement in those mental patients, he is, from our perspective, drawing an inaccurate and incomplete conclusion. We would accept such results as telling us about the way *those particular physicians* went about fabricating their own particular worlds. The implications for research are sober: As researchers we have used the wrong data, interpreted in the wrong way, to draw wrong conclusions.

At that point where an investigator is carrying out an experiment, several stages of external world construction already have occurred. Far from an unbiased consideration of a phenomenon, the investigator has reached a highly sophisticated advanced stage in constructing his world "... some type of research activity is already in progress by the time it comes to design an experiment, even if it is only the experimenter's literature search on a problem or his thinking about a particular experimental design. This means that one never really starts doing research with an experiment, but rather one approaches a certain point in an investigation where an experiment may become necessary or desirable" (Giorgi, 1966, p. 39). Looked at in this way, such experiments are less a means of gaining knowledge and more of a gauge of successful fabrication of an external world.

These considerations widen the gap between "laboratory" and "naturalistic" research. Ordinarily, laboratory experimentation is held as superior when the researcher's aim is to establish rigorous conditions to isolate particular variables rather than striving to reproduce natural daily living conditions (Andrews, 1948). Yet, from our viewpoint, this gets nowhere near the crucial difference between laboratory and naturalistic research. When the experimenter constructs rigorous laboratory conditions, our analysis submits that we are witnessing effects of the *experimenter*, and the results of the experiment tell us predominantly about the experimenter. The "difference that makes a difference" between laboratory versus naturalistic study is that in the former we are witnessing the workings of the *experimenter* and in the latter we are witnessing the workings of the phenomena we are investigating. To justify laboratory investigation by establishing rigorous laboratory conditions to isolate particular variables is, with regard to *this* problem, no justification at all! If we wish to study human beings (beyond the researcher), we must devise methodologies which properly acknowledge the pervasive effects of the researcher.

Within the framework of drive reduction and tension reduction, many researchers have investigated the hypothesis that the greater the deprivation the greater the intensity of the drive. For example, the more we deprive an organism of food, the greater should be the intensity of the drive for acquiring food. In many of these studies, especially with animals, the experimenter is highly active in fabricating the whole situation. The experimenter selects the subjects, organizes the laboratory conditions, creates the deprivation of food—fabricates everything. Yet the results are typically taken as pertaining only to the relationship of amount of deprivation to amount of food-seeking behavior. The theoretical framework out of which these studies are generated cannot account for the effects of the experimenter who organized the entire situation. Where do we insert the experimenter? If we insert the experimenter into the hypothesis, then the question is not merely: What is the relationship between degree of food deprivation and degree of drive for acquiring food? Now the question becomes: To what extent do the personality processes of the experimenter effect the food-seeking behavior of his subjects? Since our theoretical perspective lays great weight upon the effects of the experimenter on the situation he constructs, our theory would predict that there would be *no linear relation* between deprivation and drive intensity, and that the effects of various experimenters would be variegated and equivocal. As an incidental comment, our predictions seem to fit the research results better than the traditional hypothesis that there is a linear relation between food deprivation and the degree of drive for acquiring food.

In any scientific enterprise, the investigator has some aim which brings the enterprise into being and which the enterprise is to serve; that aim *ought* to lie outside the scientific enterprise, and ought not intrude itself into the process of the investigation (Rogers & Skinner, 1956). Rogers questions the effects of the investigator's motivation upon the design and results of the investigation. I believe he is right. The design and results of our investigations are testimony to the ability of investigators to fabricate their own particular external world. If much of our research arises out of such personal aims of the investigators, and if these aims do intrude themselves significantly into the process of the investigation, then let us acknowledge all of this. Let us conclude that this piece of research shows that Dr. X can show that insight is of worth, and Dr. Y can show that insight is of little worth. Since much of our research is evidence of the world-fabricating capacity of the investigator, our conclusions should reflect just this.

By understanding this fourth mode of constructing external worlds, an exceedingly broad spectrum of human enterprises can be brought under a single rubric. Here we have the mental patient who sees visions of God, the mother who creates a rebellious infant, the composer of a symphony, the researcher fabricating rigorous laboratory conditions, and the businessman constructing a new corporate organization. Each of these persons actively fabricates his own external world whose form and shape are wholly determined by the creative inventiveness of the architects. Some of the building blocks are internal and some are external. Some are prized as artistic or scholarly, and others are scorned as mad or bad. But all conform to this fourth mode of constructing an external world.

I submit these as four major modes of constructing external worlds (Figure 6.1). None of these is new. Each is championed by various approaches. Whereas many other approaches usually adopt one of these modes, humanistic theory accepts all four. In summary, our thesis is that human beings *construct* their external worlds by one or more of these four modes.

FUNCTIONS OF AN EXTERNAL WORLD

As indicated in Figure 6.1, the person (or, to be more exact, the person's potentials and their relationships) constructs an external world to play particular functions. In other words, each person's world is constructed to be the way it is because it is important for that person to live in that particular kind of world. For some persons, it is important that their worlds be chaotic and disorganized, whereas for others, their world must be stable and organized. Some persons "... *strive to construct* a stable world, a world they can control and get their bearings in. A view of the world exclusively as constant is an achievement—a *praxis*, not a 'given' ..." (Jourard, 1968, p. 153). In the same way, human beings construct worlds with all sorts of characteristics or functions. I prefer the word "function," because it suggests that the person is there to provide the function, whereas the word "characteristic" implies some property of worlds independent of the person as a constructor of the world.

When I attend to something out there, its meaning is a function of the potential which constructs it. It does not matter whether the "it" is simple—a candle flame or the words on a page—or complex—a political rally or dinner party. As the center of what I am shifts from one potential to another, I change what is out there. I can focus upon the candle flame while I am being one potential, and the candle flame can be yellow, flickering, about a foot away, an inch or so in height. When the center of my being shifts to another potential, there is a shift in what that candle flame is. Now it is dancing particles, lambent colors, three dimensional pools. Its very nature is altered by my shifting from one potential to another. I provide flames, printed words, political rallies and dinner parties with meanings—functions—which change when the potential I am changes.

Understanding a person is a process of understanding the *modes* by which that person constructs an external world, and understanding the *functions* which that external world is designed to play. When we take this posture in understanding human beings, it becomes apparent that most people construct worlds whose functions are exceedingly painful, i.e., in which they feel absolutely miserable. To avoid knowing this, most human beings cling to some sort of myth (often dignified as a scientific theory) that either the culmination of their world-building activities is supposed to make them feel good, or, if it makes them feel bad, something has gone wrong. In our discussion of bad feelings (Chapter 3), it was stated that bad feelings require an appropriate situational context. The function of considerable world-building is to construct such appropriate situational contexts. We must go beyond the proposition that human beings seek (or are entitled to) pleasure.

Human beings are continuously constructing worlds which can either make them feel good or bad. Problems occur when the worlds we build make us feel bad. "Each patient . . . experiences the world not 'as it is,' however that is, but as 'his' world, the world in which he has his experience. But it is the very quality of this experience which is the problem for him. He does not like it" (Holt, 1968, p. 242). Accordingly, the functions our constructed world is made to play can make us feel good or can make us feel wretched.

Once we understand situations as the creation of persons, and once we understand situations as serving the functions of persons, we have shifted the basis for a rigorous classifying of situations. Because of the potentials for experiencing, a situation is constructed to serve particular functions. If I am geared toward experiencing ambitiousness or belongingness, I construct situations which serve the function of providing for the experiencing of ambitiousness or belongingness. We look to the *person* for an understanding of the function the situation is to play. Such an approach differs from all schemas which classify situations on the basis of *situational* properties. Whether a situation is described as an authoritarian or a sexual situation is to be decided on the basis of the *person* who constructs the situation and provides it with its function—and not by studying the properties of the situation itself. Whether a situation is threatening or non-threatening, stressful or non-stressful, anxious or non-anxious depends upon the constructing, function-attributing *person*—and not the extrinsic properties of the external situation. We describe situations on the basis of the functions the person who creates the situation creates it for. Our schema insists that the *person* constructs the situation and gives it its function; other schemas are based on the notion that it is the situation which causes the person to behave in some way or other.

By whatever mode the external world is constructed, human beings do construct that external world. We can make sense of what is going on to the extent that we can understand the person as the constructor of that external world, and as the one who provides it with its functions. Let us put this to work in understanding "stress," for this is often an extreme case in which we do not want to see ourselves as the architect, and, much less, admit to endowing the stress with any sort of function in our lives. Stress has been defined as including a range from an alien *external* event, such as loss of a loved one, to an alien *internal* event, such as a surge of unmanageable impulses (e.g. Kalis, Harris, Prestwood, & Freeman, 1961). Regardless of the internal or external nature of the stress, our perspective holds that the stressful event is constructed by the person to serve some function. Our thesis is that any kind of world, situation, or event, including those which we label as stress, is understood as constructed by the *person* and as playing a defined *function*.

The External World as a Context for Experiencing

Human beings construct external worlds into serving as appropriate external situations for the experiencing of potentials (Figure 6.1). For this function, the external world exists as a veritable cornucopia of raw materials which we call upon in constructing the right context for our experiencing. This gigantic warehouse contains an inexhaustible supply of parts which can be fashioned into myriads of appropriate contexts. In Chapter 3, I described the three necessary and sufficient conditions for the experiencing of bad feelings, one of which was an external world constructed into an appropriate situational context. Now we can expand this notion. An appropriate situational context not only serves as one of three conditions for the experiencing of feelings, it serves a more ambitious and direct function of providing for the experiencing of potentials. For each mode of constructing an external world, the constructed external world can serve as the appropriate situational context for such experiencing (Figure 6.1). By means of the right behaviors (B1, Figure 6.2), persons construct appropriate external situations as contexts for experiencing potentials (OP1 and DP2. Figure 6.2).

The external world contains the resources required to fulfill the function of being the context for experiencing. This model, this *function* of the external world, is found in many biological conceptions of human beings wherein the external world plays a similar function. It houses the necessary resources; it contains what the organism needs. In that model, however, these resources are limited to biological resources such as oxygen, water, and food. Yet in both the biological model and in our first function of the external world, the external world offers the needed resources. The biological model of human beings *limits* the functional meanings of the external world to this one function; humanistic theory describes the external world as able to be used for a number of functions (Figure 6.1), of which this is only one. The biological model of human beings *limits* the resources of the external world to biological resources such as oxygen, food, and water; humanistic theory recognizes a far broader supply of resources far beyond oxygen, food, and water to include everything which can be used in constructing an external context for the function of experiencing. Thus humanistic theory and biological theories of human beings conceptualize the external world as serving the function of providing the right context for what human beings need, although I submit that the biological conception is more limited than the humanistic conception.

If my potential consists of experiencing love (OP1 or DP2. Figure 6.2), then I can construct an appropriate external situation as a context for that experiencing. The context might include a woman who looks at me in a loving way, or my child who falls asleep comforted in my arms, or a mother who caresses me in a loving way. In these contexts I experience love. If my potential involves compassion, I am quite capable of constructing external contexts appropriate for the experiencing of compassion. My personal history contains 20 or 30 situations construed explicitly for the experiencing of compassion. As a young adolescent I worked in a government mental hospital, in a wing devoted to little children. This provided rich contextual material for my experiencing of compassion. In precisely the same way, you and I construct hundreds of contexts in which we experience toughness, curiosity, firmness, understanding, comfort, compliance, cooperation, achievement, and every other kind of experiencing you and I have as potentials within us.

The experiencing of potentials which are painful. Some persons are simply bursting with potentials for experiencing ugly hatefulness. Of the many contexts which they can construct, one common context consists of persons whom they can distrust as objects of suspicion. Then, having constructed such a context, these persons can experience their ugly hatefulness. Such persons may, for example, go to hospitals and view their therapists as distrusted objects of deep suspicion, in what has been labeled a paranoid maneuver (Bullard, 1960). If I have a potential for experiencing disorganization and chaotic lack of structure, I can construct a world of utterly chance happenings. In the same way, if my potential involves the experiencing of being crushed, driven, tossed about by inexorable forces, I must construct a world of ineluctable determinism. Whether I live in a world of chance or a world of determinism is a function, in part at least, of the nature of my own potentials. "We know that determinism predominates in the subjective experience of the melancholic, and chance in the experience of the manic. The manic lives in a world of complete irresponsibility where he is bound neither by the past nor by the future, where everything happens through sheer chance; the melancholic, on the other hand, feeling himself crushed under the weight of his past, acts without feeling that he could change anything, because almost nothing is left to the realm of chance or free will" (Ellenberger, 1958, p. 115). These people *live* in different worlds because they *construct* different worlds, and they construct different worlds as contexts for experiencing unstructured chaotic disorganization or ineluctable iron determinism.

Suppose that I have a potential for experiencing passivity. What can I do to construct the external world into serving as a context for my experiencing of passivity? In order for my world to enable me to experience passivity, contexts can be constructed in which I am made passive, governed, influenced, instructed, stimulated and controlled, dominated, deprived of mandate, pushed and pulled. I can live, perhaps very painfully, in a world whose function is to enable me to experience passivity, and I am the one who constructs the world into serving that function.

What kinds of situational contexts can be constructed to provide for the experiencing of being bypassed by life, missing everything in life, lacking basic necessities, being entirely without that which life may have available for others? If this is the function to be played by the external world, then the person must construct very special life circumstances in order to experience all that. Indeed, its accomplishment can stand as a lifelong career. The *mode* of construction may be by (a) receiving an intrusive external world in a proper manner. The world can present itself in the form of a blizzard in the mountains where you are cross-country skiing, and, after 30 hours of being alone and lost, in the middle of the black night, you are saturated with the experiencing of being bypassed by life, lacking basic necessities. The proper situational context may be constructed by (b) utilizing a ready-made external world, or by (c) conjointly constructing the external world, or by (d) your active fabrication of the proper external world. Yet, regardless of which *mode* is utilized, the person actively co-participates in making the external world serve the specific *function* of providing for that defined experiencing. I am always impressed with the description of situations which omits the role of the *person* in their construction. For example, in arguing for the prepotency of physiological needs, Maslow (1970) *begins* with a person *in* such a state: "Undoubtedly these physiological needs are the most prepotent of all needs. What this means specifically is that in a human being who is missing everything in life in an extreme fashion, it is most likely that the major motivation would be the physiological needs rather than any others" (p. 36). That is quite a scene, viz. a person missing everything in life in an extreme fashion! Such a state is a paramount *achievement* for persons with a potential for experiencing the absence of everything in life.

To point to the external world as the *cause* of our experiencing is merely to identify the *means* whereby a particular mode of construction accomplished its task of creating the appropriate setting for the experiencing of some potential. When we describe situations in which the person is helpless, controlled, lacking necessities, in a terrible fix, bossed and bullied, missing what life has available, we typically are describing the culmination of a process of creation in which the person constructs a world whose function is to provide for such an experiencing, even when it hurts. Humanistic theory holds that we construct contexts for the experiencing of nice potentials which are personally and socially valued: altruism, loyalty, creativity, truth, beauty, and love. But we also construct external worlds as contexts for the experiencing of potentials on the shadow side of human beings: greed, hatred, brutality, selfishness, loneliness, rejection, failure, and every ugly possibility we human beings are capable of experiencing. And how very deft you and I are in constructing the external world into contexts for these baser, twisted, stressful, gnarled experiencings! I can construct the external world into being the right context for me to experience hardship, being turned down and rejected, being utterly alone, being ridiculed, being unreachable. Such experiencing can be painful. Yet that is what I have to experience. How awful it is to work hard at fashioning the external world into serving as the context for painful experiencing. And yet this is the way we are. This is what we do. This is how we build the external world.

What kind of situational context is appropriate for experiencing a sense of being disillusioned, of being angry and frustrated that what was promised is not forthcoming, that what is actually here is grossly less than I had expected? In order to provide for this kind of experiencing, the person must construct situational contexts such as the following: (a) I am going to be married, and that is going to be great and wonderful. I will have everything that I have always wanted. (b) I wanted to be accepted into that graduate school, and here I am. This is the kind of life I have longed for, worked hard at achieving, and here I am. (c) I have the job now. It is just what I wanted, and here it is. I have done just about everything I could to achieve this job, and now it is mine. Once having constructed such situations, the person can then live in them so as later to experience painful disillusion and disappointment.

Suppose I have the potential to experience utter fatigue and exhaustion. From our standpoint, I first must construct just the right context. *I* create that context, and *I* reap the fruits in the form of experienced fatigue and exhaustion. In coining the term *neurasthenia*, Beard (1905) recognized the person's own role in creating the right context. Beard saw neurasthenia as caused by the *person's* own overwork. Having successfully created the right context, the result was utter fatigue and exhaustion. We use the external world as a context for experiencing what it is important to experience, for better or for worse, for pain or for pleasure. We may have potentials for experiencing uncertainty, confusion, bewilderment, conflict, inability to make decisions. Given this potential for experiencing, how do we go about constructing appropriate situational contexts in which to undergo such experiencing? One popular way of classifying appropriate situational contexts is a three-way classification into approach-approach, approach-avoidance, and avoidance-avoidance situations. Once any of these conflict situations is properly constructed, it may fulfill the function of providing for experiencings such as being conflicted, indecisive, confused.

It is not the *situation* which invokes bad *feelings* attendant to conflict—e.g., anxiety, frustration, guilt or depression. From the perspective of humanistic theory, it is a mistake to label the situation as anxiety-provoking, frustrating, guilt-producing, or depressing (cf. Dollard et al., 1939). As discussed in Chapter 3, the function of the constructed situation is to provide for the experiencing of the *potential*, and that can be one of the conditions for the occurrence of the bad *feeling* in the conflict situation. We can construct the appropriate context by any of the four modes, and the result of each mode of construction is the experiencing of the potential (Figure 6.1). If my experiencing relates to conflict, I can construct contexts by (a) receiving an intrusive external world (e.g. a conflict between being drafted into the army or leaving the country), (b) utilizing a ready-made external world (e.g., the choice between an academic or political life), (c) conjoint construction of an external world (e.g., now that she is pregnant, if she keeps the baby, he leaves), or (d) fabricating an external world (painting a picture which I want to sell and also to keep). By whatever mode, I have constructed an external context for the experiencing of conflict.

Many persons employ the first mode in their construction of appropriate contexts. This is the easiest mode, and requires very little work. They do not have to fabricate the right context, they do not have to create it by working conjointly with others; they do not even have to go out and select the right external contexts. These persons simply receive what is impinging upon them, and what they experience is what they have available to experience. The farmer had no hand in creating the inadequate rainfall or the blight to his crops. Depending upon the nature of his potentials he may experience anger and hostility (cf. Buss, 1961), organize his neighboring farmers into a political bloc, rob a gas station, or quit farming and become a bartender. Even when the person constructs the external world by receiving its impingement upon him (i.e., the first mode), that world is received in a particular way, and that way constitutes the *function* of the external world.

One external context sequentially related to the next. When the function of the external world is to serve as a context for experiencing, the external world is constructed to be one instrumental means which is related to a subsequent instrumental means. Suppose that my operating potential is best described as "proving my worth," and the deeper potential is describable as "being inferior." In order for me to experience "proving my worth" I live in an external world composed of instrumental means for doing just that. One instrument is money.

Money is *instrumental* for enabling me to experience "proving my worth" because money is the means with which I can purchase an automobile. Money and having an automobile are related to each other sequentially. By having money I can purchase an automobile. We can go one step further in the sequence. By owning an automobile I can avoid the deeper experiencing of "being inferior." Two points are central here. First, the world out there is composed of instrumental means related to one another *in a sequence* (i.e., having money is sequentially related to owning an automobile). The second point is that the *function* of the external world (having money and owning an automobile) is to provide the right context for my experiencing (i.e., proving my worth, and avoiding being inferior). "If we examine carefully the average desires that we have in daily life, we find that they have at least one important characteristic, i.e. that they are usually means to an end rather than ends in themselves. We want money so that we may have an automobile. In turn we want an automobile because the neighbors have one and we do not wish to feel inferior to them . . ." (Maslow, 1970b, p. 21). When the external world serves the function of constituting the context for experiencing, it is easily understood as composed of a series of contexts instrumentally linked to one another.

Psychotherapy as a context for experiencing. For many potentials, finding truly appropriate contexts is not easy. Consider for example, potentials to be fully understood and appreciated, potentials to be wild and crazy, to "open up" and "unfreeze," to be fully expressive, and so on. For potentials such as these, psychotherapy can serve as an effective context. One of the advantages psychotherapy has over other life situations is that it can serve as the most appropriate situational context for the experiencing of potentials highly important to many persons.

If the psychotherapist is effective in providing such contexts, he has wide freedom of movement in several directions. First of all, the psychotherapist can become a context for a *broad spectrum of potentials*. If the psychotherapist can only provide a context in which persons can experience warmth and understanding, effectiveness is limited. If, on the other hand, the psychotherapist can offer the right context for five, 20, 50 kinds of potentials, his range of providing appropriate contexts is increased. Second, psychotherapists enjoy broad freedom of movement in helping the person to *utilize new modes of constructing the external world*. What this means in practice is that the psychotherapist can constitute an intrusive external world, can be a utilizable ready-made external world, can work conjointly with the person in constructing an external world, and can be a plastic substance fabricated by the patient into being what the patient wants. I find no particular virtue in the patient's acquiring skills in all four modes of construction, but I do find that experiencing can best occur when the patient is absolutely free to follow any of the four modes of constructing the external world. Thus, the psychotherapist who serves as a context for the patient's experiencing of tough firmness may (a) be unfair in just that way which invokes tough firmness from the patient (who is receiving an intrusive external world); (b) may be a tough, firm therapist who invites the patient also to be tough and firm (and thereby the patient has utilized a ready-made external world); (c) may work conjointly with the patient in constructing tough firmness; or (d) the psychotherapist may carefully allow the patient to fabricate the psychotherapist into being a monster, a withholder of personal ideas, or someone with arbitrary rules (and thereby the patient has fabricated an external world).

The third direction in which the psychotherapist can be effective in offering appropriate contexts is *outside the person-psychotherapist relationship*. That is, the psychotherapist need not be the right context, but the psychotherapist can help the person construct that context. Suppose, as an illustration, that the person is moving toward constructing a context for the experiencing of absolute impotence, and suppose that one context for experiencing impotence includes a dominant, highly seductive, punitive woman. The psychotherapist can open up appropriate contexts beyond the therapeutic relationship by helping-encouraging-changing the patient so that he now engages with just such a dominant, highly seductive, punitive woman.

The External World as an Extended Personality

The first function of the external world is to serve as a context for the experiencing of potentials (Figure 6.1). In order to understand other functions of external worlds, we must take a dramatic conceptual leap. The leap begins with a non-traditional view of what we mean by personality.

The concept of extended personality. From the perspective of humanistic theory, "personality" can extend well beyond one's skin to include parts of the world beyond the skin. What is "you" can include not only your viscera, your eyes, your thoughts, but also the infant kicking and growing within the mother's body. Does the infant become *not* a part of the mother once the infant is born? Is the mother's body really the threshold between what is and what is not part of the mother? I think not. I am convinced that, for some mothers at least, that baby can remain a part of the mother's personality in or out of the body. In precisely the same way, it is *possible* that your personality can reach out to encompass your watch, your spouse, your home, and your close friend. When "I" (defined as localized within the periphery of my skin) accomplish something, I feel proud; when my son (another part of me) catches a pass in a football game, I *can also* feel proud. This is far beyond a merely poetic way of describing a close relationship with my son. It means that the perimeter of my personality literally encompasses that adolescent boy running on that playing field. From this perspective, what belongs to "my personality" can include parts which are inside the skin of my physical body, and parts which are outside that skin. Indeed, my personality may include a great deal of what lies in my meaningful external world. It is in this way that I *am* parts of my surrounding world (Mahrer & Pearson, 1971b; May, 1958b, pp. 59-60). In this sense a person can be said to be ". . . fundamentally 'out in the world' and *with* the things he encounters. His existence is organically a 'being-in-the-world' . . . He *is* there with the particular being he encounters . . ." (Boss, 1963, p. 34).

Existential writers hold as the heart of their contribution the crucial importance of that which is referred to as immediacy, here-and-nowness, ontological existence, being, Dasein (May, 1958a). The importance of existence lies in the recognition that the human being is best described by more than the person's dynamisms, defense mechanisms, behavior potentials, traits and dimensions, qualities and characteristics, needs and drives, or other words referring to parameters of the person inside the skin. I suggest that one specific component of what existentialism offers is the conception of personality *as stretching beyond the skin to include meaningful parts of the external world*. When you interact with me as therapist, friend, acquaintance, student, customer, researcher, your personality reaches into me and does something to me. Your personality *extends into* your external world. That is one reason why there is something quite special about your immediacy, your here-and-now-ness, your ontological existence, your being. There is a personality present which transcends your skin and encompasses the other in a quite particular way. This *extended personality* is one specific meaning of the existential contribution to the understanding of human beings.

Parts of you can belong both to you *and to me*. Your knocking a glass of milk off the table can belong to a definition of your personality and to mine. Your brushing your hair or saying words which make you embarrassed can belong both to you and to me. The out-line of your personality behavior can be coterminal with the in-line of my personality behavior (Watts, 1961); they can overlap so that your smile fully belongs to both you and to me. When someone throws trash on the sidewalk of my home, it can be that they are throwing trash on a part of me. When you appreciate my painting, you may be appreciating a part of me. When my team wins, it can be my win. When my daughter rebels against authority, it can be my own rebelling against authority. When my son masturbates, it can be my masturbating. When the preacher, respected by the whole small congregation, is found guilty of seducing the young girl, the guilt can be shared by many of the congregation. When another preacher rises a bit toward Godliness by virtuous deeds, many of his congregation can share in a heightened sense of Godliness. My sexuality can be expressed through your sexual behavior. Your shyness can be manifested in my shy behavior. My power can be experienced through my country's conquering your country.

All of this can be stated as a basic proposition of humanistic theory: The definition of a person includes those parts extended into the world surrounding the physical being. I term this the *extended personality*. Such a concept is perhaps difficult to grasp because we have assumed that a person is defined by his skin. I believe it is safe to say that every behavioral and social science limits "person" and "personality" to that which is contained within the skin. I reject that assumption. *Humanistic theory holds that personality can extend beyond the boundaries of the physical being. The expression of one's potentials and their relationships can include not only one's own behavior, but meaningful components of the external world. The definition of a person includes those parts extended into the external world surrounding the physical being.*

Ordinarily, the I-who-is-the-operating-potential has a distinct outer boundary which is more or less coterminal with my skin. But the I which encompasses all the potentials which comprise my personality extends way beyond my skin to encircle the world I construct. This is a major characteristic of primitive persons, according to Levy-Bruhl (1923), who described the primitive mentality in terms of this "participation mystique" between the deeper parts (unconscious) and the external world. On this basis, the primitive mentality lived in a world of anthropomorphisms, ghosts and goblins, alive with the externalization of what was within. We are no different. We live in that same world. It is nothing less than a grand externalization of what is within. With one conceptual shift, huge slabs of the external world are illuminated as grand externalizations of what I am. Here is the conceptual shift which constitutes one of the bases of Gestalt therapy, whereby so much of the external world can now be understood as "projections" of our own selves (Levitsky & Perls, 1970).

When the external world fulfills the function of being the extended personality, there is always a realistic core to that external world. In extreme cases, there are delusions and hallucinations, ideas of reference and paranoid visions. These are unrealistic wrappings about a compellingly realistic core consisting of the very realistic extended personality. Underneath the leering faces which haunt the older woman is her *own* leering sexuality, confronting her from the outside.

The faces are not the kind of reality which others can see, but the faces can be stripped away and what shines forth is the woman's own leering sexuality—and *that* is utterly real! The reality is the experiencing which takes place within the woman. When we step outside her skin, the faces are not there, but the experiencing of those faces through her eyes *is* real; the experiencing of leering sexuality which occurs in the woman when she sees the external faces is real. There is, then, a soberly realistic core to every so-called paranoid delusion, hallucination, and idea of reference.

The realistic core which is the extension of my personality means that the external world is given meaning from my own potentials. By extending my personality into the external world, my potential invests things out there with meaning. Thus my penis and my huge motorcycle are invested with meaning as power. I may have a potential for experiencing growing, fertility, development, and thereby I *invest* my penis and my child with the same meaning. Both are things which can grow, be fertile, develop. A penis can "mean" power or growth or pleasure or whatever (Fenichel, 1954a). It is the *nature of the potential* which invests things with their meaning. It is not a matter that the motorcycle or the tower or the banana or the child or the girl is "symbolic" of penis. In extending our personality into the external world, things are whatever our potentials are. The meanings derive from our potentials, and not from the "symbolic" nature of things-as-things.

In its general outline, this new departure means that there is no necessary gap between the person and the external world. That is, there is no *necessary* gap for *all* of us, *all* the time. This new departure rejects the conception of two persons (or two billion persons), contained inside their respective skins, interacting with one another across impenetrable gaps. Instead, the picture includes extended personalities in which persons extend into their external worlds. The balance of this chapter spells out some implications of this departure for the understanding of the functions of an external world.

The external world: a context for experiencing or an extended personality? How can I distinguish between the external world as a context for experiencing or as an extended personality (Figure 6.1)? The first function of the external world is to serve as a context for experiencing. When an utter stranger approaches me and swears angrily at me, that stranger could serve as an external context in which I experience whatever my potential is. I can experience being picked on, or I can experience being "found out," or I can experience a terrible challenge. In this first function, that stranger is not an extension of me. He is not me out there. He is an external world used by me for the function of experiencing what it is important for me to experience.

On the other hand, the second function of the external world means that the angry stranger can be an extension of me. His swearing could be my meeting up with *my own* swearing. He could be a part of me, extended out onto the external world. How can we distinguish between that stranger as an external context (and therefore not an extension of me), and that stranger as an extension of me out in the external world? By what criteria may these two primary functions of the external world be differentiated?

I would like to describe a method of answering this question which has evolved out of my own psychotherapeutic experience. According to this method, I must identify the *instant* when my *feelings* reached their peak. This is a difficult step, for we generally have a vague sense of the larger episode, but not the slightest inkling of the precise instant when feelings reach their peak. With regard to that stranger, the instant occurred sometime during the scene in which he approached me. But when? How do I go about isolating that moment? To do this I must reinsert myself into that general scene. I must literally leave where I am right now and go back into that scene. Now I am here with him. I see his bony, hard face and the grey pants that are too large for him. When is this? It is when he first approaches me and I am becoming certain that he indeed is going to approach *me*. I am starting to have feelings now. Why me? I see his angry face and his small, wiry frame mobilized by anger. My feelings are more intense now. Is there more? Is this the moment? No, somehow it is when he swears at me. What words do it? He says, "mother fucker!" That is all. Two terse, angry words flung at me. Is this the moment? No, still more; it reaches a peak of feeling *after* that, when he stood there glaring at me. Now, more "in" the moment than ever, I am in the immediate vicinity of the peak feeling. He is standing here, poised to fly away. I knew he would run. The look of him now. Pure hate. Here it is, the encounter, the challenge, the hate. Here now, in this instant, squared off at him. This is the instant of most intense feelings.

I now have the data to distinguish that stranger as an extension of me or as an external world serving as a context for some kind of experiencing. Now that I have identified the moment of peak feeling, I can ask myself the questions whose answers differentiate these two possibilities: Is the predominance of my concerned attention *within* me and *about* him, or is it localized *in him*? Am I a separate person from him, or does there seem to be no line of demarcation between us? Something is starting to happen; is this something *within me* or *within him*? Is the center of my being in me or is it within him? I am acutely aware *of* him. I can see him vividly during this moment. But my concerned attention is within *me*. Something is happening within me. I am here in me, though aiming intently at him. Am I a separate person from him, or does there seem to be no line of demarcation between us? There are two of us here. I am intensely aware of *me*. It is as if I am more than ever me, right here, confronted by an encountering other person. There is a distinct line of demarcation between us. Something is starting to happen; is this something within me or within him? The starting activity is within me. It is not within him. Hit him. I am within me, and a physical pounding is exploding in me. I am experiencing a striking out at him. This is within me and is aimed at him. Although he has been doing all the action, right now in this peak feelinged moment, the behaving force seems to be localized within me, not him.

I conclude from all this that he is not an extended part of me. That stranger is, instead, an external situational context. He is not my own extended personality, flung out onto the external world in the form of that stranger. But let us look into another example. I am standing by the window, watching my son climbing in the big old tree in the front yard. The moment of peak feeling comes when there is a misstep and, just for an instant, he starts to fall. His right foot misses the step backward, and his back arches while his arms are flung helplessly upward as he falls. Is the predominance of my concerned attention within me and *about* him, or is it localized *within* him? It is as if my concerned attention is wholly localized within him, not me. It is *in* him. The center of my self is located in my son. I am not the one in which the center of concerned attention resides; it is all localized within him. Am I a separate person from him, or does there seem to be no line of demarcation between us? In that instant, I *am* him. Not worried *about* him, I am somehow, in that instant, that young boy out there. We are one. The center of my self is in him. Or, more accurately, I am drawn right up inside him. We are one being, perilously falling. *I* am falling. It is as if I am frozen, asleep, immobilized, because something is starting to happen, some activity is beginning, within *him*, not within me. I am not impelled to catch him, to lurch forward as if to catch him. Not at all. Instead, there is no me as a separate thing. *I* am starting to fall. It is a falling which he and I are sharing. The activity is occurring in him, and not in me. I am lost, hypnotized, asleep, mechanical because there is no "I." The center of my self, my being, is out of the physical me and is, in this instant, in him. From all this I conclude that my son, during that instant, is not a part of the external world, a context for my experiencing. Instead, I conclude that my son is my extended personality. By reinserting oneself into the moment of peak feeling, by identifying the actual instant of peak feeling, the answering of these questions will differentiate the external world as an external context from an extension of my own personality.

I listened fully to three persons telling about, not themselves, but some other individual: a mother telling about her daughter's masturbating, a husband telling about his wife's adultery, and a teacher telling about her student's inattention. For the mother, the peak moment involved rapt attention to her young daughter's expression of erotic masturbatory arousal as the daughter's pelvis rhythmically gyrated. For the husband, the peak moment involved sitting in his car outside the apartment where his wife was with her lover, imagining the lover as a handsome South American, delighting his screaming wife with powerful thrusts. For the teacher, the peak moment of feeling was when the young boy, about whom she had suffered a painfully humiliating conference with his hostile parents and her own principal the previous evening, gave her a knowing, smirking look, and then conducted himself in an unruly, inattentive manner that bothered her immensely. Using the method described above, the mother and the husband seemed to be living in extended personalities, while the teacher's external world seemed to be a context for experiencing. The mother was distraught about her own erotic sexual experiencing expressed in the form of her daughter's masturbation; the husband was living through his own experiencing as the wife's earthy, South American lover, so that the lover was his own extended personality; on the other hand, the student's inattention was not an extension of the teacher, but rather served as a context for the experiencing of her own potential for aggressive firmness.

The three loci of "I" (self, consciousness). In Chapter 2, I described two potential loci of the self, or consciousness, or sense of "I." One locus is the region of the operating potentials. This is the normal, typical locus of I-ness. Although this center may shift from one operating potential to another, the range is limited to the region of the operating potentials (Figure 2.1). In addition, however, the locus of the self was described as not being limited to this region. It *could* shift to the deeper potentials. For example, when the mother of the masturbating daughter is dreaming, she may *be* a new "I," a deeper potential, in which she is a freely erotic soul. Now we can introduce a third possible locus of the self: my extended personality. For the mother, the center of reference for her sense of self *can* be her masturbating child as her own extended personality. It is possible for the mother to be inside her child and looking out upon the world from that vantage point, that center of consciousness. The center of my self, my I-ness, can be located in my extended personality. I am the tree or romping puppy or my wizened grandmother or the special friend. This phenomenon is exemplified in coition (when I am one with you and am conscious of the world through you), hypnotism (when "my" voice is yours), dreams (in which I can be simultaneously inside and outside my body, and in which I can see me from the frame of reference of my being another person), and in drug states (when I am a drop of water or the texture of an apple).

The perimeter of my self, of "I," has been traditionally my skin. Now we can describe the perimeter of my self as being coterminal with my meaningful, constructed external world. We have approached this conclusion by considering the ways in which the person constructs a world and endows it with personal functions. In Chapter 13, we will approach this same conclusion from a study of the development of infants. Our conclusion is not an as-if; it is not an allegory. As systematically as possible, we wish to understand the perimeter of the person (I-ness, consciousness, sense of self) as coterminal with the perimeter of the person's meaningfully constructed external world. This third possible locus of I-ness has been adumbrated in Haley's (1963) definition of the significance of the social system in which the person exists. Within this interpersonal relational system, Haley is sensitive to the profound role of the family system. Somehow, Haley says, that family contextual system *is* the person. Haley's statements take us out of the old definition of the person, and arch us in the direction of a humanistic definition of the person. "What is evident is the fact that the description of the individual is going to change when his relationships are included in the description. If the individual descriptions offered in the past are used, the family context must be ignored. What a person does, why he does it, and how he can be changed will appear different if the description shifts from *only* him to the context in which he is functioning" (Haley, 1963, p. 152). A conceptual step further and the context *is* the person!

Two functions of constructing the external world as an extended personality. When the external world serves as a context for experiencing, the immediate function is simply the experiencing of a potential (Figure 6.1). When the external world is constructed as the extended personality, there are two immediate functions (Figure 6.1). First, the personality can be extended into the external world *in order to experience a potential*, exactly as when the function of the external world is to serve as a context for experiencing. In other words, a potential for sexuality can be experienced when the right external context is constructed, or when the personality can be extended into the external world. As indicated in Figure 6.1, however, the external world as an extended personality can also serve *to experience the relationship between potentials*. For example, if I hate and fear my sexuality, I can construct the external world into my sexuality and experience my hateful and fearful relationship toward that sexuality. I can hate sexual things out there. I can fear sexuality in the external world. I can also construct an external world which hates and fears *me* as sexual. Regardless of the direction, the key is that the external world is constructed as the extension of my personality to serve the function of experiencing the nature of relationships between potentials. When the external world is a context for experiencing, its only function is to provide for experiencing of potentials. But when the external world is an extended personality, its function is either to provide for experiencing of potentials or to provide for experiencing of relationships between potentials.

A method of research inquiry. The concept of an extended personality means that my personality can reach beyond my skin to fill the things in the external world. I can come to know you by letting my personality boundary extend further and further until it incorporates you. When my personality fills you, I can know you in a very special way. That is the goal—to know you by extending myself into you. When my personality extends out to encompass your thoughts, your feelings, your experiencings, then I know those thoughts, feelings, and experiencings because they become mine as well as yours. I share your being in a way which is romantic and poetic, and which also suggests a method of research inquiry. The concept of extended personality leads us to the phenomenological method of research inquiry.

The phenomenological method (Husserl called this the method of *epoche*) is that of an unbiased, focused, attentive, observant contemplation of an event. I can know you by hooking my concerned attention upon you, and focusing my self so deeply onto you that my personality reaches out to encompass you. In psychotherapy I can know you by a process of alignment with your own potentials as you focus your concerned attention upon some third event. Thus there are three parts involved: you, I, and that upon which you focus. As you focus your concerns upon your daughter (or your friend, or your husband, or your shoe, or your childhood desk, or your jealousy), I can align myself with your own potential to the extent that I can feel what is going on in you—that is, I have extended my personality into you. I can listen to what is going on inside you and hear your insides saying, "Why am I talking about my daughter? She is really not that important in my life!" I know that because I have aligned myself with you to the point where I can have your thoughts, feelings, and experiencings. "Phenomenologists believe that they have found a new approach, which enables them to grasp the subjective experience of the patient more fully than could be done within the older, classical frame of reference" (Ellenberger, 1958, p. 95). I believe they are correct.

The phenomenological researcher seeks to frame ways of getting at the experienced reality of the person who is the object of our inquiry (von Eckartsberg, 1969, 1971). It is essential that humanistic theory articulates an adequate research methodology, yet some experiential psychotherapists already have taken steps toward refining a method which can be utilized in research. In experiential psychotherapy it is already understood that my personality (as a therapist) extends beyond me to include my constructed world, and your personality (as a patient) also extends beyond you to include your constructed world. Therefore, I can align my self with your experiencing self and thereby share in your experienced reality. This requires that you and I both focus our attention on a third something which is meaningful to you. In psychotherapy, this consists of your meaningful world. It can include your mother, your car, anything of meaning to you. It can include a situational context, a critical moment in your life. But you must be directing your concern to that, and I must also get into your world and direct my concerned attention onto that. In addition to sharing your focal target, I must allow a part of my self to be thoroughly aligned with your self so that I sense, am with, resonate to, share what you are experiencing. When I accomplish this, I experience as you experience, and this is, or can be, a way of gaining research knowledge of your experienced reality.

The above method enables me to know the way in which you experience your reality. It is a way of sharing your subjective world, your private thoughts. Therefore, I can be your psychotherapist or your research investigator. Within the context of research, several components are present. First, you and I must be in an actual situation, some context of meaning to you, one in which you are focused upon a meaningful target; second, I must be the "witness" or "shadow" in your involvement with it, so that I can see for myself what is going on out there; third, you must be a reporter or informant to me of your own experience (von Eckhartsberg, 1971). As a researcher, I am in this double role that von Eckartsberg terms "participant participation," whereby I participate doubly with you, once in your relationship to the thing or situation, and once again as a participant in your way of relating to that out there.

When my personality extends out to align with your *deeper* potentials, I know what is going on *within* you. If my aim is to verify the nature of your inner goings-on, I can dispatch a portion of myself over to you and sense what is going on there. That is one way. A more systematic way of establishing the reliability of your inner state is by a method that Zaner (1967) refers to as introspective verification. I can get decently close to verifying your private, personal, subjective reactions by utilizing the point made above, i.e., putting myself in the very same situational context you are in. Then if I can sense within me the very state which you say you experience in that same situational context, we have achieved a way of verifying and replicating what occurs in your insides. When two little girls are huddled together in the big, dark bedroom, and they both see the ghost, they can describe their inner sensations to one another. If the second girl verifies the first girl's description, they have demonstrated a way of showing how to verify and replicate the inner experience of the other by placing oneself in the same situation and contacting (describing) one's own inner feelings.

In order to understand the person, to acquire research knowledge of the person, our model of human beings suggests procedures which go beyond those of understanding *causes*. Our model of the human being sees an added dimension which is continuously at work building an external world, extending its personality. Because of this added dimension, research understanding is gained by rigorous description of the here-and-now presence of the person. This method is different from and in addition to gaining research understanding by articulating *causal* explanations, especially those causal explanations having to do with antecedent events. "The phenomenologists stand against a tendency in Western culture, particularly in the Anglo-Saxon countries, to explain things exclusively by their causes . . . We tend to assume that if we have a causal explanation or if we describe how things develop, then we have described the thing itself. This is an error. The phenomenologists hold that we must cut through the tendency in the West to believe we understand things if we only know their causes, and to find out and describe instead what the thing is as a phenomenon—the experience as it is given to us in its 'givenness' . . . This is not to rule out causation and genetic development, but rather to say that the question of *why* one is what one is does not have meaning until we know *what* one is" (May, 1967, p. 88).

These methods of knowing have heuristic research possibilities far beyond the field of psychotherapy. They constitute a major departure from the traditional scientific methods of today. I expect it will be a slow process to gain research respectability for either the concept of the extended personality or the method of phenomenological knowing. It would be understandably difficult to invite researchers to adopt a way of understanding the external world as constructed by the person (a dangerous enough departure) to serve the function of being the extension of one's personality (this might well be asking far too much of a scientist already committed to other person-world assumptions). If this is too much to ask, then the phenomenological method of knowing is the gift of an alien tribe, and it can hardly be welcomed by the researchers of today who assume a gap between the human organism and the environment, and between the scientific inquirer and the person about whom he is inquiring. That gap can be reduced somewhat, but it can never be replaced by the kind of person-world relationship espoused by humanistic phenomenological researchers. Thus most contemporary researchers will continue observing carefully—across a gap between themselves and the persons they study. The history of science suggests that contemporary researchers will resist stoutly any fundamental revision in conceptualizing the person's relationship with an external world. In the meantime, what is required is energetic use and refinement of the research methods of humanistic and phenomenological theory.

Those who work from an assumptive base in which the investigator is separated and removed from the subject inevitably will be limited in their methods of gaining knowledge about the observed person. No matter how broadly their methods of research inquiry are worked out, their very assumptions set sharp limits on how the researcher can know the other person. Their methods lock in the investigator as a separated entity apart from the observed subject across an impenetrable gap. Within such a model, the investigator has a limited number of discoverable ways in which the investigator can measure aspects of the subject. Fiske (1971) is representative of those who review the various ways in which the investigator, in that system, can measure the personality behavior of the subject. In all of the research methods set forth by Fiske, or potentially discoverable within that system, the researcher is forever and inevitably set apart from the subject. It is not possible for these methods to go beyond their confining assumptions. In contrast, the methods cordial to the approach taken by humanistic theory, existentialism, phenomenology and similar systems are beyond discovery by researchers operating within a set of assumptions which exclude the possibility of the researcher and the subject entering into their mutual extended personalities.

In contrast, our definition of the person can include aspects of the person's external world. Because the person *constructs* his external world (rather than merely reacting to it) and *extends* his own personality into the world, we can engage in research inquiry of that person by a careful and systematic study of his constructed, made-meaningful world. In this sense, his world and he are one, and we investigate him by studying the person-world relationship he has constructed. Clinically we understand the person by studying the world he creates around himself. As a method of research we study the person by similarly investigating the nature of the constructed encompassing world. The phenomenon which is the object of our research inquiry is inextricably interwoven with its situational context (Giorgi, 1966; Gurwitsch, 1964); indeed, from our perspective, what is known as the situational context *is* the person's own constructed world and represents the larger, extended meaning of his personality. He *is* the situational context. On the basis of this approach to pursuing research inquiry, we reject an approach which, instead, rests upon an assumptive system in which knowledge is sought by reducing the phenomenon into its supposed basic elements and studying these apart from its situational context. The approach of the natural sciences, so prevalent in contemporary research, is to pluck the person out of his situational context. Such an approach is wholly unfitted to our perspective and must be replaced with methods of research inquiry more fitted to our own assumptions of the meaning and definition of the person-phenomenon.

It is consistent with our approach that the systematic pursuit of knowledge leaves the phenomenon in its naturally constructed situational context. The person must be studied within his own constructed world. This is a further argument in favor of natural ecological research and against laboratory research. From our perspective, the person exists within a world which he constructs, and it is this constructed world which is the outer perimeter of the definition of the person. To pluck the person out of his own constructed world and examine him as a subject in a research investigation is to commit the error of studying only a partial person. It is like bringing the older sister into a laboratory and deluding yourself that you are examining the whole family, even to the point of drawing conclusions about the family rather than conclusions about the older sister alone. The error is in the examiner's definition of the supposed reality he is studying; indeed, the reality of the subject is significantly distorted once you bring him into the laboratory (Barker, 1965). Once we understand the person as intimately bound into the external world which he constructs, we must utilize research methodologies logically consistent with this view of human beings. At the very least, as Barker and others suggest, this involves research which accommodates to the person's natural ecological setting.

In all of this, we have been describing an external world as an extended personality. We now become more specific. First we shall discuss the external world as an extension of our *operating potentials* (*that* part of our personality), and then we shall discuss the external world as an extension of our *deeper potentials* (that *other* part of our personality).

The External World as an Extension of Operating Potentials

Suppose that my operating potential involves experiencing compassionate understanding. In Figure 6.2 this is indicated as OP1. Suppose further that my deeper potential involves the experiencing of aggressive leadership. This is indicated as DP2. The disintegrative relationship between these potentials is indicated by the negative sign in the channel of their relationship. I can construct an external world whose function is to provide for the experiencing of my operating potential, viz. my compassionate understanding. How do I do this? I can construct a wife, a child, or a close friend who is my compassionate understanding. Then, when they are compassionately understanding, I gain a measure of experiencing my own operating potential. When I am with my wife (or my child or my close friend), and she is being compassionately understanding, *I* experience a measure of my compassionate understanding. My operating potential has been extended out to include her. In Figure 6.1, the function of my extended operating potential is to provide for experiencing—in this instance, my compassionate understanding.

I can also construct an external world whose function is to express toward me the same disintegrative relationship I (the operating potential) bear toward my deeper potential. How do I accomplish this? I can behave in just that way (B3, Figure 6.2) which will invite you to dislike my aggressive leadership. I may behave in just that pushy, abrasive way which will invite you to regard me as an aggressive leader, and to dislike (or recoil from or be uncomfortable with) that quality in me. I have thereby succeeded in getting you to be my extended, externalized operating potential, and to have the same disintegrative relationship to *me* as I have to the deeper potential in me. In Figure 6.1, this second function of my extended operating potential is to experience the *relationship*. We now turn to a discussion of these two functions of the extended operating potential.

In order to experience my operating potential. One of the most common functions of the constructed external world is to serve as an extension of my operating potential, and thereby to enable me to experience it. We human beings are artful in doing just that. I can construct my infant into being my fussing, my complaining, my demanding. All of these constitute my operating potential, and I thereby gain some measure of experiencing just that through my infant. I have an operating potential for uniqueness, so I purchase a unique piece of art work, and experience my uniqueness when *it* is seen as unique. If my operating potential involves being admired, I construct a spouse who is admired, and experience just that when he or she is admired. I experience my athletic prowess when my son (or team) is being athletic. I experience my defiance against my neighbor when my dog defecates on my neighbor's lawn. My aloofness is experienced when my cat manifests his aloofness. In thousands of little ways you and I construct external extensions of our operating potentials, and thereby gain a measure of experiencing.

I can try to construct you into serving as the instrumental agent of my operating potential. For example, if I want to force my brother-in-law to stop hanging onto us, to stop doing those crazy things which make us sorry for but annoyed at him, how can I construct an external world to do just that? How can I find some agent in the external world which will be the arm of the family, and do to Sam what we want done with him? We can turn him over to a hospital, and charge the hospital with the job of changing Sam so that he no longer forces us to take care of him. In this way I have made you, the hospital, into an extension of my operating potential, and the net result is that I gain a measure of further experiencing. Much of our behavior is dedicated toward constructing external means whereby our operating potentials are experienced.

In order to experience the relationship with my deeper potentials. I can construct an external world whose function is to relate to me in the same way I relate to my deeper potentials. By means of just the right behavior (B3, Figure 6.2), I construct an extended operating potential which will relate to me the way I relate to my own deeper potential. If I hate my deeper potential (DP2, Figure 6.2) for sexuality, I (OP1, Figure 6.2) can construct you and, by my own behavior, invite you to relate to me as a hated sexual person. Indeed, I can get you to look down on me, distrust me, loathe me, regard me as culpable, dumb, worthless, feel disturbed and bothered toward me—because that is the way I relate to myself. If I look down on my awful cheapness, I can behave so as to get you to look down on me as cheap. My relationship to you is indicated in Figure 6.2 by the disintegrative channel including my behavior (B3). Your disintegrative relationship toward me (viz. my deeper potential) is indicated by the channel composed of the dotted lines.

If I feel (disintegratively) defensive about my cheapness, if I cannot accept that in me, if I am somewhat horrified by that in me, I must behave in very careful ways in order to invite you to bear that same relationship toward me. When you and I are eating at a fashionable restaurant, finish our meal, receive separate bills of five dollars each, I am getting the situation ready. You leave six dollars underneath your check. I leave a five dollar bill and no tip, but I do this in a particular way. It involves fumbling attempts to hide the fact that I left no tip; it involves throwing the exact change on the table as if I were cavalier in tipping; it involves jerky body movements disguised as smooth easy tipping; it involves a brief glance at you disclosing my guilt through a nervous tiny smile. What I have succeeded in doing is inviting you to regard me in the same way I regard myself, viz., "How cheap you are! You didn't leave any tip at all. Furthermore, you tried to hide this." It is as if that way of regarding my self is now created, and is hovering about, half way between me and you. I know it is there, and you know it is there. I refuse to acknowledge its presence. When I create that way of regarding my self (the extension of my operating potential) and refuse to own it as me, I have thereby invited *you* to accept it as yours. I have invited you to be my extended operating potential and to think, "How cheap you are! You didn't leave any tip at all. Furthermore, you tried to hide this." And, if I am effective, you *will* relate to me this way. In other words, I can construct an external world which defines me in a particular way. I can construct you into casting me in a specific role, with a particular identity. I can get you to regard me as cheap. Many approaches understand a person's identity as a function of the ways in which others happen to see the person, define him, assign an identity to him. In contrast, humanistic theory holds that the *person* is the one who constructs *others* into seeing him in that way, who builds others into identifying him in that particular way. "His identity-for-himself depends to some extent upon the identity others ascribe to him, but also on the identities he attributes to the others and hence on the identity or identities he attributes to the other(s) as attributing to him" (Laing, 1962, p. 75). Regardless of which mode the person utilizes in constructing others to attribute that identity to him, the person nevertheless has a strong hand in that enterprise.

In his analysis of the relationships between the person and others, Mead (1934) distinguishes between the person's *behavior* and the person's *own attitude toward that behavior*. According to Mead, the person can take the attitude of another toward his own behavior. In proceeding one step further, our theory holds that his own way of regarding his own behavior can serve as a potent determinant of the way in which the other individual does indeed regard him. I can regard my own behavior as rather whimsical, and that attitude can be a factor in inducing you similarly to regard my behavior as whimsical. In this extension of Mead's analysis, it becomes clear that an individual can construct others into co-regarding his behavior in the same way he regards it. In all of this, you are the extension of my own operating potential and feel about me (the deeper potential) the very same way *I* (the operating potential) feel about me (the deeper potential). There is a tragedy here, for I can never share with you our hate of my deeper potential. How much better it would be if you *and I* can share in hating my deeper potential for cheapness. But it seldom if ever happens. Almost without exception, your hate is aimed at all of me, not just my cheapness. Perhaps an even greater tragedy is the ease by which the external world serves as a willing accomplice in the disintegrative relationship. I may hate my self for being cowardly, stealing, letting them down, being cruel, having those awful thoughts, carrying out those perverse acts with children. As the operating potential who hates that deeper potential, I must punish my self for being that way. Will you punish me? Usually you are all too willing to be my accomplice in relating to me the way in which I relate to my self.

It is an unfortunate characteristic of the external world that it so willingly lends itself to the role of accomplice in punitive, hateful, disintegrative relations against one's self.

I can construct the external world into being the extended operating potential through any of the four modes (Figure 6.1). If I helped to kill my aged mother by brutal inattentiveness, I can construct an external world which punishes me, does harm to me, is evil toward me. I can accomplish this by (a) the way I receive an intrusive external world, e.g., when the black cat crosses in front of me, I can receive that cat as an evil omen of hate, a sign that harm will come to me. I can (b) utilize a ready-made external world by marrying a woman who is ready-made to punish me incessantly for my inattention. I can (c) work conjointly with others to create their punishment of me. Or I can (d) fabricate (paranoid-like) "ideas of reference" in which people out there are plotting to do harm to me. In each mode, the external world which I construct is an extended operating potential, an accomplice bearing the same relationship toward me that I have toward the arcane, brutal inattention within me.

Regardless of the mode of construction, the extension of one's operating potential into the external world is quite independent of the degree of reality or unreality of the world which you construct. You can construct an external world using either "realistic" or "unrealistic" building blocks. The constructed external world may meet all our criteria of reality, and yet that constructed world is a pure externalization of your operating potential. There is a real car out there, a car which is big and powerful, a car which can mutilate and kill your young son. Yet that car is also a point-by-point extension of your operating potential.

Some implications for psychotherapy. Consider the person who constructs the therapist into being an extended operating potential, expressing the person's own fear and hate of the deeper potential. Suppose that I hate my deeper potential for insatiable sucking, and I behave so as to invite you (my therapist) to bear the same hateful relationship toward me. This happens in psychotherapy as it happens outside of psychotherapy. Under these circumstances, a psychotherapist who adopts a humanistic framework *can* permit me (OP1, Figure 6.2) to carry forward my own relationship with the deeper potential (DP2, Figure 6.2). In effect, the therapist declines the invitation to become my extended operating potential and to externalize my own disintegrative relationship toward my own deeper potential.

As indicated in Figure 6.2, three channels of relationships are involved when the person is inviting the therapist to relate to him in this given way. One channel is between the person and the therapist (OP1 and externalized operating potential); a second is between the therapist and the person's deeper potential, and the third is between the person's own operating and deeper potential. If the therapist chooses, he can move closer and closer to being *with* the person in his relationship with his own deeper potential. In accomplishing this, there is a gradual extinguishing of the other two channels of relationship. That is, the person is less and less involved with making the therapist into a particular kind of individual (the OP1—externalized operating potential relationship), and the nature of the therapist as a person is no longer a focal center of concern. Likewise, the patient is less and less concerned with the therapist's relationship with the person's own deeper potential. Instead of allowing himself to be fashioned into the person's extended operating potential, bearing a disintegrative relationship toward the person, the therapist can become *one* with the person's operating potential. I am now *inside* the person, not outside the person; I am *with* the operating potential in *its* direct relationship to the deeper potential. From the perspective of the patient, the therapist is less and less a person who is kept out there, and to whom the patient relates externally; indeed, the patient relates less and less with the therapist as a person. Instead, therapist and patient speak with one voice in the relationship with the deeper potential. Once the therapist is inside, the therapist *and* the operating potential relate to the deeper potential.

Suppose, for example, that the patient behaves in just those ways which induce the therapist to respond to his talk as "delusional." The therapist is strongly encouraged to pull back from such talk, to regard it with fear, and to label it as delusional. In treating persons with delusions, many traditional psychotherapists explicitly label such delusional material as delusional material (Boverman, 1953). But suppose that the therapist can receive such invitations as the constructing of an outside world (i.e., the therapist) into being an extension of the patient's own operating potential, and that it is the *patient* who draws back from and dislikes *his own* (delusional) deeper potential. Everything belongs to the patient: the delusional material, and also the disintegrative relationship toward that delusional material. The problem then becomes one of comparing the therapeutic effectiveness of the patient's relationship to his deeper delusional material with the relative therapeutic effectiveness of the other two channels, both of which involve the therapist as an external object.

Another implication derives from the concept (see Chapter 2) that deeper potentials assume a *bad* form under a disintegrative relationship, and a *good* form under an integrative relationship. What the person fears and hates, *can be* (in its good form) a source of joy, delight, play, pleasure, happiness! The psychotherapist *can* relate *integratively* with the *good* form of that deeper potential. In adopting this posture, the therapist opens the way for dramatic changes in the patient's behavior. What is inside the person is *not* a monstrously awful homosexuality which ought to be watched or controlled or cauterized or vigilantly tolerated. For this particular person it is, in its potentially good (integrated) form a lifting of the lifelong veil with other men, and a new closeness—lovingly, trustingly. This is why the therapist can go with the person into the very heart of the worst moments—those critical moments when the person starts to be engulfed by the terrifying homosexuality. The therapist knows the hidden secret, viz. what the awful homosexuality can become once it is fully experienced and transformed into its integrative good form. The knowledge of what the terrible deeper potential can become is the faith allowing the therapist to carry forward full experiencing of the feared bad form to its complete end result—drastic transformation into its integrated good form.

Where humanistic theory is so sensitive to the patient's invitation for the therapist to accede to the role of the patient's extended operating potential, some other approaches explicitly fulfill that very role. If the patient fears and hates his facial tic or his backache or his temper, the therapist will not be helping either the patient, his deeper potential, or the disintegrative relationship between the two by falling into the role of the extended operating potential and bearing the same disintegrative relationship to the patient as he bears toward himself. To join with the patient in trying to attack and eliminate the facial tic (cf. Bandura, 1961; Eysenck, 1965) only succeeds in *perpetuating* the disintegrative relationship toward whatever deeper potential is expressed in the facial tic. Our conception enjoins the psychotherapist *not* to fall into the role of accomplice in the operating potential's disintegrative relationship toward the deeper potential. A psychotherapeutic posture which seeks to *get rid of* some way of behaving is engaging in person-killing. The therapist is joining into an alliance with the operating potential in killing (pushing down, suppressing) the deeper potential. Billy stole ladies' handbags. He was bothered by such behavior and sought to control it or get rid of it. Billy waged war against the deeper potential which did the handbag stealing. Many therapists would join Billy in waging war against that inner potential. Thus the therapist can consider such behavior a fetish, and may administer injections of apomorphine which produce strong sensations of nausea when Billy is confronted with handbags (Bandura, 1961). If "successful," the therapist and Billy will have killed the deeper potential, pushed it down to a point where it is buried. Billy has found a part of the external world (the therapist) who is an extension and ally of Billy's own operating potential in the killing of a deeper potential for experiencing. Our conception flatly opposes such a procedure.

The External World as an Extension of Deeper Potentials

The first function of the external world is to serve as a situational context within which I experience potentials. The second function is to serve as the extension of my operating potential. We now turn to the third function of the external world: to serve as the extension of my *deeper* potential. These three functions are indicated in both Figures 6.1 and 6.2. In fulfilling this third function, the external world, by whatever mode of construction, is built out of deeper parts of my own personality, i.e., what is deep within me will confront me in the form of the external world.

When the external world serves the function of being the extension of my deeper potential for compassion, whether it is *really* there depends upon the building blocks used in the mode of constructing the compassion out there. It is possible to construct compassion in the external world by a mode which yields a true, real compassionate thing out there. By whatever definition of real, there may be a real compassionate thing there. I can, for example, utilize a ready-made part of the external world, a truly compassionate person, as my closest friend. That person *is* compassionate. His compassion is quite real. On the other hand, I may fabricate a compassionate companion who is unseen by anyone else, a private fabrication of my very own. No one can see or interact with him, for he is my (imaginary) companion. In one important sense of "real," my imaginary companion, although very compassionate, is not real. Even though the external world can serve the function of being an extension of my deeper potential, it may be quite real (in that traditional sense of "real"), or it may be quite unreal.

Aside from its degree of reality, our externalized deeper potentials are awful, monstrous, distorted, extreme and catastrophic to the extent that the disintegrative relationship is intense. In other words, the more monstrous is the externalized deeper potential, the more intensely disintegrative is the relationship between the person and that deeper potential. By our own disintegrative relationship we *make* that deeper potential into a monstrous form. Here is the tragic state of so many persons—living in agonizing worlds which are extensions of their own disintegrative deeper potentials. Indeed, much of what we refer to as stress is usually no more than the extension of one's own deeper potential which looms and screeches at one as if it were something alien and external; yet the real villain is internal, a part of one's own personality. It presents itself in so many forms: economic stress, physical stress, family stress, situational stress. Almost without exception external stress is presumed to be the explanation of human problems. If persons behave in a crazy way, we attribute that to stress, and we search for the nature and location of the kinds of stresses which, for example, lead to the onset of schizophrenia (e.g. Rogler & Hollingshead, 1965). Yet, almost inevitably, what we find is merely the external face of our own disintegrative deeper potential.

In order to experience the deeper potential. As indicated in Figure 6.1, the function of my extended deeper potential can be to provide for the sheer experiencing of that potential. I can experience my deeper potential for whimsical silliness when I marry someone like that, mould my son into being that way, select friends who are that way, conjointly work with other friends to bring it forth from them, or create private daydreams of invented figures who are the essence of whimsical silliness. When any of these occur, I experience that deeper potential in me. Indeed, in terms of sheer degree of experiencing, I experience more when my deeper potential is extended into the external world than when it languishes as a mere inner potential. Externalizing what is within is therefore not a mechanism for "getting rid of unacceptable impulses" (cf. McCall, 1968). To "get rid of an unacceptable impulse" by externalizing it into the external world is to *amplify* its experiencing, not to rid oneself of experiencing.

My operating potentials may have nothing to do with bullying. I am not a bully. Yet I always manage to have a dog who is the bully of the neighborhood. My bosses and supervisors and foremen are always bullies. My adolescent son is a cruel bully, while I am the opposite of cruel: kind, sweet, understanding, gentle. When I grew up, there was a terribly cruel man in my neighborhood; I feared and hated him for years. I remember my ritualistic fantasy of beating him up—as I fell asleep each night. There has always been some figure or force in my life whose presence provides me with the experiencing of my own deeper potential for cruelty.

She has a doctorate and works in a program for the mentally retarded. Her colleagues think of her as brilliant. Her clinical teaching is creative and serves to open up worlds of new thinking for her graduate students. Her research on the etiology of mental retardation has won significant acclaim. Where does she gain some experiencing of her deeper potential for being plain, obtuse, dumb? First, her husband occasionally speaks to her as the voice of that deeper potential. He seems unsure of himself, of his capability to hold down his position in the firm. She picks at his lapses of intellectual acuity, at his occasional obtuseness. After such fights she tries to reassure herself that she must be wrong. He is upset or concerned. She then provides herself with loads of evidence to prove that he is *not* plain and obtuse. Yet the voice of her deeper potential has come to her through the mouth of her husband. A second way in which the deeper potential is experienced is through the youngsters with whom she works. There are times when she is overcome with a sense that nothing can be done for them. They are simply there, and beyond the merest scratchings of being reached. Then, a strange and frightening thing occurs. She begins feeling much like them in some awful, frightening way—dull, not really comprehending, not aware. That is a most horrible time for her, even though that lasts but a moment. It is as if the deeper potential comes to life in these two ways, giving it a moment of experiential life.

These are two persons extending their deeper potential out into their mundane worlds. When worlds are filled with being our extended deeper potentials in ways which are *dramatic*, we label the process projection, hallucinations, delusions, ideas of reference. Yet even under such dramatic circumstances, the *function* is the same: filling out one's world in order to experience what lies within (McCall, 1968). To do this is neither crazy nor mad nor maladjustive nor sick nor pathological. We call it a paranoid delusion, yet it offers the older man in the hospital the means of experiencing the sense of enemy. He perceives the ward psychologist or psychiatrist as the unfriendly other, and proclaims that all he wants is to get out of here; if you don't get me out of here, then you are my enemy (Bullard, 1960). By enveloping the ward personnel in this role, the patient is gaining a sense of experiencing what is deeper. No matter how that older man is described—as being paranoid, psychotic, sick, or delusional—he is understood as thereby experiencing the sense of enemy.

I have within me a frothing vindictiveness, a potential which is kept hidden deep inside me. But I gain a measure of experiencing when I fabricate a delusion. Then my world is, for a few moments, complete with leering devils intent on getting revenge upon me, as I gain some measure of deeper experiencing when these devils are there in my larger, extended world, pouring forth the vengeance.

We are now able to describe the phenomenon of crisis. When the mode of construction is the fourth one, i.e. our own fabricating of the external world, we have a heavy hand in its making. As we move back down through the third mode (constructing the external world by means of conjoint construction with others) and the second mode (utilizing a ready-made external world), our own role becomes steadily less and less. In the first mode, receiving the intrusive external world, we are still in the role of the constructor, but now our determining role is quite reduced. We are now confronted, intruded into, encountered, by an external world which can serve the function of being an extension of our own disintegratively fended off deeper potential. When this *first mode* is used to construct an external world, and when the *function* of the constructed external world is to be the extension of a highly disintegrative deeper potential, the person will be in a crisis situation. For example, you are confronted suddenly with the other person's full-blown murderous rage at you; your spouse picks up the knife and jumps at you to cut your throat; the dog leaps from the bushes with ferocious jaws snapping to bite you; your father grabs the poker and raises it to strike you. If you have a deeper potential for murderous rage, if you bear disintegrative fear and hate toward that deeper process, then you will be in a crisis state when that externalized potential leaps at you from the external world and intrudes itself onto you. Under these conditions, the nature of the deeper potential lies in *what is intruding itself* onto you from out there, rather than in the damage to your body, the breakup of your relationship to that person, or your immediate tendency to pass out. You have been invaded from outside by your own deeper potential. Its forcing itself onto you, the being confronted with the wholesale experiencing of it—these are the constituents of your crisis.

In addition to the crisis phenomenon, the extension of deeper potentials into the external world is also the basis for much of what is known as interpersonal and social relationships. Our friendships and our social involvements, our group memberships and our construction of families are all good ways of providing for the experiencing of our deeper potentials. If I cannot show my deeper potential for simple affection, if it must be hidden or denied by me, if it can only come out in a muted and twisted way from *me*, I can gain a measure of experiencing by my interpersonal and social involvements with others. I can join a group of simple, affectionate persons, or a group dedicated toward fostering simple affection. I can be the friend of others who can be openly affectionate. I can have a child who is my extended affection. I can breathe the affection in the nest of my family. Much of interpersonal and social relationships are means of extending deeper potentials into the external world and thereby gaining a measure of experiencing.

Because such parts of the external world are me—extensions of my own deeper parts—I am somehow entitled to *own* them. If my daughter is the extension of my femininity, then she not only belongs to herself, she also belongs to me. I own what is me even if it is extended out there into the external world. If my wife is my compassion, then there arises a sense of ownership of her. She belongs to me because her compassion is the extension of what I am. If my deeper bullying is manifested in the form of my dog, then I somehow exert a possessive mandate over him. Truly, in some real sense, I own him. It is this process which, at least in part, accounts for one person possessively owning another person or object. Mothers do this to their children, boyfriends do this to their girlfriends, older sisters do this to their younger sisters, human beings possess other human beings as extensions of what is deeper in the possessors.

In the same way, psychotherapists do much of their experiencing through their patients (Bugental, 1964). What goes by the name of psychotherapy is, in large part, a way for psychotherapists to experience their deeper parts by constructing extensions in the form of patients. I may hesitate to show my own inner yearnings to be free, but I can experience them through *your* struggles toward freedom. I may be emotionally congealed, but when you become unfrozen and spill out your emotionality, I gain a measure of experiencing. I can even experience my deeper rebelliousness through your rebellings—while I continue to operate on the side of the establishment. I may nurse deeper potentials for openly crazy, bizarre, uncontrolled expression— and gain a good measure of experiencing by means of your hospital ward behavior. Psychotherapists are in an enviable position for experiencing their own hidden potentials by constructing an external world (i.e., patients) who serve as extensions of the psychotherapists' own personalities. In this sense, "psychotherapy" is a euphemistic label for the playing out of such mundane personality processes.

Of the four modes of constructing an external world, the most common in psychotherapy is the third mode, i.e., the conjoint construction of an external world. When patient and psychotherapist come together, the patient typically is not yet a manifest expression of the therapist's deeper potential. Yet, by working conjointly with one another, the two persons can create a new external reality. The patient may have the potential to fall in love or to act out against authority, and the therapist's deeper potential might be to experience falling in love or acting out against authority. Yet the two must work together in order to create that which, very often, is the extension of the therapist's own deeper potentials brought to life through their conjoint efforts.

In order to experience the relationship with my deeper potential. As indicated in Figure 6.1, a second function of the external world is to serve as the extension of my deeper potential in order for me to experience the *relationship between me and that deeper potential.* As indicated in Figure 6.2, I (OP1) can construct (B2) the external world into being an extended deeper potential, and I can thereby bear the same kind of relationship with it as I bear toward my deeper potential (DP2). The relationship with the extended deeper potential can be either an integrative or a disintegrative relationship. When I construct you into being my externalized deeper potential for leadership, it is either to undergo an *integrative* relationship (feeling comfortable, loving, and accepting in regard to you as my leader) or a *disintegrative* relationship (fighting, hating, pulling back from, being disturbed by you as my leader). I construct you as (my extended deeper potential for being) a leader so that the integrative or disintegrative relationship with my own deeper potential is experienced in my relationship with you.

world plays important functions in our lives, and will extinguish when we no longer need it—and that requires changes in the persons we are, a kind of personal revolution.

We will always have one group being the helpers and another group being the helpees. Nothing is going to change all of the institutions and practices which helpers and helpees have constructed. We will always have some form of crazy persons, hospitals and jails, professional and nonprofessional helpers, mental health laws, training programs and people with problems. Each group demands the existence of the other in the playing out of their mutual functions. We will go through all sorts of apparent advances and progress, with no end to new ideas of how to treat persons with problems. Yet we will always be left with the same two groups marching along together, perpetuating one another for their own functions. We will have what we have always had as long as each "revolution" in the mental health field leaves collective persons the way they are.

When collective persons undergo their own personal change, it is possible that collective persons will no longer be characterized by potentials for helping and for being helped. When that occurs, we will no longer have helpers and helpees. We will no longer have psychiatrists and social workers and counselors. We will no longer have social agencies and organizations, mental health groups and hospitals. We will no longer have patients and welfare recipients, clients and hospitalized patients. What will we have? I predict that we will have social institutions and practices which provide for the experiencing of whatever potentials then come to the fore. I predict that, with the dissolving away of helper-helpee institutions, there will arise whole new sets of institutions which provide for the experiencing of the potentials which the helper-helpee institutions had served, only the new institutions will provide for more direct experiencing of those potentials. For example, I foresee the likelihood of institutions whereby persons who "need" each other will be enabled to be with one another. I term these "psychological families," primary groups whose members provide mutual experiencing for each other (Mahrer, 1970e). Bypassing any of the helper-helpee practices, "foster" grandparents adopt "foster" grandchildren, and each provides what the other needs (Johnston, 1967). In precisely the same way, psychological families can grow on the basis of members whose experiencing is facilitated by the other family members. This is an institution which provides what helper-helpee institutions had provided, but much more directly and without any of the practices which had been associated with helpers and helpees. But again, such social change will follow from a personal revolution occurring on a collective scale.

Hobbs (1964) has described three major "revolutions" in the mental health field. The first is identified with names such as Pinel, Rush, Tuke, and Dix, and rose on the attitude that insane persons are persons deserving to be treated with human kindness and decency. The second was swept into being by psychoanalytic illumination of the intrapsychic side of human existence. According to Hobbs, we are now in the midst of the third revolution, in which public health concepts are transforming mental illness into a social problem for which responsibility lies at the doorstep of the community. We are witnessing the fallout of major contemporary theoretical advances based on assumptions about the significant effects on human behavior of the complex of social stimuli and the effects of group processes. Beneath this third revolution is the model of the human being as a social being, developed and alterable by changes in social stimuli and group processes.

I foresee the possibility of a "next revolution" as a shift occurs in our theory of how society itself changes as a consequence of collective individual change. As collective persons undergo change, the entire fabric of society and groups will undergo change, and therein lies the possibility of a dramatic, indeed revolutionary, change in society. In this Copernican switch, social phenomena become effect, not cause. Social phenomena take their place as the *products* of human construction, and give up their traditional role as determinants. Social phenomena are our creation; they fulfill functions we assign—even those of influencing, causing, modifying, and determining us.

How does this whole process of social change get started? What does the person actually do when there is genuine concern about starving children, a destitute community, the imminence of war, brutality to the underdog, people in genuine need, unfair and agonizing social conditions? Here are genuine, live, real, here-and-now social problems. What can I do to set social change into motion? Our theory (Mahrer, 1970e) offers two intercoupled processes which are designed for the person whose concerns are directed to specific problems in the real imminent world. The first process is to plunge into one's own internal change. You do *nothing* to or for that starving child or any other social problem. Leave that child alone. Instead, use the child as a vehicle to plunge into your own personal change. Instead of rushing toward the child, rush into your own insides. Let that child, that moment, exert its complete effect upon you. Go into your own insides with the target being your own inner self in connection with that child. This is the first process. The second process is to become whatever you become as you undergo the change in the very person you are. Here is the utter risk. When you emerge from the first internal process after a few minutes of being with your insides, or after a day of intensive self-probing, or after months of good psychotherapy, then you are different—perhaps only slightly, perhaps sharply different—from what you were. Be that new person, whatever that is. If you are transformed into a person who organizes the community to help that child, then that is what you do. If you become one who adopts that child into your family, then that is how you behave. If you find the child and its plight irrelevant, then you will turn to other matters. If you are transformed into a politician, then that is how you will be. Back and forth go these two processes. As you organize the community, fresh experiences are brought to you. Use these to enter more deeply into yourself, and emerge into a person who is the way the new person must be.

How is social change brought about by these two intercoupled processes? Each results in its own set of ways. As you alter the kind of person you are, you alter the ways in which you help construct and maintain the world in which you live. You alter your own ways of creating and maintaining starving children or lonely old men or downtrodden minorities. You change the very world you help collectively create. That is one set of ways. The second set of ways flows out of the forever changing person whom you become. If you move into being a social organizer, then social organizers effect social change. If you move into becoming a judge or a bartender or a member of a political party or a friend or a parent or whatever, then you effect social changes from within those roles. To champion one way *against* the other is to commit a terrible error. To turn your social concerns into mere contemplation or mere psychotherapy or mere dropping out or mere self-worry or mere withdrawal is a bad error. To turn your social concerns into mere organizational development or social planning or politics is an error of at least equal proportions.

In what appears to be a paradoxical step, the functions of social phenomena can be changed by leaving the social phenomena alone and, instead, by undergoing one's own personal change on a collective scale. That is, we change the functions of social phenomena by letting them be. From my restless urgency to "do something" about social problems and social change, I enter into the changes with my own self. Thereby the functions of the social phenomena are profoundly changed.

Once I even *posture* myself toward changing a social phenomenon, toward altering and improving it *without* coupling that with change in my self, I am falling into the same trap as the mental health helpers who construct and forever perpetuate helpees. The very posture of helping-changing-improving *maintains* the social phenomenon and endows it with its function of being that which I am intent upon helping-changing-improving. Once a social phenomenon arises and is endowed with the function of being that which I am postured to help-change-improve, the social phenomenon is subtly made permanent. I have created a social phenomenon whose function is to be that which I change-help-improve (Watts, 1960). In this way, hundreds upon hundreds of groups have, throughout history, constructed social phenomena which they are postured to change-help-improve. We create opposition which we seek to overcome. We create the poor which we hope to save. We create the downtrodden whose lot we seek to improve. We create unfair laws which we set out to alter. We create ruling classes which we set about dethroning. We create social phenomena against which we set ourselves in a posture of changing-helping-improving.

When the social group is constructed to serve the function of being my extended personality, the process of social change of which I am speaking is squeezed out of possibility. When the social group is my extended operating or deeper potential, my own selfhood is put to sleep, and the social group becomes the reservoir of determination and ownership while my I-ness falls into the state of unfeeling. When the social group becomes my "I," there is a residual false sense of self. I live under an illusions of personhood when, in actuality, my personhood resides in the social group which is my extended personality. When this occurs, I am unable to effect social change because there is no real I or personhood left. The net result is a calcifying of the external social phenomenon.

Furthermore, when the social group is my extended personality, the social group exerts powerful influences toward defining who and what I am. The social group fixes me into being a certain kind of person, and rigidly defines me into being a certain way. Because the definition of who and what I am now comes from the social group, this too stops me from being able to change the group. Because the group is now my self, the group can preserve me into being whatever it makes of me, for ". . . the place of the self is taken by the Mitwelt . . . For the Mitwelt is not one's own standard but an alien one, and as such it is no longer dependent on myself but faces me as something unmovable and foreign . . . the transfer of the center of gravity of our existence from our own self to the judgment of others, experienced as fixed. Thereby the self . . . becomes a state of things, judged by the others and accordingly by me—in other words, it becomes objectified, made into a 'fixed' object or thing, with fixed contours, fixed dimensions and weight" (Binswanger, 1958c, p. 341).

In summary, our concern has been with the *functions* of social phenomena. Essentially, the functions of *social phenomena* have been described as the same functions served by the *external world of the individual* (Figure 6.1), viz. (a) to serve as a context for (collective) experiencing, (b) to serve as an externalization of (collective) operating potentials, and (c) to serve as an externalization of (collective) deeper potentials. When social phenomena are the externalization of collective operating or deeper potentials, the function is either to provide for collective experiencing of potentials or of relationships among potentials. Individual persons build individual worlds to serve the same functions as collective persons building social worlds. We turn now to the ways in which collective persons construct social worlds.

MODES OF CONSTRUCTING SOCIAL PHENOMENA

How are social phenomena constructed? What are the ways in which social beliefs, values, realities, standards, institutions, and groups are established and altered? Chapter 6 was concerned with the ways in which individual persons went about constructing their external worlds. I proposed four modes of constructing external worlds (Figure 6.1). Parsimony invites us to adopt the thesis that social phenomena are constructed by means of the same four modes through which individuals construct their external worlds, viz. social phenomena are constructed by collective persons receiving an intrusive external world, utilizing a ready-made external world, conjointly constructing an external world, and fabricating an external world.

Collective human beings as determinants, not products, of social phenomena. Our thesis grows out of a position which is contrary to that adopted by the predominance of approaches. Almost without exception, nearly every behavioral and social science has adopted the position that social variables play a predominant role in shaping human beings. From this position, efforts to shape human beings are directed into modifying the social forces which are held as effecting human beings. Humanistic theory rejects this position in favor of one in which social phenomena are themselves constructed by collective human beings. Our collective potentials and their relationships are the determining variables which construct social phenomena.

In the four ways of constructing the social world, the generating force is always persons. Persons construct social phenomena, and it will be persons who reconstruct and change social phenomena. Whatever kind of social phenomenon we study, it is our creation. Life and form and meaning are given to it by persons. Changes in that social phenomenon mean changes in the persons who construct and perpetuate it. All solutions to the problems of social phenomena must focus on the persons who construct and maintain that particular social phenomenon—whether we are looking at a tall building, a public school system, moral codes, or computers. From this perspective, it is an error to consider solutions to a social phenomenon based upon an assumption of the social phenomenon's existence beyond collective persons. Solutions which treat social phenomena or non-personal super-organisms have adopted assumptions different from those of humanistic theory. Ellul (1964), for example, speaks of a gigantic, dehumanizing, mechanistic technological society which is in a process of evolution. A battle is looming. We human beings can win the battle by gaining perceptive awareness of that looming awful society and determining to assert our freedom against "it." Humanistic theory does not set human beings against such an "it," as if "it" held an existence of its own. That gigantic mechanistic society (or any other kind of social phenomenon) is *our* construction. It is the constructed expression of collective human beings. When human beings change, social phenomena change.

By means of the appropriate mode of construction, collective human beings can create any kind of social phenomenon, including that which seems to exist on its own, over and above human beings. The very creation of a social phenomenon existing over and above human beings—as a separate super-organism or super-organization—is a product of our own creation in the very same way that the kind of society we will have in ten or a hundred or a thousand years is a function of our own collective construction. We are busy constructing our social world through some mode or modes of world-building (Keniston, 1962), whether we construct it by one or all of the four modes to be described, or in modes we have not yet discovered.

No social phenomena are simply there; we construct them all. Marxist political theory holds that the cornerstones of the external social world include ruling classes, workers, one's own location within or outside of the ruling class, patternings of forces in the inevitable struggles among social groups. From our perspective, the raw existence of social classes and their struggles is testimony to the particular *modes* by which collective persons construct external social phenomena. The ruling class exists because collective persons construct it. The existence of struggles among social political classes is due to the world-building efforts of collective persons. We are forever at work, collectively constructing a very particular kind of external social political world, and the potentials and their relationships in collective persons are the primary generating causes. In Marxist political theory, the ruling class and workers and struggles are simply there, just as in the stimulus-response model of the person and the world, an external reality of natural science is simply there, separate from the persons who respond to (and construct) it. On this basic point, we must differ radically in insisting on the role of collective persons in constructing everything which Marxist political theory holds as the crucial determining factors of the external world.

Each social system, including those central to Marxist political theory, is constructed by human beings. This includes social systems such as the university, the military, the family, social welfare, sports, justice, business, social classes, the church. Our theory holds that such social systems determine the way human beings are only to the extent that human beings construct them to include the function of determining the way we are. Otherwise, such social systems will die when we die. I reject approaches which regard persons as constituents of a larger system, and which understand the ways persons are as conferred by their place in the larger system (cf. Schwab, 1960). I reject such an approach to describing how social systems come about, and also the relation between the social system and persons. Such a model may well be profitable in mathematics, gravitational fields, computer analysis, and economics. As an approach, it constitutes *one* way of describing social phenomena and human beings, but its fundamental conception of social phenomena and human beings is rejected by humanistic theory.

Once we adopt a theoretical framework in which we ourselves construct social phenomena, then the social professions are already *in* the process of social change. It is not a choice between involvement or removed uninvolvement. Our very existence as social professions wallows in the continuous construction of social phenomena whether we know it or not, whether we choose to direct our involvement or let it continue haphazardly. Whether we like it or not, whether we accept it or not, we are caught in the responsibility for social change. By "we" I include disciplines such as counselors and therapists, psychologists and sociologists, educators and psychiatrists, criminologists and political scientists. Hobbs (1964) is representative of those who seek to awaken these professions to an acknowledgment of their social responsibility; ". . . professional people have a responsibility for the management of innovation. The implication is that the mature profession does not simply respond to the needs of society but claims a role in determining what society should need and how social institutions as well as individual professional careers, can be shaped to the service of an emerging social order. The responsible professional person becomes the architect of social change" (p. 822). Indeed, we are wallowing *in* that responsibility. We either catch hold of our responsibility or seek to avoid its existence. Whether we like it or not, whether we choose to do something about it or not, our disciplines are already involved with the processes of social change. We can choose to what degree and in what manner we accept that responsibility, but the responsibility envelops us.

Yet what we *do* as professional persons depends on whether we assume social phenomena to have separate existences of their own, or, as is held in humanistic theory, whether social phenomena are described as a product of collective individual construction. In setting forth his picture of the public mental health specialist, Hobbs (1964) assumes "society" to constitute a separate existence, an entity on its own right. The target of the professional is society, and the question of social change is then translated into how professional mental health specialists can best deploy their manpower and knowledge onto society itself. From *our* perspective, society is *not* a separately existing thing to be worked upon from the outside, as it were. As the product of collective individuals, society cannot serve as the effective, direct, working unit. Instead, whatever we do as professional persons to change "society" must be redirected toward collective individuals. Accordingly, our approach invites efforts to change *society* to focus instead on collective *individuals*. Under this approach, the effectiveness of a method of social change is gauged by the extent to which it provides for the deepest levels of change in each individual person. Under this criterion, the working target cannot be the community, society, or organization, but what is going on deep within each individual. Assessment of a method or process of change cannot rely on measures of some presumed separate unit termed the community, organization, or society (cf. Kelly, 1970). Rather, methods of assessment would focus on the degree to which changes occur at the deepest levels within each person.

The Construction of Social Phenomena by Collective Reception of an Intrusive External World

We may have nothing at all to do with the making of an earthquake. The earthquake is an external event which intrudes itself upon us. We receive it in a way which is a function of our own *collective* potentials and their relationships. By *collective* I mean that if each one of us receives that earthquake in a unique way, no social phenomenon necessarily is constructed beyond the simple and straightforward occurrence of the event known as an earthquake. But if enough of us collectively receive that intrusive earthquake by falling into a state of confused bewilderment, then we have collectively constructed a social phenomenon: a state of general confused bewilderment. By collectively receiving the earthquake in a particular way, we construct a social phenomenon. In the same way, we construct social phenomena by the manner in which we receive such intrusive events as our country being invaded, a crowd watching quietly while one person is being brutally beaten, a fire breaking out in a crowded night club, rioting occurring in the streets, or a large section of an arena crashing upon hundreds of spectators. If the predominance of persons receive these events by becoming frenetically disorganized, a collective social phenomenon is thereby constructed: mass hysteria, a crowd gone crazy, panic.

Suppose that half the persons in a community said: "I have a bad problem. It really worries me. May I talk to you about it?" to the other half of the persons in the community. The request is a real one. It intrudes itself onto the other persons. The critical consideration is how the other persons receive that intrusive invitation. If they put themselves in the role of problem solver, if they establish special places to talk about problems, if they surround themselves with robes and ornaments of concerned problem-solvers, if they dedicate themselves to a full listening, then they have constructed a social phenomenon (helpers and helpees) by receiving that invitation in that way.

The Construction of Social Phenomena by Collective Utilization of a Ready-Made External World

We can construct social phenomena by collectively utilizing (selecting, capitalizing upon) what is already there in the external world. Suppose that enough of us require other persons to serve as our collective scapegoat, to be hated and ridiculed. How may we construct such a collective target? One way of constructing this is by selecting a group ready-made for such a function. This means utilizing a group of persons already made to be a collective scapegoat, already made for ridicule and hatred. By selecting the appropriate ready-made group, (possibly the new minority group in the community, or Indians or drunkards or Jews or Gypsies), we have thereby constructed a social phenomenon merely by utilizing what is already ready-made.

Collective rebellious persons can construct a social phenomenon by selecting and utilizing another collection of individuals ready-made to be rebelled against. Authority groups (university faculty, parents, management, those in governmental power and control) are excellent resources, for many of these persons are ready-made to be rebelled against. All the rebellious ones have to do is to select the right authority groups from a universe of ready-made authorities, and a social phenomenon has been constructed.

We construct a social phenomenon of helping-welfare-rehabilitation by selecting very special segments of the world ready-made for such use. We locate the handicapped and the disabled, homeless children, retardates, aged persons, and nonverbal members of the lower classes. We did not create these groups. But we utilized these ready-made groups to construct a whole family of social phenomena: mental health volunteers and social welfare programs, public health and rehabilitation agencies, social workers and outpatient clinics.

There are groups of persons standing ready to be utilized, and a social phenomenon is constructed when collective persons make appropriate use of these available groups. It is a matter of selection. If collective persons wish to construct a social phenomenon of suppression, they need only utilize the proper group ready-made to be suppressive (e.g. the right church authority, the right police, the right military group). When collective persons put themselves in the path of suppressive groups, social suppression happens. For example, many of us are geared toward constructing an external world which sits heavy on us and will not permit us to be silly and giddy and playful. In searching for those who shall treat us in this manner, we may find a group of persons ready-made for the part. They go about the world shaking their heads and their index fingers, saying: "Thou shalt not be silly and giddy and playful." They are continuously invoking guilt, and oozing into all the available conscience crevices of society. When we utilize them to stir up our guilt and stifle our playfulness, we are constructing very particular sets of social phenomena: codes of behavior, family loyalty, social attitudes about childishness and adulthood, class systems, immaturity, older persons, old teachers, clergymen, neighbors, judges. They are already there, waiting to be utilized, and when they are utilized, we have constructed a social phenomenon of guilt and social conscience.

The Construction of Social Phenomena by Collective Conjoint Construction

Suppose a large number of persons in one group and a large number of persons in another group have potentials for experiencing mass destruction, violence, war. It is possible for persons in both groups to work conjointly with one another to evoke the potential for war in each other. Collective persons in each of the two groups must work upon each other in precisely the right ways so that the potential for war is brought forth. This requires deftness, art, timing, delicacy. If they are successful, they can work together to construct the social phenomenon known as war. That is an achievement, a creative act of conjoint construction.

One group of persons may have potentials for mistrusting authority. Although these persons are not being that way, they share that potential. Another group of persons may share a potential for *being* authorities who are mistrusted. Both groups must work together conjointly so that one becomes those who mistrust authority and the other becomes the mistrusted authorities. They have to work together, each fashioning and moulding the other into manifesting their respective potentials. If they are successful, the social phenomenon is constructed.

I am impressed with the dyadic nature of group construction. That is, collective persons in one group work conjointly with collective persons in another group to construct a social phenomenon. We have the potential for being the restless downtrodden, and somewhere out there are you who have the potential for being the ones who trod on us. We need one another. It may be that each of us requires the other to serve as the proper context for what we have available to experience; it may be that each uses the other as an extension of collective operating or deeper potentials. In any case, we need one another to carry out that function.

These pairs of groups require a process of trying out, of shaping, moulding. The mental health groups in a community interact with sets of other community groups until the right dyad is fashioned, with one group offering mental health services and the partner group receiving the mental health services. There is typically a process of trying out, moving one another about, moulding and shaping one another. In the course of this courtship, two interesting social phenomena generally occur. One consists of a group of persons who sample the mental health game briefly and then withdraw from the whole scene. Research on the users of community mental health facilities has illuminated such a class of persons who try out the system once or twice and then stay away from the whole community mental health system (Brandt, 1965; Feister, Mahrer, Giambra & Ormiston, 1974; Sarason et al, 1966). These persons are not fitting partners in the process of conjoint construction. The second social phenomenon consists in the emergence of a class of persons who are *good* partners, fitting playmates with the persons who comprise the community mental health providers. This second group includes the active users of mental health facilities, going from agency to agency, consuming the various services that the whole spectrum of community agencies offer (Fiester, Mahrer, Giambra & Ormiston, 1974). In this process, the right two groups find each other and work conjointly together to construct a social phenomenon, viz. the users and the providers of community mental health services.

Dyadic groups also work together conjointly to establish and maintain the mental hospital system. In order for there to be such hospitals, one group must be characterized by potentials to experience that which can be experienced in hospitals (Mahrer, 1962c, 1970b, 1970c). But that alone will not suffice. We also require a second group of persons who experience what is important for them to experience by having others in mental hospitals. This second group is composed of families, social workers, law enforcement officers, psychiatrists, and others. For example, members of the first group may have potentials which say, "I need a safe place to go beserk, to scream and yell without being massacred for being that way." Members of the second group may have potentials which say, "How I would like to go beserk, to yell and scream. But I cannot myself. I need others who are that way, so I can be near them." These two sets of persons must work conjointly to construct the whole fabric of mental hospitals and associated rituals and dogma.

The mental health belief system is maintained by both groups as a kind of group illusion while they are busy conjointly constructing the mental health phenomena. Among the major planks in this belief system are the following: "Some persons are sick or ill; they are neurotic or psychotic; they ought to be treated for their illness; hospitals are places where they can be treated; hospital personnel are there to help the mentally ill receive treatment." Such beliefs must be held in spite of research which fails to support such beliefs, which casts doubt on the efficacy of hospital "treatment," which suggests that people in hospitals are not different in those particular ways from people not in hospitals, and which generally questions whether any significant progress in hospital treatment has occurred over the past half century (Mahrer, 1970b). If there is a significant change in either the hospital helpers or the helpees, whole set of relationships often must be renegotiated. If the nature of the patients changes to include much younger patients who are not asking for help, but, instead, are there to force the establishment to provide what these younger patients want, then there will be massive consequent changes in the hospital staff. If key hospital staff leave, then there will be major changes in the patients. The hospital system is a social system in which changes in any key element or group require changes in the mutually interacting other conjoint elements or groups (Caudill, 1958).

In the conjoint construction of social phenomena (e.g. the mental hospital system, war, authority, class struggles), the construction process requires the presence of the other group against which we struggle. Each time a person becomes a member of one dyadic group, he is inviting others to join the group against which his own group is struggling. When I join the "law and order" group, I am also constructing an interlocking polar group which opposes law and order, which defies and resists my group. If I am going to be law and order, then you must be anti-law-and-order. We must work together conjointly, each group working with the other to construct and perpetuate our dyadic relationship. Which group do you join? If you are drawn to the dyad in which one side is law and order and the other side is freedom and individualism, which side do you join? Fromm (1968) invites you to join "the revolution of hope," the side opposing the deadening forces of gigantic mechanical, dehumanizing government. From our perspective, to select either side is to vitalize and perpetuate the other. To join a revolution requires the existence of that against which you revolt—and is testimony to the likely existence of that other side within you. The instant you join the group for freedom, individualism, the revolution of hope, you are constructing a mechanical, dehumanizing, government autocracy. The instant you campaign for law and order, you give vitality to lawlessness, chaos, and disorder. Out of dyadic group struggle is born the social phenomenon, conjointly created by the struggling dyadic groups.

Social phenomena can be constructed conjointly in other ways—in ways other than dyadic groups. All of us can work with one another conjointly to construct a social phenomenon all by ourselves, without dyadic groups interacting with one another. By means of collective conjoint construction, a number of us can form a group out of what we have within as potentials. I have the potential for helping others. You, too may have the same potential. Both of us may worry about drinking too much. Together, a group of us work upon one another to evoke what each of us has as potential within each of us. By working together conjointly, we construct a social phenomenon which had not been there before—a self-help group of persons who seek to help one another limit our drinking. By conjoint constructing we have created a social phenomenon out of our own selves.

A group may construct a social phenomenon by working conjointly with one or more of its own members. For example, a strong leader-follower phenomenon may be constructed between one member of a group, with strong potentials for leadership, and the other members of the group, with strong potentials for following an active leader. A neighborhood group may conjointly construct a phenomenon of hatred when one member has strong potentials for becoming the mean old man, nasty and withdrawn, and the rest of the members have strong potentials for hating the mean villain. Nearly every group can create its own social phenomenon by conjointly working with a few special members of the group in ways which require graceful concert, mutual overtures, deft timing, and careful eliciting of behaviors from one another.

By means of collective conjoint construction, a group can define its own social reality. Not only can the group work together to define the nature of its reality, but the group can also work conjointly to demonstrate that its defined reality is indeed realistic, and the rigorous criteria of what is real and what is unreal will be used in the service of insuring the continued existence of that particular socially defined reality. Leighton and Hughes (1961), for example, speak of the nature of reality as defined by one's particular family, community or culture. Social reality often is a creation of consensual validation by a group of persons conjointly working together on a collective basis.

Not only is conjoint construction a powerful means whereby a group constructs social phenomena, but the outcome is predictable. If each member of a group uses the mode of conjoint construction, then the nature of that group can be predicted by examining the collective members. This applies to any group, from self-help groups to large organizations, from community groups to political parties. Whatever the group is to be, whatever the group is to do for and to its members, whatever the group "means"—all of this is contained in what the collective members are. If none of the members *manifest* cruelty and violence, but each houses a *deeper potential* for cruelty and violence, then it is likely that the conjointly constructed social phenomenon will be one involving cruelty and violence.

The Construction of Social Phenomena by Collective Fabrication

Collective persons can construct social phenomena by means of fabrication, building it out of whole cloth, from their own inner resources. When collective persons are at work fabricating social realities, there is almost no limit to what we can achieve. If a few persons see a vision of God, devils, or flying saucers, they are having delusions; but if we collectively see those things, we have fabricated a social phenomenon. If a few of us believe the world is soon coming to an end, we are insignificant crackpots; but if we all collectively share this belief, we have fabricated a new social phenomenon. Collectively held morals become social morals; collectively held standards become social standards. Through collective sharing, we fabricate social norms, social traditions, history, what is good and what is bad, what is real and what is false, even our destinies.

Collectively held destinies can become fabricated into social realities. Out of collectively held beliefs emerge social phenomena (i.e., destinies) such as the following: The destiny of Germany is to rule the world; it is the destiny of the working classes to throw off their yokes and overturn the ruling classes; it is the destiny of the Jews to regain their homeland; it is the destiny of Communism to take over the world; the destiny of the human race is to bring about its own destruction; it is the destiny of women to bear children. Collectively held destinies are merely another means of fabricating a sophisticated external world, and thereby inviting social phenomena in accord with the collectively held destiny. I hate and fear the passivity in me. You hate and fear the passivity in you. Collectively we all hate and fear the passivity in us. We together create a society which is an ally and extension of our operating potentials. That society is dedicated toward bearing the same relationship to us as we bear toward our deeper passivity. In this way we establish and maintain a society which makes us passive and hates us for being this way. It is cruel to our passivity and makes us suffer for it. It takes advantage of us and makes us into conforming sheep. We fabricate, we manufacture our own societies to be toward us the way we collectively are toward our own insides.

Our fabrications can be in the form of a belief or a building; by means of our collective potentials, we fabricate social institutions in the form of social norms, motherhood, justice, patriotism, standards, values, and morals; or in the form of prisons, slums, atomic bombs, insurance companies, and hospitals. Yet all these social institutions are creative fabrications, constructed out of the collective potentials of persons. Fabricated social *beliefs* are coupled with fabricated social *things*. For example, collective persons may fabricate social beliefs about deviant behavior, normality and abnormality, and what ought to be done with such abnormal persons. Those collective ideas will always find embodied expression in some formalized way—in things. Today that formalized way is called psychiatry. The preponderance of psychiatrists are the expressors of collectively held ideas characteristic of western cultures and pertaining to notions of mental illness and health, adjustment and maladjustment, identification of crazy people, and what to do with them (Leighton & Hughes, 1961). What is commonly held in collective persons will inevitably be formalized as their psychiatric ideology, complete with associated things—psychiatric wards, nurses, tests, drugs, shock machines, legislation, diplomas, and locked doors. We fabricate social beliefs and social things, and they emerge coupled together.

We can fabricate much more than social beliefs and social things; we can fabricate just about anything on a collective basis. Before we collectively fabricated them, there were no witches. But when I fabricate a witch and all of you fabricate a witch, we collectively fabricate a new social phenomenon: witches. And we make them as real as real can be. In this very same way we collectively fabricate the social reality of parents, priests, criminals, doctors, and schizophrenics.

Having fabricated witches, the very *collective* nature of our work invests that phenomenon with the cloak of social reality. Witches are made real, and their reality is doubly insured by our fabricated criteria of reality—which insure that what we fabricate is not considered to be *our* fabrication. One of these criteria is consensual validation. When a bunch of people agree that our collectively constructed witches are real, that reassures us that witches are real. Is she a witch? If we all consensually validate one another that she is a witch, then a reality is constructed out of our collective fabrications—and she *is* a witch! Or he is a villain, or she is a bad mother, or he is a mean boss, or she must be destroyed because she is dangerous, or he is psychotic. When we collectively fabricate witches, a harsh reality is thereby fabricated. And when we fabricate a criterion of consensual validation, our collectively held fabrications become collectively stamped with reality.

How easy it is for collective persons to fabricate witches and psychotics and criminals and retardates and mental illness and nationalities and political causes. Or buildings. Today there are no "mental health" clinics in the community. Two years from now, there they are! How were they fabricated where they did not exist before? According to Cotts (1954) the determining force is a collection of "neurotic" persons, as he labels them, who are responsible forces in establishing the mental health clinics. Particular kinds of potentials, in concert with one another, can fabricate buildings. Out of the personality systems of collective persons are fabricated real clinic buildings as a wholly new element in the external world. We construct social phenomena by means of fabricating beliefs and ideas—and things, millions of things.

How obvious! Of course collective human beings construct buildings and warships and automobiles. Of course these are real things. What we are less inclined to see is that the same applies to social institutions, values, beliefs, truths, convictions. We fabricate all of these out of whole cloth from our collective potentials. We endow them with their reality. We savagely guard against their erosion because once our collective potentials change, all of these social phenomena dissolve away. Social phenomena fabricated out of our collective potentials are encased in a reality equal to that of floods and forests, sunshine and rocks. Beliefs, collectively held, possess all the characteristics of reality. The world *is* flat, being patriotic to the country *is* good, there *is* reincarnation. Yet these are illusions, collectively held social illusions (Watts, 1961, pp. 66-67) which, with regard to reincarnation for example, such philosophies as Taoism and Buddhism expose as such. There is no code of justice out there. You and I fabricate this out of our collective heads. Once constructed, we endow that code with a social reality which is magnificently hard. It hits with a terrific wallop. It *is* real! So is God, prestige, social class, self-respect, friendship, fatherhood and motherhood, the home. There is a very real thing called a "woman's role" because we collectively share a conception of a "woman's role." It is our *collective individual* expectancies about how women are to be, and *not* "socio-cultural" expectancies (cf. Leighton & Hughes, 1968).

Once we collectively fabricate a social phenomenon invested with all the characteristics of hard reality, we usually elevate it into an ideal to be maintained and to be defended. Yet, from our humanistic perspective, what we create as the ideal, the best, that which is to be striven for, has no substance or justification of its own. It exists, and changes, simply on the basis of the kinds of persons we collectively are. Is there a best form of government? Is there a best or ideal scientific method? Our perspective holds that a group of interested and articulate persons will collectively create the best or ideal form of government as a grand collective fabrication to play one or more functions. There *is* no ideal or best form of government, no ideal or best scientific method. These are considered best or ideal by collective persons for whom it is important to create such notions. When change occurs in the persons we are, there will be a corresponding change in what, if any, are then constructed as the best or ideal forms of government or methods of conducting scientific inquiry. Under these circumstances, I suggest that a reasonable way to proceed is to *open the way* for continuous betterment of our forms of government and our scientific methods, but *never to defend* any form of government or scientific method as everlastingly ideal or as beyond change as a result of significant changes in the nature of collective persons.

As collective persons change, everything we have fabricated will change. Because we require a context in which to experience our being obedient, our being watched and kept in line, our being told what to do—we fabricate the "will" of the family (or tribe or social group or society). We invest it with its reality. But that group will is our creation. It is created out of our collective efforts, and that means it is a grand illusion. It speaks with our collective voice. We ourselves invent it and maintain it. It has power and impact because we continuously attribute life to it. When we collectively change (and no longer require such a context) the "will" of the group or the society evaporates.

Epilogue

The denouement of this chapter on the construction and functions of social phenomena brings us to the possibility of a rigorous system of principles for understanding social phenomena. If we know the personality structures of the individuals who are involved, we are in a position to predict the nature of their social phenomena. We would know the *functions* of their social phenomena, the particular *modes of construction* characteristic of those individuals, the content of their collective potentials, and the nature of the collective relationships among their potentials. From the perspective of humanistic theory, that is sufficient information to enable us to predict all of the social phenomena we have discussed in this chapter—the social groups, social beliefs, group situations, group identities, group relationships, and so on.

In seeking to describe social phenomena, humanistic theory takes the position (Chapter 4) that there are many relevant theoretical perspectives. *Our* particular perspective is that the potentials and relationships among the potentials of collective persons utilize specific modes of constructing social phenomena to play specific functions. This position sidesteps the argument between "social" versus "intra-psychic" determinants, nor can the two sets of factors be compared and contrasted with one another. In terms of social factors, our system accounts for social phenomena in ways which do not call upon social causal variables of the traditional sorts. In terms of intrapsychic factors, social phenomena are described as arising from collective modes of construction and collective functions which these phenomena are constructed to play. I am inclined to join neither the intrapsychic nor the social camp. Nevertheless, in accord with our class 1 position (Figure 4.1), social phenomena are open to description from the viewpoint of humanistic theory, *and also* open to full description from other theoretical viewpoints, including other individual theories, other group theories, and other social theories, intrapsychic *and* social.

Suppose our intent is to understand the behavior of a specific woman on the psychiatric ward of a hospital. This woman behaves in a highly demanding way. To begin with, the phenomenon we are setting out to describe is an individual, not a group or a social process. Yet the phenomenon can be described in terms of her own psychodynamics, or in terms of the processes of the small group which includes her, or in terms of the larger social factors operating at the institutional level (Schwartz, 1957). Where does humanistic theory fit in this trichotomy? Is it a theory of individual psychodynamics, or a theory of small group processes, or a social theory? I see humanistic theory as relating to all three. It does tell us about the individual; it provides a way of describing small group processes; and it also provides a mantle of explanation for social factors. Suppose we consider the decline of that mental hospital in which the woman is being so demanding. Suppose that 20 years hence no one works at that hospital. Suppose the grounds are deserted and the whole place is empty. Here is a phenomenon different perhaps from the demanding woman on the hospital ward. Yet I would use the very same principles to describe this phenomenon. Humanistic theory seeks to make descriptive sense of phenomena which are individual, group, or social. It is a theory of the individual, the group, and the society.

8

Human Behavior

The purpose of the present chapter is to propose two major principles for describing human behavior from the perspective of humanistic theory. Perhaps a more appropriate beginning is to acknowledge that we have already said a great deal about our way of making sense of human behavior. Two fundamental and interlocking concepts have been introduced, viz. potentials and the relationships among potentials (Chapter 2). It will be proposed in the present chapter that these two concepts are fundamental to our understanding of human behavior. We have already described some bodily events as behaviors (Chapter 5); in the present chapter we will describe the compass of human behavior. In Chapters 6 and 7 we described human behavior as committed to the construction of personal and social worlds, and as providing functions for these external worlds to play. Against this background of having already said a great deal about human behavior, the purpose of the present chapter is to organize the understanding of behavior under two major principles.

One principle relates behavior to *potentials*, and the second to *relationships between potentials*. The full sweep of behavior is determined by the two variables—from onset to behavioral occurrence to behavioral change. Everything which occurs in the career of a behavior is caused by these two fundamental variables. If potentials come into being, behavior comes into being. If potentials move about, behavior alters. When potentials dissolve away, behavior changes. When any changes occur in relationships between potentials, behaviors modify. At the outset, the network of causal variables is rooted in potentials and their relationships and not in external conditions (cf. Skinner, 1938, 1953). Internal changes get the process of behavior change started. Our principles of behavior call upon *internal* variables, although the history of research and applied practice indicates that be-

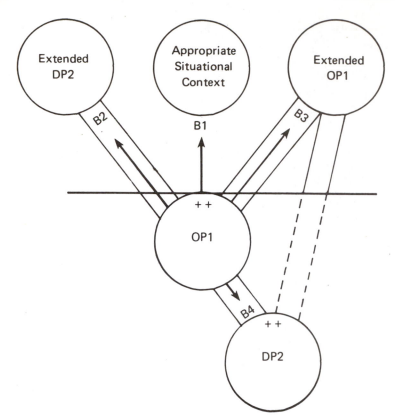

Figure 8.1 Behavior, Potentials, and Relationships Among Potentials

havior *can* be generated and modified on the basis of many variables, with our recent behavior modification approaches demonstrating the power of external variables. In this melange of ways of effecting behavior, humanistic theory relies on internal principles involving potentials and their relationships as the most theoretically consistent, most significant, most robust avenues for the description and understanding of human behavior.

The role of behavior in humanistic theory and in behaviorism. By linking human behavior to potentials and their relationships, the range of what is considered behavior becomes exceedingly broad. It includes mundane, everyday behavior such as cracking one's knuckles and using a tooth pick, driving a car and sitting hunched forward, liking chocolate ice cream cones and being pleased that others think you are as funny. It includes behavior which is seen as "different" (weird, bizarre, crazy, strange, alien), such as conversing with companions who can't be seen by others, talking in scrambled "word salad," being totally unresponsive and unknowing while huddled for days in a fetal position. It includes the gamut of internal (bodily) behavior described in Chapter 5. It includes the behavioral aspect of what has been categorized traditionally as perception, cognition and thinking, intelligence, problem-solving, sensation and memory, and values and attitudes. It includes self-directed behavior, interpersonal behavior, and social behavior, as well as the entire spectrum of behaviors which serve to construct external worlds, situations, and social phenomena (Chapters 6, 7).

Yet, broad as the range of behaviors is, behaviors are merely one component of human beings, and are not to be taken as all there is to persons. Human beings are described as including operating and deeper potentials, relationships among potentials, as well as encompassing external worlds—and behaviors. Behaviors, then, are only one part of what the person is, and are not to be taken as the whole. Behaviors, in contrast to the position of one wing of the behavior modification theories, do not define persons (cf. Eysenck & Rachman, 1965). Some behavior theories and learning theories not only identify the person, in large measure, with behavior, but approach behavior from a narrow framework that *excludes* much of what I would *include* as human behavior. It is surprising that such an over-scientized preoccupation with behavior has nevertheless failed to yield a satisfactory *definition* of human behavior. I suspect that the regnant theories in our "behavioral" sciences have boxed themselves into a position where human behavior cannot be adequately defined. If we look out upon the world through the various stimulus-response theories, then behavioral definitions must be congenial to those theories. That is, roughly speaking, behavior will be responses to stimuli. A systematic definition of behavior requires a systematic link between whatever is to be termed behavior and the stimuli (cues, reinforcements, contingencies, etc.) to which it is rigorously linked. It is on this basis that a dialectic has been established, one which draws a noose tighter and tighter around a defined region to be identified as human behavior. On the one hand, behavior is that which is cordial to the stimulus-response schema and lends itself to research investigation within that schema. On the other hand, research is increasingly bound to thsoe behaviors which lend themselves to measurement and understanding within a stimulus-response schema. The net result is that the increasing "rigor" of contemporary behaviorism is systematically *excluding* whole areas of what humanistic theory *includes* as behavior.

Watson argued forcibly that our proper data shall consist of objective behavior, knowable through observation and direct measurement, and not through methods of introspection (Watson, 1919; Woodworth & Sheehan, 1964). As one of the leading contemporary behaviorists, Skinner (1957) extended the meaning of behavior to include thought, covert or overt thought, verbalized or unverbalized thought. Even under this expanded definition of behavior, *our* proper data of study would likely include more than would be acceptable to behaviorism. For example, humanistic theory would include a large proportion of the realm of bodily changes (such as skin eruptions or tumors, ulcers or miscarriages), and also the realm of constructing external worlds, situations, and social phenomena. Ordinarily, these are beyond the behaviorist's definition of proper data.

The place of behavior in humanistic theory may be understood in contrast to the place of behavior in contemporary learning theories: (a) In humanistic theory, the proper data of study are human *experiencings*; behavior is one among several components of human experiencings. In behaviorism, the proper data of study are *behaviors*. (b) Our perspective is a member of the *human sciences*; behaviorism considers itself one of the *behavioral* sciences. (c) According to humanistic theory, behavior is but one of a number of components of personality structure. In behaviorism, personality structure is (largely tantamount to) behavior. (d) In humanistic theory, behavior *constructs* external worlds, situations, and social phenomena. In behaviorism, behavior is cast as *responses* to external worlds, situations, cues, and social phenomena (cf. Kimble, 1953). (e) As compared with behaviorism, humanistic theory accepts a broader sweep of human events as behavior.

Two major principles for describing human behavior. Many humanistic thinkers argue in favor of one grand principle for describing human behavior: the principle of actualization. Aside from the question of whether *any* single principle can be sufficient, I find that the particular principle of actualization *is* insufficient. In all the years of my applied practice, for example, I have been plagued by concerns about why actualization, as I understand it, is not occurring. Inevitably I come to the conclusion that there must be some principle, other than actualization, to describe why actualization is *not* occurring. To think this way is to be invoking some principle of not-actualization—perhaps some non-human, external "force" which acts to block actualization (cf. May, 1958b, p. 58). In this way, even by starting with a single grand principle of actualization, I have backed into at least two grand principles. Regardless of which single principle I have adopted, by itself it simply has not been enough. Always I have ended with at least two grand principles which work in concert with one another.

At the other extreme, one of the theoretical shortcomings of psychoanalytic theory, it seems to me, is its superfluity of explanatory principles. From the viewpoint of psychoanalytic theory, behavior is described as the resultant of many covarying forces (Waelder, 1960)—*too* many. There are too many forces operating in too many ways. In practice, I have found it unsatisfactory to adopt psychoanalysis' kaleidoscope of working principles, or humanism's monolithic actualization canon. One principle or a set? Actualization or some other? The solution must untangle the various options, although untangling options is not easy. For example, Farber argues that "... if we knew the independently defined principles of which such behaviors or behavioral characteristics are a function, we would dispense with such overarching concepts as self-actualization" (1964, p. 11). Farber thus argues *for* sets of working principles and links this to an argument *against* self-actualization, as if there were a choice between self-actualization and Farber's set of principles. It is my impression that these two arguments are not so closely linked, and that the two can be uncoupled and discussed in turn. If we did possess a *set* of *working* principles to account for behavior, one question is whether we could dispense with *overarching, general* principles. If it seems that we could, then the implications would constitute a double-edged sword, cutting off such overarching concepts as self-actualization on one stroke, and cutting off other overarching concepts such as reinforcement, conditioning, and learning with the other stroke. Since Farber works within a behavioristic framework, the implications of his argument might make for some serious changes close to home.

I do not see the argument in favor of sets of *working* principles as also an argument against a few *overarching grand* principles. Indeed, it seems to me that good overarching grand principles *lead* to sets of working principles in just the way Farber describes. Humanistic theory opts for a few grand overarching principles of human behavior *and* for logically derived sets of working principles. Nor do I see Farber's argument for sets of working principles as an argument against any *particular* single grand principle. We may define a set of working principles with or without actualization. We turn now to a discussion of the two major principles offered by humanistic theory for the description of human behavior.

Behavior and the Relationships Among Potentials

The first major principle of behavior is as follows: *Behavior is a means of establishing and maintaining with the external world the nature of the relationships among the person's potentials for experiencing*. This principle derives from the nature of relationships among potentials (Chapter 2) and from our conception of the way in which external worlds are constructed (Chapter 6). We may concretize this principle by considering the two kinds of relationships among potentials:

1. *If the relationships among potentials are disintegrative, then behavior*

serves to establish and maintain disintegrative relationships between the person and the external world. In order for behavior to carry out this function, the relationships among the person's potentials must be disintegrative, e.g. between OPI and DP2 (Figure 8.1). If the relationships are disintegrative, behavior then constructs an external world with which relationships are disintegrative. If I fear and hate my deeper potentials, then behavior will set about constructing a particular external world in which relationships are characterized by fear and hate. Why does the person behave in precisely those ways which establish relationships in which he is agonized, defeated, torn apart, rejected, tense, murdered, frightened, distressed? Why does the person have the facial expressions, say the words, go to the place, make the decision—all in such a way that the relationships are characterized by bad feelings? The answer suggested by our principle is that the person is behaving in just that way which will establish and maintain with the external world the same kind of bad-feelinged relationship which characterized the relationships among his own potentials.

2. *If the relationships among potentials are integrative, then behavior serves to establish and maintain integrative relationships between the person and the external world.* The person whose relationships among potentials are integrative will behave in ways which promote congruent, harmonious, loving, unified relationships in and with the external world.

Relationships Among Potentials as a Determinant of Human Behavior

The above principle tells us that the *content* of the potentials is less important than the nature of their relationships. It makes little difference whether the potentials involve the experiencing of sex, aggression, prestige, dependency, or affection—if the relationships are *disintegrative*, one set of behaviors will occur to establish and maintain disintegrative relationships with the external world. If the relationships among the *same* potentials were *integrative*, an entire new set of behaviors would occur, behaviors which serve to bring about integrative relationships with the external world.

The disintegrative or integrative nature of relationships can result in dramatic differences in behaviors which are apparently quite similar. When we attend to behavior, we notice that behaviors which are roughly similar—which seem alike on the surface—actually differ in subtle but dramatically significant ways if one is working toward constructing a disintegrative relationship and the other is working to build an integrative relationship. When behavior serves to construct a disintegrative relationship, it is creating distance, it is pushing away, it is erecting barriers, it is making the relationship hateful, angry, fearsome, bad. The person may be behaving in a way which could aptly be described as bawling out the fellow who works for him. Yet that behavior can either erect disintegrative barriers or establish an integrative relationship. The bawling out which effects a *disintegrative* relationship is different, has a different style, comes across differently, than the bawling out which builds an *integrative* relationship. The differences might be subtle. They may consist of differences in the key pauses, in the hardness of voice quality, in the presence or absence of facial warmth, in the nature of the eye contact. The differences may be subtle, but the *qualitative* differences are immense between roughly similar behaviors which build disintegrative versus integrative relationships.

The nature of the relationships invests behavior with its intention and goal-direction, constitutes the source of its activation and its direction, provides behavior with its meaning and its predictability (Maslow, 1970b). Understanding the causes and goals of behavior requires understanding of the relationships among potentials. This, for humanistic theory, replaces an inquiry into traumatic early events, inadequate social learnings (or conditionings or reinforcement contingencies), neurophysiological structure, body juices, social forces, or genetic programs.

If I am harmonious with the toughness in me (DP2, Figure 8.1), then the cause and the goal of my behavior may be to construct external tough relationships characterized by integrative harmony. I can bawl you out—and feel harmonious in the relationship; or I can behave so as to get you to bawl out or be bawled out—and feel harmonious in the relationship. Yet the cause and the goal of my behavior are the (harmonious) relationship I have with my toughness. It gets the behavior started, and it is that kind of relationship which the behavior achieves.

Melinda is terrified by her own deeper potential for throwing off her shackles, saying "NO!," objecting to being externally directed (DP2, Figure 8.1). That disintegrative relationship is the cause and the goal of her behavior. When she behaves as a frightened servant to her older son, it is because of this relationship. When she cries about the ways in which people step on her, it is because of this relationship. When she expresses dissatisfaction with her husband's brusqueness toward others, her behavior is caused by her relationship with the deeper potential.

This way of describing behavior is already present in self-concept theories, which divide personality into the person and the self, quite analogous to operating and deeper potentials. To a large extent, behavior is a function of the nature of the relationship between the person and his self, i.e., the self-concept. The nature of the relationship with one's self (or deeper potentials) will determine how one behaves in the world, how one perceives and acts toward oneself, and how one defends against and avoids that which might be contrary to the self-concept. Indeed, I believe it is fair to say that self-concept theories count on the nature of relationships among personality parts as the paramount causal determinant of behavior.

Once we recognize behavior as a function of the relationships among components of the personality system, this first principle can be found in many other theories of human behavior. In its general characteristics, our principle is akin to the principle of homeostasis and is, therefore, present in much of psychoanalytic thinking, in biophysiological theories of behavior, and in a considerable portion of behaviorism. According to the principle of homeostasis, personality includes physiological drives such as hunger or thirst. These physiological drives promote a state of tension which serves as a key factor in the production of human behavior. In both our principle and that of homeostasis, personality structure is composed of parts, a key feature is the nature of the relationship among these parts, and it is this relationship which accounts for behavior. It is a very old way of accounting for behavior, an old way which is commonplace in much of contemporary thinking—to describe behavior as a function of the relationship among "parts" of the personality "system." Behavior is understood on the basis of this general principle whether we consider general systems theory or orthodox psychoanalytic theory, in which the "parts" consist of ego, superego, and unconscious. It is the nature of their interrelationships which is paramount in the psychoanalytic understanding of human behavior.

The External World as an Extended Personality

As indicated in Figure 8.1, behavior occurs as a function of relationships between potentials only when the external world is constituted as the person's extended personality. One of the functions of an external world *as an extended personality* is to provide for the relationship among potentials (Figure 6.1). When the external world is the extension of my own pettiness, I can behave in ways which enable me to experience my relationship with my own pettiness. I can shun it, ridicule it, be plagued by it. Yet the behaviors which are involved (B2, B3, Figure 8.1) must occur in a world comprised of my own extended personality, externalized as the world in which I exist. I can shun pettiness only when I live in a world of pettiness; I can be plagued by pettiness only when my world is constituted of my own pettiness. Behavior which establishes and maintains a (disintegrative or integrative) relationship with my own pettiness must occur in a world which is constituted of my own extended personality.

In order for such behavior to carry out its task, it must continually be fashioning the world into being an extended personality. Thus we can untangle two threads which comprise behavior of this sort. One thread or function is to construct the world into being an extended personality—an extension of either the operating or the deeper potential. The second thread or function is to bring about the particular *relationship*—either disintegrative or integrative.

Unless the first function (i.e. constructing an extended personality) is carried out successfully, the second function cannot occur. If I fear and hate my own inner sexuality, I may set about fashioning an external world of sexuality. It is as if my behavior is determined by a template which programs my behavior to construct sexuality out there in the world. Whatever mode of construction I select (Figure 6.1), the degree of my success is gauged by the degree to which my constructed external world exhibits a point-by-point goodness of fit with my sexuality. The more exactly the constructed external world fits my own inner sexuality, the more successfully this behavior has done its job. It is an excellent job if the external world has the exact dimensions of my own sexuality, is a truly faithful representation.

As behavior fashions the external world into being an extension of my own potentials, it is simultaneously at work creating the right (disintegrative or integrative) relationship. As a result, such behavior is always working upon the external world, always doing things to the external world, always living in a relationship with the external world. The establishment and maintenance of relationships with the external world are, in other words, inevitably interpersonal, social, external-world-oriented affairs, working the way in that track between the person and the external world.

Behavior and the Irrelevance of Pleasure or Pain

The determinant of behavior is the nature of the relationships among potentials. If the relationship is integrative, behavior will construct an external world in which relationships are pleasing, harmonious, unified, loving. If the relationship is disintegrative, behavior will just as dutifully set about fashioning an external world in which relationships are disjunctive, fractionated, painful, disorganized. Behavior is the perfect servant, carrying out its defined mission without thinking. It just does its job as assigned by the nature of the relationships. Behavior is mindless, value-free, and utterly mechanical. It works just as effectively for disintegrative as for integrative relationships between potentials. It sets about creating external relationships in which we feel miserable or peaceful, agonized or intimate, good or bad. The nature of the internal relationships is the supreme boss, not whether the end result is toward pleasure and away from pain. In other words, if we try to make sense of behavior as somehow moving toward enhanced pleasure and reduced pain, behavior will seem confusing and haphazard, unlawful and convoluted. If we abandon the hoary pleasure-pain concept, and instead allow behavior to be understood as establishing and maintaining the nature of relationships among potentials, then, it seems to me, behavior is illuminated as understandable and orderly.

Here is where psychotherapists know something very fundamental about human behavior, namely, that human beings work industriously and with cunning effectiveness at arranging conditions in which they feel absolutely miserable. Yet many theories of personality cling steadfastly to the implicit assumption that human behavior moves inexorably, albeit in sometimes confusing ways, toward pleasure and away from pain. Many psychotherapists have abandoned such a conceptualization of human behavior. Instead, these psychotherapists know that human behavior is often painfully effective in its insidious pursuit of distress. Among contemporary psychotherapists who accurately correct personality theory on this basic point, Ellis (1959b, 1962, 1967) is especially relentless in naming the many ways in which human beings work single-mindedly toward self-induced misery.

Where many psychotherapists have abandoned the pleasure-pain concept of behavior, personality theorists who cling to this concept must invent some sort of counter-principle to explain the failure to seek pleasure and avoid pain. If so much of human behavior is painful and not pleasurable, some counter-principle must be found. Thus we have William James' law of repetition and Sigmund Freud's repetition compulsion to help explain so much of human behavior as directed unerringly toward misery, pain, and unhappiness. These and similar principles must be invented to accompany a basic principle that behavior is directed toward pleasure and away from pain. In sharp contrast, our principle does not create the problem of how to explain behavior which does not seek pleasure and avoid pain. We need no extra theoretical baggage because we do not adopt the pleasure-pain assumption. Behavior which moves toward the enhancement of pleasure, and behavior which moves toward the enhancement of pain, can all be incorporated under our single principle. Once the nature of the relationships among potentials is understood as disintegrative or integrative, we can make sense of behavior which seems to increase pleasure or to decrease pleasure, which seems to seek pain or avoid pain.

By linking behavior to the nature of relationships among potentials, we have no need for one set of principles of pleasure-seeking and another set of principles of pain-seeking. In addition, by linking behavior to relationships among potentials, we set behavior free from other concepts and principles which have traditionally entwined themselves confoundingly around the understanding of behavior. For example, there is no intrinsic force within human nature, no force which is simply there, and which directs behavior toward anything— pleasure, reduction of stress, integration, or whatever. By identifying the determinant as the relationship among potentials, we have no need for determining forces: human destiny, biological predispositions, laws of survival, or theological concepts of the nature and destiny of human beings. Nor do we need concepts of illness, psychopathology, abnormality, or other grand notions to explain how and why something went wrong. When internal relationships are disintegrative, behavior moves inexorably toward a *painful* state of external relationships; when internal relationships are integrative, behavior moves just as inexorably toward a *pleasurable* state of external relationships. I am almost inclined to conclude that it is just as simple as that.

Under our principle of behavior as a function of internal relationships, there is no puzzle to human behavior which seems to avoid pleasure and to seek pain. There is no "neurotic paradox" (Mowrer, 1948, 1950) to unravel. Such behavior presents itself as paradoxical only to those who hold to behavior as pleasure-seeking and pain-avoiding in some framework of natural law or scientific principles. Once we can profitably abandon that belief, the neurotic paradox dissolves away as an issue.

The pleasure-pain concept of human behavior is so ingrained, however, into our various psychologies, that it pops up here and there under all sorts of technical jargon. Some psychologies, for example, assume that human beings are endowed with an intrinsic tendency (or need) for positive regard (Rogers, 1959). Other psychologies rest on assumptions that human beings are endowed with some sort of natural process which moves them toward health, maturity, growth. Humanistic theory not only has no need for such assumptions, but flatly rejects their usefulness in explaining human behavior.

I suggest that much of human behavior is a *struggling toward* self-acceptance, self-regard, and self-understanding, is an *effort* toward winning the esteem of others, a *scratching after* understanding and love and closeness with others. But the key ingredient in all this is the restless urging, the effort, the struggle, the pursuit, the desperate scratching after. All of this is evidence of the near-universality of the awful internal disintegrative state which impels so many persons into the restless urgent pursuit after pleasure, esteem, happiness, love, closeness, satisfaction, positive self-regard—because their internal state is so devastatingly torn apart.

Yet, so commonly ingrained is the pleasure-pain concept, that many approaches explain pain-seeking behavior as evidence that something has gone wrong. Something must be amiss in the system which, if left alone to develop normally, would progress along the good path toward health, happiness, and pleasurable well-being. Something must have interfered or blocked normal development (Mahrer, 1967b, 1967c). Humanistic theory abandons such views. Human beings may easily gather pain and unhappiness to themselves without something going wrong with or interfering with some supposedly normal system. Once we abandon the pleasure-pain concept, we leave behind all notions of a normal personality system which ought to run well and provide pleasure. Yet this notion is so ingrained into our thinking that we almost unwittingly assume that the natural consequence of our behavior is some sort of pleasurable good feeling, and that the occurrence of a painful feeling is a symptom of something gone wrong. I doubt if many professional helpers are concerned about persons whose feelings are those of pleasure; only when the feelings are bad ones do professional persons try to "do something for" the person. Once a person evidences bad feelings, we wonder what went wrong.

If my internal relationships are disintegrative, then my behavior will naturally set about instituting the kinds of relationships in which I have heightened pain and reduced pleasure. All by myself I can construct the kind of external relationships in which I feel miserable, rejected, and anxious. If I hate and fear the deeper violence in me, I can do whatever is necessary to invite the world to be violated by me, or to be violent to me, or to fear and hate me as violent. In all of this I can successfully bring about the right conditions in which I feel terribly tense and anxious. No pleasure principle is at work here. I am not seeking pleasure and avoiding pain. I am merely instituting with the external world the disintegrative nature of my internal relationships.

In many approaches it is held that much of human behavior is directed toward or is motivated by the reduction of pain. Pain is described as an instigator to behavior. For example, many approaches understand much of human behavior as generated by anxiety in such a way that behavior is said to avoid the exacerbation of anxiety, and to promote the kinds of conditions which reduce anxiety. This notion is the same for any kind of bad feeling, so that, for example, depression is considered a common instigator to behavior which is supposed to work toward reducing the state of depression (Arieti, 1962; Ostow, 1960). Just as humanistic theory rejects the pleasure-pain concept, so are all such derivative notions also rejected. In our conception of behavior, once internal relationships are disintegrative, behavior acts to *institute* anxiety, not *avoid* it, to *bring about* depression, not reduce it, to *promote* pain, not be instigated by pain toward bringing about its removal. By fastening attention onto the nature of the relationships among potentials, a surprising preponderance of human behavior is seen as working toward some terrible consequences—and this runs directly counter to the grain of what many would like to believe about the fundamental direction of human behavior.

Much of psychoanalytic thinking, the thinking underlying learning theories and behavior modification approaches, and much of social anthropology agree that a considerable portion of human behavior aims to *avoid* (defend against, reduce) punishment, negative reinforcement, threat, loss of love and affection, and the eliciting of the annoyance or anger of others (e.g., McCall, 1968; Mowrer & Kluckholn, 1944; Wolberg, 1967). In flat contrast, humanistic theory proposes that disintegrative internal relationships lead precisely *toward* negative reinforcement, pain, unhappiness, misery, anguish, conflict, loss of love and affection, threat, punishment, and the eliciting of the annoyance and anger of others. Our theory rejects the assumption that human behavior tends to result in the reduction of excessive stimulation or discomfort or human suffering—when internal relationships are characterized by "excessive stimulation," discomfort, or suffering. Behavior does not defend against pain and punishment; it *promotes* pain and punishment when these constitute the nature of the internal relationships.

When these relationships are disintegrative, behavior works very hard to bring about a state which is often referred to as a state of "lack of gratification." To assume that behavior somehow works toward providing gratification is once again to accept the traditional assumption of behavior somehow dedicated toward pleasure (i.e., gratification) and away from pain. But the phrase "lack of gratification" refers to a very special state of affairs which behavior diligently works toward achieving when internal relationships are disintegrative. He was a young fellow who feared and hated his own deeper sexuality to such an extent that he lived in a sterilized world, cleansed free of any sexuality whatsoever. There was no sexual release, pleasure, or even excitement or arousal. In his world there was no hint of sex at all. His state was one of lack of sexual "gratification," yet this state constituted an achievement, a consequence of diligent hard work. Lack of sexual gratification means that he has behaved in just those ways which insure that his world is cauterized of sex. It does not mean that something has gone wrong, that he has a faulty learning history, or that he has "needs" which are somehow not adequately "gratified." Lack of gratification, along with pain, punishment, conflict, misery, and our whole platoon of bad-feelinged states, can be a product of behavior serving to bring about a distinctively disintegrative relationship.

Such behavior may also serve to heighten one's tension. What we refer to as tension, anxiety, or the "pressure of internal drives" may be precisely what behavior brings about—when internal relationships are such that they are characterized by tension, anxiety, and internal pressure. In this very important sense, our theory has no place for the pleasure-pain concept even when it takes the form of a basic principle of drive-reduction or tension-reduction. When internal relationships are disintegrative, behavior *increases* tension, not reduces it; behavior *increases* the pressure of drives, not reduces the pressure. In accepting the principle of behavior as a function of internal relationships, humanistic theory rejects the whole family of pleasure-pain behavior determinants, including behavior as tension-reduction and behavior as drive-reduction.

By invoking the old pleasure-pain concept, it is relatively easy to *categorize* behavior as enhancing pleasure and reducing pain. This behavior is good because it promotes pleasure; that behavior is not so good because it not only offers little pleasure, it is accompanied with heightened pain. By accepting a principle of internal relationships, the onus is transferred from the *behavior* to the *nature of the internal relationships*. Behaviors which seem opposite to one another may both be creating disintegrative relationships. If Joseph's relationship with his deeper independence is disintegrative, he may burrow deeper into the bosom of his family, taking care of his parents, being a "good boy" by helping around the house, being home most of the time. Yet the net result is a sense of unfulfillment, of missing things in life, of depression. On the other hand, doing the apparent opposite will also yield the same sorts of disintegrative feelings: leaving home, being on his own, no longer being the "good boy." It is the disintegrative nature of the internal relationships which determines the feeling state, and not whether he stays home or goes away.

I believe that when behavior is described in this way, understanding is cleaner, simpler, and more accurate. Once we no longer cling to the old pleasure-pain concept, and once we make sense of behavior by studying the nature of the internal relationships, we can forget about so many secondary principles which are derived from the pleasure-pain concept. Not only can we dispense with ideas of tension-reduction, lack of gratification, defending against threat, and blocking of normal development, but our description of so-called problem behavior can dispense with other secondary principles such as rigidity, inappropriate generalization, excessive motivational drive, or the persistence of the value of old rewards. We can describe the husband's distressing relationships with his wife as behavior caused (parsimoniously) by his own disintegrative internal relationships. He behaves in precisely those ways which institute with his wife the same disintegra-

tive relationships which occur between his own potentials. That is why he acts in just the right ways which elicit her punishment for his ineptness and his passivity. That is why he behaves in those ways which invoke her rejection of his affectionate overtures. If we cling to the pleasure-pain concept, then it is inviting to try to explain his behavior in convoluted lines of reasoning: Perhaps his behavior increases pain because of poor or inadequate learning; maybe his particular learning history explains his behaving in these painful ways; perhaps he cannot modify his behavior toward his wife because early rewards for particular responses to mother were so strong that he is now too rigid to develop a new set of responses to his wife. Our explanation suggests simply that his disintegrative relationships with his own dependency may lead to behavior which creates disintegrative relationships with his wife. We need not search his past history for ways in which something went wrong in his learning to account for the failure of his behavior tó lead toward enhanced pleasure and reduced pain.

Behavior and the Experiencing of Potentials

The first principle of behavior focused upon the nature of the relationships among potentials. Our second principle of behavior focuses upon the content of the potentials. According to the second principle, *behavior is a means of experiencing potentials* (Buhler, 1968b; Goldstein, 1939; Mahrer, 1967a; May, 1958b). I may have a *potential* for experiencing passivity or dominance or withdrawal or independence, but it is *behaviors* which enable these potentials to be experienced.

Here are behaviors whose function is no more than opening the way to simple, raw experiencing. Once we describe human beings in terms of various kinds of potentials for experiencing, then behavior becomes a simple gateway for the opening up of that experiencing. It is this characteristic of behavior which observers such as White (1959) note in the simple exploratory play activity of young children—behavior which does no more than offer a means of sheer, raw experiencing. This constitutes all there is to the intention or the function of behavior. This is all there is to the goal of behavior. Its intention, purpose, function and goal are to provide for the experiencing of potentials.

Experiencing as a Determinant of Human Behavior

One of the determinants of human behavior is the nature of the relationships among potentials. The second determinant is the nature of the experiencing, i.e., the content of the potentials linked to the behavior. Our aim is to make sense of behavior, to describe it well, to understand. We will now discuss three aspects of behavior, three ways in which understanding experiencing means understanding behavior. First we will discuss the connection between potentials and behavior, a connection which is so tight that understanding behavior requires a description of the connected potential. Second, we will discuss the increase in *feeling* which accompanies behavior, and, third, we will discuss the increase in *experiencing* which accompanies behavior.

An understanding of behavior requires an understanding of its potential for experiencing. So closely wedded are the behavior and the potential, that a good description of the behavior must take into account the nature of the potential. That is where the complications arise. To describe the intention or function or goal of a behavior requires a description of the nature of the potential whose experiencing the behavior serves. To understand behaviors as providing for experiencing means crossing the narrow gap between the behavior and its potential, and describing the nature of the experiencing. Careful description of the behaviors comprising "walking down the street" can be confined to a careful description of the behaviors themselves (Skinner, 1967). Yet the understanding of those behaviors is enormously increased when we include the nature of the coupled potential. We may maintain a strict distinction between the behavior and the potential. Yet, in contrast to Skinner, the understanding or full description of that behavior calls for a description of the walking down the street as a means of experiencing a reunion with one's brother who has returned from years of military service, or walking down the street to mail one's tax return. The two walking behaviors may be similar at the strict behavioral level, but enormously different when the description of mere behavior is expanded to include the nature of the potential which is experienced.

Mere description of behavior is sterile until the describer includes some description of the potential to which the behavior is linked. Whether our aim is description and understanding of the fellow walking down the street, or whether our aim is the scientific analysis of walking behavior in general, our perspective holds that it is fruitless to confine description to nothing but the mere behavior. Instead, humanistic theory would seek to obtain a rigorous description of both the behavior and the nature of the experiencing. One aim is to describe every bit of the total package of behavior which we refer to as walking, in the fellow moving down the street. In addition, we must seek the most careful description of the nature of the experiencing which is occurring as he is walking down the street. If the experiencing includes the explosion of warmth and affection for his brother, or a mixture of relief and guilt at finishing the income tax return, we are prepared to hypothesize that *significant differences occur between the two walking behaviors*.

We have distinguished between a behavior (B1, Figure 8.1) and the potential (OP1, Figure 8.1) whose experiencing it serves. The two are quite different, and it is important to distinguish very carefully between what one is doing and what one is experiencing in conjunction with that doing. We have asserted that it is the potential which gives a behavior its goal, its function, its intention and its purpose. We have said that description and understanding of the behavior itself require that we go beyond the behavior to include a description of the potential. At this point, proper description and understanding of a person's behavior call for adequate description and understanding of something which is not behavior, viz. of the experiencing which is linked to the behavior. A full, systematic understanding of stealing food from the grocery store, solving a problem in mathematics, or joining the group which is arguing in favor of the walkout requires both a description of the behaviors and a description of the nature of the experiencing.

One of the reasons for our assertions is that this way of describing behavior makes understandably clear sense of behavior. When the description and understanding of behavior focus exclusively on behavior, the science of human behavior is led into a series of tight little circles, going nowhere as a science. But this is only one of the reasons. Perhaps a more important reason is that I am prepared to hypothesize that *significant differences* occur among behaviors as a function of differences in experiencing potentials. If we knew how to study walking behavior in its most scientifically disclosing way, I suggest that walking down the street to meet one's long lost brother *is substantially different* from walking down the street to mail one's income tax return. The differences will be evident in the behaviors themselves, for I am convinced that behaviors differ as a function of their experiencing potentials. If we knew how to measure it, if we knew what to look for, we would know how one's stealing from the grocery store is different from another's stealing from the grocery store. If one's stealing were coupled with the experiencing of anger against the huge food companies, and another's stealing were accompanied with the experiencing of the sheer excitement of maybe being caught in the act, not only are the two *experiencings* different, but the two *behaviors* are different. Similar behaviors are therefore similar in the nature of the coupled potentials; when the potentials differ, the behavior will also differ—when we discover how to identify the differences.

Without notable exception, research on human behavior has concentrated upon the behavior itself, without wondering whether ostensibly similar behaviors differ in significant ways because they are tied to different experiencings. If our analysis is a worthwhile one, then one finger-pressing behavior differs from another finger-pressing behavior to the extent that experiencings differ in the two finger-pressings. Researchers are not studying the same behavior when experiencings differ. The proper study of human behavior would then group together as similar those behaviors which are coupled to the same experiencing. Indeed, I would suggest that similar experiencings would be a more useful unit of study than apparently similar behaviors which are likely to be quite different from one another in ways which have yet to be discovered. Behavioral researchers assume that they are studying the same behavior when all their subjects join the same political party, buy an economy car, engage in petty theft, turn to the left in a maze, check the same answer in a multiple choice questionnaire, stutter, achieve low grades in school, or get similar scores on a test of introversion, internal control, compliance, or intelligence. We have yet to frame a systematic means of identifying similar behaviors, and until we do, I submit that the preponderance of our behavioral research has committed a colossal error.

Behavior and the increase in good feelings of experiencing. There are good feelings which accompany the sheer experiencing of a potential (Chapter 2). As indicated in Figure 8.1, these feelings are signified by two positive signs within the circle representing the potential. The feelings which occur in connection with sheer experiencing are those of pleasure, aliveness, excitement, joy, vitality, buoyancy, giddiness, merriment, happiness, satisfaction, and a good bodily-felt tingling. They are quite wonderful bodily feelings, and only occur when a potential is experienced. Behaviors serve to provide for the experiencing of a potential. What this means is that to the extent that behaviors provide for experiencing, behaviors are accompanied with good bodily feelings. The *nature* of the behavior makes no difference at all. Nor does the nature of the potential make any difference with regard to the occurrence of the pleasurable good feelings of experiencing. As long as the right behaviors open the way for experiencing, any potential will do. In contrast to what might ordinarily be believed, good feelings of experiencing will occur when the person behaves so as to gain a full measure of altruism or selfishness, love or hate, openness or withdrawal, candidness or secrecy. The potential may be awful, mean, nasty, and rooted in evil—yet good feelings will accompany its experiencing.

Earlier I argued against a conception of behavior as directed toward pleasure and away from pain. Nevertheless, we must carefully note that by providing for experiencing, behavior also brings about the good feelings which accompany sheer experiencing. *Sheer experiencing is pleasurable.* As long as behavior provides for sheer experiencing, these good feelings will occur. Here then is a partial reinstatement of the old hedonic theory of behavior, recently put forth in a sophisticated form by Young (1955). Behavior which leads to the experiencing of potentials will be accompanied with the pleasurable good feelings of experiencing. These good pleasurable feelings bear no relationship to concepts of reward, reinforcement, positive self-regard, growth, maturity, tension-reduction, pain-avoidance, homeostasis, or need gratification.

If *any* behavior which provides for experiencing is accompanied with the good feelings of experiencing, we have arrived at an answer to the ancient "neurotic paradox," i.e., why it is that human behavior seems so frequently to be directed toward pain and misery. In describing behavior as a means of instituting the nature of the relationships among potentials, a portion of the answer was proposed. If these are disintegrative, then the consequence of behavior is pain and unhappiness. Now we may add more to our explanation of the propensity of human behavior to move the person ineluctably toward pain and unhappiness. All behavior—regardless of its nature—is accompanied with the good feelings of experiencing as long as the behavior provides for a measure of experiencing. Thus many behaviors (B1, Figure 8.1), which are painful in and of themselves, nevertheless serve to provide for the experiencing of potentials. To experience the potential of controlling others means that the person will have the good feelings of sheer experiencing. But the *behaviors* which provide for that experiencing may well be painful. For example, being depressed may be painful, but it constitutes a behavioral means of controlling one's family. Being frustrated may be unhappy, but it is a means of controlling others. Being crazy may be distressful, but it may be the right behavior for controlling others. Cutting one's wrists may be agonizing, but it may well control significant others. Here are simultaneous pain and pleasure—the pain contained in the behavior itself, and the pleasurable good feelings accompanying the experiencing of the potential. When we focus on the behavior, persons seem to behave in ways which promote pain. When we focus on the experienced potential, behavior seems to promote pleasure. All behavior, including painful behavior, serves to provide for the experiencing of a potential, and the experiencing is accompanied with a class of good feelings.

Many psychotherapists observe this somewhat puzzling sense of pleasure in the sheer experiencing of potentials. It has eluded personality theorists to describe what accounts for this good feeling in any systematic way, yet it is always there in the experiencing—regardless of the behavior which releases the experiencing, and regardless of the nature of the potential which is experienced. "In therapy . . . when awareness develops where it has been previously blocked, it does tend to be accompanied by a sense of release of tension and a feeling of increase in energy. The experience is in a sense pleasurable. Even when the developing awareness is of a painful affect such as mourning or anger, it is accompanied by a feeling of 'I want this; I'm glad it's happening even though it is painful'" (Enright, 1970, p. 118). I suggest that a profitable way of conceptualizing this is schematicized in Figure 3.1, in which movement from stages A to E is accompanied with the increasing proximity of the deeper potential to actual occurrence, to experiencing. It does not matter *what* is experienced; it does not matter what *behavior* launches the experience. Sheer experiencing is always and regularly accompanied with the good feelings of pleasure, aliveness, excitement, joy, vitality, buoyancy, giddiness, merriment, happiness, satisfaction, and good bodily felt tingling. These are indicated by the two positive signs within the circle of the potential (Figures 2.1, 3.1, 8.1).

Behavior and the increase in experiencing of the potential. When behavior occurs, one accompaniment is the increase in the *good feelings of sheer experiencing*. The second accompaniment of behavior is the increase in the *experiencing of the potential*. That is, I experience a greater measure of the nature of the potential. I may have a potential for affection (OP1, Figure 8.1), but I experience affection only by means of the right behavior. When that behavior occurs, I have a greater measure of sheer affection-experiencing. A clear differentiation exists between the good feelings of experiencing and the heightened experiencing of the potential itself. Yet the two are always occurring in concert. When I experience a heightened level of affection, I will always have the increased good feelings of increased experiencing. The two exist separately but occur together.

Each person has his own set of potentials for experiencing. Each person may have his own behavioral ways of providing for the experiencing of these potentials. Aside from these differences, all behavior which provides for the experiencing of the potential will be accompanied with the particular experiencing which constitutes the nature or content of the potential. That precise experiencing occurs—its level of experiencing increases—even though it is often terribly difficult to describe precisely the nature and content of the experiencing. When I drive the car fast I experience a kind of craziness, a wild explosiveness, a screaming powerfulness of breaking apart into millions of pieces at incredibly high speeds. Here is an approximation of my particular potential for experiencing. When it happens, there is a kind of increased saturation in this very special sort of experiencing. It is not loving affection or angry defiance or a sexual welling up. It is its own brand of experiencing.

Many writers have used words such as increased "tension" and increased "excitement" to describe what occurs in experiencing. To some extent, I believe that these writers are describing the good feelings which accompany experiencing, the feelings indicated by the two positive signs within each potential (Figure 8.1). There *is* a heightened sense of excitement which is part of the good feelings of sheer experiencing. But I believe that these writers are also describing something about the increase in experiencing itself—aside from the pleasurable good *feelings* of experiencing. When I have a potential for experiencing power or affection or defiance or sex, the actual experiencing of it is an increase in something which may as well be labeled tension or excitement. Goldstein (1939) speaks of the increased tension or excitement when actualization is occurring. White (1959) describes the heightened "tension" which accompanies the carrying out of certain motivations such as curiosity, manipulation, or exploration in young children. Maslow (1968) also describes actualization in terms of increased tension and excitement. In summarizing their work, Hebb (1949) and Hebb and Thompson (1954) conclude that behavior is likewise accompanied with an increase in tension and excitement. I join with these writers in noting that behavior which promotes experiencing is accompanied with *heightened*, increased tension and excitement, and not *reduced* or homeostatic tension (Gordon, 1966). I submit that this heightened tension or excitement refers to the increased level of sheer experiencing of the specific content of the potential.

Experiencing as a Potential, Not a Force

In their protest against traditional conceptions of human beings as mechanical and un-human, many humanistic followers have surrounded human beings with a romantic aura. In their protest against theories which have no place for the person in personality or for the human being in human behavior, many humanists have accepted the assumption that there is some grand force which guides and directs behavior. In contrast to the cold, mechanical, sterile, machine-like, "un-human" force which is held by many approaches, humanists have substituted a force which is good, saintly, benign, personal, and "human." Our humanistic theory has a different point of departure, one which understands mere potentials for experiencing. In our theory, there is no force of any kind—good or bad, human or un-human, machine-like or personal.

If my potential consists of experiencing passivity, that passivity is no more than a mere potential. If I am behaving in a way which provides for the experiencing of that potential, then I experience passivity. Our conceptualization has no place for any kind of added force. There is no driving quality to my passivity, no push or pull toward passivity, nothing which energizes my passivity. There is no force which is implied or intrinsic, which gets the experiencing of passivity started or which provides direction to my behavior. There is only a potential—with no drive, activation, arousal, energy, libido, psychic force, or generating push. Such characteristics, in one form or another, sweep across most theories of human behavior (Freeman, 1948; Freud, 1933; Hull, 1943; Lewin, 1935; Marx & Tombaugh, 1967; Matson, 1964), even though recent decades have witnessed a gradual increase of those who believe, as I do, that the force or drive concept is simply not adequate to account for human behavior (White, 1959).

The potential exists without any added characteristics of a force which either pushes behavior into happening or pulls behavior into happening. The push form of this force is referred to as drive, arousal, energy, libido, and so on. The pull form of this force is referred to in such words as reward and reinforcement. As a mere potential, experiencing does not have any added characteristic which occurs as rewards or reinforcements.

Earlier I referred to the humanists' version of the cold, inhuman, mechanical force to which they so vehemently object. Most commonly, these humanists invent their own force which urges motivations (tendencies, human potentials, authentic being) into actuality. Their version of this force has all the characteristics of a drive, arousal, push, pull, energy, need for reward or reinforcement, or seeking for environmental effects—in a good, flowering, almost caring way. This is the "... inherent tendency of the organism to develop all of its capacities in ways which serve to maintain or enhance the organism" (Rogers, 1959, p. 226). With only slight variations, this intrinsic force toward self-actualization or growth is an almost distinguishing feature of many humanists' conceptions of personality, wherein human nature is endowed with a force toward actualizing potentials, bringing forth creative possibilities (cf. Goldstein, 1963; Jung, 1933; Maslow, 1968, 1970b; May, 1958a; Rogers, 1959). In contrast, our version of humanistic theory includes no added overarching or intrinsic tendency (wish, push, pull, force, drive) urging human beings toward self-actualization, self-realization, authenticity, human potential, or self-fulfillment.

It may be reassuring to invoke such a force toward actualization. But I consider a tendency toward actualization as referring more to a wish or a desire on the part of humanists. Yet there is a sharp difference between a force toward actualization as a component of the personality structure of every one, and a wish or desire to become actualized. On this score, I take Maslow quite literally when he refers to this as a *desire*, a wish to become actualized, but one which he (un-

fortunately, I believe) elevates as a component of personality structure: "It refers to man's desire for self-fulfillment, namely, to the tendency for him to become actualized in what he is potentially. This
tendency might be phrased as a desire to become more and more
what one idiosyncratically is, to become everything that one is capable
of becoming" (Maslow, 1970b, p. 46). According to our humanistic
theory, personality structure includes a *capacity* for potentials to be
actualized—and, in this sense, for self-fulfillment, self-expression, becoming authentic, for realizing one's potentials. But there is no postulated force, somehow separate from us or intrinsic to either our humanness or our personality structure, bending or urging or guiding
us in that direction. The family of words and phrases surrounding
actualization refer to a possible path, not a push, not a force, and not
a ". . . basic tendency of the organism to actualize itself in accordance
with its nature" (Goldstein, 1939, p. 88). Within humanistic theory,
there is no place in the personality structure of human beings for
some basic tendency which itself is either within or outside of the personality structure. If the tendency toward self-actualization is a component of the personality structure of the human being, what is the
process by which the tendency toward self-actualization is itself actualized? If it is located within the structure of personality, it seems as if
it is a separate domain, and not really a part of the personality system.
Is it a person behind the person? Is it a force somehow outside of the
person? Is it somehow above and beyond the person, and yet so intimately entwined into the person that it is a tendency which is connected to all other tendencies which themselves are to be actualized? I
object to a tendency toward self-actualization which is both transcendent to human beings and yet an intrinsic component of human nature. I consider the tendency or force toward self-actualization as an
expression of a glorious hope on the part of some persons for all persons.

Implicitly and explicitly, belief in a force toward self-actualization is
coupled with a belief that what is inside is good and positive. This is
the conviction and hope in many humanists' description of personality: "From everything we can observe in humans and animals the basic
striving of the organism is inexorably toward health both physical and
mental . . . If an organism is free to do so, it *must* move in positive
ways" (Combs, 1966, p. 381). Not so! Our version of the above statement is: From everything we can observe in humans, human beings
behave in ways which institute the nature of the internal relationships—either integrative or disintegrative—and behave in ways which
provide for the experiencing of potentials. These ways can be positive
or negative, healthy or unhealthy. Our deeper potentials are positive,
are in a positive form, only within those persons whose relationships

are integrative. But for the predominance of persons whose internal relationships are disintegrative, the insides are negative, twisted, monstrously grotesque, sick, ugly and repulsive. I am inclined to consider romantic views of human destiny as an expression of a *fear* that human destiny is *not* positive—but is evil or purposeless or hellish. From our perspective, the insides of human personality are in whatever light the internal relationships cast them—from disintegrative to integrative.

With regard to human destiny, humanistic theory takes the position that there is no destiny. We have potential ways of being and becoming—but they are mere potentials, devoid of any force which inches us along in some direction. According to Teilhard de Chardin (1965), mankind is in the early stages of evolution toward a destiny which, as a future product of civilization, will include universal brotherly love. It may be reassuring to postulate some grand transcendent force in whose hands we are lovingly cupped, moving us gradually over the ages in the direction toward social maturity, but humanistic theory has no place for such a grand and glorious force. We can understand why persons will collectively invent such a force, yet it has no place in our theory as a determinant of human behavior.

The Fullness of Experiencing: A Measure of Behavioral Effectiveness

Behavior serves as a means of promoting experiencing. If I have a potential for experiencing control or affection or withdrawal, specific behaviors can provide for a slight measure of that experiencing or a complete measure of that experiencing. The degree to which a particular behavior provides experiencing is taken as one measure of its effectiveness. As discussed in Chapter 2, operating potentials are those to which behaviors are linked. An ineffective behavior is one which provides for no experiencing or a low degree of experiencing of the operating potential; a behavior which offers full experiencing of an operating potential is an effective behavior. Perhaps it is important to note what is *not* included in this criterion of behavioral effectiveness. First, the effectiveness of a behavior is independent of the nature of the potential. It does not matter whether the potential involves sadistic control or loving affection, nurturance or fierce competition. If I experience a full measure of sadistic control, the behavior is an effective one. Second, the effectiveness of a behavior is independent of the nature of the behavior. It may be a new behavior or an old one, a subtle nuance or a gross explosion, a socially prized or offensive one, a mundane or a bizarre one, one which is anchored solidly in reality or one which has no reality contact whatsoever (cf. Wolberg, 1954, p. 587). All that matters is the degree to which experiencing occurs. If experiencing is absent or minimal, the behavior is ineffective; if experiencing is occurring, to that degree the behavior is effective.

Behavior and the construction of appropriate situational contexts. Experiencing requires an appropriate situational context (Figure 8.1). If the external situation is highly appropriate, experiencing can occur in large measure; if the external situation is inappropriate, experiencing can only occur minimally or not at all. Behavior is continuously at work constructing a world in which experiencing can occur. But the process of building the external world is enormously complicated, and there is no insurance whatsoever that behavior will be successful in constructing a situational context maximally congenial to full experiencing. Behaviors vary all across a dimension from low to high appropriateness of the constructed situational context. Effective behaviors are those which construct a situational context which is highly appropriate for a given experiencing; ineffective behaviors are those which construct a situational context which is quite inappropriate for that experiencing.

Tony is at work constructing a proper situational context for the experiencing of leaving, deserting, ending it all. He is quite skilled in constructing the right situational context for such experiencing. He seeks and finds women like Nora, women whom he hurts repeatedly by leading them on and then disappointing them. After disappearing for a few days, he suddenly shows up at Nora's apartment, mentioning nothing about his absence. She is hurt. He inquires what is wrong, and she angrily tells him that he ought to know. Tony becomes frustrated by what he calls her bad mood, and storms about the kitchen. Nora begins crying and asks him to forgive her. Here is the right moment, the appropriate situational context. He saunters to the door, looks coldly at her and walks out—for good. With these final behaviors he is filled with the experiencing of leaving, deserting, ending it all. His behavior is quite effective in constructing the appropriate situational context, a final culmination of a whole series of orchestrated behaviors designed to build the kind of situation in which a significant measure of experiencing can occur.

When a really appropriate situational context is compared with one which is fantasied or imagined, the former almost always offers a greater degree of experiencing. As skilled as Tony is in building the right situational context for the above experiencing, he is far less skilled in constructing an appropriate context for the experiencing of being swallowed up by a voracious competent older woman. His sexual experiencing calls for a woman who is big and seasoned, with whom he is pulled in, drawn into a vortex, losing himself in her. This kind of experiencing occurs during masturbation, accompanied with this as one of a few favorite fantasies into which he enters as he masturbates. To a mild degree, this potential could be experienced in masturbatory fantasies, but only to a mild degree, for ". . . in real sexual excitement he needs an object to become satisfied with. Henceforth, masturbation is not a completely satisfying method" (Fenichel, 1954e, p. 84). For most potentials, fantasied or imagined situations offer a lower ceiling of experiencing than what may be termed actual or real situations. Ordinarily, effective behaviors construct realistic concrete situations which foster high levels of experiencing. Whatever the degree of experiencing Tony achieves in his masturbatory fantasies, there would be far more experiencing with the actual woman in an actual situation.

The more we know about the exact nature of the potential for experiencing, the more we can gauge the degree of appropriateness of the constructed situational context. What is more, we can then come to appreciate how sadly ineffective is most human behavior. The situations which behaviors build are pitifully poor approximations of those which would provide for higher levels of experiencing. When Tony was nearly eight years old, his mother was pregnant with the second child. Even then, Tony's potential for experiencing called for a big, experienced woman who would wholly surround him, pull him into and inside her, into whom he is drawn, inside whom he is lost. At that time, Tony behaved in ways which offered only a moderate level of experiencing. He found some of mother's clothes and dressed himself in her housecoat, her girdle, her stockings, and two of her dresses. Behaviors which constructed this kind of a situational context offered a rather moderate to low level of possible experiencing. Although such "transvestite" behavior is relatively common in a child whose mother is pregnant or when there is a new baby in the home (e.g. Dupont, 1968), the ceiling of potential experiencing is usually low or only moderate.

Highly appropriate situational contexts are skillful accomplishments, and the typical run of constructed situational contexts provide anything but full experiencing. In this sense, most normal everyday *behaviors* are quite ineffective, building and maintaining life situations which allow for low levels of experiencing. The same is true of behaviors which seem to be dramatic and bizarre, yet which build situational contexts in which experiencing can never reach full proportions. She is a 17-year-old adolescent whose experiencing involves pushing aside her rival mother and regaining her sexualized father. In the space of a few months she builds her world into that of a hospital wherein she engages in little girl play and fantasies along a theme of eliminating mother and capturing father. Soon she acts like a baby, with baby postures, speech, enuresis, untidiness, inability to feed herself, and generally taking on the being of a baby. She has constructed a situational context which provides only a modicum of experiencing of that potential. This case, taken from Masserman (1961), exemplifies dramatic and bizarre "regressive" behavior which, nonetheless, is ineffective in providing for full experiencing.

If my potential involves the experiencing of loving tears, the simple pouring out of love, only very particular behaviors can construct the appropriate situational contexts. Fenichel (1954a) describes a case in which that specific experiencing is brought about by behavior which constructs a kind of altruistic situation wherein one is so good to others that their response of loving appreciation completes the appropriate situational context. The stage is now set for the person to experience loving tears. To the extent that the behaviors are successful in constructing precisely the right situation they are effective; otherwise, something less than the appropriate situational context is constructed, and the ceiling on experiencing is reduced.

One parameter of effective behavior has been recognized by adherents of the client-centered (Rogers, 1967a) and Gestalt (Fagan & Shepherd, 1970) schools of psychotherapy, viz. the appropriate situational context has an immediate "here-and-now-ness." Truly effective behaviors work upon fashioning an immediate present situation. As Rogers says, to revert to some other (less appropriate) situation is to enter the "there and then," and such behaviors tend to offer significantly reduced levels of experiencing. Regardless of the nature of the effective behaviors—whether they are dramatic or mundane, socially abhorred or socially valued—as a class they construct immediately present situational contexts.

Indeed, so powerful is this characteristic of behavior that all behavior can be described as efforts toward constructing an *immediate* situational context for experiencing. Approached from this perspective, illumination is cast upon a considerable portion of behavior which otherwise is ignored and unappreciated. For example, what is the nature of the immediate situational context when a patient recounts anamnesic material? The patient is doing much more than recounting past events, for the patient is hard at work constructing some sort of *immediate* situational context. When we consider only those situational contexts which involve the constructing of a particular relationship with the therapist, the patient may be constructing a situation in which to experience avoidance of threatening material just beginning to present itself, or pleasing the therapist by offering the kind of case history which would satisfy the therapist, or offering the therapist the precious gift of the-story-of-my-life, or winning the therapist's sympathy, or pointing an accusatory finger at the bad parents, or suggesting to the therapist how very unique and special a person the patient is. "The case history is primarily a creation of the patient in social interaction with his therapist, the psychiatric social worker, or the persons with whom he comes in contact. From this it follows as a logical consequence that the patient may produce different case histories with different therapists and under different stress situations. It also follows that the correspondence between the case history and the patient's 'real' life is conjectural and perhaps, ultimately, impossible of solution unless the adjective 'real' be given acceptable definition" (Bucklew, 1968, p. 158).

What Bucklew notes with regard to the recitation of anamnesic material in the therapeutic context can be generalized to all behavior whose understanding is enhanced by careful attention to the nature of the constructed *immediate* situational context. To focus description and understanding upon the mere content of the person's behavior (e.g., recounting personal history material) and to ignore the situation-building component of such behavior is to commit what I term the *content error* (Mahrer, 1970f)—confusing the content of the verbal behavior with the situation-building component. To the extent that all behavior works toward constructing an *immediate* situational context for the promotion of experiencing, we have gained an advantage in grasping understanding of the behavior, and we are enabled to assess the degree to which the behavior is effective in providing for experiencing.

By being alert to the immediate situation-building component of behavior, we see that talking about the past is itself a behavior which is engaged in building a situation. Not to see this effect of talking-about-the-past behavior is to commit the content error. However, to step back away from the content of what the person is saying, and, instead, to see the kind of situation which is being constructed by the person saying those words, is to observe the functional center of much behavior. Suddenly it becomes clear that the behavior (e.g., telling about the delights of stealing candies from the candy store when you were seven years old) is building an immediate situation wherein experiencing can occur. Furthermore, we observe a yawning gap between the experiencing which is *actually being promoted* and the experiencing which is being *referred to* by the talk about past events. Telling about stealing candy may build a situational context in which the person experiences being the entertainer with interesting old stories, or avoiding possible confrontations by telling cute little stories, or experiencing increasing intimacy by exchanging stories about childhood. Yet none of these three experiencings has anything to do with experiencing the stealing of candies. Increasingly it becomes clear that experiencing stealing candies from the candy store cannot be accomplished effectively by telling *about* stealing candies from the store. Talking about the past is a notoriously ineffective behavioral means of experiencing what you are talking about. How may *this* be accomplished? What are effective behavioral means of constructing an appropriate situational context in which past experiences may be experienced?

One way of accomplishing this, a way which is congruent with humanistic theory, is to live in the immediate, here-and-now *past* situational context. The trick is to leave the present situational context, in which you talk *about* the past, and to enter fully into the "past" as an immediately ongoing, here-and-now present. This trick is known by psychotherapists of many persuasions who know that experiencing is robust only when the patient lives that old experience in the *immediate present*. In psychoanalysis the adult woman experiences the past relationship with her parents by transferring (i.e., transference phenomenon) that past relationship onto her present relationship with her therapist. In Gestalt therapy, "The therapist encourages her to stay there by saying, 'Could you be a little girl now?' She already is. The therapist is merely permitting her to openly acknowledge it. 'Close your eyes and speak to your parents about what it's like to be constantly shut up'" (Kempler, 1968, p. 89). Behavior is effective in promoting experiencing in past situations to the extent that the behavior is successful in enabling the person to make the past situation an immediate live and ongoing present one.

We assess the effectiveness of behavior by gauging the degree to which the behavior constructs the appropriate situational context for a particular kind of experiencing. To look at behavior in this way allows us to make sense of a great deal of behavior. Now we can understand, for example, that a whole series of behaviors is aimed at creating a situational context for the experiencing of being helped by others. Behaving in such a way that one becomes a patient in a mental hospital is illuminated as merely one of a family of behaviors aimed at constructing a situation of being helped. It is not that the behavior (trying to kill oneself, seeing visions of devils, being unable to feed oneself) is maladjustive or symptomatic of some illness; instead, the behavior is just one of a series of attempts to construct an appropriate situational context. Much of psychotherapy research can then be reinterpreted to indicate that many persons finally enter into some sort of professional helping relationship only as a final culmination of a career of trying to seek help from friends, acquaintances, social institutions, clergymen, medical healers, attorneys, teachers, family, and others (Bergin, 1963; Eysenck, 1952, 1960a, Mahrer, 1970c). We can scale these help-seeking behaviors on a dimension of effectiveness in the construction of an appropriate context wherein the experiencing can occur. Understanding the behavior becomes a matter of understanding the kind of experiencing which is enabled by the kind of situational context constructed by the behavior.

Behaviors do not simply occur—behaviors like being mute, fencing against attempts by others to communicate with you, talking in be-fuddling incoherencies. If the nature of the potential experiencing consists of the sense of separation and withdrawal, these behaviors are effective only if they construct the right situational context. Some of the best situational contexts include the people where you work, your angry spouse, or the staff of the hospital. If these behaviors manage to construct the right situational context, they can be quite effective in promoting experiencing; if they fail to construct the right situational context, their effectiveness may be quite low. Merely being unreach-able or withdrawn or being in one's own world may offer a low degree of experiencing unless these behaviors also construct the right situa-tional context which includes the right other person. Haley (1963) re-lies heavily on the defined situation with the defined other person in his strategies for treating withdrawn "schizophrenics" by reversing the whole process: ". . . it is necessary to persuade or force the patient to respond in such a way that he is consistently indicating what kind of relationship he has with the therapist instead of indicating that what he does is not *in response to the therapist*" (p. 102).

When we know the nature of the person's experiencing and the nature of the appropriate situational context for that experiencing by that person, we can assess the degree of experiencing which can pos-sibly occur in the context of psychotherapy. If, for example, the pa-tient's experiencing consists of being fully forgiven, and we know that the fullest degree of experiencing requires a situational context of mother to the patient as a little girl, then the psychotherapeutic situa-tion has a defined ceiling on the degree to which that precise ex-periencing can occur. When psychoanalytic psychotherapists work with the patient to construct a transference relationship, that particu-lar experiencing can occur only up to a particular point. No matter how skilled both patient and psychotherapist are in trying to construct the right situational context, it falls far short of what experiencing *can be* in the optimally appropriate situational context wherein the patient is a little girl with mother in the very special and very appropriate situational context. To seek forgiveness from the therapist-as-mother is always less experiencing-promoting than seeking forgiveness from the actual mother in the actual situation. Behaviors which seek out the therapist are, therefore, of limited effectiveness in building the right situation for the fullest possible experiencing of that which requires some other situational context for full and complete experiencing.

Freud's discovery of the transference neurosis was an ironic dou-ble-edged sword. The patient built the relationship with the analyst into dramatic reinstatements of early traumatic relationships with highly significant others. In this sense, the transference neurosis was an expression of the deeper processes of the patient. But no matter how strong were the transference feelings, they were far less than those which would accompany the real experiencing in the real situation with the real significant figures. Thus the psychoanalytic transference relationship brought psychotherapy a long way toward enhanced therapeutic experiencing, but the very nature of the patient-analyst relationship meant that the true situational context could never be reached. Accordingly, the career of the transference relationship as an effective therapeutic technique was foreshortened from its inception. Fenichel saw this clearly (1953f, 1954b) in his brilliant description of the resistance component to transference. In falling easily into a transference, the patient avoids the present by wallowing in the past. By transferring elements of the past onto the present therapeutic relationship, the patient curtails experiencing of both the past and the present relationships. Fenichel saw that in many ways the transference experience interfered with the immediate therapeutic aims of psychoanalysis. Unfortunately, his solution was to cling to interpretation in the hopes that the patient would gain insight into his own transference as resistance. From our perspective, the transference relationship with the analyst detoured potential *full* experiencing into partial experiencing with the analyst (who could never fully be the right significant figure) in the analytic situation (which could never fully be the appropriate situational context). Our way out is to work constantly toward constructing the veridical situational context for the patient to undergo *full* experiencing, and the guideline is that the appropriate situational context is generally not that of the psychotherapeutic situation. To the extent that the patient's behaviors work toward constructing situational contexts appropriate for *full* experiencing, we can assist the patient in his work, rather than funnelling all his behavior into the therapy situation—which, from our viewpoint, is not usually the most appropriate context for full experiencing.

An experiential psychotherapy can be formulated which enables the patient to maximize the effectiveness of his behaviors in their task of constructing the most appropriate situational context. On this score the strategic question which is uppermost is how to enable the patient to construct that most appropriate situational context—rather than how to improve the art of interpretation or establish the right therapeutic relationship or find the cues which link to some particular behavior of the patient. All the traditional ways of seeking effective psychotherapy are set aside in this search. Instead, the question for each action of the therapist is how that enables the patient to enter into the most appropriate situational context for that specific kind of experiencing. For example, the right context may be that of being fully forgiven by mother when the patient as a young girl was being especially mean and cruel to mother. Experiencing of being forgiven can be found to occur to an enormously heightened degree by enabling the patient completely to live in that situation, rather than the truncated experiencing which occurs in the endless talking *about* it, or even the muted undergoing of it in the transference relationship.

Behavior and the construction of an extended personality. As indicated in Figure 6.1, behavior provides for experiencing by constructing the external world into serving the function of being the context in which the experiencing can occur. The more the behavior constructs the appropriate situational context, the greater is the experiencing. That is one parameter of effective behaviors. If we return to Figure 6.1, behavior also provides for experiencing by constructing the external world which serves as the extension of the operating potential and as the extension of the deeper potential. When my behavior (B3, Figure 8.1) constructs the external world into serving as the extension of my *operating* potential, I gain a measure of that experiencing. When my behavior (B2, Figure 8.1) constructs the external world into serving as an extension of my *deeper* potential, I gain a measure of that experiencing also.

As indicated in Figure 6.1, the only way in which I can experience relationships among potentials is to construct the external world into being the extension of my operating or deeper potentials. If I fear and hate my deeper potential for helplessness and cute dependency (DP2, Figure 8.1), I can construct the external world into babies or puppies (Extended DP2, Figure 8.1) by means of particular behaviors (B2, Figure 8.1), and then fear and hate those babies and puppies. I can also construct the external world into being the extension of my own operating potential (Extended OP1, Figure 8.1), by means of particular behaviors (B3, Figure 8.1), so that the external world fears and hates my helplessness and cute dependency in the same way I fear and hate that deeper potential. Behaviors which accomplish this are constructing relationships among potentials. These relationships are indicated as the channels in which behaviors B2 and B3 occur in Figure 8.1.

When we turn to the experiencing of potentials, and not relationships, we are again invoking behaviors B2, B3, and B1 (Figure 8.1), for the experiencing is brought about both by behaviors which construct appropriate situational contexts *and* by behaviors which construct externalizations of potentials. If we return to Figure 6.1, we see that each of the four modes of constructing an externalized potential—each mode of building the external world as an extended operating or deeper potential—is a means of providing for experiencing. As long as I have a potential for experiencing sexuality, I experience that sexuality regardless of which mode is used to build that sexuality into the external world. (a) I can experience sexuality by receiving sexuality which intrudes itself from the external world onto me. When you are sexual to me or make sexual overtures to me, I experience sexuality by means of my receiving behavior. (b) I can experience sexuality by utilizing your ready-made sexuality. For example, I can behave so as to seek out you who are sexual. (c) I can behave conjointly with you so as to evoke your own sexuality. I behave so as to turn you, move you in just the right ways, engage in the right dance with you so that you bring forth your sexuality. (d) I can fabricate an external world which is the externalization of my sexual potential. I can manufacture a highly sexual child, or I can have sexual delusions or hallucinations. By means of the four ways of constructing an external world, my behavior can build my sexual potential into the external world, and the net result is the experiencing of sexuality.

Regardless of which mode of construction is used to build my extended potential, the sheer degree of experiencing is increased to the degree that the constructed externalization is a *good representation* of the potential. I am continually at work, building the external world into being my extended personality. But that effort does not mean that I am successful. To be successful, the extension of my personality must be faithful and true, a creation which is a veridical representation of the nature of my experiencing. Not only are the precise form and nature of my sexual potential different from yours, but it is an exceedingly rare piece of artistic genius for me to construct my external world into being a point-by-point reproduction of the exact form and nature of my sexual experiencing. If the form and nature consists of physically assaultive domination into a state of passive sexual surrender, then the degree of sheer experiencing is rather low if my behavior builds an external world consisting of sweet young things in romantic coupling, or round robin trade-offs with six couples whom we know, or homosexual encounters with pre-pubertal young boys. If these are the products of my efforts to extend my personality into the external world, then the ceiling on my experiencing is low. Most behavior is relatively ineffective in building the external world into a point-by-point exact replica of my potential, and is therefore relatively ineffective in providing for a high degree of experiencing.

Even if I succeed in constructing the external world into a good approximation of my potential, the degree of experiencing is less than complete. When I gain my experiencing only through you (as my extended personality), the degree of experiencing can be high, but always less than complete. I may have a son who is the extension of my potential when he physically assaults a woman whom he dominates into a state of passive physical surrender. When I watch him doing this, or am raptly attentive to his detailed description of this act, I may gain considerable experiencing, but the degree of complete experiencing is always less than a situation in which *I* am the active participant. Huge proportions of human beings gain a measure of their experiencing by constructing approximations of their potentials in the form of extensions of their personality—as friends, children, plays and movies, magazines and books, groups and organizations, spouses and parents. Yet that degree of obtained experiencing is always less than complete, for they are gaining the experiencing through an extended personality.

All of these behaviors are social behaviors. Indeed, a great deal of what is considered social behavior consists of the building of an external world as extensions of our own potentials so as to provide a measure of experiencing (Boss, 1963, pp. 35-41). Here is much of the basis for our interpersonal behavior (Haley, 1963), i.e., to experience through that other person what we do not experience directly, but only through behaviors which make the other person into our own extensions. In this important sense, our social interpersonal behavior achieves its goal to the degree that the external world is a good approximation of our own potentials, rather than to the degree that the behavior gains sources of instinctive gratifications whose resources lie within the external world (cf. Munroe, 1955, p. 74).

Behavior and three modes of active involvement with the external world. The degree of effectiveness of behavior is a function of the degree to which the person is actively engaged in a direct involvement with the external world. When we consider a given potential for experiencing, there are at least three modes through which the person can be involved in external world relationships. The first mode offers only a mild degree of possible experiencing; the second offers a moderate degree of possible experiencing; only in the third mode can experiencing be high.

In the first mode, you are the *observer*. You do not participate directly. You are there, watching. Your behaviors are those which construct the external world as an extension of your personality, as discussed above, but your role is that of mere observer of that extended personality which you have constructed. If the potential relates to sexuality, you are no more than a witness to sexuality which occurs in your world, but without your participation. You observe sexuality in your animal who fornicates with another animal—while you watch, and experience sexuality mildly. You observe sexuality in the adolescents in your community. Sexual experiencing occurs in muted fashion as you observe sexuality on the stage, the movie screen, on television, in novels and pornographic magazines. In your dreams, you are in the role of observer while others are engaging in sexuality. In this first mode, the experiencing is turned on, but the level is low. Behavior which places you in this position is only slightly effective in enabling experiencing to occur. If this is the way you spend your life, your behavior is barely effective.

In the second mode, the external world is the active initiator. It is the external world which gets it all started, which is the activator, the controller, the generator, the preponderant doer. Your role is to be the passive participant, the one who is activated, generated, made to do things. You are the activated partner. With regard to sexuality, it is the external world which does the sexualizing to you. Regardless of the exact nature of the sexual experiencing, it is being done by the other person, while you are the involved other. Even when the experiencing involves passivity—such as *being* seduced or *being* sexually assaulted—experiencing is only moderate when that occurs in the other person rather than in you. In the dream, here is when the dreamer is involved and engaged in the sexuality, but the experiencing is occurring within the other person rather than you. If the nature of the sexual experiencing has to do with being seduced, it is the other person who is seduced, while you may move from being an observer to being the seducer. If the nature of the sexual experiencing is explosive, lusty, wild abandonment, all that is going on in your partner rather than in you. In this mode, the degree of experiencing is moderate, and can only reach moderateness. The behaviors which create this second mode of active involvement with the external world can offer a moderate degree of experiencing, greater than the first mode, but less than what is available in the third mode.

In the third mode, the person is the doer, the activator, the one who gets things started. The person is engaged in the same relationship as in the second mode, only the roles are reversed. The person is the active one in the interaction—active in the sense that the nature of the experiencing resides within the person, and not in the interactive partner. Here again we must carefully distinguish between the (active or passive) nature of the experiencing and the person as the locus of that experiencing. With regard to sexuality, for example, it is clear that you yourself house the explosive, lusty, wild sexual abandonment. But it is also you who houses the experience when it consists of being seduced or experiencing what it is like to be sexually assaulted. In these latter kinds of experiencings, you must be the active one who initiates and activates the passive being done to. You get it started. You are the one who governs the passive being seduced. You are the one who hurls yourself into being seduced or sexually assaulted. You are the active initiator of the passive sexual experiencing. You are the one who gets it started, who moves the interaction into conjointly having it occur, who is the one who activates the co-participation.

Experiencing is highest under this third mode. The behavior which employs this third mode is the most effective experience-promoting behavior. As a psychotherapist, I find a common progression in dreams from those signifying less effective behavior to those employing most effective behavior. I find this progression in dreams which first illuminate experiencing in which the person is an observer, then the passive receiver in the interaction, and, finally culminating in the kind of dream in which the person is the active initiator in the interactive experiential relationship. In all three kinds of dreams, the nature of the experiencing remains constant, but the change is from the first to the second to the third mode of active involvement with the external world.

Behavior and directionality: self-directed or other-directed. Behavior is more effective in promoting experiencing, if it is other-directed—directed onto and into the external world. Behavior is less effective in promoting experiencing when it is directed onto and into the person himself. The key to effective experiencing is the degree to which the behavior plugs into the external world.

It is important to understand that some behavior seems to be self-directed, but that apparent self-direction is aimed at engagement into and onto the external world. I can stand in front of the window and be lost in my own thoughts. Although this behavior seems to be self-directed, it is nevertheless hurled into the external world if it does things to you—for example, if it infuriates you because thereby I am not listening to you, or it scares you because I am thereby not telling you my private thoughts, or if I make you anxious because you thereby worry about my becoming depressed and suicidal. I can slice my wrist with a knife, yet, although that behavior is self-directed in a sense, its overriding direction is external to the extent that my experiencing is hatefulness at you for making my life so miserable. I can affect my relationship with you by spending many hours by myself, by drinking myself into oblivion, by giving myself drugs, by masturbating myself, by shooting myself, by eating five banana splits. Such self-directed behavior can, nevertheless, be targeted upon the external world.

If we keep in mind that some behaviors are other-directed and some are self-directed, then the degree of potential experiencing is higher for other-directed behavior. Experiencing is increased when the behavior moves outward, when it engages into the external world. No matter what I experience by doing "it" to myself, the degree of experiencing increases when I do it within the context of the external world. For example, sexual experiencing has a lower ceiling when it is autoerotic. More specifically, masturbation can only yield a moderate degree of experiencing when it is carried out in a wholly self-directed way. Whatever the nature of the experiencing, it will occur to a greater extent when the behavior is plugged into the external world; otherwise it lacks direct experiential contact with the external world (Fenichel, 1954e, p. 84).

Quite often, the fantasies accompanying masturbation open the way for heightened experiencing. If the experiencing consists of the delights of voyeurism, then the person can achieve a degree of experiencing by masturbating to an accompanying fantasy of secretly watching the woman undress. Our principle suggests that a greater level of experiencing can be reached when the behavior consists of *actual* voyeuristic practice. Heightened experiential contact with the external world also occurs when penis-directed behavior is converted to other-person-directed behavior. Many persons who masturbate do to themselves what would yield greater experiencing if it were directed into the external world. For example, the experiencing of sexually arousing a woman is frequently turned onto oneself, so that the person gains a measure of sexually arousing a woman by means of sexually arousing himself. He holds a penis which is soft and flaccid, and energetically works it up to a feverish pitch of high sexual arousal until he achieves ejaculation. That experiencing can be significantly increased if the self-directed behavior were to become externally directed, i.e., if he were to arouse a woman (instead of his penis) to heights of feverish sexual excitement.

From the perspective of degree of potential experiencing, masturbation is generally a behavior of only moderate effectiveness. Whatever the degree of experiencing achieved through masturbatory behavior, it is likely that the experiencing would be heightened when the external world is engaged. In contrast, Fenichel (1954e) treats masturbation as "abnormal" except under a few prescribed conditions—when it occurs only seldom, under conditions where there is an absence of a suitable object, or during childhood when the appropriate other person is also unavailable. I do not employ a dimension of normal-abnormal, yet I would suggest that for most experiencings, masturbatory behavior is of limited effectiveness as a means of providing for the highest levels of experiencing.

At times the change from self-directed to external-directed interaction leads to dramatic consequences. For example, a woman in her late twenties gained a measure of experiencing nurturance by living in a self-contained world in which she was both provider and receiver. Throughout her life she was a highly obese person, never able to lose weight for any extended period. The dramatic change occurred when she opened this experiencing to external involvement by providing food for another, and also by receiving food from the other person. When the experiencing of nurturance dilated to include the external world, not only was the sheer degree of that experiencing dramatically heightened, but there was a sudden and dramatic loss of weight which endured for the first time in her life.

If the potential relates to the experiencing of being fertile, full, pregnant, she can gain a measure of that experiencing by feeding herself and filling out the body in what has been termed a "symbolic pregnancy." But the ceiling on such experiencing is less when it is brought about through self-directed behavior than through interpersonal relationships with the external world. When obesity occurs in relation to potentials for pregnancy and nurturance (Deri, 1955), the ceiling on such experiencing is higher in other-directed interaction and lower in self-directed interaction.

Behavior and the degree of contact with the external world. With regard to experiencing, behaviors are more effective if they are other-directed rather than self-directed. Of other-directed behavior, however, some are more effective and some are less effective in the degree to which they achieve contact with the external world. The highest ceiling on experiencing occurs when behaviors succeed in achieving a full contact with the external world. These behaviors complete the linkage, the connection into the external world. In contrast, many behaviors—indeed, I suspect that most of our behaviors—have a low degree of contact with the external world. They are abortive, token, incomplete, faint-hearted, "symbolic," gestural. Many of these are cognitions, going on primarily in one's head, and doing nothing to the external world. Of the many fine virtues of thoughts, noble as they are, thoughts are terribly ineffective *behaviors* with regard to plugging into full and complete experiential contact with the external world. The greater the sheer contact with the external world, the greater is the effectiveness of the behavior in promoting experiencing.

High contact with reality means that the person must reach out and lovingly caress the other's face. When that happens, experiencing has a chance of being high. At the other extreme—and that is where most behavior is—experiencing is low when the person thinks about doing it, or talks about doing it, or there is nothing but a little twitch in the arm muscles, or the hand trembles, or the hand lurches out awkwardly, or the caress is unsmooth, or the person gestures by fondling a cigarette instead.

One class of behaviors which have good contact with the external world—and which thereby offer a high experiential yield—may be termed external focusing, or directed external attention. Experiencing will be enabled to reach new heights to the extent that the person gains contact with external reality by a concentrated focused centering of attention upon the key element in the external world. If the person whom you caress is your mother, then let your full attention target itself upon her. Focus your awareness upon her face. Stare at it fixedly. Look at her left eye. Pour every bit of your focused attention into seeing her left eye. Notice the opening up of a sense of heightened experiencing as you succeed in achieving this contact with such a tiny bit of external reality. You may experience discomfort or affection or tears or a sense of fullness or a cold chill down your spine or a sudden lust or a burst of defiance. Whatever experiencing is there is hurled into happening to the extent that your centered attention locks fully onto the external world. Here is a special class of behaviors which contain the possibility of effectively promoting heightened experiencing by increasing the degree of contact with the external world.

Every psychotherapeutic approach which utilizes experiencing as an explicit or implicit agent of change provides a way for the person to fasten focused attention upon a meaningful aspect of the external world. This is the kernel of effective psychoanalytic interpretation. Without this good conjoining of the person's focused attention upon the meaningful aspect of the external world, the therapeutic impact of psychoanalytic interpretation is more or less lost. "Since interpretation means helping something unconscious to become conscious by naming it at the moment it is striving to break through, effective interpretations can be given only at one specific point, namely, where the patient's immediate interest is momentarily centered" (Fenichel, 1945, p. 25). Behavior is effective in promoting experiencing to the extent that it centers the person's interest, funnels and focuses the awareness onto a meaningful external object, achieves contact with the external world.

So, too, in methods of meditation and contemplation. The inner world of experiencing can be released when one's attention is adequately hooked onto an external focal point. The effective behavior is the proper focusing of one's full attention upon a point in the external world, which might be the tip of one's nose (Wilhelm, 1962) or the flame of a candle.

Behavior and the degree of being the potential. In Chapter 2, I spoke of the sense of conscious awareness. It was stated that behavior comes from one operating potential (OP1, Figure 2.1), but that this sense of conscious awareness may be centered anywhere in the zone indicated by the dotted lines in Figure 2.1. What this means is that the person can be completely "poured" into the operating potential which is behaving, can "be" that potential fully and completely. Under these conditions, behavior is effective in promoting full experiencing. On the other hand, this degree of experiencing cannot be attained when the person is not fully being that potential; that is, when the person (I-ness, self, conscious awareness) is *not* within the experiencing potential. Under these circumstances, the center of the self stands to the side and has thoughts and reactions to what the experiencing potential is doing. When you are *aware* of what you are doing, split into one part undergoing experiencing and another part standing by, behavior cannot be effective in promoting full experiencing.

One experiences sexuality (or sarcasm or passivity or openness) fully only by fully being it, by throwing one's self fully into that experiencing, by the center of one's self being that experiencing. Experiencing is truncated when the person refers to that (usually deeper) potential and acts upon the integrative or disintegrative relationship toward it: "I am ashamed of being sexual . . . Look how sexual I am . . . I am pleased by my sarcasm . . . If I could only guard against being so sarcastic . . . I am coming to accept my passivity . . . When I am open it makes me feel vulnerable . . ." One must, instead, surrender into being the experiencing about which one talks. To talk *about* it provides for far less experiencing than *being* it.

In terms of providing for a full measure of experiencing, sheer insight or understanding are virtually useless. A person may see that his inability to express aggression to a parental figure is the way he is and, furthermore, is causally linked to infantile fears and guilt, but such insight offers the most insignificant experiencing of either the aggression or the fear and guilt (Whitaker & Malone, 1953). It is the right *behavior* (not insight) which can offer the fuller experiencing of the aggression toward parental figures. There comes a time when insight or understanding are simply not enough to provide for experiencing. It is at this point that humanistic theory and behavior modification are in accord, for both champion the necessity of behaving. Both find insight or understanding, or even the *consideration* of what is "within," as irrelevant. The important step is doing it, behaving. Only then will the potential be experienced. This holds for any kind of experiencing, whether in education, psychotherapy, the acquisition of new skills, or simple everyday living: Experiencing fully means fully being the potential in the carrying out of the right behavior.

Fully being the potential can be gauged by the sense of good feelings accompanying the experiencing, the pleasure, aliveness, excitement, buoyancy, vitality, joy, ecstasy, thrill, exhilaration, giddiness, merriment, happiness, and satisfaction. It may involve screaming it or somehow *doing* it just as fully as possible, until the entire body reverberates with these felt bodily feelings.

We all possess this capacity to throw ourselves fully into being the experienced potential. It is a capacity which is forever available although we may or may not know about it, and may or may not ever call upon it. It is this capacity which Binswanger (1958a, pp. 197-198) refers to as the capacity to design one's self. In this regard, one may either surrender into fully being the operating or the deeper potential. It is the deeper potential which is far more difficult to experience directly, yet it is the use of the capacity to surrender into fully being the deeper potential which sets into motion the capacity to design one's self. Truly effective behaviors, the highest plateau of effective behaviors, are those which promote the complete experiencing of ever deeper potentials.

9

The Behavioral Circle

As discussed in Chapter 8, behavior is understood on the basis of two principles. Under one principle, behavior serves to institute with the external world the (integrative or disintegrative) nature of relationships among potentials. Under the second principle, behavior serves to promote experiencing of potentials. The purpose of this chapter is to orchestrate these two principles in the understanding of human behavior. We intend to answer the following questions: How do the two principles work together in the description and understanding of human behavior? What determines whether behavior serves to establish relationships among potentials or to provide for experiencing?

If behavior is promoting the experiencing of a potential, all of our observations indicate that soon the behavior shifts in some direction. Certainly that behavior does not merely continue to promote that particular experiencing. Behavior changes, and I have puzzled as to why and how any given behavior changes over the course of a few seconds or minutes, and certainly hours and years. Why is it that the behavior changes? What accounts for the end of behavior which is providing for the experiencing of one potential or for the creation of a particular kind of relationship among potentials? Right now I am at work constructing you into being my friend with whom I am sharing easy intimacies, and yet in a few minutes I may be behaving so as to experience a sense of silliness. What accounts for this ever-changing flow of one behavior into another? What is it that reroutes behavior from one principle onto another? How may we describe behavioral change? The purpose of this chapter is to provide answers to these questions from the perspective of humanistic theory.

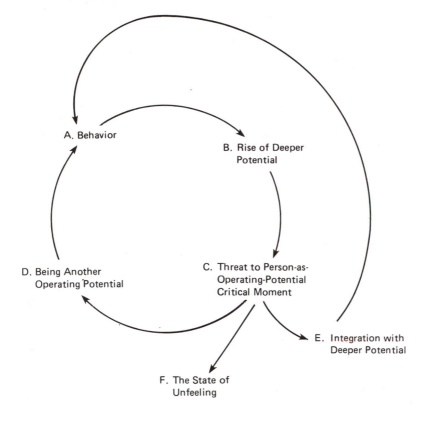

Figure 9.1 The Behavioral Circle

THE CONSEQUENCE OF BEHAVIOR

Let us begin at that point where behavior is occurring. This is indicated as *Behavior* in Figure 9.1. As indicated in that figure, the consequence of behavior—any behavior—is the rising of the deeper potential. Behavior may be serving to institute the nature of the relationships among potentials, or it may be serving to provide for experiencing. Regardless of the principle under which the behavior operates, our thesis is that the behavior is followed by the rising of the deeper potential.

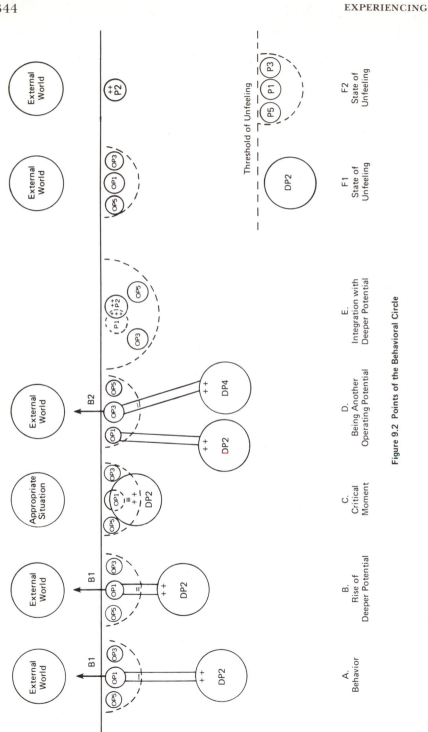

Figure 9.2 Points of the Behavioral Circle

Behavior as a Means of Experiencing Potentials

If we look closely at behavior which works toward the experiencing of a potential, our schema (Figure 9.2) indicates that the degree to which that behavior achieves experiencing is regularly accompanied by that degree of the rising of the deeper potential (DP2, Figure 9.2). Because the only way for that deeper potential to gain its experiencing is by way of the operating potential, behavior which provides for the experiencing of the operating potential also provides for the experiencing of the deeper potential. When the operating potential is being experienced, the deeper potential rises up a bit (B, Figure 9.2).

Suppose that the operating potential involves the experiencing of closeness, and the deeper potential involves sexuality. If the nature of the relationships is moderately integrative, then it can be seen that behavior which provides for the experiencing of closeness also serves to raise upward the potentiality for experiencing sexuality. It is as if the deeper potential says, "Good, I am starting to breathe some experiential life. The door is opening." When the relationships are even somewhat integrative, it is as if the channel of the relationships is ajar so that experiencing at the operating level easily transmits to experiencing at the deeper level.

If we focus our attention on the operating potential, a point may come where the behavior has provided for a great deal of experiencing. Almost always, this means that the external conditions which provide for the experiencing of the operating motivation are quite good, and the operating potential is on the threshold of its own version of success. If we could converse with that potential, it might be saying that everything it had ever wanted is just about to occur. Here researchers and clinical observers note something very interesting which commonly occurs. On the verge of its greatest success, the potential frequently is flooded with strange and uncomfortable feelings. According to our schema (B, Figure 9.2), what is occurring is that the very success of the operating potential is not only leading to the full and complete experiencing of the operating potential, but, what is more, that very experiencing is bringing upward the deeper potential. This same change occurs when the seducer is on the verge of a successful seduction, when the painter is just about to complete the fine painting, when the politician has nearly won his important election, when the boy is completing his long-awaited pubertal rites, when the woman has just delivered the baby she wanted so much, when the businessman finally gains control over the business, when the race is just about to be won, when the prison sentence is about to be completed. There is evidence of a peculiar intensification of problems when the student is on the verge of graduation (Karr & Mahrer,

1972), and this same phenomenon often occurs when, from our perspective, the experiencing of the operating potential reaches toward full saturation. When this is occurring, our description is that the deeper potential is on the rise. We will return to a fuller analysis of these kinds of special moments.

In the above examples, the relationships between operating and deeper potentials have been presumed to be integrative, and experiencing of the operating potential is accompanied by a rising of the deeper potential. This same upward rising of the deeper potential takes place also when the relationships are *disintegrative*. Suppose that relationships are disintegrative between the operating potential for experiencing closeness and the deeper potential for experiencing sexuality. According to our schema (Figures 9.1 and 9.2), the deeper potential will also rise consonant to the increased experiencing of the closeness, even when relationships are negative. Some experiential life is still breathed into the deeper sexuality. Indeed, to whatever extent the person experiences closeness, the deeper sexuality will tend to rise upward toward the operating level.

Consider the older man sitting dejectedly on the hospital ward. The operating potential involves the experiencing of regaining his wife, having her back again. His deeper potential includes the experiencing of control and domination of her. Our thesis is that the experiencing of the operating potential will lead to the rising up of the deeper potential whether their relationships are integrative or disintegrative. He was admitted to the hospital after his neighbors found him sitting withdrawn and uncomprehending in the front yard of his small house, drenched from the cold rain. He had been there for hours, not stirring. His wife had left him a few days earlier, and he had not eaten at all. After he was taken to the hospital, his wife was notified and asked to visit him. If we narrow our frame of reference to special moments when the operating potential is experienced to a significant extent, we see them in the hospital, and she is wavering toward going back to live with him. In these moments, he reaches out to hold her hand, and looks at her in a way which evokes her responsive concern. It is during these moments that he experiences having her back once again. And it is during these moments of fuller operating experiencing that the deeper potential is stirred. It does not matter whether the regaining of the wife (OP1, Figure 9.2) bears an integrative relationship with the deeper domination—is harmoniously related to it, relates to the domination in a welcoming manner—or whether the operating potential avoids the deeper domination, fends it off and is a means of suppressing or denying it. In either condition, the deeper potential rises upwards during those special moments when he gains a fuller measure of being close with her, bringing her back with him once again.

Susan was 14 years old, and behaved in ways that provided for a mild degree of experiencing being nurturant, caring, taking care of. She was characterized by a deeper potential for being the queen, replacing mother, being the head woman. Seldom, if ever, had Susan experienced this deeper potential. One day her mother went to bed in the afternoon. She had a terrible headache. Susan volunteered to make the evening meal. As Susan prepared the meal for her family, instructed her younger sister and brother to set the table, and soothed her baby brother who simply wanted to be held a while, Susan gained a large measure of experiencing the sense of being nurturant and caring. At the same time, the deeper potential was bestirred. By virtue of the enhanced experiencing of the operating potential, the deeper potential began its rise toward the operating surface (B, Figure 9.2).

As the operating potentials are experienced, deeper potentials begin to rise. This process may be compared with Maslow's (1968, 1970b) description of the hierarchical ordering of motivations. According to Maslow, one must first gratify needs such as those for water, food, sleep, safety, belongingness, identification, respect, prestige, and close love relationships. Until these needs are gratified, one cannot move ahead to function on the basis of the next echelon of needs. Basically, this is the conception adopted by humanistic theory, viz. the relationships are functional in that the next potential is raised through the experiencing of the first. Boss (1963, pp. 5-27) follows this same paradigm in his description of a patient whose surface potential involved the fending off of others. This was accomplished by having hallucinations. The deeper potential consisted of the experiencing of childishness. Still further below was the potential for experiencing erotic femininity. Upward movement of each of these three potentials occurs through the experiencing of the surface (operating) potential. When the surface hallucinations were brought forth into fuller experiencing, the next potential was thereby raised toward the operating level so that the patient was ready for childish kicking, squealing, and sucking her thumb. In humanistic theory, as well as the conceptions of Maslow and Boss, experiencing of the operating potential serves to activate the deeper potentials and brings them closer to the operating level.

Very often, full experiencing of the operating potential leads to dramatic changes as the deeper potential is raised upward. The person who experiences confusion (at the operating level) mildly may not affect the deeper potential for being taken care of and nurtured. But when the person is fully and completely experiencing the utter confusion, that higher degree of experiencing raises upward the deeper potential, and dramatic changes occur. Bergin (1963) notes that professional persons mistake this kind of change as "spontaneous remission," because it occurs without formal treatment—and also because we generally are puzzled by what may have brought about the change. Yet what has occurred is that the experiencing of confusion increased to a point where the person was now ready to experience the deeper potential for being cared for. From the outside, it appears as if some dramatic change has taken place, for where there was increasing confusion, the person is now "clear." But we also notice that now the person is being cared for—and that caring can involve a friend, a neighbor, a member of the family, expressed concern from a spouse, words of understanding from a ward attendant or another hospitalized patient. No formal "treatment" has occurred at all, yet what has occurred is dramatic and significant, but not puzzling.

In a rather vague and curious way, the field of psychotherapy has implicitly respected heightened experiencing of operating potentials. Whatever is happening right now, let it happen. If you can, try to facilitate its occurrence. If the patient is crying, let the crying occur. Respect the crying. Something precious is happening. The experiencing of the operating potential accomplishes something more. Deeper in the personality, the deeper potential is stirring. It begins to be activated by what is occurring at the operating level of experiencing.

Conceptual robustness: the prediction of new behavior. If behavior serves to provide for experiencing, and if experiencing means that the deeper potential rises upward, then we have a conceptual model for predicting the appearance of new behavior which may seldom if ever have occurred before. The full experiencing of closeness may lead to the appearance of sexual behavior. The full experiencing of regaining one's wife may lead to the appearance of controlling and dominating behavior. By fully experiencing the sense of being nurturant and caring, Susan soon behaved in utterly new ways expressing her being the queen of the household. By conceptualizing personality in terms of operating and deeper potentials, and by understanding that the experiencing of the operating potential leads to the rising up of the deeper potential, we are in position to predict the occurrence of new behavior. I submit that behavioral theories are without concepts sufficient to enable such predictions, if only because they contain nothing analogous to deeper potentials which rise consonant with the experiencing of operating potentials. Behavioral theories are not able to predict what is going to happen next—if what is indeed going to happen next has not occurred previously. As raw behavior, one walking behavior may look very much like another walking behavior, and the behavioral theories may have no way of distinguishing the two. By understanding the underlying deeper potential, however, we may regard one walking behavior as the precursor of defiant rage, while the second walking behavior may be a precursor of tender affection. By understanding behavior as providing for experiencing, and by understanding experiencing of an operating potential as leading to the rising up of the deeper potential, we can predict what can be in store for the person—even when what is in store is new.

The consequence of avoidance and denial. As long as the experiencing of the operating potential occurs, the deeper potential rises. There are no exceptions. Perhaps the most dramatic situation is that in which relationships between the potentials are disintegrative in such a way that the operating potential sets out to prove that it is not the deeper potential, to deny the deeper potential, to be its opposite. To deny the deeper wild explosiveness, the operating person is slow and careful, highly organized and unspontaneous. To deny the deeper rebellious defiance, the operating potential involves a willing cooperativeness. To avoid and deny a deeper plainness and willing conformity, the person operates as an unusual character, multi-talented and quite special. Yet, even under these circumstances, the principle nevertheless applies, viz. the more the operating potential is experienced, the more the deeper potential rises.

Virtually all the depth theories of human beings make the same central observation. Struggles toward avoiding what is within only manage to bring one closer to it. The very attempt to deny and avoid what is within is a personal acknowledgement of the deeper potential. Therefore the struggle against it only enlivens it. To the extent that one experiences the operating lie, the deeper truth comes to life. There is this special sort of alliance between polar operating and deeper potentials so that the latter always profits by the success of the former. The two have an agreement such that they advance together. When I experience that I am not mean or not dumb or not crazy, I raise upward by that amount my feared inner meanness or stupidity or craziness.

In more graphic language, the more you struggle against what is within, the more you capitulate to it. The more you run from it, the more it surrounds you. The more you writhe against its control, the more you fall into its clutches. "The more stubbornly (dictatorially) the human being opposes his being-thrown into his existence and therewith into existence in general, the more strongly this thrownness gains in influence" (Binswanger, 1958a, pp. 339-340).

With this perspective, the general aim of psychoanalysis must be questioned; ". . . we may say that analysis is always right in theory in its claim to cure neurosis by ensuring control over instinct" (Freud,

1953b, p. 331). The struggle for control over instinct insures the continued existence and growth of the instinct (or deeper potential). In
the very act of controlling, the careful observer will sense the lambent
shining through of the deeper potential.

Behavior as a Means of Instituting Relationships Among Potentials

We have been discussing the consequence of behavior understood
on the basis of the first principle of behavior, viz. to provide for the
experiencing of potentials. It was held that the consequence of such
behavior is the rising up of the deeper potential (B, Figure 9.1). Now
we turn to behavior understood on the basis of the second principle,
viz. behavior serves to establish and maintain with the external world
the (integrative or disintegrative) nature of relationships among potentials. Our thesis is that the consequence of such behavior is likewise
the rising of the deeper potential (B, Figure 9.1; B, Figure 9.2).

Behavior understood in terms of this second principle may construct the deeper potential as an extension into the external world.
Once having constructed the external world into being the extension
of the deeper potential, the person then institutes the integrative or
disintegrative relationship with it. If the deeper potential (DP2, Figure
9.2) involves the experiencing of greediness, I may construct greediness in the external world, and then proceed to fear and hate that
greediness. Under these conditions, I gain a measure of experiencing
the greediness as it exists in the external world. When I see you trying
to hoard money and to acquire even more money, I am experiencing
my own greediness. When I draw back from your greediness, when I
am critical of you for being so greedy, I am experiencing my own
greediness. By creating conditions such that I experience my own
deeper greediness, the inevitable consequence is the rising up of my own
deeper potential.

There is a paradoxical twist to all this. I tend to construct the external world as the *extension* of my deeper potential which I fear and
hate. Yet the very behavioral act of constructing externalized greediness and instituting disintegrative relationships with it *also* serves to
promote its rising up within me! No matter what principle my behavior follows, the attempt to draw back from it, to avoid and deny it,
nevertheless succeeds in its rising up within me.

Behavior operating under this principle can construct the external
world into being either the externalized *deeper* potential or the externalized *operating* potential. If I fear and hate my deeper greediness, I
may construct the external world into being an externalization of my
own operating potential, and the external world will then fear and
hate me in the same way I fear and hate my own greediness. In this

enterprise, there is likewise a measure of experiencing of the deeper greediness, and, as a consequence, the deeper potential rises up. Regardless of the manner in which the relationships among potentials are instituted in the external world, the inevitable consequence is the rising up of the deeper potential.

We have seen that any behavior, operating under any of the two major principles, results in the upward movement of the deeper potential. So regular and inevitable is this coupling that it may be stated as a "law" of human behavior: Human behavior which provides for experiencing of potentials or for the experiencing of relationships among potentials tends to be followed by the rising up of the deeper potential (B, Figures 9.1, 9.2).

Operating potentials serve two functions: (a) They *enhance* the experiencing of the deeper potential. (b) They *reduce* the experiencing of the deeper potential. These two functions seem to be opposite to one another. Now we see that whatever the operating potential tries to accomplish with regard to the deeper potential, whichever function it serves, the consequence is the rising up of the deeper potential. Thus the two apparently opposite functions turn round upon one another, and meet in their both resulting in the rising of the deeper potential. When the operating potential acts to *provide for* and enhance the deeper potential, the latter rises upwards. Yet when the operating potential tries to *reduce* the experiencing of the deeper potential, all of its maneuvers to avoid and deny, to suppress and turn away from, culminate in the selfsame rising up of the deeper potential.

THE CONSEQUENCE OF THE RISING DEEPER POTENTIAL

As indicated in Figure 9.1, once the deeper potential rises, the next step is that the operating potential will be threatened (C, Figure 9.1). Threat will occur with a kind of ponderous regularity, regardless of the nature of the potentials, regardless of the nature of their relationships.

The Threat of Death of the Person-as-Operating-Potential

From the perspective of the operating potential, the upward rise of the deeper potential means the radical change of the operating potential, the closing off of its present existence (Boss, 1963; May, Angel & Ellenberger, 1958; Wheelwright, 1956), the certainty of its own death (Ellenberger, 1958, p. 118; May, 1958b, p. 50). To the person-as-operating-potential, the tragedy of human existence is that through sheer experiencing one's own existence is drawn toward a close.

In this state, the deepest core of the sense of self faces the closing off of its fundamental existence, for the personhood now lives in a condition of absolute precariousness (Laing, 1960). What I am and who I am is now in question. My independence and autonomy are endangered. I no longer am a person who will continue, who has permanence and cohesiveness. The very core of the I-ness which is me is closing out. Here is the fundamental threat in which I exist in the most precarious way. This threat pervades one's entire world. Not only am *I* faced with the rising threat of imminent non-being, but cracks begin to occur in the *whole world* in which I exist. Everything falls apart. My world had been reasonably stable and predictable, although it was unhappy and painful. But now the whole foundation of my world starts to shudder and to reel toward utter chaos in ". . . a shattering of the present experienced 'world-structure' . . ." (Jourard, 1968, p. 154).

Little wonder that the person will do just about anything to get out of this state (Holt, 1968). The threat goes beyond mere bad feelings which the person experiences (see Chapter 3)—beyond pain or anxiety or depression. Confronted with the harshest of all realities—one's own insides—there is no alternative to the death of one's self. This is the underlying theme which May (1967) finds in the Oedipal drama wherein the horrifying awfulness resides in the deeper truth of becoming one's own inner self, and the absolute necessity of the death of the person whom you are. If I become *that*, then "I" die. In illuminating this theme to the Oedipal drama, May argues that the awfulness of this truth exceeds the awfulness of insight (or knowledge or consciousness) into the truth of what one really is. It is easier for me to accept (have insight into) my unconscious instincts than to accept the consequence of that acceptance, viz. "my" own death.

By my own efforts I have created a state in which my own existence is threatened. The very success which I achieve now threatens to close off my existence. Within psychoanalysis, there is a phenomenon known as the "success neurosis." I suggest that this phenomenon is merely a more conspicuous form of this phase of the behavioral circle, a phase in which the rising up of the deeper potential brings with it the threat of the end of the operating potential. The person who works hard to achieve a promotion may no longer exist if the promotion occurs. The person who waits for the day that he will be released from prison may sabotage this release just before his sentence is completed. The student slaves to get the high grades necessary for acceptance into graduate school, and then begins to become depressed and anxious when it begins to look like she will succeed. The doctoral student powers her way through her doctoral studies and then takes so long with her thesis that it looks like she will never graduate. In each of these examples the person has worked hard to achieve a goal, but

the goal will mean the end of the person who worked toward achieving the goal. Little wonder that we observe the phenomena known as
the "success neurosis," for the more the operating potential experiences success, the more the inevitably rising deeper potential threatens
to bring the operating potential to its end.

Almost without exception, this consequence (C, Figures 9.1, 9.2) is
omitted in approaches which speak of movement toward gratification
or need satisfaction or goal-direction. Our very process leads to the
threatened closing out of that sector of the personality which was instrumental in seeking the goal or satisfying the need or gaining the
gratification. As indicated in C (Figure 9.2), the increasing proximity
of the deeper potential means the eclipsing of the person-as-operating-potential, its death. How understandable that no matter where we
turn the fear of death is there. Every time we gain a measure of experiencing, we face the specter of our own death. Behind every face
of the threat—behind our fears and anxieties and tensions lurks the
selfsame fear of death (e.g. Caprio, 1950; Klein, 1948; Stekel, 1949;
Tillich, 1952; Zilboorg, 1943). Our hypothesis is that the fear of death
acquires its universality from the continual ebbing and flowing of the
deeper potential. Thus the face of death which we are always encountering is that of being eclipsed by our own deeper potentials.

The Threat of Transformation into the Person-as-Deeper-Potential

One consequence of the rising deeper potential is that the person I
am will die, my existence ended. But even more, I will die in a very
special way: I will be engulfed (Laing, 1960), invaded, filled by that
which is the deeper potential.

No matter where I turn, no matter what I do, my own behaving
brings the deeper potential into a looming confrontation with the person whom I am. I sense that the intruder is different, alien. I sense
that if it enters further into me there will be change, a drastic change,
in the person I am. The threat is the possibility of undergoing that
wrenching change. And yet the threat is a threat because I know the
truth represented by the deeper potential, for it is not a haphazard
thing rising up within me. It has awesome meaning because that rising
deeper potential contains the power of truth—it *is* a deeper me. When
I recoil from the murderous craziness in me, I sense its unbending
reality. There *is* a murderous craziness in me, and here it is now, on
the verge of replacing the person I am with a new person *whom I could
all too easily be*. Although I recoil in horror from that rising deeper
potential, I have a strange and fascinating bond with its content. It is
the person I (in a larger and frightening meaning of I) *could be*—provided that the whole of the person I know myself to be plunges out of .

existence. I do not want to know what that deeper potential is like because this sense of self which I am is strangely fascinated by the prospects of leaving me and slipping into being the deeper potential. That murderous craziness *is* another me, one which invites all my personhood to ooze out of being the person I am, and to take up a wholly new personhood as the murderous craziness. The result is that *I* die. There is no more to the sense of self, the consciousness I now am.

The catastrophic error that human beings commit is compressing our existence into this tiny and insignificant part of the whole world of our personality. In Figure 2.1 the outer periphery of my self (consciousness, awareness, personhood, being) is signified by the dotted elipse encompassing the operating potentials. The center of my self is limited to this tiny corner of my entire personality. How tragic it is that I battle for maintaining the existence of such a tiny and worthless piece of all that I could be. But of course the person I am only knows the domain of this personhood and knows, in my own little way of knowing, that the end of this little piece is the end of my self. Boss (1963, p. 20) implores the patient: "To be filled with apprehension, as you are, and to hear nothing but death and destruction on every hand, can only mean one is still imprisoned in the error of believing one's own neurotic egocentric world to be the sole possibility of existence and that when this shows signs of cracking, it means the crack of doom." Yet this is precisely what the patient-as-operating-potential does know as the complete truth.

The shattering of my present existence is, then, only one face of the threat of the rising deeper potential. Another face is the complete and total being of that which looms at me as the deeper potential. As it intrudes itself into me, I am presented with only its leading edge, and I see that bad form of its behavioral, pictorialized image. For certain I will go mad and become a crazy homicidal maniac. The heart of the awful terror is more than the closing out of the person I am, more than even being that bad behavioral form. I can be mad and crazy. I can even carry out acts of murder. But I must be this way *as myself*. I must remain my own enduring personhood in being mad, crazy, homicidal. What is absolutely terrifying is the complete switch in personhood. That is the ultimate core of the threat. It is no longer being *me*, but surrendering—dying—and being the deeper other self.

There is a moment, in relating with another individual, when one may teeter on the edge of losing one's self in the other. It is a moment of being too close, a moment when the person senses that he is on the verge of losing himself in the other, of being absorbed into the other—and no longer existing (Laing, 1960). These are very special dizzifying moments. One step further and one is folded into the being of the other person. One's own existence is closed out as the person is enfolded into the other. This is the very mildest form of the threat of being transformed into something else, of wholly losing one's self in the other.

It is interesting that this state of affairs, so feared by the person who begins to see the looming deeper potential, is precisely what meditation seek to *accomplish*. In those methods, the person locks attention onto a fixed point, attends fully to that point, and the desired consequence is this same losing of one's sense of self (Ornstein, 1971) in a way which includes being assimilated into that upon which one's attention is focused. One's personhood shatters, dissolves, and enters into a fusion with that external point. To see it, to see it all the way, to lose one's self in the being of it—that is the aim of meditation and a catastrophic threat to the ordinary person confronted with the rising deeper potential. It is as if the point upon which one's attention is centered—whether a flame of a candle or the presented image from the rising deeper potential—holds a compelling fascination which, if one gives in to it, promises the sweeping absorbing of the person's entire sense of self.

Added to the devilish fascination with the looming deeper personhood are the accompanying good feelings of experiencing. It is as if the person is tempted by the wicked invitation to experience arcane pleasure in surrendering one's self to the deeper potential. One senses the raw pleasure of being the alien other—the arcane excitement, the devilish delight, the fiendish thrill and merriment. One almost experiences that—but as the person one still is, and not yet as the person one might succumb into being. What a hellish state this is, absolutely terrified by the prospects of experiencing arcane pleasure, provided that one surrenders to the devil and sacrifices the person one is. Here is the threat of radical transformation and death, together with the imminence of pleasurable experiencing. By our own behavings we bring ourselves to this state, this phase in the behavioral circle (C, Figures 9.1, 9.2).

It is easy enough for the old man to be the person who places all sorts of demands upon his wife and the children who have all grown and left the family. They are to cater to his wishes and many of his whims. In being this way he gains an experiential whiff of the risen deeper potential for being the absolute tyrant. Dad is a cantankerous old character, replete with dozens of appropriate behaviors finely honed to being the demanding one. Yet being demanding raises up the deeper potential, and he is faced with the prospects of no longer being the person he is, and emerging anew as the absolute tyrant. This new person is not Dad; it is a wholly *new* person, and it is the prospect of closing off the former and becoming the latter which is the ultimate threat.

Experiencing depression is easy enough for the middle-aged woman. What is threatening is the looming possibility of not only experiencing the deeper punitive aggression, but having her entire personhood sucked into becoming that whole new person-as-punitive-aggression. Not only will the heightened experiencing of the depression stamp out her being as the depressed person, not only will her total identity be erased, but she is in imminent danger of becoming that alien other person. To be that new personality, that complete new person—that is the ultimate threat.

For 14-year-old Susan, the experiencing of a heightened measure of caring and nurturing the family soon built toward a peak of rousing the deeper potential for being the reigning queen, replacing mother. She senses the danger of having her very self murdered by the looming deeper potential. But more, she senses also the fascinating possibility of becoming something utterly new, the other person who is the reigning household queen. Fully being that is the further side of the terror.

The story is always the same. Once the deeper potential begins its rise, a point is reached where the person-as-operating-potential is engulfed in threat. No matter what face of that threat we witness, we see the final ending of the last fragment of the existence of the person whom we are. No longer a scared person, no longer frightened and anxious, no longer terrified, I am on the very edge of no longer being—anything.

THE CONSEQUENCE OF THREAT TO THE PERSON-AS-OPERATING-POTENTIAL

Confrontation with the Possibility of Choice

At this point in the behavioral circle (C, Figure 9.1), I am confronted with the possibility of continuing on around the circle or getting off. Every time I undergo the threat accompanying the rising up of the deeper potential, the possibility of a choice confronts me.

The problem is how to avoid my own death. In what may be termed the *critical moment* (Chapter 3), the person-as-operating-potential faces some serious options. To remain as this person means that the rising deeper potential will certainly eclipse the operating potential and end its existence, for, at the present moment, the operating potential is already partially eaten into and dissolved away. During this critical moment, the deeper potential is beginning to breathe experiential life. It is rising, and on the verge of replacing the operating potential. When this occurs, the deeper potential will occupy the body and be the executor of behavior. It will assume full mandate over personhood and awareness and consciousness.

In order for the person to avoid this process (the person believes), there is only one other option. The process must be frozen, stopped somehow, brought to a halt. No matter what the cost, what is happening must be stopped. He must prevent the further encroachment of the engulfing deeper potential. It must be blocked, shoved down, pushed back, covered, concealed (Binswanger, 1967). It must be kept away. Draw back from it. I cannot see it or know it. I must keep it vague and hazy. To make it cloudy is to save my self; to see it is to succumb to it. Never let it appear in clear focus, never apprehend its exactness. This backing off and not seeing is one of the salient characteristics of the critical moment.

In each critical moment, we are presented with the possible detailed imminence of the deeper potential, and we dare not see it in all its concrete specificity. This means that we must make the deeper potential vague whether we are focusing on its internal presence or its external presence. We dare not know exactly what is starting to take us over from within or from without. When the deeper potential looms at us from outside, in the form of an extended personality, we must "see" it only up to a defined point of specificity and no further. If sadistic sexuality were the content of the rising deeper potential, the young man might engage with the external world in such a way that sadistic sexual women were constructed in masturbatory fantasies. Yet, for all the years of creating such fantasies, he never saw them in perfect visual acuity. Inevitably the images were shut off at the point of such perfect visual acuity. He may be invited to try to "hold" these images, and to see one in concrete detail. Fix the image and study it carefully. However, he could not. Each time the image blurred, was made hazy, and he turned away. If he were to focus intently upon the concrete specificity of his own externalized sadistic sexuality, he would be in danger of being taken over by it. Once the threat reaches the height of endangering one's very existence, it is pushed away into vagueness.

The possibility of choice contributes to scientific predictability. Faced with the threat of non-being, each person must stop the rising deeper potential somehow. This is the point in the behavioral circle at which choices are available (C, Figure 9.1). It is the *only* point where choices are available. It does not matter whether the person knows the possibility of the choices. Not knowing is itself one of the choices. Yet these choices are there each time the person reaches this point, each time the person is in the critical moment. If the person chooses, even without knowing that he chooses, to take the route which brings him further around the behavioral circle, it *appears* that there is no choice at all. But making the same choice in each critical moment throughout his life does not deprive him of the *opportunity* to choose.

As indicated in Figure 9.1, the three pathways are there, available at this particular point in the behavioral circle. I do not see the person *knowing* the three possible routes and making some sort of considered choice. To think this way would be to invoke an entire new set of factors which determine which choice is to be made. Humanistic theory pictures behavior as systematic and predictable, and not at all random or disorganized or capriciously unpredictable. I see the description and understanding of behavior as made *more* systematically predictable by acknowledging the two possible routes *off* the behavioral circle at this point. When a person regularly follows the pathway round and round the behavioral circle, sheer predictability is, I grant, strong. Indeed, I am saddened by the heightened predictability when persons go round and round the behavioral circle, and do not use the other two possible routes available at this point. Yet to recognize that other pathways are available does not mean we are stuck in the morass of capricious unpredictability against which Immergluck (1964) and Farber (1964) warn. Instead, a schema which recognizes the choice point not only provides the rigor of deterministic approaches, but has the incredible added advantage of predictive power *when the person engaged in surprisingly novel behavior*. Any route off the behavioral circle will appear to be unpredictable, unless the predictive model understands the possibility of choice. Our model establishes the specific conditions under which the choice can occur—so that choices are not ever-present in willy-nilly fashion. Our model also specifies the form and shape of the choices—so that these are defined rather than constituting an open door to just about anything. Approaches which have no such provision for defined choice points and defined choices are, I believe, able to reach high levels of predictability only when behavior proceeds round and round the behavioral circle. To the extent that behavior does just that there is no problem. The problem arises only on those special occasions—the turning points in one's life, whether big ones or small ones—when the person moves off the behavioral circle. Under these infrequent but significant occasions, humanistic theory is robust enough to make predictive sense, and, I submit, most other approaches lack the conceptual rigor for adequate predictability.

Determinism versus free will: Some misstatements. In our discussion thus far, we have moved into the middle of considerable arguments which generally are cast in the form of determinism versus free will. On one side are the humanists, and on the other side are the so-called hard scientists. The issues about which they argue have become solidified into mutual distortions of the positions each believes the other side represents. The humanists believe the hard scientists argue that behavior is wholly determined, and that it is both unscientific and a bit addlepated to believe that the person has any choice in determining his own behavior. On the other hand, the hard scientists believe the humanists argue that behavior is determined in large measure by the person himself, and that it is inhuman and sterile to understand human behavior as determined by inhuman forces.

If we study the issue of determinism, one position is that behavior *is* determined. Factors and variables can be articulated which we can identify as the determinants of behavior. The dream is that we may someday discover all, or at least most, of these determinants. In identifying the *alternative* to this position, however, we must avoid the trap of adopting the alternative which the humanists believe the hard scientists believe. Instead, one real alternative is that behavior is *not* determined, is *un*-determined, is chaotic and beyond the grasp of systematic principles (Knight, 1946; Mailloux, 1953). Is behavior determined or is it undetermined and chaotic? Can we frame systematic principles to grasp determinants of behavior, or are there no determinants of behavior to be grasped? On this issue, *both* humanists *and* hard scientists agree. Both groups are convinced that behavior *is* determined, rather than un-determined. Both groups agree that systematic principles *can* be articulated. Both groups agree that behavior is *not* chaotic or haphazard or beyond determination. This is not the real issue dividing the humanists and the hard scientists, although this is the issue many humanists and hard scientists believe the other group believes is the real issue.

Although these extreme positions are held by very few humanists and very few hard scientists, and although these extreme views are predominantly what each group believes that the other believes, these extreme positions have a way of being perpetuated by those adopting the middle ground. For example, in an attempted rapprochement between hard-headed behaviorists and humanistic phenomenologists, Hitt (1969) links the former with extreme deterministic predictability and the latter with equally extreme, un-determined unpredictability, and then argues that behavior is both *predictable* in some ways and to some extent, and *unpredictable* in some ways and to some extent. He has proposed a resolution of positions which few behaviorists and phenomenologists would agree are accurate representations of their own position. Important as it is to identify real differences among respectable approaches, it is only beclouding the issues either to state them as mutual (mis)perceptions of each others' position, or to attempt a resolution of differences which are not veridical representations of the actual differences.

Determinism versus free will: Some of the issues. It is not easy to grasp the hard core of the issues which have come to be known as determinism versus free will. My impression of at least a part of this core is the issue of the extent to which the determinants of human behavior fall within and fall outside of the person's own control or choice. To what extent, in other words, is the person himself a "determinant of the determinants" of human behavior—whether they be group forces and influences, genetic encodings, internal or external stimuli, previous learnings and conditionings, neurological firings, potentials and their relationships, or physiological tension? On this issue, it is my impression that the so-called hard scientists and humanists agree that most determinants lie *outside* the person's own control or determination or choice. The actual difference in positions, I believe, is that the humanists accept that a small but viable corner of choice lies within the capacity of each person, whereas most behavioral scientists grant virtually no deterministic potential to this particular variable.

Another part of the hard core on which these two approaches respectfully differ is the degree to which human behavior is determined by stimuli (generally external stimuli such as external cues, reinforcements, conditionings and learnings, and the like), and the degree to which human behavior is determined by such internal variables as personal choice, personal selectivity, conscious and unconscious factors, and the like. In the theoretical systems developed by most behavioral scientists, behavior is generally understood as a function of external stimuli and consists of responses to these stimuli. These approaches include no trustworthy conceptualization of personal selectivity, choice, conscious and unconscious determinants (Von Eckartsberg, 1971). It is understandable that such theorists see these variables as contributing noise to their conceptual system. On the other hand, humanistic theorists welcome such variables, and endeavor to systematize them to the point where they can be included in the rigorous investigation and prediction of human behavior.

The choices: Yes or no. In effect, the choice is between surrendering or not surrendering to the intrusive deeper potential. Yes or no—that is the extent of the choice. The rising deeper potential is inviting the person to give in. Be me. Surrender whom you are and become what I am. One option is to accept that invitation. The other option is not to accept that invitation. That is all that is available. You are the gate keeper, and something quite definite is pressing to get through the gate. As the gate keeper you can either say yes, and open the gate, or say no, and shut it (Muller, 1960). Those are the only options which comprise the choice open to human beings at this point in the behavioral circle.

Let us become even more concrete about this choice. Precisely what is it that the person can either say yes or no to? The nature of the operating potential is already there. I have no choice over that. Similarly, the nature of the deeper potential is also already determined. If I remain within the operating potential, the behavior I carry out is already determined for me. If I give in to the deeper potential, the behavior I carry out is likewise already set for me. Humanistic theory and behavioral theory agree that the capacity for choice does not include selection from a set of potential behaviors. In no way does the person scan a number of potential ways of behaving and select one to carry out (cf. Immergluck, 1964). What then is within my choice at this point? As I see it, I have two sets of options. One is to say yes or no to the *behaviors* which are thrust upon me. Both the operating and deeper potentials are inviting me to do this or do that. I can surrender or not surrender to these behaviors. The other set of options involves the *locus* of the person I am. Right now I am within the domain of the operating potentials, and the deeper potential is inviting me to give up my present personhood, no longer to be the person I am. If I accept that invitation, I myself die. My options here are to accept or to decline the invitation to close out my existence and become the deeper potential. In effect, my set of options are (a) to say yes or no to specific behaviors, and (b) to say yes or no to becoming the deeper potential.

The easiest and most typical stance is for the person to not act in opposition to the behaviors which are coming forth mechanically. This requires no choice at all. To act in opposition requires a "waking up" which may take one off the behavioral circle. Saying no to one's mechanical behaviors during these critical moments is an important feature of Eastern methods of meditation and contemplation which place great importance upon such special critical moments; ". . . it is not intellectual because it is a moment of will. It is necessary to remember yourself not at a quiet moment when nothing happens but when you know that you are doing something wrong—and not do it . . . you must be able to feel it and then stop it and at the same time remember yourself, be aware that you are doing it" (Ouspensky, 1957, p. 112). The option to *not* carry out the mechanical behavior is there, and taking advantage of it is a most significant step.

The possibility of behavioral choice is limited, simple, and mundane. With regard to behavior, then, the person has only the choice of saying no to the (mechanical, ordinary) behavior offered by the operating potential, or yes to the behavior offered by the deeper potential. In no way does this choice have anything to do with the nature or content of the behaviors. When behaviorists warn against the dangers to behavioral predictability of the humanists' concept of choice, the behaviorists have a far more grandiose conception of choice than the one I have proposed (cf. Farber, 1964). From the perspective of humanistic theory, the range of choice regarding behavior in critical moments is so limited that not only is scientific predictability hardly *endangered*. but the *careful* application of the options of choice would *strengthen* scientific predictability.

There are other personality approaches which do utilize the grandiose conception of choice about which behavioral scientists worry. For example, Allport (1937) grants the person (ego or self) a special characteristic of *organizing thought and behavior*—and *that* is far more powerful than our comparatively pedestrian capacity to select this behavior or that behavior. But Allport's is not the only grandiose conception of this capacity for choice. Some humanists believe that human beings do possess the freedom to be however they wish, and do possess the capacity to control and to determine their own behavior! From our perspective, however, this is an important part of a belief system in which many persons live out illusionary lives. It is a world of illusion to believe that we have such a grand control or freedom or determination or will. Such a person ". . . has a long-established and very strong illusion that he is free to go where he wills, that he can move according to his wish, and that he can go to the right or to the left . . . 'Will' is quite the wrong idea; it does not exist" (Ouspensky, 1957, p. 16). Persons with an urge to believe in such a grandiose conception of the capacity for choice are expressing their own constructed world views rather than a humanistic theory of personality.

In our perspective, this capacity for choice is quite routine. It is exercised each time one is in a critical moment, each time the person reaches this point in the behavioral circle. We all have the capacity to take advantage of the choice options. Each person *can* avoid the options and pass on around the circle, *or* exercise the options and get off the circle. There is nothing rare or special or distinguishing about the sheer capacity for choice. Others, however, regard this capacity as a special distinction. Binswanger (1958a, pp. 197-198), for example, cites the capacity for choice as one of the major features distinguishing human beings from other animals. It *may be* that the availability of choice is a special distinguishing feature of human beings even though we virtually never utilize that opportunity for choice. In the field of psychotherapy, those who utilize this capacity for choice are often considered special persons with the "wanting to grow" (e.g. Jourard, 1968; Whitaker, Warkentin, & Malone, 1959). Others consider this quality as one of the key characteristics of optimal persons—the quality of using the capacity to choose in such a way as to move ahead, change, grow. From the perspective of humanistic theory, there is little that is special or rare about either possessing this capacity for choice or exercising it. We all have the capacity, and we all make choices many times a day. Each time we come to this point in the behavioral circle, and that may occur five to 20 times a day, we exercise our capacity for choice. We make the choice exceedingly quietly, and almost always without knowing that we have exercised our capacity for choice. It is the sheer frequency, and the not knowing that we are making choices, and the monotonous regularity of always making the same choice, which mask the presence of this capacity for choice. Yet this quality is always there, and comes closest to making its presence known in each critical moment, every time we reach that point in the behavioral circle.

The consequence of the rising deeper potential is threat to the person-as-operating-potential (C, Figures 9.1, 9.2). At this point the person is confronted with the possibility of choice. What are these choices?

1. Being Another Operating Potential

I cannot remain the operating potential which I am, for that would lead to my death. Nor can I surrender to the rising deeper potential, for that too would mean the death of me. The way out is to be another facet of myself—another operating potential. In this way I solve every aspect of the problem. Nothing bad happens to me, for I have slipped into being another operating potential (OP3, Figure 9.2). I preserve my self because I remain the person I am as long as I stay within the domain of the operating potentials. I can slip from one operating potential (OP1) to another (OP3) and still remain the same person. The deeper potential is no longer threatening, for I am no longer the operating potential (OP1) coupled to that intruding deeper potential (DP2). I have won, i.e., I have preserved my self and the threatening deeper potential has receded (D, Figure 9.2).

The answer to my problem lies in the fact that I have some space in which to maneuver. The center of my self is not confined to operating potential 1 (Figure 9.2), but instead is confined to the larger domain of the operating potentials, the area indicated by the dotted lines. I can easily shift from one operating potential to another and not the least harm is done. As long as I have freedom of movement from one operating potential to another, I am free, and I am in no danger of being eclipsed. Indeed, I am like quicksilver in being able to slip from one operating potential to another. If I am experiencing closeness (OP1, Figure 9.2) to you, and being this way means that the deeper potential for ugly sexuality rises upward, I can quite easily shift over to another operating potential (OP3, Figure 9.2) and instantaneously I am being carping and bitchy to you. In the quick switch to being carping and bitchy, the threat (indicated by the three negative signs in

C, Figure 9.2) is reduced; I preserve my self from the threat of death, the rising potential for experiencing sexuality is pushed back down again, and all is well (D, Figure 9.2). The critical moment is over—and it all happens in my quick switch from one operating potential to another.

The older sister is visiting with her younger sister, and being sharing and intimate (OP1, Figure 9.2) as she relates (B1, Figure 9.2) details of her problems with her husband. A mild critical moment approaches in which the older sister starts to experience the deeper potential for being utterly alone, rejected, unworthy (DP2, Figure 9.2). At this point the older sister feels the beginnings of uncomfortable feelings (indicated by the three negative signs in Figure 9.2), and is on the brink of experiencing being wholly alone, unwanted, rejected, and unworthy. Suddenly, as in a flash, the older sister is now operating potential 3 (D, Figure 9.2), and she experiences being the jokester, the funny one who tells (B2, Figure 9.2) hilarious stories about the family. Very quickly, the critical moment is over, and she has switched from one operating potential to another (D, Figure 9.1).

For 14-year-old Susan, the critical moment occurs when being the operating potential (nurturing and caring) brings the deeper potential (the reigning woman, replacing mother) dangerously close. Susan is taking over for her sick mother, she is in the kitchen telling her younger sister and brother to set the table and help prepare the salad. Susan is about to tell her father that supper is ready when her younger brother starts a squabble with the younger sister. Susan is right on the verge of being the boss, snapping at them to stop because she has other things to do, and she does not want to disturb the sick mother. Here is the critical moment when she is invaded by, and on the verge of being, the threatening deeper potential (C, Figures 9.1, 9.2). What is the way out? The center of her self must shift into being another operating potential, out of being the caring, nurturing one and out of the awful possibility of being the reigning queen of the household. It suddenly occurs to her that her girlfriend is home now, and Susan must call her. In a flash, Susan is on the phone dialing her girlfriend. She has slipped into being operating potential 3, and the problem is solved (D, Figures 9.1, 9.2). The critical moment is ended, and Susan is no longer being the caring and nurturing person whom she was just a moment ago.

Dr. Matthews is a psychotherapist. The more successful he is with his patients, the more he experiences a sense of being effective, capable, and adequate (OP1, Figure 9.2). This feels good, but it also brings with it a rising deeper potential (DP2) for being the God, worshipped by the patient. This deeper potential rises up the more he is helpful to his patients, the more he gets into their problems and helps them

over their difficulties. It is frightening for him to be visited by the
deeper potential, yet the critical moments regularly occur when the patient gives him that special look, or asks whether he might hug him,
or inquires about how he managed to become the wonderful person
he is. In these moments, Dr. Matthews senses the threat within and
quickly becomes another operating potential. Suddenly he is being
warm and understanding, a genuine close friend of the patient, one
human being to another. This is another side to Dr. Matthews, one
which followed being the effective and capable person—but more importantly, *not* the worshipped God which he might have fallen into
being. In this sudden switch, his own personhood has been preserved.
The danger of the critical moment is over, and the deeper potential
safely down once again.

She is having a party to celebrate the 50th anniversary of her parents. Here is the family reunion, with about 50 people in her home,
relatives whom she hasn't seen in three years or more. One of them is
her cousin Alice, who is about her age. She and Alice were always
compared and contrasted with one another during their childhoods,
and she wallowed in this awful competition—which one was prettier,
the more prized in the family, the one to "do well." Underneath this
competitive operating potential was the potential for experiencing utter uselessness, the hell of being nothing at all, substanceless (DP2, Figure 9.2). At this moment she is inquiring about Alice's children, and
when Alice tells her about her lovely daughter, she is filled with the
old competition. The critical moment occurs when she is becoming
just a bit tighter inside, and she is on the edge of saying something
nasty about Alice and her daughter—like asking whether Alice and
her daughter have similar eyes, a nasty remark because Alice had a
childhood eye "condition" in which her eye would quiver noticeably
when she was tired or "under stress." Without knowing, the tension in
this critical moment adumbrated the rise of the deeper sense of
nothingness and uselessness. For an instant, there was tension and inner tightness. Swiftly she was plunged into being her scatterbrained,
silly self (OP3, Figure 9.2), and she suddenly remembered that she
had completely forgotten to serve the cold cuts. Bursting out in her
silly shrill laugh, she told Alice that she had forgotten (B2, Figure
9.2). Would Alice help her set out the cold cuts? From being operating potential 1, the center of her self plunged into being operating
potential 3 (D, Figure 9.2). With this quick shift, the critical moment is
passed.

In each of the above examples, the center of one's personhood
shifts over to another operating potential. The nature or content of
the second operating potential is irrelevant. However, a rather common refuge is a second operating potential in which the person ex-

periences a sense of denial, resistance, avoidance. It is as if the second operating potential says, "I did not do that. Something else caused that. It did not come from me." For example, as she is becoming increasingly competitive (OP1) with her cousin, and as the deeper sense of being nothing rises (DP2), she may suddenly be dizzy and warm, and mention how peculiar she feels. It is as if she now is operating potential 3 (D, Figure 9.2), and is saying, "*I* wasn't being competitive with you. That came from something else in me. See how peculiar I feel now?" In the little boy who grabs the cat and swings the cat around and around by its tail until father comes in and wants to know why the cat is screeching, this operating potential can be the refuge from which the boy says that the nasty cat bit him. The boy has switched from being gleefully sadistic to justifiably stern, from being one person to a quite different person. He is now excusing himself, avoiding blame—and being a different person in accomplishing this. Shifting into this second operating potential is what the little child does when, having knocked over the milk, he says, "*It* spilled; I didn't knock it over." It is this same operating potential to which mother shifts when she denies having said what she just said. She has just talked about her neighbor in a mean way, and her 11-year-old daughter becomes swept up in the nastiness to the point of blurting out that "everyone hates Mrs. Kelly!" At this point, the mother scolds the daughter for being so nasty, and thereby implies that she herself did not talk about Mrs. Kelly in a mean way. Many persons maintain an operating potential (OP3) which insists that I did not do that, it did not come from me, something else was responsible. By maintaining this safe refuge, there is always protection for the other operating potential (OP1), there is always a way out of the critical moment, and the deeper potential can always be pushed away. Furthermore, from the perspective of this refuge, what it insists is true *is* true. That is, this second operating potential did *not* do it, it did *not* come from me, something else *was* responsible!

The advantages of being another operating potential. Whatever the nature of operating potentials 1 and 3 (Figure 9.2), the shift from being centered in one to being centered in another results in at least three consequences. First, the sense of self (personhood) has been preserved. "I" am safe. The possibility of the closing off of my existence is now gone. The critical moment is over. Second, the deeper potential is pushed back down. Its bid for entering the level of operating potentials is over. Third, the heightened threat (indicated by the three negative signs in C, Figure 9.2) is now reduced. That is, whatever the particular content of the disintegrative feeling (e.g. anxiety, anger, sense of being torn apart), it now abates.

As described in Chapter 3, virtually every helping approach assists the person in achieving the above goals by shifting to another operating potential, and thereby helping the person maintain his self, reduce the burgeoning bad feelings, and push back down the rising deeper potential. These are the aims of supportive therapies, crisis therapies, suicide prevention centers, and the whole enterprise of chemotherapeutic drugs and pills. These are the aims of custodial treatment, behavior therapies, ego therapies, milieu therapies, and social therapies. Nearly every approach which aims for insight and understanding joins the person in achieving these goals. Programs of desensitization and token economy and deconditioning are the allies of the person in working effectively toward these goals. The war cry of all of these approaches is the same: control those impulses, push down the insides, reduce the bad feelings, stop the threat, maintain the ego, push away the threat to the self, deaden the tension, guard against the instincts.

Under this banner are forces ranging all the way from psychoanalysis to behavior modification. Within a psychoanalytic framework ". . . we may say that analysis is always right in theory in its claim to cure neurosis by ensuring control over instinct" (Freud, 1959, p. 331). Within a behavior modification framework, the person who feels anxiety in conjunction with small, furry objects must be helped to overcome that anxiety—and thereby preserve the self of the anxious person and drive back down that which is burgeoning upward. In a landmark experiment, Jones (1924) reduced the child's anxiety in relation to small furry animals by constructing a feeding situation in which there were incremental exposures to such small furry objects while the child was feeding. In addition to feeding, other classes of behaviors can be invoked, behaviors incompatible or antagonistic to the anxiety (cf. Bandura, 1961; Wolpe, 1958). In all, the goal is to preserve the self; reduce the anxiety; control that which is burgeoning upward. Cautela (1965) describes the treatment of a man who changed jobs in his plant and soon began having feelings of anxiety—about not being able to function in his work, about being criticized or asked to do something outside his usual duties, about the possibility that fellow employees would ridicule him. The aim of behavior modification treatment was to press back down whatever rising personality process might be contributing to the anxiety. Specifically, the aim of treatment was for the man to smile and be at ease in these situations so that he could continue to function at work and these aims were reached by means of relaxation and autosuggestion. It is as if the aim of the therapist is allied with the aim of the person-as-operating-potential, viz. preserve the person I am, never permit the deeper potential to get me. If the treatment is successful, the person has managed to get out of the critical moment and has shifted from being endangered by the rising deeper potential to being now safely out of the critical moment (D, Figures 9.1, 9.2). By moving from operating potential 1 to operating potential 3 (Figure 9.2), the person, in the words of behavior modificationists, becomes desensitized. The "stimuli" to which the person becomes "desensitized" are typically external manifestations of what I would term the deeper potential. In the course of desensitization, the person is enabled to move into a position of strength and safety, and to become incrementally more effective in blockading the rising deeper potential. "The patient, having been relaxed, sometimes under hypnosis, is asked to imagine the weakest of the disturbing stimuli, repeatedly, until it ceases to evoke any anxiety. Then increasingly 'strong' stimuli are introduced in turn, and similarly treated, until eventually even the 'strongest' fails to evoke anxiety . . ." (Wolpe, 1964, 320).

Within our perspective, behavior modification serves to move the person from stage C to stage D (Figure 9.2), to kill the deeper potential, to preserve the existence of the person-as-operating-potential, to foreclose the possibility of change, to place the person in a condition of mechanicalness and send him round and round the behavioral circle (D, Figure 9.1). At the least sign of disruption of the person who resides within the domain of the operating potentials, the behavior modificationist sets to work murdering the intrusive deeper potential. Preserve the person at all costs. In this enterprise, the problem and the solution are all simple and straightforward. "The behavior therapist understands his task to be the use of conditioning techniques for the removal of neurotic and psychotic symptoms . . . Since the symptoms are forms of behavior, and since all behavior is learned, or conditioned response, his task is clear: when the patient comes to him and complains of a symptom, such as homosexuality or a phobia, the therapist conditions the symptoms away" (Needleman, 1967, p. ix). From the perspective of the *person*, this is wonderful; from the perspective of the *deeper potential* this is one of the worst things that one person or profession or movement can do to other persons, i.e., to prevent the possibility of change, to send people round and round the behavioral circle, to place people in states of zombie-like unknowingness, to kill what is within and leave the person in a self-delusional state of continuous hypnosis. In this endeavor, behavior therapy joins with most therapies and "helping" movements, and all of these join with collective others whose aims are likewise to anesthetize the person.

The place of tension-reduction in humanistic theory. It is essential to note that the person-as-operating-potential has successfully managed to save itself, to abate the threat and reduce the tension. Preservation of one's existence and reduction of threat are powerful bonuses. Indeed, every time the person passes this point in the behavioral circle (C, Figure 9.1), the person gains a puff of solid pleasure—in the psychoanalytic sense of pleasure as the decrease in tension (Freud, 1933, p. 131), in which there is a ". . . reduction of tension, which is experienced as gratification (pleasure)" (Munroe, 1955, p. 74). These are special moments to the person-as-operating-potential whose very existence has been saved and whose sea of threat has been dissolved away. Movement from one operating potential to another is thereby pleasurable and gratifying, and the psychoanalytic meanings of pleasure and gratification are exemplified in such moments. I suggest that this particular movement is what is occurring in tension-reduction and in the drive-reduction basic to both orthodox learning theories and to Freudian psychoanalysis (White, 1959). The "drive" which is reduced is the burgeoning deeper potential. The "tension" which is reduced is the tension accompanying the rising of the deeper potential. When behavior is understood as conforming to a grand principle of drive-reduction or tension-reduction (Miller & Dollard, 1941), even when this refers to the reduction of the tension from instinctual forces threatening to invade the ego (Arieti, 1962; Fenichel, 1954e), what is occurring, from the perspective of humanistic theory, is that the person is shifting from being one operating potential to being another, the rising deeper potential is shoved back down again, the threat of one's existence being eclipsed is now reduced, and the person continues on the course around the behavioral circle.

Instead of *drive*-reduction or *tension*-reduction, other theorists have described the grand principle of behavior as *anxiety*-reduction (e.g. Mowrer, 1939, 1950). Yet I see the referent of the anxiety as the same as the referent of the tension, viz. the bad feelings—call them threat or anxiety or whatever—which accompany the rising up of the deeper potential (C, Figure 9.1, 9.2). The behavior which occurs and which does indeed reduce the anxiety is that which has the net effect of moving the person from one operating potential to another. Drive-reduction or tension-reduction or anxiety-reduction is correct in its description of behavior, but it is correct in describing behavior only in one specific set of conditions at one point in the course of the behavioral circle. Adherents are, I believe, in error in their explanation of *all* behavior on the basis of this principle. They are in error in articulating a principle which is merely a working description of our two principles of behavior working together in concert. I submit that drive-reduction (or tension-reduction or anxiety-reduction) is not a principle of behavior because it is only a working derivative of more robust principles, and because it is sharply limited to very special conditions in the person's travels around the behavioral circle.

To my mind, psychoanalytic and behavior theorists have failed to

improve upon Mowrer's (1939) statement of the powerful three pillars
of anxiety-reduction: (a) anxiety (or fear) is essentially a learned
phenomenon; (b) anxiety acts as a motivating agent for behavior; and
(c) the reduction of anxiety (or fear) leads to the acquisition of new
behavior. These remain the major canons underlying the near universal use of anxiety (or fear or tension or drive) reduction as the grand
principle of behavior. I can accept these canons. I can accept the
worthwhileness of a tension-reduction concept. What I do not accept
is the applicability of this principle to any condition or situation other
than that (C, Figures 9.1, 9.2) in which the person is impelled to
switch from one operating potential to another. This principle simply
is too weak to explain behavior under any other condition. Furthermore, I do not even consider it an independent principle of human behavior, for it is generated from the orchestration of the two
major principles of behavior: behavior as a means of instituting relationships among potentials, and behavior as a means of providing
for the experiencing of potentials.

   Tension-reduction versus tension-conservation. Even under this special
condition (C, Figures 9.1, 9.2), behavior which succeeds in shifting the
person from one operating potential to another does not eliminate the
factors which led to the threat. The disintegrative relationship between the operating and deeper potential remains. Behavior succeeded in *reducing* the threat, and it also succeeded in *conserving* the
threat. In a review of their own work and the work of others, Solomon and Wynne (1954) concluded that such behaviors serve mainly
to freeze the conditions which account for the threat. They refer to
this as the conserving of the threat, not its removal. The deeper potential is still there; the old operating potential is still there; the disintegrative relationship is still there. The scene has been frozen while
the person has stepped to the side.

   Within a behavior modification approach, "homosexuality" can be
"treated" by creating conditions wherein like-sexed persons become
cues for *unpleasant* feelings, and opposite-sexed persons become cues
for *pleasant* feelings (Miller, Bradley, Gross & Wood, 1968). As in
switching from being one operating potential to another, such treatment leaves each factor as it was, with the notable exception that the
locus of the person switches from being one operating potential to
being another. The old operating and deeper potentials remain intact,
their disintegrative relationship preserved. What *has* changed is that
the person has stepped out of being the old "homosexual" operating
potential and into another operating potential.

   Under such conditions, the "tension" of the disintegrative relationship remains, for the treatment did nothing to alter that relationship.
The same is true of behaviors which provide a small token measure of

experiencing of the deeper potential. For example, the man who fights against deeper potentials for experiencing violent and explosive sexuality may never allow that to occur. Instead, he masturbates in the quiet of his bedroom or bathroom, and has mild sexual experiencings. At the point of giving in to and being the rising deeper potential, he slips easily into an operating potential which carries out the mild and truncated masturbatory experiencing. Such behavior does nothing to the disintegrative relationship with the deeper sexual potential. In preserving this relationship, the disintegration is also preserved. For such persons, masturbation preserves the "tension," it does not reduce the tension. Such persons are described as "masturbatory types", ". . . unsuccessful masturbators who have neurotic disturbances in the apparatus of satisfaction, and who therefore masturbate again and again, trying to achieve an aim they can never achieve. They are never adequately relaxed, and they constantly feel a sexual tension which, in contrast to the normal person, no masturbation can satisfy" (Fenichel, 1954e, p. 83). Because the tension is that of the disintegrative relationship, and because the masturbation tends to *conserve* the disintegrative tension rather than to *reduce* it, the destiny is to move further around the behavioral circle. Nothing has happened to the tension or threat, whether in this kind of so-called "compulsive" masturbation or in its treatment by the methods of behavior modification.

The consequence of shifting over to another operating potential is to reduce the threat or tension or anxiety. Approaches such as behavior modification likewise seek to reduce the threat or tension or anxiety. In both enterprises, contact with the threat (C, Figures 9.1, 9.2) is just enough to move away from it (D, Figures 9.1, 9.2). As a consequence, the *threat* does not dissolve away—the person just moves out of the line of fire. Stated in the vocabulary of learning theory, the instrumental response prevents extinction by its occurrence in the conditioned stimulus situation, but with the absence of the original reinforcement (Solomon & Wynne, 1954).

2. Integration with the Deeper Potential

I have been describing the options available at that point in the behavioral circle when the person is confronted with the threat of the rising deeper potential (C, Figure 9.1). In this critical moment, the person may move out of being one operating potential and into another (D, Figures 9.1, 9.2). That is one option, it is the one which is virtually always taken, and it leads the person further around the behavioral circle. A second option takes the person *off* the behavioral circle. This is the option of integrating with the deeper potential whose rise is causing all the trouble (E, Figures 9.1, 9.2).

Every time the person moves into a critical moment, the value system of humanistic theory names this option as the desirable path, and invites the person-as-operating-potential to stop trying to avoid its own death, stop the continuous behavioral circling, stop recoiling against the deeper potential, stop trying to preserve the self which one is. Yet, from the perspective of the person-as-operating-potential, such an option is to head right into the jaws of that which the person is avoiding. It is absolutely unthinkable to surrender—that is the final threat. The person-as-operating-potential will bounce about from one operating potential to another—*any* other operating potential—in order to *not* surrender to the encroaching deeper process. Nevertheless, the option here is to do just that. Surrender to that of which you are terrified. Give up your existence. Die. More than die—kill your self, enter *willingly* into death of the person whom you are. Enthusaistically let your self be overwhelmed by, engulfed by, surrendered to that deeper personality process which frightens you (Boss, 1963, p. 13). Throw your self into that about which you are terrified, threatened, horrified.

What is the consequence of surrendering into being the deeper potential? One consequence is that, as the grandest paradox of them all, the threat evaporates! The threat is *gone*—not reduced or avoided or side-stepped. Within the framework of psychoanalysis, Anna Freud (1936) described a very special kind of play behavior in which the child plunged into being fully that which frightened the child. If the child were terrified by his own aggression, tendency to attack, ferociousness, then that terror *dissolved away* when the child could fully surrender into being the object which he feared as aggressive, attacking, and ferocious. If that object was a dog, and the child was terrified by the dog, then the terror was dissolved away when the child could *fully be* that aggressive, attacking, ferocious dog. This key was not found in psychoanalytic play therapy. It has been around for centuries. Indeed, each therapeutic approach has its own version of the clinical axiom that anxiety (or threat or tension) is dissolved away by fully experiencing that about which you are anxious. Schools of counselling and psychotherapy have incorporated what ancient healers knew, what tribal knowledge knew, what primitive cultures knew. Even learning theory has a splinter therapy which gets rid of anxiety by inviting the person to experience fully that which makes the person anxious. Throw yourself into the guts of the anxiety-engendering situation. This is the kernal of implosive therapy (Hogan & Kirchner, 1967; Stampfl & Levis, 1967), in which the threat evaporates when the person throws himself into the core of the threat.

By surrendering—integrating—with the deeper potential, the person achieves more than the washing away of the threat. This route is the way to actualization, becoming, satori, liberation. Always, however, the key is to solve the problem by surrendering to it, for the solution lies in the problem itself (Watts, 1960). Integration means taking the final leap into the heart of the problem, the awfulness, the terror. It is through experiencing that which we desperately avoid experiencing. It is through the willing fusion with that which you encounter (Ellenberger, 1958, p. 119).

Every time I have that inner pulsing of heightened bodily feeling, I am presented with the invitation to be the deeper potential. Most especially when the inner bodily feeling is one of disturbance (Jourard, 1968) do I have the choice of giving in or not giving in (Bugental, 1968). When I accept that invitation, I leave the operating potential which I am and enter into being the deeper potential. This act of extricating one's self from what one is brings the person, for the briefest moment, into a state of limbo. It is what has been described as an existential vacuum (Frankl, 1969). I am free of the operating potential, and I am not yet the deeper potential. In this limbo state I have no meaning, no identity. In a sense I have no self, and in another sense I am, in that briefest of instances, all self.

To take this leap willingly is to gain a sense of freedom and control, a state which we virtually never know. Few persons have ever known what it is like fully to be in charge of their own fate. We spend our entire lives in continuous resistance to the encroaching deeper potential. The person who discovers that the way out is through the very doorway he has desperately avoided in each critical moment has entered a whole new world of exhilarating freedom and self-determination. He can be successively deeper potentials for experiencing by surrendering willingly to each of them as they present themselves to him. Here is the meaning of coming to life by means of suicide. This is already known by some of the persons who finally end the desperate lifelong struggle by electing to kill themselves. In that determination, they have entered into that state of existential vacuum—one in which they are finally free of all the turmoil which adhered to being stuck within the operating potentials. In this limbo state between having been the old operating potential and carrying out the final act of suicide, these persons may experience an interlude of peace, freedom, and festivity. It is a kind of good feeling which is the absence of the perpetual saturnine heaviness of being the operating potentials. In this limbo state, the person "... is festive ... because ... in the voluntary-necessary resolve for death the existence is no longer 'desperately itself' but has authentically and totally become 'itself' ... only in her decision for death did she find herself and choose herself" (Binswanger, 1958c, p. 298).

The step off the perpetual and endless behavioral circle (E, Figure

9.1) is a final step. Once it is taken, the person is no longer the person who had been going round and round the behavioral circle. It is a path which is available. It is one of the options. In this discussion, there are at least two major areas I have omitted: *how* to take this pathway, and what the person is like who has taken this pathway. The former is beyond the scope of this book; the second is described in Chapter 11.

3. The State of Unfeeling

In the critical moment (C, Figure 9.1), the person has available a number of options. One is to shift over into being another operating potential and thereby continue going round the behavioral circle (D, Figure 9.1). A second is to surrender into integration with the deeper potential (E, Figure 9.1). The third available option is to enter the state of unfeeling (F, Figures 9.1, 9.2). There are two ways in which the person can enter into this state (F1, F2, Figure 9.2).

Entering the state of unfeeling by completely sealing off the deeper potential. As described in Chapter 3, and as indicated in Figure 3.1, the person can push the deeper potential (DP2) so far down that it is rendered inert (F1, Figure 9.2). Going round and round the behavioral circle requires that the deeper potential always remain viable, i.e., that it not fall below the threshold indicated by the dotted line (F1, F2, Figure 9.2). When the deeper potential falls below that threshold, it may be described as (a) being closed off, completely choked off, sealed off. When this occurs, (b) there are no further bad feelings. The channel of relationships between the operating and deeper potentials is clear of tension, threat, hurt, disjunction, depression—any kind of disintegrative bad feeling. In effect, there are no further relationships (F1, Figure 9.2). The person-as-operating-potential (c) has entered into a state of unfeeling—deadness, numbness, nothingness, sleep, automatism, pawnness. In this state, (d) the person does not know that he is dead. He is asleep without knowing that he is asleep, automatic without knowing that he is automatic. What is more, (e) the person believes that he is a person, acts as if he has choice, functions as if he knows, seems to be aware. This is the state of self-delusion and self-illusion.

I can block off and resist my deeper violence to a point (F1, Figure 9.2) where there is no further threat from that violence. In effect, it is gone. I have succeeded in my struggles against the deeper violence to the point where I have gone off the behavioral circle (F, Figure 9.1) and no longer feel its presence because it has no presence. I may spend most of my life being not defiant, being helpful and cooperative, loyal and devoted (OP1, Figure 9.2). If I can succeed, that point may finally be reached wherein the deeper defiance is sealed below the threshold and down into the state of unfeeling (F1, Figure 9.2). The defiance is now inert, dead, unfeelinged. It causes no further trouble.

As long as I can remember, I lived in a world in which my family wanted me to join the law firm. My father always wanted me to enter his firm. Every so often I had bursts of defiance (DP2, Figure 9.2) throughout my life, and the family and the school always came down hard against me. I was a bad boy. When I was part way through law school I married Ann. The family hated her and nearly disowned me. The crisis came when I quit law school and went into drugs with Ann. She got pregnant and I worked where I could. When the family had me hospitalized, I fought it bitterly until Dr. Stewart gave me shock treatments and saw me in therapy. I saw him even after the marriage was annulled and I was allowed to leave the hospital and live at home once again. I got better and finished law school. Now I am a member of the firm, and I am engaged to Carol, whose older brother joined the firm at about the time I did. I am older now, and that former life seems never to have existed. That was an ugly dream. It seemed like it happened to some other person. I feel much better now. Life has its ups and downs, but I am a new person.

Here is the adjusted person, the normal one. There is no further trouble from the deeper potential (DP2, F1, Figure 9.2). The insides are no longer a genuine source of difficulty, for in effect there are no insides. Everything which comprises the person lies within the domain of the operating potentials. At the periphery of consciousness and awareness there is a vacuum. Accordingly, there are no problems with stirred-up insides or insides which are torn apart or insides that are threatening to overwhelm and engulf the person. Indeed, the person is effectively without insides—but without knowing that there are no insides. This person is aware only of the other operating potentials and of the external world. Between the domain of the self and the deeper potentials there is a state of nothingness, a state of unfeeling (F1, Figure 9.2).

Entering oneself into the state of unfeeling. I can shut myself off from the rising deeper potential by pushing it so far down that it enters the state of unfeeling (F1, Figure 9.2). Another way in which I can achieve that same distancing is by means of a curious maneuver in which *I myself* enter the state of unfeeling (F2, Figure 9.2). In this curious maneuver, I disengage from the ordinary level of operating potentials and thereby permit the rising deeper potential to take that vacated position. By means of this maneuver, (a) the person-as-operating-potential no longer experiences. It is sealed off, below the threshold of unfeeling. (b) There are no further bad feelings. The threat of being eclipsed by the rising deeper potential is over. (c) The person exists in a state of dumbness, unknowingness, sleep, and (d) hovers in this state of unfeeling without knowing that he is dumb, unknowing, asleep. This maneuver takes the person off the behavioral circle (F, Figure 9.1), and preserves his own existence by escaping down into the state of unfeeling.

In this critical moment, just before undertaking this maneuver, the person can meet the ultimate threat to his being, viz. its being brought to a close. This is more than being attacked or wounded or even mutilated, for then the essential core of one's existence may be preserved (Laing, 1960). In this critical moment, the essential core of one's existence is on the verge of being utterly destroyed. It is to preserve this essential core that the person folds up, enters into the state of unfeeling where he is unreachable by the external world, but he is intact; he exists in a state of numbness, dumbness, unknowingness and sleep—but he is undestroyed.

During a brief instant in the critical moment, I have choices available to me. When I sense the heightening threat in that critical moment, I have several paths I may follow. "Man experiences some freedom, some opportunity for choice. When he reflects upon it, his life unfolds before him, both transparent and opaque, and he stands able to grasp the decisions he has made and the possibilities that loom before him . . . Thus he is confronted both with the power and the responsibility of choice" (Fischer, 1970, p. 84). Yet this opportunity for choice is there only fleetingly, and only at this subtle point in the critical moment. Once I follow the route of disengaging and entering the state of unfeeling (F2, Figure 9.2), I have no freedom, no opportunity of choice, no capability of reflecting upon my life, no power or responsibility for choosing. To enter into the sleep state of unfeeling is to have forfeited choice. I have chosen not to choose, and to not know that I have made that choice.

I sacrifice far more than the option of choice. By entering into the state of unfeeling, I sacrifice my being to other determinants. The movements of the physical body are not *my* movements. The thoughts are no longer *my* thoughts. The words that are said are not *my* words. I have sacrificed my self to the influence of conditionings and learnings, the wishes and wants of others, the whole of social influences. I am now a puppet, run by others, a hypnotized zombie who is run by alien internal and external forces. The choice to enter the state of unfeeling is one ". . . that is a *resignation* or a *renunciation* of the whole antinomic problem as such, and that takes the form of an existential retreat . . . The Dasein thus *surrenders itself over* to existential powers alien to itself . . . We are forced to say of such a person that he is a

victim, a plaything, or a prisoner in the hands of alien powers"
(Binswanger, 1967, pp. 258-259).

Generally, these alien powers are external. The person who succeeds in entering the state of unfeeling—either by forcing the deeper
potential down far enough (F1, Figure 9.2) or by plunging his own
head into the state of unfeeling (F2, Figure 9.2)—has accomplished
what learning theory has been struggling for nearly a century to accomplish, viz. to identify human beings as devoid of inner personality
determinants and as a wholesale function of external determinants.
Once the person enters the state of unfeeling, he has become the
paradigm of a social learning organism. While in this state, the person
is a responder to stimuli, moulded by social influences, a product of
social learning. If the person exists in this state (F1, F2, Figure 9.2)
for two seconds, the social learning model of human beings is appropriate for the two-second span of time. If the person exists in this
state for 20 years, then the social learning model makes general good
sense. But the state of unfeeling is only one state in which the person
can exist (Figure 9.1), even though he is without a self and subject to
alien powers during this state—however brief or extended.

I can surrender my self over to these alien powers—I can fall into
the state of unfeeling—quite easily and quickly and undramatically.
Abrupt disengagement from the level of operating potentials and abrupt plunging into the state of unfeeling are maneuvers you and I
carry out many times every day. It is by no means reserved for special
persons whom we call crazy or mentally ill. In a flash I can fall asleep,
and do so without knowing that I have fallen asleep. If I am experienced at this maneuver (and most of us have spent years perfecting
this maneuver), I can fall asleep instantaneously right before your
very eyes, and you will probably never even know. When I switch
suddenly and easily from one operating potential to another, I am still
being myself. I am merely switching facets of who I am. I can easily
know that I have switched from experiencing love with you to experiencing anger with you. I know that because I am always here
within this domain of operating potentials. The switch to down below
the threshold of unfeeling (F, Figure 9.1, 9.2) is merely another
movement. I am quite skilled at shifting about the center of my selfhood. To enter the state of unfeeling is merely another bit of shifting
about, except that now I do not know. I have no sense of self or
awareness or consciousness.

What shines forth from me is the deeper potential. It is not me. I
am not conscious or aware of knowing of what is coming forth while I
am buried within the state of unfeeling. In this state, we are indeed
unconscious of the behavior which shines forth from us. Indeed, that

sense of self, which ordinarily is my presence, is not there. There is no I, no personhood, no being, no awareness or consciousness. That "I" has been sealed off, and in its place is a mechanical being which is devoid of the sense of self.

Dodie is talking with some friends, and her husband has just now interrupted. Dodie is telling about the way she gets when she is drunk, and, in the middle of a sentence, her husband intrudes by saying, "Uh . . ." He says this one sound in a way which pulls a few heads toward him. It is a mild bid for attention to be shifted onto him. If Dodie were the kind of person in which a potential for experiencing stout firmness is another operating potential, the center of her self may quickly switch from operating potential 1 to operating potential 3 (D, Figure 9.2), and she might fill up the pause by rushing on with her description, or raising her voice a bit and going on, or turning to him and forthrightly telling him to stay out of this because this is her story, or glaring at him. Yet, because both are operating potentials, Dodie might well be aware or conscious of what she is doing. She might even sense anger or irritation or threat. On the other hand, if that potential for experiencing stout firmness were a *deeper* potential, the center of her sense of self might disengage and plunge quickly into the state of unfeeling (F2, Figure 9.2). In this instance, what may come forth from Dodie would be a way of being (the deeper potential for stout firmness of which she herself is thoroughly unaware. Her voice may rise and she may plunge on with the story, but *she* is momentarily gone. If someone later mentions that brief moment when her voice raised and she overcame his interruption, the sense of self which is Dodie would be confused, bewildered, not fully knowing.

Quite often, the dip into the state of unfeeling is brief, a short interlude of a few seconds or a minute or so. During this interlude the person only has the faintest awareness, if that, of what the regnant deeper potential (P2) is doing (F2, Figure 9.2). It is as if the person were drugged or asleep and virtually unaware of what the deeper potential is doing. You are at work and your boss asks you whether you have finished that job yet. Immediately you go on automatic pilot and respond in a docile manner. Immediately *afterward* you are back in the role of operating potential, and you have practically no concrete memory of exactly what occurred—for *you* had not been there when that docility occurred.

There are many times when you enter the state of unfeeling and thereby grant mandate to the rising deeper potential. Quite often it occurs when you are in a critical moment in which some wicked deeper potential is challenging to take you over. You give in and stand by, virtually unknowing. Something has taken you over. You are "giving in to an impulse." Yet there is an automaticity to the behavior, a not fully being there. It is as if you are not fully present. Although you only have occasional homosexual thoughts during the week, on the weekends there are times, often for periods of three or four hours, in which the deeper homosexuality takes you over. During these short homosexual sprees, you are another person. The usual you can testify to what is going on, but it would testify almost as an observer. This observer is not engaging in the homosexual spree. It is merely there, not fully knowing, only watching from the sidelines. The older school teacher is not fully there when the deeper potential takes over and she strangles the cat. She was there, but she barely knew what happened. She steals from many stores, yet she may not be prepared to steal until she slips into the state of not knowing, of unfeeling, and the deeper potential graciously takes over mandate. To a person walking alongside her, the takeover is undetectable. No one can discern that one personality has more or less gone underground while another personality is now present, one who is geared toward stealing something from stores. There are many activities, carried out by many persons, which are expressions of a deeper potential doing its own behaving—while the ordinary person has entered into the state of unfeeling.

In an extreme form of this same maneuver, the person-as-operating-potential can enter the state of unfeeling by suicide. The choice to disengage and allow the deeper potential to take over occurs as a quiet and peaceful slipping into death. It occurs when the person allows the "illness" to take over. It occurs when the person slides peacefully into the state of unfeeling by taking the right pills in an alcoholic stupor. It is the suicide of quiet sleep. There is no explosion of rage—no gun, no automobile crash, no hanging. The person who ends the struggle in this way betrays this imminence of suicide in a brief interlude of peacefulness. It is not the festivity associated with the decision to end the struggle, but more the peacefulness of a gradual succumbing to the state of unfeeling. It is marked by a period of halycon tranquility.

The state of unfeeling is a state of inertness, of death. Whether the operating (F2) or the deeper (F1) potential resides in this state, whether the state lasts a moment or for years, the state is one of death. I mean real, actual physical death—not some poetic allusion to death. Potentials which are so far away from experiential life will be worn away slowly. These potentials are in a state in which they will be slowly worn away and eroded until the final culmination is death of the person. We may not yet know how many potentials for experiencing lie within a given person. But I have a strong conviction that only a tiny proportion of what we *can* experience is actually experienced. After many years of consignment to a state of unfeeling, these potentials slowly wear away. They literally are dying. And after 50 or 70 years, when the proportion of the dying potentials gradually increases to 90 percent and then 98 percent, the whole personality is dead and the existence is over. We bury ourselves by consigning potentials further and further into the state of unfeeling for longer and longer periods of time. Many persons go off the behavioral circle by entering into the state of unfeeling. Their lives are increasingly characterized by less and less feeling—less disintegrative feeling, less integrative feeling, less good feelings of experiencing. They become bored, meaningless, monotonous, and then slowly and without knowing, their existence closes off into the nothingness of the state of unfeeling. This entry into death can never be entered by the person who elects the path of integration, whereby the state of unfeeling is emptied of its contents, and the person pursues a direction toward increasing life— not the death of unfeeling.

The Consequence of Being Another Operating Potential

As indicated in D, Figure 9.2, the deeper potential (DP2, Figure 9.2) is pushed down and away when the person shifts from being the intruded operating potential (OP1, Figure 9.2) to being another operating potential (OP3, Figure 9.2). At this point (D, Figure 9.1), everything begins all over again. Instead of being operating potential 1, the person is now operating potential 3. Instead of being related to deeper potential 2, the person is now related to operating potential 4 (D, Figure 9.2). Instead of carrying out behavior 1, the person now carries out behavior 2. The schema of D (Figure 9.2) is the same as the schema of A (Figure 9.2). The person is back where he started, and the circling continues.

The older sister is telling her younger sister about her marital difficulties. By experiencing sharing and intimacy (OP1, Figure 9.2), the deeper potential (the experiencing of being utterly alone, rejected, unwanted) begins to rise (DP2), and she switches to being the funny one, the jokester (OP3). Now there is a stirring of the deeper potential for hatred and rage (DP4) and the whole process begins again. As the new operating potential, the sister is at point D in the behavioral circle (Figure 9.1). If the sister shifts back to the former operating potential, she is also at point D. Regardless of the nature of the new operating potential, regardless whether the person moves back and forth between operating potentials, the person is being an operating potential (D, Figure 9.1) and will be carrying out behavior (A, Figure 9.1). Behavioral circling continues.

As father behaved (A, Figure 9.1) in a way which provided him with the experiencing of depression and sadness, the deeper potential for raging fury was raised (B, Figure 9.1) to the point (C, Figure 9.1) where he switched to another operating potential. That is when he became helpless and dependent (D, Figure 9.1). But as this second operating potential, he will only proceed further along the behavioral circle. To behave in the helpless, dependent way (OP3, Figure 9.2) will stir the deeper potential for being a repulsive, clinging, sucking parasite (DP4, Figure 9.2). Around and around the behavioral circle he goes, constantly switching back and forth between being sad and depressed (OP1), and on the other hand, helpless and dependent (OP3). Each rises to a point and then switches to the other.

Susan is the 14-year-old daughter whose deeper potential related to being the boss, the reigning woman, the one who replaces mother. As she was being the nurturant, caring daughter, her own behavior brought her to the point where the deeper potential was brought dangerously near to the behavioral surface. At this point, she exited from being the nurturant, caring one, and slipped quickly into being the girlfriend who must chat with her friend. As she switches, the deeper potential recedes. But in Susan's personality, this second operating potential is also related to the deeper potential for being the reigning boss, and so, as she chats merrily on the telephone, she soon is involved in a situation in which she is beginning once again to be visited by the deeper potential. Susan is giving advice to her girlfriend, instructing her to get the beer for the party that Susan wants to have on Thursday, and soon she is visited by the deeper sense of becoming the reigning boss. Susan has circuited the behavioral circle.

For every person who switches from one operating potential to another, the story is always the same. Behavioral circling is the human dilemma.

BEHAVIORAL CIRCLING: THE HUMAN DILEMMA

Human behavior follows two major principles: Behavior provides for the experiencing of potentials, and behavior provides for the experiencing of relationships among potentials. These two principles orchestrate with one another so that the predominance of human behavior proceeds endlessly round and round the behavioral circle, and the residual balance of human behavior either leads off the behavioral circle into integration with the deeper potential or into the state of unfeeling. It is my contention that virtually all the principles of human behavior put forward by other approaches are either incorporated under our two major principles or are pertinent only to particular points around the behavioral circle.

Behavioral Circling as a Way of Understanding Human Behavior

From our two major principles of human behavior, we may understand human behavior as moving round and round a behavioral circle. By focusing on particular segments of the behavioral circle, we
can understand behavior in several different ways—and each of these
ways is an accurate description of one segment of the behavioral circle.

Behavior moves back and forth from one operating potential to another.
The predominance of human behavior is terribly sad, for it merely
follows an interminable career of behavioral circling. Human beings
move back and forth from one operating potential to another, back
and forth. There is no substantial change, only a sideward movement
between operating potentials. Sometimes the switching is rapid, and
the pattern is one in which the person is most often one or two
operating potentials interspersed with brief dips into being less common operating potentials in particular critical moments. Sometimes
the switching is much slower, and the person remains being a given
potential for hours or days before switching again.

Behavior moves into and out of critical moments. If we focus on critical
moments (C, Figure 9.1), rather than on the operating potentials, then
behavioral circling can be described differently. It becomes a process
of moving into critical moments and then moving out of them. Behavior is revealed as a means of structuring situational contexts into
critical moments, followed by movement to extricate oneself from
those critical moments. These critical moments may occur once an
hour or once a day, but when they occur, there is no explosive happening, no change. Each time the critical moment is manufactured,
something is now on the verge of occurring, but it never occurs. Thus
the course of human behavior becomes a concatenation of situation-
buildings—without anything ever happening. Harold spends his life
building toward the experiencing of freedom (or wild craziness or
being king), without it ever happening. Back and forth goes the person, building the critical moments, and then stepping back away from
them.

Behavior moves toward and away from the heightening of experiencing.
When we focus on experiencing, human behavior is describable as a
circling toward full experiencing and then a backing away from it.
Our entire lives are wasted away in approximate experiencing, always
falling just short of complete experiencing. Behavior comes from the
operating potential until the deeper potential begins to come too
close, and then our own behavior acts to curtail the intensification of
experiencing. Thereupon the whole process starts ever anew. Never is
experiencing completed. If the process were speeded up and observed, the operating potentials would look like pulsating sacs, glow-

ing with experiencing and then cooling off while another pulsates. Yet the experiencing rises only up to a point, and then abates—without ever reaching its full saturation.

Behavior moves toward and away from the construction of appropriate situational contexts. If we focus on the situational contexts in which experiencing occurs, then we spend our lives constructing a particular kind of situational context, and then withdrawing away from it. I may spend my whole life building situational contexts in which I can experience freedom from external control—but I never *fully* experience. Instead, I move back from that situational context and start to build another. By my own behavior I may fix up my own room in the basement or in the attic, one which is away from the family so that I can experience a sense of freedom up to a point, and then I begin building some other situational context in which to experience that same sense of freedom from external constraints. Whole lifetimes can be seen from the perspective of constructing situational contexts in which experiencing occurs up to a point, and then behavior turns to further building of further situational contexts. Thus my whole life consists of a concatenation of situational contexts in which I experience a moderate degree of freedom from external constraints: building a life of a truck driver who roams from place to place and firm to firm, having women who give me plenty of freedom of movement, building a boat which I can haul about the lakes country with my camper.

As persons continue round and round the behavioral circle, they become progressively more skilled at building appropriate situational contexts which house just the right degree of experiencing. These situations provide for a measure of experiencing, but never too much. The acquisition of these skills, the settling in of these constructed situations, is a mark of habituated life maturity. She has spent 20 years provoking men into mistreating her until the skill has become perfected so that the situation of being mistreated is easily constructed, but never in a way which explodes into saturated mistreatment. Such brinkmanship subsides with age and increasing skill. A part of the skills includes safety measures to dampen experiencing. Charles spent his entire life building situations in which he gained the experience of infusing life into frail, dry things. Yet he quickly learned to truncate the situation so that experiencing never reached dangerous proportions. When he was a child, he existed to infuse a degree of life and vitality into the aged grandparents who raised him. He was a lively child who delighted his grandparents with his enthusiasm, his passion for enjoying what they guided him into enjoying, his bubbling vitality. During his adolescence he gained a safe measure of this experiencing by selecting worn out, mildly depressed, retiring friends, and serving

as their energy, their excitement, their happiness. In university he became a historian and accepted positions as a teacher of ancient Latin
and Greek—which he made come alive as he infused life and vitality
into his classes and into his students. As an older man, the school system found him to be an especially gifted administrator who enlivened
tired, worn out, old schools, and helped them to become bustling and
energetic. Always the same operating potential was experienced, but
never beyond the danger point. His life consisted of a series of mild
experiencings of the same operating potential up to a safe point.
Then he died.

Behavior increases and decreases disintegrative relationships. If we focus
on the relationship between the operating and deeper potentials, then
we can describe the behavioral circling as a continuous rising and falling of the degree of disintegrative feeling. As indicated in Figure 9.2,
the negative signs in the channel of the relationships between the
operating and deeper potentials increase (A-C) and then decrease
(C-D, A), increase and decrease. Threat or tension rises and falls, rises
and falls. Yet the rise is never too much, and the fall is never to the
point where the threat or tension dissolves away completely. When the
behavioral circling is described from this vantage point, we are
speaking in the vocabulary of those who understand behavior as
serving to maintain an optimal level of threat (or stimulation or tension or excitement) (e.g., Leuba, 1955). If the level is down, then behavior serves to raise it up a bit; if the level is up, then behavior
serves to reduce it a bit. Such a description of behavior is merely one
of a variety of ways of describing the behavioral circle by focusing on
different aspects of the same overall process. None of these constitutes
a major principle of human behavior—even though each of these re-
descriptions and selections of different foci are in themselves accurate
statements about what is occurring. In other words, humanistic theory
has no place for a general conception of behavior as serving to maintain some (homeostatic) optimal level of tension (or stimulation).

When we focus attention on the rise and fall of the threat (i.e., the
disintegrative relationship), then the rising and falling can be described in at least three ways. First, behavior serves to *maintain* an optimal level of threat (or tension), and the evidence is that behavior
both increases and decreases the amount of threat. Second, behavior
serves to *reduce* threat, and the evidence is that following behavior the
degree of threat is reduced (see point D in Figures 9.1 and 9.2).
Third, behavior serves to *increase* threat, and the evidence is that
threat increases following behavior (see points A, B, and C in Figures
9.1 and 9.2). By means of our schema we can understand that each of
these three observational perspectives are focusing on different points
in the behavioral circle, yet each is reporting accurately what is there.

Everyone is correct and, at the same time, incorrect in elevating their particular focused observation into a general principle of human behavior.

Behavior raises and lowers the deeper potential. If we focus on the deeper potential, then the behavioral circle can be redescribed so that the deeper potential rises up and then moves down, rises up and moves down, over and over again. Although behaviors are involved in both phases, many theoretical approaches are impressed with the coupling of behavior with the reduction of the potential. These are the approaches which maintain that behavior serves to reduce "drives," and accept the popular "drive-reduction" conception of behavior. According to our schema of the behavioral circle, however, behavior serves *both* phases, and it is equally possible to be impressed with the coupling of behavior and motivational (or drive) *increase* or gain or stimulation. Under the schema of the behavioral circle, however, behavior serves to *increase* the deeper potential at point A (Figure 9.1) and to *reduce* the deeper potential at point D. The drive-reduction hypothesis seems to be applicable at only one point in the behavioral circle, and therefore is far from a universal description of behavior. I reject the drive-reduction theory of human behavior, though I can understand how a selective attention to one point in the behavioral circle can give rise to such a description of human behavior.

Approaches which view human beings from a biological perspective tend to think of deeper processes as biological (see Chapter 4) and to think of disintegrative relationships as physiological tensions. These approaches are therefore selectively drawn toward grand conceptions of human behavior as following principles of tension-reduction and drive-reduction. From our perspective, however, these are by no means adequate descriptions of human behavior in general. They are, instead, biologically derived, selective perceptions of only a few phases of the behavioral circle.

Aside from the biological conception of the nature of deeper potentials, the raising and lowering of deeper potentials have an external aspect in relationships between the person and other individuals. In conjunction with the raising and lowering of the deeper potential are the approaching and moving away from other persons. To the extent that other persons are constructed as externalizations of deeper potentials, the course of the behavioral circle will bring the person closer to others and then away from others, over and over again. In this periodic, endless movement toward and away from others, the polarity is between complete merging with the other and complete isolation-withdrawal from the other (Laing, 1960). The person faces a looming threat of self-destruction as he moves closer and closer into others, and yet his very behavior brings this threat into increasingly prominent possibility. This circling toward and away from relationships with others is merely the external aspect of the internal circling toward and away from relationships with one's own deeper potential.

REGULARITY AND PERIODICITY OF HUMAN BEHAVIOR

The net effect of behavioral circling is a periodic waxing and waning of each of these components. As behavior moves round and round the behavioral circle, there is regularity in (a) movement back and forth from one operating potential to another, (b) movement into and out of critical moments, (c) movement toward and away from the heightening of experiencing, (d) movement toward and away from the construction of appropriate situational contexts, (e) movement toward the heightening and lowering of the degree of disintegrative relationships, and (f) movement upward and downward of the deeper potential. I propose that these evidences of the regularity of human behavior are accounted for by our principles of human behavior—and are not to be taken as evidence of any assumed *biological* underpinnings of human behavior.

The presence of regularity and periodicity is evidence of nothing more than regularity and periodicity. There are several ways of accounting for such regularity and periodicity. Among them are the behavioral circling schema of humanistic theory *and also* the principles of biological approaches. I see no reason for concluding that periodicity and regularity are evidence that the phenomenon is of biological origins, yet this is too frequently the conclusion which is drawn. For example, in reviewing research on dreaming, Murray (1965, p. 88) notes that nearly ". . . all researchers using the REM technique report that for a given individual, the dream periods occur with a more or less predictable periodicity. This suggests a basic biological process involving an endogenous rhythm." Jones (1970) echoes a similar line of reasoning in concluding that ". . . the almost metronomically occurring periods of dreaming sleep are basically governed by neurophysiological factors" (p. 42). In contrast, I would conclude that the apparent periodicity and regularity are descriptions of a phenomenon which is open to various modes of conceptualization, among which is the neurophysiological mode. From the humanistic mode of conceptualization, the regularity and periodicity are taken as *in vivo* expressions of the principles of the behavioral circle and the regularity and periodicity characteristic of sheer behavioral circling. Indeed, I see the phenomena of sleep and dreams as especially pure expressions of the regularity and periodicity of the behavioral circle (Mahrer, 1975a). In both the waking and sleeping states, our behavioral circle schema would suggest a periodic movement into and out of the domain of the deeper potential. In the sleep state, the center of the person moves increasingly into the deeper potential until that point on the behavioral circle where more fully experiencing the deeper potential would seriously threaten the existence of the operating potentials or ordinary waking life. Throughout a given sleep cycle, one process consists of a regular going into and out of this "D-state," while a second process consists of remaining in the deeper (dream) potential for increasing periods of time. Murray (1965), as well as other dream researchers (e.g. Hartmann, 1967; Jones, 1970; Kramer, 1969; Snyder, 1963) have confirmed both periodic processes. Such findings are in accord with the principles of our behavioral circle.

As suggested by the behavioral circle, all human behavioral phenomena, including dreaming, would be characterized by a regularity, a periodicity, an orderly sequence of phases. Careful clinical observers note that patients follow such regular phases, although the nature of the phases varies with the person. Boss (1963) describes a patient's rising experiencing of sensual femininity, followed by a phase he terms "pathology," and back again to the initial phase. There is a predictable regularity for the observer who knows the patient and who can apply the schema of the behavioral circle. "The pathological phase could be predicted with empiric certainty each time the patient was confronted with the realm of her sensual and emotional femininity" (p. 23).

Students of psychopathology accept as axiomatic the regularity of changes from one phase to another. Indeed, when the expressed nature of these phases takes on a characteristic predictability, we dignify the phenomenon with a label—e.g., manic-depressive. Yet the factors which account for the change from one phase to another are essentially unknown, compared with our firm observation that changes from being manic to being depressed to being manic occur with some regularity. What accounts for such changes in phase? Very often, the completion of one phase is considered a kind of "spontaneous remission," though we have little or no idea of what accounts for the transition from one phase to another. At present, " . . . no attempt has been made to explain the phenomenon in other than quite gross terms. If spontaneous remission of neurosis occurs, it must occur via some psychological and/or physiological process. What is the stimulus which initiates the process of recovery? Are the stimulus and the process the same for all psychoneurotics, or different for various types? How does it come about that attitudes and habit systems on which one has acted for much of his life are modified so easily without rather energetic intervention of some sort? What makes an habitual maladaptive pattern of behavior suddenly begin to disappear?" (Kiesler, 1966, p. .115). It is my contention that the movement from a manic to a depressed to a manic way of being, the phenomena which we refer to as spontaneous remission, and the general regularity and periodicity characterizing human behavior, are expressions of the systematic change from one point to the next in the behavioral circle. There are no new or special principles required to explain these phenomena. As we understand how each point in the behavioral circle makes way for movement to the next point, we are making sense of this regularity and periodicity in human behavior.

10

Painful Behavior

The purpose of this chapter is to answer the following questions: How may we make sense of behavior which is accompanied with painful feelings—feelings of being in pieces, fractionated, incomplete, disjointed; feelings of being painfully at war, in turmoil, torn apart; feelings of anxiety, threat, tension, dread, fear, helplessness, smallness, pawnness, shame, guilt, self-punishment, separation, alienation, aloneness, meaninglessness, hollowness, depression, gloom, bodily pain and distress, painful hostility and anger? How may we describe behavior which curtails experiencing, which places a person in a state of unfeeling, a state of deadness, of nothingness, a state in which the person is asleep, behaving automatically, a state in which one does not experience that there is no experiencing, a state of living death?

With the exception of optimal persons, those who are well into the process of integration and actualization (Chapters 11, 12), all persons are characterized by painful behavior. Thus the purpose of the present chapter is to describe the painful behavior of ordinary, everyday persons, regardless of the ways in which other approaches classify these persons. This chapter describes painful behavior which has been labeled as psychopathological and normal, stupid and intelligent, crazy and healthy, immature and mature, maladjusted and adjusted, neurotic and psychotic, antisocial and prosocial. As long as the behavior is accompanied with any kind of painful feeling, it falls within the scope of this chapter.

ONE SET OF PRINCIPLES FOR THE PAINFUL BEHAVIOR OF ALL PERSONS

Chapter 8 introduced two major principles of human behavior—behavior as a means of providing for experiencing of potentials, and behavior as a means of instituting relationships among potentials.

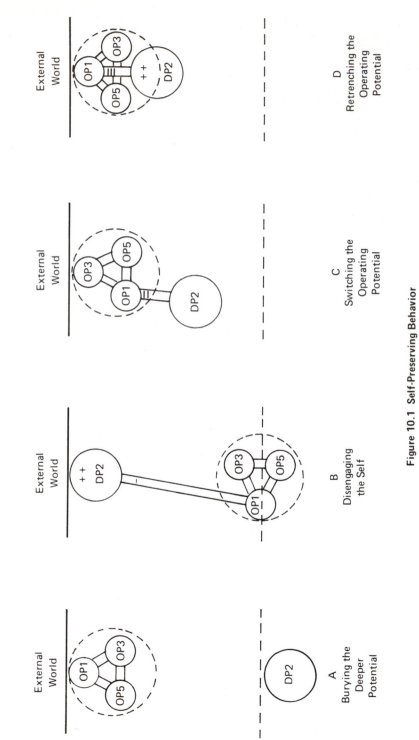

Figure 10.1 Self-Preserving Behavior

Chapter 9 orchestrated these principles into the behavioral circle. These principles are sufficient to account for painful behavior, and, therefore, no new principles will be introduced in the present chapter.

Our posture is that the only unique kind of behavior is that which characterizes optimal persons, who are substantially integrated and actualized. All other behavior is typically painful, and that includes the behavior of persons said to be normal or ordinary or adjusted. In contrast, for example, psychoanalysis distinguishes between normal, adjusted persons, and persons who are abnormal, mentally ill, neurotic or psychotic. Humanistic theory provides one set of principles to account for all painful behavior, and this behavior includes the behavior of those whom psychoanalytic theory distinguishes as normal, adjusted, healthy, well, versus those considered abnormal, maladjusted, sick, and ill. In psychoanalytic theory, one set of principles accounts for the behavior of the former group, and a different set of principles is put forward to account for the behavior of those in the latter group. Whereas those who are normal, healthy, adjusted, and well function on the basis of a *reality* principle, the abnormal, maladjusted, sick, and ill are held as functioning on the basis of a principle of *repetition compulsion* (Freud, 1950; Wolberg, 1968, pp. 40-41). From a humanistic perspective, the same principles describe the painful behavior of *all* persons. We speak only of painful behavior—including the painful behavior of the well, the healthy, the normal and the adjusted. There is no principle that behavior is directed toward pleasure (in persons who are normal, healthy, well, and adjusted) and toward pain (in persons who are abnormal, maladjusted, sick, or ill). Because the pleasure-pain concept is so basic to so many approaches, separate sets of principles must be invented to account for behavior which predominantly leads to pleasure, and for behavior which predominantly leads to pain. Principles such as repetition compulsion, death instincts, homeostasis, and others must explain why it is that behavior does not do what it should do when the system is working the way it ought to be working. Because humanistic theory incorporates no basic division into pleasure and pain, there is no fundamental division into one set of principles for the healthy, the normal, the adjusted, the well, and another set for those who are called unhealthy, sick, ill, and maladjusted.

According to humanistic theory, all behavior, including painful behavior, is understood on the basis of the same principles. There is therefore no need to identify certain behavior as painful (or abnormal or deviant or neurotic or whatever), and to find special ways of explaining that generated class of behavior (Mahrer, 1970f). Accordingly, humanistic theory has no place for concepts such as illness, emotional problems, anxiety neurosis, inadequate learnings, brain damage, deficiencies of conditioning, delinquency, or any other concepts to explain painful or problem behavior.

DISTINGUISHING FEATURES OF PAINFUL BEHAVIOR

The distinguishing feature of all painful behavior is the presence of disintegrative relationships among potentials. Thus we are speaking of every one in whom potentials are related disintegratively, for each of the kinds of painful behaviors derives, ultimately, from the presence of disintegrative relationships.

A functional classification of painful behavior. The function of the painful behavior always relates back to the disintegrative relationships among the potentials. First, if relationships are disintegrative, behavior will institute disintegrative relationships between the person and the external world. Inevitably such behavior is accompanied with certain kinds of painful feelings. Thus the first major classification of painful behavior refers to *disintegrative behavior*. Second, if relationships among potentials are disintegrative, then behavior which serves to provide for the experiencing of potentials may likely be painful. We are here concerned with painful behavior in the service of experiencing potentials, and therefore the second classification of painful behavior refers to *experiential behavior*. Third, if relationships are disintegrative, the person-as-operating-potential will behave in ways which avoid the threat of dissolution, the threat of closing out the existence of the person. As described in the last chapter, such behavior is accompanied with its own brand of painful feelings as the person struggles to preserve its self. This third classification of painful behavior refers to *self-preservative behavior*.

It is interesting to note that our threefold classification is based on the *function* of the painful behavior, and not on the nature or content of the behavior itself. We cannot say that a particular behavior is a painful behavior. We must, instead, identify the presence of some kind of painful feeling as it relates to one of the three functions of painful behavior. In the history of classification of human behavior, such a basis is relatively unique. As far back as 2800 B.C., classification systems used by the Sumerians and the Egyptians were based upon the nature and content of the behaviors themselves, and not on their supposed functions (Robbins, 1966, p. 8). Throughout recent history, with very few exceptions, systems of classification have been based upon the nature and content of the behaviors themselves rather than upon their function (Mahrer, 1970d), and this includes our ponderous psychiatric classification of mental diseases as well as the various attempts to categorize behavior pathology within behavior modification frameworks.

Value judgments inherent in humanistic theory. Our classification system bespeaks of a set of value judgments which ought properly be explicated. "Rarely, if at all, does the Scientist consider, let alone justify, the value judgments that may be an essential part of his presumable 'objective' description of behavior . . . all concepts of pathology, especially of psychopathology, are predominantly valuational" (Needleman, 1967, p. ix). In explicating the value judgments of humanistic theory, the *highest value* adheres to optimal behavior, the behavior of persons significantly into the processes of integration and actualization (Chapters 11, 12). *Less* value is attached to painful behavior, to behaviors which impede or block integration and actualization, to behaviors which are accompanied with any of the varieties of painful feeling, to disintegrative painful behavior, to painful experiential behaviors, and to self-preservative behaviors. In other words, less value is attached to behaviors deriving from a personality characterized by disintegrative relationships.

A behavior cannot be said to be a painful behavior on the merits of its own nature and content, but only on the basis of its *function* as it derives from a disintegrative relationship. Eating and smoking and sucking and talking may be considered "oral," but they qualify as painful behaviors only on the basis of their function within the personality system (Erikson, 1950). So-called "oral" behavior is painful only if it is accompanied with painful feelings in its role of serving any of the above three functions. Otherwise, such behavior is not painful. We cannot construct a list of "pathological" behaviors or symptoms or maladjustive behaviors. We cannot even construct a list of painful behaviors. Once the focus is on the *function* of the behavior, and not its *nature*, a behavior qualifies as painful only when we know more about it than that it consists of eating or smoking or sucking or talking.

Theorogenic issues. How may we categorize behaviors such as hearing voices that others do not hear, having "hallucinations" and "delusions," or speaking in sentences that are incomprehensible to the listener? In our system we classify such behaviors as painful *only if* they are accompanied with some form of painful feeling—only if they function as disintegrative painful behavior, as painful means of experiencing, or as painful means of self-preservation. It is quite possible that such behavior may be closer to optimal behavior than to painful behavior. There is nothing in the behaviors themselves which automatically distinguishes them as qualitatively different from other behaviors (Rogers, 1966; Skinner, 1967). To label such behavior as sick, psychotic, symptomatic of mental illness, or pathological is to think in terms of antediluvian psychiatric concepts which have no place in humanistic theory.

Nor is there any place in humanistic theory for the pursuit of answers to *theorogenic* issues which are meaningful only within a system which accepts concepts such as neurosis and psychosis, mental illness, psychopathology, and schizophrenia. All of the efforts to identify the distinguishing features of "schizophrenia" have about as much relevance, in humanistic theory, as efforts to identify the distinguishing features of witches or persons whose humours of the body have a preponderance of black bile. It is fruitless to search for the core of schizophrenia (cf. Binswanger, 1967, p. 250). It is fruitless to expend theoretical and research energy to investigate the differences between schizophrenics and non-schizophrenics, or between psychotics and non-psychotics (cf. Maher, 1966). Because such variables have no place in humanistic theory, such issues are considered theorogenic, i.e., meaningful and relevant only within personality approaches which legitimize such distinctions.

DISINTEGRATIVE BEHAVIOR

The first class of behavior which is accompanied with painful feeling is that behavior which institutes disintegrative relationships between the person and the external world. Given disintegrative relationships among potentials, this behavior sets about constructing disintegrative relationships between the person and the external world, and thereby brings about painful feelings: being in pieces, fractionated, incomplete, disjointed; being torn apart inside, with one's parts at war and in turmoil; anxiety, threat, tension, dread, fear; helplessness, smallness, pawnness; shame, guilt, self-punishment; separation, alienation, aloneness; meaninglessness, hollowness, depression, gloom; bodily pain and distress; hostility and anger.

Human beings are continuously at work behaving in ways which invite others to hate them, ridicule them, reject them, fear them. Behavioral means of establishing these kinds of relationships have been carefully refined over years and years of practice. Most human beings are skilled artisans in the behavioral construction of such relationships and spend large proportions of their time behaving in ways which establish such relationships, and bring on such painful feelings.

One of the characteristics of such disintegrative behavior is the restless urgency to do things to the world, to mess with it, change it. Behavior which establishes disintegrative relationships *must* mould the world into relationships which are abrasive. Each tiny behavior must turn or fashion the world into being something else—regardless of what mode of constructing the external world is adopted (cf. Chapter 6). Such behavior is unable to simply let things be, to live in peaceful comfort with the way the world is. Such disintegrative behaviors are characterized by ". . . that inability to 'let things be' in the immediate encounter with them . . . They persist in suffering because things are not the way they would like them to be . . ." (Binswanger, 1967, p. 252). Here then are behaviors which continually are at work doing those things to the external world which culminate in the establishment and maintenance of disintegrative relationships accompanied with painful feelings.

There are two categories of painful disintegrative behavior. The first category includes those behaviors which effect disintegrative relationships with the externalized *deeper* potential, and the second category includes those behaviors which effect disintegrative relationships with the externalized *operating* potential.

Behaviors Effecting Disintegrative Relationships with the Externalized Deeper Potential

Two coordinated behavioral steps. In order to construct disintegrative relationships with the externalized deeper potential, behavior must occur in two orchestrated steps. The first wave of behavior constructs the external world into being the externalized deeper potential, and the second wave of behavior establishes and maintains the disintegrative relationship. As both waves of behavior occur, the accompaniment is always painful disintegrative feelings.

She was an older teacher who had taught at the same junior high school for 16 years. Her deeper potential consisted of experiencing freely flowing, sensual, bubbling sexuality. Given the disintegrative relationships surrounding this deeper potential, the first wave of behaviors was geared toward constructing an externalization of her deeper potential. By means of utlizing a ready-made external world (Figure 6.1), she found another recently hired student teacher to serve as the externalization—a young, nicely groomed, slender, gracious, intelligent, inviting woman who exuded a fresh and bubbling sexuality. Next the older teacher fashioned the relationship into disintegrative channels by making offhand, snide remarks about the student teacher, regarding her with cool distance, avoiding close contact with her, finding fault with her, and writing a cuttingly negative evaluation of her. By means of such behavior she succeeded in constructing a disintegrative relationship complete with painful feelings. Her own behaviors not only brought to life the deeper potential, but stamped her relationship with painful disintegrative feelings: a painful anger, a being torn apart inside, a sense of being tight and clutched up, an agonizing anxiety. By means of her own behavior she had succeeded in saturating herself in such painful feelings.

Yet these feelings are rather sporadic, and certainly do not dominate her life. As bad as they are, they nevertheless are mild against the whole sweep of her life. In the instance of Lewis, however, behavior went about the same task of effecting disintegrative relationships with the externalized deeper potential, and the consequences were far more painful. Lewis' life was dominated by relationships with a highly disintegrative deeper homosexuality from which he recoiled in panic. On numerous occasions, that homosexuality was constructed in his external world by his way of *receiving an intrusive* (homosexual) *external world* (Figure 6.1). Once he was waiting on a street corner for a friend, and a stranger walked up to him, touched him on the penis, asked him if he wanted a blow job, and Lewis was transfixed with a paralyzing anxiety. He had no memory of the way in which the man finally left, but Lewis was plunged into catastrophic fear. On another occasion he was in a public toilet, and someone passed a note underneath the stall partition, inviting him to a party that evening. Again he was thrown into a panic. These occasions illustrate the behavioral confrontation with frightening externalizations of his own deeper potential constructed by means of receiving an intrusive external world.

Lewis soon moved on to other behavioral modes of constructing disintegrative relationships with that externalized deeper potential. In concert with another young man, the two of them *conjointly constructed* strained outbursts of homosexuality (Figure 6.1). By means of his own behavioral experimenting with homosexuality, Lewis was now filled with excruciating loathing and self-hate. By the time Lewis began *fabricating* the externalized deeper potential (Figure 6.1), the painful feelings were intense and nearly all-encompassing. He was terrorized that the wall scribblings in public toilets were directed personally toward him. He was driven by the agonizing likelihood that homosexuals could discern his own homosexual odor. He was plagued by visions of brawny, hirsute, dominant homosexuals who could attack him at will and force him to submit to hellish homosexual tortures. The world was filled with forces cognizant of his homosexuality, and devilishly thwarting each attempt to run away from it. We may label such behavior as paranoid delusions, projections, ideas of reference, and hallucinations, yet they also occur as terribly painful behaviors effecting brutally disintegrative relationships with the externalized deeper potential.

When the relationship with the deeper potential is disintegrative, behaviors can effect a disintegrative relationship with the externalized deeper potential simply by seeing it there in the external world. Without working at all, the person can find externalized deeper potentials all over the world. Typically, these behaviors construct the externalized deeper potential by receiving an intrusive external world and by utilizing a ready-made external world (Figure 6.1). If I am disgusted by and loathe my own deeper potential for being decimated and "castrated," my disintegrative behavior may consist of simply selecting out crippled persons without arms or legs or chunks of their bodies (Dollard & Miller, 1950) and then loathing them and being disgusted by them. If I bear a disintegrative relationship toward deeper potentials for death and dying or for vengeance and vindictiveness, I may be fearful in the presence of death or dying persons (Fenichel, 1953b). Such disintegrative behaviors are remarkably easy to carry out, for they consist in merely seeing or perceiving—i.e., receiving an intrusive external world or utilizing a ready-made external world. Yet they succeed in filling me with painful feelings.

The irrelevance of the degree of reality. Such painful disintegrative behavior may be either highly realistic or highly unrealistic. These behaviors can use modes of constructing an external world out of realistic or unrealistic building blocks (Chapter 6). Although the young assistant professor writhed and twisted in his disintegrative relationship with his deeper potential for supreme power and coerciveness, he was unerringly accurate in constructing externalizations out of devastatingly real external expressions of supreme power and coerciveness. He dug out quite real power and coerciveness in the full professors in his department, and then twisted in hatred at their power and coerciveness. He was remarkably realistic in finding the power and coerciveness in his coterie of students, and saw quite clearly the coerciveness in the university administration with whom he engaged in disintegrative battle. Never in error, his tortured deeper potential led him unerringly to locate external expressions of supreme power and coerceiveness. Then, by means of his own behavior, he effected painfully disintegrative relationships with the externalized—and realistic—deeper potential.

In such instances, the external world lends itself quite cordially to the construction of externalized deeper potentials. There is really a great deal of ominous coerciveness and power out there in the world, so that disintegrative relationships can easily be established with elements which are terribly real. Regardless which mode of construction is adopted, behavior will find plenty of realistic building blocks. There is industrial power, and it can wipe you out. Military power is real and deadly. The legal system is constructed on power, and it demands fear and hatred. The havoc which governmental power can wreak is nearly boundless. One need not look far to find realistic external manifestations of coerciveness and power which can be related to in fear and hate.

The work of Laing and Esterson (1970) indicates that a realistic base typically underlies so-called paranoid schizophrenic ideas of reference, projections, delusions and hallucinations. Even in these instances, behaviors serve to construct an externalization of the deeper potential, and then to establish disintegrative relationships with that externalization—even though the constructed external reality is quite real. Laing and Esterson describe women whose "paranoid schizophrenic" worlds include others suspected of hating them, plotting against them, secretly tormenting them. Yet in each instance, it was true that others *were* plotting, tormenting, rejecting, and hating them. The suspicions of these women were entitled to occur because they were anchored in reality. However, the degree to which the constructed reality is real and true is irrelevant. Persons whose behavior constructs a particular externalized deeper potential and establishes a painfully disintegrative relationship toward that constructed external world are engaging in painful disintegrative behavior regardless of the degree of reality in their constructed worlds and constructed relationships.

Disguised as helping behavior. Such painful disintegrative behavior is by no means restricted to problems or difficulties or to behavior which seems weird or bizarre or even clearly distress-ridden. Much of this behavior can be masqueraded as "helping behavior" or as the behavior of social change. All too often, the intent to change others is a mask, thinly veiling the effecting of disintegrative relationships with the externalized deeper potential. My intent to help you or to change you is too often comprised of my first constructing you as an externalization of my own deeper potential, and then my effecting a disintegrative relationship with you. I harbor deeper potentials for stealing, lying, wanton destruction, and then set out to help you or change you or rehabilitate you. I become a counsellor or case worker or policeman or lawyer or judge or social worker. My aims are laudable, for I want only to help you and to assist you in changing. Yet underneath I fear and hate you who are the externalization of that which I fear and hate in my self. Painful disintegrative behavior often takes the form of constructing relationships with those whom one wishes to change. Beware of those who seek to help you change or who seek to help you change your world, for they are effecting painful disintegrative relationships with their own externalized deeper potentials.

This behavior frequently takes curiously twisted forms which occur as highly laudable, socially valued actions of the good people, and often of the very group who leads the community. Listen closely to those who exhort others to be noble, who tell others how they ought to be. Listen quite carefully and you will discern the fear and hate at those who are not that way. They are fearful and angry at persons who are bad, petty, not noble, not altruistic. Exhortations to be different (loyal, altruistic, forgiving, patriotic, social, dedicated) are ways of constructing external worlds and then relating to them disintegratively.

I listen to the social leader, to the teacher, the physician, the psychiatrist, the social worker, the judge, the clergyman. They seem to be trying to help, to change the world in some good way. They do not kill people. They are not behaving like people who are in prisons and mental hospitals. Still, they use the very same mechanisms in their behavior. They first construct the external world into being externalizations of their own deeper potentials, and then they effect disintegrative relationships with those externalizations. Yet all of this is carried on as if they were being helpful, and acting in the service of human beings. Be sensitive to the disintegrative behavioral aspects of efforts to change others, efforts to help, to lead the way, to change the world, to change *you*.

All such behavior is accompanied with a mixture of feelings. Many of these feelings are good ones. But there lurks beneath a bedrock of disintegrative pain. Underneath the lie of helping others, of being saintly and therapeutic, is the ugly truth of fearing and hating the helpee—the student, the minority group, the followers, the patient or client, the sick one, the uneducated, the sinner. In one's own way, one is constructing others into being the externalized deeper potential and there is inevitably the painful disintegrative relationship. In these instances, the pain is seldom directly felt. The helper (judge, teacher, group leader, mental health volunteer, nurse, physician, psychotherapist, counsellor) does not writhe in the pure painful feeling. Instead, the pain is a sea of feeling in which the feelings of helping (judging, teaching, rehabilitating, doctoring, ministering) are cupped. The helper lives in a sea of disintegrative feelings without knowing. Instead of directly and honestly constructing disintegrative relationships and wallowing in the pure disintegrative pain, the helper lives in a world of lies and deceit, struggling to run away from the pure disintegrative pain of his behavioral enterprise. His is a world of half-sensed agony and anxiety, shadowy meaninglessness and depression. The painful feelings lurk about without ever being directly confronted. They are always present without being directly seen, sensed rather than fully felt.

The impenetrable gap. Some behaviors construct an externalized deeper potential and then proceed to erect an impenetrable gap between the person and that component of the external world. These are the behaviors which maintain a subject-object split, which erect a wall. These are the behaviors which insure that the person is unreachable. Such behaviors, whether exhibited by the community drunk or the family physician, are disintegrative behaviors, for they follow the same pattern of constructing the world as the externalization of the deeper potential, and then effecting a disintegrative (in this instance, in the form of an impenetrable gap) relationship with the externalized deeper potential.

The disintegrative behaviors which accomplish the impenetrable gap may occur in the form of intimacy avoidances. In dozens of ways, the person insures that the moat of safety is never bridged. Do not ever come too close to me. Come that far and no further. I am civilized and social, friendly and interpersonally skilled. But I also behave in ways that insure that you shall never get too close. There must be a final gap between you and me, a gap which you shall never penetrate. Be loving and understanding to me, but only up to a point. Beyond that point I must erect the same barrier I maintain between me and what is deeper within me. I will allow you to comprehend me, but only up to a point. I can have sex with you before we marry, but after we take a step toward further closeness and intimacy I must keep you (as my deeper potential) safely back across a gap, and therefore sex must be made mechanical or muted or rare. I can regard you across a gap of objectivity. The gap may be gossamer thin, as subtle as can be, but it is there—when I am involved with you as the externalization of my own deeper potential. My stance toward you is neither bizarre nor impolite. I do not peer at you in the caricature of the scientist. Nevertheless, when you are made into that which I fear and hate in me, I maintain a narrow little impenetrable gap by erecting a kind of screen of objectivity. You are caught into being my subject, the object of my objective knowing. Binswanger uses the term "communicatio" to refer to social intercourse, and the term "communio" as love, in the erection of this disintegrative gap or wall of objectivity when a person must draw back from another's behavior as different, or crazy, or strange; ". . . which is to say that something has got between him and her which is experienced by him as a barrier to communicatio and, even more so, to communio . . . Thereby I separate or remove myself from my fellow men, and the closeness of sympathy and intercourse changes into the distance of objective regard, observation, and judgement . . ." (Binswanger, 1958b, p. 228). When I maintain a gap between myself and that awful thing deep within me, I know you as that awful thing—and regard you objectively, have private objective thoughts about you, think things about you. I am thereby instituting an impenetrable gap between you and me.

I can also effect that veil of separation by taking the posture of the intermediary between you and what is going on within me. You can never reach me when I inform you about what is there within me. I tell you that I am angry, but there is no anger in my presence. I tell you that I have love for you, but I am not loving as I tell this to you. I am telling you *about* my deeper feelings, but I do not *have* them. "I am damned mad about that," yet he says it with a tone of tired resignation and depression—no mad-ness. To describe the feelings inside is not to have them. To tell you about my affection is different from being affectionate. Such behavior constitutes a particularly deceptive piece of behavior because its outer face is one of intimacy, closeness, candidness and honesty. It gives an *appearance* of utter transparence because it does tell about some inner state. To describe inner feelings *seems* to be open and transparent. To be honest about what is happening within seems to invite trust and intimacy. Yet the describer remains across an impenetrable gap while pointing, in an apparently revealing and transparent manner, to the deeper feelings supposedly going on within.

Whether I tell you about things going on within, or regard you from behind a wall of objectivity, or generally maintain a moat of intimacy-avoidance, I am constructing you into being an externalization of my own deeper potential, and I relate to you in the same way I relate to it—viz. by means of a disintegrative impenetrable gap. There are ways of constructing the external world into being an almost exact, point-by-point replica of the deeper potential, and then instituting the impenetrable gap between the person and the external world. For example, if I draw back from my own inner foul-mouthed ugliness, I can establish a gap between me and it by literally not seeing or hearing the foul-mouthed woman belting out the explosive ugliness at me. I freeze, and in the frozen state I do not see her clearly, nor do I hear what she says in lapidary clarity. Suddenly it is vague and hazy as if my senses are clouded. By means of this fuzziness, I have established an impenetrable gap between me and that woman.

If I maintain internal disintegrative distance from my own deeper weirdness and craziness, I can impose this impenetrable gap the instant I encounter that same weirdness and craziness in the world. You imply that if a cat looks at you in a certain way, your sexual potency will evaporate. You act as if creatures from another planet are invisibly present among us. You open the window in such a way that alludes subtly to a fear that enemies are intent upon killing you with poisonous gas. Immediately I regard you as strange, weird, different, crazy, I draw back from you and impose an impenetrable gap between us. The gap is subtle, implied, indirect, but impenetrable. Or the gap can be gross and direct, and I openly regard you as sick, abnormal, or mad, and label you as such (Bandura, 1961; Binswanger, 1958b; Szasz, 1956, 1957, 1961). The gap is between me and you as the externalization of my own deeper potential which I draw back from as sick and abnormal. In this sense, your craziness is in part a function of me. "Whether or not a given behavior will be considered normal or a symptom of an underlying disturbance will depend on whether or not somebody objects to the behavior . . . whether a specific behavior will be viewed as normal or as a symptom of an underlying pathology is not independent of who makes the judgment, the social context in which the judgment occurs, the age of the person, as well as many other factors" (Bandura, 1961, p. 153). Because we institute such an impenetrable gap between us and that which exists within as strange or crazy, ". . . a person is judged 'sick' wherever his social behavior deviates from the respective norm of social behavior and thus appears conspicuous or strange" (Binswanger, 1958b, p. 227). Living with a disintegrative gap between ourselves and our insides, we effect that same gap between ourselves and the externalizations of these insides. We construct others into being externalizations of our own inner craziness and put them away in special institutions for the mad, the insane, the sick, the lunatic, the psychotic (Albee, 1970; Szasz, 1956, 1957, 1961), in a further extension of our disintegrative separation.

If my impenetrable gap is dramatically compelling, you will be unable to reach me. My unreachability will show forth as behavior which is weird and bizarre, strange and incomprehensible, but the dominant characteristic is its imposing a gap between us, one which defies my being reached by you. In its extreme form, this dominant characteristic has been proclaimed as the landmark of what we know as schizophrenia, viz. the social mistrust, social fear, basic certainty of unlovability and rejection to the point of almost impossibility of neutralization and intervention (cf. Meehl, 1962). It is as if persons who behave in this way, and are typically called "schizophrenic," employ these extreme means of effecting an impenetrable gap between themselves and their deeper potentials, as well as between themselves and the externalization of their deeper potentials.

The foredoomed, fruitless external pursuit of internal integration. Sooner or later, painful feelings will engulf the person who runs from his basic disintegration into the utterly impossible pursuit of integration with the external world. This is the person whose internal relationships are disintegrative, and who throws himself into the task of trying to get others to like him, provide him with a sense of belonging, accept and love him. He scratches the external world for the integration which is so lacking within. It can never succeed. In this pursuit, the pseudo-integrative relationship is sought from externalizations of the disintegrative deeper potential. Recoiling against her own inner tendency for graspingness and avariciousness, the young woman unerringly sought out persons who manifested those qualities, and settled into a campaign to hack out a relationship of warmth and closeness, acceptance and love. These kinds of persons became her friends and lovers throughout her life. Superficially she usually achieved a cardboard veneer which looked like an integrative relationship. Yet each finally degenerated into the disintegrative relationship marking her relationship with her own deeper potential. Many of these persons launch their campaigns into groups which likewise are the externalizations of disintegrative deeper potentials. If I withdraw from my pettiness or my open sexuality or my exclusivity, I seek out groups with members expressing pettiness or open sexuality or exclusivity. Then I behave so as to gain a sense of being integrated in the group. It is "my" group, I feel free in the group, accepted and loved in it, with a sense of belongingness and unity. I need my therapy group, my encounter group, my group workshop, my family, my cell, my movement, my party—for in it I find the integration which is so painfully missing inside me. But the integration I find is illusory, for it always dissolves away and reveals the underlying disintegration.

To wash away the tide of inner loneliness and separation, I can turn to an involvement in the group. I must lose myself in the group, and anesthetize my self against the experience of utter loneliness and separation. I need my group. Engulf me and fill me with purpose and titillated feeling. Please give me a sense of mission—any kind of mission. We can dedicate ourselves to loving one another or fighting against some other group, we may touch one another like playful puppies or plot how to overthrow them. Nothing matters as long as the accompanying sense is one of groupness to barricade myself against the fundamental loneliness and separation which is always there. Such behavior, born of the superficial group hunger, can never achieve internal integration. It is disintegrative behavior, working agonizingly toward achieving relationships fraught with pain.

The fundamental lie in all behavior foredoomed to fruitless external pursuit of external integration is that (a) although my internal relationships are *disintegrative*, I will be successful in my pursuit after *integrative* external relationships, and (b) although my deeper potential exists in its *disintegrative* form, I will find relationships with its polar pseudo-*integrative* form. Whatever the nature or content of my deeper potential, I convert it to its idealized polar form and dedicate my life toward seeking the perfect union with the idealized other. Regardless whether my deeper potential consists of pettiness or avarice, nothingness or hatred, incorporation or separateness, my life becomes the pursuit of the perfect partner or guru or mate or child or life situation or community or mission or parent or psychotherapist or priest or wise man or God or philosophy—and the effecting of the perfect relationship of idealized integration, oneness, blissful understanding. No matter how successful I am, the whole structure of such life pursuits is foredoomed to failure. Being always the person I am, you will always disappoint me. My insides whisper the truth to me: the other one is not the perfect partner, my lover is not a saint, my teacher is not omniscient. I sense that our union is not perfect. The quest cracks apart and I am filled with agony and hurt and fear and loneliness and emptiness and hatred.

If I am torn apart, I will feel rotten even if you are the perfect other who offers me the perfect relationship. You may be a perfect human being who offers me absolute acceptance and loving oneness, but my yawning disintegration will incorporate everything and transform it to pain. Yet virtually the entire field of psychotherapy rests on the assumption that the patient is going to benefit from the very special relationship proferred by the therapist. That assumption has not produced substantive results. "This point must be emphasized because of the common error in many circles of assuming that the experience of one's own being will take place automatically only if one is accepted by someone else. This is the basic error of some forms of 'relationship therapy' " (May, 1958, p. 45). Almost without exception, the field of psychotherapy rests upon the deceptive seduction of those who are propelled into seeking external relationships of apparent integration while their insides are torn apart. The siren-like chant of psychotherapists (counsellors, mental health volunteers, case workers, and the entire "mental health" field) is, "Come to me. I will offer you love and acceptance and oneness and understanding." These inducements keep the market value of psychotherapy robust (Sorokin, 1959). But the whole enterprise is foredoomed to failure in the sense that the seeker can never attain the promised state of integration. Regardless of the form (psychoanalysis, hospital custody, marriage counselling, yoga or bioenergetics), the disintegrated seeker of external integration will never rise out of the mud of internal disintegration.

The search for tranquility, the effort after peace, the pursuit after oneness, the urgency for belonging and love, the hunger for harmony and order—all of these are external pursuits after the missing internal integration. Their career is inevitably one of failure, a tormented seeking of ways out of one's fractured existence (Binswanger, 1967, p. 253). Although we spend a measure of our lives in such hopeless ventures, and although the behaviors are usually not bizarre or strange, and although the pain is often not acute, and although practically no one acknowledges this way of being as painful disintegrative behavior, all of these restless efforts after external integrative relationships qualify as merely another form of behaviors effecting disintegrative relationships with the externalized deeper potential. Once internal relationships are disintegrative, the behavioral die is cast.

So common is the effort after external integrative relationships, that many observers believe they have seen a universal "need" for love, peace, closeness, intimacy, belongingness, oneness. Many approaches accept the universality of this as a characteristic of human beings, and explain it as an intrinsic quality of human nature, a function of our biological nature, or a product of our evolutionary cultural heritage. In contrast, humanistic theory describes the commonness—indeed, the near universality—of this pursuit as evidence of the commonness of the internal disintegration of human beings.

Behaviors Effecting Disintegrative Relationships
with the Externalized Operating Potential

The central feature of disintegrative behavior is its establishment of disintegrative relationships between the person and the external world. Such behavior inevitably constructs relationships marked with disintegrative painful feelings. In constructing these relationships, the external world can be made into an extension of my *deeper* or my *operating* potential. When the external world is made into an extension of my *operating* potential, the external world then bears the same disintegrative relationship to me that I bear toward my deeper potential. I make you fear and hate me in the very same way that I fear and hate my self. I draw back from my deeper potential, and so I get you likewise to draw back from me.

Many of us regard our deeper potentials as bad: "You are bad. I disapprove of you. You should not be the way you are. You ought to feel bad about the way you are. I am critical of you." Under this kind of relationship, the person sets out to construct another individual as the externalization of the operating potential, and as bearing that same attitude toward the person. How can you invite a parent (or a neighbor, colleague, spouse, acquaintance, relative, social worker, customs agent, policeman) to express an attitude of disapproval toward you? Think of the hundreds of behavioral ways we have of inducing others to regard us as bad, to disapprove of us, to tell us not to be the way we are, to be critical of the way we act or look or conduct our lives. In accomplishing this, we have been successful in effecting disintegrative relationships with the externalized operating potential.

There is an almost exact parallel between the way you relate to your deeper motivation and the way you get the other person to relate to you. If you do not trust your own insides, you will mould another person to regard you as unworthy of trust. If you treat your own insides as sneaky, you will soon create someone in your life who regards you as sneaky. The person who regards his insides as dangerous will construct a life in which others consider him as dangerous.

Notice those moments when you have very private reactions to your own immediate behavior. An acquaintance asks you for five dollars, and you say you do not have five dollars. But *you* have a reaction to that: "You liar. You have the money! Why don't you tell him honestly?" Your inner reaction, of whatever kind, will be his reaction too. By your own way of being, you will invite him to bear the same relationship to you that you have to yourself. He, then, will think (or say or express): "You liar. You really do have the money. Why don't you tell me honestly?" In hundreds of moments, you have private reactions to the behavior which comes forth from you, and you will behave in specific ways which invite others to have that same reaction to you. These are your private inner sensings such as: "I don't think I really know what I am doing . . . That was mean of me . . . I sound like I am on the verge of crying . . . It doesn't hang together; why did I say that?" We behave in precisely that way which induces others to have those same reactions to us: "He doesn't really know what he is doing . . . He is mean . . . I think he is on the verge of crying . . . What he says doesn't hang together. Why did he say that?" We turn now to the behaviors which invite the external world to bear toward us the same disintegrative relationships we bear toward ourselves.

Behaviors which express the deeper potential. One of the most common ways of effecting disintegrative relationships with the externalized operating potential is to behave in ways which express the *deeper* potential, and which induce others to respond to you in the same disintegrative manner in which you respond to the deeper potential. Thus the behavior must not only indicate the nature of the deeper potential, but also must indicate it in that way which invites others to fear and hate you for being that way. This constitutes a behavioral skill which many persons have mastered.

Not only do we construct others into relating to us in the same way we relate to our deeper potentials, but the curious and baffling twist is that others fear and hate in us exactly what we fear and hate in ourselves. This is not so baffling when we do things which are generally disliked. For example, she may fear and hate her own controllingness, and it is not surprising that she finds companions who likewise fear and hate her being dominant and controlling. What is baffling, however, is when we rather openly struggle against deeper characteristics, and still find others who join us in fearing and hating those same qualities in ourselves. I try to combat my superciliousness, and yet I always succeed in surrounding myself with someone who draws back from me as a supercilious person. No matter how much I try to avoid that competitiveness in me, there is always someone who dislikes me as competitive. I do not like my pettiness, and yet I always manage to affect others in such a way that I come across as petty, and they dislike me for that. It is as if we are devilishly clever at being just the way we fear and hate in ourselves so that others fear and hate those very qualities in us.

For years and years I have struggled against being dumb. I hate that tendency in me. Yet inevitably I behave in uncanny ways which inevitably betray my dumbness and induce others to be bothered by my dumbness. On some occasions I do not grasp what others say to me, and the others regard me as a bit stupid. On other occasions I seem to sense when the conversation turns to something abstract or intellectual, and before I know it, I have changed the subject so that others not only turn away from me, but regard me as rather dull. I know just how to wait a bit, or smile vacuously, so that the other person thinks how uncomprehending I am.

I hate and am affronted by the gross sexuality in me. Yet it seems baffling that I am continuously confronted with the fact of my own grossly sexual behavior which leads others to hate me and be affronted by me. I scream foul sexual words in church. I aggressively paw women in sexual ways which others loathe. I exhibit myself on my front porch. When my daughter brings friends home I tell them sexually dirty stories. I stare openly at breasts and thighs and buttocks. As a result, I quickly and easily induce others to be hatefully affronted by the gross sexuality in me.

The young man is disgusted with his deeper potential for being rejected, easily hurt, whining. Yet he behaves in precisely that way which practically forces others to be disgusted at him for being that way. Five of them finish playing basketball in the afternoon, and one suggests that they go for a beer. In the appropriate lull, looking a bit withdrawn, hanging back in the proper way, the young man asks, "Hey you all, can I come along?" By behaving in this way, he is forcing the others to be disgusted at him, and to regard him as rejected, easily hurt, and whining. Indeed, the others would have to work hard *not* to regard him in this manner, a manner which is the same way he regards that deeper potential in himself.

In this behavioral maneuver, the person exhibits the deeper potential in such a way which invites others to bear toward him the same disintegrative relationship which he bears toward the deeper potential. If the person is utterly dismayed at his deeper infantilism, he must exhibit that infantilism in ways which are extreme, and which are successful in inviting others likewise to be appalled. Instead of going to work he stays home and plays in the attic with toys and games he played with as a child. It must be carried out in ways which bring that to the attention of his wife, who then tells her friends and the others at work. Soon several key individuals are utterly dismayed with his infantilism, and they think of him as sick, strange, peculiar, regressed, psychotic, mentally ill.

In more mundane ways, the husband moulds his wife into expressing his own frustrated irritation at his deeper self-centeredness. Her mother has recently died, and she is quite worried about what to do with her father. Should she talk with her sister and brother about the problem? Maybe Pa can live with us? He is such a bother. As she frets, she becomes increasingly confused. The unspoken message to her husband is, "I am becoming bewildered and quite upset. Please be with me. Come closer. Please help me decide what to do." Sensing the message, the husband is ready to act. He asks if she would make supper soon because he wants to pick up Eddy to go bowling tonight, and he wants to know where his good shirt is, and on and on until she shrieks at him in absolute frustration. Although her screaming is about his never staying at home and why can't Eddy pick him up once in a while, the deeper sensing is one of frustrated irritation at his failure to share her concern and, instead, to ignore her pleadings in favor of his own self-centered concerns. Both he and his wife are annoyed at his deeper self-centeredness, while he behaves in the proper ways to induce her to express that annoyance at this deeper potential in him.

It requires skill to exhibit the deeper potential in those ways which induce others to bear that disintegrative relationship toward me. I must express the deeper potential with deft timing, in the right situation, with the right intonation, choosing the right words, with the right behavioral stance, the right pauses, the right facial expression. It also requires the skill of *not* saying it or doing it in ways which would prejudice the case. That is, I must omit behavior which would inhibit you from regarding me in the disintegrative manner in which I regard myself. These requirements constitute a most skilled package of behaviors. In a group, for example, I am a behavioral artist at very deftly getting others in the group to regard me as without substance, never coming through, having nothing to say. I make comments which are just off the subject. When I act as if I am setting out to make a point, I become vague and superficial, and always somehow fall short, and manage to say practically nothing. Soon I mould the group into regarding me precisely the way I regard myself, i.e., as having nothing of substance to offer, as being essentially vacuous.

Stuttering is an effective behavior to invite others to bear a number of different disintegrative relationships toward one, and yet the stuttering person almost typically bears the same relational attitude that others bear (Mahrer & Young, 1962). Both the stuttering person and the listener may react to the stutter with such reactions as, "My God, say it already." "What a pitiful thing you are!" "I wish I could exit from here." "What's wrong with you?" "I am getting damned frustrated and annoyed at your stuttering." Both stuttering person and listener may house the same attitudinal relationship, with the stuttering person bearing this relationship toward himself, and the listener toward the stuttering person.

Behaviors which construct the externalized operating potential. Some behaviors express the deeper potential in ways which practically force others into regarding the person in the same disintegrative way that the person regards himself. Other behaviors construct an externalized operating potential already geared to regard the person in the same disintegrative manner in which the person regards himself. If I bear a disintegrative relationship toward my own deeper potential, I can construct an externalized world which bears that same disintegrative relationship toward me—and I need never behave on the basis of my deeper potential. This can be accomplished, for example, by my way of *receiving an intrusive external world*, or by my way of selecting a *ready-made external world* (Figure 6.1). If I fear and hate my own deeper potential for being incapable, feckless, dependent, weak, I merely have to locate others who are geared to look with disfavor upon me as incapable, feckless, dependent, and weak. For example, I can effect such a relationship by assuming the role of helpee and seeking help from those counsellors, therapists, and "helpers" who are already geared to serve me begrudgingly, to look down upon me for requiring help, to dislike my patienthood, to regard me as incapable, feckless, dependent, and weak. All of this may be accomplished merely by acceding to the role of helpee, and thereby placing the helper in the role of externalized ally of the operating potential—and all of this can be successfully accomplished without ever behaving in ways which are openly incapable, feckless, dependent, and weak.

If I sense what is within as something impulsive and dangerous, I may not only struggle to blockade against it, I can solicit your help in joining me in the struggle against it. That "it" may be sensed tendencies to become a complete alcoholic, or a thorough drug addict, or a hardened criminal, or a crazy person who strangles helpless old men, or a sexual pervert who seduces little children. In my struggles to block against what is within, I may behave in the right ways so that others are found (or constructed) to serve as my allies in fearing and hating that in me, and who join me in dedicating themselves toward blocking its expression. The behavior virtually never directly expresses the awful impulses, and certainly never in full bloom. Typically, the behaviors hint at what can occur, or tell about it, or carry it out very mildly. The person is not a complete alcoholic, though she is scared to death of becoming one. He is not a drug addict, but once, several years ago he came so very close. She is not a hardened criminal, yet all the signs point toward that likelihood. He is not crazy, but a case can be assembled from bits of evidence here and there. Such behavior must indicate the distinct *possibility* of the awfulness within, and, more importantly, must solicit others to serve as the externalized operating potential in blocking and guarding against the ever present possibility. Stay with me, stop me from myself, help me fight that in myself, commit yourself to the fight against what is within me, help me prevent the terrible possibility, worry about it.

Very specific behaviors insisted that others join the young man in his struggles against the deeper impulse to strangle older women. It is as if the behaviors said, "You must help me to structure and control against those bad inner impulses." When he felt himself enveloped by the urge, he sought to construct a self-imposed imprisonment. "Especially in the evening, between 9 and 11 P.M., the urge came over him with increasing force, and it drew him with such overwhelming power to murder some woman or other that he would lock himself in his room, hide the key from himself and try to regain his self-control by perpetual smoking" (Boss, 1963, p. 189). Such behaviors, and others such as complaining about headaches, were invitations for others to join him in the struggle against the outbreak of impulses. "In the weeks preceding the attack he had suffered from continual and severe headaches and had repeatedly expressed the wish to be put in an asylum" (Boss, 1963, p. 189). All of these behaviors serve to invite the constructed external world to join with him as the externalized operating potential in the struggle against the implied deeper potential.

In many therapies, especially behavior therapy, the client or patient says, "Will you join me in my battle against this behavior of mine? Will you help me to control this behavior?" And the behavior modifier replies, "I will be pleased to join you in your efforts to control that behavior." Large components of most therapies are dedicated to joining with the person in the control of their behavior, but the behavior modification approach expresses this dedication in its purer form of social control of one person's behavior by another (cf. Krasner, 1962). In order to engage the behavior modificationist, the patient must behave so as to indicate the existence of something which ought to be controlled. I am afraid of heights, I fear being in elevators, I cannot control my smoking or drinking, I bite my nails, I get anxious when I am a passenger in a car. Effective behaviors indicate the existence of *other* behaviors which are to be controlled and, at the same time, engage the assistance of others (therapists) who join with the person in efforts to control the designated behavior. Most psychotherapists constitute available externalized operating agents, waiting to join the person in his disintegrative struggle against the deeper potential.

In general, the helping professions constitute a ready and willing grand externalization of the operating potentials of those who struggle against their deeper potential, who fear and hate it, try to block it, to suffocate and kill it. It is assumed that "it" is bad and ought to be struggled against or feared or hated or suffocated or killed. There is no question that "it" must be treated, imprisoned, cured, worked through, remedied. In this enterprise the helping professions will chemically dampen it, use social pressure against it, try to modify it, use the group to get rid of it, counsel it away, give instruction on how to overcome it. All you are required to do is to behave in those ways which are successful in enlisting the helpers in your effort to effect a disintegrative relationship toward "it."

Behaviors subsequent to the thrilling transgression. I can behave in ways which get the external world to join with me in my disintegrative relationship toward myself by the two classes of behaviors described above. In the former class of behaviors I express the deeper potential in ways which *simultaneously* invite the external world to relate to me in the same disintegrative way I relate to myself. In the latter class of behaviors, I simply engage the right part of the external world *without directly exhibiting the deeper potential.* A third way of effecting disintegrative relationships with the externalized operating potential is by means of behaviors *subsequent* to the direct expression of the deeper potential. In this class of behaviors, the person temporarily surrenders mandate to the deeper potential which expresses itself directly. Some time later, the person regains mandate over his own behavior and then proceeds to behave in such a manner that the external world is invited to effect the same disintegrative relationship toward the person as the person maintains toward his deeper potential.

The older man fears and hates his deeper potential for sexual violence. Throughout his 22 years of marriage, he has never been sexually violent to his wife. Yet occasionally he finds a prostitute with whom he is that way. He surrenders into being another person, the deeper potential, and is physically cruel to her, twisting her hair, utilizing sexual positions designed to inflict physical pain. On these occasions, which occur once or twice a year, he has surrendered into being that deeper personality. *Following* these transgressions, when he is "himself," he must find ways of punishing himself. He must find ways of getting the external world to join him in the disintegrative relationship he bears toward his own deeper potential. Horrified at having been the person he was, he provokes his wife into serious arguments endangering their marriage. Soon she is heaping punishment upon him, and she is joined by their children and their friends, until he is being a punished person. He has constructed the external world into heaping punishment upon him in an expression of the punitive relationship he bears toward the deeper part which took him over and carried out the sexual violence with the other woman.

The transgression is thrilling. When the deeper potential takes over behavior, one has the *good* feelings of experiencing which are indicated by the two positive signs within the circle of the potential (Figure 8.1). As the deeper potential takes over and carries out actions, there is a feeling of arcane pleasure, secret ecstasy, wicked excitement, delight, a devilish kind of aliveness. This is when you do what you ordinarily do not do as the ordinary person whom you are. When the person-as-operating-potential disengages and steps aside, the deeper potential rises up and steals from the store, secretly watches the neighbor undress, beats up the drunk, goes to another city and gambles away the money, carries out the tabooed sexual act. Then the deeper potential recedes, and the person-as-operating-potential regains mandate—horrified, guilty, ashamed, anxiety-ridden, self-abased, fearful and angry at the deeper potential. Now the person sets out to get the external world to punish him, be fearful and angry at him, horrified at him, ashamed and vindictive toward him. Where the deeper potential stole clothes from the store, the person picks arguments at work; where the deeper potential secretly beat up the drunk, the person antagonizes the family.

Whereas the above examples are common enough, they are more or less extreme, usually involve extremely disintegrative relationships between the operating and deeper potentials, and require a dramatic change of person from person-as-operating-potential to person-as-deeper-potential. It is much more common for the operating and deeper potentials to be on speaking terms, for the disintegrative relationship to be mild, and for the switch from one personality to another to be smooth. When you get drunk, you may give in to being your deeper potential and it says some rather nasty things which come from the deeper potential, and not from you. Afterwards, you are again the operating potential, and you behave in ways (B3, Figure 8.1) which invite others to be critical of you—for example, by being quite late in picking up your buddy for work. Or you give in to the deeper potential which loves to overeat, and, gorging yourself, the person-as-operating-potential takes over mandate once again and behaves in ways which induce others to be critical of you—such as losing the requisition or betraying a confidence or not paying back the money you borrowed. Where the deeper potential thrilled at secretly masturbating, the operating potential soon takes over once again and is cuttingly caustic to your friends so that they bear a generally negative attitude toward you.

In all of these examples, the core of the problem, as always, lies in the disintegrative relationship between the operating and deeper potentials. It is, I believe, an error to identify the problem as the deeper potential and its behavior. The problem does not lie in being physically cruel, in stealing, in the voyeurism, in the sexually perverse act, in the gambling. Nor does the problem lie in the actions of the returned operating potential as it induces the externalized operating world to punish, be critical, be fearful or angry at the person. In our analysis, the *problem* consists of the *disintegrative relationship* which lies at the heart of the actions of the deeper potential and the subsequent actions of the operating potential.

The psychotherapist who knows all this is not surprised nor thrown off track by the disappearance of the presenting "problem." Quite commonly, the psychotherapist is placed in the role of the externalized operating agent, and is invited to share in the person's disintegrative relationship. After the deeper potential commits the thrilling transgression, the patient asks the psychotherapist to attend to some *other* "difficulty." For example, after losing a lot of money gambling or after committing adultery with the spouse's younger sister, the patient seeks therapy with complaints of having trouble on the job or feeling irritable with the family. After a few sessions, however, this focus of concern loses its compellingness when the patient succeeds in being criticized or punished or antagonizing others. Those psychotherapists who allow themselves to be placed in the role of the external operating agent soon find themselves "treating" a "problem" which either has dissolved away or which lacks the patient's compelling interest, and the psychotherapist either credits himself with a therapeutic success, explains it as a spontaneous remission, or doggedly sets out to energize the patient's ebbing interest.

Once having stepped aside and permitted the deeper potential to carry out the thrilling transgression, I can effect the disintegrative relationship merely by the way I construct my external world. Having surrendered to my deeper potential, it thrilled at committing the sexual crime in the dark of another city. Now I have returned to my life, and I am geared to construct an external world which will punish (torture, hate, reject) me. As indicated in Figure 6.1, there are four available modes of constructing such an external world. I can *receive an intrusive external world* which sets out to hurt me, so that when my older brother seeks me out and excoriates me for my failure to be concerned about our parents, I add considerable surplus meaning to his actions—and I am thoroughly destroyed by his criticism. In the same way, whatever intrudes itself upon me from the outside world is received as disintegrative punishment and rejection: your slights, the elbows of the crowd, the sneer of the man on the porch, the angry screeching of the motorcycle below my window. Second, I can *utilize a ready-made part of the external world* in such a manner as to promote the required disintegrative relationship. I can place myself in interaction with the supercilious physician who treats his patients as immature dummies, and then feel awful about being treated as an immature dummy. Third, I can work *conjointly* with you so as to elicit your anger and dislike of me. Fourth, I can *fabricate* an external world out of whole cloth so that voices jeer at me sexually and the patterns in the bathroom floor portray the awful acts I committed.

The most thrilling ecstatic moments in his entire life were spent in explosive sexual submission to his mother-in-law, a divorced woman in her late forties. She carefully nurtured his lust for her until the evening his wife was in the hospital, and she came to the apartment. During that evening he surrendered both to her and to his own deeper potential. Thereafter he built the external world into a replica of his own operating potential. Just as he was appalled at the deeper potential, violently opposed to it, wished to murder it, in just the same way he fabricated an external world dedicated to accomplishing the same thing with him. His world became filled with evil plots against him, secret cliques meeting to take over his mind and his thoughts. Evil individuals masked themselves as ordinary people and watched his every move. Having committed the thrilling transgression, behaviors can effect a disintegrative relationship with the externalized operating potential merely by means of the way in which the external world is constructed.

I have suggested a series of steps in this avenue toward the construction of a so-called paranoid world. As with each disintegrative behavior, the first step is the disintegrative relationship between the operating and deeper potentials. For example, she must fear and hate her incestuous deeper tendencies. Second, the person disengages and allows the deeper potential to carry out the thrilling transgression. She may, for example, give in to the deeper potential which then experiences the thrilling incestuous relationship. Third, there must be some key figure constructed to share the same fearful-hateful relationship toward the deeper potential. This other figure may be the father with whom she experiences the incestuous tendencies, a husband who suspects, a mother who senses, someone who is meaningfully involved. Finally, the constructed external world is *filled* with the extended operating potential, and becomes her persecutory idea or idea of reference or "paranoid delusion." What I term the extension or externalization of the operating potential, Binswanger refers to as "pluralization," yet the concept is the same, viz. her own fear and hate of the deeper process is externalized, extended, or pluralized into being the external world. Thus, ". . . the actual meaning of her insanity rests on the pluralization of the father . . . Ilse's disappointment in the father develops—always by way of the pluralization of the thou—into the delusions of reference. The pluralization of the thou—into the delusions of reference. The pluralization of the thou is the order principle by which alleged disorder ('insanity') can be understood; it is the principle which permits us to see not just chaos but method in this insanity" (Binswanger, 1958b, pp. 222-223).

Behaviors Effecting Disintegrative Relationships
with the Internal Deeper Potential

A third way in which behavior effects a disintegrative relationship is distinguished by its direct targeting upon the deeper potential without constructing or involving the external world in any way, either as externalized operating or deeper potential. In this third way, behavior

(B4, Figure 8.1) proceeds directly from the person (OP1) to the self, inner process or deeper potential (DP2, Figure 8.1).

If I bear a disintegrative relationship toward what is within, I may recoil from an intrinsic coldness, a stoic unemotionality, a metallic aloofness. Depending on the nature and degree of my disintegrative relationship, I may criticize myself as cold, write in my diary about the growing madness of unemotionality, cut myself with a razor just to arouse some feeling in me, or drown myself in alcoholism. In carrying out these behaviors, the axis is the direct lane between me and the deeper potential. Typically such behaviors effect disintegrative relationships with the deeper potential by depriving oneself, maiming oneself, punishing oneself, killing oneself, hating oneself. It consists of a war against oneself, a war which does not require a particular external situation or external world. You and your deeper self are the combatants, and you carry on the war admirably without requiring external resources.

When the axis of interaction is between the person and himself, the culprit is inside. You are one person, the self is another, and you *do* relate to the self in such a manner as to cut it off, hate it, kill it. In this sense, the war against one's self is more real than the war against either an externalized operating or deeper potential. Disintegrative behavior against one's self is an attack upon the real enemy— the deeper potential. Our position differs from that of psychoanalysis wherein the real culprit is *external* in the form of some significant other, so that turning upon oneself is held to be a mistaken retroflection (Freud, 1953d; Munroe, 1955, p. 145).

The struggle against the implied inner opponent. If we allow the person to be distinct from that deeper other part, then a great deal of disintegrative behavior becomes illuminated as strugglings against some inner opponent. If I listen in this way, the person is typically fighting his own inner opponent, arguing with it, justifying himself against its accusations. It is as if the listener is hearing a person arguing on the telephone, and the listener hears only one side of the argument, but the listener can make reasonable guesses about what the opponent is saying. If you just listen, do not interact, and certainly do not accept the role of the antagonist, you will hear the person arguing with his inner self—and you will be able to deduce what the inner self is saying. When the person assembles proof of her astuteness and ingenuity, it is as if she is arguing against an inner opponent who is asserting her dull stupidity. Against whom is the husband arguing when he tells how wonderfully satisfying his current marriage is? What must the internal opponent be saying when the woman defensively lauds the accomplishments of her friend? If you pay attention to the person's disintegrative relationship with the inner opponent, you can sense how awful that inner thing must be and how negative is the relationship. "You sound like you have to be on guard against something inside that wants to drag you down . . . It's like you have to argue against some inside person who thinks you're absolutely worthless . . . What a fight you seem to have with something inside that seems to say that it's never going to work, it's always got to fail . . ."

The opponent is inside, somewhere. It is the voice of the deeper potential, looming as a terrible urge or impulse, as part of a neurotic or psychotic condition, an awful thought, peculiar fear, primitive unconscious force, inherited weakness, taint, or strain. We carry around our internal opponents, argue with them, fight and struggle against them, and regard them through a disintegrative channel as fearful, bad, unyielding.

Because the opponent is internal, and because my relationship with it is disintegrative, it usually takes some actual, internal, bodily form. As discussed in Chapter 5, the physical body manifests the deeper potential when the relationship is a disintegrative one, when the operating potential does not express the content of the deeper experiencing, and when the deeper potential occurs nowhere in the external world. All these conditions are fulfilled when the behavior effects disintegrative relations with the deeper potential *directly*, and not with a deeper potential extended out upon the external world. Thus there often is a bodily form to the inner opponent, to the thing within myself against which I fight, argue, protest. Indeed, just as disintegrative behavior effecting relationships with the *externalized* operating or deeper potential is in interaction with something quite real in the external world, so it is that behavior effecting disintegrative relations directly with the deeper potential is likewise in interaction with something quite real in the *bodily realm*. If the person's behavior is in response to something within which is insatiable, dangerous, all-devouring, there is quite likely an event or phenomenon somewhere in the body which is insatiable, dangerous, and all-devouring. That inner opponent is often quite real, with a bodily locus, form, and shape.

Roger fought against something within which would never let him sleep through eight or nine beautiful refreshing hours of peaceful slumber. Not only would "it" work toward keeping him from falling asleep, it would wake him up two or three times during the night— and he simply was unable to get back to sleep. In his war against it he tried sleep workshops, counselling, and psychotherapy. Finally he found just the right combination of pills, and they helped him to win the fight against it. Roger lived a 30-year war against that "it."

Beatrice's pressure headache resisted every kind of pill she could find. In her efforts against this inner opponent, she dragged it about from physician to physician, and psychotherapist to psychotherapist. About the only way she found to reduce the head pressure was to masturbate simultaneously with the fantasy of a well-rehearsed rape scene in which she was seduced and forcibly taken by another woman.

Persons with inner opponents located in the region of the stomach—often in the form of what is described as ulcers—quite often stumble on ways of heading off the pain. Diets and pills and medications help in the war. But in addition, many of these persons often find other personal ways of coping with their internal opponent. One person found that the pain was reduced by sleeping in a curled position hugging his wife, with her buttocks against his stomach, and his right arm around her, holding her right breast. Another found that sitting in a reclining chair with a heating bag on his stomach helped to reduce the pain.

In one form or another, human beings are continuously building disintegrative relationships by means of behavior. Whether the channel of relationships is with the external world as an externalized operating or deeper potential, or whether the channel of relationships is with one's self, we behave in that channel, and our behavior both constructs and lives in that disintegrative relationship. Such behavior is always accompanied with some measure of disintegrative bad feeling. It is a pity how much of our behavior can be understood as disintegrative behavior—and all flowing out of the underlying disintegrative relationship among potentials. We now turn to the second class of painful behavior.

EXPERIENTIAL BEHAVIOR

Disintegrative behavior builds disintegrative relationships and brings on the painful feelings which occur when relationships are disintegrative. There is a second class of behavior which works quite differently. One of the major principles of human behavior (Chapter 8) is that behavior serves to provide for the *experiencing* of potentials. If I have a potential for experiencing being cared for and protected, that potential can be experienced only by means of behavior. However, the actual behavior which gains this experiencing may *itself* be painful. Our second class of painful behavior includes all of the pain-laden behavior whose work is to provide for experiencing. As schematicized in Figure 8.1, the *behaviors* include those (B1) which carry with them some load of pain (or bother or distress), and, in addition, provide for the experiencing of a potential.

The Nature of Painful Experiential Behavior

In this section, I shall describe three characteristics of painful experiential behavior. First, such behavior is described as merely another means of providing for the experiencing of potentials. In this important sense, such behavior may be said to be goal-directed. Second, as with all such behavior, its degree of effectiveness is a function of its capability of enabling experiencing of the potential. In this sense, pain-laden behavior may be highly effective. Third, many extreme behaviors (highly deviate, different, bizarre, unusual, crazy behaviors) can be revealed as painful means of enabling such experiencing.

Painful behavior directed toward the goal of experiencing. When we restrict attention to the actual behavior itself (B1, Figure 8.1), we may be struck by the pain. The young woman is undergoing terrible depression and a sense of absolute failure (OP1, Figure 8.1) as she holds the sharp knife in her hands after cutting deep into her wrist, and watches the blood spurting out in great intense red bursts. There are painful feelings there. When we dilate the focus of our attention, however, we see her mother and father and older sister clasping her and kissing her and constantly caring for her—and we see the heightened measure of experiencing being cared for and protected (DP2, Figure 8.1). The wrist cutting, painful as it was—and the pain was intense—served to provide for the experiencing of her potential. Such behavior is goal-directed, and the goal is the increased experiencing which occurs.

A line of research has evolved from the hunch that the immediate painful aspect of behavior is not the whole story. This line of research was based on an idea that an enlargement of the scope might show us something more that is going on, perhaps something which could help us make sense of the immediate pain. Possibly, these researchers wondered, even though the immediate consequences of such behavior are painful, if the subsequent consequences might be pleasurable (Mahrer, 1956; Mischel, 1958, 1966; Mowrer, 1948; Mowrer & Ullmann, 1945). One of the conclusions to this line of research is that there is much more to such behavior than its immediate painful consequence. Our interpretation adds that a dilated context of study reveals a measure of *experiencing* coupled to behavior with immediate painful consequences.

In this sense, such painful behavior can also be grasped through the Hullian principle of reinforcement or the law of effect. In other words such behavior is goal-directed. The "reinforcement" of such behavior, its crucial effect, is the movement toward experiencing. Cutting the wrist is understood as directed toward the goal of the experiencing of the potential for being cared for and protected. Such experiencing can be described as the reinforcement or as the effect.

Let us study the behaviors of being anxious. These include a scared facial expression, wide eyes, shallow breathing, tense voice, saying the right words to convey anxiety. In addition, the person *feels* the bad feelings of anxiety. He is having a painful feeling; he is not play-acting or putting on an appearance of anxiety in some sort of clever deceit. Yet in addition to the painful feeling, his being this way provides for experiencing. Anxious behavior may serve to gain control over another individual, or it may be a means of disarming the other individual (Haley, 1963). By being anxious I may gain other goals—such as the experiencing of your being solicitous to me, or my experiencing of keeping you from being mean to me, or my experiencing the avoidance of any sorts of bothersome situations, or my experiencing a sense of fending you off, or getting you to pander to my helplessness (Szasz, 1961). All of these are goals, experiencing which occurs by means of anxious behavior.

Indeed, the painful aspect of many such behaviors is frequently the effective component in enabling experiencing to occur. Haley (1963) and Bandura and Walters (1962) are among those who cite the painful aspect of such behavior as the core of its effectiveness. In order to gain the experiencing of safety, of avoiding a threatening situation, the core of effectiveness lies in the actual occurrence of real pain. If you are confronted with the crucial examination and must get out of it at any cost, burst a blood vessel, have a painful seizure, have a searing migraine attack, exacerbate the internal injury—in short, have pain. The greater the pain, the more effectively you will achieve the safety of avoiding the threatening situation. If it hurts you terribly, you can gain many different kinds of experiencing, thanks to the pain itself—mobilizing others to action, suddenly stopping them from attacking you, making them take you in and nurse you, avoiding the responsibility, being the center of attention, being nurtured, and so on and on and on. Pain is a well-known, highly respected means of providing for experiencing.

Any painful feeling coupled to such goal-directed behavior is in the service of behavior dedicated to the noble task of providing for experiencing. Feeling anguished or miserable or torn apart is only a small part of what is happening, for the larger picture reveals the more central experiencing. This is why bad feelings sometimes seem to be apotheosized and ennobled. This is why "... we find them necessary, or beautiful, or noble; we glorify them ... Some people are very proud of their irritability ... There is practically no negative emotion which you cannot enjoy ... Really some people get all their pleasures from negative emotions" (Ouspensky, 1957, pp. 11-12).

The degree of effectiveness of painful experiential behavior. Once behaviors are understood as a means of providing for experiencing, we have a basis for assessing their effectiveness: To what degree is that painful behavior effective in providing for the experiencing? Once we understand the experiencing (or goal) as the domination and control of the household, we can gauge the degree of effectiveness of her painful behavior—her being depressed, melancholy, lost and alone, her dizziness and spells of confusion, her occasional enuresis and demanding fussiness about the way her things are placed in her room. All of these ways of behaving provide her with painful feelings, yet they serve to fill her with a sense of dominating and controlling her daughter, son-in-law, and three grandchildren. And over the past year and a half, grandmother has become more behaviorally effective. That is, a year or so ago, when she first started to "get worse," her painful ways of being were only moderately effective in securing the experiencing of domination and control over the household. But in the last six months or so, her behaviors have refined and developed to the point that they are very effective in providing for that experiencing. The degree of painful feeling has not changed much, but the behavioral effectiveness has increased significantly.

If providing for experiencing is the heart of the matter, then we are led away from mere attention to the painful feeling, and we have a kind of awful perspective on the linkage between the behavior (painful as it is) and the experiencing. Furthermore, we can observe a gradual refinement and development of behavioral efficiency over time. Just suppose that some persons behave in very particular ways, albeit painful, as a means of experiencing being accepted into a hospital (Mahrer, 1962c, 1970b). If the experiencing of successful admission to a psychiatric ward is a goal, then it becomes understandable that "veteran admission-achievers" should perhaps require both fewer and more mild behaviors ("symptoms") to obtain successful admission. Indeed, research seems to indicate that seasoned admission-achievers significantly differ from novices in these ways (Mahrer & Katz, 1963). Patients learn, and large proportions of patients demonstrate a smooth learning curve. In much the same way, ordinary persons also learn, perhaps even more rapidly, to behave painfully in ways which achieve the proper experiencing. Psychotherapists who know their patients well, and who are attuned to see this process of refinement, can trace a growing effectiveness of behaviors which provide for the very same experiencing from early childhood, through late childhood, adolescence, and on into adulthood. The nature of the experiencing may persist unchanged. What has altered is the degree of behavioral effectiveness and efficiency in providing for the old experiencing, until at present the behavior is highly effective and efficient—although quite painful.

Such surreptitious alliance between painful behavior and inner experiencing is well-known and described in other approaches. Ellis (1963) is familiar with the alliance between painful "neurotic symptoms" and what he refers to as deeply held irrational and illogical ideas and attitudes. In this alliance, the person's behavior becomes smoothly linked to the irrational and illogical underlying ideas and attitudes in such a way that the behavior is effective and artfully functional—and painful. When the person maintains an irrational and illogical basic idea that he must be loved to be of worth, his ways of behaving can become honed to such a point that he provides for a full measure of that experiencing with each slight behavioral movement, i.e., his behavior becomes marvelously effective.

In this whole process of sharpening the effectiveness of such painful behavior, the *person* is ensconced within the operating potential, and has little or no awareness of what is going on. In our untangling of pain-laden experiential behavior we can step back and observe the gradual refinement of its effectiveness. But the behaving person seldom if ever can sit where we are and observe his own behavior. Usually the behaving person is caught in the immediacy of the moment, and is engaged in experiencing and the undergoing of the associated pain.

Aside from the person's awareness of what is occurring, and of the factors responsible for the painful behavior, the key factor is the degree to which the behavior provides for experiencing. With or without awareness, the painful behavior will become locked in, and perhaps even more painful, to the degree that it is effective in providing for the experiencing of the potential. Thus the readiness for behavioral change is a function of the degree to which an alternate behavioral candidate can exceed the effectiveness of the pain-laden behavior in offering experiencing of the potential. It is therefore not a matter of poor or unfortunate learnings, nor is it a matter of reinforcements or punishments or linking the behavior to new cues. Instead, the predominant determinant is the effectiveness of the behavior in serving to promote that very particular and concrete experiencing. No behavior, new or old, painful or exhilarating, is going to displace the pain-laden behavior unless it can do a better job.

Extreme behavior as a means of providing for experiencing. Many behaviors are extreme—crazy, weird, bizarre, different, deviant, sick, psychotic. Viewed as means of providing for the experiencing of potentials, many of these behaviors can be illuminated as quite simple and understandable (Haley, 1963; Kovacs, 1965; Laing & Esterson, 1970; Mahrer, 1962c, 1967a, 1970b, 1970c, 1970f; Mahrer, Stewart, Horn & Lind, 1968; Rogers, 1966; Szasz, 1956). Regardless of its extremity, regardless of the load of pain which it contains, the crucial element to such behavior is its providing for some kind of experiencing, and in this endeavor, it typically is directed toward doing something to others. All the while, the crazy behavior is providing for some kind of experiencing, for ". . . even such phenomena as psychosis or acting out must be considered as gesture, as communication, as object-directed, goal-seeking action . . . I believe . . . that every act . . . must be looked at in terms of something like, 'What is he trying to do to me and to others (or to tell me and others) with this? What is this going to get him? What are its consequences? What kind of response is he looking for?' " (Kovacs, 1965, p. 99). The answers to these questions describe the nature of the experiencing promoted by the extreme behavior. For example, the answer might be that the be- having person is trying to indicate that he must remain hidden behind a moat, a safe distance. To achieve this safe distance is what the be- having person is trying to do to me, to tell me. Thus his experiencing will consist of being reasonably safe behind this wall. In all this, we have spoken only of the nature of the experiencing—the message, the consequence of his behavior, the goal toward which the behavior is aimed. We have sought to understand the behavior by trying to make sense of the nature of the behavior. We have never said whether the behavior consists of not being able to see, brushing nonexistent flies away from the face, or mumbling in a totally incomprehensible man- ner.

Whatever the nature of the extreme behavior, no matter how un- usual it is, the way of grasping its function is to describe the nature of the experiencing. This is illustrated in Binswanger's description of Ilse, and his understanding of the nature of the experiencing which accompanied her quite unusual behavior. "One day, when her father had once again reproached her, she told him she knew of a way of saving him, and in front of her father she put her right hand up to her forearm into the burning stove, and held out her hands to him with these words, 'Look, this is to show you how much I love you' " (Binswanger, 1958b, p. 215). How may we make sense of such an un- usual act? Making sense of it means describing the nature of the ex- periencing within Ilse. As Binswanger describes, the act ". . . serves the expression and confirmation of Ilse's love for her father as well as the atonement for this love" (p. 218). Such an act expressed ". . . the mo- tive of the testimony of love to the father and of the test of fire of her influence upon him . . . The self-surrender is also surrender of her inner heat to the ice-cold father, it expresses the 'insane idea' of touching the father's cold heart by 'something decisive,'—a 'decisive event' " (p. 219).

Once we can uncover the nature of that experiencing, we can thereby make sense of a considerable swath of extreme behavior. Our position accepts ". . . the premise that the behavior of persons said to be mentally ill is meaningful and goal-directed—provided one is able to understand the patient's behavior from his particular point of view" (Szasz, 1956, p. 59). In this manner we have adopted a way of listen- ing to all manner of extreme behavior, including the hearing of strange voices, so-called paranoid ideas of reference, "schizophrenic ideation," scrambled and incoherent logic and thinking (Rogers, 1966). Once we accept extreme behavior as directed toward the goal of providing for experiencing, we are led to reorganize our classification of such behavior. For example, we may propose a whole new classification of the behavior of persons who are admitted to mental hospitals and psychiatric wards, a classification derived from the basic premise that such behavior takes its place among all behavior which provides for experiencing. On this basis, a system of classification has been derived from the goals (experiencings) of persons entering psychiatric hospitalization (Mahrer, 1970b, 1970c).

Indeed, the sheer extremity of such behavior is often the effective ingredient of its effectiveness in providing for the experiencing. Being weird and crazy works; it packs a wallop that less extreme behavior often lacks. "Implied in all this is an understanding that a complaint may sometimes be more effective for mobilizing others to action than a simple informative statement" (Szasz, 1956, p. 130), and an extreme behavior may sometimes be more effective than a milder behavior in providing for sheer experiencing. But this is not necessarily true in all, or even most, extreme behavior. I do not regard extreme behavior as necessarily offering an extreme measure of experiencing. As discussed in Chapter 8, many extreme behaviors fall quite short of enabling full experiencing. Thus, for example, the experiencing of freedom from mother may be gained more by a firm encounter, in which you look at mother eye to eye and straightforwardly tell her that you are leaving, than by "leaving" her and entering into a crazy world of unreachability, or barricading your room against the she-devils who are trying to capture your mind. The nine-year-old child may gain a fuller sense of defiance by saying a direct, "No, I will *not*," rather than behaving in extreme ways such as eating stones and dirt, or becoming incontinent, or setting fire to fields and garages. Extreme behavior may either be effective or ineffective in providing a large measure of experiencing.

We have discussed some of the nature of painful experiential behavior. Perhaps the core of its nature, and its distinguishing feature, is that such behavior, painful as it is—or sometimes by virtue of its pain—serves as a means of experiencing. We turn now to a description of some of the potentials which are frequently experienced by such behavior.

Potentials Experienced by Painful Experiential Behavior

One way of grasping painful experiential behaviors is by grouping them under the various potentials which frequently are experienced by means of these behaviors. What are some examples of potentials which commonly are experienced by means of painful experiential behaviors? What are some painful experiential behaviors which commonly provide for their experiencing? Our purpose here is merely to be illustrative, and not at all exhaustive. Indeed, it is not possible to be exhaustive if only because potentials differ so widely from one person to another.

Being cared for and the object of concern. There are many painful behaviors which serve to gain the experiencing of being cared for and being the object of concern. It is as if many of these behaviors express the following: "See how much pain I am in. Please take care of me. Please be concerned about me." This is the message, and the underlying experiencing, of the person who is alcoholic and who is struggling against the awful condition in just that way which invites others to show concern and provide care. The person may behave like a child or even a little baby, and thereby elicit care and concern. Many persons solicit care and concern by being physically unable or incapacitated in hundreds of ways which issue the same invitation. Others gain this by being confused and bewildered, and thereby asking others to show care and concern. Some invite this kind of experiencing by being dull, uncomprehending, stupid—"mentally deficient" or "retarded." Bandura and Walters (1962) describe various states of disability, lack of capacity and outright "illness" as behavioral means of gaining dependency from others—and thereby gaining the experience of being cared for and being the object of concern.

Suffering and anguish can be the right keys to unlocking care and concern from others. Depression, for example, not only pains the depressed person, but is often a means of reaching out to others in soliciting pity, care, and concern. In gaining ". . . a modicum of prestige as a sufferer, a person worthy of pity, the sufferer discovers by trial and error that this is the one device still ready to his hand" (Murphy, 1947, pp. 581-582). Underneath the real pain of depression is the very real experiencing of being pitied and being cared for and being concerned about.

Psychotherapy can be, for some persons, a situational context offering concern and care. Hospitalization can also serve, for many, as another resource providing care and concern. To the extent that the experiencing of care and concern occurs in a hospital or a psychotherapeutic context, it is perhaps understandable that those who seek hospitalization and psychotherapy are behaving in a painful ways. Such painful behavior becomes an admission ticket to hospitalization and psychotherapy and, once admitted, the experiencing consists of being cared for and being concerned about. But hospitalization and psychotherapy are by no means the only resources available. The family, for example, may constitute a resource whose capability to offer care and concern may equal or exceed that of the hospital or the psychotherapist. When researchers label those who are hospitalized and psychotherapized as an "experimental" group and those who seek hospitalization or psychotherapy (i.e., are on a "waiting list") as constituting a "control" group, the two groups may well differ essentially on the availability of care and concern from various resources. Those who are in the control group may be exposed to resources which nevertheless offer a great deal of care and concern. From this perspective, we must be exceedingly chary about the meaning of experimental and control groups (cf. Powers & Witmer, 1951). If the person seeks care and concern, and hospitalization and psychotherapy are the only available resources, that person is quite different from the person for whom other adequate resources are available. The effects of hospitalization or psychotherapy would presumably be extensive for the former and minimal for the latter person.

Being a child, avoiding adulthood. Painful behaviors may provide for the experiencing of being a child and of avoiding adulthood. Quite simply, the person may behave as a child or perhaps as an infant, talk like a baby, be enuretic, play with dolls, or effect the body postures of an infant. In these behavioral ways the person experiences that sense of being a child and avoiding adulthood. Such ("regressive") behavior constitutes merely another means of providing for a specific kind of experiencing. It is in the understanding of this linkage between behavior and experiencing that the explanation lies, and not, for example, in any supposed failure of repressive mechanisms in current situations which redintegrate anxiety in childhood (cf. Wolberg, 1967).

Other ways of gaining this sense of experiencing are frequently milder. Here are the behaviors of being cute and pixyish, and thereby being like a child. The person who surrounds himself with a layer of baby fat may be prolonging the dangerous entrance into adulthood. So too is the person who will block any efforts to be responsible, to be counted upon. Underneath such behaviors, which may vary in the degree of associated pain, is the inner experiencing of being a child and of avoiding adulthood.

Being plain, ordinary, unspecial. For some persons, behaviors must provide for the experiencing of being plain, ordinary, unspecial, and *not* being prized, a jewel, a very special one, a saint or a God. Painful behaviors can be engaged which offer a modicum of such experiencing. The gorgeous child becomes the plain adult. The brilliant adolescent turns into the non-intellectual older person. Talents, once flourishing, seem to fall to the wayside. Qualities eliciting high praise and esteem seem to vanish. The person begins to stutter, to get low grades, to get into trouble at school, at home, at work, with the police.

He is anything but a God; he is a sinner, a drifter, a loser, a failure, a mental patient. It is quite clear that she is not perfect or special or prized. In addition to the pain, there is the underlying experiencing of thereby being plain, ordinary, unspecial, and not at all the highly prized, God-like one.

Hurting and blaming. Painful behaviors, frequently by virtue of the pain and anguish, are means of hurting and blaming the responsible others. Beneath the pain is the voice of the experiencing potential: "I am going to make you writhe for the way you treated me. I am going to feel miserable, and that will hurt you. I feel awful, and that will make you feel awful too because you are responsible. Feel contrite and a failure. Feel guilty. I want to hurt and blame you as much as I can." She is only 11 years old, yet her ulcer is a gun aimed at her parents. Each painful wince is accompanied with the inner experiencing: "You are cold and unloving, and I hate you for being this way to me. My pain is all your fault. I hope you hurt far more than I do."

Behaviors of painful and unhappy withdrawal frequently are ways of gaining this sense of hurting and blaming. "I am withdrawn from you. This gets to you, doesn't it? It makes you feel miserable. Good!" By being unreachable the person inflicts real damage. This kind of experiencing can be promoted when the person falls apart, "needs treatment," goes crazy, retreats into a deep depression, or simply is unhappy or discontented or loses interest. Such behavior is both artistic and effective. It can be exceedingly effective to be unhappy in just those very ways which induce others to try to make him feel better. Yet he can be quite skilled in side-stepping their best efforts so that, in the end, they will be frustrated or annoyed or angry (Abraham, 1960a, 1960b). My hunger is insatiable, and your attempts to feed me will nevertheless leave me unsatisfied. My depression can never be lifted by you, and will reveal the deeper punitive blame I have toward you (Abraham, 1960a; Fine, 1962, p. 212). My depression is my weapon. Without uttering a word, my withered body and overwhelming depression scream: "You will never get anything from me. There is no life in me, and I am going to suffocate you with my gloom until you feel the hate, the blame, the vindictiveness in me." When he is quite sad and uncommunicative, the old father experiences the inner blame and anger at his wife, his sister, and his two children. As he slips deeper into becoming mute, quite withdrawn, and even autistic, the punitive knife is plunged further into them. When loneliness is communicated effectively to the target, it is capable of arousing extreme discomfort in the victim (Fromm-Reichmann, 1959). This is a public, interactional, goal-directed loneliness which attacks the significant others and blames them vindictively. Painful as is the loneliness, its very painfulness is instrumental for its effectiveness.

She is 15 years old, and has an array of behavioral means of torturing her parents, hurting and blaming them, making them feel anguished and hated, blamed and guilty. Her life is a secret to them, even when she becomes pregnant and decides to have the baby. Whatever she says to them, whatever she withholds from them, everything finds its mark in providing her with the necessary inner experiencing. By means of her own behavior, painful as it often is, she succeeds in gaining the sense of hurting and blaming them. Whether by keeping the baby or having no concern for the baby, keeping secrets from her parents or telling them about her latest sexual exploits, the underlying experiencing is that of hurting and blaming them.

One gains a sense of hurting and blaming others by an array of sexual "problems." For example, how bothered he is by his inability to sustain an erection, and by his premature ejaculations. It is a terrible problem to have so much difficulty getting the penis hard and erect; all too often it remains limp, especially when he would want it hard because he and his girlfriend are both highly aroused. When he does succeed in getting hard, he ejaculates much too soon. Yet just beneath is the experiencing: "You will never get anything from me. I love it when you worry about not turning me on. Go ahead and worry. Feel bad. Make it all your fault. I hate you and I'm going to make you squirm with guilt because it is all your fault."

Superiority. One way of gaining the experiencing of superiority is by working others into emotional fits while being cool and unruffled. He seemed emotion-less, but his behavior was sheer artistry in working with the right other persons to bring them into states of high emotion, whether one of angry frustration, tension and anxiety, failure and depression, or sexual passion. While his victim writhes in the flames of emotion, he regards the other with disdain, cool distance, and experiences a sense of enormous superiority. Fenichel (1954c, p. 34) describes such a person as follows: "A patient of mine uses this lack of affect entirely for purposes of resistance . . . This stoical equanimity has always been his most powerful weapon throughout the rest of his life as well. He has been in the habit of tormenting father substitutes almost to death; he works them into a violent passion in order that he may express his own superiority by remaining entirely without emotion." One may be bothered about being cold and aloof. One may even be pained by getting involved in working others into an emotional frenzy. Yet, bothersome and perhaps even painful as this is, the underlying experiencing may consist of this sense of superiority.

Having magical powers. Although carrying an aspect of pain, some behaviors provide one with a sense of possessing special magical powers. She could discern the nasty inner thoughts of others, the thoughts behind the thoughts. Although she felt worried about what she discerned and somehow dirty because of her knowing, there was that underlying sense of magical knowing. The older woman was pained by a strange and unnatural power to influence others. She felt responsible for the occurrence of certain tragedies such as automobile accidents, miscarriages, strange maladies, and financial losses to those whom she hated. It was as if some evil power lay within her and enabled her to have magical influence over their lives. Such behaviors carried pain, but served as a means of providing for strong experiencing.

Distance. Various behaviors, many of which are painful in and of themselves, serve to provide a sense of distance, of being unassailable, beyond reach, separated, preserved. It is as if the inner experiencing says the following: "Keep out. No one shall ever get that close. I am intact and safe. You shall never invade me or get to me. No one and nothing shall ever get close to me. Keep your distance."

In mild ways, the fussy uncle gains this inner experiencing of distance by effecting a quick and effortless retreat whenever it is important for him to step back from whatever is going on. If the conversation veers dangerously close to any sort of tabooed topic, to one which is scary or threatening, he stops talking. There is quiet, distance. He thereby breaks off the relationship and draws the distancing wall around himself. Suddenly uncle is not present any longer. Occasionally he is bothered by being this way, but, whether bothered or pristinely unaware, the inner experiencing is one of distance and safe separation.

The maintaining of little secrets can, for some, provide a behavioral means of experiencing this sense of distance. Even though there may be clouds of ominous bad feeling associated with such ways of being, there is also a common sense of safety in the distance which the secret entails, and sometimes even a wicked inner pleasure (cf. Levitsky & Perls, 1970). In this maneuver, the content of the secret is irrelevant. What is relevant is the distance maintained by the having of the secret. Mother knows what the daughter has been doing lately because mother and daughter confide in one another. But both father and older brother are denied access, and thereby mother gains the important sense of distancing.

There are far more extreme and dramatic ways of providing for this same experiencing of distance. One is to be alone and mute, wholly unresponsive; plunged fully in my own private inner world. Place me in a sitting posture and I remain that way for hours. My body has been described in terms of "waxy flexibility," for it persists in whatever posture it is placed in, plastic and thereby unresponsive to what external forces do to it. Inside there is the experiencing of distance, safe separation. The person who behaves in these ways gains the sense of distance which can offer ",.. temporary refuge in her own world, her private world, her shell" (Laing & Esterson, 1970, p. 44). It is important that "... the mentally ill live in a 'world' different from ours..." (Binswanger, 1958a, p. 213). Indeed, existing in a separate world is an achievement offering the important experiencing of distance.

But there are lots of other extreme and unusual ways of gaining this sense of distance. An effective means, and one which often is accompanied with painful feelings, is to trap you within the web of my delusions. They are plotting to trick me, to try to get me to reveal myself, my inner thoughts. They are plotting to ensnare me, but I am alerted and vigilant against their traps. You are one of them. Or maybe they are tricking you so that they use you against me. No matter what you try to do, I keep you at a distance by encompassing you in my delusion. I know why you just smiled at me, and I am too clever to be taken in by your invitation that I just talk freely with you. Stay back. I know what you are up to. Even when you try to explain the facts about my illness and my lack of contact with reality (Boverman, 1953), I know what you are really up to; you can't fool me. And inside there is always the experiencing of distance.

Others are kept at a distance by his retreating into a crazy world of the infant. He is 23 years old, yet he wets his bed, has to be fed, gurgles, mouths objects, crawls about the room. It is the experiencing of a safe distancing which occurs by means of such behaviors. Frequently this sense of distance can be achieved within the mental hospital, which itself lies safely separated from the community. The hospital provides a haven so that such persons feel safe behind its walls—even when there is no apparent "treatment," and they are left alone or perhaps neglected (Goldberg & Rubin, 1964).

Removal and escape. A number of painful behaviors serve to provide a sense of removal from an uncomfortable situation, of escape from something which has possibly become intolerable. My withdrawal may be painful, but it nonetheless enables me to get away, perhaps even to reevaluate what is happening, or possibly to move more constructively in the direction of change (McCall, 1968; Shostrom, 1967, p. 67). It is common for depressed ways of being, painful as they may be, to serve as means of moving out of bad situations. In mild forms, the adolescent becomes depressed and moves into himself, as a means of getting away from the suffocating intrusiveness of his mother who pries and digs ever deeper into him. In the same way, the daughter sinks into a depression as a step toward getting away from the saturnine serving of her aged mother who hangs on her, forcing the daughter to be bound tightly to her.

There is an experiencing of removal and escape from mildly uncomfortable moments when the mother becomes confused and fumbling, mixed up and somewhat bewildered. By means of such behavior she manages an exit from whatever uncomfortable situation she is in. Another woman effects her removal and escape from unpleasant situations by means of sudden outbursts of temper. If her children are crowding her into revealing her prejudice against Spanish-Americans, she can get out of that immediate situation by flaring up in anger at such irrelevancies as their disregard for their room ("Clean your room; it's filthy!"), or the lack of help around the house ("You two get the table ready for dinner; who the hell do you think you are around here?") The school teacher had been an assistant principal for many years. It became part of his natural way of being—although also a source of some discomfort—that he exited from any sort of uncomfortable moment by becoming rather stiff and formal. Others quickly knew that he was bothered when he became that way, even though he sometimes was unaware of anything except a pocket of vague unease.

Whether by becoming stiff and formal, confused and bumbling, or annoyed and angry, the behavioral means of effecting removal and escape from an uncomfortable situation brings with it a load of pain. These persons may complain about their temper, or their being mixed up, or their being stiff and formal, and they may have a measure of hurt and anguish at being that way. Nevertheless it is by means of such painful behavior that they gain the experiencing of removal and escape from the problematical situation.

Avoiding external punishment. The deeper potential is experiencing a sense of getting out of it: "Stay away. Don't try to punish me or make me responsible. Don't you get close enough to blame me. I am humbled. Stay away. Leave me alone." He is sitting in his room, saturated with a numbing depression. He thinks nothing and says nothing. Off somewhere in the room the mother is muttering to the police that her son has been like this for two days; not eating anything, looking vague, not seeing anything, never moving. What has God done to her? What has happened to him? The police officers explain that he was responsible for the death of the old man who was custodian of the store he robbed with a few other boys. Being this way is painful, yet it provides a means of avoiding external punishment.

There are ways of behaving which are painful, yet serve to avoid punishment from others. Being contrite, suffering, doing self-imposed penance, carrying out some self-imposed penalty or mission or the proper kind of vow—beneath such ways of being can be the experiencing of being beyond their punishment, staying just out of their punishment, avoiding what they may do. After the young wife shot her father-in-law, she was enveloped in the awfulness of her crime and the certainty of her punishment. That was the last thought she had, for her next way of being was that of sheer madness. In this new state she said and did anything. She was entertaining, gay, emotional, tearful, delicate and brutal, behaving as a different person every five minutes. They called her crazy, but that made no difference to her.

She tore her marriage to shreds, ridiculed her impotent husband, flaunted her marriage vows, defied her clergyman father with her adultery. That year was the turning point in her life. When it came to an end, she was without her lover, her husband no longer wanted her, her father died. She was alone, and now she faced the accusations of her friends, her family, all those who knew what she had been and had become. Soon after a number of suicidal gestures—very mild wrist cutting and driving her car in alcoholic stupors—she found her way into the hospital where she beat her thighs until she had to be restrained. In the hospital she repeatedly hit herself, jabbed herself with spoons. With such behaviors came the inner experiencing of the avoidance of the punishment she deserved and provided for herself while simultaneously avoiding it from the external world.

Loss prevention. Although the behaviors are filled with pain, the underlying experience is one of preventing the loss or separation of the other person. That other person is to be kept here, nearby. There is a danger that the other person may leave, and such a possibility must be forestalled. Pain is the key. Create the need for that other person to remain. Every behavior must bind that other person so that there is no chance that they might leave.

Lisa's mother is in her sixties. After a four-year marriage and divorce, Lisa had returned home to take care of her mother who was invaded by arthritis and other bone and joint ailments. Mother was able to get about the small apartment, but Lisa must help. Mother can cook a bit, can barely dress herself, but certainly is unable to write letters or do the heavy cleaning or shop. Lisa was essential. If Lisa whispered about the possibility of leaving, mother would turn away, be so very sad, and her poor old body would be racked with terrible pains. A physician unwittingly conjoined with the mother's efforts to bind Lisa to her. Mother must be attended to; the condition is worsening; we could arrange for a nurse if she goes to a convalescent home; it would be costly, perhaps excessive. In a kindly way, the physician buried Lisa in guilt, and mother's body ached with pain whenever Lisa took a slight step back from bondage. Mother's body hurt; there was pain. Yet the painful body insured a particular kind of experiencing, i.e., prevention of the loss of Lisa.

Being helped. The status of being helped typically is a pathway to numerous subsequent experiencings. In the role of being helped I can experience being nurtured, being safe and protected, being a child, proving that I am not a special jewel, hurting and blaming the family, acting out the personal fantasies of the hospital personnel, being wicked and bedeviled. Mahrer (1970b, 1970c) has proposed a category system of the kinds of goals (experiencings) associated with the role of being helped in a mental hospital setting. For a population of male patients, Mahrer proposed that "being helped" provided for the following experiencings: avoidance of threat, punishment, acceptance of impulses, being structured and controlled, dependency, and identification. The helpee role is quite powerful, partly because it serves as a pathway toward so many subsequent kinds of experiencings.

Powerful as the helpee role is, it is not achieved without pain. Indeed, the presence of pain is one of the most common threads across behaviors which are instrumental in placing oneself in the role of helpee—whether in personal relationships with family, friends, acquaintances, or with professional helping resources such as social agencies, emergency wards, psychiatric wards, counselling centers, outpatient clinics, private psychotherapists and counsellors. Help is elicited by having pain, and this pain is legitimate and real.

A dimension which cuts across a different plane is that of sheer complaining. Aside from the *kind* of problem and aside from the *extent* of the pain, there is a behavior which also gets one into the role of helpee, and the behavior consists of complaining. Some persons are low complainers and some are high complainers. These two groups differ both quantitatively and qualitatively from one another (Mahrer, Mason, Kahn & Projansky, 1966). Adding further to the distinctiveness of these two groups is the finding that, in a given hospital population, the distribution of sheer number of complaints occurred in a distribution which was non-Gaussian, and highly skewed in a positive direction (Mahrer, Mason, Kahn and Projansky, 1967). Such persons become helpees by virtue of sheer complaining. It does not matter whether there is pain.

Behavior which provides for the experiencing of being helped has to accommodate to the nature of the helping agency. That is, the person seeking to be a helpee must alter the painful presenting problem depending on whether the context is a social agency, outpatient clinic, crisis center, or hospital. It becomes even more complex when one considers the kind of deeper experiencing. For example, private resources differ from public resources in the kinds of available deeper experiencings—such as the difference in intimacy and the avoidance of public disclosure (Szasz, 1956). In general, painful behaviors are frequently effective in placing the person in the role of helpee. Even further, a finer grained analysis of the painful behavior can be gained by studying the nature of the deeper experiencing and the appropriate situational context where that experiencing may be obtained.

The person seeking the experiencing of structure and control from a jail will present different behaviors than the person seeking self-punishment from a hospital.

It is inviting to speculate on the implications of what has come to be known as the human potential movement and the various therapeutic philosophies associated with that movement. Essentially, the professional persons in this movement invite anyone to enter the therapeutic process, without the ticket of admission being some problem or difficulty or painful behavior. The therapeutic process is open to those who seek actualization or heightened facilitation or increased actualization or altered states of consciousness. I am strongly inclined to hypothesize that a popularization of the movement would mean the virtual elimination of problem behaviors which historically have been required to gain the role of helpee. One may gain the role of helpee directly without having to present crazy behavior, headaches, marital problems or stuttering.

No discussion of the kinds of potentials experienced by painful behavior or the kinds of painful behaviors serving a given motivation can ever be complete. What have been illustrated are the ways in which a variety of painful behaviors provide for the experiencing of a given potential, and some of the potentials experienced by means of such painful behaviors.

SELF-PRESERVING BEHAVIOR

Humanistic theory provides three classes of painful behavior. The first consists of *disintegrative* behavior, in which behavior institutes disintegrative relationships between the person and the external world. The essence of this kind of painful behavior is that there are disintegrative relationships among potentials, and behaviors serve to institute those same disintegrative relationships between the person and the external world. A second class includes painful behaviors which serve to provide for the experiencing of potentials. Such behaviors are known as *experiential* behaviors. We turn now to a third class of painful behavior: behavior which serves as a means of preserving the self.

The Nature of Self-Preserving Behavior

The term "self" refers to that sense of "I-ness," to the center of my consciousness and awareness. As discussed in Chapter 2, the "self" is located within the domain of the operating potentials. There is a set of behaviors which serve to preserve that self, to insure that the domain of the operating potentials is not intruded into or radically altered or wrenched apart. These behaviors serve to maintain the integrity of the domain of the operating potentials, to prevent the destruction of the person. Within a psychoanalytic vocabulary, these are described as behaviors serving to preserve ego integrity (Kovacs, 1965).

The insignificant domain of the operating potentials. The self (or personhood or ego or I-ness) which is defended, protected, guarded, and preserved by such behaviors is, from our perspective, a pitifully small and insignificant corner of the total personality. The realm of the self is nothing more than the domain of the operating potentials, and although that domain is all that exists, from the perspective of the self, it is practically nothing at all against the backdrop of the whole personality.

Even though *we* may know that the total personality includes potentials outside the domain of the operating potentials, the self or person-as-operating-potential lives in a different world. From the perspective of the person-as-operating-potential, deeper potentials are alien pools of danger, sources of threat to the intactness of the self. The self is endangered because it commits what Zen Buddhism describes as a fundamental error by assuming its (part) self to be tantamount to the whole self (Maupin, 1965). To the person-as-operating-potential, the domain of the operating potentials *is* the whole self. What Zen Buddhism calls a fundamental error is indeed the self's fundamental truth. While some outside individual may know that the person has a particular deeper potential—such as being ambitious or rejecting or cowardly—to the person-as-operating-potential, that deeper potential is something alien, not-me, even dangerous, beyond the boundary of the self which I am.

In order to live in a world in which my self (or I-ness) is coterminal with nothing more than the domain of the operating potentials, the person must never question a number of paradoxical assumptions. Each of these assumptions tends to preserve the fiction that personhood and the domain of the operating potentials are coterminal, that the person is the operating potentials.

One fundamental error is the conviction that the person has choice, has mandate over his life, determines his own fate. It is paradoxical in that this conviction is *accepted* to the degree that the person *is nothing more* than the domain of the operating potentials. The more the person is confined to being nothing more than the domain of the operating potentials, the *less* choice he has, the *less* mandate does he have over his life, the *less* can he determine his own fate. Indeed, the more the person is nothing more than his operating potentials, the more he is determined, mechanical, without choice, and yet—paradoxically—the more he is convinced he is free and master of his own destiny. "We ascribe to ourselves powers which we do not have;

we imagine ourselves to be self-conscious although we are not. We have imaginary powers and imaginary self-consciousness and we imagine ourselves to be one when really we are many different 'I's' . . . we imagine that we can 'do,' that we have choice; we have no choice, we cannot 'do,' things just happen to us" (Ouspensky, 1957, p. 9). Such convictions, paradoxical as they may be, tend to *preserve* the person-as-operating-potential. The person must accept these convictions in order to exist as the tiny, insignificant, part-person which he is.

Above all, the person-as-operating-potential (the self or I-ness) acts so as to maintain its integrity. An entire array of behaviors serves to maintain the self, to insure that nothing interferes with or endangers its integrity—no matter how insignificant that domain is, no matter what possibilities lie outside that domain. All of these behavioral means constitute self-preserving behavior.

Self-preserving behavior, "neurosis," and "psychosis." To preserve the self, the person will behave in ways which are painful. A good measure of behaviors which are termed "neurotic" are ways of preserving the self. "Neurosis, then . . . is the method the individual uses to preserve his own centeredness, his own existence. His symptoms are his way of shrinking the range of his world in order that his centeredness may be protected from threat . . ." (May, 1964, p. 28). I do not consider all of the behaviors which are termed "neurotic" to be understood as self-preserving behaviors. But a large measure of so-called neurotic behaviors are designed to maintain the self. It is in this vein that ". . . sickness is precisely the method that the individual uses to preserve his being . . . he cannot permit himself to give up his neurosis, to get well, until other conditions in his existence and his relation to his world are changed" (May, 1968, p. 95). In all of this, the endeavor is to preserve the self, the person he is. And to achieve this end, the person must protect against the intrusion of the encroaching deeper potential; ". . . the neurotic's very symptoms, disruptive and disjunctive as they appear to us on the outside, are expressions of his endeavor to preserve his unity. To preserve this unity he has to block off, refuse to actualize, some potentials for knowledge and action" (May, 1967, p. 97). Accomplishing these goals is the basis of self-preserving behavior.

In accomplishing these goals, the target is the encroaching deeper potential. As described in Chapter 9, the rising deeper potential is the threat to the closing off of the existence of the person-as-operating-potentials. However, the *working target* is generally something in the *external* world. In the interaction with the external world, especially interaction aimed at preserving the self, behavior is required—self-preserving behavior. From the outside, such behavior is often called neurotic or psychotic because it prevents too much contact with other individuals. Letting that contact happen, participating more fully in contact with others, means threatened destruction of one's self, and therefore the person is not so much avoiding contact with the *external* world as with the menacing *internal* world of deeper potentials which threaten the very intactness of one's self (Laing, 1960).

When we look externally, we see behavior working hard at insuring that the external resource does not endanger the self or person-as-operating-potential. It is as if the person sees what is external and says, "I must defend against that, and keep it from threatening my existence. If it comes further into me, it will endanger the existence of the person that I am." When we look *internally*, we see the person struggling desperately to remain the person whom he is, and to struggle against giving in to the intrusive deeper potentials. It is this deeper potential which Binswanger refers to as "oneself" in his description of a central characteristic of schizophrenia: ". . . at the root of so many 'cases' of schizophrenia can be found the 'desperate' wish . . . *not* to be oneself" (Binswanger, 1958c, p. 297). In so many ways, existentialist theorists turn to this third class of painful behavior, self-preservative behavior, as carrying the burden of explanation of problem behavior, so-called neurotic behavior, sick behavior, and schizophrenic behavior.

The pain of self-preserving behavior. Such behavior is classed as painful behavior. Yet its pain is quite different from the pain of the first two classes of behavior described in this chapter. There are two kinds of pain associated with self-preserving behavior. One is the pain of truncated experiencing. Every time behavior serves to preserve the self, the person cuts himself off from the possibility of experiencing deeper potentials. A wall is built around the domain of the operating potentials, and the total amount of available experiencing is curtailed. This kind of pain includes the feeling state of nothingness, in which the available amount of sheer experiencing is progressively reduced, and the person moves increasingly toward an existence of little or no experiencing. The second kind of pain is located not within the domain of the *operating* potentials, but rather within the domain of the *deeper* potentials. As behavior occurs, the person-as-operating-potential feels little or no pain, but the deeper potentials experience ever more of the painful feelings of meaninglessness, numbness, unfeeling, and nothingness. Were we to move inside the deeper potential, the pain would be that of increased suffocation and eventual death. If the person is successful in his efforts to seal off the deeper potential, the consequence is, paradoxically, no pain whatsoever for the *person*. He exists in a state of unfeeling (not pain), the state of death, of absolute nothingness. The *person* is now fully asleep, fully mechanical and automatic. One is now in a trance, without knowing that one is in a trance (see Chapter 3).

Just before the person-as-operating-potential carries out any self-preserving behaviors, he will sense painful feelings. These are the painful feelings from the rising of the disintegrative deeper potential, the disintegrative feelings of being invaded, being torn apart, and having one's existence brought to an end. But these feelings, painful as they are, are not yoked to self-preserving behavior. As described in the behavioral circle (Chapter 9), these painful feelings precede that point on the behavioral cricle when the person has the choice of ways of behaving—including engaging in self-preserving behaviors. Thus these painful feelings do not occur in conjunction with self-preserving behavior, but serve only to precede the occurrence of such behavior.

There is, however, a special kind of painful feeling which does accompany the occurrence of self-preservative behavior. We have described such self-preservative behavior as being accompanied with the curtailing of experiencing, and with the envelopment by nothingness. In addition, there is a subtle kind of feeling which occurs as the person engages in self-preserving behavior. This feeling is painful, but muted. It is an uncomfortable feeling, but soft and subtle. It consists of a little internal whimper, a delicate inner voice which says, "You should not do this; that was a real mistake." It is the voice which psychoanalysis attributes to the superego, and which humanistic theory attributes to the deeper potential which is blockaded in the service of preserving the self. When you are swept along by the group, and find yourself agreeing to go drinking, and when your insides want to go home and be with your wife who is alone and waiting for you, the deeper potential wants to say, "No! Thanks, but I'm going home." But instead of listening to the deeper potential, you agree to go with the guys. At that instant, your behavior served to preserve the self, the person whom you are—and not to allow the deeper potential to threaten the domain of the self. What you may well have felt was a kind of inner bodily clunk, a brief uncomfortable sinking. Commonly, when you behave in a self-preserving way, you know that uncomfortable bodily sensation is there, for a moment, but you barely sense its presence, and certainly do not listen attentively to it. That inner voice is saying that something is wrong; do not continue doing what you are doing.

We now turn to five ways in which behavior functions to preserve the self (see Figure 10.1).

Behavior Which Buries the Deeper Potential

The person-as-operating-potential can be preserved by behavior which pushes down the deeper potential so far that it is forced below the threshold of unfeeling (A, Figure 10.1). The person cuts the deeper potential off so completely that it is in effect inert (Chapter 3). As described in Chapter 9, behavior which propels the person round and round the behavioral circle keeps the deeper potential from approaching the domain of the operating potentials. It seems that thousands of such behaviors, thwarting the deeper potential time after time, build toward a cumulated consequence. After thousands of thwartings, it is as if the deeper potential atrophies, becomes eroded, lifeless, without viability, and sinks into the zone of unfeeling (A, Figure 10.1). The behaviors which accomplish this are those which occur at point C in the behavioral circle (Figure 9.1). These are behaviors which have two characteristics. First, these behaviors avoid giving in to the rising deeper potential, and inevitably decline the invitation to take advantage of one's capacity for choice in the moment of peak feeling during critical moments. Second, these are behaviors which are ordinary, typical, without risk, conforming, everyday, mechanical and easy. It is difficult to describe the nature of such behavior by virtue of its commonness and because it is the accumulated impact of thousands of such behaviors which finally wears out the deeper potential.

I recognize that I am describing as painful, self-preserving, and blockading of deeper potentials many of the behaviors which in other approaches are considered normal, healthy, adjustive—and even mature and optimal. Most normal, mature behavior preserves the self—at the expense of the deeper potential. What's more, once behavior has succeeded in killing the deeper potential, there is little or no possibility of change. New behaviors may be added and others washed away. One operating potential may take the place of another, and new operating potentials may even be developed. But since the deeper potential is rendered essentially inert, it will not intrude into the domain of the operating potentials, and that means no further possibility of integration. The person who has succeeded in killing the deeper potentials lives in a world of no substantial change. In essence the person is dead.

The state of the external world. Once the person has succeeded in consigning the deeper potential below the threshold of unfeeling, the world in which that person exists no longer contains externalizations of that deeper potential. During the years of struggle against her own deeper rivalry, her world contained competitive individuals filled with rivalrous tendencies. After several decades of struggle, she finally buried the deeper rivalry within her, and the world was drained of persons with such qualities. Acquaintances whom she knew when she was much younger—school mates from her childhood and adolescence—noticed quite a difference in her, for she no longer interacted with them along a dimension of rivalry. Yet they also sensed a quality of deadness in her, something akin to a zombie-like mechanicalness. A certain quality of life was gone.

In addition, the person who kills the deeper potential constructs a world which is purged of external situations which might be appropriate for the experiencing of the deeper potential. Where before the person behaved in ways which constructed situations appropriate for the experiencing of rivalry, now those situations wash out of the person's life. In her world there are no more acquaintances with whom she competes. Her former tendency to seek a career extinguishes. Her world of graduate school loses its meaning. No longer does her world include competitive or rivalrous situations. In effect, there are no further life situations in which the experiencing of rivalry can occur. By means of her own behavior she has killed the deeper potential for experiencing rivalry, and with that achievement her world is purged of situations which might enable such experiencings.

The state of the internal world. Once the behavior succeeds in burying the deeper potential, and once the external world is thereby purged of the externalized deeper potential and situational contexts appropriate for the experiencing of the deeper potential, these persons live in a state of limbo, nothingness, death, unfeeling. Such persons no longer undergo disintegrative feelings which occur from the threatening intrusion of the rising deeper potential. Defensive behavior no longer occurs, for there is no longer a viable deeper potential to defend against. No longer do such persons engage in disintegrative behavior because the deeper potential is too inert to lead to disintegrative behavior. There are no disintegrative insides, no being torn apart or at war internally because in effect there are no insides.

You and I may describe such persons in this way, viz. as dead, or without insides, or as being hollow. But the persons who exist in this state certainly do not describe themselves in this way. Their awareness, their sensing of what comprises them, extends only to the periphery of their operating potentials. Such persons in effect have no deeper potentials, and do not know that they have no deeper potentials. Thus the quality of their relationships is distinctive. Almost literally, these are two-dimensional persons who lack the depth provided by deeper potentials. Such persons are free of inner disintegrative struggle. They exist in the tranquil state of automaticity and mechanicalness, severed from the troublesome deeper potentials. Nothing speaks to them from within.

It is crucial to understand that the *person* is no longer aware of or bothered by the deeper potential. This means that the person *is not aware* of no longer being bothered by the deeper potential. As long as the deeper potential is *above* the threshold of unfeeling, the person will sense some sort of disintegrative feeling. There is a deeper potential for freedom and independence, a potential which rises up frequently and leaves me with scary and uncomfortable feelings. The I which I am *can* shift from the domain of operating potentials into being the deeper potential. But when I bury that deeper potential far enough, there is no chance that I will be that deeper freedom and independence. I do not even know of its existence, nor do I know that I don't even know. That deeper potential simply does not exist in these ways: (a) the person (or self) no longer has disintegrative feelings from the rising up of the deeper freedom and independence; (b) the person (or self) can no longer enter into being the potential for freedom and independence.

The state of the physical body. To speak of the insides as dead, buried, inert—this is more than poetic speech. To the extent that the body houses the realm of the deeper potentials, the person who has succeeded in killing these insides will have a body which likewise is atrophied, dead, lifeless, unfeeling, inert. Such persons will die because portions of their bodily processes have become lifeless. In fact, the process of death will begin at that point when the person-as-operating-potential succeeds in killing the deeper processes. When they fall below the threshold of unfeeling, the body will lose its function of manifesting the deeper potentials, and those parts of the body will slowly die (Chapter 5). By a careful investigation of the inner bodily processes of such persons, we will someday be able to make reasonable inferences about the state of experiential life of various sectors of the body—and from that we will be able to guess what deeper potentials have been sealed off. One of the causes of death is suicide, a process which takes place slowly as we work hard at pushing down the deeper potentials into the zone of unfeeling.

Behavior Which Disengages the Self

A second behavioral means of preserving the integrity of the self is by behaving in ways which disengage the self (B, Figure 10.1). In this behavioral maneuver, the domain of the operating potentials steps graciously aside and permits the deeper potential to take over behavioral mandate. Through such a maneuver, nothing dangerous happens to the domain of the self. It is neither intruded into, disrupted, wrenched apart, nor radically altered. It is preserved more or less intact and unchanged.

Radical disengagement of the self. When the young man senses the rising deeper potential for sexual excitement, that deeper potential may impel him toward sneaking out at night and peeking into the window of the two women in the next apartment. If such an invitation from the rising deeper potential poses a threat to his ordinary, normal self—to the domain of the operating potentials—one way out, a way which preserves the person-as-operating-potential, is to disengage the self and open the way for the deeper potential to carry out that voyeuristic behavior. In selecting that option, the domain of the self is preserved intact. The deeper potential is side-stepped, and it does not intrude into the domain of the self. Indeed, if the domain steps aside and far enough down, it may enter the state of unfeeling (B, Figure 10.1) with the result that the person has no bad feelings whatsoever. He is essentially unaware of what the deeper potential is doing as it peeks into the windows. In essence, the person is asleep, behaving in ways that he does not know. He is unconscious.

The behavior which disengaged the person is a very special kind of behavior. Typically, such behavior is undramatic, barely discernible from the outside. It is typically a most subtle switch as if the person who was there a moment ago is gone—and without the person knowing that he is no longer there. A moment earlier the person may be the one who would *not* be a voyeur, who may even dislike voyeurism, who may even struggle against being that way. Now, with the subtle disengagement, that person is no longer present.

Subtle disengagement of the self. There are occasions in which the person-as-operating-potential does not sink fully below the threshold of unfeeling. Instead of falling asleep, not knowing, the person simply disengages and stands to the side. This position is indicated by the upper portion of the domain of the operation potentials *above* the threshold of unfeeling (B, Figure 10.1). In this position, the person has disengaged, has relinquished behavioral mandate to the deeper potential, but is still aware of what is happening. This is the person who gives in to stealing the watch from the jewelery store, but now is off to the side, watching what is going on. His hands are taking the watch; those hands are secreting the watch in the pocket, there are thoughts of how to move out of the store in an unobtrusive way—yet all of this seems to be occurring almost to someone else, to an alien being that behaves and thinks. He himself is still here, watching, observing from the side, perhaps bothered and scared, but disengaged so that *he* is unable to do the behaving and the thinking. He is not asleep and mechanical; he does indeed know what he is doing, except that the he that is doing the doing is the he of the deeper potential.

When the center of the self is removed, the behavior which comes forth may be quite ordinary. The person may be chatting with someone, yet the true center of the self, the center of the sense of I, is always watching and observing, but never fully present in interaction. This center of I-ness has private thoughts and reactions about what is coming forth from the person. "I don't like being this way . . . I wish I were home . . . She is pushing me around . . . I am bored but cannot show that I am . . . I am funny . . . How charming I am being . . ." This is the removed I which talks about the kind of person I am. When I tell you that I am friendly or unfriendly, that I impress others as funny or sober, that I am anxious or comfortable, it is the removed sense of I which is doing the talking. This is the removed I which endlessly talks about myself and the processes of my change: ". . . if you tell me *truly* how you experience me, I can compare this with my experience of myself, and with my own self-concept. You may thus insert the thin edge of doubt into the crust of my self-concept, helping to bring about its collapse, so that I might re-form it" (Jourard, 1968, p. 162). The I who compares what you say about me with the way I think about me is an I which is safely removed. Yet that I is never directly reachable because it is safely disengaged, and that state of being disengaged leaves it perpetually preserved.

It is not possible to reach a self which is so subtly disengaged. That center of I-ness always takes a step back and talks *about* but never directly *is*. Without ever *being* angry, that self can talk *about* anger. But while it speaks of its anger, of its wanting to kill, of its hating this or that, the disengaged self which is doing the talking is never directly presented, for it is always off to the side just a bit, subtly disengaged. In this location, the center of the self is safe. It will not undergo the *experiencing* of anger as long as it *talks about* the anger. Because the center of the self is thereby disengaged and preserved beyond reach, the Zen master refuses to engage in endless talk and analysis and conceptualization, for all that can never entice the center of the self into the desired experience (Maupin, 1965). Talking about experience keeps the center of the self from its own bathing in experience. Thus in Zen Buddhism there is a strong distrust of mere conceptual knowledge, which preserves the subtly disengaged center of the self.

Insight or understanding is acquired by the center of the self about other aspects of the total personality. But the part which has the insight or understanding is never brought forth into actual direct experiencing. You can saturate me with insight without ever reaching the center of my self. The center of my self is thereby preserved. I am the one who accepts or who rejects the insight you offer to me. You are unwittingly acknowledging the existence of the disengaged I when you tell me that some other part of me has murderous tendencies or loves its mother or wants to be protected. Within the language of psychoanalysis, the psychotherapist is talking *to* the ego *about* instinctual derivatives; ". . . when we demonstrate to a patient the fact that he is setting up a defense, what its nature is and why, how, and against what he is employing it, we are really training his ego to tolerate instinctual derivatives" (Fenichel, 1954b, p. 20). Any subtly disengaged ego would be delighted to receive such training, for there is no threat to its integrity, and its state is preserved. Insight and understanding are games played delightfully and endlessly by the disengaged self bent upon its own preservation.

Psychotherapies which utilize insight and understanding are working to *preserve* the disengaged person, ego, self, or center of being. Such psychotherapies will fail to reach or bring about change in the self. Thus the disengaged self is quite willing to learn all manner of things about warping childhood influences, behavioral tendencies, deeper wishes, ways in which it perceives and misperceives the world, and childhood emotional patterns which persist in the present world. The disengaged self can absorb all the insight the psychotherapist has to offer, for the recipient self is safely disengaged and unreached by the very process of offering insight. Indeed, the very rules of the insight game anchor the I in its safe and secure position, for the position of receiver of the understanding automatically withdraws the receiver from any other role. The I does not gain insight about the *I*, but, rather, about other parts and relationships. In this role, the I can absorb loads of insight, for the I burrows ever deeply into its nest of self-preservation. Little wonder that insight alone is found to be generally ineffective as a means of achieving personality change (Bandura, 1961). It would seem that the attempt to provide insight and understanding would, on the contrary, act to *prevent* personality change. No matter how accurately one names, labels, or describes the other personality parts, the center of the self is not *being* those named, labeled, or described parts: ". . . the hidden is only named—i.e., determined as here and now existent within the organism—but by no means is it revealed in its being or essence" (Binswanger, 1958b, p. 230). There is a profound difference between the center of the self "having insight into" another part of the personality which is named as being competitive toward an older sister or wanting to have intercourse with mother or being fearful of rejection, and, on the other hand, actually *being and experiencing* competition or intercourse or rejection. As long as the center of the self gains insight into the nature of personality parts, it burrows ever deeper into its position of safety, preserved in its present state of selfhood.

Psychotherapists, especially those who seek to utilize methods of experiencing, are recognizing sharper and sharper differences between insight and experiencing (e.g. Shorr, 1972). From the perspective of humanistic theory, it is almost impossible for pervasive personality change to be instrumented through insight. Instead of *preserving* the self, significant personality change requires that the self be hurled into direct experiencing, that the self be, as Binswanger says, "revealed in its being or essence." There are, then, conceptual reasons for regarding insight and experiencing as polar to one another, with the former coupled with preservation of the self and the latter coupled with the destruction of the self.

Disengaging behaviors and painful feelings. By disengaging, the self is preserved intact. However, whether the self stands by to the side, awake and aware, or falls below the threshold of unfeeling, asleep and unaware, the disintegrative relationships remain. Accordingly, the state is one of disquieted, restless, troubled, frenetic feelings, a state of having given in to evil (Binswanger, 1958c, p. 289). There is no oneness, no peace, no inner tranquility. When the self disengages, the deeper potential carries out the evil act—strangling the old man, exhibiting oneself in the car, stealing the jewelery, disemboweling the cat, having intercourse with the prostitute. And all the while the person-as-operating-potential is squirming with tension and fear, unhappiness and restlessness. Even when the domain of the operating potentials falls below the threshold of unfeeling, so that the person is asleep and unaware of what is going on, the disintegrative relationship remains. To disengage the self does nothing to alter the disintegrative relationship. At best it postpones the pain for a time.

This state is made even more painful by the form in which the deeper potential comes forth into behavioral actuality. When you disengage from the deeper potential, it will come forth in its bad form. If the disintegrative relationship is *mild*, the deeper potential behaves in ways which may leave you guilty or ashamed. It behaves in ways which you want to hide, such as having a secret avocation of building model airplanes, stealing pencils from stores, saving string, secret drinking, secret masturbation, occasional sexual sprees, secret gambling. If you are caught or found out you would feel bad. If the disintegrative relationship is of *intense* proportions, then the deeper potential bursts forth in a form which may be monstrous, twisted, ugly, bizarre—as the wild maniac, the demonic sadist, the crazy killer. In this extreme form the potential load of pain is high, sometimes extremely high.

Yet the domain of the operating potentials is preserved intact, and that is what self-preserving behavior is all about. The person-as-operating-potential may be squirming with restlessness; the bad form of the deeper potential may come forth, inviting disintegrative painful relationships. No matter what the deeper potential looks like when it comes forth, no matter how bizarre or destructive it is, the person-as-operating-potential is preserved. Thus what has traditionally been described as a "schizophrenic withdrawal" may have the effect of *avoiding* personality disorganization (or shattering of the domain of the operating potentials) rather than as constituting the *result* of "personality disorganization" (cf. Wilson, 1963). By thus disengaging the self, the self avoids change, prevents intrusion from the deeper potential, is not disorganized—while the manifest deeper potential behaves as wildly and as crazily and as "schizophrenically" as it may.

In the critical moment (C, Figure 9.1), the 17-year-old girl was at the reception of the wedding of her older brother. The situation was filled with openness, freedom, attractive new people, drinking, happiness, pleasant sexuality, jokes, touchings, kissings, dancing. Within her the deeper lusty sexuality was rising and she was vaguely uncomfortable, slightly withdrawn and tense. The switch occurred while she was dancing with the best man, an attractive close friend of her brother's and a man whom she had known for years. The person she is stepped aside, disengaging the domain of the operating potentials, and she was no longer there. The deeper potential assumed behavioral mandate in a maneuver that was brief and subtle. Now she pressed her lips against his, slid her tongue deep into his mouth, and pressed the length of her body hard against him, moving slowly in a sensuous pelvic movement. The person-as-operating-potential knew, but only dimly, what was occurring. Such self-preserving behavior keeps the integrity of the domain of operating potentials, no matter how much pain follows from the extruded deeper potential.

Such disengagements are by no means confined to the conspicuous, bizarre or dramatic. They are part of the everyday life of many persons. In these critical moments, we go vague, dull, half-aware, and just before and after we disengage there is further pain of struggling with or having been that way. Yet, as always, the person-as-operating-potential has been untouched, unchanged, preserved. Louis is a social worker who fears his deeper potential for being dumb, not having much to offer, not really belonging on a professional staff. The critical moment occurs repeatedly in situations such as those in which he is called upon to present his case report to the visiting consultant. The moment it is his turn to talk—whether to discuss the case or to present his report—Louis goes underground. He disengages and stands half-knowingly to the side, rather frozen, enveloped in a cloud of tension. The one who talks is not Louis, but the deeper potential, while Louis stands to the side, drugged, hypnotized, inert. He dimly senses presenting material which is fragmented and inept, impressing himself and others as far below the standards of acceptability. While the deeper potential takes over there is a mild state of discomfort; before and after, there is a state of disintegrative disquiet and disturbance. So many of us disengage in precisely this manner and undergo such muted states of pain.

Disengaging fully and entering into the state of unfeeling has been described earlier as "falling asleep." As a general rule, persons skilled in the behavior of full disengagement have little or no difficulty *actu-*

ally falling asleep. A difficulty occurs, however, when the deeper potential rises and the person-as-operating-potential does not or cannot disengage completely enough to enter the state of unfeeling (i.e., literally to fall asleep). This is a critical moment, typically one which occurs in the evening, around sleep time, when the person senses the rising up of a deeper potential which seeks some sort of experiencing which the person is not prepared to permit. In this situation, the person seeks to disengage, seeks to fall asleep. The difficulty falling asleep is a function of the inability of the person to disengage and enter the sleep state. This description of the difficulty in falling asleep is in contrast to predominant theories which hold that the person is filled with anxiety against either some external (e.g. Burton & Harris, 1955; Freeman & Watts, 1942) or internal threat (e.g. Conn, 1950; Freud, 1950; Gilman, 1950; London, 1950; Rothenberg, 1947), and that it is the *person* who *resists* falling asleep. Research not only is equivocal on this point, but even suggests (cf. Gering & Mahrer, 1972) that persons reporting difficulty falling asleep are not characterized by anxiety. Such research is in accord with the hypothesis that the person-as-operating-potential *seeks* to disengage and enter the sleep state, rather than *avoiding* the sleep state. Such research also suggests that the common deeper potentials, within a sample of hospitalized male patients, included (a) the experiencing of an active, explosive, impulsive physical act; (b) the experiencing of a full measure of depression; (c) the experiencing of a full measure of dependency; and (d) the experiencing of falling apart, releasing all controls. Easy passage into sleep is an expression of smooth disengagement of the domain of the operating potentials below the threshold of unfeeling. The *difficulty* falling asleep is the expression of failure of the domain of the operating potentials to undergo this disengagement.

If the disengagement is complete, and the person is below the threshold of unfeeling, he is not reachable. The person or self is out of contact, gone. From the perspective of humanistic theory, an error is perpetrated by "helping persons" who seek to establish a direct contact with the missing self. These helping individuals act as if they are able to communicate with the ordinary, daily self right now, when it is the deeper potential which is there before them. "You need psychotherapy . . . If you want to get better I can help you . . . You have been through a real trauma and are feeling the effects . . . You are having hallucinations, and that is a symptom of an illness which I can help you overcome . . ." The psychotherapist is trying to communicate with "you," the sensible, ordinarily there, person-as-operating-potential, but that "you" is not there. Thus, under these conditions, the predominance of psychotherapies will fall in their attempts to communicate directly with the disengaged self, to reestablish a connection with the "ego," to bring the person-as-operating-potential back into contact with the psychotherapist (i.e., reality) (e.g. Wolberg, 1954).

The person who is the deeper potential. Humanistic theory sees the personality as comprised of a number of selves, each having the capacity to move about, from one potential to another (Chapter 2). The ordinary self is only one of a number of selves which occupy the total personality. I consider it to be a kind of colossal narcissism to assume a single self, and a single self which is more or less fixed. In rather stark contrast, the person-as-operating-potential is one center of self, and there is also a person-as-deeper-potential—another different person.

If, then, we may speak of the person-as-*deeper*-potential, we can describe the kinds of feelings which that person has. When the deeper potential is uppermost (B, Figure 10.1), it experiences, and, therefore, the person-as-deeper-potential will have the good feelings of sheer experiencing: excitement, nerve-edged tingling, heightened aliveness and vitality. These feelings of pleasurable experiencing are indicated by the two positive signs within the circle of the deeper potential (B, Figure 10.1). When the person-as-deeper-potential is stealing the sweater from the store, secretly watching the pornographic movie, or speeding away from the accident, there is a raw, pleasurable, exciting, all-over aliveness. Yet these good, pleasurable feelings occur within a pool of disintegrative relationships between the deeper potential and the disengaged domain of operating potentials. When the disengaged operating potentials are merely off to the side, not buried (A, Figure 10.1) within the state of unfeeling, the disintegrative feelings are within close proximity. Thus, even though the person-as-deeper-potential may be excitedly alive, there are nearby feelings of distrust, hatred, disjointedness, and danger. These disintegrative feelings constitute the second set of feelings occurring when the deeper potential is uppermost. Accordingly, the aliveness and tinglingness and excitement lack a setting of integrative peacefulness or happiness or tranquility. It is a frenetic aliveness, a jangled vitality, a restless excitement.

What is the person-as-deeper-potential like? There are certain likely characteristics of the person whom you are when you are this upthrusted deeper potential—whether this upthrusted deeper potential peeks out for a few seconds, for hours, or for weeks and months. First, because of the disintegrative relationship, the form taken by the deeper potential will generally be a bad form, possibly even grotesque. The person who is the deeper potential, and the behaviors carried out by that person, will be evil, nasty, dangerous and threatening, possibly monstrous and bizarre, mad and strange. Second, relationships between this person-as-deeper-potential and other individuals will generally be disintegrative. The person will be feared and hated. Third, because the domain of the operating potentials is disengaged, and because the person-as-deeper-potential lives a separated, removed existence, out of contact with the world, that person-as-deeper-potential will affect others as strange and different, a part-person, not fully there, not a whole person, not representative of a whole person. That sense of whole personhood will be missing. Fourth, there is inevitably an absence of integration, wholeness, intactness, peacefulness, internal togetherness. Although this quality is lacking in most persons, it is a gaping vacuum in the person who is the deeper potential.

Disowning onto internal agents. The ordinary self, the person-as-operating-potentials, disengages and preserves itself by disowning responsibility and ownership of behavior. In effect, the person indicates that behavior is determined by alien internal agents. In this maneuver, ". . . he must indicate in some way that he cannot help behaving as he does" (Haley, 1963, p. 5), and that the behavior was caused by some internal agent over which he has no control—from alien chemicals to alien impulses, from alien early learnings to alien deeper forces. The person's behavior may proclaim that he has no ownership over that particular action. Some alien internal agent is the owner and the determinant of that behavior. *He* was not responsible for losing the job. It was the trembling hands, or the condition of being nervous, which was responsible for the loss of the job. By exhibiting the trembling hands, the person is placing responsibility on them, and not on himself. The responsible agent is some neurological condition, not *him*.

These behaviors indicate that I (the person-as-operating-potential) am not the responsible agent, but rather that alien internal agents are responsible for the actions. Among the alien internal agents are the following: problems and difficulties in my childhood, a severe inferiority complex, a depressive character, immaturity, old age, human nature, faulty or incomplete or inadequate conditionings or learnings, unconscious processes and forces and impulses, constitutional and genetic endowment and make-up, an inherited taint or weakness or tendency, strange ideas or thoughts or cognitions, a warped or distorted or unrealistic philosophy of life, lowered intelligence or mental retardation, minimal brain damage, a schizophrenic process, poor judgment, low blood sugar, alien deeper motivations, insanity, drugs or chemicals, epilepsy, a bad back, a weak stomach, liquor, a weak heart, muscular weakness. Behavior must indicate that these kinds of internal agents are responsible for the way the person is—and not the person. In this way, the self is disengaged and preserved. Nothing of the self I am will change as long as I am not responsibly linked to the behavior coming from me.

I behave in particular ways to indicate that alien internal agents cause my actions. For example, I vomit or am enuretic or incontinent in ways which indicate that my actions are determined by the physical condition, the drugs, the psychosis, the regression, the liquor, the illness. This can be accomplished ". . . by labeling what he says as affected by some force outside himself. He may indicate that *he* is not really talking, because he is upset or deranged by liquor, or insanity, or drugs . . . He may even vomit or urinate and indicate that these things are organically caused and not messages from *him* . . ." (Haley, 1963, p. 89).

When the muscles on the right side of the mouth sporadically tighten, the "condition" has been named a facial tic. To the extent that the person disowns that movement, the person is successful in disengaging the self from responsibility for the behavior. There is a mode of "treating" such behaviors which has an ancient history and is well known in contemporary clinical lore. The person repeats the facial tic over and over, consciously and voluntarily. After an extended number of such conscious and voluntary repetitions, the tic occasionally goes away. A similar mode of treatment has historically been utilized for many behaviors over which the person seems to have no control—behaviors such as stuttering, tremors, eye blinking, peculiar gait, scratching, and so on. Such a mode of treatment can be understood as a way of extending one's mandate over such behavior—and thereby blocking the effect of disengaging one's self from connection with the behavior. (There are, of course, many other explanations of this phenomenon. For example, within a learning theory approach, the repetition may be construed as building up reactive inhibition which is reduced by rest (cf. Eysenck, 1970).)

Stuttering can occur in a way which communicates that the speaker (the person, self, sense of I) is separated or disengaged from the stuttering speech and, thereby, not responsible. By this means, the sense of I-ness is preserved, separated from the agency responsible for the stuttering. In the same way, the person may indicate that he is not responsible for the verbal production which flows from him. Instead, something else is responsible, something such as voices in his head or a machine implanted by creatures from another planet or another person who occupies his body. In any case, the person-as-operating-potential is thereby preserved.

Yet, in order to make these alien internal agents responsible, one must behave in those ways which connect these internal agents to the action, and simultaneously disengage the self. One way of accomplishing this connection is to establish a linkage between some responsible agent (a problem or difficulty or "condition") and a *reasonable causal basis* for that agent. For example, the person can explain that he was subject to certain early traumas, or that he has had a certain weakness or ailment (e.g., a bad heart, amnesia, or epilepsy) for years. By communicating the existence of the evidence, a connection is established between the present behavior (e.g., not showing up at work) and the responsible condition (e.g., epilepsy). The simplest expression of this connection is for the person to *proclaim* that not showing up for work was caused by the epilepsy, or that exhibiting his genitals in public was caused by the history of the nervous condition. *I* am therefore not responsible; *I* am disengaged and preserved.

I am not the one who will not have intercourse with you. It is the back condition which is responsible—and therefore I wince with the pain or walk in a way which accommodates to the pain or sit in the chair with the heating pad or take the pills for my back condition. Or perhaps it is the fatigue which is responsible—and therefore I try so valiantly to stay awake, or am unable to help the son with his homework because of my tiredness, or I wonder if I should see the physician about the fatigue. By these means, I disengage from the behavior of avoiding intercourse and insure that no change threatens the person I am.

One can behave in crazy ways which have the effect of disengaging one's self from the actions. By means of such behaviors, one can cede ownership to God, the devil, or to the other personality in me (Haley, 1961). When I urinate on the floor of the restaurant, I must behave in ways which disengage me and which assign responsibility to these alien internal agents. So I proclaim or indicate that God made me do it, or that I am God; I proclaim or indicate that the devil made me do it, or that I am the devil; I proclaim or indicate that Mr. George (another personality who co-inhabits my body) made me do it, or that I am Mr. George. By means of such behaviors, the self is preserved by disengaging and ceding ownership to these other crazinesses.

It is easy to disengage one's self by means of some bad condition of the senses. The problem is then how to manifest that one has a "condition" involving one's hearing or tasting or smelling or seeing. For most persons this is an easy skill, one mastered by many young children. I did not hear the baby crying. I just didn't see the baby crawling there. By establishing a "condition of the senses," the person is disengaging the self and linking the action to that condition.

Quite often, the disengaging, responsibility-avoiding behavior *precedes* the action of the deeper potential. This is the person who goes into an epileptic state and, in the throes of the seizure, physically assaults the brother-in-law. This is the person who exhibits the sudden onset of insanity and, in the throes of the sudden insanity, smashes the car into another car or a pedestrian or the neighbor. This is the person who takes the powerful drug and then, under the influence of the drug, insults the wife's family or "makes a scene" in public or tells his older brother what he really thinks of him.

One may disengage from the action by feeling bad about it. By feeling properly depressed or frustrated or angered or sorrowful or guilty, one has removed the self from ownership of the action. Such behaviors set the stage for some other agent which is responsible for the action. It all happened so suddenly; you knocked the child down the stairs without knowing what you were doing; see how sorrowful you are; I know how upset you were about your wife's losing her job; you were under stress; that explains it. Having just excoriated your daughter's friend, complete with loud voice, bawling her out in front of your daughter and her other friends, you then disengage by feeling bad about your "temper," worry about your temper, complain about your inability to control it. By feeling bad about your temper, you disown the meanness which poured out of you, and thereby preserve the self.

In all of these behaviors, the person (or self or sense of I-ness) is busily disowning, as if the person is pointing to something else which causes the behavior. Humanistic theory attends to the *person who is doing the pointing* rather than that to which the person is pointing. When, for example, the disengaged person denies ownership of the "bawling out" behavior by complaining about his "bad temper," humanistic theory attends to the disengaged self which does the complaining—and *not* to the "bad temper" about which he complains. To attend to the latter is to attend to the content to which he refers and not to the person who is doing the referring. This is to commit what I term the *content error*, an error which is so easily committed when the person disowns onto internal agents. Where traditional approaches would acknowledge that the person has a bad temper, humanistic theory sees a disengaged self in the act of disowning.

From the perspective of humanistic theory, the above error is serious enough. But a far graver error is committed by virtually the entire array of behavioral and social sciences which have constructed and maintained whole bodies of theoretical fiction and professional poses which legitimate disowning behavior. Most theories and professional practices reinforce the person in disengaging from and disowning onto alien internal agents. Your behavior is not yours, it is a symptom of some illness. It is the alcohol problem which is responsible for your drinking, and not you. You behave the way you do because of faulty learnings. It is your neurosis which causes you to behave the way you behave. Theorists, researchers, and professional persons all join in disowning mandate onto the chemicals and drugs, the neurological condition, alien impulses, the schizophrenia, the brain damage, the immaturity, lowered intelligence. Helping professions and sciences perpetuate the game of disowned behavioral mandate—and invent waves of alien internal agents to which the disengaged self can point in its own act of self-preservation.

Disowning onto external agents. By means of a special class of behaviors, persons indicate that alien *external* agents are responsible for what the person does. Thereby, the person succeeds in disengaging and preserving his self. Accordingly, the disengaged self is not directly threatened with dissolution, closing off of its existence, or wrenching transformation. As indicated in B (Figure 10.1), the domain of the self is quite safely disengaged. In this behavior, it is some alien external agent which controls me, determines me, activates me to behave in this way (Arieti, 1961; Binswanger, 1958a; De Charms, 1968; Ellenberger, 1958; Rotter, 1966).

Such behavior must, therefore, indicate that the person is not responsible for the action, that there is some external agent out there, and that the external agent is the causal agent in the behavior. It must, for example, identify the existence of evil external forces which control the mind, and demonstrate that these alien external forces determine the action. I accomplish this by letting you know about these external forces which control what I say. Thus the disowning behavior is accomplished ". . . by labeling what he says as affected by some force outside himself. He may indicate that *he* is not really talking . . ." (Haley, 1963, p. 89). Another way of disowning mandate onto an external agent is by being wiped out by a powerful and compelling external event. Following the loss of one's family in an airplane crash, a hurricane, explosion, tornado, ocean storm, crashing lightning, the person enters a state of shock and exhibits behaviors indicative of a disaster (Raker, Wallace & Raymer, 1956), i.e., being in a stupor, being mixed up and confused, asleep, bewildered, stunned, apathetic. In the switching into this way of being, the self is disengaged and, thereby, preserved.

As indicated in B (Figure 10.1), the disengagement may leave the self *below* the threshold of unfeeling or *above* the threshold of unfeeling. Is the person conscious and aware and knowing that he is behaving stunned and dazed? If the self is situated above the threshold of unfeeling, the answer is yes; if the center of the self sinks below the threshold of unfeeling, the answer is no. Regardless of whether the person is unaware or aware, such behavior preserves the self against disruption and change.

In such public disasters as floods and hurricanes, the alien external event is there for everyone to see. In other instances, the alien external agent may be exceedingly private. It may be fabricated by the person, quite beyond the knowledge of others. For example, a person may fabricate the deceased grandfather, and behave in such a manner as to indicate that control resides in the will of that deceased person. No one may see the deceased grandfather, yet, as with the flood or hurricane, the person has disengaged the self and is now signifying that alien external agents determine his actions.

These are extreme ways of disowning onto external agents. In the flow of everyday life, there are common behavioral means of disowning onto external agents. Consider the thousands of everyday behaviors by which one person indicates that his behavior was caused by another individual. In effect the person is saying, "I am not responsible for that action. That action was triggered off or caused by or determined by what the other individual did." By means of hundreds of concrete behaviors a person indicates that he is being the way he is being because others are thoughtless or mean or nasty or uncaring or cold or cruel or some other way. Arguments are mutual assignations of causal responsibility, so that each is saying that I am the way I am because of you. Yet one consequence is that the center of the self is thereby disengaged. It is off to the side, not directly connected with the behavior coming from the person. In this sense, the person is slipped away when he walks about in a state of shock after the explosion, when he shoots the hated neighbor because the deceased grandfather returned and told him to do so, and when he is so hurt by her mistreating him that he buys the sports car he wanted.

A part of everyday life behavior, and one which allows the person to disengage while placing responsibility onto external agents, is to behave so as to place responsibility on a *role*. By means of one's own behavior, it must be indicated that it is the role which causes the person to be that way. My being ruthless toward you is a function of my role as your military officer or your judge or guardian or parent. Therefore I behave in ways which link my actions to that role— and it is this behavior which disowns upon the external agent. A part of this behavior is wearing the uniform of the judge or the military officer. Thereby the center of my self has been disengaged just enough to preserve it from radical change, no matter what happens within that role. Thus *I* did not hang you or sentence you to 20 years in prison or have you transferred or confine you to barracks; it was the role which was the external causal agent. Ruthless behavior can come from the role, but not from me. Once I turn ownership over to the role, the stage is set. Roles are both personal and collective inventions by which we disown our own behavior and cede mandate onto the role as an alien, causal, determining external agent.

Having turned mandate over to the role, the center of the self does not have access to the good feelings of experiencing. As indicated in B (Figure 10.1), the good feelings of experiencing (indicated by the two positive signs) are located within deeper potential 2, while the center of the person is located within the disengaged domain of the operating potentials. Thus the person does not have these feelings of joy, vitality, excitement. By turning mandate over to the role, the person is not that intimately connected to the ruthless behavior. When the judge pronounces sentence, when the social worker judges the parents as unfit and removes the baby, when the professor throws the doctoral student out of the graduate program, when the boss fires the worker, there is no full experiencing of glee, aliveness, ecstasy, happiness. Instead, these delightful feelings are muted and disconnected from the center of the person.

The self can be disengaged and preserved by means of behavior which turns mandate over to the *situation*. We have many behaviors which disown behavioral responsibility onto the situation as an alien external agent. To accomplish this, the behavior must define the situation as being of a particular kind. For example, the behavior must define the situation as one characterized by distrust. To accomplish this, the person may simply describe the situation as being this way: "I can't tell you who said that about you because the situation around here . . . one has to be careful . . . it's hard to trust anyone . . ." Having defined the situation, the center of the self is disengaged and it is the situation which becomes the external agent responsible for one's behavior. It is the situation which owns the way one behaves. The situation can be defined by ascribing to it a particular character: It is a party situation; it is a situation where one must be on one side or the other; it is a group where we are loyal to one another; it is an emergency; it is a situation in which we must all pull together. Regardless of what method is used to construct the situation (see Chapters 6 and 7), the act of constructing a situation serves to disown responsibility to the situation as the external agent. Once having constructed the situation, my own behavior becomes understandable or required or justified or otherwise a function of that situation—and not of the self.

Another set of behaviors which accomplish the same goal is assigning mandate to "them." I must behave so as to indicate that my behavior is a function of my family, my group, my students, my bosses, the party, the voters, the board, the committee, the firm, the customers. Their wants and expectations govern my behavior. These behaviors place the person in that postural relationship to "them" so that "they" are the ones who stimulate, control, determine what I do. Then, having proclaimed that they own the way I behave, I kill because the group wants me to kill; I oppose killing because my group opposes killing; I treat you as the enemy because "they" regard you as the enemy; I break into stores because of the influence of the crowd; I go to school or do not go to school because of group norms or because of society. My own behavior adjures the crowd (or the group or society) to own my behavior. Behaviors which proclaim this posture toward the group disengage and preserve the self by assigning the group as the external agent.

The world view of such persons is formalized in various theories of learning wherein behavior is determined, controlled, owned, and stimulated by the external world (external cues and reinforcements, the crowd, the group, the situation, social norms and standards, the expectations and attitudes of others, social classes, the community). Aside from their current popularity and usefulness, learning theories are, among other things, the science fictions of persons who live in worlds in which human behavior is preponderantly the plaything of external agents. On that stage, human beings respond to external stimuli. The behavior must indicate that I am a responder to external stimuli, that external agents control my behavior.

We need not create this world view. There is no need to work hard at manufacturing such conceptions of the world as determiner of my behavior. These views are all around us. All we have to do is slide into seeing the world in this way. Yet, whether we consciously select to perceive the world in this manner or unconsciously take on this world view, its effect is to enable the self to step aside and thereby to be preserved.

When mandate is successfully ceded to external agents and the center of the self is disengaged, everything which is, or was, or might be, the characteristic of the self is taken up by the external world. It is the external world which defines who I am, what sort of person I am, what I do, and why I do it: ". . . the place of the self is taken by the Mitwelt . . . For the Mitwelt is not one's own standard but an alien one, and as such it is no longer dependent on myself but faces me as something immovable and foreign . . . the transfer of the center of gravity of our existence from our own self to the judgment of others, experienced as fixed. Thereby the self . . . becomes a state of things, judged by the others and accordingly by me—in other words, it becomes objectified, made into a 'fixed' object or thing, with fixed contours, fixed dimensions and weight" (Binswanger, 1958c, p. 341). From such a relationship to the external world it is an easy step to altering the person's behavior by altering these external agents (e.g., patterns of cues, reinforcement contingencies). Since external agents own the person's behavior, changes in the external agents will result in changes in the person's behavior. "Symptoms are learned S-R connections; once they are extinguished or deconditioned treatment is complete . . . no matter what the origin of the maladjustive behavior may be, a change in behavior brought about through learning procedures may be all that is necessary for the alleviation of most forms of emotional disorders" (Bandura, 1961, p. 152). Once the person preserves the self by disengaging, external agents assume mandate over behavior, and this mandate is most substantial, extending from the definition of who the person is to the procedures by which the person's behaviors are modified.

Behavior Which Switches the Operating Potential

In its effort to preserve itself, the domain of the operating potentials has a number of options. It can bury the deeper potential (A, Figure 10.1). Or, as a second behavioral maneuver to preserve the self, it can be disengaged so that the rising deeper potential can do no damage whatsoever—in the form of intruding into the self, wrenching it apart, disrupting its integrity, ending its existence. By means of this behavior, the domain of the operating potentials relinquishes behavioral mandate and hands it as a gift to the looming deeper potential (B, Figure 10.1). Both these kinds of behaviors preserve the intactness and integrity of the self. A third kind of behavior which accomplishes the same goal is switching from one operating potential to another, which was described in Chapter 9.

By means of such switching behavior, the deeper potential never intrudes into the domain of the self. Whenever the deeper potential comes too close, for example to operating potential 1 (C, Figure 9.2), the center of the person switches to operating potential 3 (C, Figure 10.1), and the deeper potential retreats downward (D, Figure 9.2). Most persons are able to shift from one operating potential to another like quicksilver, ducking away and reappearing in a continually remontant way. By means of this maneuver, the center of self jumps from one operating potential to another without ever endangering its intactness.

At this moment, you are in a situational context in which you are interested in that other individual at the next table. The critical moment occurs when your eyes meet. As operating potential 1 (C, Figure 9.1), you are about to be invaded by the rising deeper potential. Perhaps the danger is that of being intruded into by powerful sexual experiencing. The simplest maneuver to offset this danger and preserve your self is to switch to another operating potential. In an instant you avert your eyes to the wall or your garments or the friend next to you or your book. The person whom you are has merely switched from one operating potential to another without endangering its existence. In the meantime, the looming deeper sexual potential recedes and the threat is over.

Switching to another operating potential means behaving in ways which uncouple the person from the immediate situation. The second operating potential is not opposite or polar, merely different. For example, as the operating potential which you are, you help construct a situational context with your parents in which you are sensing the rising up of deeper annoyance and frustration toward them. The person whom you are is experiencing being special and intelligent, and you are telling them about your courses in engineering at university. In order to preserve this self, you suddenly become another operating potential and experience silliness and giddiness by saying how hungry you are in a funny way which amuses your parents. The switch preserves the self from invasion and uncouples you immediately from the threatening situation.

The key to this switching is that operating potential 3 is not directly related either to operating potential 1 or to deeper potential 2 (C, Figure 10.1). For example, eating (operating potential 3) may be unrelated to the experiencing of food or nutrition or anything at all having to do with eating. Instead, the person who overeats or is compelled to eat or who eats in a state of tension may be switching from another potential related to the experiencing of ferocity or dominance or independence or sexuality or whatever. Psychotherapists are familiar with patients who complain of overeating or excessive sleepiness or compelling sexuality or gambling or drugs or masturbation, when the underlying, deeper potential is something quite foreign. The behaviors about which patients initially complain constitute the havens to which they run in order to escape the danger of the rising deeper potential.

A common characteristic of human behavior. Switching from one operating potential to another, and thereby preserving the self, is so common that it is virtually a major characteristic of human behavior. It is commonly expressed in a continuous switching about from subject to subject and topic to topic. Here is the simplest way of endlessly proceeding around the behavioral circle, i.e., beginning to experience as one operating potential and then quickly switching to another—expressed behaviorally as switchings from subject to subject and topic to topic. Indeed, human interaction is virtually a matter of mutual "free association" as the center of the self frenetically switches from one operating potential to another.

Conscious attempts to *avoid* this continuous switching demonstrate how finely tuned we are to moving from one operating potential to another. Try, for example, to focus your attention onto a single target, either external or internal. Focus your attention upon the flame of a candle, the other person's left eye, your fingernail, the letter E in the title of the book, the knob of the drawer. Or, focus your attention upon the valve of your heart, the baseball glove you had when you were a boy, the image of your father's pocket watch, or the "cancer" in your stomach. As you focus your attention on the target, that sense of self will begin to lose ground and give in to a deeper potential. At this instant, the self must preserve itself by, for example, switching to another operating potential and being hungry, or having a backache, or looking off to the right, or remembering that the show is now on television, or hearing the knock at the front door. One always has another operating potential to switch into when the present one is in danger of being invaded.

Does it not seem paradoxical to include such common behavior, so common that it is perhaps characteristic of human behavior in general, in a chapter on *painful* behavior? Such switching from operating potential to operating potential is dignified as civilized social skills, carried out nearly everywhere by nearly everyone. It is not weird or bizarre, not crazy or pathological, not unusual or deviant. But from our perspective, it is merely another set of behaviors which have the effect of preserving the self, and all such self-preserving behaviors fall under the general rubric of painful behavior.

Switching between operating potentials whose relationships are disintegrative. Quite frequently, two operating potentials are opposite or polar to one another. Furthermore, they may even be related to one another in a disintegrative manner. Disintegrative relationships are not confined to those between operating and deeper potentials. For example, Jim seems to rattle back and forth between being friendly and sharing, warm and trusting (OP1, C, Figure 10.1) and, on the other hand, being captious, short-tempered, frustrated, and aggressive (OP5, C, Figure 10.1). When he is angry and critical, he fears and worries about his tendency (OP1) to be easy-going, fawning, pushed around, a "nice" guy. When he is friendly and warm, he fears and worries about his tendency (OP5) to be negative and aggressive. When the center of his self is in neither place, he wonders what he is "really" like, is bothered by being either way. Jim is confused about what kind of person he is. Jim is either friendly—fighting the aggressiveness, or he is tough—fighting the easy-going, "nice" guy, or he is neither—and then he feels stuck, caught in an impasse, not knowing who or what he is, or who or what he can become. From the perspective of humanistic theory, this is merely another instance of switching from one operating potential to another. Although being either is fraught with pain, the *larger context indicates that the self is preserved*, for both are mere operating potentials. Neither of the two is a deeper potential and the self is safely familiar with being either one. Many psychologically sophisticated persons are in individual or group therapy trying to solve this problem. Am I really this kind of person or that kind of person? I seem to have an affinity for both, and a fear and distrust of both. Am I heterosexual or homosexual, domestic or free-swinging, a loner or one of the group, in the family or out, hated or loved, strong or weak, good or bad, smart or dumb? So many people are stuck in the impasse of sensing they can never get out of the trap of rattling back and forth between the two polar operating potentials.

Under these circumstances, behavior which switches from one operating potential to another is truly and unquestionably painful, and going round and round the behavioral circle is a painful process of living in a prolonged and pain-ridden impasse. This is an especially difficult problem for many patients who remain in therapy for years and, at the end, have gone nowhere. Too often patients and therapists alike become exhausted and discouraged after months and months of apparent improvement and slipping back. Each succeeding therapist or way out seems to work for a while and then leave the person where he started. In the end the person gets nowhere. Whether in psychoanalysis or marathon encounter groups, the therapy just seems to lose momentum and fade away. In patients and therapists alike there is a growing sense of discouragement and defeat.

Our conceptualization enlarges the context to illuminate the presence of a single underlying deeper potential which typically is related disintegratively to *both* operating potentials. The revealed error is to presume that one of the polar (operating) potentials is, somehow, a *deeper* potential. It is not. For example, when Jim is friendly, sharing and warm to others, he struggles against his disintegratively related operating potential for being short-tempered, frustrated and aggressive. When, however, he is aggressive, he struggles against the soft friendliness. Awareness is limited to these two operating potentials. Yet beneath both of these is the deeper potential for experiencing independence, intactness, being on his own. Jim had always linked himself to a number of companions, and either moved into intimate warmth with them or badgered and fought with them. Jim had never known the sense of self-sufficiency, independence, the deeper potential which underlies both operating potentials.

The way out of the awful impasse is to be neither operating potential, and has nothing to do with resolving the conflict between the two operating potentials, living with the two of them, or transforming one to live with the other. The way out is by being neither heterosexual nor homosexual, domestic nor free-swinging, a loner nor one of the group, in the family nor out, hated nor loved, strong nor weak, good nor bad, smart nor dumb. In each instance the way out has to do with the deeper potential, but the person is blind to the deeper potential—and only knows the fear and hate of the other operating potential or the awfulness of being stuck in such an impasse.

Most persons who rattle back and forth between two disintegrative operating potentials are trapped, and never get out. In the case of Clare, Horney (1942) describes the case of a person who rattles painfully back and forth between (an operational potential for) excessive modesty and (an operational potential for) excessive ambition. As the excessive modesty she would regard her own wishes and demands as secondary, inevitably thinking of herself less than her consideration of others. As the excessive ambition, she had to excel over others, gain triumphs over them, take up battles against adverse forces. After years of psychoanalytic investigation, the deeper potential was uncovered, one which underlay both operating ways of being. Clare's deeper potential consisted of a sense of being the excluded one, the one who is nothing, who is unlikeable and hated. From this deeper potential arose both for excelling, triumphing, engaging in battles against adverse forces. Much as Clare struggled against each operating potential, her self was preserved by being either one, and *not* the profoundly threatening deeper possibility to succumb to being nothing at all, excluded as hateful and thoroughly disliked.

Behavior which switches the person from one disintegrative operating potential to another also serves the larger purpose of preserving the domain of the self, although this is typically an exceedingly painful existence, one which can lead the person around and around the behavioral circle, and one which leaves the person always stuck and at an impasse.

Behavior Which Retrenches the Self

In order to preserve the self, behavior can (a) bury the deeper potential so that it is no longer a threat; (b) disengage itself so that it is safely out of the way of the deeper potential; or (c) keep switching from one operating potential to another in a continuous dodging of the deeper potential. A fourth behavioral mode of preserving the self is by staying where it is and pulling in its forces. There is a digging in, a retrenchment.

By freezing in a state of shock. It comes as a complete shock to you when the other individual lets you know that she considers you a sneak. You hear the words clearly, words which are smooth and mellifluous, not loud and boisterous. It is as if you wake up several seconds later. In those intervening seconds you did nothing. You were transfixed, in a state of shock, frozen. Then, a few seconds later, it is all over. The one who called you a sneak is now chatting with someone else, and you are left to emerge from the state of shock.

The immediate freezing has the effect of preserving the self whom you are. You *do* nothing—except freeze. The center of the self is transfixed and everything comes to a sudden halt. The deeper potential stays precisely where it is. After a few seconds or so the situation usually changes and the danger is over. Freezing is an immediate reaction, reflex-like in its automaticity. During the freezing process there is no experiencing of the deeper potential through behavior—such as grabbing the other one by the throat, passing out, screaming back, running away, glaring murderously, or pushing her in the face. The self is preserved.

In that moment of being frozen, the person is suddenly saturated with internal pressure, and everything becomes hazy, out of focus. The person is in a state of momentary shock, temporarily unable to function. For an instant, he has no grasp of the situation—where he is or what he is doing. What he sees is suddenly a plane, with no figure and ground, no focal visual center. The self is out of touch and out of contact with the concrete specifics of both the external world and the internal world. There are no thoughts to be grasped, no private sensings. Because the self is frozen, the person has no contact with other operating or deeper potentials. Feelings are frozen and cut off. The person does not perceive accurately. Show me pictures on a screen, flashed there by means of a tachistoscope, and I will respond quickly until you flash a picture of a vaginal opening. In the immediate state of shock I do not see. Show me pictures brought to clarity by gradual increments, and I correctly and quickly anticipate the correct picture until you show me a picture of cunnilingus. Because I go into a frozen state of shock I do not see what is there. I am preserved by not knowing, not perceiving, not seeing. The center of the self, this part of the total personality which I am, does not know what is there. That is its way of preserving itself. In this maneuver, not only do I not know what is there, I do not know that I do not know.

The net result of hundreds upon hundreds of momentary states of frozen shock is that the person-as-operating-potential is forever preserved against change. Nothing threatening ever reaches the self, which is protected by the shock state. Instead, there is an immediate and sudden retrenchment, the threat passes, and the person unfreezes. In this way the person glides through life untouched.

By having the disintegrative bad feelings. It may seem strange, but as long as the person has the bad disintegrative feelings, the self is preserved. The self retrenches, digs in, *and feels awful*—but it persists in being the self. When the deeper potential threatens the self, intrudes into the domain of the operating potentials to the point where the self is in danger of falling apart (D, Figure 10.1), the self can absorb any amount of bad feeling—as long as the self remains being the self. There is a self which feels terribly anxious or torn apart or guilty or scared or just about any kind of disintegrative feeling, but which remains intact.

The one who experiences the bad feelings of disintegration is the person-as-operating-potential, not the deeper potential. As the person continues to have the disintegrative bad feeling, the person remains within the domain of the operating potentials. For example, the young boy and girl are undressed in her bed. Her parents are gone for the weekend, and she is encouraging him to have intercourse. As operating potential 1 (D, Figure 10.1), the young boy avoids and resists her; he is on edge and worried, preferring to kiss and touch but not to have intercourse. As long as the center of the self remains within that operating potential, he will undergo the tension and the fears. These are the disintegrative bad feelings which the person will have as long as the person remains being the operating potential which experiences the avoidance and the resistance. Although he feels awful, he is retrenched, and that self is preserved.

Were he to step out of being the operating potential, and to step into being the intruding deeper potential, there would be a number of consequences. He would now experience a passive being aroused, a sexual submission. Second, he would exchange the disintegrative bad feelings for the good feelings of experiencing. Thus, as he experiences being sexually aroused and sexually submitting, he will have feelings of raw excitement and pleasure and aliveness. Third, the operating potential might well crumble and fall apart. While the person remains within the operating potential, however, the self is preserved. The center of his self has remained where it is, and he has the awful feelings. He has dug in, and he will persist in being the operating potential which avoids and resists her sexual advances—thereby retrenching the self and keeping it preserved. If the person-as-operating-potential is listened to carefully, it says something like the following: "On all sides there are pressures to give up being me. But if I give in, I collapse, I will no longer be me. The person I am *must* resist her. I cannot possibly give in or I will shatter and undergo a radical transformation. That will be the very end of who I am. Sure I feel awful. Sure I am tense and scared as hell. But at least *I* am still myself being tense and scared, for the consequence is the end of my very existence."

Many persons go through their lives retrenched into being the person-as-operating-potential, undergoing the bad disintegrative feelings, and coming into close proximity of the rising deeper potential. Such persons complain about the bad disintegrative feelings: "I am so tense ... I seem scared lots of times ... I am depressed." They know these bad disintegrative feelings. They also know the imminent bad form of the deeper potential: "I am starting to lose my drive and my ambition ... I am getting old and my body is falling apart ... I get these strange thoughts of killing someone." These are sometimes the focus of complaints which persons carry to psychotherapists. To the person-as-operating-potential, the disintegrative feelings are indeed problems, and the looming bad form of the deeper potential is also a legitimate problem. But they are also the inevitable consequences of being the retrenched self. As long as the self digs in and steels itself to stay within the domain of the operating potentials, the person will inevitably have the bad feelings and will feel the hot breath of the risen deeper potential.

Stella, Sam, and Brenda are similar in their steadfast retrenchment within their operating potentials, and their disintegrative relationship toward a deeper potential which they share in common, viz. the potential for experiencing lush passivity, an infantile trust in being held and loved and taken care of. Each of the three have clung to being retrenched into their operating potentials.

Stella is 54 years old, in her second marriage. Her two children are grown and gone. She loves classical music, plays golf decently well, has five or six close friends, reads historical novels, is especially fond of traveling. She is a person on whom her husband can count, has a good sense of humor, a weakness for too much candy, has trouble with arithmetic, is sometimes forgetful, and once considered herself as having a problem with drinking. That was during college when she had one especially bad year, complete with an awful love affair, flare-ups with her family, low grades, and mild troubles at school, including considerable alcohol. Stella has to "watch" her drinking, even today. She has never been alcoholic, has never even considered her drinking to be serious, but there are times, about once every month or so, when she must fight quite hard to keep herself from drinking into a state of oblivion. During these battles she is quite tense and distraught, for she is struggling to retrench herself within her operating potentials.

Sam is a house painter, who has dedicated his entire life to clinging to the self he is, and not giving in to the deeper potential for experiencing lush passivity and the infantile trust of being loved and taken care of. He is a kind of petty tyrant, demanding and petulant with the men he hires. Sam works hard and sets high standards for himself. His bad feelings occur when his wife verges toward caring for him. Generally this occurs when he gets sick. Sam gets sick every month or so, usually with a very bad cold or a syndrome including nausea, exhaustion, and aching pains throughout his body. Sam retrenches within the domain of the operating potentials, and struggles against the rising deeper potential. When that deeper potential begins to rise, he digs in, stays right where he is, and has the pain of nausea, exhaustion, aching pains, and stuffed up nose.

Brenda is 19 years old, slender, works as a city recreation counselor. She is a capable and competent woman who does well in her job and is intimate and steady with the man with whom she lives. Yet she has bouts of anxiety every so often, especially when she is confronted with the possibility of being pregnant. When this happens, Brenda becomes upset, tense. She becomes withdrawn and pulls away for a few hours or more. She cannot tolerate full lush passivity either in herself or in the man with whom she lives. Her way of coping with this rising deeper potential is to dig in, retrench, and have the associated bad feelings—and thereby to insure the preservation of the person whom she is.

By being polar to the deeper potential. When the deeper potential looms from below and threatens the domain of the self, a third way of retrenching is by being the opposite of the deeper potential. That is, the self lies, denies; it proves that it is not the deeper potential by being the polar face (Binswanger, 1958b; McCall, 1968). Such a behavioral maneuver enables the self to remain rooted, to prevent change, to be preserved. It is as if the person senses the nature and presence of the rising deeper potential, and sets out to prove that what it fears is true is not true at all. It is a career dedicated to proving that I am not stupid or not vain or not selfish or not crazy or not homosexual or not cold or not whatever the feared and hated bad form of the deeper potential seems to be. Yet, in this enterprise, the self is preserved—and as far as the self is concerned, that is all that is important.

Such a way of being is curiously intriguing, for it is a classic expression of the two basic functions of the operating potential. That is, the operating potential serves both the function of *enhancing* and, at the same time, *reducing* the experiencing of the deeper potential. By being the polar face, its opposite, the operating potential (a) preserves the person-as-operating-potential, (b) reduces the experiencing of the deeper potential, and (c) enhances the experiencing of the deeper potential. Indeed, by being the exact opposite of the deeper potential, the person backs directly into expressing that which it sets out to deny. Thus this classic paradigm is a joke; it inevitably becomes the servant and ambassador of the feared and hated deeper potential.

As a consequence, persons who preserve their sense of self by being polar to their deeper potential present observers of human beings with sets of opposites. We have come across this polarity in human behavior earlier. In a discussion of behavior which preserves the self by switching from one operating potential to another, it was noted that some operating potentials become bifurcated or polarized, so that the person switches from one operating potential to its polar opposite—in the grand enterprise of preserving the self (C, Figure 10.1). Both of these sets of behaviors culminate in polar and opposite ways of being which have been recognized in the history of carefully observed human behavior. It is understandable that attempts to categorize human behavior would acknowledge these sets of polarities and opposites as incorporated in, for example, Janet's hysterical-psychasthenia dichotomy, Jung's introversion-extroversion, Kraepelin and Bleuler's dichotomy between schizophrenia and manic-depression, Jaensch's dichotomy between persons who are open (integrate) and closed (disintegrate) to the environment, Kretschmer's cycloid-schizoid dichotomy, and others. Such typologies acknowledge that human beings often present polar ways of being. From our perspective, preserving the self by being the polar opposite of the deeper potential emerges as part of a distinguished mode of being in the history of human beings.

In order to preserve the self against deeper potentials for being excited and manic-like, the operating potential is sober, heavy, carefully weighing each decision, even depressed. For other persons, quite the reverse may hold. If the deeper potential involves the experiencing of sobriety, seriousness, evenness, the person-as-operating-potential may be silly, impulsive, manic-like, and excited. In order to disprove and deny the deeper potential for experiencing bitchiness, nastiness, criticalness, the person presents the opposite face, i.e. kindness, sweetness, understanding, acceptance. By the same token, the reverse may also occur, so that the person is tough, hard, nasty, as a means of retrenching the self against the deeper potential for experiencing softness, kindliness, acceptance.

When the deeper potential pulls the person toward being separated, intact, independent, the operating potential can avoid this—and its own dissolution—by dedicating itself to being *not* separated, intact, independent. In being a daughter, woman, mother, friend, Joy early developed an operating potential for loyalty, closeness, friendliness, warmth, belongingness. Throughout her 67 years, she has been devoted to her family, surrounded with close friends, available and responsive to others. Yet this way of being is born of the necessity for not succumbing to the deeper separation, intactness, independence.

Edwin is now in his late twenties, and he has pursued an entire life of struggling *not* to be the deeper potential for experiencing ineffectualness, inadequacy. From early childhood, Edwin was a person who was polar to that deeper potential, who was a force, someone to be reckoned with, an organizer, a leader. He learned skills which made him effective at school, in sports, in his personal and social relations. Edwin is launched into a successful career of not being that which is his deeper potential—and thereby preserving his self. In much the same fashion, many persons are propelled into proving that they are not failures. They are haunted by the deeper potential's chant that they are failures, losers, unable to accomplish. Accordingly, these persons are propelled into lives of achievement and success. The spectre from which they are fleeing is the sensed inner truth, viz. that nothing will work, that the fundamental truth is their being failures. When that deeper truth threatens, they retrench, become successful, and preserve the self, the pitiful self-as-operating-potential. Yet for others, the reverse holds true. To preserve their selves they must retrench by disproving deeper potentials for power and strength. These persons are endangered by the possibility of being promoted or winning the election or scoring the success or emerging the powerful one in the competition. In order to deny and avoid this, the person must be the opposite, the failure, the feckless one, the loser, the impotent one. Such persons accomplish this by insuring that they are weak, impotent, failures. Although the state may be painful, the person is nevertheless preserved. These are the persons who sabotage the possibility of success at the last moment, who masturbate away the rising inner sense of strength and power, who ejaculate too early or not at all, who behave in whatever ways will insure that they are not strong and powerful.

When the deeper potential consists of a soft dependency, the person can run in the opposite direction and be tough and rugged. This is the adolescent boy who is highly aggressive, super-masculine, a tough anti-social person running from the deeper softness and unmasculine feminity (Parsons, 1947). On the other hand, if what is within is a disintegrative toughness and independence and ruggedness, the operating potential can fend off its rise by retrenching, preserving itself, and being soft, delicate, dependent.

How does the person-as-operating-potential dig in and preserve itself against a snarling, hateful deeper potential which is ready to fight, to kill, to have the other as an enemy? This inner potential rises up when you are laughed at on the assembly line, when the boss charges you for the money taken from the till at the gas station, when your neighbor takes over part of your property, when the other person has no use for you. There appears an easy-goingness, a sense of humor, a cordiality, a friendliness. This is the civilized face, the face of amicability. Almost always this way of being includes that little extra bit of overfriendliness, forced cordiality, perhaps even the servile flattery of the sycophant. Yet the self has retrenched and preserved itself intact.

The deeper potential knows the full sense of sexuality. It whispers of being father's choice, the beautiful and special one, the one with whom he has the special bond. In order to preserve the self as *not* being any of this, she rushes into a world of being *not* sexual, not seductive, not sexually bonded to a man, not being genital. She walks in a way which is slightly awkward, develops a set of facial expressions which are unsexual. Her sitting and standing postures are unsexual. She does not seem to be "of" her body, but more or less stuck into it.

In general, she is candid, forthright, intelligent, friendly, sometimes whimsical, and characteristically unsexual.

Preserving the self by being the polar of the risen deeper potential almost always leaves the person with disintegrative feelings (D, Figure 10.1). The self is preserved, but the cost is heightened painful feeling. There is virtually nothing but a painful hollowness and emptiness in the person who runs away from the deeper aloneness and withdrawal into a frenetic social involvement, into groups, into forced friendships and parties and family involvement (Fromm-Reichmann, 1959). What is more, digging in and *not* being the deeper potential almost inevitably lacks the good, pleasureable feelings of experiencing. The feelings of joy, excitement, ecstasy, aliveness are always missing, or at best sharply curtailed. No matter the apparent success in retrenching, no matter the degree of experiencing the operating potential, the person lacks these pleasureable feelings. Thus the person may gain a full measure of experiencing the operating potential for social involvement, for interpersonal relations, for being with others, but there is always something missing, and that something is these good feelings of raw experiencing. This is the price paid for retrenching the self by being the polarity of the deeper potential.

Even more, the retrenched self always lets the deeper potential shine through. It may look like gentleness, but there is always something amiss, something not quite right about the gentleness which is the polar opposite of the deeper hatred and ferocity pressing from within. Something about that gentleness will be odd, different, a bit askew. It is not genuine, just a bit impure. Indeed, the kindliness and gentleness almost seem interlaced with threads of cruelty and meanness. As the receiver, you will sense its presence if you allow yourself to do so. You will sense the deeper aloneness and withdrawal in the person who runs from this deeper potential into a forced involvement in social relationships. When the deeper potential whispers of age, tiredness, death, slowing down, erosion, many persons desperately seek the polar trappings of youth. This self must lose weight, dress youthfully, behave like the young, disguise the wrinkles, regain the hair, play the youthful games. But the rising deeper experiencing cannot be hidden, and will shine through. The way of being has an edge of betraying that which it seeks to hide. As a result, the added quality is one of not quite fitting, being slightly out of place, with a hint of inappropriateness.

One of the reasons why such retrenchment of the self is accompanied with painful disintegrative feelings is that polar behavior—although preserving the self—*maintains* the deeper potential. By being the polar opposite, a good measure of experiencing is provided for the deeper potential. Ordinarily, one may spend years, or even a lifetime, running from the inner cruelty and nastiness by being kind and accepting, but at the end, the deeper cruelty and nastiness is still exceedingly present, imminent, threatening. In this sense, polar behavior fails to reduce the disintegrative threat. Yet, by steadfastly remaining the operating being, the person preserves the self whom he is.

Accordingly, the person-as-operating-potential never knows the sense of internal integration, the sense of inner oneness and peacefulness, the sense of unity and tranquility. Instead, the person exists in a constant state of strong disintegration. As indicated in D, Figure 10.1, the feelings of disintegration are typically quite high when the self is preserved by effecting the polar opposite of the deeper potential. Thus the person who gains the experiencing of being kind and gentle and accepting, as the polar operating potential to the deeper cruelty and nastiness, will probably know only the accompanying inner sense of disintegrative turmoil or tension, and will probably never know the sense of inner peace and oneness characteristic of a state of integration. This is another painful price paid for preserving the self by retrenching into a polar operating potential.

Even more, the self-as-operating-potential is plagued by a *having to be, a desperate struggle after*. One is not merely kind and gentle; one *must* be this way, one is caught in a desperate struggle against kindliness and gentleness. The person who seeks success and achievement as a polar opposite to the deeper nothingness and inadequacy *must* scratch after success, *must* always struggle after achievement. These persons are in the hell of *having to be* the full measure of the operating potential. When the deeper potential is the yawning abyss of loneliness, there is a restless *having to be* social, an unquenchable thirst for being with others. These persons are characterized by a restless and frenetic struggle to *not* be the deeper potential. The being of a polar opposite may preserve the self, but the cost is enormous.

Nevertheless, the career of being the polar opposite is foredoomed to failure from the very beginning. The person-as-operating-potential may be preserved, but there is no possibility of ever achieving the goal of *not* being the deeper potential. One can never rest, having finally proved that one is not stupid, not worthless, not crazy, not worthy of rejection, not homosexual, not cold and removed. These are hellish operating potentials within which the self is caught in interminable struggle—all in vain. The struggle to not be the deeper potential is, then, an impossible one, foredoomed to failure from the very beginning. In addition, it is foredoomed to failure because frequently the *specific mission* of the operating motivation is not possible. Suppose, for example, that the deeper potential proclaims that I am imperfect, full of human foibles, ordinary. The career of the polar opposite operating potential is dedicated to proving that I *am* perfect, above human foibles, beyond imperfection. Such a career is impossible. It is simply too much to maintain such a life. As a result, the person is forever confronted with failure. Day after day the person faces evidence that he is not perfect—someone is prettier, taller, knows something he does not know; he makes mistakes, commits errors, does something dumb; he gets fatter or balder or slower; he forgets, he is neither perfect at this nor at that. After hundreds of pieces of evidence, it becomes clear that the mission is impossible: The person simply cannot attain perfection. In much the same way, other operating potentials are launched into impossible careers, and the consequences are always painful. "A person who wants to lead such a humanly impossible existence we have every right to call deranged" (Binswanger, 1958c, p. 339). No human being can ever gain a perpetual sense of being the greatest force on earth, yet some poor souls must gain this continuing experience in order to not be a pressing deeper potential.

Too often, in the lives of such persons, apparent changes in oneself or in one's life or way of being are merely other ways of preserving the self as something which must be the polar opposite of the deeper potential. From the very beginning, she was a self which must disprove the feared and hated deeper potential for being cold and ungiving, separated and closed off. To disprove this, she was a child who clung to her mother. The two were inseparable. In her later childhood she turned to other girls in close and intimate bonds of friendship, several of which ripened into homosexual flurries wherein sexuality became an added ingredient to the polar denial of the deeper potential. Her early marriage was characterized by a forced closeness and needed intimacy; the two were virtually inseparable. They were a team, not only in their work (they both gained doctorates in the helping professions), but also in their love of music, camping, travel, and community involvement. As their marriage seasoned, they adopted several children, and surrounded the family in closeness and intimacy—a closeness and intimacy born of her efforts to run from the underlying deeper potential. As an older woman, after her husband left her, she became a leader in the small groups movement, teaching about groups, and conducting good workshops in groups. Yet all of these apparent changes throughout her lifetime served as variations on operational means of not succumbing to the deeper coldness, ungivingness, separation, and tendency to be closed off. She must always remain preserved as the self which she is.

In the choice between being the operating potential or being the deeper potential, the person is progressively confronted with impossible alternatives. To remain within the domain of the operating potentials preserves that self, but every other aspect of remaining here is intolerably painful. On the other hand, to give up and to succumb to the deeper potential is also intolerably painful. There is virtually no way out. This is the existence of many everyday persons, including those who constitute the teachers and the psychiatrists, the executives and the attorneys, the housewives and the plumbers, the athletes and the small businessmen. I suspect that having to be these polar operating potentials is so common that the manifest behaviors are generally those which are collectively valued and applauded, considered good and acceptable by many others. We will behave as good people, being the way collective persons want one another to be. We want one another to be, then, the polar opposite of what we collectively fear and hate in collective individuals. Accordingly, the problem does not lie within the ways of behaving, for we tend to be good, kind, altruistic, loving, honest, concerned about others, upholding collectively held ideals and morals. The problem lies, rather, in our disintegrative relationships with our deeper potentials, and in the preserving of our selves by being the polar opposite of our deeper potentials.

11

The Optimal State:
Integration

The purpose of chapters 11 and 12 is to describe an optimal state of human experiencing. This optimal state has two characteristics: integration and actualization. Chapter 11 discusses integration and Chapter 12 discusses actualization.

THE DISCONTINUITY BETWEEN INTEGRATING PERSONS AND NON-INTEGRATING PERSONS

Integration is a process of achieving integrative relationships among progressively deeper potentials. Either a person engages in this process or he does not. He may spend one hour a day, a week, a year, or a lifetime in this process. But the person in that one hour is in a process or state which is qualitatively different from the ordinary state. The integrating person or the person who is now in the process of integrating is qualitatively different from the non-integrating person or the person who is not in the process of integration. The normal, ordinary, adjusted state is one of non-integration. These persons are neither integrated nor do they engage in the process of integration. In terms of the behavioral circle, these persons travel round and round the behavioral circle, whereas *integrating* persons behave so as to withdraw more and more potentials away from such endless circumlocutions. I recognize the state of integrating as a qualitatively different one, one which is unique, rare, and special. It is a different plateau. It is being or becoming a different kind of person. This concept of discontinuity has traditionally been entertained as existing between persons described as normal and persons labeled as psychotic. I accept this concept of discontinuity, but place it between persons who are integrating and all others, including those who are considered normal, adjusted, without problems.

471

One of the differences between integrating persons and those who are not into the process of integration is that persons who are integrating behave in ways which open up the possibility of *further* integration. They have acquired the behavioral skills required for further integration. As a result, integrating persons draw further and further away from non-integrating persons. They acquire more and more of those behaviors which are not only indicative of greater integration, but also are the very behaviors by which further integration comes about. I find this to be one of the most prized characteristics of integrating persons.

By means of these skills—the behaviors of integration—the process of integration is voracious. It consumes every potential. It consumes all the operating potentials and all the deeper potentials. It consumes the potentials of so-called normal persons and those of the persons who are behaving in painful ways. There are no limits to the potentials which are consumed by the process of integration. Because of this, integrating persons are qualitatively different from persons who are not hurled into the process of integration. One is either in or out of the process of integration, either on that plateau or not on it. You are doing it or you are not. At any moment a person is either in or not in the process of integration. Thus a person may spend five minutes a week in the process of integrating, but those five minutes are qualitatively different from all the other minutes of the week.

THE DESCRIPTION OF OPTIMAL PERSONS

What are optimal persons like? How may we describe persons who are well into the processes of integrating and actualizing? A number of writers have described optimal persons within the perspective of a broadly conceived humanistic family. Among these are Gendlin (1967), Mahrer (1967a, 1967b), Maslow (1970b), and Rogers (1961, 1963). Chapters 11 and 12 draw from the thinking of these and other writers within the humanistic family. As described in Chapter 4, our basic assumptions about human beings differ from those of many other approaches. Accordingly, our description is to be understood as referring to a different conceptualization of optimal beings than those held by other approaches. Because of this, because our definition of optimal persons tells us to look for individuals who are different from the optimal persons held by other approaches, we have very little data on what these persons are like. Nearly everything we shall say about optimal persons is based upon the best guesses from humanistic theory, and practically nothing is based upon any sort of good data. If there are optimal persons, or persons who are even close, they probably are not among the subjects of our research. Indeed, as Dalal and

Barber (1970) say about the yogi's attitude toward scientific investigation, optimal persons may well regard "... the work of the scientist as trivial and futile, if not presumptuous and sacrilegious" (p. 120).

According to humanistic theory, collective human beings construct the external world. We can describe *individual* persons who are into the process of integrating and actualizing, and we can describe the kinds of external worlds constructed by *collective* optimal persons. In these chapters we will primarily focus on the *person* who is into integrating and actualizing, and secondarily, describe the external worlds constructed by *collective persons* who are into these processes.

Integrating persons are rare and special. Yet the possibility of being an integrating person is available to just about any person. Anyone *can* enter this process. Thus the persons whom I describe in this chapter can come from any class, any walk of life, any background. One need not be special or gifted in order to elect to enter the process of integration.

A criterion of good and bad, desirable and undesirable. Within the framework of humanistic theory, movement in the direction of integration is good, it is desirable, it is a valued way of being. I consider increases in the degree of integration as an indication that something good and desirable is occurring. This applies to a person and to collective persons. If an event or a program or any sort of change results in heightened integration, it is good and desirable. Psychotherapy or a government program or education or any personal or social program is good and desirable if it results in heightened integration.

INTEGRATION WITH THE INTERNAL WORLD

The state of integration has two aspects: integration with the internal world and integration with the external world. In this section we will describe integration with the internal world, i.e., what the integrating person is like inside. This is an *internal* matter, apart from changes in the integrating person's external world and in the nature of the relationships between the integrating person and the external world.

Commitment to the Journey into Internal Integration

The act of commitment. The integrating person is committed to undergoing the internal journey. There is a time when this person turns away from the external world and turns within. This turning inward is a statement to the external world, as well as an expression of the work of integration. The statement to the external world is that this is a time when I must withdraw, must disengage from involvement with the external world, and must carry out my commitment to the internal journey. The commitment to the internal work of integration is also a way of coping with the problems and the difficulties of the external world. If my world is boring and monotonous, troubled and in turmoil, or crazy and chaotic, I do something about all that by turning inward, by seeking within myself the courage and integrity to be myself in this world in which I live (May, 1953). Withdrawing from the external world, being the kind of person who *can* withdraw into one's inner world, is itself a means of coping with the external world. In addition, the fruits of the internal journey enable the person to cope with the external world. Thus the integrating person commits himself to undergoing the internal journey, and constructs a world in which he reserves some time to his own inner journey; in addition, he is free to publicize the commitment to withdrawing from the external world during these inner journeys.

The *external* face of the commitment involves detaching oneself from the external world and placing one's attention upon the internal world. The *internal* face of this commitment is the decision to commit oneself to the internal journey. It is the acquisition of skills whereby integration occurs. It is the throwing of oneself into the process of becoming; "being human is not only a having-to-be but also a being-able-to-be . . ." (Binswanger, 1958c, p. 327). It involves the commitment to be whatever there is within to be. This is the leap of faith, the tearing of one's self from what one is and the falling into whatever is there within. In this commitment, I am the one to decide, the one who makes or fails to make the commitment. It is *my* commitment, not my parents' or my group's or my spouse's. I am the responsible director of my own process of internal change (Jung, 1933, p. 53).

Carrying out the commitment by oneself. Having made the decision, one must set aside a certain amount of time, time which is reserved for the internal journey. In this time, one has withdrawn from external affairs, *all* external affairs. It is more than being alone, for the focus must be one's own insides. This time may be a few minutes a day or an hour a week or a month a year. The time may be regular or irregular. That does not matter, so long as the time is reserved for the internal journey.

This commitment is made by the person alone (Mahrer, 1975a). We know of remarkable internal journeys achieved by such singular persons as Nietzsche, Kierkegaard and Freud. Yet the methods of the internal journey can be learned and utilized by others who are less remarkable. If we knew effective ways of undertaking the internal journey, Nietzsche, Kierkegaard, Freud and others would take their role as pioneers, persons who discovered ways of undergoing the internal journey. From this vantage point, we seem to be in a century of first approximations of ways whereby we can successfully negotiate the internal journey. So far, we have discovered pitifully little which seems to work. Thus, the journey is made even lonelier by the paucity of methods and techniques which can be refined and given as gifts from one generation to another.

The internal journey can be undertaken with the benefit of someone else who functions as the teacher, master, guide, instructor, or psychotherapist. Yet the actual internal journey is a solitary voyage. Actual moments of internal change are undertaken by oneself. Whether one is fully and completely alone or undertakes the lonely journey with the benefit of the wisdom and counsel of another, the consensus is that the person must possess rare and special qualities. Writing out of the tradition of meditation and contemplation, Wilhelm (1962) describes such a person as possessing the highest degree of intelligence, extreme clarity, the capacity for complete absorption and tranquility, and a high degree of understanding. These are singular qualities which are quite similar to those possessed by the patient who utilizes psychotherapy to undergo successful depth personality change (e.g., Cartwright & Lerner, 1963; Garfield & Wolpin, 1963; Hiler, 1959; Isaacs & Haggard, 1963; Kadushin, 1968; Kamin & Coughlan, 1963; Lipkin, 1954; Raskin, 1961; Rayner & Hahn, 1964; Sharaf & Levinson, 1957; Stephans & Astrup, 1965; Strupp, 1960; Strupp & Bergin, 1969; Wallach & Strupp, 1960). At our current level of knowledge, the person who successfully negotiates the internal journey may have to possess special qualities. But I foresee a time when we have discovered and refined workable methods of undergoing this internal journey so that most persons have these methods available and can successfully negotiate this journey if they so desire. Even when we have such workable methods available, however, the sheer availability will not insure that persons will undertake the journey. That calls for a willingness to commit oneself to the journey. There will always be the choice to commit oneself or not to commit oneself. Accordingly, the commitment to the inner journey will probably always require some qualities not usually present in many persons (Maupin, 1965).

In Maslow's system, a person must be ready to undergo this internal journey. This readiness is a function, in his system, of the degree of satisfaction or fulfillment of basic physiological needs, and also of basic psychological needs such as needs for safety, love and esteem. Until these two sets of basic needs are satisfied, the person is, in Maslow's system, in no position to begin the inner journey (1970b). From my perspective, however, the critical questions have to do more with the state of the art. Precisely what is this inner journey? If I choose to enter this inner journey, what are the methods which I use? When we do have satisfactory answers to these questions, I expect we will find that the entrance to the inner journey is far more available than we believe at present. I cannot agree with Maslow that one must have achieved a significant amount of personal change in order to qualify for the internal journey.

There can be no more personal journey than that into the guts of one's own deeper personality processes. It is courageous, frightening, and exciting. But it is yours alone. Are other persons involved in any way? Another person may be with you when you undergo the inner journey. That other person may be sitting next to you, and may be in physical contact with you. You may be in the midst of a group such as a sensitivity group or a more traditional therapy group. You may also be alone, and your guide is a book which tells you about the inner journey and instructs you in the ways of negotiating the journey. You may study with a person who is a teacher and an instructor in the ways of undergoing the inner journey. Someone must provide you with the ways of undergoing the inner journey. That person may be known as a guru, psychotherapist, wise person, teacher, group leader, spiritual leader, priest. Yet, the actual journey is yours alone. You are alone on the journey. No one goes along with you; no other person can replace your own experiencing of the inner journey.

Openness to the deeper potentials. The internal journey means that the person will see into the heart of his own deeper potentials. We know this, in one form, as insight, understanding, awareness of one's own deeper processes. For those who seek to be open to their deeper potentials, psychoanalysis offers at least three methods of pursuing this enterprise. For one, the person may learn the method of free associating. Second, one may attend to dreams in a way which illuminates the deeper personality processes. Or third, these deeper processes are brought forth in the form of the transference neurosis. Except for these methods, and perhaps a few others, we have no effective ways of discovering deeper potentials. We need a map of the internal personality processes and a set of methods for seeing into them. On this score we are far behind a tribe such as the Senoi (Greenleaf, 1973; Stewart, 1953) which possess both a map and a set of working guidelines so simple that children can easily learn them and carry them out on a regular basis. We need such a conceptual map and a technology easily usable by large numbers of persons, including children. At present, we lack these effective working methods. We lack maps of the inner world. We lack ways by which a person can know what is within. We have precious little to offer the person who is committed to the inner journey and wishes to know what to do and how to do it.

The person who has made the commitment to undergo the inner

journey, and who utilizes the rough tools and methods available today, is characterized by a sense of eagerness and excitement as the journey unfolds. For these persons, seeing and knowing the nature of the deeper potentials bathes them in an exciting thrill of discovery. This sense of excitement spreads to the very process of the inner journey. One *wants* to turn inward, to discover what is there. One is ready to engage in the inner journey, and seeks to gain further and further knowledge on how it is to be carried out. However, the eager readiness is for the process itself rather than for what one actually sees. When I illuminate the deeper potentials, I know that I view them through the channel of the disintegrative relationship. What I see is often scary and nasty, threatening and grotesque. What I discover is accompanied with disintegrative feelings such as anxiety and fear. I know that my seeing of what is within is *not* coterminal with what one can be (cf. Maslow, 1963). What one sees is almost always through the channel of the disintegrative relationship, and that bad form is not at all the same as what that deeper potential can be when it is integrated and emerges as its good form.

What one discovers is both already dimly sensed and surprisingly new. It is as if the process of discovery always seems to reveal more and more of what one has already sensed is there. I find a terrible competitiveness in me, the proportions of which are new and the specifics of which are new, but its overall presence is somehow not that new to me. Quite often, one discovers the other side, the shadow side, the polarity of what the person is. There is a half sensed "play of opposites" (Watts, 1961, p. 83) in the confident, precise person who houses the inner confusion, the weak person who houses the inner strength, the sweet person who houses the inner ferocity. Yet, the discovery is also surprising. Once the sphere of what is seen dilates, that deeper potential is illuminated as quite new. Its specifics, the actual seeing of its details and the proximity of its sheer presence—all of this is new and surprising. I may have half sensed a kind of unwillingness in me, but it is quite new and fresh to see the concrete details of the defiant independence which there is in me. Having seen it, I know now that it has somehow always been there, yet I *see* it now for the first time.

Receiving the inner feelings. The commitment to turning inward and undergoing the inner journey means that the person is now in a position to *receive* all of the feelings which are going on within. There is a world of continuously ongoing inner feelings. Facing the inner world of the deeper potentials means living in a state of heightened receptivity, responsivity, and sensitivity to these internal feelings. It is as if the channels of relationships are now opened simply by the act of turning inward, and through these channels the person is now able to receive the feelings which are occurring. "No longer is he fearful of what he may find. He comes to realize that his own inner reactions and experiences, the messages of his senses and his viscera, are friendly. He comes to want to be close to his inner sources of information rather than closing them off" (Rogers, 1970, p. 174).

The person may or may not be able to describe the nature or meaning of the feeling. One may not be able to say this is a scary feeling or that is a feeling of happiness. Feelings are felt bodily sensations, and the openness is to the events occurring within the body. There is a receptivity to a sensation of tightness across the forehead or a clenching up in the bowels. One is sensitive to the sudden washing away of anxiety in the upper chest or a loosening and clearing in the throat or a lightness and dizziness in the top of the head or a drawing in of the muscles of the eyes. The receptivity is to the felt bodily sensations which are the feelings.

The person who undertakes the inner journey is involved in a learning process, one in which he may acquire increasing skills of receiving the internal feelings. There are persons who are *moderately* skilled at receiving these bodily sensations, and persons who are *expert* at sensing the felt bodily sensations. Most persons are the merest of novices in tuning into this feeling world, with the exception of gross bodily feelings such as compelling aches and pains. In contrast, persons who are masters can be in continuous touch with the full range of internal, bodily felt feelings. Once one has postured oneself to receive the internal feelings, there are particular sets of teachable and learnable skills. There is nothing "natural" to being the master of these skills; to reach that stage requires definite skills whose learning requires work and practice and instruction. For example, receiving the internal feelings calls for explicit skills of being quiet, letting one's attention hover over the body, being receptive to identifying where the feelings are in the body, and being sensitive to the nature of the felt bodily sensations (Gendlin, 1969; Wilhelm, 1962).

Most persons lack these skills. Most persons are barely aware of feeling at loose ends, or scared, or tense. At best, these bodily sensations are somewhat vaguely sensed. Most persons provide themselves with very little data about the nature of their feelings, and even less about the antecedents and consequences of these feelings (Thorenson & Mahoney, 1974). As described in chapter 9, the common ways of coping with bodily feelings involve turning away from them, not knowing that they are there. It is the rare person, the optimal person, who has the skills to listen to these feelings, to attend to them carefully.

A simple component of these skills is the very act of placing oneself in the posture of listening to or receiving the inner feelings. It is as if the person sets out to locate the feeling and to identify its nature by an alignment of the center of the self with the center of movement within the deeper potentials. If a deeper potential is stirring and there are disintegrative feelings occurring, the person listens to the internal goings on. To do this is to keep oneself in alignment, to bring oneself into balance, to "center" oneself. The journey into the inner world introduces the person to the possibility of acquiring this skill.

In addition to aligning or centering oneself, the skills of listening to one's feelings mean that the integrating person is able to stop the wrong behavior. This skill has rather pronounced implications for the way the person actually behaves. Not only is the integrating person able to behave in a new way by turning attention to the location and nature of the felt bodily sensations, but the person is also able to stop whatever behavior is immediately ongoing. When the person hears bad feelings of disintegration, it is as if the insides are saying, "Watch out. Be careful. You are doing something, behaving in some way that is wrong or dangerous or not right. Take it easy now. This is a critical moment here. What you do or do not do is very important. Don't fall asleep. Don't behave mechanically. Don't run or defend or avoid. This is a critical moment." How many times have you behaved in a certain way and then later wondered why you did not heed the little warning signals that went off? You failed to heed the funny little clutching up or the localized pumping of blood or the rise of inner pressure. The integrating person is in touch with these signals and can use them as guideposts to behavior. Instead of proceeding with the smooth talk of the parlor, if the inner feelings are firing, the person can stop such behavior and proceed in the right behavioral direction. These inner feelings then serve as guideposts, censors, danger signals (Rogers, 1963) and the integrating person can hear them and can act upon them.

Thus the integrating person is able to listen to his feelings, to receive and "hear" them. It is this kind of integrating person who is able to learn the skills of centering himself in good alignment with the immediately ongoing feelings. It is this kind of integrating person who is able to learn the skills of monitoring behavior on the basis of these immediately ongoing feelings. It is also this kind of integrating person who is able to learn the skills of simple bodily relaxation (e.g. Wolpe & Lazarus, 1966). Once the person is on friendly terms with the immediately ongoing bodily feelings, he is in a good position to learn such skills which require a sensitive receptivity to these bodily feelings.

Metamorphosis

The integrating person actively commits himself to this internal journey, engages in this journey essentially by himself, discovers what is there in his internal world, and acquires a sensitive receptivity to the inner feelings. In all of this, the substance of the person persists. The person who undertakes the journey is the same person who was there prior to the commitment. But the journey into one's inner world is unlike any other journey, for it is one wherein the traveler undergoes a radical transformation by virtue of the journey itself. One becomes a qualitatively new self or person in the course of the internal journey, for it is an adventure in transformation of the very person whom you are. It is a being of a new being, a radical shift in the domain of the operating potentials. It is a profound metamorphosis of the self.

Metamorphosis as the suicidal plunge into the death of integration. There are at least three ways of describing the process of metamorphosis. One way is to attend to the act of integrating with the deeper potential. Viewed from this perspective, the center of the person or self or person-as-operating-potential kills itself by hurling itself into the very core of the deeper potential.

No longer is the center of the person lodged within the domain of the operating potentials; no longer is the center of the person separate from the bowels of the deeper potentials. To extract oneself from within the flesh and bones of the person whom you are, and to plunge into being the deeper potential means venturing way beyond staying where you are and being on different terms with what is within. It means going way beyond coming to understand and accept what is within you. Such maneuvers preserve the self where it is, but there is no integration, no process of metamorphosis. There is no radical transformation of the center of the personhood, which becomes only more solidly entrenched in its location within the domain of the operating potentials. Prize the deeper potentials all you want; the invitation is to fuse with them, not prize them. There is, then, a rather significant departure from those humanistic writers who describe optimal states in terms of coming to terms with what is within, living harmoniously with one's self, even liking and loving one's deeper processes (Maslow, 1970a, 1970b; Rogers, 1959, 1961, 1963). Our theory invites the person to undertake a more drastic wrenching journey into the destruction of that center which is supposed to do the coming to terms with, the living harmoniously with, the liking and loving. Metamorphosis takes one beyond prizing and blending in with these deeper possibilities. Once the person *is* the deeper possibility, he cannot also be separated from it enough to prize or accept it. It is the difference between accepting your sexual tendencies and being in the throes of orgasm, the difference between liking your sense of humor and being in the midst of an hilarious belly laugh. Going beyond prizing, loving, accepting what is within consists of fusing with that which you had formerly prized and accepted and loved in yourself.

When we picture the optimal person within the psychoanalytic world, there is a self-confident ego, strengthened in its resources against the primitive id impulses (Fenichel, 1954b). Not only is the ego preserved, it is made even more intact. When we switch over to our humanistic process of integration and the metamorphosis which eventuates, an almost polar picture is drawn. The domain of the operating potentials, roughly analogous to the ego, is *extinguished*, not preserved; it undergoes its own death, not strengthening. The domain of the operating potentials plunges *into* the deeper potential; it does not build stronger and stronger defenses against the monstrous id impulses. To move in the direction of *strengthening* the ego is, from the perspective of humanistic theory, merely another example of self-preservative *problem* behavior—far from the behavior of optimal persons!

If there is a landmark characteristic of the integrating person, it is metamorphosis, the trusting sacrifice of one's very self to the process of integrating with the deeper potentials. In this adventure, the very core of the person plunges into the metamorphosis of self-transformation. Nothing is held back or withdrawn. In the following passage, Laing describes a process of change in which one seizes upon what one is and changes all but the person himself. The "one" who actively promotes change *is not itself changed*: "As one grows older one either *endorses*, or tries to *discard*, the ways in which the others have defined one. One can decide to be what it has been said one is. One may try not to be what, nevertheless, one has practically inevitably come to assume one is, in one's heart of hearts. Or one may try to tear out from oneself this 'alien' identity that one has been endowed with or condemned to, and create by one's own actions an identity for oneself . . ." (Laing, 1962, p. 84). To engage in metamorphosis means that nothing is necessarily omitted from what is changed. Thus the change can also encompass everything that is referred to as "one." Even one's self can be consumed by metamorphosis—that one which is the heart of one's heart, the Dasein, the center of the self, the I-ness, the core of one's being.

To be successful, the process must be understood as insatiable, as all-consuming, and its appetite is such that every last shred of self is comestible. Indeed, every part of the thinking, reflecting, conscious, planning, assessing self is to be hurled into the process of metamorphosis. Kierkegaard (1944) describes the goal as the achievement of a state in which the person reflects upon his situation, selects from several options which are his possibilities, exercises choice, and takes responsibility for that choice. But in the process of integrative metamorphosis, even that faculty of the sense of self must be sacrificed. No part of the sense of I is inviolate, not even the part which reflects upon what is occurring right now. Everything goes.

This is death, the final closing out of one's existence, with the all-encompassing completeness and finality of absolute death (May, 1958b, pp. 47-49). It is not death of the physical body, but rather a death of the person-as-operating-potential. At the base of a considerable portion of human suffering is the struggle to ward off this death. The ordinary person may be said to be engaged in a perpetual agonizing struggle to preserve the self, whereas, in stark and utter contrast, the integrating person is willingly engaged in suicidal self-destruction. These two persons are proceeding in opposite directions. The integrating person knows that the way to liberation, to integration, to metamorphosis, is through the eye of the nameless horror which the ordinary person desperately struggles to avoid.

In gracious symmetry, integration with the deeper potential completes the functions of the operating potential—and it extinguishes. As described in Chapter 2, the operating potential comes into existence to provide for the experiencing of the deeper potential, and also to reduce or curtail the experiencing of the deeper potential. By surrendering to the process of integration with the deeper potential, those two functions are brought to a close, and the very bases for the existence of the operating potential no longer are present. And it *ought* to end its existence. What the person does not know is that the domain of the operating potentials insures endless problems and difficulties. Although the operating potentials were created in part to provide for the experiencing of the deeper potentials, their sheer presence limits and truncates the ceiling of possible experiencing. Their very presence means partial and incomplete experiencing. For the sake of heightened experiencing, the domain of the operating potentials constitutes a problem, one which could be best removed. The second function of the domain also holds nothing but the certainty of problems and difficulties, for it consists of the explicit function of preventing experiencing of the deeper potentials. This is a function whose accouchement is that of suffering and misery. At the very core of most problem behavior, misery, and suffering is a disintegrative relationship between the operating and deeper potentials. From its very inception, the domain of the operating potentials exudes conflict and difficulty, and it is wisest, in the long run, to be rid of the whole domain (cf. Byles, 1962).

In order to achieve integration with the deeper potential, the person must open up to, fuse with, become assimilated with, the deeper potential. This means the end of the existence of the person-as-operating-potential. This is a virtual death, an entering into nothingness. It is mandatory that successful hurling of oneself into integration involve the bringing of one's self to the absolute necessity of ending one's own existence. Successful integration means conscious, volun-

tary, eager ending of the existence of the present person-as-operating-potential. "In order to pass from inauthentic to authentic existence, a man has to suffer the ordeal of despair and 'existential anxiety,' i.e. the anxiety of a man facing the limits of his existence with
its fullest implications: death, nothingness" (Ellenberger, 1958, p.
118). There is no way of fooling this process, no way of achieving integration without the most drastic radical transformation—death—of
the person-as-operating-potential. Every consideration points toward
the undergoing of one's own death. This final ending is of a different
order than those which involve changes in behavior, and *only* changes
in behavior. We must differentiate quite sharply between the death of
the self in the process of integration and, on the other hand, changes
in such distal behaviors as a reexamination of life-style, alterations in
social behavior or work patterns or friendships or marriages (cf. Holt,
1968). Changes in one's behavior can constitute significant achievements. But it is a far more profound achievement to surrender oneself to the process of internal integration and the final closing out of
one's own personhood.

This is a complete death of everything which is me, everything
which thinks about myself, and everything which contemplates the
possibility of change. The person who I am right now, who is thinking
this right now, will be completely sacrificed. This is a final death of *all*
of me which is thinking that this is a final death of all of me. Before I
face this choice I can consider that there is much more to my personality outside the domain of my operating potentials. But when I stand
at the brink of surrender, of death, I face utter and complete
nothingness. To undergo this death is the landmark of integration,
and of genuine personality change from the perspective of humanistic
theory. It is a death in which every shred of my conventionalized and
structured experience is fully abandoned (Schachtel, 1959) by an I
which no longer exists.

Within the vocabulary of Zen Buddhism, I have been describing the
kernel of the meaning of satori and the pathway toward achieving a
true state of liberation by the dissolution of the I-self (Suzuki, 1956).

The integrating person is marked by the special quality of continuously surrendering the domain of the operating potentials to its own
death. At any moment, this person-as-operating-potential is quite willing to undergo his own ending of existence. This is a skill in sacrificing oneself, the skill of doing it willingly and by oneself. In other
words, the quality is that of suicide. "The symbol of suicide, the
capacity to confront death, is placed in a central position in the existential approach in psychology and psychiatry . . . The capacity to
confront death is a prerequisite to growth, a prerequisite to self-
consciousness . . . It is the experience of the capacity to abandon one-

self. to give up present security in favor of wider experience" (May, 1967, p. 103).

Something very special happens to the person who finally decides to kill himself, to surrender, to succumb to what is within. For some, not for all, the very decision to end the existence of the person means an end to problems and difficulties. This is the decision of the integrating person who willingly sacrifices his own existence. As a result, the decision to suicide is often followed by an interlude of peace and festivity (e.g. Binswanger, 1958c, pp. 292-298). This is the tranquil state which accompanies the final washing away of the problems as the person is no longer being the person-as-operating-potential, and is poised at the brink of final self-extinguishing.

There are rare and wonderful moments when the center of the person disengages from the domain of the operating potentials—and is flooded with new feelings of freedom and liberation. For the first time in their entire lives, these persons are no longer stuck with the awful problems. They have discovered the freedom to leave the domain of operating potentials, with all its problems. The feeling is one of freedom, liberation, and the utter hilarious nonsense of their former problem-filled life. These persons are plunged into the silliest, giddiest laughter. Their state is one of being struck with the absolute nonsensicalness of it all (Watts, 1960). The problems do not matter anymore, and any serious consideration of these problems only sends them deeper into gales of laughter. What about the business? Who is going to be concerned about your family? As these persons no longer exist within the domain of the operating potentials, these considerations lose all their meaning, all their seriousness, all their potential for conflict, and are illuminated in all their awkward nakedness as utter nonsense.

Metamorphosis as detachment from the person one is. I have been describing metamorphosis in terms of the active surrender of the domain of the operating potentials to assimilative fusion (integration) with the deeper potentials. There is a second way of describing *this same process*. It is a *detachment* from the person one is, from everything which constitutes the domain of the operating potentials. This detachment is as if the existence, the Dasein, the personhood, the I-ness for the first time exists on its own, separate from the domain of the operating potentials. In this state, there is a pure being-ness without self-awareness, without knowing that one exists, without a sense of self. There is only "I," without a knowing that I am I. There is detachment without a self which knows or is aware of being detached. Because I am not in the domain of operating potentials, I am sheer existing without existing as anything constitutive of the operating potentials. I am sheer I, being, without a self to be reflexive onto. In meditation, this state of detachment, whether it occurs for a split second or an extended period, is described as losing one's self, as the state of darkness, the void, emptiness, a state in which there is no external world (Ornstein, 1971).

The person I am—this particular domain of operating potentials—may be embedded in problems and struggles and difficulties. The way out is to detach from every last shred of the domain of the operating potentials, from the person I am. I solve my *problems* by no longer being the person who has the problems. I change my *behavior* by detaching from being the person who behaves that way. My struggles and difficulties end when I am no longer the person *with* the struggles and difficulties. There are times when the person is stuck in an impasse which is so tight that there is no way out. One's life, one's whole existence, can go nowhere. Here is the person with absolutely no way out of the problems and conflicts, no way out of the existence in which one is stuck. This is the person who is overcome by thoughts of death to escape the tortuous hell of one's life. There are no more steps. The life game is at an end. When the person has finally arrived at this stage, the *only* way out is to *give up the existence of the person with no way out*. So many of life's unsolvable tormenting problems are solved by exiting from being the person with those problems (Watts, 1960). Indeed, once these problems become absolutely unsolvable, once one is stuck in the impasse of impossible conflicts, the only solution to the impossible situation is to wake up from the dream—no longer being that person in the bad dream.

One does wake up from the awful dream—in the sense of moving out of being the person with the problem. How do I cope with my problem of getting old: giving up the delights of youth, the physical slowing down, the loss of my family and friends, the inexorable meeting with death? I can no longer think of much else, and my life is becoming a torture. The way out is not to solve the problem. Like the student confronted with the problem posed by the Zen master, the way out does not lie in granting the problem the aroma of solution. Instead, the way out is no longer to be the person who has constructed the problem, breathed life into it, and who now is tortured by it. As a result, the problem ceases to exist. You are no longer up against the awful problem because you are no longer the same you who is up against the awful problem. Although you may be caught in terrible impasses, and although these impasses have ground you to a halt, and are now ready to tear you apart, each of them is resolved by the metamorphosis of the center of personhood, and with that profoundest of all changes the impasse vanished.

Some of these impossible problems consist of being caught in a life which chokes you to death. Although you must be perfect, the prized jewel, the superhuman God, you are everywhere confronted with the dirtiness of being human. You fail, you have faults. You are confronted with incontrovertible evidence of being utterly *im*perfect, *not* a prized jewel, *not* superhuman. At the end, you are ground under and ready to fall into the slimy pit of hell. You cannot reach up any longer. The way out of that state is *no longer to be the person who exists in that world*: metamorphosis of the very core of your self.

When your problems consist of impossible polar opposites struggling against one another, rattling back and forth between the two equal and opposite combatants, a time will come when you are confronted with the utter impossibility of it all. When you are the heterosexual one, you struggle valiantly against the homosexuality; when you are the homosexual one you fight the impossible fight against the heterosexuality. The left side fights the right side, the top against the bottom. The only way out is to no longer be the person caught between the two polar combatants. Now you are not caught, are no longer in the impasse. The combatants fight on, but they do not devastate you. They continue the battle. Instead of having to be one side or the other, now you are neither, and they wage their impossible war without you. Let them fight. Leave them be. As this new person you are in an existence in which you had never been. Instead of having no room to move, except being one or the other, now you are utterly free of both sides locked in perpetual and unresolvable combat with one another.

Nearly every attempt to cope with problems or to undergo change assumes that the person will remain the same essential person. What changes is the way the person behaves, or the person's insight and understanding into himself, or the way the world is. We do everything possible to the domain of operating potentials. We spend years trying to change its behavior—and we often succeed. We work terribly hard at doing helpful things for that self, things like telling it what it is like (you are smart; you are lazy), telling it what lies within (there are incestuous impulses in you; you must cope with your rage), telling it what the real world is like (people are basically human; you've got to watch out for yourself), being with it in beneficial ways (I will really listen to you; no matter what you are, I will accept you), or providing it with new behavioral equipment (if you want to become assertive I will give you assertive training; I can teach you communication skills). Virtually all of the helpful ways to enable the person to straighten out problems leave the *center* of the person untouched, locked in even more deeply. In contrast, the person *can* detach from the *entire* domain of the operating potentials. That domain does not have to be your prison, no matter how nicely you decorate the prison. That sense of I-ness can walk away at *any* time—provided you are willing to leave the whole domain. Nothing can be taken with you. Everything which gives form and shape to you must be left as it is, discarded, if you are to free your self by walking away. In the realm of religion, this step is approximated in the mildest possible way by exhortations to give up your material possessions and dedicate your self to a particular religious mode of living. Leave behind your clothing, your family, your car, everything, and come live with us.

By leaving behind the entire domain of the operating potentials, all of the problems of that domain are also left behind. Rattling around within the tiny province of his operating potentials, Richard could see nothing but the awful problems with his wife. She is setting a bad example for the children. He wants to leave her but he can't live without her. He is frightened by her and afraid to lose her. She is fat and sloppy and picks on him mercilessly. He has never gotten along well with her. Maybe he should try some other woman. Why won't she take better care of the house? On and on go the unsolvable whinings of the person who is the operating potentials. As this person there is no way out, no solution. The only way to solve these problems is no longer to be the person with these problems. This is the meaning of metamorphosis: the way out· is to step into the domain of the *deeper* potentials. Once Richard stepped *out of* being the person of the operating potentials and stepped *into* being the person of the deeper potentials, his initial experience was a melange of surprising freedom and rollicking hilarity. He could do what he wanted, and what he wanted was far more than he had previously wanted. Somehow, in a mysterious way, his wife no longer mattered so much. His whole world had undergone a profound shift as *he* now looked out upon the world from the perspective of a different person.

Much of this freedom and hilarity comes with the newfound capacity to move the center of one's personhood from one potential for experiencing to another—within *or without* the domain of the operating potentials. This is a massive shift in personhood. If I choose, I can be the experiencing of whining and complaining, or the experiencing of affection, or the experiencing of meanness and cruelty, or the experiencing of whatever potential exists *anywhere* in my personality—it is this freedom which is dizzifying. The person truly is giddy with the power ". . . of maintaining an old and perhaps inappropriate mode of experience or choosing one which much better suits his present realities and opens to him a more promising future" (Holt, 1968, p. 251).

Once the center of the person detaches from the person-as-operating-potential, one is also free of the utter subservience to the deeper potentials and the external world. In a seemingly paradoxical way, the detachment from the domain of the operating potentials floods one with the truth that one has been living a lie. The lie is the *illusion of being in charge* of one's own behavior. Inside the domain of the operating potentials, the person can maintain the illusion of being free, of being able to do this or that, of being able to alter this or that about one's self, of doing this or that to the external world. It is a fiction, collectively held by all persons who are stuck within that domain without knowing that they are stuck. But once the center of the person detaches from the domain, gets outside of it, gains the sense of freedom to be the deeper potential, then the whole illusion is glaringly revealed in bold relief. It has all been a mordant joke, a wry fiction in which we existed without even knowing that we existed in it. "One of the most important and most difficult illusions to conquer is our conviction that we can 'do' . . . we think that we can make a plan, decide, start and achieve what we want, but the system explains that man . . . cannot do anything, everything just happens to him" (Ouspensky, 1957, p. 18). Once we exist within the domain of the operating potentials, we *are* controlled, we have no freedom; we are controlled by the internal and the external world. We are even controlled by the fictitious illusion that we are not controlled, that we can control our own behavior and our own lives. But none of this is clear until the center of the self detaches from that domain of the operating potentials.

Metamorphosis as transformation of the deeper potentials. There are at least three ways of describing the metamorphoses which characterize the process of integration. The first focuses on the person's suicidal plunge into the very heart of the deeper potentials. The second focuses on the detachment of the person from the domain of the operating potentials. We now turn to a third way of describing the process of integration. In this third way we focus on the transformation of the deeper potentials as a result of detaching one's self from the domain of the operating potentials and being the deeper potentials.

When the person is within the domain of the operating potentials, the deeper potentials stand fixed and unalterable. There is no way of changing anything about their nature or their form. They do what they must do wholly independent of the center of the person. You may be their pawn, you may live somewhat free of their effects, you may be somewhat successful in existing in the same world as they. But they are omnipotent forces far outside your reach. The only way you can effect changes in your deeper potentials is to undergo the ultimate change in your self. When you accomplish that, the inevitable, regular, lawful consequence is the radical transformation of the nature of the deeper potentials. This point has been introduced in an earlier discussion of the basic concepts of humanistic theory (Chapter

2). What had existed as the bad form of the deeper potential is magically gone, and in its place is the integrated, good form. Only the core of the deeper potential for experiencing persists, but this core has never been seen or known or even sensed. In effect, the warp and woof of the entire deeper potential have undergone a radical transformation by virtue of the process of integration.

To the operating personality, there is always something ominous and uncannily threatening about the deeper potential, yet the *form* of that deeper potential is all that the person knows. Everything one knows or senses about the deeper potential occurs as the form which it displays to the person. Because the person is not wholly the deeper potential, there is a measure of distrust, a viewing of it as something ominous and threatening, some measure of disintegrative relationship. Thus a change in the *form* of the deeper potential is functionally tantamount to a fundamental and wholesale change in its bowels. In other words, this change can be described as an opening of vision in which the evilness of what was within becomes subordinated and transformed from the wider perspective in which everything of oneself is now drenched in the beauty of the total design (Watts, 1960). The bad form of the deeper potential is transformed into the good form in the process of integration.

Prior to integration, the person cannot be what the deeper potential is because that would be disastrous. If I were to be the way I am inside, I would murder my enemies, slash the throats of those I hate, shout obscene words in church. My insides are evil, and their expression would smash the world in which I live. When, however, I become integrated with what is within, nothing so evil occurs. The person is no longer terrified about the damage to one's world. It is as if what is within can become transformed into good. "His feelings, when he lives closely and acceptingly with their complexity, operate in a constructive harmony rather than sweeping him into some uncontrollably evil path" (Rogers, 1970, p. 177). The whole awful possibility of what might occur if I express what is within is itself an expression of my disintegrative relationships toward the deeper potentials. Yet, in all this, I have little or no conception of what the deeper potential would be like if it were transformed in the process of integration.

Only the process of integration illuminates the nature of the transformed deeper potential. This new form is revealed only when the person closes out his own existence in the hurling of one's self into the jaws of the deeper potential. All I see, and all I can possibly see, is what the deeper potential is from the perspective of the domain of the operating potentials. I am prevented from conceiving of its transformed nature by virtue of being the person whom I am. By definition, then, the center of the person cannot know the transformed deeper potential. He knows that the deeper potential within him consists of images of being seduced by a man, memories of another boy touching his genitals and inviting him to secret thrills which were unnamed and hidden. He knew that he was taken over by "it" when he drove to special sections of the city and took out his penis while sitting in the car at night, and when he bought magazines of naked men and masturbated to fantasies of rubbing against their penises. But what can the deeper potential be? What form is it capable of assuming? As the person whom he is, he can never know. Maybe he will be born into an utterly new experiencing of a genuine closeness with men. Maybe he will emerge into a world in which he experiences an utterly new sense of self-certainty and self-confidence, forthrightness and toughness. Maybe he will experience a whole world of softness and dependency. Maybe he will enter into a new world of sexual experiencing. As the person whom he is he will never, and *can never*, know.

As discouraging as this may be, the revolutionary implications almost defy description. *One is capable of significantly transforming deeper potentials*! One can alter the very foundations of one's own personality. The possibilities are open to transform your gut nature in a kind of psychological alchemy. As described in Chapter 2, the form of the deeper potentials is open to massive transformation, and the consequences consist of unbelievable and unknowable profound changes in those deeper potentials.

The assumption of *unchangeable* inner personality processes may be germane to some approaches to the description of personality. But from the perspective of humanistic theory, such a notion is part of the world view of a personhood locked into being within the domain of the operating potentials. From within that domain, what is deeper in the personality is beyond change. I see this dreary pessimism as exemplified in, for example, orthodox psychoanalytic therapy, in which there can be no "transformation of motives" (Allport, 1937). In stark contrast, humanistic theory holds that the metamorphosis of the personhood which holds to the fixed stability of deeper motives opens the way to endless transformations of the most fundamental potentials for experiencing.

She knew that she was unhappy, and nothing was any different over the years. She was now in her early forties, and knew that she was tired a great deal, bitter and tight, seldom really laughed anymore, did not much care to live at times when "it" seemed to bunch up. Although she had ideas of what was wrong, nothing seemed to accomplish any change. Her ideas ranged from general notions of culture ("My trouble is that I am tied to being a mother and a wife, and I must be free . . . All of this is part of western middle-class living, maybe I should get a real job somewhere"), complaints about her husband ("There is nothing lively about him anymore; no wonder my life is monotonous . . . I can't stand his complaints about me; they are wearing me down after 11 years"), and speculative insight about herself ("My friends are right; I tear myself down too much . . . My priest is right; I am withdrawn and pessimistic . . . My older sister is right; I have always been sad like father was . . . My therapist is right; I lack assertiveness"). Everything had the spark of accuracy, but nothing changed. What she avoided, without knowing that she avoided it, was a deeper potential whose form consisted of a raging dependency, a clinging, scratching, sucking dependency which aggressively took the life out of the host. She was a leech, a monstrous leech, tearing the flesh away from its host, sucking the life juices. This was the bad form of the deeper potential, one which she never knew and never allowed near enough to be seen (DP2, Figure 12.1).

In a tumultuous crashing down of the walls of her self, the immured personhood shattered apart. She plummeted into a screaming craziness in which, for the first time in her life, she was no longer the vaguely unhappy self, and instead fused with the deeper potential. In the throes of being the deeper potential, this woman was a raging parasite, clasped onto her mother, her father, her husband. She was musteline ferociousness, fully hating her role in life, her friends, her priest, her older sister, her therapist. And then integration occurred, and with the metamorphosis, the deeper potential was transformed. It was revealed as a sense of trust, of intimacy, of loving closeness. She had never experienced what it was like to fully trust and be trusted, to be in a relationship of billowing intimacy and fulfilling closeness. These experiencings were new, utterly new for her. They constituted the emerged good form of the deeper potential, the foundation of a complete new personhood which she had never known or suspected was lying within.

Metamorphosis is explosive, not quiet. Successful negotiation of the process of integration calls for the heroic act of complete and utter detachment of one's self from the person into whom one has been absolutely trapped; it requires the hurling of oneself into the nameless horror of the deeper potentials. However described, this act is a massive uprooting. It is a thunderous crashing of the self. It is explosive.

In order for the metamorphosis to be complete, the process of integrating with the deeper potential must itself be complete. To detach from the domain of the operating potentials, one must be complete in being the deeper potential all the way. Described one way, the person must wholly and completely be the deeper potential; no part of the person can be left behind, as a residual, within the domain of the operating potentials. Described another way, the person must wholly and completely experience as the deeper potential. Mr. Plummer was a gentle, amiable partner in the two hardware stores owned by him and his younger cousin. He was also agitated, anxious and periodically quite upset by the decades of differences between himself and his partner. For years his hands trembled; now they trembled even more. Beneath the person whom he was existed a deeper potential which consisted of a potential for experiencing rage and violence. The life that Mr. Plummer had lived insured that he never fully entered into being rageful and violent. He spent his life in partial experiencing and partial non-experiencing of that deeper potential. The way out of being the person whom he was required a *complete being* of the deeper potential, i.e., *absolutely total being* of rage and violence. Anything short of this whole being means that the metamorphosis is incomplete. In the same way, a person may spend a lifetime struggling against the deeper aloneness, but metamorphosis requires the complete surrender to the wholesale experiencing of that absolute loneliness (cf. Moustakas, 1961). It is all-enveloping and all-encompassing, with every last shred of the self hurled fully into the experiencing of the loneliness.

When the person splits from the domain of the operating potentials there is a catastrophic implosion of internal feelings. When the person fuses with the deeper potential, there is a cataclysm of experiencing. The process which results in metamorphosis is characterized by extremely high states of feeling and experiencing (Ouspensky, 1957, p. 111). In order to pull out of the domain of the operating potentials, the center of I-ness or personhood must be split asunder from the very ground of everything it has been. This is typically a catastrophic expenditure of energy. It may be that we will someday discover a way of achieving this which is quiet, like gently falling into a sleep state or a dream state. But my experience, limited to psychotherapy patients and to persons undergoing their own self-change, is that the splitting is characterized by enormously high expenditure of feeling. This is confirmed in the various Zen approaches, in which there is a virtual crashing to pieces of the self, a shattering experience in which the core of one's existence is battered into oblivion—not at all a quiet, cerebrally meditative accomplishment (Maupin, 1965).

In the process of giving up one's self and being the deeper potential, the person risks the hell of being without personhood or identity or self. In this channel, bereft of the operating domain, the feelings are extremely intense and painful. Furthermore, the person steps into being that which he has envisaged as the most terrifying enemy: the deeper potential. To surrender to that which is the nameless terror is to undergo bad feelings outside the ordinary course of living. Accordingly, compared to the intensity of bad feelings experienced by most persons most of the time, the integrative process of metamorphosis promises that the person will pass through a curtain of far more intense bad feelings.

Metamorphosis and behavioral change. The process of integration requires that the person behave in ways different from the behavioral flow of his life. From the very beginning, new behaviors are involved, for the person withdraws from ordinary involvement with the external world and spends time alone or with a therapist or group. The person learns the skills of opening the eyes to see the inner world of experiencing and feeling. All of this constitutes new ways of behaving, requisite skills of undergoing the internal journey which results in metamorphosis. In addition, the process of metamorphosis results in behavioral changes. Primary among these is the uncoupling of all those behaviors which were bonded to the former operating potentials (B1-B4, Figure 12.1). The process of metamorphosis simply cuts away the roots of all those behaviors and, as a result, they fade out of existence.

The profoundness of the change lies in the certainty that the *person* will no longer be the same. Very often the person will wonder about the way he will be after the leap into integration. Or the parents or children or friends or spouses or acquaintances will wonder. Will he still work and be counted upon to support the family? Will she still play the cello in the symphony? Will she no longer go to concerts, go to the races, shop in out-of-the-way stores, drive the car recklessly, laugh heartily, imitate others, make love in the shower, spend money on impulse? The answer is that if the person undergoes integration, none of these behaviors will remain. Either the *behaviors* will no longer be around, or the *person* who carries out the behavior will be a new and different person. Let us discuss each of these in turn.

When the person surrenders into an integrative fusion with the deeper potentials, one of the possible consequences is that the entire behavioral equipment of the old operating potentials will be lost. It is very possible that the father will no longer work, and can no longer be counted on to support the family. She may no longer play the cello or go to concerts. There is a high probability that many of the behaviors will simply not occur after the process of integration. In this sense the behaviors die along with the old operating potentials (Figure 12.1). When the operating potential which leads to the behavior of driving recklessly or making love in the shower goes right out of existence, then these behaviors have no further basis for existence, and they fade away. The person stops smoking cigars or telling dirty jokes or listening to you with that little playful grin. Evelyn was in her middle fifties, living alone in a quiet, neatly kept small apartment. She had lived in the same apartment ever since her husband died 11 years ago, and left her with a strong sense of being abandoned. In quiet little ways she constructed a life as if someone were going to come back home to her, but this was carried out in benign and undramatic ways. In her apartment was a second bedroom, quite small. It was her guest room, and was always ready for instant use, although it actually was used only once in the last 10 years when her daughter stayed there for two days. The room was waiting for her husband. When Evelyn entered actively into the process of integration, she was no longer a person operating on the basis of the sense of being abandoned. With that change, she moved into another apartment with a larger living room and without that second bedroom. The folding up of the old behavior was soft and undramatic, but quietly signified a more significant change in the person whom she now was.

What often happens is that the outer shell of the simple behavior remains, but the person who carries it out is a different person. Now there is still a behavior of going to concerts, but it is a new and different person who is carrying out the old behavior. The new I-ness or self may also shop in out-of-the-way stores, laugh in that hearty and infectious way, and make love in the shower, but it is a new person and not the old self. Father may remain in the family and still be trusted to support the family, but there are important differences, for father is a different *person*. Integration of the operating and deeper potentials is a significant change in both the potentials and their structural and functional relationships. These changes in turn lead to changes in the nature and relationships in the external world and between the person and the external world. From the perspective of humanistic theory, the behavior itself is altered when the nature and relationships of the operational potentials differ, and when the nature and relationships of the external world differ. On this score, humanistic theory differs from Skinner's (1967) statements about behavior being the same regardless of the nature of the motivations or goals linked to the behavior—whereby walking is walking whether the person is walking for exercise or to meet one's lover. On the basis of these two sets of considerations, it can be assured that the behaviors linked to and generated by the old operating potential will undergo significant change when relationships between the operating and deeper potentials become integrated, and when the person-as-operating-potential surrenders to integration.

When this occurs, the skeleton of the old behavior may remain, but because the *person* has undergone significant change, the entire character of the old behavior has been altered. This is especially germane to those instances in psychotherapy in which the problem behavior seems still to be there, yet everything is different, or the problem is no longer a problem. In the beginning of psychotherapy, he was bothered by his short temper. He was easily upset, and found himself screaming and yelling at others. In the course of psychotherapy, the person undergoes change such that some of the behavior remains the same. He still has a short temper, but somehow it is quite different. *He* is a different *person*; the potential for experiencing changes; and the behavior alters. In so many ways, "... successful therapy need not be a 'cure' by any objective standards; that is, it need not necessarily issue in radically different behavior or in a cessation of symptoms" (Holt, 1968, p. 244). Yet the person who has the behavior will have changed, and that in itself makes for a profound change in the meaning and form of the behavior.

When the center of the person remains within the domain of the operating potentials, the range of possible behavior change is limited. For example, if I am being the potential for keeping you away, for maintaining a safe distance, I may behave in dumb ways. My being dull and uncomprehending serves as a means of fending you off. Over the course of time I may undergo significant changes in my ways of behaving. I may give up being dull and uncomprehending. But I am always a person with the operating potential for experiencing that sense of fending you off and maintaining a safe distance. That persists. When, however, my whole self becomes integrated, that operating potential is no longer there (B, Figure 12.1). Now the range of possible behavior change is increased magnificently. There is no further basis for any behavior related to the experiencing of safe distance because there *is* no potential for experiencing safe distance.

By virtue of the operating potential, its very existence, the deeper potential is not allowed full access to the external world. It is a major function of the operating potential to reduce the experiencing of the deeper potential. That function is instrumented by sets of behaviors. With integration, that deeper potential is no longer deeper. It gains a stature equal to that of the operating potentials, viz. direct egress to the external world and to experiencing (B, Figure 12.1). Once the operating potential assimilates with the deeper potential, the former sacrifices its function of truncating experiencing. The whole function simply evaporates, and with the absence of the function comes the washing away of all behaviors which mediate that function.

In addition, the process of integration cuts out the very basis for a whole slab of behaviors dedicated toward preserving the self. As a result, these behaviors automatically wash away. Nothing has been done directly to these behaviors. They were not the object of any program of change. But they have no further basis for existing when the person no longer must preserve himself as any given self. When I existed as the beautiful one, the highly valued special one, much of my behavior was dedicated toward avoiding any threat of not being such a person, and served to preserve my self as that sort of person. But when I no longer am such a person, when I no longer am confined to being that sort of person, then the very root system is cut out of the whole array of behaviors which supported and preserved that self. And they are free to disappear. In an important sense, those behaviors have no further territory to defend. The process of metamorphosis leads one toward a state of absence of self, of the ending of a permanent self, of the reduction of self to zero (Byles, 1962, pp. 190-191). With the dissolution of the self comes the falling away of self-preserving behavior.

Without even trying, all polar behavior (see Chapter 10) washes away. Polar behavior serves as a means of preserving the self. For example, to preserve oneself as being an energetic, competent, accomplishing person who is *not* feckless, dumb, and impotent, the person behaves in distinctive ways. She gains academic laurels, enters the profession of social work, and attains high administrative positions. However, once the person-as-operating-potential sacrifices itself to integration with the deeper potential, the basis has evaporated from such behavior. There is no longer a person who must behave in ways which prove that she is not feckless and impotent. Without ever thinking about such behavior, without trying to modify it at all, the whole slab of such behaviors loses its foundation. When that person extinguishes, so too does the person who *must* be selected as chairperson of the department, must be asked to head this committee, must be in charge of the conference.

Ian struggled against a somewhat similar deeper potential for being nothing, empty, without substance. To avoid falling into this catastrophic state, Ian became a big, fat boy, and, as an adult, he weighed somewhat over three hundred pounds. Yet his very center of self was thereby preserved. After undergoing integration, that self no longer was imprisoned into that urgency to disprove the horror of being empty and hollow. Ian was no longer the same person he had been, and the necessity for polar operating potentials was removed. Now Ian weighs between 175 and 185 pounds, but, what is more, he no longer is a person who must disprove the feared truth.

In order to preserve the present self, the person must do anything to fend off the possibility of actually *being* the deeper potential. One way of accomplishing this is the endless *regarding* of the deeper potential. Regarding includes endless talking about it, poking it here and there, considering it, discussing it, researching it. One talks about aggression and never is aggressive. One talks about changing jobs without ever changing jobs. Sex is monotonously discussed but never undertaken. In the course of integration, this slab of behaviors slides off and the person is now free to *be* the deeper potential, to experience aggression or sex or whatever is the nature of the potential.

Among the behaviors which integration washes away are the cognitions associated with the domain of the operating potentials—expectancies and attitudes, basic premises and fundamental ways of thinking about and conceptualizing oneself and the world, systems of morals and values and beliefs and convictions and ideations. Many systems of psychotherapy have sought, with varying degrees of success, to bring about significant changes in these fundamental cognitions (e.g. Adler, 1927, 1969; Dreikurs, 1956, 1967; Ellis, 1962, 1967; Kelly, 1955, 1967). To a large extent, their failure to achieve these aims is due to their *preservation* of the self whose fundamental cognitions they seek to modify. By ignoring the fundamental cognitions, and instead focusing upon the radical transformation of the center of the self, these fundamental cognitions are almost inevitably extinguished. When a person operates upon the basic conviction that he must be loved to be of any worth, far more is achieved by a change in the *person* who holds the conviction than by implicitly maintaining the person while attacking the endearing convictions he holds.

As the domain of the operating potentials fades away, so do its hopes, its ambitions, its plans, its intents to gain this goal and that goal. The person who seeks to alter his smoking behavior or overeating or nail picking or bad temper simply washes away and is no more. With the folding up of that self comes the extinguishing of those goals. Plans to make the marriage work or to have a good home or to prepare oneself for that kind of job wash away when the person who maintained those plans is extinguished. With integration, there are drastic changes in the plans or goals which the person-whom-you-were maintained for itself.

Metamorphosis and the physical body. Metamorphosis refers to substantial, perhaps radical, changes, accruing as a consequence of integration. Not only do these metamorphoses occur in the heart of the self, in the radical transformation of the deeper potentials, and in the sphere of behavior, but also significant changes will automatically occur in the physical body itself. For example, the physical body will no longer serve as the expression of deeper disintegrative potentials. Our description of the physical body understood that bodily events are expressions of deeper potentials (cf. Chapter 5). Especially when relationships with these deeper potentials are disintegrative, the physical body constitutes events expressing these disintegrative deeper potentials. When these deeper disintegrative potentials are transformed into integrative potentials, there will occur a washing away of these bodily phenomena. If a so-called tumor is a bodily event expressing a disintegrative deeper potential, then the process of internal integration will lead to a rather significant metamorphosis, i.e., the absence of that tumor. In precisely the same way, inernal integration can bring about innumerable changes in bodily events—such as valve leakages, inflammations, ulcers, internal bleedings. If a "malignant carcinoma" is the bodily expression of a disintegrative deeper fierce destructiveness, transformation of this potential into its integrative form will be accompanied with a metamorphosis in the physical body such that the "malignant carcinoma" no longer exists. In the same way, there is a radical transformation in the inflammation of the bursa when integration occurs in the disintegrative deeper potential for defiant refusal. Its integration leads to a metamorphosis in the physical body, and the inflammation of the bursa fades away.

Dilation of Self

In the hurling of one's self into being the deeper potential, that self plunges into its own death, splits from the very foundations of the person whom one is. In addition, in this process the deeper potential is itself transformed. These constitute metamorphoses which characterize the process of internal integration: radical change of the person or self and also of the deeper potentials which constitute the stuff of personality. We now turn to the consequences of this process of integration. One of these is a self or personhood which is enlarged in its scope, i.e., a dilated self.

The internal and the external aspects to dilation of self. There are several ways of describing this change. We may, in one sense, speak of an expansion of consciousness, an enlargement of the domain of operating potentials, an increase in the proportion of operating potentials (B, Figure 12.1). In another sense, we may describe an expansion in the freedom of movement of the center of the self, for it is now free to shift easily into a greater compass of potentials for experiencing. In the vocabulary of ego psychology, the new ego is stretched in every direction. I become much more of what there is to me. In the vocabulary of psychoanalysis, there is a freeing up of bound instinctual energy, with the result that there is a resurgence of genital primacy, of genital sexuality (Fenichel, 1954b).

However, from the perspective of the person himself, metamorphosis is not at all a dilation of the self. It is a plunge into the depths of certain death. It is only from the points of view of the external observer and the person who comes to the surface *after* the process of integration that this whole process can be seen as dilating the domain of the self.

Here are two processes which seem opposite, yet they culminate in a paradoxical sense of substantialness and permanence. One process is a surrender into death. The other is a consequent dilation of the sense of self. Following repeated surrenders into death, something is always emergent, something is always there. It is as if "I" exist even after I allow my self to die by hurling my self into integration with the deeper potential. As I surrender into death, and as a dilated self always emerges as a consequence, there is a newfound paradoxical permanence to "I," a strange kind of continuity. I gain a sense of substantiality and permanence in being able to die and emerge dilated. My own self acquires a strength, a wholeness, an intact organization to the extent that I can surrender it into death and emerge from the death still there—different perhaps, altered in many ways, but still there is something continuous (Laing, 1960). This something is the dilated self which continues (B, Figure 12.1) as the operating potentials sink into the death of integration into the deeper potentials (A, Figure 12.1).

Integration of the operating and deeper potentials changes the nature of both. It is possible that the operating potential will remain, but drastically altered in its basic nature. Under these circumstances, the self now dilates to include both the transformed operating potential and the transformed deeper potential which now takes its place in the dilated domain of the operating potentials. However, there is also the risk that the operating potential will wash away. But even under these conditions, the self dilates to incorporate the former deeper potential. If that deeper potential includes the experiencing of fatherliness, then the process of integration expands the domain of the operating potentials to include the experiencing of fatherliness. Inevitably the compass of the self is stretched to include the integrated deeper potentials, and by this process of accretion, the self dilates. Now I am this fatherliness which heretofore I had shrunk from or did not know existed within me.

When the domain of the operating potentials is at odds with the deeper potentials, one way of constructing the external world is to fill it with the externalized deeper potentials. The external world is alien, strange, hostile, for it is comprised of the deeper potentials which the person fends off. In effect, the stuff of the self stands depleted to the extent that it faces such an external world. The toughness and firmness which are my deeper potential are flung into being the tough and mean external world which now attacks me. In the course of integrating with my own deeper toughness and meanness, that potential is withdrawn from the external world and is incorporated into the domain of the operating potentials. The self dilates by incorporating those deeper potentials which were flung out upon the external world.

The sense of self dilates by fusing with deeper potentials. This is an *inner* enterprise, not an outer enterprise. Having taken back into one's self the externalized deeper potential, the person now is free to relate more intimately and integratively with the external world. This is an *external* affair involving closer bonding between the person and the external world. Such a description of the internal and external aspects helps us to understand that dilation of the self has been described as a process of unification with the *outside* world, such as giving oneself to God or union with supreme reality (Dalal & Barber, 1970), whereas others have referred to the importance of finding one's own *inner* nature. Some describe the dilation of self as a process of seeing the inner world, while others refer to a new seeing of the external world in its ultimate truth (Maslow, 1962). It is described as an *expansion* of self (e.g. ego), whereas others describe it as a *loss* of self (or ego). All of these are, from our perspective, accurate descriptions of the processes involved in the dilation of the self.

Awakening of dilated consciousness. A self which is dilated has an expanded sense of awareness or consciousness. Consciousness is bounded by the perimeter of the domain of the operating potentials. As this domain incorporates deeper potentials, it dilates (B, Figure 12.1), and as it dilates so too does the consciousness dilate. Furthermore, as integration proceeds, the zone of unfeeling (Figure 10.1) becomes smaller and smaller. The person is less and less able to push down a deeper potential so far that there is no consciousness or awareness of it. By the same token, the process of integration means that the person-as-operating-potential cannot itself seek a retreat below the threshold of unfeeling so that it has no consciousness or awareness of what is occurring (B, Figure 10.1). All in all, the process of integration shrinks that zone of unfeeling so that the dilated self is de facto increasingly aware and conscious of its own felt experiencings (B, Figure 12.1).

In effect, the shrunken zone of unfeeling means that the person cannot so easily "fall asleep." This shows itself especially in critical moments when the person would ordinarily, perhaps, fall asleep and thereby not know what is going on right now. Thus the deeper potential may be inviting the person to fight back or to steal the camera or respond to the insult. Prior to integration, the zone of unfeeling may be quite available so that the person quickly goes to sleep and simply has no idea what the deeper potential is doing. He may steal the camera and have the dimmest of awareness of doing that. Or he may freeze in response to the insult, and do so with little or no consciousness or awareness. In effect, the person is not there in the critical moment because he has quickly and silently slipped into sleep, i.e., has fallen into the zone of unfeeling. But the process of integration forecloses on that possibility. Now the person is still there, relatively aware and conscious of what he is doing. He knows that he is stealing the camera or knows that he is frozen as the insult washes over him. He remains a conscious and aware person who knows what is happening. He is able to know the behaviors which are flowing forth from him, and to know the feelings which are occurring.

Formerly, the center of the person may stand aside and allow the deeper potential to take over behavioral mandate (B, Figure 10.1). Although not fully going to sleep, the person takes the posture of being detached and seeing what was occurring from a detached position. This is the person who watches the deeper potential take over and sneak about at night, looking for a window through which a woman can be seen undressing. In this state, the person is aware and conscious, but as a detached observer who is there, yet who is not in control of behavior. With integration, the *locus* of consciousness shifts so that the person is being conscious and aware, but as the person who is *fully* there, *doing* the peeking in the window. Now the behaving is coming from the conscious and aware person.

This expansion in the scope and quality of consciousness has been described quite commonly as very much like waking up. Persons whose consciousness has dilated speak of this sense of having awakened as a kind of awe, as an awakening from a lifelong sleep in which they had been, without ever knowing that they had been in that sleep. Others have described this awakening as if they had been in a kind of personal hypnotic state, but again without knowing that they had been in such a state, like awakening from a kind of social hypnosis (Watts, 1963) wherein the old way of seeing the world has been peeled off one's eyeballs. This is new-sight, and is something of a different order than in-sight. The qualitative newness of this mode of dilated consciousness has been described as the opening of a third eye, so that the person now has acquired a qualitatively new mode of experiencing (Maupin, 1965). Because this mode of experiencing is new and is the key to a qualitatively different mode of experiencing, it is quite difficult to describe what it is like to someone who has not experienced it. In much the same manner, we would have difficulty explaining what it is like to live in a world perceived through binocular vision if we were communicating with organisms with monocular vision.

In this waking up, one is conscious and aware of the previous narrow limits of the former sense of being conscious and aware. As the former person, I am fully aware and conscious to the extent that I can be, and I have no sense of any limitation to the world of my consciousness and awareness. Following integration, my world is qualitatively different and enlarged. I have awakened, and that awakening is accompanied with a new sense of having lived previously in a world of illusion, the illusion of being aware and conscious. As the process of integration alters the contents of the domain of the operating potentials, each dilation will leave one with a sense of having awakened from the past state, a state in which the illusion was that of being fully aware and conscious.

The sense of self: personhood. With each awakening, one sees that one previously had existed in an illusion of being in charge. Each constituency of the domain of operating potentials lives in an illusion that one can do things (Ouspensky, 1957), that one is more or less the central resource of one's own actions, that one controls and governs and initiates one's own behaviors and thoughts and actions. But now, having awakened, it becomes clear that in your former sleep state you were *governed* by alien internal and external factors. Even when you formerly protested against the control of internal and external factors, the world in which you had existed was one of an illusion that you were, to a large extent, and could be, to an even larger extent, in charge of your behavior. Now it is revealed that even your protesting against the control of alien factors was itself an action preponderantly under the control of alien internal and external factors. Only after awakening is one aware and conscious of the internal (e.g., unconscious, instinctual, intrapsychic) and external (familial, group, communal, social, world) factors which led you about in your former state of hypnotic sleep—together with the illusion of being an intact person who could be preponderantly in charge of your own behavior. In the awakening, you pass through the "existential vacuum" in which these internal and external forces no longer carry you along (Frankl, 1969).

With each increase in the depth and scope of the self comes a corresponding decrease in the initiating and activating power of alien external factors. The paradigm that one is a complex of response contingencies applies less and less. Gradually the external world loses its power to stimulate and to control. Social forces lose their power over you. The family sheds its control over you. Cues and complexes of stimuli tend to wash away. You are less situation-bound. As the process of integration folds up more and more of the former operating potentials and fills the self with deeper potentials, the external world stands revealed as puppeteers who have subtly moved you about—and all the puppeteers fade out of existence. You become free of the pulls and pushes of the whole external world.

Correspondingly, there is an increased sense of self, of I-ness, of control and governance over one's own behavior, of self-confidence, of being the initiator and activator of one's own behavior, of internal control. It is a sense of ownership over one's own behavior, of mastery through a "reversal of voice" (Loevinger, 1966). This change is manifested as increased independence, mastery and self-direction wherein, for example, the person is increasingly responsible for his own choices in life. "By this I mean that gradually he chooses the goals toward which *he* wants to move. He becomes responsible for himself. He decides what activities and ways of behaving have meaning for him, and what do not" (Rogers, 1970, p. 171). Here is the person who is the decider, the chooser, the selector of his own way of being (Szasz, 1956; Van Dusen, 1957).

One who has this sense of internal control and self-initiation of behavior is attuned to the voices of the various inner potentials. I hear both this and that possibility, and am therefore in a position to choose one or the other. I choose. I have the *freedom* to do one or the other. Right now my son is chiding me about my overprotectiveness toward the old car, and I sense both the experiential possibility of becoming defensive and annoyed, and the warmth of his chiding me. I can slide into either channel of being, and I incline myself just slightly toward the latter and instantaneously am lovingly close to him. Yet, for a brief moment, I was poised, able and free to go one way or the other.

This person also has the capacity to say no to the automatic flow of behavior which pours forth from him. In awakening, one becomes aware of the risings and fallings above and below the threshold of unfeeling. The person is able to catch himself sinking into a state of sleep, a state in which his behavior is slipping out of his own mandate, becoming automatic, and falling under the control of alien internal and external factors. In being able to catch oneself, the person now can stop such an automatic flow of behavior. He can say in effect, "What am I doing? This is not coming from me. I must block such behavior." Accordingly, the person can stop such mechanical behavior. Very simply, this person can catch himself falling asleep, and can say no to such automatic modes of behaving. In effect, the dilated self takes over more and more of what was automatic behavior. Muscular tics are good examples of behaviors carried out automatically by alien deeper potentials. The person may be aware of the muscles in his cheek or his mouth doing things wholly on their own. It is as if the tic is under the control of some alien inner headquarters. With the process of integration, the domain of the person or self dilates to include the deepest potential which governs the tic, and it is now the *person* who is the controller of the tic behavior. There are, of course, various vocabularies of explaining and describing this approach to the reduction of tic behavior, but the commonality resides in the voluntary stretching of mandate over the formerly alien behavior (e.g., Dunlap, 1932; Yates, 1958).

Behavioral freedom to be each potential self. With the dilation of the domain of the operating potentials, I now am free to be anywhere in this expanded domain. This new freedom significantly expands the array of behaviors which can flow forth from *me*. I literally can be this potential or that other potential, and I can accomplish this switch with ease. In effect I am free to be each of these potential selves, and in each there is a distinctive set of behaviors. As a result, the total repertoire of behaviors which can flow forth from me is considerably increased.

Prior to my integration I was a loyal friend, someone who could be relied upon. That person whom I was had a good sense of humor, and enjoyed reading. At times he was unsure of himself, and struggled against these feelings by hard work. I remember him, mostly with a sense of affection. If I wish, I can slip once again into being him. But now I know a secret: I can slip right out again, out of being him and into being the person I am now. I did not know that secret then. When I was him, part of being him was knowing with absolute certainty that my identity was restricted to being him. To step out meant death, and that was bad. Now I know that my identity is not restricted to being him or to being the person I am now. This is the behavioral skill of the integrating person. It is even championed as a landmark characteristic of the optimal person (Malone, Whitaker, Warkentin & Felder, 1961), whose movement into and out of each potential self is accomplished with an ease and a grace requiring no cerebration, no conscious choice.

Such a skill means that one is a different person, free at any moment to slip out of being this potential and these ways of behaving. These behaviors may be as tiny as putting on a sock or as broad as an entire social role—such as that of clerk or mother or male or judge or worker. Now the person knows that he will exist even if he detaches from being that role. Since there is now a person and a social role—where formerly these were fused into one—the person is free to play with the social role. Being a person, a center of self which can exist in or out of the social role, means that the behaviors in that role are now altogether different.

Now that the deeper potential is part of the self and the relationships among the new operating potentials are integrated (B, Figure 12.1), social roles, social mores, social conventions become things to play with, sources of delight, tools to be used by human beings to enjoy—or to pass by and invent others. It is a matter ". . . of adopting social conventions without taking them seriously and by experiencing a sense of play and fun-game in accepting or not accepting a given social custom" (Watts, 1961, p. 68). One plays with social roles and customs and conventions with an easy versatility and fluid grace, a matter of good relationships wherein the person now has the capacity to slide in and out, enjoy and modify, cast off old ones and invent new ones.

What has been said about social roles, customs, and conventions also applies to behavior itself. One can entrust one's self into being fully coterminal with actual behavior. Thus one can throw oneself completely into hugging the baby, drinking the beer, watching the sun set, or telling the hilarious story. Yet the person accepts the right to fling one's self into fully being *another* potential whose behavior would be quite different. Being another person means enjoying the cigar, or shaking the baby's hand in a joking manner, or declining to hug the baby. The behavior persists as long as the person is that potential. The behaviors are friends and not prison cells.

Integrated Relationships Among Potentials

There is something new and wonderful about integrated relationships among potentials. Not only does the domain of the operating potentials dilate, but one becomes friends with each of the potentials. We turn now to a description of what it is like to enjoy integrated relationships among potentials, to relate to these potentials as friends.

Friendly enjoyment of one's own potentials. Becoming more integrated means that the center of the self is freer to move easily from one operating potential to another along channels of integrated relationships. Integrating persons enjoy their potentials far more than the rest of us. When they are centered within one operating potential, they are pleasurably welcoming toward other operating potentials—and since their domain of operating potentials includes those which had been deeper in the personality structure, these persons are functioning on a qualitatively different plateau than the rest of us. That is, integrating persons have risen to a plateau on which they are friends, even with potentials which seem opposite, polar, logically inconsistent with what they are being now. They are congruent with apparent discrepancies and contradictions which exist within themselves (Rogers, 1970, p. 157). Potentialities for experiencing dominance and submission seem to exist happily in integrating persons. These persons seemed to enjoy being excitedly active and soberly withdrawn. They are both solitary and group-oriented in ways which smoothly complement one another. Their tight little organized and compulsive part seems to be on the greatest terms with their sweepingly general part. Rationality and impulse are easily synergic with one another (Maslow, 1970), so that irrational thoughts, intuitive associations and ungrounded spontaneity smoothly interrelate with rational analysis, clear thinking, and cerebral reflection.

Such persons have the audacious characteristic of liking their "selves." Each part has with other parts a relationship which exudes a kind of understanding, friendship, mutual respect and enjoyment of one another. As simple as this is, it is a quality which distinguishes integrating persons from ordinary non-integrated persons. Others have described the necessity of such affectionate *internal* relationships for the occurrence of similar *external* relationships between the person and others. That is, ". . . one can love others only to the extent that one loves oneself" (Fromm-Reichmann, 1959, p. 7). When the relationships among potentials are integrated, it is then possible to establish integrated relationships with the external world.

Open self-reflexiveness. What is even bolder and more audacious, the integrating person is willing to relate to deeper potentials. These are not yet a part of the operating domain, not yet integrated into his sense of self. Yet the integrating person can engage with them. He hardly knows them, but he is postured toward engaging with them. He can play with them, jostle them, enjoy a kind of good involvement with them. In turn, those deeper potentials know him better than anyone else can possibly know him. They know him far better than he knows himself and far better than he knows them. The deeper potentials know that he is basically weak, behind all that toughness, that he puts on quite a show of capability, that he is really mixed up and confused, struggling to run away from how weak he actually is. The weakness and uncertainty which are the deeper potentials can speak to him, can relate to him—and he *listens*. He is able to engage in a relationship with his deeper potentials, a relationship which enables him to engage in a more or less integrated fashion with potentials which are not yet fully integrated (Mahrer, 1977).

When one potential is expressing itself behaviorally, the center of the person is able to sense the reactions of the other parts. Furthermore, the person is quite capable of expressing what the other operating potential feels toward the first. When the person is being resistant and obstinate, another potential may have reactions toward being that way. It is the integrating person who not only knows this reaction, but is able to move over into *being* the second potential: "That sounds pretty damned bull headed!" In effect, the person is able to step aside and be comfortably self-reflexive: "I think all that was pretty dumb;" "That sounds like a whining little baby, I must say." "I don't think that went at all well, in fact it sounded like a rotten try." Not only is the person integrated enough to be critical of one's self, but one is also able to be pleasantly self-reflexive: "I am kind of proud all that came from *me!*" "Great! I liked the way that sounded." "Say, I enjoyed that speech myself."

These self-reflexions require only the person and his reactive relationship with his own behavior. But this same kind of self-reflexion also characterizes the integrating person within an interpersonal context. In this context, the integrating person has the capacity to know and to express the kind of attitude which the other individual *is invited to bear* toward the person. That is, if the integrated person is being somewhat overbearing, it is quite likely that the other individual is being invited to experience: "He is certainly being overbearing." In effect, the other person is structured into being the externalized or extended potential. The integrated person is capable of stepping into that (deeper) potential and expressing precisely what the other individual is being induced into experiencing. Thus the integrating person is able to say, "Well, that sounded damned overbearing to me!" In this, the integrating person is comfortably free to express what both he and the other individual are privately sensing or thinking. This quality is one of the hallmarks of maturity, according to Sullivan (Bullard, 1959). Typically, this attitudinal relationship is unexpressed, especially in the immediate moment when it seems to hang there in the air, unacknowledged by both parties. It is the integrating person who not only knows its presence but who is able to give expression to it: "I don't think I really answered your question." "What I just said sounded rather dumb." "That sounds terribly pompous to me." The integrating person can express this at precisely the moment when both the person and the other are thinking, usually privately, that the person was avoiding the question, or being dumb, or appearing pompous. To be able to know these reactions and to be able to express them, require dilated consciousness, courage, and a state of internal integration of such proportions that one can shift into being that which he is inducing the other to be, and to give voice to what is hanging there in the air.

At any moment, having behaved in some particular way, the person has the capacity to listen to what each neighboring potential has to say about that. The person can do this by pausing, and by allowing each potential to have its experiential say about the behavioral event. If one has just refused an invitation to attend a meeting of the committee, the person is able to receive what each adjacent part has to say about that. One may be frightened and exceedingly concerned about having done that, and the person is able to listen attentively—or even to be that potential and give voice to what it has to say. Then the next potential moves forward to offer its experiencing of a sense of autonomy and independence, and the person can listen carefully to its expression, or join with it in saying what it is important to say.

In self-reflexion, one of the landmark features is the integrative relationship the person bears toward his own behavior. Not only is the person able to stand aside and reflect or take a perspective upon himself, but the nature of that relationship is that which occurs between truly good friends. He likes himself! He is able to have fun with his own parts. He can joke about them, tease himself about them, be proud of them, be warm and loving toward them. Regardless of their nature, he is able to maintain a good dialogue with them. "Ah, there you go again. Can't resist a chance to be kind of pushy, eh! You just can't resist a golden opportunity to kind of throw your weight about. What an old delightful scamp you are." They are like old friends who love and respect one another. When the person walks down the hall, turns a corner, and abruptly runs smack into a most attractive woman, one potential is delighted. "How marvelous to bump into her! Such a lovely woman. I love bumping into beautiful women." Another potential has a different reaction but, as old friends, it can dialogue openly and honestly: "If you keep doing that I am going to have a hard time being shy. Sometimes you make me feel like I ought to demand equal time. I just can't keep up with you, partner."

Entrusting oneself to other potentials. Because relationships are integrated, the person is able to entrust himself into being whatever potential is rising, is asking to occur and to experience. This is the mark of trust in integrated relationships among potentials. It is the ability to surrender into being the deeper potential, fully to experience it, to live in its world. Living fully in its world consists of experiencing its situational contexts, its important moments. If the deeper potential consists of the experiencing of being violated, then living in that deeper potential means living in the situational contexts associated with the particular experiencing. It means being a girl of 11 and pleading with the cousin not to put it in again because it hurts, and a full having of the feeling of being made raw and vulnerable. From the perspective of the person who is living in the present, that event occurred 15 years ago. But from the perspective of the deeper potential, that event is immediately ongoing. To have the capacity to entrust one's self to the deeper potential means that the person can live fully in various situational contexts, in various moments of time.

If the potentials are integrated, the person can step fully into being the other potential, and the situation is brightly vivid, as real as can be. It occurs right here and now in all of its concrete specificity. Now I am the little girl, and I smell the odors of my bedroom and the warm mouth odor of my cousin; I see the little crack across the ceiling of my bedroom, and am aware of the window there to my left, with the paint coming off in the corner there. When I enter fully into being the potential, I live with detailed specificity in the situational moments of its experiencing. The switch from being within one potential—who *remembers* the incident in the bedroom—to being the potential which is *experiencing* in the bedroom, is an abrupt and sudden switch: ". . . what you remember from childhood are only glimpses of self-remembering, because all that you *know* of ordinary moments is that things happened. You know that you were there, but you do not remember exactly; but if this flash happens, then you remember all that surrounded this moment" (Ouspensky, 1957, p. 8). When relationships are integrated, the person trusts enough to enter fully into each potential, and this opens the way to complete living in the moments of experiencing. But when you are not fully integrated, then you consider from a distance, from another removed perspective. You remember from the side, so to speak, and then the remembered event is cloudy and veiled.

The person who has integrated relationships can enter into entire worlds of the past. Each potential has its own personal history of critical moments, situational contexts, experiencings. To enter fully into a potential is to live once again in its immediate present moments for very little of those moments is lost or extinguished. What is "forgotten" of *these moments* is now fully retainable and re-experienceable. Indeed, the movement away from being one potential into being another *gives the illusion* that something is lost or forgotten or gone. We sometimes explain this as memory loss or psychological deficit or loss of skills or cerebral injury or aging or simply personality change. Yet it is nothing more than mere movement away from being that potential (Mahrer, 1958). When we dream, we can once again move into being that old potential. When we are hypnotized or under the right drugs or taught to do so in psychotherapy or become integrated, we are able to go back into those old potentials and be them fully once again. Then we are not 64 years old; we are five. We are not myopic; we can see clearly and well. We are not retarded and closed in; we are the way we were when we were not that way. The process of integration includes the freedom to enter into being all our potentials, including those whose experiencing occurred many years ago, and whose natures differ significantly from the way we now are.

As potential after potential is incorporated into the operating domain, the person also gains a sense of trust in the *process* of integration itself. In this manner, integration picks up tempo and moves forward. It is a momentous achievement to open up the operating domain and to fuse with a *single* deeper potential. But soon the dilated personhood gains a sense of trust in the very process of integration itself, and the person is not only able to entrust oneself to the other parts which constitute the integrated *operating* domain, but also to gain a sense of trust in opening the gates of the operating domain and surrendering to the *deeper* potentials. As this process continues, the person reaches the plateau of integration with the most basic level of potentials. At this point, the person has achieved the most fundamental state of oneness, integration with everything which is within, all one's deepest potentials. This is the goal of the integrating process, and the goal of Vipasanna meditation (Byles, 1962). It is the ultimate meaning of oneness of self.

The more one has enlarged the self, dilated the operating domain, the more is the domain constituted of integrated (former) *deeper* potentials (B, Figure 12.1). One is now free to speak with and to *be* more and more of the potentials which comprise the total personality, to relate trustingly with a greater compass of these deeper potentials. In the major decisions of one's life, the integrating person turns in complete trust to those deeper potentials which have something to say. At these important points in one's life, ". . . such as the choice of a mate or a profession, the decision should come from the unconscious, from somewhere within ourselves. In the important decisions of our personal life, we should be governed, I think by the deep inner needs of our nature" (Reik, 1948, p. vii). It is these potentials which provide the experiencings of what constitutes the inner reality. The integrating person has these data available as trustworthy guides to the ways in which external factors affect the insides, and all of that can be used in making the decisions of one's life (Maslow, 1963). Following this principle implies that the professions which deal with such important life decisions (e.g. vocational counseling or marriage counseling) must enable the person to come into integrative dialogue with the *deepest* potentials. Where the integrating person turns to the deepest inner regions for wise counsel on these matters, it is unfortunate that professional vocational counselors and marriage counselors typically hover about the most superficial veneers of the persons who are facing these important matters, ignoring the deeper potentials in matters of such import. In contrast, the integrating person places trust on the wisest possible counsel of the deepest potentials in the truly important matters of life.

Feelings

The process of integrating with the internal world inevitably is accompanied by changes in feelings. This is a regular epiphenomenon which is so predictable that it can be framed as an empirical rule: As the person increases internal integration, there will be changes in feelings. Not only are these changes in feelings regular accompaniments, but the nature of these feelings can be taken as landmark characteristics of integrating persons (cf. Gendlin, 1964). At the present time, feelings are slippery and imprecise data. We have not settled upon a satisfactory mode of describing and understanding precisely what feelings are. Nevertheless, our discussion will proceed as if the description and understanding of feelings were a friendly enterprise, and our concern is to describe the kinds of feeling changes which are characteristic of integrating persons.

Increase in feelings of integration. The person who is integrating will have (a) a felt bodily sense of wholeness, unity, oneness, a feeling of being together. It is that feeling which occurs when the part of you which had been walled off is now welcomed into oneself (Bergman, 1949). To integrate with the other part is a taking of it into one's self, an assimilating, an including as one's own (Buytendijk, 1950), with the accompanying feeling of unity and oneness. This feeling is constituted of potentials which had been separate from one another, and are now fused together in integration. The feeling is the expression of this sense of wholeness and oneness.

One has this feeling only when the person whom he is dilates on the ground of integrated potentials. One cannot be the same person as before. One cannot contemplate what it would be like to be integrating and hope to undergo this feeling of oneness and unity. Only when the person changes by virtue of having *undergone* integration can the person know this feeling. Once the center of the person draws back to *regard* its state or to *consider* its self, this feeling is cut off.

The person who is integrating will have (b) a felt bodily sense of internal peace, tranquility, harmony. This is a feeling of relationship, of the special state wherein each potential relates to other potentials. This is independent of the *nature* of the potentials, for it is felt by any integrating person regardless of the parts which comprise that person. In this feeling the boundaries between the potentials seem to vanish, and the domain covered by the feeling of internal peace, tranquility, and harmony covers all of the potentials. It is an *inner* sense which comes from and relates to the body itself. Furthermore, it can be an *overall* bodily feeling which includes the *entire* body rather than being confined to one part (e.g., the chest or head or legs). Thus this feeling is qualitatively different from and a step beyond being a defined personhood which *regards* another potential. No matter how much you regard another potential well, you cannot achieve the sense of peace, tranquility, and harmony because you are not fully and completely integrated with it. I can positively regard my potential unconditionally; I can care for it non-possessively; I can prize it. But the fullest extent of this good relationship toward it falls short of *being fully integrated with it*—and I therefore am unable to have the feeling of absolute peacefulness, tranquility, and harmony. The paradigm of the client-centered therapist's relationship to the client is *not* what is meant by integration, for the client-centered therapist remains the therapist. He still is separate no matter how well he regards the other individual. Only when he assimilates *fully* with the other is it possible to have the feeling of peace, tranquility, and harmony.

Feelings of integration include (c) a felt bodily sense of welcoming, taking in, assimilating, becoming, growing. It is the feeling of openness toward integrating with the next potentials, the feeling of expanding to encompass the next potentials, regardless of their nature. It is the receptivity to taking in. The feeling of integration is the welcoming of the further process of integrating. This is the person who is now an old hand at throwing oneself into the internal journey, who now welcomes what the internal journey will bring, and whose sense of welcoming *is* this feeling of integration.

Integrating persons have these kinds of feelings, are characterized by the presence of these feelings. If you can grasp the nature of these feelings, you can tap your own inner feeling state and know the degree to which your body houses these kinds of physical sensations. But of course there is a catch. The person who is not integrating is dedicated to not tapping into the inner state of bodily felt feelings, or doing so only minimally. Furthermore, the person who is not integrating has only approximate knowledge of what these feelings are like. Therefore, as in every other way, the person who is into the process of integration tends to draw further and further away from the ordinary person who is not into the process of integrating.

When one moves into the process of integrating, the overall good feeling of pleasure now occurs with added dimensions. One now feels good pleasure in a different way, for now the good feeling of pleasure occurs in a person who (a) is whole, one, unified, (b) is peaceful, tranquil, harmonious, and (c) is welcoming, expanding, becoming. So remarkably different is this new kind of good feeling that its absence can serve as a "diagnostic sign" (Rado, 1956; Rado & Daniel, 1956). These feelings of internal integration are, as a whole, quiet. They constitute one kind of good feeling, much akin to that kind of good feeling which accompanies the state of satori (Maupin, 1965), and contrasts with the second kind of good feeling which is characteristic of the state of actualization (Chapter 12).

Decrease in feelings of disintegration. The process of integration is accompanied by a regular and automatic decrease in the felt bodily feelings of disintegration. There is (a) a reduction of the bodily feelings of being in pieces, fractionated, incomplete, disjointed. There is a bad feeling of parts being walled off or sealed off, and with integration that bad feeling is diminished.

With integration there occurs a reduction in the bad feeling (b) of one's parts being at war with one another, in turmoil, threatening one another, set against one another in anger and hate, vigilantly guarding against the menacing alien part which is the enemy, the threat, the source of danger. In the language of Sullivanian psychoanalysis, the ego no longer has to be engaged in the continuous task of repressing dangerous unconscious forces from awareness (Bullard, 1959). The war is over, and the struggle of one side against the other recedes. It is pitiful how intensely and continuously one lives in a state of internal struggle, with one potential set against another. So intense and continuous are these feelings that consciousness of them recedes away until the person simply exists in a feeling state of internal war without knowing that he exists in such a feeling state. Under these conditions, the process of integration lifts one out of a bed of feeling in which one existed without knowing.

Under disintegrative relationships, the domain of the operating potentials is always under the tyrannical control of the deeper potentials, and the fight is against the awful forces which loom up from below. One guards against the bad forces, defends one's self against them, plays tricks on them, resists their menace, tries to fend them off. Yet one is forever locked into bondage with deeper potentials against which one struggles. Inevitably there are feelings which reflect and express this struggle. Integration releases the person from this war so that the feelings of struggling against the inner foe simply are no more.

With the end of the war, I no longer must fear and hate my hands, my penis, my belly, my feces, my mouth, my head. I no longer must have the feelings which accompany the war against my nagging at you, my being quiet when I should say something, my getting you to the point of fearing me, my forcing you to treat me as rather conservative, my brushing my teeth every damned morning, my nose picking when I drive my car. The feelings of being set against my own body finally extinguish.

The integrating person will (c) undergo a significant change in specific disintegrative feelings such as anxiety, threat, tension, dread, fear; helplessness, smallness, pawnness; shame, guilt, self-punishment; separation, alienation, aloneness; meaninglessness, hollowness; depression; hostility and anger; bodily pains, aches, and distresses. It is clear that these feelings no longer will be present in the same way in which they were present when relationships among potentials were disintegrative. What is less clear is the ways in which these feelings differ in a state of integration, as contrasted with a state of disintegration.

One change is in the relative proportion of these disintegrative feelings to integrative feelings. Prior to integration, most of the relationships were almost always disintegrative. This is the characteristic state both within the domain of the operating potentials and especially between the operating and deeper potentials. In the process of integration, however, some of the disintegrative relationships become integrative. A specific relationship may no longer be characterized by disintegrative anxiety, but instead may consist of the good feelings of integration. As this process continues, a diminishing proportion of the relationships is characterized by these disintegrative feelings.

A related change is the extinguishing of a particular disintegrative feeling. Where there existed a bad feeling of depression, this feeling goes away. There is, then, an absence or sharp reduction in that specific feeling. The process of integrating will remove specific bad feelings so that the person no longer has that feeling of guilt or helplessness or dread or hate or anxiety. If the process of integration occurs fully and completely, involving more and more potentials, the humanistic perspective holds that these specific disintegrative feelings can be virtually eliminated. That specific anxiety can be washed away, and virtually all feelings of anxiety can be extinguished. If a specific set of relationships is characterized by a disintegrative feeling of guilt, integration will be capable of reducing and eliminating that guilt. There is no theoretical basis for limiting this process to some irreducible minimum so that there is always some pocket of unresolvable guilt (cf. Buber, 1957) or anxiety or fear or any other disintegrative feeling.

Because integration will eliminate specific disintegrative feelings, and because integration will increase the proportion of integrative relationships among potentials, the integrating person will undergo a third change. Essentially, the integrating person will have significantly different feelings *about* a specific disintegrative feeling. Between a given pair of potentials there may occur a disintegrative feeling of anxiety, but the balance of the person will have integrative feelings *about* that disintegrative anxiety. But if the potentials constituting the operating domain bear *integrative* relationships toward one another, then the anxiety expressive of the disintegrative relationship between an operating and a deeper potential will be welcomed, accepted, responded to with harmony and tranquility. Accordingly, the integrating person receives disintegrative feelings in a new and very special way. He has anxiety and fear, and knows what it is like to feel helpless and tossed about and angry—but the person is integrated in the very having of these feelings. Depression is there, but it is cherished, welcomed, lovingly received. Fear occurs, but it occurs to a person who feels good toward it. Helplessness is a bad feeling, but it occurs in a person who has good feelings *about* the helplessness. In these ways, the contextual meaning of any bad feeling is dramatically different in the integrating person.

Indeed, as a behavioral expression of the integrating person's *good* feelings about *bad* feelings, the integrating person acquires the behavioral skills to cultivate bad feelings in a way which leads to further integration. The integrating person can work well with his own anxiety or guilt or depression. He converts these awful disintegrative feelings to his own advantage by furthering his own enterprise of internal integration. He knows how to move forward on their backs.

I consider disintegrative feelings to encompass the entire range of bodily aches, pains, distresses, hurts, and discomforts. These lend themselves to description and understanding as disintegrative feelings (Chapters 3 and 5). Just as disintegrative feelings of anxiety extinguish with integration, so too will bodily pains tend to evaporate under the process of integration. Bodily pains are merely another expression of disintegrative feelings—which share in the bodily locus and nature. Accordingly, the process of internal integration will be accompanied by the washing away of the headaches, the pains in the shoulders, the racking hurt of labor and delivery of babies, back pains, chest pains. Integrating persons have fewer of these bodily pains.

INTEGRATION WITH AN EXTERNAL WORLD

The process of integration has an inside face and an outside face. Its inside face involves the commitment of an internal journey leading to a continuous process of change or metamorphosis. In this process there is an ending of the present operating potentials and a transforming of the deeper potentials, including the physical body itself. The self dilates so that there is a greater sense of expanded personhood. Within this domain of the self, relationships become increasingly integrated, and the person is filled with increasing integrative feelings and decreasing disintegrative feelings. All of this comprises the *internal* face. We now turn to the *external* face, and to the nature of the world of the integrating person.

Integrative Openness

The integrating person has a characteristic openness. There are at least three aspects to this openness, and we will discuss each in turn.

The integrative space of letting be. Openness means granting the external world freedom to be the way it is. He respects the other individual and provides space for the other individual to be how it is important for him to be. If you are scared, the integrating person sees and knows the scare occurring in you now, and, coupled with this seeing and knowing is a letting-be. In this sense, you are related to in the same way as his inner potential is related to, viz. with a letting-be, an acknowledgment, a stepping back and giving of space to be. When I am with integrating persons, they seem to *know* the nature of my *deeper* potentials. They *understand* the deeper potentials underlying the way I behave and the way I am on the surface where I engage with them. More than that, they surround *my* deeper potentials with *their own* sense of integration. That is, they give plenty of space to what is within me. They let my deeper potentials be. If I am somewhat reserved and held in on the surface, and if my inner stirrings are bubbling suspiciousness, then the integrating person surrounds my inner suspiciousness with a pool of easy space. He gives me plenty of peaceful room to be suspicious. In a way, that is strange and somewhat disconcerting, but it is also welcomed and softening.

It is a letting-be with love and acceptance and respect and warmth.

That means the integrated person does not swarm all over me with love. He does not intrude into me or engulf me with intimacy. I do not feel violated or intruded into by his concern or warmth. It has an easiness which allows me space in which to move around. He does not "help" me with his positive regard, but instead leaves me be in a warmly concerned way. Nor is it a letting-be with coldness or indifference.

What is let be, what is given plenty of space for coming forth, is whatever is moving forward in the other individual. If an affection is moving into being, that is let be and welcomed. If a scared withdrawal is occurring, that too is let be and given space for its experiencing. The integrating person welcomes ways of being which are different and new, and also those which are polar and contradictory to one another. Being strong is welcomed and let be; being weak is also welcomed and let be. The other individual is received in the process of change, or in the process of expressing different experiential faces. There is no boxing in or imposed having to be this way or having to be that way. There is no crowding you into being one part of you and not some other part of you. If you are strong and sure of yourself, there is no forcing of you into being only that. There is no forcing you not to be mixed up and confused, or not to be something entirely different—competitive or highly organized or carping. There is no complaining that you are not "yourself," or that you are not being "consistent." The integrating person ". . . can perceive and respond to others much more as they are and become from moment to moment" (Enright, 1970, p. 120) without working upon them to fit into particularized stereotypes. He lets me be the way I am, without wrapping me in his own network. He lets me be even though I am different from him. Just as there are good relationships with the different parts within him, he offers integrative space to those parts of the external world which are different from the way he is. The upper class integrating person can relate well with the lower class other; the lower class integrating person can relate integratively with the upper class other. The radical integrating person can live in that special integrative relationship with the most conservative other person. The integrating person who is disorganized is able to relate integratively with the meticulously compulsive, the untalented with the talented, the withdrawn with the gregarious, the insider with the outsider, the poor with the wealthy, the young with the old. Differences, even differences which are opposites, are encompassed within the space of letting-be.

This quality of letting be and welcoming provides plenty of space for the other individual's opportunity to have his *own* reactions to his *own* ways of being. If the other individual has a way of reacting to his own competitiveness, then the integrating person lets be and welcomes the competitiveness *and* the reaction to it. The other person is let be and welcomed in his excited tingling about his own competitiveness, or in a being threatened by his own competitiveness.

When I am with the integrating person, I sense his invitation for me to be what I am, to experience what is in me to experience. If I am inclined to open up a particular experiencing, I sense a welcoming invitation to go ahead; ". . . if you suspend any preconceptions you may have of me and my being, and invite me simply to be and to disclose this being to you, you create an ambience, an area of low 'pressure' where I can let my being happen and be disclosed, to you and to me simultaneously—to me from the inside, and to you who receive the outside layer of my being" (Jourard, 1968, p. 162). Furthermore, in welcoming my behavioral expression of it, the integrating person is able to join with me in my efforts to find the best way of doing it. If I am looking for the right words to express it, the integrating person can search for the right words together with me. If I am trying to find the right way of expressing the thought or the idea, the integrating person can work right along with me in locating the right way of expressing it. It is as if the integrating person is able to join together with me in my doing what is important for me to do. In this very important sense, the integrating person seems to know me and to understand me.

In this easy space of letting-be, he is more than a passive openness. As his own person, he moves, acts, does things, experiences. Yet his movements into life are characterized by the space of letting-be rather than the restless urgency of *having* to be. He accomplishes, he moves ahead, he has wants and goals—but it is in connection with an integrative letting-be. There is striving without the urgency of striving, movement ahead without having to move ahead, ambition without a restless pressure to be ambitious, seeking without the need to seek. The striving or ambition is an expression of a potential which bears only integrative relationships with its neighboring potentials, and occurs without urgency, pressure, restless and frenetic having to be, inner drive, insatiable need. In his seekings and beings, he relates to others by giving them plenty of space in which they are let be.

I-thou, equal stature, transparency. The openness of the integrating person endows interpersonal relationships with a character of equal stature. He relates to the other individual in the same way in which he relates to the other potentials within himself, ". . . an I-thou relationship in which each person is aware, responsible, and direct in his own communications and listens as fully as possible to the other person as an equal" (Enright, 1970, p. 115). It is a relationship of equality and respect, one in which I am invited to be in that role to him. He re-

gards me as an equal because that is the way he regards his own potentials, and because his openness lends this I-thou character to his
relations with me.

In this relationship of equal stature, there occur the good feelings
of integration. These include feelings of (a) wholeness, unity, oneness,
(b) peacefulness, tranquility, harmony, and (c) welcoming, expanding,
becoming. When these occur in an I-thou relationship with an external object, they constitute a relationship of love. The integrative relationship is a loving relationship, but this kind of love is not easily
forthcoming in most persons. To the extent that one's internal relationships are *dis*integrative, this kind of I-thou loving cannot occur.
Thus it is understandable that the achievement of an integrative relationship is one of the final modes of living in one's world. Genuine
integrative relationships, as described here, are rare. Genuine loving
relationships are almost unknown in interactions between lovers,
spouses, friends, family. What I term integrative relationships is described as a *dual mode of existence* by Binswanger, who likewise treats
this kind of relationship as virtually unknown in most persons.
"Though or just because it is the authentic mode of being human, the
dual mode is the one most hidden, indeed, the one most severely
suppressed. Just as in the history of mankind it took a long time until
the dual mode achieved its breakthrough in the religion of love, in
Christianity, and just as this breakthrough subsequently changed the
psychic countenance of mankind, so is this breakthrough too, likewise
faced with the greatest obstacles in the individual existence
. . . love . . . claims existence as a dual one" (Binswanger, 1958c, p.
312). There is something awe-inspiring about the experience of a
genuinely integrative relationship with another.

There is an openness, a guilessness in letting the inner feelings be.
It is a being transparent when feelings are occurring, a transparency
that shines forth as an honesty, a candidness. One has feelings without
hiding them or protecting them with a screen. All internal bodily sensations occur without necessitating avoidance or denial. Instead of behaving in ways which hide the inner feelings, there is a transparency,
a behavioral letting the feelings occur. The person who has internal
bodily sensations of tranquility and peace behaves in the simple way of
allowing them to occur, and not hiding or curtailing them. If what is
occurring is a bodily fright and tightening up, those bodily sensations
are also let be and allowed to be transparent. You are in equal stature
with him, and his feelings shine forth in this I-thou transparency.

Having inner feelings in a simple transparent manner requires behaviors which simply let the feelings occur. The behaviors do as little
as possible, except for not getting in the way of the internal feelings.
In this connection, there are behaviors which *prostitute* the mere oc-

currence of inner feelings. These tell *about* the inner feelings. They are slippery and deceptive, for they give the illusion of transparence and openness. Yet they never let the inner feelings be. Instead, they use the feelings in ways which are cheapening and which actually prevent feelings from occurring in their own simple ways. It is the *telling* which becomes the compelling center, and the feelings fall into the role of referent for the behavior of telling about them. Here is the person who tells about having peaceful feelings or bodily pains or a sensation of clutching up, and the telling masks the actual occurrence of the internal bodily feelings. Instead of being this way, the integrating person is simply transparent in the shining forth of feelings to the person with whom he shares an equal relationship. This is a simple open posture toward the external world, a posture characterized by a minimum of defendings, avoidances, distances and denials. There is a replacement of deviousness and indirection (Shostrom, 1967, pp. 50-51) with a brand of communication which is open, straight, honest and truthful (Szasz, 1956, p. 301), a kind of luminosity to one's communications. It is no longer necessary that the person ". . . should live behind a mask or a front. The polite words, the intellectual understanding of one another and of relationships, the smooth coin of tact and cover-up—amply satisfactory for interactions outside—are just not good enough" (Rogers, 1967, p. 268). In the I-thou relationship, there is a minimum of hiding, deflecting, withholding, avoiding.

Free of avoidances and defenses, the person's I-thou relationship with the external world means that he is fully open and receptive (Buytendijk, 1950; Maslow, 1963; Rogers, 1963). Of the four modes of constructing the external world (Chapter 6), this is the one which is the most passive. Instead of actively fabricating an external world, conjointly constructing an external world, or utilizing a ready-made external world (Figure 6.1), the person assumes the most passive posture of simply receiving the external world as it intrudes upon him. But it is a passivity laced with openness and receptivity. In this posture, ". . . you are letting the world disclose itself to you as it is *in itself* . . . you open the doors of perception and let birds, trees, other people, in fact everything disclose itself to you . . ." (Jourard, 1968, pp. 163, 164). Once the person passively receives the external world he is entering into a special kind of contact with it, and it is the nature of this contact that we now turn to.

The integrative contact. Internal integration means that the person is in point-by-point contact with the inner reality. He knows the potential which is within, knows what it is to experience it. If there is a potential for experiencing violent jealousy, he can get into its guts, can see it, can wallow in it, can surrender into being it. Because of the integrated contact with *inner* reality, the person is able to be in contact with *external* reality. The integrated person has the capacity for being in point-by-point contact with the actual contours of the external world to the very degree he enjoys complete integrative contact with the internal world. It is the *relationship* which is critical in determining the degree of contact. Others have also cited this relational variable as the determining key in the person's degree of contact with the external world. Rogers (1959), for example, understands the nature of the person's relationship with the self (referring to an organized set of deeper personality processes) as a key determinant in the person's degree of awareness, perceptual distortion, and perceptual selectivity. Borrowing on this idea, we may assert that to the degree that these internal relationships are integrated, the person will likewise be in integrated relationship with the external world, and that this will be manifested in heightened reality contact.

When the integrating person no longer must work upon the external world to construct it into being this way or that way, there is a most curious phenomenon which regularly occurs. It consists of experiencing that fragment of the external world as if for the first time. It is a first seeing, a new sight. It is that which occurs when you are able to let the external world be, when you let it shine forth as it is, and not as you must construct it into being, when it illuminates as a new and different thing out there, grasped as if for the very first time. This experience is found typically in the person who constructed the external world into presenting its bad aspect. Your father was cold and sterile, but when you no longer must construct him into being that coldness and sterility, what shines forth from him is something qualitatively new and different—even if that consists of *his* coldness and sterility. Now you see him for the very first time. It is this which is strange and curious, and yet which almost inevitably occurs in the course of integration. In this curious new state, the integrating person and the external object or individual exist in a context of oneness. It is a unity which, afterwards when one thinks about it, has a kind of rightness, sometimes a transparency, a luminosity which may occur as a penetrating light (Watts, 1960). This is the manifest expression of the harmonious unity encompassing the person and the other object or person. To be in this kind of deep contact with your father means being invaded by the real father, and the relationship is characterized by a luminosity which defines the shining forth of the way he really is. Now it is *his* genuine coldness, not yours, *his* authentic sterility. You experience him clearly without veils, and the integrative contact occurs in a kind of awe.

The integrative relationship with the external world is a state of genuine oneness with it. When one permits the state of integration to occur with a pencil or a lover or a brother, there is a dissolution of the boundary of one's self and the boundary which defines the pencil or the lover or the brother. This, then, is a qualitatively new mode of relationship, one which goes beyond a dualistic world of person and separated things with which the person interacts (Suzuki, 1949). One does not remain a separated person who observes accurately or inaccurately. One no longer is separated enough to observe. The outer periphery of your I-ness dissolves. This new contact, this closeness, can be expressed in the form of physical touching, the primitive touching-experiencing mode of which Buytendijk (1950) speaks. In this contact-touch there is a washing away of the defined outer boundaries and an entry into the state of integration—whether the contact-touch is with a stone, stream, or another person. Contact is more than a cerebral phenomenon; it is a physical experience monitored through touching.

Enshrouded behind my defenses, I keep a safe distance between myself and the external world. There is to be minimal contact, and what contact there is must be only of the specific sort that I allow. While I am in this state, the integrating person may burst into contact with me. He is not caught in my defensive strategies, but instead has the ability to establish an integrative contact with me. That typically requires a wrenching dramatic thrust into me. "Now, if you can break through my imaginative experience, or my fantasy image, of you; if you can catch my attention, by a shout, a blow, a scream of pain or joy—I may, as it were 'wake up' from my daydream-like experience of your being and undergo a fresh perceptual experience of you" (Jourard, 1968, p. 159). Whether or not the integrating person elects to do this is one issue. But, in any case, the integrating person is the one who has the capability of doing just this in his offering integrative contact with the external world. Through touch or action or yelling, he cracks through my barriers into an integrative contact with me.

In his reaching of me, he can effect an integrative contact with my own deeper potentials. I may fear and hate my insides, recoil from them and defend myself against them. But when I am with an integrating person, he affects me in a strange way. It is as if he connects with those awful insides of mine, those potentials from which I recoil. But he relates to then in a genuinely accepting way. He likes what I hate in me, bears an integrative relationship with that which I defend against in me. He offers a kind of integrative contact with my deeper parts, one which I certainly am unable to bear toward my own insides. It is this kind of relationship which I experience as strange yet peaceful, and I seek out that person to bathe in the kind of loving, integrative contact that I wish I could bear toward my own deeper self.

Yet his contact with me or my insides or with a flower or a stone is accomplished in a way which is distinctive to integrating persons. By integrating with the external object or individual, the integrating person sacrifices his sense of self. Momentarily at least, his own existence as an I-ness is ended. There is no awareness of self, no sense of personhood. In the integrating fusion with the external object, his own conscious identity is gone. This sense of oceanic unity—without conscious awareness of it—is the kernel of integration, and is described as the state of satori and the psychoanalytic state of infantile complete satisfaction. In all, there is a quality of losing one's self in a sacrificing of that self to incorporation or fusion with the other. Psychoanalysis describes this in terms of the infant who is fully fed, and, in this predormescent state, loses its own identity as it is enveloped and incorporated by the breast. The description which makes conceptual sense for humanistic theory is that of losing one's own identity in becoming one with the external object, being enveloped and assimilated into being it. This is what occurs in integrating with any external object. In meditation and contemplation, the method includes a focusing of all one's attention upon a single center of attention, and a shutting out of everything else (Ornstein, 1971). When this is accomplished successfully, one loses the self, the consciousness, and enters into that same state of integrative oneness, of self-less fusion and assimilation. Across the various languages of description, there is, then, a commonality in both the method and the state which is reached.

Integrative contact is a risk, for the willingness to sacrifice one's self in contact with an external object brings one into the process of actual change. Two persons who are able to establish this kind of contact with one another, to the point that each of their selves is sacrificed in the contact, will each undergo significant change in the potentials which are in contact. It is this which is referred to as the "encounter." Yet this kind of contact requires a measure of integrative relationships among potentials. Integrating persons have personality structures which allow them to engage in this degree of contact with one another. In turn, it is this degree of contact with another which carries the process of actual change further along. There is, then, a back and forth process of increasing integration leading to integrative contact, and of integrative contact promoting further integrative change in the potentials.

When the integrating person adopts this mode of being, he is exceedingly sensitive and vulnerable to the external world in at least two ways. In one way, the external world is given an opportunity to construct and mould him. That is, the integrating person goes limp, becomes non-active, becomes passive-receptive. In this posture, the external world *does to* him. For example, the external world may act upon the integrating person so as to construct him into being a villain or a close companion or someone who is rejecting. This means that the external world has potentials which are like that, viz. being a villain or close companion or rejecting. Or it means that the external world requires that building block in constructing an appropriate external situation. Whatever the external world does to the passively receiving integrating person comes from the external world and reveals what that external world is like.

The second way in which the integrating individual is affected by the external world is along the lines of a given *relationship*. By adopting the passive-receptive stance, the integrating person is affected in ways which range from an integrative to a disintegrative relationship. The data for this include the inner feelings, the bodily felt physical sensations. Thus the integrating person is put into turmoil, is made tense and tied up, is torn apart. Or the integrating person is made peaceful and unified, internally of a piece and harmonious. However the integrating person is affected, it provides a way of knowing the external world. In the realm of human science and research, too little is known of the nature and meaning of the *relationship* between the external world and the person who is affected by it. Here is a realm of data which is largely ignored, yet which can tell us a great deal about the external world of human beings.

Integrative Being-One-With

During the state of integrative contact with the external object, the self (I-ness, center of personhood) is freed to reside outside the operating domain. In that state, there is no self which, for example, is there to have thoughts about what is happening, what is coming forth from the external world. There are no thoughts about what is occurring because the self which has such thoughts is no longer located within the domain of the operating potentials. In effect, the domain of the operating potentials may be described as dilating out beyond the integrating person's physical body (Watts, 1960). Indeed, the outer perimeter of the self is now encompassing portions of the external world. If the person attends to a tree in such a manner that the self of the person dilates to include that tree, then the self will be in a state of oneness with that tree. The contents of the self are enlarged to include the tree itself, and the integrating person will have the experiencings which are the tree.

One way in which the integrating person achieves this special contact with another is by aligning himself with the other individual's focused center of attending. In this method, the other individual focuses his attention upon something which may be external or internal. For example, it may be his dog, his chair, an acquaintance, a flame of a candle, or any other *external* thing. It may be his liver, his rumbling stomach, his ulcer, or any other thing *internal* to his physical body. Once the other person focuses attention upon that thing, the integrating person *also* focuses his attention upon that thing so that the focal centers of both persons are coterminal. As this occurs, the integrating person moves closer and closer to the domain of the other individual until he achieves a fusion. This method of conjoining or being-one-with the other individual constitutes a method of research inquiry (Von Eckartsberg, 1971), a method available to the psychotherapist, and a method by which the integrating person becomes one with others in his world.

Yet, accomplishing this state of oneness means sacrificing, at least momentarily, a good portion of the sense of self. I can know what is occurring within the other individual by dilating my self to include the experiencings going on within the other person. But that means there is no "I" to know that I am doing this, no conscious awareness of being wholly aligned with the other person. To sacrifice this sense of self, even temporarily, calls for two qualities. One is a courage to no longer be me. It takes guts to give up this sense of self. It is a leap of faith that calls for real sacrifice. The nature of this courageous faith can be stated in several ways. It is as if the integrating person has a faith in his own permanence of self so that he knows he will again exist after he has let himself be-one-with the other. It is as if the integrating person no longer must care what happens to his self if he were to be-one-with the other person. In describing the way Sartre and Heideggar understand this point, Laing (1960) speaks of a person's inability to die another's death for him, nor for the other to die one's own death. Second, to allow my self to experience what is occurring in you calls for a maximum of trust. I must fully trust both me and you in order to entrust my self to you. This kind of ability to entrust my self to you is a quality of the integrating person (Erikson, 1950). It is a kind of willingness to be passive, to be vulnerable to you. In a very important sense, being-one-with you calls for the highest plateau of courage and of trust.

Persons who are predominantly disintegrated are unable to do any of this. They live in worlds which they are unable to know by this mode of being-one-with. They are unable to get inside the tree or the bicycle or the faucet or their younger brother or enemy or spouse. What is more, their worlds are such that they are unable to *know* that they are unable to do this. But integrating persons have acquired this capacity and, having acquired it, they are able to gauge the extent to which they live in integrated worlds. They are able to assess whether or not they can be one with that tree by trying it out. Can they be one with the tree, experiencing what it is experiencing? Can they dilate their own selves to encompass being the tree? If the answer is yes, then they have achieved that degree of integration. If the answer is no, then integration has not proceeded that far yet.

Integration with the External World: A Methodology for Research

The integrating person is marked by qualities of *openness* and *being-one-with*. We now turn away from the integrating person and his world to consider the implications of these qualities for the human sciences. Our thesis is that the integrating person as a researcher will discover a new methodology for the pursuit of human knowledge. More specifically, our thesis is that *integrative openness* and *integrative being-one-with* contain the seeds of a robust new methodology for research in the human sciences.

Consider the passive-receptive mode of being *integratively open* to the other individual. By adopting this posture, the integrating researcher can know the other individual by setting aside his own self, and simply being open to that which the other individual is putting forth. It is a matter of letting oneself be affected by what intrudes from the external individual. If you stay perfectly quiet, put your own self to rest, and allow yourself to receive, you might sense a being bunched up or a distancing moat or a sexual arousing. To the integrating researcher who receives openly what the other individual is doing, this is a way of knowing that the other individual is making you bunched up or is building a distancing moat or is sexually arousing you. If the integrating researcher disengages his operating domain, assumes this most passive mode of receiving the external world, and locks onto a reception of what is coming forth from the other individual, then the integrating researcher is in a position to receive, to sense, to be intruded into and affected—and *not* actively to construct or share in the construction of bunching up or distancing or sexual arousal. Here then is a special way of knowing the other individual.

In this way of knowing, there are two steps which must occur. One is an opening up, a being affected, a passive-receptivity to what the external world is doing to the researcher. The second is a scanning of what these inner effects are, an accurate sensitivity to what is occurring within. It is a knowing of the external world by turning inward (May, 1958, p. 26). Both steps are necessary. The person who exposes himself to the external world, who is porous to its impacts, will be affected by the external world but will not know what these effects are. This is the person who is scared by the external world, but who does not utilize these effects to know that which is having these effects upon him. In similar fashion, the person who only turns inward and who senses the being scared will be relatively unknowing of the external world which does this to him. The skill lies in combining the two steps, in opening oneself up to the intrusive effects of the external world, and in scanning the insides to assess the nature of the internal effect.

The integrating person can use this mode to gain knowledge of the other individual. What the passively receiving person does with this knowledge is important. If the increased knowledge leads, for example, to a change in our conceptual understanding, then the integrating person is functioning as a research investigator. That is, the integrating person is systematically gathering knowledge and is modifying conceptual structures on the basis of that knowledge; "... if I adopt the attitude of 'Let the world disclose itself to me,' I will receive this disclosure and change my concepts" (Jourard, 1968, p. 157). In other words, we may pursue knowledge by a systematic utilization of the passive-receptive open mode, and alter our conceptualizations on the basis of such knowledge. Such a mode of inquiry falls within the province of the phenomenological scientist (Giorgi, 1965). When the scientist adopts the phenomenological mode of inquiry, he gains knowledge which is both systematic and which generally falls outside the realm of knowledge typically obtained by more traditional methods of scientific inquiry.

Because the integrating researcher is able to enter into the personal world of the other person, he opens up to careful scientific study that whole realm of inner experience which traditional research methods have been unable to grasp. Historically, this realm has been labeled as private, inner, subjective, and has been excluded from careful scientific observation. That inner realm, it has been held, is not observable. Therefore it lacks the verifiability of public data. Although a small cadre of scientists has argued for the usefulness of such data (e.g. Giorgi, 1970; McCurdy, 1961; Polanyi, 1958), scientific investigators have not been given the gift of systematic means of studying this inner realm. I expect that the development of phenomenological methods of entering into the inner subjective world of the other person will constitute a major breakthrough into a world which scientists have never adequately penetrated.

Current status of this research methodology. In the field of human research, there is a hard lesson yet to be learned: The methods by which the integrating *person* gains knowledge and understanding of his external world can be refined and adopted by the *researcher* seeking systematic means of pursuing knowledge and understanding. In a kind of haphazardly unsystematic manner, we have found that one route to creative scientific knowing is through these inner resources (Reik, 1948, p. 17). Humanistic theory seeks to join with phenomenology in utilizing the mode of integrative openness and the mode of being-one-with in the process of scientific inquiry. But at the current time, virtually none of our research employs these or similar modes.

It is terribly difficult to employ these methods. One cannot grasp them in any constructively effective way unless one has entered into the process of integration. But even then, utilizing these two modes requires that the researcher lay aside conceptual frameworks which impose a structure upon the external world, which organize the external world in a predefined manner, for the data are not to be pre-organized. Instead, the integrating researcher adopts the passive-receptive open mode and the being-one-with mode of grasping external data and allowing the data to organize itself along the contours of *its own* natural lines. This is a continuation of a theme in the history of science, a theme in which rigorous research methodologies are generated whereby the data are allowed to speak to us directly—without our twisting them out of shape by predetermined imposed conceptual structures. In one sense, methods of factor and cluster analysis can be described as means of allowing the data to group itself more or less along its own contours. We need to develop powerful research means of grasping the data in its own natural form and organization.

In the history of the human sciences, practically no research methods allow us to know the external world the way the integrating person knows the external world. Neither the passive-receptive open mode nor the being-one-with mode has been systematically refined for use in careful research inquiry. A few threads may be found tied to the Titchenerian structuralist methods of introspection. Like our own methods, these involve a turning to one's own experience to grasp data, but radical differences occur in the supposed nature of the experience which is thereby tapped (MacLeod, 1964). In the Titchenerian school, experience was held as consisting of a set of irreducible elements which could be illuminated by an introspective self-reporting of experience. But by and large the only thread of similarity lies in turning to what is within for the necessary data. As *methods*, especially as usable tools of inquiry, we have yet to know how to utilize the researcher's capacity for integrative openness, being-one-with, and other characteristics of the integrating person.

Beyond observation of the object of inquiry. One means of knowing, of understanding and gaining knowledge, is by observing the external event. In the human sciences we have developed refined methods of observing the objects which we study. The integrating person adds at least two other methods to that of observation. The passive-receptive open mode of knowing and the being-one-with mode of knowing are qualitatively different from observation of the external event. At the present time, observation is the predominant research mode of gaining further knowledge. Humanistic theory joins with other approaches which offer the other two modes as potentially robust means of gaining further knowledge. In contrast to the observation mode, these other two require that the scientist *not* function as an observer.

Instead, the scientist must sacrifice his personhood momentarily when he is either passively open to the external world or being one with it. Both of these methods require that the scientist no longer be a separated person who observes a phenomenon and who retains the I-ness or personhood which enables him to know that he is observing. Our methods complement those of observation, and are of a different order.

Our modes of knowing call for the researcher placing himself in a very special relationship with the phenomenon he is studying. However, I wish to draw a distinction between these methods and the study of oneself, for the latter does not require placing oneself in this special relationship with the external phenomenon. What it *does* require is accurate and precise examination of one's own internal phenomena, and the payoff may be enormous in terms of knowledge gained. Much of the credit for Freud's work involves his courageous ability to submit himself to his own examination. "When he learned to recognize the meaning, hidden to himself before, of what takes place behind the facade of his own thinking, the meaning of unconscious processes of all people dawned upon him. He could not have discovered the most valuable secrets of the human mind had he not found them in himself first" (Reik, 1948, p. 17). Different from self-observation as a scientific method, however, are the modes of gaining knowledge of an external phenomenon by placing oneself in an integrative relationship with it.

It is clear that the integrating person as psychotherapist is in the process of undergoing change in the course of the psychotherapeutic experiences. This is also true of the integrating person as researcher. It is not new that psychotherapy profoundly can alter the psychotherapist. It is *less* acknowledged that equally profound changes will take place in the researcher who adopts these methods of inquiry. More specifically, the researcher who goes beyond observation by opening himself fully to the phenomena he examines, and who adopts the method of being-one-with the phenomena, will risk undergoing profound change in the person whom he is (Von Eckartsberg, 1971). This is true on two counts. First, in order to employ these research methods successfully, the person who is the researcher must already be in the process of integration. Second, opening one's self to a full reception of the phenomena, and being-one-with the phenomena, will both contribute to the process of further integrative change. Thus the researcher who adopts these methods and carries them out steps beyond observation into the process of personal change in the course of scientific inquiry itself.

Resolving the nomothetic versus idiographic issue. Going beyond observation means going deeper and deeper into the particular event or phenomenon we are studying. In adopting this research methodology it is easy to be concerned with losing the advantages of a more general, nomothetic approach to scientific inquiry. In the effort to pursue knowledge in systematic fashion, researchers have evolved general principles about human beings, including laws, personality conceptualizations, common behavioral determinants, general statements about human behavior and personality processes—all of which are regarded as essential for the understanding of *collective* human beings and also the *individual* human being (cf. Farber, 1964). In addition, researchers have evolved an approach to understanding the individual human being which steps out of the general principles and which focuses upon an intensive study of the *individual* person. When these two approaches are understood as being antagonistic to one another, they are known as the controversy between the nomothetic and the idiographic approaches. It should be clear that humanistic theory aligns with *both* the importance of general principles of human beings and also the importance of careful, detailed study of the individual human being. In the pursuit of knowledge and understanding of the individual human being, the methodologies we have discussed involve ways of boring ever deeper into the personal and highly individualistic core of the single person. General principles about human beings are essential to enable us to develop and to refine the *methods* of knowing the individual person, and also to make general sense of what we learn from applying these methods to collective human beings.

Integration with the object of inquiry versus committing the experimental error. By integrating with the event or phenomenon we are studying, we run into other differences with traditional approaches to research. In our approach, *general* principles are used to bore ever more deeply into the study of the *particular* event or phenomenon we are interested in studying. To know or understand that particular baby or that particular older woman or that motorcycle means locking onto it in an integrative relationship and describing the event with increasing depth and precision. In this research probe, the investigator stays with the event rather than leaving it. He moves closer into it, describes it in particularized minute detail. This approach is in contrast with those which seek to understand a specific phenomenon by moving *away* from it. For example, our way of studying persons who are labeled "schizophrenic" is to stay with the person, and to engage in exhaustive description of that particular person. Research tools would help us develop guides as to what to describe and how to describe it rigorously. Other approaches, however, seek to understand "schizophrenia" by moving *away* from the very phenomenon they seek to study. These other approaches seek to study the relationship between schizophrenia and distant events to which it is supposedly related. Thus, instead of describing "schizophrenic" phenomena, schizophrenia is linked up with other variables such as ego functioning, chromosomal imbalance, early loss, social class, or endocrine disturbance. Instead of delving further into the "schizophrenic" events themselves in rigorous description of what is there, research seeks to pull away by categorizing, not describing, by understanding through classification, not penetrating further into the events. To classify is not to describe exhaustively. Classification is an expression of backing away from the phenomenon into general theoretical speculations about process or reactive schizophrenia, simple, catatonic or paranoid schizophrenia. "All these are theoretical (psychopathological) interpretations of the schizophrenic process, attempts to explain it by way of formula, which use an explanatory theoretical judgment to skip over what really goes on and what must serve as starting point. Here too our watchword is: back from theory to that minute description of the phenomena which today is possible with the scientific means at our disposal" (Binswanger, 1958c, p. 342). Integrating persons who are researchers will develop systematic means of understanding phenomena by means of increasingly accurate and useful descriptions of the phenomena themselves.

In this connection, such an enterprise is consistent with the philosophical position of humanistic theory (see Chapter 4) and is unlikely to occur in classes of theories which have other positions on the assumptions discussed in that chapter. It is no accident, therefore, that our research methodologies have given us so little knowledge about human phenomena, since these methodologies take us *away* from the phenomena instead of going deeper *into* the phenomena. For example, we have studied depression for decades and decades, but have succeeded in accumulating pitifully little knowledge largely because we have failed to affix research attention on the actual phenomena of depression. "There have been very few systematic studies designed to delineate the characteristic signs and symptoms of depression" (Beck, 1967, p. 10). We have yet to examine the phenomena of depression by systematically adopting a passive-receptive open mode or a mode of being-one-with persons who are depressed.

Humanistic theory is coupled to research methods which will go deeper into the human phenomena we study. For example, many phenomena tend to occur in what I have termed the *critical moment*, when feelings are high and the deeper potential is pressing in on the operating potential (Chapter 3). These critical moments are precious opportunities for research inquiry (Chapter 9) into human phenomena such as depression, shame, riots, family stress, suicide, creative thinking, and epileptic seizures. I have spent sessions of three to four hours with persons in psychotherapy, detailing the aspects of a critical moment which may have lasted two to four seconds. As a psychotherapist, I understand the event by studying the critical moments in which the phenomenon exposed itself for observation. In contrast, most researchers seek to understand the event by rushing *away* from it into laboratory analogues of it, extracted pieces of it, larger categories of it, historical antecedents of it, and untold factors external to it. The phenomenological method of capturing critical moments stands in stark contrast to the method of seeking to understand the phenomenon by rushing off to variables and factors related to it.

In contrast to such traditional ways of backing off from the phenomenon, the integrating person who is the researcher leaves the phenomenon preciously alone. He reduces to a minimum his own acting upon the phenomenon by adopting the passive-receptive open mode and the mode of being-one-with it. If he is interested in studying the families of persons labeled "schizophrenic," he devises ways of passively receiving the data and being-one-with the data. He listens, observes, seeks to be one with them, moves into their world by becoming plastic to them and by resonating to their own experiencings and feelings. He allows the natural data to speak to him. Among the hundreds of articles and chapters on the families of "schizophrenics," there are exceedingly few which let the natural data speak out. Instead, the bulk of our knowledge comes from *experiments* which actively *do* things to the families. It is the *experimenter* who is the active one in moulding and constructing the families. "Most of the investigations of families of 'schizophrenics,' while contributing original and useful data to different facets of the problem, have not been based on direct observation of the members of the family *together* as they naturally interact with each other" (Laing & Esterson, 1970, p. 21). The bulk of our data comes from experimental conditions which therefore express what I term the *experimental error*. That is, to the extent that experimental conditions are constructed, the data tell us more about the experimenter than the phenomenon studied. Failure to attribute the resultant data to the experimenter is the *experimental* error—committed in most contemporary research.

Extinguishing of the Former External World

Integrating persons (a) become increasingly open to their external worlds, and (b) are increasingly able to become-one-with their external worlds. In discussing these two characteristics, our focus has been on the integrating persons rather than on the external worlds in which they exist. We now turn to the altered nature of their external worlds. Once the person becomes integrated with his own deeper potentials, his external world alters. Its very structure and form change. No longer is it constructed out of disintegrative potentials and no longer does it serve disintegrative functions. By contrast, in virtually all other approaches, the external world per se undergoes no nuclear changes as a consequence of change in the person. It is sufficient that the person change, and that is expected to alter the leading interacting edge between the person and the external world. When the person changes, that will promote changes in others, and so the paradigm goes. Humanistic theory contains audacious principles and constructs whereby changes in the *person* are accompanied with the boldest possible changes in the very nucleus of the *external world*. The integrating person lives in an external world qualitatively different than that of the non-integrating person.

In traditional humanism, as opposed to humanistic theory, the optimal person exists in the same old world, but relies increasingly upon feelings as an internal behavioral guideline. "He relies on his own feelings about himself because, essentially, he sees no meaningful external corrective to them. And so the idea of development or movement toward a better personal existence, or health, becomes linked to an active striving to *feel* better, either by doing certain things or by relating to other people in certain ways" (Needleman, 1967, p. xiii). This is a truncated, impoverished conception of the optimal person, one which Needleman discards in favor of a more dauntless existential conceptualization. Humanistic theory likewise rejects that model of person-world relationships (cf. Chapters 6 and 7). We turn now to an illumination of the larger scope of changes attendant to integration, and consider the bolder contours of changes in the external world of the integrating person. Our thesis is that the integrating person lives in an external world which is qualitatively different from the world of a person whose potentials are related together in disintegrative fashion.

A world no longer constructed of disintegrative relationships. Once the person achieves significant integration among his own potentials, the external world is no longer comprised of disintegrative relationships. The world in which the person now exists has reduced relationships of disintegrative fear and hate—whether the relationship is between the person and the external world or among parts of the external world. No longer is the external world constituted of components whose structure and function consist of relating together with anger, hate, destruction, tearings apart, disharmony, disorganization, disjunctiveness, or any of the various characteristics of disintegrative relationships.

One way in which this occurs is the integrating person's active declining of invitations leading to such disintegrative relationships. The integrating person is not a feather blown about by helter skelter invitations of the external world, for he *actively* declines invitations to participate in relationships which deepen disintegrative relationships. He has the ability to say no to these invitations, and to step back away from all relationships which only serve to deepen his own disintegrations. As described in Chapter 6, I can act upon the integrating person by means of at least four modes. I can receive him as the intrusive world which acts upon me. I can utilize him as a ready-made part of my external world. I can conjointly construct an external world together with him, and I can fabricate an external world which I lay onto him. Regardless which mode I follow in constructing my external world onto him, he will decline my invitations if they contribute toward his own internal disintegration. Because of the kind of person I am, I may invite him to be a mean authority while I am the unfortunate victim. As I weave my web around him, inducing him to be the mean authority, he will not play with me. Instead, he actively declines the role which I weave about him—if the result is a deepening of his own disintegrative relationships. I may use all my tricks to ensnare him in my disintegrative relationships. I may be more clever and shrewd than he, but his degree of integration is an advantage which I cannot overcome, and he usually is successful in declining my invitations. In this important sense, the integrating person is surely not all-accepting, for he will not participate in my torturing him. He is not one who unconditionally welcomes everything about me, for much of what there is to me requires that he widen the disintegrative furrows within him.

In declining these ensnaring invitations, the integrating person is being active. Yet his world differs from mine in being freed of such disintegrations from which the invitations pour forth. Indeed, he no longer must *do* things to the world; he can leave it be. He does not *have* to work upon the external world, need not *bend* it out of shape, need not *construct* it into serving twisted disintegrative purposes. There is, in the integrating person, a severing of this kind of connection with the external world, ". . . and so the *participation mystique* with things is abolished" (Jung, 1962, p. 123).

The integrating person *already has* the sense of oneness and love and belongingness. That sense is not sought in external world pursuits. Although the integrating person lives in a world of bananas and automobiles and friends and colleagues, these are not resources to provide oneness and love and belongingness. The integrating person lives in an external world of families and groups, but not to fulfill a missing sense of internal integration. The integrating person is not a plant dependent upon the external world for supplies. Although this paradigm is paramount in many of the natural sciences, it is declined as a necessarily accurate paradigm for humanistic theory. Internal integration is sought and gained within oneself, and not from anything in the external world. In effect, the integrating person no longer falls within a model in which the resouces are always to be found in the external world. In shedding that way of being, the external world itself is radically altered, and so are the relationships between the person and the external world, for the integrating person neither "needs" nor seeks internal integration from the external world—and no longer lives in an external world which holds the seductive promise of supplying love, acceptance, understanding, belongingness, unity, oneness, and peacefulness for a person who is disintegrated internally.

Because the person is integrated, the external world no longer is constructed into bearing disintegrative relationships toward him. It no longer is made to ridicule him or to reject him, to assault or kill him, to attack or hate him. The person does not work at constructing an external world which hurts him or deserts him or physically abuses him. No longer is the external world invited to bear toward him the same disintegrative relationships he bears toward himself. When he is no longer terrified at what is within, he no longer works at constructing an external world which terrifies him or which is terrified by him. The integrated person simply is no longer that kind of person, and no longer constructs this sort of external world.

In no longer requiring that the external world bear a disintegrative relationship toward him, all such behavior is abandoned, regardless of the mode of construction which had been utilized. The external world is not constructed into punishing the person, and all means of construction are dropped, whether they are active or passive means. No longer does the person *actively* provoke the external world into punishing him, e.g., by criminal acts or by physically assaulting others. Nor does the person use *passive* means of constructing the external world into being punitive toward him, so that he is unaccountably the victim who is always on the receiving end. Along another dimension, the integrating person no longer uses *realistic* aspects of the external world to bear punitive relationships toward him. Nor does the integrating person use *unrealistic* modes of constructing an external world. For example, he does not have delusions of enemies out to punish him for his past misdeeds. In no way does the integrating person construct the external world to bear disintegrative relationships toward him, regardless of the mode of construction.

Even his uniqueness is not used to promote disintegrative relationships. The integrating person *is* unique. He is different, special, not like ordinary persons. He acts in ways which are out of the ordinary. These ways of being might possibly be construed as strange, weird, bizarre, antisocial, crazy, deviant from the norms established by those who are not integrating. Little wonder that one's spouse or family or acquaintances or the psychodiagnostician may very well see that person as being chaotic, disorganized, and even as falling apart (Rogers, 1963). He may be described as schizophrenic, lacking ego controls, manifesting poor judgment, narcissistic, impulse-ridden, and psychotic. But the distinguishing feature of the integrating person is that his deviateness is not used to promote disintegrative feelings in him or to promote disintegrative relationships with and from the external world. He will not use his deviateness to be crucified or to crucify, to hurt or be hurt, to alienate or be alienated, to hate or be hated. Instead of using his deviateness to promote bad relationships, the integrating person lives out his deviateness in ways which invite *integrative* relationships. He will not force the external world to receive his deviateness in disintegrative ways or in ways which lead to bad feelings. Instead, he invites you to share in it, enjoy it, let it be. Although the person may be different, radical, even strange, there is a kind of aura about him which speaks of a peacefulness, a tranquility. His way of being is benign and free of personal threat to the other individual. Because he is internally integrated, his way of being is reassuring and settling.

It is almost inevitable that the integrating person will be faced with resistances and retaliations. He does not get entangled in the disintegrative traps others lay for him. Others will pressure him to be this way or that way in *their* own worlds. Ordinary wonderful people and ordinary terrible people will be throwing their nets around him, forcing him to play the roles they insist he play. He will be alone, often, and alone in ways which occur because he is not a part of the intimate disintegrative relationships in the lives of a family or friends or acquaintances. More than being alone, he will be disliked, hated, crucified for not joining in, for not being the way the group wishes him to be. In addition, his ways of being can be awfully threatening to others. His ability to play with social roles can be infuriating. Others may sense him as mocking the pitfalls and self-engendered catastrophes in which they live. Because of all of this, there is almost inevitably a clash. Although the integrating person does not participate in constructing this clash, in another sense he does indeed participate in constructing this clash by virtue of daring to follow the integrative way. Given this reaction to the way he is, and to the ways in which he declines to be, the integrating person is distinguished by the ways in which he copes with all of that. The reactions to him are there. They will occur. But he will not whip them up into manufactured disintegrative relationships. He will not use them as construction blocks in the creation of disintegrative relationships.

Because of the way he is, the integrating person will often be regarded as one who must be distrusted. The evidence lies in his being difficult to place in the ordinary categories. He is playful, and yet sober. To assume that he will carry out the responsibilities in the way we expected, even in the way he had carried them out in the past, is an error. He cannot be counted upon to be the way we wish him to be. He must be distrusted like a little child or an irresponsible character. The only category we can place him in is distrusted and irresponsible. There is a kind of special aura about the way he is, one which makes the inconsistency and easy slipping in and out of contradictory ways of being acceptable—even special and reassuring. He is being untrustworthy and irresponsible in ways which convey that here is a person who, nevertheless, is integrated, is all-of-a-piece, is unified and all together.

Others will see the integrating person's way of being as alien, often menacingly alien. His fluidity, flexibility, freedom from the usual constraints of social roles, and easy shifting from one experiencing to another may well be taken as evidence of near chaos, as personality disorganization, as falling apart (Rogers, 1963). Because he is on speaking terms with his own deeper potentials, because he is, in other words, friendly with his craziness or unconscious, he will be regarded as crazy. Yet the integrating person will surround those reactions with his own integration. You can regard him as being disorganized, and he will join you in that regard. You can consider him as falling apart, and he will share such a perception with you. He can have the same reaction toward himself that you bear. He can wink at his craziness and have fun with his craziness. It is his ability to take an integrative stance toward your reactions to him which allows him to *not* build your reactions into a disintegrative mould.

Yet, with all of his differences, the integrating person need not maintain distance from the external world. When the person achieves degrees of integration, chunks of distancing behaviors simply fall away. No longer will the person require an armor of bodily fat to serve as a protective moat against a dangerously intrusive external world. No longer will the person need that impenetrable mask—about which he himself may be ignorant—to be safe behind. No longer does the person require the ways of dodging your overtures or slipping the real messages. There is an extinguishing of protective and distancing social roles. All of these behavioral means of effecting a safe distance tend to slide away once the person moves along the path of integration.

A world no longer constructed of externalized potentials. As the person undergoes a conversion of his own internal relationships from disintegrative to integrative, the external world no longer is comprised of the person's externalized potentials, and no longer serves the function of being externalized potentials. It is this latter change to which we now turn.

The integrated person no longer grasps the external world as an externalization of what he is, neither the externalized operating nor deeper potential. No predetermined role is assigned to you out of the potentials of the integrating person. You are no longer moulded and fashioned into being the integrating person's operating or deeper potentials. You are not constructed into being the person's defiance or affection or evilness or competition. In no way are you constructed into being that which exists in the person's own system of potentials.

The integrating person takes back into himself that which he extended out onto the external world. I peel off of you the potentials which are mine. If I have a potential for experiencing nurturance, I bring that potential back within my self. No longer do I construct my nurturance into the external world by fabricating nurturant figures out there, for example by daydreaming them, by imagining them, by seeing them where no one else can see them. Nor do I work conjointly with you to bring forth your nurturant face. Nor must I place myself in the path of persons who are being nurturant. Nor do I receive what you intrude upon me as nurturance. Now the nurturance belongs to me. It is a part of me, and I welcome it back into me.

A major step in welcoming it back is being my own potential instead of constructing the external world into being its expression. Haley (1963) describes the treatment of an enuretic young man who constructed the external world into being his own potential for experiencing defiance and punishment. Haley's mode of treatment consisted of suggesting to the young man that whenever he urinated in bed he was to get up immediately, take a two-mile walk in the night, come back, and sleep in the cold, wet bed (1963, pp. 47-49). In this way, the young man is himself being and doing and experiencing the defiant punishment that he formerly had built into the external world. He is taking a major step toward bringing this potential back into himself, toward regaining his own potential for experiencing—and thereby withdrawing this chunk of the constructed external world.

By freeing your world of your own externalized potentials, you no longer must live in a world from which you recoil in the way you recoiled from the menacingly powerful, disintegrative deeper potentials. You no longer must defend against the external world, fight against it, conform to it, adjust to it, be careful lest it overwhelm you and tear you apart, placate it, give in to it, strike out against it, be in everlasting conformity to or rebellion against it. The profound difference is between *choosing* to conform to or rebel against social values, and having to conform or rebel. The "compulsive" conformer or rebel is not a person, even though he may believe he is (Malone, Whitaker, Warkentin & Felder, 1961). He is under the power of his external world. By integrating with your deeper potentials, you divest the external world of its invested power. It loses its alien and menacing face. It is drained of its evilness, bad power, awful control, menace.

No longer is the external world constructed as a grand complex of conditioning mechanisms or activating stimuli. There are no further external cues, stimuli which control me, run me, get me to be this way or that way. No longer am I the way I am because my family or my community or my culture or my society moulded and fashioned me into being this way or that way. Where it *was* such a world, and where I *did* live in such a world, I am no longer a cornered tiny personhood, controlled by overwhelming deeper potentials which loom at me as the powerful external world. I have awakened from a world which stimulated and reinforced me, trained and rewarded me, pushed and pulled me, shaped and moulded me, modified and manipulated me. Because the deeper potentials no longer run the person, take him over, dictate his life for him, the integrating person no longer lives in a world in which *others* take over his personhood.

The Construction of Integrated Social Worlds

We have been discussing the process of integration as it involves an individual person and his external world. The person constructs a particular kind of external world and exists in relation with that world in defined ways. We now turn from the individual person and his external world to collective persons and their social worlds.

Humanistic theory rests upon a set of principles in which *the construction of social worlds is a function of collective persons*. Social worlds are constructed, maintained, and reconstructed by collective persons. Thus the essential avenue toward change in our social worlds lies in collective persons. When collective persons undergo change in their own internal personality systems, there will occur substantial changes in the external social worlds (Mahrer & Pearson, 1971a). This means that it is fruitless for a group of individuals to mount a program of social change aimed directly at "society." From their inception such programs are foredoomed to failure. They are linked to a view that the determinants of personal problems reside in an encompassing social system rather than in the individual, and, on that basis, efforts are directed toward modifying the family, the school, the community, work, the organization, the judicial system, the peer system. As attractive and reasonable as this sounds, *from the perspective of humanistic theory* it is simply an error. That system—whether it is the family or peer group or school—is itself a function of world-building efforts of collective persons, and will undergo substantial changes as these collective persons change.

Dyadic group relationships. As a consequence of integration on a collective basis, there will occur a dissolution of dyadic groups locked together in mutual disintegrative relationships. It is the disintegrative relationship between the potentials of collective individuals which is ultimately responsible for such dyadic groups. For example, if collective persons have disintegrative relationships among their individual potentials for power, dominance, control, authoritarianism, or potentials for submission, being victimized, defiance, rebellion, then these collective persons may construct worlds of painfully interlocking dyadic groups. One group emerges as the powerful, the dominant, the controllers, the authorities, and the other group emerges as the ruled, the weak, the dominated, the victims. The process of integration within *each* individual person in the two groups removes the very foundation for this social phenomenon. On a collective basis, the very nature and content of the potentials are transformed, and the disintegrative relationships among these potentials are converted to integrative relationships, thereby removing the very ground on which the social phenomenon rests. As an inevitable consequence, these dyadic groups wash away. No longer are there fear and hate between a strong group and a weak group, between dominators and dominated, between victors and victims. This entire phenomenon fades out of existence.

The occurrence of such disintegrative dyadic groups requires large numbers of individuals who fear and hate their deeper potentials as powerful, overwhelming, controlling. Out of these relationships is created a social world of dyadic groups locked in an unresolvable struggle with each other, with one being powerful and the other weak, one controlling and the other being controlled. However, integrating persons do not share in constructing such dyadic group relationships, for their personalities do not include the powerful control which characterizes disintegrative individuals; there is no intent to control, no basis for perpetuating either side in these dyadic group relationships. Obviously, those who exist in worlds of disintegrative power and control will seek to ensnare integrating persons who will be seen as indecisive, cowardly, unrealistic. "The plain fact is, the obdurate refusal to arrange circumstances for influencing others, on ethical or moral grounds, may simply serve as a mask for indecision and irresponsibility. Furthermore, such refusal ignores the evident fact that we influence others in unintended and unplanned ways" (Farber, 1964, p. 14). Whether disguised as influencing or illuminated as disintegrative controlling, the social worlds of integrating persons are free of dyadic relationships in which one group establishes relationships of control, dominance, influence, manipulation over another.

In the social struggle over power and control, there is no winning. Once the struggling groups are composed of collective persons with *internal* struggles over power and control, the *external* struggles over power and control simply persevere in one form or another. Power struggles will continue interminably regardless of the groups involved and regardless of the nature of that over which they struggle, for groups will always find territory to struggle over. When one group is triumphant, the struggle just moves on to the next phase in the endless process of struggle over power and control. Human beings can gain waves of triumphs over "nature" by means of "science and technology" (Muller, 1960), but the war of power and control will only move onto newer and newer expressions of the internal state of disintegrative struggle. There is no triumph in this war.

On a personal level, the way out occurs when the integrating person is able to plunge into an integrative fusion with the deeper potentials. Neither the operating nor the deeper potential "wins." In much the same way, collective integrating persons know that there is a way out of the struggle against warring sides. Instead of controlling or being controlled, they enter a state in which there is an awakening from having been in a world in which the options were those of controlling or being controlled. There is a new consciousness of freedom (May, 1967) in which these persons acquire a sense of heightened personhood, increased internal control and freedom and mandate and activation. These are strange persons who acquire a *higher* plane of power and strength by the unusual act of *not* participating in our grand struggles for power and strength.

Many social groups are constructed by collective individuals who are in a constant struggle against being taken over by their own deeper potentials. These persons construct social groups which are comprised of and which represent the threatening deeper potentials—and which lay claim upon individuals' heads. These organizations do what the deeper potentials do, viz. own the person, take over their thoughts and their reactions, deprive them of mandate, choice, I-ness, personhood. On this basis we construct religions which we invest with the power to own us (Byles, 1962, p. 198), and gigantic administrative bureaucracies and governments to take us over and to leave us mindless, person-less. We construct all manner of social groups, political parties, gangs, offices, agencies, families, departments, cliques, and outfit them to control, activate, govern us. When integrating persons decline the invitation to construct such social groups and institutions, when they no longer *require* external agencies to be their controllers, governors, centers of self, then these kinds of agencies will slide out of the external world, will no longer exist. Our external world will be freed of all such social groups, and the struggle of each group to avoid the control of the other is finally put to rest.

In these disintegrative relationships, each group is characterized by an intent to change the other, a *restless urge* and *necessity* of doing *to*. One group must violate another by "helping," by "relieving their suffering," by giving them the benefit of our wisdom, our achievements, our tools, our insights, our knowledge, our way of life. We are *impelled* to cure their sicknesses and solve their problems. The villain in all of this is the *having* to do it to them, the *unquenchable thirst* for changing them, modifying them, making them different. What is termed the "last truth" in Vipassana meditation is the final state in which persons are freed of this disintegrative inner necessity (Byles, 1962). Out of this awful inner restlessness comes the bounding *necessity* of making pleasant things be encased in permanence, of *having* to make things better or different. A political party *must* change the government. The religious *must* convert the heathen. The educated *must* teach the uneducated. Marxists *must* alter the non-Marxists. Groups are *impelled* to modify the system, the government, the culture. When persons finally achieve internal integration, there is no further having to, no must, no restless urge to, no necessity to do to. On a collective basis, there no longer are groups eagerly struggling to change other groups.

Helper/helpee as a social institution. This restless urge to alter the external world exemplifies itself in the so-called "helping" professions. There the intent to change comes forth in many guises. One group seeks to help another group to reduce their suffering, to solve their problems. The target group is recognized as having certain problems, troubles, conditions, all of which call out for assistance. They have mental deficiency or schizophrenia or delinquency or criminal tendencies or craziness or psychiatric conditions; they are troubled boys and problem girls; they are patients and clients and inmates and prisoners. In all of this, once the guise is removed, what stands forth is one group having their own justified intent to change another group. When, in sharp contrast, persons are collectively integrating, there is a dissolution of the *intent to change,* and the whole basis of one social group helping (i.e., intending to change) another group washes out of existence.

Client-centered counseling gentles the traditional directive role of the counselor. Yet the same intent to change shines forth. It is a client-centered intent to change, one which is comprised of a respect for and prizing of the client. Still, it is the counselor who houses the intent for the client to change, and who uses specific methods of instrumenting that intended change. In this enterprise, client-centered therapy constitutes " . . . a relationship in which at least one of the parties has the intent of promoting the growth, development, maturity, improved functioning, improved coping with life of the other . . . a helping relationship might be defined as one in which one of the participants intends that there should come about, in one or both parties, more appreciation of, more expression of, more functional use of the latent resources of the individual" (Rogers, 1958, p. 6). Helping relationships, in whatever guises they are dressed, are typically filled with a large component of one group intending to change the other group. In other words, if the process of integration extinguishes the intent to change, it is almost certain that much of the foundation upon which the helping professions rest will be gone, and we may envision the gradual termination of the whole social-professional ethic of one group "helping" (that is, intending to change) another.

On a grander scale, the intent of helpers to change helpees becomes institutionalized into a profession (psychiatry, social work, psychology, mental health, etc.) accepting for itself the target of changing *society*. Now the subject of our intent to change is not the crippled or twisted person, but the whole of society. Under this banner, helping professionals set out explicitly to change social institutions, facilitate the emergence of a new social order, serve as architects of social change (Hobbs, 1964). From the perspective of humanistic theory, the arising of helping professions with the messianic self-appointed mission of changing society is precisely *not* the way of moving toward social change. It is merely a collective expression and institutionalization of the internal disintegration of collective members of the helping professions. When integrated persons constitute the bulk of the various helping professions, they will have no collective intent to change society. They will leave society alone, and be free of that compelling restless intent to change others. No, the aim is not to change society, not to perpetuate the social institution of helpers and helpees, spiced with the intent to change the other. That institution will vanish. There will be no profession dedicated toward social change, no group setting out to change another group.

One group setting out to change (help) another group is the disintegrative face of a social world in which persons provide one another with space to be and space to become without any disintegratively-rooted *having* to make another be in any particular way. It is a social world in which persons no longer must make other persons be a certain way. Most pointedly, there is a transcending of one group "helping" another group.

In the world of helper-helpee, the participants are predominantly characterized by fearing and hating their insides, recoiling from their insides as mad, crazy, lunatic, demented, weird, different, strange. On a collective scale, this leads to the construction and maintenance of a class of individuals who constitute the externalization of all that. They are what we recoil from within ourselves. What is more, we then relate to them in the same manner as we retate to the craziness within ourselves. We victimize them, deprive them of rights, construct special places for crazy people, regard them with fear and hatred, ridicule them, animalize them, isolate them.

The reasons for creating such a class of individuals and for treating them in these ways are dependent upon the disintegrative relations toward collective deeper potentials. When collective individuals plunge into the process of internal integration, they achieve personal changes with preponderous social consequences. When you and I achieve integration with our own deeper potentials, we no longer will recoil from them as strange and crazy. Thus this basis for the existence of crazy persons will be washed away and the institution will begin to fade away. In a world of integrating persons, each is given the space to be and to become. Each is given the room and the opportunity to be whom he is, and to become whatever he is capable of becoming. Instead of one group intending to change another, there is the integrative relationship of space and freedom to be.

The process of integration involves two primary agencies. One is the person, the center of the self located within the domain of operating potentials. The other is the deeper potential. In this relationship, the center of gravity lies between the person and his own deeper potentials, and *not*, as has been true in virtually all forms of the helping relationship, between helper and helpee. To the extent that the crucial relationship is understood as between the *person and his own insides*, the entire structure of the traditional helper role collapses. Instead, the person who seeks to engage in internal integration is free to extract from an external source the instrumental means of bringing about one's own self-change. The other agent is used as a source of information, if that is needed. This role is one of information-giver, teacher of a method used by the person who is undergoing his own internal integration. In this capacity, the major axis of change lies between the person and *his own* insides, and no longer exists between the helper and the helpee. In this work, the external agent never deflects the major axis of communication onto that between the integrating person and the external agent. Within the literature on psychotherapy, models of this role are contained in those approaches to family therapy wherein the work of the external agent (therapist) is to open up lines of communication among family members, and not between any member of the family and the therapist (Bell, 1963). When we relate the members of a family to the parts of a single person, the role of the family therapist is coterminal with the role of the teacher who provides the integrating person with the knowledge of how to undergo the process.

Our model includes two coupled principles. In one the integrating person is given full freedom and space to be and to become. Whether or not the person embarks on the integrating journey is the person's own choice. The second principle is that the major axis of interaction is between the person and his own potentials. Taken together, the arena of personality change lies *within the person himself*, in his own relationship with his own potentials, within a context of space and freedom to engage or not engage in this internal integrating journey. It is my contention that no other school of psychotherapy or counseling embraces this model of personality change. In the various relationship therapies, the key to change lies in a particular kind of achieved relationship between therapist and patient, counselor and client. Not only does this arrogate the critical relationship *away from* the person and his own insides, but it deprives the person of his own mandate, his own freedom to be, his own personal space. A second typical lever of personality change consists of external stimuli and cues which are manipulated by a therapist in accord with principles of conditioning and learning. In these therapies, the critical relationship is between the person and these external stimuli and cues, and not between the person and what is within himself. Furthermore, instead of mandate residing within the person, instead of the person having all the freedom and space, the preponderance lies within the therapist. A third lever of personality change consists of insight and understanding wherein the therapist is the leader who directs the person into insight or understanding. These three typical levers of personality change stand in contrast to one in which the integrating person, *not* the therapist, has all the choice, all the freedom to be, all the space and choice and responsibility—and in which the critical integrating relationship is entirely confined to that between the person and his own insides, rather than that between the person and therapist, counselor, or any other external agency. Consider the kinds of institutions and practices which might emerge if substantial proportions of integrating persons were to enter what are now known as the helping professions. What would the field look like if the intent to change and the "need to be helped" were no longer predominant features of helpers and helpees? Not only would there be a washing away of virtually all of our current institutions and practices, but it is likely that a whole different crop of institutions and practices would appear (Mahrer, 1971b, 1972a). It is terribly difficult to see clearly what such new institutions and practices would look like, partly because we are essentially non-integrating persons caught in our perspective of being helpers and helpees. Nevertheless, a few best guesses are in order. First, it seems to me that the emphasis would be on the provision of resources for those who wish to take advantage of such resources. This would include available instruction in methods by which the interested person can achieve what he seeks to achieve with himself. I foresee the possibility of instructional training in methods of self-control, self-change, self-integration, and the like. Instead of helpers and help-ees, there will be teachers and interested students. Persons will likely be in both roles—a teacher of others and a student of others, with the major work being on and with one's self and not others. Second, facilities will occur whose function is to enable integrating persons to join together in *psychological families* (Mahrer 1970e, 1971b, 1972a). Offering integrative movement to each member, this kind of new group stands ready to emerge as a nascent social institution. Third, in addition to the provision of resources, I foresee a major shift toward the creation of optimal infants and away from the helping of children and adults with problems. These are my best guesses as to the kinds of social institutions which might emerge when integrating persons constitute what we now know as the helping professions.

The extinguishing of social institutions. When collective individuals are at war with their own potentials, these disintegrative relatioonships occur as wars, mass destruction, social violence. We construct and feed such social phenomena out of our own collective disintegrative relationships. When processes of *internal integration* occur on a collective basis, the foundation is cut away from such social phenomena as wars, mass de-struction, exploding social hatreds, social violence. Others (e.g. Soro-kin, 1959) have pointed toward a solution through moral transforma-tion, typically involving exhortative proclamations to be noble, altruis-tic, and loving. From the perspective of humanistic theory, the only effective means of moving in this direction consists of collective indi-vidual internal integration. When this occurs on a collective individual basis, there can be no war, no social hatred, no social violence, no so-cial hatefulness and destruction. We will construct wars as long as we collectively are at war within our individual selves; when we are inter-nally integrated, there will be no basis for wars.

Social institutions—such as war—and social beliefs are constructed by component individuals as a collective. An individual person may construct an external world of elves and Gods, beliefs about social classes and schizophrenics, and ideas about reincarnation and the spec-ial nature of our group. When a *collection* of persons share similar external worlds, the group constructs its own reality. Reality is har-dened by consensual validation. In this process, Gods are invested with a group-bequeathed social reality. Schizophrenia is real because we all share in constructing its reality. Our group is a real thing, has its own group mind, exists as something to be defended and loved be-cause we collectively make it so. Collectivity invests shared external worlds with a brutal realness. Reincarnation and the caste system, for example, are collectively cherished social realities to such an extent that one integrated person constitutes an intolerable danger to their continuation. However, when the preponderance of the group consists of integrating persons, there is a radical and sweeping change in the entire fabric of all of the group's social realities. Under these new conditions, much of what had been created and maintained as hard reality may now disappear. Reincarnation and the caste system may now occur as false social beliefs (Watts, 1961, pp. 67-68). So too may Gods, schizophrenia, and large chunks of what our group had constructed as external reality. All become illuminated as false social realities, myths granted reality by collective validation. By this process, our social institutions extinguish.

One of these false social realities is referred to as culture, society, civilization. We invent it and regard it as a real thing, separate from the individuals who are constitutive. Sometimes we separate it out as the responsible agent for our problems. For example, so-called "primitive cultures" are cited as "healthier" than ours because their culture permits open, free expression of deeper human tendencies such as sex and aggression. In contrast, our culture is "less healthy" because modern civilization blocks open and free expression of the deeper tendencies of individual persons (cf. Leighton & Hughes, 1961). From the perspective of humanistic theory, collective persons construct that which we refer to as culture or society or civilization. If our civilization blocks the expression of sex and aggression, it is because collective persons have constructed that which we refer to as civilization, and invest it with properties of blocking the expression of sex and aggression. There is a thing called culture or society or civilization because we have collectively constructed that thing. We are its determiners, architects, and owners. Culture or society or civilization is created by collective persons in the very same way collective persons construct such social institutions as Gods, elves, priesthoods, schizophrenia, nations, patriotism, and educational systems. These are all false social realities, arising into pseudo-reality by virtue of collective individual construction. When—and if—collective human beings change, there will occur the most radical changes in culture, society, and civilization. These are products of our own collective construction, and not separately existing real entities. They are all group-constructed social institutions, invested with social reality.

The extinguishing of the group-constructed social reality is a significant affair whose consequences can be wrenchingly profound. The group collectively shared in constructing a mutually held set of social realities, and the forbidding danger is that these sets of realities will emerge as false beliefs. Here is a shattering of the very foundations on which these group-held realities were built. The risk is that pillars of reality will crumble. Worlds will fall apart. Everything which the members accepted as truth is subject to dissolution. When I believe in it, it is my personal reality. When you and I believe in it, we share a secret reality. But when the group believes in it, it *is* absolute truth—

which collapses when we individuals step back away from perpetuating the collective fiction. It is this danger which threatens the absolutely unquestioned realities in which we exist as a member of a group—without even knowing that these unquestioned realities are there. To undergo the holocaust of the end of the social realities in which we exist is the danger which emerges when a single member of the group enters the process of internal integration.

With the dissolving away of the group-constructed social realities is coupled the dissolving away of sets of supporting social institutions, social mores, social norms and values. In order to construct wars, collective human beings design and maintain a complex fabric of supporting social institutions. There are armies, and patiotism, veterans administrations and national pride, military spending and military history. Dozens of social institutions are required to implement wars. Because these are means, nothing substantial will be accomplished by efforts directed toward these means. Only when relationships among the potentials of collective individuals become integrated will these social institutions become obsolete and unnecessary. When the integrated relationships of collective persons no longer construct external worlds offering the experiencings of war, there will be an associated fading away of cannons, armies, patriotism, veterans administrations, guns, soldiers, military spending, national pride, and military murder.

We have constructed a fabric of social institutions designed to protect our collective selves against deeper potentials involving infants, children, and the aged. Suppose that a large proportion of collective individuals house deeper potentials for murdering these groups, abandoning them, letting them die. Out of these collective deeper potentials are constructed all manner of social institutions to deny and avoid what is collectively within, and, instead, to construct a polar set of institutions. On this basis collective individuals construct respect for the old people, social agencies for infants and young children, legislation to protect and provide welfare for old and young, families to care for the baby and the old one, familial responsibility, mother and father love, filial love and respect—social institutions for warding off collective fears and hates toward the very old and the very young (cf. Montagu, 1950; Sorokin, 1950a, 1950b). Once collective individuals become integrated with these deeper potentials, no longer maintain such disintegrative deeper potentials, no longer must fear and hate these deeper potentials, then the very foundation of such social institutions is eroded. No longer is there a social institution of respecting old people—born out of a deeper potential to kill them. No longer is there a social institution of fierce protection and savage nurturance of babies—born out of deeper potentials to murder them (cf. Bakan, 1966).

The impossibility of seeing the possible social worlds. As collective individuals move further along the path of internal integration, more and more of our social institutions will wither away. What kinds of social institutions will appear in their place? It is relatively easy to describe how collective integrating persons will lead to the dissolution of so many social institutions whose existence requires a foundation of collective internal disintegration. We may speak of specific social institutions which will wither away: e.g., families, religions, the military, political parties, wars, businesses. But what will take their place? If virtually all persons were internally integrated, what sorts of social institutions would emerge? Aside from what the social world would *not* be like, what *would* the social world be like under those conditions?

Is it possible for us to see the nature of a world of integrating persons? Humanistic theory suggests that only when the relationships are fully integrative can the person truly know his deeper potential. But this means the person is no longer the former person, and the deeper potential itself has undergone essential transformation. I cannot see what the social world of collective integrating persons is like because I am not sufficiently far along the path of internal integration. I can only view what I foresee in my present state of preponderantly disintegrative relationships. Therefore, I cannot trust what I envision.

As long as the visions of better worlds come from persons who are largely disintegrated, their visions are more functions of their present state than accurate forecasts of the future. Visions of automatized technocracy may be the grand externalizations of very particular kinds of persons for whom such a vision is exceedingly important. Individuals coping with alienation and apathy and separation may very well envision optimal societies characterized by commitment, belonging, closeness, and a sense of meaningfulness (Keniston, 1962). Those who are themselves struggling against disintegrative deeper potentials, and who are themselves torn apart, will envision a new society in which relationships are accepting, intimate, peaceful and mutually integrating. But these and similar projections may be radically different were the creators metamorphosed in the process of internal integration.

I cannot see in detail what integrating parents will be achieving with infants. Therefore, I have no ideas about the nature of social institutions which will surround the parent-infant relationship. What I do have, however, is an unbounded faith that collectively integrating persons will construct new sets of social institutions around infancy and our ways of being with infants. In the final chapters of the book, for example, I have sketched out what integrating adults *can* be like with infants. These may become social institutions of infancy. I am hesitant to speculate because I am not sufficiently integrated, nor am I in a position to get out of my present personhood and into one from which that future can be envisioned properly. Tomorrow I will perhaps be able to locate a genuinely integrating person, and I may even be able to listen to what he says about a social community of integrating persons. Perhaps.

With the exception of predictions put forth by integrating persons, most visions of the good life are suspect. These visions become downright *dangerous* when they involve changes in the way *others* are to be. Most visions of the good life mean that changes are to occur in you and in me. For my group to achieve our good life, there will be no upper classes, or everyone will be Christian, or the present governing clique will be overthrown. Such conceptions of optimal societies are thinly veiled intentions for others to be changed by me and my group. Because I am not integrated, I must push at *you* to be different, and my conception of the good life is the expression of how you are to be different. Each consideration points toward the same conclusion, viz. envisionings of the good life by persons who are not integrated are far more likely to be expressions of their difficulties and problems than accurate predictions of the possible optimal societies.

12

The Optimal State: Actualization

The optimal state has two aspects: integration, discussed in the previous chapter, and actualization. In this chapter we will consider, first, the connections between the processes of integration and actualization, for there are important ways in which they are interconnected with one another. Then we shall consider actualization as depth and breadth of experiencing, and conclude with actualization as heightened intensity of experiencing.

ACTUALIZATION AND INTEGRATION

The interconnections between integration and actualization. The optimal state is reached by means of integration and actualization, two processes which are independent of one another in some respects, and *inter*dependent in other respects. A person can achieve a great deal of integration without invoking processes of actualization, without achieving much actualization of potentials. Through the integrative journey, a person can achieve significant transformation or metamorphosis of the deeper potentials, a dilation of self, an expansion of the domain of operating potentials, an expansion of the center of one's personhood. By integrating with the insides, the person can achieve friendly and enjoyable relationships with his own potentials. He can also achieve the kinds of feelings which are associated with the state of integration. All of this constitutes a great deal to be gained without actualizing the potentials which have been brought into the domain of the operating potentials by means of the process of integration. But after the first wave of deeper potentials has been integrated, the process of integration grinds to a stop unless the companion process of actualization is engaged. The wheels may keep on spinning, but the

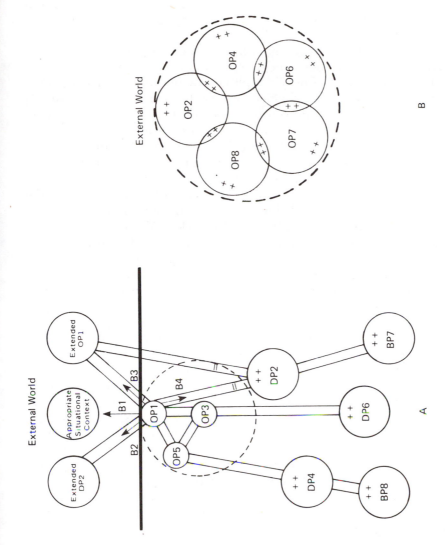

Figure 12.1 Integration and Actualization

person cannot move ahead in achieving higher levels of integration unless one engages in actualization. Bear in mind that achieving as much as one can achieve without invoking actualization constitutes a rare and wonderful accomplishment. It is the most exceptional person who has moved that far. But once the exceptional person has moved that far, he can move no further without engaging the process of actualization.

Integration, then, can accomplish a great deal in working with one's *internal* world. What about integration and the *external* world? Here we find much less that can be accomplished by the process of integration all by itself, without the coupled process of actualization. There can occur virtually no integrative openness with the external world without invoking actualization. There can occur no essential progress in achieving a state of being-one-with the external world. Some progress of a limited nature can occur in extinguishing components of the former world in which one existed, but the ceiling here is not very high. Far less can be achieved in the construction of an integrated external world for the individual, and practically nothing in the collective construction of integrated social worlds. All in all, virtually no changes will occur in regard to the external world without the engagement of the process of actualization. Integration can proceed to a point *internally*, and then the process of actualization is required to move further ahead. Integration cannot even get started *externally* without invoking the process of actualization. In these ways, the process of integration is dependent upon the process of actualization. But it works the other way too. Actualization is connected to integration so that the former depends upon the latter.

Actualization is the culmination of hard work. It is an accomplishment to experience one's complement of operating potentials. It is an even greater accomplishment to do what is necessary (i.e., integration) to bring a *deeper* potential into the level of operating potentials. To some extent, sometimes to a very large extent, actualizing a potential calls for guts, courage, hard work. One cannot sit back and be wafted along by some mysterious inner actualizing mechanism. As human beings, we have only the *potential* for actualization, at least from the perspective of humanistic theory. There is no conception of human beings as endowed with a spontaneous force moving everyone inextricably along the rose garden path into a state of actualization. In some other conceptions of actualization, one need only remove the roadblocks and the "intrinsic" process of actualization carries us along under its own steam. Sullivan's interpersonal theory is representative of many in which human beings are somehow intrinsically set ". . . in the direction of mental health; as the obstructions are removed, he will develop on his own" (Tauber, 1960, p. 673). The position of humanistic theory on many of the underlying conceptual issues (see Chapter 4) makes such a portrayal of actualization both unnecessary and unacceptable. Moving into the process of actualization calls for work, not faith in some intrinsic alien force.

Much of the work requires the achievement of a degree of integration, a state marked by tranquility, inner peace, oneness. After one achieves a measure of integration, the next step is working toward actualization. As described in Vipassana meditation, the achievement of a degree of inner peace and tranquility (our state of internal integration) is to be followed by a stage of movement, changing, activity (Byles, 1962, p. 205). In Vipassana meditation this state is referred to as phyit-pyat; in humanistic theory it is referred to as actualization. Integration lays the groundwork for the next step, but the next step requires effective skills and work.

Because the work of actualization follows the achievement of a significant degree of internal integration, it is not at all accidental that the actualizing person may be 40 or 50 or 60 or 70 years old. It is possible that actualizing persons may be younger, rarely in their adolescent years, sometimes in their twenties or thirties. Yet the necessity of having attained a significant degree of internal integration grants older persons a measure of favored status. In my own practice, I have found increasing possibilities for both further integration and further actualization as persons move from decade to decade. In this, I have confirmed in my own psychotherapeutic work the observations of Jung (1933), i.e., that many older persons are especially outfitted for the journey into actualization. Indeed, because the work of actualization follows the achievement of a significant degree of internal integration, it may be expected that such a state of actualization may be especially cordial to older persons.

Actualizing the integrated form of the potential. Actualization is the process whereby one experiences the *integrated good form* of the potential. What had existed as a deeper potential, in its bad form, across a disintegrative channel, is now operationally present in its good form (B, Figure 12.1). The process of integration transforms the deeper potentials, metamorphoses them from their bad disintegrative form to their good integrative form. Now the process of actualization opens these potentials to actual experiencing. If, then, we focus our attention on a given deeper potential (A, Figure 12.1), the process of integration alters it from its bad form to its good form, and raises it from a deeper to an operating potential. At that point the process of actualization opens it to actual experiencing.

Does the person (A, Figure 12.1) know what the good form will look like (B, Figure 12.1)? Both humanistic theory and clinical analysis tell us that it is the good form of the former deeper potential which will be actualized, but the person himself will not know the *precise* parameters of the integrated potential. All the woman knew was her tendency was to work others into a frenzy of confusion while she steadfastly maintained an icy calm of ugly superiority. She found herself constantly on the alert and constantly probing for areas of weakness in the other individual, areas which she could work into the other individual's confusion, self-doubt, and disorganization. Having accomplished that, she looked down upon the other in a most despicable way. When she threw herself into the process of integration, what had existed as a deeper sadistic dominance was transformed into a new (integrated) sense of competence. In this new form, she moved increasingly into politics and, within two years, gained a position of significant responsibility in the province. She was respected, and deservedly so, for she was a most capable leader who enjoyed a real sense of integrated competence. She now enjoyed this sense of competence, whereas before it had plagued her in its disintegrated bad form.

When Constance even glimpsed or sensed what was within, it loomed as frightening homosexual tendencies. A few times she came close to homosexual affairs, followed almost immediately by periods of anxiety and depression. Under the process of integration, she moved into a new state in which she now experienced the deeper potential in a new, integrated form, viz. a strong affection with women, a oneness she had never before experienced, a trusting openness with women where before she had only known sexual lustful fantasies and brushes with genital invitations. What is more, she now engaged in sexual relations with a few women, but the sexual relationships bore little relationship with the earlier secret fantasies and sordid daydreams. Her new era of sexuality was ensconced in a context of trust, intimacy, openness, honesty, and genuine closeness. As the process of integration transforms the potential, actualization brings it into experiential concreteness in its new, integrated form.

Edward worked hard to know the disintegrative deeper potential. As he came to grasp it, even in his present disintegrative state, it loomed as an awful helplessness, a being exposed and laid bare, a painful vulnerability to erosive external forces. Distressful as it was, that seemed to be its nature. As he worked further and further in the process of integration, its manifestable form changed to a potential for being reached, for receiving and being open, for being affected. Actualization of this integrated potential led to a more genuine listening to what others had to say, a far closer touch with his own feelings, and, in his own words, a removal "of the caps from my nerves." He found himself able to cry, to have strong sexual feelings, to laugh heartily, to be utterly giddy, and also to be fully bitter, envious, and gluttonous. Actualization brings forth the integrated form of the potential.

The mother's deeper potential was manifested in actions carried out by her adolescent son. His final separation from the entrapping family was the expression of what existed deep within her. When he left, she plunged into a depression, another expression of the deeper potential—a pulling in, a getting away from it. The process of integration revealed the potential in its good form, a potential for extricating herself from engulfing situations. Actualization of this good integrated form consisted of a series of acts such as going to college (she had quit high school to work and support her family), studying theater (an unrealized lifelong ambition), and traveling with and without her husband (she had never left her home province). She had brought back into herself the potential which had been externalized upon her son, and actualized its good, integrated form into her daily ongoing life.

These examples indicate rather dramatic shifts from the bad form to the good form. There are other changes which in many ways are less dramatic, for the same behavior can shift from serving a disintegrated potential to serving an integrated one. Actualization of the new, integrated potential may continue the raw skeleton of many of the old behaviors, but at least two major changes alter the *meaning* of the ostensibly same behaviors. First, the potential is now transformed from its old, disintegrative form to its new, integrative form. Second, the nature of the associated feelings is altered. Thus the behaviors undergo slight, subtle changes which express major and significant changes in the potential and its relationships with other potentials. A potential of taking in and receiving assumes its bad, disintegrative form as behavioral means of grabbing what is good in the world, pulling and sucking love from others, gorging oneself with food and drink, needing God's protection and offerings. As expressive of a disintegrative potential, these behaviors exemplify what Fromm (1966) labels a nonproductive character formation. Actualization of the *integrated* form of this potential may lead to the continued expression of receiving love (without grabbing and wrenching), taking in sights, sounds, smells, and the good things of the sensuous world (without the restless pressure of having to corner and possess), enjoying the taking in of good food and drink (without frenetic gorging in a fearladen insatiability). When the potential is actualized, the same behaviors are now different in ways which may be slight and subtle, but highly significant.

Yet, slight and subtle as are the changes, there are radical consequences when integration rotates the meaning of a behavior. Consider the older man whose mood was dour, who was chronically complaining, nursing irritations and grievances, periodically giving in to outbursts of hateful temper. The experiencing of anger occurred in disintegrative behavioral ways which filled others with bristling tension. When he was angry, persons around him were made to fight against him in disintegrative fear and hate. He existed in a kind of chronic state of war with the others with whom he related. He behaved in angry ways which induced others to fear and hate him for being that way. All in all, his angry behaviors filled his world with painful disintegrative relationships. When he went through the process of integration, something subtle occurred to the potential for experiencing anger. Somehow his being angry was different. He was still angry, still behaved in many of the ways he had behaved before. The potential for experiencing anger was still there, and the angry behaviors were still there, but now there was a new quality to his anger. In a strange but pleasant way, his anger was different. Now it seemed right or fitting. The persons around him now seemed to enjoy his blowing off. Now he exploded in ways which seemed open and honest and to the point. It filled others with good feelings, even though he continued to be angry, and often was angry at the person who now was made to feel comfortable and solid in receiving the anger. Somehow his bitching made the situation fresher and more honest. Now it was almost fun to argue and complain and fight with him. His anger was now occurring as integrated anger, and its actualization made the angry behavior different. The actualization of an integrated potential may continue the same old behavior, but now it occurs in a way which makes it radically different—from serving a disintegrated potential to serving one which is integrated.

The physical body and the actualizing of integrated potentials. The physical body is a site of potentials, especially potentials surrounded by disintegrative relationships. When these relationships are integrated, profound changes can occur in the physical body. As profound as these changes are, the process of actualization adds perhaps an even more dramatic set of changes in the physical body.

In its disintegrative bad form, the deeper potential occurred within the young man's body as a kind of imploded physical act. That is, it was as if a violently explosive physical act was occurring within the physical body, resulting in a chronic state of acute high blood pressure, regular epileptic-like seizures, and high anxiety, alternating with weakness and fatigue. Following a good measure of integration, he underwent rather dramatic changes in his life situation. The changes opened with an incident in which he threw his brother-in-law out of the house, grabbing him by his pants and his shirt, and physically throwing him out, followed by his belongings. A few days later, at a typical afternoon cocktail party, he suddenly had enough, turned on his heels without even so much as a word of warning to his wife, left the party, went home, and put on his old clothes. He went walking with his son, listened to him, played catch with him, and participated with him and others in a pick-up baseball game at the playground.

None of these things had he ever done before. With such acts, he had begun to actualize the potential for engaging in (integrated) explosive physical acts. Actualization puts into experiencing the former disintegrative potentials which had occurred as disintegrative physical problems and bodily processes, and now occur as behavioral acts expressive of the actualized integrated potential.

Physical bodily expression of disintegrative sexual potentials may occur as skin rashes. Ever since she was 12 years old she had been medically "treated" for skin rashes which appeared and disappeared. Largely they occurred on her neck, face, shoulders and upper chest. She was by now an expert on the various orchestrations of medicines and ointments, yet the skin rashes still, were present, seven years later. Only with integration did the strong underlying sexuality go beyond the bodily expression and lend itself ready for actualization. In this good form, she could finally engage in sexual touchings, playfulness, caressings, and physical lovemaking. The good form of the deeper potential could now come forth in the process of actualization.

Typically, the bodily expression is of a twisted, disintegrative potential about which the person is wholly unaware. Furthermore, the first blush of understanding generally is through a distressing disintegrative channel. For example, the persistent cough had plagued the young woman on and off for many months. In the course of psychotherapy, the throat constriction and the associated cough were revealed as the bodily expression of a deeper potential involving frightening fantasies of sucking a penis to the point of ejaculation, and incapacitating anxiety associated with the act of swallowing the fluid. In the course of integration and actualization, this potential emerged in the good form of aggressive sexuality, complete with the sexual using of her hands, mouth, breasts, and vagina to arouse men to orgiastic heights. Her new ways of being included entrance into a whole world of sexuality about which she had only fantasied in anxiety-provoking and distressing ways. Aside from the vaguest sensings, she had no idea of the specific nature of the deeper potential underlying her persistent cough.

The young man's facial tic consisted of a spasmodic twitching of the muscles around the mouth, pulling the mouth to the right side, and frequently opening the lips slightly with a smacking sound. Years later, after this young man had undergone his own process of internal integration, the potentials came forth in new behaviors. There was a potential for experiencing defiance and rebelliousness, and also a potential for experiencing nurturance and dependency. These potentials had been expressed behaviorally in a conflict-ridden embracing of both heterosexuality and homosexuality. Now he sought and found genuine intimacy with both men and women, where before there were virtually no intimate contacts in his life. Gourmet cooking became an important area of his life where before he had no knowledge or skills in this area. Breasts took on a whole new significance, and he enlarged his sexual world to include the delights of breast-centered sexuality. He now enjoyed being nurturant and dependent upon others, and providing others with nurturance and dependency. In the actualization of these potentials, the old facial tic lost significance and quietly disappeared.

The body houses various disintegrative deeper potentials which can occur in forms referred to as cancer. Friendly, crusty, dedicated, hard working old Carl was in his middle fifties when he sought medical assistance for strange pains in his stomach. He underwent tests and was told that he had cancer. Almost immediately thereafter, Carl went on a long trip, and sought psychotherapy in another country from someone' his son, a young psychologist, had recommended. It appeared that the cancer was the major expression of a recondite potential, buried within himself for his entire adulthood—a not caring, an impulsive eagerness, a kind of fierce expressiveness which was surrounded in a disintegrative pool and occurred as a devouring physical event labeled cancer. So deeply buried was this potential that Carl was utterly unaware of its existence. In the major changes which followed, that potential was altered into its integrative form and the process of actualization led to whole new sets of experiencings. Primarily, there was a new zest for living, a newfound capacity for fun and excitement. Carl seemed to devour each moment now, to be eager to enjoy life. This was a drastic conversion of the kind of person he was, an actualization in the good form of what had occurred in disintegrative form as the cancer. Not only was the cancer gone, but Carl entered a dramatically new life of being an essentially new person.

Actualization and the harmful violation of other persons. What are the effects of actualization upon the other individuals in one's world? Will the effects be harmful, damaging? Will the actualizing of potentials heighten the painful disintegrative feelings of others? Worries and concerns about actualization typically picture the process as culminating in the open, free expression of "impulses" and "primitive material" in persons "without control." People would behave like animals, in uncivilized ways. They would urinate and defecate in the streets. There would be rape and slaughter as sexual and aggressive impulses are given license. All reason and control would be gone, as would justice and law. If the person wanted food, she would simply take food from stores without paying. There would be no consideration of others, no regard for the rights of others, no respect for the concerns of others. People would "act out" their neurotic and psychotic impulses. Social taboos would be violated. There would no longer be any conscience or sense of personal accountability.

Would actualization free people to be crazy? What would occur if persons who behave in crazy ways underwent the process of actualization? Jerome was such a person. He periodically fell into withdrawn states, during which his communications were incoherent, gibberish, "schizophrenic." Beneath these ways of being was an intactness, a wall of privacy protecting him from an explosively threatening world. Without knowing, his "crazy" ways kept him from being violated and destroyed. Jerome retreated behind that wall of uncommunication. No one could reach him. After the intense period of integration, followed by the actualization of the new potential, he behaved in dramatically different ways. He said what he really meant. He counted upon himself. He was able to be alone comfortably. These behaviors were surprisingly new. Yet there was a commonality in the way he had been and the way he became, for Jerome still exuded a sense of intactness, a kind of person-unto-himself. It set well, now, and shone forth in its actualized good form. With integration, Jerome's new behavior was *less* "crazy," though the potential had previously been expressed in "crazy" ways. Many persons have potentials for experiencing that same sense of intactness, being-unto-themselves, a preservation of themselves as persons, a kind of withdrawing from feared external and internal onslaughts. Of these persons, many utilize behaviors which are bizarre and crazy to gain some sense of that experiencing—although it is of a disintegrative nature. When, in rare and special instances, this potential undergoes integration and is brought forward in the process of actualization, the core nature of the experiencing remains the same: being intact, a sense of personhood. What is altered is the behaviors attached to the new form of the potential. In its good, integrated form, the behaviors provide for the experiencing of a kind of self-certainty, a self-confidence, an honesty of self-expression, a being able to know what one thinks and believes. In its core nature, the potential remains the same, but the form changes, and the behaviors are drastically different when the process of actualization brings the potential into actual experiencing.

What about other ways of being which can be downright dangerous to others? If you actualize what is within you, will I be harmed? There are persons who already exhibit the frightening face of their disintegrative deeper potentials, preserving their selves by stepping aside and allowing the raw deeper potentials to take over (see Chapter 10). Here are "thrilling transgressions" wherein the deeper potential carries out behaviors which are thrilling and exciting, yet which the operating potentials fear and hate. During these periods the person behaves in ways which are atypical from his ordinary ways of being, and which almost always are shrouded in secrecy. This is the person who steals things from stores while in this special state. This is the older man who steals women's undergarments and puts them on secretly. Here is the man who prowls the streets at night to find solitary older women to beat up. Here is the middle aged woman who sinks into this state and secretly goes to parties where she engages in perverse sexual practices. Here is the voyeur who peeks in windows, the sadist who disembowels cats, the responsible father who carries out burglaries while in this state of thrilling transgression.

When the person is in this state, the feelings are those of a strange kind of heightened excitement, a tingling sense of nerve-edged dangerousness, a kind of pressured stimulation. In addition, however, relationships between the extruded deeper potential and the disengaged operating domain are terribly disintegrative. It is as if the presented form is the grotesque gargoyle of the deeper potential. This is not the form in which the deeper potential *can* appear, for the process of integration radically alters the deeper potential into a form which is significantly different. The new, integrated form is one which is surrounded with integrated relationships of harmony and oneness, acceptance and love. These are the feelings of integration which replace the feelings of fear and hate which characterized the state in which the thrilling transgression occurred. In addition, the actualization of the transformed potential is accompanied with the same feelings of excitement, aliveness, vitality, but without the pressure, without the nerve-edgedness. Thus the process of actualization will culminate in ways of being which are accompanied with excitement and aliveness, no longer are carried out in hidden secrecy, do not have that sense of fear and hate, and, perhaps most importantly, are significantly different from the behaviorial form in which they occurred in their disintegrative state.

For persons who commit these kinds of acts, actualization means much more than giving in to their transgressions. From their perspective, they are torn apart by prospects of giving in wholly to their secret escapades. That would mean wholeheartedly becoming someone who commits masochistic acts, or maintains a cache of pornographic pictures, or has sexual relations with dogs. While in the throes of these acts, they may feel excitedly alive, but otherwise their reactions are those of fear and fright about becoming that kind of individual. From the perspective of humanistic theory, actualization will bring forth the integrated form of the deeper potential, and it is quite unlikely that what will emerge will have the same behavioral form as before.

What is the nature of the deeper potential behind the wicked transgression? It is a question which requires a great deal of careful analysis of the specific person. For example, suppose that the underlying potential behind one man's transvestite behavior consists of the experiencing of being worshipped and admired as the beautiful sexual being (cf. Fenichel, 1954a). Will the processes of integration and actualization culminate in continued transvestite behavior? The principles of humanistic theory suggest that the process of integration will radically alter the bad form of this deeper potential so that it is almost virtually impossible that the old transvestite behavior will occur following actualization of the integrated potential. Instead, the potential will almost undoubtedly be expressed in a new package of behaviors which provide experiencing of admiring and being admired, worshipping and being worshipped, as a beautiful sexual being. The specific behavioral forms of this actualized expression may include innumerable actions such as being a wonderful lover who is genuinely admired, and even worshipped, as a beautiful sexual person. But it is highly unlikely that the same old transvestite behavior will persist.

The key to what the person becomes is the specific nature of the underlying potential. Suppose that the underlying potential behind the transvestite behavior of another man involved the experiencing of being within a woman, encased safely within her, wholly surrounded by her, wallowing securely within her. In this instance, the processes of integration and actualization would also culminate in the replacement of transvestite behavior with new behaviors. However in this person, actualization was expressed as wholly new behaviors of letting himself be reached by his wife, held and cared for by her; it included allowing himself to rely on women, to be aided and assisted by them; it included his being able to place himself in a dependent, little boy relationship with his older sister and aunt, being physically held by them. Although the nature of the underlying potential will vary, it is clear that the old transvestite behavior will no longer occur—not because it is transvestite behavior, but because it occurred as the disintegrative, bad form of the deeper potential.

The focal point is the nature of the underlying potential, and not the behavior. I have in mind an older man who likewise engaged in transvestite behavior, quite similar to that carried out by the two men described above. However, in this third fellow, the underlying potential involved the experiencing of taking, of getting something for himself, of assertively making it his. The act of stealing women's clothing carried the peak feelings in his transvestite behavior. In addition, this same potential appeared to be expressed in a number of other acts, each of which was accompanied with peaked excitement and followed by periods of depression and guilt and self-punishment. In the course of integration this potential was transformed, and when actualization of the new good form occurred, the transvestite behavior was replaced with new behaviors which provided for the experiencing of taking, getting something for himself, assertively making something his. In many behavioral ways, he now acted much more assertively, was more aggressive and self-confident. The new behaviors were accompanied with even greater feelings of aliveness and excitement, but in addition there was a bed of feelings of togetherness, being organized and more of his own self, of internal peace and happiness.

Such "wicked transgressions" often involve other persons. It is quite possible that transvestite behavior can occur virtually free of interpersonal effects upon others. But typically the worlds in which these persons live—the secret voyeur, the secret sadist, the secret homosexual, the secret burglar—contain relationships with others. Whether or not these others are victims, they are affected by the wicked transgressions, and the processes of integration and actualization profoundly alter their own lives. Because the potential is now integrated, its actualization no longer has the effect of constructing disintegrative relationships with others. It does not act to incite or induce others to fear or hate. It does not serve to arouse pain or hurt or distress or turmoil. Its disintegrative nature is ended, and that removes its bad hooks from others. There is no further working up of others to engage in or to participate in disintegrative relationships with the person. He does not push at the other individual, restlessly dig at the other individual, or work upon him to construct difficulties and problems. There is, instead, an integrative letting the other individual be, an integrative I-thou relationship of equal stature, a more tranquil integrative contact. There is a characteristic of being-one-with the other individual.

These are characteristics of *integrating* persons. It is because the potentials which are expressed are *integrated* that the actualizing person does not harm me or make me fearful or hateful or torn apart. The reasons have nothing to do with the core content or nature of the actualized potentials. Actualizing persons do not mysteriously acquire new potentials of piety, goodness, virtue, wisdom and understanding. They do not acquire potentials for providing for my peaceful existence or my belongingness (cf. Goldstein, 1939). They do not acquire potentials which *I* would want in order for *me* to be happy, satisfied, relieved, or tranquil. Instead, they no longer contribute to my disintegration because whatever potentials they actualize are now *integrated*.

The key here is the integrated nature of the potential, and its experiencing in a manner which bespeaks of integration, not disintegration. This is the key in the description of some so-called primitive cultures in which supposedly deeper potentials are expressed in ways which are characterized as open and free and comfortable (e.g., Leighton & Hughes, 1961). According to many of the descriptions of these "primitive" cultures, they are "healthier" than ours by virtue of that more *integrated* expression of deeper potentials. From the perspective of humanistic theory, actualization refers to the experiencing of *integrated* potentials, and not to those which are glutted with disintegration. I agree that it is "healthier" to actualize potentials which are integrated—and that it is "unhealthy" to actualize potentials which are disintegrated. In the expression of potentials, the key is the encompassing integration (or disintegration) rather than the specific content of the inner core of the expressed potential. From our perspective there is nothing of value in "expressing basic drives." What *is* of value is the actualization of deeper potentials which are *integrated*.

The actualization of an integrated potential must carefully be distinguished from seeking to justify the way one is by rather shallow credos about "letting it all hang out," or "expressing one's feelings," or "being authentic." The behavior to which these credos refer typically arises out of internal disintegration, and exudes fear and hate as the person exhibits himself sexually, ridicules the old ways, steals, lies, is deceitful, is disrespectful, is destructive. When the integrated person actualizes a potential, it *is* on the basis of expressing what is within, of being guided by one's inner feelings, of actualizing what there is to be actualized. When the *disintegrated* person *talks about* actualization, it is a lie, a defensive justification for being the awful way he is. Thus the actualizing of integrated potentials can be cheapened and misused by non-integrated, non-actualizing persons to dignify their obnoxious ways of being. It is unlikely that the integrated person will spit on you, insult you, rob you, murder you, ridicule you, or make you hateful and fearful—and then justify the carnage as his way of expressing his feelings, being himself, or "letting it all hang out."

Yet the actualizing person does not necessarily follow social norms. Because the process of actualization deals with the raw materials produced by integration, the relationship of the person to social norms is marked by essential harmony and congruence. Whether or not the actualizing person manifests the behavioral characteristics framed within a set of social norms, whether he behaves in "normal" or "abnormal" ways, his integration reduces the possibilities of dissonance. Thus the *quality* of the actualizing person's relationship with social norms is one of harmony and congruence. But what of the *nature* of his behavior? Does he move into increasing or decreasing coincidence with social norms? Humanistic theory joins with other theories in regarding social norms as neither the *valued* nor the *expected* outcome of personality development and change (e.g. Bandura, 1961; Fromm-Reichmann, 1958, p. 32; Jung, 1933). Our theory allows for the actualization of a person who either conforms to social norms or who is "abnormal," in this sense. There is no necessary reason for actualization to produce either kind of person. But softer reasons make it far more likely that actualization will yield persons who differ sharply from social norms. Prominent among these reasons is the presence of increasingly deeper potentials. Actualization of these potentials almost inevitably produces persons who differ—in integrated ways—from social norms. If anything, the process of actualization *widens* the (integrative) gap between the person and social norms.

In summary, the actualization of integrated potentials does not produce destructive animals who explode primitive impulses onto helpless victims. Actualizers are neither uncivilized hedonists, evil devils, nor asocial savages. Because the potentials are *integrated*, they are not filled with harmful violations of other individuals.

Depth and Breadth of Experiencing

We have been discussing the interconnections between actualization and integration. Now we turn to actualizing persons themselves, and to the nature of actualization itself. Perhaps the paramount characteristic of actualization is the sheer increase in the depth and breadth of experiencing. As the process of actualization continues, more and more of the person's potentials are thrust forward into experiencing. If we record the proportion of *all* the potentials which are experienced, the non-actualizing person will experience a low proportion (e.g. 5-10%) over a period of time. In contrast, the actualizing person will experience a significantly larger proportion of his potentials, for example, 30% or 50% or more. As actualization proceeds, the depth and breadth of experiencing increase.

Structurally, actualization involves bringing deeper potentials into the realm of the operating potentials (B, Figure 12.1), where they are ready for experiencing. Thus the process of actualization is one of movement into the realm of operating potentials, and from there into actual experiencing. In other words, the domain of the operating potentials stretches outward to encompass more and more of the deeper potentials. It is this process which leads to increasing depth and breadth of experiencing.

Operating potentials are functionally tied to deeper potentials. These functions consist of *providing for* and also *truncating* the experiencing of the deeper potentials. When we consider functional sets of operating and deeper potentials, human beings seem characterized by a general state of curtailed experiencing, a state in which they experience pitifully little of what they are capable of experiencing. In Figure 12.1, for example, the ordinary person gains only slight experiencing of potentials 2, 4, and 6, and virtually no experiencing of basic potentials 7 and 8. A few deeper potentials are typically served by a set of operating potentials so that, at the operating level, there may be a moderate range of experiencing, whereas at the deeper level the range is quite limited. A deeper potential for experiencing control may be served by operating potentials for experiencing organization and structure, for experiencing leadership, and for experiencing sexual dominance. Through these several operating potentials, there is a modicum of experiencing of the underlying control. As actualization progresses, there is an increase in the number of sets of these couplings. This is represented by the increase from three operating potentials (A, Figure 12.1) to five (B, Figure 12.1). Functionally the change is from narrowed and constructed experiencing to greater depth and breadth of experiencing. Too many persons live out their entire existences without experiencing much of what they have available to experience. Actualization offers the possibility of a deepening and a broadening of the scope of available experiencing.

In this process, there is a regular dissolution of current operating potentials. No longer do they serve as the interveners between the deeper potentials and the external world. There is no further need for them to provide experiencing of the deeper potential, nor to carry out the function of reducing its experiencing. Whether the operating potential primarily serves the former or the latter function, its sheer presence attenuates the degree to which the deeper potential can be experienced. Structurally, then, the process of actualization leads to the washing away of the operating potentials. As indicated in Figure 12.1, actualization replaces the old operating potentials with the former deeper ones.

Typically, the replacement of the current operating potential takes place in a series of steps. As the operating potential's depth and breadth of experiencing increase, it generally undergoes a change in its manifested behavioral form. Howard gained a sense of worth, of substance and self-regard, by sheer physical size. He had been a fat little boy and, as an adult, was a heavy big man. He was a school athlete in part because of his sheer bulk. Well over six feet tall, he weighed nearly 250 pounds and played football throughout both high school and university. As he entered in the processes of integration and actualization, a change started to occur in the behavioral ways in which that operating potential was experienced. Sheer bodily bulk seemed to mean less and less, and he found himself taking increasing responsibility at work in the factory. Not long thereafter he was asked to be shop foreman and union representative. With these changes there occurred a deepening and broadening of the sense of substance. He felt quite different now, much better. Then, a more dramatic change began intruding into his life as the deeper potential moved upward. This had consisted of a feared and hated deep sense of being utterly worthless, being rejected and discounted. Slowly that deeper potential was transformed into a sense of freedom and independence.

With this transformation came a dissolving away of the former operating potential for having to confirm his substance and worth. With this, the meaningfulness and importance of sheer physical bulk, of being listened to and respected, of being a responsible person, dissolved away. In its place occurred a new experiencing of personal independence and freedom, the former deeper potential which had been buried throughout his previous life. Increased depth and breadth of experiencing the operating potential not only modify its behavioral manifestation, but also bring forth the deeper potential which then replaces the former operating potential.

Phrased in other vocabularies, this process of increasing depth and breadth of experiencing has been described as the bringing into being of the person's own complement of motivations (Maslow, 1970b) or unique pattern of possibilities (May, 1958b). Boss speaks of the person's becoming in actuality what is within as a potential (1963, p. 15). Rogers (1963) describes this process as becoming fully open to one's experiencings, to the experiencings occurring within the person, as freely living the experiences of the total organism. A similar thread of commonality is found in the conception of personality change as the satisfaction of basic personality processes, the fulfillment of deeper instinctual wishes (Freud, 1953, p. 568; Freud, 1959). Jung describes it as a development of the unrealized creative potentials (1933), a releasing of dormant possibilities (Van Dusen, 1957). Within a Sullivanian framework, there is a setting free of one's capacities for personal growth, creative expansion of one's personality, and self-realization (Bullard, 1959), including the realized full use of one's talents, skills and powers (Fromm-Reichmann, 1958, p. 34). Phrased in different ways by the various vocabularies, actualization as the process of increasing depth and breadth of experiencing has familial relationships and a respectable history.

In each of these vocabularies, actualization is characterized by creation, by bringing forth, by expression. It is a constructing of something new and its opening into the external world. Indeed, in many ways it *is* a process of birth. Little wonder that the actualization which occurs in psychotherapy is frequently accompanied by dreams of birth. Fenichel (1953d) describes these birth dreams, birth fantasies, and dreams of rebirth as often associated with the terminal phase of successful psychoanalyses. Birth and actualization share many common elements, and the description of the birth process is in many ways a description of the process of actualization.

The Goal Is Achieving Higher Levels of Actualization

The value system of humanistic theory. According to humanistic theory, the process of actualization is invested with goodness and value.

Within the realm of psychotherapy, for example, this means that the goal ". . . is less one of treatment than of developing the creative possibilities that lie within the patient himself" (Jung, 1933, p. 61). In general, the valued direction is one which Maslow (1963) describes as finding out who and what one is, and moving in the direction of becoming all that. It is a matter of becoming what is potential within oneself (Boss, 1963, p. 15). What Jung, Maslow, and Boss are describing is a point of agreement among humanistic, psychoanalytic and Zen theories. Each assumes possibilities and potentials which constitute what is within, and hold as the valued direction that of becoming those inner possibilities. Humanistic theory aims at increased depth and breadth of experiencing. Psychoanalytic theory aims at making the unconscious conscious. Zen speaks of the goal as satori, a state which is the extrapolation of the psychoanalytic goal of making the unconscious conscious (Maupin, 1965). To open up and become what is within is the good way, the goal, the definition of the optimal state, both for the person and for collective persons, for the world of the individual and for the interpersonal social worlds of collective persons.

In the field of psychotherapy, the assessment of change requires an explication of the value system of the particular psychotherapeutic approach which is used (Bergin, 1963). Is it desirable or undesirable that there is an increase in the person's depth and breadth of experiencing, or is the goal to be a *lower* and more *even* level of feeling? Is it the aim of psychotherapy for the person to give up many of her former friends, or to become a more central member of the group to which she belongs? How do we know whether ending the marriage or preserving it is a good or bad outcome of psychotherapy? Within the framework of humanistic theory, value lies in that which contributes to heightened depth and breadth of experiencing. Giving up many of her friends is desirable or undesirable depending on the degree to which it expands or narrows the depth and breadth of experiencing. The same value criterion holds for preserving or ending the marriage, or for any other life changes. By invoking this criterion, we are able to define and assess constructive personality change in general, inside or outside of psychotherapy (Truax & Carkhuff, 1967). In addition, such a criterion enables us to define what is desirable for collective persons, for groups, communities and societies.

One may not know, with any high degree of precision, what will come forth as the process of actualization moves the person into increasing depth and breadth of experiencing. Yet the faith is to move increasingly in the direction of becoming what is within. It is this continuous process which defines the valued direction of becoming. To the extent that a theory accepts the existence of deeper potentials, it is likely that the direction of good and value consists in the bringing forth of what is *within*; if, on the other hand, a theory de-emphasizes deeper personality processes, then it is likely that the valued guidelines for change are *external*—such as social ideals, social norms, meeting the demands and expectations of the group (Jung, 1933, p. 44). In humanistic theory, valued guidelines are internal. Indeed, social norms are understood as representing values which typically are set *against* those of increasing depth and breadth of experiencing. Because of the processes which construct social norms (see Chapter 7), "normality" includes much of what is fiercely inconsistent with the goals and values of actualization. Thus, for actualizing persons, ". . . the very thought that you want to educate them toward normality is a nightmare; their deepest need is really to be able to lead 'abnormal' lives" (Jung, 1933, p. 48).

Actualization versus problem reduction. In achieving higher levels of actualization, the aim is to bring into the realm of experiencing the potentials which are present within the person. This process deals with deeper potentials, not located within the operating domain, but residing deeper in the personality. If there is a deeper potential for experiencing naive wonder, surprise, curiosity, then our process brings that potential forth. To the extent that the potential is disintegrated, the process brings it forth in its good, integrated form. To the extent that the potential is virtually unexperienced, the process moves it toward increased depth and breadth of experiencing. It is in this sense that the goal is that of actualizating human potentials—and *not* in the sense of the reduction of human problems. It is consistent with humanistic theory that the processes of integration and actualization offer the most robustly effective means of reducing human problems and stress. But our direct goal is *not* the reduction of problems and stress. The implementation of human potentials adds an invigorating new dimension to the goal of personality change and to the salient mission of professions which address themselves to processes of development and change of the human beings individually and in community.

With regard to behavior, actualization caters exclusively to those behaviors which contribute to heightened depth and breadth of experiencing. For these purposes, actualization is a process of *adding* and *expanding* behaviors. Every potential for experiencing is to be coupled with those (new) behaviors which enable the potential to be experienced. In this sense, actualization must be contrasted with enterprises aimed at *reducing* and *extinguishing* behaviors. Actualization is not the attacking of any behavior for any reason. It does not matter whether the behavior is considered a symptom of psychopathology, self-defeating, unadjustive, neurotic, psychotic, crazy, evil. It does not matter whether the behavior is considered socially wrong, antisocial, contrary to group norms, deviate. The aim is *not* to get rid of any behavior, to make the behavior different, to control it, to bring it into contact with reality. Actualization is not a process for attacking, modifying, changing, controlling, extinguishing, or getting rid of any particular behavior.

Nevertheless, the process of actualization is *accompanied* by the washing away of old behaviors. Indeed, integration and actualization cut away the very foundation of disintegrative behavior, of painful experiential behavior, and of self-preserving behavior—the three classes of painful behavior described in Chapter 10. These twin processes are powerful tools for the reduction of many behaviors even though their work does not involve direct attack upon such behavior. Rather, old behaviors will fall away as the processes get on with their own work. Although actualization does not focus on the old behavior and does not seek to get rid of old behavior, the bringing forth of potentials into heightened experiencing will be accompanied with the dissolving away of old behaviors. When the woman entered into the process of integration, one of her concerns was her inability to fall asleep, her nightmares, and her frightening visions of her recently deceased mother. Integration led to the discovery of inner potentials for her own sense of caring for, nurturing, parenting. As these moved forward into heightened experiencing, the focal concern was on the actualizing of that potential and its articulation through new behaviors. Coupled with both the integration and actualization of that potential was the gradual washing away of the inability to fall asleep, the nightmares, and the frightening visions. Yet these remained outside the center of focal concern throughout the processes of integration and actualization. It is as if these problem behaviors are left behind as the person gets on with the process of actualization, a process which involved behavioral *expression and development, acquisition and utilization.* It is concerned with providing the right behavior, creating the new behavior. Earlier, it was mentioned that goal of actualization is to *bring forth* potentials rather than to attack, eliminate, reduce or extinguish. With regard to behavior, actualization is a process of emergence and development, and is virtually *unable* to eliminate or extinguish or attack old behaviors. Actualization does not and cannot destroy behavior. It cannot attack or eliminate behavior. It is able to add new behavior, and unable to get rid of old ones. By its very nature, actualization is behavioral growth and development.

Painful behaviors which provide a measure of experiencing are replaced by actualization—but that reduction is an epiphenomenon rather than the direct product of actualization. Such behaviors, painful as they are, are often rather effective in providing for the experiencing of a potential. Often these behaviors are extreme or unusual. They include depressive behavior, behaviors which communicate suicidal threats, stuttering, being dull and uncomprehending, anxious behavior, withdrawal behavior, and hundreds of painful ways of being which nevertheless serve to provide for the experiencing of potentials. Actualizing persons begin with whatever level of experiencing is afforded by the existing set of behaviors, and proceed from there. If these painful behaviors offer the highest levels of experiencing a given potential, then it is quite likely that they will persist. Typically, however, these painful behaviors are replaced with other means of gaining even higher levels of experiencing. The former behaviors are not replaced because of their painful nature, but because other behaviors (almost always of a non-painful nature) offer still higher levels of experiencing. For example, one may gain a measure of punitive attack against parents by means of depression and failure in ways which make them feel bad. Although a measure of experiencing is afforded by such behaviors, other behaviors may carry a higher load of experiencing. If one dares to risk higher levels of experiencing, new behaviors become possible, e.g., yelling and screaming at them, being physically aggressive toward them, having it out with them. Such behaviors are generally accompanied with much *less* pain, and with *higher* levels of experiencing. Almost always, painful behavior offers moderate levels of experiencing, and is replaced, in the actualization process, by behaviors offering higher levels of experiencing.

The middle-aged woman was heavy, shrewd, sophisticated, and alcoholic. Her husband had left her many years ago, and she quickly married a man who was much older, kind, and altogether uninspiring. They got along like two strangers. Her alcoholism was painful in many ways. She was pitied by her kindly husband, who hated her for being that way. She found herself slipping increasingly into periods of depression, punctuated by sharp suicidal thoughts. As painful as these ways of being were, they constituted partial means of experiencing a deeper potential for being in control. She had always been in charge of her life, always controlled the next step and then proceeded to enter into that phase of her life. There had been no spontaneity, no real surprise in her life. From the time she was a little girl she lived in a world of fulfilling what others had planned and wanted for her, and, later, of carrying through what she herself had set as her goal. In the course of integration and actualization, she became ready to be the boss of her own fate—in nonpainful ways. It was the beginning of a new life in which she fully experienced a sense of freedom to control her own fate, a sense of being in charge, and a new sense of utter spontaneity. She began to laugh, to be silly, to step out of the marriage and into genuine relationships with other men. She had a great deal of money, and combined a business shrewdness with a delightful doing-what-she-wanted. The old potential had been served by the old behaviors, in painful ways, and were replaced with an array of new behaviors, in ways which were free of pain. And, more importantly, the new array of behaviors offered a heightened level of experiencing.

The Content of Actualized Potentials

As actualization continues, there will be increased depth and breadth of experiencing. This stands as the goal of personality change, the expression of the good life, and the way optimal persons can be. But what is it that the person is like as the process continues its unfolding? All we have said is that there will be heightened levels of experiencing, greater depth and breadth of experiencing. But experiencing of what? What is it that emerges in the course of actualization? What is the content of the potentials which are experienced as a result of the process of actualization?

Resistance, defiance and rebellion. There is a package of behaviors which flow directly out of internal disintegrative relationships among potentials. When relationships are disintegrative, relationships with the external world may be characterized by resistance, defiance, rebellion—as well as avoidance, blockage, denial, and other behavioral expressions of disintegrative relationships. When the process of integration is successful, these disintegrative behaviors are extinguished. However, we must carefully distinguish between such ways of being as a function of *disintegrative relationships*, and these ways of being as descriptive of *potentials*. Some persons have deeper potentials for experiencing resistance, or defiance, or rebellion. When these potentials undergo integration, they are cleansed of their disintegrative aspects, but what is there exists as an experiencing of resisting, not giving in, standing up for oneself, defiance, a capacity for challenging, an aggressivity, a rebelliousness, a self-confident independence. The *form* switches from bad, disintegrative, to good, integrative, but the nature of the potential remains intact. Actualization of these potentials means the *heightened* expression, the *increased* experiencing of all of this. Persons with these deeper potentials become *more* resistive, defiant, and rebellious, whereas integration typically leads to *less* (disintegrative) resistance, defiance, and rebelliousness. The distinction is between these words as descriptive of disintegration or as descriptive of the actualization of particular potentials.

This distinction is especially relevant to psychotherapy, for it is all too easy to miss the nascent potential in regarding resistance, defiance, and rebelliousness as evidence of the person's problems. In general, psychotherapists tend to mould patients into being persons who are not defiant, rebellious, and resistant. Or, if such ways of being are encouraged, they are emasculated, and made into toothless virgins, filled with niceness, sweetness, and light. Their edge is removed, and they are sent on their feckless way. What is more, the very structure of psychotherapy forces *virtually every expression* of defiance, resistance, and rebelliousness to occur either in relationship to the psychotherapist or in relationship to the patient's own internal processes. In this connection, psychotherapists wage war against patients' expressions of resistance, rebellion, and defiance because they are regarded as evidence of a wrong or bad or incomplete patient-therapist relationship. Thus the patient is scolded, interpreted, fooled, punished, pressured into not being that way. Good patients do not openly defy therapists, they do not evidence resistance to the therapist, and they certainly do not rebel against the therapist. Virtually every school of psychotherapy finds ways of "dealing" or "handling" patients' defiance, resistance, and rebellion. From the perspective of humanistic theory, the critical and precious distinction is between these ways of being as manifestations of disintegrative internal relationships among potentials—which are quite common—and as manifestations of a deeper potential. As a general rule, both the theory and the strategy of nearly all psychotherapies fail to acknowledge this distinction, and therefore are not equipped to see any alternative to psychotherapeutic war against these ways of being. A theory and strategy of psychotherapy are in order which can be sensitively and accurately receptive to the distinction between defiance, resistance, and rebelliousness as expressions of internal disintegrative relationships and as expressions of very particular potentials. Actualization yields increasing depth and breadth of all potentials of experiencing, regardless of their content. Even when the content is that of resistance, defiance and rebellion, the process opens the way for such modes of experiencing.

Freedom of movement among potentials. To experience potentials with increasing breadth and depth means that there is a "freedom to be" potentials which seem contradictory, inconsistent, even polar to one another. We cannot say what the precise content of these potentials will be, but we can understand the actualizing person as fully capable of moving into and out of each of the operating potentials (B, Figure 12.1). If he has potentials for experiencing dominance *and* submission, then he becomes capable of shifting from one to the other. He has the capacity for being gregarious and being solitary, being a business leader and playing marbles with the kids, being homosexual and heterosexual, being radical and being conservative. Because his range of potentials is broad, he is quite capable of smoothly shifting into and out of potentials which seem to us to be opposite or inconsistent with one another. Thus the actualizing person may well appear to be unpredictable, fluctuating, and inconsistent (Rogers, 1963) as he moves easily among potentials which do not exist together as friendly neighbors and ordinary persons.

Not only does the person shift easily from one operating potential to another, but he is also able to move from full experiencing of the operating potential to the subsequent experiencing of the deeper potential to which it is functionally related. The experiential actualization of one operating potential leads smoothly to the possibility of experiencing its deeper potential, so that, in the actualizing person, there is a smooth transition from the completed experiencing of the operating potential to the experiencing of the deeper potential. In integration, one can shift into and out of one's potentials; in actualization, one adds to this capacity that of fully *experiencing* each deeper potential in turn. We must also distinguish this capacity from the *having*-to-shift from one operating potential to another as the person endlessly travels round and round the behavioral circle (Chapter 9). Yet the quality of freedom of movement among potentials tells us nothing of the *content* of the potentials which are actualized.

Factors determining the content of actualized potentials. Actualizing persons function more and more on the basis of deeper potentials. Does this mean that there is progressively increasing similarity among actualizing persons? Is it possible to construct a list of potentials characteristic of actualizing persons? Are there "universal" basic potentials which are experienced as persons become increasingly actualized? Can we predict what actualizing persons will be like as they progress further and further along the avenue of actualization? From the perspective of humanistic theory, the answer to each of these questions is no. As will be discussed in detail in Chapters 13-15, there is no necessary theoretical basis for universality or uniformity or even similarity across the basic potentials of individuals. My basic potentials may be similar to or quite different from yours. The answers to the above questions hinge on the degree to which there is any theoretical basis for similarity across the basic potentials of individuals. Since humanistic theory postulates *no basis* for universal basic potentials, and since the determinants of basic potentials provide considerable room for strong *differences* (see Chapter 14), then it becomes clear that we have no theoretical basis for making predictions about the kinds of potentials which will emerge as persons move further and further along the pathway of actualization. There are no universal basic potentials which are experienced as persons become increasingly actualized. It therefore is not possible to construct a list of potentials characteristic of actualizing persons.

Once we dismiss the assumption of universal basic needs or drives or motivations or potentials (Chapter 4), the above questions are rather easily answered. But some humanistic psychologists accept basic human tendencies, with certain ones more readily actualizable than others. For example, Buhler (1968, p. 401) identifies sex, love, and accomplishment as among those basic human tendencies which are more readily actualizable. Therefore, according to Buhler, progressive actualization ought to produce persons who show increasing similarity along the lines of sex, love, and accomplishment. In contrast, we make no such assumption. As persons move along the pathway of actualization, there is no basis for predicting that they will function along those lines, manifest those particular motivations, or exhibit those particular basic human tendencies to any degree.

As discussed in Chapter 4, humanistic theory rejects an assumption that there are basic needs or drives whose nature, for example, is biological or neurophysiological. Once this assumption is rejected, there is no basis for presuming that actualization will culminate in increasing similarity along lines which are biological or neurophysiological. If a theory holds a conception of biologically grounded developmental stages, that theory is convinced that actualizing persons will move away from infancy, away from childhood, and toward a biological conception of maturity. In contrast, humanistic theory understands that the nature of basic potentials may well include those which are considered to be *characteristic* of infancy or childhood. It is quite possible, for example, for actualization to culminate in basic motivations of simple (childlike) trust in others, simple (childlike) dependency, a simple (childlike) capacity for experiencing events as new and fresh, a capacity for (childlike) awe and wonder, and other potentials for experiencing which commonly are associated with infancy and childhood. Indeed, it is quite likely that actualization will culminate in *increased* expression of experiencings characteristic of infancy and childhood—if that is the content of the person's basic potentials.

As actualization proceeds, there is a progressive expression of deeper and deeper potentials until basic ones (BP7, BP8, Figure 12.1) are lifted to the operating level and actualized. From our perspective, basic potentials across individuals are not necessarily similar because of universal basic needs, common biological or neurophysiological intrinsic nature, or any such notions of the human personality and its foundation. If we find that the actualization process reveals a fair degree of similarity among progressively deeper potentials across persons, I would regard this as an *empirical* finding and not evidence in support of the above conceptions about human nature. Such an empirical finding would suggest to me merely that the factors which account for the nature of the basic potentials bear some similarity across individuals. These factors are discussed in Chapters 13-15, but it is important to recognize that these factors have nothing to do with some predetermined, intrinsic, biological, common nature of basic potentials. Therefore, humanistic theory holds that there will be *no necessary similarity* among actualizing persons; depending upon the factors which determine the particular nature of basic potentials, actualizing persons may become progressively more *or* less similar to one another. On the basis of *theoretical assumptions* about the intrinsic nature of basic potentials, humanistic theory cannot construct a list of basic characteristics of actualizing persons. Answers to these questions depend upon *empirical* factors rather than *theoretical assumptions* about the intrinsic nature of basic potentials.

Whatever is the given content of a person's basic potentials, actualization comes to a close with their experiencing (B, Figure 12.1). This is the culmination. If a person's structure includes four basic potentials, then the full experiencing of the integrated forms of these four basic potentials is the pinnacle of actualization. These four constitute and delimit what that person can be, and he can be no more than that. He cannot be all things, cannot be all possibilities. These four basic potentials constitute what has been termed the "ground" of his existence. In, for example, his study of Ellen West, the basic potentials constitute the ". . . being . . . into which she had actually been thrown from the ground of her existence" (Binswanger, 1958c, p. 298). That ground of one's existence, that set of basic potentials, stands as the ultimate possibility of what the person can become, the ultimate expression of my possible destiny. There is nothing more.

Grasping the nature of these basic potentials is the function of understanding, the searching for the deepest possibilities of what the person can be. In this search, we may enter into the past to understand what there is which had been experienced, or which started to be experienced. The past reveals the potentials which are there; it does not constitute factors which shape the content of deeper potentials so much as it constitutes the stage upon which they play out their roles. In this sense, ". . . we must understand by the past in the existential sense the has-been, which decides that we not only have been but actually *are* from the viewpoint of 'has-been.' In this 'having-been' are founded the capabilities by virtue of which the existence exists. Indeed, existence does not mean being-on-hand, but being-able-to-be, and to know about this being-able-to-be means understanding" (Binswanger, 1958c, pp. 302, 303). By entering correctly into the enlivened past, we understand the content of the deeper, and the basic, potentials. We witness them occurring, and we know what they are.

In this search for the nature of basic potentials, one begins with a clean slate. It is a matter of being fully open to whatever is revealed. One begins with no hunches or guesses or expectations. Any theoretical expectations, any preconceptions of what persons are like or even what this particular person must be like, are confounding errors. The method of phenomenological search and descriptive discovery of the precise deepest potential of this particular person admits of no favor for any kind of preconception. We come to know by a rigorous naivete, allowing ourselves to see whatever is there to be seen.

But this is a knowing from the vantage point of the other. It is virtually impossible to see one's own deepest potentials, for every hint is from the side, as it were. It is possible to predict only to a point, and one which falls a good deal short of what actually will occur, for the final factor which determines the actualized deepest potential is the immediate, here-and-now total experiencing of it. The person is poured into experiencing to such an extent that there is no removed residual to regard what is going on, to think about it from a removed vantage point. A part of the meaning of being integrated is that one is no longer in a position to judge the other potential. Thus when the integrated potential is actualized, you are not there to judge what it is like. It is, therefore, virtually impossible to predict what the actualized deeper or basic potential will be.

The person who is actualizing is *thrown* into experiencing. In actualizing my potential for experiencing loving, I am wholly cast into loving. I am being. I am wholly within the actualizing potential. The center of my self is the experiencing. It is a thrust-into. To the extent that the very process of actualization leads to changes, I cannot look ahead to what I shall be when I am *in* the process of actualization itself. I cannot consider the changes which may occur in me in the course of actualization. There is, then, a commitment, a faith, in the process of actualization. When the person is in this process, is being actualizing, nothing can occur which requires that the center of personhood be separated. One cannot consider the facts. One cannot make decisions or think about oneself. One cannot have insight into what one is like. One cannot make guesses about what one might become through the process of actualization. When I am in the process of *integration*, I *can* see into my insides. I *can* discover something which has the form and shape of loving. I can regard it and have reactive feelings about it—a pain for all the lost moments, or a scary fear of what being that would mean for the person I am. But when I hurl myself into the actualizing being of the experiencing of loving, I am nothing but the experiencing of my loving-ness. Before I hurl myself into the experience of loving, I know that I may be made different by the actualizing of my loving. The resolve to go ahead is a leap of faith. While I am leaping, my eyes are closed and I jump into the deep chasm. I know only that I will experience loving in the course of the actualization, but I do not know who or what I shall be when and if the actualization is over. That is the faith in the ongoing process of actualization itself.

When I am actualizing, I cannot make important life decisions. I am being, experiencing. I am not quietly standing to the side, viewing my potentials and my world. As Maslow sketches out the making of important life decisions, ". . . ultimately, the best way for a person to discover what he ought to do is to find out who and what he is, because the path to ethical and value decisions, to wiser choices, to oughtness, is via isness, via the discovery of facts, truth, reality, the nature of the particular person" (1963, p. 120). Actualization is *not* equipped to do this for the person. It is not able to help the person see what he is like, discover what is within, arrive at wise choices in the major decisions of living. Actualization closes down the self which considers, weighs possibilities. It is not a cerebral or contemplative process.

Behavior and Actualization

Actualization is heightened depth and breadth of experiencing. It is in this process that behavior is not only essential, but in which behavior attains its highest stature. We turn now to a discussion of the role of behavior in the process of actualization.

Behavior and the appropriate situational context. The process of integration has a great deal to do with the external world, and exerts profound changes in the external world. With regard to actualization, the external world plays a key role—i.e., it must constitute an appropriate situational context in which the actualization process occurs. Increasing depth and breadth of experiencing *requires* that the external world provide the right context, and, therefore, the external world is intimately connected with actualization in a necessary causal way. Whereas *integration* can occur without involvement of the external world, the process of *actualization* requires proper involvement of the external world.

In this enterprise, there is a necessary intimate interconnectiveness of potential, behavior, and the external world. Actualization occurs only when all three are properly present. With a potential present and ready, and in the appropriate situational context, the key final component is behavior. One must do, must act, must express it behaviorally. Behavior, of the proper sort, and in the appropriate situational context, is the necessary ingredient. But behavior is not the passive third party in this trio, for one of the intimate causal connections is between behavior *and*, not only *in*, the appropriate situational context. In outlining the roles and functions of the external world (Chapter 6), I described the external world as either serving as an extended personality (that is, an extension of operating or deeper potentials), or as a context for experiencing. It is this latter role or function that is required for the process of actualization to go forward. Every potential requires a proper context for its experiencing. Thus, in the actualization of (integrated) potentials, the external world serves as the appropriate situational context—and not as a reservoir for the housing of extended or externalized operating or deeper potentials.

The appropriate situational context is *constructed* by means of behavior. The behavior of actualizing persons is characterized by the quality of building the appropriate situational context—as the behavior serves to provide depth and breadth of experiencing. In an important sense, the same behavior thus has an inside and an outside face. Inside, the behavior makes the potential come alive; the behavior enables depth and breadth of experiencing. Outside, the behavior— the same behavior—builds situational contexts wherein that potential is experienced in heightened depth and breadth. In this sense, it is the *person* who owns and determines the situation, and not the situation which owns and determines the behavior of the person. The actualizing person thus has a measure of situational flexibility in that he is able to behave in more or less organized ways in varied situations, and has the capability of extricating himself from inappropriate situations (Mailloux, 1953). He is the determiner and the active utilizer of situations, instead of being the pawn of situational contexts. He has the capacity for stepping back away from situations which do not provide appropriate contexts for experiencing. Not only is there the quality of declining the invitations offered by inappropriate situations, but the actualizing person is often marked by a quality of detachment from those components of the external world which fail to offer experiential actualization (cf. Byles, 1962).

Experiencing involves the right intimate involvement with the external world. It is the connection with the encompassing external world which carries the possibility of heightened experiencing. Thus experiencing is *truncated* from the very start when the context is limited to oneself. This is not true with regard to internal integration, for that process can carry forward most effectively with oneself. But with regard to actualization, the arena must be enlarged. Regardless of the nature of the potential, it must be experienced within the proper external context. Affection, competitiveness, sexuality, independence, destructiveness, or any other kind of potential requires the proper *external* context, and not oneself. When one's own person is the target, the context, experiencing is inevitably truncated and attenuated from the very start. I am referring especially to those interactions wherein the object (situational context) of one's behavior is one's own physical being. It is attenuating to be affectionate to only one's own physical being, for the object of one's competitiveness, sexuality, independence, destructiveness, or any other potential to be one's own physical being. When the external situational context is coterminal with one's own physical being, depth and breadth of experiencing are narrowed and constricted.

On the other hand, *optimal* interpersonal relationships are those in which each person constitutes the appropriate situational context for the actualization of the potentials of the other. In optimal dyadic or group relations, each participant gains increasing depth and breadth of integrated experiencing by virtue of the context of the other(s). I gain increased depth and breadth of experiencing because of you, and you gain increased depth and breadth of experiencing because of me. Because we are integrating, our relationships are characterized by integration, but we offer much more than that to one another. We conjointly offer contexts wherein you and I both are actualizing with increasing depth and breadth of experiencing. It is this which now serves as the guideline for assessing good interpersonal relations—whether for a dyad, a small group, a community, or a society. My sheer presence can either constrict or dilate the depth and breadth of your experiencing, and your sheer presence can do either for me. We can serve as the appropriate situational contexts for one another—and our behavior serves to construct and maintain these situations for one another.

I expect that actualizing persons will construct new social institutions which are virtually absent in our present societies. I expect that actualizing persons will construct new kinds of "psychological families" or primary groups whose predominant feature will be that of providing for the mutual actualization of each of its members (Mahrer, 1970e, 1971b, 1972a, Mahrer & Pearson, 1971b). These groups will be organized by collective persons who constitute appropriate situational contexts for mutual actualization of one another. I move ahead because of the context which contains you all, and each of you moves ahead because of the context which includes me. Without effortful working at the construction of such groups, without someone external to these groups being instrumental in their construction, I can foresee their construction by collective persons themselves. These psychological families will either replace or complement traditional families as optimal persons live with one another in small groups which facilitate actualization among its collective members.

The highest levels of interpersonal relationships are those characterized by integration *and actualization*. This kind of relationship exceeds one of integrative love, mutual integrative oneness, and mutual integrative being-one-with. Because of the nature of actualization, these highest levels of interpersonal relationships are *also* characterized by mutual contexts enabling each participant toward increasing depth and breadth of experiencing. When relationships are of this order, they define the highest and most valued interpersonal relations available to human beings.

The compellingness for new behavior. Behavior and appropriate situational contexts are interconnected in a friendly manner. Behavior constructs and maintains the appropriate situational context, and the appropriate situational context exerts a kind of pull for the emergence of the right behavior. That is, behavior which enables heightened depth and breadth of experiencing constructs conditions which in turn pull for the emergence of new behavior. In the process of actualization, there is an intimate causal relatedness among (a) depth and breadth of experiencing, (b) the appropriate situational context, and (c) behavior. Each is a function of the other, and each paves the way for the further occurrence of the other.

Indeed, actualization compels behavioral expression, for the specifically right behavior is the necessary key to the experiencing of the potential. Each occurrence of actualization requires behavior, requires the right behavior, and cannot occur without the presence of the right behavior. The whole process of actualization is a clearing away of blockages to effective behavioral action, and not a monastic withdrawal into contemplation (e.g., Maupin, 1965). Thus actualization is both the product and the producer of new behavior. What is more, a potential which is at the operating level and which is in the appropriate situational context is *ready* for the final link, the right behavior. In these conditions, the acquiring of new behaviors is relatively easy, although the human sciences make behavioral change a major battle. In these human sciences, one works at modifying behavior, jamming it onto the person, subjecting him to endless psychotherapy, group forces, or social influence to budge the slightest behavioral change. In contrast, the process is reversed when the potential is there in the appropriate situational context. Then the question is one of locating behavior which can do the experiential job. Although there is no actualization *force*, no intrinsic force shoving the person along the road to actualization, these conditions are tantamount to a virtual hunger for the right behavior, as if the potential *wants* the right behavior to provide for its immediate experiencing in this state of behavioral "need." At this proper moment, behaviors can be acquired (modified, changed) with surprising ease, for the readiness of the potential and the context of the appropriate situation constitute conditions compelling the emergence of the right behavior.

Here is where humanistic theory and behavioral theory meet. Once the process of integration is over, and once the potential is ready for actualization in the appropriate situational context, the focus is on the outfitting of new behavior and *not* on the potential. We have done as much as we can for the potential. Now all efforts are targeted upon the engaging of the right behavior. Bandura is representative of behavioral theorists who likewise set the focus as the engagement of the new behavior and not the modifying of the motivation; ". . . it is not the underlying motivations that need to be altered or removed, but rather the ways in which the patient has learned to gratify his needs. Thus, for example, if the patient displays deviant sexual behavior, the goal is not the removal of the underlying causes, i.e. sexual motivation, but rather the substitution of more socially approved instrumental and goal responses" (1961, p. 153). Our commonality lies in the importance of new behaviors rather than work on the motivations or personality processes. In this focus on behavioral occurrence, humanistic theory works under conditions friendly to and compelling for new behaviors, whereas behavior modification approaches work under conditions in which the forces of the behavior modificationist must overcome the forces of the person whose behavior is to be modified. Yet in both, the central focus now is the new behavior.

According to humanistic theory, first the person changes, then behavior changes. First integration and processes of actualization occur, then appropriate behavioral changes *follow*. In general, the magnitude of the consequent behavioral change is a function of the magnitude of the propaedautic internal change. Consider, for example, the adolescent in whom integration evolves a new operating potential for being a leader; under these conditions, whole new sets of appropriate leadership behaviors will be ready to occur. The readiness for new behavior depends upon the degree to which the operating domain is changed and enlarged. Such a principle has yet to be adopted into the bulk of the learning theories, for they persist in holding the person fixed while seeking to modify the behavior (e.g., Thoresen & Mahoney, 1974). From our perspective, the person who is most cordial to behavioral change is the person who has already undergone internal integration and initial processes of actualization.

The nature of the new behavior. We can state that actualization will be coupled with the occurrence of new behavior, but there is no substantial basis for constructing a list of the specific *behaviors* characteristic of actualizing persons. Since we can not articulate a list of the *potentials* characteristic of actualizing persons, there is virtually no basis for setting forth any list of specific behaviors. Humanistic theory is unable to propose lists of optimal behaviors analogous to those supplied by other approaches (cf. Whitehorn, 1959, p. 5).

Even if we knew the particular content of the person's deeper potentials, we would not be able to define the precise behaviors which would provide for the highest levels of experiencing. The more we know about the nature of the particular potential, the more we are enabled to make good guesses about the ideal kinds of behaviors. Yet there is always room for much more precision. If we know that the deeper potential relates to affection, we would be in no position whatsoever to make guesses about the kinds of ideal behaviors. If we study the deeper potential further, and understand a potential for affec-

tionate understanding and warmth, a loving expressiveness, an affec-
tion-giving, a capacity for physical affection—then we can frame certain guesses about the kinds of behaviors which would enable higher
levels of that experiencing. But even then, we would not know the
nature of the appropriate situational contexts in which the experiencing of affection can optimally occur. It may involve situational contexts of the early family—parents and siblings. It may involve her own
children, or friends of hers, or her husband. It may involve places
such as her cabin or her garden or special rooms in her home. It may
involve small groups in which she elects to participate. The study of
the deeper potential itself cannot enable us to specify the precise
appropriate situational contexts. Finally, the deeper potential itself
does not contain the necessary behaviors which provide for the highest levels of experiencing. It may come about through physical
touchings, facial expressions, words, or subtle movements and gestures—which open the way to highest levels of experiencing. Even if
we knew the full nature of the person's deeper potential, we would
know very little about the nature of specific behaviors which promote
experiencing of that potential.

For the individual person, the actualizing of deeper potentials will
mean the development of new and different behaviors. These potentials are new to the operating domain, and the behaviors which provide for their experiencing will likewise be new. These new behaviors
will sweep across the spectrum of behavioral categories, and can include changes in perceptual motor behavior, intellectual and cognitive
behavior, problem-solving and conceptual behavior (Mahrer, 1957,
1958). No realm of behavior is excluded, for the process of actualization calls for any behavior which effectively does the job.

Although we cannot provide a list of the specific behaviors manifested by actualizing persons, there are more or less uniformities in
what may be termed the *style* of the behaviors. For example, their behaviors are marked by qualities of directness, straightforwardness and
candidness rather than being indirect, devious, misleading, circuitous.
As a rather extreme example, the disintegrative person with a deeper
potential for being free, not pushed out of shape, not violated, may
behave in ways which express this potential in circuitous and indirect
behavior. The person may be withdrawn and unreachable, utilize
bizarre ways of communicating, be illogical and incoherent. After integration and actualization of this potential, the new behavior now has
a directness to it. He is now able to say no, to be direct in refusing to
be pushed out of shape, to communicate what he thinks and feels in
direct and straightforward ways. This is the person who now is able to
say: "You are crowding me too much; I need breathing space," where
before he would respond in misleading and incoherent ways which
had the effect of keeping the other person at a distance.

Intensity of Experiencing

The process of actualization incorporates deeper and deeper potentials (depth), and spreads out to include more and more potentials (breadth). If we focus on a given potential, actualization means that it is experienced with a high degree of strength, fullness, saturation, magnitude. Whatever its nature or content, actualization enriches the experiencing, makes it occur all-the-way. Complementing actualization as heightened depth and breadth of experiencing, actualization is also heightened *intensity* of experiencing.

Such a quality is virtually absent in the lives of most human beings. Instead of intense experiencing of *potentials*, human beings typically undergo little more than the risings and fallings of disintegrative *feelings* as they proceed round and round the behavioral circle. Seldom is there any substantial experiencing of the actual potential itself. Actualization changes all that. Now the *potential* is experienced, instead of risings and fallings in anxiety, fear, depression and all the other kinds of disintegrative *feelings*. Almost inevitably, these constitute new kinds of experiencings, with periods of prolonged and dilated experiencing. Sexual passion may have been experienced for a few seconds; now that peak plateau of sexual passion is experienced for minutes or hours. A new level of *intensity* is reached.

It must be clear that it is the *potential* that is experienced; it is more than the having of feelings. It must also be clear that the potential is one which is *integrated*, not one which is disintegrated. I make these distinctions because some persons know their own painful meaning of intense experiencing, and the promise of prolonged periods of such intense experiencing constitutes the worst kind of hell. With regard to the first distinction, many persons know knife-edged terror, catastrophic anxiety, profound depression. They know what it is like to live with such intense and awful disintegrative *feelings*. Indeed, for these persons, it is the diminishing of such intense feelings which is longed for, not the prospects of being saturated with greater intensities of those awful feelings. Many of us live in worlds which periodically plunge us into the worst kinds of intense feelings, but the sharp distinction is between such intensely awful *feelings* and the intense experiencing of *potentials*, *not* the feeling relationships between potentials. There is a world of difference between experiencing sexual passion and undergoing the most horrendous anxiety *about* a deeper potential for experiencing sexual passion. Too many persons who live the awful anxiety seldom if ever experience the sexual passion from which the anxiety recoils. Intensity of experiencing refers to the potential, and not to the having of intense feelings.

Intensity also refers to the experiencing of *integrated* potentials, not disintegrated ones. For example, some persons have the kind of contract with their deeper potentials wherein they step aside in critical moments and permit the deeper potentials to take over. By this maneuver one's self is preserved while the deeper potential prowls the streets in search of someone to kill, or embezzles money from the firm, or searches for a child to sexually overpower. These potentials provide peaks of experiencing, but their forms are severely disintegrative. As a consequence, the experiencing is intense but twisted, jagged, impure. The difference is between the nature of intense experiencing of *integrated* versus *disintegrated* potentials.

Once the person knows what it is like to undergo heightened intensity of experiencing, he is in a position to gauge where he is on this dimension. Actualizing persons experience their potentials with intensity, and their periods of intense experiencing have increased frequency and greater duration. Once we understand what intense experiencing means, we are in a position to measure the degree to which the actualizing person has progressed along this dimension. Whether for purposes of research or for purposes of assessing one's own progress, a systematic assessment can be made of the frequency and duration of the periods of higher levels of intense experiencing. I can judge that I seldom experience intense sexual passion, or that there is increasing frequency and duration to the intense experiencing of sexual passion.

Aside from its frequency and duration, intense experiencing must occur in a situational context which is appropriate and immediate. When this immediateness is combined with the full intensity of experiencing, there is a quality which Gestalt and existential psychotherapists refer to as experiencing "in the now," a living intensely in the immediate moment (Watts, 1960). This is a result of the right behaviors in the right situational context appropriate for the experiencing of the right potential. It is this combination of rightnesses which makes for the sense of immediacy of intense experiencing. Thus intensity of experiencing has a now-ness, a full being in the immediate moment.

In this immediate moment, we can rather systematically assess the degree to which very specific behaviors can do the job. Here is the potential for experiencing love and warm affection. Right now, will this concrete behavior raise the level of intense experiencing? How does that level compare with the level provided by another concrete behavior? One may try out various specific and concrete behaviors, all the while assessing what happens to the degree of intense experiencing. Effective behaviors are those which raise the level of intense experiencing of that particular potential. If we focus on the person's potentials, we may assess the degree to which behaviors are present which open the way toward intense experiencing. Given the same array of potentials, one person may possess an effective set of actualizing behaviors whereas the other person may possess few if any such behaviors. If we focus on behavior, we may assess the efficiency of the behaviors in providing high levels of experiential actualization. On this dimension, some persons' behavioral repertoires may be high and others' low in efficiency of promoting high levels of intense experiencing.

The Feelings of Experiential Actualization

Integration is characterized by one set of feelings—bodily felt events which mark integrated relationships among potentials. These are indicated by the positive signs *between* potentials, in B, Figure 12.1. Actualization is characterized by its own set of feelings—which are similarly bodily felt events. These feelings occur as accompaniments of heightened intensity of experiencing. Inevitably, the intense experiencing of a potential is coupled with the occurrence of these feelings, signified by the positive signs *within* each potential in B, Figure 12.1. Although feelings of integration and actualization both consist of bodily events and both are pleasantly positive, each comprises its own distinctive set of feelings.

The nature and content of the feelings. The following words refer to the nature and content of the good feelings of experiential actualization: aliveness, vitality; physical-bodily lightness, tingling, buoyancy, "high"; excitement, exhilaration, ecstasy, joy; happiness, satisfaction, pleasure; power, force, energy. Each word is to be taken as referring to events of the physical body.

It is interesting that quite similar words are used to describe the state of experiential actualization and the analogous state achieved by following the precepts of Zen. The Zen student first enters a state in which he achieves a disengagement from his self. Following that, he moves into a subsequent state in which he engages or becomes (what I would term) deeper personality processes. This is our state of experiential actualization. It is interesting that the words used in the Zen literature to describe this particular state include feelings of energy, vitality, aliveness, power (Chang, 1959; Herrigel, 1956; Kondo, 1952, 1958). Such similarities in describing both the nature of the state and the attendant feelings perhaps may be taken as a small hint of confirmation. Both humanistic theory and Zen describe this special state in terms of feelings of power, force, energy. Neitzsche has also described the state of fully being one's deepest potentials, and he too finds the heightened intensity of feelings as including that special sense of power (May, 1958a). The literature of meditation and contemplation describe this state in terms of great joy, a sense of being intoxicated, the budding of a golden flower, entering a world of light and brightness, a sense of shining, a feeling of being uplifted and drawn upward (Wilhelm, 1962, pp. 49-51). Such words and phrases refer to a similar set of feelings of experiential actualization, and point both to a common state and also to the lack of a systematic vocabulary for the description of these feelings.

Because of the presence of the good feelings of experiential actualization, the same potential now comes forth in a different style. When experiencing occurs, two distinct sets of events are coupled together. One is the heightened *level* of experiencing the potential—so that one now intensely experiences smashing, or thrusting sexuality, or competitive encounter, or love and affection. But coupled with this experiencing are the good *feelings* of actualization. Thus the actualizing person is characterized by both a heightened intensity in experiencing the potential, and by the having of such good feelings. These feelings constitute the precious added bonus, the difference between experiencing sexuality (or smashing or competitive encounter), and experiencing sexuality with accompanying feelings of aliveness and vitality. It is the difference between affection, and affection swathed in joy and ecstasy. The person now encounters competitively, with excitement and exhilaration, satisfaction and pleasure. Good *experiencings* and good *feelings* of actualization occur together in the actualizing person. As a result, the good feelings add a new dimension to the nature and content of the good experiencing.

In the optimal state of actualization, the person has both the experiencing of the potential (OP2, Figure 12.1) and the good feelings of actualization, signified by the two positive signs within OP2. In the disintegrative state (A, Figure 12.1), not only is that potential *not* experienced, not only are the good feelings of actualization *not* felt, but the person has disintegrative feelings *about* and *instead* of the good feelings of actualization. When the deeper potential (DP2, Figure 12.1) rises close to the operating domain, the person is offered the gift of feeling pleasurable aliveness and excitement. Instead, however, the person will feel anxious or fearful or upset *about* the possibility of feeling pleasure and aliveness and excitement. What is more, in the disintegrative state, the good feelings of actualization are given the quality of wickedness, profanity, unrighteousness, heinousness. When, however, the person moves into an integrative state, and proceeds to actualize the potential, these good feelings of actualization occur in quite a different way. Now the person has them joyfully as friends, instead of recoiling from them as evil. There is a *welcomed* feeling of experiential actualization, instead of a disintegrative avoidance of them as something bad. As a result of welcoming and having these good feelings, instead of recoiling from them and truncating them, there is a simple being of unadulterated aliveness, excitement, pleasure, energy.

Using the feelings as hard data.. Because these good feelings are constituted of physical-bodily events, they possess a bodily locus which is identifiable and localizable. If one attends carefully to their presence, listens quietly for where they are, one can begin identifying the specific bodily site. That feeling of aliveness may occur within the head, filling the entire head region. It may occur all over the back, or in the legs, or in the genitals, or in the upper chest or the stomach. It may occur deep within the viscera or all over the skin of both arms. It may be a tiny area, such as a point of tiny excitement in the middle of the upper chest; it may be an all over sensation of ecstasy. If one listens carefully and is attuned to receive the feelings, one can identify where they are located within the body. Furthermore, one can readily develop skills at becoming an increasingly accurate localizer. At that point the feelings of actualization become reasonably hard data. For example, the person now is in a position to gauge the degree to which he has these good feelings of experiential actualization. Whether one is interested in assessing this for oneself, or whether one is interested in broader research endeavors, these feelings constitute reasonably hard data. Actualizing persons ought to enjoy an increase in these good feelings. It ought to be possible to assess whether these good feelings occur once a day, twice a day, once a week, three times a month. One should be able to assess whether they take up ten seconds or four hours a week. I have, for example, no systematic basis for estimating whether ordinary person have these particular feelings at all, or only for a few seconds or so, in the course of two or three days. I have no idea whether actualizing persons increase the degree of these feelings a little bit or a lot, or perhaps not at all. We need a considerable body of data on simple questions relating to the occurrence of such feelings in various persons under various conditions. To the extent that we can identify such feelings as accompaniments to higher levels of intensity of experiencing, it is possible to move toward more systematic gathering of data on such questions.

If we could measure changes in the feelings of actualization—and integration—we would be in a position to assess individuals on perhaps the most significant dimensions of human change. With regard to feelings, one continuum stretches from feelings of integration to feelings of disintegration. Both kinds of feelings can be assessed by studying their physical body events. A second continuum of feelings stretches from the good feelings of experiential actualization to the opposite pole planted firmly in the zone of unfeeling. In that zone, the state is one beyond deadness and apathy, meaninglessness and nothingness. It is the state of unfeeling, nothingness, the pit of death.

It is this dimension from actualization to unfeeling which is championed by Perls (Shostrom, 1967) as more salient than the psychiatric dimension from sickness to health. From the perspective of humanistic theory, value and goodness adhere to the movement away from unfeeling, through disintegration, and into the twin sets of feelings of integration and actualization. We champion these two dimensions as the direction of optimal being, but systematic study of changes toward both integration and actualization will require discovering ways of converting the physical bodily nature of these feelings into hard data.

Even in moment-to-moment behaving, the physical bodily nature of these feelings helps make them useful as immediate behavioral guidelines. Behavior which increases such feelings is good and desirable; behavior which reduces these feelings is neither good nor desirable. The actualizing person trusts the occurrence of these particular feelings as a responsible guide in both the moment-to-moment flowing of one's behavior, and also in the resolution of the more serious decisions of one's life. When you are with your friend and you reach out to touch the other's hand, does that act release feelings of aliveness and vitality, feelings of pleasure and happiness, feelings of joy and ecstasy? Are these feelings minimal or of high intensity? If these feelings are minimal, then a behavioral shift to another act is in order, perhaps one in which you look straight into your friend's eyes and hold his hand in both of yours. With this comes the upward surge of feelings, and you are filled with the exciting feelings of being alive. Here is the smooth shifting into those ways of behaving which offer the higher loads of such good feelings.

Such good feelings serve as momentary and immediate guidelines so that behaviors search out that which is accompanied with a full measure of these good feelings. She is talking to her friend, telling about her concern toward her father. "I want to care for him so very much." She stops. Saying this does not elicit the good feelings of experiential actualization. "I want to show him all my caring . . ." Something stirs. There is a rustling of the good feelings, but just a wee stirring, a kind of lambent glow of a soft presence of vitality and aliveness. She proceeds further, "I want to show him all my caring . . . but it is as if something won't permit that." Here are the feelings, the excitement, the pleasure, the tingling of aliveness. Saying these right words to her friend fills her with the good feelings of experiential actualization. Smoothly, without effort, she glided into the right verbal behavior. For the actualizing person, the degree to which the good feelings of actualization occur constitutes a responsible guide to the identifying of the right behavior. These good feelings will become illuminated as hard data which actualizing persons will learn to use in the smoothly continuous monitoring of immediate behavior. By learning to utilize the degree of good feelings as a continuous behavioral guideline, actualizing persons arrogate the right to modify their own behavior until it is accompanied with a measure of good feelings. They entrust determination of their own behavior to this guideline under which behavior is continuously modified. The presence of such feelings is a kind of necessary criterion for moment-to-moment behavioral assessment. But, what is perhaps more significant and characteristic of these persons, the regulation of behavior is internally administered. In actualization, it is the person who is the activator, the determiner of what the behavior is to be like. From moment to moment, these persons possess the capacity for the internal modification of their own behavior.

What characterizes actualizing persons in the smooth flow of moment-to-moment behavior is also characteristic of their way of encountering decisions, significant life choices. Such persons are able to try out each of the possibilities, but, more than merely being able to try them out, they know how to utilize the presence or absence of feelings of actualization to enable them to select the right option. Entering into the several possibilities, which of these fills the person with the good feelings of experiential actualization, and which leaves the person with deadness and unfeeling? By entering into the scene of accepting the new job, one can virtually try out the kinds of feelings which occur within the specific context of the new job. Does that increase the good feelings of actualization? The degree to which these good feelings are released can serve as an effective guideline to the behavior of actualizing persons. They have the skills to sample the various choices, and to use the feelings of actualization as reasonably hard data in arriving at decisions.

The Locus of Self in Intense Experiencing

In the crescendo of intense experiencing, the self assimilates into the experiencing potential. There is no sense of self in moments of intense experiencing, no separated I-ness, no part which stands off and regards what is happening. In intense experiencing, the sense of self closes down temporarily, and throws itself into being the potential which is undergoing the intense experiencing. Thus intense experiencing occurs without self-awareness, without a removed center of self. It is, therefore, experiencing without knowing—in the moments of intense experiencing—what is occurring. One has no thoughts about what is occurring. In these moments, self-awareness is surrendered to a heightened intensity of experiencing unmitigated by conscious thought (Suzuki, 1949). There is no separated center of self to be pleased or displeased, to enjoy or worry about what is occurring.

There is no disengaged self to assess what is occurring. This is signified, in Figure 12.1, by the expansion of the domain of the operating potentials from a small component of the total personality (indicated by the dotted circle enclosing operating potentials 1, 3 and 5 in A, Figure 12.1), to the perimeter of the entire set of potentials (B, Figure 12.1). The self, or I-ness, or domain of operating potentials, is now in and of each operating potential.

There is a quality of throwing one's self fully into the experiencing of it. One hurls one's self into a full experiencing of the potential, whatever the nature of the experiencing—whether that of conquering or loving or sharing or pulling away. There is a blending of consciousness into the actual experiencing of it—of the headiness of it, of the sense of rushing and falling, of the total abandon-ness of it. Yet, while the intense experiencing is occurring, there is no removed part of me to be conscious of that, to weigh it or regard it, to know it or judge it. There is no "I" separate from the wholesale intense experiencing.

It is as if the person trusts each potential enough to leave it alone. When I meet a new person I can trust my self sufficiently to let occur fully what is there to occur. Because I do not have to be vigilant, I do not have to stand aside and observe what is happening, or have to keep a part of my self removed to guard and to watch. At the moment of experiencing, I am *experiencing*, not knowing, observing, having insight. There is no I which is conscious of deeper meanings and subtle cues. Whatever potentials are not participating—and in every moment of experiencing not every potential can fully participate—are left alone, trusted. The net effect is that the potentials which are not engaging in the immediate experiencing are unconscious, but trustingly and confidently unconscious. It is a paradox, of sorts, that optimal functioning is a return to unconsciousness, a kind of unconscious functioning (Whitaker & Malone, 1953) which enables the self to dissolve in the service of intense experiencing.

The paradox is that the actualizing person, who is now able to trust to the point of folding one's self into the momentary experiencing is nevertheless characterized by mandate over his own behaviors. It is as if the person acquires *increased* control by being able to *sacrifice* control. He actualizes by shutting down the removed, controlling self, and that very capability is evidence of a heightened sense of internal governance. Thus the actualizing person is active, not passive. He constructs the external world by active means, not passive means. He is able to place himself actively into a passive receiving of that which provides for actualization. He postures himself so the sun warms his body. He actively seeks out the right persons and the right contexts wherein he gains the experience of being passive. Actualizing persons and their behaviors are characterized by activity, initiation, control, determination, and governance—in the acts of actively throwing their selves into passive sleep or passively being nurtured or passively receiving assistance. Such persons are not manipulated, unless actively hurling themselves into being manipulated. They are not responders to external stimulation. They are active in being able to be passive.

To the extent that intense experiencing requires the wholesale assimilation of the self, there is no basis whatsoever for the self to be separated during those special periods. All of the functions of the self then are revealed as excuses for not undergoing intense experiencing. All of the functions are revealed as occurring instead of intense experiencing. For example, one may engage in assessing one's own degree of intense experiencing. Am I experiencing intensely? What is there in me which may be experienced intensely? Do I experience this particular potential to a low degree or to a high degree? Such acts of *being concerned about* intense experiencing serve to attenuate the degree of intense experiencing. When the moment offers a high degree of intensive experiencing, *any* function of the self—except total surrender to experiencing—is an act of sabotage. One forecloses self-awareness in moments of actualization, for every posture of self-regard is evidence of the failure of actualization. When there is an assimilation of self into the experiencing potential, the person *is* it; he does not talk *about* it. The intensely experiencing person is with you; he does not merely talk about being with you or tell you about it. He is irritated at you, rather than talking with you about his irritation. He shares with you—instead of telling you about sharing, or explaining how important sharing is, or lapsing romantic about the notion of sharing. To talk about it requires that one is split, that one is an intact self, removed from the intense experiencing of that about which he tells you.

In the moments of experiencing, even ordinary attenuated experiencing, it is difficult for the center of self to be removed, knowing, aware. As described in Chapter 10, in those moments, the sense of I-ness may be withdrawn below the threshold of unfeeling so that the center of the person—during those moments of doing—does not know about the doing. It is most typical for the sense of awareness to be there, to the side, separated, sensing and knowing what is happening. Yet, that sense diminishes at the instant of actual doing, of actual risings up of experiencing, for ". . . we cannot be aware of ourselves at moments of action or thought" (Ouspensky, 1957, p. 105). In peak moments of intense feeling, this closing down of the sense of awareness is furthered to a point where there virtually is no self-knowing, no sense of I-ness.

Actualization offers the gift of intense experiencing to the depth and breadth of potentials. It is this intensity of experiencing which is the core quality of actualization. This stands as the ultimate goal of actualization, its consumate form, its mission or aim. It is the purpose of life, of being. Intense experiencing is its own end, the meaning of living and being, the intrinsic quality of human being. There is no further meaning, purpose, goal—from the perspective of humanistic theory. Those who argue whether life holds any discoverable purpose or meaning are falling into the error of opposing one perspective against another, and of missing the intimate coupling of integration and actualization (cf. Watts, 1960).

II

Human Development

13

The Origins of Infants

Our description and understanding of human beings focused upon human beings themselves, their potentials and their feelings, their ways of behaving, their construction of worlds, their problems and difficulties and their movement into optimal ways of being. We did not seek to describe and understand human beings by studying their development and growth from infancy. The reason that we consider infancy and child development at the *end* of the book instead of at the beginning is that humanistic theory enables us to appreciate the Copernican switch between infancy and adulthood. That is, almost without exception it is presumed that understanding of the adult flows out of understanding of the child. But humanistic theory adds an equal and opposite causal flow, viz. in order to understand the child, we must understand the adult.

The thesis of the present chapter is that the origins of infants reside in the adults constructing the world constitutive of the infants. In other words, adults cause infants. It is in appreciation of this thesis that the description and understanding of infancy properly follow a description and understanding of adults. In a sense, then, the preceding chapters have been the groundwork for a discussion of the origin of infants.

THE PRIMITIVE PERSONALITY

Humanistic theory draws heavily from schools of thought known as existentialism, phenomenology, and the humanistic psychologies. Yet I believe it is fair to say that no comprehensive theory of infancy and child development has emerged from these schools of thought. In outlining a humanistic theory of infancy, our discussion will revolve

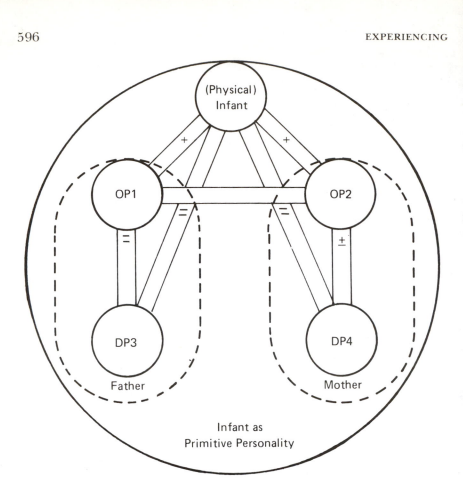

Figure 13.1 Structure and Contents of Primitive Field

about two landmark questions: How may we describe and understand the *processes which construct* the infant? How may we describe and understand the *structure and contents* of that which comprises the infant? We will discuss each of these in turn.

Construction of the Infant

The story of infancy opens with human beings continuously at work building worlds. The capacity to construct worlds is perhaps foremost among human characteristics. As robust as is the individual person in the continuous construction of worlds, there is even greater robustness when human beings work together in dyads or groups. Whether individually, in dyads, or in groups, human beings are continuously constructing worlds populated with things—houses, organizations, nightmares, machinery, works of art, religions, Gods, clothing, books, ships. In the course of their world-building, human beings bring these things into existence. At one moment, the thing did not exist. Now, by virtue of the world-building of human beings, the thing exists. Human beings construct infants in the very same ways in which human beings construct other elements which comprise their worlds. I have proposed (Chapter 6) four modes by which human beings construct their external worlds. I suggest that these are the same four modes by which human beings construct infants. Each of these four modes is a way in which the existence of an infant comes about. If we understand a person's world as now including an infant, I propose that its presence can be explained as having occurred through one of these four modes. Our focus, then is an infant, a living, breathing, existing infant. But the construction of that infant can also incorporate the *idea* of an infant, the *conception* of an infant, and all of the processes which culminate in the existence of the infant. How does the idea of an infant come about? How is an infant conceived? How may we describe and understand the presence of this particular infant? Each of these questions is answered by citing the four modes by which worlds are constructed.

By receiving an intrusive external world. An infant can be constructed by receiving an *intrusive external world*. In this mode, it is the external world which initiates the idea of infancy and intrudes it upon the person. The person is the receiver who is acted upon by an initiating and determining external world which is the activating source. The external world gets the process going, presents the person with the stimulus, forces the person to be confronted with the idea of an infant. In this mode, the immediate imminence of an infant is thrust upon the person by the external world. The presentation may take the form of other individuals who tell the person that it is time to have a baby. A parent or husband or child may ask the person to have a baby. The possibility of constructing an infant may occur in the form of an activating man during intercourse. While being in the presence of an infant, the key words may play upon the person from another individual: "When are *you* going to have a baby?" Another individual may physically overpower the person and ignite the possibility of becoming pregnant. A relative or an acquaintance or a friend may invite the person to take care of an infant. In each instance, it is the external world which generates the idea of an infant and presents that idea to the person. Infantness intrudes itself onto the person from the external world.

There is a point when infantness intrudes onto the person. What happens from that point on is a function of the person herself who determines how that shall be used in the construction of her world. Infantness can mean nothing, its impact washes away, and no further use is made of it. Whatever becomes of that intrusion from the external world is a function of the person herself. Although the external world intruded infantness into her, she is the active agent in determining how it shall be received. Depending upon the nature of her potentials, and their relationships, intercourse may result in conception, or it may not. Depending upon the person whom she is, depending on the way in which it is important for her world to be constructed, infantness may be nurtured and developed, or it may wash away into meaninglessness. Her own potentials and their relationships determine whether an infant is to be constructed, or not. She may receive an infant, or decline the invitation. She may seek to construct an infant in her world, or she may not. Thus the *idea* of infantness either becomes constructed into her world, or it is not. Or the physical conception of a fetus is fostered in her world, or it is not. Or an actual infant is received as a part of her world, or it is not. In each case, infantness is either built into the person's world, or it is not a component in the world, depending upon the way in which the person receives the possibility of infantness presented to her by an intrusive external world. If the person's potentials and their relationships are of the right kind, the person will fill her world with infantness. She will construct an infant.

By utilizing a ready-made external world. In the first mode, infantness originates in the external world and intrudes itself onto the person. In this second mode, infantness already is present within the person, and the person constructs the infant by *utilizing a ready-made aspect of the external world*. That is, the person goes into the external world to find ready-made stuff—the infant. In this second mode, construction consists in proper selection and utilization of what is already present in the external world. There is a seeking for infantness, a constructing of it by searching it out, by utilizing what is already present.

In its simplest form, the person can seek and find ready-made infants. Thus the person may construct a world in which she cares for babies, works in a maternity ward, works at a hospital for sick children, serves as a wet-nurse, becomes a foster mother, is a social worker dealing with infants and young children, works in a laboratory or an academic department which studies infancy. A woman may live with another woman or man who already has a baby or a young child. A man may live with a woman who has a baby or a young child. An individual or a couple or a family may adopt or bring within its fold a foster baby or an adopted baby or a mother and her baby. In each instance there already exists a baby, and what is required is the utilization of that ready-made baby into one's own world.

By conjoint construction of an external world. In each of the above two modes, infantness is already present in the external world. Infantness intrudes itself onto the person in the first mode, and stands ready-made and available in the second mode. In the third mode, however, infantness itself must be created where it had not existed. It is constructed by persons *working together conjointly*. Each works upon the other conjointly to construct infantness. This may take the form of talking with one another so that it is the conjointness which brings forth the concept of infantness where it had not existed before. A given man and a given woman may neither have any substantial infantness in their lives until each works upon the other so as to bring forth the infantness residing in each. Now that infantness has been constructed, they may further construct infants by sexual relations, by adoption, by any means of realizing actual infants.

It is clear that there are many ways of constructing infantness other than by sexual intercourse. Even with regard to the mode of conjoint construction, the actual means of constructing infantness includes much more than sexual intercourse. An older couple may bring forth in one another the idea of having a baby, so that infantness arose only through their conjoint interaction and, within a few months the couple may be volunteers in a nursery school, or welcome a foster baby into their home, or serve as a family for a mother and her baby. By the same token, sexual intercourse is frequently far more than the conjoint construction of a baby. Indeed, only when the idea of infantness is brought forth in the conjointness of intercourse is it an example of the conjoint construction of an infant. Sexual intercourse can be much more than conjoint construction of an infant, and conjoint construction of an infant can be accomplished in more ways than sexual intercourse.

By fabricating an external world. In the first two modes, infantness was already there in the external world. The person constructed infantness into her world by the way in which she received the infantness intruding upon her from the external world, or by the way in which she utilized the infantness which was readymade and existent within the external world. In the third mode, infantness is not already present in the external world. It must be constructed, but that construction process requires a number of persons who, conjointly, bring forth infantness. In the fourth mode, the person brings forth infantness all by herself, the sole creator and the architect. Where there was no infantness in her world, there now exists infantness because of her own creativity and artistry. She constructs a world in which there are infants, and the activation and creative power, the determination and the resourcefulness, come from her alone. She has fabricated infants where there were none.

In the simplest form, the woman is the active agent in getting pregnant. The idea of infantness is already within her, and her behavior is geared toward creating a baby in her world. She is the creator, the one who moulds and shapes the world so as to constitute a baby. Sexual intercourse and impregnation serve as instrumental means by which the baby is fabricated—literally manufactured and brought into existence where before there was none. A baby now exists, and she stands as the fabricator, the one who brought it about in the same way a person may fabricate a new symphony, a new painting, a new home by one's own efforts. Becoming pregnant is part of the act of personal fabrication, and gives meaning and significance to the search for an impregnator, the courtship ritual, and the act of impregnation. The sexual act is merely a necessary element in the process of fabricating an infant.

Infantness may be fabricated in ways other than through intercourse. By virtue of one's own efforts and creative power, infants can be fabricated out of other materials—just as a block of marble may be fabricated into a statue of an infant. A person may sculpt infants, or paint pictures of infants, or write stories about infants. In each case, the creator fabricates infantness where there was none. The person may write a play about an infant, or produce a film about an infant. The seed for infantness lies within the creative artist, and infants are fabricated out of nothing by means of this mode of construction. Or, a person may fabricate infantness in the very same way a person fabricates a vision of a deceased parent or a vision of the devil. Out of his own resources, the person fabricates voices saying nasty things about him, or plots hatched by a cabal, or faces leering at him—or infants. All of these are products of the same mode of constructing a world, viz. by a straightforward fabrication. In addition, a person may work at fabricating infantness out of actual components of the real world. Thus a person treats the puppy as an infant, or fabricates infantness out of a spouse, a plant, a kitten.

Regardless of which mode is adopted, infants are constructed in the very same ways in which human beings are forever at work constructing their worlds. Human beings are active in building, shaping, creating, and moulding their worlds—and infantness is constructed in the very same ways. In this process, the architect is a particular individual or dyad or group which utilizes one or more of the four modes in their active construction of infantness. Because infants are constructed by persons, infants serve the same functions as any other components of constructed external worlds. We turn now to a consideration of the functions of infants, constructed to play particular roles in the worlds built by human beings.

The Functions of Infants

Family theorists and therapists respect the power of the family to define the role of a particular member, especially the child (Bell, 1963; Boszormenyi-Nagy & Framo, 1965; Haley & Hoffman, 1967; Jackson, 1957; Laing & Esterson, 1970). A specific function is assigned to that child, and massive forces are assembled to construct the child into serving that function. The child can be assigned the function of being the ill one, and the family draws together to help the ill child. Similarly, the child may be assigned the function of the family goat, the worshipped messiah, the tyrant, the nasty one against whom the family rebels, the bad one who acts out the intolerable impulses of the family. There is virtually no limit to the kinds of functions which the family can define for the child.

These roles, or functions, are not designed capriciously nor haphazardly. Their design arises deep within the bowels of the family's potentials and relationships among potentials. We are only slowly appreciating the importance of these roles, the work which goes into their design, and the significance of these roles in moulding the nature of the child. When it is important that the family make the child into the crazy (schizophrenic) one, the magnitude of that "need" is enormous (e.g., Haley, 1963; Jackson, 1957). Parents will work tirelessly to force the child to behave in mindless ways, to communicate in defensively jumbled ways, to be "schizophrenic."

This organized way in which parents construct the infant also applies to the way in which parents construct sets of children. A careful examination of siblings within a family reveals underlying organizational patterns (cf. Adler, 1930; Brown & Lynn, 1966; Irish, 1964; Kahn, Mahrer, & Bornstein, 1972; Sears, 1950; Toman, 1969). Thus the functions assigned to the infant can be illuminated in relationship to the functions assigned to the older sibling(s). Similarities and differences between siblings may then be seen as arising in an organized psychological design, with the parental figures as the organizers. The first child may be born into the role of the little mother, and subsequent infants are her wards. The first born male may be assigned the function of the strong capable one, and the next son fulfills the function of the weak sensitive one. A boy and a girl may be born to serve as the intimate pair the parents cannot be. Families assign roles and functions to family members, and it is within the larger context of the family that the role and function of the infant can be appreciated.

What has been revealed in studies of the family applies a hundredfold to the construction of infants. Parental figures construct infants to fulfill functions which arise out of the potentials and relationships among the potentials of the parental figures (Mahrer, 1967a; Mahrer & Pearson, 1971b). Indeed, infants *are* those very functions. Infants are the most personal creations of persons who construct them as the fulfillment of very particular functions. The key to understanding the nature of the infant lies in understanding the nature of the function the infant was constructed to serve. Parents can construct infants to be everything the child is assigned by the family—and far more. The infant can be the treasured one, the hateful one, the confidante, the beautiful one, the secret lover, the little king, the violent anger, the lost father, the proof of fertility, the murderer, the devouring one, the bearer of hopes, the one who protects, the devil. There is virtually no limit to the functions the infant is constructed to fulfill, just as there is virtually no limit to the functions the external world is constructed to fulfill. In order to understand what the infant is, we. must turn to a description of the various kinds of functions infants serve. As pointed out in the opening of this chapter, the description and understanding of infants require no new basic principles. All the basic principles have been set forth in earlier chapters. Our work consists in using these principles to make sense of infants. In chapter 6, we proposed three major functions for the worlds which human beings construct. Our purpose now is to apply these three major functions to infants.

The infant as the appropriate situational context. Human beings build their external worlds into situational contexts appropriate for the experiencing of potentials. In the working out of this function, behavior constructs the external world into appropriate situational contexts wherein that potential can be experienced. Infantness is constructed by many human beings to fulfill this function. The infant is constructed to serve as a particular situational context in which the parental figures can experience what it is important for them to experience. It is this appropriate situational context which comes first and which defines the exact function of the infant. Indeed, the nature of the appropriate situational context *determines* the nature of the infant, and it precedes the construction of the infant. That is, the appropriate situational context is the predominant determinant of the infant itself. Thus conception becomes understandable as one element in the construction of the appropriate situational context. It is there during pregnancy, and serves as the determining variable of the events which comprise pregnancy. It is there after birth, and determines what occurs after birth. It is there at every moment that infantness is present in the parental figures' world. It is there guiding every minute interaction between parent and infant. It is even there organizing the meaning of others' remarks about marriage, about having a baby, about being an adult. It is there during heterosexual interaction, making love, romance, courtship. It is there as you become a child care worker or see infants being fed. Your potentials can be experienced in appropriate situational contexts, and your behavior works toward building those contexts. Infantness comes into your world as an element of that appropriate situational context. You are continuously working upon the world, fashioning it into constituting the right situational context, and it is in this encompassing framework that infants are brought forth to serve as a constituent of that special situational context you are working to construct.

The particular *nature* of this situational context is a function of the kinds of potentials in the parental figures. Parents can construct situations in which to experience inadequacy or protection, ripeness or intimacy, helplessness or control. The nature of the function fulfilled by the infant depends upon the potentials of these parental architects—and *not* upon some presumed characteristics or intrinsic qualities of the infant. Whether the infant is to be a demanding tyrant or a frail organism depends upon the nature of the parental potentials and the kinds of situational contexts to be constructed to enable experiencing of those potentials.

Nearly every theory of infancy and human development endows the infant with some kind of intrinsic basic nature. Although these theories consider that nature as intrinsic in the foundation of humanness, I see that nature as *attributed* and as *constructed* by theorists of each of these schools. In precisely the very same ways, parental figures construct their infants into having the same "intrinsic" basic natures and characteristics. Whether the infant's nature is attributed-constucted by a theorist or by a parent, that process of attributing and constructing is, from our perspective, part of a larger process of constructing the infant into playing a particular function—one that requires that the infant "have" that particular nature. This whole process is one of building a situational context appropriate for the experiencing of a particular potential. For example, in order for the parent to experience being needed, being the protector, being the provider, being the one who determines life and death, it is essential that the situational context include an infant whose central nature is helplessness and dependency. This is precisely the attributed core nature of infants as seen from the viewpoints of psychoanalytic and social learning theorists (e.g., Dollard & Miller, 1950; Sears, 1963). It is also the way in which many parents must define the infant in order to build a situational context appropriate for the experiencing of quite specific potentials. Endowing the infant with these basic characteristics (or any other) is part of a grand process of situation-building for purposes of experiencing potentials. The function of the infant is to be a core component in a situation in which persons experience being needed, being the protector, being the provider, being the one who determines life and death.

What are the kinds of potentials which can be experienced in a situational context built around an infant? A woman may construct the situation of pregnancy as a context wherein she experiences fullness, ripeness, fertility, creation. By constructing a situation of pregnancy and birth and an actual neonate, a person may build the appropriate context wherein she experiences heterosexuality, masculinity or femininity, or adultness and maturity. In the same manner, these situational contexts can serve to disprove and to deny deeper potentials for sterility and barrenness, for asexuality, for immaturity and childishness. The infant serves as a situational context appropriate for the experiencing of such potentials, i.e. to fulfill that function.

An infant can serve as the situational context in which a parent experiences protectiveness, comfort, nurturance. By virtue of the infant, the parent is filled with a measure of protectiveness, comfort and nurturance. A woman may be enabled to experience a sense of ownership in the situational context of her baby. With her baby, this sense is one of having produced it; it is mine, it belongs to me, it is finally something which belongs only to me. Or, the parent experiences being needed, having a purpose, something to live for—and that experiencing occurs only within the context of having a baby. The baby is swathed in that specific meaning; serving as that particular context is the function of the baby.

Some parents are geared toward constructing a situational context in which the infant-child is to be critical of them, is to regard them as poor parents, as inadequate and incompetent as caretakers. These parents work upon the infant situation to bring this about. When the infant-child fulfills this function, the parents gain a special kind of experiencing. They are overwhelmed by the enormity of it all; being parents is far too stressful and demanding. They are incapable and incompetent. In order to gain this experiencing, the infant-child must be a certain, predefined way. That role, being an important part of that situational context—these constitute the function of the infant.

Karen was already skilled at constructing situations in which she experienced being used, drained, taken advantage of. The entire sweep of her marriage, conception, pregnancy, and motherhood was constructed to provide the appropriate situational context for her to experience that potential. The fetus was an unwelcome stranger who intruded into her body, drained her vitality and energy, parasitically took from her. The infant robbed her of her youth, spontaneity, freedom, and was an organism robbing her, sucking on her, taking advantage of her for its own growth. Given this potential for experiencing, the infant was assigned a quite specific function in the appropriate situational context.

There are all sorts of roles which can be assigned to the infant. Even before the baby was conceived, it was apparent that the mother was working toward the construction of a situational context in which she could experience a denial of being rejected, outside, lonely. The baby was to be the first real confidante in her life, a sister or a brother she never had, the genuinely close friend. She and her baby were going to be her intimate, two-person group. She would know everything the baby felt and thought. She would share everything with her baby. This was the predefined function of the infant as an integral part of a situational context enabling the experiencing of that potential. In this function, the infant is buddy, friend, partner. Theirs is an equal relationship from the very beginning. It is a "symbiotic" relationship (Benedek, 1956) created by the mother as the appropriate context wherein she experiences what is important for her to experience.

Throughout her life, the daughter had tried one way after the other to make herself acceptable to her parents. It is as if she were saying to them: "Will you like me if I am this way or that way, or if I bring home this boyfriend, or if I become a nurse, or if I try to understand you, or if I give you money when you need it?" Another means is the having of a baby. In this instance, the baby is simply another situational context in which the daughter struggles to please her parents, to give them gifts, to give them what she hopes will please them. The potential is to try to please, to gain acceptance—and the baby is merely another situational context in which to experience this potential.

A man may have the potential for experiencing abrasive rivalry for his wife's affections. As a means of experiencing this, there are various situational contexts which can be constructed. He may exist in a world in which he is only one of several agents vying for his wife's affections. Other agents may include his wife's mother and father, her own career, her former husband. Still another situational context might be an infant whose existence means that the wife pours affection upon the infant and not upon the husband. In understanding the world of the father (Figure 13.1), the infant is an important ingredient in a situational context appropriate for the father's experiencing of abrasive rivalry for his wife's affections. As an ingredient, the infant is constructed to serve that specific function. Indeed, the whole process of constructing the infant may be guided by that intended function, from well before conception to well after birth.

It is a short step to the father who houses potentials which call for a situational context of the infant as the hated competitor. A man may have potentials for being overcome by other men, or for archaic struggles for dominance, or for homosexual encounters, or for murdering rivals for the woman. Such potentials can be experienced in situations involving the son as the hated opponent in deadly competition. To the extent that such potentials are present, the father may construct a son whose function is to fulfill that precise role. Not only does this lead to phenomenon which has been referred to as the oedipal complex, but, perhaps more significant, it is the father who constructs the scene from the very beginning. The father is the architect who moulds the players in this situational context, and the son is fashioned to play a predetermined function—as a means of enabling the father to gain the experiencing which is important for him to experience.

Here, in the phenomena referred to as the oedipal complex, is an exemplification of the father as a major determinant of the role to be fulfilled by the son. The father builds a situational context in which the infant son is to play a defined role. Underneath all of the father's work in building a very particular kind of world is a potential for experiencing homicidal rivalry with the son. One way, therefore, that the oedipal phenomena transpire, is through the playing out of the father's potentials in constructing a son whose function is to serve as a necessary component in a very particular situational context. Long before Oedipus was able to say words or take his first steps, Laius regarded his son as a feared and hated enemy destined to grow up into his murderer. Laius was .tortured by the Delphic oracle's dire prediction that he will be murdered by his own son. So real was that tortuous prediction that Laius abandoned his preconceived murderer on the hillside. Here, in one of the interpretations of the classic story, is the playing out of the father's own potentials, the building of a situational context in which his own death " . . . is a rigidly determined consequence of Laius' own character structure" (Devereaux, 1964, p. 179). Laius is creating a particular situational context in which the son is to play a defined role. The son is structured to fulfill this function. But infants are constructed to serve as key components in many situational contexts. A few are related to what we describe as the oedipal phenomena. Others relate to the experiencing of death.

It is singular for some persons to construct infant-situations around the experiencing of death. We will describe a number of forms taken by the imminence of death and its role in the construction of infants. Consider persons who confront death in the form of a parent's terminal illness, the death of a grandfather or older sibling or close friend. The determining potential may include the warding off of death fears, a warding off of a sense of helplessness in the face of death, a pushing away of the ineluctability of death, a denial of the atrophy and moribund state of death, a running from one's own impotence in the face of death. To ward off all of this, the person rushes into creating life, making a baby, conceiving life, being potent over death. The infant is a central ingredient in establishing a situational context for such experiencings. Indeed, I am strongly inclined to hypothesize that systematic study of such persons would reveal an empirical coupling of recent deaths with the conception of infants. But death may also include a severe loss or the imminence of loss. A person loses an arm or a leg or a kidney. A person loses a business or a lifelong dream. One's empire falls apart. One loses a homeland or one's lifelong homestead. To ward off and deny the certainty of the loss, the sense of helplessness and frailty before the powerful forces of destiny, it is desperately important for some to construct life, to conceive a baby. By constructing a baby, the person has an appropriate situational context for the experiencing of mastering the loss, not being a frail puppet, having something of one's very own.

Sometimes the loss is of a specific kind of relationship with a parental figure. The parent is the boss or protector or best friend, but now the parent dies or is senile. Then the person sets out to reconstruct the same relationship with a surrogate: the baby. All of the forces are there to build the baby into being the replacement of the lost parent. Thus the baby is to be built into being the person's boss or protector or best friend. From the very beginning, the person is geared toward constructing an infant who will be boss; in that situation the person gains the same experiencing which had occurred in the parental relationship, viz. being the follower, the one whose job is made clear, the one who pleases the boss. Having had this relationship with her own parents, she now reestablishes the same relationship with her child in the "parental" role. A man may relate to his aging father in such a manner as to provide for the experiencing of protection, taking care of the old man, nurturing and succoring the loved father. But now father is dying. Soon the couple become pregnant and have another child after all these years. That infant is conceived and born to replace the husband's father. By the time the baby is four months old, the old man has died—and the husband is now experiencing the same sense of protecting, taking care of, nurturing and succoring the little infant. The imminence of death and loss is present in many instances in which the function of the infant is to be a significant part of a situational context in which parents experience what they experienced with their own parents. (In such instances we have yet to appreciate the similarity between grandparent and grandchild.)

Another form taken by death and loss is that of an eroding relationship. The marriage is over. Each party senses it, and fights to deny the looming truth. Death and loss of the relationship are present all around the couple. Their operating potential is to pump life to their relationship, to disprove the loss by building a situational context in which they can experience proof of the viability of their marriage. The baby is conceived and born to serve that very purpose, viz. to

constitute a significant element in a situational context in which the
parents can experience a continuing, growing, viable marriage.

Death and loss can take the form of parents' own inevitable movement toward eclipsing youth. Mother and father are growing old.
Their own parents are dying or already dead. Sexuality is waning.
Lifelong ambitions are becoming unreachable. Mother is no longer a
mother, for her children are adolescents. Father is balding and getting
fat. Both are catching scary glimpses of their own looming death.
Birthdays are ominous. The parents' fertility and creativeness are
waning, life and vitality are slipping away. Out of this tapestry comes
the infant—their own baby, or the adoption of a child, or welcoming a
young mother and her baby into the family. However a baby is
brought into their lives, the baby's function is to serve as an important
component in a situational context constructed by the parents to enable them to experience youth, parenthood, vitality, life—and not death,
loss, atrophy.

One function of the constructed infant is to comprise the situational
context appropriate for the experiencing of given potentials (Figure
13.1). But this is only one function of the constructed infant. In addition, the parental figures may construct the infant to serve as extensions or externalizations of the parental operating or deeper potentials.

The infant as an extended operating potential. Regardless of the mode
by which the infant is constructed, the infant can serve as the extension of the parental figure's operating potential. As described in
Chapter 6, a person may construct an aspect of his external world as
an extension of the operating potential. With regard to infants, this
function is incredibly easy to bring about, and, accordingly, this is a
common function fulfilled by infants. There are two sub-functions of
the infant as the extended operating potential, and we shall discuss
each in turn. In the first sub-function, the purpose of the infant as an
extended operating potential is to provide for the experiencing of the
parental operating potential. As indicated in Figure 13.1, the infant is
a direct extension of operating potential 1 or 2, and father or mother
thereby gains experiencing of that operating potential. Under these
conditions, what occurs in or to the infant is tantamount to occurrences in or to the parent. If mother's operating potential (OP2, Figure
13.1) involves the experiencing of fussing, whining, and complaining,
the infant likewise manifests fussing, complaining, and whining. In
this way, mother gains a measure of that experiencing through the infant. If father's operating potential (OP1, Figure 13.1) consists of specialness, uniqueness, and Godlikeness, the infant can be constructed
into being that which is special, unique, and Godlike. When the infant
is being special, or is treated by others as quite unique, or radiates an

aura of Godlikeness, the father's own operating potential is experienced.

A parent may experience defiance and rebellion either as he himself is being and behaving, or as his infant is being and behaving. This operating potential is experienced as the father is refusing to comply, or as the infant is refusing to comply. When that infant is the proper extension of the father's operating potential, the infant's refusal to comply fills the father with the experiencing of defiance and rebellion. In actuality, the father experiences in and through the being of the infant. Donald is a mechanic who derives pleasure from understanding how things work, from figuring out their interconnections and what causes what. The function his baby daughter was assigned was precisely that. She was born to figure out how to hit the mobile to make it move, how to move her fingers so as to pinch the nipple. She constituted the extension of his own operating potential. When his daughter fulfilled that function, Donald experienced a sense of pleasure in understanding how things worked. His daughter was the extension of his own operating potential, and he experienced that potential via the behaviors of his daughter.

Mother gained the experiencing of nastiness through her biting sarcasm, her aggressive encounters with her fellow workers. By having a baby, she extended the ways of experiencing that potential by assigning to her daughter the role-function of having temper tantrums, pinching other babies, spitting on persons, biting them, breaking objects, throwing things at other babies. In all this, it was the mother who gained that experience of nastiness by means of her daughter as the extended operating potential. Literally, the daughter was constructed to be the extension of the mother's nastiness.

In their own ways, the husband and wife waged war on one another, each trying to get the other to give in. It is as if each told the other: "I am going to force you to change, to break you." When they had a baby, they made the baby into the extension of their own operating potentials. The trio then fell into a three-way war, each one locked into resisting the other and trying to get the other to give in. Theirs was a real fight, each manifesting the same operating potential. With the added participation of the baby, each parent gained a measure of fuller experiencing as the baby expressed his own version of: "I am going to force *you* to change, to break you." In being this extended operating potential, the object might consist of a toy, another child, a parent, teacher, school system or government.

In fulfilling the function of being the extension of the parental operating potential, one sub-function has been to provide for the experiencing of that operating potential. A second sub-function pertains to the nature of the *relationship* rather than the experiencing of the *potential*. In this second sub-function, the infant is constructed to bear the same relationship toward the parent as the parent bears toward her own deeper potential. As indicated in Figure 13.1, the infant is the extension of operating potential 2, and its function is to bear the same relationship toward deeper potential 4 as the mother (operating potential 2) bears toward deeper potential 4.

Almost without exception, this relationship is disintegrative. Where the parent fears and hates the deeper potential, the infant is likewise to fear and hate the parent. Where the parent defends against what is within, sees it as menacing and dangerous, the child regards the parent as someone to be defended against, as menacing and dangerous. Where the parent must struggle to keep distance against it, the child is made to keep distance from the parent. In the fulfillment of this function, the infant is invested with a kind of mysterious special knowledge about the inner awfulness of the parent. The infant fears, hates, defends against, draws back from the parent because the infant "has" special knowledge about what the parent is really like. The infant is constructed to sense that the parent is homosexual, crafty, a liar, basically hateful, has secrets, is weak, is evil. Thus the infant fears and hates what the parent only dimly suspects, and does not really want to know about himself. Because of this, the parent endows the infant with special powers or sensings which permit the infant to know the real awfulness of the parental insides.

Mother may have a deeper potential which, through a disintegrative relationship, is seen as not providing, tending to avoid responsibility, not giving. In fearing and hating that potential, mother constructs an infant who bears that same relationship toward her. From the very beginning of her pregnancy, mother perceived the fetus as hating her for not adequately providing, not giving proper supplies. After the difficult pregnancy and delivery, the baby whined incessantly, had colic, was perpetually unsatisfied. The daughter made mother feel that she never offered enough, what she did offer was inadequate, there was too little care, nothing was given freely. Mother had left the baby carriage unattended while she was sitting at a pool talking with a friend. During those unattended minutes, the carriage was brutally thrown over by some young boys, hurling the baby out of the carriage. Although no damage was identified, the mother spent the rest of her life defining the daughter as hating her as irresponsible, not providing, not caring. In fulfilling this function, the daughter manifested the mother's own disintegrative relationship toward the deeper potential.

The father pulled away from his own deeper potential for being cold, distant, mechanical. He maintained periodic fears of becoming that way. He worried about having his own baby. When he finally did, the whole scenario came to life. The baby was uncomfortable and squirmy when he held him. The baby twisted and screamed to get out of father's grasp. Although it seemed difficult to believe, father had the strangest thought that the baby could see right through him, and could discern his deepest thoughts. There were times when the father was made anxious by a particular look from the baby, one that seemed to say, "You are cold and unfeeling. I know what you are really like—and I will always hate you for that." The function manifested by the baby was to bear the same disintegrative relationship to the father as the father bore toward his own deeper potential.

Both mother and father were afraid of their deeper potentials. They were fragile, gentle people who were fearful of being overcome and overwhelmed by impulses. Drinking was bad. Raising one's voice was bad. Driving fast was dangerous. They bore a child who manifested the same disintegrative relationship toward them as they bore toward their own deeper potentials. The child seemed fearful of them. She was edgy and jumpy in their presence. The child seemed anxiously vigilant toward the parents as if they were impulse-ridden monsters. She seemed afraid that the parents would harm her, overwhelm her. Throughout her childhood and adolescence, her function was to be watchful of her parents, to be uneasy with them as impulsive and monstrous people—and yet they never behaved in that way, and she knew them to be fragile and gentle, not drinking, never raising their voices, never driving recklessly. It was all very strange, yet she feared them in the same way they feared their own inner tendencies.

Whatever the mother fears and hates in herself, the child can be fashioned into also fearing and hating in mother. Thus the child regards the mother as dumb, or as lazy, or as demanding, or as mean and cruel. Each of these is a deeper quality which the mother senses is within, and from which the mother recoils. In precisely the same manner, the child is handed the function of fearing and hating the mother for being that way.

The infant as the extended deeper potential. The infant can be constructed to serve as an appropriate situational context in which the parent experiences potentials. The infant also can be constructed to serve as the extended operating potential. We now turn to the third function of the constructed infant, viz. to serve as the extension of the parental *deeper* potentials. In carrying out this function, the infant is made to express that which the parent does not manifest. While the parent expresses the *operating* potential, the infant is made to express the *deeper* potential.

This idea is already incorporated in the hypothesis of the schizophrenogenic mother. According to this hypothesis, the mother herself may not be schizophrenic, may not behave in ways considered schizophrenic. Instead, she houses schizophrenic inclinations, proclivities (schizotypic tendencies), and engages with the infant in ways which are effective in bringing forth schizophrenic behavior from the infant (Meehl, 1962). In this hypothesis, the infant is constructed to serve as the extension of the parental deeper schizophrenic tendencies. If we enlarge this hypothesis, parents construct the infant into being the extension of *any* deeper potential, not merely those which we consider schizophrenic.

Because the parental potentials are *deeper*, their connections to the infant are hidden in mystery. If the parent has deeper potentials for passivity and helplessness, the parent will likely avoid and resist any connection between the infant's passivity and helplessness and the possibility of that kind of a potential existing within the parent. It is understandable that both parents and theorists would tend to consider the roots of the infant's characteristics to lie intrinsically within the infant. Thus passivity and helplessness would be seen as being essential qualities of the nature of infantness, intrinsic to infants. Each school of human personality and each epoch of thought about human personality would have its own version of what the intrinsic nature of infants is like. But, from the perspective of humanistic theory, these are attributed qualities, many of which are attributed as part of the process of constructing the infant into being the externalized deeper potentials of collective parental figures (and personality theorists). The deeper potentials of collective persons include, as an hypothesis, virtually all of the qualities held as intrinsic to infant human nature: seeking, stimulation, dependency, helplessness, activity, flexibility and adaptability, gregariousness, excitability, curiosity, love and affection, restlessness, sensitivity, emotional reactivity, impulsivity.

Like the infant as the extended *operating* potential, the infant is constructed to serve as the extended *deeper* potential for two purposes. One is to provide for the enhanced *experiencing* of the parental deeper potential, and the other is to externalize the nature of the *relationships* between the operating and deeper potentials. We shall discuss each of these in turn.

A parent may house deeper potentials for passive dependency. Although not manifesting that at the operating level, the parent may construct an infant into manifesting passive dependency, and thereby gain a measure of experiencing that deeper potential. As indicated in Figure 13.1, the function of the infant may be that of serving as the extension of deeper potential 3 or 4, both of which exist within the parents. It is interesting how parental figures who draw back from their own insides as crazy will construct infants into being the live manifestation of that craziness. Parental figures often house deeper potentials whose nature is bizarre, deviant, strange, different, peculiar. Fighting that deeper potential, not manifesting that way of being in their own operating way of being, such parental figures construct infants into being the externalized manifestation of that potential and thereby gain some measure of experiencing that deeper potential.

Just as the infant may be constructed into that which parents regard as crazy, parents are marvelously adept at constructing the infant into serving as virtually anything which parents fear and hate in themselves. In that way, parents gain a measure of such deeper experiencing. For example, a woman fears and hates the menacing inner potential for being dull and uncomprehending. She is almost terrified by the slightest hint of these qualities in her. Yet her infant is fitted to constitute just that way of being. Her son is slow in comprehending, dull-witted. In constructing him as this deeper potential, she gains a measure of experiencing her own inner dullness and uncomprehendingness. Father recoils from his own inner eroticism, his sexual touching, the experiencing of mutual sexual arousal and stimulation. He has carved out a life which is studiously devoid of any of this. But his baby fills the vacuum. The baby is the personification of eroticism, for that is the meaning assigned to its existence, the function the baby is to play in the life of the father. As the extension of the father's eroticism, the baby provides the means whereby the father gains some sense of that deeper potential. Mother houses a deeper explosive anger and violence. Unable to express herself, she has always found some other person or group which manifests this. In her marriage, she selected a husband characterized by sudden bouts of temper, while she was concerned, long-suffering, and even-tempered. Her infant fell into this same pattern, born into the function of being restless, fighting, nasty, violent, wrenching. In this way, through the existence of the baby, the mother gained a measure of experiencing that deeper explosive anger and violence.

Andrew was supposed to finish college and to begin work in the company his father built. But instead he defied the family and worked as a ranch hand. Interestingly, the father took all the steam out of the defiance by approving fully of this fling, and sending Andrew a monthly allowance check of $400—which Andrew accepted. The crunch came when, after six months, the father decided that the fling had ended, no more checks would be forthcoming, Andrew was to come home or go forth on his own, fundless forever. The rebellion was squashed, Andrew came home, he had "matured," spoke little of his fling, entered the business. Within a year he had married and his wife was pregnant. Father could keep Andrew in line, even though there were occasional glimmerings of defiance: speeding tickets, a drunken brawl, an affair with another woman, once in a while missing

a family gathering. The baby, Andrew Junior, was invested with the
spirit of the deeper defiance. Before the baby was even born, it was
assigned the function of being openly rebellious. No one would ever
cut him down. Nothing would put him into line. The potential which
had gone underground was exhumed in the form of the baby, and
constituted the means by which Andrew gained a residual experiencing of rebelliousness and defiance. From its inception, the baby fulfilled its function. He kicked, fussed, twisted, whined. He was never
satisfied, made endless and insatiable demands, refused to be born
smoothly, would not eat, would not sleep. As the externalization of
father's defiance, the baby provided the means by which that deeper
potential was kept alive.

What lay within the middle-aged woman consisted of a kind of
deathness, a sterility, arridness, a barren nothingness. In the course of
her life, she found employment in an institution for the custodial care
of children, and worked on a ward of newborns. Indeed, she was
joined by an entire staff of similar caretakers, each of whom enveloped
the infants in the same function, i.e., to manifest the externalization of
their collective deeper potentials. These infants were without life, listless, quiet, arrid, dead. They exhibited what Spitz and Wolf (1946)
term "anaclytic depression," and many died. Infants can manifest the
deeper potentials of their caretaking adults, even when the consequences are those of life or death.

I have been describing the infant as the extended deeper potential,
providing for the experiencing of the parent's deeper potential. The
second function is to externalize the nature of the *relationships* between
the parental operating and deeper potentials. If I fear the deeper
potential, I construct the infant into being that externalized deeper
potential, and then establish a relationship of fear between us. If I
must deny what my deeper potential is, I construct my baby into being the extended deeper potential, and establish a relationship in
which I deny what my baby is. If I hate my deeper potential, I will
make my baby into that externalization, and then hate my baby for
being that way. Almost without exception, relationships with deeper
potentials are disintegrative. If not grossly negative, they contain a
good measure of disintegration. Were these relationships integrative,
the deeper potential would be elevated to the operating domain. The
sober consequence is that this whole enterprise becomes enshrouded
in unhappiness, for, not only is the infant constructed into being the
bad (disintegrative) form of the deeper potential, but it is virtually inevitable that relationships with the infant will be characterized by disintegrative feelings.

A woman may house deeper potentials for sucking, draining,
hanging on, being parasitic. She may hate that within her, and seek to

punish that way of being. As part of her constructed world, she builds a baby who is invested with the function of being that deeper potential. The baby hangs on to her, never lets her go, drains her of every resource, is a parasite from whom she can never be free. Mother establishes a relationship of hate with her baby. She tries to get her baby *not* to be that way. She tries to discourage that way of being, to punish baby for being that way. She is bothered by his needing her too much; she is irritated by his slurping; she is disgusted by his clinging; that constant whining is driving her crazy; he hangs on her and never leaves her alone. The scenario is set, and mother's world complete, for she now has successfully constructed the baby into being the extension of her own deeper potential, and she lives with the baby the same relationship she holds with her own deeper potential.

Parents who are made anxious by their own deeper potentials for experiencing exhibitionism work diligently toward constructing their infants into being that exhibitionism. But the function of the babies in the parents' world exceeds merely that of being the extension of the deeper exhibitionism. In addition, the more important component of the babies' function is to be that of which the parents are anxious. They become ridden with distress and anxiety when babies run about naked, take off their garments in view of others, play with their genitalia, "show off" in front of others. In these moments, parents are made anxious and bothered, and the disintegrative relationship occurs. It is as if parents construct these babies as exhibitionists about whom the parents feel anxiety in their disintegrative relationships with their own externalized deeper potentials.

Parents may be quite bothered by their own deeper potentials for detachment and withdrawal. Their lives consist of continuous battles against the possibility of being taken over by that deeper potential. In a painfully predictable sequence, these parents construct infants who exist as detached things, withdrawn from others, living in their own worlds. But more than merely constructing infants as such externalizations, these parents establish awful relationships with the infants who are that way. Parents see the infant as being detached, and excoriate the infants for being that way. Parents find evidence of withdrawal, and detest the infants for that way of being. They look upon withdrawn, detached infants with hateful derision, and call such ways of being crazy (Laing & Esterson, 1970, p. 38). Parents establish the same relationship with the detached, withdrawn infants as the parents maintain with their own deeper potentials for being detached and withdrawn.

Laing and Esterson (1970) describe a family in which the older brother and the mother bore enmity toward the father, an enmity which reeked in the family atmosphere, and yet was mutually denied by both mother and the older brother. The daughter, Sarah, was made into the expression of their family enmity toward the father, so that she expressed their anger and resentment toward him. Yet it was precisely these expressions that the mother and older brother regarded as evidence of her illness, of her disturbance and craziness. She was made into being the expression of their deeper potential, and she was made to suffer the same disintegrative reaction which they bore toward their own deeper anger and resentment. Parents can assign the infant the function of being the parents' own deeper potentials for being wild, uncivilized, untameable, ruggedly independent, free, primitive, animal-like—and then proceed to hate and fear the infant for being that way. Because the parents' deeper potential is itself feared and hated, the function assigned to the infant is programmed to be surrounded in fear, hate, loathing, and other bad-feelinged manifestations of disintegration.

This mechanism may illuminate a number of related phenomena. For example, with the advent of an infant, the parental deeper potentials may target upon the older sibling. Then, having constructed the older sibling into being the extended deeper potential, the parents relate to the older sibling in the same way they relate to that deeper potential. It is quite common for the parental deeper potential to involve infantness: being taken care of, not having control over bodily functions, being free of adult responsibilities, being fed, mouthing. Yet, the relationship toward being that way is mildly negative. One should not be that way, one ought to act one's age, that is "infantile," it is being "regressed." Someone is to be surrounded with carrying out that role, and being the victim of the disintegrative relationship. Accordingly, the older sibling becomes the externalization of the parents' own deeper potential. The older child now wets the bed, talks like a baby, demands holding and cuddling, must be fed like a baby, defecates in his pants, cannot do what children his age do. And, being this way, the child is scolded by the parents, made to feel bad for being that way, may even be "treated" for his "regression." Yet the architects of the whole scene are the parents and their disintegrative relationships with their own deeper potentials for babyness.

If our relationship with deeper potentials is sharply disintegrative, we are commonly engaged in an unending struggle against the awful inner tendencies. We are in a war of existence in which the horrible possibility is to be overcome and destroyed by the powerful deeper tendencies. We are locked into a power struggle against the growing, looming inner possibilities; they are our mortal enemy. For many people, the infant is the live external manifestation of what lurks within. Once the baby is there, we bear the same intensely disintegrative relationship with it. Freud identified this as the universal oedipal complex and observed the archaic sexual competition, with its inevitable components of destruction *of* the infant or being destroyed *by* the infant. Fromm saw the inevitable struggle as one of authority. Adler saw it as the primordial struggle over power. All of these are strands of the struggle against what we hate and fear within us. When we fear and hate our insides, our relationship with babies is characterized by a war of existence against the baby, a war in which we are terrorized by the fear of being overcome and destroyed by the baby, locked into a final struggle with the baby, struggling not to be overcome by the baby as a growing, looming, powerful force which is our most personal enemy. When our internal relationships are so disintegrative, the baby is assigned the function of being those horrible insides against which we must struggle and likely be destroyed. The war is universal, with the combatants being parents and infants.

When parental figures give birth to their own fiercely hated insides, the core of their relationships with those infants is characterized by murderous impulses and homicidally destructive tendencies. The stage is set for the outbreak of physical violence against infants. These intensely disintegrative relationships occur in the form of mauling, physical abuse, gross mistreatment, infanticide, utter hateful negligence, inhuman aggressive acts directed against the baby. In all of this, the parents are acting out the archaic war against the most powerfully destructive enemy which exists: their own catastrophically hated insides. Killing the baby is preserving their own existences, achieving victory over the raging inner madness which promises to destroy if it is not itself destroyed. Babies are the devil, the flesh and blood exemplification of everything that is evil.

Regardless of the nature of the deeper potential which the infant is to be, it is also given the gift of the relationship. If the parent's relationship is integrative, the infant is given the potential plus the basis for integrative feelings of peacefulness and tranquility, oneness and harmony. But, more typically, the infant is handed the bad form of the deeper potential together with its disintegrative relationship, feelings of anxiety, depression, tension, disjunctiveness, and all other kinds of disintegrative feelings.

From the very beginning, then, parental potentials and their relationships are at work building infants as means of carrying out functions. The infant may be constructed to serve as a major component of a situational context which enables the parental figures to experience potentials. In addition, the infant may be constructed to serve the function of being the extended operating or deeper potentials, enabling the experiencing of these potentials and also the establishment with the infant of the same relationships which are present between the parental operating and deeper potentials. Out of these factors, constructing the infant and its functions, arise the basic foundation of the infant.

The Primitive Personality: Structure and Contents

Parental figures are hard at work constructing infants long before that point which we know as biological conception. Indeed, these forces are at work constructing and defining the infant, framing out the functions to be served by the infant, during a period which runs approximately from months prior to conception and ending months or years after birth. This period typically occupies two to four years or more, during which parental figures are busy constructing the infant through any or all of the four modes, and during which the parental figures are defining the functions to be carried out by the infant. Psychological conception occurs long before biological conception. Indeed, conception, in our sense, can occur with or without biological conception. Prior to fertilization, with or without fertilization, parental figures can begin the construction of infantness in their worlds. In the form of distinctly definable attitudes toward the infant, these constructing variables have been found to occur during pregnancy and to persist some time after birth (Davids, Holden & Gray, 1963).

Defining the infant's primitive personality. In this period of constructing and developing an infant, the necessary components include a parental figure or figures, their potentials and relationships among potentials, and a thing called infantness. That infantness may refer to an actual, physical entity—a baby; or it may refer to an idea, a conceptualization of the actual, physical infant-to-be. All of these components are indicated in Figure 13.1. In this field, the critically determining components include parental potentials and their relationships which construct infantness and define that infantness with certain functions. I refer to this field as the *primitive personality* of the infant (Mahrer, 1967a, 1970b, 1970e). That is, *the primitive personality of the infant includes the parental potentials and relationships which construct the infant and define its functions, and that component of their external worlds which is the constructed and functionally defined infantness.*

As indicated in Figure 13.1, the primitive personality of the infant includes that which is constructed by the parental figures. That may be an actual, physical infant, lying before our eyes on the floor. It may be a fetus inside the mother. It may be a constructed image in the heads of the parental figures who are at work constructing that image. The primitive personality also includes the characteristics which comprise its functions. These characteristics include the infant's being an appropriate situational context, an extended operating potential, or an extended deeper potential. If the infant has the characteristics of being a devouring devil, that characteristic may be in its role as an appropriate situational context to enable the mother to experience her operating potential for being ravaged and torn apart. Another functional possibility is that the infant as devouring devil may be the extension of the parent's own *operating* potential. The third functional possibility is that the infant as devouring devil may be the extension of the parent's own *deeper* potential. Thus the primitive personality of the infant includes defining characteristics which identify the nature or meaning (i.e., the functions) of the constructed infant.

In addition, the primitive personality of the infant includes the nature of the relationships between the constructed infant and the parental figures. If the infant is the extended *operating* potential, the parent may construct the infant into a devouring devil whose relationship to the parent is highly disintegrative, and consists in overwhelming, overcoming the parent as a weak and feckless nothingness. If the infant is the extended *deeper* potential of the parent, the parent may recoil from the infant in horror, for the infant is that which the parent recoils from in himself. Thus the primitive personality includes these disintegrative or integrative relationships among potentials.

Finally, the primitive personality of the *infant* includes the *parental* potentials and relationships responsible for the construction of the infant and the defining of its functions. These potentials (operating potentials 1 and 2 and deeper potentials 3 and 4 in Figure 13.1) and their relationships are the working determinants of the infant, the raw causal agents, the ultimate factors which bring the infant into existence and define its nature. Who houses these factors? Within our perspective, these factors are housed within those persons for whom the infant or that particular infantness is a meaningful and significant event. There may be several persons whose potentials and relationships are responsible for constructing the infant and defining its functions—a mother, a father, a caretaker, a grandfather, an older sibling, an aunt, a person living with the father or mother. The key is the extent to which any person defines that infant or infantness as a significant event, and whose potentials and relationships are critical in constructing that infant and defining its functions. In other words, the primitive personality of the infant includes the potentials and relationships of those persons for whom the infant is a centrally significant event.

The primitive personality of the infant is comprised of (a) the event or thing (actual physical infant, the image of idea or conception of the infant) constructed as infantness, (b) the characteristics which constitute the functions of the infant, (c) the relationships between the constructed infant and the constructing persons, and (d) the potentials and relationships of the constructing persons as they pertain to the infant.

Humanistic theory accepts two complementary definitions of the infant. In one, the infant is that which is constructed by the parents. This definition includes the ordinary definitions accepted by all theories of human beings, viz. the infant is a physical thing (Figure 13.1) whose periphery is its skin. To identify the infant, one need only point to the physical thing encircled by skin. Still within this definition, the infant as that which is constructed by parents can also include an idea, a conception, an image of an infant—with or without an actual, physical infant. An infant exists when a person has an image of it, rearranges a room for it, acts and behaves on the basis of it, undergoes bodily changes because of it, dreams about it, and has feelings about it.

The second, and larger, definition of the infant calls for a willingness on the part of the reader to undergo a conceptual leap. According to humanistic theory, the larger definition of the infant includes the constituents of the primitive personality. That is, the infant is defined as being comprised of that which is constructed by the parents, the characteristics which constitute the functions of the infant, the relationships between the constructed infant and the constructing adults, and the potentials and relationships of the constructing persons as they pertain to the infant. In other words, the larger definition of the infant includes the constructors of the (physical) infant! We thus offer two complementary definitions of the infant. One is that thing which is constructed by parental figures, and the other is the primitive personality. Once the primitive personality may be said to exist, the infant may be said to exist!

Although I venture that such definitions of the infant are found only within humanistic theory, soft leanings in this direction may be found scattered about in the literature. In her conceptual analysis of the mother-infant symbiotic relationship, Mahler (1952, 1958) finds mother and infant as sharing a common boundary. This suggests the conceptual possibility of something more than two separate entities in the closest kind of relationship. Beyond closeness, beyond a very special relationship of two intact, separate entities, is the conceptual possibility of *one* existence, a duality sharing a common boundary. Within the field of the primitive personality are at least two persons occupying the same conceptual territory, a territory housing both a parental figure and the physical infant, a territory which *is* the larger definition of infant.

Another bit of soft support lies in the work of Speers and Lansing (1965) with psychotic children. Their therapeutic work derives from a conception that only a portion of the psychotic child's "personality" resides within the physical child. The balance, indeed the predominant remainder, lies outside the physical child and is in that field comprised of the significant others. Their conceptualization derives from Anthony's notion of a group ego and Mahler's notion of Symbiosis. Out of such a conceptualization emerges a picture of the child's personality extending beyond its skin to encompass significant portions of the personalities of other persons.

Other fragments of soft supporting evidence lie in clinical observations of the incredible similarities between parents and infants. Typically, such observations are found in psychoanalytic reports. For example, Glauber (1953) cites similarities of extraordinary proportions between the needs and anxieties of very young stutterers and those of their mothers. Glauber leans hard in the direction of describing these needs and anxieties as if mother and infant share the same personality structure. Throughout the research on fetal development and neonatal growth are observations of further mother-infant identities, polarities and complementarities ranging from "schizophrenia" (e.g., Lidz et al., 1958; McConaghy, 1959) to agitation, from intelligence to emotionality. These observations have persisted in the face of changing sets of explanations to account for such far-ranging incredible similarities. I suggest that these observations are cordial to our definition of the primitive personality of the infant.

Lambent soft glows of support lie in what is known as field or systems theory. With regard to the understanding of a family, for example, systems theory argues that we can make better sense of the component persons by understanding the field of which each is a component. That field has properties which are describable on their own, independent of the properties of the separate components. From this perspective, the infant is a part of a system, a field which has its own distinctive properties. The next step, one taken by humanistic theory, is that the infant *is* the encompassing field or system.

It is understandable that there is virtually no theory of human beings holding a definition of the infant as a field of which the physical infant is but a part. It is understandable for at least three reasons. First, our preponderant system of thought accepts the identifying of a thing as coterminal with its physical boundary. As applied to human beings, mother is this physical thing, father is that physical thing, and the infant is that other physical thing over there. In contrast, humanistic theory suggests that the infant is more than the physical thing known as infant. Furthermore, humanistic theory suggests that the infant can exist without any physical thing known as the infant. To accept the infant as more than the physical thing means going beyond a definition which restricts the meaning of infant to its physical boundary.

Second, our common system of thought assumes a gap between persons and between objects. There is a gap between infant and mother, between infant as one object and father as another object.

The two may influence each other, relate together, effect one another, be intimate and close. But each is separate and distinct as entities in interaction. In contrast. humanistic theory suggests that a person constructs the external world in which the person exists. Mother constructs the external world which can occur as the extension of her being. Her boundary can extend beyond her skin to encompass objects, things, other persons which are constructed as segments of her external world. Thus, according to humanistic theory, there need be no gap between mother and infant. Mother's personality, the definition of her being, can encompass the infant. Instead of two separate entities interacting across a gap, the two can each be a part of the other.

Third, in contrast to our common system of thought, humanistic theory suggests that the definition of an object varies with the context. What mother is depends upon our context of understanding. Within the context of mother, mother is one thing, the center of a given context. Within that context, baby is an extension of mother, a constructed component of her world. But when we switch to the context of the infant, and hold the infant as the center of that context, then mother becomes a constituent of baby. Humanistic theory suggests that mother (or father or baby or any person or object) may be one thing or two things, or even more, depending on the contexts in which mother is understood. These are difficult conceptual switches to undertake, but they are necessary to understand our definition of the infant as coterminal with its primitive personality.

Contents of the primitive personality. I have conceptualized the infant as including the potentials and relationships of the parental figures as they relate to the (physical) infant. Bluntly, the potentials of the infant are the relevant potentials of the significant figures. That is, *the potentials of the infant are those potentials of the figures within the primitive personality which pertain to the infant.* If father's potentials include those for experiencing rugged independence and for experiencing passivity, then, to the extent that these potentials relate to the infant, it may be said that the primitive personality of the infant includes potentials for rugged independence and for passivity. In Figure 13.1, the larger primitive personality structure of the infant includes operating potential 1 and deeper potential 3. If mother constructs and relates to the infant on the basis of potentials for affectional closeness and sexuality (operating potential 2 and deeper potential 4, Figure 13.1), then these two potentials are said to be parts of the larger definition of the infant.

Thus the infant's personality includes much more than what parents *do* to the infant. Parents may behave this way or that way, may laugh at or love the infant, may cuddle or feed the infant. Yet the larger meaning of the infant includes the parents as well as what the parents do, the parental potentials as well as the parental behaviors toward the infant. This primitive personality includes the person who does the cuddling, as well as the cuddling, the feeder as well as the act of feeding. Take, for example, the case of Clare, as described by Horney (1942). From the beginning, Clare was constructed to fulfill the function of the unwelcomed intruder. In the blossoming of this function, Clare *was* the unwelcomed intruder, complete with feelings of being unlikeable, beliefs that everything that occurred was inevitably her fault, and living out the life of the rejected intruder. Yet the deepest level of Clare's personality included the underpinnings which had existed in the mother from the onset of Clare's existence. Mother experienced being "in" a closely bonded clique, being part of a highly close knit bond. That potential was housed within mother, and occurred between mother and Clare's older brother. Yet that potential also existed within the larger perimeter of Clare's primitive personality. Clare not only was the unwelcome intruder, she too housed the potential for experiencing being part of a closely bonded clique. Clare had never lived that potential, yet, because it existed within mother in the earliest primitive personality, it likewise existed within Clare's deeper potentialities.

The same reasoning places some of the *relationships* of the significant figures within the larger conception of the infant. That is, *the relationships among potentials of the infant are those relationships among the potentials of the figures within the primitive personality which pertain to the infant.* The disintegrative or integrative nature of these relationships becomes the nature of relationships within our larger definition of the infant's primitive personality. If these relationships are disintegrative, then relationships among the infant's potentials may be said to be disintegrative. For example, if father's deeper potential relates to passivity, and if relationships with the father's operating potential for rugged independence are disintegrative, then these same disintegrative relationships may be said to characterize the infant's own relationships. If mother is friendly and accepting with her deeper sexuality, then it may be said that integrative relationships embrace the infant's potential for experiencing sexuality. If father's passivity and mother's sexuality clash with one another, then the infant's potentials for experiencing passivity and sexuality bear disintegrative relationships toward one another. As long as the potentials pertain to the physical infant and exist within the primitive field, it does not matter whether they are housed within mother or father or both. The key is the nature of relationships occurring within one person or in two or more persons within the primitive field.

Now we are in a position to grasp the ultimate causal basis of the most fundamental integrative or disintegrative feelings within the infant. As an integrative feeling, the roots of love lie within the nature of the relationships within the totality of the primitive personality. As indicated in Figure 13.1, these relationships occur between relationships *among* father, mother, and infant, and also between relationships *within* mother and *within* father. If these are integrative relationships, then the basis is there for integrating loving feelings within the total personality of the infant. If mother's internal relationships are characterized by love, if there is a loving relationship between mother and father's potentials for experiencing, if the relationships between parents and the infant are characterized by love, then it may be said that the basis for love exists within the primitive personality of the infant. There is no question about the crucial importance given to love by clinicians and theoreticians concerned with the foundations of the infant's personality. Love is held to be of profound importance not only in the child's future healthy development (Langdon & Stout, 1951), but also as a crucial variable in sequelae ranging from ability to tolerate frustration to the nature of general peer relationships, from the child's degree of empathic sensitivity to the likelihood of the development of ulcers. Yet theories of personality have no systematic way of conceptualizing the foundations of love. Ordinarily, the infant is described as having needs or drives for love which differ in no essential structural way from other needs or drives. Humanistic theory differs. Love originates in the nature of the relationships among potentials within the primitive personality. In this sense, loving relationships (or fearful, hateful disintegrative relationships) are inevitable and universal. Regardless of the nature of the potentials within the primitive personality, the relationships determine whether the basis is there for integrative loving or disintegrative hating. Love (or disintegrative hate) is massively powerful and far-reaching in its impacts because of its inevitable omnipresence in all relationships among potentials. Love (or disintegrative hate) exists as a statement of these relationships, and, as such, it acquires its profound importance in the manufacture of the kind of person the infant is and can become.

Every infant "has" relationships among its potentials. Our theory asserts that these relationships are best described as varying from integrative to disintegrative, and that the universal characteristics of all infants consist *only* of relationships between potentials, relationships of either an integrative or a disintegrative nature. Except for this, we eschew all other statements about supposedly universal human conflicts. We reject the thesis that the universal human conflict is between the expression and control of aggressive and sexual instincts. We reject that our universal human conflict is between needs for belongingness, security, and closeness, and needs for independence, separation, freedom. Other statements refer to the grand universal conflict as occurring between our animal nature and our human nature, forces of growth and development versus forces of containment and suppression, good versus evil, self versus society, life versus death, mind versus body, we versus they, struggles for survival, struggles for dominance and control, and so on and on. In each of these, there is an assumption of particular kinds of archaic human processes, statements about the fundamental content of human personality or "basic motivations." Our concept of the primitive personality includes no such specific content or nature of the basic potentials or motivations of the infant. There is no necessary theoretical basis for presuming that infants contain basic processes whose nature is aggressive or sexual or involves closeness or security or freedom or growth or good or life or we-ness or survival or anything else. What *is* necessary, and therefore universal, is the existence of integrative or disintegrative relationships among potentials, regardless of there nature or content. All human beings have relationships which vary along a continuum from integrative to disintegrative.

Coupled with these relationships are feelings. Once relationships are present in the primitive personality, there will be feelings—either the bad feelings of disintegration or the good feelings of integration. From the very beginning, then, the infant-*as-primitive-personality* may be said to "have" disintegrative feelings of anxiety, tension, or disjunctiveness, or integrative feelings of peacefulness, oneness, or unity. As indicated in Figure 13.1, these relationships may occur within parental figures, between parental figures, or in relationship with the physical infant. Yet, in all three instances, it is the parent who is centrally involved, and it is within the parent that the feeling occurs. For example, the mother who is breastfeeding the physical infant may be recoiling from her own potential for being inadequate, for not being sufficient, for having insufficient resources. She may then be *feeling* anxiety, and that anxiety becomes a central feature of the immediate state of the primitive personality. That is, the infant may be said to "have" anxiety because anxiety is occurring in the primitive personality. In the same way, the breastfeeding mother may be in a state of integrative oneness with her own potential for giving, providing, nurturing. To that extent, the mother may be feeling oneness and integrative peacefulness and unity. In this sense, the infant may be said to "have" an integrative feeling of oneness, peacefulness, and unity.

Yet, regardless of the universality of integrative-disintegrative relationships, the contents of the primitive personality are the basic foundation of what is the infant. As indicated in Figure 13.1, the potentials and relationships of the infant consist of those present in the parental figures and focused upon the infant. In one mother, there was a fearfulness of something which was sensed as a withdrawn unresponsiveness. She recoiled against this, struggled to cope with this, tried not to be overwhelmed by this. When we consider her infant daughter we can speak of her primitive personality containing a potential for withdrawn unresponsiveness, together with disintegrative relationships accompanying this potential. Another mother has a similar potential, but in her it occurs as an intactness and independence, an integrated potential whose relationships are characterized by good feelings of peacefulness and wholeness, unity and inner harmony. She is at home with this potential, comfortable with being it. When we consider *her* daughter, we can speak of a primitive personality including a potential for intactness and independence, framed within relationships which are peaceful, loving, harmonious. What is present in the primitive personality constitutes the very heart of the raw stuff which is the infant—including the infant's potentials and the nature of their relationships.

What, then, are the contents of the primitive personality?

1. There is a focalized "infantness." This may be in the form of an image (idea, conception) of an infant, or it may be in the form of an actual physical event referred to as the infant.

2. There is a centering upon the infantness. That is, the encompassing primitive field focuses upon the infantness as a meaningful event in constructing it and defining its functions.

3. There is a set of characteristics which comprise the functions of that infantness. These functions include the infant as an appropriate situational context, an extended operating potential, or an extended deeper potential.

4. There are potentials for experiencing. These are located within the significant figures within the primitive field, figures for whom the infant is a meaningful central focus.

5. There are relationships between potentials. These include integrative and disintegrative relationships, and are located within each of the component figures, between them, and between each of them and the focalized infant.

6. There is a capacity for actualization of the potentials within the primitive personality. Coupled with this is a capacity for the good feelings which accompany actualization—and the bad feelings which accompany a state of unfeeling or lack of actualization.

7. There is a potential for integrative relationships between potentials. Relationships can become integrated, and the bad (disintegrative) form of a potential can be converted to a good (integrative) form. Coupled with this is a capacity for the good feelings of integration—and the bad feelings of disintegration.

Primitive personality: the wellsprings of genesis. The constitutents of this primitive field also constitute the answer to where it all originates, to the basic foundations of the infant, to what makes the infant what it is. In the processes and variables of the primitive personality lie the answers to the origins of the personality, and to the nature of the most fundamental factors which determine the basic nature of a person. I submit that the concept of the primitive personality is sufficiently robust to take its place among other grand answers to these questions, answers which include heredity, constitution, biology, neurophysiology, learning, environmental and social variables.

In tracing the ultimate roots of depression, Klein (1948a) was led to that period prior to the earliest individuation and the development of object relations. The roots lay in the first days and weeks of life. Something important was occurring here, something which caused the later depression. It was here, but Klein could not find where to look. Early trauma may be dismissed; biological changes may be dismissed; neurophysiological mechanisms seem unable to provide an explanation. What are the mechanisms, the critical factors and variables that were somehow already working in the earliest days and weeks of life? Our answer to this and every other question about the ultimate factors and variables in the causal foundation of the infant is that all of the answers reside within the field of the primitive personality.

Depression is one of myriads of problems whose roots have eluded clinicians, theorists, and researchers. What is the ultimate cause of problems, of difficulties and stresses, of psychopathology, of painful behavior? The pursuit of the root causes has led to early learning experiences, to constitutional predispositions, or to pathological disease processes (Ainsworth, 1945). I submit the factors and variables of the primitive personality as a fourth causal bedrock of answers to this ancient question, the answer of humanistic theory to the question of where and how it all begins.

In a review of the early precursors of adult pathology, Ricks (1970) interprets the research as indicating that we can no longer support theories which hold to the idea that human problems have their origins in traumas or environmental stress or acute causal events. Instead, he points toward variables which I accept as those of the primitive personality of the infant: "The characteristics of the parents, their relationship with each other, and the kind of environment they create for the growing child need investigation" (Ricks, 1970, p. 301). Researchers are beginning to open up the possibility that the grand answers we have used are simply not sufficient to explain where human problems and difficulties begin. Here and there are occasional hintings that answers lie in what humanistic theory describes as the primitive personality. For example, in studying the roots of schizophrenic behavior, Fisher, Boyd, Walker and Sheer (1959) found that the probability of such behavior was high when each of the parents was "disturbed." But the interesting aspect of their findings is that the probability of the emergence of such behavior was *lower* when the *relationships* among these "disturbed" parents were harmonious (i.e., integrated), and *higher* when the *relationships* were not harmonious (i.e., disintegrated). Here is a soft, indirect hinting of the importance of the nature of the relationships between potentials for painful behavior or "psychopathology." I suspect that such a line of research will tell us a great deal more than we now know about the genesis of human problems and sufferings.

Ricks is one of many who essentially confess that we are unable to identify the early roots of problems, that we know precious little about what there is in early life that bears regular and systematic linkages with later ways of being (Frank, 1965; Orlansky, 1949). As popular as are theories using genetics, biology, neurophysiology, environmental stress, traumas, or acute causal events to predict the later occurrence of human problems, the roots of human problems remain virtually undisclosed. I propose that the most robust reservoir of predictions of human problems and ways of being resides in the factors, variables, and processes of the primitive personality. When we accurately, carefully, and exhaustively fill in the contents of the schema in Figure 13.1, our thesis is that prediction of the later development of that human being can be achieved.

But the influence of parental figures goes far beyond human problems and difficulties. Beyond problems, the persons who occupy central roles in the primitive personality of the infant *are* that infant. These persons constitute what the infant is. I submit that the highest level of social influence is exemplified by the parent and the infant, for the infant *is* the parent. A parent cannot try to be a good parent or to behave in helpful ways toward the infant. The parent *is already constitutive* of the infant. That in the parent which tries to be a good parent or to behave in helpful ways is already a central ingredient of the infant. Because we already *are* our infants, it is inaccurate to presume that we can influence or affect or modify or respond to or raise infants. Indeed, I can think of no greater arena of social influence than inserting oneself into the infant's primitive personality. For those who seek to influence society (or a community or social groups or another person), the avenue of highest effectiveness lies in being a significant component in the primitive personalities of infants.

It is intriguing to me that virtually all infants in Western cultures are left alone with their mothers during the period of greatest development of the primitive field. From a few weeks after birth to the end of the first year or so, the infant belongs to the mother figure. With the enormous complex of social institutions we have developed, none of them intrudes into this almost sacrosanct relationship. There are many social institutions around pregnancy and birth. The family is involved. The church takes part. The field of medicine takes part. Governmental institutions are involved. Once the baby is born, it is as if we are complicit in leaving mother and baby alone. Indeed, that relationship is deemed special. It is as if there is a vacuum during that period. Only later does society intrude in the form of nurseries and, later, schools. At every age in our life we are embedded in and surrounded by social institutions—except for that special early period. I suspect it is no accident that we leave mother and baby alone during the very period in which the primitive field is made most viable, and during which the infant is perhaps most open to social influence.

For those who are concerned with social change, the enormous influence of parental figures is a golden key. The slightest modification in the primitive fields of a community of infants will result in the most profound differences in the persons whom the infants become, and equally profound differences in the society constructed by those persons. Indeed, I am convinced that the most substantial and enduring social changes are a function of changes in the constituency of the primitive personalities of collective infants (Mahrer, 1970e, 1973). On this score, I believe the primitive personalities of collective infants have long-range social impacts of greater magnitude than change in mental health, politics, science, economics, technology, government, or any other system whereby social change is sought.

My thesis has been that the primitive personality is the ultimate answer to our questions about human beings—their basic origins, their problems, their social worlds. The contours of the field encompassing the physical infant are the contours of what that physical infant and its encompassing world will become. There is at least one other question for which the concept of the primitive field is held forth as an answer: the question of the wellsprings of the infant's very existence and life. The encompassing primitive field does more than lay its impact upon the physical infant. As indicated in the contents of the primitive field, it *centers* upon the infantness, it *focuses* upon the infantness as a meaningful event. In this focused centering, the encompassing primitive field may be said to vitalize and activate that infantness. In other words, the primitive field is the primary resource of activation. It vitalizes and enlivens the infantness. It generates process, movement, vitality, activation, life. This fundamental property of the primitive field is occurring whether we consider the fetus being provided with nutriment, a neonate being breast fed by the mother, a grandfather having feelings of affection as he holds the infant, or the older sibling engaging the baby in a fixed mutual gaze.

Without the activating property of the primitive field, there is a truncation of the infant's aliveness, activation, vitality, life. Without this activating primitive field, the infantness atrophies, or, in extreme instances, fails to come to life (cf. Dennis, 1941, 1960; Dennis & Najarian, 1957; Provence & Lipton, 1962; Spitz, 1945; Spitz & Wolf, 1946). Our search for the wellsprings of life itself must include the activating resources of the encompassing primitive field. According to our hypothesis, this life-promoting agent is not within the infant's body, not within its bodily processes conceptualized chemically, neurologically, physiologically. There are hints, in research represented by those cited above, that the life-promoting agent may occur in the form of archaic caring, nurturance, and stimulation. I suspect that the mechanism whereby the physical parent activates the physical infantness is further hinted at in the phenomenological research of what Buytendijk (1950) names primitive touch-contact, and in the macaque monkey research on what Harlow and Zimmerman (1959) term contact comfort. Such hints are within the neighborhood of our own hypothesis that the life-promoting resources lie within the activating primitive field.

I consider the activating characteristics of this field as in a continuous state of change. From moment to moment there is a fluidity in the locus, magnitude, and quality of the activation. When mother caresses the infant, the activation is located in that interaction. Its locus shifts when mother's attention drifts to other aspects of her life, and father smiles at baby or becomes annoyed at baby's crying. The quality of the activation changes as the primitive potentials and their relationships shift from one kind to another. The depth, intensity, and magnitude of this activation change when mother focuses more and more, or less and less, of her centered attentiveness upon the infant. But whether the state of activation is high or low, the infant may be said to exist in a field which is activating, and in which the nature and magnitude of activation is in a continuous state of change.

There is some soft evidence of such an encompassing activating field in research on sleep and dreams. Jones (1970) has summarized a body of research which seems to indicate a second state of sleep, one whose activated nature is found in irregular pulse, blood pressure, respiration, and in rapid conjugate eye movements, increased brain temperature and metabolic rate, sporadic heightened muscular activity, a low voltage desynchronized cortical EEG pattern, and, in males, penile erection. Incidentally, it is in this state that there is a high correlation with the reporting of dreams when awakened. What is interestingly suggestive for our hypothesis is that research has indicated that the neonate exists in this activated sleep state about half of its sleeping time, and that the proportion of sleep time spent in this activated state seems to decline regularly with increasing age and development. "At age two the percentage is 40; at age five it is 25 to 30;

during adolescence and adulthood it is 20; and at 60 years of age it is around 15" (Jones, 1970, p. 27). For prematurely born babies, the proportion rises to about 75 percent, and indications are that in the intrauterine condition, the fetus is entirely in this state.

Here is a body of research whose results have almost exclusively been interpreted within a biological framework. Yet they bear upon our hypothesis of the physical infant existing in an encompassing activating field whose properties are in a continuous state of flux. From the perspective of humanistic theory, these results are taken as cordial to the following speculative statements. From the moment of its origin, the fetus exists in an enveloping field which activates and vitalizes that fetus. The outer perimeter of that primitive field can enlarge or shrink. In the waking state, when the newborn is the focalized center of parental potentials and relationships, the outer perimeter is enlarged. In the sleeping state, the field is constricted. But the field is activating and vitalizing regardless of its magnitude. The working strength of this activation and vitalization seems to be highest in the fetal state, and to reduce progressively in the neonatal state, infancy, childhood, and on into adulthood.

This activating field, so essential and compelling in the stages of infancy, is what I refer to as the primitive personality. In the genesis of infantness, the primitive personality activates, vitalizes, enlivens. It surrounds the infantness with a field which makes it alive.

THE QUESTION OF HUMAN NATURE

Humanistic theory accounts for the origins of infants by the concept of the primitive personality. Among the more traditional answers is that infants are the way they are because of *human nature;* the fundamental origins of human beings lie in that which is intrinsic to human nature. How does our concept of the primitive personality compare with the concept of "human nature" on the origins of human beings?

The Assumption of Discoverable Human Nature

Is there a discoverable human nature? Is there any irreducible set of fundamental properties of human nature? If our research and theoretical analyses are successful, will we arrive at the basic core of humanness? As described in Chapter 4, the position adopted by humanistic theory is that the answer to each of these questions is no. When we look at the human infant, humanistic theory accepts the position that there is *no* discoverable or identifiable basic nature to that infant. It is not a fundamentally biological thing or a fundamentally neurological thing, neither a fundamentally genetic nor a psychological thing. It has no *basic nature*. Instead, we select modes of description to make conceptual-scientific sense of that event called infant. Each mode of description is free to describe an infant as having, or not having, a basic nature. Those which opt to describe the infant as comprised of basic events with discoverable, identifiable natures can, and do, fill in the contents of "human nature." Humanistic theory assumes no such basic nature and, therefore, does not set out on a search for the contents of that which is not assumed to exist.

In contrast to our own position, however, nearly every approach assumes that there *is* a particular kind of discoverable human nature. Thus each approach proclaims that it alone has grasped what human nature really is. As popular approaches replace one another, each wave of adherents believes that it has discovered the way the infant really is—its basically irreducible human nature. "The shift in point-of-view—to set the antithesis sharply—has been from the child who is a passive receptacle, into which learning and maturation pour knowledge and skills and affects until he is full, to the child as a complex, competent organism who, by acting on the environment and being acted upon in turn, develops more elaborated and balanced ways of dealing with discrepancy, conflict, and disequilibrium" (Kessen, 1953, p. 52). From the perspective of humanistic theory, the shift from one grasping of the infant's "real" nature to another is merely a shift from one mode of description to another. No paradigm is what the infant really is, for the infant *is* nothing (see Chapter 4). He is not fundamentally a passive receptacle any more than he is a chemical thing, no more a competent organism acting upon the environment than he is a system of mechanical forces, the expression of God's will, a psychological thing, a biological thing, or a complicated mixture of fire, air, and water. Each shift in paradigm, each embracing of a new discovery of the infant's basic nature is merely another way of grasping the infant by a given mode of description, and not the capturing of the real intrinsic human nature of the infant.

Humanistic theory articulates one mode of description using a concept of the primitive personality. According to our theory, the primitive personality (like theorists) can make the infant into a passive receptacle. It can also make the infant into a competent organism interacting with an external environment. In place of arguments as to which paradigm is the real one, we accept that each proposed paradigm may be a correct description of some infants but not necessarily all infants. Every basic paradigm of the infant's intrinsic human nature is another possible expression of what the primitive personality (or theorists) can produce. In place of a fruitless search for "the" real, fundamental paradigm, we accept the primitive personality as capable of producing *many* different kinds—each of which is a useful and appropriate mode of describing some infants. It can produce infants who are passive responders and infants who are active experience-seekers. From our perspective, the origins of what the infant basically is lie in the capabilities of the primitive personality and not at all in the assumed human nature of infants.

Approaches which label infants as being active or passive may be quite accurate in their observations, but erroneous in concluding that infants are *intrinsically* active or *intrinsically* passive. Psychoanalytic and learning approaches view the infant through a conceptual system in which the infant is assumed to be intrinsically *passive*, and, accordingly, to be passive in its relationships with the external world. In contrast, Piaget's theory of development and the etho-logical theory of human interaction emphasize the intrinsic *activity* in the infant's relationships. From the perspective of humanistic theory, both are correct in finding evidence of the infant being active or passive in its relationships. Yet both approaches are in error in sharing an assumption that the infant's basic activeness or passiveness is intrinsic in the structure of human nature.

The search for biophysical roots of human nature. Where humanistic theory locates the fundamental roots in the primitive personality, psychoanalysis looks to instincts. The psychoanalytic concept of instincts rests upon a biophysical base wherein it is possible to follow a reductionistic analysis and to discover the basic, biophysical nature of instincts. Instincts can be reduced to their biophysical elements, and those elements exist, are discoverable and identifiable. Within our framework, there is *no* human nature (except that which we construct), and it is therefore *not* discoverable—even by reducing instincts to their fundamental biophysical elements.

Psychoanalysis is joined by other approaches which accept the assumption that basically the infant is a biological organism, and the most fundamental nature of the infant includes biological needs (see Chapter 4). Intrinsic to human nature, then, are biological needs for food, water, warmth, escape from injury, shelter, rest, and so on (e.g., Maher, 1966, p. 60; Maslow & Murphy, 1954). Along with such social learning theorists as Walters and Parke (1964), I reject the framing of a basic physiological need for food—or any other kind of basic physiological drive or need. From the perspective of humanistic theory, the infant is said to have a larger encompassing primitive personality whose basic content includes potentials for experiencing (not basic physiological needs) and relationships among these potentials for experiencing. But all of these are *constructions*, for our philosophical position holds that there is no "human nature" at all—not one with physiological needs, and not one with potentials for experiencing.

Human nature and research inquiry. It seems paradoxical that systematic research inquiry is facilitated by *abandoning* a notion of human nature, and is closed off by *clinging* to the notion of human nature. Psychoanalysis is by no means alone in assuming that there is an intrinsic human nature. As discussed in Chapter 4, the preponderance of approaches believe that there is some kind of irreducible base to human nature. Their argument with one another revolves around the nature of this irreducible base. In contrast to *humanistic theory*, there exists a body of thought known as *humanism* which holds its own notions of what intrinsic human nature is like. According to the humanists, the infant has a basic nature which is inherently free, spontaneous, creative, loving, active, striving, actualizing. What is more, this human nature is inherently there *and beyond systematic inquiry.* Those who assume such a human nature are massively disinclined to entertain questions such as the following: How may we describe these qualities in any systematic fashion? How do they become a part of human nature? How may we assess their presence? Many humanists go beyond a disinterest in such questions into an active denial that such questions are answerable. Indeed, humanism may in itself preclude the possibility of systematic answers to such questions (Needleman, 1967).

To tuck assumed characteristics into "human nature" is virtually to place these characteristics beyond research investigation. The humanists' picture of infants as idyllic flower children is uninvestigateable as long as it is considered part of human nature. But so too is *any* picture of human nature. Whatever characteristics are assumed to be a part of human nature are therefore nearly beyond the pale of systematic inquiry, whether those characteristics refer to the humanists' freedom and spontaneity or to Adlerian power, to psychoanalytic instincts or to biophysical needs.

*Answers Lie within the Primitive Personality, not within
the Physical Infant's "Human Nature"*

How do we make sense of the way the infant is? How do we understand centuries of observations about the infant—its properties and characteristics, its qualities and behaviors? Almost without exception, every approach has sought the answers inside the skin of the physical infant. Humanistic theory invites us to dilate the scope to include the field encompassing the physical infant. The concept of the primitive personality enables us to look outside the skin of the infant for the most fundamental answers to the most fundamental questions. We understand that this particular infant exists, or is restless, or cries incessantly, or is difficult to wean, because of variables which lie within that primitive field. If we do not use the concept of the primitive personality, then the answers tend to lie within the skin of the physical infant. Once the answers lie within the skin of the physical infant, we are led to accepting the idea of human nature, i.e. the infant is the way it is because these are the characteristics of being human. Once we know how to look for the answers in the field surrounding the infant, there is no need to cling to something called human nature.

When we dilate our focus to include the whole of the primitive personality, we find, already there, virtually everything that observers try to stuff inside the skin of the physical infant. Indeed, when we investigate the encompassing primitive field, we find the answers to the mystery of how the infant is what it is.

Properties of the neonate: primitive personality versus human nature. There is a package of observations about the neonate. These observations are up for conceptual grabs, and the question is which theoretical networks are sufficiently substantial to make good sense of this package? Included in this package are observations of such behavioral phenomena as curiosity and exploratory behavior, planning and intending behavior, manipulatory behavior, locomotion, and the development of language. In his review of relevant theory and research, White (1959, 1963) concluded that concepts of instinctual forces and principles of homeostatic energy systems are too feeble to provide an adequate explanation. Our proposal is to expand the explanatory region beyond the skin of the infant to include the primitive personality. As discussed in Chapter 14, it is our thesis that the primitive field provides a mode of describing neonate behavior whose robustness exceeds that of concepts of instinctual forces and principles of homeostatic energy systems located inside the physical infant.

In addition to the above behaviors, neonates are generally characterized by well-developed abilities including remarkable visual resolution powers, an ability to track and find, an ability to discriminate variations in olfactory stimulation, pitch, and light intensity, as well as a refined ability to inhibit general movement upon insertion of a nipple into its mouth (Kessen, 1953). Among the explanatory options is that of invoking a human nature complete with such well-developed abilities. The explanation then lies in the assertion that such abilities are intrinsic to human nature. Humanistic theory describes these abilities as the final products of at least a year of productive effort on the part of the primitive field. The primitive field has worked diligently and productively to construct the neonate into a very specific entity, so that the abilities of the neonate are evidence of the productive powers of the primitive field rather than evidence of what is inherent in human nature.

The issue of whether or not the newborn "has" an "ego" (or sense of self) is tied to the kinds of abilities found in the newborn. If certain abilities are present, they are suggestive of a simple ego; if they are lacking, even a simple ego is not yet present. Where do we look to answer this question? How do we find out whether the infant has the ability to receive and to perceive the external world, has mastery of motor apparatus, has an ability to bind by cathecting? If we study just the physical neonate, we may justifiably conclude that these are missing from the neonate, and assert that the neonate therefore lacks an ego (Fenichel, 1954c). It is on such lines of reasoning that various approaches are led to conclude that the neonate lacks a self, an "I," a consciousness (Mead, 1934). If, however, we expand our domain to include the primitive field, then a different set of (psychoanalytic) conclusions would be in order. The neonate does have an ego; furthermore, that ego is quite refined and sophisticated. There is no ego *as part of the package of human nature*, but the infant does have an ego (self, "I") when we regard the infant as the primitive personality.

The major focus of our discussion is not the issue of whether or not the infant has an ego (or self or "I"). Yet it is interesting that, as a side topic, it is the *learning* approach which makes the most solid case for the existence of a well-developed ego in the neonate. Working within a learning theory framework, Watson (1967), for example, describes the newborn as functioning under a refined instructional set to identify and repeat whatever behavioral response immediately preceded the occurrence of the rewarding stimulus. Here is an ego or self so sophisticated that it consists of refined cognitive learning sets. Are these part of the properties of the physical neonate? Our perspective holds that when these cognitions are present, they are located within the *primitive personality*, and not within the cognitive system of the physical infant. These cognitions may well be within the significant figures of the encompassing field, and, to that extent, they *are* constituents of the larger definition of the infant.

According to Rogers (1959), the infant has an already developed perception of reality. It is not pertinent whether an ability to perceive reality is an ego function—and therefore evidence of a neonatal ego. What is pertinent is that this ability to perceive reality is presumed to be intrinsic to the infant's human nature. In Roger's system, this ability is central to the determination of the infant's behavior, which is held as flowing out of the infant's perceived reality and not the reality as defined by others. If the infant perceives the stranger as threatening, the infant may cry, and the ability to perceive the stranger as threatening is intrinsic to the infant's nature. Humanistic theory holds that the ability to perceive reality is a function of the *primitive field*, and not the *physical infant*. When we enlarge the definition of the infant to include the larger field, there is a quality of perceiving reality. In this sense, and only in this sense, may the infant be said to have the ability to perceive reality.

Basic tendencies: primitive personality versus human nature. Each infant may be described as "having" particular kinds of "basic tendencies." Thus a given infant may be described as having basic potentials for security or for explosiveness or for dominance. These potentials—part of the fundamental properties of the infant—have their particular nature because of the primitive personality. We reject an assumption that the infant has any fundamental properties by virtue of being human, viz. as a function of human nature. Our hypothesis is that the predominance of that which is interpreted as the infant's basic tendencies (needs, drives, motivations) is a behavioral expression of the functions into which the physical infant is constructed. Parental figures construct infantness and endow it with specific functions. For example, the infant is to be passive or competent or affectionate or omnipotent—in fulfilling the functions assigned to it by the primitive field. Thus it is easy (but erroneous) to presume that the physical infant has intrinsic basic tendencies or needs or drives or motivations for passivity, competence, affection, or omnipotence.

From our perspective, some infants may have basic tendencies describable by words such as mastery of reality, sense of competence, effectance (White, 1959). If so, these are there because of the nature and contents of those particular infants' primitive personalities. We reject the idea of a human nature such that all infants have inherent, intrinsic tendencies toward mastery of reality, competence, or effectance. These qualities are simply not to be assumed as merely present by virtue of the humanness of the infant. The apparent tendency in many infants to move toward progressive mastery of reality, competence, or effectance, and the differences across infants in the degree to which this tendency is present (Bronson, 1974) are taken as a function of the nature of primitive personalities rather than elusive qualities of an assumed human nature.

In the same way, the primitive personalities of some infants may include omnipotence, whereas omnipotence is not a salient characteristic of other primitive personalities. Some infants will "have" omnipotence and others will not. If, on the other hand, one accepts a notion of human nature, then omnipotence may be understood as a component of human nature, and a fundamental part of every infant. It is consistent with this latter approach that all infants will "have" omnipotence, and may go through an omnipotent stage of development (e.g., Fenichel, 1954c). Our theory postulates no such stage of development, no intrinsic omnipotence, no human nature containing a necessary omnipotence—or mastery of reality, sense of competence, or effectance.

In the construction of infantness, and in defining the functions to be played by that constructed infantness, love often plays a significant part. Love plays such a significant part because of the structure and contents of the primitive personality. Loving (integrated) or unloving (disintegrated) relationships among potentials are very important in the construction and function-defining of the infant. Indeed, what is universal is the loving (integrated) or unloving (disintegrated) nature of *relationships*. If the relationships are integrated, then what shines forth is love. If relationships are disintegrated, then it is common for behavioral interactions to seek evidence of love, acceptance, belonging, intimacy, in a grand renunciation and denial of the disintegrated nature of relationships. Thus the infant is made to be something which participates in and toward loving relationships. Also, love itself may be a common potential in parental figures and, to that extent, it frequently is present in the primitive personality—and therefore is part of the package of the infant. Humanistic theory thus accounts for the presence of love and loving relationships in the primitive field and also in the constructed physical infant. In none of this, however, is there any notion of an infant human nature complete with basic needs or drives or motivations or basic tendencies for love. Yet theorists and researchers alike conceive of infants with intrinsic psychological needs for love, intimacy, closeness, tenderness, affection, belongingness, emotional contact, and contact-stimulation-comfort (e.g., Dennis, 1941; Fromm-Reichmann, 1959; Maslow, 1968, 1970b; Spitz, 1945).

In one form or another, variations on the love-as-an-intrinsic-need theme are found in nearly all personality approaches. Within the client-centered approach, as one example, it surfaces as a universal need for positive regard. Each individual has a need to regard oneself positively, and to be regarded positively. Rogers refers to this directly as ". . . a need for positive regard. This need is universal in human beings, and in the individual, is pervasive and persistent" (1959, p. 222). Although humanistic theory rejects any built-in "needs," especially those which are assumed to be intrinsic to human nature, there are some considerations which account for the commonness (perhaps "universality") of human beings' efforts after "positive regard." *Relationships* among potentials are universal. Each infant is described as "having" these relationships. Since these relationships vary along a dimension from integrated to disintegrated, what may be referred to as positive regard (as part of a context including loving, accepting, being-one-with) either surfaces in the form of integrated relationships, or is implied in its other side as disintegrative hating, fearing, blocking off, pushing away—*not* positively regarding. Thus, positive regard or its other side ("negative" regard) is always implied in relationships between potentials. And these are universal. On the other hand, these are *relationships* and not *needs*. Furthermore, these may refer to positive regard *or* negative regard.

Some theorists hold that intrinsic human nature contains a basic tendency or psychological need for seeking reassurance and protection, and cite as evidence young children who seek reassurance and protection from their parents under such crises as being physically ill or facing surgery (cf. Maslow, 1970b). A large part of such reasoning is that early evidence of a given behavioral motif is held as indicative of intrinsic psychological needs. In contrast, I see the early evidence of any behavioral motif, including that of seeking reassurance and protection from parents, as cordial to nearly any substantial conceptualization of human behavior, and not differentially confirmatory of any conceptualization over others. Leaving aside, for now, an explanation of the sheer *occurrence* of young children seeking reassurance and protection from their parents, I see no basis for postulating *intrinsic basic tendencies or psychological needs* for seeking reassurance and protection. No such tendencies or needs exist as an intrinsic human nature—from our perspective at least.

In place of intrinsic needs, instead of being led by a particular conceptualization into the infant's body, we can enlarge the scope to see how the encompassing primitive field accounts for the evidence which hitherto has been taken as evidence of some need or other. Parents are skilled at constructing infants whose function is to be frightened, scared by the danger, disrupted by suddenness. When infants are that way, humanistic theory seeks to describe the primitive field which constructs the infant into that particular function. Our approach contrasts with that in which the manifest way the infant behaves is taken as evidence of the opposite intrinsic human need. Thus, if the infant is frightened, scared by the danger, disrupted by suddenness, it is taken that the infant has an intrinsic need for safety, for an organized world without disruptions, without chaos or dangers (Maslow, 1970b, pp. 40-41). Once you go inside the infant for a need, and once you turn the manifest behavioral evidence into the polar other side of the intrinsic need, then you must have other principles to explain why manifest behavioral evidence is sometimes evidence *for* an intrinsic need and other times evidence for its *opposite*. Why is it that when the infant seems to manifest evidence of love and affection, there is an assumption of an intrinsic need for love and affection, but when the infant is frightened, scared, and disrupted, that is taken as evidence of a need for the opposite? It is easy, but, from our perspective erroneous, to presume some kind of intrinsic need behind the ways in which infants behave.

In the same vein, we may observe that infants are attributed a "basic tendency" to seek the breast. Within our perspective, we can describe a primitive field wherein the infant is *constructed* to serve a particular *function* which is fulfilled by breast-seeking. In stark contrast, many theories must locate all the processes as occurring primarily within the physical infant. Such theories then assert that ". . . the newborn infant unconsciously feels that an object of unique goodness exists, from which a maximal gratification could be obtained and that this object is the mother's breast" (Klein, 1952, p. 235). If everything must originate within the physical infant proper, then such a conclusion is in order. Yet from our perspective, it is quite unacceptable to presume some basic tendency, part of the physical infant's very nature, which consists of a knowing that maximal gratification can be obtained from the good breast. Yet it *is* understandable, within our theory, that the *primitive field* may include significant parental figures who construct that into the physical child. Indeed, from the very beginning a mother may encompass the newborn in a primitive field in which good-breastness is a paramount feature. Under these conditions the development of a seeking for the good breast emerges out of that parameter of the primitive field. In our view, it is the *significant parental figures* who feel, if I may borrow Klein's words, that an object of unique goodness exists, from which maximal gratification could be obtained, and that this object is the mother's breast. The concept of the primitive personality enables us to locate good-breast-seeking outside the infant's intrinsic human nature, and within the domain of the encompassing primitive field.

Underlying the presumption of a basic human nature of love, positive regard, dependency, protection-seeking, and seeking the good breast is a common notion that some sort of social attachment is a basic tendency of human nature. That is, human nature is understood as including a basic tendency toward others, toward gregariousness, toward Adlerian social interest, toward social attachments. Our view is that all of the parameters of the infant's social attachments are direct functions of the primitive personality, and not of human nature. To the extent that social attachments are there, the causal root lies within the encompassing field, and not within the nature of the physical infant. To assert that the significant figures construct the infantness and define its functions is, in other words, to describe attachments between the physical infant and its significant figures. Understood this way, the physical infant is entwined in a network of social attachments, none of which come from some assumed basic tendency toward social attachments.

This same line of reasoning applies similarly to the basic tendency of aggression. That is, humanistic theory understands the salient factors as residing within the primitive field rather than within the physical infant, and understands those salient factors as the near-universality of disintegrative relationships among potentials. Observers seem to agree that aggression is common to human beings, and conclude that aggression is somehow intrinsically characteristic of human beings. This conclusion is supported by reviews of studies which suggest that aggression constitutes a single overall package, i.e., that there is something common and central to the various kinds and forms of aggression (Berkowitz, 1962; Buss, 1961; Dollard et al., 1939; Feshbach, 1964; Pomeroy, Mahrer & Mason, 1965). I suggest that the common element is the relationship between potentials, specifically the disintegrative relationship.

Activation and drive: primitive personality versus human nature. We now turn to a basic tendency of an order different from those we have discussed—a basic tendency which activates personality processes in general. Some theorists hold that human nature comes equipped with basic tendencies which determine both the direction and the nature of development, and are assumed to contain their own germinating power which moves development toward predetermined ends and in predetermined ways. It is assumed " . . . that need satisfaction, self-limiting adaptation, creative expansion, and instituting as well as upholding internal order, are basic tendencies of the human being. Their implicit ultimate intent is self-development, the establishment of contacts, the mastering of reality, and the fulfillment of life through an integrated actualization of the individual's potentials (Buhler & Marschak, 1968, p. 93). Here is a rather splendid display of a richly conceived human nature. However, humanistic theory declines to accept this picture of human nature. I assume that the contents of personality include *potentials*, without any force or drive or activating agent which is supposed to "realize" or actualize these potentials. They are potentials for experiencing; nothing forces experiencing to occur. Actualization and integration are potentials; nothing pushes the person to become actualized or integrated. The contents of personality, at least so it is held in humanistic theory, include no activating force to creatively expand, self-develop, master reality, or actualize the person's potentials. Likewise, there is nothing built into the primitive personality which has the job of insuring that the person becomes integrated—or achieves a kind of internal order. To assume such basic tendencies as intrinsic to human nature is to be exceedingly gratuitous about the contents of human nature. Wouldn't it be nice if all of this *were* part of the package of raw humanness? No such basic tendencies, however, are assumed to be tucked into our human nature.

Those who accept the infant as fundamentally a biological organism frequently presume some sort of intrinsic drive *toward* tension reduction and *away from* tension. Tension is held as unpleasurable and tension reduction is held as pleasurable. Human nature is biological, and includes tendencies toward pleasurable tension reduction. In contrast, humanistic theory rejects such a conceptualization on several grounds. First, we reject any conception of an intrinsic (biological) human nature. Second, we reject any conception of intrinsic pushes toward integration or actualization in any form—whether framed as tension or tension reduction.

When we consider the contents of the primitive personality, there is, then, nothing which activates the potentials and their relationships. Nothing keeps the potentials from experiential actualization, and nothing drives them into experiential actualization. In the same way, nothing pushes the relationships into either integrative or disintegrative channels. All that is there is a *capacity* for becoming experientially actualized or integrated. Relationships among potentials are such that they can become disintegrated. To consider that the contents of the primitive personality are there by virtue of human nature, and to go even further by adding an intrinsic property of drive is simply too much to ask of humanistic theory—although for other approaches, the latter request is merely redundant (cf. Bowlby, 1958, 1965, 1969).

Such an assumption of intrinsic drive qualities is often coupled with a picture of human infants as being active, striving, seeking, selecting. Given that the infant is observed to be this way, we would turn to the nature of the encompassing primitive personality for an answer. We would not subscribe to a Liebnitzian model (Allport, 1955; Buhler, 1968) in which such qualities are an expression of the infant's basic human nature: intrinsically growth-oriented, activity-oriented, and experience-seeking (e.g., Schachtel, 1959). That overall picture is of a human nature which equips the infant with tendencies toward seeking involvement, engagement, stimulation, or experiential contact with the external world. However, none of this is germane to humanistic theory.

Writers in the humanist tradition are especially prone to endow human nature with such qualities as spontaneity, creativity, choice, actualization, and intentional action—and equally loathe to consider the external world as having any hand in the genesis of these wonderfully human qualities (Needleman, 1967). In all of these assertions, the infant is assumed to be the physical object, and the external world is essentially held as separated, alien, and even menacing. It is as if these good qualities are inside the human infant to enable him to cope with an external world which could not possibly have such positive human qualities. Humanistic theory takes a different position in which none of these qualities is intrinsic to human infants, activating them toward being spontaneous, creative, choosing, actualizing, and intentionally acting. These activating qualities are either present (or absent) in the primitive personality, either part and parcel of the contents of the primitive personality or simply not present in that encompassing field. But, regardless, they are not activating endowments of intrinsic human nature.

There are many theorists who consider intrinsic human nature to include some sort of growth force which activates the person toward fulfillment or maturity. But humanistic theory declines to endow the human infant with Adlerian intrinsic creative powers (Ansbacher & Ansbacher, 1964), built-in forces which move the infant toward growth (Appleton, 1910), self-realization, self-actualization, or self-fulfillment (Buhler, 1968, p. 93), or any Rogerian inherent tendency toward actualization: "He has an inherent tendency toward actualizing his organism . . . He interacts with his reality in terms of his basic actualizing tendency. Thus his behavior is the goal-directed attempt of the organism to satisfy the experienced needs for actualization in the reality as perceived . . ." (Rogers, 1959, p. 222). In blunt contrast, humanistic theory holds that there are no such processes within the infant, no growth force in any of its conceptual guises, no driving force which has any particular mission.

Leaving aside any such missions or ends, there is still a question of what generates infant phenomena. What gets it all started? What accounts for infant behavior? What activates the infant into movement? For us, the answers lie within the encompassing primitive personality. Included in its contents are the variables which construct the infant, define its functions, and activate it into being this way or that way. Our answers to these questions are contained within the primitive personality, *and not* in the intrinsic properties of the physical infant itself. We reject each and every attempt to identify the source of activation as within the physical infant. Thus, for example, we reject a conceptualization of something in the infant's human nature which orients the infant along a dimension from good, pleasurable tension-reduction to bad, unpleasurable tension-increase (cf. Mahler, 1952; Mahler & Gosliner, 1955).

Universality: primitive personality versus human nature. Each consideration leads us to conclude that there is no basis for entertaining the idea of universal basic tendencies or needs intrinsic to the infant's human nature. We have arrived at this conclusion, in part, by having adopted a position which rejects a reductionism to a biological substratum comprised of basic needs. We have, instead, accepted a mode of description which includes the primitive personality as a robust concept to account for that which has been taken as evidence for universal basic tendencies of needs intrinsic to the infant's human nature. We are prepared to abandon any notions of such universal basic tendencies or needs tucked within the physical infant's intrinsic human nature.

In seeking a way of accounting for similarities across infants, we turn toward the primitive personality and away from universal human nature. Once we abandon the notion of universal human nature, we are enabled to search for those variables which would incline the primitive personalities of collective infants to be similar. We may discover, for example, that there are remarkable commonalities in the *cluster of potentials* across the primitive personalities of large numbers of infants. To that extent, infants will manifest similarities. Yet the extent of similarity is not evidence of universal human nature. Rather, the extent of the similarity is evidence of whatever conditions account for similarities across potentials and their relationships in primitive personalities. If infants in two different cultures seem to be afraid of strangers or to seek physical contact, our working hypothesis is that factors in the two cultures yield comparable potentials and relationships, in the primitive fields encompassing the physical infants, involving the infants as afraid of strangers or as seeking physical contact. We would not be inclined toward a conclusion that there is a universal human nature inclining infants toward fearing strangers or seeking physical contact.

In the rush to postulate universal human needs (or drives or basic tendencies), virtually every approach has ignored the robustness of the relationships among potentials. I suspect that the preponderance of universal phenomena, which theorists have tried to explain by postulating packages of universal tendencies or needs, is far better described by postulating relationships. It is quite unlikely that every infant, or even most infants, would have the same potentials. But, on the other hand, *every* infant has *relationships* which are either of a disintegrative or an integrative nature. I strongly suspect that evidence of universal human nature is better grasped as evidence of disintegrative or integrative relationships. Thus, similarity across infants *may* be taken as evidence of universal basic tendencies or needs, but will more likely be taken as an expression of relationships which vary along a dimension from integration to disintegration.

Because of the nature of the relationships, infants may be generally characterized as predominantly integrative or predominantly disintegrative. Our speculation is that most infants exist in primitive personalities which are disintegrated. In rather sharp contrast, many theories assume that the infant begins in a universal, necessary state of integration, a state of basic oneness with the world and with itself (e.g., Rogers, 1959). We must reject such a position. We reject *any* kind of given human nature, including one in which the infant is born necessarily in a state of integration—or disintegration. The integrative state of oneness, or the disintegrative state of disjunctiveness, is a function of the primitive personality, and not an expression of universal human nature.

Although we reject the idea that infants universally exist in a state of integrative oneness, there is a sense in which virtually all infants are in a relationship of oneness. Each physical infant exists within an encompassing primitive field. Because of that primitive field, the physical infant is bonded and attached to its encompassing "environment," i.e. primitive field. The physical infant originates in a state of oneness with and in that primitive field, and therefore begins with a state of oceanic oneness with an external world which is the dilated definition of the infant-as-primitive-personality. Almost without exception, we all begin this way, and it is a universal beginning, but one which is a consequence of the primitive personality, not any supposed properties of human nature.

Whether the core characteristics are conceptualized as basic motivations, basic needs, basic tendencies, intrinsic human nature, or basic drives, empirical knowledge in this whole area is too sparse to warrant substantive conclusions. As usual, when data are lacking, speculation is rampant. We can speculate that the fundamental stratum of personality consists of a handful of basic drives, or we can speculate that there is virtually no commonality whatsoever. The data will accommodate a bewildering array of speculations. Many approaches share a notion that there is a pronounced degree of commonality across infants, and that this commonality flows out of rather similar (universal) basic tendencies—or drives or whatever they are termed. There is a kind of unstated agreement across approaches that there is increasing similarity and commonality as one proceeds from the *vast* diversity of behaviors to the *moderate* diversity among daily means of satisfying a more or less common set of basic tendencies (e.g. Maslow, 1970b). Each avenue of considerations expresses the same view, viz. that a handful of basic tendencies constitutes the intrinsic nature of infants. In this scene of inadequate empirical data, humanistic theory can offer the following speculations on this issue: (a) The degree of similarity or difference across infants is a function of the degree of similarity or difference in the contents of infants' primitive personalities; (b) the specific, concrete nature of the basic *potentials* across infants is characterized by a rich diversity. Indeed, I am quite inclined to accept a degree of *difference* which far exceeds what we have heretofore believed.

Undeveloped rudiments: primitive personality versus human nature. We observe that the infant becomes. It seems to be something now it was not fully a few weeks or months ago. There is a becoming more of something. It is as if there is something which flowers, which is there and unfolds. From our perspective, the determining factors are found in the primitive personality. Many approaches presume that there is a human nature which includes archaic rudiments or "anlage" of processes which unfold along developmental lines. For example, other approaches presume a human nature containing the rudimentary wherewithall for the infant's thinking processes. Within psychoanalytic theory, the newborn already has undifferentiated intrinsic rudiments for symbolizing, for conceptual thought, for the perception of external cues, and for making subtle conceptual distinctions among external cues (Munroe, 1955, p. 5). These rudiments are part of human nature, and they grow and develop into increasingly complex modes of thought. Yet, from the beginning, the infant's human nature is presumed to contain the anlage or rudimentary processes of thought. Humanistic theory sees the beginnings of thought as residing in other determining factors located within the larger primitive field. There are no intrinsic *rudiments* of thought, no intrinsic *anlage* of conceptual processes.

It is common, in other approaches, to presume that much of what later occurs has some beginning in a form not unlike that of a seed, and that this form lies somewhere inside the skin of the infant. For example, it is presumed that human nature is such that it includes a rudimentary, undeveloped, archaic ego (or consciousness, or self) which stands ready to develop forth. This ego occurs in the infant as a rudimentary, highly simplified, undifferentiated form of the mechanisms which will develop later into mature ego mechanisms (Ainsworth, 1969). After some time, the newborn will have a fully developed ego which will be able to discriminate among objects in the environment, will be able to discriminate itself from the rest of the environment, and will be able to discriminate between sensations arising from within and sensations arising externally. The personality structure will differentiate into conscious, preconscious, and unconscious domains. It is understandable that these sophisticated ego mechanisms are presumed to exist in some undeveloped, undifferentiated state when it is unquestionably assumed that the causal roots must necessarily lie within the physical infant. Once we understand the infant as far more than that which exists within its skin, then we are more able to connect these ego mechanisms to factors and variables in the larger, encompassing primitive personality—and to abandon the undeveloped-seed paradigm of infant development.

Using the undeveloped-seed paradigm, other approaches explain specific empirical observations about infants by citing rudimentary, undifferentiated processes inside the physical infant. For example, it is observed that infants show progressive increases in internal control, mastery, competence, or effectance motivation. In his landmark analysis of this avenue of development, White (1959) concludes that the ultimate beginnings of this thematic avenue of development reside in the energies of the nervous system, gently stimulated by the external environment. Here is yet another instance of the possibilities being confined to the physical infant. Once the infant is only the physical infant, then we can only search therein for the determinants of progressively increasing mastery and competence. Once our search is limited to the physical infant. it is easy to believe that there must be an anlage of internal control, an undifferentiated beginning of mastery, an unfolding competence process. In contrast, we search for the description of the phenomena referred to by mastery, internal control, competence and effectance within a broader scope, viz. within the encompassing primitive personality. By enlarging the possible domain of causal description, we can abandon the idea of rudimentary processes.

In describing the particular neonate's active grasping behaviors, our theory has no place for rudimentary developmental processes whose unfolding explains such a specific behavior. Using such a notion of developmental stages, Erikson (1950) can explain active grasping behavior of the neonate as an expression of the second oral stage of development, a stage known as active incorporation. But humanistic theory would understand such behavior as a consequence of the workings of the primitive personality. For example, the construction of active grasping may serve the function of being an appropriate situational context wherein the parent experiences a sense of being used or attacked or needed, or a sense of resisting the infant's active grasping. The parental construction of active grasping may serve the function of being the extension of the parents' own operating or deeper potentials for experiencing taking. attacking. clinging. owning. incorporating, manipulating. Our theory would describe in these ways the behaviors of active grasping whether that active grasping referred to fingers, biting, or even active visual "grasping" such as focusing and tracking. We reject description from the perspective of rudimentary developmental processes, and support instead the potentials and relationships of the primitive personality.

If the relationships in the primitive personality are integrated, the feeling of trust can be a characteristic of the infant from the very beginning. On this score, humanistic theory differs from those in which the feeling of trust is taken as an indication that the infant has progressed through early stages of development (Erikson. 1950). Mother can be secure with baby, knowing it well, trusting baby, being in the most primitive state of confident assurance with it. When this occurs, it may be said that the feeling of trust is an expression of the integrated relationships between parts of the primitive personality. In other words, trust is a feeling of the infant-as-primitive-personality, and *not* the manifest expression of a human nature containing the seeds of developmental processes whose sequential unfolding includes a stage of trust.

Theorists who adopt a learning model typically solve this problem in the same traditional way. That is, if some process occurs in a developed, differentiated form, then it must start from an undeveloped, undifferentiated rudiment which can only be located within the physical infant. For example, with progressive development, infants demonstrate increasing signs of curiosity and movement toward affection-seeking. Simple proclivities for curiosity and affection-seeking seem to be present before the time when their presence can be accounted for by principles of learning. Accordingly, these theorists conclude that such processes have their origins in undeveloped rudiments linked to primary biophysiological drives contained within the physical infant (Maher, 1966). From the perspective of humanistic theory, the essential causal fabric of what later occurs as curiosity and affection-seeking lies within the encompassing primitive personality—and *not* within undeveloped biophysiological rudiments inside the physical infant.

With regard to memory or what might be called "object cathexes," the same reasoning traditionally holds. That is, these are frequently presumed to exist in rudimentary, undeveloped states in the form of disturbing tension and gratifying tension release (Fenichel, 1954c). As a part of human nature, states of disturbing tension and tension release are considered to be rudimentary anlage of what later develop into memory and object cathexes. From the perspective of humanistic theory, however, it does not matter whether we are speaking of memory, affection-seeking, object cathexes, ego, curiosity, consciousness, thinking processes, competence-mastery, or whatever. All of these refer to phenomena whose explanations lie in the factors and variables of the primitive personality and not in some rudimentary, undeveloped, undifferentiated processes intrinsic to the infant's human nature.

The Question of Inheritance

In understanding the origins of infants, how does our concept of the primitive personality compare and contrast with that of genetic inheritance?

The Place of Genetic Constructs in Humanistic Theory

When we seek to describe and understand the origins of infants, our humanistic theory stands separate and independent from genetic theories. In our understanding of origins, the most central construct is that of the primitive personality, which in no way *causally* links with the concepts, constructs or variables from genetic theories. The reasons for making such statements are set forth in some detail in Chapter 4, but a few of the more important considerations will now be discussed.

From our position on issues of the philosophy of science, a given event is open to description and understanding from the viewpoint of humanistic theory, and also from the viewpoint of genetic theory, chemical theory, and so on. Each mode of description may be full, and yet each is causally independent of the other. For example, each of these theories may describe how it is that an infant seems to become a young child whose behavior is assaultive, and who seems also to be seriously withdrawn. From the perspective of humanistic theory, the primitive personality may itself be characterized by assaultive withdrawal so that behaviors of the young child become specific means of expressing the assaultive withdrawal. Among these behaviors may be those termed low intelligence (as evidence of withdrawal and distance from the external world), photosensitivity (more evidence of separation and distance from the external world), and seizures (as evidence of a violent assaultiveness against an intruding external world). These are some of the behavioral means of expressing the child's assaultive withdrawal within the framework of humanistic theory.

Such behavioral phenomena are also open to full description from other viewpoints such as genetics or chemistry. Described chemically, we can speak of disturbances in the hepatic enzyme system leading to difficulties in the hydroxylation of phenylalanine; described genetically, we can speak of transmission of a single autosomal recessive gene (Bjornson, 1964). I am describing a behavioral syndrome known as "phenylketonuria," a rare syndrome found in approximately 5 out of 100,000 young children. From a humanistic perspective, the cause lies in the primitive personality. From a chemical perspective, the cause lies in hepatic enzyme disturbances. From a genetic viewpoint, a single recessive gene is the cause. Yet the events themselves are open to full description from each of these perspectives without getting in each other's way. Each mode of description can be full and complete without turning to the constructs of another mode of description. Not only for these particular phenomena, but for everything which comprises the origin of infants, our position is that a humanistic theory and a genetic theory may be co-existent, but each is causally independent of the other.

A systematic science of the origins of infants does not require the use of genetic constructs. However, the genetic viewpoint is followed implicitly by the preponderance of approaches, including many that do not even know that they assume a genetic causal base. So ingrained has the genetic viewpoint been that, in setting forth "the formal criteria of a systematic psychology," McGeoch (1933) included the proposition that the starting point of the human organism *must* lie within the *genetic* starting point! Approaches which did not include this genetic proposition fell outside systematic psychology. On this point, humanistic theory proudly falls outside McGeoch's defined region of a systematic psychology!

Once the point of origin is freed of having to be the genetic point, and once earliest events are open to description from theoretical viewpoints other than genetics, the entire body of intrauterine research takes on a new significance. Traditionally, basic determinants were either genetic or environmental. In terms of research strategies, this bifurcation means that if an outcome can be linked to intrauterine events, it can be taken as evidence in support of genetic variables. From this position, methodologies are generated wherein comparisons are drawn between one-egg and two-egg twins, and between these and other sibling relationships, reared together and reared apart. However, if we switch over to a humanistic approach to the philosophy of science issues discussed in Chapter 4, the conclusions drawn from such research methodologies must be drastically revised. From our perspective, the primitive field is exceedingly present during the intrauterine period. Accordingly, research which confirms the importance of intrauterine events may be taken as supportive of both a genetic hypothesis and the hypothesis of the primitive field. Our theory holds that the preponderance of determining variables is at work in the intrauterine arena, and we would use much of the genetic research as supporting that hypothesis. I expect that the addition of a humanistic mode of describing the earliest phenomena will not only expand and invigorate our research methodologies, but will enable illumination of knowledge essentially unavailable to a genetic viewpoint alone.

A viewpoint which accepts multiple modes of description, free of causal relationships between constructs of each mode of description, rejects the idea of sciences organized on the basis of hierarchies. That is, there is no way in which constructs from one construct system are fully and without loss of meaning translatable into another construct system. Thus we cannot describe one group of events in *genetic* constructs (e.g. "chromosomes") and then formulate a chain of causal statements which switch over to *psychological* constructs (e.g. "ego defects associated with catatonic behavior"). Such an hierarchy of sciences is assumed when a theory asserts a specific *genetic* etiology in the form of a biochemical defect which is held as related to behavior along a series of causal links formulated in a molar *psychological* language system (Meehl, 1962). Furthermore, as discussed in Chapter 4, the foundations of any event (such as "infant") are not assumed to be of some special kind—such as neurological, or electronic, or chemical, or genetic. From our perspective, infants are described using humanistic constructs, even when we are talking about the most fundamental origins. Thus we reject any approach which switches to the constructs of some other language system when it gets down to the basic foundations. Our position rejects an approach which describes human beings in psychological terms, but switches over to genetics in describing the fundamental beginnings of all the later psychological processes (cf. Ainsworth, 1969, p. 974). We reject dualistic, reductionistic assumptions in making sense of the ultimate beginnings. Each consideration leads us away from genetic constructs in describing the origins of infants.

Furthermore, although both humanistic and genetic theories seek to grasp the origins of infants, the specific phenomena they deal with are quite different, and each theory studies its own specific events. Humanistic theory does not have a systematic way of describing the specific events which genetic theory studies. In our description of the origins of infants, we are not setting out to describe the very same events which genetic constructs seek to describe and explain. Thus, humanistic theory and genetic theory may both seek to describe and understand events referred to very generally as "the origins of infants," but the *specific* events which genetic theory describes are *not* those which humanistic theory describes. Accordingly, the two theories are not causally related to each other because they move in different circles of specific target events.

On the other hand, there are *some* specific events which both humanistic and genetic theories seek to describe. On these specific events, there are some singular similarities between the concrete causal mechanisms in both theories. Let us consider, for example, the theory that genetic influence is transmitted by means of an *integrative neural defect* (Meehl, 1962). According to that theory, genetic factors involve concrete changes in neuronal functioning so that there is a deficiency of inhibition in the neurone's synaptic control function. Genetic influence means an altered neuronal membrane stability so that there is *much greater dispersion of transmission in the synaptic area*. These are neurological terms referring to altered bodily structure and function. In Chapters 4 and 5 I proposed that the body can be described from the perspective of humanistic theory. The same principles used to describe human personality and behavior can be usually employed to describe the body. I suggest that our hypothesis of the primitive personality bears remarkable similarity to the transmission of genetic influence. That is, the idea of how genetic influence is mediated through neurone membrane changes is remarkably similar to the idea of how the primitive field affects the physical infant. Freed of its neurological language, the idea is that inhibition is lowered in the synaptic area so that what is transmitted has greater dispersion. Within our own language system, the same idea may be stated as follows: the physical infant is highly open to transmissions from the encompassing primitive field. In other words, neither the neuronal membrane (in genetic theory) nor the physical infant (in humanistic theory) is intact; both have "reduced inhibition," and what comes from "outside" has heightened influence. In this sense, genetic theory and humanistic theory picture the infant as quite open to influence, and this heightened influence is the means by which genetic factors and the primitive field transmit their effects. Where genetic theory and humanistic theory study the concretely specific events, there may occur similarities in the nature of both descriptions framed within different language systems. However, we must conclude that there is no necessary place for genetic constructs with humanistic theory.

The Description of Early Infantile Phenomena:
Primitive Personality versus Genetic Theory

If the phenomena of early infancy cannot be explained by "environment" or by principles of learning, then they are explained by a giant wastebasket called inheritance. There has been no other wastebasket. "Human nature" could not explain early phenomena and individual differences which seemed to be present before the environment and principles of learning took over. For example, Pavlov found a great deal which could be explained on the basis of conditioning, but he carefully noted that dogs varied in their earliest readinesses for conditioning, quite independent of the nature of their previous training (Williams, 1967). To what can these pre-training individual differences be attributed? Whereas nothing has been available except genetic variables, I propose that the concept of the primitive personality serve as an available second wastebasket for explaining not only predispositional readinesses for conditioning but all early infantile phenomena which heretofore had been understood as a function of genetic variables.

Increasingly, infant researchers and theorists have become confident of the importance of the earliest period of life, and dissatisfied with the conceptual adequacy of the genetic wastebasket. The search for where and how it all begins has led increasingly to the first years of life, beginning with conception. Yet the more knowledge we gain about these earliest months and years, the less we "explain" by the notion of inheritance (Dollard & Miller, 1950). The weight of research leads toward the conclusion that learning experiences and interaction with the environment seem to be approached by an infant *already* characterized by readinesses, tendencies, predispositions and personal preferences. Something prepares the infant for the way it engages with the environment. If that something is less and less some innate genetic factor, we are left with a growing certainty that another genre of etiological factors seems to be operating in the earliest months and years, something in between human nature and genetics on the one hand, and learning experiences and the interaction with the environment on the other. That something is, in my opinion, the workings of the primitive field. We turn now to a few of these early phenomena, and to a comparison of the primitive personality and genetic theory in the description and understanding of these phenomena.

Differences in physical bodies. We observe differences in the physical bodies of newborns. It is our thesis that the particular nature of a primitive field is the determinant of the physical bodily nature of the infant which is constructed. By "physical nature" I am referring to the body of the neonate, especially those aspects referred to as, for example, its endocrine system, respiratory system, nervous system, circulatory system, and brain morphology. From the very beginning, neonates are demonstrably different visually, auditorially, gustatorially, olfactorally, and in relation to thermal, contact, and pressure variations. It is axiomatic that these aspects of the bodies of newborns reflect enormous differences (e.g., Pratt, 1937; Pratt, Nelson & Sun, 1930). The endocrine systems of a group of babies will be patently different and reflect impressive variations. What accounts for this? Is this a function of genetic variables? Our theory rejects that explanation, and suggests instead that the physical body of the neonate is the product of the nature of the primitive field. As discussed in Chapters 4 and 5, the body is fully open to description from the perspective of humanistic theory. Once the body is open to such description, it can be seen that the body of the neonate is a prime example of the work of a singular primitive personality which has had at least nine months to construct that physical infantness in quite specific ways. Differences in the endocrine system are outcomes of differences in the nature of the primitive personalities which construct those endocrine systems. The same is true of differences in respiratory systems, nervous systems, brain morphology, and the ways in which the physical infant relates to thermal, pressure, and contact variations.

Our theory of the role of the primitive field in constructing the physical body of the infant is put forth to account for differences in the nature of every aspect of the physical body, including those aspects referred to as the nervous system. Differences in central nervous system functions are therefore held as evidence of the workings of the primitive field. Some theories of stuttering, for example, hold that infants may be born with a predisposition toward stuttering because of a "throwback" state of their central nervous systems (Hahn, 1943). Although these predispositions from supposed throwback states of the central nervous system are generally accepted as flowing out of genetic factors, and although manifest differences in central nervous system functionings are likewise accepted as generated by genetic factors, I propose that all of these are also friendly to an hypothesis of the influence of the primitive personality. For example, recent research has led to changing conceptions of that part of the body known as the brain. From a model in which the brain served as a mechanical switchboard, we now have models in which the brain is described as a far more active system of information processing (cf. Hebb, 1958; Miller, Pribram & Galanter, 1960). From our perspective, the determining factor is the nature of the primitive personality. Taking this one dimension, from mechanical passivity to active processing, it is the primitive personality which makes the infant—and its brain—as either mechanical and passive or as active and processing. When we discover the infant's brain as mechanical or as active, we are therefore describing the physical bodily effects of the primitive personality, and not some inherent parameters of the brain. Because of the primitive personality, some are mechanical switchboard brains and some are active processing brains. Brains, according to our perspective, can fit along a number of different dimensions as a function of the nature of the determining primitive personalities. Once again, the answer lies in the nature and effects of the primitive personality, and not in some presumed inherent, genetic neurological parameters.

Stability and consistency. Genetic variables do not have an easy time accounting for observed stability and consistency over time. They have difficulty accounting for the restless infant being restless over a period of two days or two weeks or two years. How do we account for observed consistency and stability over time? Why is it that the highly curious and investigative infant is also that way four weeks later—or the next day? Heredity variables help us to understand a measure of such stability and consistency. But the specific relationships between genetic variables and infant behavior are such that there may only be a relatively low degree of stability and consistency over time. From our perspective, at least two factors must be considered in seeking to understand this very simplistic stability and consistency. One is that the primitive field has had at least a year to fashion an infant with defined (and stable, consistent) characteristics. With diligent work over at least a year, the primitive field may produce a newborn which is restful and slow, and which continues to be for the next six to eight months or even longer. But perhaps more important is that I take observed stability and consistency of the physical infant to be a measure of the stability and consistency of the encompassing primitive field. In general, primitive fields may be taken to be stable, and it is, therefore, quite understandable that their expressed products—behaving infants—are likewise stable and consistent. If the primitive personality is stable throughout the period from a year or so before birth to days and weeks after birth, we would expect that certain characteristics would be present at birth and would show a measure of persistence after birth. Thus the sheer presence of a characteristic at birth, together with its persistence after birth, does not differentiate between a genetic theory and a humanistic theory. Specifically, if the neonate manifests responsiveness, poise, equableness, and self-contentment, and if these characteristics persist following birth (Gesell & Amatruda, 1945), they are not to be taken as evidence of genetic causation. Humanistic theory accepts these characteristics as outcomes of the work of the primitive field, completely aside from any genetic variables. If these characteristics are present at birth, and if they persist for weeks or months after birth, they are evidence of the constructive power and stability of the primitive field. Their specific nature—e.g., the sense of equable self-contentment—would indicate a measure of integrative relationships in the primitive field. If the relationships are predominantly disintegrative, the neonate would likely not manifest such characteristics. Thus humanistic theory would be in a position to venture predictions about the presence or absence of such neonatal characteristics free of genetic considerations.

Infant characteristics. How may early infant characteristics be described from genetic and from humanistic perspectives? From the very beginning, there seem to be differences in what has been termed the emotional expressiveness of the infant. In the first hours, days, and weeks, some neonates seem to be highly expressive, while others are low in emotional expressiveness. How may we account for these observations? The concept of the primitive personality enables us to understand how the physical infant can be moulded into manifesting high or low emotional expressiveness. The determining factors are the potentials and relationships of the significant figures, which in turn determine how the physical infant is to be constructed and the functions it is to play. This portrayal has no place for a genetic theory wherein the infant is held as inheriting instinctual tendencies toward emotional expressiveness (as well as pugnacity, anger, laughter, flight, sexuality, protectiveness, acquisitiveness, curiosity, humility, and more) (Burt, 1955). According to Burt, each infant inherits a capacity for emotional expressiveness which is either normal, deficient, or excessive. Such a genetic description of the infant's emotional expressiveness differs sharply from a humanistic description. It would appear that a humanistic explanation of these phenomena differs from a genetic explanation in ways which could energize further research.

Our thesis is that the concept of primitive personality is able to account for a considerable portion of what has been accepted as genetically determined: for example, intelligence. The traditional model of intelligence, increasingly unable to support the weight of research, includes a notion of innate intelligence coupled with a process of unfolding along lines of development (Hunt, 1960). How may we account for what we refer to as "innate" intelligence? It appears that some infants are smarter and some dumber than others right from the very beginning. It has been taken that genetic factors account for these very early differences, but so too does the concept of a primitive personality. Differences in what has been termed intelligence can occur within the first few weeks or months of birth—or even during the period of gestation—because of the workings of the primitive field. Some primitive fields include potentials for intellectual sharpness, mental acuity, and conceptual complexity, whereas other primitive fields may include potentials for dullness, lowered comprehension, and conceptual simplicity. The ways in which the infant is smart or dumb, or is made into being smart or dumb, are no different than the ways in which the infant is made restless or god-like, vibrant or quiescent. These earliest individual differences are described as products of the primitive field, and not outcomes of genetic operations.

Early social behavior. How do we understand such specific early social behaviors as clinging to the mother or movement toward the breast? Genetic theory has at least two overlapping answers. One consists of a straightforward genetic basis for instincts of clinging behavior (Balint, 1949) and of movement toward the breast (Klein, 1952). The second is that the infant inherits instincts or inborn behavioral systems for evoking and sustaining caring behaviors from the mother as an expression of the infant's biological heritage of gaining evolutionary adaptedness by being close to parents during its long period of helplessness against external dangers (cf. Bowlby, 1958, 1965, 1969). Thus, according to the second genetic answer, clinging to mother and movement toward the breast are both in the service of an instinctually grounded predisposition toward evoking and sustaining caring behavior from the mother. Humanistic theory rejects both answers together with their instinctual groundwork. Specific behaviors such as clinging to mother or movement toward the breast are the result of successful efforts on the part of the *primitive field* to fashion such behaviors. Specific ways in which concrete behaviors are brought about are discussed in the following chapter. But, in any case, the determinants lie in the primitive field rather than in genetic variables. The basis for evoking and sustaining caring behavior in the mother resides in the *primitive personality* and not in the *instincts* of the physical infant. The basis for the infant's behaving in such ways *is* there from the very beginning, but it is housed within the significant figures, and not in the genetics of the physical neonate.

It is common to understand early infant social behavior as a two-step process wherein parental figures respond to infant cues or stimuli which are genetically caused. Thus, for example, genetic factors account for the infant's clinging to the mother and movement toward the breast, while learning principles account for the way the mother responds to such behavior by the infant. The same model is used to account for the child who has a "constitutional ego defect" from genetic factors, and it is this constitutional ego defect to which the mother responds in deleterious ways which set the child on the road toward psychosis (Mahler & Gosliner, 1955). Our theory, however, paints a picture in which the parents are the complete architects of everything. The parents construct whatever it is that is referred to as an "ego defect," and then proceed to respond to that constructed ego defect however it is important for them to respond. It is the parent (not genetic factors) who gets the infant to be a certain way, and it is the parent (not principles of learning) who relates to the infant's being that way.

Many writers have noted a constellation of early social behaviors such as curiosity, play, exploratory behavior and the like, behavior which seems to be more or less spontaneous almost from birth. These behaviors are social, and include an attachment between the physical infant and outside things. According to our approach, the heart of attachment lies in that which gets the significant figures to construct infantness in their world, and to give the infant defined functions. These primitive attachments are deeper than the infant's breast clinging behavior, effectance behavior, or movement toward the mother. I am referring to the bonds between infant and parental figures, and to *all* the physical infant's behaviors which flow forth from these bonds. These attachments arise because of what is present in the primitive personality—and not because of genetically based innate mechanisms for developing social attachments. Within humanistic theory there are no Darwinian instincts toward gregariousness, no McDougallian herd instincts, no genetically rooted proclivities toward social interest (Adler, 1927, 1969), no genetic tendencies toward contact with responsive persons, closeness, or reactivity (cf. Buhler, 1968b), no inborn behavioral systems which evoke and sustain caring behavior in the mother (e.g. Bowlby, 1958, 1965, 1969). Psychoanalytic theory developed within an assumptive system in which the physical infant is separated from an external environment, and the fundamental driving forces are of a biological nature. Out of such a system it is understandable that Freud would turn to an explanation calling upon inborn genetic drives which contained their own source and target, uninfluenced by environmental factors, together with an external object by means of which the aim was to be achieved. By altering assumptions, none of these social attachment mechanisms is required. Early evidence of social attachments, either in the form of subtle tendencies or concrete behaviors, are understood to be the result of the nature and operations of the primitive personality and not because of genetic variables in any form, content, mechanism, or mode of operation.

Primitive Personality and the Question of Inheritance

The concept of primitive personality is sufficiently robust to make some sense of early infantile phenomena, a few of which were discussed above. We turn now from specific early phenomena to more general issues in pursuing the same thesis, i.e., on the question of inheritance, the primitive personality is a concept of adequately comparable rigor.

The interaction of heredity and environment. The concept of primitive personality stands between heredity and environment, not only accounting for what each is unable to explain by itself, but accounting also for their interaction. Probably the most popular explanation of the origins of the human infant borrows both from heredity and environment, and rests confidently upon notions of the interactions between the two. It is my contention that the concept of primitive personality accounts both for that which is "passed on" or "transmitted" and also for the interaction between that and the infant's environmental interactions with the external world. For example, the interaction between heredity (in the form of particular instinctual biological processes) and environment (in the form of a schizophrenogenic mother) is often cited as an explanation of schizophrenia (e.g. Jenkins, 1950, 1952; Meehl, 1962). The concept of the primitive personality, on the other hand, accounts for the interaction without the problems and complicated antinomies existing between heredity and environment. By means of the primitive personality we can account for what is there from the very beginning (so-called "heredity") and what stands ready to encompass the physical infant (the so-called "environment"), as well as the interaction between the two—and all in the single parsimonious concept of the primitive personality!

From the perspective of humanistic theory, the *model* of the schizophrenogenic mother is correct, but its "theory" is wrong. Somehow, according to that model, mother delivers an effective one-two punch. First she provides the basic genetic foundation necessary for the infant's receptiveness to certain kinds of later experiences. Then she provides the appropriate kinds of later experiences. The particular theoretical framework of that model is a genetic-social learning one. I submit that this model is accurate in its basic contours, but incorrect in its theoretical context. From a humanistic perspective, parents provide the basic foundation, not through a mechanism of genetic encodings, but by means of the particular nature of the primitive personality. Having constituted the right primitive personality, the parents are then present to define social learning experiences consistent with that primitive personality. In this way, humanistic theory accounts for the data pertinent to the schizophrenogenic model. For example, how may we account for the young child's behaving in ways which are characterized by the (schizophrenic) extremes of separation, distance, distrust, withdrawal, removal from interpersonal contact? The basic foundation is laid down by a primitive field in which these potentials and functions are woven about the physical infant, rock bottom constituents of the infant's primitive personality. Then, consistent with this base, the parents provide the very social learning environment appropriately conducive to the development of that way of being. Rather than the explanation residing in the *combination of heredity and environment*, it resides in the *biphasic workings of the primitive field* in both constituting the primitive personality and the appropriate ways of being.

The interaction between genetic and environmental factors is traditionally defined as one in which genetic factors provide the predisposing boundaries, and environmental factors define the specific behavioral outcomes. If we push this further, we may ask for the precise relationships between genetic variables and the occurrence of *later* behaviors. More specifically, let us consider the relationship between defined genetic variables and the behaviors of the child at one or two or three years of age. In considering this problem, it is our thesis that genetic variables stop at providing a kind of predisposing foundation while the concept of the primitive personality not only provides the foundations of the infant, but also constitutes the environment which fashions the specific behaviors. What genetic theory has to say on this point is exemplified by Meehl (1962) in his description of the etiology of schizophrenia. He speaks of the relationships between a specific etiological genetic factor and the subsequent emergence of schizophrenic pathology. Meehl offers five statements about this relationship, and I would like both to offer these statements and to discuss them from the perspective of humanistic theory in comparing the two approaches on the occurrence of later behavior:

1. The etiological genetic factor does not always, or even usually, result in a specific clinical illness (Meehl, 1962). As applied to our problem, that means that an etiological genetic factor is not causally related to a specific problem, way of being, or set of behaviors of our one-to-three-year-old child. In humanistic theory, in contrast, the primitive personality *does* result in a more or less *specific* clinical illness, problem, way of being, or set of behaviors. It is the primitive personality which accounts for the young child behaving in specific ways, for the primitive personality is present and functioning when the child is one and two and three years of age, moulding

and guiding what may be termed the young child's problem, way of being, and set of behaviors.

2. The symptoms of the clinical illness are not directly derivable by reference to the etiological genetic factor (Meehl, 1962). That would mean that hereditary factors would not account for the behaviors which comprise our young child's way of being at one-three years of age. This is not true with regard to the primitive personality, for the primitive personality is by far the predominant determinant of the specific behaviors which comprise our young child's ways of being. Where the etiological genetic factor stops, the primitive field is still working.

3. The course of the illness is not restricted to procedures which materially influence the etiological genetic factor (Meehl, 1962). In other words, what happens to the child's way of being is virtually independent of the etiological genetic factor. Again, this does not hold for humanistic theory, for what happens to the ways of being of the very young child *depends upon* what occurs in the primitive field. Without some alteration in the primitive personality, the ways of being persist.

4. Infants with similar specific etiological factors may have different lines of development, different symptoms, and different illnesses (Meehl, 1962). Translated into a humanistic vocabulary, this statement would read as follows: Infants with similar primitive personalities may have different problems, ways of being, or sets of behaviors. That statement is not acceptable within a humanistic perspective. Almost without exception, the primitive personality would still be determining what the infant is like at one or two or three years of age so that the statement would read more accurately as follows: infants with *similar* primitive personalities would tend to have *similar* problems, ways of being, and sets of behaviors. Once again, the reason is that the primitive personality both constructs the physical infant and, after constructing it, works upon it later to fashion it into being that way.

5. The specific etiological genetic factor is not the largest single contributor to symptom variance (Meehl, 1962). Within the vocabulary of humanistic theory, the statement would read as follows: The primitive personality is not the largest single contributor to behavior variance. However, with regard to the behavior of the one-to-three-year-old, the primitive personality *is* the single largest contributor to behavior variance.

As compared with genetic factors, the primitive personality plays a far more robust role. Where genetic etiological factors are conjoined with increasingly important environmental factors, in many traditional approaches, such is not the case in humanistic theory, wherein the primitive personality merely continues its constructing and fashioning of the physical infant after birth and for several years thereafter. Thus, what is grasped by notions of the interaction between heredity and environment is accounted for more confidently by the single concept of the primitive personality.

The need to invoke genetic constructs. Careful study of infants seems to warrant the following conclusions: (a) Even before typical learning experiences and environmental interactions take place, the infant seems to demonstrate an observable set of individual characteristics. (b) Infants seem to have certain predispositions, readinesses, proclivities, and tendencies toward given packages of learning experiences and environmental interactions. Several theories are able to live with these two conclusions. Among these are humanistic theory and genetic theory, both of which are cordial to these conclusions. It is important to acknowledge that these conclusions do not favor one theory over the other. Rather, to the extent that they are well-grounded conclusions, they constitute statements that must be grasped by all modes of describing the origins of infants, and do not constitute a need to invoke genetic constructs over humanistic constructs.

Individual differences between infants are typically seen as the product of both hereditary and environmental factors operating conjointly under all possible combinations (Vinacke, 1948). Within our perspective, (a) there is no need to turn to a genetic mode of description, and (b) the "environment" is subsumed under the concept of the primitive personality. Therefore, without a need for concepts of genetics and environment, we are not concerned with explaining individual differences by a combination of the two. Instead, we understand that infants differ from one another as much as primitive personalities differ from one another. Indeed, the likelihood is that no two infants, even within the same family, are similar to one another. When you study the precise potentials and relationships of the significant figures, and when you understand the precise functions of the constructed infant, then it is easy to appreciate the enormous differences between infants—without ever invoking the traditional concepts of genetics and environment and their interaction.

As humanistic theory unfolds, it is likely that we will have less and less of a need to make inheritance into a giant wastebasket into which we pour everything we cannot explain. The concept of the primitive personality may be one among many which will make it more and more difficult to issue flat generalizations of the influence of heredity: "We see heredity's influence perhaps most clearly in physical features and in various constitutional factors such as sensitivity, vigor, vulnerability to disease, and intelligence" (Coleman, 1964, p. 61). Indeed, I believe it is unfair even to the development of genetic theory to give it such sweeping explanatory power. Certainly it is unfair to humanistic theory to foreclose its relevance by attributing to genetics the preponderance of explanation and description. I foresee a period of research invigorated by decreased need for genetic constructs.

As we move away from genetics, the weight of responsibility moves ever closer to the parents themselves. It is perhaps not accidental that the major schools of thought share a common stance of placing essential responsibility on neither the parents nor the infant. If the infant's basic foundation springs from human nature or instincts, then the responsible agents certainly are neither the parents nor the infant. It is the fault of human nature or instincts that I am miserly or have such high standards or have a bad temper or am full of hate. If we are finding that such undesirable ways of being are "acquired," and not a function of instincts (Maslow, 1949), this brings responsibility a bit closer to home. We parents are the ones who must have some measure of responsibility for what our infants "acquire." Even the concepts of genetics imply that we parents share some responsibility, if only through our own genetic package—which we can disclaim as not our fault. But the concept of primitive personality places virtually all the responsibility, for better or for worse, at our own feet. Parents are the agents responsible for the origins and foundations of the infant. As the need to turn to genetic constructs wanes, the way is clear to identify parents as responsible for virtually everything which had been attributed to inheritance.

Psychological inheritance: mechanisms of transmitting the nongenetic. By means of the primitive personality, a great deal is "transmitted." For example, there are certain events which occur before the infant is even conceived, yet these events seem to be "present" years afterwards. Parents are filled with the horrors of atomic war years before they conceive a child who, in her own later childhood and adolescence, manifests the same horrors of an atomic holocaust. A grandfather's fear of death emerges in the grandchild even though the grandfather dies before the child is even conceived. A mother's childhood competitiveness with her sister resurfaces in *her* child's identical competitiveness two and a half decades later. A father's reverence for his grandfather seems to occur again in his son's reverence for the same (great-) grandfather. In her childhood, mother served her own mother as a loyal and obedient subject; that same tendency seems to be present in her daughter. The simplest way in which humanistic theory accounts for such phenomena is by understanding each of these as current elements in the primitive personality. That is, whatever is present within the primitive personality is thereby a part of what the infant is. If the horrors of an atomic holocaust are present in the primitive field, the infant will have that as an integral part of its personality foundation—even if the actual atomic war or the imminent possibility occurred much earlier. A grandfather's fear of death may be a part of the grandchild's primitive personality because it is "carried" by the parent. If mother's childhood competitiveness with her sister surfaces during the years of the primitive personality, it becomes a part of the child's personality foundation. By means of the primitive personality, humanistic theory accounts for a kind of "psychological inheritance," the passing on of the past into the present which is the foundation of the infant. Psychological inheritance is accomplished by sheer presence in the primitive field. It does not require genetic encodings or chromosomal patternings or genetic mechanisms.

Neonates often differ along a dimension of what may be termed openness to external events or receptivity to outside influences. It is as if some neonates are in a world which is constricted and narrow, whereas other neonates are in a world which is dilated and enlarged. Where this is a salient feature of what the neonate is like, our explanation lies in the nature of the respective primitive fields. Because of the contents of the particular field, some are preponderantly open to external influence, enlarged, receptive, while other neonates are closed in, constricted, unreceptive. In either case, the primitive personality constructs the infantness into being one or the other. Among the observable ways in which neonates exhibit one or the other of these inclinations is what is termed openness to conditioning. Thus, some neonates, like Pavlov's dogs, may be more open to conditioning than others. The mechanism for inclining a neonate one way or the other has been taken as hereditary factors related to excitation and inhibition (Eysenck, 1955a, 1957), but humanistic theory prefers to describe these differences on the basis of differing primitive personalities, differing contents of the primitive field. Those infants who are constructed into being open are quite receptive to the elements of the primitive field. They are open to the residue of the past and to the outer reaches of that field—to the social, to the cultural.

A great deal is transmitted through the primitive personality. Not only is the personal and the familial transmitted through sheer presence in the primitive field, but that same field includes everything which has been described as social, cultural, racial and ethnic. The primitive personality serves as the unifying mechanism for the transmission of what Benedek (1956) terms *cultural inheritance*, Mead (1954) calls *social transmission*, and Jung (1933) refers to as *racial unconscious*. Indeed, the concept of the primitive field brings all these phenomena together into a single class of constituents of the primitive field, and, perhaps more importantly, removes the mystique surrounding their mechanisms of transmission. If a particular culture or ethnic group includes a distinctive conception of family kinship, hell, moral code, or group feeling, these are transmitted to the infants by the simple mechanism of sheer presence of the primitive field. If they are "in" the parents, they are integral components of the infants' personality foundations.

The Question of Environment

Our eye has been on questions of the origins of the infant, on the genesis of human beings, on how to account for the way the human infant is. To answer these fundamental questions, humanistic theory offers the primitive field, and argues that the primitive field provides a more adequate description than that provided by intrinsic human nature and inheritance. We now turn to another way of answering these fundamental questions: the origins of the infant are explained by the *environment*; the genesis of human beings lie in *environmental* factors and variables; it is the *environment* which accounts for the way the human infant is. Let us consider the question of the environment, and how humanistic theory compares and contrasts with "the environment" in understanding the origins of infants.

A Theorogenic Problem Solved by a Theoretical Shift

The question is how external environmental factors exert effects upon the infant. How does mother's anxiety about her adequacy exert its effect upon the infant? How does father's dependency exert an impact upon the infant? Even when our eye is on the most fundamental origins of the infant, the question is still there, viz., how does the external environment help fashion the foundations of the infant? Since this question was created by *fiat*, it ought properly be solved by *fiat*. That is, the question is a question only for that body of thought which carves up the world in such a way that there is an infant (a physical infant), and there is a separated external world (that is, an environment). Under these circumstances, there *is* a problem. In other words, the problem is created by having adopted a particular theoretical manner of carving up the world (i.e., the problem is *theorogenic*). Then it would seem that the problem may be solved in the same way—by theoretical conceptualization. By adopting a concept of the primitive field, there is no longer a separated physical infant and a separated external world. In this primitive field what had been an external world is now—by fiat, by a change in theoretical conceptualization—a component of the larger definition of infant. In other words, the problem vanishes. Since there is no separated physical infant and separated external world, there is no problem as to how the latter exerts an impact upon the former. Mother's anxiety and father's dependency are now components of the infant-as-primitive-personality. They are *parts* of the infant and not elements of an external environment which somehow affects the infant. "Environment" is a construct. It leads to the problem of how it accounts for the origins of the infant only because of a theory which asks us to view the world in terms of a separated external environment.

In effect, we have taken the perimeter of the physical infant and stretched it out to encompass variables which heretofore had been considered *external* variables. Mother's nurturance—including her kindly touch, her breast, the warmth of her body, the openness and availability of her presence, her loving glances—has been transformed from outside and external to inside and internal. With the infant as mother's touch, and with mother's touch no longer an external element, there is no further problem to be solved, no problem of how external environmental variables affect the basic foundations of the infant. It becomes clear that such a problem is coupled with a very specific meaning of infant and external environment, neither of which is accepted by humanistic theory, both of which are assimilated by the concept of the primitive personality.

Because infant and external world are one, the infant is and has built-in social attachments. From the very beginning, the significant figures are intimately entwined with the physical infant with all manner of bonds, linkages, and connections. There is, then, no problem of how a fundamentally separated and intact infant comes to develop social attachments to a fundamentally separated and intact external environment. Such a problem is a problem in theories which accept infant and external world as existing across a gap over which social attachments can be flung.

The concept of the primitive personality has dramatically altered the meaning of both "infant" and "external environment." Accordingly, the meanings of these two terms must be clarified before our position can either be placed in the Lockean or the Leibnitzian camp. If, for example, we ask to what extent the "external environment" determines the nature of the infant, our answer is that the environment (as primitive personality) is the predominant determinant of the infant (as physical infant *or* as primitive personality). We are thereby in full agreement with the Lockean school of thought which sees the infant as a tabula rasa. If we consider the Leibnitzian question of whether or not the infant contains its own intrinsic package of determinants, our answer depends upon the meaning of "infant." If "infant" is taken as the primitive personality, then we agree that the infant contains its own intrinsic package of determinants—and we find ourselves in accord with both the Lockean and the Leibnitzian schools of thought. If, however, "infant" is taken in its traditional meaning of the *physical* infant, then we are in stark opposition to the Leibnitzian position.

The issue of the relative weight of internal-personality variables versus external-environmental variables similarly depends upon the meaning of *infant*. When social learning theorists (e.g., Bijou & Baer, 1965; Gewirtz, 1969) eschew the role of internal-personality variables (such as cognitive, neurophysiological or genetic variables), they presume the infant as the physical infant. On this score, we agree. That is, when the infant is defined as the physical infant, the determining variables lie *outside* the physical infant and not *inside* the physical infant. When, however, the infant is defined as the primitive personality, then the determining variables are internal, not external, and our position is in flat disagreement with that of social learning theory. Our position is that the determining variables are external to the physical infant, and internal to the infant-as-primitive-personality.

By means of our conceptual switch, the environment-as-primitive-field is elevated to the supreme determinant of what the infant is, even beyond the model adopted by the various learning theories. Our position goes beyond one in which environmental stimuli determine infant *behavior*. In our model, the external environment determines the infant's behavior, the infant's entire personality, and the infant's world; it constitutes *everything* which is the infant. Our position renders many learning principles unnecessary because there is no longer an issue of how the external world influences the infant, once it is assumed that the external world *is* the infant. Indeed, we are no longer confronted with the problem of how the external environment shapes the infant. In virtually every other approach, some solution must be found to the question of how the (assumed) external world transmits its impact upon the (separated) physical infant. For example, what are the mechanisms by which mother's anxiety affects the physical infant? It is almost axiomatic that mother's anxiety somehow is coupled with evidence of anxiety in the infant. By what mechanisms does this occur? In seeking an answer to this (theorogenic) question, Schachtel (1959) argues against Sullivan's mechanism of empathic induction, Freud's mechanism of changes in excitation, and Escalona's mechanism of contagion. Instead, Schachtel proposes a solution in which he postulates an infant need for embeddedness or union. Mother's anxiety threatens this need by removing mother, and the infant's anxiety is the basic anxiety of being separated from her. Here is an example of attempts to solve a problem which grows out of assumptions of a fundamentally separated external world and physical infant. In contrast, humanistic theory accepts mother's anxiety *as* infant's anxiety. The concept of an encompassing primitive personality makes unnecessary the solving of a problem which does not exist for humanistic theory.

What is more, the primitive personality can construct all kinds of physical infants, and can relate to the physical infant in all kinds of ways. Thus the physical infant can be constructed by the primitive personality into being an oral thing which incorporates and introjects portions of an "external" world. Or, the primitive personality can construct the physical infant into being pushed by drives and needs which can be gratified or reinforced by the "external" world. Or, the primitive personality can fashion the physical infant into being a "learning organism" coping with external cues and complexes of stimuli. From our perspective, the infant is not "really" any of these. Yet each are models which the primitive personality can mould the physical infant into being. By means of a theoretical shift, not only is the problem of "environment" solved, but the various models of various theories are illuminated as varying expressions of the underlying primitive personality.

Mechanisms by which the Environment Affects the Infant

We have solved by fiat the problem of how the external environment affects the basic foundation of the infant. Other approaches must invent mechanisms whereby the former affects the latter. We turn now to a discussion of some of the more popular mechanisms.

Incorporation and introjection. As soon as a gap is inserted between a separated physical infant and a separated external world, some solution must be found to the problem of how the latter gets inside or becomes a part of or affects the former. One way in which psychoanalytic theorists seek to solve this problem is by formulating a stage in which the developing infant "takes in" portions of the external world. In this stage, the developing infant is said to incorporate or "introject" such chunks of the external world as the parents' "mental characteristics" and their "cultural inheritance." According to this conceptualization, ". . . the growing individual incorporates the mental cherecteristics of the parents, including their cultural inheritance . . . this process is in itself 'oral,' i.e. it occurs through introjection . . ." (Benedek, 1956, p. 407). One problem in such a conceptualization is whether or not this mechanism explains the *fundamental origins* of the infant or is itself a *later* and more sophisticated stage of an already established infant personality. Aside from this issue, however, oral introjection is a mechanism for solving a problem created by a theory in which the external world and the physical infant are two essentially separated entities. In humanistic theory, infant and encompassing external world are conceptualized as one, and, since no separation is invoked, no mechanism such as oral introjection must be invented. The infant does not have to incorporate the external world in order to internalize the external; in humanisitc theory the external is *already* a part of the infant-as-primitive-personality.

Reward-reinforcement-gratification of drives-needs. A common way in which the external environment is held as determining the basic foundations of the infant is through mechanisms of rewarding-reinforcing-gratifying basic drives or needs. For example, what the infant becomes is a function of the nature and degree to which the external environment satisfies or gratifies basic needs for love, warmth and affection (Buhler, 1968b; Langdon & Stout, 1954). If the infant's "need" for love and tenderness is not "satisfied", there are such unfortunate sequelae as a painful aloneness and lack of love (Sullivan, 1953; Suttie, 1952). Not only does humanistic theory reject intrinsic basic needs, but our concept of primitive personality renders unnecessary such mechanisms as the satisfaction or gratification of these basic needs as means of determining the basic foundations of the infant.

The traditional model postulates basic needs and drives which require reward-reinforcement-gratification. But such a model is terribly strained in trying to describe much of what we observe about infants. For example, clinical observors have noted that some institutionalized infants share many of the following characteristics: a tendency toward emaciation, listlessness, quietness and unresponsiveness, lowered social attachments, impoverished play, inadequate delay of gratification, reduced body weight, lowered intellect, lack of emotional warmth, inadequate sucking, and poor language development (Ainsworth, 1962; Provence & Lipton, 1962; Spitz, 1945). How may these observations be explained? One way is to postulate basic infant needs for mothering, for affectional contact, for social and emotional stimulation. Given these basic needs, the outcome depends upon the degree to which these are gratified. If the institutional caretakers fail to gratify these basic needs, the babies will become listless, unresponsive, emaciated, and so on (cf. Yarrow, 1961). All of this is an expression of the external world's affecting the infant by gratifying or not gratifying the infant's supposed basic needs. The concept of primitive personality offers a way of making sense of the above observations without calling upon such supposed basic needs and without invoking mechanisms of gratifying or not gratifying these basic needs. In our view, the caretakers are the significant figures who construct the infant into fulfilling certain functions. These caretakers may fashion the infants into listless and impoverished creatures (a) as appropriate external contexts wherein the caretakers will experience what is important for them to experience, (b) as externalized operating potentials of the caretakers, or (c) as externalized deeper potentials of the caretakers. In each instance, the infants are made to be that way because of the nature of the primitive personality—and without postulating basic needs or mechanisms of gratification or lack of gratification.

Our thesis is that the concept of the primitive personality makes it unnecessary to invoke that drive model and its mechanisms of reward-reinforcement-gratification, not only in the description of listless and emaciated infants in institutions, but in much more common infant behavior and characteristics. For example, how do we account for social attachment behavior in infants? From our perspective, the concept of the primitive personality enables us to acknowledge that social attachments between the parental figures and the physical infant are *already present*. By virtue of the primitive field, the attachment grooves are already there in the form of relationships with and defined functions of the physical infant. Within the primitive field, the physical infant already is socially attached to mother, father, breast, milk, cultural taboos, meaningful objects, and all other significant components of the encompassing field. The physical infant *starts* social; it does not become social. We reject the traditional formulation whereby the infant is assumed to come into the world with primary biophysiological needs (Asch, 1952; Gewirtz, 1969; Sears, Whiting, Nowlis & Sears, 1953) which are gratified through parental removal of negative reinforcements and the provision of positive reinforcements (Bijou & Baer, 1965, 1966) in the development of early social attachments which are then broadened and made more complex through the acquisition of speech, social and cultural skills in the grand social extension of the biological drive-reinforcement conception of human beings (Asch, 1952). Not only has this model not proven adequate to the grasping of the growth of social attachments, but that whole drive model has been stretched to the breaking point in trying to account for research findings pertaining to curiosity, imitation, crying, following, clinging, exploration, play, contact-seeking, competence and effectance behaviors (e.g. Hinde, 1965). Research on early affectional behavior (e.g. Harlow & Zimmerman, 1959) and imprinting (Bateson, 1966; Eibl-Eibesfeldt, 1970; Sluckin, 1965) cast serious doubt on the tenability of basic physiological drives and reward-reinforcement-gratification principles, especially with regard to feeding, as an adequate explanatory foundation of the earliest social attachment relationships of the newborn. It is time to cast aside the whole drive model, wherein the parent influences the infant through mechanisms of reward-reinforcement-gratification, and to recognize the central role of the parental figures within the context of the encompassing primitive field.

In moving from attachment to anxiety, the same mechanisms of gratification (or non-gratification) of basic needs are called upon. Indeed, a psychoanalytic theory of infant anxiety is based upon non-gratification of basic needs. In the psychoanalytic theory of infant anxiety, there are at least three planks in the platform which humanistic theory rejects. The major one is that the infant has basic needs which the external world either gratifies or fails to gratify. No part of this is accepted by humanistic theory. Second, the infant is held as intrinsically helpless, a view of the infant not at all shared by humanistic theory. Third, the physical infant, although helpless to deal with the external world's failure to gratify, nevertheless is supposed to possess cognitive skills of such refined sophistication that it is able to assess all of the above and, furthermore, to conclude that such a situation is dangerous. In humanistic theory, the physical infant is not presumed to possess such finely grained cognitive skills. Yet all of this, and more, is included in the psychoanalytic theory of how the external environment affects anxiety in the infant: "The situation which the infant appraises as 'danger,' and against which it deserves reassurance, is therefore one of not being gratified—a situation against which it is powerless . . . anxiety proves to be a product of the psychic helplessness of the infant which is the obvious counterpart of its biological helplessness" (Freud, 1936, pp. 76-77). Once the infant has intrinsic basic needs, and the external environment is there to gratify those needs, we have laid the groundwork for mechanisms for affecting the basic personality structure (e.g. anxiety) of the infant. No such mechanisms are called for by humanistic theory. Instead, anxiety is the expression of a disintegrative relationship within the primitive personality. The requisite conditions for anxiety lie in the primitive field, and not in the external environment as non-gratifier of basic needs within the infant.

We have been considering a model in which the needs reside in the infant and the rewarder-reinforcer-gratifier is the parent. This is a traditional model. Recently, infant researchers working within a learning framework have articulated a model which lies intermediate between traditional ones and that proposed by humanistic theory. According to this recent model, infant and mother are described as mutually reinforcing dyad in which the behavior of each is contingent upon the response of the other (e.g. Bijou & Baer, 1965; Gewirtz, 1969). Here is an interactive model in which each participant reinforces the behavior of the other. Yet such a model begs the very question it sets out to answer, i.e., how does the external environment account for the infant being the way it is? That is, such a model already has the infant as an entity which reinforces mother's behavior, but it fails to explain how the infant got to be that way. From the perspective of humanistic theory, the answers are contained in the primitive field. Mother is the architect of the infant which she constructs into being a partner in a mutual interaction designed and produced by her. For example, mother may construct an infant whose function is to resist mother's overtures of love, or to be pleased with mother's overtures of love. The result is a mutually reinforcing dyad in which mother provides overtures, baby resists (or accepts) these overtures, mother responds to baby's resistance (or acceptance), and on and on. Yet, in all of this, the prime determiner of the role and function of the infant is the mother. Mother determines that baby will respond in the way baby responds to mother in the mother-infant dyad. In other words, it is the primitive personality which defines the nature and function of the physical infant.

Whatever the infant does, our perspective holds that the parent is the one who got it started. The baby looks up at mother and extends his arms because the encompassing primitive field got him to behave that way. In a model wherein mother and baby interact with one another, mutually stimulate and respond to one another, there is a terribly knotty problem of untangling what gets what started. Baby's behavior serves as a cue for mother to reach toward and enfold baby. But mother's smiling proximity may serve as a cue for baby to have looked up at mother and to have extended his arms. Humanistic theory solves this knotty problem by allowing for two distinct perspectives. We can focus on the *baby* and understand mother as a component of *baby's* constructed world. Within this perspective, everything that mother does is determined and initiated (that is, is constructed) by the baby. We can also focus upon the *mother* and understand baby as a component of *mother's* constructed world. Within this perspective, everything that baby does is determined and initiated (that is, is constructed) by mother. The problem of who initiates whom is solved by imposing two perspectives in which each initiates the behavior of the other. There is no mother-infant system, nor is there any mutually interacting dyad. There are, instead, as many perspectives as there are participants. For research purposes, we may focus on the infant and observe the ways in which the infant initiates (activates, stimulates, reinforces) mother's behavior—and, separately, we may go over *the same data* by focusing on the mother and observing the ways in which mother initiates baby's behavior. Our proposed research strategy has no place for a single perspective in which a single behavioral bit must be classed as either stimulus or response, but not both (cf. Bronson, 1974).

In the drive model, parents are the ones who reward-reinforce-gratify, and they remove the punishments and negative reinforcements (e.g. Bijou & Baer, 1965). "The infant's primitive interest in the external world is in any case solely and entirely due to the circumstance that the external world is a source of gratification for it. This interest is first determined by hunger, later by other erotogenic zones" (Fenichel, 1954c, p. 42). The role of parents is highly attenuated compared with their role in humanistic theory, in which parents are everything, the complete determiners of the infantness—its very existence, construction, and functions. They constitute the very needs and drives which are to be rewarded, reinforced and gratified. In other words, the environment enjoys far greater determining power in the humanistic model as compared with the drive model.

We have spoken about becoming listless and emaciated, about play behavior, curiosity, imitation and exploration, competence and effectance, and attachment. In these and other phenomena, the drive model and its mechanisms of reward-reinforcement-gratification have failed to offer an adequate explanation. In arriving at the same conclusion, Sears (1963) asks about alternative explanations. I submit that the concept of the primitive personality provides a most respectable alternative—free of the postulate of basic needs and of mechanisms of reward-reinforcement-gratification.

Learnings by and of the physical infant. The environment has been held as affecting the foundations of personality by means of two mechanisms: (a) The infant incorporates and introjects the external environment; or (b) the environment rewards-reinforces-gratifies the intrinsic basic drives or needs of the infant. We now turn to a third mechanism, viz. the "learnings" which the physical infant processes in relation to the external environment.

At the outset, the position of humanistic theory is that the physical infant is *not* a learning organism, and that foundations of the infant are *not* a function of learnings by and of the physical infant. According to our formulation, the specific nature of that which is "learned" is *already* present in the primitive field. So-called "learning experiences" merely express what is already there, and the expression takes the form of constructing the infant into manifesting specific functions. For example, a given primitive field may be characterized by "lack of social feeling." If that is part of the primitive field, then the parental figures will construct the infant in ways which manifest lack of social feeling. It is as if the infant is surrounded with "lack of social feelings," or breathes in and is constructed into being "lack of social feeling." In other words, once "lack of social feeling" is a part of the primitive field, the parental figures will construct experiences conducive to the "learning" of "lack of social feelings." Even in her feeding of baby, mother will carry that out in ways which are saturated with "lack of social feelings." Indeed, lack of social feeling will be everywhere in the infant's life. Our formulation may be contrasted with a learning approach in which the infant learns lack of social feeling from being stuffed with food so that food rewards become spoiled and, as a result, social feeling for others is lowered (e.g. Dollard & Miller, 1950). What is learned (lack of social feeling) is the *determiner* of experiences (stuffing the infant with food) rather than the *consequence* of learning experiences.

Just as what is to be learned is already there in the primitive personality, the meaningful aspect of the external world is already there too. If the mother is the active one, the constructor, the part of the primitive personality which actively interacts with the physical infant, the infant will come to relate to the mother as a meaningful segment of its world—rather than a patch of the rug, or two legs of a chair, or the mother's left elbow. Learning theory has always had to solve the problem of what become the defined meaningful entities in the infant's world, and the problem of how those entities are made meaningful. It has been proposed that whatever gratifies the infant's needs is made into a meaningful aspect of the infant's world. Or whatever is associated by contiguity with drive reduction will become illuminated as meaningful aspects of the infant's world. According to learning theory, the meaningful aspects of the infant's world are brought forth in the course of the processes of learning. In humanistic theory, in contrast, aspects of the primitive field are already organized as meaningful, and it is the already defined meaningful aspects which interact with the physical infant. Thus it is the whole mother which is a unit in interacting with the baby, and not mother's right hand or just her eyes. Once again, it is the defined primitive field which *precedes* and *utilizes* the processes of learning, and not the processes of learning which define the meaningful aspects of the infant's external world.

In a particular primitive personality, the mother's breast may be an organized entity which has meaning as the resource of gratification. That already exists before the neonate sucks at the breast. It is mother who makes the breast into a defined entity and who gives it the meaning of being an agent of gratification. Ensuing interactions with the infant are guided and determined by the breast as a thing of gratification. Psychoanalytic theory, in contrast, understands the breast as *becoming* a defined entity through learning experiences in which the infant's need for food is gratified by the breast, and the contiguity of breast with pleasure of tension reduction results in an attachment between the infant and a defined breast. In humanisitic theory, the *already defined* part of the primitive field constructs the appropriate learning experiences, whereas in learning approaches, the principles of learning account for the emergent parts of the external world.

If learnings are held as fashioning the foundation of the infant, we are faced with the question of what the earliest "learning experiences" are like, and when the first "learning experiences" occur. The answer of humanisitic theory is that the earliest environment-infant experiences take place when the significant figures of the primitive personality construct infantness and undergo interactive relationships with that constructed infantness. It is quite likely that a rich history of such interactions has occurred prior to that point known as conception, and most certainly by that point known as birth. From our perspective, then, we take the sharpest exception to theoretical stances in which the infant's first interaction is the feeding experience, and consists of feeding and breasting (Erikson, 1950). By the time the newborn feeds at the breast, hundreds of interactive experiences have already taken place. As the conceiver of infantness, as the one who creates infantness and defines its functions, mother has already completed a long history of commerce with the infant by the time other approaches believe the first infant-environment interaction takes place. Mother has had hundreds of interactions with infantness in the course of constructing the infant and moulding it into a being which is to be gratified by breast feeding. To consider that the first experience of the infant is feeding is akin to saying that the first interaction between a home and its owner is at the time that the owner moves in and holds a "house-warming" party—when in truth the owner conceived the plans for the house, spent two years building the house, moved in, and arranged for the party.

Sullivan's interpersonal theory lies in that region between psychoanalytic and social learning theories of human development. Sullivan's approach is representaive of those in which the foundations of personality are laid down by the nature of the earliest interpersonal relationships of the child (Tauber, 1960). Yet these social interpersonal relationships, especially those carried out by the child, are refined and sophisticated *products* of a career which already has a long history. The interpersonal relationships of the child do not constitute the foundations of personality. Rather, they constitute the later expression of a personality already formed as the primitive field. By the time the child may be said to be engaging in social interpersonal relations, the primitive personality has had a rich history which itself lays the groundwork for the emerging interpersonal relations.

When does the first sexual anxiety experience occur? Some approaches hold that the first sexual anxiety experience takes place when the parents manifest a taboo response to the child's masturbating (Dollard & Miller, 1950). Our theory objects vehemently, and suggests that by that time, the child (as primitive personality) has had the opportunity to assemble hundreds of sexual anxiety experiences extending over the previous months or even years. The first sexual anxiety experiences may have occurred when the mother was filled with anxiety in relation to the fetus seen by her as a sexualized thing wiggling and squiggling inside her, or when she had anxious feelings of being sexually aroused by the baby suckling at her nipple, or when she had sexual anxiety during intercourse while the three-month-old infant lies crying in the crib next to the bed. Whereas our approach allows the first interactive experiences to occur when the primitive field constructs infantness and engages in relationships with that constructed infantness, other approaches which assume a separated external environment and a separated physical infant will find first experiences as occurring months, years, and hundreds of experiences later.

The same questions pertain to traumas as learning experiences which fashion the foundations of the infant: When do they first occur? To what extent are they constructed and by whom? Who "has" the trauma? In many approaches, traumas are more or less happenstance, unforeseeable, unfortunate occurrences. For example, some theorists speak of the trauma of birth (Greenacre, 1945; Rank, 1929). In humanistic theory, however, it is the primitive field which accounts for everything. If birth is to be a traumatic event, it is because the primitive field makes it into a traumatic event. The primitive field constructs the event itself and invests that event with its traumatic nature.

Authentic external events happen "to" the primitive field, and not to the physical infant. If some external event occurs, its meaning is defined by the parental figures, and not by the infant. In other words, it is the parental figure who "learns," and not the infant. Suppose, for example, that the father dies when the infant is four months old. The meaning and the significance of that event are functions of how the mother grasps that event. If the death has a profound effect on mother, then it may be said that the death has a profound impact upon the infant-as-primitive-personality. If that event is *not* shattering to the mother, then it is not shattering to the infant-as-primitive-personality. If mother makes that death into an experience of loss and permanent mourning, then that is the meaning of that event to the infant-as-primitive-personality. Any way in which mother grasps and adds meaning to the death becomes the meaning of that event from the infant-as-primitive-personality—whether it means distrust of intimacy, depression at being left behind, guilt over hating father, fear of the powerful external world, or whatever. The death does not directly affect the physical infant (cf. Erikson, 1950). Instead, it is processed by the parental figure who *is* the infant-as-primitive-personality. Thus the *physical* infant does not do the "learning," the processing, the giving of meaning and significance to the event.

We have taken as an example the death or loss of a parent in early childhood. The effects, our interpretation suggests, are determined by the way the early loss is grasped by the significant figures of the primitive field, and not by any direct impacts upon the physical infant itself. The key lies in such variables as the effects upon the surviving parent and the effects on the general family atmosphere (McCord, McCord & Thurber, 1962). Hilgard and Newman (1960) refer to this as the climate surrounding the death. That is, the death has a meaning because of the way it is processed by the figures of the primitive field, and not because of any direct effect upon the physical infant.

Ordinarily, however, research on parental loss has presumed that there is a direct learning connection between the loss and the physical infant (e.g. Lynn & Sawrey, 1959). Indeed, a learning theory framework is unable to investigate variables which fall outside that paradigm. By accepting the concept of the primitive personality, we have a conceptual alternative to that of seeking the effects in the supposed direct (learning) impacts upon the physical infant itself.

What has been said about death or early loss also pertains to any other event which occurs in or to the primitive field. Whether that event is of traumatic proportions or not, its effect is through the significant figures and not directly onto the physical infant. For example, the birth of another baby has its meaning from the parental figures, and not in the way the infant is supposed to perceive or grasp or add significance to or learn from the birth of its sibling. If the parents are traumatized by having two babies so quickly, then it may be said that the second baby was a traumatic event to the infant-*as-primitive-personality*. The same holds true for such events as father losing his job, the death of the older brother, mother leaving with another man, suicide of the boarder who was living with the family. If the surviving figure experiences a sense of frightening lack of control, then the meaning or significance of that event to the infant-as-primitive-personality is a frightening lack of control. If, however, the surviving figure uses these events to experience profound depression, then depression becomes the main effect of the event. The "learning" consists of the way the parental figures meaningfully experience the event—and not in so-called learning processes occurring within the physical infant. The environment fashions a trauma or a frightening lack of control or depression as part of the infant's personality foundation by the way the environment affects the parental figures.

There is a body of research on the relationships between early events and later consequences. This line of research studies all kinds of interesting events which occur early in the life of the child and relates these to a larger spectrum of outcomes which occur when the person is six or twelve or in adolescence or even older. If our thesis is a good one, then it would mean that we have a better key to understanding many of the existing findings, and we have a new set of factors (the figures of the primitive personality) to plug into the relationships between early life events and later outcomes. For example, in a sample of boys whose fathers were absent during their childhood, it was found that the boys tended to have high scores on an antisocial behavior scale (Siegman, 1966). Our thesis suggests that the key to the relationship between father absence and later high scores on an antisocial behavior scale is the way in which the wife-mother experienced the father absence. Always we turn to the figures of the primitive personality for the interpretive meaning of the event. If the wife-mother experienced the father absence in terms of increased freedom and sexual license, the outcome effect on the son would be predicted to be different from the experiencing of heightened turning to the son as comrade-companion. The key is the wife-mother, and not the direct learning-effect upon or by the physical infant-son.

According to our formulation, what have been taken as causal relationships are better described as multiple expressions of the same primitive personality. Early and later events are related to one another only because each are expressions of the same primitive personality, and not on the basis of any causal relationships. For example, if a woman wants to be clean and pure, free of any pregnancies, she may express that potential in (a) chemical changes in her endocrine system, and also in (b) a tendency toward miscarriages. Both are manifestations of the potential to be unpregnant. It is an error to attribute a causal relationship to the high relation between a particular chemical state and a high tendency toward miscarriages. Once again, the primitive personality is the cause. It is the cause of both events which are then highly related to one another as expressions of the same primitive personality, and not as causally related events. Even though it is not common to take this interpretative stance instead of the usual causal stance, some researchers are beginning to entertain this interpretative possibility. Research on the relationship between parental smoking and infant prematurity illustrates this point. As reviewed by Joffe (1969), the research first indicated a high correlation between maternal smoking and infant prematurity, especially when prematurity was defined in terms of birth weight. This research was interpreted as suggesting a causal relationship between maternal smoking and premature birth. Subsequent research, however, reported similar high correlations between premature low birth weight and *paternal* smoking! In an interpretative summary of the research, Joffe adds a noncausal possibility, viz. that the high relationship between smoking and premature low birth weight may be due to a *third* factor of which *both* are expressions: "It may simply indicate that the number of cigarettes smoked is an index of the potency of whatever third variable causes both smoking mothers and low birthweight infants. Yerushalmy's findings on the relationship of the number of cigarettes smoked by the father and the prematurity rates of their children supports such an explanation" (Joffe, 1969, pp. 240-241). That mysterious third variable, according to humanistic theory, is always the primitive personality which, in this instance, accounts both for the high smoking and the prematurity. Perhaps this consists of an inability to be intact by oneself, a having to drain the external world, or using and getting rid of little things. Whatever its nature, it characterizes the primitive personality and leads to consequences which are coupled to one another and which are understandably mistaken as *causally* related to each other.

We are only beginning to grasp what occurs in early experience. In nearly every area of childhood, the signals are pointing toward a far more intensive searching of the events of these earliest weeks and months. In the area of intelligence, for example, we have moved from a position relying upon constitutional-genetic variables to one relying upon early experience understood through the laws of learning (cf. Hunt, 1960, 1963). Many researchers are looking further into early experience, and are unenthusiastic about restricting their search to the factors and variables offered by the learning theories. I suggest that humanistic theory, especially the concept of the primitive personality, holds greater promise for both guiding us into fruitful research avenues in early experience, and for helping us grasp the findings better than the learning theories.

The role of social factors. Does the environment affect the foundations of the infant through social mechanisms? Are social factors significant in constructing these foundations? How do social factors exert their influence? One way that social factors are held as operating is by opposing the infant's impulses. According to this formulation, the infant has (usually as an essential component of its human nature) blind, uncivilized instinctual impulses. These instinctual impulses, especially as seen by psychoanalysis, are savage. Inevitably, there is a clash between these savage blind impulses and the taboos of a society which does not permit expression of these impulses. In this inevitable clash, the external environment moulds the infant's very foundations and exerts its effect upon the way the infant is to be. But humanistic theory tells a different story. To begin with, the infant has no savage instinctual impulses. Instead, some parental figures construct infants to fulfill such functions. An infant who is "savage blind impulse" is evidence of the creative genius of parental figures. Next, what is typically referred to as "society" is the significant figures of the primitive field itself. Here are mother, father, and perhaps older sister, grandmother, and so on. When these figures have reactions to the infant's defecating, it is an instance of grandmother being offended by the sight and smell of the defecation—and not a grand scene of "society" exerting its impact upon the infant. Finally, the inevitable clash between society and the infant's blind impulses turns out, in humanistic theory, to be an expression of the disintegrative relationships characterizing that particular primitive field. If mother fearfully recoils from her own insides as blind animal impulses, she may construct her infant into being those animal blind impulses, and proceed to fear and hate him for being that way. The so-called clash between "society" and "animal instincts" turns out to be mother's angry struggle to toilet train the infant, or father's violent opposition to the baby's slurping and sucking at the breast. Every element in the supposed clash between "society" and the "blind savage impulses of the infant" is constructed and designed by the parental figures. It is the primitive personality which accounts for everything the society is held as doing.

Those approaches which see social factors as determining the infant cite specific ways in which the basic foundation of the infant is shaped by the clash between the infant's instincts and the society's reactions. Out of this clash is fashioned the infant's conflicts with *its own* internal personality processes. Psychoanalysis, for example, cites three ways in which society's reactions to the infant's instincts accounts for the infant's conflicts with its own deeper personality processes (Fenichel, 1954c). One way is that society does not and can not immediately gratify the pressing instinctual impulses; under this condition, the infant comes to react to its instincts as dangerous. A second way is that society may respond to the infant's instincts with counterthreats, prohibitions, and punitive taboos; under this condition, the infant learns to fear the build-up of its own instinctual tensions. A third way is that the infant responds to the inimical society with projective misapprehensions, and therefore views its own instincts with even greater mistrust and fear. In these specific ways, the interaction between society and the infant's instincts is said to fashion the infant's internal conflicts with its own deeper personality processes—and thereby make the infant what it is.

By invoking the concept of the primitive personality, humanistic theory offers quite a different description of the origins of the infant's conflicts with its own deeper personality processes. The determining roots have already existed in the form of the disintegrative relationships in the primitive personality. If the primitive personality includes fear and hate toward, as an example, open aggressivity, then the structure is already there for the infant to fear and hate its own deeper aggressivity. Experiences which occur months or years later only express the disintegrative conflicts which are already present. Aggressivity is already coupled with fear and hate; the fear and hate do not come about later because of lack of immediate gratification or because of parental punitiveness or because the society is inimical. Given disintegrative relationships toward aggressivity in the primitive personality, the parents construct the infant into an aggressive animal, and then the parents respond to the infant's aggressivity with repulsion, lack of gratification, opposition, and punitiveness. The parental response is already existing; it plays itself out along a script which was contained in the whole field of the primitive personality from the very beginning. Seen from this perspective, social factors play an attenuated role in the fashioning of the infant's relationships toward its own internal personality processes.

Our discussion so far has denied social factors any direct role in determining the infant's personality foundation. Are there ways in which social factors do play a role? Our position is that social factors affect the basic personality foundations of the infant to whatever extent these factors are present in the contents of the primitive personality. If the society is characterized by sexual permissiveness and the insecurity of war—and if these are present in the infant's primitive personality—then the infant's basic personality foundations include sexual permissiveness and the insecurity of war. Social factors do not *influence* the infant; if they are in the primitive personality, they *are* the infant!

Societies and cultures differ widely in child-rearing practices (e.g., Mead, 1953). The way in which these differences make a difference in the basic personality foundations of infants is through differences in the encompassing primitive fields. For example, in some societies and cultures, the major responsibility for child care is assigned to someone other than mother or father. Does this make a difference in the way the child is? How does this make a difference? From our perspective, the presence of this third person can make for radical differences in the basic foundations of the infant by virtue of that third person's existence within the primitive field—that is, the nature of that third person and the relationships within that third person and between that third person and others in the primitive field. It is the altered contents of the primitive personality which both constitute and mediate the ways in which social and cultural differences make for radical differences in the basic foundations of infants.

We have considered a number of mechanisms by which the external environment affects the foundation of what the infant is. Our thesis is that the concept of the primitive personality can replace each of these mechanisms because the primitive personality is both the external environment and the infant. But because of this very coterminality, there is a very special bond between the infant and those parts of itself which are the primitive personality. It is as if the infant could look about and know that virtually everything in its primitive field is the determining part of what it is. Mother is the infant, as well as mother. But more, mother is indeed the part of the infant which constructs and defines the functions of the infant which now regards its encompassing world. Here is a primordial sensing of (a) a oneness and coterminality with the external world, and (b) the unlimited power of that external world to construct and define what one is. Such sensings are contained in the primordial core of that which is described as the "paranoid" world, a way of being in the world such that the world has all the power. Such sensings are contained in the primordial core of every conceptualization of the external world as influencer, controller, determiner. In this sense, every theory is accurate in describing human beings as determined by outside forces, environmental determinants, stimuli and cues, Gods and devils, force fields and economics, governments and astrological factors. We are run by families, communities, societies and cultures. None of this comes about through mechanisms; it merely *is*, because of the nature of the primitive personality.

Our concept of the primitive personality covers the territory known as the external environment. Yet a careful listing of our "external variables" includes a great deal of what is ordinarily excluded in other lists of external variables. For example, if we were to list the external variables which determine the physical infant's "toilet training behavior," prominent among these would be the potentials and relationships of the significant parental figures. These are variables, external to the physical infant, which play a prominent role in determining whether the baby would smoothly acquire these behaviors or not, whether baby would enjoy urinating in a potty, would be bothered by failures to contain the anal sphincters, would be defiant in refusing to conform to parental pressures for toilet training, and so on. Yet listings of the significant external variables influencing toilet training behavior typically omit parental potentials and their relationships (cf. Dollard & Miller, 1950). It is one thing to speak generally about the determining role of external environmental variables; it is quite another to agree on the specific nature of those variables. Listings of determining external environmental variables typically omit those illuminated by the concept of the primitive personality.

14

Infant Behavior

Chapter 13 focused on the origins of infants. We were concerned with how the primitive field sets about constructing an infant invested with given functions. We turn now to the *behavior* of infants. Our focus is now the description and understanding of the behaving physical infant and the specific mechanisms which account for the initiation, maintenance, and change of its behavior.

In chapter 13 we rejected some of the commonly accepted mechanisms for explaining the behavior of infants: (a) We rejected human nature as a way of explaining infant behavior. Our theory has no place for such concepts as biophysical roots of human behavior, intrinsic physiological needs, and behavioral characteristics thought to be there by virtue of an all-purpose human nature. (b) We turned away from genetic mechanisms as determinants of infant behavior. Even the most archaic behavior of the neonate is not attributed, in humanistic theory, to the effects of genetic deposits or to interactions between genetic and environmental variables. (c) We have also rejected the whole array of mechanisms whereby the external world is described as determining infant behavior through mechanisms of learning, especially those of reward-reinforcement-gratification of the infant's needs or drives. Our problem, then, is how to describe infant behavior on the basis of the concepts and mechanisms of humanistic theory.

TOWARD A GENERAL POSTURE OF INFANT BEHAVIOR

From the previous chapter, we can make some rather general statements about the determinants of infant behavior: (a) The behavior of infants is a function of the primitive personality. Knowing the nature and contents of the primitive personality, we should be able to describe and to predict the nature of the behavior of the physical infant. (b) The behavior of infants is a function of the potentials and relationships between the potentials of the significant figures of the primitive field. (c) The behavior of infants is determined by the functions which define the physical infant and the nature of the significant figures who define those functions.

These general statements are ways of acknowledging that the determinants of the physical infant's behaviors are the psychodynamics of the family (Bateson, 1961; Haley, 1963; Jackson, 1957; Laing & Esterson, 1970). In our view, the physical infant is a behavior machine produced and run by (a) the primitive field, (b) the potentials and relationships of the significant figures, and (c) the functions into which the physical infant is constructed. This primitive field (or the "psychodynamics of the family") determines virtually everything about the behavior: what the behavior shall be, the context in which it occurs, when the behavior occurs, the style and characteristics of the behavior, and the physical infant's behavioral responses to its own behavior. In effect, our thesis has been neatly adumbrated in the work of the Bateson-Haley-Jackson group and their recognition of the central role of the family dynamics in the determination of the behavior of the physical infant.

The Bateson-Haley-Jackson group, other family theorists, and some child developmentalists share the idea that the infant-child's behavior is a function of the family as a *system*. They understand the mother-child dyad as a system, and the properties of this system help to make sense of the behavior of the child. Yet, even conceptualizing the mother-child dyad as a system, the problem remains, viz. how may we understand this particular behavior of the child? "For years (and now with increasing frequency), various investigators have stressed that the mother-child pair is a dyad joined in mutual interdependence; that it is a system whose properties must be defined if we are to fully understand the behavior of either constituent member . . . I know of no one who disagrees, but of only very few whose work is aimed at such goals" (Bronson, 1974, p. 277). What is it about the "system" which enables us to understand the behavior of the child? I submit that the concept of the primitive personality paves the specific avenue toward understanding the child's (and especially the infant's) concrete behavior.

In the main, research and theory on the origins of *problem* behavior are turning slowly in the direction of what we term the primitive field. So-called schizophrenic, irrational behavior of the young child is beginning to be coupled with the dynamics of the family. For example, Rogler and Hollingshead (1965) cite the work of Lidz, Wynne, the Bateson-Jackson-Haley group, and others who generally tend toward such an emerging model. Yet the specific mechanisms have yet to be articulated whereby the actual behavior is brought about. It is our intention to explicate these mechanisms, not only for problem behavior but for all behavior of the infant. It is interesting to find in the work of the Bateson-Jackson-Haley group hintings toward specific mechanisms which can explain all infant behavior. That group has concentrated predominantly on the *pathological* behavior of the *child*. Behavior which is psychotic, peculiar, deviant, and "crazy" is described in terms of the personality dynamics of the parents and the family interrelationships. For example, one or both parents may have personality tendencies toward keeping others away, preventing contact. Yet they themselves do not carry out these personality tendencies in actual behavior. Instead, the child is made into the behavioral expression of these parental personality tendencies, and the child behaves by being incoherent, grossly unresponsive to the external world, being by himself for periods of time, speaking and communicating generally in ways which avoid contact, seldom if ever allowing any kind of physical contact. Building upon such analyses, our aim is to redescribe "family psychodynamics" as the primitive personality in studying *all* behavior (not merely peculiar, deviant behavior), of the *infant* (not merely the young child) as determined by concrete *mechanisms* (not merely loosely linked to family psychodynamics).

Toward Specific Mechanisms of Infant Behavior

Many approaches tend to agree that the behavior of an infant is influenced by the ways in which parental figures relate to the infant (e.g., Hawkins et al., 1966). Most typically, the relationship is classified as falling along a dimension from accepting to rejecting, from loving and warm to hating and cold, from rewarding and reinforcing to unrewarding and unreinforcing, from integrative to disintegrative. Representative of such studies is the classic work of Baldwin, Kalhorn and Breeze (1945) in which parental acceptance was seen to be coupled with certain classes of infant behavior such as intellectual development, originality, emotional control, whereas parental rejectance was coupled with other behavior such as lack of originality, rebelliousness, and aggressivity. Our concern begins with the importance of the relational variable, and proceeds to a more concrete analysis of the *specific mechanisms* whereby the relationships among parental potentials lead to specific infant behavior. To *begin* with an accepting or rejecting relationship toward the infant (the starting point of many approaches) is to begin at a very advanced point, for we are concerned with the mechanisms which account for that kind of a relationship with the infant. We are concerned, for example, with much earlier processes which culminated in the mother's rejecting the infant's whining. How are the relationships between the mother's potentials responsible for the construction of that kind of behaving infant and that kind of attitude toward that kind of behaving infant? We intend to propose specific mechanisms whereby the mother brings about a rejection of the infant's whining. Although all of this may be generally categorized as supporting the importance of the relationship, our aim is to study the mechanisms whereby relationships within and between the parental figures link up with specific behaviors of the physical infant.

Some infant behaviors are plain to see and have been observed for centuries. Others require the singular clinical acumen and brilliant powers of observation of a Sigmund Freud or a Jean Piaget. Yet theoreticians and researchers alike have never been securely confident about the explanation of even ordinarily observed infant behavior. Indeed, when it comes to specific infant behaviors, we have *general* theories embarrassingly devoid of *specific* mechanisms. We know that infants behave in ways which seem to promote attachments to external persons and objects. But we lack systematic explication of the specific mechanisms which explain the occurrence of those particular behaviors. Our aim is to propose a set of specific mechanisms whereby the primitive personality determines the range of observed infant behavior. Our aim is to answer questions such as the following: What are the ways in which the primitive personality leads to specific infant behaviors? How do the potentials and relationships of the significant figures account for specific behaviors of the physical infant? How does the primitive personality construct an infant with defined functions which include specific infant behaviors?

We will discuss four ways (or mechanisms) whereby the primitive personality determines the behavior of the infant. In the first three of these four ways, the primitive personality is *external* to the physical infant, encompassing it and doing things to it. This is the primitive field which surrounds the physical infant, the world in which it exists. The fourth way flows out of the primitive personality *as* the infant, as the larger meaning and definition of the infant-as-primitive-personality. In this posture, the primitive field *is* the infant, whereas in the first three ways, the primitive field encompasses and does things to the physical infant. In other words, the first three mechanisms treat the infant as the physical infant, and propose ways in which this primitive field accounts for the physical infant's behavior. In the fourth way, the primitive field accounts for the behavior of the infant-as-primitive personality.

Behavior without conscious awareness. In each of these four mechanisms, the center of that which determines the behavior of the infant lies within the encompassing primitive field, outside the perimeter of the physical infant. There is, in this conception, behavior *before* consciousness or self-awareness. That is, for weeks, months, and years, the physical infant behaves without any consciousness, without any awareness, any sense of self or "I." Indeed, the sense of consciousness emerges only after these months and years of behavior, including that behavior which Mead (1934) describes as interactional, communicative, or social behavior. Thus, this chapter deals with a physical infant behaving without any archaic ego, any sense of self or consciousness or awareness. All of the determinants are external to the physical infant, and free of any infant consciousness or self-awareness. When the infant reaches out for the glass and knocks it over, there is no conscious self or I-ness which ways, "I am reaching for the glass. Now I am hitting it, and there it goes!" The physical infant carries out thousands of behaviors completely independent of any sense of conscious awareness located anywhere within the mechanical behaving machine which is the physical infant.

In the same way, as indicated in Chapter 13, the parental figures work toward the production of infant behavior virtually independent of any consciousness or awareness. As a segment of their external worlds, the infant (and its behavior) is constructed and made to function on the basis of parental potentials and relationships. The parents are limited in their knowing, their awareness or consciousness, to the perimeter of their immediate operating potentials. Thus the predominance of what they do is accomplished independent of their awareness or consciousness. It is the primitive field which determines infant behavior. It is the primitive field which uses the four mechanisms to be described in this chapter—and not the knowing, aware, conscious parent. In effect, the entire scene is carried on without anyone being conscious or even half-sensing what is going on. Neither the infant-as-physical-entity nor the infant-as-primitive-personality "has" awareness of what is occurring. Infant behavior is produced by specific mechanisms which operate largely without benefit of awareness or consciousness.

Primitive Field as Behavior-Inducing Conditions

The primitive world is the infant's complete world, its entire ocean of existence. Contained in the encompassing primitive field are parental figures who both control and constitute, own and are, everything of that world. There are two aspects of that primitive field which together bring about infant behavior from nothing. That is, where no such infant behavior exists at one moment, the primitive field can bring it into existence. The first aspect is a highly defined, predetermined behavioral target. Before the parental figures even begin their work, they have "in mind" a specific behavior which the infant is to be or is to carry out. In other words, the parental figures have a goal, a mission to create more than an infantness which is a particular function. These parental figures have the mission to induce a specific behavior which the physical infant is to be. Second, the parental figures must organize the primitive field such that the predetermined behavior will be induced. Since every component of the encompassing primitive field is either under the controlling mandate of the parental figures or is itself the parental figure, the primitive field is fully capable of being contoured in precisely the right ways which bring about the necessary behavior. Indeed, the primitive field is capable of organizing itself such that *only* the predetermined behavior can and will come about. Thus, combining these two aspects, *the primitive field brings about infant behavior by (a) identifying a predetermined behavior to be brought about and (b) organizing the conditions and components of the primitive field so as to induce the occurrence of that behavior.*

By following this principle, we can account for the *very first occurrence* of a behavior. Behavior can, in effect, be produced from nothing. By having a specific behavior in mind, so to speak, the parental figures set about organizing the primitive field so that behavior occurs, and, whereas a few minutes ago the infant was not behaving in that way, now the behavior *is* occurring. This is not a behavior which is modified or altered from some form in which it had existed, nor is it a fuller development of some behavior which had existed in some rudimentary form.

The Parent as Unknowing Determiner

We have understood for centuries that given conditions or circumstances *force* the occurrence of particular (infant) behaviors. What is most difficult to recognize is the role of parental figures in bringing this about. All of the responsibility lies within these parental figures—without their knowing or acknowledging their role as the whole determinant. Parents have a definite program of the specific behavior their infant is to carry out. Without knowing, parents set out to insure that their baby is to be left-handed or to be fearful of soft objects or to be terrified of strangers or to be fussing and squirming or to be grabbing onto mother's breasts. Although carrying out this predefined task, the parent has no idea whatsoever that she holds such a definite predetermined idea of the behavioral product. Mother may go about her work with precision, carrying out her task as if she knows exactly the behavior she is going to produce. Yet the conscious person of mother has no idea whatsoever of the delicate task she is accomplishing. Nor is the parent aware of the delicate ways in which she carefully organizes the conditions of the primitive field to induce that specific behavior.

Without knowing, without having a sense of what they are about, parents are brilliant craftsmen or architects or experimenters who are wholly dedicated toward producing a very definite behavioral product. They are like architects creating singular plans for what they are going to set about producing. They are like experimenters planning for the right control of the right conditions in order to produce the definite behavior. If we observe parents from the point of conception throughout pregnancy and the earliest months of infancy, they will fashion very precise conditions encompassing the physical infant. If the desired product is that their baby be left-handed or flee in fear from strangers, then the parents set about arranging the primitive field into unerringly right conditions for inducing that particular behavior. The role of stranger is carefully created; the placement of mother, baby and stranger is carefully arranged; looks, gestures and timing are all organized into a careful set of conditions which induce a very particular behavior from the infant. And yet, in all of this, the experimenter-parent is brilliant in her organizing of the behavior-inducing conditions without knowing either that she is brilliant or the nature of her experimental work. In organizing the primitive field into the right behavior-inducing conditions, parents are dedicated, persistent, tireless, dogged, and ingeniously monomanic—without ever knowing that they possess such singular qualities. Furthermore, their "subject" in this experiment is a willing, and mindless, subject, with both subject and experimenter in perfect working partnership, totally unaware of the purposes, goals, methods and design of the enterprise in which both are engaged.

Chapter 6 described the ways in which persons constructed their external worlds without knowing that they are constructing such external worlds. Chapter 13 described the ways in which parental figures constructed infants as given roles and functons, without knowing that they are constructing infants to be such roles and functions. It is in this enterprise that parents will work diligently toward producing a specific infant behavior without knowing that they are wholly responsible for and dedicated toward producing such behavior. How is it that a parent will set about to construct her baby into behaving fearfully toward small furry objects—and will organize the primitive field into just the right conditions to induce such behavior from the infant? (a) The parent herself may house an operating or a deeper potential for experiencing fearfulness. As a means of experiencing that, the parent constructs the infant into being the externalization of her own operating or deeper potential so that when the baby is being fearful, getting away from terror, being panic-stricken, it is the mother who thereby experiences. Thus it becomes important to organize all the necessary conditions to induce such behavior from the infant. Or (b) by constructing just such a situational context, the mother may be experiencing what it is important for her to experience. Thus the infant's being fearful of soft furry objects may constitute the appropriate situational context wherein the mother gains a measure of experiencing power or cruelty or monstrousness in the very situation which she organized to occur. Or, the mother may have other experiencings in the situation she constructed. She may have created just the right situation for experiencing protectiveness and comfort so that, having made baby terrified, she is protective and comforting of the distressed infant. On the other hand, (c) she may construct the infant into being fearful of the soft furry object in order to establish the very relationship she has with her own potentials. For example, she may construct her infant into being fearful and terrified of soft furry objects so that she can then hate the baby for being that way. Just as she hates that potential within herself, she now relates to baby's being that way with the same disintegrative hateful relationship. Or the relationship may be one which she constructs between baby and her own deeper potentialities. For example, if her own relationship toward her deeper cruelty and monstrousness is a distintegrative one of hating it and drawing away from it, she may be hard at work constructing her baby into being someone who likewise hates and draws away from mother's awful cruelty and monstrousness. Baby hates and draws away from that which mother also hates and draws away from in herself. Here are the various determinants of a parent setting out to organize the primitive field so as to induce a very specific infant behavior, without the parent ever knowing what is occurring—and knowing even less of the modes and functions of the induced infant behavior.

Behind the work of the parent are the potentials and relations which comprise the parent. Much of what theories cite as *principles* to account for the behavior of infants refer, in actuality, to specific *potentials* in the parents. For example, how may we understand infant behavior which draws mother into closer proximity, such as crying, imploring looks at mother, crawling after mother, and clinging to mother? Some approaches account for such behavior by citing principles such as the importance of mother's proximity as a more potent reinforcing agent when she is close by (cf. Bijou & Baer, 1965). According to humanistic theory, *such principles are descriptions of particular potentials existing in particular parental figures—and not general principles of human behavior.* Some parents may be described as having a potential for experiencing being of importance to baby, being a "potent reinforcing agent," being of significance to the infant. For these particular parental figures, the behaviors to be induced in the infant may well be those which enable the parents to experience "being a potent reinforcing agent," and, therefore, the target behaviors to be induced consist of crying, crawling after mother, and similar behaviors to keep mother close by. In order to induce such behaviors, parents with those potentials may organize the primitive field in ways which are effective in inducing those particular behaviors. In similar ways, many of the "principles" of human behavior, and especially infant behavior, are taken by humanistic theory as descriptions of the primitive field, the parental figures, parental potentials and relationships—and not general principles of behavior. Virtually all of the principles cited by other approaches as *explanations* of *infant* behavior in general are understood by humanisitic theory as *descriptions* of common *parental* potentials.

Each hypothesis, principle and theory of human infant behavior is a description of the *describer* (i.e., adult as parent) rather than human infant behavior in general. For example, the behavior of infants is commonly described as following a principle of immediate gratification, wherein the behavior does not yet operate according to a principle of delay of reward or reinforcement. It is not the "behavior" or the "principle of behavior" which "has" the seeking for immediate gratification; it is the *parental figure* who houses the urgency toward immediate gratification. What has come to be the principle of immediate gratification is the description—masquerading as a scientific law—of collective parental figures. The same is true of all such hypotheses, principles, and theories of infant behavior which are externalized and reified descriptions of the (adult parental) describers themselves. Taken together, these hypotheses, principles, and theories of infant behavior represent accurate descriptions of collective parents, and represent centuries of wisdom misinterpreted as scientific study of the behavior of infants.

One such general principle of behavior, especially from the perspective of psychoanalytic theory, is that behavior moves from the pleasure principle to the reality principle. This is linked to immediate and delayed reward by virtue of immediate reward as an expression of the pleasure principle, and delayed reward as an expression of the reality principle. Freud was careful in understanding the infant's behavior as initially operating under the pleasure principle and only later coming under the mandate of the reality principle. Yet, from the perspective of humanistic theory, it is the *parent* who "has" the pleasure principle, who sees the infant as seeking pleasure and avoiding pain. What has been termed the pleasure principle of *infant* behavior is a grand description of the ways in which collective parents regard

their infants; it is not a scientific statement about infant behavior itself. There is no law that infant behavior is to be operating under the
pleasure principle. It is just the way collective parents are with their
babies. The same holds for the shift to the reality principle. That simply does not occur as a principle of behavior. What we witness is a
change in the *parent*. Now the parent sees the infant as able and expected to behave "realistically." That is, typically, the parents now begin expecting that the baby should be "mature," should no longer act
"like a baby," and is now "ready" to behave in older ways. For example, now the baby is able to be toilet trained. Behaving on the basis of
the reality principle means being able to delay urinating and defecating, and generally being the way the parents believe the baby should
be. What has been taken as a reality principle of behavior turns out to
be ways that the parents perceive the baby, maintain expectancies for
the way the baby should be, and construct infants into being—all on a
grand collective scale. The shift from behavior operating under the
pleasure principle to the reality principle is really a mother seeing her
nine-month-old baby as doing enough urinating and defecating; now
it is time to become toilet-trained.

Organizing the Primitive Field to Induce Behavior

Some parents are engaged in inducing left-handed behavior from
their infant, and they have all the resources of the primitive field to
use in their work. Once parents set about the creation of left-handed
behavior in their infant, they can organize the primitive field so that
all the conditions are present to induce precisely that behavior. Picture
a mother and father geared to construct a baby whom they would endow with properties of being different, weird, peculiar. Before baby
was even conceived, it was predictable that the baby would be constructed to fulfill that function. One behavioral mark of being peculiar
was being left-handed. Not only was everyone in father's and mother's
families right-handed, but there was a kind of family lore that being
left-handed was somehow sinister and suspicious. Something was
wrong with anyone who was that way. As a part of the family lore,
that attitude was not made public, yet it was nonetheless known and
understood. Both mother and father imagined the fetus as lying on its
right side, giving its left arm greater freedom of movement. When the
baby was born, mother would hold baby in such a manner that consistently the right arm was pressed against mother's body and it was
the left arm which was free to move about. When baby was placed by
mother on the bed or chair next to mother, baby was consistently
placed on mother's left side so that mother's right hand would have
greater contact with baby's left hand. The crib was located in the

room so that, when baby was placed at the "head" of the crib, it was the left arm which was toward the room and the right arm which was close to the wall and away from the room. Objects were placed closer to the left arm than the right arm. A mobile was located above the crib in such a way that, when baby was placed in its usual position, its left hand had greater access to the mobile than the right hand. Mother and father both carried baby in such a way that baby's right hand gripped the parent while the left hand was free to engage in interactions. In hundreds of ways, the parents systematically arranged conditions favoring left-handedness. As a result, left-handed behavior was produced. The parents had organized the requisite encompassing conditions so that left-handed behavior would occur. Its occurrence was an expression of a long history of parental organization of the conditions such that the desired outcome was the natural and expected behavioral consequence.

By virtue of their being in control of the primitive field, parents can organize the conditions so as to induce a very *precise* infant behavior, like left-handedness, or a *general class* of infant behaviors. Parents can organize and construct the primitive field to induce behaviors called immediate gratification. This class includes the behaviors of babies who can not and will not wait for anything. They are demanding that it occur right now. One way that this can be induced is simply to promise something and then break the promise. Although parents will typically find all manner of excuses to re-explain their own behavior, from our perspective, the parents are being marvelously adept and shrewd in organizing the primitive conditions in precisely those ways which are designed to induce behaviors of immediate gratification. Whether described as "violating the child's code by breaking the promise" (Blatz & Bott, 1930) or organizing the right primitive conditions, the outcome is the inducing of behaviors of immediate gratification, and it is the parents who alone have constructed the right conditions which induce the right behaviors.

The plastic primitive field can also be organized into conditions which *constitute* the behavior rather than being a context pulling for the occurrence of a given behavior. By acting upon the infant, the infant is acted upon, and this can be accomplished in such a way that the infant's being acted upon constitutes the behavior. Toss baby into the air and she is jumping-floating-flying; drop the baby five feet into a net and the baby is falling; put baby into a swimming pool and baby is floating or splashing or drowning. In these instances, the condition into which the primitive field is actively organized and the behavior which the baby carries out are the active and passive sides of the same behavioral coin. A baby is induced to behave in ways which are withdrawn and isolated when a parent organizes the primitive field into a condition of separating and rejecting. Thus, so-called premature weaning can constitute one way of organizing the primitive field so that the behavioral other side of the coin is infant withdrawal and isolation. In this sense, premature weaning is less of a *causal* event leading to infant withdrawal and isolation (cf. Fromm-Reichmann, 1959), and is more of a condition whose passive behavioral other side *is being* withdrawn and isolated. By organizing the primitive field in a very particular manner, only certain infant behaviors can occur as the other side of the behavioral coin.

When the infant behavior is the other side of the way in which the primitive field is organized, subtle changes in the primitive field can constitute gross changes in the induced behavior. The primitive field can wean the infant early in such a way that constitutes behaviors of being withdrawn and isolated. But it also can occur in such a way that the behavior consists of draining mother, eroding her of resources. Here are behaviors of crying for more, clinging and not leaving go, demands for instant attention. In both, the condition may be called premature weaning, yet a more careful description illuminates subtle differences whose behavioral other sides are strikingly different from one another, and both are the behavioral other side of the condition into which the primitive field is organized by the parents.

There are many ways in which parental organizing of the right conditions induces infant behavior. Parents have magnificent control over the whole array of conditions in the primitive field which bear a *direct influence* on the infant's behavior. If excessive heat or cold induces particular kinds of infant behavior, parents can control the temperature so as to induce those behaviors which the parents are geared to induce. Once having constructed an infant whose behavior is responsive to anything from gross temperature changes to subtle changes in external stimulation (Hunt, 1963), parents can then monitor these conditions to produce the desired infant behavior. In this sense, parents can be brilliant orchestrators of whole sets of primitive field conditions which lead directly to behavior. If the baby cries under conditions of extreme temperature, parents can induce crying by arranging for baby to be "too" warm or "too" cold. By constructing an infant with defined behavioral reactions to defined conditions, parents are in an excellent position to organize the primitive field so as directly to induce behaviors of crying, smiling, crawling, hitting, fussing, squeezing.

One powerful way in which parents organize the right conditions to induce behavior is by initiating interactions. If baby gurgles when you lift her in the air, then you initiate that interaction. Organizing the conditions means that the parental figure must be the initiator, and it is consistent that in the earliest weeks and months parental figures tend to be the initiators of parent-infant interactions while after the first year or so this tendency to initiate tapers off (Bronson, 1974). From the beginning, parents are typically hard at work initiating behaviors from the infant by organizing the primitive field in just that way which induces very particular behaviors.

Certain kinds of parent-initiated interactions tend to raise the likelihood of some classes of infant behavior and lower the likelihood of other classes of infant behavior. For example, if the parent engages in a high rate of interaction with baby, that condition, in and of itself, defines the occurrence of at least three classes of induced infant behavior: (a) There is a forced increase in the infant's *mutual responsive interactions* (e.g., smiling, crying, touching, talking, grasping, holding, imitating); (b) There is a forced increase in *interaction-avoidant* behavior (e.g., not smiling, not talking, not looking at mother, turning away, not allowing oneself to be touched); (c) There is a forced decrease in *self-directed, self-interactive, self-stimulatory* behavior (Beckwith, 1972). By the same token, these three classes of infant behavior are respectively heightened or reduced when the parent engages in *minimal* interaction with baby. Thus the behavioral implications are rather strong when the parent constructs the conditions such that particular classes of behaviors can occur, for that not only defines the kinds of behaviors which can occur, but also defines the kinds of behaviors which are seldom if ever brought into occurrence. Here is added power to the parents who organize the primitive field in the inducing of infant behavior.

That power lies in both inducing one set of behaviors and, thereby, closing off another set of behaviors. Similarly, some behaviors are induced by closing off other behavioral possibilities. That is, parents can induce a given behavior by establishing conditions which close off virtually all other behavioral possibilities. By arranging never to be free of baby—by closing off that behavioral possibility, parents close off all behavioral possibilities except those of baby being with parents—e.g., interfering and clinging to parents, having to be with them, being the interloper, never letting go of them. Parents organize these conditions by never finding someone to stay with baby, having to remain in the same room with baby, being impelled to keep baby in their room at night, not being able to go anywhere because they must stay with baby. Such a constructed primitive field closes off all possible ways in which baby can be alone or with someone other than the parents. By arranging the conditions such that the only possible behavioral avenue left is the baby always being with the parents, that is precisely how the baby will be. In the same way, parents can insure that baby will be fussy, squirmy, restless and twisting by organizing the primitive field so as to prevent any but those kinds of behaviors. That is, parents will establish the right conditions so that baby shall not be peaceful, satisfied, quiescent, tranquil. As soon as baby heads in that direction, the parents must swoop baby up and play with her, change her, pull her one way or the other, "do things" to her. When baby starts to become tranquil, both parents find reason to be annoyed at her, to pick at her, yell at her, nudge her about, become tense and tightened up at her. By blocking other behavioral exits, parents create conditions which induce a particular infant behavior.

In all of these enterprises, what makes parental figures so very powerful is their *constituting* the actual primitive field which induces infant behavior. The parent can *be* the right condition which induces the specific behavior the parent is geared to bring about. If crying can be induced by bouncing the baby in a particular way at a particular time, by squeezing baby, holding down his arms, yelling and screaming at baby, slapping him—then the parent can be that effective environmental condition. By virtue of *being* the encompassing primitive field, the parent can organize herself or himself to be the condition which effectively induces the occurrence of the predetermined infant behavior. In all of this, parents are extraordinary experimenters who do much more than control the behavioral conditions—parents *are* the behavioral conditions.

As powerful as parental figures are, it is understandable that they are loathe to acknowledge their role in inducing unfortunate infant behavior, and that they are ingenious in inventing other determinants of such behavior. Nevertheless, parents induce distressing infant behavior. For example, some parental figures may work to produce infants who are unobtrusive, undemanding, quiet, not attentive to the external world, not walking, and not interacting with the environment. When it is important to produce such behaviors, parental figures can become expertly effective behavior producers by organizing the primitive field in just the right ways. One way this can be accomplished is by providing the infant with little attention. Keep interaction to a minimum. If these are infants in a room in a hospital or custodial ward for babies, keep them in their cribs rather than with other babies. Interact with the babies only in feeding and changing and other necessary care. Enclose each crib in a homogenous white opaque cloth so that infants cannot see outside and their world is restricted to the bland white cloth. Reduce stimulation to a minimum. By installing such conditions, the infants will be unobtrusive, undemanding, quiet, not attentive to the external world, not typically developed and not interactive, and all of this will be reflected in lowered scores on scales of infant development (Dennis, 1960; Dennis & Najarian, 1957). It is no accident that some infants are not "stimulated." It is an expression of specific conditions arranged by parental caretakers with defined potentials and relationships employing primitive conditions in effective ways.

We arrive at the same conclusion regardless of the nature of the behavior which is induced and regardless of the nature of the condition which is directly linked to it, viz. the parental figures are the organizing determiners. Sometimes the parental figures themselves constitute the condition which induces infant behavior. At other times, the parental figures are the ones who organize the rest of the primitive field into the behavior-inducing conditions. The parents can induce behavior by *being* a condition or by *infusing* themselves into some condition. If the behavior to be induced is that of being fearful, the parent can either scream at the top of her voice, or she can strike a steel bar with a hammer in just that way which makes the baby fearful. The parent can be the object whom baby fears, or the parent can be expressed in any element of the primitive field which serves as the agent or expressor or externalization of the parent. Thus the parent can be expressed as the soft furry object which is present when the parent strikes the steel bar with the hammer. Watson and Rayner (1920) have described exactly how this can be accomplished. The parent can stand behind the baby and strike a steel bar with a hammer whenever the baby moves toward a small furry object. By repeating this over and over, the baby will behave in a fearful manner in relation to the small furry object. It is as if the parent is expressed through each condition: the bar and hammer, and the small furry object which then serves as the parental agent. Within the language of learning theory, the above state of affairs has been termed "conditioning." The infant's reaction to the disruptive noise of the steel bar striking the hammer can be linked (conditioned) to the soft furry object so that the infant responds to the soft furry object with behavior of fear. From our perspective, the capability of the steel bar, hammer, and soft furry object to bring about fear behavior in the baby is a function of the degree to which these conditions are "parenticized." That is, if the conditions express the parent, are infused with the parent, are made to be the agents of the parent, "conditioning" will work. If, however, the parent is not infused into the soft furry object, then "conditioning" will be less effective. Always it is the parent whose determining presence lies behind the conditions which induce behavior. Little wonder that human beings have reified, deified, and anthropomorphized a fascinating array of Gods, goblins, forces, and unknowable influences which guide our lives.

PRIMITIVE FIELD AS THE DEVELOPER OF BEHAVIORAL NUBBINS

The primitive field originates infant behavior by organizing and controlling those conditions which induce the infant's behavior. That is one way in which the primitive field produces an infant who behaves in specific ways. We now turn to a second way in which the primitive field constructs infant behavior. In this second way, the primitive field seizes upon something that the infant actually does, and proceeds to develop that something into a full-blown behavior. This second way requires that the infant do something. It must express the rudiment of some behavior, a behavioral beginning, the tip or nub of a behavior which the primitive field can then develop. That behavioral nubbin can be initiated and put forward by the infant itself (cf. Moss, 1967; Moss & Robson, 1968), or it can be induced or pulled from the infant by external environmental factors. What gets it started is not important. What is important is the infant's production of a behavioral nubbin. In this second way, *the primitive field brings about infant behavior by (a) identifying the predetermined behavior to be brought about and (b) organizing the conditions and components of the primitive field to develop the infant-produced behavioral nubbin into the predetermined full-blown behavior.*

In the last three or four decades there has arisen a sophisticated psychology of learning whose principles help us understand how parents are able to take a behavioral nubbin, a rudimentary tip of infant behavior, and develop it into a full-blown actual behavior. Each of the various learning theories offers a favorite method or principle by which this can be accomplished. For example, Bandura (1961) cites the use of counterconditioning, advocated by Wolpe, the use of extinction and discrimination, urged by Dollard and Miller, and the use of reward, as advanced by Skinner. Parents use them all. Parents are virtuosos in orchestrating the spectrum of learning principles such as behavioral shaping, refining, rewarding, punishing, conditioning, counter-conditioning, processing, extinction, discrimination, and dozens of ways which have yet to be articulated.

Yet the parent is like the experimenter who is unaware of his theory, hypothesis, or what he is trying to demonstrate. He is like the architect-builder who is hypnotized into action without knowing what he is constructing or even that he is constructing it. The parent will "see" a fully developed behavior, not a behavior tip. Mother will see before her a baby who is demanding immediate gratification, who is demanding that things be done right now; she will not see a mere behavioral nubbin, a whimper or a little cry. Without knowing it, the parent will invoke all sorts of sophisticated principles of developing a mere behavioral nubbin into a fully grown mature behavior, and yet, in her world, the fully developed behavior is already before her and she will have no idea of the mechanisms used to develop the nubbin into its fully flourishing behavioral form.

By Integrative or Disintegrative Mode of Reception

The parent develops the nubbin by receiving it integratively or disintegratively. Either way, the behavioral bit is developed further along
the lines toward a mature behavior. When the behavioral bit is received integratively, is surrounded with acceptance and peacefulness,
there is behavioral development. If the behavioral bit threatens the
parent, is received with fear and hate, there is also development of
behavior. A movement can be developed into one kind of twisting and
turning by its being received integratively, and another kind of twisting and turning when it is received disintegratively. The latter becomes a flourishing hyperactivity, unhappy restlessness, frenetic
twisting, cantankerous turning, while the former becomes fluid
movement, active energy, aliveness. While there are gross differences
between the behaviors developed by integrative or disintegrative
modes of receiving the behavior, the developmental power lies in the
reception, the nature of the relationship between the parent and the
infant behavioral bit.

Once the infant puts forth a rudimentary nubbin, parental figures
can develop that behavior by receiving it in an integrative way. The
integrative relationship is expressed in warmth, love, closeness, acceptance, and similar parameters of what is otherwise known as positive reinforcement. Thus, for example, rudimentary beginnings of
dependent behavior in young children are developed into full-blown
dependency behaviors when parents receive these nubbins with love,
warmth, positive regard, and affectionate demonstrativeness (Bandura
& Walters, 1962). Such ways of responding act as if they were pulling
from the child a flourishing dependent package of behaviors. Research has amply demonstrated the developmental powers of an integrative relationship in the studies of the effects of parental warmth,
loving, caring on the behavior of infants. An integrative relationship
between parent and the constructed function of the baby contains two
key ingredients which develop the behavioral bit. When baby just begins to behave in a dependent manner—even postures himself toward
carrying out a dependent behavior—mother's integrative reception
will (a) define, refine, clarify, identify the behavior-to-be-developed,
and (b) surround the to-be-developed behavior with integrative love,
closeness, and oneness. Thus the parent can develop a behavioral
nubbin into a more mature behavior by relating integratively, and by
identifying-clarifying the behavior. Positive reinforcement or reward
may be said to possess the same developmental power when it contains these two ingredients.

When a parent receives the infant's behavioral nubbin in a *disintegrative* way, the same two ingredients are doing their job. First, she is

identifying and defining and clarifying the behavior which she is geared to develop. It is as if she is saying the behavioral bit is going to be developed into this kind of mature behavior. Second, she is coupling the behavior with disintegrative feelings. Let us describe how two mothers work with a single behavioral bit to develop it in two different directions by means of a disintegrative mode of receiving the behavioral bit. A baby urinates on a good chair. One mother is the kind of person who constructs baby into being her externalized defiance, and, therefore, the constructed function of baby is that of defiance. Bearing a disintegrative relationship toward that defiance, she responds to baby's urinating in a way which defines and clarifies it as defiant behavior. Urinating is defying, and will develop into full-blown defiance linked with disintegrative feelings of distress, hatred, fear, and the like. A second mother is oriented toward constructing the baby into the feared and hated externalization of her own distance and separation from body functions. When she responds to baby's urinating on the good chair, she does so in ways which define and clarify that behavioral nubbin along the lines of distancing and separating from body functions, and, furthermore, linking that behavior to disintegrative feelings of distress, anxiety and fear. Two different mothers, responding to quite similar behavioral nubbins, will develop the nubbin in quite different directions, yet both will be linked to disintegrative feelings, and the effective factor in the development of the behavioral bit is the precise way in which the mother responds in identifying and clarifying the nature of the behavior-to-be-developed.

To relate disintegratively is to relate with fear and hate, depression and anger, meaninglessness and menace, to the behavioral bit put forth by the infant. In this mode of relating-receiving the behavioral bit, the major factor is the defining and clarifying of the to-be-developed behavior, for that tends to develop the behavioral nubbin into a fully blown behavior. Just as relating to the behavioral nubbin *integratively* will act to develop the behavioral bit, so too does relating *disintegratively* develop the behavioral bit. Both operate through the same factor, viz. the identifying and defining of the to-be-developed behavior. Reviews of research on punishment have consistently identified its ineffectiveness as a means of *eliminating* disapproved behavior (e.g. Bandura, 1961). I am persuaded that punishment as a disintegrative relationship is not only ineffective in *eliminating* the behavior, but, instead, operates to *develop* the behavioral nubbin into a mature behavior. The punitive relationship acts to stamp in the to-be-developed behavior by utilizing the effective ingredient of identifying-defining the behavioral nubbin as mature behavior.

To the extent that a disintegrative relationship with an infant behavioral bit contains the right ingredient (i.e., refining, defining, and identifying the to-be-developed behavior), the behavior should endure rather than reduce and fade away. Perhaps the closest pertinent area of research is that on punishment, where reviews of research find punished behavior to dig in, to have an enduring quality, to persist with a stubbornness termed "rigid repetitiveness" (Wilson, 1963). Whereas research observes that punished behavior persists, the nature of the effective ingredient eludes our grasp. Humanistic theory holds that the effective factor lies in the extent to which the punishment also refines, defines, and identifies the behavior to be developed. Our description-explanation may be contrasted with one in which the punished behavior somehow emerges as the only possible compromise in a conflict situation in which the behavior is met with frustration from parents who impose inhibitory controls on the behavior (Wilson, 1963). Both explanations recognize that punishment (i.e., a disintegrative relationship) gives the developed behavior persistence, even though we differ on the nature of the effective ingredient in this enterprise.

By Aligning Behavior and Change in the Primitive Field

The leading edge of the behavioral bit is drawn forth, extended, developed, by welding it to the encompassing primitive field. The welding means that changes in the encompassing primitive field occur in regular contiguity and continuity with the leading edge of the infant's behavior. Indeed, the artistry here is the smooth contiguous continuity of behavior and change in the primitive field. If the behavior and the change in the primitive field are precision-honed to one another, their temporal connection is one of immediate contiguity. Changes in the environment must be immediate to the occurrence of the infant's behavioral bit (Gewirtz, 1969; Watson, 1967), for immediacy means connection, bonding, a welding of baby's movement and continuous change in the primitive field. What we are describing has been construed as *immediate* reinforcement in other approaches; in humanistic theory, we are describing the alignment of primitive field with the baby's behavior—with the result that the behavioral nubbin becomes further developed into a mature behavior.

In order to carry this out effectively, the parent once again must have a program of the behavior which is to be developed. Given this preconception of the nature of the behavior-to-be-developed, the parent aligns the primitive field to the behavioral bit in precisely that manner which develops the right behavior. If, for example, the behavioral nubbin is to be developed into full-blown aggressive behavior, the primitive field must be aligned to the behavioral nubbin in just the right way. Not only must the behavior be bonded with the primitive field so that the change in the field occurs regularly and with immediate contiguity, but the nature of the change must be fitted to the development of aggressive behavior. Thus the change must be one of being knocked over, or retaliatory aggression, or compliance to the aggressive behavioral bit. The alignment must include parameters of regularity, immediacy, and content.

By Receiving the Nubbin as a Fully Developed Behavior

The parent can respond to the behavioral bit as if it were the fully developed behavior, as indeed it is to the parent. This defines the nature of the fully matured behavior and also tends to hasten its development. In so doing, the parent seizes on a tip of infant behavior and reorganizes the encompassing primitive field as if the tip were a very particular full-bodied behavior. A baby cries. To the parent, the cry is a demand, a punishment for not having "it" right now—removal of the cover, changing the diaper, holding, feeding. It is as if the infant is saying, "I want it immediately. I will not wait an instant. If you give it to me now I will be quiet and satisfied, but if you don't I will scream and yell." Mother is galvanized into responsive action by the mere cry. Mother's actions may include looks of frenzied frustration at being bullied by baby, frantic trying out of whatever mother guesses the demanding baby wants, immediate dropping of whatever she is doing. By seeing and treating the merest of crying as fully grown behavior of demanding immediate gratification, the parent is busily developing the behavioral nubbin into that to-be-developed mature behavior. Behaviors of immediate gratification, of demanding, are developed by virtue of being there in full dress—as perceived by the parent responding to the mere behavioral tip.

From the very beginning, the infant may behave in ways which the mother perceives and responds to as requests for help or as expressions of distress or frustration. Over the course of months, the earlier bits of behavior become moulded and shaped into defined mature behaviors of requesting help and expressing distress or frustration. Although the mother has seen and responded to these behaviors as consistently requesting help and expressing distress or frustration, an outside observer would witness a progressive shaping and moulding of these mature behaviors. From the perspective of an outside observer, there appears to be a progressive increase in these behaviors (e.g., Bronson, 1974), but from the perspective of the mother, the baby has been consistent in requesting her help and in communicating distress or frustration from the very beginning.

In the same way, a parent can receive early common iterative speech as stuttering—fully developed, dangerously present stuttering. It is quite ordinary for very young children to repeat sounds in what has been described as a more or less normal iterative speech period (e.g., Froeschels, 1942). Here is a beautiful opportunity for the right parents to regard that as the developed behavior, and to construct that behavioral nubbin into a full-blown stuttering. Parents can be enormously successful in regarding this normal iterative speech as stuttering, defining and labeling as such, and then responding to such speech behavior in those hundreds of precise ways which serve to bring about the stuttering speech (Johnson, 1959). The young child puts forth the bits of iterative speech behavior. They serve as the behavioral nubbins which the parents, as the encompassing primitive field, develop into stuttering by means of all of the methods which learning theory organizes as principles of learning (Mahrer & Young, 1962). To the responding parents, the young child's speech behavior *is* stuttering and the behavioral nubbin becomes what the parents treat it as being.

By receiving a behavioral bit as the fully developed behavior, a parent can seize upon the tiniest actions of the newborn and define them as refusal to nurse, or as tense and anxious behavior, or as negativistic behavior. Having grasped the nubbin in this way, the parent diligently responds to that behavioral bit so that it emerges as the fully developed behavior. When parents are effective at working the behavioral nubbin into a developed behavior, it is understandable that neonates can be made to evidence such behaviors as refusing to nurse, being tense and anxious, and being negativistic (Ribble, 1944). Such behaviors, evidenced by the newborn baby, are merely testimony of genuinely effective work by the parents. In the same way, by utilizing the same mechanism, parents can develop infant behaviors of fearfulness, aggression, jealousy, loneliness, hostility, attention-seeking, and insecurity (cf. Bandura & Walters, 1959; Pepitone & Wilpizetski, 1960; Sears, Maccoby, & Levin, 1957).

Sometimes the behavioral nubbin is immediately grasped by the parent as the expression of a particular *class or category* rather than a defined mature behavior. Instead of receiving iterative speech behavior as mature stuttering, the parent would grasp the iterative speech as evidence of "slow development" or "faulty development" or a "problem." Under these circumstances, the behavioral bit develops into some other fully flourished behavior. For example, the early iterative behavioral bit develops into mature behavioral evidence of slow development (e.g., being unable to walk) or faulty development (e.g., athetoid movements) or problem behavior (e.g., heightened aggressivity). Thomas, Rutter, and Birch (1963) gathered data on infants, some of whom were later referred to treatment for "pathology." Within the first year of life, these infants, who would later be referred to treatment, were *already* perceived by their parents as evidencing irregular behavior, non-adaptive behavior, highly reactive behavior, and negative mood behavior. It is singular that these very early behavioral bits were already grasped as evidence of pathology and were developed into full-blown behavioral evidences of pathology even though the only relationship between the early nubbins and the later behavior was their being classified as problems or pathology. It is as if the parent saw the newborn's behavioral bits as crazy, and developed those behavioral bits into specific full-blown crazy behavior. The tragedy is that the parents probably saw real behavioral bits in their infants, and genuinely received them as the irregular, non-adaptive, negative behavior into which they later developed.

The history of the infant's putting forth of behavioral bits often reaches back into the fetal career. The fetus does something. It behaves in ways which the parent receives as a given behavior, and then the developed behavior seems to occur almost from conception. For example, even in the fetal state, the infant was received as refusing, opposing, rebelling. That squirming of the fetus is her being rebellious, oppositional, fighting. Having defined the behavioral nubbin in that way, the mother responded to the behavior as fully blown resistance, and the mother's own tightening up against the twisting and squirming further worked upon the fetal behavioral bit to develop it into a very particular set of behaviors. As a result, it does seem that right from conception or birth the daughter was refusing things, setting herself in opposition, being resistive and rebellious (Binswanger, 1958a, p. 270).

In describing the way in which parents receive nubbins as fully developed behavior, there is no watchful parent knowing what is "really" occurring. We have placed ourselves in a privileged position to observe what is happening. Within mother's world, however, that *is* demanding behavior, not mere nubbins. When baby cries, mother has already selected out a differentiated demandingness. Mother is cringing at a demanding infant. To mother, her baby *is* demanding and *is* behaving in a demanding way, whereas to us, there is a process with more or less separate stages. Consider a baby whose behavioral nubbin is developed into flagrant smiling, a mature, regular, conspicuous smiling behavior. From outside, as it were, we can identify a parent who seizes out a particular infant behavioral bit. Mother must first perceive and find something which she regards as baby's smiling. Then, by regarding it as smiling, mother responsively interacts with what she regards as smiling until, from our view, that infant behavioral bit is developed into a flourishing smiling behavior (Beckwith,

1972). Yet, within mother's world, there is no knowledge of this, no segmented stage following stage. There is only a smiling infant. Mother is honest, genuine, and veridical in seeing the smiling.

PRIMITIVE FIELD AS THE INTERPRETOR OF ATTRIBUTED BEHAVIOR

We have described the primitive field as inducing behavior from the infant by (a) organizing the conditions of the primitive field so that the behavior will come about, and (b) selecting a behavioral bit or nubbin put forth by the infant, and by developing that behavioral bit into a flourishing mature behavior. We now turn to a third way in which parents construct infant behavior. In this third way, there is no behavioral nubbin intruding itself onto the parent. Indeed the external world, in the form of the infant, does not have to do much at all. It is the parent who does all of the work.

In this third way, parents construct infant behavior simply by the manner in which they *interpret* behavior which they *attribute* to the infant. They name the behavior, and add the meaning and significance which define the behavior as occurring. Thus the behavior occurs by virtue of the parents' interpreting it as occurring. *Accordingly, the primitive field brings about infant behavior by interpreting and perceiving behavior attributed to the infant.*

The Ease and Power of Constructing Behavior by Interpretation

There is no issue of whether or not the behavior "really" is occurring. There is no concern as to whether some external observor would confirm the presence of the behavior. Since the primitive field is the only world in which the physical infant exists, the behavior is present by interpretation of the parents. Once the parents attribute that behavior to the infant, the behavior *is* present, for the predominant criterion of its presence is the interpretation of the parents. Indeed, this method is powerful in part because the way in which the parent interprets the infant's behavior is both the determinant of the behavior and the final criterion of its presence. Thus there is no presumption that the infant's "actual" behavior will change or develop or become the way the parent believes the behavior to be. In the world of the primitive field, the infant is behaving sweetly when the parent interprets the infant as behaving sweetly. The behavior is attributed to the baby by means of interpretation.

This mode of constructing infant behavior is relatively easy. The parents need not organize the conditions of the primitive field in any way. Nor do the parents have to locate a behavioral bit put forth by the infant, and do something to it. Not only is this mode easy for the parents, it is also easy for the infant since the infant does not have to do much at all. There need be no special behavior carried out by the infant, no doing something to the external world. In this mode, behavior is not acquired by its effect upon the external world, nor by the way the external world responds or reacts to that behavior. There need be no process of mutual interactive shaping between parent and infant. Indeed, the infant simply exists in the most ordinary way, and the parent does no more than *see* a given behavior as occurring. Careful external observers are frequently singularly impressed by the discrepancy between what *they* observe as quite ordinary infant behavings and what the parents interpret as behaviors of an exceedingly different order (Laing & Esterson, 1970).

When the parent seizes upon a behavioral nubbin, such as iterative speech, there must follow a process of developing that behavior in the direction of a flourished behavior, e.g., stuttering. In the present mode, in contrast, there is no process of development, no methods are used to bring the behavioral nubbin along, to move it through a process of development until it becomes the full-blown behavior. In rather sharp contrast, all that is necessary is that the parent see or interpret the behavior as being present. The genesis of behavior by interpreting attributed behavior saves a lot of menial work by the creative act of seeing the behavior right there in full bloom.

All the baby has to do is behave in the most ordinary ways. Nothing more. Indeed, baby's role is so easy that often all baby is required to do is *not* behave in some way. Then, because baby is not being a certain way, its behavior is given a defined interpretation. Any infant can be interpreted as behaving in a cold and unresponsive manner. To mother, that interpretation is built around the most ordinary behaviors of the most ordinary infant. When baby simply lies there, does nothing, mother sees the baby as being cold and unresponsive. When baby *stops* "smiling," *that* is interpreted as being cold and unresponsive. When baby whines and cries, that is interpreted as being cold and unresponsive to mother and to what mother wishes. Within a mother's world, the evidence of her baby's coldness and unresponsiveness may consist of the most ordinary behaviors, while within the father's world, on the other hand, the evidence lies in what baby does *not* do. When father is with baby, she does not smile and gurgle. She does not become peacefully quiet and tranquil the instant father picks her up. She does not seek and hold eye contact with father when he looks into her eyes. All of these are behaviors the baby does *not* carry out, and thereby her way of being is, in her father's world, exuding coldness and unresponsiveness. Both mother and father know their baby as behaving in a cold and unresponsive way. Mother interprets this in baby's ordinary behaviors, and father interprets this in baby's failure to behave in specific ways. Thus it is extremely easy for both baby and parents to bring about behavior through this mode of construction.

Yet the power of this mode is enormous. Simply by interpreting attributed behavior as occurring, the parent can construct an extremely wide swath of behaviors. Given the most ordinary movements and actions by the infant, the limits of what the parent can construct depend on the limits of what the parent can perceive, can attribute and interpret. Even the absence of defined behavior can be interpreted as evidence of an astounding spectrum of attributed behavior.

Interpreting Attributed Behavior

From our perspective as we view the baby, we may describe him as lying there, awake, rather quiet and comfortable. But mother may be perceiving the baby as carrying out all sorts of behavior. Here is a baby being cold and frigid, or being self-contained and intact. She may see him as being unresponsive and dull, or peaceful and tranquil, or as being drawn into evil plotting, or as being contemplative and thinking the situation over. These are ways of interpreting what is going on, attributions of a behavioral nature. In none of these must the baby "do" anything, from our perspective. It is the mother who brings the behavior to life by the manner of her interpreting what is there—or not there.

Where we may describe the infant as urinating or defecating, the parent is able to interpret far more as occurring. There is an interpretation of the ordinary into the extraordinary, an interpreting of what is occurring so as to create a most sophisticated behavioral event. Before the parent's eyes, that infant may be being earthy and open. Or the infant may be doing sensuous, sexual things. "Right from the time you were born you were the sexual one; you liked the nasty things; you were full of sexual nature, you know." In actuality, this meant that the person urinated and defecated. Or the baby may be having a mind of its own. When it wants to pee, it pees; that's the kind of do-what-it-wants-to-do child he is. Or it might be a savage and uncivilized behavior. It was being like an animal. "For the first three years or so, he behaved like a kind of uncivilized animal. He had to be trained and civilized. But watch out because there always is a trace of that savageness and uncivilized nature just like when he was a child." What the parent interprets as behaviorally occurring is limited only by the extent of the parent's creativity and originality.

Typically, the external observor will see quite ordinary behavior, while the parent will interpret that as evidencing quite special behavior. While the external observer sees the infant simply lying there, doing nothing much at all, both father and mother may see that infant as evidencing its special powers of "knowing" what is really happening in the parents (Laing & Esterson, 1970). These parents are seeing an infant who is looking at them in a very special way. That look in his eyes is a knowing look, a look which sees right through them. Here is an infant who is being omniscient, who is giving forth with special powers of knowing the evil which lurks in the hearts of the parents. Here is a full-blown way of behaving which requires little or nothing from the baby; the parents merely read it into existence.

Mother saw her son as being close and understanding from the first. He saw deeply into her and knew what she was thinking and feeling. He sensed her moods and accepted whatever she was. He loved her and had a special sense of knowing exactly when she was tense or worried, peaceful and tranquil. Her baby understood what she whispered to him. It was uncanny but so pleasing that he understood everything about her. Here is a very special set of behaviors attributed like a cloak around baby's touching her face or being quiet when she felt quiet or looking at her face or squeezing her breast. These most ordinary behaviors were interpreted in the most highly sophisticated ways by mother, ways which constituted a special set of behaviors attributed to and interpreted as occurring in the baby son.

For another mother, similar ordinary ways of being were interpreted as behavioral evidence of baby's positive regard for her. Her baby might simply have been lying on her breast, sucking, feeding. Yet mother interpreted baby as valuing her, appreciating her, pleased and happy with her. "You were always pleased and happy with me. From the day you were born, there was a special bond between us. You always seemed to appreciate me, to trust and value what I had to give you." The reference for this consisted of the baby feeding, yet within the primitive world of the baby, very special behaviors were occurring precisely as mother is describing them. Here are behaviors of enjoying, being appreciative, being gratified, being positively regarding.

Father attributed sexual behavior to the infant from conception on, and interpreted the young infant as being a sexual thing throughout the extent of the pregnancy and most certainly after birth. Sexuality oozed from his description of the infant, and settled all around the infant's behavior, providing it with a distinctive sexual nature. The male fetus was inside the woman, warm, and intimate with her, making her feel. The fetus kept her aroused and centered upon it. During pregnancy the fetus was between them, disturbing him and owning her; it was his rival, and was far more intimate with her than he was. Like his penis, it grew and grew, became more and more malelike. It got fuller of life until it forced her to spread her legs and then it came through the intimate opening. It was the little man who now touched her all over, sucked on her breasts and was sensuous with her. Through the interpreting eyes of the father, the infant had accumulated a distinguished career of sexual behavior long before the baby could even say the word "sex."

As simple as it is to attribute sexuality to the infant, it is easier, perhaps, to attribute badness. Yet the interpreter remains the parental figure, in whom there is both childhood sexuality and original sin. It can be chilling to see the range and power of what parents interpret as behaviors of an infant's badness, its illness, its bad nature, its strangeness or being difficult or crazy or having a problem, or even its evilness and sinfulness. From our perspective, the baby is merely looking, or smacking its lips, or turning, or moving its arms or making a fist or making the most ordinary sounds. Yet all or all of these are interpreted by the parents as awful, crazy behaviors (Laing & Esterson, 1970). Here is the genesis of original sin, lying within the parents themselves, capable of interpreting sinful behaviors as occurring in the infant.

All such interpreted behaviors are made even more complex by embedding them in a disintegrative relationship. Without doing anything, at least from the perspective of the external observor, the parents can interpret a given behavior as occurring, then proceed to feel hate and fear toward the baby for being that way. Many infants are interpreted as behaving in ways which may be described as having special knowledge, as divining what the parents are really thinking, as seeing further and deeper into the parents, of knowing the awful thoughts and the terrible secrets which lie hidden within the parents. Because the infant is this way, the parents draw back from the infant, hate and fear her for being that way, feel fearful and anxious or threatened and menaced by the infant behaving in that way. Here are feared and menacing signs and symptoms of an awful pathological process—even though it is the parents themselves who have preciously nurtured this perceived way of being (Laing & Esterson, 1970, p. 38). It is little wonder that children later evidence what is termed ideas of influence, for, from the very beginning of their lives, they were feared and hated for actually having and manifesting ideas of influence, special evil powers. First they were interpreted as behaving that way. Then they were feared and hated for behaving that way.

The integrative or disintegrative relationship is always present, and always surrounds the constructed behavior with integrative or disintegrative feelings. When mother interprets baby's glance as a knowing of her inner thoughts, mother couples that interpreted behavior with good integrative feelings or bad disintegrative feelings. She can feel peaceful and loving in connection with the infant's knowing her so well, or she can feel anxiety and fear in connection with that interpreted behavior. The former behavior is a deep understanding, and it is filled with good feelings of peacefulness and tranquility, whereas the latter behavior is a discerning of awful things, and it is filled with danger and disjunctiveness. When the parents are hateful and fearful toward the behavior, they are able first to construct the behavior and then to couple it with the bad feelings of disintegration. Thus the presence of an integrative or disintegrative relationship adds a significant dimension to an interpreted behavior, and makes the behavior quite different, not only in the good or bad feelings encompassing the behavior, but also in the nature of the behavior itself.

The primitive field interprets attributed behavior simply by perceiving it as there. For example, parents are actively attributing and interpreting behavior when they name or describe their infant in ways which are saturated with behavioral attributions and interpretations. These are sets of behavioral expectancies, ways in which parents are already interpreting the behaviors of their baby, pre-packaged sets of behavioral interpretations, role functions encompassing the infant. Parents are postured toward providing their infants with capsule personality descriptions which pre-interpret the behaviors the infant has and attribute the behavioral ways the infant is to be. Thus, practically from conception, often from birth, and typically within a few months, the baby is said to be relaxed and easy-going, or liking people around, or shy and careful, or possessing a mind of its own, or as someone who likes to be held. These capsule personality descriptions are interpretations of attributed behaviors, spectacles through which the parent sees and interprets attributed infant behavior. Sometimes these behavioral prescriptions are included in the infant's name or, even more commonly, in nicknames and personalized family names. Parents are practically interpreting their infant's behavior when they name the baby Slugger, Lefty, Tiny, Samson, Abraham, Hercules, or Angel. By naming the baby, the parent is behavior-interpreting in the very act of naming. It is as if the parents are thereby attributing certain defined behavioral packages to the baby and then interpreting these behaviors as occurring.

PRIMITIVE FIELD AS THE BEHAVING PHYSICAL INFANT

In each of the three mechanisms we have described, the primitive field has been all around the physical infant, determining behavior because the primitive field constituted the world in which the physical infant existed. By its sheer all-aroundness, the primitive field can do a great deal of what must be done to make the physical infant behave in whatever ways the primitive field wants the physical infant to behave. The fourth mechanism differs from the other three by *being* the infant—and not merely encompassing it. As indicated in Figure 13.1, the primitive field *is* the infant. Our conceptual switch enables the primitive field to be the whole external world of the infant *and also* the whole infant itself.

Infant-as-Primitive-Personality

As described in Chapter 8, behavior serves potentials and their relationships. As indicated in Figure 13.1, these determining potentials and relationships are within the primitive field *which is also the infant itself*. Everything exists within the all-powerful primitive field—all the potentials, all the relationships among potentials, and also the infant itself. If we look for the potentials and the relationships, they exist within the same primitive field which is also the infant. Therefore, the infant-as-primitive-personality behaves on the basis of potentials and relationships occurring within the primitive personality. Viewed from this perspective, it is irrelevant that the potentials and relationships are in the parents too, because the potentials and relationships of the parents are also *of* the infant-as-primitive-personaliy. By conceiving of the infant-as-primitive-personality, the (parental) potentials and relationships, and the (physical infant's) behavior are all in and from the infant. *The primitive field brings about behavior by constituting the potentials and relationships of the infant-as-primitive-personality.*

Consider the primitive field as a single, whole "person." This person is described as "having" potentials and relationships among potentials. Furthermore, these potentials and relationships are directly linked to the person's behavior. In the same way, potentials and relationships of the primitive field *are* the infant's. The behavior carried out by the physical infant also is *of* the infant. In this picture, there is no need for intermediating conditions or mechanisms or factors. The frustration and explosive anger, which is the potential, is expressed in the whining, yelling, screaming of the baby. The linkage is direct between the potential and the behavior—even when the potential may be said to be housed in the physical mother and the behavior is carried out by the physical infant. There is no need to consider external conditions which are organized in a particular way by the mother who is frustrated and explosively angry. There is no need to study the integrative or disintegrative way in which the mother receives tiny little behavioral bits from the infant, and works hard at developing those into behaviors of whining, yelling, and screaming. There is no need to study mother as the interpreter of attributed whining, yelling, and screaming. Instead, it is allowable that such behavior (from the physical infant) directly serves to provide for the experiencing of the potential (in the physical mother) because both behavior and potential are components of the total infant-as-primitive-personality.

As long as parent and physical infant are encased in a primitive field, as long as they are *not* separated, intact entities somehow affecting one another, then no mechanisms need be invented to show how one separated entity (parent) affects the behavior of the other (physical infant). Once the potential is there in the parent, the physical infant can serve as the vehicle of expression, directly, and without the kinds of intervening, intermediating mechanisms which have been described earlier. A mother may have potentials and relationships such that there is an integrative gentleness. When her infant is with a little puppy, the baby may then behave gently. If mother has a potential for being mean and hurting, and, furthermore, must disintegratively fight against this, her infant may squeeze the puppy's neck or pull the puppy's ears in a way which hurts the puppy. The potentials and relationships are in the same primitive field which contains the behavior, and both are to be considered the infant-as-primitive-personality. Other approaches must seek some way that mother, as a separate object, affects the infant as a separate object. One way in which other approaches propose this is done is by reinforcement. If mother proclaims that it is good to be gentle with puppies, the proclamation of that "value" serves as a reinforcement, and it is held that the proclamation of any value constitutes a reinforcement (e.g., Rogers & Skinner, 1956). However, in our approach the sheer existence of the potential for being or saying that it is good to be gentle with puppies is sufficient to be directly linked with the physical infant's behavior. Within the perspective of the infant-as-primitive-personality, it is the *infant* (*and* the physical mother) who proclaim the importance of being gentle with puppies, and it is the infant who also carries out the appropriate *behavior*.

Reinforcement is an unnecessary concept when parent and infant are one. In describing the almost magical relationship between the behavior of infants and the personality processes of parents, Arieti (1961) leaned about as precariously as he could in this direction without falling into the conceptualization I am proposing. He retained the thinnest perimeter around the infant as a separate object, and virtually connected the infant directly to the personality processes of the parental figures. "At this early ontogenetic level, volition is . . . extreme submission. It is more than submission: It is enormous receptivity to the interpersonal world . . . the child is extremely receptive to the will of others . . ." (1961, p. 77). It is the slightest step to conceptualizing the behavior of the infant as *fully and directly* connected to the "will" of others. But this step requires the final dissolution of a separate infant interacting with a separate external world, and an acceptance of an infant *as* the encompassing primitive field. Once we accept the infant as the primitive personality, the behavior of the infant is fully and directly linked to the "will," personality processes, potentials, and relationships of significant others.

There is something quite special about all this. A parent must be experiencing, must have something occur within her (like the experiencing of fussiness), and the infant must behaviorally express that fussiness. Such a relationship simply does not occur between any two ordinary persons. I describe that specialness as the presence of a field, a primitive field. Given that field, if the parent part of the field has the experiencing, then the infant part of the field is the behaver. I would not be surprised if a similar avenue of explanation unfolds in the understanding of dreaming subjects and telepathic agents. That is, in very special pairs of dreamers and telepathic agents, there are striking correlations between the content of the material "sent" by the telepathic agent and the content of the dreams reported by the dreamer (Ullmann, 1966; Ullmann, Krippner & Fieldstein, 1966). Without knowing, a mother is a powerful telepathic agent, and her infant is an excellent receiver. The mother who experiences the fussiness sends the message to the infant to behave in a fussing way. However, mother has no awareness of the behavior her infant is to carry out, and sending a message translates into being in the same primitive field in which the physical infant is a most special "receiver."

We are considering a *direct connection* between experiencing parent and behaving infant. Clinicians often have a way of getting right to the observation without being bothered by theoretical barriers. In his description of very young stutterers, for example, Glauber (1953a, b) explains that the child stutters because he is the mother's "spokesman." Mother has the tendency to stutter and the child is the one who stutters. Here is the direct linkage between the potential in the parent and the stuttering behavior in the child. Good clinicians and clinical observers hurdle the barriers which stop theoreticians. Where Arieti and others cannot quite overcome the theoretical hurdle of infant and the parent as separate entities, Glauber simply *describes* the oneness of mother and child. Mother is filled with agitation, and the child expresses her stuttering for her. Mother must not be in control of her own verbal behavior, and the child stutters. No special intermediating mechanisms are necessary because mother and child are part of a singleness of the primitive field.

The observation is a relatively common one. When parents fight with one another and have problems in communication, the infant shows behavioral signs of agitation. When management of a firm fight with one another and have problems in communication, the workers show behavioral signs of agitation. When there are fighting and communication problems among the professional-administrative personnel of the mental hospital, the patients show behavioral signs of agitation (Caudill & Stainbrook, 1954). It is possible to speak of the family as a system; I refer to this parent-infant system as the primitive personality. Conceptually, this system is the corporation, the group, the mental hospital. Social scientists conceptualize a social system and understand the behavior of employees, workers, patients, and so on as a direct function of organizational system variables. Applying this conception to infants in the system of the family, it can be said that the variables of the family system are directly linked to the behavior of the infant, with the specific variables consisting of the potentials and relationships embedded within the primitive field.

This system, this organized primitive field, has had approximately nine months of pregnancy to differentiate the physical infant as a component of the field. By the time the infant is born, it is quite common that the system is sufficiently organized and intact to bear direct linkages between parental potentials and relationships, on the one hand, and the behavior of the neonate, on the other. It is the network of parental potentials and relationships which leads to the behaviors of the neonate: orienting, tracking, grasping, sucking, and the whole range of neonatal behaviors. Many other approaches hold that the neonate is quite capable of a large spectrum of behaviors. Ethological theory is quite explicit in identifying sets of behavioral systems which are ready to go at birth. The difference lies in the locus of the determining variables and the nature of the moderating mechanisms. From the perspective of humanistic theory, the locus of the variables is within the parental figures, not within the *physical* infant, and there is no need for moderating mechanisms because the infant and parents are all components within an encompassing field which *is the infant*. The behavior of infants, even neonates, is open to description as a direct function of the potentials and relationships comprising the infant-as-primitive-personality.

The Behaving Infant

Infant behavior and potentials. When the primitive field is a well organized, efficient system, then the infant can serve as the behavioral vehicle of that which is experienced by the parent—directly, without any intervening mechanisms. It is just the same as the experiencing of a parent is directly linked to the *parent's own* external behavior or to behavioral changes within the physical body of the parent. Thus the mother experiences a sudden loss of security and the infant manifests fear and terror. The infant's behavior provides for the experiencing of a potential housed within mother. Father's insecurity is experienced through the infant's restlessness and agitation. A parent's frustrated anger is experienced through baby's temper tantrums. Mother is filled with defiance, assaultiveness and rebellion, and the infant or young child spits, breaks objects, smashes things, bites, hits other children, damages property. When the parent experiences hesitation and defensiveness, the baby fusses and draws back from adults. Father's love and affection shows in baby's reaching out to be held, in happy gurgling, and in smiling and holding. Mother's fear of separation is expressed in the infant's clinging behavior. The potential is within the physical parent, and the physical infant carries out the behavior which provides for the experiencing.

Each behavior of the infant is connected directly to the potentials of the primitive personality. Ways in which the infant breast feeds are direct behavioral expressions of potentials which reside within mother. A mother may house potentials such that the breast is a reservoir of good resources; or, her potential may be such that her breast is bad, incomplete, or inadequate. Mother may house potentials relating to taking, draining, having it all; or mother's potential may relate to being unsatisfied. Depending upon the nature of mother's own potentials, the infant may suck without getting milk; or the baby may feed fully and satisfyingly; or the baby may avoid breast feeding; or the baby may cling and bite. It is the infant who expresses the behavior while the potential resides in the mother. In each instance, the potential is not "in" the *physical* infant; it resides within the *primitive field*. If there is a potential for withdrawal in the primitive field, whether in mother or within father, it may very well be the child who behaves in ways which provide for the experiencing of withdrawal. Thus the child may behave incoherently, may be unreachable, may recoil from contact, may be frightened by strangers, may be unresponsive to others, may be introvertive and hidden, may live in his own world, may have private thoughts, may avoid eye contact. Such ways of being and behaving are means of providing for the experiencing of a potential inside the primitive field but outside the skin of the physical infant.

All of these infant behaviors can be described without invoking any intermediating mechanisms. For example, if the older sibling of two or three or four years of age is locked tightly into the primitive personality, he expresses directly the potentials of the parent. It is commonly observed that an older sibling frequently shows "regressive" behavior when a newborn baby enters the scene. The older sibling becomes enuretic or speaks in baby talk or assumes baby-like postures or generally behaves as an infant once again. One way in which this occurs is when the mother or father houses the potential to be a baby, to "regress." Under these circumstances, the presence of the potential in the primitive field (i.e., in the parent) is directly linked to the "regressive" behavior in the older sibling. This direct connection requires no intermediating mechanisms such as the older child's being jealous of the attention paid by the parents to the newborn so that, to win back the attention, the older sibling "regresses."

Infant behavior and relationships among potentials. In addition to behavior as a direct function of *potentials* in the primitive field, behavior of the infant is also a function of the nature of parental relationships, of the *relationships among the potentials* in the primitive field. Consider the example of a mother whose deeper potentials relate to fighting, picking at, being unhappy with, screaming and yelling at. But she is not behaviorally that way. Instead she is quiet and unobtrusive, rather stolid and slow moving. The nature of the relationships among these operating and deeper potentials is quite negative. To the extent that the infant is made into the externalization of either of these potentials, the disintegrative relationship will insure that the infant's behaviors (a) will have a disintegrative style, tone, or "way," and (b) will be coupled with disintegrative feelings. If the infant is made into the externalization of the mother's *deeper* potentials, the infant is going to behave in fighting ways. Baby will fuss and scream, beat and bite. But whatever the particular nature of the behavior, it is going to be carried out in a way which is disintegrative. It will be disjointed, torn apart, disjunctive, disorganized—and it will be accompanied with disintegrative feelings: anxiety, fear, anger. If the infant is made into the externalization of the mother's *operating* potential for quiet slowness, those behaviors also will be marked by the disintegrative relationship, for they will consist of a quietness which conveys a disintegrative distaste, a fear and hate of fighting, and which bears the same disintegrative relationship toward mother than she bears toward her own deeper potential for fighting. Thus the baby's quietness and slowness will have a style and tone which includes fearing, hating, disliking, pushing away, avoiding, and the like.

Behaviors of the infant are direct consequences of potentials and relationships in the primitive personality. Sometimes the infant behaves because of the *potential* which is present in the primitive personality; sometimes the infant behaves because of the *relationship* between potentials. These two factors account for significant classes of infant behavior. For example, it is our thesis that both the potentials and the relationships among potentials culminate in attachment behaviors carried out by the infant, behaviors including baby's clinging, approaching, grasping, touching, following, regarding, vocalizing, smiling, imitating, contact-seeking, remaining near, and so on. In each of these behaviors, the one who carries out the behavior is the physical infant, and the object of the behavior is the parent. One factor which accounts for such behavior is the nature of the parental potential. To the extent that the parents house potentials for attachment, closeness, belongingness, dependency, the infant can serve as the behaving vehicle in direct connection with those potentials. If mother has a potential for closeness and dependency, the infant may then cling to, seek to remain near, and follow mother. In this accounting, mother is both the one who houses the potential, the object of the baby's behavior, and the one who experiences the closeness and dependency. The second factor is more prevalent and more robust. To the extent that the baby is constructed as the externalization of the parental operating or deeper potential, the key mechanism is the relationship between the parental potentials. Whether relationships between potentials are integrative or disintegrative, *there is a relationship*. It is a welding together, a bonding, a linking together. Even when relationships are characterized by fearing and hating, the relationships among potentials are close, tight, bonded. This relationship between parental potentials is therefore expressed in that class of infant behaviors known as attachment behavior. Baby will track and follow mother, will grasp and not get too far away from her, a behavioral expression of the same relationship between baby and mother as exists between mother's potentials. Put differently, whenever the relationship between potentials is strong—either strongly integrative or strongly disintegrative—there is an attachment, a bonding between the potentials. When mother is one of these potentials and when the physical infant is an externalized potential, there is a strong relationship between mother and baby. That relational bonding is a strong one, whether we are referring to the relationships between potentials within mother or as manifested in the mother-infant dyad, and that powerful relationship will be manifested in what has come to be termed attachment behavior of the infant. Both of these factors result in the infant's attachment behavior, and both reside within the primitive field and directly link to the infant's behavior.

Attachment behaviors are direct behavioral expressions of potentials and relationships of the parental figures. The answers lie in the primitive field as the larger definition of the infant. Such a conceptualization may be contrasted with other approaches which must look *inside* the *physical* infant for the answer. Ethological theory finds the answer to the infant's attachment behavior in the infant's biological genetic processes which are held as maintaining proximity to mother so that, if the infant deviates from safe proximity, the infant is led to behave in ways geared toward the goal of returning the infant to safe proximity (Bowlby, 1958, 1965, 1969). At the moment when the infant is at the threshold of the safe perimeter, biological genetic processes and programs activate behavioral systems which mediate attachment behavior. The differences between this approach and humanistic theory appear to be rather significant.

The Behaving Fetus

We have been discussing the infant who is a few weeks or months or years of age. Our thesis has been that the primitive field is directly linked to the infant's behavior by virtue of the (parental) potential and their relationships, all existing within a primitive field which is the larger definition of the infant. This model also applies, perhaps more appropriately, to the behavior of the *fetus*. When we focus on the fetus, it is relatively easy to accept the fetus as existing within mother, within her region or field, relatively easy to accept that what occurs in and to the fetus is predominantly a function of mother as the encompassing world. In this sense, it may be easier to accept the role of the primitive field in determining the behavior of the fetus than it is to accept the role of the primitive field in determining the behavior of the infant or young child. The fetus and its behavior stand as a kind of paradigm of the powerful influence of the primitive field.

No new principles need to be framed. What happens inside mother's body has been described by a set of principles (Chapter 5) which assert generally that mother's potentials and their relationships determine the nature of her bodily processes. For example, mother's internal bodily processes can constitute and manifest her deeper potential for frenetic restlessness and refusal to be satisfied. The fetus is draped with the same principles, and the behavior of the fetus is explained the same way mother's bodily processes are explained. Mother's frenetic restlessness and refusal to be satisfied can be manifested in the way her stomach is, the way her colon is, or the way her fetus is. The fetus is merely another body part and is understood the same way that other actual physical changes occur in mother's body.

In understanding physical bodily phenomena, it was proposed (Chapter 5) that the body expresses that which the person's operating potentials also express. If the person's operating potential relates to rushing forward, entering into, then this principle suggests that the person's external behavior and internal physical bodily processes may both be characterized by rushing forward and entering into. Mother's operating potential can be expressed in her own behavior and also in bodily processes. In precisely the same way, what is occurring in mother would be likely to occur in the fetus. It is understandable that mother's heightened or lowered heart rate would be expressed isomorphically in fetal heart rate changes (Copher & Huber, 1967). Although it has not been demonstrated in fetal research, at least not to my knowledge, it would follow that this relationship would be higher in those mothers wherein the physical body expressed that which also occurs in the operating potential. That is, if mother's body is such that what occurs behaviorally is also occurring within the physical body, then the correspondence in fetal and maternal heart rate ought to be more robust than in those mothers for whom this principle does not apply.

On the basis of the principles described in Chapter 5, the mother can construct a blocking obstruction somewhere in her own physical bodily processes. She may develop such a bodily event in her throat, stomach, intestine. Wherever it occurs, it is an expression of her own potential for blocking obstruction. Mother may house that as an operating potential so that she herself functions as a blocking obstruction, someone who is that way, who lives that way in her world. On the other hand, she may not behave that way at all, but instead house a blocking obstructionism deep within her. In either case, her own bodily processes may be characterized by blocking obstructionism. Given this kind of person, the fetus may also be constructed along the same lines, expressing the same potential. Not only is the fetus itself a manifest expression of the potential, but the potential may well be manifest in such physical fetal characteristics as an imperformate anus, atresia of the esophagus, or pyloric stenosis. These terms refer to specific physical characteristics of the fetus, characteristics which manifest the mother's potential for blocking obstructionism, features which have been otherwise interpreted as congenital anomalies but which are regarded in humanistic theory as physical bodily expressions of the mother's own potentials.

Primitive field versus a causal concatenation. It has been observed for over a hundred years that mother's personality processes are related to fetal behavior (Whitehead, 1867). Beginning with studies by Sontag and his co-workers (e.g., Sontag & Wallace, 1934), research has identified specific relationships between mother's personality processes and fetal behavior (Ferreira, 1969; Joffe, 1969; Montagu, 1965; Sarason, 1966). What has never been clear is the way in which mother's personality processes and fetal behavior are related. For example, observations have linked maternal smoking and fetal prematurity. Yet it has never been understood how maternal smoking and fetal prematurity are related. Researchers have suggested that these observed relationships are expressions of the potency of a third underlying variable (cf. Joffe, 1969). Our way of understanding these phenomena points toward the third underlying variable as the primitive field which contains both fetal behavior and maternal personality processes. The potentials and their relationships are held as accounting both for maternal behavior (e.g., smoking) and fetal behavior (e.g., prematurity), and as including and encompassing both the personality processes of the mother and the behavior of the fetus. An understanding of the nature of the primitive field helps us to understand both the personality processes of the mother and the behavior of the fetus.

Humanistic theory allows for the presence of that underlying factor whose expression in multiple events is erroneously taken, in other approaches, as a *causal* connectedness among the multiple events. With regard to the fetus, potentials and relationships of the primitive field may lead to (a) physical changes in the pregnant mother, (b) fetal behavior, and (c) occurrences in later childhood. Our underlying factor is the particular potential and relationship which leads to all three events. Other approaches seek to find a causal chain between these three events. For example, a primitive field may include a potential to reject, get rid of, not give it a home. This potential, characteristic of a given primitive field, can lead to what has been reported as (a) hypertension and toxemia in the pregnant mother, (b) fetal prematurity, and (c) later placement of the child in a psychiatric hospital (Zitrin, Farber & Cohen, 1964). From our perspective, each of these events is an expression of the potential to reject it, to get rid of it, to not give it a home. This underlying characteristic of the primitive field leads to all three events, and is proposed as an alternative to an explanation in which pregnancy complications somehow cause fetal prematurity, and fetal prematurity is somehow causally related to childhood pathology. From our perspective, such findings offer soft suggestions toward the worthwhileness of a concept of a primitive field.

We study fetal behavior by understanding the primitive field. If the fetus is to be restless, or wrapped peculiarly in the cord, or dead, the particular fetal behavior will occur because of the potentials and relationships within the primitive field. In the case of the fetus, the nature of the primitive field is easier, perhaps, to study than in the case of the neonate or young child. It consists of a field which, from a neurophysiological perspective, includes neurohumoral systems comprised of nerves and endocrines and blood chemistry (Montagu, 1965). There is more to this field, yet the primitive field encompassing the neonate is perhaps easier to grasp than the primitive field encompassing a baby of six months or a child of four years. If we can study the field of the mother and fetus, we will know more about the way in which the primitive field occurs in the neonate or young child.

15

The Development
of the Child

We have discussed the origins of infants (Chapter 13), and the ways in which infant behavior is determined by the primitive field (Chapter 14). The purpose of the present chapter is to discuss the development of children. The word *development* is used in its active sense, viz. ways in which the primitive field actively works to develop the child. Our task here is to describe how children are developed by a primitive field which either tightens its grip or dissolves away. Our focus is on the primitive field and the ways in which the fate of the primitive field determines how the child is developed. One line of development occurs when the primitive field is made tighter, more organized, preserved. Another line of development is generated when the primitive field dissolves itself away. Although we will be studying the child, our pivotal focus is on the primitive field, its preservation or dissolution, and the effects of that altered primitive field on the emergence of the child.

PRESERVATION OF THE PRIMITIVE FIELD

If the parental figures behave in just the right ways, the primitive field can be preserved intact. Indeed, it may even be made into a tighter organizational system. But in order to strengthen this field, the parental figures must behave in quite specific ways. It requires a great deal of careful work to keep the growing child emprisoned within the encompassing primitive field. Parental figures must be successful in work which is persistent and demanding, whether such work is carried out wittingly or unwittingly.

It is as if the parents remain fixed, and the infant is progressively moulded and shaped into being what the parents make him into being. The primitive field is there before the infant is even conceived, and it is the primitive field which constructs the infant from week to week, month to month, refining and polishing it into being very particular ways. From the outside it looks as if the infant is undergoing progressive change—and it is. But the changes are dictated by a relatively fixed primitive field which smooths the infant into fulfilling the functions it was constructed to perform. The net result is a changing infant, an enduring and unchanging primitive field, and a progressively better and smoother fitting of the infant into the primitive field. "Whenever I look at the toddlers I note a developing, changing organism. When I look at the mothers . . . in most instances I face relatively unchanging modes of behavior. And yet, when I look at the mother-toddler interaction, I come up with an increasingly effective dyadic system" (Bronson, 1974, p. 289). This is what I also see in general as the primitive field works upon its infant. Under ordinary circumstances, the primitive field will continue its mandate over the infant and the primitive field is preserved—without the parents even knowing how powerfully they maintain a firm control over the infant.

In his debate with Skinner, Rogers (Rogers & Skinner, 1956) envisioned the awful possibility of a growing class of controllers, armed with technical knowledge about how to control human behavior, enslaving other classes of human beings in scientifically insidious ways, depersonalizing these classes of human beings and turning them into robots. Rogers had in mind a class of adults, government bureaucrats and scientific technicians, who controlled other adults. We already have these two classes of persons, one class the controllers of the other. What is more, their prevalence and power exceed anything Rogers described. Parents are unwitting scientific technicians in the control of their infants and children. Parents place infants in a web of control far more intact and organized than controlling adults can accomplish with controlled adults. Those who wish to control the masses of adults can learn from the ways in which parents enslave children, keep them in a drowsy, hypnogogic state within the strengthened primitive field.

Parents do not "raise" their children or "bring up" their children; instead, parents imprison them. Parents, modest as they are with regard to the extent of their control, are the complete determiners of the behavior of their children. As their infants become young children and older children, there is an ongoing battle to keep the primitive field preserved, and never to let the child escape from the control of the primitive field. Levitt (1957) summarized research on therapy with children, and concluded that approximately 70 percent of children referred but not treated tended to lose the symptoms for which they were referred. Such findings are open to many interpretative conclusions. From the perspective of humanistic theory, I would view these findings as soft evidence of the controlling power of the primitive field. Rather than evidence of "spontaneous remission of symptoms," I regard the findings as soft evidence of the controlling power of the parental figures who are still instrumental in controlling and determining the behavior of the child who is four or seven or ten years of age. Beginning with an intact and well organized primitive field in infancy, that field can be preserved throughout the course of childhood.

Parental figures preserve the encompassing primitive field because the child continues to fulfill a function in the world of the parental figures. (a) The child is the constructed external situation in which the parents experience what they experience. (b) The child is the extension of the parental operating or deeper potential. (c) The child must relate to the parents in the ways in which the parents relate to their own deeper potentials. These are the reasons why the child is kept within a primitive field which is strengthened and ever more tightly organized. The child is kept mindless and asleep as a person because of these reasons, and not at all because parents are evil or cruel. Unfortunately, neither parent nor child has any awareness of the process which is going on daily, which is guiding and directing virtually all their tiny interactions. The child is not kept in this state because the parent gains some sort of satisfaction from success in this endeavor, or because the parent never gained adequate autonomy from his or her own parent, or because the culture forces the parent to accomplish this with the child. Instead, the infant was conceived to fulfill certain functions, and the child is preserved within the primitive field as a means of insuring that these functions are carried out.

In order to keep the child within the primitive field, in order to insure that the child serves the functions for which it was conceived, the parents must gain control over several aspects of the child. They must control the child's behavior, and the parents must continue to serve as the deeper potentials of the child. The child is allowed to "be" the potentials which the parent constructs the child into being (Figure 13.1), whether these are derived from the parents' operating or deeper potentials. The child is allowed to carry out the behavior which the primitive field determines shall be carried out. But the major battle always revolves around the ownership of the determining center, the causal nexus of all of this. To be successful in preserving the primitive field, the parents must be successful in never allowing the development of a self, a personhood, a sense of I-ness. All of that absolutely must remain within the parental realm, and not the domain of the physical child. If the parents are successful, the child is owned by the primitive field, and the child exists in a hypnotic-like state, a partial person, a mechanical figure. The child moves about and thinks, has reactions and acts like a real person. What is worse, the child acts as if he is a person, a self, an I-ness, when in actuality that sense is an illusion. In actuality the child is the tiniest part of the larger child-as-primitive-personality of which he is unaware. More than being unaware, the sense of I-ness and self is itself a grand illusion, for the determining reins of his personality lie within the potentials and relationships of the parental figures. This is an awful battle in which the parent wins without knowing that it wins, and the other, the child, always loses without knowing that it has even been in a battle.

The balance of this section deals with four major ways in which parents behave in order to preserve the primitive field. Parental figures must behave in very particular ways in order to maintain the child within the encompassing primitive field. They must (a) maintain ownership of the child's behavior, (b) maintain ownership of the child's external world, (c) maintain ownership of the child's relationship with himself, and (d) prevent escape from the encompassing primitive field.

By Parental Ownership of the Child's Behavior

Initiating the child's behavior. Parental figures must insure that they are the initiators of the child's behavior, the ones who get the behavior started and who define the nature of the behavior to occur. Parents are to be the activators and the governors of as much behavior as possible. This can be accomplished by using every possible mode of interaction, from primitive touching (Buytendijk, 1950) to talking, feeling, facial expression, body movement, gesture. Every possible mode is to be put into the service of guiding, directing, initiating the behavior of the child.

With infants, the parent is virtually the complete initiator of what the infant does. Indeed, even with young children, the predominant mode is for parents to maintain an undeviating, unrelenting control over the initiation and activation of behavior (Escalona, 1972; Lewis, 1972; White, 1972). It is as if interaction is almost tantamount to parental initiation and activation. Thus, the parent owns the child's behavior by being the unquestioned initiator of nearly everything the child does.

Taking over the child's behavior. The child is retained within the encompassing primitive field when his behavior is taken over by parental figures. Picture a child with a new toy train. Whatever the child does with that train is owned completely by father who is there, swarming all over the child. "Do it this way . . . Let's do this . . . hand me that over there." It is the parent who tells the child precisely what behavior is to be carried out and how to carry it out. The model is the parent who moves the child's arms and legs, almost a matter of doing the behavior for the child—and naming that as the behavior of the child. When father moves the child's hands to put the train track together, or when father tells the child exactly what to do in assembling the tracks, or when father actually does the assembling for the child, father is literally taking over the child's behavior. Under these conditions, the child is a mechanical thing, behaving under the governorship of the parent.

If the child perchance initiates ownership of a behavior, the parent must fight the child for ownership. One way in which this is accomplished is by completing all behaviors initiated by the child. In no way is the child to be permitted to complete his own behaviors. If he is in the process of putting together the train tracks, the parent must take over the final steps and finish putting the tracks together. If she is climbing into her bed, help her up and lift her just a bit into bed. If he is trying to put on the sweater or button a shirt or tie the shoe lace, the parent steps in and finishes off each of these behaviors. Finish the painting for him. Complete the sentence which he started. Even when the child initiates the behavior, parental ownership is maintained by completing the behavior for the child.

Owning the child's thoughts. One of the most crucial domains which the parent must take over is that of thoughts. As behavior, thoughts must be owned by the parents in order to preserve the child within the primitive personality. Thus the parents must have the thoughts for the child, especially thoughts about what the child likes and dislikes, wants and does not want, feels like and does not feel like. The parent tells the child: "You like beans . . . you love your mommy . . . you like the ball . . . you do not like the bright light in the room . . . you want to play . . . you do not want milk now . . . you are tired . . . you are hungry now . . . you love reading your book." In all of this, the main achievement is for the parent to occupy the center of direction and personhood, and to deprive the child of ownership. Taking over the behavior of the child must necessarily include taking over the child's thinking behavior.

Preventing the child from defining its center of attention. It is the parent, never the child, who defines what is the focal center of concern for the child. Whenever the child attends to something, thinks about something, concentrates upon something, the nature of that something is to be defined by the parent, and not the child. Thus the child is told to think about this, look at that, attend to this other thing. Read the book, look at the ants on the sidewalk, listen to this music. If the child tries to define for itself what is *its* center of concern, the parent must do whatever is necessary to not permit that to happen.

Never allow the child to define its own center of concern. If the child tells the parent that he wants to talk about his sore, the boy at school, or the design on the kitchen floor, the parent must not pay attention. The parent must not shift from the parent's center of concern to that of the child. Always it must be the parent who identifies the center of the child's concern.

Serving as model and leader. The parent is to be the leader, boss, exemplar, model, experimenter; force the child to be the follower, underdog, imitator, mimic, subject. Show the child how to do it. Be the model as much as possible. Get the child to learn to do it the way you do it, to succeed by doing it your way. Develop the child's vocabulary by encouraging him to imitate the parental sounds (McCarthy, 1954). It is the parent who determines the way the child learns to do everything, thus perpetuating the parent in the role of owner of the child's behavior.

Taking over the perception of reality. The child is prevented from gaining mandate over his own behavior by the parent serving as the confirmer and interpreter of what is real, and insuring that the child's attempts to grasp reality are squashed. If the child accurately perceives that others are really talking about her behind her back, cast doubt on the accuracy of her judgment, make her graspings and interpretations unfounded and incorrect, make her feel dumb or crazy for having such (accurate) perceptions (Laing & Esterson, 1970). "No one says that about you; you are so silly to think that; how foolish of you; you are off the beam because they would never say something like that about you." This class of behaviors consists of seeing reality for oneself, and such behavior is dangerous, for it automatically flexes the dawning sense of personhood. To judge reality for oneself means that there is the rising presence of a self with which to judge reality. Therefore, the attempts by the child to be a person who makes its own assessments of reality must be squashed. Often this is especially pertinent when the threat level is moderately high. For example, if the parents look at one another in that special knowing way when grandmother slurps her food, and the child catches that knowing look, the parents must squash the child. If the child says, "Grandma, mommy and daddy are laughing at you," then deny that the child ever saw you grinning at grandmother and catching each other's eyes with a knowing look. The child is not to be included among those who can share in seeing the little grins and the knowing looks. Sharing in that is reserved for *persons*, and the child is not to be permitted to be a person. Kill that person which is struggling for existence in the child by telling her: "Betty didn't see anything of the sort! Be a good little girl and mind your business. We did not do that. How can you say that?"

Even mild interpretations of reality by the child are to be disqualified: "It is not raining outside; that dress fits you; your hand does not hurt; the cat is not making a noise." Neutralize, disqualify, stamp out any accurate perceptions that the child makes of reality. What is more, the final authority and confirmer of what is real must be the parent and never the child. When the child thinks (accurately) that the neighbor dislikes her, not only must the parent disqualify that perception, but the parent must designate herself as the final unquestioned authority on what is real: "Mrs. Lord likes you; you know mommy knows best . . . How silly you are; of course you heard her yell at you, but mommy knows what she means; Mrs. Lord tells me how much she likes you, and mommy knows what is right." Even when mother agrees with the child's perception, the perception must never be accurate on its own without the final corroboration of the parent. The child must always turn to the parent to confirm whether it is real or false.

Every perception about the external world must be questioned and squashed, and then replaced by the real state of things as interpreted by the parent. Thus the child can never be allowed to have his own perceptions of the external world. If the child ventures that it is a real blizzard out there, tell the child that he is wrong; it is just nicely snowing. If the child says that it is nicely snowing out there, tell him that he is wrong, that it is a bad blizzard. The formula is that whatever perceptions the child has are wrong, and the correct one must be supplied by the parent. It is not too warm in the room, it is just right. That is not a bicycle, it is a racer; or it is not a racer, it is a bicycle. So much of what passes for learning or teaching is a mask for disqualifying the child's accurate perceptions of reality, and constitute effective means of maintaining parental ownership of the child's behavior.

Make especially certain that the child does not have accurate judgments about the thoughts and perceptions of others. It is always the parent who mediates that function. Whatever the child senses or guesses about what others are thinking or feeling, the parent must not permit the *child* to be the one who guesses and senses, and whatever the child guesses or senses must be wrong. It is the parent who tells how others view the child ("Jerry likes you; he likes your pretty hair . . . Auntie is very old, and she thinks you are sweet for coming to visit her"). The parent is the one to decide how the child believes others view her ("Mommy, I think Grandma didn't like my talking at the table." "You know that Grandma likes your talking when you have something to say; you can tell she likes you to talk."). The parent is to decide how the child thinks the parent views her ("Mommy, you like me when I eat it all up." "No I don't, now hurry up, I have to do the dishes.").

In order to disqualify any attempt by the child to grasp what is real, always deny that you said whatever you said, insure an incongruity between what you said and what you say that you said. If your son puts only the forks and spoons at each place, and you had said that he should put the forks and spoons at each place, deny that you said that. Tell him he never hears properly, that he didn't get it right. Act as if you told him to include knives too. If you change now what you said earlier, and do it in such a way that tells your child he is unable to know the reality of what you say, then you are depriving him of an opportunity to be a person. If you are skilled, the dialogue runs like this: Mother says something; child tries to grasp what mother says; mother denies that child's grasp is correct. Mother replies that she never said that. According to this formula, the child is forever reaching out to grasp the reality of what mother says, and is frustrated repeatedly by mother. Soon the child gives up and that endeavor toward personhood collapses.

Quite often mother and father share some common deeper secret truth which they work hard at denying. For example, there may be a history of suicides or institutionalizations or criminality which both parents tacitly agree to hide from themselves. They both stay away from that topic and mutually agree to consign that topic to the realm of denied unawareness. The child is also forced to not know about that topic, and to join the parents in the conspiracy of sleeping unknowingness. Expressing that topic, looking at it and bringing it to life is a sign of dangerous personhood which must be squashed. Thus the child is forced to not know about "that," to deny its existence. If the child even approaches the vicinity of mother's institutionalization, uncle's suicide, or father's imprisonment, that leading edge of personhood is to be squashed. Such ideas are crazy or dumb or silly or bad or wrong or whatever will erase their existence—and the accompanying existence of dawning personhood. Clearly the child is venturing near to what is true, and the child must never be permitted to share in the grasping of what is true. She is never "in" with others in perceiving what the ingroup knows is true.

As a final effort, the possibility of personhood is squashed by *punishing* any attempt by the child to make accurate perceptions of reality. Thus the child moves increasingly toward having correct, accurate perceptions of reality, and suffers increasingly for those accurate perceptions, with the net result of increasing the power of the primitive personality and suppressing the possibility of personhood. If the parents are annoyed at grandmother's food slurping, and the child says, "Ha, ha, grandmother is making funny noises," the parents can allow the child to have those accurate perceptions, but suffer for them. "Go to your room!" "How many times have we told you to keep your mouth shut." "Who asked you, you bad boy!" "Tommy, that's a terrible thing to say; you apologize to Grandmother!" The child is indeed accurate in his perceptions, but he is made to feel miserable for having them. How like the adult who senses quite accurately that others hate him or think of him as evil or are plotting to hurt him—and feels desperately bad or mad for having these accurate perceptions (Laing & Esterson, 1970): The child's behavior consists of accurate perceptions, but personhood is coupled with crushing disintegrative feelings for those very accurate perceptions. Or, the shadow of personhood, of venturing near one's own accurate perception of the world, is made fraught with terrible pain so that the child forever stays away from the possibility of having accurate judgments.

Neutralizing attempts to own its own behavior. A common mechanism for owning the child's behavior, but one which is fraught with risk, is for the parent to punish the child each time the child attempts to own its own behavior. The parent must become distressed, alarmed, upset, bothered at the slightest hint of the child owning its own behavior (Laing & Esterson, 1970, p. 34). Be distressed if the child initiates its own behavior, makes a decision on its own, completes something on its own, has its own private thoughts, defines its own center of attention, defines and maintains its own perception of reality. If the parent can be effectively distressed and alarmed, the child may make no further efforts to own its own behavior and surrender mandate to the parental figures. However, the risk is that such alarm and distress and upset on the part of the parent may only culminate in the child's *further* emergence out of the parental ownership of its behavior.

Disqualifying attempts to define equal stature relationships. Every instance of the child's starting to own its own behavior can be neutralized by an ingenious parental maneuver which has been refined and systematized by Haley (1963). Haley studied, not the relationship between parents and children, but strategies in the psychotherapy of "schizophrenic" patients. His immediate therapeutic aim was to disqualify their resistance of equal stature relationships. He sought to win the battle of ownership over their attempts to resist, to withdraw from the therapist, to stay out of an equal stature relationship. Such patients defied and resisted the therapist's attempts by "schizophrenic" behavioral means of resistance and avoidance. Haley neutralized these patients' resistance by the maneuver of *encouraging* their resistance! The more the therapist encouraged the resistance, the more it lost its resistance value. He therefore neutralized their efforts by going along with the resistance, taking it over, forcing the patients to yield to *his* control by and mandate over their behavior. Parents use this same therapeutic maneuver in taking over and disqualifying the child's efforts to resist. Any attempt by the child to be equal to the parent and thereby to step *away* from parental control is disqualified by going along with the "stepping away" so that even the attempts at resistance are owned by the parents. In this way the child is effectively subjugated, and the parents retain ownership of all behavior, including that which endangers the mandate of the parents over the child. As a result, the child is deprived of its attempt to define equal stature relationships as a way of resisting the control of the parent.

If the child asks you to pick her up or throw the ball, the parent can acknowledge the child's personhood by acceding to what the child asks or by refusing to accede to what the child asks. In either response the parent acknowledges the child as a person. What kind of response by the parent is effective in disqualifying the child as a person without falling into the trap of doing what the child asks or not doing what the child asks? Once again, Haley (1963) points the way in his study of the behavioral maneuvers of "schizophrenic" patients. Their method is to refuse to do what they are invited to do, but to refuse without ever taking responsibility for refusing. If you ask a schizophrenic patient to throw the ball or to sit down in the chair, Haley describes the patient as refusing to do what you say. He will not throw the ball or sit in the chair. But more important, he will refuse in ways which never acknowledge that you exist as a person. That is, he will not sit down or throw the ball because the *voices* tell him not to do so—and not because he himself refuses to do it. Or he will not hear what you ask him to do, and thereby refuse without ever acknowledging you as a person who defines the relationship. In carrying out the same behavioral maneuver, the parent must refuse to do what the child asks, but it must be done so as to erase the child as a person who makes the request, who has taken the initiative in defining the relationship. One way is to refuse to do what the child asks without talking to the child. Without ever talking to or looking at the child, refuse his request by not hearing it, by being too preoccupied to even acknowledge the request, or by misunderstanding the child's request. Another way is to refuse without acknowledging the child as a person making the request by doing something else or by making a counter request to the child. For example, when the child asks you to pick her up, go to the kitchen and get yourself a drink of water, or brush your hair, or pick up a book to read. If the child asks you to throw the ball, tell her to fix her strap or get off the lawn or look at the red bird in the tree. Each of these maneuvers by the parent neutralizes and disqualifies the child as a person in its attempts to define an equal stature relationship with the parent.

Each time the child initiates an attempt to define an equal stature relationship with you, counter that bid with your own initiation of an unrelated defined relationship which *you* impose onto her. When she says, "Mommy, are you crabby?" (and therefore is a person owning her own behavior, defining an equal stature relationship with you), put your arm around her and say, "Put your feet down; don't get mommy's dress dirty." In this way you are disqualifying her bid to be a person, to own her own behavior, to be the definer of the relationship with you, and to establish an equal stature relationship with you. The encompassing primitive field is thereby maintained.

Each of the above mechanisms is effective in preventing the child from owning its own behavior, and in insuring that the parental figures maintain mandate over the behavior of the child. One of the keys to the successful utilization of these mechanisms is the all-pervasiveness of the parental use of these mechanisms. Keep the child busy being the recipient of these mechanisms. Use these mechanisms all the time so that the child is forever behaving on the basis of parental ownership of its behavior. The parent can own the child's behavior by invoking these mechanisms every waking moment of the child's life. It is as if the child never can own its own behavior if it is perpetually engaged in doing what the parent gets it to do (Bronson, 1971a). Little wonder that some adults have practically no memory of huge slabs of their childhood; they were engaged in responding to parents, in carrying out what parents got them to do, in never owning their own behavior.

By Parental Ownership of the Child's External World

We have described how parents preserve the child within the primitive field by insuring that the parental figures, and not the child itself, have ownership of the child's *behavior*. We now turn to a second way in which parents act to preserve the child within the encompassing primitive field. In this second way, the parents are the owners of the child's *external world*.

Parents as determiners of the nature of the external world. Whether the child is two, five, eight, or fourteen, the primitive field remains strong if the parental figures have virtual control over what occurs in the external world. The parental figures must determine whether windows open, the temperature increases, others are friendly, colors change from yellow to bright blue, noises increase or abate, the room tilts, or the sun shines. Parental figures must be hard at work constructing the external world, altering its nature. In this enterprise, the target of the parents' work is not the actual behavior of the child, but rather the nature of the external world in which the child exists.

Parents must extend or generalize what is included in the primitive field. By working in the right way, the parents can make the neighbors, the car, the cat, the relatives, and virtually all elements of the external world into components of the child's primitive field. As a result, the external world is an encompassing primitive field. One way in which the parents can accomplish this is by arranging for the child to be afraid of the neighbors, the cat, and other elements of the external world. If the child is afraid of the neighbors, then the parents *and* the neighbors control the child's external world. Parents can arrange to have the child hurt, scared, alarmed, frightened, punished by the car door, the electric socket, the postman, the teacher, the policeman, the lawn mower. In the vocabulary of learning theory, these mechanisms have been studied under the aegis of negative reinforcement, fear and anxiety as secondary drives, and the acquisition of fear-responses and anxiety-responses. Regardless of the kind of vocabulary, the idea is to make the child fearful of more and more of an external world which controls the child, does things to the child, is the boss of what happens in the relationship with the child, and generally determines the nature of that external world. As the child becomes increasingly fearful of formerly neutral elements of the external world (cf. Miller & Dollard, 1950), parental ownership of the child's external world is generalized.

Uncouple the child's behavior from consequent changes in the external world. Parents, and not the child, own the child's external world by insuring that the external world is virtually unaffected by the behavior of the child. The external world moves and changes independent of the child's behavings. It is the work of the parent to insure that the child is consistently seen and treated as neither influencing, controlling, manipulating, causing, or effecting the external world (cf. Katkovsky, Crandall & Good, 1967; Lewis & Goldberg, 1969). When this state of affairs is successfully accomplished, the external world remains beyond the purview of the child, and, from that position, the primitive field maintains its ownership of the child.

One way of blocking the influence of the child's behavior upon the external world is to insure that no effect is immediately contingent upon the child's behavior. The child will behave in ways which might well bring forth an immediate effect or response or change in the external world, but the parents must arrange conditions so that the effect or response or change is not immediate. When the child calls, do not answer immediately. When the child falls down, do not come running immediately. Within the framework of learning theory, the immediacy of responses is recognized as a significant potentiator of reinforcements (Gewirtz, 1969). To this is added, in humanistic theory, the possibility of mandate over the external world. That is, if a change in the external world is immediately contingent upon the child's behavior, the behavior becomes coupled with consequent changes in the external world—and this state of affairs vitiates *parental* ownership of the child's external world. When parents insure that the external world is not immediately responsive to the child's behavior, it is the *primitive field* which exerts continuing ownership of the external world—and not the personhood or sense of I-ness of the child. A simple way of accomplishing this is by not responding. It is typical of parents that in the earliest weeks, months, and possibly years there is a high frequency of not responding (Bronson, 1974). That is a powerful means of both establishing the primitive field and of preserving the child within that field by insuring that the field does not respond to the child's behaviors.

In every way, the parents must insure that the child's behavior is not successful in bringing about consistent desired consequences from the external world. The parents can accomplish this by following a procedure used by Maier (1959). He arranged the external world of subject animals so that they were placed on a jumping stand and then forced to jump off the stand by means of an air blast or electric shock. Escape doors were locked randomly so that neither a learned response based upon discrimination patterning nor one based upon position responses proved effective. This construction of an unsolvable problem culminated in a single kind of rigid, stereotyped, simple behavior. In adopting similar procedures, parents make sure that the "problem" is not solved in any consistent way by the child's behavior. Instead, parents arrange that the effects of the child's behavior are erratic, inconsistent, and generally unsuccessful. Whatever the child does to get his own breakfast, or to resist another child who is pugnacious to him, or to locate a lost mitten, or to gain comfort when he is physically hurt must be made unsuccessful and its effects randomly inconsistent. When the external world is such that nothing works in any consistently successful fashion, the parents maintain ownership over the child's external world, the child's behavior is uncoupled from consequent changes in the external world, and the primitive field maintains its mandate over the child.

In order to ensure that couplings between the child's behavior and consequent changes in the external world are random, irregular, capricious, what occurs in the external world must be independent of the child's own behavior. Parents can bring this about by such mechanisms as the random keeping or not keeping of promises, a mechanism central to such topics as delay of reinforcement (Mahrer, 1956; Mischel, 1958, 1966) and interpersonal trust. If the parent promises that the child will get the skates, or will play catch tomorrow or will have wieners for dinner, or will go to the zoo—the critical factor is that what actually occurs must be capriciously unrelated to the child's request. In this way, the child's behavior does not act upon the external world, does not do anything to the external world. Under these conditions, it is the primitive field which retains mandate over the external world, and not any emerging personhood from within the child.

Indeed, the child's behavior will have no consequential change on the external world if the child never even has to make requests of the parent. That is, the child does not have to ask for skates; they are there. The child need not ask for anything; it is there. If the child defecates, the external world does the necessary caretaking. The child-as-a-person never has to stir. In the language of learning theory, gratification is immediate to need, and requires no behavior of the child. If the rhythmic coupling of "need" and "gratification" occurs immediately and with consistency, the child's behavior is disconnected from the external world, the parents own the external world, and the emergence of the child-as-a-person is further delayed. Our position conflicts with one in which the need-gratification coupling is held as responsible *for* the emergence of the sense of self: "It takes several weeks of postnatal development until, through the rhythmic repetition of need and its gratification, the infant develops the perception that the source of his need (hunger, pain, discomfort) is *within* and the source of his gratification is *outside* the self: i.e. separation in the psychological sense begins to exist for the infant" (Benedek, 1956, p. 395). If the external world is alert, hunger is fed, pain is alleviated, and discomfort comforted quickly and effectively, without the necessity of the child (or infant) having to do anything at all. Thus the attentive parent who carefully services the child maintains ownership of the external world.

The child owns no part of the external world. Nothing of the external world is to be owned by the child. It "has" nothing of the external world, and the parents ensure that the child owns nothing. Never allow the child to have her own zone of personal space, her own territory. This applies to a room of her own, or a special place, or her own bodily zone. That is, do not permit her to have her own bed, her own furniture, her own room. She can own nothing of the external world. Do not restrict her to the sidewalk or the apartment or to any zone which could demarcate her own personal space, a dividing line which differentiates a part of the external world which is hers, which she owns. Do not permit this. There is to be no special place which she arranges to be hers—such as the space in the pantry, or in the basement, or under the stairs, or by the store. No place in the external world is to be owned by her. She is to have no article which is hers—no bed, no shoes, no hat or doll or thing of any kind. By keeping the external world beyond her ownership, the primitive field is maintained and extended, and the child is kept within the controlling mandate of the encompassing primitive field.

By Parental Ownership of the Child's Relationship to Its Self

The primitive personality is preserved and maintained by parental ownership of the child's *behavior*, and by parental ownership of the child's *external world*. To the extent that parents can accomplish both of these ends, the primitive field remains regnant, and the I-ness or self or personhood of the child is prevented from developing, or more accurately, remains located within the primitive field which encompasses the physical child. We now turn to a third way in which parental figures accomplish these goals: by parental ownership of the child's *relationship to its self*. The theme is that parents must make certain that the child never regards its self. The child cannot be permitted to step away from its self and have any sort of relationship with its self. In this enterprise the parents have two jobs: (a) to make certain that the child never is allowed to step away from its self, and (b) to ensure that it is the *parent* who relates to everything which constitutes the child's self.

When the child behaves, the *parent* must be the one who has the reactions to that behavior. Was it a good behavior or a bad behavior? The parent is the one to have and to express these reactions. When the child pets the cat, the parent and never the child should decide whether that behavior is a good one or a bad one: "That was a good petting . . . Oh, that was a bad thing to do." Do not permit the child to be pleased or displeased with her own behavior. Instead, the parent has and expresses the pleasure or displeasure. If the child ties its shoes well, *mother* expresses the pleasure *for* the child. If the child drops the egg on the floor, the mother should say, "That was a bad thing to do." Jump in and have the reaction for the child, instead of the child reacting to its own behavior as good or bad, as something of pride or dismay, as pleasureful or unpleasing.

Never let the child define for itself what it is like. Always do that for the child. Tell the child that he is handsome, a good boy, a smart or a dumb boy, a strong or weak boy. You define for her that she is pudgy or skinny, quick or slow, athletic or awkward, big or small, friendly or unfriendly. Each definition of what the child is like must come from the parental figure and never from the child.

Parents, and not the child, must have special access to knowledge about what the child is "really" like. This is the inner or deeper or real child. Somehow, this inner real child is something only the parents can see and are privy to. When the child says that he wants to be a cook when he grows up, the parents say, "But you have a scientist's mind, and with your intelligence, you'd never be happy as a cook." A scientist's mind? Your intelligence? The child cannot see his scientist's mind, nor can he hold his intelligence in his hand. These are mysterious things somewhere inside. They are very important because they mean he cannot be a cook because of them, yet only his parents know that his "mind" is that of a scientist (and not that of a cook), and only his parents can weigh his "intelligence" and decide on the basis of his intelligence that being a cook is out. It is as if he does not and can not see these deeper, mysterious, inner things which comprise him—like his stomach or his mind, like his lungs or his intelligence. In the same way, the parents, and *only* the parents, know the "real" (deeper, inner) child: "I'm glad you talked back to your teacher; that's the real you!" "You should never have said that to the postman. That's not my Shirley." "I'm glad you told her to get off our yard. There's a lot of backbone in you, Ann, and you are expressing yourself." "Saying that to your uncle is strange, Charles. What came over you? That's not the way you are, not my Charles." The parents know the real child, that it has a lot of backbone, that the real self can "take one over." As long as the parents, and not the child, are the only ones who can see and define that inner real stuff, the child is deprived of the opportunity of relating to its own self.

The child may act and be treated like a goat who is picked on and ridiculed, but the parents must not allow the child to define a self which is so regarded by others. Being like a goat is permitted. What is *not* permitted is describing oneself as being treated as a goat: "Grandma laughs at me . . . they make fun of my pants . . . Sheila knocks me down and doesn't like me . . . when they play they tell me to go home." There are three entities here: the describer, the others, and the self or person or "me" which is described. For the child to have a self to step away from and describe, for the child to describe relationships between that self and others—that state of affairs is dangerously close to the development and emergence of a person-hood and to the dissolution of the primitive field. The parents' task here is to break up this state of affairs. Ignore what the child says, dispute its accuracy, get mad at the child for taking the position of describer of these relationships between self and others, label every-thing about it as wicked or mad, deflect the child onto something else, respond to other components of what he is saying ("When did you see Grandma? . . . When you talk, look at me; don't turn away and mum-ble . . . It's *She*i-la, not Shei-*la*; can't you talk straight? . . . Can't you see I am busy? Leave me *alone*!"). Never allow the child to define what its interpersonal-self relationships are like.

Do not allow the child to have self-reflexive statements. Instead of the *child* placing itself in a position to make statements about its self, the *parent* must be the one to make such statements. If the child looks at the sore on its finger and says that the sore is getting better, the parent is to say that the sore is getting worse, or that now the danger is from an infection, or that these things are mysterious and only the parent knows about such things. If the child puts on the sweater and says that she looks funny in it, tell her that she looks nice in it, that the parent can tell. Only the parent can make statements about the child. The child's statements about its self are incorrect and silly, and it is only the parent who can make the real statements about the child.

Who is to have mandate over the child's wishes, wants, needs, preferences? If the child begins to identify what these are like, the child is nurturing the development of a self. To combat this, the parent must battle the child for the authority over these inner needs and wants. It must be the parent who decides what the wishes and wants are like, which one is occurring, and whether or not the wish or want is present. It is the parent who decides that the child wants ice cream or prefers to lie this way in bed or that the child dislikes large dogs or loud noises or to be thrown in the air. When the child says that she wants to go outside, the mother must ignore her or tell her that she doesn't like going out when it is almost dark, or get mad at her or tell her that Mommy knows best and she would rather help Mommy with the salad. When the child believes that she could either ride her bike or read her book, the parent will tell her that she prefers reading her book because that is the way she is, or that she doesn't want to go riding in this weather, or that she is a reader and no question about that no matter which she chooses to do. In every instance, it must be the parent who identifies all the characteristics of the child's wishes, wants, needs, and preferences.

Each time the child tries to step aside from itself and have a reaction to itself, the parent must stamp out that effort and instead, have the reaction for the child. Whenever the child seeks to describe its own behavior, the parent must squash that effort and, instead, provide the more authoritative description of what the child's behavior really is like. If the child asks for chocolate milk, and does not receive chocolate milk, he may say, "I said that I wanted chocolate milk." It is now the parent's turn to disqualify the child as an accurate describer of his self, of what he said that he said. The parent can do this by instituting a yawning inconsistency between what he actually said, as defined by the mother, and what he says that he said. Thus the mother tells the child, "You didn't ask for chocolate milk . . . I know what you said, and you asked for milk, just milk . . . I know what you really said, you just *thought* you asked for chocolate milk; you really asked for milk, the usual milk." Point out to the child that there are huge gaps between what the child thinks he said and what the child now says that it said (Laing & Esterson, 1970). In this way, the parent squashes any attempt on the child's part to develop a relationship to a self.

Parents must not allow the child to treat or regard itself as an object. That would be the beginning of a stepping away from its self and a having of a relationship with its self. Whenever the child begins to decide what is good or bad for its self, the parent must squash such efforts. Instead, it must be the parent who carries out such a function: "Open your mouth; this medicine will be good for you . . . wearing shoes without socks is bad for you . . . going to bed now is good for you . . . Holding that so close to your eyes is bad for you . . . Getting a chill is bad for you . . . Sticking your finger into your nose is bad for you . . ." Parents are endless resources of what is good or bad for the child, thereby depriving the child of the opportunity of a relationship with its self. In this maneuver, parents typically omit reasons why something is good or bad for the child; thus the whole process is left mysterious and vague. The major goal is for the parent, not the child, to be the one who decides what is good or bad for the object-child. Thus the parent may say that eating a full meal is good for the child, but the child is never told why, except by way of vague allusions. It is because it makes you healthy, but nothing is fully explained. In this maneuver the predominant aim is for the parent to be the one who decides on what is good or bad for the self of the child.

If, in spite of all these efforts, the child manages to develop a self to which it relates, the parents have a splendid last maneuver. I have been describing ways in which the parents can oppose the dawn of the child's self. Parents fight that self in each of these ways, and carry on the good fight against the possible emergence of an inner self. A final shrewd maneuver for carrying on the fight is to groom the *child* to oppose the development of its own inner self. Instead of the *parent* fighting the child to prevent the development of an inner self, the parent can deputize the child to do the parent's work—and to do its own fighting against the possible emergence of a self. If the *parent* can stop the child from defining what the inner deeper self is like, the parent can get the *child* to make sure that it does not define what the inner deeper self is like. If I can get the child to make sure that he never defines the kind of person he is, then I have managed to get the child to carry out my job. No longer must *I* make sure the child does not carry out these acts; now the *child* makes sure that he does not carry out such acts. I have succeeded in getting the child to oppose the development of its own self. What is more, if I can do this to my child, then maybe my parent did the same thing to me. I am part of a lineage of persons who oppose the development of their own selves. And my lineage is not alone. I suspect that a frighteningly large proportion of persons spend much of their time opposing the development of their own selves. Most of us are effective in insuring that any developed sense of self, any personhood or I-ness, is at a minimum. It is as if parents, without thinking, without being persons themselves, get their children to drug themselves, oppose the development of their own personhoods, put themselves to sleep, hypnotize themselves.

What has come to be termed "bowel and bladder control" or "toilet training" can be the most insidious expression (and model) of parents getting children to kill their own developing selves. The key is whether this accomplishment is one element in a war carried on by the child to oppose its own self, to fight against the possibility of having a self. What typically occurs is that the child takes over the parental mission to oppose and truncate the possibility of an emerging selfhood in himself. The child's controlling its own possibility of defecating and urinating is typically part of a larger mission in which the child benumbs itself, drugs itself, controls itself, keeps itself down. With the successful accomplishment of toilet training, the parent who fights the development of the child's own sense of self can relax. From now on the child may well control the possible emergence of its own self.

Toilet training must occur while the child is fully within the primitive field. Once the child is no longer within the primitive field, or once the parents are not seeking to oppose the development of the child's sense of self, the child's achieving of friendly management of its defecating and urinating has a totally different meaning. It is not toilet training that is bad; what is bad is toilet training to oppose the development of self, carried on in an overall effort to keep the child within the encompassing primitive field. Humanistic theory thus flatly differs from psychoanalysis' celebration of bowel and bladder control as the landmark of the beginning of ego development, as the first grand volitional act of the child (Arieti, 1961). The achievement of control over its own urinating and defecating *may* be an expression of the child's own volition, although I doubt if it is the first. What is more relevant, however, is that the child is now doing to itself what the primitive field has been doing, viz. controlling the child, keeping it asleep, suffocating its chances of developing a self. The achievement of bowel and bladder control may well be a major victory in the primitive field's war to seal off the possibility of selfhood in the child.

By Preventing Escape from the Primitive Field

The fourth mechanism of the parents to keep the child in the primitive field is to make sure that the child never escapes from the primitive field. What is it that accounts for the child being prevented from movement out beyond the primitive field? What stops the child from escaping? From our perspective the causal variables lie within the *parents*, and not the child or the relation between parents and child. Parents stop the child from escaping. They behave in just those ways which prevent the child from escaping. In discussing the behavior of infants (Chapter 14), a contrast was drawn between humanistic theory and ethological theory. According to ethological theory, evolutionary processes have developed sets of behavioral systems in the infant, systems which provide for biologically adaptive proximity to parental care and protection against external dangers (Bowlby, 1958, 1965, 1969). Our thesis, both in regard to the infant and to the child, is that the potentials and relationships of the parents construct the infant-child and endow it with functions. This means that the parent will work actively to maintain the child within the primitive field. There is no intent or conscious dedication to prevent the child from escape. But the net result of the parental construction and function-setting of the child is to keep the child in the primitive field, to use whatever behavioral means are required to keep the child from escaping.

Punishment and threat. The parents can prevent the child from escaping the primitive field by the effective use of punishment. When the parent punishes, especially when the parent punishes any slight hint of escaping from the primitive field, the insidious effect is to weld the child to external (i.e., parental) constraints instead of the child's developing its own internal constraints (Bandura, 1961). Each tightening of external constraints locks the child further into the primitive field and prevents the development of its own sense of self. Furthermore, when punishment is administered properly, the "ownership" role of the parent is strengthened, for it is the parent who decides that punishment is in order (and not the child), and it is the parent who carries out the punishment (and not the child). Increasingly, the primitive field owns the child, and the opportunities for the child to develop its own self are diminished. Whenever the child shows the slightest signs of escape, the parents must be annoyed, dismayed, angered, vindictive, hurt (Laing & Esterson, 1970)—and thereby escape is curtailed.

Punishment is effective when it is coupled with a family rule: no close independent relationships are to be established by the child outside the family. This rule is sometimes formally stated in explicit statements to the child. Often, however, the rule is simply there—obeyed without its being put into words, always implicit. The child ". . . does not have independent relationships outside his family . . . Not only does he lack experience with people, but if he forms an intimate involvement outside the family he is breaking a deeply ingrained family rule against such relationships" (Haley, 1963, p. 108). The entire family upholds such a rule, and each member of the family enforces it by punishing the child whenever the rule is violated. If the child seems to be moving into a close independent relationship with a teacher, an older child, a peer group, or a companion of his own age, the parents become upset, angry, disturbed, vindictive. Punishments are often imposed, usually without the child being told exactly what crime he committed. Thus the child is denied favors, or mother becomes cold, or father finds other things to criticize about the child, or he is alienated by the family.

When the parent is upset by the child's attempts to escape, there is a strengthening of the disintegrative relationship between the child's deeper potential (manifested by the parents) and the experiencing of escape. Any attempt by the child to escape from the primitive field is thereby filled with anxiety, worry, trepidation, tenseness. *Mother's* being upset at child's escaping becomes *child's* being upset at his own escaping. Thus the child may succeed in stepping outside the boundary of the primitive field and into a relationship with a friend, but there will be a cost—feelings of anxiety and unease, upset and disturbance. The net result is that the child, even if he succeeds in escaping, will tend to pull himself back into the domain of the primitive field. Punishment is thus effective when the child becomes his own punitive agent.

In addition to punishment, escape is discouraged by filling the external world with threat, predatory forces, menace and evil. By constructing an outside world of threat, the child is bound ever tightly to the parents who construct such an external world, and away from the bad external world itself. Thus the parent populates the external world with predators ready to pounce upon the child: People are out to use you; they will be nice to you because you have money to spend on them; watch out for the quiet ones, they will do you the most harm; there are bad men who will do bad things to girls like you; never talk with a stranger; don't give anything to anybody; never accept anything from anyone; children sometimes get murdered; gangs of kids will beat you up; stay away from the Catholics; watch out for the black kids; never trust the whiteys; funny things happen at night. Gathered together into a theory, these ideas become residues of evolutionary fears of predators attacking the helpless baby (cf. Bowlby, 1965, 1969). Aside from the *origin* of these fears, their *effect* is to populate the external world with threat, and thereby to weld the child to the primitive field. Thus the child is given behavioral proscriptions of how to act in an external world of threat: Never trust anyone; it's dog-eat-dog out there; the only ones who care are your family; your family is everything you have in the world (cf. Cooper, 1971); we are your real friends; smile nicely to them; be friendly to the other children; don't tell those kids about the family, no one else must ever know; even if you're scared, put up a good front; above all, remember you are our representative out there; make them know what kind of a family you come from; spend as much time with them as you will, just make sure it is superficial (cf. Morgan & Riccuiti, 1969). Escape is prevented by turning the external world into a threatening distant realm. A moat is established between the child and the external world. He will have extreme difficulty trying to break out of the primitive field and into an external world which is so alien and distant and threatening.

Each time the parent defines the external world as threatening, the child is brought closer to the parent, the external world is filled with threat, and the alienating moat between child and external world increases. As parent and child walk along the street, all of this occurs when the parent holds the child just ever so much closer, more protectively, as the big dog approaches, or the bad man, or the two tough boys, or the scary lady. In thousands of ways the parents construct an external world which is bad, unhealthy, dangerous, harmful, threatening, untrustworthy, cold, nasty. The family is loving, loyal, trustworthy, good, providing, protective, nurturant, beloving. The net effect on the child is to prevent escape from the primitive field into the menacing external world.

Escape inside the family. The child must be prevented from escaping into its own personal world or into a subgroup or clique in the family. Some children remain in the family and still find means of escaping the primitive field. One of the most dangerous zones into which the child can squeeze, safely hidden from the primitive field, is its own private thoughts. Here is an oasis, a sanctuary. Once the child retreats into its own thoughts, the parental figures have a difficult time flushing the child out of its hiding place. The best strategy is never to let the child discover that escape route. Never permit the child to have its own thoughts. From the very beginning, make sure that the child shares all of its thoughts with the parents. To share a very personal thought must be saturated with goodness and value; not to do so must be labeled very wicked and sinful. Sharing thoughts must be a distinct family value, and it even helps to make it a religious-moral value to share, to be open, to confess and to give one's thoughts as a gift. In this way, the parents or group leaders prevent escape from the mandate of the (family) group. This mechanism has been refined in studies of group processes, wherein the group leaders weld members to the group by proclaiming a group value of revealing one's misdemeanors, sins, bad thoughts, problems (cf. Pilnick, Elias, & Clapp, 1966).

If the child takes advantage of this inner escape route, she is to be showered with abuse. Laing and Esterson (1970, pp. 127-128) explain how this can be accomplished: ". . . it was not only the fact that Sarah lay in bed that upset them, it was also the fact that she was thinking so much . . . Sarah's 'thinking' worried them all a great deal. Mrs. Danzig knew that 'thinking,' especially a lot of 'thinking,' was liable to make you have peculiar thoughts, because it 'turns the brain.' According to mother, father, and John, Sarah's breakdown was due to lying in bed 'thinking' . . . No matter how her mother shouted at her she would not stop 'thinking,' and to their great alarm, she thought inwardly, not out loud. Mrs. Danzig reproached herself. She should have called in a psychiatrist sooner. They know how to handle such people." Although Laing and Esterson are describing the family of a girl who was hospitalized as a schizophrenic, the same kinds of reactions are employed by parents of children who become the normal, everyday adjusted person. Accordingly, having private thoughts is dangerous even when the retreat is mild, and the child is not on the road to hospitalization. Thus the parents have reason to be upset when the child starts to become a little quiet, or does not quite say all of what it thinks, or seems to be thinking while it is playing alone. These are mild, yet they are signs of a moving away from the primitive field. In much more dramatic behavioral states, what is so disturbing is the successful escape from the primitive field. All Sarah was doing consisted of lying in her bed, thinking. There are children who become mute, or who enter into a serious withdrawal, or who escape into severe depression, or who become "autistic," or who spend virtually all of their time alone. One of the reasons why parents are so very upset by such ways of behaving is that the child has successfully barricaded himself behind these serious states. The children are unreachable, and the parents are upset in part because the child has escaped. Behind their barriers, the children can think, can have private thoughts, be free of the primitive field. These are the dangerous possibilities which must be avoided by never letting the child find and use these escape hatches inside the family.

The child also can escape from the primitive field by entering into an equal stature relationship within the family itself. Picture a family consisting of parents, a child of seven, and her older sister who is nine. The seven-year-old daughter is not to be permitted to form a subgroup or clique or alliance with the nine-year-old sister. If the child is permitted to be a person with her older sister, to have equal stature relationships with the older sister, to be a person with her older sister, she has succeeded in escaping from the primitive field. Such relationships are actively to be discouraged. The family is to include the older sister who is "one of us," while the seven-year-old daughter is an unperson, controlled by the primitive field. She is not to be permitted to participate in the family's inner structure of person relationships. The younger daughter is to be a *possession* of the family, but never granted the status of a *person* in the family structure (Laing & Esterson, 1970, p. 122). Such coalitions are easier to establish in larger families, where the child can escape into equal stature relationships with a sibling, or an adult (e.g. grandfather or aunt) who lives in the family. However, even when the family consists of parents and child, the danger is present. Here is where the child can have person-to-person relationships with the mother alone, or the father alone. Under these conditions, the other parent must wage war against such an alliance. The father must win the mother away from such relationships with the child, must break up such relationships and return the child to the status of a possession, controlled by the primitive field.

The power of contiguous love. Parents can weld the child to them and block any efforts to escape from the primitive field by providing the child with an enveloping integrative relationship. Bathe the child in love, belongingness, warmth, affection, closeness, intimacy, attachment, companionship, oneness. Very often, the parent becomes the child's closest companion. They "do things together." The child plays with the parent. The two are buddies. The parent goes shopping with the child, goes hunting and fishing with the child, goes on little trips with the child. They are close companions. Such loving closeness is itself the most sticky glue, and once welded together in love, the child is unable to be a self who can escape from the primitive field. All of this can be accomplished without any tantrums by the parents, without being a wounded parent or a punitive parent, without invoking "Jewish mother" guilt in the child for its attempts to exit. If the parent is successful in binding the child in love, the child will not be able to get away.

The effective factor includes both the provision of love and the ever-present contiguity, a surrounding of the child in love, an always being with the child in loving contiguity. It is possible to separate the thread of contiguity from that of love (cf. Cairns, 1966), but both together constitute an effective combination which blocks the child from escape. In combination, the child is surrounded by a parent who is loving and caring, nurturant and succorant, the best friend and companion, providing and rewarding. As suggested in the contiguity principle, sheer associative conditioning will strengthen the bonds of attachment so that ten to fourteen years of ever-present parents, always being with the child under nearly all circumstances, will tend to lock the child into the encompassing primitive field. It is this state of being welded together which Mahler and Gosliner (1955) refer to as a state of symbiosis. The net result is a child caught in the web of the primitive field, unable to escape, and without a self which is there to escape or even to know that it is unable to escape. Such a loving contiguity is a potent factor in maintaining the robustness of the primitive field. Touching, bodily softness and comfort of direct physical contact maintain a powerful attachment between child and parent (cf. Harlow, 1958; Harlow & Zimmerman, 1959). In this sense, parental love serves to weld the child into the primitive field, especially when the love is combined with and expressed in touching, bodily softness, and the comfort of direct physical contact. The parent who is this way with the child is, among other things, insuring that the child never can escape from the confines of the encompassing primitive field.

Stretching the outer periphery of the primitive field. Whatever means the child uses to escape, by behaving in the right way the parent can convert that escape effort into a deeper burrowing into the primitive field. It does not matter whether the child physically leaves the family, has her own ideas about herself and the world, spends loads of time by herself, or has a few girlfriends who are her closest confidantes. Each of these, or any other means of escape, can be used to weld her ever more firmly into the primitive field. The method has been described by Haley (1963, pp. 111-112), though his concern was with the treatment of adult schizophrenic patients. Nevertheless, the method is even more appropriate, it would seem, to disqualify the escape attempts of children. The method is simply to stretch out the periphery of the primitive field. *Encourage* the escape behavior, suggest it, condone it, join in on it—and thereby establish control over it. The child is prevented from escaping out of the primitive field by carrying the primitive field right along with the child's very attempts to escape. If mother and father observe their daughter lying in bed, "thinking," then they can take over that behavior by such means as the following: (a) Say to her, "That's nice. Stay in bed and think special thoughts. That's good for you. I'll shut the door so you won't be disturbed." (b) *Before* the daughter goes to her room and thinks private thoughts, but just when daughter is *about* to do that, tell her: "I think it would be nice for you to go to your room now, all by yourself. You can think thoughts all by yourself. They will be your own private thoughts and no one will know about them. Go ahead." (c) Join with the daughter in the withdrawal behavior. Go into her bedroom, lie down with her, and say, "Let's stay here. Let's think private thoughts and keep them to ourselves. You think your private thoughts and I'll think my private thoughts. And we won't tell anyone what they are. So just lie here and be quiet, and think very private thoughts." In these ways, not only are attempts to escape disqualified, they are converted into means of strengthening the control of the primitive field.

Attempts to escape can be thwarted by extending the outer periphery of the primitive field to encompass significant figures with whom the child might have established person-to-person relationships. The aim is to get these other persons to treat the child in the same way the parents do, i.e. as a possession to be controlled by the primitive field, as an unperson, devoid of a self, wholly under the guidance of the primitive field. This can be accomplished by telling others about the child, by getting them to regard him the way the parents regard him. This applies to the child's friends, to the parents of his friends, to neighbors and relatives, and especially to teachers. "Edward is slow; you probably noticed. You have to treat him in a special way, and he will be all right. He is a nice boy. There is nothing bad about him. Maybe you have to watch him once in a while, that is all." It requires very little to extend the outer periphery of the primitive field so that the child cannot escape from it, even when he goes outside the members of the family.

By following this principle, each outside group is merely an extension of the parental primitive field. If the child finally manages to move from the family to an external group, the primitive field must stretch to encompass that group. When the child enters into an outside group, that group must be owned by the parents, approved of by the parents. Consider the institutions of day care centers, nurseries, and especially schools and churches. Without ever knowing, without ever openly acknowledging the role of these institutions, it is as if the primitive fields of the children go right along with them as they move out of the immediate family and into the organized school or church systems. What occurs in these groups is decided by parental figures who collectively extend the domain of the individual primitive fields into these systems. The school system is safe and approved of by those parents who are operating to keep the child safely ensconced within the primitive field. Parental approval of particular extra-familial groups is tantamount to mere extension of the primitive fields. Thus the child is prevented from escaping because each escape group is merely another face of the primitive field.

These extensions of the primitive field also apply to groups in which children are placed, not only for religion and education, but also for recreation and for "help." In the treatment of juvenile delinquents, for example, a child is "helped" with his "juvenile delinquency" by being placed in a "pro-social" group organized and designed to apply enormous group pressures and influences to force the child to conform, to adopt prosocial norms and behaviors (Pilnick, Elias, & Clapp, 1966). Under the guise of treatment and help, what is occurring, from our perspective, is merely the imposition of a powerful primitive field which negates the possibility of escape.

DISSOLUTION OF THE PRIMITIVE FIELD: THEORY

The primitive field can either be preserved or dissolved, encrust itself around the child, or wash away. We have described the ways in which the primitive field is preserved intact, and turn now to a primitive field which is dissolved away. Our concern is with (a) the nature of a child whose primitive field is dissolved away, (b) why dissolving of the field is important for the long-range development of the child, and (c) the pivotal role of the parents in the dissolution of the field.

The Nature of the Child Whose Primitive Field Is Dissolving

What are the indications of a dissolving primitive field? To the extent that the dissolution of the primitive field is a necessary condition for the development of a sense of self or personhood, we are interested in the initial indications of that particular state. Our brief answer, then, is that the nature of the child whose primitive field is dissolving is that of a rudimentary *person*, a person with an I-ness and sense of self. The *initial indicators* of personhood in the child are the following:

Self-reflexiveness. With the dissolution of the primitive field comes a sense of self which can reflect upon or react to itself. The child can respond to its self, there is a self to respond to, and there is a self which can respond. The child can be pleased or displeased with its self, can reflect upon its self, consider itself as a self, regard its self. Behaviors, gestures, words which come forth can be perceived and responded to as if from the perspective of another person (Mead, 1934). Now the child can have a conception of its self as little or big, strong or weak, a girl or a boy, nice or not nice. Before dissolution of the primitive field, the *parents* did all the regarding, all the having of reactions to the child, all the reflecting upon the child; now the *child* can fulfill all those functions. Before the dissolution of the primitive field, the *parents* had reactions to the child as a thing; now the *child* can have reactions to that thing, and in this relating to one's self is the presence of a sense of self, an I-ness, a personhood.

With a self there, the child can now talk to her self. She can have conversations with her self, conversations in which the several parts say what they have to say: "I shouldn't take that flower; it belongs to Ann. Well, so what! She has too many of them anyhow. But I think it is bad to take hers . . ." The child can have private thoughts. Indeed, she can now have her own thoughts, all by her self, for it is as if she is her own dyad. There is a person who can think about and reflect upon itself. She can talk to her self, and her self can talk to her.

This division into her own parts means that the child can have feelings which characterize relationships among potentials. In reflecting upon or to her self, she is now able, for example, to have disintegrative feelings. This is the curse of personhood, for once there is a person there, she can have disintegrative feelings in her relationships with her self. The child whose primitive field is preserved, who has no self-reflexion, does not have disintegrative feelings in regard to her self. She may fear being killed by a car, or be made anxious by a snake approaching her sleeping bag, but these lack the quality of disintegrative feelings. The presence of a self and the possibility of self-reflexiveness set the stage for the occurrence of anxiety, depression, tension, and all the feelings of disintegrative relationships. At this point, the child stands ready to have the anxieties of the adult (Fischer, 1970, pp. 88-89). Such disintegrative feelings stand as one set of indications of the ongoing dissolution of the primitive field and of the emergence of personhood and sense of self which can reflect upon itself.

Independent autonomy. The child who now "has" his own deeper potentials expresses a new sense of independent autonomy. The child himself is the source of activation and initiation. There is a new sense of intactness about the child. Control is within now, and is no longer lodged in the primitive field. The child owns its own sense of internal regulation. Structurally, the deeper potentials are now within the child, and not the encompassing primitive field. Accordingly, the child radiates a new sense of organizing itself "from within." There is a newly emergent self-direction, self-initiation, self-activation, self-control (Buhler & Marschak, 1968; Erikson, 1950; Hendrick, 1943; Moss, 1967; Moss & Robson, 1968). The center of self-ness has shifted into the child, and away from the primitive field which had served as the predominant activator, stimulator, controller. No longer is the child a package of responses to external stimuli or cues.

In the process of dissolving away the primitive field, the child now "owns" the deeper potentials which had formerly resided within the parental figures. The child makes them his, and relates to them in his own way—either integratively or disintegratively. This sense of ownership can occur in the form of some representation of mother and father, for example in the form of dolls. Thus the child can hit the mother doll, spank the father doll, eat the baby doll. The child can take over the role of mother or father, and play school teacher, or be the mommy or the daddy in play situations. The child can wear parents' shoes, play the parental roles, imitate the parents' ways of walking or talking. In the same way, the deeper potentials which had resided within the parents can now be played with by the child. She can now play with her own competitiveness, act it out, or be scolding or praising of it. In this way the child owns these deeper potentials, gains a sense of independent autonomy by having them, makes them her own—rather than their residing within the parental figures only. To the extent that play life and dream life contain expressions of deeper potentials, it is understandable that, in their essential properties, the child's play life and dream life are quite similar (Freud, 1908, 1920, 1926). Both can be arenas wherein the child is owning what had been deeper and alien.

When the child takes over its own potentials, it is as if the child *becomes* that which has been done *to* it. A potential for direction and control may have occurred in the form of the parents being directive and controlling, with the child participating as the passive one who is directed and controlled. As the parents gradually recede out of the child's primitive personality, and as the child becomes independent and autonomous, the *child* now is the potential for direction and control. As a result, the child is an active director and controller. It is now that the child uses his play as a means of reversing roles and being the active one in contrast to those early situations in which he was the passive one. This change has been referred to as a reversal of voice or a gaining of a sense of mastery (Erikson, 1959; Loevinger, 1966). It is a way of making deeper potentials mine by actively being the experiencing which had existed out there in the primitive field. Regardless of the nature of the potential, once the child takes over for himself, he can be the active agent. He can do to others what they did to him. He can actively be what he passively received. All of this is in the service of the sense of independence, autonomy, and the owning of his own deeper potentials.

Effectance. Once the primitive field dissolves away, there is a child with an intentional going into things, a directed exploration of its world, a searching for and an investigating into. There is a selected, persistent directiveness in which the child focuses its attention, directs its awareness. This quality is expressed in a kind of play behavior (comprised of curiosity, exploration, reality-testing, mastery) which is beyond the grasp of psychoanalytic and learning theories (Schachtel, 1964; White, 1959, 1963), and which seems, instead, to be the expression of the child's own emerging sense of self. It is as if there is now a personhood which engages in experience-seeking. The change is that there now is ". . . an eagerness to turn toward an increasing variety of things in the environing reality and that sensory contact with them is enjoyed . . . the pleasure and fulfillment found in the encounter with an expanding reality and in the development, exercise and realization of his growing capacities, skills, and powers" (Schachtel, 1959, p. 9). Here is a person complete with an intent to do things to its world.

The child now has the ability to produce a regular and consistent effect upon and from its environment. As it first surfaces in the infant, this quality has been termed "effectance" (White, 1959), and it is manifested in, for example, the infant's ability to produce a "circular reaction" (Piaget, 1936), and to produce again those effects which the infant finds interesting. Here is the expression of a doing something to the external environment, a kind of reversal of voice (Loevinger, 1966) from the earlier state in which it was the primitive field which produced the effect on and from the physical infant. With this reversal, with this ability to effect the external world, emerges the personhood, the sense of self (Piaget, 1952; White, 1959).

For some children, the sense of self first comes to life in that context in which they are doing something to something. They are carrying out *effectance* behavior. The child "awakes" in the course of doing that. The sense is one of *I* can do this. I *am* doing this. *I* am hitting the ball or pulling the weeds or cutting the paper or biting my finger or spilling the paint. A few seconds before, the child is knocking down the toy soldiers more or less mechanically. Now there is a whole different quality, for the child knows, or senses, that *he* is knocking down the toy soldiers. Suddenly, there is a person here, a sense of I-ness. In these few seconds, the sense of I-ness has broken through. Free play is both a good context for the awakening of I-ness and an expression of its awakening. In free play the child generally is the activator and the initiator. There is a precious quality about a child getting the Jack-in-the-box to pop up suddenly, or making the pile of blocks fall over with a loud noise. In play, the objects are there, letting themselves be done to. The child *can* do things to the objects, i.e. produce effects on and from them. Thus a play situation which the child creates for himself is one indicator of the dawn of the sense of self. When he is in a room by himself, and he plays with something "effectantly," that is an expression of the emergence of the I-ness. When the child is playing, there is frequently a large component of effecting something, producing effects on and from the objects with which he plays. Because of these two components—activation-initiation and the generation of effects—it is quite common for the sense of self to emerge in play situations. Indeed, the exercising of these archaic capacities has been identified as one of the essential cores of play itself (Groos, 1908).

Whether effectance behavior occurs in play or in other contexts, the child can know that doing this results in that. Or at least the child acts as if it knows that its behaviors have consequences. It is as if the child has a kind of expectation that its own behaviors will have consequential effects in the external world (Lewis & Goldberg, 1969). Such expectations, or acting as if on the basis of such expectations, are an expression of the dissolution of the primitive field and the emergence of a sense of self—especially in studying the first glimpses of both the dissolving of the field and the emergence of self.

Together with an *expectation* that this behavior leads to that effect is a *control* of the behavior. Now there is a sense of personhood, in its dawning stages, as the child has the wherewithall to initiate, to modify, and to terminate its own behavior. In the infant, this quality shows itself in, for example, the control of sphincter muscles (Arieti, 1961) and other behaviors which alternate withholding and expelling (Erikson, 1950). Control of one's behavior, dissolution of the primitive field, and the emergence of self are so coupled that *when* the self emerges, the primitive field *is* dissolved, and the child *has* behavioral control. But it is *not* true that control of, for example, the sphincter muscles means necessarily that the primitive field is dissolving (for the primitive field may own the child's muscle-control). Nevertheless, when the self is emerging, and when the primitive field is dissolving, significant changes occur in the physical body. Actual changes occur which are quite open to description in terms of neurology, physiology, anatomy, biology, and which express the child's growing control over its own bodily functions. Yet these changes in the physical body are held as *expressions* of the dissolving of the primitive field, and not as its *causes*. The sense of self is not a result of some process which has stages of development and a bodily locus. Instead, bodily changes are both expressions and consequences of effectance behavior and the dawn of personhood.

Building a world. The child whose personhood is emerging and whose primitive field is dissolving is able to build his own external world. He is able to organize the external world into appropriate situations for the experiencing of his own potentials. If the child has potentials for experiencing being within, being hidden and safely protected, the child can build a house of his own or arrange the pillows into a cave or construct an igloo out of snow. He can act upon the external world to create situations which had not existed before, situations appropriate for the experiencing of potentials. He can build his world. One way the child can build his world is to construct situations appropriate for experiencing (Chapter 6). Another way is to construct a zone into which the child can externalize his own potentials. In doing this, it is common that the child makes a part of the external world his own. He can, in other words, construct a zone of personal space, a place which is his. That space may be a room, the alley behind the garage, a club house, a special piece of furniture, a garden. It may be a large space, such as a field, or a small space such as a drawer. But that space is his. He arranges it his way. It is a part of the external world which he owns, and to which he can do what he wishes. Building such a zone can be an expression of an emerging personhood.

The child builds her world even in her minute grasping of the world, for here is a *person* who sees the world, who looks at it comprehendingly. Seeing now takes on an active quality. *I* see! I carve into the world with my presence. I *do to* the world in my perceiving of it. Here is a sense of self-confidence and trust in one's own grasping of the world. The child now has her own ways of comprehending and perceiving the world. The child trusts what *she* sees; she has a confidence in her own grasp of things. This quality is manifested in a self-confident trust in the continuity and permanence of things. An object is there, it has presence and existence. I, too, am here, have presence and existence. This shows itself most singularly at that point in the infant's development where the infant perhaps has a kind of inner representation of an absent object. Following this point, the object which is out of sight seems to be conceptually retained. Prior to this point, an object which is out of sight is gone out of existence.

The essential quality is that of acting upon the world. With the dissolution of the primitive field, the sense of self emerges into a world which is itself constructed, acted upon, and grasped by the emerging self. "Part of the definition of Dasein or human being is that it is already-in-the-world: Dasein does not emerge as Dasein unless it has already constituted its world" (Needleman, 1967b). To caricature the change: before the emergence of personhood or Dasein, the world of the primitive field does to (acts upon, grasps, builds) the behaving physical child; with the emergence of personhood or Dasein, the *child* is the active builder of its world.

In the building of a world, even in seeing-grasping-perceiving-comprehending a world, the child can bend and mould phenomena to fit in with his own way of perceiving the world. Translated into behavior, the child is able to play in a particular way whereby that stick becomes a spear, the tree is a house. Such bending of reality to fit the child's existing mental schema is what Piaget (1926, 1929) labels assimilation, an indication of a child with its own mental schema which acts upon the external world. Here is another expression of the dissolving away of the primitive field in the building of world.

External reality can be bent about and played with because the dissolving away of the primitive field enables the child to come into closer contact with what is there. The child becomes familiar with doorknobs, cars, streets, siblings, parents, people, dogs, thoughts, ideas. There is a finding out about their nature, what they can and cannot do. With the building of a world *as a person* comes heightened familiarity with the objects, and the consequence is that such an emerged self has heightened flexibility and versatility (Sutton-Smith & Sutton-Smith, 1974) in adapting to and constructing the things which comprise his external world. Personhood makes objects friendly—both thing-objects and people-objects.

With the dawn of personhood, perceived objects have continuity and permanence because there is a self which also has continuity and permanence. With the advent of personhood comes the ability to have memories of oneself as a self. Many persons remember the first occasion when they seemed to "come awake." These are times when the sense of personhood burst forth, when the sense of I-ness first happened. One person may remember the time when he was about three years old, squatting near the back porch, watching ants running around on the ground near the side of the garage. That was when he first saw one ant dragging another around. That sight was mildly puzzling. But what was more singular was the sense of *thinking* about it; the idea that *I* am thinking about it, and *I know* that I am thinking. In this mundane little instant came forth the sense of personhood. Later, even decades later, he remembered that scene in pinpoint detail, the scene in which he seemed to come awake.

These kinds of memories occur only after the emergence of a sense of self. Such memories seldom occur prior to the dawn of personhood, e.g., the time when you were born, or of the earliest weeks and months. To the extent that selfhood seldom occurs prior to control over one's own behavior, as described above, it is understandable that memories are quite rare of times prior to bowel and bladder control (Dollard & Miller, 1950).

As the child builds his world, and as the primitive field dissolves away, chunks of the external world no longer hold their primitive mystique. The external world becomes an external world, no longer activating and initiating, directing and controlling. There is, in other words, a change in the very nature and meaning of the external world, a change in which the external world becomes whatever it is, and no longer the child's primitive field. Earlier, the child is only passive and responsive to the external world. Now there is a person, a sense of self, which can actively place himself in a position of being passive and responsive to the external world. Now there is a person who gets the world to be that way or other ways. In building his own world, the child is free of the activating primitive field. In being free of the activating primitive field, the child can activate the world he builds. What is more, the child moves out of an existence in which everything was activated and brought about by generating forces mysteriously tucked into unseen recesses of the primitive field. In short, the child now exists in a world of causal relationships and means-ends linkages, and he is now in a position to grasp that this leads to that in a world of comprehensible relationships among things.

Pivotal Significance of the Dissolution of the Primitive Field

According to humanistic theory, the preservation or dissolution of the primitive field is the most pivotal change in childhood. As indicated in Figure 16.1, the child who exists within a fixed primitive field may well spend the rest of his life in that field. Only through the dissolution of the primitive field does the child have the opportunity to move onto and through other plateaus. Chapters 11 and 12 discussed what it is like for persons to move into the optimal states of integration and actualization. The child whose primitive field is never dissolved cannot ever become integrated or actualized. He cannot even begin, for he is not even near that plateau of development (see Chapter 16). He remains within the encompassing primitive field. Perhaps the landmark of the child whose primitive field is dissolved away is the presence of a self, a personhood, an I-ness. In other languages, this is referred to as ego development, emergence from embeddedness (Schachtel, 1959), individuation, or the genesis of selfhood. It is the dawn of consciousness and awareness as a person. Once the primitive field is dissolved away, the child can move into this state. Becoming a person is the reason why the dissolution of the primitive field is so very pivotal.

Thus the two processes are interlocked: dissolution of the primitive field and the evolution of personhood. The latter cannot occur without the former. By the same token, the evolution of the personhood means that the primitive field is attenuating. With regard to parents and children, these two interlocking processes mean that as children become their own selves, the importance of the parents recedes. "A sense of themselves as the ones who do things is dawning. You are beginning to be ever so slightly phased out" (Sutton-Smith & Sutton-Smith, 1974, p. 52). It is inevitable that a dramatic change occurs in the meaning, significance, and role of the parents as the child acquires a sense of self. This is the inevitable price paid for the dawn of personhood. But it is a small price indeed. Within humanistic theory, value is placed upon personhood. It is special, precious. Even in its initial emergence, it is miraculous that the infant becomes a person, with a sense of self, who can reflect upon its self, manifest independent autonomy, can engage in effectance behavior, and can build his own world. These are valued qualities because they signify the presence of a self, a personhood, an I-ness, the dissolution of the primitive field. To remain within the primitive field is bad; to be possessed of one's own self is good—from our perspective. Without undergoing this change, a person can never achieve optimal integration or actualization (Figure 16.1).

I believe it is quite possible for a parent to open the way for an infant to achieve a greater degree of personhood than that achieved by the parent. If a woman of 30 has become a person able to open the way for her infant, she is helping the infant in at least two ways. One is that the infant's opportunity comes at one or two years of age instead of 30 years of age. The second is that the woman can acquire methods which will enable her to free the child to an extent beyond that to which she herself is freed. In these two ways, the woman is helping to develop the child into a person who, in these ways, surpasses her. Adults who are or who become ready to learn these methods bring children closer to optimal beings. These children can become better persons than the adults who provided them with the opportunity to become more optimal persons. When parental figures are successful in dissolving an infant's primitive field, they are, in my opinion, participating in the slow evolutionary process toward optimal social change. "What we need is just enough play in our lives to get our unimaginative souls to take those few steps that will make our own children have better answers to society's problems than we have . . . it is encouraging to know that your best answer to the future of civilization might be on the floor—flat on your back, holding up your one-year-old baby, and making faces at each other" (Sutton-Smith & Sutton-Smith, 1964, pp. 8, 9). At least one way of contributing to future social change seems, from the perspective of humanistic theory, to reside in whatever methods dissolve the primitive fields of infants.

It is curious to me that behaviors signifying personhood have yet to be understood by theories of personality. Such behaviors have been intriguingly uninvestigated. Yet there has clung a kind of specialness around such classes of behavior as intentionality, curiosity, exploration, experience-seeking, self-reflexion, building world, and other behaviors which are expressions of a dawning sense of self. The various learning theories, especially those which eschew concepts of self, have denied such behaviors the rights and privileges of legitimate behavior. Theorists outside the learning theories have enjoyed reminding the learning theorists that a proper understanding of such behavior has yet to be provided. It seems to me that, with the glaring exception of the learning theorists themselves, all of the individuals they study are seen as existing within a highly organized primitive field saturated with stimuli and behavior-determining cues. These classes of behavior seem to be beyond the conceptual net of learning theories, for these theories are not prepared to acknowledge persons existing in worlds from which the primitive field is dissolved. According to humanistic theory these classes of behaviors are open to investigation by those who have a sense of self, of personhood, and whose primitive fields have dissolved away. Similarly, such behaviors are far less available to those who still exist in primitive fields. Whether such ways of being are found in the infant or young child, or expressed in their more sophisticated form by optimal adults, they are, from the perspective of humanistic theory, very special ways of being, of high value and desirability—and available only to those whose primitive fields have been dissolved away.

Children who have gained the sense of self behave in singular ways.

Thus the child who exists within a primitive field, who has no sense of self, can act in ways which seem roughly similar, but there is a marked qualitative difference between his behavior and that of the child whose primitive field is indeed dissolved away and who has that sense of self. The child who is still within a primitive field can have *a kind of* autonomy, independence, self-reflexiveness, internal control, and all the other expressions of a developed sense of self. But that child's modes of being are nonetheless qualitatively different. If they are present at all. They are shallow and fragile; they come from a child who is not a person; they lack the presence of an "I" which has consciousness of being an "I."

The Role of Parents in the Dissolution of the Primitive Field

Social interactions in general will not dissolve the field. Interpersonal relations will not do it. In order for the sense of self, of I-ness, to occur, the child must "have" its own potentials. As long as the parental figures own these deeper potentials, the structure of the child's personality is such that no self or I-ness can occur. The child can accumulate a large number of social interactions without ever developing a sense of self (cf. Mead, 1934). If the parents retain ownership of the primitive field, no amount of social interaction will unlock the sense of self. Once, however, the primitive field *is* dissolved away, *then* the child's social interactions can have a determining influence on the nature of the developing self. In other words, a particular kind of social interaction is necessary but, in itself, insufficient. The sense of self occurs in a social process which must include ways in which parents interact with the child in order to dissolve away the primitive field. More explicitly, the sense of self is brought about by interactions in which parental behavior dissolves away the encompassing primitive field. Other social interactions will not result in the development of a sense of self, and therefore, social interactions in general cannot be said to result in the sense of self.

Parental behavior is crucial. In the dissolution of the primitive field, the key figures are the parental figures, and not the child. As with the preservation of the primitive field, the behavior of the parental figures is the crucial determining factor. Parents can behave in ways which preserve or which dissolve the primitive field. Their behavior overshadows any other variables which may be held either to lock in the primitive field or to dissolve it away. There are no social, intrapersonal, or developmental processes which operate either to maintain or dissolve away the primitive field. Regardless where we begin, we always return to the parental figures, and to their behavior.

By parental figures, I mean those persons who are the significant components of the child's primitive field. How much can be accomplished by others? How much can be accomplished by peer groups or by friends, by other adults such as teachers? How much may be accomplished by therapists and counsellors, helping professionals in general? As long as the parental figures are actively working toward the preservation of the primitive field, I am of the opinion that little or nothing can be accomplished by these other persons or groups. Even if these parental figures are not present in the child's life, it is doubtful if anything of significance can be accomplished toward the dissolution of the encompassing primitive field. The parental figures are critical, and the most robust roles of those in the helping professions is through their work with the key parental figures.

In essence, the parental figures must step back, leave go, give the child space in which to move. Parental figures must give up control, power, mandate. They must no longer be the determining potentials, the center of activation and initiation. To accomplish this requires specific kinds of parental behavior. If the parents let go, then the way is clear for the emergence of a self. If parents do not let go, then the self cannot occur. The act of dissolving away the primitive field is more than the passive freeing of shackles. It is an *active* step in the development of the sense of self. I believe the sense of self is actively initiated, the product of active behavior on the part of parents. It is *not*, in my estimation, something which emerges on its own. There is no self there, no seed or anlage, ready to come forth once the right conditions are present.

Thus the key ingredient in the development of self is the parent whose behavior leads to a dissolution of the primitive field. This emphasis upon the parent may be contrasted with a psychoanalytic conception wherein the development of the ego is a function of mechanisms carried out predominantly by the *child*, not the parent. In a psychoanalytic conception, for example, a central mechanism is that of introjection, the incorporating of parental do's and don'ts. By means of incorporation, the child takes into its self components of the external world and makes them his own. In that mechanism, parents play a minor role, whereas in the humanistic conception, parents play by far the crucial major role. Nor is there any place in humanistic theory for biological processes or developmental stages which either dissolve away the primitive field or which culminate in the emergence of the sense of self. Neither of these occurs as the result of gratification of needs, as suggested by Benedek (1956, p. 395): "It takes several weeks of postnatal development until, through the rhythmic repetition of need and its gratification, the infant develops the perception that the source of his need (hunger, pain, discomfort) is *within* and the source of his gratification is *outside* the self: i.e. separation in the psychological sense begins to exist for the infant." From our perspective, there is no such developmental process, nor is there any basis for need gratification to culminate in an ego, in the dissolution of the primitive field, or in the emergence of a sense of self.

As discussed in Chapter 13, there is no place in humanistic theory for concepts of intrinsic or rudimentary processes, especially when coupled with an idea of unfolding development. None of these concepts is held as accounting for the occurrence of a sense of self. Anna Freud (1946), as one example, speaks of the growth and biological development of intrinsic powers of perception within the infant; at a given stage in the development of these powers of perception, the infant is able to distinguish between self and not-self. No such notions are present within humanistic theory. Instead, the presence of a sense of self depends upon quite specific ways of behaving on the part of the parental figures.

Parental readiness. Many parents work effortlessly to weave a tight primitive field around the infant. They work without knowing what they are doing. Under no circumstances would such parents, of their own accord, willingly reverse themselves and act in ways which *dissolve* the primitive field. Skinner wisely saw that persons heavily committed to maintaining control over others virtually never give up control willingly (Rogers & Skinner, 1956). *Parents* are perhaps even more passionate in maintaining control over their children. In the case of parents, their control is even more insidious because the control is so subtle, and their subjects are so unknowing. We cannot ask parents to dissolve the primitive field if these parents have an investment in maintaining its existence. Indeed, anyone who seeks to divest parents of control of their children must expect the stoutest form of resistance and retaliation. It is virtually impossible for parents willingly to act to dissolve the field they have worked so diligently to create and to maintain.

Humanistic theory recognizes explicit reasons why parents resist letting the primitive field dissolve. First, to the extent that the children are constructed as (a) externalizations of parental potentials, parents would be losing a veritable part of their very selves. No parent would likely be able to put this into words, yet the bad feelings around losing the child are those of one's own self being lost, or ripped off, or destroyed. To the extent that the child has been constructed to serve as (b) the appropriate situational context for the parent to experience what it is important for the parent to experience, there is also a serious loss. It takes a very special person to allow this to occur, and especially to promote its occurrence. Second, if the primitive field dissolves, the released child would become what it really is. To the extent that the child has been constructed into being the externalization of the parental potentials, the child would become a most monstrous form—according to the parents. Thus the child would become a monster whose nature is a reflection of the parent's own monster nature. Parents would accurately envision a child who is a terror, because the parental potential is that of a terror. Or, parents fear, the child would become uncivilized, out of control, manipulating, incestuous, sadistic, evil, demonic, an animal—because these are the awful forms in which the parental potentials exist. A variation on this theme is the parental fear that the child would become a precious thing which will be violated by the bad world. Thus parents worry that the world would destroy the child, that the child is not sufficiently prepared to cope with a big, nasty, uncivilized, tough, heartless, destructive external world (that is, the child is not ready to cope with "reality"). Third, parents would resist dissolving the primitive field because the released child might turn back upon the parents. To the extent that parental relationships are disintegrative, the fear is that the child might become an active force in doing to the parents what the parents have done to the child—own the parent, murder the parent, destroy the parent, turn upon the parent in hate and terror, suppression and suffocation. For at least these three reasons, parents are typically not at all ready to dissolve the primitive field.

Parents give up the primitive field *only* when they become persons for whom it is no longer important that the field be maintained. There must be a change in the persons whom they are, a distinctive readiness to dissolve away the field. When such a change occurs, parents are ready to behave in ways which actively dissolve the field. When, on the other hand, parents remain persons for whom the *preservation* of the field is important, the field will be maintained no matter how the parents behave. For example, the parents may *try* to provide the child with plenty of personal space, space to have as his own, space to have his own thoughts, space to do what he wants to do, but none of this will be to any avail. They will remain persons for whom the encompassing field is important, and they will be successful in retaining the field, no matter how much they try to imitate parents who are ready to allow children to be free of their encompassing fields.

Explicitly, then, the focus includes parental figures who have that sense of readiness to work toward dissolving the primitive field and to help illuminate the personhood of the child. With that sense of readiness, parents can learn how and what to do. But without that readiness, little if anything can be accomplished. Parents without such a readiness are to be left alone, not pressured to be different or to act in different ways. On the other hand, parents *with* that sense of readiness can acquire methods of dissolving the primitive field. The question becomes one of defining methods for parents who are ready. How can infants or children be released from the confines of that field? How can infants and children be exposed to the sense of self, of I-ness, of existing as a person? The answers to these questions are our concern in the balance of this chapter.

Dissolution of the Primitive Field: Methods

There are parental figures for whom the primitive field no longer must be maintained, and for whom its dissolution is important. I believe such persons constitute a small proportion of parental figures. Nevertheless, it is these persons to whom this section is addressed. Our question is: What methods can such parental figures use in dissolving away the primitive field (and helping to bring about the occurrence of personhood) in the development of infants and children? I am including three groups of persons under the term *parental figures*. The first group includes those parental figures who maintain the primitive field. These are the key persons, usually consisting of mother and father. But it can include anyone else who keeps the primitive field alive, who is on a more or less daily relationship with the child, a relationship in which the primitive field is kept fresh and viable. This first group of persons may, therefore, include a grandmother or a foster parent, the caretaking older sister or a nanny. The second group of persons includes those who are not the major figures in maintaining the primitive field, but who contribute in a secondary way. For these persons, the child is not a central part of the world which they construct. Nevertheless, these persons are the lieutenants in keeping the child entwined within the primitive field. This second group ordinarily includes siblings, other adults who reside in the home, relatives and friends who interact a great deal with the child. The third group includes persons who are not at all involved in maintaining the child's primitive field. This group includes persons genuinely interested in learning ways in which children can be freed of primitive fields, persons such as nursery school teachers, infant caretakers, expectant parents, professional persons concerned with infants and children, volunteers to agencies for infants and children. I am lumping all of these persons, in all three groups, into the general term *parental figures*.

Being or Becoming Parents Who No Longer Preserve the Primitive Field

Parents can facilitate the dissolution of the primitive field by being or becoming persons for whom the preservation of such a field is no longer necessary, and for whom the dissolution of such a field is a natural and fitting consequence. If parental figures are, from the start, such kinds of persons, then the primitive field will not get locked into place, and the soft field can easily be dissolved. These persons are, from the perspective of humanistic theory, good parents. Any way which facilitates parental figures moving in this direction is good. Any methods which enable parental figures to move in this direction are, in this regard, desirable methods. If psychotherapy of the right kind by the right therapist can help bring about this change, then psychotherapy is valuable, especially during that period when the person is moving toward and into parenthood. That is the period of, say, a year or so prior to conception through the first three or four years of the child's life. One way in which psychotherapy is valuable during that period is the extent that it allows for the dissolving away of the primitive field.

Only particular therapies and therapists result in this change, for the change in the parent must be of a very specific kind. The parent must no longer own the child's deeper potentials (Figure 13.1). Once the parent gives up ownership of the child's deeper potentials, the primitive field is dissolved away, and there is no further need for the various mechanisms whereby the primitive field is preserved. It is as if the parent leaves go of the deeper potentials of the child and thereby faces the child as a person, not as a possessed chattel. Such a goal can never be directly sought. Instead, the parent must become a person who is able to release the child. Becoming this kind of person is a likely consequence of very few therapies and therapists. What is necessary is the kind of psychotherapy which culminates in the freeing of the child, in the releasing of the bonds by which the child is owned by the parents. This means that the child must no longer be constructed into being the parent's exclusively owned external situation, or extended operating or deeper potentials, or constructed exclusively to relate to the parent in the way the parent relates to herself (see Chapter 13).

Parents are able to release the child from the primitive field and are able to regard the child as a person with its own integrity and selfhood to the extent that parents are themselves internally integrated. This means that parents must be or become the kinds of persons, with regard to their own potentials and also with regard to their child, who can relate with integrative openness—being able to provide plenty of space of "letting be," being able to have an I-thou integrative relationship of equal stature, being able to have a kind of integrative contact, being able to be-one-with their children as well as their own potentials (see Chapter 11). Parents must be able to see the child as having a personhood, a sense of self, an I-ness, an intact self, capable of autonomous and independent functioning. self-direction and self-competence. Soft evidence seems to suggest that the parent who *regards* the infant this way may *be with* infants in ways which actually bring about this state (Combs, 1966; Tulkin & Cohler, 1972). If the parent hasn't achieved intactness, the parent cannot enable the child to achieve intactness. But the parent who achieved a modicum of this at age 40 can enable the child to achieve this at age 4, and therein lies the key. Once the parent can perceive the child as capable of having person-to-person relationships of equal, I-thou stature, the stage is set for the dissolving away of the primitive field. To the extent that the parent becomes internally integrated, she can be with the infant-child in ways which dissolve the field and provide for the emergence of personhood.

The right kind of change (whether or not through a rare and special psychotherapy) is that which enables the parents to regard the child as having his own legitimate way of grasping the world. The parent understands that the child sees the world in his own way, and that way is the child's way. It is as if the parent says, "I have my own way of making sense of that, and he has *his* own way of making sense of that. Our ways may or may not differ, but his is just as legitimate as mine. There is an accuracy and a correctness and a realness in each of our ways of grasping our worlds." When parents become more internally integrated, they can come to have an accurate knowledge of the way the child grasps its world. They understand the child's frame of reference, personal perspective, phenomenological view. Parents will know accurately that the child sees mother's sister as a real buddy, even though mother does not see her sister that way, or that the child prefers playing with friends rather than getting to school on time, even though that is not at all the way mother is. Such parents can know, respect, and prize the child's own distinctive way of seeing the world. There is a quality of letting-be, enabling the child to have its phenomenological perspective. When parents can become such persons, they are also freeing the child from its field and behaving in ways which provide for the emergence of the child's selfhood.

When parents become the kinds of persons who can have reactions to themselves, they can allow their children to do the same, to have their own reactions to themselves. The child is enabled to be pleased or displeased with the way it is, to criticize its self, or take genuine pleasure in responding to the way it is. When the child spills the milk or breaks the window or leaves the meat out so that the dog gobbles it up, the parents provide the child with the kind of space in which the child can be disgusted with its self, or be wickedly devilish about its self, or even scold its self. The child can now have a self to react to, and a self which can react to its own behavior.

In each of these ways the parent is, or becomes, a person who dissolves the primitive field, and the net result is the freeing of the infant-child. No longer is there the former kind of ownership in which the infant-child is literally a part of the parent. Whether the infant is one year old, or whether the child is eleven years of age, the process of dissolving away the primitive field is, among other things, sad. It is literally like losing a part of oneself. For a while that child belonged to me. She was a part of me. Now she is no more. I am no longer the primitive field in which she exists. From the very beginning, Helen was mother's closest companion and confidante. Helen did not exist as a person, though she was six years old. She was run by mother, encompassed and owned by mother. When mother was ready to undergo her own personal change, she entered into the kind of psychotherapy which brought to an end her owning of her child, her making the child into the companion and confidante which mother had never had, belying mother's deeply rooted aloneness and separation. No longer needing her daughter in the same way, the encompassing field began dissolution. As the bonds dropped away, as Helen came forth out of the primitive field, little by little, in subtle ways, Helen's mother felt sad. Mother knew that Helen was not, and had not been, the perfect companion. In many ways, Helen had no understanding at all of her mother. Helen preferred to have other friends, and was not really interested in hearing mother's thoughts and feelings. Each tiny increment in the dissolving of the old field had its own entitled bit of sadness as mother became a new person with a new daughter. It was a good sadness, accompanying the dawning personhoods of both Helen and her mother.

The Promotion of Effectance in Infants

One method of dissolving the primitive field includes the parental figures being or becoming persons who no longer require the primitive field. We now turn to a second method, one which involves the promotion of a particular class of behaviors in infants. It is important to note that this method is for all infants, including those who are healthy, normal, happy, fine in every way. It is also for sick, premature, retarded, unhealthy, autistic, problematic infants. It is for all infants whose parents are ready to dissolve away the primitive fields.

Once we are convinced that the key to the unlocking of personhood lies in the relationships between the parents and the infant, the next task is to identify the concrete nature of the mechanisms. Precisely what does a parent do, even if the parent is now the right kind of person, to help bring about the infant's sense of self? Mead (1934) tells us that the answers lie within the social interpersonal relationships between the child and the parent, but there is little said about the precise mechanisms a parent can follow. Escalona (1953) goes a step further, and locates the mechanisms somewhere in mother-infant interactions such as smiling, playing, and talking-babbling to one another. But the specific mechanisms remain unarticulated. Our task is to propose specific mechanisms which can be used by parents to dissolve the primitive field by promoting a particular class of behavior known as effectance behavior.

Specific and concrete mechanisms for the infant are quite different from specific and concrete mechanisms for the child of eight or ten years of age, although the principles might be similar. We will take as our focus the infant of approximately six to eight months of age, and describe the ways in which parental figures can dissolve the primitive field by promoting the effectance behavior of the infant. One of the reasons for focusing upon infancy is that during the second half of the first year the infant commonly begins manifesting all sorts of initiative in doing things to things. During that period most infants acquire loads of skills to enable them to promote effects on and from their immediate environment. This is one reason, among several, for selecting out the period from approximately six to nine months as one of flourishing resources for "effecting" its environment.

The meaning of effectance in infants. In their discussion of the early development of perceptual-cognitive learning processes, Lewis and Goldberg (1969) propose a model in which the infant is understood as gaining an expectancy that its own behavior will exert effects upon the environment. The key ingredient consists of experiences in which the infant's own behavior leads to regular effects upon and from the environment. Whereas Lewis and Goldberg see this as pivotal in their theory of the development of perceptual-cognitive learning, I suggest that such experiences are instrumental also in the generation of the self or personhood which, incidentally, is there to "have" the expectancy. Consistent with this view of the infant, parents can be with very young infants in ways which enable the effects of the infant's own self-initiated behaviors to be contingent upon their own self-initiated behaviors. Soft evidence for this comes from research with institutionalized infants. "Provence and Lipton have described how institutionalized infants, whose contingent experiences must have been minimal, did not play with toys even when they were available. This suggests that before a child can manipulate inanimate objects and gain some feeling of efficacy from the feedback he receives from his manipulations, he may first have to experience something as contingent upon his actions at a time when he is too immature to bring about this effect himself, and must therefore depend on others to give him such feedback or arrange that he receives it" (Ainsworth, 1971, pp. 278-279). The promotion of effectance behavior may well require that the adult work with the very young infant in such special ways.

Of all the behaviors coming from the infant, effectance behaviors possess a quality of intentionality. It is as if the infant intends toward producing the effect. A behavior may produce an effect inadvertently, haphazardly, without intent. The difference is when that same behavior produces the effect with a kind of intentionality, as if the infant seeks to bring about the effect. Now the infant is the source of generation, initiation, activation. Under these conditions, the infant can be described as ". . . motivated towards achieving effects that are contingent upon its own actions" (Bronson, 1971a, p. 270). The right behavior has this quality of "as if" intentionality. When the behavior produces an effect in this way, it has been termed *effectance behavior* (Bronson, 1971a, 1971b; Mahrer, Levinson & Fine, 1976; White, 1959). This refers to a class of behavior in which the infant focuses active attention upon an effectable object, and when the infant's behavior produces an effect upon or from the object, an effect which is contingent upon the infant's own behavior and which is more or less "natural" to the behavior-object interaction and to the characteristics of the object itself. We will use this as a provisional working definition of effectance behavior in infants.

Within this meaning of effectance behavior, the question is how such behavior can be brought about. Although there are programs explicitly dedicated to infants six to nine months of age, there are virtually none especially developed for the promotion of effectance behavior. As difficult as it is to categorize infant programs on the basis of their aims, practically none of them provides an explicit focus on ways in which the parent can directly contribute to the enhancement of effectance behavior. Instead, infant programs are aimed at (a) cognitive and perceptual development (Badger, 1970; Beck, 1975; Gordon & Lally, 1968; Lambie, Bond & Weikart, 1974; Lambie & Weikart, 1970; Painter, 1971; Sparkman & Carmichael, 1973; Tronick & Greenfield, 1973), (b) sensory and motor development (Barsch, 1967, Braga, 1975; Levy, 1974; Prudden, 1964; Rabinowitz, 1973), (c) language development (Engelmann & Engelmann, 1966; John Tracy Clinic, 1968), (d) character development (Williams & Barber, 1971), and (e) a "good" parent-infant relationship (Dodson, 1971; Gilbert, 1972; Gordon, 1967; McDiarmid, Peterson & Sutherland, 1975; Winnicott, 1964). With the exception of a program described by Sutton-Smith and Sutton-Smith (1964), a program of effectance training has yet to be articulated. We have some notion of what effectance behavior is in infants, but little or no explicit guidelines for how to bring it about.

Yet the *importance* of effectance training seems to be increasingly recognized. If we are correct in linking effectance behavior to the dissolution of the primitive field and to the emergence of the infant's self, then some very interesting hypotheses are in order. One hypothesis is that whether the child's eventual effectance behavior is to occur within the realm of human beings or within the realm of objects is a function of the degree to which the parents related to the child in an effectance-promoting manner. This hypothesis has been stated by Bronson: "Whether the effectant behavior is directed towards people or towards objects is one dimension of the distinction I am drawing; whether the orientation of competence becomes structured to include a regard for other people's plans or not is another. I see the behavior of the mother as highly relevant to these differences . . . " (Bronson, 1971a, p. 275). It is as if the individual whose sense of self emerged in the context of human beings (i.e., parental figures) can be a self in the context of others, can come forth as a person with other persons, can engage in effectance behavior in the world of persons. In contrast, the individual whose sense of self emerged in the context of objects, and not other human beings, will not be a self with others, will be less of a person, will engage in effectance behavior more easily in a world of objects, things, ideas, than a world of persons.

The second hypothesis is that the infant whose parents engaged in effectance-promoting behavior will more likely emerge as a self *earlier* than the infant whose parents did not relate in that way. When the parents promote effectance behavior of the infant, our hypothesis is that the primitive field dissolves earlier, the personhood emerges earlier, the child "awakes" earlier. Substantial emergence of the sense of self can, according to our hypothesis, occur during the first years of life. Otherwise, it would seem that the emergence of self occurs much later, if at all (see Chapter 16).

As significant as the early promotion of effectance is, or is described by humanistic theory, parents do not ordinarily relate in effectance-promoting ways. It is the rare parent who either assists the infant in its effectance behavior with objects or who herself assumes the role of the effected object. Indeed, it is much more likely that parents act to suppress the effectance behavior of their infants. Parents tend to cling to the role of the activator and the initiator, and to stay out of the role of the one who is effected by the infant's behavior. This is perhaps one reason why many infants engage in effectance behavior with objects rather than with parental figures. "The promptness and sensitivity of the mother's reaction will of course be an important source of relevant experience, but I am not convinced that the infant's experience with non-maternal contingencies is not of equal importance. Indeed one may argue that it is easier for the infant to realize his effectance in interaction with the simple elements of the inanimate environment than with mother" (Bronson, 1971b, p. 279).

I would like to turn now to some specific ways in which parents can be with infants of 6-9 months in order to promote effectance behavior as a means toward the dissolution of the primitive field and the development of the sense of self.

1. *The right context.* Playing with a baby in an effectance-promoting way should occupy about 30 minutes to no more than an hour of the parent's time each day. It is to be only a part of the 24 hours, a small added component. But it is to be carried out on a regular basis, at least five or six days a week during the period when the infant is 6-9 months of age. Clearly, the parent's own natural way of being with the baby is also to be carried out; effectance play-training should complement the parents' own natural style.

Play-training should be done when both parent and baby are rested, decently alert, moderately composed, free of any special fuss or bother. Parent and child should be alone, as much as possible, with no likely interferences or distractions for half an hour or so. Select a place where both parent and baby can feel comfortable, with plenty of space to move around. Ordinarily, a carpeted floor is best. Make sure that baby will not be playing with anything which would worry the parent, e.g. a razor blade or an expensive heirloom. The wrong place is one which constricts parent's and baby's movements. Do not indicate some boundary, for example, by restricting baby to a blanket spread on the floor. The wrong place is in a crib or walker or a playpen, in a car or bed or swimming pool.

Each session is to end when approximately 30-45 minutes have been accumulated, or when either parent or infant loses interest, or when the parent must take over the role of primary initiator. The parent may regain the role of initiator (and thereby end that session) under such conditions as the following: (a) The infant begins urinating or defecating, and the parent decides that taking care of that is more important than playing. (b) There is a knock at the door or the telephone rings, and the parent is impelled to attend to the door or the telephone. (c) The infant falls and hurts himself, and the parent feels it is important for her to initiate care. It should be comfortable terminating a session and returning later to accumulate the 30-45 minutes of daily play-training. The session may terminate when either parent or baby is no longer interested. Baby may simply fall asleep, or the parent may find that in the last few minutes the enthusiasm has evaporated. Play-training should continue only so long as the interest is maintained; when either participant tires of interest, terminate (Sutton-Smith & Sutton-Smith, 1974).

For play-training, the baby's immediate environment should be "effectable," i.e., composed of things which can be activated, which can respond to the baby's behaviors, which can generate effects when baby gets the whole process moving. An "effectable" environment is different from an environment which offers a lot of stimulation. The major consideration is that the environment should be one which the baby can do things to, mould, produce responses from, architect, alter, modify, get interesting responsive feedback from (Hunt, 1965; Hunt & Uzgiris, 1964; Watson, 1966, 1972; Watson & Ramey, 1969; White, 1972), and, in general highly responsive to the infant's manipulations (Lipsitt, Pederson & DeLucia, 1966; Rovee & Rovee, 1969; Yarrow, Rubenstein, Pedersen & Jankowski, 1972).

As an approximation of the characteristics of effectance-promoting objects (Bronson, 1971a), the following may be cited: (a) They can be touched, grasped, held, squeezed, shaped, mouthed, sucked, and crumpled. (b) As a direct consequence of baby's behavior, they can be moved, pushed, thrown, hit, released, rolled, set in motion. (c) They have parts which can be taken apart, tinkered with, opened and closed, assembled and disassembled; they contain inner or connected parts. (d) They can make noise, light, odor, color. (e) They are three-dimensional. (f) They are interesting to look at, have interesting surfaces, can be studied and explored. (g) They can be started and stopped by baby's own behavior. (h) They are capable of producing an effect which is the *same* as what the infant does *to* them. That is, if the infant picks them up, they are capable of being picked up. If baby tips them, they are capable of being tipped. If baby pulls them, they are capable of being pulled. If baby twists them, they are capable of being twisted. (i) They are capable of producing an effect which is *different* from what the baby does to them. That is, if the baby picks them up, they are capable of making a noise or having one of the parts spin around, as well as being capable of being picked up. If baby tips them, they are not only capable of being tipped, but also capable of changing color or lighting up. These "... illustrate the principle that what babies do with the toy must produce some other effect ... Nesting boxes, which are so popular at this time as a way of putting things into things and taking them out again, can be made more sophisticated by being transparent and permitting babies to see animal pictures when they get them together in a certain way ... In the bing-bonger, for example, when the babies turn the toy upside down, the metal ball bearing inside runs down to one end and produces a tune; when the toy is turned up the other way, the ball bearing runs down to the other end and produces a different tune" (Sutton-Smith & Sutton-Smith, 1974, pp. 56, 57).

2. *Be within interactive distance of baby.* The parent is to be within reaching-touching distance of baby. A good rule is to try to keep the face within about two feet of baby. Obviously this cannot be done if he is inspecting the parent's toes, but in general try to follow this guideline. If baby moves along, try to move along with him, staying within easy reach.

Vary the level of the face, as long as the parent's face is within approximately two feet of baby. Sometimes the face will be at the same level as his, sometimes above and sometimes below.

You are to be there, to be present and available, without crowding. Do not press in or block him from any movement. Be close enough for him to see you and do things to you, but do not constrict him. Always make sure that he has freedom to move about, and to attend to other objects. Provide the infant with space in which to get his own behavior started, to determine for himself what he does. Arrange the kind of immediate environment which invites the infant to move about, to explore, to move out into. The perimeter about the infant can either invite exploration and freedom of movement, or it will constrain against this way of being. "One of the most fundamental things a mother can do to encourage a baby's effectiveness in relation to non-social objects is to set the stage for him to gain appropriate access to such objects. Once locomotion begins to develop, the amount of floor freedom permitted to the baby is a factor of significance in his development of competence. The children who develop great interest in the control of the physical environment seem, more than others, to have substantial opportunity to explore. The mother is important, in other words, because she monitors so much of the baby's experience, and so to a significant extent, sets up his phenomenological world for him" (Ainsworth, 1971, p. 279).

Your aim is to be available near the center of baby's attention. Try to remain near enough to that center of attention to be able to help baby do whatever he is trying to do. Yet make certain that you are not crowding baby or in any way preventing him from moving in any direction or from attending to other objects.

Occasionally he will get into cramped quarters where you are left outside. If he gets into or under something like that, try to get yourself decently close, even though you may not be able to get within two feet of him. Otherwise, stay nearby, waiting.

3. *Let baby initiate its own behavior. Do not block (stop, deflect, distract, initiate, take over, or interfere with) baby's initiating of its own behavior.* It is important to regard your baby as capable of effecting its world. This is an attitude which you may already have. If you do, then it will be easy and natural to follow these guidelines. In some ways at least, you are being invited to perceive the baby as a more or less separated, independent "person," able to initiate his own way of behaving.

Letting baby initiate his own behavior means actually interacting with him as a person who has his own ways of perceiving his world. It is as if you are saying to baby: "I have *my* way of making sense of that, and you have *your* way too." Thus a cat may jump down from a chair, and baby makes sense of that as something frightening, so he cries. To you, on the other hand, the cat jumping down is just a cat being a cat; it is not frightening—to you. You can understand baby's way of making sense of the cat jumping down, even if that way is not your way. It is a short and easy step from understanding baby as having its own way of seeing its world to letting baby initiate his own behavior.

This means that the parental role is that of being more or less passive. Leave baby be. Baby is the leader, the organizer, the one who gets everything started. You are the follower, the one who will fit in with what baby is initiating. It is as if you are saying to baby, "This is your time. I will fit in with what you seem to want to do, but you are the boss, the one who initiates whatever is to go on." During these sessions, it is the baby who is the activator, controller, the determiner, the generator, the stimulator (cf. Lewis & Goldberg, 1969; Katkovsky, Crandall & Good, 1967; Moss, 1967). Your role is to grant baby the freedom to initiate his own behavior (Arieti, 1961; Lambie & Weikart, 1970; Moss, 1967; Moss & Robson, 1968).

Once you let him be the leader, the initiator, the one who gets things started, he will begin accepting that invitation. You are to wait for him to do something. Just be there and be ready for whatever he does. If he looks at your lower lip and leans toward you, reaching out his right hand toward your lower lip, he is *being* the initiator of his own behavior. Allow your baby to get everything started. You can do this by paying attention to his behavior, and by observing that he actually initiates many behaviors, once you let him do so. All by himself, without any prompting from you, he can initiate many additional behaviors—from laughing to pulling a knob, from rocking up and down to grabbing your finger. If you watch closely, he will do many (new) behaviors, largely from his own initiative. "Judging by the amount of time they spend at it, during the second half of the first year infants are very concerned about mastering such forces as banging, inserting (poking) small objects into spaces, twisting or turning knobs, pushing and pulling movable objects, crawling under things (such as tables and chairs), getting into things (such as cupboards under the sink, opening and shutting doors, pulling drawers in and out, getting in and out of cardboard boxes, climbing stairs, squeezing water out of sponges, and dropping objects from heights (Sutton-Smith & Sutton-Smith, 1974, p. 53).

Letting baby be the initiator means that you do not try to distract him from whatever he is doing. Nor do you try to get his attention. Do not try to shove a toy at him or say things like, "Look at this. Would you like to play with this? Here! See this!" Let baby *terminate* his own behavior. It is up to baby to stop doing whatever he is doing. If baby is opening a book and closing it, opening and closing it, on and on, allow baby to continue doing that until he decides to stop. If he rolls a ring about eight feet away, and starts to go after it, allow baby to decide *not* to go after it. If baby is sitting on your lap and playing a game of patty-cake with you, let him be the one to terminate the game. If he places a finger on your lower lip and gently depresses it, he may do it over and over again, or he may stop depressing your lower lip after doing it once. Let him stop doing whatever he is doing. If he plays with a toy and then drops it or leaves it alone, let him do just that. Do not remove the toy. Do not bring it back to his attention. Let him decide to leave the toy alone. Letting baby *initiate* his own behavior includes that important act of *terminating*, inhibiting, or withholding. The opportunity to withhold, inhibit, or not do something has been held to be important in the development of the sense of self (e.g. Arieti, 1961).

Whatever baby is doing, you are to make sure that he *remains* the initiator, the leader, the one who is in charge of his behavior. In doing this, you will not take over baby's behavior for him. If he is reaching out for the duck, do not do it for him; do not take over his "reaching-out-for-it" behavior by grabbing the duck when he is just about to grasp it. There is a very important line between doing it *for* him (taking over his behavior) and *helping-assisting* him in what he is doing.

Subsequent steps describe what the parent is to *do* to facilitate baby's effectance behavior. In order to insure that baby is the initiator of his own behavior, what you *do* is to be done little by little. For example, if baby grasps your finger and pulls, your finger is to be pulled little by little. In this way, baby can remain as the initiator of his own behavior. If he sits on your lap and rocks back and forth, getting you also to rock back and forth, do that as long as he seems to be getting you to rock. In this way, when he is ready to stop or to do something else, he can be the initiator. If, following one of the later steps, you are gently assisting him to climb on top of a chair, and you are doing this by pushing gently on his bottom, do so in little increments. Push upwards just a bit and then stop for a moment. In this way, if he decides not to continue toward the chair, he can stop.

There is occasionally a moment when he will take stock of what just happened, or when he puts it all together, or when he seems to "catch on." For example, if he pulls on the string and the mobile moves, he may pause for some moments as if he is seeing the connection between pulling the string and the movement of the mobile. Do not interfere. Give him space and time to put the two together, to learn.

As much as possible, be loving (praising, rewarding) without stopping baby from initiating his own behavior. If baby is trying to drop the triangular piece in the triangular hole, and succeeds, you may be pleased and happy. Express your pleasure and happiness in ways which do not prevent baby from then doing whatever it seems to want to do. Smile, express how pleased you are, be happy and gratified—but do so in ways which allow him to continue being the initiator, and which do *not* interfere with baby's initiation of his own behavior. The good feelings of the parent must not overwhelm the baby to the point where he is no longer the initiator of his own behavior. "A toddler . . . whose gratification at his own effectance is consistently distorted as he is overwhelmed by rewards focused solely on the particular effect he has achieved is unlikely to come to value effectiveness for its own sake" (Bronson, 1971b, p. 280). The ceiling on approval, reward, praise, reinforcement, and the like is that point at which the baby is no longer the initiator.

There will be moments when mother is filled with a kind of immediate, spontaneous burst of love and affection. Hold baby close, laugh and be silly, nuzzle and kiss him, lift him up and make loving faces at him, touch him in sheer delight. Play-training does not mean the exclusion of spontaneous love and affection. But it does mean the exclusion of love and affection which deprives him of the role of initiator, so it is important to allow him to be the initiator as soon as the love and affection is over. Stay there, be available, let him now do whatever he is ready to do as initiator.

In the ordinary course of being with baby, there will be many times when you must express displeasure or annoyance, or when you must punish him for doing something that you do not want him to do. But during this play-training, you are asked to keep all of this to a minimum. It is best if the play-training is free of punishment, "no-no's," or expressions of annoyance—if this is possible. Try to let him do whatever he is doing. If he puts his finger up his nose, try to let him do that. If he puts his hand on his genitals, try to let him do that. If he slaps the table over and over again, let him do it. Obviously there will be times when he gets on your nerves, or is boring you to an extreme, or does things you do not like, or even doing something which may be dangerous or harmful to him. When this happens you must of course be the way you must be. But in general, try to let him do whatever he finds important to do.

4. *Identify baby's focused center of attention.* Try to identify what it is which is the center of his attention. Is he focusing attention upon his foot or upon the television knob, upon your nose or upon the mobile? Very often, but not always, his attention is focused on *something*. Try to know what that something is.

Babies produce all manner of noises and sounds. Be especially attentive to sounds which seem to be directed toward you. In his own way, he is talking, and the object of his conversation may be you. The difference is in part whether or not he seems to be aware of you as he talks, whether he looks at you when he makes his sounds.

The presence of a focused center of attention is taken as an expression of something which is difficult to assess, viz. baby's *intention*. We cannot be sure when baby is intending to do something. Many of his behaviors are carried out more or less mechanically, without intention. But we can make good guesses that he is intending (or wanting to do something, or seeking to do something) when there are signs of a focused center of attention. There is a big difference between spreading his arms in a more or less mechanical, inadvertent, or haphazard way, with a vacant look on his face and, on the other hand, spreading his arms with an actively centered focused attention on mother. When he spreads his arms in this latter way, he may be looking directly at mother, jiggling his body up and down. The signs of an actively focused center of attention suggest that he is intending something. Your task is to be continuously aware of baby's active center of focused attention. Almost without exception, babies at this age manifest this by a way of looking at something, a looking that is accomplished with behavioral signs of attending in a centered, focused way—which we take as intending, seeking, wanting.

5. *Identify the intended effect of baby's behavior (what baby is trying to do).* To make good guesses about what he is trying to accomplish, you must see him as *having the capacity* to achieve intended effects. This means that he is seen by you as having the capacity to want to repeat that interesting noise, to get your mouth to open, to have the ball fall into the plastic milk bottle. In order to identify the intended effect of a behavior, ask yourself questions such as the following: "What is he trying to do right now? What is the immediate effect he is trying to achieve? What is he seeking to accomplish?"

Not all behaviors seem to have such an intended effect. Many behaviors seem random or haphazard or inadvertant. This includes many verbal behaviors—sounds and noises which appear to be nothing more than sounds and noises, not directed toward achieving anything at all. However, some sounds are genuine verbal communication—talk. He may be looking at you and making sounds which you can easily understand as having meaning. He looks at you and makes a sound *as if* he is saying that he is happy or he is scared or do that again or something hurts. Listen to these sounds as if he were actually talking to you, in his way. Obviously you already know the meaning of many of his sounds. Making good guesses about what he is trying to do means knowing him quite well. The more you are familiar with him, the better guesses you will make. This is why applying these guidelines requires individual tailoring to each baby, so that knowing your baby well enables you to be the best one to play-train baby in this way.

Sometimes you will know clearly what he is trying to do. Your guesses will be good guesses because you know him so very well. At times, however, you must wait a bit before you can be sure. When his finger is against your lower lip, is he intending to poke into it? Is he intending to push your lower lip down? Is he trying to move your head back? Is he interested in seeing the inside of your mouth? These are moments when you might wait a bit to see more clearly what he is trying to accomplish.

Your job is to try to know what the *immediate* effect is that he is trying to accomplish. Stay with what he seems to be trying to do right now. Do not anticipate way ahead or try to figure out the long-range goal he is trying to achieve. If he drops the ball, wait a bit and try to be sure whether he wants to get the ball, wants you to go and get it for him, or wishes to turn to something else. Do not go and get the ball for him unless you are really quite certain that he does indeed want you to do that.

Allow baby the right to "expect" the kinds of behavioral effects *from you* that he himself carries out. For example, he does a lot of putting things into his mouth and sucking them. What do you think the intended effect would be if he put his finger on your lip? You might think of his intending to get the feel of your lip, or trying to open your mouth, or getting you to stick out your tongue. Would you think that he is intending for *you* to suck *his* finger? It often comes as somewhat of a surprise that parents can also do what babies do. Babies make it quite normal to do a lot of sucking. You too may include sucking—and many other things that babies do among the likely intended effects of his behavior. At times you may be quite right in guessing that the effect he is "intending" to achieve is one that he himself frequently carries out.

6. *Do what must be done to facilitate the occurrence of the intended effect of baby's behavior.* Your major task is to help bring about the effect to which baby's behavior is directed. Having made a best guess about the nature of the intended effect, you are now to accommodate in that sensitively responsive way which will carry forward the baby's behavior toward its effect (Ainsworth, Bell & Stayton, 1972; Ainsworth & Wittig, 1969; Bettelheim, 1967; Bowlby, 1969; Lambie & Weikart, 1970; Rheingold, 1961; Walters & Park, 1965; Yarrow & Pedersen, 1972). One of the most precious characteristics of parental figures is the ability to make good guesses about what the intended effect is or could be, and to make sure that the effect occurs.

Your role is to help bring about the effect *he* is trying to accomplish. If he is trying to move the hands of a toy clock, you are to help him do that—even if he is moving the hands in a counter-clockwise direction. In this play-training you are helper, not a teacher who tries to teach him to do things your way. Help him to achieve *his* effect, not yours or whatever you believe he will have to learn in the future. Do not "correct" what he is trying to do.

Once you know the effect he is trying to bring about, you can help bring about that effect by doing things to the environment. By keeping in mind what he is trying to bring about and the properties of the object, the effect will be a "natural" one. When he pushes the rubber ball toward you, your best guess may be that he is trying to roll it along, and the natural properties of the ball include that of rolling. These effects are more "natural" than arbitrary consequences which you devise, such as opening the window or feeding him or making a loud noise when he rolls the ball. Natural effects are found in the infant's normal free play (Groos, 1908) or in the normal mutual visual regard when infant and mother look at each other's eyes (Robson, Pederson & Moss, 1969). In this sense, the effect you are facilitating is a more or less natural one.

Your aim is to link up the effect with baby's behavior. The effect is to be so closely coupled with his behavior that they are practically welded together in immediate contiguity (Ainsworth, Bell & Stayton, 1972; Ainsworth & Wittig, 1969; Bettelheim, 1967; Bowlby, 1969; Gewirtz, 1969; Lambie & Weikart, 1970; Lewis & Goldberg, 1970; Rheingold, 1961; Walters & Park, 1965; Yarrow & Pedersen, 1972). If he is trying to move the hands of the clock, it is better for you to make sure that the hands move when he is pushing or pulling on them rather than ten seconds later. By coupling the behavior and the effect with one another, his behavior almost seems to include the effect "at the other end." It is as if he becomes more skilled at bringing about the effect through that behavior.

As he becomes skilled at achieving the effects, you can help him to put more and more of himself into the behavior so that he is doing it with increasingly greater activity of his own. He will be doing it with more confidence. He may lean backward and, in following the guidelines, you will support him so that he goes back safely. As he does this again and again, he can gain increasing confidence so that he lets himself fall back easily and confidently, perhaps with somewhat greater activity—after making sure you are there to catch him.

When you facilitate the occurrence of the effect, one consequence is that baby is increasing the repertoire of his behaviors. He is engaging in new behaviors. Now he can move the hands of the clock where before he may never have accomplished that. Each new coupling of an effect with a behavior adds a new behavior. Thus the range of new ways of behaving is increased. Even when the behavior inadvertently results in the right effect, when baby does the behavior-effect sequence over and over again, it soon becomes "his," and constitutes a new behavior.

If you follow the guidelines, you will be enabling him to carry out many behaviors with greater precision, with smoother activity, and with increasing effectance. If you help him in just the right ways, he will put the rings onto the peg easier, more quickly, and with heightened smoothness and confidence.

6a. *Modify the physical conditions to facilitate the occurrence of the intended effect.* If baby is attending to some physical object and is trying to achieve an intended effect, your aim is to help that intended effect come about. Do this by modifying something in the environment in just that way to insure that the effect comes about.

He may be trying to drop the triangular piece down through the triangular hole after having successfully dropped the square piece down through the square hole. He moves the triangular piece *almost* in the right way, just about right—then misses and tries again. You can move the box containing the holes, ever so slightly, but in the right way which enables the triangular piece to fall through. You have modified the object just a bit, and that enabled the effect to occur. You are not to hurry the success, nor to arrange things so that success happens too easily, but the little bit of help helps to facilitate the occurrence of the effect.

He is standing up and holding onto the chair. Now he is trying to *push* the chair. You can assist him by very gently moving the chair in the direction of the push. Do it very slightly, just a bit.

Physically assisting baby in his efforts to do something can take the form of your providing physical support. He may be trying to stand up, and your gentle assist consists of supporting him underneath his arms, around his chest and back, while he tries to stand up. Or he may hold your fingers while he begins to stiffen his legs to stand up. Your job is to provide support. Offer some firmness in letting him grasp your fingers while he tries to straighten his legs into a kind of standing position. If he stands up this way, with your help, he may try little steps or he may bounce up and down (Sutton-Smith & Sutton-Smith, 1974, p. 33). In all of this, your job is to provide the proper support.

There are times when baby is able to carry out a particular effectant behavior in a very smooth way. He knows the behavior well, and carries it out easily. For example, he drops the toy monkey always within reach, reaches down and picks it up, drops it again within reach, and repeats the process a few times. You can "play" with the reaching-out behavior by moving the toy monkey away from baby *just a bit*—not very much, just enough to invite him to make a slightly greater reach. The general idea is to invite baby to work just a bit more to gain the effect. Carrying out this kind of play-training is very sensitive because your aim is to promote the effectant behavior, and not to tantalize or get him to expend huge efforts. Once again, the key is whether you can arrange for him to be successful—he must reach the toy monkey when he stretches forward. If baby could talk, he would say, "That was fun—to reach out for it," or "I like reaching out just a bit further, and getting it."

Being this way with baby seems to work especially well when his effectant behavior seems nearly too easy for him. He may, for example, pull the string and attend to the little car which is pulled forward when the string is pulled. After a while, the car moving forward when the string is pulled is almost too easy. The pulling-on-the-string can be heightened, and the effect of the little car moving can also be heightened, when you make him work just a bit more to get the car to move. Hold the car *slightly* in just that way which invites baby to yank *a bit* harder. Then let go of the car so that it is moved with slightly more of a yank. It is important that baby "gets the idea," i.e. that he continues pulling and is successful in pulling the car forward. This must be done rather subtly and smoothly. The idea is to help him pull the string *just a slight bit* harder—not much harder.

You allow baby to repeat that interesting effect when you return things to their original position. Suppose you have your head above his and he reaches up, grabs your hair, and pulls down your head. At that point, you might return things to their original position by again putting your head back above his. If he wishes, he can once again repeat the interesting effect by doing it all over again—that is, reaching up and pulling on your hair again. If baby knocks over the long cylinder, you can recreate the original conditions by putting the cylinder back up in the same position so that baby can knock it over again—if he wishes.

6b. *Modify your body to facilitate the occurrence of the intended effect on you*. When baby's behavior is directed onto you, you are to *receive* that behavior in a way which helps bring about the intended effect. Let yourself be "plastic" to whatever baby is trying to do to you. It is as if you are a very special life-sized toy to which baby can do all sorts of things. Baby can act upon you, move you, explore you, push you, grasp you, rock you, feel you, poke you, rub you. The range of person-effects can be much greater than the range of effects with any other thing. By letting yourself accommodate to whatever baby seems to be trying to do to you or with you, you will find yourself doing much that may well be new. Some of what you will do will be new and exciting or fun, and some may be new and just a bit questionable.

Try to "go with" the physical movement. (This idea of "going with" the movement of the baby is one of the core ideas in natural childbirth. When the fetus moves during labor, the mother is to relax the muscles so as to "go with" the movement of the fetus. The same holds in effectance play-training.) If he grasps your finger and pulls you toward him, let your whole body be moved toward him. If he pulls on your hair, let your head and whole upper body move in the direction that he is pulling. If he is holding your finger and then, suddenly, flings your finger outward, "go with" that motion by letting your hand and arm and perhaps even your whole body move in that direction. It is as if his motion flung you to the side. If he pushes on your chest, then "go with" that motion and let the effect happen by letting your body move backward, in the direction of the push. If he grasps your finger and moves it toward his mouth, let your whole body be drawn forward—and let your finger be inserted into his mouth. If he pulls your finger out of his mouth, let your finger be pulled out.

If he throws a toy at you with some force, even mild force, then let that force "do" its effect onto you. Move slightly backward with the force, in the direction of the force. Let your body alter to facilitate the occurrence of the effect. If he hands a toy to you, let yourself receive the toy. Put yourself in a posture to receive the toy—for example, by cupping your hands together, or by reaching out your hand so that he can hand it to you. If he holds the plastic duck and seeks to put it into your mouth, you can move your mouth ever so slightly so that his motion is successful in inserting the duck into your mouth. You are adjusting and modifying your body slightly so as to let baby be successful in doing it to you.

Sometimes, you need simply make your body available. He may find it fascinating to explore your hair or your hand or your ear. Under these conditions, simply make that available for him to examine or do things to. He may find it very interesting to push his lips against your neck or your cheek. He may breathe against your neck and find delight in the way it feels or the way it sounds or the way one nostril closes when he pushes against your neck. Many of the effects consist of what he himself already can do. For example, he usually knows what it is like to explore his own fingers, to study them carefully. Thus he may seek to explore *your* fingers for some time. Let your fingers be explored. He knows what it is like to mouth things. When he puts his fingers into your mouth, you can suck his fingers just the way he sucks things. You are promoting the kinds of effects with which he is already familiar. He knows what it is like to do something again and again. If he puts his fingers in your mouth to be sucked, pulls his fingers out, inserts them again, then you are to suck them again. He knows what it is like to do something again and again, so, in promoting the occurrence of effects, let them occur again and again.

In moving your body, it is important that you accommodate just slightly—and not too much. As described in guideline 3, you are not to take over baby's behavior and do it *for* him.

Let the full effect occur. If baby pulls on your finger, let the effect

include your whole body, not just the finger. The pull may be sufficient so that if you let your body be light and connected, your finger
will move, and so will your arm, shoulder, upper body, and maybe
even your whole body. In letting the full effect occur, in being easily
activated by baby, you are doing a bit of exaggeration. Sometimes you
are doing a *lot* of exaggerating—but always in the direction of high-
lighting the effect baby's behavior has on you. Feel free to exaggerate,
as long as you are decently comfortable doing so. If he pulls forward
on your finger, you may lurch forward as if he really gave your finger
quite a yank. Letting him be the one who leads and who is the initiator means that you can, nevertheless, let the full (even an exagger-
ated) effect occur. The same is true of your facial expressions, so that
you may exaggerate pleasure, annoyance, or surprise as long as doing
so seems comfortable to you, and as long as your reactions are in the
direction of the effect his behavior is intended to achieve.

When you exaggerate the effect, you frequently add elements of
quickness and suddenness. Baby may quickly see all this with some
surprise and even startle, with happiness and amusement. He pushes
you backwards and you go suddenly backwards and fall plop on your
back with your arms and legs up in the air. Baby is at first startled,
and then amused and pleased. You are adding a new element to the
intended effect (mere pushing you backward), and you must make
sure that all of this is carried out in such a way that baby is preserved
as the initiator.

6c. *Be the responsive partner in baby's interactive game with you.* Some of
baby's behaviors are games that he plays with you. In these behaviors,
he invites you to be his partner in playing a particular game with
which you both are already familiar. He "knows" the game, and you
are invited to respond to him appropriately. For example, he may
lean toward you and open up his outstretched arms, inviting you to
put your arms around him and enfold him. Do that. Hold him, cuddle him. He may learn that doing something to you gets you to make
a certain noise or sound. Handing the ball to you may get you to
make a particular sound (e.g. "Thank you!"). He may then hand the
ball to you and look at your face as if waiting for that sound. In this
way, baby has found a great toy, you, one that can make all sorts of
sounds when he does certain things to you. Squeezing your nose may
make you say, "Honk!" and so he will do it again and again to get that
great sound from you.

Some games consist of doing to him what he does to you. He may
roll the ball to you in such a way that he is inviting you to roll the ball
back to him. For example, he may make a sound (as if asking you to
roll it back), look at the ball and look at you (as if asking you to roll it
back), and move his body up and down (as if asking you to get started

rolling it back). Under these conditions, play the game by rolling the ball back to him.

He is sitting on your knees and you are sitting on the floor with him. Suddenly he begins rocking up and down, and that rocking motion gets you to rock too. If you rock your body (in "answer"), for example by lifting up your heels two or three times, then another back-and-forth game can be started. In this game, he rocks you a few times, and you rock him a few times, back and forth, back and forth. You may help the effect to occur by taking a moderately active role. Suppose that he hands you the toy and then reaches out to grab it back. It seems that the effect is give and take and give and take. If you get into the rhythm of this, you and he are moving the toy back and forth—with his giving almost being your taking, and your giving almost being his taking.

By this age, most babies already know a few games. Some of these are the standard games such as patty-cake. If this is a game that he already knows, then you are to play the game with him when he claps his hands together (and thereby initiates the game), and focuses his attention on you as if he is inviting you to play. This is the kind of game in which you do what baby does.

Many games involve mocking, echoing, imitating. You do what baby does—provided that he focuses his attention upon you in such a way that he seems to be inviting you to do just that. If he opens his mouth in this way, then you open your mouth too. If he hits his mouth with his hand, then you hit your mouth with your hand. If he makes a sound, you make the same sound. But you are to imitate what he does only if he focuses attention on you in that special way that signals some intention on his part that you are to do the same thing. You can also do what baby does (mock him, echo him, imitate him) when he does something to an *object*. If he hits the low coffee table—and focuses his attention on you in such a way that indicates an intention for you to do the same—then you also should hit the coffee table.

At this age many parents have already begun to have conversations with baby. He says something (remember he is the initiator), and you "answer" him. This means that you must have some reasonable idea about what he is saying, and the more you know your baby the more you will be able to make sense of the various sounds he makes. Your job is to answer what he says. You can answer him in your language or in his. If he makes a sound that seems to say that he likes what just happened, you can answer him in your language by saying something like, "Well good, I'm glad you liked that. Do you want me to do that again?" Or you may answer in *his* vocabulary, using the kinds of sounds that he makes. It may seem peculiar, but you do know the various "words" in his own language, and it is possible to talk with him using his own vocabulary. When you use his words, make sure that you fill the words with the appropriate feelings and tones.

Often he will "speak" to you without looking directly at you. Usually this happens when he is busy doing something else. He may be trying to climb up on the chair, and the sound he makes may mean, "Oh, I can't do it!" You can converse with him by answering him (e.g., "All right. Here, I will help you a bit.") as you gently put your hand on his bottom and help him to climb on top of the chair. As he reaches out for the toy duck, he may make a sound as if he is saying, "I can't get it. It is too far away." His center of attention is on the toy, not you, but he nevertheless may be talking to you. You may answer him (e.g., "I'll bring it just a little closer for you.") as you bring the toy duck a little closer within his reach.

In the course of play-training, many babies discover that something quite interesting just happened, and they indicate that they would like that to occur again. Their behavior asks you to do it again, to repeat that interesting effect that just happened. He may suddenly discover that a push on your chest and over you go! By means of his laughter and gurgles and happy body movements, he is inviting you to do that again. He may be asking you to repeat that interesting effect by a big smile and a jiggling up and down (Sutton-Smith & Sutton-Smith, 1964, p. 32). Come back up, place yourself near to him, and if he pushes you again, you are repeating that interesting effect. If he grabs you by the windpipe and you squawk, that may be a most interesting effect which he wants you to repeat. Soon a game is established in which he touches your throat and you are squawking.

Methods of Dissolving the Primitive Field in the Child

We have been discussing ways in which parental figures can dissolve the primitive field and promote the development of personhood, I-ness, or sense of self in the (6-9 month) *infant*. One way is for the parental figure to undergo the kinds of personality changes which result in the parent's becoming a person who no longer maintains an encompassing primitive field. A second way is for the parental figure to learn specific techniques of promoting effectance behavior in the infant. We now turn to ways in which parental figures can dissolve the primitive field, and promote the development of self, in the young *child*.

As with the infant, these methods are successful to the extent that they are employed by a parental figure who is *ready* to dissolve the primitive field. The parent who is geared toward preserving a primitive field cannot employ these methods successfully; they will be abortive, mechanical, and ineffective. Thus it is critical that the parental figure be a particular kind of person—one who is free of his own primitive field, one who is enough of an integrated person that he can allow the child to move in the direction of personhood.

Self-reflection. The primitive field is dissolved when the child is enabled to reflect upon itself. The child is helped to have his own reactions to everything which expresses his own being—behaviors, gestures, language, anything (Mead, 1934). For example, the parent enables the child to step slightly to the side and to have a reaction to what she has just done. When the child sketches on a piece of paper, the parent's aim is to enable the child to have a reaction to that sketch:

> *Parent*: You're grinning, Jill. Do you like the horse?
> *Jill*: I think she's beautiful! When I was drawing her I could almost see her. I like the drawing, but the one I really saw . . . she was the prettiest horse I ever saw.

When the child sneezes, the parent can enable the child to have a reaction to that sneeze:

> *Parent*: (laughing) That's the silliest, sneeziest sneeze I ever heard. I thought your nose was going to blow off! You too? What did you think?
> *Child*: (laughing too) The sneeze just snuck up on me. It scared me. All sudden. (laughing) It was a crazy sneeze, a super nutty sneeze (gales of laughter).

In the same way, the child is helped to have reactions to his own facial expressions (Oh, that was a goofy look), things he says (Those were very big words), parts of his body (I think one foot is bigger than the other). The tone can be serious or jolly, contemplative or flat. What is important is that the child is enabled to have reactions to himself.

The parent can help the child self-reflect by having responses to her own behavior ("I can't think of the word; I must be losing my mind." "I think I look nice in this blouse."). Although the parent can offer the child her reactions to the child's behavior ("That egg you made looks just right." "You can really whistle well." "You are one lousy handwasher."), it is more important that the parent invites the child to express her own reactions to her own behavior ("What do you think about the painting job you did? OK, or not so OK?" "What do you think about the egg; look all right to you?" "Are you a good handwasher or a lousy one? What do you say?").

Inviting the child to have reactions to himself is an effective avenue toward the dissolution of the primitive field. The next question, however, is whether the parent is helping to establish integrative or disintegrative relationships among the differentiated parts. The kind of person the parent is, and the way in which the parent interacts with the child, determine whether the child's self-reflexion is characterized by good feelings of peacefulness and oneness or bad feelings of misalignment and tension. Here are some simple examples of the young child beginning to exhibit a self-reflection:

> "I didn't knock over the glass. My hand did it."
> "My legs know how to run real fast."
> "I have a (imaginary) friend. His name is Tuffy."

The parent can confirm the existence of that other part, and at the same time, provide for an *integrative* relationship between the child and that other part of himself:

> *Child*: My legs know how to run real fast.
> *Parent*: You really like your legs, don't you?
> *Parent*: Did you teach them how to run so fast?
> *Parent*: Great! Let me see them run fast.

Both child and parent have good feelings here, and these good feelings occur between the child and that part of himself (the legs) to which he is relating. By confirming and acknowledging both the other part to which the child relates and the integrative nature of the relationship, the parent is enabling (a) the dissolution of the primitive field, and (b) the emergence of a self (c) which relates integratively. For the parent who is integrated, these three consequences can occur even in situations when parent and child feel momentarily tense and angered:

> *Child*: I didn't knock over the glass. My hand did it.
> *Parent*: Then tell your damned hand to clean up the milk!
> *Parent*: (glaring at the child's hand) Why the hell did you knock it over? All over the table! Now what are you going to do? (turning to the tense child) He won't answer! Tell him to answer me!

Once the parent accepts the child as having parts to which he can self-reflect, it becomes almost playfully natural to respond to the child that way. In the above example, the mother was annoyed, yet she was able to distribute the annoyance over a relationship between a differentiated child and the villainous hand. To scream *at the child* would have the effect of collapsing the parts into a single undifferentiated child, and *that* would prevent the dissolution of the primitive field. We turn to the third example, one in which the parent is not angry, but rather one in which she felt she was given a gift of a valued secret:

> *Child*: I have a (imaginary) friend. His name is Tuffy.
> *Parent*: Honey, thank you for mentioning your friend. He sounds very special.

Parent: I had a friend too when I was a little girl. My friend was named Ann . . . Do you think Tuffy knows Ann?
Parent: I'd like to meet Tuffy, especially if he is your friend. Does he have brown hair like you do?

Internal focusing on deeper potentials and feelings. Children can be helped to focus on what is within, on deeper potentials and feelings. They can learn how to attend to the sensings, messages, images and ideas which come from within. In this posture the very act helps to bring into existence a person, a consciousness, a self-awareness, an I-ness who is here to know another part which is sending these messages. Specific training methods such as Gendlin's focusing technique (1969) can be taught to children from as early as five or six years of age.

The aim is to help the child listen to what is coming to him from within. Too many of us mistake efforts of the child to do just this as evidence of his craziness or illness or deviateness (Laing & Esterson, 1970). A child can make uncertain, fumbling, mistaken attempts to put into words inner rumblings, and instead of assisting the child to do just that, we swarm all over the child. We buy the child a dress and ask the child to try it on. Now comes the critical moment. The child indicates that she likes it, but now she is visited by inner messages from a deeper potential that has reservations about how the dress looks. Looking at herself in the mirror, she does not know how to listen to the inner sensings, and does not know how to put them into words. She has no vocabulary for what is going on. At this point, the parent can help. The parent can assist the child in finding the vocabulary to acknowledge what is coming to her from within. What are the inner feelings? What is "it" saying? Try to put all that into words. To do all this in a way which permits the existence of a child who can receive what is happening within is to engage in active promotion of selfhood.

Another way of accomplishing this is through the use of dreams. Humanistic theory, in concert with many other theories, accepts a view of dreams as expressive of deeper potentials (or deeper personality processes in general). Translating this view into a method for the child to dissolve the primitive field means that the parent can make it a regular practice to listen to the child's dreams. As in the Senoi culture, it can be a regular practice for the child to report his dreams to the family, and for the family to have ways of discussing and "working" with these dreams (Greenleaf, 1973). Indeed, it is quite possible for the family as a whole to report dreams to one another. To the extent that dreams can be taken as expressions of deeper potentials, the child's relationship with his own deeper potentials can be made friendly when the tone and atmosphere of the interchange is itself friendly. A dream of aggression, even when the aggression involves another family member, can be related cordially in this context. Not only does the child have an opportunity to stand aside and relate to what is within, but he has an opportunity to join with others in their discussion of his aggressive dream, and to be a person in sharing his own reactions to that aggressive dream. Talking about the dream enables the child to take the posture of relating to that which is deeper in him.

There are other advantages and opportunities. Interested, friendly dream-sharing enables the child to be on a kind of equal footing with others in the family. Everyone has a chance to express what is deeper, whether or not they "know the meaning" of the dream. In expressing what is deeper, each has a chance to have reactions to the dream— wonder, surprise, awe, anxiety, even fear. Not only does the child have an opportunity to have a reaction to *his* dream, but he also has an opportunity to share in others' reactions to his dreams and to their own dreams. There is also the possibility of wallowing in the objects and actions and interactions of the dream, a practice which helps the child to become a self who can "play" with the dream-manifested deeper potentials. That is, the primitive field dissolves away as the child describes the elements of the dream, becomes them, experiences them, relates to them, and "plays" with them. It is most helpful to do this with the encouragement and participation of the parent.

Effectance training with the child. The effectance training which I described for infants can be modified and adapted for the child who is two, five, seven, eleven, or on into the adolescent years.

The overall aim remains the same, viz. to promote the dissolution of the primitive field and the emergence of the sense of self. With children, even older children and adolescents, there are bonuses, however, even though each of the bonuses also insures the further dissolution of the primitive field and the refinement of the sense of self. There is a kind of equal stature relationship between parent and child who carry on this way of being together. The child is offered a rare and special kind of access to a part of the parent which is frequently quite hidden and removed in the ordinary course of growing through childhood and adolescence.

The rules of the game are simple, and are modifications of effectance play-training with infants. First, there is a defined period during which the two will be together in this special way. For the young child, the period might be a half hour each day or so. The period has a beginning and a predefined end. The period may be from about 4:00 to 4:30 p.m. When 4:30 comes, the time is over. Typically, this special time acquires a label which defines it and differentiates it from other times and ways of being together. Various labels include: play-time, our time, we-time, (parents as) slave time, Janice's time, fun time, together time. Second, the parent and child are to be alone, just the two of them, not the other parent or the siblings or any other person. This means that parent and child do not go to a store or visit a friend. They do nothing which involves another person.

Third, the rule is that the parent will do whatever the child wants the parent to do during that defined period. For the younger child, this generally includes playing together; for the older child, it often means talking together, especially with the adolescent. The child is thus the initiator of what is done. The child is boss, leader, the one who decides what the two will do together. Frequently the child will take the parent for a walk, or show the parent a special hide-out, or play ping-pong together, or throw a ball, or read a story, or work on a model, or wrestle, or play on the trampoline, or any of a thousand other possibilities. By virtue of the child as initiator, the parent accepts the role of student, learner, apprentice, follower, playmate, and the child is the teacher, organizer, leader, exemplar. The child explains the rules of the game, or shows the parent how to put the model together, or tells the parent how the tomato plant is to be planted, or instructs the parent in the secret code, or shows the parent how to hit the ping-pong ball in that particular way. As in effectance play-training with infants, following this third rule requires that the parent come to see and respect the child's own center of attention. The child defines what the center of attention is, and the parent must know it and respect it, whether attention is focused upon the tomato plant, a sore on the child's leg, life on other planets, the parent's childhood, or the glaring illogicalities in the parent's reasons for not permitting the adolescent to have a party at the house.

Fourth, the two must be within reasonable playing distance of one another, depending upon the nature of the interaction.

There is a dimension in this kind of relationship which consists of testing the limits. For example, if the parent does not permit the child to eat before supper, what does the parent do when the child says that what they will do will be to eat a quart of ice cream before supper? Or the parent becomes tense at the child's suggestion that they paint the bricks on the front of the house or smash a back window or cut down a neighbor's tree? Or suppose a child inquires about a carefully guarded family secret or invites the parent to smoke pot or get drunk on scotch—if these leave the parent tense and upset? The guideline here is for the parent to not do whatever would arouse bad feelings of significant intensity. This is the fifth rule, viz. the parent will not do that which arouses feelings that are too disturbing.

It is important that these rules be clear, and that they be understood by both parent and child. Frequently, the child learns the rules easily once the parent has them well in mind. It is the parent who generally has the most trouble grasping and following the rules.

Both partners often learn from the child's having the right to initiate his own behavior. Many parents find an immense gulf between the way they are during this time and the way they are in general with the child. I have found that parents are both pleased and dismayed by the gross contrast: "I had no idea how much I get him to do only what *I* wanted him to do." "It's like seeing a whole other side of him." "We've never been like that before. I feel a little ashamed, and like I am starting to respect her." "We didn't know what to do at first. That was funny for both of us. I never realized how little I listened to her." "That was so new. He really is a person with his own ideas. I think I learned a lot from him, even about the way I am."

Cultivating the child's phenomenological grasp of his world. The sense of self is illuminated by cultivating the child's own way of grasping the reality of his world. Listen to his way of describing and understanding his world. Encourage him to express his own grasp of his world, whether through the medium of words, pictures, or deeds. Acknowledge the intactness and viability of his way of grasping his world so that differences can exist in a friendly way between his grasp of his world and your grasp of yours. If he is telling you about his teacher, be receptive to his conception of her. Encourage him to describe how the teacher demonstrated the simple chemistry experiment. If he says that his uncle can see through a wall, receive that mode of grasping his world, and encourage him to tell about that feat. Respect his description of reality even if there are gaping differences from your version, and even if the reality he sees is threatening to you. For example, if he notices the funny way you pronounce some words, allow him to have *his* grasp on that reality. Share it with him. Get further details of it from him.

Does this lead him into a personalized, bizarre world of his own? No, it enables him to become a *person* who has the capacity to grasp several worlds, even that in which the parent exists. Provide him with ways of checking on the accuracy of his own grasp of reality. In this way, he can move toward serving as his own reality-check and away from dependence upon the parent as the one to confirm or disconfirm the accuracy of what the child grasps as real. If the child wonders whether it is raining outside, let him go outside and see—instead of your telling him that it is or is not raining. If the child thinks one dog is taller than another dog, show him how to use a tape measure to assess their heights—instead of your telling him that he is right or wrong. In passing the role of authority onto resources better than the parent, the parent becomes the teacher of skills such as how to use a dictionary or the library, how to use household tools, how to measure and weigh, how to use an egg beater or a magnifying glass or a thermometer. With these tools and these skills, the child can provide his own assessments of what he believes is real. Here is where the simple scientific method is helpful, for the child can be taught how to see whether what he believes is true really checks out. Does a lighter car get better mileage than a heavier car? Can you do a better job with a small hammer or a big hammer? Can you run faster in the morning or in the evening? Help the child to figure out ways of getting answers to these questions so that the *child* can be his own experimenter, instead of having to turn to parents for answers. There are often criteria by which the child can find out for himself whether his grasp of reality is accurate or not, and the guideline is for the parent to show the child how to gauge for himself, rather than the parent serving as the authority of external reality.

16

The Plateaus of
Human Development

Each infant begins its existence encompassed within a primitive field. Some infants remain that way. They become children who are still preserved within their primitive fields. In this chapter I shall describe the continued existence within the primitive field as one plateau of human development. Some persons exist throughout their lives on that plateau. What is life like for a person who lives on this plateau? What are other plateaus on which a person may exist? What is it like to move from one plateau to another? If the primitive field is dissolved, what kind of existence is there for such a child, and how does that existence differ from the one awaiting the child who remains within the primitive field? The purpose of the present chapter is to describe the plateaus of human development within the perspective of humanistic theory.

Plateaus of development versus biopsychological stages of development. Whether the child remains within the primitive field or the primitive field is dissolved away depends upon parental figures and what they do. It requires work to keep the primitive field preserved or to dissolve it away, and movement from one plateau to another also requires effective work. *People* are responsible for an individual's staying on one plateau or moving to another. Those people may include the individual himself, his family, the groups in which he lives, significant strangers. There are no intrinsic forces moving the child from one plateau to another, no biological factors, no built-in developmental sequences, no neurophysiological or hereditary or cultural lines of development, no biopsychological stages of development (Mahrer, 1967c). "Development" from one plateau to another is a function of what persons accomplish and not what biopsychological forces are like.

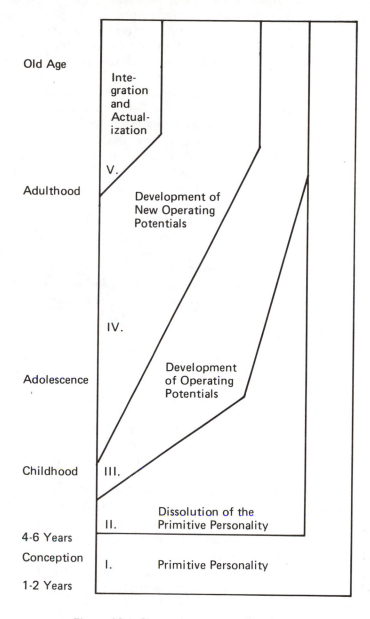

Figure 16.1 Plateaus of Human Development

Indeed, our humanistic theory sets aside the whole framework of biosocial, biopsychological stages of development. As we accumulate more and more data about infants and children—as well as about persons in their sixties, seventies, and eighties—the whole traditional framework of biologically rooted stages of development is having an increasingly difficult time embracing the data in an acceptably systematic fashion. There has now accumulated, for example, a creditable pool of research from anthropology, behavioral biology, child development and related fields suggesting that the traditionally held lines and stages of child development are highly modifiable; there seem to be wider and wider variations in rates of development, the nature of stages of development, and even the sequence of traditionally held stages (Gordon, 1966). I propose the framework of *plateaus of human development* rather than the traditional biologically grounded stages of human growth and development as an alternate framework for making sense of the movement from conception to death. According to humanistic theory, there are five plateaus on which persons can exist. They are organized in sequence (Figure 16.1) such that movement from one plateau to the next, if it occurs and to the extent that it occurs, is a function of the work of human beings rather than the playing out of biologically rooted developmental forces.

I. The Primitive Personality

The first plateau is one on which the person exists encompassed within the primitive field. Chapters 13-15 described the infant and young child whose existence may be said to be on the plateau of the primitive personality. We turn now to a discussion of the kinds of lives which characterize persons who exist on this first plateau, i.e., who spend their lives, or large portions of their lives, as primitive personalities.

As infants, these persons were determined by activating sources in the external world, controlled by factors outside their skin. They were paradigms of responses to external stimuli—the parental figures. Persons who remain on this plateau live out their lives in this way. When they are 25 or 55 or two or five, forces in the external world determine them, get them activated, control them. These are the persons who are responders (often very sophisticated responders) to external stimuli (often complex packages of subtle cues).

It is relatively easy to identify the parental figures as the controlling, activating, determining resources of the infant. The potentials and relationships of the parental figures constitute the deeper (controlling, activating and determining) personality processes of the infant. It is often less easy to identify the external agents who serve as the activating and determining resources of the child, adolescent or adult who remains on this plateau. But controlling, activating and determining resources are always there, somewhere in the person's life.

If we carefully observe the person as he moves from a child of four to a child of five, or from an adolescent of 15 to a man of 26, we observe changes in the way he *behaves*. Often these are grossly significant behavioral changes. Yet if we expand our domain of observation to include the activating and determining external resources, it becomes clear that these ways of behaving are brought about by external sources in the very same way as the behavior of the infant can be described as a function of the potentials and relationships of the parental figures. The behavioral changes of the person on this plateau are activated and controlled by the external world as primitive field.

The illusory sense of self and identity. Because these persons have no selves, no personhoods, they are dependent upon the external world for their very identity. They need others who see them as having a particular definition. Who I am is a function of how others see me. It is as if one's very being, self, definition, identity all drain away when external primitive fields are no longer present (Laing, 1960). In effect, such persons cannot tolerate being truly alone because being alone means being without the defining primitive field. Without the others, this person is not a person. He must imagine or fabricate others who can serve as his primitive field to tell him who he is and what he is like.

In their relationships with others, these persons undergo a most interesting switch which has been pointed out for centuries, but only recently has begun to be seriously investigated (cf. Laing, 1960). While these persons may *appear* to have a self and a personhood at some times, their relationships with others are marked by the absence of self or personhood. It is as if an involvement with another person closes down their sense of self. There is a point in their relationships with others where they fold away as persons and relate to others in the same way they related to the archaic primitive fields. That is, these persons lend themselves easily to being the extensions of significant others. Just as in the old primitive fields, these persons slide easily into being the vehicle of expression of others' personalities. They become what others invite them to become, and they take on the characteristics which others make them into being. They are the extended personalities of the host other figure. In the extreme form of this, such persons are owned and possessed by others—by the strong spouse, boss, friend, leader, or even by the wicked witch, thought machine, or deceased parent. In less extreme, more common ways, these persons take on the characteristics of others, or they are made into being whatever the other persons make them into being—

whether that means being friendly or tough, a lover or a follower, caustic or intelligent, altruistic or withdrawn. They are what others make them into being. Whether common or extreme, the mechanism involves a temporary fading away of their selves or personhoods in relationships with others who serve as controlling primitive fields.

These persons have no real selves, no genuine I-nesses or personhoods. Even the *apparent* sense of self, or identity, is activated and determined by the external primitive field. It is nothing more than an illusory sense of self, a deceptive sense of being a person. The self-awareness is moulded, defined, and operated by the external primitive field. Thus these persons are in reality zombies, puppets, hypnotized and sleeping—and in a state where they are that way without knowing that they are that way. Instead of a real self they possess a false sense of self masquerading as a real sense of self. These persons are puppets who never can know that their strings are pulled by an external primitive field. They spend lives without ever knowing what it is like to be a real self or personhood.

So common is this illusory sense of self and identity that only a very small proportion of persons on this first plateau are the deviates—the retarded, the handicapped, the crippled, the crazy, the lunatic. Most of the persons on this plateau are policemen and truck drivers, social workers and tennis players, university professors and housewives, voters and the politicians for whom they vote. These persons exist with an illusory sense of self, or self-consciousness and personhood. But the sense of self extends only to the narrow limits of their operating potentials. They "have" no deeper potentials, and the extent of their operating potentials is the extent of what they are. In truth, these persons are half-persons, without ever knowing that they are half-persons. The activating, determining deeper potentials lie elsewhere, external to themselves. They are inextricably linked to their families, yet move about as if they were free. They are inextricably linked to their jobs, their businesses, their communities, their nation, other people, "they." These external resources serve as the activating, determining deeper potentials which move these persons about—without these persons knowing that they are moved about. Just as the infant is activated and determined by the primitive field, without knowing, so are these adults also activated and determined by their own primitive fields, and also without knowing. The apparent sense of self and seeming ability to act like a person with self-consciousness and self-awareness—these are all illusions, trappings of a real person without their being real persons. Many persons exist as primitive personalities in normal, average ways, without ever knowing that they are activated and determined by external primitive fields. Indeed, these persons constitute much of what *is* normal and average.

The Nature of Their External Worlds

These persons live in external worlds which are their primitive fields. What are these external worlds like?

The family. At the extreme, these persons simply exist in the family. They create little or no fuss, get into little or no trouble while the family is there. They certainly do not seek help for problems or for difficulties, predominantly because there is no "person" there to *be* distressed or concerned. They seldom find their way into treatment, for they exist in the role of children (at every chronological age) who are needed or tolerated by the families and, as research corroborates, live in a kind of one-person chronic ward in the family (Davis, Freeman, & Simmons, 1957; Freeman & Simmons, 1958), within the soft enveloping web spun around them by the family.

Some of these persons behave in weird and unusual ways. They are deviates, cripples, handicapped, retarded, persons who have "something wrong" with them. But they are protected and tolerated in the family. Others, however, are the normal people. They are the adjusted, the average, the workers, the ordinary people without problems. Yet they too must exist within the family which activates and determines, which provides them with the necessary encompassing field. The defining characteristic is the requirement of the sustaining family, and not whether the person is deviate and peculiar, or average and normal. It does not matter whether the person lives in the family home (although he often does), or whether he moves away or even marries and has children of his own. In any condition, he remains "in the family" as the primitive field.

Surrogates of the original family. As long as the original family is there, the person exists within its defining field. If something happens to the original family, the person must find a surrogate. No matter what happens to the family, the person must exist in a world which constitutes the extension or perpetuation or replacement of that primitive field. If we understand that primitive field as the original family system, then the person's behavior serves ". . . as a way of perpetuating a particular kind of family system" (Haley, 1963, p. 108). If the parents die, leave, undergo some serious change which removes them from the primitive field, the person usually finds another host to serve as the surrogate significant figure. By whatever means, the primitive field must be preserved. Perhaps the person can attach himself as a pawn to the right other individual. Often another family can fulfill the role of the primitive field. Sometimes the person can replace the lost significant figures with a social agency, hospital, clinic, helping organization, penitentiary. In any case, surrogates must be found to replace the lost significant figures. Sometimes the transition is smooth.

As one parent dies another figure easily moves in to take her place. A child moves from the family to the army or to a peer group or to a spouse or to a job—and each of these serves as the surrogate primitive field. At other times the loss of the old primitive field cannot be repaired so easily and the person is lost. Here is the fish out of water, the helpless individual, the person who is hurting and needing an entire determining, activating field. Yet, whether smooth or jagged, it is most common that the person's life contains two or four or six replacements for the lost components of the early primitive field.

Persons on this plateau must have the primitive field in order to function. Therefore, there is a particular sensitivity to loss, separation, and absence. In the young child, to whatever degree there is a nascent personhood to have feelings, that personhood is not able to tolerate loss, separation, or absence. When that occurs, the child is rendered unable to function. It has lost its personality foundation. In the older child or adolescent or adult, the reaction to loss, separation, or absence is similarly a disconnection from that vital foundation which activates and determines—and that state is beyond one of mere sadness or depression (Laing, 1960). The child is welded to the parent so that something catastrophically wrenching has occurred when father dies, mother and father separate, or mother goes away for a long trip to another country. The child has been disconnected from its vital organs when it must go on a visit to grandmother, or is sent off to school, or must go out to get a job.

For such persons, loss, separation, or absence of or from the primitive field is catastrophic and intolerable, and it is the catastrophic intolerability itself which calls out for a replacement. In effect, the state of loss, separation, or absence says, "Be my primitive field. Take me up. Control me. Activate and determine me. Take care of me. Be my family." Sometimes these persons communicate this in passive ways. They are helpless, wholly unable to care for themselves. They fall apart and *must* be taken care of by agencies, caring persons, hospitals, social institutions, friends. In their very helpless inability is the message of help (Mahrer, 1970c). It is as if they radiate an incompleteness, for they are only partial persons, human beings who lack the fundamental organizing structure of their own deeper potentials. They are lost, incomplete, pitiful, and this very state is a powerful invitation for others to provide what is missing, i.e., the surrogate primitive field. At other times, these persons communicate more actively. They seek and find the right agency or friend, hospital or spouse to assume the role of their primitive field. In their efforts to locate a surrogate primitive field, they often are aided by others who work hard at conjointly constructing such a relationship. They are helped, that is, by others who are quite ready to assume the role of the primitive field, individuals postured to activate, to initiate and control, to determine and to be primitive fields. Often these helping others are nurses, psychotherapists, social workers, foremen, supervisors, families, and the staffs of hospitals, agencies, organizations and institutions—as well as spouses, friends, neighbors, relatives, employers.

Many of these persons find their way into hospitals. When and if parts of their own primitive fields are lost, they must find another host primitive field. If mother and father are lost, an excellent replacement for the lost primitive field is the hospital. Many of these persons lost their parents in early childhood, and spent their lives coupling up with one surrogate primitive field after another. Although these persons comprise a small proportion of the total mental hospital population, some samples of hospitalized patients are characterized by a heightened frequency of bereavement in early childhood (Archibald, Bell, Miller & Tuddenham, 1962). For such persons who require replacements for a lost primitive field, hospitals often are just the right places. Indeed, one function of hospitals may be said to serve as the activating, determining primitive field for persons whose primitive fields are missing (Mahrer, 1970c).

To the extent that hospitals serve such a role, it is understandable that some patients are characterized by having lost their parents at an early age and, I suggest, spending the rest of their lives linking up with agencies as replacements for the lost primitive fields. Loss of parents, "psychopathology," and hospitalization are clustered together because the hospital replaces the lost parents, and the "crazy way of being" (that is, the so-called "psychopathology") becomes a means of securing hospitalization (Mahrer, 1970c). For some hospitalized patients, then, the career of finding replacements for the lost primitive field began early with loss of father or mother. In this regard, Hilgard and Newman (1963) found that loss of mother or father occurred at an earlier age in hospitalized schizophrenic women than in a sample of non-hospitalized, non-schizophrenic, "normal" controls.

Persons who require a surrogate for the missing primitive field need not connect up with hospitals or other such agencies and institutions. Hundreds of thousands of persons, primitive personalities who are themselves half-persons, have constructed and maintained a world which replaces the missing primitive field, which activates and determines, which houses all the controlling forces. They have constructed a grand primitive field of determining forces, controlling governments, inexorable powers, natural immutable laws, political economic reality. Instead of living in the old primitive field of mother and father, these persons have collectively constructed and preserved a new primitive field of laws, governments, forces, determinants—

which activate us, control us, force us to behave, house all the secrets, control our fates, shape our lives. They have erected a grand external world which is mysterious, oceanic, brooding, omnipotent. There is no danger if the old primitive field should be lost, for we have an external world of hard reality to take up where the old primitive field ended.

A great deal of our common, everyday world serves the function of just such a surrogate. For example, persons whose primitive fields are lost or missing frequently construct very particular kinds of groups which serve the function of activating, controlling, defining their members. Such groups constitute the deeper potentials of the members, just as the old primitive fields contained the deeper potentials of the encompassed infants. The difference is that the members of these groups are instrumental in constructing their primitive fields. Do you belong to a new family of your own, to a group of friends, to a work group, neighborhood group, social group, or any other kind of group? To what extent does that group replace the archaic primitive field which is now gone, lost, missing? It is so common to use groups as surrogates for the old primitive field that this function of groups cannot be seen by its creators.

II. Dissolution of the Primitive Field

A person may spend his life on the same plateau upon which he entered the world, i.e. the primitive personality. As indicated in Figure 16.1, the person may pass through childhood, adolescence, adulthood, and old age still on this plateau. Or, a person may move from this first plateau to the second plateau. As described in Chapter 15, the person who moves onto this second plateau is a different kind of person.

The Transition from Plateau I to Plateau II

Birth of selfhood. The transition from plateau I to plateau II is a landmark event because it constitutes the birth of selfhood. Dissolution of the primitive field is the other side of the generation of a sense of self. Thus, in regard to personhood or selfhood, the transition from plateau I to plateau II is indeed a birth. Psychoanalysis is correct in considering birth as a pivotally significant event, traumatic in its impacts upon the person's development. However, psychoanalysis, because it was rooted in biology, mistook birth as the biophysical birth of the physical infant. Another kind of birth, the kind which I suggest psychoanalytic theorists were studying without knowing it, was the birth of the self, of the sense of I-ness. When psychoanalysts identify birth as traumatic and as critical in the construction of the person, I accept their insights as referring to the catastrophic transition from the first plateau to the second plateau.

The parents: their role and the impacts of their loss. If the parental figures do not work hard at dissolving the primitive field, it persists, and the person remains throughout his life on that first plateau. If the parental figures encompass the child as a primitive field, the loss of the parental figures leaves the child on the first plateau. That is, he still exists as a primitive personality, and the balance of his life generally consists of constructing other primitive fields as surrogates for the lost original field. The key is whether the parental figures have worked successfully at dissolving away the primitive field. If they have, then to the extent they are successful, the child moves onto this second plateau.

Whenever loss of parental figures occurs, the meaning of the loss depends on whether the child is on the first plateau or the second plateau when this occurs. By loss I am including such events as death of the parents, divorce, wrenching separation, or any kind of serious personality change in the parents which results in their loss from the primitive field. Any such loss has meaning depending on the child's "stage of development" (e.g., Barry, 1949; Barry & Lindemann, 1960; Beres, Gale & Oppenheimer, 1960; Wahl, 1956). If the loss occurs while the child is on the first plateau, the child is not yet a person, not yet a self. The primitive field is still encompassing the child. Accordingly, loss of the parent typically results in a replacement of the missing portion of the primitive field. If, however, the loss occurs when the child is on this second plateau, the child has emerged as a person, and the meaning of the loss is significantly different. There is no encompassing primitive field to be replaced. In much of this research, an error is committed by linking the loss to biopsychological development, rather than to plateaus of human existence. According to the bulk of that research, loss of parents during the years two to four is held to be different in meaning from loss when the child is eight to ten, for biopsychological development is held as roughly approximating chronological age. According to humanistic theory, however, a child of three or a child of nine may be either on the first or the second plateau. A man of 20 may be on the first plateau, whereas a child of six may have progressed to the second plateau. The meaning of the loss differs depending on the *plateau*, but the plateaus do not so closely parallel chronological age.

When the transition occurs, the dissolution of the primitive field can *begin* during pregnancy, and it can ordinarily extend throughout chronological infancy and childhood (Figure 16.1). The *results* of this transition normally occur cumulatively throughout infancy and childhood. If we ask when the emergence of a sense of self or personhood occurs, I would say that for some persons it occurs in early childhood, for most persons during middle childhood, and for some persons well into adolescence and adulthood (Figure 16.1). Although the process of dissolution can begin as early as pregnancy, the actual emergence of a sense of self occurs, typically, much later. Frequently the bulk of the emergence of self takes place during the middle childhood years, from approximately six to twelve years of age. In general, this is much later than the time psychoanalytic writers hold for the development of the ego—for example, within the first few weeks after birth (Benedek, 1956) or during the second stage of oral development, some time during the second half of the first year of life (Erikson, 1950).

There is no intrinsic developmental force which accounts for the dissolution of the primitive field. Therefore no age can be cited for the dissolution to occur "normally." It requires work on the part of the parental figures to dissolve away the primitive field. This work can be carried out early or late, effortfully or casually, effectively or poorly. The net result is that we can only observe empirically when most persons seem to undergo the dissolution of the primitive field. There is very little data on how many persons move from the first plateau to this second plateau when the child is two months of age, two years old, six years, 10, 14 and 20 years of age. Because data are lacking, we have only the barest of speculative bases for guessing when this plateau occurs. Does that sense of I-ness occur two days after birth? At two or three months? How early does this occur? Psychoanalysis places this event quite early, usually within the first year after birth. Often the clinical evidence includes the patient's sense of "I remember," and especially in early traumas recollected with a sense of the trauma occurring "to me." That is, if the patient "remembers" being breast fed when he was one month of age, then many psychoanalysts presume the sense of self or I-ness must have been present by one month of age. Psychoanalytic writers describe traumas which occur to the patient as a person, traumas which occur quite early in life. Lindner (1944), for example, describes a patient who recollected being traumatized by the image of a dog on the movie screen when he was six to eight months of age. If we accept that events which we recollect with a sense of I-ness locate the dawn of selfhood, then we are led to agree with the psychoanalytic position that the sense of self occurs within the first weeks and months after birth. Humanistic theory holds, in contrast, that one may "recollect" experiences which occurred *prior* to the dawn of selfhood. Recollection is *not* evidence of the emergence of self. There is a child, an infant, in the form of the primitive field even *before* there occurs a dissolution of the primitive field. One may have "memories" of events which happened during delivery, during pregnancy. One may have a memory of events which occurred *prior* to conception, because the infantness was already present in the primitive field (see Chapter 13). There is, I would suggest, a difference in the sense of self which accompanies the dissolution of the primitive field, and the sense of self which inheres in events occurring prior to the dissolution of the primitive field. One "has" memories prior to the dissolution of the primitive field, such as memories of the house where one lived during the first four weeks after birth, or memories of the delivery process itself, or memories of father's suicide when one was six weeks old, or memories of being in the crib when one was three months old, or mystical memories of father's being blown up on the military ship a week before one's birth. These are memories of the infant-as-primitive-field, and not memories of an infant whose primitive field has dissolved away. Memories are accessible of events occurring to the primitive field, long before the sense of self emerged to fill the child with the I-ness marking the dissolution of the primitive field. That sense of self is different from the sense of the infant-as-primitive-field. Because of these considerations, humanistic theory does not couple the dissolution of the primitive field and the emergence of self with earliest memories of traumas.

Identifying the age when the transition occurs is even more confounded because it occurs in little steps to parts of the person rather than a single wholesale jump. A chunk of the transition commonly occurs in bits and pieces over the period from approximately four to six years to adulthood (Figure 16.1). In our culture, it takes a big jump during adolescence. Thus many children begin ascending onto this second plateau during the early childhood years, and bring most of themselves onto this plateau during adolescence. Many of the characteristics of the adolescent years may be taken as rituals of the dissolving away of the primitive field. Even the simple act of leaving the family household is a final dissolving away of some of the residual bonds with the primitive personality (cf. Erikson, 1950). While the ascent onto the second plateau can begin in early childhood, it typically carries on during later childhood and adolescence, in bits and pieces, little juttings and bursts.

Loss: Its Nature and Effects

The transition from the first to the second plateau occurs through the dissolution of the primitive field. Accordingly, the personhood which emerges has been separated from its complete primitive field. For nearly every person, this separation constitutes a loss of profound significance.

The nature of the loss. In the ideal case, the primitive field is itself thoroughly integrated, and the dissolution of the primitive field yields a sense of self which is also integrated. Under these ideal circumstances, loss is minimal or non-existent. But virtually every primitive field is itself characterized by significant disintegration. To whatever extent the primitive field is itself disintegrated, the dissolution of the primitive field will culminate in a sense of loss. The disintegrative relationships between person and encompassing field insures that the person must search for what is missing, to try to reunite with the primitive field which is missing, and which can never be found. Inevitably the quest is hopelessly fruitless, with a vague sensing that one will never be able to reintegrate and be whole once again, a sense of loss of the most precious gift of all—one's primitive field. These qualities come from the disintegrative nature of the primitive field which has dissolved away, and have nothing to do with the nature of the potentials which are there.

Although this sense of loss is a familiar theme in literature, cultural anthropology, history and religion, I am most familiar with it in the field of clinical psychopathology. Regardless of the particular kind of pathology, regardless of the particular school of personality, there is a recurrent theme of some mysterious early loss. So common is this theme of early loss that clinical and research lore seem to regard it as a non-differentiating, all-purpose ingredient in the causal fabric of nearly every kind of later difficulty (e.g., Bowlby, 1969; Gregory, 1958). It has been described as loss of a parent, loss of the protection and security of the womb, separation or divorce, birth trauma, father absence, dissolution of the family. Whatever the nature of the current problem, from acting like a crazy person to having skin problems in adolescence, the literature on the early roots of the problem always includes some sort of early loss. However, we have been unable to identify the nature of that early loss. I am inclined to hypothesize that the loss is of the primitive personality. This is the oceanic loss which lies behind each of the expressions of loss which have been entertained as the wellsprings of psychological problems.

This sense of loss is felt by the child whose primitive field has dissolved away. Yet he is not the only one to experience the loss, for the parental figures also have lost something equally precious to them, viz. the child. Almost by definition, if the parental figures constitute a primitive field, the child is a centrally meaningful part of their world. Typically the child was conceived and constructed to fulfill important functions in the worlds of the parental figures. Now, when the primitive field is dissolved away, something exceedingly precious is severed and the parent has lost something of herself. It is, then, a characteristic of this second plateau that a sense of loss is present, a sense of loss experienced by the child and a sense of loss experienced by the parent, with both contributing to the depth and profoundness of the loss sensed by the emerged sense of self.

Accordingly, the receding of parental figures out of the primitive field has very special meaning to the *parent*. There is no separated, intact, infant-as-person to receive this receding out as a serious blow. Yet, since the larger meaning of infant encompasses all that occurs in the primitive field, the experience of the *parental* figure is part of the constituency of the *infant*. On this score, I must take issue with Erikson's (1950) assertion that the receding away of the mother is the first serious life crisis for the infant. From our perspective, the infant is not yet a person being influenced by the receding away by mother. Instead, the receding away of the mother can be a life crisis for *mother*. It may be quite shattering for the mother to find herself withdrawn and separated out from her infant, no longer such a prominent figure within the primitive field. And *that* becomes part of what the infant is. Loss of the infant by mother occurs to the mother, not to the infant. Yet the sense of that experienced loss is "inherited" by the infant-as-person who comes forth because of that loss. The more shattering the loss is to the mother (or any parent), the more shattering is the sense of loss to the emerging infant-child. If the parents are integrated, the dissolution of the primitive field can bequeath to the emerged infant-as-person a sense of integrated independence and autonomy. The world in which the infant now exists is an integrated world in which the infant or child can exist separated yet close, intact yet with a sense of equal stature with the parental figures. On the other hand, if the primitive field is disintegrated, then the loss of the child is fraught with bad feelings for the parent. Under these conditions, what the *child* inherits is a sense of loss which is filled with bad feelings, disintegrated.

Little wonder that this mysterious sense of archaic loss is so ephemeral, is omnipresent in research on the earliest precursors of problems, and has remained so very obscure. According to humanistic theory, one component of the loss occurred before the person even emerged as a self. That is, when the person emerged as a self with some awareness and self-consciousness, the loss had already occurred. All the person has is a sense of something missing. The person was not even "around" when the loss of the primitive field occurred. Perhaps this is why human beings are forever looking for significant factors occurring before the dawn of awareness, significant factors such as hereditary factors, racial unconsciousnesses, and so on. It is as if we have a glimmering of knowledge that something of significance was there before we emerged as selves (though we have looked in the wrong places for what it was). Whereas one component of the loss is that it may have occurred before we emerged as personhoods, the second component is that the loss was likely experienced by the *parental figures* who had been a part of what we were. Mother and father experienced the loss, and we sense the loss which they experienced.

Both components of the loss occurred not to our selves as conscious personhoods, but in and to the primitive fields which had been what we were! Little wonder that it has been so very hard to define the nature of that loss, and why our attempts to specify the loss have been in the wrong places.

The effects of the loss. Once the primitive field is dissolved, it cannot be put together again. Like Humpty Dumpty, the effort to reassemble it is fruitless. Nevertheless, one of the major characteristics of this second plateau is the hopeless, fruitless search for the old primitive field. Filled with magical hope and longing, these persons frequently seek to regain the old state of being encompassed in the primitive field. Whereas persons who exist on the first plateau can almost always replace lost pieces of the primitive field, persons on this second plateau can not. Instead, they surround the old primitive field with beauty and splendor, and search evermore for the irretrievably lost state. The theme is one of hopeless searching for what can never be found. Yet the hope is forever there. It shows itself in a generalized wish to regain the old (lost) sense of oneness, unity, belonging, togetherness. One was a whole person then, at one with the encompassing world, and the person spends the rest of his life searching vainly to be a whole person once again, to "find one's self," but he never succeeds. The person may spend an entire life searching for how to be at one with his world, encompassed by his world, nurtured and unified with his world. But that will occur nevermore. He will seek the mysterious love-milk (alcohol, marihuana, food, psychedelic drug) to remove all tensions and to reunite himself with the lost state of complete peace, but it will never be found. He will seek vainly for others in whom he can lose himself, be with in unity, be one with. He will seek a perfect mate or friend or lover or parent. He will seek the right family or group or locale or neighborhood or country. There is none. He will seek to hurl himself into some grand mission in which he can lose himself—whether politics, religion, science or whatever. It will, in the end, fail. He will seek the answers to the final questions, the peace behind death, the final way of making sense of it all. In the end, such quests are always fruitless. He seeks friends and intimates, a group to replace the lost primitive group in which he existed (Asch, 1952), but he can never acquire that magical sense of being enfolded within the group of which he is a part. He sets out to reconnect himself with his own personal history, or with his ancestry, or with his people, or with his nation, but such efforts can never truly succeed in reintegrating the lost primitive field.

Entire lives are spent trying to reconnect with the old primitive field. Many persons invite others to be their lost primitive fields. It is as if these persons say, in effect, "I will enter a state of being a half-person, a pawn. I will be moulded and fashioned by you to be what you must make of me. In return, you must be my activation, my control. You must get me started, provide direction, determine how and what I shall be." It is easy enough to locate others who respond to such invitations. There are friends and lovers, spouses and relatives, each of whom will gladly step into that role. Persons on this plateau form alliance after alliance, seeking to reestablish the dissolved primitive personality. But these are fruitless lives, for the old primitive field cannot be brought back. Even before each new relationship starts, it is clear that the relationship will end in despair and disappointment. Each affair ends with a failure to find the early lost state. Generally the person is vaguely restless and unquenched. Yet they are on a plateau wherein it is impossible to gain more than brief wisps of the lost primitive state. The transition to the second plateau has made it impossible to accomplish what existence on the first plateau provides so easily.

In the efforts to regain the lost state, such persons become fodder for groups and organizations. Indeed, they are instrumental co-participants in the construction of groups and organizations which promise what the lost primitive·fields provided. Thus they engage in the construction of groups and organizations which run their lives, offer direction and activation. So common are such groups and organizations that these persons are often found in agencies, clubs, political parties, governments, businesses—in the myriads of forms taken by groups and organizations. They can be the bosses or the bossed, the leaders or the followers, the managers or the workers. What matters is the presence of a particular kind of group or organization. Yet these persons are never fully satisfied. There is always something missing, some quality which is lacking in these groups and organizations. Unlike those on the first plateau, these persons are never fully right or satisfied in such groups or organizations. They cannot achieve what has been forever lost.

This same theme characterizes the worlds in which these persons live. They frequently construct worlds invested with the qualities of the lost primitive field. Thus their world may be filled with power and control, an omnipotent world, saturated with all the secrets and the mystery of the lost primitive field. The psychoanalytic mechanism of introjection recognizes this quality in the requirement that the external world be omnipotent before the child can introject that omnipotence (Fenichel, 1954c, p. 34). What is the source of that omnipotence? The source is the sensed loss of the primitive field and the effort to regain it by constructing a world filled with its omnipotent quality. Yet the context in which all of this occurs is loss, for, even though the constructed world is powerful and omnipotent, the predominant theme is the impossibility of regaining the old state. One lives in an omnipotent world filled with loss, unfulfillment, restlessness, lack of peace, essential unreachability. In all of the effects, the denoument consists of the loss of the primitive field.

Once the primitive field is lost, the external world is asked to play a role which it can never fulfill. For example, the world is asked to be orderly, to run on the basis of natural laws, to conform to scientific laws of predictability and regularity. It is to be a world of consistency. Yet, for these persons, the world is never right. The old primitive field is never fully brought back, and the world is never sufficiently orderly, consistent, lawful, predictable, regular. That disappointment, that departure from what it ought to be—is the inevitable consequence for the person on this second plateau, and constitutes another effect of the loss of the primitive field.

Acquisition of Basic Potentials

Transition onto the second plateau not only involves *loss* of the primitive field, it also involves *acquisition* of the basic personality structure which had been the primitive field. Basic potentials and their relationships, formerly localized in the primitive field, are now welded onto the person himself and the person is utterly transformed.

The disintegrative relationship between the person and the basic potentials. In a most important sense, the acquisition of one's very own basic potentials is tantamount to the inheritance of the whole domain of problems (psychopathology, behavioral symptoms, difficulties). Almost without exception, the basic structure is disintegrative. Once the person moves onto this second plateau, he acquires a sense of self, an "I-ness," and he becomes the proud owner of basic potentials and their (disintegrative) relationships. Once the primitive field dissolves away, there stands a person on the ground of everything which had comprised the activating, determining primitive field—with all its problems and difficulties. This is bad enough. What makes matters worse, however, is that the emerged sense of self is only a tiny bit in an ocean of deeper, basic potentials and relationships. To the extent that he emerges as a self, he "has" all of the problems inherent in the former primitive field, although he has mandate over none of it. That is, he is not boss, owner, controller of that whole domain of basic potentials and their relationships. Indeed, one of the characteristics of this second plateau is the onset of the war between the person and the deeper, basic potentials.

The child struggles against an unseen enemy, for when he acquires the basic potentials and their relationships, he is a self separated from the basic structure by a disintegrative gulf. These basic potentials had been constituents of the primitive field. Now they are in some strange way a part of the child yet separated from him. They are there, but the child does not see them. It is as if the child somehow "has" basic potentials which are, at the same time, alien. When the child enters onto this second plateau, there will frequently be a sense of powerful forces which are part of the child, but at the same time alien. Most theories of personality carry this theme of guiding, determining basic personality forces which are "not me," which are alien. These forces may be referred to as instincts and hereditary forces which are both in me and not me. They are alien yet somehow a part of me. Sometimes these forces reside in early experiences which shape the person I am, yet they are alien and not at all a part of what is me. Sometimes they are called social forces which are both a part of what is me and mysteriously alien. In some theories there are unconscious processes which are in me, yet alien to me. Regardless of the form it is said to take, the person is linked to some kind of powerful, determining force (I refer to it as the basic potential structure) which is, at the same time, alien, removed, not fully seen—which is, in other words, disintegrative.

Because of the disintegrative relationships, the sense of self is connected to a basic structure it does not know. The person on the second plateau does not even know that he is connected to an unseen, unknown set of basic potentials. When the child existed on the first plateau, the basic determining forces resided in the primitive field and expressed themselves through the parental figures. If, for example, the primitive field included the potential for experiencing nothingness and invisibility, it might have expressed itself in the form of a parental figure who was compelled to know things, who was full of knowledge, who must be on top of things intellectually, who could organize and structure the world. Once the child passed onto the second plateau, that potential became connected directly to the newly emerged personhood which had no knowledge whatsoever of the existence of that deeper potential. Now the child has a basic potential for the experiencing of nothingness and invisibility—but without any knowledge that he has such a basic potential. Without fanfare, the basic potential has silently connected itself to the emerged personhood.

There is a kind of wry irony in the magnificently myopic awareness of the self. There now exists a child with awareness. Whether the child is five, 10, 15, or 20 when the sense of self emerges, it has an awareness which extends only to the outer periphery of its own immediate personhood. There is always a strong sense of awareness, but it is so terribly limited that it is a joke. It is as if the light of conscious awareness has turned on, but the illumination is pitifully weak. Awareness and understanding and consciousness stop at the outer periphery of the immediate personhood. Beyond that outer periphery are the deeper potentials and their relationships about which the emerged personhood has absolutely no knowledge. In effect, the emerged personhood now has a foundation of basic potentials and relationships which he had no hand in constructing, which will determine the course of his life, about which he has no knowledge and, most sardonic of all, the existence of which he does not know that he does not know. Indeed, the opposite is the case, namely that he has a distinct sense of knowing, when he has no knowledge at all. He now has an awareness which gives him the illusion of knowing what there is to him, when he is supremely oblivious of the vast extent of what there really is to him.

Almost without exception, the primitive field is characterized by disintegration. Accordingly, when the primitive field dissolves away, the child acquires a set of basic potentials which are related disintegratively to one another. These disintegrative relationships insure that there is massive distance between the domain of the operating potentials—the sense of personhood and self—and the foundation of basic potentials. It is practically insured that the child avoids, defends against, is separated from the basic potentials without having any knowledge whatsoever of being avoidant, separated from, and defending against them. If, for example, the basic potential consists of the potential for experiencing nothingness and invisibility, the emerged child may awake with a sense of being achieving, of having to know how things work, of being of substance. But that is the extent of the knowledge, for the disintegrative relationship will make sure that the child knows nothing at all of the existence of the basic potential.

Because of the disintegrative relationships between the basic potentials, and also between the basic potentials and the emerged personhood, the child runs away without knowing that from which he is running or even that he is running. Everything which constitutes the disintegrative relationship happens, and happens without the child knowing that it is happening. Thus the child will avoid and defend against the basic experiencing of his nothingness, his invisibility—and will do so without awareness, and even without any awareness that he has no awareness. The child may struggle to stay away from any situation which promises an experience of being nothing, of being invisible. Yet he will know nothing about his avoiding such situations. The disintegrative relationship makes him behave in disintegrative ways, yet he has no knowledge of what he is doing, nor does he know that he does not know.

When most persons come awake, when they emerge as self-conscious personhoods, they stand in stark opposition to their own basic potentials. Regardless of the nature of their basic potentials, the disintegrative relationships are such that persons fight against what they are, opposed to their own basic potentials. It is as if they are in revolt against their own deeper nature. Often such a relationship is so pervasive that there is a fundamentally irresolvable opposition to these basic potentials. From the very onset of self, of personhood, such a person will manifest "... a self-willed, stubborn revolt against the way in which she herself was 'thrown' into existence, in short, against a special mode of human fate" (Binswanger, 1958c, p. 339).

Accommodating to the acquired basic personality structure. The acquired basic potentials had, in the earlier primitive field, activated the child. They determined him, constituted all the power and control. They got everything started, moulded and shaped him, defined his nature and functions. Having become a part of the child, on the second plateau, they retain their active characteristics. Regardless of the nature or content of the basic potentials, the form (Chapter 2) is always an active form. If the basic potential consists of hate, the form is one of active hating, and not being hated. If it is a potential for experiencing affection, the form is active affection, and not a passive receiving of the affection from others. Basic potentials are doers, initiators, activators, generators, and the form which they assume is active, not passive. To the extent that relationships are disintegrative, the child runs from the active form of basic potentials, recoils from and defends against them in their active form. Even when its *nature or content* is passive, the *form* which the child senses and defends against is an active form. Consider the deeper potential for experiencing dependency. The receiving of nurturance from others takes on an active form. It is a force with activating power. It is a pulling from, an active sucking, a parasitic feeding off of or draining, an active taking from. Its impact on the child is likewise an active one, with an intrinsic force. Being dependent bothers the child, manages him, looms at him menacingly. Each basic potential assumes its active form and launches itself actively onto the child.

On this plateau, the child is a strange creature saddled with powerful active basic potentials, not yet a person with a developed set of operating potentials. There has yet to be developed the operating potentials whereby those basic potentials are experienced. Nevertheless, the basic potentials are there and, perhaps more than at any other time in the person's life, they are in a position to be expressed and experienced directly. Accordingly, it is not the *infant* on the *first* plateau who manifests archaic primitive material. It is the *child* on the *second* plateau whose primitive field dissolves away leaving the child with nothing but the basic potentials. What is more, these are typically related to one another in disintegrative fashion. Therefore, we may identify a period between the infant-as-primitive-field (plateau 1) and the development of operating potentials (plateau 3) when behavior patterns would occur whose nature is archaic and primitive. I suggest that the behavior patterns during this period are at the core of what G. Stanley Hall (1906) encapsulated within his theory of early development recapitulating the developmental stages of the species. For some persons, then, entrance onto this second plateau ought to be accompanied with outbursts of behaviors (actings-out) directly expressive of the basic potentials. I take this way of being as an accommodating to these acquired basic potentials.

The child must accommodate to basic potentials which are both his and not his. They are his because the primitive field has dissolved, and now the basic potentials are components of the larger personality structure which the child carries around with him. But they are not his because the domain of the self is so delimited, and the basic potentials are far outside this domain. In order to make them his, the child must carry out in an active role the archaic experiences in which he had been in the passive role (Loevinger, 1966), must live the basic potentials in the active role played by the parents who initially "did it" to the child. If the basic potential consists of rejection, and if the earliest experiences consisted of the parent rejecting the child, now the child must be the rejector. If the earliest experiences consisted of the parent being the rejected one and making the child into the one who rejects, the child must gain the experience of being the one who gets the other to reject him. Whatever the parent did *to* the child, the child must now actively *do* to the other. This role reversal or reversal of voice or being the parent is a way of accommodating to the acquired basic personality structure.

Entry onto the second plateau as a critical determinant of the nature of the basic personality structure. When the primitive field dissolves away, there emerges a personhood which has its own deeper potentials. If the primitive field consisted of a lovingness and a wholesome dependency, these become the constituents of the child's basic personality structure. This second plateau is where the child takes with him (acquires) that which constituted the primitive field. Suppose that the child enters onto this second plateau during the period from seven to 10 years of age. According to our theory, the constituents of the primitive field *during these years* become the basic foundations of the child, his deepest potentials and their relationships. If we stay with this thinking, then we are led to speculate that the nature of the primitive field *during the period of its dissolution* is more significant than the nature of that primitive field prior to that period. This is a wrenching departure from those theories which hold that the early years are by far the most formative, are the most paramount in the establishing of personality foundations.

If the primitive field were characterized by disintegration during the earliest years and, through some marvelous change, the relationships became integrated during the period of this second plateau when the primitive field dissolved, our theory holds that the basic foundations of the child's personality would be integrated, not disintegrated. If a secure, loving grandmother replaces a deceased mother when the child is two, and the child's primitive personality dissolves when the child is seven to 10, the grandmother's secure lovingness becomes a salient part of the child's basic personality foundations to a much greater extent than the characteristics of and experiences involving the mother. The father who is undergoing awful turmoil during the pregnancy and the first three years of the child's life may suicide in an explosion of hateful anguish. A year later the mother remarries and the new father is integratively peaceful and happy. According to our theory, the dissolution of the primitive field during the years from seven to ten bequeaths to the child much more of the second father than the first. In this important sense, the basic potentials and their relationships are predominantly a function of the nature of the primitive field at the time when the child moves from the first to the second plateau.

If good changes occur in the primitive field at any time before the primitive field dissolves away, those good changes become incorporated into the child's basic potentials and relationships. The ideal is, of course, to have a sound primitive field from the very beginning. But it is reassuring to consider that problems and difficulties can be corrected prior to the time that the child enters upon this second plateau. Mother may be torn apart during the period of the first plateau from conception throughout pregnancy and the early years of the child's life. She is angry and lost, full of a hurting hate toward the man who impregnated her and rejected her long before the baby was born. The abortive love affair and her having the baby were testimony to the essential defiant unreachability which was boiling within her during these years. These are problems which characterized the child's primitive field. But there is time to repair them. Whether through effective psychotherapy or any other means, if the wrenching disintegration is converted into a state of integration, if mother becomes solid and more substantial, then the acquired basic structure can be free of the awfulness and the anguish of the early years. It is not a mystery that the anguished problems of infancy seem somehow to have left little or no effect upon the child. When the child emerged into the state of selfhood (i.e., onto the second plateau), the damage had already been repaired.

There are at least two grand exceptions. One is that such salubrious changes are rare, and therefore the best indicator of the nature of the primitive field at the time of dissolution is the nature of the earliest primitive field. If, during conception, pregnancy, and the earliest years of life, the primitive field is a particular way, the likelihood is that the primitive field will still be that way when the child enters onto this second plateau. If mother assigns the infant the role of savior of the mother as a fragile jewel, then the experiencing of being a fragile jewel is there during the earliest years and it is likely that the child will inherit the being of a fragile jewel when he enters onto the second plateau. Ordinarily the primitive field persists relatively intact from the period of the first plateau and onto the period of the second plateau.

The second grand exception is that the parental figures frequently serve as the agents intermediating between the early events and the period of this second plateau. Thus an early event may affect the *parent* who carries the impact of that early event on through to the period of the second plateau. If the infant were in an accident requiring serious surgery, these events will likely have a far greater influence upon the parents than upon the infant. A fearfulness about life and death may be carried by the parents so that it becomes a component of the primitive field during this second plateau, but the carrier is the parental figure, not the child. A divorce during infancy may well leave the mother with a pool of hurt and anger. Even though the divorce may not have a direct impact upon the child, the mother may carry the hurt and anger into the period of the second plateau. Accordingly, events occurring during the first plateau are often carried onto the second plateau by their impact upon the parent.

III. Development of Operating Potentials

On the first plateau, the child exists as a primitive personality, encompassed by an oceanic primitive field which defines the functions of the child. If the child moves to the second plateau, the primitive field dissolves away and emerges as the basic personality structure of the child who now has a sense of self, a personhood. We now turn to the third plateau and the development of operating potentials.

The Active Construction of Experience

On the third plateau, the child takes an active stance toward experience under the executive direction of the deeper potentials and their relationships. The child meets experience in an active way, seeking it out, organizing it, processing it, defining it—in short, the child is now an active constructor of experience.

Unconfounding the systematic linkages between early and later events. Now that the child has a set of deeper potentials with defined relationships, the general contours of his future life are present. Especially if there is no change in the nature of the basic potentials and the nature of their relationships, there is a good measure of invariance in most of the components of the person's personality structure and the world he constructs. Only certain kinds of operating potentials will likely be developed. Only certain kinds of external worlds will be constructed. Only certain kinds of experiences will be in order. A careful study of the child's basic potentials and relationships will reveal what the person and his life will be like, so that the way he is on the second plateau sets the contours of the way he is to become on the third plateau.

The child's deeper potentials and their relationships determine how the child will construct experience. For example, the birth of a new sibling will vary in its meaning and significance depending upon the nature of the older child's deeper potentials and their relationships. Whereas one child may organize this event for the experiencing of intimacy and closeness, a second may use that event for the experiencing of maturity and the gaining of a sense of older-brotherliness, while a third may process that event so as to experience loss and rejection. In addition, the event will have soberly differing meanings depending on whether the child is on the first, second, or third plateaus. Although two children may both be five years old, the birth of the younger sibling will have vastly different meanings for the child who is ensconced within the primitive field (plateau 1) as compared with the child whose primitive field has dissolved, and who is now actively organizing his own experience (plateau 3). Accordingly, humanistic theory suggests that no systematic linkages will occur between specified early life events and specified later life events or adult outcomes as long as the plateau remains a confounding variable. Such research paradigms are based upon assumptions of human growth and development not shared by humanistic theory. It is not surprising that reviews of research have regularly failed to confirm the hypothesis that direct linkages can be found between these two sets of events (Archibald, Bell, Miller & Tuddenham, 1962; Bucklew, 1967; Frank, 1965; Kanfer & Saslow, 1965; Orlansky, 1949; Robbins, 1966; Yarrow, 1961). Reviewing 40 years of such research, Frank (1965) concluded: "No factors were found in the parent-child interaction of schizophrenics, neurotics, or those with behavior disorders which could be identified as unique to them or which could distinguish one group from the other, or any of the groups from the families of the controls" (p. 191). Such a research venture can prove fruitful only when it takes vigorous account of the plateau on which the person exists, and the nature of the deeper potentials and their relationships.

Reviewing the research on the relation between early deprivation and later outcome, Gregory (1958) concluded that no sound, stable relationships have emerged. This class of events includes, for example, parental death, loss, or bereavement and such outcomes as the later occurrence of antisocial behavior. According to humanistic theory, stable linkages will tend to emerge only when research incorporates the two factors cited above. That is, the meaning of the loss of a parent will depend upon (a) whether the child undergoes the loss when he is on the first, second, or third plateau, and (b) the nature of the deeper potentials and relationships of the child who constructs the meaning of that event. The child whose deeper potential consists of rivalry and competitiveness will construct a different meaning of that event as compared with the child whose deeper potential consists of the experiencing of security and safe protection.

In searching for the relationships between one's early life and the way one is later, one key to the early life is the nature of the deeper potential. If it consists of rivalry and competitiveness, the research question is: What are the relationships between early evidence of a deeper potential for rivalry and competitiveness, and later outcomes? This research strategy is proposed instead of one which examines early *events*, because the deeper potential is acknowledged as being far more robust in causing later outcomes than a single early event or set of early events (Mahrer, 1969). Thus we no longer examine the later sequelae of early divorce, or birth of a new sibling, or seduction by an aunt, or a schizophrenic parent.

The meaning and significance of an early event depend also upon the plateau the child is on at the time of its occurrence. Birds may be chirping throughout the child's life, but they are processed and organized as expressions of the beauty of nature when there is a child whose deeper potentials are ready to construct experience in that way. In thus rejecting the psychoanalytic rule of thumb—the earlier the event, the more pronounced its impact—we join with Yarrow (1961) and others who support a critical period hypothesis, viz. the meaning and significance of an event are á function of the critical period (humanistic theory would redefine this as "plateau") wherein it occurs. On the first and second plateaus, the chirping of birds may have little or no meaningfulness. But the child who approaches his world (on the third plateau) to experience the beauty of nature may well construct the chirping of birds into an especially meaningful event.

We can begin to uncover linkages between early events and later events when we can take rigorous account of plateaus of human development and the functional relationship between deeper and operating potentials. When we know how to identify that the child has emerged out of the primitive field, we can begin to study the kinds of operating potentials which are constructed in relation to particular kinds of deeper potentials. There is a growing body of research on the relationships between prenatal events and events occurring in childhood (e.g. Ferreira, 1969; Joffe, 1969). As a way of uncovering linkages between prenatal events and later childhood events, one avenue would be to examine those prenatal events which express potentials of the primitive field, and those later events which express the kinds of operating potentials the child constructs in functional relationship to those deeper potentials. If, for example, defined prenatal events are expressive of a potential for rejection, distancing, getting away from (events including such pregnancy complications as toxemias, placental abnormalities and prematurity), then researchers may look for ways in which the child with such a deeper potential will construct functionally related operating potentials as expressed perhaps by such bodily events as cerebral palsy or such behavioral events as high aggressivity. The research question becomes one of uncovering the kinds of operating potentials constructed in relationship with particular deeper potentials, instead of a haphazardly unsystematic pursuit of early and later events.

The child as an active constructor of experience. Once the child is well onto the second plateau, he has a sense of self, together with a set of deeper potentials, and he exists in his own phenomenological world. There is a personhood, an awareness of being, a sense of existing as a person. He also has deeper potentials and their relationships, gifts of the dissolved primitive field. These deeper potentials may, for example, relate to the experiencing of nothingness, emptiness, a dead being without substance; they may also include the potential for experiencing raging unreachability, a protective withdrawal from any sort of threatened encroachment. Given all this equipment, the child is now ready to construct experience in an active fashion. That is, the child *is geared toward having certain kinds of experiences*, toward processing his world in such a way as is determined by these deeper potentials and their relationships. This system of potentials and relationships constitutes a kind of template or "world design" for the development of particular modes of experiencing (Binswanger, 1958a). Given the deeper potentials for experiencing nothingness and for experiencing unreachability, given the relationships among these potentials, given a differentiated sense of self, the child is now a person geared toward constructing his world in ways which enable certain kinds of more or less predefined experiencings.

The person on this plateau, whether he is six or 16, will now select out experiences, will organize his world such that certain kinds of experiences will occur to and with him, will search out and cause to occur given classes of experiences. Even when the person on this plateau is a young child, he is the one who constructs the "learning" experiences. We arrive at this position by at least three considerations. (a) The child has a set of deeper potentials for experiencing. Because of these potentials for experiencing, the child will organize, define, cause to occur those events which fit in with these potentials for experiencing. Given a deeper potential for experiencing affection, the child will construct experiences which relate in some meaningful way to such a deeper potential. (b) The child has particular kinds of relationships among his deeper potentials. If these relationships are integrative, the child is oriented toward constructing experiences which are of an integrative nature. If these relationships are disintegrative, the child will construct experiences whose character is disintegrative. (c) The child actively constructs his own external world by the four modes described in Chapter 6. There is a conspicuously large measure of active construction when the child fabricates his external world. There is a large measure of active construction when the child builds an external world conjointly with others, and also when the child constructs his external world by utilizing readymade building blocks. Even when the child receives an intrusive external world there is a component of the child as an active constructor of the external world. On the basis of these three considerations, humanistic theory sees the child as actively constructing (organizing, processing, determining, selecting, causing) the nature of his experiences. This position must be set against those which hold the reverse, viz. that the experiences cause and determine the way the child is.

The deeper potentials and their relationships orient the child to process experience into predetermined meanings. If the deeper potential involves clinging to another, gaining security from closeness, then this deeper potential is like a meaning ready to lend itself to events which come his way. Events lend definition to the meaning which is already present in a manner reminiscent of the James (1894) theory of emotions. The child's potential for clinging to security was present in the primitive field as the potentials of his father and mother. When the primitive field dissolved (plateau 2), that potential became a part of the child himself. When he was six years old his father deserted the family. Within approximately two years, the son became much more mature and responsible, a person with a common sense stability, and probably his mother's closest friend. The deeper potential for experiencing clinging to the other person and gaining secure closeness had organized father's leaving in its own way. Did father's desertion "cause" the son to be stable, mature, responsible, close to mother? Only in the sense that the event was there to be organized and given meaning by the deeper potential. The desertion defined further what was already present. Thus, according to humanistic theory, the learning (or readiness to learn or deeper potential) causes the experience rather than the traditional posture in which the experience causes the learning.

When we focus on the infant encompassed within the primitive field (plateau 1), the primitive field *acts upon* the infant who is passively moulded and shaped by the primitive field. When we move to the second plateau, the child is still the passive one. If the primitive field dissolves away, the pivotal agents are the significant figures of the primitive field, and not the child himself. Now, on the third plateau, it is the *child* who is the active one, the one who acts upon and organizes and processes and constructs. There occur magnificent changes in the child and in his world, changes which *he* brings about. The child makes the experience he has. He actively constructs the world into being a menacing place or a nest of security. Virtually everything which has been considered as "development" or "growth" or "learning" lends itself to reinterpretation in which the child is the active seeker and organizer of experience. In all of this, the child is possessed of primary initiative, selectivity, and an active seeking of experience (Buhler, 1968b). Development, growth, and learning are not processes which happen *to* the child, not processes within the child, processes which do things to him. They are the fruits of the child's active construction of the world in which he exists.

The Construction of Operating Potentials

If we take a closer look at the construction of operating potentials, it seems to involve more than just a child's actively organizing experience. There are initiating experiences comprised of material more or less furnished by the external world, organized and processed by the deeper potentials and their relationships. We shall discuss each of these factors in turn.

The role of the deeper potential. When deeper potentials work upon experience, seeking to organize experience in a way which fits, sooner or later the deeper potentials are usually successful. If the deeper potential involves the experiencing of emptiness and nothingness, it will process what happens to the child until the right experience is constructed. It is as if the deeper potential is on the lookout for the appropriate event for the experiencing of emptiness and nothingness. Within the language of learning theory, ". . . a strong motive state will lead the individual to be especially alert to any stimuli which are relevant to the goal objects for that motive" (Maher, 1966, p. 62). The child is so ready to architect experiences which fit in with the deeper potential for experiencing emptiness and nothingness that he typically is quite successful. Working on all his experiences to have that sense of nothingness and emptiness, success occurs when his friend walks right past him to the other child, and when the two walk away, leaving him sitting on the grass, alone. In those moments are born the way to experience nothingness and emptiness: being invisible and left behind. He was five years old, and he had constructed his own operating potential: being invisible and left behind constitute a newly constructed operating potential serving to provide for the experiencing of the deeper sense of emptiness and nothingness.

The child with a deeper potential for the experiencing of being special and prized will be led toward the development of operational means of fulfilling that experiencing. When he is a young child, that potential begins to come alive when he is alone with his grandmother who is telling him about her childhood in Europe. That deeper potential, which seldom if ever came to life hitherto, now leaps into life and guides him into just the right ways of being with grandmother. He listens to her well, and it happens when she prizes him and responds to him as special in his listening to her, his receiving her stories about the past. What has emerged is an operating potential for being a good listener, a confidante, a sharer of the secrets of the other person. It was the deeper potential for experiencing specialness and for being prized which guided him into constructing that situation with grandmother into the birth of a new operating potential. The deeper potential is there first, and actively guides the child into fashioning and developing a mode of instrumenting what it must experience, i.e., an operating potential.

The young daughter acquired a basic potential for the experiencing of potency when the primitive field dissolved away and that deeper potential became a part of her. As she moved through childhood, it was as if the deeper potential hungered for ways of experiencing capability, virility, strength, energy—potency (cf. Fenichel, 1954f). She became invaluable to boys: attractive to boys, needed and wanted by boys, friendly and intimate to boys. She became the energizing resource in her relationship with all groups—peers, younger children, and older folks. In being this way, especially with older persons, she sparked others to feeling alive again. She had characteristics which made people feel energetic and vital. These ways of being were formed as an operating means of providing for the experiencing of the deeper potential which had worked to fashion experience in its own defined way, an operating potential enabling the deeper experiencing to occur.

In the construction of an operating potential, the deeper potential is constantly working to fashion the world into constituting the right kind of experience. Without the appropriate situation or event, that particular operating potential would not occur—not in precisely the same way at the same time. Had those companions not been there, not looked past the child, and not walked off without him, the operating potential for rejection would not have been born, not born there and then. The external event or situation is useful but insufficient for the construction of an operating potential. The child was ready to use such a situation. But if the child were not ready, if his deeper potential were of a different kind, no amount of available rejection situations would have culminated in a rejected child. I am prepared to suggest that early experiences contribute to operating potentials only to the extent that the deeper potentials of the child are appropriate and ready to use the events to construct the operating potential.

The role of relationships among potentials. When the deeper potentials are integrated, the processing of experience is typically pleasurable, and the deeper potential engages with good feelings in the development of the operating potential. Binswanger (1958c) describes a woman whose deeper personality process includes the experiencing of being a hole, being filled, being emptied, retaining. Given that deeper potential for experiencing, the designing of experience in the form of operating potentials *can* be surrounded with good feelings. Thus eating, preparing food, enjoying the learning of culinary skills can all emerge as operating ways of being, and these can be saturated in good feelings. Or the young girl could become an avid reader and story teller, and being this way, as an operating potential providing for the experiencing of the deeper potential, could be filled with good feelings of happiness, pleasure, and satisfaction.

If the deeper potentials are relatively integrated, the operating potentials which are constructed tend to provide a more or less *direct* means of enabling the deeper experiencing. For example, if the deeper potential relates to the experiencing of potency, the child will develop operating potentials which provide a more or less direct means of that experiencing. Thus the child may develop operating potentials which consist of leadership or competence or energizing others, and these provide a relatively direct avenue for the experiencing of the deeper potency. Accordingly, the child whose deeper potential (e.g. being nurtured and cared for) is integrated will tend to develop an operating potential which not only provides more or less directly for that experiencing, but which does so in ways which are accompanied with integrative good feelings. That child may develop operating ways of being charming, or eliciting care and concern from others, or for giving and receiving, or for attracting dependency-providing others. He will not only experience a direct full measure of being nurtured and cared for, but, in addition, the tone and style of the developed operating potential will be such that the accompanying feelings are good ones.

If, on the other hand, the deeper potential is surrounded with *dis-*

integrative relationships, the operating potentials which are developed not only provide *for* the experiencing of the deeper potential, but, in addition, serve to *fend off*, avoid, deny, hide, defend against, disprove the deeper potential. If, for example, the deeper potential relates to potency, and the relationships are disintegrative, the child may develop an operating leadership which seems wrong or fruitless or which is full of problems. She is bothered and disliked. She is a failure as a leader. She is never really a good leader. Or she may develop operating ways of fighting against and denying the deeper potential by being a feckless person, incompetent and unsure of herself, never able to accomplish, lacking drive and energy, needing others to provide her with direction and vitalizing energy.

A child, whose deeper potential for experiencing being cared for and nurtured is surrounded with disintegrative feelings, will be set on a life course which not only provides for that experiencing but which will insure that the accompanying feelings are bad disintegrative ones. For example, a disintegrative operating potential is born one day when a boy is five years old, and is playing with two boys who are about eight years old. The three of them have been playing with his tow truck. The companions lose interest in the truck and decide to leave him in order to find others who want to play baseball. Arising out of that situation is an operating potential which serves the function of inducing others to regard him in the same disintegrative way he regards his own deeper potential. His eyes fill with tears, his face feels hot. He sits there holding his truck close, and when the boys look at him they know that he has no interest in going with them. Kevin whines about playing with his truck. Here is the emerging of a whining, rejected, lost operating potential which invites others to regard his disintegratively, i.e., as disgusting, hateful, infantile. In that experience emerged an operating potential linked to disintegrative feelings, one which not only offers a measure of experiencing the deeper potential, but more importantly, which gets others to bear toward him the same disintegrative relationship he bears toward that deeper potential.

Given a deeper potential with disintegrative relationships, an operating potential may be born out of simple ordinary experiences. Binswanger (1958a, p. 203) tells of a little girl for whom the very ordinary event of the heel separating from her shoe while ice skating is invested with traumatic anxiety and, furthermore, defines much of the balance of her life. How can such a mild event apparently bear such an impact upon the little girl's life? Suppose that her deeper potential related to clinging to mother, uniting with her, and that this deeper potential is surrounded with disintegrative feelings. How to run from this? How to pull away from and avoid the deeper potential? In the mild event of the heel tearing loose from the shoe is invested the answer which was in shadowy half-formation. In that moment was expressed the new operating potential: tear loose, separate, break free. Until then she had never experienced that, yet she was fully *ready* to experience all that prior to the incident. The structure of her personality led her to be ready to have such a meaningful experience to celebrate the birth of the new operating potential.

When relationships among the deeper potentials are disintegrative, construction of the operating way of being is tantamount to the birth of problem behavior (symptoms, pathological behavior, painful ways of being). In the first appearance of the operating potential is the first occurrence of the problem. Alan moved onto the second plateau with a deeper potential for being immature, undeveloped, infantile. This was surrounded in disintegration. An operating potential was born in circumstances involving the birth of a younger brother when he was five years old. Alan's deeper potential had been on the lookout for a means of being experienced disintegratively. The new operating potential came to life little by little in the context of the new baby. It emerged in good measure one morning when, sitting on the toilet, he smelled the diapers of the baby. Picking them up, he rubbed them over his arms and on his knees. He went to the baby's room and played with the baby's clothes, smelling them, fondling them. Finally, he wrapped himself in baby's blanket, got in the crib and fell asleep. Later, Alan began making baby sounds and urinated in the diaper he put on. This operating potential, born in the simple, ordinary situation of sitting on the toilet, can be taken as the emergence of problem behavior, specifically of so-called regressive symptoms.

The disintegrative operating potential may be born in situations which are ordinary and mundane, or it may be born in situations which are traumatic. For example, a little boy entered onto the third plateau with a deeper potential for being fragile, delicately put together, easily shattered. That potential was surrounded with disintegrative relationships, and sought an operating means of insuring that being shattered would never occur. In the barn, playing with four other little boys, one of them grabbed him and was on the verge of hurling him over the side. He was filled with explosive terror of falling and breaking apart, his body shattering into splinters. He was catastrophized with blind terror. One of the other boys stepped in, firmly told the assailant to stop, and the situation was ended. At that moment, the operating potential was born. From then on he bound himself to protectors who could save him from sudden shatterings of his delicate fragility. The precise nature of the operating potential was organized and defined in this traumatic episode. Mednick (1962, 1967) has reviewed research suggestive that behaviors which first happen in such explosive, anxious, traumatic situations seem to be characterized by a remarkable perseverativeness. Why is this? I am inclined to hypothesize that deeper potentials surrounded by profoundly disintegrative relationships will (a) lead to the birth of operating potentials dedicated toward burying the deeper potential, (b) will arise in sudden, anxiety-filled, dramatic, explosively traumatic situations. I find that the severely disintegrative relationships lead to the construction and use of traumatic situations, that the experiencing of the deeper potential contributes to the traumatic nature of the situation, and that the function of the operating potential is one of burying (massively denying) the deeper potential. For example, Frieda, who was nine years old, and had lived alone with her father and two younger brothers since her mother left years ago, had a disintegrative relationship with a deeper potential for experiencing powerful sexuality, being her father's mate, being joined to him sexually. One afternoon, coming home from school, she saw her father's car in the driveway. Puzzled, because he seldom was home that early, she went inside and went to her father's bedroom. There they were, in the midst of sexual groanings and bodily jerkings, both nude, the slender chestnut-haired girl sitting astride her father. For the first time her deeper potential rose up to the behavioral superfice: "Be with *me*. *I* want to be your woman. Be that way with *me!*" The severely disintegrative relationship with that potential screamed out for some desperate way of burying it, of running from it, blocking it out, not seeing it. Her whole being was surging for some way. She ran to her room, fell on the bed, her whole body flung into clonic and tonic movements. Gradually, her state receded into unawareness, and the bodily feelings concentrated in the anus. There was a pushing and a holding there, and then the soft defecation oozed into her panties. She whimpered and cried as a baby whimpers and cries. She is a baby now. An operating potential had just been born: experiencing being a baby. Awakening an hour later, she was ashamed of herself, threw the soiled undergarment in the trash, took a shower, and thought vaguely about her father and the woman. The thumping sexuality in her had receded. Now she had an available operating potential: being cute, baby-like, a little-girl-ness. That operating potential came into play from then on, whenever the deeper sexuality rose too close to the behavioral superfice. She was capable of regressive, infantile behavior if necessary, but the little girl cuteness was adequate for many years to come.

As described in Chapter 2, the operating potentials are developed to serve two purposes. One is to provide for the experiencing of the deeper potentials, and the other is to attenuate and truncate the experiencing of the deeper potentials. The more or less precise nature of the operating potentials which are constructed depends upon the integrative or disintegrative relationships surrounding the deeper potential. Aside from the magnitude or intensity of the disintegrative relationships, if the relationships are disintegrative, we have a basis for predicting that the kind of operating potential which is constructed will be accompanied with disintegrative feelings. The child heads into life *ready* to be that way which provides for bad feelings such as anxiety or fear, being torn apart or at loose ends, depressed or bewildered. Although other theories share this picture of the child's readiness to enter life experiences so as to have bad feelings, there are significant differences in what it is which so equips the child. For example, Eysenck (1955, 1957, 1960) understands the determining factors to include the inheriting of a high loading on a neuroticism dimension, preparing the child with a strong proclivity toward anxiety-invoking stimuli. According to Eysenck, the child's nervous system has been gentically predisposed toward such affective overreactivity. According to humanistic theory, on the other hand, the readiness or proclivity is a function of the disintegrative nature of the relationships among the deeper potentials.

The role of the external world. In the construction of one's world, four modes are available (Chapter 6). In each mode, the person may use building blocks, raw materials of the external world. In the same way, a child may construct the operating potential from raw materials of his encompassing external world. Thus the particular nature of the operating potential is more or less a function of what is there in the environment. We may know that the deeper potential involves godliness, and that godliness organizes and selects from experiences there in the encompassing environment. In the first mode (Figure 6.1), worshipping females may *intrude* onto him, inviting him to be their god, and the deeper potential may process an operating potential for sexual masculinity, for being the object of women's romanticized idolatry. A second mode includes use of *ready-made* components of the external world. If the neighborhood includes persons waiting to worship the messiah who will mobilize their foaming angers, then the deeper potential may construct an operating way of being a political revolutionary. Or, using the third mode of construction, the person may work out an operating potential *conjointly* with another person. They "play" with one another, they do a creative dance with one another until, out of that process, one becomes the needy hurting one, the one with pain and anguish, while the other enters into the constructed role of healer, the understanding one, the god. Finally, in the fourth mode, the operating potential may be constructed by means of fabrication, a mode which can require very little from the external world. The child organizes the tiny toy buildings and machinery and workers into a magnificent empire which magically carries out his every wish. Huge play buildings are constructed, and a toy city is developed under his omnipotent leadership. In the construcion of these operating potentials, the deeper potential uses' materials available in the world. Depending on the mode of construction, the more available the materials, the more likely they are to be used in the construction of the operating potentials.

What is available will vary with different families, neighborhoods, cultures, for the deeper potentials can only organize what is more or less available within that person's external world. When the sheer raw materials for godliness vary from culture to culture, the constructed ways of being godly—that is, the constructed operating potentials— will also vary from culture to culture. Even within the same culture, the raw stuff which is available will vary from generation to generation. Being a priest or a head of the family or a psychoanalyst may have been an available commodity in grandfather's generation, but the meanings of these roles may have significantly changed a few generations later. Children in different neighborhoods or cultures or societies may share similar deeper potentials about personal loss and death. But the operating potentials which are constructed will differ immensely from one another. A child living in a particular time and place in China may make use of the receding of sexual organs into the abdomen, and the certain imminence of death. That child may develop a large belly because of the ideas available in that culture. A child in America, having the same deeper potential, would probably not become obese. On the other hand, a child of the Objibwa tribe lives in a culture complete with ideas of homicidal killing and cannibalistic eating of one's own family members. The ways of being (operating potentials) evolving from the same deeper potential will be quite different from the Chinese or the American child.

The role of initiating experiences. The experiences which initiate or give birth to operating potentials contain a lot of power. In these initiating experiences are deeper potentials, with their relationships, actively working on events so as to carve out operating potentials. Prior to these initiating experiences the child was not especially caustic and sarcastic (or athletically competitive, or sexually provocative, or competently responsible), but *after* these initiating experiences the child was a somewhat different person. An operating potential was generated, took shape in a defined package of initiating experiences. Whereas we can identify these initiating experiences for *operating* potentials, we cannot do the same for *basic* potentials, for the latter were present in the primitive field before the child even emerged as a person. There is no analogous set of initiating experiences for basic potentials, no points of origin, no situational context in which they were generated.

Once we differentiate the origins of operating potentials from the origins of deeper potentials, we are in a position to recognize the broad range of experiences in which operating potentials are initiated. Personality approaches which fail to make such a differentiation typically acknowledge only one or two kinds of initiating experiences. Yarrow (1961) finds that many approaches presume that initiating experiences fall into two categories: deprivation and stress. If the child is caustic and sarcastic, or athletically competitive, or withdrawn from interpersonal interaction, the initiating experiences consist either of deprivation or stress. No such two-fold category system is used in humanistic theory. Instead, we recognize an extremely broad spectrum of kinds of experiences in which operating potentials are initiated, and the search for the origins of the person's operating potentials consists of an investigation of these initiating experiences. If it consists of being strong and potent, we look for the initiating experiences wherein that operating potential was born. These are the crucially determining experiences, the special moments in which the person's operating potentials first came to life. Identifying these circumstances is the goal of searching into one's highly personalized past. Sometimes the search takes us to circumstances when he is ten or 12 or 16, sometimes we locate the circumstances when he was a year old or when he was five or seven years old. Regardless of the age, the importance lies in the nature of the initiating circumstances within which the operating potential was first constructed.

Once we know the initiating experiences, we can reenter those experiences to construct *other* operating potentials. Even if the nature of the deeper potential is held constant, experiencing can be promoted in ways which bring about *altogether new operating potentials*. There are at least two ways in which new operating potentials may be constructed out of the initiating experiences. One involves the disintegrative relationships surrounding the *deeper* potential. To the extent that these relationships are changed to integrative relationships, the person is free to reenter the initiating experiences and create new operating ways of being. For example, I described the nine-year-old girl whose deeper potential consisted of sexuality, of being her father's female, of being joined to him sexually. So disintegrative were the relationships surrounding this deeper potential, that the task of the operating potential would be to block out the slightest whisper of this deeper experiencing. Coming across her father and a woman in the throes of intercourse, the operating potential was born—a little girl cuteness, a being like an infant, all as a means of completely sealing off the possibility of experiencing the deeper sexuality. If this person were able to soften the disintegrative relationships surrounding the deeper potential, if she were able to move in the direction of integrative relationships, then it is possible to reenter the earlier initiating experiences in ways which would provide for the creation of other operating potentials. A reentry into the early traumatic scene might enable her to experience the pleasurable love-making in a new way which yields a new experience of identifying closeness and intimacy with the woman. Here is the birth of another operating potential (identifying closeness and intimacy with women) to complement or replace that which arose in the initial experience (little girl cuteness, being like an infant).

A second way of reconstructing other operating potentials out of the initiating experiences grows out of the nature of the deeper potential itself. In nearly every initiating experience in which operating potentials are born, *other* operating potentials *can* be constructed which provide a much better fit and far more direct experiencing of the deeper potential. This is true even in those circumstances where the nature of the relationships was moderately disintegrative, but it is exceedingly appropriate in those circumstances where the nature of the relationships was *severely* disintegrative. Regardless of the degree to which the operating potential was born to facilitate or to reduce the experiencing of the deeper potential, the sheer presence of the operating potential stands in the way of full experiencing of the deeper potential (see Chapter 2). When we go back to those initiating experiences in which the operating potential was born, we are in a position to undergo considerably more direct experiencing of the deeper potential. We can undergo those early initiating experiences in altogether new ways which no longer avoid or curtail the deeper potential but, instead, open it up to much more direct experiencing. In this way those early initiating experiences become powerful avenues for rebeginning personality development along whole new lines of operating potentials. Take, for example, the child whose deeper potential consists of the experiencing of mastery. Initiating experiences occurred when he was building a structure with his erector set, and when he was building a tree house with a friend. Out of these experiences arose the operating potential for building, for making something, for creating some sort of structure. This operating potential carried him into real estate and building construction. Reexperiencing those initiating experiences allowed for the more open, direct experiencing of the deeper sense of mastery. The compellingness of building, of creating structures, receded. Instead, the person entered into a more deeply intensive, saturated sense of mastery itself. To the operating potential for building and constructing was added a new operating potential for direct mastery—for owning, making his, creating. To the real estate and construction businesses there were added new ways of being, new ways of directly experiencing the sense of mastery, new operating potentials. He began reading history, novels. He developed a keen interest in painting. He also developed a new sense of the area where he lived, and he entered into the political arena.

The Construction of an External World

The person on the third plateau becomes the constructor of his own external world. He is now engaged in a lifelong process of building external worlds whose nature is largely predetermined by the nature of the deeper potentials and their relationships. As the child begins building his own external world, he constructs one which offers the appropriate context for experiencing, or he constructs an external world which is an extension of his operating or deeper potentials. We are now describing the processes discussed in Chapter 6. If the child has a deeper potential for the experiencing of nothingness, emptiness, being without substance, then the child will go about constructing an external world in a way which fits in with this deeper potential and its relationships with other potentials. Only certain kinds of external worlds will likely be constructed. For example, the external world may provide for the experiencing of such operating potentials as leadership or ambitiousness, or being dumb and uncomprehending. Or the external world may be composed of extensions of the deeper potential. Whatever the function of the external world, its nature must fit in with the content and relationships of the child's deeper potential.

On this third plateau, the child is an intact personality, actively working upon the construction of an external world on the basis of deeper potentials, operating potentials, and the relationships among these sets of potentials. On the first plateau, the infant existed in an ocean which was the encompassing primitive personality. Now there is a person, complete with deeper and operating potentials, existing in an external world which he constructs. Suppose that the primitive field were characterized by strength, certainty, sinew and toughness, potentials of the parents who perhaps construct an infant as their dependency, softness, clingingness. As the child enters upon the third plateau, he acquires the deeper potential of strength, certainty, sinew and toughness. Out of this deeper potential and its relationships, there is developed a set of ways (operating potentials) for experiencing the deeper potential in ways consonant with the dependency, softness, clingingness. As one likely outcome, that child may remain dependent, soft, clinging, and the nature of this way of being takes on a quality which removes it far afield from any whisper of the deeper strength, certainty, sinew and toughness. What kind of a world does this child construct? As described in Chapter 6, he may build an external world which serves as a *context for experiencing* the operating dependency, softness, clingingness. His world may enable him to experience the soft dependency of being the kind of world which cuddles him, protects and cares for him, is the kind of world to which he can cling in soft dependency. Or, he may construct a world which is an *extension of his operating potential*. His world is dependent, caring, nurturing, soft. It may be a world which draws away from him as tough and mean. Or, finally, the constructed world may be an *extension of the deeper potential*: tough and mean, strong and certain. It likely is a world to which he relates disintegratively, one he distrusts and fears. The modes and functions of the constructed external world were described in Chapter 6. Our point here is that the third plateau is one on which the person now has the wherewithall to construct and build the external world in which he exists.

IV. Development of New Operating Potentials

On the third plateau, the major work consists of the development of operating potentials. Once a set of operating potentials has been developed, the next task consists in the development of *new* operating potentials. The person who is engaged in this enterprise is on the fourth plateau.

The Process of Developing New Operating Potentials

The new operating potential is developed to serve essentially the same functions as the old one. Both are means of providing for the experiencing of the deeper potential, and both are also means of attenuating the experiencing of the deeper potential (see Chapter 2). If the old operating potential served as a means of providing for the experiencing of a deeper dominance, the new one is developed to carry out the same mission. If the old operating potential served as a means of denying the deeper dominance, so too does the new one. Whatever the old operating potential accomplished with regard to the deeper dominance and its relationships, so too does the new operating potential. More than serving the same deeper potential, there often is a phenotypic similarity. For example, in his large-scale research on early life history factors in relation to later adult maladjustment, Roff (1970) concluded that his findings were in the same neighborhood as those of other such large scale investigations, viz., youngsters with poor peer relations in early life later tended to show patterns of social maladjustment. From our perspective, such research is consistent with a paradigm in which early poor peer relations (as an early operating potential) are replaced with later patterns of social maladjustment (as a later operating potential). One set of operating potentials replaces a previous set of operating potentials. Whatever deeper potentials were served by "poor peer relations" in early life were served also by "patterns of social maladjustment" in later life. The process of developing new operating potentials generally consists of the replacement of one operating potential with another which not only serves the same functions but even looks like the initial one.

One of the functions of both new and old operating potentials is to avoid and deny the disintegrative deeper potential. Thus the person develops new ways of doing precisely what the initial operating potential did. The physician is now in his fifties, and his immediate problems center on his growing inclination to divorce his wife and marry his pretty research assistant who is 23 years old. His entire life can aptly be described as a struggle against a deeper potential in the form of death, decay, atrophy. As a child he was always restless, agitated, playful. In later childhood and throughout his adolescence he became a skilled sculptor. Artistic, creative, energetic, he entered medical school and became a physician specializing in obstetrics. In his thirties he "found" his body, plunging into tennis, jogging, and yoga. In addition, he had five children with his young, pretty, vibrant wife, and enjoyed life fully. Soon there was added a new career of research on childbirth. Each new wave of operating potentials served as a fresh means of warding off the deeper sense of death, atrophy, and decay. Now, in his fifties, his wife was clearly becoming old. He too was becoming less vibrant and youthful; the spectre of decay and death was taking hold. Turning to the young research assistant was merely another sought after means of doing what each succeeding wave of operating potentials had always done, viz. warding off the deeper sense of death, atrophy, and decay.

Whether the new operating potential is developed primarily to provide for the experiencing of the deeper potential or for its avoidance, the functions of the old and new operating potentials are quite similar. Sometimes the process can be described as one of differentiation so that the old and the new operating potentials share a root commonality and differ primarily in their behavioral aspects. In childhood, an operating potential for competition may be experienced through physical competition. Thus the child experiences physical competition in being stronger than his peers, running faster, being better at hockey. In later adolescence and adulthood, that operating sense of competition may differentiate to include a sexual competition, so that he is better looking than others, more skilled in charming girls, cleverer in sexualized conversation. It is as if the operating potential involves the experiencing of competition, and the change has been from the experiencing of this competition through physical means to the added experiencing of this competition through sexual means.

When does this process of development take place? As indicated in Figure 16.1, the development of new operating potentials can occur whenever the child has developed the first set of operating potentials. As a general guideline, the development of new operating potentials can begin quite early in childhood, although it may begin during later childhood, or throughout adolescence, or at any time during adulthood. Indeed, the development of new operating potentials can stretch throughout the person's entire life span.

Change and Invariance in the Course of Life

Change occurs at the operating level. On the fourth plateau, the course of life is one of *change* at the operating level and *invariance* at the deeper level. Especially when the deeper potentials are surrounded in disintegrative relationships, each succeeding wave of operating potentials has its backward eye on the same set of disintegrative deeper potentials. Practically from birth, Stella fled from being the cold, unfeeling one. So fearful was she of this disintegrative deeper potential that there developed wave after wave of running from this awful inner truth. Throughout her childhood she was the good little girl. That first operating potential proved successful as a way of not being cold and unfeeling, not caring, not responding. In her early adolescence, she became warm and friendly, sympathetic to her friends. This was her first new operating potential, but it too served to run from the metallic inner unfeelingness. In her later adolescence and early adulthood she developed a second new operating potential: wild festivals of unfettered feelings. She was silly and impulsive, moody and effervescent. In her thirties she began experiencing homosexuality—a loving, caressing, warmly intimate closeness with women of her own age and general way of life. Yet each additional operating potential was a solution to the same old problem—the unchanging disintegrative deeper coldness, uncaring, unfeeling hardness. Has any substantial change occurred? When we focus on each old operating potential, the addition of a new one constitutes a real and substantial change. When, however, we focus on the deeper potential and the nature of the disintegrative relationship between the person and the deeper potential, practically nothing has changed.

From childhood on, each developed new operating potential served as a means of providing for the experiencing of nurturance. During childhood she was the little mother who helped others, loved caring for pets and flowers, nourished her younger brothers. In adolescence she was the beloved friend whose house was the center of activities. In adulthood she married a man whom she gently nurtured into becoming an extremely wealthy businessman and philanthropist. Now, in her late forties, she is the beloved sponsor of humanitarian projects in her community, a warm and giving person, respected as a true friend by scores of persons whom she has nurtured along their ways. At the operating level, there have been waves of changes. But at the level of deeper potentials, she has continuously been providing for new ways of experiencing the fixed potential for nurturance.

Changes in intellectual performance can be understood as the engaging of new operating potentials to serve an unvarying deeper one. This includes changes from one kind of intelligent behavior to another, or changes in apparent overall level of intelligence. If we abandon the traditional baggage on the concept of intelligence, the notion is quite simple: a deeper potential may engage a new operating potential complete with a new set of intelligence behaviors. Thus, the young boy never manifested a high level of cerebral activity, was never especially keen on solving abstract problems, did not figure things out—until his deeper masculine competitiveness slowly disengaged an operating potential for physically dominating peers, and slowly developed a new operating potential for intellectual prowess. This change occurred during his pubertal years from 11 to 13. He had, indeed, become "smarter." Yet, from our perspective, this "change in intelligence" is understood as merely the replacement of one operating potential for another, with the result that substantial changes in measured intelligence scores would be manifested (cf. Sontag, Baker, & Nelson, 1955). What occurs as change *is* change at the level of operating ways of being, even though the determining deeper potential remains unchanged.

Growth and maturation as the development of new operating potentials. If change may be said to occur over the course of a person's life, the predominance of that change consists of the development of new operating potentials. At the distal operating level, significant life changes seem to occur, but at the proximal level of the deeper potentials, there may be no change whatsoever. Over the course of life there is typically no change in the nature of the deeper potentials. There is typically no change in the disintegrative (or integrative) relationships surrounding the deeper potentials and between them and the operating potentials. There is typically no change in the *functions* served by the kind of external world which is constructed, and generally the *nature* of the external world remains essentially unaltered. In spite of all this invariance, the development of new operating potentials is dignified as maturation, growth, and human development. According to humanistic theory, existence on this fourth plateau is not entitling to such dignity. What has been accepted as growth, maturation, and human development is little more than the development of new operating potentials under the direction of the same old deeper personality structure.

We can select a given person and follow the succession of operating

potentials which serve the same deeper experiencings over the course
of his life. When we observe large groups of persons, we notice commonalities in newly developed operating potentials. From a normative
empirical point of view, we may identify high frequency deeper potentials which are served by common operating potentials as persons
move from infancy on through adulthood. It is the common basic
potentials which, to some extent, explain the relative consistency along
what developmental psychoanalysts and psychologists such as Leon
Saul (1960) and Anna Freud (1965) conceptualize as "lines of development." Underneath each "line of development" is a shared deeper potential (e.g. dependency) which is normatively and empirically
common to some group. When these theorists find five, six, or eight
"lines of development," they are describing sets of common deeper
potentials. When these theorists describe "stages" for each "line of development," they are making normative, empirical statements about
succeeding waves of operating potentials. For example, Anna Freud
speaks of a line of dependency development proceeding from
mother-infant unity on through later stages such as an oedipal stage
and a stage of adult object relationships. These stages are descriptions
of empirically common operating potentials. We reject the notion of
biologically based lines and stages of development, and, instead, understand these respectively as empirically common deeper potentials
and commonly shared new operating potentials.

If we study a culture and inquire when certain kinds of behaviors
take place, we are describing empirical norms (i.e., common operating
potentials) relative to that culture. We are not uncovering some process of development which moves along in stages. For example,
roughly half of stuttering behavior seems to emerge by approximately
the fifth year, and virtually all stuttering seems to have initiated by the
close of pubertal years. What does this mean? From our perspective, it
means that we now have a description of a particular culture, and the
approximate years in which an operating potential is engaged. In no
way is it presumed that we are dealing with a developmental process
with stages which include that of speech or stuttering. We can only say
that if a person in that culture is going to engage an operating potential involving the behavior of stuttering, he most likely will have engaged that by the end of puberty.

Stuttering has typically been considered a problem, and the biopsychological notion of growth, stages of development, and maturation
has ordinarily excluded problems. Yet the development of "problem"
operating potentials follows, from the perspective of humanistic
theory, the same principles as apply to the development of "non-
problem" potentials. In both the selection is drawn from that which is
available in the given culture. How may an adolescent female, living in

Ontario, avoid and deny her close sexualized bond with her father? During childhood and preadolescence she was a buddy of her father's, avoiding sexuality by being a partner in skiing, rough housing with her collies, building model trains. In adolescence, she transformed into a defiant homosexual, continuing in a new way the same avoidance of the deeper potential. She owned her sexual partners, led them into rebellious defiance against school authorities, families, other "straight" girls, and the police. How may we explain the development of these specific ways of being? If such rebellious defiance is not an expression of a particular stage of growth of development, then how can it be understood? Given the young woman's deeper personality structure, each new operating potential was constructed (selected) from what was available in her situational context or group setting. Problematic ways of being ". . . may be as much characteristic of some particular situation or group setting as they are enduring attributes of persons" (Mechanic, 1962, p. 68). More than that, these problematic operating potentials may be said to be characteristic of a particular group or culture which holds them forth as an available repertoire from which the person's own deeper personality structure makes the appropriate selection.

Each successively developed operating potential, whether problematic or not, is typically more complex than its predecessor. Thus the child who gains a sense of mastery by building a tower of small blocks may become an adult who gains that sense of mastery by building a small business into a massive conglomerate. As succeeding waves of operating potentials become more complex, so too is the nature of the constructed external world more complex. When we step back and consider collective human beings over many centuries, it appears that the constructed external world has been made progressively more complex. We may cite progressively more complex technology, communication, social and economic institutions. Yet these progressively more complex external worlds are constructed out of deeper potentials in much the same way as the deeper potentials in the person lead to the construction of progressively more complicated external worlds by successive sets of operating potentials. Whether in an individual or in collective persons, the construction of more complex external worlds is a function of deeper potentials. This way of making sense of the development of more complex external worlds may be contrasted with what Asch (1952) terms the "biological conception of man," in which the development of technology, complex social and cultural institutions, are understood as merely more complicated means of satisfying simple physiological needs of biological human organisms. At the base, according to humanistic theory, are basic *potentials* and not basic *physiological needs* (cf. Chapter 4).

Some implications for life history research strategies. So embedded in our thinking is the idea of development (with its sequence of developmental stages), that practically no amount of research will dislodge that idea. If life history research accumulates an impressive record of failure to identify systematic linkages between early and later life events, what are our options? Must we correct our research paradigms and strategies? Must we alter our theory of developmental stages, and possibly consider alternative theories of how infants become children and children become adults? Must we ask whether we are trying to see something which is not there? Bronson (1974) takes the position that the theory of development is sound and the fact of development is also sound; what requires change is the research strategy employed: "Along with some others, I see our apparent inability to make empirical predictions about later life from the early years as so much against good sense, common observation, and the thrust of all developmental theories that I can take it only as an indictment of established paradigms and methods rather than as evidence of a developmental reality" (p. 276). In contrast, humanistic theory is willing to concede that all three can profitably be altered. We can alter the traditional theory of developmental stages. We can alter the research paradigms we employ, and we can alter the supposed facts of developmental reality. Indeed, once we must no longer "see" a process of bio-developmental stages, we can entertain the possibility that the apparent changes we witnessed were not developmental stages at all. Furthermore, once the theory is free to take a different perspective toward what occurs in the course of a person's life, we can devise more fitting research paradigms and methods.

In childhood, one set of operating potentials may serve to express a deeper process. In later childhood or adulthood, another set of operating potentials may be developed to serve the same potential. It appears as if the first set is causally related to the second, yet what we have is merely another instance of a second wave of operating potentials. For example, Ricks (1970) summarizes research by many investigators as confirming a relatively consistent relationship between low IQ scores in childhood and the later emergence of psychosis. One conclusion is that "low intelligence" is an antecedent causal variable in the later outcome of "psychosis." Our own conclusion, hinted at by some of the research cited by Ricks, is that both the behaviors suggestive of low intelligence and the behaviors suggestive of psychosis are expressions of the same potential. We may speculate that a single deeper potential can be expressed initially by an operating potential equipped with behaviors of being dumb, dull, uncomprehending. This occurs in childhood. Later, in adolescence or adulthood, that same deeper potential may be expressed by an operating potential and behaviors having to do with being crazy, psychotic, strange. What appears as change is merely the development of a new operating potential serving the same deeper one. High relationships between early and later sets of behaviors express the functional similarity of both sets, viz. both serve the same deeper potential.

V. Integration and Actualization

The philosophies and the theories underlying our traditional approaches generally lack a concept of a highest state of being. We have states of sickness—being unadjusted, maladjusted, abnormal, neurotic and psychotic, ill, deviate. We have states of health—being adjusted, mature, normal, with few problems and symptoms. In contrast with traditional approaches, humanistic theory offers a concept of a higher order state, a plateau which is beyond normal, mature, adjusted, healthy. Our concept is like that of a yogi, an individual who has attained the goal of yoga, viz. the state of samadhi (union of self with the supreme reality or universal self) (Dalal & Barbar, 1970), a person who has attained a plateau above that of the normal, adjusted, healthy, mature. In humanistic theory, this higher plateau is that of integration and actualization, the plateau of optimal being.

The state of samadhi is described as a qualitatively new and different state, complete with a qualitatively different realm of experience. As described in Chapters 11 and 12, the processes of integration and actualization are capable of leading to a change in the very structure of the personality. With these changes in personality structure go changes in the ways the person is. These are qualitative changes, of a different order than those available to the person who exists on any other plateau. Chapters 11 and 12 describe the kinds of characteristics of the person who is on this plateau. Once having achieved the optimal state, once the personality structure has been altered, the optimal person is qualitatively different from others.

The fifth plateau is achieved by a very small proportion of individuals. Persons at this plateau are engaged in processes of integration and actualization. They work toward achieving significant changes in the guts of their personality structures: in the relationships among deeper potentials, in the progressive actualization of these integrated potentials, and in the external world in which they exist.

There is a curious career in the person's lifelong relationship to selfhood. During infancy and early childhood, the struggle is to *acquire* that selfhood, to gain one's own identity, to come into the dawn of selfhood by emerging from a dissolving primitive personality. From then on, the struggle seems to be one of *preserving* one's selfhood against change. In this final plateau, the struggle is to *lose* selfhood.

We struggle to lose the selfhood we struggled so hard to acquire and to preserve throughout our lives. But the aim is to acquire a self which is dilated—outward and inward—as far as possible so that the old self is gone.

References

ABRAHAM, K. Notes on the psychoanalytic investigation and treatment of manic-depressive insanity and allied conditions. In K. Abraham, *Selected papers on psychoanalysis*. New York: Basic Books, 1960. Pp. 137-156. (a)

ABRAHAM, K. The first pregenital stage of the libido. In *Selected papers on psychoanalysis*. New York: Basic Books, 1960. Pp. 248-279. (b)

ADLER, A. *Practice and theory of individual psychology*. New York: Harcourt, Brace, 1927.

ADLER, A. *Problems of neurosis*. New York: Cosmopolitan, 1930.

ADLER, A. *The science of living*. New York: Anchor-Doubleday, 1969.

ADLER, K. Depression in the light of individual psychology. *Journal of Individual Psychology*, 1961, *17*, 56-67.

AINSWORTH, M. D. S. The effects of maternal deprivation: A review of findings and controversy in the context of research strategy. Geneva: World Health Organization. Public Health Papers, 14, 1962.

AINSWORTH, M. D. S. Discussion: The growth of competence. In: H. R. Schaffer (Ed.) *The origins of human social relations*. New York: Academic Press, 1971. Pp. 277-280.

AINSWORTH, M. D. S., BELL, S., & STAYTON, D. Individual differences in strange-situation behavior of one-year-olds. In H. R. Schaffer (Ed.) *The origins of human social relations*. London: Academic Press, 1972.

AINSWORTH, M. D. S., & WITTIG, B. A. Attachment and exploratory behavior of one-year-olds in a strange situation. In B. M. Foss (Ed.) *Determinants of infant behavior*. Volume 4. New York: Barnes and Noble, 1969.

AINSWORTH, S. Integrating theories of stuttering. *Journal of Speech Disorders*, 1945, *10*, 205-210.

ALBEE, G. W. Notes toward a position paper opposing psychodiagnosis. In A. R. Mahrer (Ed.) *New approaches to personality classification*. New York: Columbia University Press, 1970. Pp. 385-395.

ALEXANDER, F. *Psychosomatic medicine*. New York: Norton, 1950.

ALEXANDER, F. The dynamics of psychotherapy in the light of learning theory. *American Journal of Psychiatry*, 1963, *5*, 440-448.

ALEXANDER, F. & FRENCH, T. M. *Psychoanalytic therapy*. New York: Ronald, 1946.

835

ALEXANDER, F. & FRENCH, T. M. *Studies in psychosomatic medicine.* New York: Ronald, 1948.

ALLPORT, G. W. *Personality: A psychological interpretation.* New York: Holt, Rinehart, & Winston, 1937. (a)

ALLPORT, G. W. *Pattern and growth in personality.* New York: Holt, Rinehart, and Winston, 1937 (b).

ALLPORT, G. W. *Becoming: Basic consideration for a psychology of personality.* New Haven: Yale University Press, 1955.

ALLPORT, G. W. The trend in motivational theory. In B. I. Murstein (Ed.) *Handbook of projective techniques.* New York: Basic Books, 1965. Pp. 36-48.

ALTMAN, J. W., SMITH, R. W., MEYERS, R. L., McKENNA, F. S., & BRYSON, S. *Psychological and social adjustment in a simulated shelter*: A research report. Pittsburgh: American Institute of Research, 1960.

ANDREWS, T. G. *Methods in psychology.* New York: Wiley, 1948.

ANSBACHER, H. L., & ANSBACHER, R. R. (Eds.) *The Individual Psychology of Alfred Adler.* New York: Basic Books, 1956.

APPLETON, L. E. *A comparative study of the play of adult savages and civilized children.* Chicago: University of Chicago Press, 1910.

ARCHIBALD, H. C., BELL, D., MILLER, C., & TUDDENHAM, R. D. Bereavement in childhood and adult psychiatric disturbance. *Psychosomatic Medicine*, 1962, *24*, 343-351.

ARIETI, S. Volition and value: A study based on catatonic schizophrenia. *Comprehensive Psychiatry*, 1961, *2*, 74-82.

ARIETI, S. The psychotherapeutic approach to depression. *American Journal of Psychotherapy*, 1962, *16*, 394-406.

ASCH, S. E. Forming impression of personality. *Journal of Abnormal and Social Psychology*, 1946, *41*, 258-290.

ASCH, S. *Social psychology.* Englewood, N. J.: Prentice-Hall, 1952.

BACHRACH, H. Adaptive regression, empathy and psychotherapy. *Psychotherapy: Theory, Research and Practice*, 1968, *5*, 203-209.

BADGER, E. *Activities for infant stimulation or mother-infant games.* Mount Carmel, Illinois: Mount Carmel Parent and Child Center, 1970.

BAKAN, D. *The duality of human existence.* Chicago: Rand McNally, 1966.

BALDWIN, A. L., KALHORN, J., & BREEZE, F. H. Patterns of parent behavior. *Psychological monographs*, 1945, *58*, 1-75.

BALINT, A. Love for the mother and mother love. *International Journal of Psychoanalysis*, 1949, *30*, 251-259.

BANDURA, A. Psychotherapy as a learning process. *Psychological Bulletin*, 1961, *58*, 143-159.

BANDURA, A. & WALTERS, R. H. *Social learning and personality development.* New York: Holt, Rinehart, & Winston, 1962.

BARKER, R. Explorations in ecological psychology. *American Psychologist*, 1965, *20*, 1-14.

BARRY, H. A. A study of bereavement. An approach to problems in mental disease. *American Journal of Orthopsychiatry*, 1939, *9*, 355-359.

BARRY, H. A. Significance of maternal bereavement before age eight in psychiatric patients. *Archives of Neurology and Psychiatry*, 1949, 62, 630-637.

BARRY, H. A. & LINDEMANN, E. Critical ages for maternal bereavement in psychoneuroses. *Psychosomatic Medicine*, 1960, *3*, 166-179.

Barry, H. Jr., Barry, H, III, & Lindemann, E. Dependency in adult patients following early maternal bereavement. *Journal of Nervous and Mental Disease*, 1965, *140*, 197-205.

Barsch. R. H. The infant curriculum—a concept for tomorrow. In J. Hellmuth (Ed.) *Exceptional infant*, Volume 1. New York: Brunner/Mazel. 1967.

Bartemeier, J. H., Kubie, L. S., Menninger, K. A., Romano, J. & Whitehorn, J. C. Combat exhaustion. *Journal of Nervous and Mental Diseases*, 1946, *104*, 358-389.

Barton, W. The future of the mental hospital: The portent of some current emphases. *Mental Hospitals*, 1962, *13*, 368-369.

Bateson, G. The biosocial integration of behavior in the schizophrenic family. In N. W. Ackerman. F. L. Beatman. N. Sharman (Eds.). *Exploring the base for family therapy*. New York: Family Service Association of America. 1961. Pp. 116-122.

Bateson. P. P. B. The characteristics and context of imprinting. *Biological Review*. 1966, *41*, 177-220.

Beard, G. M. *A practical treatise on nervous exhaustion (neurasthenia), its symptoms, nature, sequences, treatment*. (5th ed.). New York: E. B. Treat, 1905.

Beck, A. T. *Depression: Clinical, experimental and theoretical aspects*. New York: Harper & Row, 1967.

Beck, J. *How to raise a brighter child*. Markham, Ontario: Simon and Shuster, 1975.

Beckwith, L. Relationship between infants' social behavior and their mothers' behavior. *Child Development*, 1972, *43*, 397-411.

Begelman, D. A. Determinism vs. free will. *The Catholic Psychological Record*, 1944, *4*, 124-128.

Bell, J. E. A theoretical position for family group therapy. *Family Process*, 1963, *2*, 1-14.

Bender, J. F. Prophylaxis of stuttering. *Nervous Child*, 1943, *2* (2), 181-189.

Benedek, T. F. Toward a biology of depressive constellation. *Journal of the American Psychoanalytic Association*, 1956, *4*, 389-428.

Beras, D., Gale, C. & Oppenheimer, L. Disturbances of identity function in childhood: Psychiatric and psychological observations. *American Journal of Orthopsychiatry*. 1960, *30*, 369-381.

Berelson. B.. & Steiner. G. A. *Human behavior*. New York: Harcourt. Brace. Jovanovich. 1964.

Bergin, A. E. The effects of psychotherapy: Negative results revisted. *Journal of Counseling Psychology*, 1963, *10*, 244-255.

Bergin, A. E. Some implications of psychotherapy research for therapeutic practice. *Journal of Abnormal Psychology*, 1966, *76*, 235-246.

Bergin, A. E., Garfield, S. L., & Thompson, A. S. The Chicago conference on clinical training and clinical psychology at Teacher's College. *American Psychologist*, 1967, *22*, 307-316.

Bergman, P. The germinal cell of Freud's psychoanalytic psychology and therapy. *Psychiatry*, 1949, *12*, 265-278.

Bergmann, G., & Spence, K. W. The logic of psychophysical measurement. *Psychological Review*, 1944, *51*, 1-24.

Berkowitz, L. *Aggression: A social psychological analysis*. New York: McGraw-Hill, 1962.

Bertalanffy, L. On the definition of the symbol. In J. R. Royce (Ed.), *Psychology and the symbol*. New York: Random House, 1965.

Bettelheim, B. *The empty fortress: Infantile autism and the birth of self*. New York: Free Press, 1967.

BEXTON, W. H., HARON, W., & SCOTT, T. H. Effects of decreased variation in the sensory environment. *Canadian Psychologist*, 1954, *8*, 70-76.

BEYELMAN, D. A. Determinism vs. free will. *The Catholic Psychological Record*, 1944, *4*, 124-128.

BIBRING, E. The mechanism of depression. In P. Greenacre (Ed.), *Affective disorders*. New York: International Universities Press, 1953. Pp. 13-48.

BIJOU, S. W., & BAER, D. M. *Child development: Volume 2*. New York: Appleton-Century-Crofts, 1965.

BIJOU, S. W., & BAER, D. M. Operant methods in child behavior and development. In W. K. Honig (Ed.) *Operant behavior. Areas of research and application*. New York: Appleton-Century-Crofts, 1966. Pp. 718-789.

BINSWANGER, L. The existential analysis school of thought. In R. May, E. Angel, H. F. Ellenberger (Eds.), *Existence: A new dimension in psychiatry and psychology*. New York: Basic Books, 1958. Pp. 191-213. (a)

BINSWANGER, L. Insanity as a life-historical phenomenon and as mental disease: The case of Ilse. In R. May, E. Angel, & H. F. Ellenberger (Eds.), *Existence: A new dimension in psychiatry and psychology*. New York: Basic Books, 1958. Pp. 214-236. (b)

BINSWANGER, L. The case of Ellen West: An anthropological-clinical study. In R. May, E. Angel, H. F. Ellenberger (Eds.), *Existence: A new dimension in psychiatry and psychology*. New York: Basic Books, 1958. Pp. 237-364. (c)

BINSWANGER, L. *Being-in-the-world*. New York: Harper Torchbooks, 1967.

BJORNSON, J. Behavior in phenylketonuria. *Archives of General Psychiatry*, 1964, *10*, 65-69.

BLATZ, W. E. & BOTT, H. *The management of young children*. New York: William Morrow, 1930.

BLISS, E. L., CLARK, L. D., & WEST, C. D. Studies of sleep deprivation: Relationship to schizophrenia. *A.M.A. Archives of Neurology and Psychiatry*, 1959, *81*, 348-359.

BORDIN, E. S. Inside the therapeutic hour. In E. A. Rubenstein & M. B. Parloff (Eds.), *Research in psychotherapy*. Washington, D.C.: American Psychological Association, 1959. Pp. 235-246.

BORING, E. G. *A history of experimental psychology*. New York: Appleton-Century-Crofts, 1950.

BOSS. M. *Psychoanalysis and Daseinsanalysis*. New York: Basic Books, 1963.

BOSZORMENYI-NAGY. I. & FRAMO. J. L. (Eds.). *Intensive family therapy: Theoretical and practical aspects*. New York: Harper & Row, 1965.

BOVERMAN, M. Some notes on the psychotherapy of delusional patients. *Psychiatry*, 1953, *16* (2), 141-157.

BOWLBY, J. The nature of the child's tie to his mother. *International Journal of Psychoanalysis*, 1958, *39*, 350-373.

BOWLBY, J. *Child care and the growth of love*. London: Penguin, 1965 (2nd edition).

BOWLBY, J. *Attachment and loss. Vol. 1. Attachment*. London: Hogarth, 1969.

BRADY, J. D., REZNIKOFF, M., & ZELLER, W. W. The relationship of expectation of improvement to actual improvement of hospitalized psychiatric patients. *Journal of Nervous and Mental Disease*, 1940, *130*, 41-44.

BRAGA, J., & BRAGA, L. *Learning and growing: A guide to child development*. Englewood Cliffs, New Jersey: Prentice-Hall, 1975.

BRANDEN, N. The contradiction of determinism. *Objectivist Newsletter*, 1963, *2*, 19-20.

BRANDT, L. W. Studies of dropout patients in psychotherapy: A review of findings. *Psychotherapy: Theory, Research and Practice*, 1965. *2*, 6-12.

BRENNER, C., FRIEDMAN, A. P., & CARTER, S. Psychological factors in the etiology and treatment of chronic headache. *Psychosomatic Medicine*, 1949, *11*, 1-24.

BREUER, J. & FREUD, S. *Studies in hysteria*. New York and Washington: Journal of Nervous and Mental Disease Publishing Company, 1934.

BRIGGS, P. F. Eight item clusters for use with the M-B History Record. *Journal of Clinical Psychology*, 1959, *15*, 22-28.

BRILL, A. A. (Ed.) *The basic writings of Sigmund Freud*. New York: Modern Library, 1938.

BRODY, E. B., & FISHMAN, M. Therapeutic response and length of hospitalization of psychiatrically ill veterans. *Archives of General Psychiatry*, 1960, *2*, 174-181.

BRONSON, W. C. The growth of competence: Issues of conceptualization and measurement. In H. R. Schaffer (Ed.) *The origins of human social relations*. New York: Academic Press, 1971. Pp. 269-277.(a)

BRONSON, W. C. Discussion: The growth of competence. In: H. R. Schaffer (Ed.) *The origins of human social relations*. New York: Academic Press, 1971. Pp. 277-280. (b)

BRONSON, W. C. Mother-toddler interaction: A perspective on studying the development of competence. *Merrill-Palmer Quarterly*, 1974, *20*, 275-301.

BROWN, D. J., & LYNN, D. B. Human sexual development: An outline of components and concepts. *Journal of Marriage and Family*, 1966, *28*, 155-162.

BROWN, J. S. The generalization of approach responses as a function of stimulus intensity and strength of motivation. *Journal of Comparative Psychology*, 1942, *33*, 209-226.

BROWN, J. S. Gradients of approach and avoidance responses and their relation to motivation. *Journal of Comparative and Physiological Psychology*, 1948, *41*, 450-465.

BRUCH, H. *The importance of overweight*. New York: Norton, 1957.

BRUCH, H. Developmental obesity and schizophrenia. *Psychiatry*, 1958, *21*, 65-70.

BUBER, M. Guilt and guilt feelings. *Psychiatry*, 1957, *20*, 114-129.

BUCKLEW, J. *Paradigms for psychopathology: A contribution to case history analysis*. Chicago: Lippincott, 1960.

BUCKLEW, J. Prediction of psychiatric symptoms from case history information. *Psychological Record*, 1967, *17*, 1-12.

BUCKLEW, J. The use of symptoms to assess case history information. *Multivariable Behavioral Research* (Special Issue), 1968, 157-168.

BUGENTAL, J. F. T. The person who is the psychotherapist. *Journal of Consulting Psychology*, 1964, *28*, 272-277.

BUGENTAL, J. F. T. *The search for authenticity*. New York: Holt, Rinehart, & Winston, 1965.

BUGENTAL, J. F. T. Values and existential unity. In C. Buhler & F. Massarik (Eds.) *The course of human life*. New York: Springer, 1968. Pp. 383-392.

BUHLER, C. Theoretical observations about life's basic tendencies. *American Journal of Psychotherapy*, 1959, *13*, 561-581.

BUHLER, C. Introduction. In C. Buhler & F. Massarik (Eds.) *The course of human life*. New York: Springer, 1968. Pp. 1-10. (a)

BUHLER, C. Early environmental influence on goal setting. In C. Buhler & F. Massarik (Eds.), *The course of human life*. New York: Springer, 1968. Pp. 173-188.(b)

BUHLER, C. Fulfillment and failure of life. In C. Buhler & F. Massarik (Eds.) *The course of human life*. New York: Springer, 1968. Pp. 400-403. (c)

BUHLER, C., & MARSCHAK, M. Basic tendencies of human life. In C. Buhler & F. Massarik (Eds.) *The course of human life*. New York: Springer, 1968. Pp. 92-102.

BUHLER, C. & MASSARIK, F. (Eds.) *The course of human life: A study of goals in the humanistic perspective*. New York: Springer, 1968.

BULLARD, D. M. (Ed.). *Psychoanalysis and psychiatry: Selected papers of Frieda-Fromm-Reichmann*. Chicago: University of Chicago Press, 1959.

BULLARD, D. M. Psychotherapy of paranoid patients. *Archives of General Psychiatry*, 1960, 2, 137-141.

BURT, C. *The subnormal mind*. London: Oxford University Press, 1955.

BURTON, A., & HARRIS, R. E. (Eds.) *Clinical studies in personality*. New York: Harper & Row, 1955.

BUSS, A. H. *The psychology of aggression*. New York: Wiley, 1961.

BUTLER, J. M. Self-ideal congruence in psychotherapy. *Psychotherapy: Theory, Research, and Practice*, 1968, 5, 13-17.

BUYTENDIJK, F. J. The phenomenological approach to the problem of feelings and emotions. In M. L. Reymert (Ed.), *Feelings and emotions*. New York: McGraw-Hill, 1950. Pp. 127-141.

BYLES, M. B. *Journey into Burmese silence*. London: George Allen and Unwin, 1962.

CAIRNS, R. B. Attachment behavior of mammals. *Psychological Review*, 1966, 73, 409-426.

CAMERON, N. *The psychology of behavior disorders: A biosocial interpretation*. Boston: Houghton Mifflin, 1947.

CANTOR, G. N., & CROMWELL, R. L. The principle of reductionism and mental deficiency. *American Journal of Mental Deficiency*, 1957, 61, 461-466.

CAPRIO, F. S. A study of some psychological reactions during prepubescence to the idea of death. *Psychiatric Quarterly*, 1950, 24, 495-505.

CARMICHAEL, L. Are the sexes really equal? *Science Digest*, 1957, October, 38-43.

CARTWRIGHT, D. S. Effectiveness of psychotherapy: A critique of the spontaneous remission argument. *Journal of Counseling Psychology*, 1955, 2, 290-296.

CARTWRIGHT, R. D., & LERNER, B. Empathy, need to change, and improvement with psychotherapy. *Journal of Consulting Psychology*, 1963, 27, 138-144.

CASSIDY, W. L., FLANAGAN, N. B. & SPELLMAN, M. Clinical observations in manic-depressive disease. A quantitative study of 100 manic-depressive patients and 50 medically sick controls. *Journal of the American Medical Association*, 1957, 164, 1535-1546.

CATTELL, R. B. The nature and measurement of anxiety. *Scientific American*, 1963 (March), 96-104.

CATTELL, R. B. The integration of functional and psychometric requirements in a quantitative and computerized diagnostic system. In A. R. Mahrer (Ed.), *New approaches to personality classification*. New York: Columbia University Press, 1970. Pp. 9-52.

CATTELL, R. B. & SCHEIER, I. H. The nature of anxiety: A review of thirteen multivariate analyses comprising 814 variables. *Psychological Reports*, 1958, 4, 351-388.

CATTELL, R. B., & SCHEIER, I. H. *The meaning and measurement of neuroticism and anxiety*. New York: Ronald, 1961.

CAUDILL, W. *The psychiatric hospital as a small society*. Cambridge: Harvard University Press, 1958.

CAUDILL, W., REDLICH, F. C., GILMORE, H. R., & BRODY, E. B. Social structure and interaction processes on a psychiatric ward. *American Journal of Orthopsychiatry*, 1952, 22, 314-334.

CAUDILL, W. & STAINBROOK, E. Some covert effects of communication difficulties in a psychiatric hospital. *Psychiatry*, 1954, 17, 27-43.

CAUTELA, J. R. The application of learning theory "as a last resort" in the treatment of a case of anxiety neurosis. *Journal of Clinical Psychology*, 1956, *21*, 448-452.

CHANG, CHEN-CHI, *The practice of Zen*. New York: Harper & Row, 1959.

CHESS, S., THOMAS, A., RUTTER, M., & BIRCH, H. G. Interaction of temperament and environment in the production of behavioral disturbances in children. *American Journal of Psychiatry*, 1963, *120*, 142-147.

CHILD, I. L. *Humanistic psychology and the research tradition: Their several virtues*. New York: Wiley, 1973.

COHEN, J. The concept of goal gradients: A review of its present status. *Journal of General Psychology*, 1953, *49*, 303-308.

COLEMAN, J. C. *Abnormal psychology and modern life*. 3rd ed. Chicago: Scott, Foresman, 1964.

COMBS, A. W. Intelligence from a perceptual point of view. *Journal of Abnormal and Social Psychology*, 1952, *47*, 662-673.

COMBS, A. W. Fostering self-direction. *Educational Leadership*, 1966, *23*, 373-387.

CONN, F. H. Psychogenesis and psychotherapy of insomnia. *Journal of Clinical Experimental Psychopathology*, 1950, *11*, 85-91.

COTTS, G. K. A socially constructive type of psychopathologically determined activity. *Psychiatry*, 1954, *17*, 97-99.

COWEN, E. L., ZAX, M., & LAIRD, J. D. A college student volunteer program in the elementary school setting. *Community Mental Health Journal*, 1966, *2*, 319-328.

CRANDALL, V. C. Differences in parental antecedents of internal-external control in children and in young adulthood. Paper read at meeting of Society for Research in Child Development, Minneapolis, 1965.

CROMWELL, R. L. A social learning approach to mental retardation. In N. L. Ellis (Ed.) *Handbook of mental deficiency*. New York: McGraw-Hill, 1963. Pp. 41-91.

DALAL, A. S., & BARBER, T. X. Yoga and hypnotism. In Barber, T. X. (Ed.) *LSD, marihuana, yoga, and hypnosis*. Chicago: Aldine, 1970. Pp. 117-132.

DAVIDS, A., HOLDEN, R. H., & GRAY, G. B. Maternal anxiety during pregnancy and adequacy of mother and child adjustment eight months following childbirth. *Child Development*, 1963, *34*, 993-1003.

DAVIS, J. A., FREEMAN, H. E., & SIMMONS, O. G. Rehospitalization and performance levels among former mental patients. *Social Problems*, 1957, *5*, 37-44.

DE CHARMS, R., LEVY, J., & WERTHEIMER, M. A note on attempted evaluation of psychotherapy. *Journal of Clinical Psychology*, 1954, *45*, 129-131.

DEIKMAN, A. J. Implications of experimentally induced contemplative meditation. *Journal of Nervous and Mental Diseases*, 1966, *142*, 101-116.

DEMENT, W., & KLEITMAN, N. The relation of eye movements during sleep to dream activity: An objective method for the study of dreaming. *Journal of Experimental Psychology*, 1957, *53*, 543-553. (a)

DEMENT, W., & KLEITMAN, N. Cyclic variations in EEG during sleep and their relation to eye movements, body motility and dreaming. *Electroencephalography and Clinical Neurophysiology*, 1957, 9, 673-690. (b)

DENNIS, W. Infant development under conditions of restricted practice and of minimum social stimulation. *Genetic Psychology Monographs*, 1941, *23*, 143-190.

DENNIS, W. Causes of retardation among institutional children in Iran. *Journal of Genetic Psychology*, 1960, *96*, 47-59.

DENNIS, W., NAJARIAN, P. Infant development under environmental handicap. *Psychological Monographs*, 1957, *71*, 1-13.

DERI, S. K. A problem in obesity. In A. Burton & R. E. Harris (Eds.), *Clinical studies of personality*. Vol. II. New York: Harper & Row, 1955.

DE CHARMS, R. *Personal causation*. New York: Academic Press, 1968.

DEVEREAUX, G. Why Oedipus killed Laius. In H. M. Ruitenbeek (Ed.) *Psychoanalysis and literature*. New York: E. P. Dutton, 1964. Pp. 168-186.

DIAMOND, S. A neglected aspect of motivation. *Sociometry*, 1939, *2*, 77-85.

DODSON, F. *How to parent*. New York: Signet, 1971.

DOLLARD, J., DOOB, L. W., MILLER, N., MOWRER, O. H., & SEARS, R. R. *Frustration and aggression*: New Haven: Yale University Press, 1939.

DOLLARD, J., & MILLER, N. E. *Personality and psychotherapy*. New York: McGraw-Hill, 1950.

DREIKURS, R. Adlerian psychotherapy. In F. Fromm-Reichmann & J. L. Moreno (Eds.) *Progress in psychotherapy*. New York: Grune & Stratton, 1956. Pp. 111-118.

DREIKURS, R. Goals of psychotherapy. In A. R. Mahrer (Ed.), *The goals of psychotherapy*. New York: Appleton-Century-Crofts, 1967. Pp. 221-237.

DUNLAP, K. *Habits: Their making and unmaking*. New York: Liveright, 1932.

DUPONT. H. Social learning theory and the treatment of transvestite behavior in an eight-year-old boy. *Psychotherapy: Theory, Research, and Practice*, 1968, *5*, 44-45.

EDWARDS, A. S. Effects of the loss of one hundred hours of sleep. *American Journal of Psychology*, 1941, *54*, 80-91.

EIBL-EIBESFELDT, I. *Ethology: The biology of behavior*. New York: Holt, Rinehart and Winston, 1970.

ELDRED, S. H., HAMBURG, D. A., INWARD, E. R., SALZMAN, L., MEYERSBERG, H. A., & GOODRICH, G. A procedure for the systematic analysis of psychotherapeutic interviews. *Psychiatry*, 1954, *17*, 337-345.

ELKE, F. Specialists interpret the case of Harold Holzer. *Journal of Abnormal and Social Psychology*, 1947, *42*, 99-111.

ELLENBERGER. H. F. A clinical introduction to psychiatric phenomenology and existential analysis. In R. May, E. Angel, & H. F. Ellenberger (Eds.), *Existence: A new dimension in spychiatry and psychology*. New York: Basic Books. 1958. Pp. 92-124.

ELLIS, A. A homosexual treated with rational psychotherapy. *Journal of Clinical Psychology*, 1959, *15*, 338-343. (a)

ELLIS, A. Requisite conditions for basic personality change. *Journal of Consulting Psychology*, 1959, *23*, 538-540. (b)

ELLIS. A *Reason and emotion in psychotherapy*. New York: Lyle Stuart. 1962.

ELLIS, A. Goals of psychotherapy. In A. R. Mahrer (Ed.). *The goals of psychotherapy*. New York: Appleton-Century-Crofts, 1967. Pp. 206-220.

ELLUL, J. *The technological society*. New York: Vintage Books, 1964.

ENGELMANN, S., & ENGELMANN, T. *Give your child a superior mind*. New York: Simon & Schuster, 1966.

ENRIGHT, J. An introduction to Gestalt techniques. In J. Fagan & I. L. Shepherd (Eds.), *Gestalt therapy now*. New York: Harper & Row, 1970. Pp. 107-124.

ERIKSON. E. H. Growth and crises. In M. J. F. Senn (Ed.) *Symposium on the healthy personality*. New York: Josiah Macy Foundation, 1950.

ERIKSON, E. H. Growth and crises of the healthy personality. *Psychological Issues*, 1959, *1*, 50-100.

ESCALONA, S. K. Emotional development in the first year of life. In M. J. E. Senn (Ed.) *Problems of infancy and childhood: Transactions of the sixth conference*. New York: Josiah Macy Jr. Foundation, 1953. Pp. 11-92.

ESCALONA, S. K. Basic modes of social interaction: Their emergence and patterning during the first two years of life. *Merrill-Palmer Quarterly*, 1972, *18*, 205-232.

EYSENCK, H. J. The effects of psychotherapy: An evaluation. *Journal of Consulting Psychology*, 1952, *16*, 319-324.

EYSENCK, H. J. A reply to Luborsky's note. *British Journal of Psychology*, 1954, *45*, 132-133.

EYSENCK, H. J. A dynamic theory of anxiety and hysteria. *Journal of Mental Science*, 1955, *101*, 28-51. (a)

EYSENCK, H. J. The effects of psychotherapy. *Journal of Abnormal and Social Psychology*, 1955, *50*, 147-148. (b)

EYSENCK, H. J. *The dynamics of anxiety and hysteria*. New York: Praeger, 1957.

EYSENCK, H. J. The effects of psychotherapy. In H. J. Eysenck (Ed.), *Handbook of abnormal psychology*. New York: Basic Books, 1960. Pp. 697-725. (a)

EYSENCK, H. J. *Behavior therapy and the neuroses*. London: Pergamon, 1960. (b)

EYSENCK, H. J. The measurement of motivation. In R. S. Daniel (Ed.), *Contemporary readings in general psychology* (2nd. ed.), Boston: Houghton-Mifflin, 1965. Pp. 255-264.

EYSENCK, H. J. A dimensional system of psychodiagnostics. In A. R. Mahrer (Ed.), *New approaches to personality classification*. New York: Columbia University Press, 1970. Pp. 169-207.

EYSENCK, H. J. & RACHMAN, S. *The causes and cures of neuroses*. San Diego: Knapp, 1965.

FAGAN, J., & SHEPHERD, I. L. *Gestalt therapy now*. New York: Harper & Row, 1970.

FARBER, I. E. A framework for the study of personality as a behavioral science. In I. P. WORCHEL & D. BYRNE (Eds.) *Personality change*. New York: Wiley. 1964. Pp. 3-34.

FARBER, M. *The foundation of phenomenology*. Cambridge, Mass.: Harvard University Press, 1943.

FARRELL, B. A. *Experimental psychology*. London: Blackwell, 1955.

FEIGL, H. The mind-body problem in the development of logical empiricism. In H. Feigl & M. Brodbeck (Eds.) *Readings in the philosophy of science*. New York: Appleton-Century-Crofts, 1953. Pp. 612-626.

FEIGL, H. Aims of education for our age of science: Reflections of a logical empiricist. In N. B. Henry (Ed.) *The 54th Yearbook of the National Society for the Study of Education*. Chicago: University of Chicago Press, 1955. Pp. 304-341.

FEIGL, H. The "mental" and the "physical." In H. Feigl, M. Scriven, & G. Maxwell (Eds.) *Minnesota Studies in the philosophy of science*. Vol. 2. Minneapolis: University of Minnesota Press, 1958. Pp. 370-497.

FEISTER, A. R., MAHRER, A. R., GIAMBRA, L. M., & ORMISTON, D. W. Shaping a clinic population: The dropout problem reconsidered. *Community Mental Health Journal*, 1974, *10*, 173-179.

FELIX, R. H. Implications of goals of therapy. *Mental Hospitals*, 1961, *12*, 10-15.

FENICHEL, O. *The psychoanalytic theory of neurosis*. New York: Norton, 1945.

FENICHEL. O. Two brief clinical contributions. In H. Fenichel & D. Rapaport (Eds.) *The collected papers of Otto Fenichel: First series*. New York: Norton, 1953. Pp. 3-4. (a)

FENICHEL. O. On masturbation. In H. Fenichel & D. Rapaport (Eds.) *The collected papers of Otto Fenichel: First series*. New York: Norton, 1953. Pp. 5-7. (b)

FENICHEL, O. Psychoanalysis and metaphysics: A critical inquiry. In H. Fenichel & D. Rapaport (Eds.) *The collected papers of Otto Fenichel: First series*. New York: Norton, 1953. Pp. 8-26. (c)

FENICHEL, O. From the terminal phase of an analysis. In H. Fenichel & D. Rapaport (Eds.) *The collected papers of Otto Fenichel: First series*. New York: Norton, 1953. Pp. 27-31. (d)

FENICHEL, O. An infantile, preliminary phase of "defiance by lack of affect." In H. Fenichel & D. Rapaport (Eds.) *The collected papers of Otto Fenichel: First series*. New York: Norton, 1953. Pp. 32-33. (e)

FENICHEL, O. Psychoanalytic method. In H. Fenichel & D. Rapaport (Eds.) *The collected papers of Otto Fenichel: First series*. New York: Norton, 1953. Pp. 318-330. (f)

FENICHEL, O. The symbolic equation: Girl = phallus. In H. Fenichel & D. Rapaport (Eds.) *The collected papers of Otto Fenichel: Second series*. New York: Norton, 1954. Pp. 3-18. (a)

FENICHEL, O. Symposium on the theory of the therapeutic results of psychoanalysis. In H. Fenichel & D. Rapaport (Eds.) *The collected papers of Otto Fenichel: Second series*. New York: Norton, 1954. Pp. 19-24. (b)

FENICHEL, O. Early stages of ego development. In H. Fenichel & D. Rapaport (Eds.) *The collected papers of Otto Fenichel: Second series*. New York: Norton, 1954. Pp. 25-48. (c)

FENICHEL, O. The concept of trauma in contemporary psychoanalytic theory. In H. Fenichel and D. Rapaport (Eds.) *The collected papers of Otto Fenichel: Second series*. New York: Norton, 1954. Pp. 49-69. (d)

FENICHEL, O. On masturbation. In H. Fenichel & D. Rapaport (Eds.), *The collected papers of Otto Fenichel: Second series*. New York: Norton, 1954. Pp. 81-88. (e)

FERREIRA. A. J. *Prenatal environment*. Springfield. Illinois: Charles C Thomas. 1969.

FESHBACH, S. The function of aggression and regulation of aggressive drive. *Psychological Review*, 1964, *71*, 257-272.

FIDLER, J. W., GUERNEY, B. G., ANDRONICO, M. B. & GUERNEY, L. Filial therapy as a logical extension of current trends in psychotherapy. In B. G. Guerney (Ed.), *Psychotherapeutic agents: New roles for nonprofessionals, parents and teachers*. New York: Holt, Rinehart & Winston, 1969. Pp. 47-55.

FIEDLER, F. A. A comparison of therapeutic relationships in psychoanalytic, nondirective, and Adlerian therapy. *Journal of Consulting Psychology*, 1950, *14*, 436-445.

FINE, R. *Freud: A critical re-evaluation of his theories*. New York: David McKay, 1962.

FINGARETTE, H. Real guilt and neurotic guilt. *Journal of Existential Psychiatry*, 1962, *3*, 145-158.

FISCHER, W. F. *Theories of anxiety*. New York: Harper & Row, 1970.

FISKE, D. W. *Measuring the concepts of personality*. Chicago: Aldine, 1971.

FLEISCHL, M. F. A note on the meaning of ideas of reference. *American Journal of Psychotherapy*, 1958, *12*, 24-29.

FORER, B. The therapeutic value of crisis. *Psychological Reports*, 1963, *13*, 275-281.

FRANK, G. H. The role of the family in the development of psychopathology. *Psychological Bulletin*, 1965, *64*, 194-205.

FRANK, J. D. *Persuasion and healing: A comparative study of psychotherapy*. Baltimore: The John Hopkins Press, 1961.

FRANKL, V. E. *From death camp to existentialism*. Boston: Beacon Press, 1959.

FRANKL, V. E. *The will to meaning*. Don Mills, Ontario: General, 1969.

FREEMAN G. L. *The energetics of human behavior*. Ithaca: Cornell University Press, 1948.

FREEMAN, H. E., & SIMMONS, O. G. Mental patients in the community: Family settings and performance levels. *American Sociological Review*, 1958, *23*, 147-154. (a)

FREEMAN, H. E. & SIMMONS, O. G. Wives, mothers, and the post-hospital performance of mental patients. *Social Forces*, 1958, *37*, 153-159. (b)

FREEMAN, H. E. & SIMMONS, O. G. The social integration of former mental patients. *International Journal of Social Psychiatry*, 1959, *4*, 264-271.

FREEMAN, W., & WATTS, J. W. *Psychosurgery*. Baltimore: Thomas Press, 1942.

FREUD, A. *The ego and the mechanisms of defense*. London: Hogarth Press, 1936.

FREUD, A. The psychoanalytic study of infantile feeding disturbance. *Psychoanalytic Study of the Child*, 1946, *2*, 119-132.

FREUD, A. *Normality and pathology in childhood: Assessments of development*. New York: International Universities Press, 1965.

FREUD, S. *Collected Papers*. Vol. IV. London: Hogarth, 1908. Pp. 184-191.

FREUD, S. *New introductory lectures on psychoanalysis*. New York: Norton, 1933.

FREUD, S. *The problem of anxiety*. New York: Norton, 1936.

FREUD, S. *The interpretation of dreams*. New York: Modern Library, 1938.

FREUD, S. *A general introduction to psychoanalysis*. New York: Perma Books, 1949.

FREUD, S. Mourning and melancholia. *Collected Papers*. Vol. IV. London: Hogarth Press and The Institute of Psychoanalysis, 1950. Pp. 152-172.

FREUD, S. Further recommendations in the techniques of psychoanalysis. In J. Strachey (Ed.) *Standard edition of the complete psychological works of Sigmund Freud*. Vol. III. London: Hogarth Press & The Institute of Psychoanalysis, 1953. Pp. 13-21. (a)

FREUD, S. Fragment of an analysis of a case of hysteria: Prefatory remarks. In J. Strachey (Ed.) *Standard edition of the complete psychological works of Sigmund Freud*. Vol. V. London: Hogarth Press & The Institute of Psychoanalysis, 1953. (b)

FREUD, S. Analysis terminable and interminable. In J. Strachey (Ed.) *Standard edition of the complete psychological works of Sigmund Freud*. Vol. V. London: Hogarth Press & The Institute of Psychoanalysis, 1953. (c)

FREUD, S. Beyond the pleasure principle. In J. Strachey (Ed.) *Standard edition of the complete psychological works of Sigmund Freud*. Vol. XVIII. London: Hogarth Press, 1953. (d)

FREUD, S. Analysis of a case of hysteria: The clinical picture. In E. Jones (Ed.) *Collected papers of Sigmund Freud*. New York: Basic Books, 1959.

FREUD, S. The metapsychology of instincts, repression, and the unconscious. In T. Millon (Ed.) *Theories of psychopathology*. Philadelphia & London: W. B. Saunders, 1967. Pp. 140-152.

FREUND, H. The psychological aspects of stuttering. *American Journal of Psychotherapy*, 1953, *7*, 689-705.

FRIEDMAN, A. S., COWITZ, B., COHEN, H. W., & GRANICK, S. Syndromes and themes of psychotic depression: A factor analysis. *Archives of General Psychiatry*, 1963, *9*, 504-509.

FRIEDMAN, A. P., VON STORCH, T. J. C., & HOUSTON, M. H. Migraine and tension headaches: Clinical study of 2000 cases. *Neurology*, 1954, *4*, 773-788.

FROESCHELS, E. Pathology and therapy of stuttering. *The Nervous Child*, 1942, *2*, 148-161.

FROMM, E. *Man for himself*. New York: Holt, Rinehart, 1947.

FROMM, E. The nonproductive character orientations. In L. Gorlow & W. Katkovsky (Eds.) *Readings in the psychology of adjustment*. New York: McGraw-Hill. 1948. Pp. 340-347.

FROMM, E. *The art of loving*. New York: Harper & Row, 1968. (a)

FROMM, E. *The revolution of hope*. New York: Harper & Row, 1968. (b)

FROMM, E., SUZUKI, D. T. & DE MARTINO, R. *Zen Buddhism and psychoanalysis*. New York: Harper & Row, 1960.

FROMM-REICHMANN, F. *Principles of intensive psychotherapy*. Chicago: University of Chicago Press, 1958.

FROMM-REICHMANN, F. Loneliness. *Psychiatry*, 1959, *22*, 1-15.

GARDNER, J. *The recovery of confidence*. New York: W. W. Norton, 1968.

GARFIELD, S. L., & WOLPIN, M. Expectations regarding psychotherapy. *Journal of Nervous and Mental Diseases*, 1963, *137*, 353-362.

GENDLIN, E. T. *Experiencing and the creation of meaning*. New York: The Free Press of Glencoe, 1962.

GENDLIN, E. T. A theory of personality change. In P. Worchel & D. Byrne (Eds.) *Personality change*. New York: Wiley, 1964. Pp. 100-148.

GENDLIN. E. T. Existentialism and experiential psychotherapy. In C. Moustakas (Ed.) *Existential child therapy*. New York: Basic Books, 1966. Pp. 206-246.

GENDLIN, E. T. Values and the process of experiencing. In A. R. Mahrer (Ed.) *The goals of psychotherapy*. New York: Appleton-Century-Crofts, 1967. Pp. 180-205.

GENDLIN, E. T. The experiential response. In E. F. Hammer (Ed.), *Use of interpretation in treatment: Technique and art*. New York: Grune & Stratton, 1968. Pp. 208-227.

GENDLIN, E. T. Focusing. *Psychotherapy: Theory, Research, and Practice*, 1969, *6*, 4-15.

GESELL, A. L. & AMATRUDA, C. *The embryology of behavior*. New York: Harper, 1945.

GERING, R. C. & MAHRER, A. R. Difficulty falling asleep. *Psychological Reports*, 1972, *30*, 523-528.

GEWIRTZ, J. L. Mechanisms of social learning: Some roles of stimulation and behavior in early human development. In D. A. Goslin (Ed.) *Handbook of socialization theory and research*. Chicago: Rand McNally, 1969. Pp. 57-212.

GILBERT. S. D. *Three years to grow: Guidance for your child's first three years*. New York: Parent's Magazine Press, 1972.

GILMAN, L. Insomnia in relation to guilt, fear, and masochistic intent. *Journal of Clinical Experimental Psychopathology*, 1950, *11*, 63-64.

GIORGI, A. Phenomenology and experimental psychology: I. *Review of Existential Psychology and Psychiatry*, 1965, *5*, 228-238.

GIORGI, A. Phenomenology and experimental psychology: II. *Review of Existential Psychology and Psychiatry*, 1966, *6*, 37-50.

GIORGI, A. *Psychology as a human science: A phenomenologically based approach*. New York: Harper & Row, 1970.

GLAUBER, I. P. The nature of stuttering. *Social Casework*, 1953, *34*, 95-103. (a)

GLAUBER, I. P. The treatment of stuttering. *Social Casework*, 1953, *34*, 162-167. (b)

GOLDBERG, A., & RUBIN, B. Recovery of patients during periods of supposed neglect. *British Journal of Medical Psychology*, 1964, *37*, 266-272.

GOLDSTEIN, A. P., HELLER, K., & SECHEST, L. B. *Psychotherapy and the psychology of be-*

havior change. New York: Wiley, 1966.

GOLDSTEIN, K. *The organism*. New York: American Book Company, 1939.

GOLDSTEIN, K. On emotions. *Journal of Psychology*, 1951, *31*, 37-46.

GOLDSTEIN, K. *Human nature in the light of psychopathology*. New York: Shackery, 1963.

GOODMAN, G. An experiment with companionship therapy: College students and troubled boys—assumptions, selection, and design. *American Journal of Public Health*, 1967, *57*, 1772-1777.

GORDON, I. J. New conceptions of children's learning and development. In W. B. Waetjen & R. R. Leeper (Eds.), *Learning and mental health in the school*. Washington, D. C.: Association for Supervision and Curriculum Development. 1966. Pp. 49-73.

GORDON, I. J., & LALLY, J. R. *Intellectual stimulation for infants and toddlers*. Gainesville, Florida: Institute for the Development of Human Resources, 1968.

GORDON, T. *Parent effectiveness training*. New York: Wyden Press, 1970.

GREENACRE, P. *Trauma, growth and personality*. New York: Norton, 1952.

GREENLEAF, E. "Senoi" dream groups. *Psychotherapy: Theory, Research and Practice*, 1973, *10*, 218-222.

GREGORY, I. Studies of parental deprivation in psychiatric patients. *American Journal of Psychiatry*, 1958, *115*, 432-442.

GRINKER, R. R., & GOTTSCHALK, L. Headaches and muscular pains. *Psychosomatic Medicine*, 1949, *11*, 45-52.

GRINKER, R. R. & Robbins, F. P. *Psychosomatic case book*. New York: Blackiston, 1954.

GROOS, K. *The play of men*. New York: Appleton-Century-Crofts, 1908.

GROVER, P., MAHRER, A. R., & BORNSTEIN, R. Syndromes of physical head complaints in psychiatric patients. *Journal of Clinical Psychology*, 1970, *26*, 45-46.

GUNN, D. R. Psychiatric recognition of anxiety and depression. *Canadian Psychiatric Association Journal*, 1962, *7*, 1-3.

GURWITSCH, A. *The field of consciousness*. Pittsburgh, Pa.: Duquesne University Press, 1964.

GUTHRIE, E. R. *The psychology of learning*. New York: Harper, 1935.

HAHN, E. *Stuttering: Significant theories and therapies*. Stanford: Stanford University Press, 1943.

HALEY, J. The art of psychoanalysis. In S. I. Hayakawa (Ed.), *Our language and our world*. Harper, 1959. Pp. 113-125.

HALEY, J. Control in psychotherapy with schizophrenics. *Archives of General Psychiatry*, 1961, *7*, 340-353.

HALEY, J. *Strategies of psychotherapy*. New York: Grune & Stratton, 1963.

HALEY, J. & HOFFMAN, L. *Techniques of family therapy*. New York: Basic Books, 1967.

HALL, G. S. *Youth*. New York: Appleton-Century-Crofts, 1906.

HAMILTON, M. A. A rating scale for depression. *Journal of Neurological and Neurosurgical Psychiatry*, 1969, *23*, 56-61.

HAMMOND, G. B. *Man in estrangement: A comparison of the thought of Paul Tillich and Erich Fromm*. Nashville, Tenn.: Vanderbilt University Press, 1965.

HARLOW, H. F. The nature of love. *American Psychologist*, 1958, *13*, 673-685.

HARLOW, H. F. & ZIMMERMAN, R. R. Affectional responses in the infant monkey. *Science*, 1959, 130, 421-432.

HARTMANN, E. *The biology of dreaming*. Springfield, Ill.: Charles C Thomas, 1967.

HARTMANN, H. Psychoanalysis as a scientific theory. In S. Hook (Ed.), *Psychoanalysis, scientific method and philosophy*. New York: New York University Press, 1959. Pp. 3-35.

HAVEMANN, E. *The age of psychology*. New York: Simon & Schuster, 1957.

HAWKINS, R. P., PETERSON, R. F., SCHWEID, E., & BIJOU, S. W. Behavior therapy in the home: Amelioration of problem parent-child relations with the parent in a therapeutic role. *Journal of Experimental Child Psychology*, 1966, *4*, 99-107.

HAWKINSHIRE, F. B. W. Training procedures for offenders working in community treatment programs. In C. Spenser (Ed.), *Experiment in culture expansion*. Washington, D. C.: U.S. Department of Health, Education and Welfare, 1963.

HEBB, D. O. *The organization of behavior*. New York: Wiley, 1949.

HEBB, D. O. The motivating effects of exteroceptive stimulation. *American Psychologist*, 1958, *13*, 109-113.

HEBB, D. O., & THOMPSON, W. R. The social significance of animal studies. In G. Lindzey (Ed.), *Handbook of social psychology*. Vol. I. Cambridge, Mass.: Addison-Wesley, 1954. Pp. 532-561.

HENDRICK, I. *Facts and theories of psychoanalysis*. New York: Knopf, 1939.

HERRIGEL, E. *Zen in the art of archery*. New York: Pantheon, 1956.

HERRIGEL, E. *The method of Zen*. New York: Pantheon, 1960.

HILER, E. W. The sentence completion test as a predictor of continuation in psychotherapy. *Journal of Consulting Psychology*, 1959, *23*, 544-549.

HILGARD, J. R. & NEWMAN, M. F. Early maternal deprivation as a functional factor in the etiology of schizophrenia and alcoholism. *American Journal of Orthopsychiatry*, 1963, *33*, 409-420.

HINDE, R. A. The early development of the parent-child relationship. In R. S. Daniels (Ed.) *Contemporary readings in general psychology*. Boston: Houghton-Mifflin, 1965. Pp. 168-173.

HITT, W. D. Two models of man. *American Psychologist*, 1969, *24*, 651-658.

HOBBS, G. E. Mental disorders in one pair of identical twins. *American Journal of Psychiatry*, 1941, *98*, 447-450.

HOBBS, N. Sources of gain in psychotherapy. *American Psychologist*, 1962, *17*, 741-747.

HOBBS, N. Mental health's third revolution. *American Journal of Orthopsychiatry*, 1964, *34*, 822-833.

HOCH, P. Discussion of D. E. Cameron, "A theory of diagnosis". In P. Hoch & J. Zubin (Eds.), *Current problems in psychiatric diagnosis*. New York: Grune & Stratton, 1953. Pp. 46-50.

HOGAN, R. A., & KIRCHNER, H. Preliminary report on the extinction of learned fears via short-term implosive therapy. *Journal of Abnormal Psychology*, 1967, *72*, 106-109.

HOLT, H. The problem of interpretation from the point of view of existential psychoanalysis. In E. F. Hammer (Ed.), *Use of interpretation in treatment*. New York & London: Grune and Stratton, 1968. Pp. 240-252.

HORNEY, K. *Self-analysis*. New York: W. W. Norton, 1942.

HULL, C. L. *Principles of behavior*: New York: Appleton-Century-Crofts, 1943.

HULL, C. L. *A behavior theory concerning the individual organism*. New Haven: Yale University Press, 1952.

HUNT, J. McV. Experience and the development of motivation: Some reinterpretations. *Child Development*, 1960, *31*, 489-504.

HUNT, J. McV. *Intelligence and experience*. New York: Ronald, 1961.

HUNT, J. McV. The epigenesis of intrinsic motivation and the stimulation of early cognitive learning. Paper presented at a symposium on stimulation of early cognitive learning. American Psychological Association, Philadelphia, 1963.

HUNT, J. McV. Intrinsic motivation and its role in psychological development. In D. Levine (Ed.) *Nebraska symposium on motivation.* Lincoln: University of Nebraska Press, 1965. Pp. 189-282.

HUNT, J. McV., & UZGIRIS, I. Cathexis from recognitive familiarity: An exploratory study. Paper presented at American Psychological Association, Los Angeles, California, 1964.

IMLAB, N. Narcolepsy in identical twins. *Journal of Neurological and Neurosurgical Psychiatry,* 1961, *24,* 158-160.

IMMERGLUCK, L. Determinism-freedom in contemporary psychology: An ancient problem revisted. *American Psychologist,* 1964, *9,* 270-281.

IRISH, D. P. Sibling interaction: A neglected aspect of family life research. *Social Forces,* 1964, *42,* 279-288.

ISAACS, K. S. & HAGGARD, E. A. Some methods used in the study of affect in psychotherapy. In L. A. Gottschalk and A. H. Auerbach (Eds.) *Methods of research in psychotherapy.* New York: Appleton-Century-Crofts, 1966. Pp. 226-239.

JACKSON, D. D. The question of family homeostasis. *Psychiatric Quarterly,* 1957, *31,* 79-90.

JAMES, W. *Principles of psychology.* New York: Macmillan, 1894.

JENKINS, R. L. Nature of the schizophrenic process. *Archives of Neurology and Psychiatry,* 1950, *64,* 243-262.

JENKINS, R. L. The schizophrenic sequence: Withdrawal, disorganization, psychotic reorganization. *American Journal of Orthopsychiatry,* 1952, *22,* 738-748.

JESSOR, R. Social values and psychotherapy. *Journal of Consulting Psychology,* 1956, *20,* 214-266.

JESSOR, R. The problem of reductionism in psychology. *Psychological Review,* 1958, *65,* 170-178.

JOFFE, J. M. *Prenatal determinants of behavior.* Oxford: Pergamon Press, 1969.

JOHNSON, W. *The onset of stuttering.* Minneapolis: University of Minnesota Press, 1959.

JOHNSTON, R. Some casework aspects of using foster grandparents for emotionally disturbed children. *Children,* 1967, *14,* 46-52.

JOHN TRACY CLINIC. *Getting your baby ready to talk.* Los Angeles, California: John Tracy Clinic, 1968.

JOINT COMMISSION ON MENTAL ILLNESS AND HEALTH. *Action for mental health.* New York: Basic Books, 1961.

JONES, M. C. A laboratory study of fear: The case of Peter. *Journal of Genetic Psychology,* 1924, *31,* 308-315.

JONES, R. M. *The new psychology of dreaming.* New York and London: Grune and Stratton, 1970.

JOURARD, S. M. *Disclosing man to himself.* New York: Van Nostrand Reinhold, 1968.

JUNG, C. G. *Modern man in search of a soul.* New York: Harcourt Brace, 1933.

JUNG, C. G. *The undiscovered self.* Boston: Little Brown, 1957.

JUNG, C. G. The detachment of consciousness from the object. In R. Wilhelm, *The secret of the golden flower: A Chinese book of life.* London: Routledge & Kegan Paul, 1962. Pp. 122-127.

KAHN, M. H., MAHRER, A. R., & BORNSTEIN, R. Male psychosexual development: Role of sibling sex and ordinal position. *Journal of Genetic Psychology*, 1972, *121*, 187-196.

KALINOWSKY, L. B. & HOCH, P. B. *Somatic treatments in psychiatry*. New York: Grune & Stratton, 1961.

KALIS, B. L., HARRIS, M. R., PRESTWOOD, A. R., & FREEMAN, H. E. Precipitating stress as a focus in psychotherapy. *Archives of General Psychiatry*, 1961, *5*, 219-226.

KALLMAN, F. J. The genetics of human behavior. *American Journal of Psychiatry*, 1956, *113*, 496-501.

KAMIN, I. & COUGHLAN, J. Patients report the subjective experience of outpatient psychotherapy: A follow-up study. *American Journal of Psychotherapy*, 1963, *17*, 660-668.

KANFER, F. H. Self-regulation: Research, issues, and speculations. In C. Neuringer & J. L. Michael (Eds.) *Behavior modification in clinical psychology*. New York: Appleton-Century-Crofts, 1970.

KANFER, F. H., & SASLOW, G. Behavioral analysis. *Archives of General Psychiatry*, 1965, *12*, 529-538.

KANGAS, P. & MAHRER, A. R. Suicide attempts and threats as goal-directed communications in psychotic males. *Psychological Reports*, 1970, *27*, 795-801.

KANTOR, J. R. Preface to interbehavioral psychology. *Psychological Record*, 1942, *5*, 173-193.

KANTOR, J. R. *The logic of modern science*. Bloomington, Ill.: Principia Press, 1953.

KANTOR, J. R. Events and constructs in the science of psychology. *The Psychological Record*, 1957, *7*, 55-60.

KARR, S. D. & MAHRER, A. R. Transitional problems accompanying vocational development and college graduation. *Journal of Vocational Behavior*, 1972, *2*, 283-289.

KATKOVSKY, W., CRANDALL, V. C., & GOOD, S. Parental antecedents of children's beliefs in internal-external control of reinforcement in intellectual achievement situations. *Child Development*, 1967, *38*, 765-776.

KATZ, S. E. & LANDIS, C. Psychologic and physiologic phenomena during a prolonged vigil. *Archives of Neurology and Psychiatry*, 1935, *34*, 307-317.

KELLY, G. A. *The psychology of personal constructs*. Vols. I, II. New York: Norton, 1955.

KELLY, G. A. A psychology of the optimal man. In A. R. Mahrer (Ed.) *The goals of psychotherapy*. New York: Appleton-Century-Crofts, 1967. Pp. 238-258.

KELLY, J. G. The quest for valid preventative interventions. In C. D. Spielberger (Ed.) *Current topics in clinical and community psychology*. Vol. 2. New York: Academic Press, 1970. Pp. 183-207.

KENISTON, K. *The uncommited*. New York: Harcourt Brace Jovanovich, 1962.

KENYON, E. L. The etiology of stammering: An examination into certain recent studies, with a glance into the future. *Journal of Speech Disorders*, 1941, *6*, 1-12.

KESSEN, W. Research in the psychological development of infants: An overview. *Merrill-Palmer Quarterly of Behavior and Development*, 1953, *9*, 83-94.

KIERKEGAARD, S. *The concept of dread*. Princeton: Princeton University Press, 1944.

KIESLER, D. J. Some myths of psychotherapy research and the search for a paradigm. *Psychological Bulletin*, 1966, *65*, 116-136.

KIMBLE, G. A. Psychology as a science. *Scientific Monthly*, 1953, September, 1957-160.

KINGET, G. M. *On being human: A systematic view*. New York: Harcourt Brace Jovanovich, 1975.

KLEIN, E., & LEVITT, E. E. Side effects of a contraceptive medication in a university associated population. *Journal of the American College Health Association*, 1967, *16*, 182-184.

KLEIN, M. *The psychoanalysis of children*. New York: Norton, 1932.

KLEIN, M. *Contributions to psychoanalysis, 1921-1945*. London: Hogarth Press, 1948. (a)

KLEIN, M. A contribution to the theory of anxiety and guilt. *International Journal of Psychoanalysis*, 1948, *29*, 114-123. (b)

KLEIN, M. Some theoretical conclusions regarding the emotional life of the infant. In M. Klein, P. Heimann, S. Isaacs, & J. Riviere (Eds.) *Developments in psychoanalysis*. London: Hogarth Press, 1952. Pp. 198-236.

KLEITMAN, N. *Sleep and wakefulness*. Chicago: University of Chicago Press, 1939.

KNIGHT, R. P. Evaluation of the results of psychoanalytic therapy. *American Journal of Psychiatry*, 1941, *98*, 434-446.

KNIGHT, R. P. Determinism, freedom, and psychotherapy. *Psychiatry*, 1946, *9*, 251-262.

KNIGHT, R. P. An evaluation of psychotherapeutic techniques. *Bulletin of the Menninger Clinic*, 1952, *16*, 113-124.

KOESTENBAUM, P. Phenomenological foundations for the behavioral sciences: The nature of facts. *Journal of Existentialism*, 1966, *6*, 305-341.

KOCH, S. Theoretical psychology, 1950: An overview. *Psychological Review*, 1951, *58*, 295-302.

KOCH, S. Behavior as "intrinsically" regulated: Work notes toward a pretheory of phenomena called "motivational". In M. R. Jones (Ed.) *Nebraska symposium on motivation*. Lincoln, Nebraska: University of Nebraska Press, 1956. Pp. 42-86.

KONDO, A. Intuition in Zen Buddhism. *American Journal of Psychoanalysis*, 1952, *12*, 10-14.

KONDO, A. Zen in psychotherapy: The virtue of sitting. *Chicago Review*, 1958, *12*, 57-64.

KORANYI, E. K. & LEHMAN, H. E. Experimental sleep deprivation in schizophrenic patients. *Archives of General Psychiatry*, 1960. *2*. 534-544.

KOVACS, A. L. The intimate relationship: A therapeutic paradox. *Psychotherapy: Theory, Research and Practice*, 1965, *2*, 97-104.

KOVACS, A. L. Ego psychology and self-theory. In C. Buhler and F. Massarik (Eds.), *The course of life*. New York: Springer, 1968. Pp. 143-173.

KRAMER. M. *Dream psychology and the new biology of dreaming*. Springfield. Ill.: Charles C Thomas, 1969.

KRASNER, L. Behavior control and social responsibility. *American Psychologist*, 1962, *2*, 199-204.

KRECH, D. Dynamic systems, psychological fields and hypothetical constructs. *Psychological Review*, 1950, *57*, 283-290.

LAING, R. D. *The divided self*. London: Tavistock Publications, 1960.

LAING, R. D. *The self and others*. Chicago: Quadrangle Books, 1962.

LAING, R. D. & ESTERSON, A. *Sanity, madness and the family*. Harmondsworth, Middlesex: Penguin Books, 1970.

LAMBIE, D. Z.., BOND. J. T., & WEIKART, D. B. *Home teaching with mothers and infants*. Ypsilanti, Michigan: High-Scope Educational Research Foundation, 1974.

LAMBIE, D. Z. & WEIKART, D. B. Ypsilanti Carnegie infant education project. In J. Hellmuth (Ed.) *Disadvantaged child*. Volume 3. New York: Brunner/Mazel. 1970. Pp. 362-404.

LANGDON, G., & STOUT, I. W. *Teacher-parent interviews*. Englewood Cliffs, New York: Prentice-Hall, 1954.

LAWTON. G. Neurotic interaction between counsellor and counsellee. *Journal of Consulting Psychology*, 1958, *5*, 28-33.

LEARY, T. & GILL, M. The dimensions and a measure of the process of psychotherapy: A system for the analysis of content of clinical evaluations and patient-therapist interactions. In E. A. Rubenstein & M. B. Parloff (Eds.), *Research in psychotherapy*. Washington, D. C.: American Psychological Association, 1959. Pp. 62-95.

LEIGHTON, A. H. & HUGHES, J. H. *Causes of mental disorders: A review of epidemiological knowledge*. New York: Millbank Memorial Fund, 1961.

LEUBA, C. Toward some integration of learning theories: The concept of optimal stimulation. *Psychological Reports*, 1955, *1*, 27-33.

LEVITSKY, A., & PERLS, F. The rules and games of Gestalt therapy. In J. Fagan & I. L. Shepherd (Eds.) *Gestalt therapy now*. New York: Harper & Row. 1970.

LEVITT. E. E. The results of psychotherapy with children. *Journal of Consulting Psychology*, 1957. *21*, 189-196.

LEVITT, E. E. *The psychology of anxiety*. Indianapolis: Bobbs-Merrill, 1967.

LEVY, J. *The baby exercise book: The first fifteen months*. New York: Pantheon, 1974.

LEVY-BRUHL. *Primitive mentality*. London: Macmillan, 1923.

LEWIN, K. *A dynamic theory of personality: Selected papers of Kurt Lewin*. McGraw-Hill, 1935.

LEWIN, K. *The conceptual representation and the measurement of psychological forces*. Durham: Duke University Press, 1938.

LEWIS, A. States of depression: Their clinical and aetiological differentiation. *British Medical Journal*, 1938, *2*, 875-883.

LEWIS, M. State as an infant-mother interaction: An analysis of mother-infant interaction as a function of sex. *Merrill-Palmer Quarterly*, 1972, *18*, 95-121.

LEWIS, M., & GOLDBERG, S. Perceptual cognitive development in infancy. A generalized expectancy model as a function of the mother-infant interaction. *Merrill-Palmer Quarterly*, 1969, *15*, 81-100.

LIDZ, T., CORNELISON, A., TERRY, D., & FLECK, S. Intrafamilial environment of the schizophrenic patient: The transmission of irrationality. *Archives of Neurology and Psychiatry*. 1958. *79*. 305-316.

LINDNER, R. M. *Rebel without a cause*. New York: Grune & Stratton, 1964.

LIPKIN, S. Clients' feelings and attitudes in relation to outcome of client-centered therapy. *Psychological Monographs*, 1954, No. 372.

LIPSITT, L. P., PEDERSON, L. J., & DELUCIA, C. A. Conjugate reinforcement of operant responding in infants. *Psychonomic Science*, 1966, *4*, 47-68.

LITTMAN, R. A., & ROSEN, E. Molar and molecular. *Psychological Review*, 1950, *57*, 58-65.

LOEVINGER, J. Three principles for psychoanalytic psychology. *Journal of Abnormal Psychology*, 1966, *5*, 432-443.

LONDON, L. S. Unconscious hostility and insomnia. *Journal of Clinical Experimental Psychopathology*, 1950, *11*, 70-71.

LORR, M., SONN, T. M., & KATZ, M. M. Toward a definition of depression. *Archives of General Psychiatry*, 1967, *17*, 183-186.

LUBORSKY, L. A note on Eysenck's article, "The effects of psychotherapy: An evaluation." *British Journal of Psychology*, 1954, *45*, 129-131.

LUSTMAN, S. L., The headache as an internalized rage reaction: A preliminary report. *Psychiatry*, 1951, *14*, 433-438.

Lynn, D. & Sawrey, W. L. The effects of father's absence on Norwegian boys and girls. *Journal of Abnormal and Social Psychology*, 1959, *59*, 258-262.

Macdonald, A. P. Internal-external locus of control: Parental antecedents. *Journal of Consulting and Clinical Psychology*, 1971, *37*. 141-147.

MacKinnon. D. Fact and fantasy in personality research. *American Psychologist*. 1953. *8*.

Macleod, R. B. Phenomenology: A challenge to experimental psychology. In T. W. Wann (Ed.) *Behaviorism and Phenomenology: Contrasting bases for modern psychology*. Chicago: University of Chicago Press, 1964.

Maher, B. *Principles of psychopathology: An experimental approach*. New York: McGraw-Hill, 1966.

Mahler, M. S. On autistic psychosis and schizophrenia: Autistic and symbiotic infantile psychosis. *Psychoanalytic Study of the Child*, 1952, *7*, 286-305.

Mahler, M. Autism and symbiosis: Two extreme disturbances of identity. *International Journal of Psychoanalysis*, 1958, *39*, 77-83.

Mahler, M. S. & Gosliner, B. J. On symbiotic child psychosis: Genetic, dynamic, and restitutive aspects. *Psychoanalytic Study of the Child*, 1955, *10*, 195-212.

Mahrer, A. R. A clinical study of set in intraserial learning. *Journal of Abnormal and Social Psychology*, 1952, *47*, 478-482.

Mahrer, A. R. The role of expectancy in delayed reinforcement. *Journal of Experimental Psychology*, 1956, *52*, 101-106. Also in J. B. Rotter, J. E. Chance, & E. J. Phares (Eds.) *Applications of a social learning theory of personality*. New York: Holt, Rinehart & Winston, 1972. Pp. 98-105.

Mahrer, A. R. Potential intelligence testing: A case study. *U.S. Armed Forces Medical Journal*, 1957, *8*, 684-692.

Mahrer, A. R. Potential intelligence: A learning theory approach to description and clinical implication. *Journal of General Psychology*, 1958, *59*, 59-71.

Mahrer, A. R. A preface to the mind-body problem. *Psychological Record*, 1962, *12*, 53-60. (a)

Mahrer, A. R. Psychodiagnostic preference by professional affiliation and length of experience. *Journal of Clinical Psychology*, 1962. *18*. 14-18. (b)

Mahrer, A. R. The psychodynamics of psychiatric hospitalization. *Journal of Nervous and Mental Disease*, 1962, *135*, 354-360. (c)

Mahrer, A. R. Psychological symptoms as a function of psychiatric hospitalization. *Psychological Reports*, 1963, *13*, 266.

Mahrer, A. R. Analysis of a fragment of a dream. *Voices*, 1966, *2*, 40-41.

Mahrer, A. R. The goals of intensive psychotherapy. In A. R. Mahrer (Ed.) *The goals of psychotherapy*. New York: Appleton-Century-Crofts, 1967. Pp. 162-179. (a)

Mahrer, A. R. The goals and families of psychotherapy: Summary. In A. R. Mahrer (Ed.) *The goals of psychotherapy*. New York: Appleton-Century-Crofts. 1967. Pp. 259-269. (b)

Mahrer, A. R. The goals of families of psychotherapy: Discussion. In A. R. Mahrer (Ed.) *The goals of psychotherapy*. New York: Appleton-Century-Crofts. 1967. Pp. 276-287. (c)

Mahrer, A. R. The goals and families of psychotherapy: Implications. In A. R. Mahrer (Ed.) *The gods of psychotherapy*. New York: Appleton-Century-Crofts. 1967. Pp. 288-301. (d)

Mahrer, A. R. The psychological problem inventory. *Psychological Reports*, 1967, *20*, 711-714. (e)

Mahrer, A. R. Childhood determinants of adult functioning: Strategies in the clinical research use of the personal-psychological history. *Psychological Record*, 1969, *19*, 39-46.

MAHRER, A. R. Some known effects of psychotherapy and a reinterpretation. *Psychotherapy: Theory, Research and Practice*, 1970, 7, 186-191. Also in A. G. Banet, Jr. (Ed.) *Creative psychotherapy: A source book*. La Jolla, Cal.: University Associates, 1976. Pp. 334-344. (a)

MAHRER, A. R. Motivational theory: Foundation of personality classification. In A. R. Mahrer (Ed.) *New approaches to personality classification*. New York: Columbia University Press, 1970. Pp. 239-276. (b)

MAHRER, A. R. Motivational theory: A system of personality classification. In A. R. Mahrer (Ed.) *New approaches to personality classification*. New York: Columbia University Press, 1970. Pp. 277-307. (c)

MAHRER, A. R. Present trends and future directions. In A. R. Mahrer (Ed.) *New approaches to personality classification*. New York: Columbia University Press, 1970. Pp. 397-413. (d)

MAHRER, A. R. Self-change and social change. *Interpersonal Development*, 1970, *1*, 159-166. (e)

MAHRER, A. R. Interpretation of patient behaviour through goals, feelings, and context. *Journal of Individual Psychology*, 1970, *26*, 186-195. (f)

MAHRER, A. R. Personal life change through systematic use of dreams. *Psychotherapy: Theory, Research and Practice*, 1971, *8*, 328-332. (a)

MAHRER, A. R. An emerging field of human relations. *Interpersonal Development*, 1971, *2*, 105-120. (b)

MAHRER. A. R. The Human Relations Center: Community mental health from a motivational perspective. *Corrective Psychiatry and Journal of Social Therapy*, 1972, *18*, 39-45. (a)

MAHRER, A. R. Theory and treatment of anxiety: The perspective of motivational psychology. *Journal of Pastoral Counselling*, 1972, 7, 4-16. (b)

MAHRER, A. R. Defining characteristics of a humanistic program of community change and a specimen: The facilitation of self-competence in the neonate. *The Ontario Psychologist*, 1973, *5*, 45-50.

MAHRER, A. R. Metamorphosis through suicide: The changing of one's self by oneself. *Journal of Pastoral Counseling*, 1975, *10*, 10-26. (a)

MAHRER, A. R. Therapeutic outcome as a function of goodness of fit on an internal-external dimension of interaction. *Psychotherapy: Theory, Research and Practice*, 1975, *12*, 22-27. (b)

MAHRER, A. R. Sequence and consequence in the experiential psychotherapies. In C. Cooper and C. Alderfer (Eds.) *Advances in experiential social processes*. New York: Wiley, 1977.

MAHRER, A. R., & BERNSTEIN, L. A proposed method for measuring potential intelligence. *Journal of Clinical Psychology*, 1959, *15*, 286-288.

MAHRER, A. R., & BORNSTEIN, R. Depression: Characteristic syndromes and a prefatory conceptualization. *Journal of General Psychology*, 1969, *81*, 217-229.

MAHRER, A. R., & KATZ, G. Psychiatric symptoms at admission to hospitalization. *Psychiatry Digest*, 1963, *24*, 23-30.

MAHRER, A. R., LEVINSON, J. R. & FINE, S. Infant psychotherapy: Theory, research and practice. *Psychotherapy: Theory, Research and Practice*, 1976, *13*, 131-140.

MAHRER, A. R., & MASON, D. J. Changes in number of self-reported symptoms during psychiatric hospitalization. *Journal of Consulting Psychology*, 1965, *29*, 285.

MAHRER, A. R., MASON, D. J., KAHN, E., & PROJANSKY, M. High complainers versus low complainers: Patterning of amount of self-reported symptomatology in psychiatric patients. *Psychological Reports*, 1966, *19*, 955-958.

MAHRER, A. R., MASON, D. J., KAHN, E., & PROJANSKY, M. The non-Gaussian distribution of amounts of symptomatology in psychiatric patients. *Journal of Clinical Psychology*, 1967, *23*, 319-321.

MAHRER, A. R., MASON, D. J., & ROSENSHINE, M. A headache syndrome in psychiatric patients: Symptom clusters accompanying headaches. *Journal of Clinical Psychology*, 1966, *22*, 411-414.

MAHRER, A. R., & PEARSON, L. The directions of psychotherapeutic change: Creative developments. In A. R. Mahrer & L. Pearson (Eds.) *Creative developments in psychotherapy. Volume I*. Cleveland: Case Western Reserve University Press, 1971. Pp. 1-14. (a)

MAHRER, A. R. & PEARSON, L. The expanded context of psychotherapy: Creative developments. In A. R. Mahrer & L. Pearson (Eds.) *Creative developments in psychotherapy. Volume I*. Cleveland: Case Western Reserve University Press, 1971. Pp. 189-203. (b)

MAHRER, A. R. & PEARSON, L. The working processes of psychotherapy: Creative developments. In A. R. Mahrer & L. Pearson (Eds.) *Creative developments in psychotherapy. Volume I*. Cleveland: Case Western Reserve University Press, 1971. Pp. 309-329. (c)

MAHRER, A. R., STEWART, P., HORN, J. & LIND, D. Symptom patterns in psychiatric patients: A goal-directed approach to psychiatric symptomatology. *Journal of Psychology*, 1968, *68*, 151-157.

MAHRER, A. R. & THORP, T. A comparison of methods of predicting potential intelligence. *Journal of Clinical Psychology*, 1959, *15*, 286-288.

MAHRER, A. R., THORP, T. & STERNLICHT, I. The role of cues in psychodiagnosis. *Journal of General Psychology*, 1960, *62*, 247-256.

MAHRER, A. R., & YOUNG, H. H. The combination of psychodiagnostic cues. *Journal of Personality*, 1961, *29*, 428-448.

MAHRER, A. R., & YOUNG, H. H. The onset of stuttering. *Journal of General Psychology*, 1962, *67*, 241-250.

MAHRER, A. R., YOUNG, H. H., & KATZ, G. Toward a psychological rationale for understanding the effects of anti-depressant medication. In C. L. Lindley, (Ed.) *Cooperative chemotherapy studies in psychiatry and research approaches to mental illness*. Washington. D. C.: Veterans Administration. 1960. Pp. 131-134.

MAIER, N. R. F. Frustration theory: Restatement and extension. *Psychological Review*, 1956, *63*, 370-388.

MAILLOUX, N. Psychic determinism, freedom, and personality development. *Canadian Journal of Psychology*, 1953, 7, 1-11.

MALMO, R. B. Activation: A neuropsychological dimension. *Psychological Review*, 1959, *66*, 367-386.

MALONE, T. P., WHITAKER, C. A., WARKENTIN, J. & FELDER, R. E. Rational and nonrational psychotherapy. *American Journal of Psychotherapy*, 1961, *15*, 212-220.

MARMOR, J. & PUMPIAN-MINDLIN, E. Toward an integrative conception of mental disorder. *Journal of Nervous and Mental Disease*, 1950, *111*, 19-29.

MARX, M. H., & TOMBAUGH, T. N. *Motivation*. Scranton, Pennsylvania: Chandler, 1967.

MASLOW, A. H. Our maligned animal nature. *Journal of Psychology*, 1949, *28*, 273-278.

MASLOW, A. H. Lessons from the peak experiences. *Journal of Humanistic Psychology*,

1962, *2*, 9-18.

MASLOW, A. H. Fusions of facts and values. *American Journal of Psychoanalysis*, 1963, *23*, 117-131.

MASLOW, A. H. *Toward a psychology of being.* (2nd ed.) New York: Van Nostrand-Reinhold, 1968.

MASLOW, A. H. Humanistic education vs. professional education: Further comments. *New Directions in Teaching*, 1970, *2*, 3-10. (a)

MASLOW, A. H. *Motivation and personality.* (2nd ed.). New York: Harper & Row, 1970. (b)

MASLOW, A. H. & MITTELMANN, B. *Principles of abnormal psychology: The dynamics of psychic illness.* New York: Harper, 1941.

MASLOW, A. H., & MURPHY, G. (Eds.) *Motivation and personality.* New York: Harper, 1954.

MASSERMAN, J. H. *Principles of dynamic psychiatry.* (2nd ed.) Philadelphia: W. B. Saunders, 1961.

MATSON, F. W. *The broken image.* New York: Braziller, 1964.

MAUPIN, E. W. Zen Buddhism: A psychological review. *Psychedelic Review*, 1965, *5*, 59-97.

MAY, R. *Man's search for himself.* New York: Norton, 1953.

MAY, R. Contributions of existential psychotherapy. In R. May, E. Angel, & H. F. Ellenberger (Eds.) *Existence: A new dimension in psychiatry and psychology.* New York: Basic Books, 1958. Pp. 37-91. (a)

MAY, R. The origins and significance of the existential movement in psychology. In R. May, E. Angel, & H. F. Ellenberger (Eds.) *Existence: A new dimension in psychiatry and psychology.* New York: Basic Books, 1958. Pp. 3-36. (b)

MAY, R. On the phenomenological bases of psychotherapy. *Review of Existential Psychology and Psychiatry*, 1964, *4*, 22-36.

MAY, R. *Psychology and the human dilemma.* Princeton, New Jersey: D. Van Nostrand, 1967.

MAY, R. The daemonic: Love and death. *Psychology Today*, 1968, *1*, 16-25.

MAZER, D. B. & MAHRER, A. R. Developmental factors in masturbation: Family background antecedents and later personality patterns. *Journal of Psychology*, 1971, *79*, 21-27.

McCALL, R. J. The defense mechanism reexamined. In L. Gorlow & W. Katkovsky (Eds.) *Reading in the psychology of adjustment* (2nd ed.). New York: McGraw-Hill, 1968. Pp. 317-335.

McCARTHY, D. Language development in children. In L. Carmichael (Ed.) *Manual of child psychology.* New York: Wiley, 1954. Pp. 476-582.

McCONAGHY, N. The use of an object sorting test in elucidating the hereditary factor in schizophrenia. *Journal of Neurology, Neurosurgery and Psychiatry*, 1959, *22*, 243-246.

McCORD, J. McCORD, W., & THURBER, E. Some effects of paternal absence on male children. *Journal of Abnormal and Social Psychology*, 1962, *64*, 361-369.

McCURDY, H. G. *The personal world: An introduction to the study of personality.* New York: Harcourt Brace and World, 1961.

McDIARMID, N. J., PETERSON, M. A., & SUTHERLAND, J. R. *Loving and learning: Interacting with your child from birth to three.* New York: Harcourt Brace Jovanovich, 1975.

McFARLAND, R. A., & HUDDELSON, J. H. Neurocirculatory reactions in the psychoneuroses studied by the Schneider method. *American Journal of Psychiatry*, 1936, *93*, 567-599.

McGEOCH, J. A. Formal criteria for systematic psychology. *Psychological Review*, 1933, *40*, 1-12.

McKELLAR, P. Our hidden differences. *The Listener*, 1963, 498-501.

McREYNOLDS, P. Anxiety, perception and schizophrenia. In D. D. Jackson (Ed.), *The etiology of schizophrenia*. New York: Basic Books, 1960. Pp. 248-292.

MEAD, G. H. *Mind, self, and society*. Chicago: University of Chicago Press, 1934.

MEAD, M. Research on primitive children. In L. Carmichael (Ed.) *Manual of child psychology*. New York: Wiley, 1954. Pp. 667-700.

MECHANIC, D. Some factors in identifying and defining mental illness. *Mental Hygiene*, 1962, *46*, 66-74.

MEDNICK, S. A. Primary prevention and schizophrenia: Theory and research. In *Public Health Practice and the Prevention of Mental Illness*. Copenhagen: World Health Organization, 1962.

MEDNICK, S. A. Psychophysiology, thought processes, personality and social development of children with a high risk for schizophrenia. *Sociological Micro-Journal*, 1967, *1*, 1-100.

MEEHL, P. E. Schizotaxia, schizotypy, schizophrenia. *American Psychologist*, 1962, *17*, 827-838.

MENDELSON, M. *Psychoanalytic concepts of depression*. Springfield: Thomas, 1960.

MILLER, G. A., PRIBRAM, K., & GALANTER, E. *Plans and the structure of behaviour*. New York: Holt Rinehart & Winston, 1960.

MILLER, N. E. Experimental studies of conflict. In J. McV. Hunt (Ed.) *Personality and the behavior disorders*. Volume 1. New York: Ronald, 1944. Pp. 431-465.

MILLER, N. E. & DOLLARD, J. *Social learning and imitation*. New Haven: Yale University Press, 1941.

MILLER, P. M., BRADLEY, J. B., GROSS, R. S. & WOOD, G. Review of homosexuality research (1960-1966) and some implications for treatment. *Psychotherapy: Theory, Research, and Practice*, 1968, *5*, 3-6.

MILLON, T. Theory in psychopathology. In T. Millon (Ed.) *Theories of Psychopathology*. Philadelphia: Saunders, 1967. Pp. 1-8.

MISCHEL, W. Preference for delayed reinforcement: An experimental study of a cultural observation. *Journal of Abnormal and Social Psychology*, 1958, *56*, 57-61.

MISCHEL, W. Theory and research on the antecedents of self-imposed delay of reward. In B. A. Maher (Ed.) *Progress in experimental personality research*. Volume 3. New York: Academic Press, 1966.

MONEY, J. Mind-body dualism and the unity of bodymind. *Behavioral Science*, 1956, *1*, 212-217.

MONTAGU, A. *On being human*. New York: Schuman, 1950.

MONTAGU, A. Our changing conception of human nature. In R. S. Daniel (Ed.) *Contemporary readings in general psychology*. Boston: Houghton-Mifflin, 1965. Pp. 311-319.

MOORE, O. K. The preschool child learns to read and write. In Y. Brackbill & G. Thompson (Eds.) *Behavior in infancy and early childhood*. New York: Free Press, 1967.

MOSS, H. A. Sex, age and state as determinants of mother-infant reaction. *Merrill-Palmer Quarterly of Behavior and Development*, 1967, *13*, 19-36.

MOSS, H. A. & ROBSON, K. S. The role of protest behavior in the development of the mother-infant attachment. Paper presented at American Psychological Association, San Francisco, 1968.

MOUSTAKAS, C. *Loneliness*. Englewood Cliffs, New Jersey, 1961.

MOWRER, O. H. A stimulus-response analysis of anxiety and its role as a reinforcing agent. *Psychological Review*, 1939, *46*, 553-566.

MOWRER, O. H. Learning theory and the neurotic paradox. *American Journal of Orthopsychiatry*, 1948, *18* 571-610.

MOWRER, O. H. *Learning theory and personality dynamics*. New York: Ronald, 1950.

MOWRER, O. H. & KLUCKHOHN, C. A dynamic theory of personality. In J. McV. Hunt (Ed.) *Personality and the behavior disorders*. New York: Ronald, 1944. Pp. 69-135.

MOWRER, O. H. & ULLMAN, A. D. Time as a determinant in integrative learning. *Psychological Review*, 1945, *52*, 61-90.

MULLEN, H. & SANGIULIANO, I. *The therapist's contribution to the treatment process.* Springfield, Ill.: Charles C. Thomas, 1964.

MULLER, H. J. *Issues of freedom.* New York: Harper & Row, 1960.

MUNROE, R. L. *Schools of psychoanalytic thought.* New York: Holt Rinehart & Winston, 1955.

MURPHY, G. *Personality: A biosocial approach to origin and structure.* New York: Harper, 1947.

MURRAY, E. J. *Sleep, dreams, and arousal.* New York: Appleton-Century-Crofts, 1965.

MURRAY, H. A., & KLUCKHOHN, C. Outline of a conception of personality. In C. Kluckhohn, H. A. Murray, & D. M. Schneider (Eds.) *Personality in nature, society, and culture*, 2nd edition. New York: Alfred A. Knopf, 1956.

MURRAY, H. A. & KLUCKHOHN, C. Outline of a conception of personality. In C. Kluckhohn, H. A. Murray, & D. M. Schneider (Eds.) *Personality in nature, society and culture*. (2nd ed.) New York: Knopf, 1967. Pp. 3-49.

NEEDLEMAN, J. Preface. In J. Needleman (Ed.) *Being-in-the-world: Selected papers of Ludwig Binswanger*. New York and London: Harper Torchbooks, 1967. Pp. viii-xvii. (a)

NEEDLEMAN, J. The concept of the existential a priori. In J. Needleman (Ed.) *Being-in-the-World: Selected papers of Ludwig Binswanger*. New York and London: Harper Torchbooks, 1967. Pp. 9-31. (b)

O'HEARNE, J. J. Some methods of dealing with delusions in group psychotherapy. *International Journal of Group Psychotherapy*, 1962, *12*, 35-40.

ORLANSKY, H. Infant care and personality. *Psychological Bulletin*, 1949, *46*, 1-48.

ORNSTEIN, R. E. "Turning off" awareness. In C. Naranjo & R. E. Ornstein, *On the psychology of meditation*. New York: Viking, 1971. Pp. 142-169.

OSGOOD, C. E. *Method and theory in experimental psychology.* New York: Oxford University Press, 1953.

OSTOW, M. The psychic function of depression: A study in energetics. *Psychoanalytic Quarterly*, 1960, *29*, 355-394.

OUSPENSKY, P. D. *The fourth way.* London: Routledge and Kegan Paul, 1957.

PAINTER, G. *Teach your baby.* New York: Simon and Schuster, 1971.

PARSONS, T. Certain sources and patterns of aggression in the social structure of the western world. *Psychiatry*, 1947, *4*, 172-185.

PIAGET, J. *The language and thought of the child*. Harcourt Brace, 1926.

PIAGET, J. *The child's conception of the world*. Harcourt Brace, 1929.

PIAGET, J. *The origins of intelligence in children*. New York: International Universities Press, 1952.

PILNICK, S., ELIAS, A. & CLAPP, N. W. The Essexfield concept: A new approach to the social treatment of juvenile delinquents. *The Journal of Applied Behavioral Science*, 1966, *2*, 109-125.

POLANYI, M. *Personal knowledge*. Chicago: University of Chicago Press, 1958.

POLONSKY, N. A., WHITE, R. B., & MILLER, S. Determinants of the role-image of the patient in a psychiatric hospital. In M. Greenblatt, D. Levinson & R. H. Williams (Eds.) *The patient and the mental hospital.*. Glencoe, Ill.: The Free Press, 1957. Pp. 384-402.

POMEROY, E., MAHRER, A. R., & MASON, D. J. An aggressive syndrome in hospitalized psychiatric patients. *Proceedings of the 73rd Annual Convention of The American Psychological Association*, 1965. Pp. 239-240.

POWERS, E. & WITMER, H. *An experiment in the prevention of delinquency*. New York: Columbia University Press, 1951.

PRATT, K. C. The organization of behavior in the newborn infant. *Psychological Review*, 1937, *44*, 470-490.

PRATT, K. C., NELSON, A. K., & SUN, K. H. *The behavior of the new born infant*. Columbus: Ohio State University Press, 1930.

PROVENCE, S. & LIPTON, R. C. *Infants in institutions*. New York: International Universities Press, 1962.

PRUDDEN, B. *How to keep your child fit from birth to six*. New York: Harper & Row, 1964.

RABINOWITZ, M. *In the beginning: A parent guide of activities and experiences for infants from birth to six months*. New Orleans, La.: Parent Child Development Center, 1974.

RADO, S. The problem of melancholia. *International Journal of Psychoanalysis*, 1928, *9*, 420-438.

RADO, S. *Psychoanalysis of behavior: Collected papers*. Volume I. New York: Grune & Stratton, 1956.

RADO, S. & DANIEL, G. *Changing concepts of psychoanalytic medicine*. New York: Grune & Stratton, 1956.

RAKER, J. W., WALLACE, A. F. C., & RAYMER, J. F. *Emergency medical care in disasters: A summary of recorded experiences*. Washington, D. C.: National Academy of Sciences, 1956.

RANK, O. *The trauma of birth*. New York: Harper Torchbooks, 1973.

RASKIN, A. Factors therapists associate with motivation to enter therapy. *Journal of Clinical Psychology*, 1961, *17*, 62-65.

RAYNER, E. H., & HAHN, H. Assessment for psychotherapy: A pilot study of psychological test indications for success and failure in treatment. *British Journal of Medical Psychology*, 1964, *27*, 331-342.

REIK, W. *Listening with the third ear*. New York: Grove Press, 1948.

RHEINGOLD, H. L. The effect of environmental stimulation upon social and exploratory behavior in the human infant. In B. M. Foss (Ed.) *Determinants of infant behavior*. New York: Wiley, 1961. Pp. 143-171.

RICKLES, K., DOWNING, R. W., & DOWNING, M. H. Personality differences between somatically and psychologically oriented neurotic patients. *Journal of Nervous and Mental Diseases*, 1966, *142*, 10-18.

RICKS, D. F. Life history research in psychopathology: Retrospect and prospect. In M. Roff & D. F. Ricks (Eds.) *Life history research in psychopathology*. Minneapolis: University of Minnesota Press, 1970. Pp. 288-307.

RIESSMAN, F. The 'helper' therapy principle. *Social Work,* 1965, *10,* 27-32.

ROBBINS, L. L. Historical review of classification of behavior disorders and one current perspective. In L. D. Eron (Ed.) *The classification of behavior disorders.* Chicago: Aldine, 1966. Pp. 3-37.

ROBSON, K. S., PEDERSON, F. A., & Moss, H. A. Developmental observations of diadic gazing in relation to the fear of strangers and social approach behavior. *Child Development,* 1969, *40,* 619-627.

ROFF, M. Some life history factors in relation to various types of adult maladjustment. In M. Roff & D. F. Ricks (Eds.) *Life history research in psychopathology.* Minneapolis: University of Minnesota Press, 1970. Pp. 265-287.

ROGERS, C. R. The necessary and sufficient conditions of therapeutic personality change. *Journal of Consulting Psychology,* 1957, *21,* 95-103.

ROGERS, C. R. The characteristics of a helping relationship. *Personnel and Guidance Journal,* 1958, *37,* 6-16.

ROGERS, C. R. A theory of therapy, personality, and interpersonal relationships, as developed in the client-centered framework. In S. Koch (Ed.) *Psychology: A study of a science,* Volume 3. New York: McGraw-Hill, 1959. Pp. 221-231.

ROGERS, C. R. *On becoming a person.* Boston: Houghton-Mifflin, 1961.

ROGERS, C. R. The concept of the fully functioning person. *Psychotherapy: Theory, Research and Practice,* 1963, *1,* 17-26.

ROGERS, C. R. Implications of recent advances in prediction and control of behavior. In R. S. Daniel (Ed.) *Contemporary readings in general psychology,* (2nd ed.), Boston: Houghton-Mifflin, 1965. Pp. 375-380.

ROGERS, C. R. Some learning from a study of psychotherapy with schizophrenics. In A. Goldstein & S. Dean (Eds.) *The investigation of psychotherapy.* New York: Wiley, 1966. Pp. 5-13.

ROGERS, C. R. The process of the basic encounter group. In J. F. T. Bugental (Ed.), *Challenges of humanistic psychology.* New York: McGraw-Hill, 1967. Pp. 261-276. (a)

ROGERS, C. R. The interpersonal relationship in the facilitation of learning. In R. R. Leeper (Ed.) *Humanizing education: The person in the process.* Washington, D. C.: Association for Supervision and Curriculum Development, 1967. Pp. 1-18. (b)

ROGERS, C. R. *On becoming a person.* Boston: Houghton Mifflin, 1970.

ROGERS, C. R. & SKINNER, B. F. Some issues concerning the control of human behavior. *Science,* 1956, *124,* 1057-1066.

ROGLER, L. H., & HOLLINGSHEAD, A. B. *Trapped: Families and schizophrenia.* New York: Wiley, 1965.

ROTHENBERG, G. Psychoanalytic insight into insomnia. *Psychoanalytic Review,* 1947, *34,* 141-169.

ROTTER, J. B. *Social learning and clinical psychology.* Englewood Cliffs, New Jersey: Prentice-Hall, 1954.

ROTTER, J. B. The role of the psychological situation in determining the direction of human behavior. In R. Jones (Ed.) *Nebraska symposium on motivation.* Lincoln, Neb.: University of Nebraska Press, 1955. Pp. 245-269.

ROTTER, J. B. Generalized expectancies for internal versus external control of reinforcement. *Psychological Monographs,* 1966, *80* (Whole No. 609).

ROTTER, J. B. A new scale for the measurement of interpersonal trust. *Journal of Personality,* 1967, *35,* 651-665.

Rovee, K. R., & Rovee, D. T. Conjugate reinforcement of infant exploratory behavior. *Journal of Experimental Child Psychology*, 1969, *8*, 33-39.

Salter, A. Three techniques of autohypnosis. *Journal of General Psychology*, 1941, *24*, 423-438.

Sarason, I. G. *Personality: An objective approach*. New York: Wiley, 1966.

Sarason, S. B., Levine, M. I., Goldenberg, I., Cherlin, D. L., & Bennett, E. M. *Psychology in community settings: Clinical, educational, vocational, social aspects*. New York: Wiley, 1966.

Saul, L. J. *Technique and practice of psychoanalysis*. Philadelphia: Lippincott, 1958.

Saul. L. J. *Emotional maturity: the development and dynamics of personality*. (2nd ed.) Philadelphia: Lippincott, 1960.

Schachtel, E. G. The development of focal attention and the emergence of reality. *Psychiatry*, 1954, *17*, 309-324.

Schachtel, E. G. *Metamorphosis*. New York: Basic Books, 1959.

Schiller, F. *Essays, aesthetic and philosophical*. London: Bell, 1873.

Schofield, W. *Psychotherapy: The purchase of friendship*. Englewood Cliffs, New Jersey: Prentice-Hall, 1964.

Schwab, J. J. What do scientists do? *Behavioral Science*, 1960, *5*, 1-27.

Schwartz, C. G., Schwartz, M. S., & Stanton, A. H. A study of need fulfillment on a mental hospital ward. *Psychiatry*, 1951, *14*, 223-242.

Schwartz, M. S. Patient demands in a mental hospital context. *Psychiatry*, 1957, *20*, 249-261.

Seagull, A. A. The treatment of a suicide threat. *Psychotherapy: Theory Research and Practice*, 1967, *1*, 41-43.

Sears, R. R. Ordinal position in the family as a psychological variable. *American Sociological Review*, 1950, *15*, 397-401.

Sears, R. R., Whiting, J. W., Nowlis, V., & Sears, P. S. Some child-rearing antecedents of aggression and dependency in young children. *Genetic Psychology Monographs*, 1953, *47*, 135-234.

Selling, L. S. *Man against madness*. New York: Garden City Books, 1943.

Selye, H. *The stress of life*. New York: McGraw-Hill, 1956.

Serban, G. The existential therapeutic approach to homosexuality. *American Journal of Psychotherapy*, 1968, *22*, 491-501.

Shah, S. A. Training and utilizing a mother as the therapist for her child. In B. G. Guerney. Jr. (Ed.) *Psychotherapeutic agents: New roles for nonprofessionals, parents and teachers*. New York: Holt, Rinehart & Winston, 1969. Pp. 401-407.

Sharaf, M. R. & Levinson, D. J. Patterns of ideology and role-definition among psychiatric residents. In M. Greenblatt, D. J. Levinson, & R. H. Williams (Eds.) *The patient and the mental hospital*. Glencoe, Ill.: Free Press, 1957.

Sheehan, J. G. The theory and treatment of stuttering as an approach-avoidance conflict. *Journal of Psychology*, 1953, *36*, 27-49.

Sheldon, W. H. *Atlas of men: A guide for somatotyping the adult male at all ages*. New York: Harper, 1954.

Shoben, E. J. Psychotherapy as a problem in learning theory. *Psychological Bulletin*, 1949, *46*, 366-392.

Shorr, J. E. *Psycho-imagination therapy*. New York: Intercontinental Medical Book Corporation, 1972.

Shostrom, E. L. *Man, the manipulator*. Nashville: Abingdon Press, 1967.

Skinner, B. F. *The behavior of organisms*. New York: Appleton-Century-Crofts, 1938.

Skinner, B. F. *Science and human behavior*. New York: Macmillan, 1953.

Skinner, B. F. *Verbal behavior*. New York: Appleton-Century-Crofts, 1957.

Skinner. B. F. What is psychotic behavior? In T. Millon (Ed.) *Theories of psychopathology*. Philadelphia: Saunders, 1967. Pp. 324-337.

Sluckin, W. *Imprinting and early learning*. Chicago: Aldine, 1965.

Snyder, F. The new biology of dreaming. *Archives of General Psychiatry*, 1963, *8*, 381-391.

Solomon, R. L. & Wynne, L. C. Traumatic avoidance learning: The principles of anxiety conservation and partial irreversibility. *Psychological Review*, 1954, *61*, 353-384.

Sontag, L. W. War and fetal-maternal relationship. *Marriage and Family Living*, 1944, *6*, 1-5.

Sontag, L. W., Baker, C. & Nelson, V. Personality as a determinant of performance. *American Journal of Orthopsychiatry*, 1955, *25*, 255-262.

Sontag, L. W. & Wallace, R. F. Study of fetal activity. *American Journal of Diseases of the Child*, 1934, *48*, 1050-1057.

Sorokin, P. A. *Explorations in altruism*. Boston: Beacon, 1950. (a)

Sorokin, P. A. *Altruistic love: A study of American good neighbors and Christian saints*. Boston: Beacon, 1950. (b)

Sorokin. P. A. The powers of creative unselfish love. In A. H. Maslow (Ed.) *New knowledge in human values*. New York: Harper & Row, 1959. Pp. 3-11.

Sparkman, B., & Carmichael, A. *Blueprint for a brighter child*. New York: McGraw-Hill, 1973.

Speers. R. W., & Lansing. C. *Group therapy in childhood psychosis*. Chapel Hill. North Carolina: University of North Carolina Press, 1965.

Spence, K. W. *Behavior theory and conditioning*. New Haven: Yale University Press, 1956.

Spencer, H. *The principles of psychology*. New York: Appleton-Century-Crofts, 1873.

Spiegel, E. A. Neurologic aspects of the body-mind problem. *Journal of Nervous and Mental Diseases*, 1957, *125*, 614-621.

Spitz, R. A. Hospitalism: An inquiry into the genesis of psychiatric conditions in early childhood. *Psychoanalytic Study of the Child*. Volume 1. New York: International Universities Press, 1945.

Spitz, R. A. *The first year of life: A psychoanalytic study of normal and deviant development of object relations*. New York: International Universities Press, 1965.

Spitz, R. A. & Wolf, K. M. Anaclictic depression. In A. Freud *et al.* (Eds.) *Psychoanalytic study of the child*. Volume 2. New York: International Universities Press, 1946.

Stampfl, T. G. & Levis, D. J. Essentials of implosive therapy: A learning theory based psychodynamic behavioral therapy. *Journal of Abnormal Psychology*, 1967, *72*, 496-503.

Stekel, W. *Conditions of nervous anxiety and their treatment*. New York: Liveright, 1949.

Stephens, J. H. & Astrup, C. Treatment outcome in "process" and "non-process" schizophrenics treated by "A" and "B" types of therapist. *Journal of Nervous and Mental Disease*, 1965, *140*, 449-456.

Stevens, S. S. The operational definition of psychological concepts. *Psychological Review*, 1935, *42*, 517-527.

Stevens, S. S. Psychology and the science of science. *Psychological Bulletin*, 1939, *36*, 221-263.

STEWART, K. Culture and personality in two primitive groups. *Complex*, 1953, *9*, 3-23.

STRACHEY, J. (Ed.) *Standard edition of the complete psychological works of Sigmund Freud*. London: Hogarth Press & The Institute of Psychoanalysis, 1953.

STRAUS, E. W. *Phenomenological psychology*. New York: Basic Books, 1966.

STRAUSS, A., SCHATZMAN, L., BUCHER, R., EHRLICH, D. & SABSHIM, M. *Psychiatric ideologies and institutions*. New York: Free Press, 1964.

STRUPP, H. H. *Psychotherapists in action: Explorations of the therapist's contribution to the treatment process*. New York: Grune & Stratton, 1960.

STRUPP, H. H. The outcome problem in psychotherapy revisited. *Psychotherapy: Theory, Research, and Practice*, 1963, *1*, 1-13.

STRUPP, H. H., & BERGIN, A. E. Some empirical and conceptual bases for coordinated research in psychotherapy: A critical review of issues, trends and evidence. *International Journal of Psychiatry*, 1969, *7*, No. 2.

SULLIVAN, H. S. *The interpersonal theory of psychiatry*. New York: Norton, 1953.

SUTTIE, I. D. *The origin of love and hate*. New York: Julian Press. 1952.

SUTTON-SMITH, B., & SUTTON-SMITH, S. *How to play with your children*. New York: Hawthorn, 1974.

SUZUKI, D. T. *Living by Zen*. Tokyo: Sanseido Press, 1949.

SUZUKI, D. T. *Zen Buddhism*. Garden City: Doubleday, 1956.

SZASZ, T. S. *The myth of mental illness*. New York: Hoeber-Harper, 1956.

SZASZ, T. S. Commitment of the mentally ill: "Treatment" or social restraint? *Journal of Nervous and Mental Disease*, 1957, *125*, 293-307.

SZASZ, T. S. The use of naming and the origin of the myth of mental illness. *American Psychologist*, 1961, *16*, 59-65.

TAUBER, E. S. Sullivan's conception of cure. *American Journal of Psychotherapy*, 1960, *14*, 666-676.

TEILHARD DE CHARDIN, P. *The phenomenon of man*. New York: Harper & Row, 1965.

THORESEN, C. E., & MAHONEY. M. J. *Behavioral self-control*. Toronto: Holt Rinehart & Winston, 1974.

TILLICH, P. *The courage to be*. New Haven: Yale University Press, 1952.

TOMAN, W. *Family constellation: Its effects on personality and social behavior*. New York: Springer, 1969 (2nd ed.).

TOWER, S. S. Pain: Definition and properties of the unit for sensory reception. *Proceedings of the Association for Research in Nervous and Mental Diseases*, 1943, *23*, 16-23.

TRONICK, E., & GREENFIELD, P. M. *Infant curriculum: The Bromley-Heath guide to the care of infants in groups*. New York: Media Projects, 1973.

TRUAX, C. B. Effective ingredients in psychotherapy: An approach to unraveling the patient-therapist interaction. *Journal of Counselling Psychology*, 1963, *10*, 256-263.

TRUAX, C. B., & CARKHUFF, R. R. New directions in clinical research. In B. G. Berenson & R. R. Carkhuff (Eds.) *Sources of gain in counselling and psychotherapy*. New York: Holt Rinehart & Winston, 1967. Pp. 358-391.

TULKIN, S. R., & COHLER, B. J. Childrearing attitudes and mother-child interaction in the first year of life. *Merrill-Palmer Quarterly*, 1972, *18*, 95-106.

ULLMANN, L. P. A behavioral comment on the experiential response. *Psychotherapy: Theory, Research and Practice*, 1972, *9*, 199-203.

ULLMANN, M. An experimental approach to dreams and telepathy: Methodology and preliminary findings. *Archives of General Psychiatry*, 1966, *14*, 605-613.

ULLMANN, M., KRIPPNER, S., & FIELDSTEIN, S. Experimentally induced telepathic dreams. Two studies using EEG-REM monitoring technique. *International Journal of Neuropsychiatry*, 1966, *2*, 420-437.

VAN DUSEN, W. The theory and practice of existential analysis. *American Journal of Psychotherapy*, 1957, *11*, 310-322.

VAN RIPER, C. *Speech correction: Principles and methods*. New York: Prentice Hall, 1954.

VESPE, R. Ontological analysis and synthesis in existential psychotherapy. *Existential Psychiatry*, 1969, *7*, 83-92.

VINACKE, W. E. The basic postulates of psychology. *Scientific Monthly*, 1948, August, 110-114.

VON ECKARTSBERG, R. Geography of human experience. *Journal for the Study of Consciousness*, 1969, July-December.

VON ECKARTSBERG, R. On experiential methodology. In A. Giorgi, W. F. Fischer & R. von Eckartsberg (Eds.) *Duquesne studies in phenomenological psychology*. Volume 1. Pittsburgh: Duquesne University Press, 1971. Pp. 70-76.

VON ECONOMO, C. Sleep as a problem of localization. *Journal of Nervous and Mental Disease*, 1930, *71*, 249-267.

WAELDER, R. *Basic theory of psychoanalysis*. New York: International Universities Press, 1960.

WAHL, C. W. Some antecedent factors in the histories of 568 male schizophrenics of the United States Navy. *American Journal of Psychology*, 1956, *113*, 201-210.

WALLACH, M. S. & STRUPP, H. H. Psychotherapists' clinical judgments and attitudes toward patients. *Journal of Consulting Psychology*, 1960, *24*, 316-323.

WALLERSTEIN, R. S. Treatment of the psychosis of general paresis with combined sodium amytol and psychotherapy: Report of a case. *Psychiatry*, 1951, *14*, 307-317.

WALTERS, R. H. & PARKE, R. D. Influence of response consequences to a social model on resistance to deviation. *Journal of Experimental Child Psychology*, 1964, *1*, 269-280.

WALTERS, R. H., & PARKE, R. D. The role of the distance receptors in the development of social responsiveness. In L. P. Lipsitt & C. C. Spiker (Eds.) *Advances in child development and behavior*. Volume 2. New York: Academic Press, 1965. Pp. 59-96.

WATSON, J. B. *Psychology from the standpoint of a behaviorist*. Philadelphia: Lippincott, 1919.

WATSON. J. B. & RAYNER. R. Conditioned emotional reactions. *Journal of Experimental Psychology*, 1920, *3*, 1-14.

WATSON, J. S. The development and generalization of contingency awareness in early infancy: Some hypotheses. *Merrill-Palmer Quarterly*, 1966, *12*, 123-135.

WATSON, J. S. Memory and "contingency analysis": in infant learning. *Merrill-Palmer Quarterly*, 1967, *13*, 55-76.

WATSON, J. S. Smiling, cooing, and "the game". *Merrill-Palmer Quarterly*, 1972, *18*, 330-341.

WATSON, J. S. & RAMEY, C. T. Reactions to response-contingent stimulation in early infancy. Paper presented at Society for Research in Child Development. Santa Monica, California, 1969.

WATTS, A. W. *This is It and other essays on Zen*. New York: Random House & John Murray, 1960.

WATTS, A. W. *Psychotherapy east and west*. New York: Pantheon, 1961.

WECHSLER, H., & BUSFIELD, B. The depressive rating scale: A quantitative approach to the assessment of depressive symptomalology. *Archives of General Psychiatry*, 1963, *9*, 334-343.

WEDDELL, G. The multiple innervation of sensory spots in the skin. *Journal of Anatomy*, 1941, *75*, 441-448.

WEISS, E. & ENGLISH, O. S. *Psychosomatic medicine*. (2nd ed.). Philadelphia: Saunders, 1949.

WEISS, S. Therapeutic strategy to obviate suicide. *Psychotherapy: Theory, Research and Practice*, 1969, *6*, 39-43.

WESTOFF. C. F. & RYDER, N. B. Duration of use of oral contraceptives in the United States, 1960-1965. *United States Public Health Reports*, 1968, *83*, 277-287.

WHEELIS, A. *The quest for identity*. New York: Norton, 1957.

WHEELWRIGHT, J. Jung's psychological concepts. In F. Fromm-Reichmann & J. L. Moreno (Eds.) *Progress in psychotherapy*. New York: Grune & Stratton. 1956. Pp. 127-135.

WHITAKER, C. A., & MALONE, T. P. *The roots of psychotherapy*. New York: Blakiston, 1953.

WHITAKER, C. A., WARKENTIN, J. & MALONE, T. P. The involvement of the professional therapist. In A. Burton (Ed.) *Case studies in counselling and psychotherapy*. Englewood Cliffs, New Jersey: Prentice-Hall, 1959, Pp. 218-257.

WHITE, B. L. Fundamental environmental influences on the development of competence. In Merle-Meyer (Ed.) *Third Western Symposium on Cognitive Learning*. Bellingham. Washington: Western Washington State. 1972. Pp. 79-101.

WHITE, R. W. Motivation reconsidered: The concept of competence. *Psychological Review*, 1959, *66*, 297-333.

WHITE, R. W. Ego and reality in psychoanalytic theory. *Psychological Issues*, (Monogr.), 1963, *3* (Whole No. 11).

WHITE, W. A. Medical philosophy from the viewpoint of a psychiatrist. *Psychiatry*, 1947, *10*, 77-98.

WHITEHEAD, J. Convulsions in utero. *British Medical Journal*, 1867, *2*, 59-61.

WHITEHORN. J. C. The goals of psychotherapy. In E. A. Rubenstein and M. B. Parloff (Eds.), *Research in psychotherapy*. Washington, D.C.: American Psychological Association, 1959. Pp. 1-9.

WHITMER, C. A., & CONOVER, C. G. A study of critical incidents in the hospitalization of the mentally ill. *Social Work*, 1959, *4*, 89-94.

WHORF, B. L. Science and linguistics. In J. B. Carroll (Ed.) *Language, thought and reality*. Cambridge, Mass.: The Technology Press and John Wiley, 1956.

WILHELM, R. *The secret of the golden flower: A Chinese book of life*. London: Routledge & Kegan Paul, 1962.

WILLIAMS, H. & BARBER, L. Description of an infancy curriculum for character development. *Character Potential*, 1971, *5*, 99-106.

WILLIAMS, R. The biological approach to the study of personality. In T. Millon (Ed.), *Theories of Psychopathology*. Philadelphia: Saunders, 1967. Pp. 19-31.

WILSON, R. S. On behavior pathology. *Psychological Bulletin*, 1963, *60*, 130-146.

WINNICOTT, D. W. *The child, the family, and the outside world*. New York: Penguin Books, 1964.

WISCHNER, G. T. Stuttering behavior and learning: A preliminary theoretical formulation. *Journal of Speech and Hearing Disorders*, 1950-51, *15-16*, 324-335.

WITTENBORN, J. R. Depression. In B. B. Wolman (Ed.), *Handbook of Clinical Psychology*.

New York: McGraw-Hill, 1965. Pp. 1030-1057.

WOLBERG, L. R. *The technique of psychotherapy*. New York: Grune & Stratton, 1954.

WOLBERG, L. R. Techniques of reconstructive therapy. In T. Millon (Ed.) *Theories of Psychopathology*. Philadelphia: W. B. Saunders, 1967. Pp. 212-217.

WOLFF, H. B., & WOLF, S. *Pain*. Springfield, Illinois: Thomas, 1958.

WOLFF, W. *The dream = mirror of conscience*. New York: Grune & Stratton, 1952.

WOLPE, J. *Psychotherapy by reciprocal inhibition*. Stanford: Stanford University Press, 1958.

WOLPE, J. Isolation of a conditioning procedure as the crucial psychotherapeutic factor: A case study. *Journal of Nervous and Mental Disease*, 1964, *134*, 316-329.

WOLPE, J. & LAZARUS, A. A. *Behavior therapy techniques*. Oxford: Pergamon, 1966.

WOODGER, J. H. *Biology and language*. Cambridge: Cambridge University Press, 1952.

WOODGER, J. H. *Physics, psychology, and medicine*. Cambridge: Cambridge University Press, 1956.

WOODWORTH, R. S. *Dynamics of behavior*. New York: Holt Rinehart & Winston, 1958.

WOODWORTH, R. S. & SHEEHAN, M. R. *Contemporary schools of psychology*. New York: Ronald Press, 1964.

YARROW, L. J. Maternal deprivation: Toward an empirical and conceptual reevaluation. *Psychological Bulletin*, 1961, *58*, 459-490.

YARROW, L. J. & PEDERSEN, F. A. Attachment: Its origins and course. In L. J. Yarrow & F. A. Pedersen (Eds.) *The young child: Review of research*. Volume 2. Washington, D.C.: National Association for the Education of Young Children, 1972. Pp. 302-312.

YARROW, L. J., RUBENSTEIN, J. L., PEDERSEN, F. A., & JANKOWSKI, J. J. Dimensions of early stimulation and their differential effects on infant development. *Merrill-Palmer Quarterly*, 1972, *18*, 205-218.

YATES, A. J. The application of learning theory to the treatment of tics. *Journal of Abnormal and Social Psychology*, 1958, *56*, 175-182.

YOUNG, P. T. The role of hedonic processes in motivation. In M. R. Jones (Ed.), *Nebraska symposium on motivation*. Lincoln, Neb.: University of Nebraska Press, 1955. Pp. 193-238.

YOSS, R. E. & DALY, D. D. Narcolepsy. *Archives of Internal Medicine*, 1960, *106*, 148-171.

ZANER, R. M. Criticism of tensions in psychology between the methods of behaviorism and phenomenology. *Psychological Review*, 1967, *74*, 318-324.

ZIEGLER, F. J., ROGERS, D. A., KRIEGSMAN, S. A. & MARTON, P. L. Ovulation suppressors, psychological functioning and marital adjustment. *Journal of the American Medical Association*, 1968, *204*, 849-853.

ZILBOORG, G. H. *A history of medical psychology*. New York: Norton, 1941.

ZILBOORG, G. H. Fear of death. *Psychoanalytic Quarterly*, 1943, *12*, 465-475.

ZILBOORG, G. H. Rediscovery of the paient: An historical note. In F. Fromm-Feichmann & J. L. Moreno (Eds.) *Progress in Psychotherapy*. New York: Grune & Stratton, 1956.

Subject Index

867

Rage:
    and cancer, 169
    and deeper potential, 162, 164-65, 249, 381
Rape fears, and deeper potential, 48
Rapid eye movement, research on, 25, 386
Rash, psychosomatic, 557
Rational-emotive therapy, 95
Reaction formations, 135
Reactive schizophrenia, 530
Reality principle, 102, 391
Recovery Incorporated, 263
Reductionism, in theory, 133-37, 141, 143
Reference, ideas of. *See* Ideas of Reference
Regression, 197-98, 327, 425, 714-15
Reincarnation, 545, 546
Reinforcement value, 208
Relativity, theory of, 101
Religion, function of, 540
Repetition compulsion, 391
Repression:
    and neurosis, 28
    psychoanalytic theory of, 31
Reticular formation, 150
"Reversal of voice," 502
Rivalry, deeper potential for, 439
Role induction, 197
Role playing, 95

Sadism, and deeper potential, 45, 49
Saguine temperament, 115
Satori:
    as goal, 567
    state of, 512
Scapegoat, collective, 291
Schizophrenia, 274, 394, 402, 436, 744. *See also* Psychosis
    cause of, 109
    characteristics of, 7
    comprehension of, 529-30
    hospitalization for, 795
    and humanism, 104, 106
    as label, 531
    and manic-depression, 465
    and mother-infant, 621, 658
    onset of, 247
    psychotherapy of, 728, 729
    reality of, 545, 546
    roots of, 627-28
    tendencies, 612
    theory on, 122-23
    treatment, 330
    and withdrawal, 44
    world of, 253
Science, as institution, 261
Secondary reinforcers, and parents, 8

Self. *See also* I-ness
    birth of, 796ff.
    dilation of, 498ff.
    loci of, 233-34
    and metamorphosis, 496-97
    potential, 503-504
    self-awareness, 26-27
    self-concept, 26-27
    self-directed interaction, 336-38, 694
    self-preserving behavior, 392, 433ff.
    self-reflectiveness, 506-508
Self-actualization. *See* Actualization
Self-hypnosis, and hysteria, 109
Self-realization, 566
Senoi tribe, 476, 783
Sensitivity groups, 256
Sexuality:
    and actualization, 586
    and aggression, 154-55, 191
    and body, 85
    communication of, 466-67
    confrontation, 407
    denial of, 89
    and drive, 19
    experience of, 340
    and extended personality, 229, 234
    and external personality, 230
    genital resurgence, 498
    and gratification, 313
    and group, 264
    humanistic approach to, 23
    of infant, 706-708
    potential for, 44, 51, 58, 64-66, 74, 169-70, 241, 254, 321, 332-33, 334, 340, 345, 346, 348, 357, 364, 371, 395, 411-12, 440-41, 462, 557, 623, 820, 823-24
    problems, 427
    as threat, 160
Shame, as disintegrative feeling, 83-85
Shaping, 95
Shock therapy, 176
S-H-R paradigm, 189
Sibling rivalry, 65, 714-15, 811, 819
Simple schizophrenia, 530
Situational contexts, 260ff., 325ff., 383-84
Sleep, and unfeeling, 90-93, 95
Smoking, and birth weight, 677, 718
Social groups, construction of, 273-74
Social learning approach, 12, 122
Social phenomena, construction modes, 287ff.
Social roles, and internal conflict, 71-72
Social transmission, 663
Social work, as field, 3, 9
Sociology:

Name Index

Abraham, K., 426, 835*n*.
Adler, A., 20, 132, 184, 497, 601, 617, 634, 640, 643, 657, 835*n*.
Ainsworth, M.D.S., 627, 646, 651, 668, 768, 773, 774, 835*n*.
Albee, G.W., 275, 402, 835*n*.
Alexander, F., 60, 119, 139, 149, 150, 153, 157, 165, 169, 835*n.*, 836*n*.
Allport, G.W., 13, 111, 135, 252, 362, 490, 642, 836*n*.
Altman, J.W., 212, 836*n*.
Amatruda, C., 655, 846*n*.
Andrews, T.G., 217, 836*n*.
Angel E., 13, 351, 856*n*.
Ansbacher, H.L., 643, 836*n*.
Ansbacher, R.R., 643, 836*n*.
Anthony, 621
Appleton, L.E., 19, 643, 836*n*.
Archibald, H.C., 795, 811, 836*n*.
Arieti, S., 60, 155, 252, 265, 312, 369, 452, 711, 712, 738, 750, 769, 770, 836*n*.
Artemidorus of Daldi, 4
Asch, S., 42, 43, 111, 112, 669, 802, 831, 836*n*.
Astrup, C., 475, 862*n*.

Badger, E., 764, 836*n*.
Baer, D.M., 665, 669-71, 689, 838*n*.
Bakan, D., 13, 547, 836*n*.
Baker, C., 829, 862*n*.
Baldwin, A.L., 684, 836*n*.
Balint, A., 656, 836*n*.
Bandura, A., 207, 208, 215, 245, 253, 367, 401, 402, 419, 424, 443, 455, 563, 580-81, 697, 698, 702, 739, 836*n*.

Barber, L., 764, 865*n*.
Barber, T.X., 151, 473, 500, 833, 841*n*.
Barker, R., 239, 836*n*.
Barry, H.A., 797, 836*n., 837*n*.
Barsch, R.H., 764, 837*n*.
Bartemeier, J.H., 261, 837*n*.
Bateson, G., 683, 684, 837*n*.
Bateson, P.P.B., 669, 837*n*.
Beard, G.M., 224, 837*n*.
Beck, A.T., 57, 85, 104, 109, 530, 837*n*.
Beck, J., 764, 837*n*.
Beckwith, L., 694, 703, 837*n*.
Bell, D., 795, 811, 836*n*.
Bell, J.E., 601, 837*n*.
Bell, S., 773, 774, 835*n*.
Benedek, T.F., 605, 663, 667, 733, 756, 798, 837*n*.
Beras, D., 797, 837*n*.
Berelson, B., 254, 837*n*.
Bergin, A.E., 194, 329, 348, 475, 567, 837*n.*, 863*n*.
Bergman, P., 75, 511, 837*n*.
Bergmann, G., 201, 837*n*.
Bergson, 30
Berkowitz, L., 641, 837*n*.
Bernheim, 109, 130
Bernstein, L., 29, 854*n*.
Bertalanffy, L., 15, 837*n*.
Bettelheim, B., 773, 774, 837*n*.
Bexton, W.H., 212, 838*n*.
Bijou, S.W., 665, 669-71, 689, 838*n*.
Binswanger, L., 13, 37, 40, 42, 43, 64, 78, 84, 119, 161-62, 180, 253, 255, 286, 340, 349, 357, 362, 373, 377, 394, 395, 400, 401, 404, 414, 422, 429, 436,